HUMAN RESOURCE MANAGEMENT

AN EXPERIENTIAL APPROACH

SECOND EDITION

H. JOHN BERNARDIN
Department of Management and International Business
Florida Atlantic University

JOYCE E. A. RUSSELL
Department of Management
The University of Tennessee

Irwin McGraw-Hill

Boston   Burr Ridge, IL   Dubuque, IA   Madison, WI   New York   San Francisco   St. Louis
Bangkok   Bogotá   Caracas   Lisbon   London   Madrid
Mexico City   Milan   New Delhi   Seoul   Singapore   Sydney   Taipei   Toronto

Irwin/McGraw-Hill

A Division of The McGraw-Hill Companies

HUMAN RESOURCE MANAGEMENT: AN EXPERIENTIAL APPROACH, 2/e

Copyright © 1998 by The McGraw-Hill Companies, Inc. All rights reserved. Previous edition © 1993. Printed in the United States of America. Except as permitted under the United States Copyright Act of 1976, no part of this publication may be reproduced or distributed in any form or by any means, or stored in a data base or retrieval system, without the prior written permission of the publisher.

This book is printed on acid-free paper.

1 2 3 4 5 6 7 8 9 0 QPD/QPD 9 0 9 8 7

ISBN 0-07-005846-6

Vice president and editorial director: *Michael W. Junior*
Publisher: *Craig S. Beytien*
Senior sponsoring editor: *John E. Biernat*
Editorial assistant: *Erin Riley*
Marketing manager: *Ellen Cleary*
Project manager: *Maggie Rathke*
Production supervisor: *Lori Koetters*
Designer: *AM Design/Michael Warrell*
Compositor: *ElectraGraphics, Inc.*
Typeface: *10/12 Times Roman*
Printer: *Quebecor Printing Book Group/Dubuque (QPD)*

Library of Congress Cataloging-in-Publication Data

Bernardin, H. John.
   Human resource management : an experiential approach / H. John
Bernardin, Joyce E. A. Russell. — 2nd ed.
     p. cm.
   Includes bibliographical references and index.
   ISBN 0-07-005846-6
   1. Personnel management—United States.   I. Russell, Joyce E. A.
II. Title.
HF5549.2.U5B456   1998
658.3—dc21   97-32386

www.mhhe.com

ABOUT THE AUTHORS

H. John Bernardin, a mountain of a man, is also University Professor of Research in the College of Business at Florida Atlantic University. He earned his Ph.D. in industrial and organizational psychology from Bowling Green State University in 1976. Professor Bernardin was the coeditor of the *Human Resource Management Review* and has had editorial board appointments on the *Academy of Management Review, Human Resource Planning,* and *Human Resources Management.* He has authored or edited six books and published over 130 articles. He has consulted for numerous organizations and served as an expert witness in many employment discrimination cases. Dr. Bernardin is former chair of the Division of Personnel/Human Resources of the National Academy of Management.

Joyce E. A. Russell is a Professor of Management at The University of Tennessee. She earned her Ph.D. in industrial and organizational psychology from The University of Akron in 1982. Dr. Russell serves on the editorial boards of *Journal of Applied Psychology, Journal of Vocational Behavior, Human Resource Management Review* and *Performance Improvement Quarterly.* She also serves as a reviewer for numerous other journals, including *Personnel Psychology, Performance Improvement Quarterly, Sex Roles,* and *Leadership Quarterly.* She has published over 50 articles, proceedings, book chapters or reviews, and has presented papers at national and regional conferences. Her primary areas for research, teaching, and applied work include: training, leadership and management development, career development, work teams, change management, quality improvements, and workforce diversity issues. She has provided human resource management consulting to a number of private and public sector organizations.

PREFACE

This text differs from other human resource management (HRM) texts in providing theoretical and experiential approaches to the study of HRM while focusing on the enhancement of student personal competencies. Students are given the conceptual background and content necessary to understand the relevant issues in HRM. In addition, they participate in individual and group exercises that require the application of chapter content to specific problems designed to develop critical personal competencies.

Our book is the first attempt to directly link student learning experiences in HRM with assessed competencies judged by experts to be essential for graduating business students. As we discuss in Chapter 1, recent studies have been critical of the readiness of business graduates for work, noting deficiencies in a number of areas, including communication skills, analytical thinking, decision-making ability, and leadership potential. While other experiential texts are available, this is the first to attempt to provide adequate coverage of the subject matter in each of the vital areas of HRM while preparing the student to "learn by doing." This is also the first attempt among HRM texts to provide a research-based methodology for the assessment of the critical competencies and to provide a process by which students may evaluate the extent to which they have improved their competencies as they progress through the course.

All the experiential exercises in this book were designed to enhance some or all of the critical personal competencies in the context of HRM subject matter. We introduce the student to these competencies in the first chapter and attempt to develop them all the way through the text. To do so, we use participation in experiential exercises requiring the application of the HRM knowledge expected of practicing managers. The experiential exercises were developed so as to facilitate greater learning through class interaction and projects. There is usually an individual writing component to the exercise followed by group interaction and consensus building. A 1991 study by Dr. Richard Light at Harvard University found that this approach to undergraduate education is superior to the standard straight lecture approach.

Successful completion of these field-tested exercises, combined with the assessment processes described in Appendix A, should foster student development in all the areas experts believe to be critical in preparing business students for their first "real jobs."

Studies show that the majority of business graduates will ultimately manage or supervise employees. Research in this area shows that the two areas that prove to be the most troublesome and crucial for managers are performance management and dealing with an increasing diverse workforce in the context of equal employment opportunity law. Our objective with this book is to emphasize knowledge and direct experience in these areas without compromising treatment of the other domains of HRM.

Procedures are available in this text to require students to evaluate their own performance and that of peer group members after completion of most of the experiential exercises. The first chapter provides an exercise that requires students to collect performance information on competencies from people who have worked with them. As we discuss in Chapter 9, this multirater, "360-degree" approach provides more valid information about performance and is a useful frame of reference for monitoring performance improvements. Research also shows that the more experience a person has had with the performance management process, the more effective that individual is in fulfilling this important managerial responsibility.

We have incorporated exercises and discussion questions throughout the text that require the student to consider equal employment opportunity laws in particular HRM contexts. So, unlike the standard HRM text, which covers EEO in one chapter, this book compels the student to weigh the EEO implications of HRM activities such as job analysis (Chapter 4), downsizing programs (Chapter 5), personnel selection processes (Chapter 6), employee training and development (Chapter 7), performance appraisal (Chapter 9), compensation (Chapters 10 and 11), and other major HRM activities.

We do not shy away from any of the significant, yet controversial issues of the day. For example, among the topics we cover and for which we have critical thinking and experiential exercises are ethnic score differences on employee screening devices, affirmative action programs and preferential treatment, binding arbitration agreements, sexual harassment and sexual orientation, employment at will, random drug testing with no probable cause, smoking in the workplace, executive compensation, employee rights of privacy, employee assistance programs, and equal pay for work of comparable worth.

Another distinctive feature of this book is that the chapters from the first edition were written by experts in the HRM field. Our experts were selected on the basis of their experience, knowledge, and research accomplishments in a particular area of HRM and/or their experience with well-tested, experiential exercises that foster learning in a critical HRM content area. Since HRM is strongly influenced by a number of disciplines (e.g., law, economics, psychology, sociology, strategic management), we sought out expertise to represent these varied orientations. We believe the finished product represents a broader perspective than a book prepared by authors from only one of those disciplines. The second edition is an extension of the first edition but attempts to establish more continuity by relying mainly on the two authors to integrate the chapters.

A few other distinguishing features of this text should also be noted. First, international issues are discussed in most chapters to illustrate both the special and common characteristics of international HRM. Given today's competitive global marketplace, HR professionals need to increasingly understand international strategies if they are to provide meaningful assistance to their firms. We have also devoted separate chapters to the issues of "quality" and competitive advantage. Interwoven in each chapter is an underlying theme of improving quality and increasing competitive advantage with more effective HRM practices.

ACKNOWLEDGMENTS

A number of people have made valuable contributions to this book. First, we would like to thank the various editors and staff members with whom we have worked at McGraw-Hill. We would also like to acknowledge the many reviewers from various universities and colleges who provided helpful comments and suggestions: Jarold Abbott and Barry Axe, Florida Atlantic University, Debra A. Arvanites, Villanova University; Dan Braunstein, Oakland University; Robert L. Cardy, Arizona State University; Herschel N. Chait, Indiana State University; Joan G. Dahl, California State University, Northridge; Randy L. DeSimone, Rhode Island College; William L. Eslin, Glassboro State College; Nancy Johnson, University of Kentucky; Katherine Karl, Western Michigan University; John F. P. Konarski, Florida International University; Jacqueline Landau, Suffolk University; Robert M. Madigan, Virginia Polytechnic Institute; Herff L. Moore, University of Central Arkansas; James S. Russell, Lewis and Clark College; Janet Stern Solomon, Towson State University; Lee Stepina, Florida State University; Charles M. Vance, Loyola Marymount University; Richard A. Wald, Eastern Washington University; Elizabeth C. Wesman, Syracuse University; Kenneth M. York, Oakland University; and Mary D. Zalesny, University of Missouri—St. Louis.

Contributors of chapters or portions of chapters were: David O. Ulrich, Barbara A. Lee, Scott A. Snell, Chris Hagan, Monica Favia, Michael M. Harris, Barbara K. Brown, Joan E. Pynes, P. Christopher Earley, Diana Deadrick, Philip J. Decker, Barry R. Nathan, Nancy McKinney, Jeffrey S. Kane, Sabrine Maetzke, Lee P. Stepina, James R. Harris, Alan Cabelly, E. Brian Peach, M. Ronald Buckley, Nancy Brown Johnson, Joseph G. Clark, Jr., Roger L. Cole, Lauen J. Lispi, Harriette S. McCaul, Fred E. Schuster, Thomas Becker, Susan M. Burroughs, and Peter Villanova. Contributors of experiential exercises were: Sue A. Dahmus, Jeffrey D. Kudisch, Marilyn A. Perkins, Lori Spina, Jarold Abbott, Mary E. Wilson, Joan E. Pynes, Peter Villanova, M. Ronald Buckley, Robert W. Eder, J. R. Biddle, Patrick Wright, James A. Brcaugh, Barbara Hassell, Lee P. Stepina, James R. Harris, Jeffrey S. Kane, Kimberly F. Kane, Roger L. Cole, Christine M. Hagan, Scott A. Snell, Ann M. Herd, Larry A. Pace, Caroline C. Wilhelm, Sheila Kennelly-McGinnis, Stephanie D. Myers, Paul Guglielmino, Lucy Guglielmino, Fred E. Schuster, E. Brian Peach, Brenda E. Richey, Steven M. Barnard, Steve Long, Lillian T. Eby, Kathaleena Bernardin, Sharon L. Wagner, Richard G. Moffett III, Catherine M. Westerberry, Esther J. Long, Joseph G. Clark, Jr., Susan M. Burroughs, and Nancy Brown Johnson.

Many colleagues have provided enormous assistance on this revised edition—by contributing their comments on earlier drafts, reviewing exercises, or furnishing extensive reference materials. We truly appreciate the efforts of Lauren Lispi, Danielle Adams, Bryan Anderson, Jennifer D. Burgess, Joseph Clark, Stephen H. Gaby, Michael C. Rush, Lynn B. Curtis, Laura A. Davenport, Aaron T. Fausz, Jeffrey D. Kudisch, Ann Rigel, and Christine Hagan. We would also like to thank our departments for their assistance during these difficult budget times. Special thanks go to Oscar S. Fowler, Carolyn Alfrey, Maggie Bakalar, Jackie Cook, and June Trbovich from the Management Department at The University of Tennessee. Carol Annunziato provided impeccable clerical assistance on Professor Bernardin's behalf.

We would also like to express our deepest appreciation to our families for their support, encouragement, and patience throughout this entire process. Thanks to Michael, Gerri, Bruce, Colleen, Kathy, Chuck, Suzanne, Erin, Toni, Kelly, Patrick, Brian, Kitty, Manny, Rosie, Kathleen, Liesa, and Maude.

Bernardin thanks Mary E. Wilson for work on just about everything.

H. John Bernardin
Joyce E. A. Russell

BRIEF CONTENTS

CONTENTS

ix

HRM IN A CHANGING ENVIRONMENT

OVERVIEW

The CEO of a medium-sized manufacturing company once confided that, not too long ago, the major responsibility of the personnel director was to organize the annual company picnic. The executive claimed that the personnel officer always carried the watermelon.

While this is an obvious exaggeration, there is no question that the personnel officer often served as the "Rodney Dangerfield" of corporate activity and, as the comedian says, got "no respect." One personnel manager even referred to the personnel department as "the dumping ground for people who couldn't hack it in operations . . . people basically failed their way into personnel." The role was often viewed as clerical, with the personnel department overseeing basic tasks such as recordkeeping, regulatory compliance, and payroll.

A lot has changed, including the name that summarizes the activities. The personnel function has become human resources. Human resource management, or HRM, concerns a broad range of important company functions, including the recruitment, selection, training, development, compensation, retention, evaluation, and promotion of personnel within an organization. Responsibilities have expanded and greater prestige is associated with the leading HR positions. The majority of top HRM executives now report directly to the CEO, and half of *Fortune* 500 firms assigned the top HR professional to a vice president position. Many HR executives now serve on major strategy and policy committees for corporations (e.g., GE, IBM, GM, Xerox, Coca-Cola, Microsoft, Merck, Sun Microsystems, Wal-Mart). More importantly, progressive HRM activities are now considered to be major sources of competitive advantage and a growing body of research supports this view.

While there is still plenty of room for improvement, the status of HRM activities has clearly changed and is continuing to improve in the United States. We believe that HR processes such as hiring and maintaining the most effective and efficient workforce are growing in importance relative to other potential sources of competitive advantage for an organization. We are not alone in this belief. Stanford University scholar Jeffrey Pfeffer notes, "Traditional sources of success (e.g., speed to market, financial, technological) can still provide competitive leverage, but to a lesser degree now than in the

1

past, leaving organizational culture and capabilities, derived from how people are managed, as comparatively more vital."[1]

How people are managed *is* the human resource management function. The human resources of an organization consist of all people who perform its activities. In a sense, *all* decisions that affect the workforce concern the organization's HRM function. Regardless of the size—or existence—of a formal HRM or Personnel Department, the activities involved in HRM are pervasive throughout the organization. Line managers, for example, spend most of their time involved in human resource activities. The effectiveness with which line management performs HRM functions with the tools, data, and processes provided by HRM specialists is the key to competitive advantage through HRM. This principle generalizes from very small businesses to the very largest global enterprises.

Those individuals classified within an HRM functional unit provide or endorse products and services for the organization. These products and services may include the provision of, or recommendation for, systems or processes that facilitate organizational restructuring, personnel planning, recruitment, hiring, evaluating, training, promoting, compensating, and terminating. A goal of this book is to provide information and experiences that will improve the student's future involvement and effectiveness in these HRM activities. Our thesis is that the most effective HRM programs, policies, and practices are established, maintained, and improved with the organization's mission and strategic plan in mind. This mission and strategic plan should focus on attracting, maintaining, and, in most circumstances, expanding a customer base for the organization's products or services. This focus should in turn drive an increase in shareholder value. All HRM activities should be evaluated in this context using meaningful and measurable criteria.

Unfortunately, this is not how HRM is typically carried out in U.S. organizations. HRM activities are often faddish and disjointed, giving little consideration to the organization's mission or goals and the ultimate effect on customer satisfaction. Companies often adopt some procedure simply because they learn that some competitor or successful company was using it. Many HR systems and activities are not systematically evaluated. The damaging effects of such practices are well documented.

Many organizations do not assess either the short-term or the long-term consequences of their HRM program or activities in terms of meaningful criteria. Many decision makers in HRM are neither qualified nor motivated to properly evaluate the effectiveness of an HRM program, system, or activity. Stanford professor Pfeffer considers measurement to be one key to competitive advantage. His book, *Competitive Advantage Through People,* cites measurement as one of the 16 HRM practices that contribute to competitive advantage.[2] Yet research indicates that a minority of HRM programs or activities are subjected to any systematic evaluation using carefully defined outcomes or criteria.[3]

A growing number of organizations look at HRM functions and systems as major contributors to accomplishing the organization's mission. We believe, as we head toward the 21st century, this new conceptualization is essential for American business. Dave Ulrich's excellent new book, *Human Resource Champions,* calls for focusing our attention on what HR professionals *deliver;* that is, the outcomes and results of HR work. The 21st century HR roles are that of strategic partner, administrative expert, employee champion, and change agent.[4] The responsibilities are to provide deliverables in all four areas. These deliverables must be responsive to an increasingly competitive and global marketplace and must be closely linked to business strategic plans. Ulrich, Pfeffer, and others conclude that the most effective companies are serious about treating their employees as assets—assets to be invested in the real and potential customer base. Scott Adams, creator of the cartoon strip "Dilbert," considers "the first great lie of management to be 'employees are our most valuable asset'" because "money is our most valuable asset. Employees are ninth . . . carbon paper is eight." Adams's point is that many companies pay lip service to treating employees as assets.[5] The most reliably effective companies do not.

In their book, *Megatrends 2000,* John Naisbitt and Patricia Aburdene emphasize the role of HRM in preparing America for the millennium.

> It will require a tremendous human resources effort to transform corporate America into the decentralized, customer-oriented model of the information society. Yet that is what is needed for the United States to fully participate in the blooming global economy. With new markets, with a single-market Europe, and with new competitors from Asian countries, corporations need people who can think critically, plan strategically, and adapt to change.[6]

This statement was written *before* the remarkable advances in the information highway and communications technology. (There is little discussion of the Internet in *Megatrends 2000.*) Like virtually all areas of business today, these technological changes necessitate flexibility in corporate structure and HR. As Microsoft founder Bill Gates concluded in *The Road Ahead,* "Technological progress will force all of society to confront tough new problems, only some of which we can foresee. The pace of technological change is so fast that sometimes it seems the world will be completely different from one day to the next. It won't. But we should be prepared for change."[7] One major responsibility of HR is to foresee as many of these challenges as possible and to react in order to exploit them for competitive advantage. Flexibility is a key to meeting this responsibility.

OBJECTIVES

After studying this chapter, you should be able to:

1. Describe the field of HRM and its increasing importance for competitive advantage.

2. Describe the discrepancy between HRM practice and recommendations from academic research.

3. Describe the major activities performed by HRM professionals in the context of eight HR domains.

4. Discuss the role of employee involvement in designing and implementing effective HRM programs in the context of the critical HRM constituencies.

5. Explain the trends relevant to the growing importance for HRM, including the concern about productivity measures, changes in the global marketplace and technology, greater global competition, the increasing role of regulations and lawsuits, and the changing demographics of the workforce.

6. Emphasize the importance of measurement for effective HRM.

A growing body of research shows that progressive HRM practices can have a profound effect on corporate performance.[8] Studies now document the relationship between specific HR practices and critical outcome measures such as productivity, product and service quality, and cost control. Sophisticated staffing and job design methods are related to higher productivity and reduced costs.[9] Better training and development programs have been shown to improve the performance of current employees.[10] Certain incentive and compensation systems translate into higher productivity and performance.[11] The fair treatment of employees results in greater loyalty, higher performance, and reduced costs.[12] As depicted in Figure 1.1, the critical feature of these HRM practices is that they must be linked to the firm's business and strategic objectives.

Companies are more fully recognizing that their workforces can be their greatest strength. But this belief does not mean pouring millions of dollars in overhead into a large HR bureaucracy. As Ken Alvares, vice president of human resources for Sun Microsystems, puts it: "The bottom-line business of human resources must be the delivery and/or development of human capital that enable the enterprise to become more competitive, to operate for maximum effectiveness, and to execute its business strategies successfully."[13] This can be accomplished only by a lean but very knowledgeable HR staff and line management personnel who are convinced that HR practices are vital for competitive advantage.

HRM personnel typically participate in the development and implementation of HR systems and processes that are then carried out by line managers. For example, with the assistance of HRM specialists and outside consultants, AT&T developed a system for its massive restructuring and downsizing in 1996. HRM specialists developed all the systems used to make decisions about personnel. Line managers made the actual decisions regarding the people who would be retained and the people who would be terminated. HRM specialists critiqued the proposed decisions made by line management, paying particular attention to possible violations of equal employment opportunity law. The long-term effects of the AT&T downsizing depend on the manner in which these line managers did their jobs. When Miami Dolphin owner Wayne Huizenga launched his huge used-car business in 1996, he hired a personnel specialist to develop systems for hiring and training sales managers. The ultimate hiring decision was made by the sales manager, and the sales training was done by an outside sales training organization.

Managers in smaller organizations are more likely to have direct responsibility for the major HR functions. Even franchised businesses of large corporations give store managers great discretion. For example, franchise owners of major fast food outlets such as Wendy's, Arby's, Subway Subs, and Domino's Pizza have primary responsibilities for determining staffing needs, recruiting employees, hiring, and determining compensation policy.

Progressive HRM requires sophisticated HRM spe-

FIGURE 1.1
A MODEL OF THE HR–SHAREHOLDER VALUE RELATIONSHIP

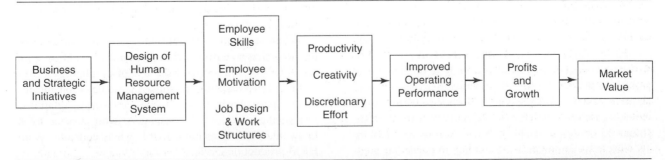

Source: HR as a source of shareholder value: Research and recommendations, B. E. Becker, M. A. Huselid, P. S. Pickus and M. F. Spratt, *Human Resource Management,* copyright © 1997. Reprinted by permission of John Wiley and Sons, inc.

cialists who develop or adopt the best systems and then line managers who effectively use the systems. As we shall emphasize later and throughout the book, this cooperative and intelligent approach to HRM is not common, regardless of the size (or reputation) of the company.

Greater demands are now being made on HRM professionals to respond to contemporary trends in the business environment. Today, the HRM function must be conceptualized in a business capacity, constantly focusing on the strategy and the core competencies of the organization. HR professionals must show how they can make a difference in the company's bottom line. As IBM's James G. Parkel suggests, "Today, HRM professionals are much more concerned with business management functions, government relations, and international issues—issues beyond human resources . . . HR professionals will be judged on their ability to be innovative and cost-effective, along with their ability to get the job done in conjunction with line management."[14]

Many corporate strategy specialists maintain that the key to sustained competitive advantage is building and sustaining core competencies within the organization and maintaining flexibility in order to react quickly to the changing global marketplace and the incredible advances in technology. As illustrated in Figure 1.1, the primary role of HRM should be to facilitate this process. Business and strategic initiatives should drive the design of the HRM system.

Line management must also recognize the importance of the HRM function and that achieving results through people, the basic purpose of line management, is best achieved with good, efficient, and progressive HRM practices. HRM specialists must be trained and qualified to either develop such practices or select those products or services that can deliver such practices at the lowest possible cost.

DISCREPANCIES BETWEEN ACADEMIC RESEARCH AND HRM PRACTICE

While HRM executives and managers are more educated and professional than the days when they were in charge only of the company picnic, the level of knowledge and sophistication in actual HRM is another story. Many companies, large and small, hire MBAs for HRM jobs when not one HRM course is required in the typical MBA curriculum. The 85,000-member Society for Human Resource Management (http://www.shrm.org), which established the Human Resource Certification Institute, formally recognizes human resource professionals who have demonstrated expertise in particular areas of HR. But only 11 percent of Society members have received this certification. The level of knowledge and sophistication appears to be related to company size as well. While larger companies tend to have well-trained HR decision makers, small to medium-size companies tend to be staffed with less-educated and less-well-trained HR specialists who may have more difficulty either developing or adopting the most progressive and effective approaches to HRM.[15] As one would expect, small and medium-size companies, the fastest growing segment of the U.S. economy, are also much less likely to use progressive HRM programs.

Many HRM activities are directed at correcting problems, rather than anticipating and planning to avoid problems. A serious lawsuit or the desire to keep up with the competition should not be the impetus to initiate a program. One Florida bank found this out when it implemented an expensive computer-based managerial training program simply because its major competitor used it. Unfortunately, no one attempted to assess the actual need for the training. Another company attempted to determine whether a test it was using actually predicted performance on the job *after* the company had been sued for discrimination because of the test.

Universities have been under attack in recent years for allowing faculty to spend too little time teaching and too much time conducting research. It is said that academic research has little or no relevance to the real world. While some academic research is clearly trivial, irrelevant, and insignificant, there is also a great deal of carefully crafted research that is not only relevant but also provides clear guidelines to the "real" world. This is particularly true for research in HRM. For example, academic research has identified **high performance work systems (HPWS),** which have been linked to firm value.[16] Comprehensive recruiting and selection systems, incentive compensation and performance management, and extensive employee involvement go into defining HPWS. While the research that went into defining HPWS has been around for a long time, the extent of use of the HR practices comprising HPWS is low.

Many HRM managers either ignore relevant academic research or are unaware of it when making decisions regarding HRM systems and practices. A 1996 issue of *INC.* magazine, for example, discussed the growing popularity of handwriting analysis in determining a person's potential job performance.[17] The academic literature has clearly established that handwriting analysis does not predict performance.[18]

Companies that use this staffing method instead of methods that actually work will ultimately end up with less effective workers. Yet the use of graphology in selecting and promoting personnel is actually on the increase, particularly in small companies with relatively less sophisticated HRM managers who do not even know the right questions to ask when considering an HRM product or service.[19]

Figure 1.2 presents a few examples of discrepancies between the current state of HR practice and what the academic literature clearly recommends. We will cover

FIGURE 1.2
SAMPLE OF DISCREPANCIES BETWEEN ACADEMIC RESEARCH FINDINGS AND HRM PRACTICES

ACADEMIC RESEARCH FINDINGS	HRM PRACTICE
RECRUITMENT	
Quantitative analysis of recruitment sources using yield ratios can facilitate efficiencies in recruitment.	Less than 5% calculate yield ratios. Less than 20% know how.
STAFFING	
Realistic job previews (RJP) can reduce turnover.	Less than 5% of companies use RJPs in high turnover jobs.
Weighted application blanks (WAB) reduce turnover.	Less than 10% know what a WAB is; less than 1% use WABS.
Structured, behavioral, or situational interviews are more valid.	18% of companies use structured interviews.
Use statistical model of prediction with multiple selection devices.	Less than 5% use actuarial.
Graphology is invalid and should not be used.	Use is on the increase in the United States.
PERFORMANCE APPRAISAL	
Do not use traits on rating forms.	More than 75% still use traits.
Train performance raters (for accuracy, observation bias).	Less than 24% train raters.
Make appraisal process important element of job.	Less than 30% of managers are evaluated on performance appraisal.
COMPENSATION	
Merit-based systems should not be tied into a base salary.	More than 75% tie merit pay into base.
Gainsharing is an effective PFP system.	Less than 5% of companies use it where they could.

each of these examples and many others as we cover specific HR activities.

Throughout the book, we will emphasize the most glaring discrepancies between the way HRM is being practiced and what academic research has to say about those particular practices. The failure on the part of practicing HRM personnel to either be aware of the research or to understand it can have a profound effect on an organization's bottom line. Although line management plays a critical role in the successful implementation and execution of HRM programs, these programs are typically either developed or purchased by HRM specialists. Although some research has been around for years, recent research has established the relationship between the use of progressive and effective HRM practices and bottom-line corporate performance measures, such as return on equity, profit, profit growth, and stock price.[20]

HRM professionals should possess up-to-date knowledge about the relative effectiveness of the various HR programs and activities such as HR planning, job design, employee compensation, performance management, personnel staffing, information systems, equal employment opportunity, recruitment, health and safety issues, and employee training. HRM professionals should also be capable of conducting their own research to determine the relative effectiveness of a program or activity. Unfortunately, some HR professionals adopt programs based either on effective marketing from vendors selling HR materials and programs or on what other companies are doing.

When bottom-line questions arise later—as they inevitably do—HR departments are caught off guard because costly and relatively ineffective programs have

been adopted. A careful study of the program with the effectiveness criteria in mind might reveal negligible or no impact at a high cost. Many HR specialists today operate with a "best practices" perspective based on "benchmarking" the way the best companies do things (see http://shrm.org/hrlinks/manage.htm). While this research is helpful, the characteristics of HPWS will only be effective to the extent that *the measurement processes of these activities are aligned with business and strategic initiatives.*

Many HR professionals are not even trained to ask the right questions and conduct the appropriate study of a given HR program or activity. One HR vice president of a *Fortune* 500 retail company adopted a very expensive computerized testing program that the publisher claimed would reduce employee turnover by 50 percent. The vice president did not request the research that purported to document this effect and later admitted that he was unqualified to assess the test's usefulness since he could not even ask the most fundamental of measurement questions that should be the focus of any evaluation of such a product or service. (You'll be able to ask those questions after you have read this book!)

One great value of academic research is the objective evaluation of activities or programs using controlled experimental designs, which allow for unambiguous assessments of effects. For example, a reference text exists that provides test evaluations written by qualified academics who have no vested interest in the tests themselves. Had the retail company vice president consulted this text, he would have found two highly critical reviews, which were based on asking the right questions of the publisher and getting unsatisfactory answers.

Convincing Line Management about the Value of HRM Activities

Practicing HR specialists must be aware of relevant research and weigh it appropriately when considering various HRM policy and practice options. Line managers must carry out required HRM activities with the conviction that a conscientious job will improve the bottom line. HRM professionals must be able to convince line managers of the value of these activities for meeting organizational goals. The change agent role of the HR manager is best facilitated through data. Line managers tend to resist new HR programs or activities. In general, they are more convinced that a particular program or activity should be adopted when the HR professional justifies it with the same type of effectiveness criteria for which line management is accountable.

Successful HR practice requires instilling in line managers and employees a sense of ownership in HRM activities. If management is motivated by an agenda that is incompatible with the agenda of the HRM function, the effectiveness of the HRM system is in serious jeopardy. It is not enough that the HRM departmental staff possesses up-to-date knowledge of HRM practices. Line management must also recognize the importance of these activities and behave accordingly. HR professionals will have a better chance of enlisting line management cooperation by showing results or outcomes from HR programs and their linkage to critical outcome measures directly relevant to the organization's mission.

THE ACTIVITIES OF HUMAN RESOURCE MANAGEMENT

Intense competition pressures organizations to carefully examine their costs and to exploit every possible source of competitive advantage. Edward Lawler, a prominent management author and consultant, states, "All staff departments are being asked to justify their cost structures on a competitive basis . . . head-count comparisons are being made by corporations to check the ratio of employees to members of the HR department."[21] Whether the organization is facing increasing international competition or simply more intense pressure to improve the bottom line, HR has a great opportunity to meet new and old challenges as a business partner. Lawler sees the most pressing need in the area of corporate strategy. "The HR function must become a partner in developing an organization's strategic plan, for human resources are a key consideration in determining strategies that are both practical and feasible."[22] This HR partnership must evolve out of the major activities of the HR function. So what are the major activities and how do they relate to contemporary trends in the business environment?

Figure 1.3 presents a listing of the most commonly performed activities by HRM professionals. These HRM activities fall under eight major human resource policy domains:

1. Organizational design.
2. Staffing.
3. Employee and organizational development.
4. Performance appraisal and management.
5. Reward systems and benefits.
6. Productivity improvement.
7. Employee/employer relationships, including labor relations.
8. Health and safety.

The activities subsumed under these domains are at least conceptually interdependent, although many organizations pursue various activities and domains as if they had no implications for any of the other domains. For example, many organizations have reduced or eliminated health care benefits without considering the effects of the new compensation package on staffing and employee retention. Companies have installed new staffing procedures without considering the effects on its diversity or affirmative action program. Complementary HRM activities are also considered to be a key to competitive advantage. As one recent article concluded, "If the HRM system is not properly aligned, these individual best practices can potentially be in conflict within the HRM system and actually diminish firm performance."[23] Let us introduce the eight domains next.

Organizational design involves the arrangement of work tasks based on the interaction of people, technology, and the tasks to be performed in the context of the mission, goals, and strategic plan of the organization. HRM activities such as human resources planning, job analysis, organizational restructuring, job design, computerization, and worker-machine interfaces are under this policy area. Corporate downsizing efforts often begin with human resource planning in the context of a strategic plan and a critical analysis of how products or services could be delivered more efficiently. We will emphasize these design issues in Chapters 2, 4, and 5.

After the organization is structured and jobs are clearly defined in terms of the necessary knowledge, skills, and abilities, positions must be staffed. **Staffing** has to do with the flow of people into, through, and out of the organization. Recruitment, employee orientation, staffing, promotion, and outplacement, which is assistance for terminated employees, are among the functions that fit into this domain. Of all the HR domains, staffing is probably the one most likely affected by litigation. Chapters 5 and 6 cover this critical area after we introduce you to the laws that are the basis of this litigation (see Chapter 3).

Employee training and organizational development programs are concerned with establishing, foster-

FIGURE 1.3
MAJOR DOMAINS/ACTIVITIES OF HUMAN RESOURCE MANAGEMENT

ORGANIZATIONAL DESIGN

Human resource planning
Job analysis
Job design
Socio-technical systems
Information systems

STAFFING

Recruiting/interviewing/hiring
Affirmative action
Promotion/transfer/separation
Induction/orientation
Employee selection methods

PERFORMANCE APPRAISAL AND MANAGEMENT

Management appraisal/management by objectives
Customer-focused performance appraisal

HEALTH AND SAFETY

OSHA compliance
Accident prevention
Stress reduction
Wellness programs
Employee assistance/counseling programs

REWARD SYSTEMS AND BENEFITS

Safety Programs/OSHA compliance
Health/medical services
Complaint/disciplinary procedures
Compensation administration
EEO compliance
Wage/salary administration
Insurance benefits administration
Unemployment compensation administration
Pension/profit sharing plans
Outplacement services

EMPLOYEE TRAINING AND ORGANIZATIONAL DEVELOPMENT

Management/supervisory development
Career planning/development
Skill training

EMPLOYER/EMPLOYEE RELATIONS

Labor relations
Collective bargaining
Employee grievances
Alternative dispute systems
Attitude surveys
Employee communications/publications

PRODUCTIVITY IMPROVEMENT PROGRAMS

TQM programs
Productivity/enhancement programs
Suggestion systems
Quality circles
Team-building

Source: Organizational Capability Competing from the Inside Out, D. Ulrich and D. Lake, Copyright © 1987. Reprinted by permission of John Wiley and Sons, Inc.

ing, and maintaining employee skills based on organizational and employee needs. Developmental activities may include specialized training, career development plans, self-directed learning, and retirement programs. Chapters 7 and 8 will cover the vital areas of training and career development.

Performance appraisal and management activities include assessments of individual, unit, or other levels of performance to measure and improve, work performance. This domain includes employee discipline. Chapter 9 will deal with these subjects, which are also the focus of numerous lawsuits. A lawsuit can occur if the organization maintains that an employee was terminated, not promoted, or not given a merit raise because of performance and the employee believes that negative personnel action was because of his or her gender, race, age, disability, or some other characteristic. An employee can also claim an unlawful discharge based on an alleged contract or implied contract violation. Obviously, merit pay systems require accurate measures of employee performance.

Reward systems and benefits have to do with any type of reward or benefit available to employees. Direct and indirect compensation, merit pay, profit sharing, health care, parental leave programs, vacation leave, and pensions are among the critical areas within this domain. The activities also include domestic and international compliance requirements from local, state, and federal agencies. We address these issues in Chapters 10 and 11.

Productivity improvement programs have become a major emphasis of HR activity as companies pursue a variety of different programs designed to increase effectiveness and efficiency. The total quality movement (TQM) is subsumed in this discussion, which is covered in Chapter 12.

The **employee/employer relationships** domain concerns labor relations law and compliance and procedures designed to maintain good working relationships between employees and employers. A critical part of HRM is the establishment and maintenance of a good working relationship with employees. Communications is an important component of this domain. This domain include the negotiation of collective bargaining agreements, which require employers to negotiate with unionized workers over the conditions of employment. We cover this area in Chapter 13.

The final domain is **employee health and safety** and includes compliance with a number of laws and regulations concerned with the work environment and its effect on workers and the general public. This area is explored in Chapter 14.

All these domains are concerned with sharing information among employees, management, and outside constituents, including customers. Information systems, personnel research, attitude surveys, and company publications are all included here. The manner in which the organization treats its employees, pays its executives, outsources work and to whom, promotes workforce diversity, and uses its workers can affect customer satisfaction and is thus an important HR activity. Discussion of these critical issues are nested within each of the chapters of the book.

How Are Employees Involved in HRM Activities?

Underlying all the HRM activities presented in Figure 1.3 is the extent of employee involvement or influence. According to Harvard professor Michael Beer and colleagues, the essential question in this area is, "How much responsibility, authority, and power should the organization voluntarily delegate and to whom?"[24] Will management seek to minimize the power and influence of employees or will influence be shared in critical areas related to employee welfare, such as reward systems, appraisal, and staffing? The critical task for management is to determine the extent to which employees will be involved in organizational decision making.

Senior management can adopt an implicit policy of little or no employee influence or a participatory culture of high levels of employee involvement. Attitude surveys, open-door policies, ombudsmen, quality-of-work-life programs, and self-managing teams are examples of high participatory HRM practices. One survey found an increase in such activities in American organizations.[25]

A policy regarding the degree of employee influence is related to the general philosophy management has about the quality of working life for its employees. Some organizations set an objective of establishing and maintaining a high quality of working life for its employees, regardless of the effect on corporate performance or productivity. These organizations are more likely to adopt programs and policies that facilitate employee influence. For example, IBM, Hewlett-Packard, McCormick & Co., and S.C. Johnson Wax have corporate mission statements that reflect a high quality of working life for their employees. Other organizations consider a higher quality of working life as a means to a desired end. These companies have determined or hypothesized that programs such as quality circles, team building, attitude surveys, and other forms of employee involvement have

an impact on the bottom line and should thus be maintained. With this perspective, such programs are sustained only when it is believed that they affect important indicators of organizational performance. Still other organizations allow employee participation only to the extent that it is legislated or mandated through collective bargaining. With this philosophy, management often considers stockholders as the only major constituent to which it is responsible.

Some organizations do not clearly fit into one of these three philosophical categories. Some have had either positive or negative experiences with employee involvement programs and might have changed philosophies accordingly. Many U.S. companies are unsure about the effects of such programs yet are willing to try them in order to assess their impact empirically. The number of such companies willing to try worker involvement programs is increasing steadily as more organizations seek a competitive edge in an increasingly competitive world. Chapter 12 addresses this in more detail.

The management philosophy regarding employee influence will have a great deal to do with the activities pursued within all eight HRM domains. For example, the process by which personnel are promoted could be the traditional "top-down" assessment. Input also could be gathered from peers, subordinates, or the work team. GM Saturn plant workers participate in the selection of team members and the promotion of team leaders. The same thing is true for the extent of participation in the allocation of rewards. Management may assume complete control over the design and administration of these programs, or they may be compelled to negotiate these procedures through collective bargaining or they can choose to involve employees to a lesser or greater extent.

What Should Be the Ultimate Focus for the Long-Term Success of an Organization?

While management must recognize employees as an important constituency group, with legitimate interests in organizational functioning, executives must attempt to integrate employee interests with the interests of the stockholders, customers, suppliers, and the community at large. A company's competitiveness depends on a long-term financial relationship with all major stakeholders. Customers require high-quality products and services at a competitive price. Workers require competitive compensation and a high quality of working life. Suppliers have financial claims. And shareholders want higher stock prices and bigger dividends.

Long-term financial success depends on the ability of senior management to enhance the organization's competitive position by focusing on meeting or exceeding customer requirements and expanding the customer base. And since customers also prefer lower prices, cost control is one element of this customer-based focus. If the organization loses this focus, the long-term prospects for the stockholder are not favorable. HRM practices and policies that overemphasize cost reduction may initially get a favorable response from the stockmarket but in the long run may cripple the organization.[26]

The focus on customers will depend to a large extent on whether management can convince all employees of the virtues of this philosophy. This ultimate goal should foster the long-term interests of all constituent groups. HRM professionals are increasingly called on to assist in this critical endeavor. Dave Ulrich and many other HR experts believe this customer-based orientation should be driven deep within the organization by viewing employee relationships as customers and suppliers as well. Says Ulrich, "When HR practices are aligned with the needs of internal and external customers, firms are more likely to succeed. HR departments must be held to a higher standard than they have been until now. They must move their HR professionals beyond the roles of policy police and regulatory watchdogs to become partners, players, and pioneers in delivering value."[27]

The evaluation of the effects of the various HRM activities should have this customer focus. HRM has taken on increased importance in recent years because of several trends affecting and defining the business environment. We examine those trends next.

TRENDS RELATED TO THE INCREASED IMPORTANCE OF HUMAN RESOURCE MANAGEMENT

As we said at the outset of this chapter, there is an increasing realization that the manner in which an organization conducts its HR activities will help create and sustain a competitive advantage. The contemporary trends and challenges in the business environment necessitate that even greater attention be given to HRM as we head toward the 21st century. Let us examine these trends next and relate each to particular HRM activities. Figure 1.4 presents a summary of the major trends.

There are a number of reasons for senior management's increasing focus on human resources. The most significant are concerns over productivity, cost control, and a growing competitive work environment with a premium on product and service quality. In addition, there is a need to be more flexible today due to the incredible pace of change in markets and technology. HRM can facilitate this flexibility. The growth and proliferation of lawsuits related to HR and changes in workforce characteristics have also had a big impact on HRM. Also, many in the workforce lack the necessary knowledge, skills, abilities, and employees to do their jobs well. We will discuss each of these trends next.

FIGURE 1.4
CONTEMPORARY TRENDS THAT AFFECT HRM

Trend 1: Concern over productivity
Slow U.S. growth rates
Increasing evidence that HRM can increase productivity
Trend 2: The need to be flexible in response to changing business environments
Outsourcing and downsizing; temporary employees
Trend 3: Increasing international competition and the expanding global economy
Increasing competition for U.S. products and services
Opportunity for expansion
Trend 4: Increase in litigation related to HRM
Federal, state, and municipal lawsuits on the increase
Wrongful discharge; claims of negligent hiring, retention, referral
Trend 5: Changing characteristics of the workforce
Growing workforce diversity
Changing attitudes; less loyalty, more demands
Labor shortages/ aging workforce
Job skills gap; poor match between skills and corporate needs

Trend 1: Concern over Productivity

A team of leading scientists, engineers, and economists from the Massachusetts Institute of Technology concluded their comprehensive 1989 review of American productivity with this ominous statement: "Relative to other nations and relative to its own history, America does indeed have a serious productivity problem . . . it is manifested by sluggish productivity growth and by shortcomings in the quality and innovativeness of the national products."[28] In the 10 years since this dismal report, American corporations have responded nicely and HRM practices deserve a great deal of the credit.[29]

But we still need to pick it up. Since 1973, U.S. productivity has grown at an average rate of a little over 1 percent a year, less than half the historical rate. While growth improved in the late 90s, growth is still considered slow by most experts. Even the most optimistic growth rates for the United States do not match favorably with many nations providing comparable data. While U.S. productivity has improved in recent years for all sectors of the economy, most experts believe we could still do a lot better.[30]

In the United States, services represent about 75 percent of the workforce and close to 70 percent of the gross national product. Experts predict in the next 20 years 9 out of every 10 new jobs will be in the services sector. Productivity figures show a steady improvement in the late 1990s in services but a disappointing 10-year record.

WHY ARE PRODUCTIVITY FIGURES SO IMPORTANT? Productivity is the major correlate of a nation's standard of living and the best measure of economic performance. History shows a nation that is the productivity leader eventually becomes the dominant world leader—economically, militarily, and politically. Given this, there is little wonder that corporate leaders are deeply concerned about productivity. This concern translates into organizational decisions related to HRM functions. The most important reason for the increased interest in HRM is the perceived connection between HRM activities and productivity and the related criticism of the quality of our products and services. A sizable portion of corporate America realizes that competing in an increasingly global environment requires constant vigilance over productivity and customer satisfaction. A smaller but growing percentage of managers recognize the importance of human resources in dealing with these issues. Indeed, a great deal of the recent corporate downsizing can be linked to some technological improvement and estimates of productivity improvements with HRM and the interacting technological changes. Companies such as Chrysler and General Electric have successfully followed a formula of cutting personnel costs while investing in automated equipment. In 1996, for example, Chrysler made 1.8 million cars, slightly more than it made in 1988, but with 9,000 fewer workers.

More organizations are now evaluating their human resources and labor costs in the context of available technologies, based on the theory that products and services can be delivered more effectively (and efficiently) through an optimal combination of people, software, and equipment. This optimal combination should affect productivity. Recent evidence shows that it does. Today, more companies are carefully evaluating the role of organizational structure, technology, and human resources for providing more and higher quality products and services to the customer at a lower price. This pricing is at least partially achieved by controlling the cost of labor while not losing the focus on meeting customer definitions of quality. Of course, the ultimate goal is to maximize profit margins while sustaining customer values.

Trend 2: The Need to Be Flexible in Response to Changing Business Environments

Being innovative and responsive to changing business environments requires great flexibility. The trend toward the "elastic" company is affecting the HR function, too. More companies are focusing on their core competencies—what they do best and what is the essence of their business. They outsource other work, use temporary or leased employees to perform valuable services or work on specific projects, even at the professional level, and replace personnel with new technology. These so-called modular companies such as Nike and Dell Computers

can be highly successful if they have reliable vendors and suppliers and a hot product.

HR departments and the employees within them are not exempt from this trend toward outsourcing. A proliferation of consulting firms compete for HR projects and programs previously performed within the company by company employees. Towers Perrin, one of the largest of these consulting firms, provides a service called People Strategy, which "enables client companies to determine specifically how people should be managed and deployed to help achieve competitive advantage."[31]

One strong trend in the United States is toward hiring temporary employees through one of the thriving temporary employment agencies such as Interim, Kelly Services, or Manpower. These organizations provide companies with skilled and unskilled employees on an "as needed" basis and take care of all aspects of the hiring, placement, and assessment of those employees. This trend toward outsourcing some of the personnel function supports the thesis of many experts that the HRM functions must be very lean so that companies can react quickly to the changing world. Many HRM departments are now mandated to assess the need for any expense, personnel included, in the context of the primary functions of the organization and its competitive strategy.

While HR activities are being seen as increasingly important as a source of competitive advantage, HR departments have been downsizing targets themselves. Substantial portions of HR functions are now often outsourced to another company that specializes in particular HRM activities. For example, an increasing number of companies outsource their payroll function. Many companies rely on outside recruiting services for all or part of their staffing needs. Many consulting firms now recruit new college graduates who perform HR services for companies that were performed by full-time employees a few years ago. Internet services and software have now replaced company-developed systems for many HR activities. Some HR services are now available on the Internet.[32]

How lean can you get in HR? Nucor, a steel company with 6,000 employees, has an HR staff of four at its headquarters. Most of the HR work is farmed out to HR consultants and run by a very lean HR divisional staff. Some experts argue that the most efficient and perhaps most effective HRM functions primarily select the best and least costly outside contractors for HRM products and services, make certain these products or services are being used properly, and then evaluate these products and services to make certain they are working effectively and efficiently.

DO WE ACTUALLY NEED AN HRM DEPARTMENT? If companies can maintain a leaner and more flexible and cost-effective structure by outsourcing, and can purchase HRM products and services through consulting and/ or the Internet, where will that leave the HR department in the future? According to Thomas Stewart's 1996 somewhat tongue-in-cheek *Fortune* magazine article, "Why not blow the sucker up?"[33] In the article, titled "The Last Bureaucracy," Stewart maintains that the entire HR function can be outsourced with considerable cost savings for the company. The effect of such a policy on HR product and service quality is another question and the extent to which a company actually saves money by outsourcing HR activities has not been clearly established (see the following Critical Thinking Exercise 1.1).

CRITICAL THINKING EXERCISE 1.1

Resolution: Close down the Human Resources Department

A great deal of research indicates that it is line management which will determine whether or not human resources can create and sustain a competitive advantage for organizations. While HR staff develop, purchase and administer HR activities, the proper use of these activities by line management has the most to do with their effectiveness. *Fortune* magazine's Thomas Stewart argues that outsourcing those HR functions that can be outsourced will ultimately save the company money and thus facilitate a competitive advantage through reducing costs.[1] This cost reduction could then increase profits and/or help the company compete on price.

Some HR departments are already responding by outsourcing many functions traditionally done by full-time employees. Compensation and executive recruiting are two of a growing number of areas which are extensively being outsourced, and other functional areas may follow.

Stewart argues that an in-house HR department will probably cost the company much more money and since it's line management (not the HR staff) which really determine HR effectiveness, the use of outsourced personnel to perform HR activities should have little impact on effectiveness. For example, instead of using full-time HR staff to develop and implement a new performance management system, the company could contract with a company to do this work.

Stewart refers the reader to the Washington, D.C.-based Corporate Leadership Council which concluded that indirect compensation (benefits), personnel record-keeping, and employee services such as outplacement and retirement counseling, and health and safety issues (drug testing, wellness programs, workers' compensation) could all be outsourced to save money.

Stewart goes beyond the Council's recommendation. He argues that many HR functions can now be purchased from vendors with considerable savings and no loss in quality. For example, recruiting can be done through "head-hunters" now for even low-level jobs. Personnel testing, performance management and pay-for-performance systems can be purchased from consulting firms with impressive expertise in these areas. He cites Nucor Steel which has an HR staff of four for its 6,000 person operation. Nucor farms out most of its HR work.

Assignment

Generate a list of reasons why there may be another side to this story. What key questions would you want to ask Mr. Stewart and others who are making these recommendations? Compile a list of advantages and disadvantages to outsourcing that could help a company make a decision about the best decision to make.

[1] Stewart, T. A. (January 15, 1996). Taking on the last bureaucracy. *Fortune*, 105–108.

The key here in terms of competitive advantage is the adoption and proper use of effective and progressive HRM practices. Thus, while the Internet and the plethora of HR consulting firms may offer a myriad of "solutions," or "people strategies" in the form of products and services, someone within the organization must be capable of distinguishing between what constitutes progressive, cost-effective HRM practices and what is pure "snake oil." Some evidence suggests that practicing managers, including HRM managers, may not be particularly good at this. Management must always be aware that the consulting firms performing work previously done in-house are in the business of making money. Remember earlier when we discussed *expanding* the customer base. Consulting firms are trying to sell their clients products, services, and person-hours. This motivation does not usually exist when work is done in-house. Management must always be aware that simple head-count reduction does not always translate into increased productivity or effectiveness. Outsourcing does not necessarily decrease your costs.

WHAT DO TECHNOLOGICAL CHANGES HAVE TO DO WITH HRM? The need to be flexible is driven by the uncertainty in global markets. The remarkable change in technology is affecting virtually all aspects of business. Corporate downsizing efforts and improvements in technology are credited with improving productivity in recent years. More than 75 percent of the *Fortune* 200 corporations reduced workforce size from 1990 to 1996. One study found that improved communications and technology facilitated most downsizing efforts but that reorganization was the key to competitive advantage. One consultant sees corporate anorexia setting in because companies have actually cut too much and are unable to grow the "revenue line." Reorganization calls for changing the way employees work with the new technology.[34]

Most of us are familiar with such technology. Instead of speaking to a customer service representative at NationsBank to discuss your account, you can interact with an automated system programmed to handle almost any problem for which you call. With the automated system, NationsBank is able to shed customer service representatives, thereby reducing labor costs. As more people use this service and the automated teller machines (ATMs), there is less need for supervision. Customers, as a result, pay less in service charges, may earn more interest on their money, and could be more satisfied with the service, even though they are not dealing with an actual person.

In a similar manner, organizations are taking advantage of the Internet, or World Wide Web. Wal-Mart enables you to shop from your home computer through the Internet (http://www.wal-mart.com). This convenience reduces Wal-Mart's need for in-store associates. And customers, who would otherwise not have the time or inclination to shop at Wal-Mart, appreciate and use the service. Numerous other organizations now do business on the Internet via their individual Web sites. Companies conduct internal international business as well. Motorola employs computer programmers in India who work on a program over a Web site while the U.S.-based programmers are sleeping in a different time zone. The results of such activity are a substantial savings in costs and a reduced product development cycle.

Bill Gates's book *The Road Ahead* discusses the power of the computer and the World Wide Web to change forever the way customers learn about products and services.[35] The effect of technology on HR activities should also be profound. Stocks are now routinely bought and sold on the Internet without a stockbroker. The amount of business transactions conducted on the Internet in 1996 was 400 percent higher than in 1995. On-line grocery shopping is becoming more and more common. New York-based Peapod takes grocery orders over the Internet and delivers the order to the customer within hours (http://www.peapod.com). The day is not far off when we will even "surf" through our virtual reality grocery store and take our "cart" down each aisle all while sitting at home. We select our products and a short time later they arrive at our front door (if they could only figure out how to put the stuff on our shelves).

WHAT WILL BE THE IMPACT OF THE INTERNET ON HRM ACTIVITIES? The Internet has already had an impact on HR, but the effect will be much greater in the future. The following scenario is not far off: a manager or supervisor gets authorization to

hire someone. The manager goes into a "node" on the Internet and completes a standardized job description for the new position that establishes critical information regarding the job, including the necessary knowledge, ability, skills, and other critical characteristics. The job description is then used to conduct a "keyword" computer search of a potential applicant pool in order to match the job requirements with the standardized résumés in the database. Out pops a number of potential candidates for the job. The manager then immediately sends out the job vacancy announcement to all the potential candidates in the database through electronic mail. Interested candidates respond back through the electronic mail. The manager then selects the "short list" of candidates who would compete for the job (see http://intellimatch.com).

The same job analysis information could also be used to construct or retrieve job-related tests or questions for an employment interview. The manager might even have a state-of-the-art video computer and could conduct the testing and "face-to-face" interviewing of the candidate as soon as the contact is made (assuming the candidate also has access to a camera-based computer). The entire process could take less than a day.

Once this system is up and running, the role of the full-time HR recruiting specialist is limited to selecting the best job analysis and selection methods and ensuring legal compliance in the hiring process. Although this system is not yet available, software and CD-ROM is now available for every major HRM activity, and systems similar to this are now being developed. We are only a few years away from being able to download many kinds of HR software from the Internet and then adapting it for our purposes. The key for HR specialists is selecting (or developing) the most effective and efficient systems for their particular work situations (see http:///www.resumix.com).

Employee recruiting, particularly for "hot jobs" in technology, has already been profoundly affected by the Internet. Some of the most successful high-tech companies today rely on the Internet for fast, convenient, and efficient recruiting of their core personnel (see http://www.cisco.com). Even the CIA does some of its recruiting on the Internet (try www.odci.gov/cia if you'd like to be a spy).

Trend 3: Increasing International Competition and the Expanding Global Economy

While productivity figures are probably the most important reason for the increased interest in HRM, there are other important and related trends that may also explain the increased importance being placed on HRM. One of these trends is the increasing international competition

FIGURE 1.5
UNIQUE HRM CHALLENGES IN INTERNATIONAL JOINT VENTURES

HR ACTIVITY	HRM CHALLENGES
Staffing	Host country may demand staffing policies contrary to maximizing profits.
Decision making	Conflicts among diverse constituent groups; complexity of decision processes.
Communication	Interpersonal problems due to geographical dispersion and cultural differences.
Compensation	Perceived and real compensation differences.
Career planning	Perceptions regarding value of overseas assignments; difficulties in reentry.
Performance management	Differences in standards; difficulties in measuring performance across countries.
Training	Special training for functioning in international joint venture (IJV) structure.

Source: Adapted from O. Shenkar and Y. Zeira. Human resource management in international joint ventures: Directions for research. *Academy of Management Review, 12,* 1987, 546–557. Reprinted with permission.

for U.S. products and services and the expanding global economy. U.S. exports, for example, now generate one in six jobs, an increase of over 20 percent in just 10 years.

McDonald's opened its first non-U.S. restaurant in Canada in 1967. Total sales outside the United States contributed over 50 percent of the firm's operating income in 1997. Two-thirds of its new stores are opened outside the United States each year (See Critical Thinking Exercise 2 for more detail on McDonald's). While McDonald's has moved more quickly than other U.S. firms, many other U.S. companies are now expanding rapidly both in terms of new countries and new markets. The majority of new restaurants opened by Burger King, KFC, and Wendy's in 1997, for example, were opened in an international market.

As one expert put it, "There is nothing that any American organization does that is not directly affected by developments throughout the world. The emerging technologies, the competition, and the opportunities are global . . . all organizations, regardless of locales, soon must evaluate workforce skills, costs, and availability on a global basis."[36] The chances are better than ever that you may work for a foreign corporation in your own community. The majority of 1997 Hondas driven in the United States were actually manufactured in the United States. More than 200 German businesses have moved to North or South Carolina in the last 10 years. Even Mercedes-Benz cars are manufactured in the United States.

While there is also a higher probability now than 10 years ago that you will work for a large American company, there is also a higher probability that you will have an overseas assignment or that your company will have some type of joint venture with a foreign corporation. Businessland, for example, one of the biggest U.S. dealers of personal computers, moved into Japan with the help of Japan's four largest electronics firms. There are estimates that over 80 percent of U.S. businesses could market their products or services overseas if they knew something about exports. Since U.S. markets are regarded as mature or "soft" in many product lines, in-

ternational markets appear to have more potential for substantial growth. Coca-Cola, like McDonald's, is a good example of the potential global economy for U.S. corporations. In 1996, while Coca-Cola had 7 percent growth in U.S. sales, it had 10 percent average growth internationally and almost 30 percent growth in Eastern Europe. This growth put great pressure on the company's international HR operations. Coca-Cola is not alone. Growth in international markets has exceeded domestic growth for numerous other major U.S. corporations, including IBM, GM, AT&T, Marriott, and GE. In 1997, Wal-Mart planned to open 40 new discount stores in Brazil, Canada, China, Indonesia, Mexico, and Puerto Rico. The first Wal-Mart in China opened its doors in August 1996.

All these scenarios place a heavy burden on HRM professionals. Figure 1.5 presents a summary of HRM activities and challenges related to international joint ventures. Critical Thinking Exercise 1.2 that follows presents some examples of how McDonald's has dealt with the challenges. We will consider international HRM in every chapter in the book since we can best understand the similarities and differences between domestic and international HRM in the context of particular HRM activities and domains.

| CRITICAL THINKING EXERCISE 1.2 |

International HR: How about a Le Big Mac?

You can get a Le Big Mac in Paris. And you can get a glass of wine to go with your fries. By the end of 1996, McDonald's had added an additional 2,019 restaurants for a total of 20,921 in 91 countries. Expansion plans will increase the McDonald's workforce to 2 million by the year 2000. Most of the expansion plans are international. McDonald's opened its first foreign restaurant in British Columbia in 1967 and has not looked back. It is now the world's largest food service retailer. Given the domestic competition (e.g., the 99 cent Whopper is beating up on the Big Mac), McDonald's plans to the year 2000 emphasize international growth, particularly in the Latin American, European, and Asian/Pacific regions. It plans to open 50 restaurants in Central America by 2000.

The key to McDonald's international success has been adapting its main product line to the target customer. The first McDonald's opened in India in 1996 and serves no beef. The Big Mac and Quarter Pounder are made with lamb and mutton. McDonald's serves kosher beef in Israel, beer in Germany, McSpaghetti in the Philippines, and Mango shakes in Hong Kong. This diversified menu is not unlike the diversification strategy of the domestic menu over the years. After considerable research, McDonald's introduced the Big Mac in 1968, the Egg McMuffin in 1973, and Chicken McNuggets in 1983. In what can only be described as a shock to the Colonel and his fans, McDonald's (not KFC, not Kenny Rogers, not Chicken Delight) is the largest retailer of prepared chicken.

McDonald's combined sales exceeds that of the four companies ranked immediately below it. Net income grew 16 percent in 1996 and systemwide sales exceeded $30 billion, a 15 percent annual increase. Foreign operations contributed over 50 percent of operating income in 1996 and 1997. The most successful operations were in Australia, Hong Kong, Japan, Taiwan, France, Germany, Spain, and Brazil. The first Romanian outlet broke the central European record with over 15,000 orders in one day. Needless to say, McDonald's continued international aspirations make great business sense.

Due to the company's highly sophisticated infrastructure, international expansion is relatively easy (it opens a new restaurant every three hours). McDonald's relies on joint ventures in many markets, particularly the Far East where knowledge of local customs, food preferences, and markets is vital.

So what are the critical HR issues with regard to McDonald's international goals? What are the key questions that must be asked once research has determined the market is going to be profitable in a particular country? In terms of the eight HR domains discussed in Chapter 1, what answers are required before getting too far along in plans to open another restaurant? Write down what you regard as the top five most important questions for which you need answers. Select a country that you believe would be a good opportunity for a McDonald's restaurant. Then think about the variables you considered in selecting that country. Write down those variables. Do you have any opinions regarding the country you have selected and the five HR questions for which you need answers? Your instructor will compare your answers to those of McDonald's international HR directors.

UNIQUE INTERNATIONAL HRM CHALLENGES

Another response to increasing global competition is restructuring/downsizing, as described earlier. Apple Computer, Sears, AT&T, ARCO, CBS, Du Pont, GM, Eastman Kodak, and IBM are among the many corporate behemoths that have reduced their workforces by more than 10 percent in the last decade. HRM departments are often required to assist in organizational restructuring, make layoff decisions, conduct counseling for those who are displaced, and assist in developing new staffing plans as a result of the downsizing. As we will describe in more detail in later chapters, HR managers are also asked to help in the development of a legal defense against allegations of discrimination related to the corporate downsizing. Unfortunately, this HR involvement with corporate downsizing often occurs only after decisions and possible discrimination have occurred.

The effects of increased international competition cannot be separated from the productivity concerns. As the MIT group put it, productivity problems could "impoverish America relative to other nations that have adapted more quickly and effectively to pervasive changes in technology and markets."[37] Over 80 percent of the U.S. economy is now exposed to some form of international competition. Free and open markets are readily available for commerce through the General Agreement on Tariffs and Trade (GATT), the North American Free Trade Agreement (NAFTA), and other trade agreements. On one side of the coin, the result has been great opportunities for American companies; on the other, there have been difficulties for sectors of the American economy dealing with national defense and in industries where U.S. labor costs are substantially higher than in other countries. One result of this trend, when combined with slow economic growth, is a decline in the annual income of working Americans.

Trend 4: Increases in Litigation Related to HRM

In addition to the growing concerns over productivity, changes in technology, and increases in global competition, another important trend affecting the status of HRM is the proliferation of regulations and lawsuits related to HR. According to one bad statistician, by the year 2010, there will be more lawyers in this country than people. While this is obviously a joke, there is no question that the proliferation and creativity of lawyers and their brethren lawmakers has fostered our highly litigious society. There is no sign of this activity letting up. In fact, federal lawsuits charging violations of labor laws have increased faster (up more than 125 percent since 1991) than any other area of civil rights legislation.[38]

In general, these laws and regulations reflect societal responses to economic, social, or political issues.

For example, the Civil Rights Act of 1964, which prohibits job discrimination on the basis of race, sex, religion, or national origin, was passed primarily in response to the tremendous differences in economic outcomes between blacks and whites. The 1990 Americans with Disabilities Act (ADA) was passed to promote equal opportunity for handicapped and disabled Americans. Another example is the proliferation of state laws regarding corporate acquisitions and mergers, laws protecting AIDS victims and homosexuals from employment discrimination, and even regulations regarding family leave benefits and video display terminals.

Organizations are bound by a plethora of federal, state, and local laws, regulations, executive orders, and rules that have an impact on virtually every type of personnel decision. There are health and safety regulations, laws regarding employee pensions and other compensation programs, plant closures, mergers and acquisitions, new immigration laws, and a growing number of equal opportunity laws and guidelines. Today's HRM professionals and line managers must be familiar with the ADEA, OFCCP, OSHA, EEOC, ADA, and ERISA—among other acronyms. Each represents a major regulatory effort. Organizations spend considerable time and expense to comply with these laws and regulations and/or to defend against allegations regarding violations. Line managers who do not understand the implications of their actions in the context of these laws can cost a company dearly.

Sometimes companies learn the hard way. Mitsubishi was sued by the Equal Employment Opportunity Commission (EEOC) in 1996 on behalf of 400 women who claimed they were victims of sexual harassment at the company's Normal, Illinois, plant. The suit may cost the company millions of dollars. Rayford Hudson was awarded $7.6 million in 1995 by a California jury after being told he was the "wrong color" for a job with a subsidiary of Waste Management Systems. Texaco settled a race discrimination lawsuit for $176 million in 1996. Baker and McKenzie, the largest law firm in the United States, was assessed $3.5 million in punitive damages for sexual harassment committed by one partner at the firm. The EEOC settled a similar suit with Honda of America for $6 million. Westinghouse Electric Corporation agreed to a $35 million settlement in an age discrimination suit involving 4,000 employees affected by the company's reorganization. A judge in California returned a $5.3 million judgment against Shell Oil for dismissing an executive solely because he was a homosexual, a violation of California state law. An accounting firm recently lost a $43 million case involving an unlawful discharge. This increasingly common lawsuit challenges the long-held principle of employment-at-will—the rule that employers could terminate employees at will as long as it did not violate some other law, regulation, or collective bargaining agreement. There are an estimated 10,000 wrongful discharge cases per year with the rate increasing every year.

Employers can now be sued for "negligent referral" if they know a former employee is dangerous and don't say so or make a reference to the contrary. Of course, employers can also be sued for libel if they say something about an employee that is judged to be libelous and without merit. (In other words, you may be damned if you do or damned if you don't!)

One of the most common lawsuits today is brought under the Age Discrimination in Employment Act (ADEA), which prohibits job discrimination against people older than 39. Many such individuals are claiming violations of this law when they are terminated under a corporate downsizing effort. Fifty people sued Pratt and Whitney, a division of United Technology, under ADEA, claiming they were terminated due to their age and salary as part of a downsizing program. Pratt maintained that the terminations were based on company needs and employee performance. We will elaborate on the critical issues of HRM and equal employment opportunity in Chapter 3.

Trend 5: Changing Characteristics of the Workforce

Several trends regarding the future of the American workforce underscore the challenges to and the importance of the human resource function. Compared to 10 years ago, American workers are more ethnically diverse, more educated, more cynical toward work and organizations, getting older and, for a growing number, becoming less prepared to handle the challenges of work today. Let us examine each of these issues next.

WHY IS THE GROWING DIVERSITY OF THE WORKFORCE IMPORTANT FOR HRM? The composition of the workforce is changing drastically and these changes are affecting HRM policies and practices. Increasing diversity creates the need for more diverse HRM systems and practices and increases the probability of the litigation just discussed. In the next decade, 39 million workers will enter the U.S. labor force; one third will be minorities.[39] A greater number of women and minorities have entered the workforce and are beginning to move into previously white, male-dominated positions, including those of managers, lawyers, accountants, medical doctors, and professors. It is estimated that nearly 90 percent of the growth in the workforce for the remainder of this century will be women, immigrants, blacks, and people of Hispanic or Asian origin. In addition, greater percentages of dual-career couples comprise the labor force. The "typical" worker in the past was a male—often white—who was a member of a single-earner household. Fewer than 20 percent of today's employees fit this description. The proportion of Americans who were born elsewhere was near 10 percent in 1996. From 1990 to 1995, 5.1 million immigrants entered the United States—almost as many as for the entire decade of the 1970s.[40]

An increasing number of disabled workers are entering the workforce for the first time due to passage of the American with Disabilities Act. Compliance with the ADA is usually the responsibility of the HR department. Such compliance requires a careful consideration of the law in the context of several HRM domains, particularly **organizational design** and **staffing.**

As a result of these changes in workforce composition, organizations are implementing programs on diversity, more flexible work schedules, better training programs, child care arrangements, and career development strategies, so that work and nonwork responsibilities can be more easily integrated. Building and sustaining a quality workforce from this diversity may be one of the greatest challenges for HRM and practicing managers. Such diversity may also prove to be an important asset in international business.[41]

While increasing diversity translates into a greater probability of EEOC legal actions, many experts also argue that the diversity of the workforce must match the population or the organization is vulnerable to public criticism, which can hurt the business. Most large U.S. companies include a goal of increasing the diversity of their workforce as a priority for the new year. As we will discuss in later chapters, the diversity goals of corporations can have an impact on the less diverse but older part of the workforce, particularly in downsizing situations. Such scenarios create great difficulties for corporations.

WHY DO MORE EDUCATED WORKERS INCREASE THE IMPORTANCE OF HRM? By the year 2000, 25 percent of the workforce will have a college degree. These employees have the potential to contribute to the improvement of organizational effectiveness. Educated workers are also demanding more involvement in corporate decision making; they seek a greater voice in corporate affairs and due process issues. The shift from manual to knowledge work means that we can no longer rely on people for their physical horsepower alone; rather, we will rely more on their intellectual horsepower. Consequently, greater demands are placed on the HR function to meet more demanding employee needs for innovative programs in training, compensation, performance measurement, and career development.

HOW DO CHANGING ATTITUDES TOWARD WORK AFFECT HRM? American workers are changing their attitudes toward work. Employees now demand better coordination between lifestyle needs, including family and leisure, and employment needs.

Leisure pursuits have become more highly valued than work goals. Even previously loyal employees have become cynical of the corporate world. This cynicism has spawned a new interest in organized labor and collective bargaining, even among professionals. The popularity of cartoonist Scott Adams, author of the Dilbert books, underscores this cynicism. Figure 1.6 is one cartoon that could easily represent the attitudes of corporate survivors and victims of continued downsizing.

Du Pont Corporation recently reported that its surveys suggest that family obligations play a greater role in career choices for both men and women. American workers are more interested in jobs with meaningful work, which allow for self-fulfillment and work satisfaction. They want jobs that provide greater challenges and enable them to use more skills and knowledge. These changes in employee attitudes and values require the use of different HR strategies in organizations.

Gone are the days when organizations simply used pay and promotion as the primary motivators for performance. Instead, organizations must develop new staffing plans and restructure jobs to offer opportunities for employees who seek personal fulfillment from their work. Companies must further recognize the impact that plant closings, reductions in force, mergers, and acquisitions have on employees' commitment to their jobs and the organization.

In defending AT&T's huge 1996 downsizing, James Meadows, an HR vice president, stated, "People need to look at themselves as self-employed, as vendors who come to this company to sell their skills . . . we have to promote the concept of the workforce being contingent . . . jobs are being replaced by projects and fields of work."[42] Statements like these contribute to the growing cynicism of the American workforce and the decreasing loyalty toward employers, particularly in light of the downsizing trends and the obscene salaries being drawn by corporate executives. This change in attitude and loyalty can translate into less effective performance and high turnover among employees with external marketability.[43] HRM must attempt to counteract this more cynical attitude toward corporate America.

HOW DO LABOR SHORTAGES AND THE AGING OF THE WORKFORCE AFFECT HRM? The U.S. workforce is aging. The shortage of young workers in the United States is already a problem in the fast food, retail, and hotel industries. This shrinking young workforce is beginning to hurt small business. By the year 2000, the median age in the United States will be 35 and more than 40 percent of the workforce will be older than 40.[44]

HR professionals will need to become more actively involved in dealing with potential discrimination issues, including age discrimination. As we discussed earlier, the age of 40 is critical in that people older than 39 are

FIGURE 1.6
THE DOWN SIDE OF DOWNSIZING

Source: DILBERT reprinted by permission of United Feature Syndicate, Inc.

covered by the Age Discrimination in Employment Act (ADEA), which prohibits age discrimination in the workplace. It is projected that the number of lawsuits brought under ADEA will increase substantially in the years ahead due to the aging of the huge baby boomer population. As companies continue to downsize, plaintiffs' attorneys will market their services, and older employees will become more aware of their rights.

Another issue created by the aging workforce and downsizing is the increased incidence of midcareer **plateauing.** This describes workers who are stuck in the same job with few prospects for promotion. Plateauing can often result in feelings of stagnation, alienation, and boredom. To help stop this cycle, HR professionals and management will need to design alternative methods of career development and build more satisfaction and achievement into individual jobs.

HRM professionals and managers continue to face difficulties in recruiting qualified workers for entry-level jobs. As a result, employers need to expand their labor markets. McDonald's and Burger King now actively, and successfully, recruit senior citizens as counter personnel. The Marriott Corporation employs many mentally disabled persons for a variety of hard-to-fill positions. Companies are now recruiting in inner-city minority and immigrant neighborhoods and providing transportation to jobs in the suburbs. More part-time workers are being hired and a variety of enticements are being offered to attract workers. More flexible hours, college tuition, and referral pay are three examples of the enticements. Outsourcing jobs not at the core of the business has become a strong trend for both skilled and unskilled labor.

It is little wonder that many companies outsource jobs to employee leasing companies or temporary agencies, such as Kelly, Manpower, or Interim Services. After Office Depot struggled for years to hire and retain qualified counter associates, it contracted with Interim Services, which was responsible for providing the new associates and monitoring their behavior. Office Depot believes it is saving money using Interim to furnish some of its associates.

The aging of the workforce, the downsizing trends, and the increasing diversity of the workforce often create great difficulty for organizations attempting to cut costs while not violating labor laws. In many downsizing cases, for example, maintaining the diversity goals of the company could ultimately affect the status of older workers.

WHAT IS THE JOB SKILLS GAP AND HOW DOES IT AFFECT HRM?   David Kearns, former CEO of Xerox, calls it "the making of a national disaster." Brad Butler, former CEO of Procter & Gamble, fears the development of a "third world within our own country." James Burke, CEO of Johnson and Johnson, referred to it as "the American dream turned nightmare." These executives are referring to the growing problem of structural unemployment in the United States. Structural unemployment refers to the inability of the labor market to match workers with the available jobs. Projections call for increased demand for technological skills while scores on standardized tests in math and science are going down. Most entry-level positions require some computer skills and assembly-line work calls for a sophisticated understanding of mathematics.

More than 50 percent of jobs in the year 2000 will

require some college or technical training beyond high school. As the need for more highly trained people grows, the percentage of the potential working population that is adequately prepared for technological training is on the decrease. According to one report, by 2005, as many as 90 percent of all jobs in American organizations will be altered by some form of expert, technological system or some other form of artificial intelligence.[45] With advances in automation and information technology, there is likely to be a growing percentage of the population that reflects nearly an irreversible status of structural unemployment.

American business is more involved in education today in an attempt to reverse this ominous trend. Some companies have taken matters into their own hands. Polaroid, Hewlett-Packard, Motorola, and Unisys are among the many companies that provide in-house training in basic math, reading, and writing. The 1996 federal Welfare Reform Bill provides financial incentives for companies that employ former welfare recipients. Many of these individuals will require special training to prepare them for work. This will be the responsibility of HRM specialists.

The report card on college-educated workers is not particularly flattering either. The Department of Labor established a special commission to identify "foundation skills" for the 21st century American workforce. Communication skills were at the top of the list. Another report from a panel of business school deans and senior business executives concluded that too many business school graduates are ill-prepared to manage in this global economy. The report stressed the need to enhance communications skills and critical thinking with a more practical focus in business education.[46]

THE IMPORTANCE OF HRM MEASUREMENT IN RESPONDING TO ENVIRONMENTAL TRENDS

All these trends are having a profound effect on the way HR is conducted. The changing demographics and cultural diversity of the workforce, the increased number of lawsuits and regulations, and the growing demands on American workers to improve U.S. productivity and establish a competitive edge all create a situation that will challenge HRM professionals and line management into the 21st century. Through better coordination with organizational planning and strategy, human resources can be used to create and sustain an organization's advantage in an increasingly changing and competitive world. The most recent research indicates that anticipating and reacting favorably to these trends is facilitated by sound measurement techniques. As we stated earlier, Pfeffer's research identified measurement as one of the progressive HRM practices most related to corporate success,

including classic Wall Street measures of corporate performance.[47]

HR consultant Jac Fitz-enz summarized the importance of measurement for HRM: "HR employees gain respect when they begin to prove their value, manage HR like a business, and learn to use data to forecast outcomes. There is no better way to become a strategic business partner."[48] While Fitz-enz, Stanford's Pfeffer, and other experts emphasize the need for serious measurement, their discussion focuses on the role of measurement at the macro-level for assessing HRM interventions. We also believe that measurement and precision in measurement is critical for the effectiveness of particular HRM activities summarized in Figure 1.3. For example, research has established that more precision in the development of measurement criteria for employment interviews and precision in the measurement of managerial potential will ultimately increase the probability that more effective employees will be selected.[49] Precision in the measurement of employee and unit work performance has also been shown to increase the effectiveness of the performance management system.[50]

A recurring theme throughout this book is that human resource policies and practices can enhance productivity, product and service quality, and customer satisfaction and create and sustain a competitive advantage. We will focus on efforts that have most successfully met these goals. The most important measurement criteria for assessing HRM interventions are measures of individual or unit level performance, productivity, or product/service quality; measures of customer behavior, including satisfaction, employee absenteeism, turnover, or accidents, employee aberrant behavior such as theft, substance abuse, or violence; and employee attitudes toward work, coworkers, and management. Research has established that the results of HRM programs that are measured in terms of these criteria can be directly linked to substantial cost savings, financial performance, and increased productivity. Following are illustrations of recent HRM activities directed at these criteria.

Frito-Lay recently instituted a training program through its HRM division to cross-train workers for several jobs in an effort to reduce downtime from employee vacancies. The downtime could be operationally defined in terms of dollars, and the training program saved the company $250,000 in the first year. AMC Theaters developed a battery of applicant tests to identify individuals most likely to perform effectively and to stay with the company longer. The reduction in turnover saved the company $175,000 in the first year. Blockbuster Video tried an applicant test that purported to help reduce employee theft and developed a new performance management system for all employees. It estimated savings at $450,000. Owens-Corning Fiberglas trained all its managers in statistical quality analysis as a part of its total quality management program. Trainees were made accountable for improving the quality at Owens-Corning and the program worked. Reduction in rejected materials saved over $1 million. John Hancock Insurance installed a new managerial pay-for-performance system in order to increase regional sales and decrease employee turnover. J. Walter Thompson developed a new incentive system to promote creative advertising ideas from its consumer research and accounting units. RJR Nabisco replaced a fixed-rate commission with a new compensation system that linked ad agency compensation to the success of the advertising campaign. Concerned about the quality of one managerial level, Office Depot developed a managerial assessment center to select district managers. It then determined the extent to which the quality of management improved as a function of the new screening method. A major clothing retailer installed a "360 degree" performance appraisal system for its managers (i.e., formal appraisal by customers, employees, peers, and supervisors). It then evaluated the extent to which store and managerial performance improved because of the 360-degree appraisal system.

In the past, these types of HRM interventions were rarely linked to macro productivity or cost figures in order to show a reliable financial benefit. This inability to link HRM practices to the "big picture" might explain why personnel departments had so little clout. While marketing departments were reporting the bottom line impact of a new marketing strategy in terms of market share or sales volume, personnel could only show that absenteeism or turnover was reduced by some percentage, rarely assessing the relationship between these reductions and a specific financial benefit. As Peter Drucker once said, "The constant worry of all personnel administrators is their inability to prove that they are making a contribution to the enterprise."[51] Stanford professor Pfeffer summed it up: "In a world in which financial results are measured, a failure to measure human resource policy and practice implementation dooms this to second-class status, oversight neglect, and potential failure. The feedback from the measurements is essential to refine and further develop implementation ideas as well as to learn how well the practices are actually achieving their intended results."[52]

Human resource researchers have developed a number of useful statistical tools that can yield reliable dollar values for virtually all HRM activities. For example, a study of the effects of preemployment drug testing for the U.S. Postal Service showed not only a 59 percent higher rate of absenteeism for applicants who tested positive and a 47 percent higher rate of involuntary turnover, but also a cost-savings estimate in excess of $4 million each year if applicants were screened using the test. Another study showed a net return to a bank of more than $148,000 during five years as a function of a training program for only 65 supervisors.

Academic research has also established a reliable connection between many HRM programs and activities and more critical bottom-line figures. As we said at the beginning of this chapter, specific HRM activities have been shown to be directly linked to corporate performance indicators, such as return on investment and return on equity. One recent study found that a 34 percent increase in the use of *HPWS* factors was associated with a $42,000 *per employee* increase in market value.[53]

Developing clear criteria that define effectiveness is not only one of the biggest challenges facing HRM, but it is also one of the more difficult problems facing practicing managers. In general, and regardless of the job, the *most effective employees are those who provide the highest possible quantity and quality of a product or service at the lowest possible cost and in the most timely fashion, with a maximum of positive impact on co-workers, organizational units, and the client/customer population.* This statement of effectiveness also applies to all HR activities, products, and services. The effectiveness criteria are simply aggregated across workers. We will focus on these criteria throughout the book.

HRM professionals and practicing managers spend considerable time developing, administering, and maintaining employee and unit performance management systems that attempt to measure and improve these criteria of effectiveness. While the relative weights to be applied to these criteria should be directly linked to strategic business objectives (e.g., sales, customer satisfaction), they rarely are. Most organizations have difficulty even measuring overall performance in a reliable manner, and few systematically relate individual performance to performance of the unit or some other organizational level. For example, while numerous companies have adopted the 360-degree performance appraisal systems we described earlier, almost no companies have evaluated whether this complicated system accomplishes anything other than taking up time and paying consultants who market and administer the program.

The most effective organizations get down to specifics about all important criteria and these are directly linked to key objectives or desired outcomes for the organization. This prescription applies to HR like any other business function and applies to all HRM activities regardless of the size of the organization. Whether we're talking about a mom-and-pop corner store or IBM, the principle is the same: *Good practice requires good measurement.* Wayne Keegan, vice president of HR for toymaker ERTL in Dyresville, Iowa, clearly represented the bottom line for HR: "HR managers should strive to quantify all facets of HR to determine what works and what doesn't."[54] Dave Ulrich's 1997 book, *Human Resource Champions,* echoes this theme. Says Ulrich in looking at the challenges of technology and globalization, HR must add "measurable value" and the HR functions must "deliver business results." Such an orientation to HR in the context of the new competitive reality "will require new ways of thinking about HR practices, functions, and professionals."[55]

SUMMARY

Human resource management is to some extent concerned with any organizational decision that has an impact on the workforce or the potential workforce. The trends we described in Chapter 1 underscore the importance of HR to meet these challenges. We contend that progressive HRM methods can meet these challenges and create competitive advantage. We further contend that many of the HRM activities that have been identified as the most effective are not actually practiced. HRM professionals need to be aware of these progressive methods and qualified to assess the extent to which they would be (or are) effective for their particular circumstances.

While there is typically a human resource or personnel department in middle to large corporations, line management is still primarily responsible for applying HRM policies and practices. There are critical competencies for general management and HRM professionals. An organization needs both competent personnel trained in HRM and motivated managers who recognize the importance of HRM activities and apply optimal procedures. HR managers are more likely to convince line managers of the value of HR programs by focusing on measurement and effectiveness criteria that are clearly understood by management. Personnel/HR functions are often perceived by line managers to be out of step with the real bottom-line outcome measures for the organization.

The most effective human resource departments are those in which HRM policy and activities are established in congruence with the mission and objectives of the organization with a focus on creating, maintaining, and expanding the customer base. This perspective will ultimately drive corporate profits and maximization of profits. HRM should assist management in the difficult task of integrating and coordinating the interests of the various organizational constituencies with the ultimate criterion being to enhance the organization's competitive position by focusing on meeting or exceeding customer requirements and expanding the customer base. Research shows HRM can play a significant role in this endeavor, particularly when HRM activities are aligned with the strategic objectives of the firm.[56]

Our next chapter will explore the critical competencies required of general management and HRM professionals to create and sustain a competitive advantage. These competencies include knowing the business, being aware of current HR developments, managing the process of change, and integrating these roles. We will elaborate on this notion that HRM systems and activities must complement the objectives of the business.

DISCUSSION QUESTIONS

1. Describe the changing status of HRM. What factors have led to these changes?

2. How do productivity concerns influence organizational policies and procedures regarding HRM activities?

3. Describe the major HRM activities conducted in an organization. Provide an example of each from a company with which you are familiar.

4. How has the composition of the workforce changed in recent years? What impact should these changes have on HRM practices or activities? What future trends do you see that will influence HRM activities? Why is the growing cultural diversity of the workforce a management challenge?

5. Why is the support of line management critical to the effective functioning of HRM practices in an organization? Provide some suggestions to ensure that this support is maintained.

6. Why is measurement so important for effective HRM?

NOTES

1. Pfeffer, J. (1994). *Competitive advantage through people*. Boston: Harvard Business School Press, p. 6.

2. See note 1; see also, Martinez, M. N. (October 1996). Three strategies for successful business partners. *HR Magazine*, pp. 1–4; Burrows, D. M. (September 1996). Increase HR's contributions to profits. *HR Magazine*, pp. 103–110; Anderson, R. W. (1997). The future of human resources: Forging ahead or falling behind? *Human Resource Management, 36* (1), 17–22; Brown M. G. (1996). *Keeping score: Using the right metrics to drive world-class performance*. New York: Quality Resources.

3. Fitz-enz, J. (1995). *How to measure human resource management*. New York: McGraw-Hill; see also, Bernardin, H. J.; Buckley, M. R.; and Ferris, G. (May 1998). Discrepancies between academic research findings and human resource management practices. Paper presented at the annual meeting of the American Psychological Society. Washington, DC; Hope, T., and Hope, J. (1996). *Transforming the bottom line: Managing performance with the real numbers*. Boston: Harvard Business School.

4. Ulrich, D. (1997). *Human resource champions*. Boston: Harvard Business School Press; see also, Ulrich, D. (1997) HR of the future: Conclusions and observations. *Human Resource Management, 36* (1), 175–179; Ulrich, D. (1997). Judge me more by my future than by my past. *Human Resource Management, 36,* 5–8.

5. Drucker, P. (1996). *Managing in a time of great change*. New York: Truman Books; see also, Adams, S. (1996). *The Dilbert Principle*. New York: HarperCollins; Beer, M. (1997). The transformation of the human resource

function: resolving the tension between a traditional administrative and a new strategic role. *Human Resource Management, 36* (1), 49–56; Bowen, D. E., and Siehl, C. (1997). The future of human resource management: March and Simon (1958) revisited. *Human Resource Management, 36* (1), 57–64.

6. Naisbitt, J., and Aburdene, P. (1992). *Megatrends 2000.* New York: William Morrow, p. 47.

7. Gates, W. (1995). *The Road Ahead.* New York: Penguin Books, p. 251; Brockbank, W. (1997). HR's future on the way to a presence. *Human Resource Management, 36* (1), 65–70; Ehrlich, C. J. (1997). Human resource management: A changing script for a changing world. *Human Resource Management, 36* (1), 85–90.

8. Becker, B. E.; Huselid, M. A.; Pickus, P.S.; and Spratt, M. F. (1997). HR as a source of shareholder value: Research and recommendations. *Human Resource Management, 36,* (1) 39–48; Becker, B., and Gerhart, B. (1996). The impact of human resource management on organizational performance: Progress and prospects. *The Academy of Management Journal, 39,* 779–801; see also, Huselid, M. A. (1995). The impact of human resource management practices on turnover, productivity, and corporate financial performance. *Academy of Management Journal, 38,* 635–670; Waterman, R. H. (1994). *What America does right.* New York: W.W. Norton.

9. See note 8; see also, Becker, B. E., and Huselid, M. A. (1992). Direct estimates of SD, and the implications for utility analysis. *Journal of Applied Psychology, 77,* 227–233; Heskett, J. L., and Schlesinger, L. A. (1997). Leading the high-capability organization: challenges for the twenty-first century. *Human Resource Management, 36*(1), 105–114; Tziner, A., and Birati, A. (1996). Assessing employee turnover costs: A revised approach. *Human Resource Management Review, 6*(2), 113–122.

10. Bartel, A. P. (1994). Productivity gains from the implementation of employee training programs. *Industrial Relations, 33,* 411–425; Knoke, D., and Kalleberg, A. L. (1994). Job training in U.S. organizations. *American Sociological Review, 59,* 537–546.

11. Banker, R. D.; Lee, S.; and Potter, G. (1996). A field study of the impact of a performance-based incentive plan. *Journal of Accounting and Economics, 21*(2), 195–226; Gerhard, B., and Milkovich, G. T. (1992). Employee compensation: Research and practice. In M. D. Dunnette and L. M. Hough (eds.), *Handbook of industrial and organizational psychology* (vol. 3). Palo Alto, CA: Consulting Psychologists Press, pp. 481–569.

12. Ichniowski, C. (1986). The effects of grievance activity on productivity. *Industrial and Labor Relations Review, 40,* 75–89.

13. Alvares, K. M. (1997). The business of human resources. *Human Resource Management, 36*(1), 9–15.

14. Finney, M. I. (1988). Leading the way into HR's new age. *Personnel Administrator, 33,* 42–49; McKee, K. D. (1997). The human resource profession: Insurrection of resurrection? *Human Resource Management, 36*(1), 151–156; Pucik, V. (1997). Human resources in the future: An obstacle or a champion of globalization? *Human Resource Management, 36*(1), 163–168; and Rucci, A. J. (1997). Should HR survive: A profession at the crossroads. *Human Resource Management, 36*(1), 169–174.

15. Bernardin, H. J., and McKinney, N. (1998). A survey of HRM practices among small and medium sized companies: The widest discrepancy between research and practice. Unpublished manuscript, Florida Atlantic University, Boca Raton; see also, Christenson, R. (1997). Where is HR? *Human Resource Management, 36*(1), 81–84; Losey, M. R. (1997). The future HR professional: Competency buttressed by advocacy and ethics. *Human Resource Management, 36*(1), 147–150.

16. Huselid, M. (1995). The impact of human resource management practices on turnover, productivity, and corporate financial performance. *Academy of Management Journal, 38,* 635–672; see also, Neal, J. A., and Tromley, C. L. (1995). From incremental change to retrofit: Creating high performance work systems. *Academy of Management Executive, 9,* 42–54. See also, note 9.

17. Bianchi, A. (February 1996). The character-revealing handwriting analysis. *Inc. Magazine,* pp. 77–92.

18. Beyerstein, B. L., and Beyerstein, D. F. (1992). *The write stuff: Evaluations of graphology, the study of handwriting analysis.* Buffalo, NY: Prometheus; see also, Driver, R. W., Buckley, M. R., Frink, D. (1996). Should we write off graphology? *International Journal of Selection and Assessment, 4,* 78–86.

19. See note 15.

20. Professor Fred Schuster of Florida Atlantic University was one of the first to document this relationship. Read Schuster, F. (1986). *The Schuster Report: The proven connection between people and profits.* New York: Wiley; see also notes 8 and 9.

21. Lawler III, E. E., and Mohrman, S. A. (1997). Transforming the human resource function. *Human Resource Management, 36*(1), 157–162; Lawler, E. E. (1988). HRM: Meeting the new challenges. *Personnel,* August, p. 24.

22. See note 21.

23. See note 8; Becker, Huselid, Pickus, and Spratt (1997), p. 41.

24. Beer, M.; Spector, B.; Lawrence, P. R.; Mills, D. Q.; and Walton, R. E. (1985). *Human resource management.* New York: The Free Press: p. 24; Ellig, B. R. (1997). Is the human resource neglecting the employees? *Human Resource Management, 36*(1), 91–96; Kochan, T. A. (1997). Rebalancing the role of human resources. *Human Resource Management, 36*(1), 121–128; Lobel, S. A. (1997). In praise of the "soft" stuff: A vision for human resource leadership. *Human Resource Management, 36*(1), 135–140.

25. American Productivity and Quality Center (1990). *Putting strategy to work: Tools for cost and quality management.* Palo Alto, CA: Electric Power Research Institute.

26. Harrison, J. S., and St. John, C. H. (1996). Downsizing the firm: Answering the strategic questions. *Academy of Management Executive, 10,* 46–60; see also, Cascio, W.

F. (1993). Downsizing: What do we know? What have we learned. *Academy of Management Executive, 7,* 95–104.

27. See note 4, p. viii; see also, Johnson, J. W. (1996). Linking employee perceptions of service climate to customer satisfaction. *Personnel Psychology, 49*(4), 831–842; Paradise-Tornow, C. (1991). Management effectiveness, service quality, and organizational performance in banks. *Human Resource Planning, 14,* 129–140.

28. Detouzos, M. L., Lester, R. K., and Solow, R. M. (1989). *Made in America: Regaining the competitive edge.* Cambridge, MA: The MIT Press, p. 166.

29. Author (Oct. 9, 1995). Riding high: Corporate America has an edge over its global rivals. *Business Week,* 13; see also, Farell, C. (Oct. 9, 1995). Why the productivity tide will lift all boats. *Business Week,* pp. 136, 137; Madrick, J. (Jan. 16, 1996). Post-1973, the era of slow growths. *New York Times,* p. A15; Tornow, W., and Wiley, J. (1991). Service quality and management practices: A look at employee attitudes, customer satisfaction, and bottom-line consequences. *Human Resource Planning, 14,* 105–116.

30. Uchitelle, L. (May 12, 1996). We're leaner, meaner and going nowhere faster. *New York Times,* Sec. 4, pp. 1,4; see also, Nasar, S. (Oct. 10, 1992). U.S. rate of output called best. *New York Times,* pp. C1, C16; see also Kupfer, A. (1992). How American industry stacks up. *Fortune,* May, p. 30.

31. Towers Perrin (1992). Priorities for competitive advantage: An IBM study conducted by Towers Perrin.

32. Hall, G., and Allen, G. (1997). *The Internet guide for human resources.* Cincinnati, OH: South-Western.

33. Stewart, T. A. (Jan. 15, 1996). Taking on the last bureaucracy. *Fortune,* pp. 105–108.

34. Uchitelle, L. (June 18, 1996). Layoffs are out; hiring is back. *New York Times,* pp. C1, C6.

35. See note 7, p. 25.

36. Hallett, J. J. (1987). *Worklife visions.* Alexandria, VA: American Society for Personnel Administration, pp. 45–46.

37. See note 27.

38. Ferguson, T. W. (Nov. 4, 1996). Boss harassment. *Forbes,* pp. 150, 151.

39. Edmondson, B. (1996). Work slowdown. *American Demographics,* March, 5–7; Goddard, R. W. (1989). Workforce 2000, *Personnel Journal,* October, 65–71. See also, Jamieson, D., and O'Mara, J. (1991). *Managing Workforce 2000: Gaining the diversity advantage.* San Francisco, CA: Jossey-Bass.

40. Immigration and Naturalization Service (1995). *Annual Report.*

41. Milliken, F., and Martins, L. L. (1996). Searching for common threads: Understanding the multiple effects of diversity in organizational groups. *Academy of Management Review, 21,* 402–433; Kerr, S., and Von Glinow, M.

A. (1997). The future of HR: Plus ca change, plus c'est la meme chose. *Human Resource Management, 36*(1), 115–120.

42. Andrews, E. L. (1996). Don't go away mad, just go away: AT&T's gentle but firm effort to cut 40,000 jobs. *New York Times,* pp. C1, C4.

43. Gordon, D. M. (1996). *Fat and mean: The corporate squeeze of working Americans and the myth of managerial "downsizing."* New York: Martin Kessler Books/The Free Press.

44. Burke, W. W. (1997). What human resource practitioners need to know for the twenty-first century. *Human Resource Management, 36*(1), 71–80.

45. Fiske, C. (Sept. 25, 1989). Impending U.S. jobs disaster: Work force unqualified to work. *New York Times,* p. 1. See also, Kantrowitz, B., and Wingert, P. (Sept. 25, 1992). An "F" in world competition. *Newsweek,* p. 57.

46. Secretary's Commission on Achieving Necessary Skills (SCANS) (1992). *Skills and Tasks for Jobs.* Washington, DC: US Government Printing Office; Fuchsberg, G. (June 6, 1990). Business schools get bad grades. *Wall Street Journal,* pp. B1, B2.

47. See notes 1 and 2.

48. Sheley, E. (June 1996). Share your worth: Talking numbers with the CEO. *HR Magazine,* pp. 86–95; Fitz-enz, J. (1997). The truth about best practices: What they are and how to apply them. *Human Resource Management, 36*(1), 97–104.

49. Latham, G. and Sue-Chan, C. (1997). Meta-analysis of the situational interview. Paper presented at the annual meeting of the Society of Industrial and Organizational Psychologists. St. Louis, MO, April. See also, Maurer, S. D. (1997). Situational interview accuracy in a multiple rating context. *Academy of Management Best Paper Proceedings,* August, 149–153.

50. Bernardin, H. J.; Hagan, C.; Kane, J.; and Villanova, P. (1998). Effective performance management: Precision in measurement with a focus on customers and situational constraints. In J. Smither (ed.), *Performance appraisal: State-of-the-art in practice.* San-Francisco: Jossey-Bass.

51. See note 5 (Drucker, p. 158).

52. See note 2, p. 57.

53. Huselid, M. A. and Becker, B. E. (1997). The impact of high performance work systems, implementation effectiveness, and alignment with strategy on shareholder wealth. *Academy of Management Best Paper Proceedings,* August, 144–148.

54. See note 48.

55. See note 4, Ulrich (1997), p. 2.

56. See note 53; see also, *Futures Study: HR's survival depends on developing competencies to manage future issues* (June 1996). Washington, DC: SHRM/CCM; Alvares, K. M. (1997). The business of human resources. *Human Resource Management, 36*(1), 9–16.

C H A P T E R

COMPETITIVE ADVANTAGE THROUGH HUMAN RESOURCES*

OVERVIEW

As we noted in Chapter 1, because organizations face increasing competition and more critical scrutiny from investors, managers have been confronted with greater challenges in securing organizational survival and competitive advantage. Today's managers face a conflicting set of demands—they are expected to minimize costs while increasing quality and fostering innovation and creativity. Consequently, they have sought strategies and practices to meet outside pressures. Mergers and acquisitions, strategic alliances, downsizing, reengineering, outsourcing, and restructuring have been common responses to the new challenges facing organizations. Companies can choose from an array of alternatives in trying to achieve improved performance, including such options as pyramid flattening, empowerment, total quality management, continuous improvement, paradigm

shifting, searching for "white space opportunities," and becoming "learning organizations." In the 1990s, the importance of developing an organizational strategy, or a vision of the organization's long-term direction, became a major focus of top management.

The most effective approach to strategic planning involves people from all levels of the organization, as well as key suppliers and customers, in a process oriented toward transforming the organization and changing the rules of its industry to its own advantage. The effective use of human resources should be an integral part of organizational strategy.[1] A company that seeks to achieve competitive advantage must align its human resource management processes with its business strategies. This is one of the most critical tasks facing management today.

This chapter will discuss how the effective utilization of human resources can assist organizations in achieving competitive advantage through the development and implementation of organizational strategy. We will describe several organizations that have pursued competitive advantage by using their human resources to

---

*Contributed by Dave Ulrich.

leverage potential sources of strength. We will also identify the skills needed by managers and human resource professionals to help organizations to become more competitive through the eight human resource policy domains introduced in Chapter 1.

OBJECTIVES

After studying this chapter, you should be able to:

1. Understand what is meant by competitive advantage, and why it is important for organizations to maintain.
2. Understand the two major principles of competitive advantage: Customer value and uniqueness.
3. Describe how human resource activities may provide businesses with a competitive advantage.
3. Identify the competencies that general managers and HRM professionals need to assist organizations in becoming competitive.

Personnel Assessment Systems, Inc., (PAS) was a highly successful, privately held psychological screening company doing business all over the United States. Its core business was psychological assessment of job applicants and other personnel using scientifically valid, copyrighted paper and pencil tests to assist companies in personnel decisions. PAS's business has grown by 15 percent per year over 10 years and profits have been steady although not spectacular (averaging 6.3 percent). To increase profits, the company decided to develop and copyright its own tests which would then be used for screening. PAS executives also believed it was time to expand into the growing international market, assisting multinational companies in personnel selection matters, including expatriate placement. The company conducted the appropriate research to justify the use of its own test. PAS also believed that one test might have mass-market appeal to the huge "self-help" segment. It began exploring the idea of marketing the test to the general public either through the Internet or some other source such as an automated 800 or 900 telephone number. The organization was at a crossroads since the core business was holding steady with reliable and satisfied customers and there were no major threats to the business except for the inevitable increase in testing using the Internet. Serious revenue growth appeared to be on the international front and in the mass-marketing of its test.

Borg-Warner was a successful, diversified company with four major core products: automotive parts, chemicals, protective services, and credit reporting. These products had been brought together to balance diverse business cycles; when one industry was flat, the other industries would be peaking. In early 1987, Borg-Warner

executives faced a serious challenge. The stock of the company was selling for approximately $35 per share. Analysts believed the "breakup" value of Borg-Warner was closer to $55 per share. The breakup value indicates the sum of how much each of the four businesses could be independently sold for to separate buyers. This gap between actual and breakup value meant Borg-Warner was not effectively utilizing its assets. A number of major investors and takeover artists began to buy Borg-Warner stock.

To avoid being taken over and broken up by investors, Borg-Warner managers decided to work with Merrill Lynch to buy back stock through a leveraged buyout (LBO). With Merrill Lynch support, Borg-Warner borrowed approximately $4 billion and purchased all of its stock, making it a private firm, not traded on Wall Street. Unfortunately, by borrowing $4 billion, the organization now incurred an enormous debt payment (approximately $400 million per year) that exceeded annual profits of about $240 million. This meant managers had to find ways to earn an additional $160 million in profits in 1988 and in each subsequent year just to break even. One short-term solution was to sell some of the businesses. In 1988, Borg-Warner sold the credit reporting business to TRW and the chemicals business to General Electric. The remaining protective service and automotive businesses still had to earn enormous cash to cover the debt.

The executives of Borg-Warner concluded that the key to their success was to change the mind-set of the managers. That is, they wanted to change the way managers thought about their role in the organization. If managers could begin to think as if they were owners, they might begin making decisions to emphasize efficiency. To help managers think like owners, the company asked managers throughout the organization to invest in the new company. Managers were required to invest from $50,000 to $1 million in Borg-Warner. Many managers tapped into their personal savings or pension plans to make this investment. In addition, all managers in the company were offered training to help them understand the implications of the LBO. With such personal investment and because of training efforts, Borg-Warner managers began to change their mind-set, and the company was able to generate enough profit to make payments on its debt.[2] In competitive environments such as the one that firms such as Borg-Warner face, managers are rightfully concerned about how they can continue to be successful.[3] One major agenda for most firms facing technological, social, and competitive change is to create a sustainable competitive advantage.[4]

WHAT IS COMPETITIVE ADVANTAGE?

Competitive advantage refers to the ability of an organization to formulate strategies that place it at a favorable position relative to other companies in the industry.[5] Companies achieve competitive advantage through effectively leveraging their capabilities. A firm's capabilities include all of its physical and financial assets as well as all capabilities, competencies, organizational processes, firm attributes, information, knowledge, and so forth that are controlled by the firm and that enable the firm to both design and implement its competitive strategy. One highly regarded **core competency** model by Hamel and Prahalad calls for reconceptualizing the organization into a portfolio of underlying functions, or core competencies.[6] Core competencies are essentially what the organization does, or could do, best.

Two major principles—perceived customer value and uniqueness—describe the extent to which an organization has a competitive advantage. We examine these principles next.

Competitive Advantage Principle 1: Customer Value

These unique capabilities or core competencies can help build competitive advantage by improving the value that customers receive—or perceive that they receive—from the company's goods and services. When a company fails to take advantage of its unique capabilities, the results can be disastrous. IBM virtually owned the computer industry from its inception through the 1970s. By failing to identify and perceive the importance of the emerging personal computer market, IBM lost as much as $90 billion in market capitalization and was forced to undertake drastic repositioning and organizational restructuring actions. An emphasis on customer value as the framework for sustained competitive advantage has a great deal to do with the human resources of an organization. Understanding customer value and building HRM programs with a customer orientation in the context of core competencies may be the underlying glue of the HRM function.

Competitive advantage occurs if customers perceive that they receive more value from their transaction with an organization than from its competitors. Price has a lot to do with value. Burger King launched a 99 cent special for its Whopper in 1996 based on focus group studies involving comparisons to Wendy's and McDonald's Big Mac. The focus group research showed that 99 cents was magical in its ability to clearly distinguish the Whopper in customer value relative to its major competitors and a decision to even purchase fast food.

Procter & Gamble made a strategic decision in 1992 to compete on the basis of low prices, even for its premium brands. Customer research had indicated price was becoming relatively more important in the buying decision. That data drove a strategic decision to cut costs throughout the organization. The result was an increase in profit margins of more than 5 percent despite reducing prices on several major brands.

But customer value is far more complicated than a simple assessment of product quality relative to price. One *Harvard Business Review* article asks how Dell Computer was able to overcome IBM and Compaq; how Home Depot came from nowhere to capture market share; and how upstart Nike overwhelmed Adidas and other competitors.[7] The authors argue that these companies redefined value for customers in their markets and then built cohesive systems that could deliver more value. By doing this, these companies raised customers' expectations and actually changed what customers valued. The concept of *value* includes price and quality but also convenience of purchase, after-sale service, and dependability.

The authors maintain that the Home Depots and Nikes have succeeded because they have narrowed their focus on defining value according to one of three value disciplines: operational excellence, customer intimacy, or product leadership. Operational excellence means providing customers with reliable products or services at competitive prices (such as Dell). Customer intimacy means segmenting and targeting markets precisely (Home Depot). Product leadership means offering leading-edge products or services (Nike products).

Strategy should be directed at configuring the organization's resources based on a thorough understanding of its customers' and potential customers' priorities and expectations. Ensuring that customers receive value from transacting with a business requires that all employees be focused on understanding customer needs and expectations. This can occur if customer data are used in the designing of products or service processes and customer value is used as the major criterion of interest. Many companies (e.g., Met Life, Weyerhaeuser, 3M, Chevron, Xerox) have now pushed a customer and marketing orientation deep into the organization with HRM systems based on models of internal customers and suppliers and how they relate to external customers.[8] Performance management and reward systems are designed with this marketing orientation.

DOES CORPORATE IMAGE AFFECT CUSTOMER VALUE? The notion of customer value is more complicated than it may seem to the uninitiated. For example, many customers seek out products and services to some extent as a function of the reputation of the organization selling the product or service in matters not directly related to the cost or quality of the particular product or service. One reason companies (and politicians) wrap themselves around the Olympics every four years is because they believe the basic sense of American pride and excellence that goes with the Olympics tends to rub off onto the company. Marketing research shows that perception of product quality is positively affected by affiliation with the Olympics. Thus, the theory is that customer value is affected by this connection.

Likewise, the reputation of companies' environmental policies as well as the use of child labor or pitiful labor conditions in international facilities affects the decision making of some consumers. For example, when Kathie Lee Gifford was accused of exploiting child labor in Honduran clothing plants, some consumers avoided her line of clothing. Nike was accused by the chairman of the Made in the USA Foundation of using child labor in Indonesia to make its athletic shoes. Nike's business was affected to the extent that consumers consider these allegations when they buy sneakers. Jesse Jackson launched a boycott against Mitsubishi in 1996 to "encourage" the company to put more women and minorities in executive positions. Many people still avoid Texaco stations because of the extensive reporting on an audiotape in which Texaco executives made highly offensive and racist remarks.

Many consumers use "Newman's Own" products (as in Paul Newman) not only because they like the products but also because all profits are donated to "educational and charitable purposes." Sure Newman's Sockarooni spaghetti sauce is tasty, but does the taste account for all of the customer value when the sauce typically costs almost twice as much as other sauces? Ben and Jerry's, the Body Shop, and Stonyfield Farm are among the growing number of companies that also enjoy socially responsible reputations.

Customer value can be complicated. Jessie Jackson and Burger King were aware of this when Burger King agreed to special financing and support for minority-owned franchises. Burger King considered the positive and negative public relations that would result from its discussions with Mr. Jackson. Knowledge regarding Burger King's policy toward minorities could affect some consumers' fast food decision. Many out-of-court settlements in EEO matters are mainly driven by fear of the anticipated negative publicity relating to the lawsuit and the effect of this publicity on customer behavior. For example, Texaco not only lost some customers, but it also took some stock price hits and encountered recruiting difficulties.

An organization's reputation regarding issues such as corporate ethics or social responsibility, pro-family policies, or affirmative action/diversity practices can go into a "customer value" assessment at least for some customers. Such issues not only affect customer behavior but also, perhaps just as important, the ability of an organization to recruit and retain valuable employees. For years, Dow Chemical in Midland, Michigan, had a negative reputation on college campuses because of napalm, a chemical agent it produced that was used in the Vietnam War. Dow had a terrible time recruiting chemists and other vital professionals because of this one product. Dow launched a public relations campaign to enhance its reputation. It focused advertising on the many agricultural products it produced and marketed. The result was a profound improvement in Dow's ability to recruit on college campuses. Obviously, Dow's ability to recruit and retain the best chemists was vital to its competitiveness.

One hot issue related to the complicated equation that is "customer value" is the way in which a company treats its employees. AT&T, for example, took a terrible public relations beating in 1996 when it announced that 40,000 employees would be terminated while almost simultaneously divulging that it was paying CEO Robert Allen in excess of $7 million for one year of work. Former Secretary of Labor and Harvard professor Robert Reich gave a speech asking two loaded questions: "(1) Do companies have obligations beyond the bottom-line? and (2) Do they owe anything to their workers, their workers' families, and their communities?" In a not-so-veiled reference to AT&T, he asked these questions at a time when "one of the largest and most profitable companies in the U.S. will permanently lay off tens of thousands of employees."[9] The way in which consumers answer these questions could affect customer value. AT&T competitors seem to be aware of this. MCI responded with an ad about how it treats employees. After "60 Minutes" ran a piece on CEO pay that focused on Mr. Allen's compensation package and AT&T's poor stock performance, many people switched their long-distance telephone service to an AT&T competitor. AT&T lost 28 percent of its stock value in 1996.

Professor Reich and others argue that corporate social responsibility makes good economic sense and clearly affects employees, recruiting, and retention. Says Reich, "The debate that sounds as if it's about maximizing shareholder returns versus being socially responsible usually comes down to whether a top manager is paying attention only to very short-term performance or is taking a longer-term view."[10]

There is no question that corporate image has an impact on organizations' ability to attract and retain qualified workers. This is one reason companies compete so vigorously to make the various socially desirable lists that appear on the covers of popular magazines. "Whether motivated by altruism, profit, public opinion, or some combination thereof, even General Motors is among hundreds of corporations that participate in organizations like Business for Social Responsibility, the Coalition for Environmentally Responsible Economies, and the Council on Economic Priorities, which bestows 'corporate conscience' awards to deserving companies at its annual ceremony."[11]

Companies that rank high on lists for diversity programs or pro-family policies receive almost immediate reinforcement for this designation in the form of more and better applicants for their positions. To a lesser extent, customers are also more favorably disposed toward these corporate winners. The fast food industry, for example, is well aware of the connection between diversity image and the ability to both recruit minorities to sell the burgers and fries and also to buy them (the proportion of Burger King, Wendy's, and KFC customers who are minorities is higher than in the population as a whole).

Some politicians recommend legislation to make corporations more accountable for the social implications of their actions. Activist consumers, by calling attention to possible corporate greed, may foster more social responsibility by simply affecting the complicated variable of the "customer value" equation. Other commentators on this subject believe corporations should keep things as simple as possible. Chainsaw Al Dunlap, for example, who acquired his nickname because of his tactic of slashing the workforce of companies he takes over, doesn't believe in any corporate charity. This is the business of the individual, *not* the corporation, according to Dunlap. Dunlap's position is that if he or anyone else wants to give money to a charity, that's that person's business. As CEO, he does not have the right to spend the shareholder's money in the name of "corporate social responsibility." This is an old argument most clearly articulated by Nobel Prize winner Milton Friedman who argued that the "social responsibility of business is to increase its profits."[12] But Friedman's essay was careful to qualify his position by conceding that what is considered to be corporate social responsibility may be simply rational corporate behavior that can ultimately affect consumer behavior and corporate profits (see the Critical Thinking Exercise).

While consumers undoubtedly place greater weight on the quality of the particular product or service they are considering relative to its cost, there is no question that "customer value" can include tangential variables such as corporate responsibility, environmental impacts, diversity policies, political issues, and affiliations with other products or services. Thus, a company's business strategy must include consideration of these important environmental factors.

CRITICAL THINKING EXERCISE 2.1

What Is the Value of Corporate Social Responsibility?

In his 1996 book *Mean Business*, Sunbeam CEO Al Dunlap echoes the neoclassic theory of Nobel Laureate Milton Friedman regarding CEO obligations.[1] Says Friedman, management's job is "to make as much money as possible while conforming to the basic rules of society, both those embodied in the law and those embodied in ethical customs."[2] Like Friedman, Dunlap only sees corporate social responsibility in the context of returns to stockholders. Dunlap argues that the CEO's focus should always be on maximizing return for the company's stockholders. Corporate social responsibility only becomes important when the issue has an impact on the purchase behavior of the consumer and thus the potential profitability of the company.

This neoclassic view can be contrasted with the "stakeholder model" which stipulates that the CEO should consider all major stakeholders in making decisions.[3] With this model, employees, suppliers, customers and, of course, stockholders are all important and any stakeholder may be given priority at some point. Thus, corporations can make contributions to charities or community projects regardless of the impact of this behavior on the "bottom line." This model does, however, assume that corporate social responsibility may be important to some consumers.[4] Thus, companies should pursue such socially responsible behaviors because they in turn may affect consumer behavior.

Mr. Dunlap would argue that "corporate citizenship" must be linked to bottom-line corporate performance indicators. Management decisions to spend company money on corporate social responsibility can only be justified with this connection and maximizing return to stockholders should always be paramount. Dunlap closed or sold inefficient plants and operations for Sunbeam when he took over. He gave little consideration to the impact of his decisions on the employee or community stakeholders. He states that he was brought in to make the company profitable (and he succeeded).

Assignment

As a consumer, to what extent do you take a company's social responsibility into consideration when buying a product or service? As a CEO, how would you handle the barrage of solicitors who seek charitable contributions from your company? To what extent would you consider corporate social responsibility when applying for jobs? To what extent would you consider a company's corporate social responsibility when buying stock? As a stockholder, would you approve of socially responsible behavior which could not be linked to the bottom line in some way? Identify at least one company which you regard as socially responsible and explain how this image has affected your consumer behavior.

[1] Dunlap, Al. (1996). *Mean Business*. Boston: Random House.

[2] Friedman, M. (1970)

[3] Clarkson, M.B.E. (1995). A stakeholder framework for analyzing and evaluating corporate social performance. *Academy of Management Review, 20*, 92–117.

[4] Owen, C. L., and Scherer, R. F. (1993). Social responsibility and market share. *Review of Business, 15*, 11–16; see also, Smith, S. M., and Alcorn, D. S. (1991). Cause marketing: A new direction in the marketing of corporate responsibility. *Journal of Consumer Marketing, 8*, 19–35.

Competitive Advantage Principle 2: Maintaining Uniqueness

The second principle of competitive advantage derives from offering a product or service that your competitor cannot easily imitate or copy. For example, if you open a restaurant and serve hamburgers, and a competitor moves in next to you and also serves hamburgers that taste, cost, and are prepared just like yours, unless you quickly offer something unique in your restaurant, you may lose a large part of your business to your competitor. Your restaurant needs to have something that is unique to continue to attract customers. Competitive advantage comes to a business when it adds value to customers through some form of uniqueness.

SOURCES OF UNIQUENESS. A key to any business's sustained competitive advantage is to ensure that its uniqueness lasts. Three traditional types of resources exist to offer customers uniqueness. These three resources are **financial capital, physical capital,** and **human capital.** In addition to these three resources, businesses may offer customers uniqueness through a nontraditional capability, namely, **organizational capability.** The four mechanisms for offering uniqueness are described below.

First, a business needs **financial,** or **economic, capital.** This uniqueness comes when a business receives special access to financial funding or is able to produce a good or service cheaper than someone else. If, in your hamburger restaurant, you have received a financial gift from family or friends to build the restaurant, without repayment of the gift, you may be able to charge less for your product than a competitor who borrowed money from a bank or financial institution. Your cheaper hamburgers would then become a source of uniqueness that customers value. Large organizations are frequently at an advantage over smaller competitors in terms of their access to financial capital. For example, Microsoft has benefited from the financial capital it has acquired through its sales of operating and software products. Microsoft's available financial capital has allowed it to launch an aggressive strategy for its Internet browsing software, including spending millions of dollars on free subscriptions. PAS, the small, psychological testing company, had considerable financial capability to explore and perhaps expand its business into other areas.

The second source of uniqueness rests in the organization's **physical capital.** This includes all the company's plants and equipment as well as its ability to purchase necessary supplies. Specific examples of physical capital that could be used to create competitive advantage include specialized computer hardware and software, robotic manufacturing systems, and control of prime geographic locations. Physical capital helps create competitive advantage by allowing the company to de-

velop a unique technological or operational capability. That is, a business can have a distinctive way of building or delivering its product or service. In the hamburger restaurant, the different types of cooking used to prepare the hamburgers may distinguish restaurants from each other (broiled versus flame-grilled). Customers may prefer one technological (cooking) process over another, and thus continue to patronize one restaurant. For PAS, its physical capital advantage was a scientifically sound, copyrighted test that could predict success and job satisfaction in numerous occupations and that could also predict satisfaction in romantic relationships.

In more complex businesses, technological capability may include research and development, engineering, patents, computer systems, and manufacturing facilities. Microsoft has thrived in this area by getting consumers to purchase and get comfortable with one of its products so they are then more attracted to future products related to their technological capability. Microsoft practically gave away its Windows 95 software so it could sell the more profitable products that worked off of it.

Retailers are scrambling for a technological edge on the Internet. Spiegel, the giant catalogue company, anticipates a loss in revenue from its high overhead catalogue business in favor of buying on the 'Net. It has a temporary technological competitive advantage because of the ease in which a consumer can now purchase something off Spiegel's Web site relative to other retail competitors (http:/www.spiegel.com). Bookstores such as Borders, Walden, and Barnes and Noble are also trying to differentiate themselves from book retailers such as Amazon.com that only sell books off their Web sites on the Internet. Overhead is a problem when Borders tries to compete with "virtual bookstores" such as Amazon.com, which claims to be "earth's biggest bookstore" while having no retail square footage. A "virtual bookstore" enables the consumer to sit at home and not only peruse the books available on a given topic but also read the first few pages of a book before deciding whether to buy. Amazon.com, for example, has served over a half million customers in 100 countries. Borders has a problem to the extent that the consumer favors this approach to buying books and it has not developed the technology to compete. PAS was moving toward an Internet option for its core business and thought the Internet could also be used as an option for its potential mass-market product and entry into international personnel decisions.

The third source of uniqueness that an organization can use to achieve competitive advantage is its **human capital.** Human capital refers to the skill and abilities of the individual members of the organization, including their training, expertise, experience, creativity, and relationships. Many examples exist of organizations that have succeeded because of the skills and abilities of their human assets. The importance of Bill Gates's entrepreneurial and technical skills cannot be understated in assessing Microsoft's success. Microsoft's reputation also fosters an almost overwhelming pool of potential contributing engineers and programmers for the Microsoft cause. Ben & Jerry's Homemade Ice Cream carved out a highly profitable niche among many large competitors because of Ben Cohen's unique leadership style and vision. The importance of individual skills and abilities is not limited to those at the very top of the organization. W.L. Gore and Associates, inventor and manufacturer of Gore-Tex fabric and apparel, has achieved success because of the individual contributions of "entrepreneurs" at every level in the organization. Employees at W.L. Gore and Associates choose their own work assignments and receive regular performance feedback and coaching from "sponsors" who replace the traditional organizational hierarchy.

PAS had expertise in the area of psychological testing and a highly regarded president who had maintained close working relationships with all 55 major clients who used the company's services for screening applicants or promoting personnel to managerial positions.

A fourth but related source of uniqueness helping a company gain competitive advantage may be derived from **organizational capability.** While human capital refers to the skills and abilities of individual members of the company, organizational capability refers to the synergies that they create collectively. Organizational capability represents the business's ability to manage organizational systems and people in order to match customer and strategic needs.[13] Organizational capability helps a company achieve competitive advantage because the manner in which it contributes value to the organization's products or services is rare, hard to substitute for, and difficult to imitate.[14] A competitor cannot reverse-engineer organizational capability and create a copy of it as it can an end product because organizational capability is so closely matched to the unique characteristics of the company. Human capital and organizational capacity have a great deal to do with the organization's "core competencies"—what the organization does best and how it differentiates itself from the competition.[15] Dave Ulrich, University of Michigan professor, and editor of the *Human Resource Management Journal,* believes organizational capability is the key to competitive advantage today. In his book *Human Resource Champions,* Ulrich states, "The increased pace of change required by technology, globalization, profitable growth, and customer demands places workforce competence and organizational capabilities at center stage."[16]

PAS's core competence was efficient, customer-friendly psychological testing with a proven track record for assisting companies in personnel decisions. Technology, through the Internet, and globalization, through the hiring and placement of personnel in overseas assignments, were viewed as major challenges for the future.

In a complex, dynamic, uncertain, and turbulent en-vironment (e.g., changing customers, technology, suppliers, relevant laws and regulations), organizational capability derives from the organization's flexibility, adaptiveness, and responsiveness. In less dynamic environments, organizational capability derives from maintaining continuity and stability of organization practices. In a restaurant, organizational capability may be derived from having employees who ensure that when customers enter the restaurant, their customer requirements are better met than when the customers go to a competitor's restaurant. That is, employees will want to ensure that customers are served promptly and pleasantly and that the food is well prepared.

PAS had stability in its core business with the only apparent threat being the growth of the Internet as a testing option. The business expansions it was considering were complex and uncertain but had great potential based on a cursory study of the mass market for such testing and the increase in the globalization of its reliable domestic customers. While organizational capability had a great deal to do with PAS's success to date, the extent to which this capability would help them expand their business was a key question.

HOW DOES STRATEGY EVOLVE FROM UNIQUENESS? The creation of strategy requires an alignment between the organization's environment and its unique capabilities. HRM is critical for exploiting these capabilities, some of which may interact. For example, Microsoft is awash in cash (financial capital) and technological advantages that enable the organization to attract even more talent (human capital) for the 21st century. To create this alignment, human resource managers need to understand the company's strategy, identify the necessary skills and capabilities required to implement this strategy, and create the needed human resource systems. These systems help determine how people are hired, trained, evaluated, motivated, treated, and integrated into the organization.[17] Many experts maintain that organizational capability may be the most important source of sustained competitive advantage. An organization's ability to sustain competitive advantage depends on its ability to attract and retain those individuals with the skills needed to give the organization the edge. Attracting and retaining individuals with skills related to the core competencies of the organization are key HR activities directly relevant to organizational capability. Developing other HR systems to take full advantage of the potential competitive advantages are also critical to sustained advantage.

Stanford professor Jeffrey Pfeffer has identified organizational capability as the main reason the five companies with the highest returns from 1972 to 1992 prospered (Southwest Airlines, Wal-Mart, Tyson Foods, Circuit City, and Plenum Publishing). These organizations are in industries with no other reliable strategic advantage. Says Pfeffer, "What these five successful firms tend to have in common is that for their sustained advantage, they rely not on technology, patents, or strategic position, but how they manage their workforce."[18]

HRM practices represent the set of organizational activities that directly affect the human resources of an organization. As noted in Chapter 1, eight domains of HRM activities have been identified. Figure 2.1 lists some of the critical issues and activities that should be considered and choices that should be made in each of these domains. As these activities are adapted to conditions confronting organizations and evaluated in the con-

FIGURE 2.1
STRATEGIC ACTIVITIES WITHIN HRM DOMAINS

ORGANIZATIONAL DESIGN

- Human Resource Planning in the context of strategic *theories* for the organization.
- Extent the organization should formalize how work is to be accomplished through a set of standardized operating procedures, formal chains of command, extensive rules and regulations, and detailed job descriptions.
- Extent different organization units maintain their independence and responsiveness to their unique market niches while integrating their work with other organizational units through liaison teams, matrix organizations, etc.
- Design of jobs so that individuals within the organization work on tasks that are rewarding and self-reinforcing.
- Design of organization in context of strategy and sources of uniqueness.
- Processes used to shape the organizational structure (e.g., how decisions are made, how widely accountability is distributed, how clearly roles and responsibilities are defined).
- Extent the marketing orientation is employed within the organization.

STAFFING

- Compliance with EEO laws and regulations.
- Type of criteria to set for bringing in new employees (e.g., short-term versus long-term, full-time, part-time, contract/leased employees, job versus career focused, customer perspective).
- Processes for succession planning (e.g., formalized systems, involvement of senior managers, integration with strategic planning, link to developmental programs, emphasis on internal versus external candidates).
- Types of programs for terminated employees (e.g., during layoffs, downsizing, early retirements).

EMPLOYEE TRAINING AND ORGANIZATIONAL DEVELOPMENT

- Desired outcomes of development (e.g., conceptual understanding, competency-based, skill building, attitude change, team building, problem solving) with customer focus.
- Types of participants for developmental programs (e.g., new employees, first-line supervisors, middle-level managers, top executives, part of diversity, affirmative action programs).
- Nature of the content built into developmental programs, and how programs are integrated with the strategic direction of firms.
- Delivery of training programs (e.g., internal versus external faculty and facilities, using line managers).
- Evaluation of programs to assess changes in employee or organizational performance, effects on customers.
- Alternatives to development used to create organizational competencies (e.g., cross-functional career moves, special assignments).

PERFORMANCE MANAGEMENT

- Types of standards set for employees or units (e.g., behavioral versus outcome focused, short versus long term, explicit versus implicit, linked to individual versus strategic performance or plans).
- Types of performance review feedback sessions offered (e.g., frequency, nature of feedback, monitoring of feedback sessions, forms used, formal reporting systems in existence, managerial accountability).
- Role of customers and customer satisfaction data in development of criteria, outcome measures, deliverables.
- Processes used to ensure that feedback occurs continually (e.g., quarterly reviews).
- Performance management and legal environment.

REWARD SYSTEMS

- Types of financial incentives existing (e.g., short versus long term, base versus incentive pay, pay for performance versus pay for seniority).
- Extent reward systems are linked to strategic plans and encourage employees to work toward accomplishing business needs.
- Extent rewards are based on individual versus group or corporate performance.
- Structure of nonfinancial rewards (e.g., recognition programs, titles, informal status symbols).
- Linkage of reward systems to customer data and customer requirements.

PRODUCTIVITY IMPROVEMENT PROGRAMS (PIPS)

- TQM or other HRM activities.
- Specific PIPs and design issues.
- Assessments of outcomes/deliverables.
- Customer-based focus of PIPs.

EMPLOYEE/EMPLOYER RELATIONSHIPS

- Compliance with labor relations law.
- Efforts to prevent unionization.
- Alternative dispute resolution effects.
- Efforts to establish and maintain employee morale and job satisfaction.

HEALTH AND SAFETY ISSUES

- Compliance with health and safety (e.g., OSHA).
- Efforts to reduce stress levels among workers.
- Efforts to reduce illnesses and accidents in the workplace.

text of other potential sources of competitive advantage, businesses should gain and sustain competitive advantage. In fact, at companies such as the five cited by Pfeffer, research has shown that the use of High Performance Work Systems (HPWS) had a great deal to do with the firms' sustained financial successes.[19] Strategic success, however, requires adherence to a chronology of interventions with regard to HRM activities. For example, for organizations undergoing substantial change in strategy because of new or lost revenues or new technologies, organizational design activities are probably the first to be implemented. Whether an organization is considering downsizing or expansion, the activities within the *organizational design* domain are excellent initial steps.

At PAS, organizational capability was critical to create and coordinate the new line of business so as to not disrupt the core business. Work needed to be redesigned to take advantage of the technological advantage of the valid and copyrighted test and the working financial capital, but the organization lacked human capital to market the new product and experienced some difficulties entering the new business due to the increasing demands of the current customers. Expanding to a new and different customer base could prove difficult and could even jeopardize the solid base of the core business. HRM was a key to successfully carrying out the strategy.

HUMAN RESOURCE MANAGEMENT AS A COMPETITIVE ADVANTAGE

The previous discussion provides a basis for thinking about human resources as a competitive advantage. Below, we review three specific ways that human resource management activities can build organizational capability and sustain a business's competitive advantage. These three are: implementing a strategy, dealing with change, and building strategic unity.[20]

Human Resource Management and Strategy Implementation: Analysis of Strengths, Weaknesses, Opportunities, and Threats (SWOT Analysis)*

Pratt & Whitney, a jet engine division of United Technologies, faced a major threat as the 21st century approached. Its marketing projections for the year 2000 anticipated lower demand due primarily to decreases in defense spending and increased competition from General Electric and Rolls-Royce. Pratt also had identified a serious weakness in its organization—administrative or overhead expenses had increased faster in the last five years than had other areas of operations. Pratt realized it

had to make significant changes in its internal organization to respond to the threats presented by a more competitive environment.

Pratt developed a strategy based on an understanding of these external threats and internal weaknesses. A reduction in administrative costs was considered to be strategically vital to make the company more competitive and to prepare it for the 21st century. Based on a study of major competitors, P&W concluded that a 30 percent reduction in costs was necessary to improve the company's competitive position. Organizational design and human resource planning was considered a critical component of this cost-reduction process since personnel costs were the primary area where cuts could be made.

Strategy is defined as "a process through which the basic mission and objectives of the organization are set and a process through which the organization uses its resources to achieve its objectives."[21] Strategy deals with the future, providing the organization with answers to such questions as:

1. What opportunities are available to us now and in the foreseeable future?

2. What threats do we face from our competitors, regulatory bodies, technological change, or shifts in customer preferences?

3. What are our unique strengths and internal abilities and how should we leverage them in developing competitive advantage?

4. What are our weaknesses, and how can we improve these areas?

Organizations with a "well-articulated strategic vision" are more likely to achieve sustained competitive advantage over organizations that lack such a vision.[22] Strategies pursued without thorough answers to all four of these questions are more likely to fail.

Implementation of strategy requires the involvement of people from every functional area and level. As we discussed in Chapter 1, an organization can perform at its maximum capability only when the HR strategic planning process is fully integrated with the organization's strategy in a form of *reciprocal interdependence*. This should be the first consideration within the organizational design domain of HRM.

The development of a human resource strategy requires future thinking, integrated decision making, formalized procedures, and programming, all done in the context of the organization's overall mission and, ideally, in the context of the potential sources of uniqueness. Human resource planning (HRP) incorporates each of these components as well in the context of this strategy. While we typically focus on the particular techniques used by HR planners, these techniques are simply tools for solving internal organizational problems related to the strategy of the organization.[23]

---

*This section contributed by S. Snell, P. Wright and N. McKinney.

The identification and analysis of strengths, weaknesses, opportunities, and threats (SWOTs) is central to the strategic planning process. SWOT analysis involves developing a strategy that responds to external threats and opportunities by exploiting internal strengths and avoiding or improving internal weaknesses. Effective SWOT analysis include most of the organizational design activities listed in Figure 2.1. An organization employing the SWOT approach would first analyze its competitive environment to identify potential opportunities and threats and then match these opportunities and threats to its internal strengths and weaknesses. The perceived fit between external conditions and internal capabilities articulates the organization's strategy. Figure 2.2 depicts the SWOT approach. A SWOT analysis should involve many of the activities in Figure 2.1. Effective HRP closes the gap from the current to the desired state of affairs in the context of the SWOT analysis.

IDENTIFYING ENVIRONMENTAL OPPORTUNITIES AND THREATS. Strategy development is an analytic exercise, requiring research and assessment of the threats and opportunities presented by the company's external environment. The organization must view its competitive environment as a business ecosystem, complete with opportunities to form mutually beneficial alliances and partnerships as well as threats from aggressive competitors. The successful organization must accurately discern and respond to the environmental changes that will most directly affect the organization's future. One approach to identifying potential threats and opportunities is *environmental scanning.* Environmental scanning involves studying and interpreting social, economic, political, regulatory, and technological trends

that can affect competition in the industry. Generally, environmental scanning addresses the overall economic conditions in the industry, driving forces that are changing industry conditions, the nature of competition in the industry, and regulatory and social trends.

Environmental scanning helps strategic planners identify and anticipate sources of threats and opportunities.[24] The "big picture" of scanning should focus on the future customer base. This focus provides a better understanding of the context in which HR decisions are or will be made. On the one hand, environmental scanning is used to analyze, or tease apart, the individual sources of threats and opportunities. At first glance the environment is a muddled array of positive (opportunities) and negative (threats) events. Whether a problem is viewed positively (e.g., opportunity) or negatively (e.g., threat) has a great deal to do with the solution adopted. Some of the best planners are those who can turn a threat into an opportunity. For example, while most companies in smoke-stack industries view unions as a serious threat to performance, the executives at National Intergroup, Inc., (formerly National Steel) work side by side with the unions to improve quality and productivity. In this case, a potential threat became an opportunity. Southwest Airlines is another example of a company that has turned the union threat into an opportunity. Despite one of the most unionized workforces, Southwest has outperformed all other airlines over the last 10 years.

The environmental scan of future markets and competitor positions by Pratt & Whitney provided relatively clear opportunities and threats for the future. Analysis of competitors' characteristics (e.g., costs, overhead, pricing, quality, image, reputation, safety, etc.) is a critical part of the environmental scan. At PAS, the threat of the use of the Internet for testing could be turned into an opportunity with the development of a Web site for the company and the new option of testing personnel using the Internet site rather than the traditional paper and pencil method. In addition, the increased globalization of PAS's customer base indicated that its products would have to be assessed in terms of the HR decisions required for increased globalization. The key to PAS's growth plans was to turn the globalization challenge into an opportunity. The mass marketing of one of its tests required an extensive study of this *possible* opportunity.

On the other hand, environmental analysis is also used to synthesize the wide variety of threats and opportunities into an integrated whole. The variety of demands placed on the organization requires some method for tying them together to assess their joint effects. At Quaker Oats, for example, HR planners were able to synthesize more than 50 HRM programs into a list of 10 that were of top priority to the firm in the context of its strategic plan.[25] In addition to their variety, some of these threats and opportunities place competing demands on the firm. For example, the need for efficiency and the need for in-

FIGURE 2.2
AN ANALYSIS OF STRENGTHS, WEAKNESSES, OPPORTUNITIES AND THREATS (SWOT)

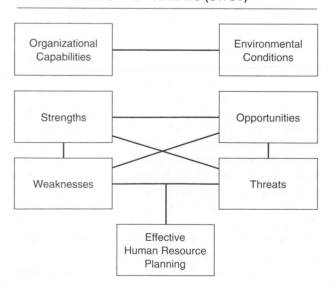

novation sometimes lead to inconsistent HR policies. Environmental scanning helps strategic planners set priorities, find synergies among activities, and create future opportunities. Some examples of the kinds of issues addressed by environmental scanning are discussed below. We will return to environmental scanning issues in Chapter 5.

Industry competition has a profound impact on HR strategic planning. The U.S. auto industry, faced with increasing competition from the Japanese in the 1980s, had to change technological and human resource management approaches. Adoption of such techniques as total quality management, just-in-time inventory control systems, benchmarking, and robotic production lines can be attributed largely to pressure from increasing competition. An increase in outsourcing for parts also reduced the cost of production. The reduction of labor costs through plant closures and relocations would have a great impact on competitive pricing.

Changes in labor supply and demand are also a critical consideration. As argued above, businesses must utilize their human capital and organizational capabilities as effectively as their financial and physical capital. Given the importance of managing for competitive advantage, organizations are increasingly aware that talented employees are vital to their success. America Online, the access company, realized an annual growth rate of 215 percent in 1996 and tripled its number of subscribers. The company's ability to succeed against very aggressive competition in this emerging industry was largely due to its ability to attract and motivate the highly talented multimedia software engineers who develop their unique online programs. Apple Computer problems in the '90s were attributed to its "brain drain," the loss of many of its top computer engineers.

Since labor can constitute as much as 80 percent of operating expenses, and since most businesses compete at least partly on a price/cost basis, managing the labor market is a crucial HR activity. In fact, the control of labor costs in the context of the supply and demand for labor is considered by some experts to be one of the most important components of environmental scanning for competitive advantage.[26]

Government regulations and labor laws also influence HR strategy and planning and must be carefully considered in any effort to reduce the cost of labor or increase productivity. Virtually every decision made by a business owner, a supervisor, or a manager that involves personnel could have legal consequences. Hiring employees, firing employees, the terms and conditions of their employment, the monitoring of their behavior at work, discrimination, disability, unemployment benefits, and labor union issues are just some areas where there are legal minefields for decision makers. Equal employment opportunity legislation such as Title VII of the Civil Rights Act, the 1991 Civil Rights Act, the Age Dis-

crimination in Employment Act, and the 1990 Americans with Disabilities Act requires that companies pay close attention to the manner in which they treat employees and job applicants. State and local laws regulating personnel practice must also be closely monitored. For example, many states now have laws that govern how employees are treated in mergers and acquisitions and that protect workers' rights of privacy. Of course, any international expansion requires a thorough understanding of labor laws where expansion is being considered. PAS, for example, needed to know about all laws related to personnel testing in their potential international markets.

Many companies provide extensive training in labor law for their decision makers. For example, Pratt & Whitney developed an extensive training program on government regulations with emphasis on age discrimination as part of its cost-reduction efforts that it knew would involve employee transfers and terminations. PAS contracted with a labor law expert who rendered opinions about the legality of using PAS tests in European countries.

Among the other important federal laws related to human resource strategy and planning are the Workers Adjustment Retraining Notification Act (WARN) of 1988 and the Immigration Act of 1990. WARN requires employers to give 60-days' notice of plant closings and mass layoffs that result in employment losses. The Immigration Act has expanded opportunities for companies to transfer multinational executives and managers while at the same time restricting the ability of U.S. corporations to hire foreign national professionals.

IDENTIFYING INTERNAL STRENGTHS AND WEAKNESSES. External threats and opportunities do not, in themselves, define a company's ability to achieve competitive advantage. Wal-Mart, for example, exists in a highly competitive industry that is threatened by the emergence of on-line shopping through the Internet. Several discount retailers have declared bankruptcy in recent years and others are struggling. Nevertheless, Wal-Mart has achieved a return on sales that is consistently higher than the industry average. Perhaps the major reason Wal-Mart has been so successful is its distribution system, which was developed by employees who have been with the company since it started. The organizational capability that has fostered the Wal-Mart culture has established a nearly unprecedented level of corporate loyalty among the key personnel who developed and sustain the incredible Wal-Mart system of product distribution (the Wal-Mart distribution goal is to never "own" a product; to sell a product before it has paid for it). Wal-Mart's distribution system is an excellent example of a "core competence," the determination of which should be a focus of the SWOT analysis.

As stated above, the most effective organizations

blend HR planning with the organization's overall strategy to ensure that the goals and resource deployments of HR work in concert with those of the organization as a whole. Issues related to the internal environment are often related to the external environment. For example, mergers and acquisitions require redesign of structures and jobs. Geographic expansion and consolidation require managerial succession planning and development and an assessment of labor markets in the areas planned for expansion. International expansion represents an extreme case of this type of business growth. But expansion does not always mean concurrent growth in employment. For example, during the 1990s many firms had aggressive plans for business growth, while either reducing or holding head count constant. Instead of requiring new employees, this type of strategy required job redesign, retraining, outsourcing, and reassignment of human resources.

Some competitive strategies may require considerable employee downsizing or redeployment; these types of HR activities are evident in a host of companies such as AT&T, IBM, HRB Singer, Honeywell, Control Data, and Ford Motor Company.[27] For AT&T to position itself after passage of the 1996 Communications Act, it had to reorganize and divest. The substantial restructuring and downsizing effort was designed with the company's strategic plan in mind. AT&T understood that rapid response to environmental change required a lean, flexible organization. The company had to be reduced in size, layers of hierarchy had to be eliminated, and business units spun off to operate as autonomous divisions.

Another example of a company that may have required downsizing is Sunbeam, the manufacturer of household goods. When Al Dunlap took over as CEO in July 1996, the company's stock was taking a real beating in a market that was generally flourishing. Dunlap eliminated 6,000 jobs, closed facilities, and redesigned the organization around its core competencies. In less than one year, Sunbeam's stock had tripled in value and stockholders were ecstatic. In this case, the huge downsizing probably saved the company from bankruptcy. Dunlap's method of downsizing, in the context of a restructuring and based on an assessment of core competencies, is one successful model for strategic HRM action.

Other corporate and business strategies suggest different HR requirements. While downsizing was at an all-time high in 1996, the rhetoric regarding restructuring changed because of adverse publicity regarding job elimination and evidence that some companies may be overdoing their workforce reductions and ultimately hurting revenue growth. It is becoming more and more obvious that downsizing must be done carefully and with a long-term perspective. Growth strategy is now making a comeback. As a recent *Business Week* article put it, "Strategy gurus with new prospects are in."[28]

In addition to human capital, technology evokes an important set of potential internal strengths and weaknesses for HR strategy. Industry investment in automation has nearly quadrupled since 1980 to almost $60 billion. Researchers have shown that technological change may affect both the number as well as the kind of jobs in a firm.[29] Other HR changes may emanate from technology as well. For example, technology allows U.S. corporations such as IBM and Compaq to outsource some engineering functions to companies in India and South Korea because the work can be carefully monitored and delivered quickly.[30]

The internal strengths and weaknesses of an organization may reflect its culture. During the merger of Baxter Travenol and American Hospital Supply, HR planners were concerned about blending two very different corporate cultures. American Hospital Supply executives ran their own divisions without interference, whereas Baxter was centrally managed. American's philosophy involved working very closely with its customers, while Baxter stressed technology development and managing its own people. This represented a potential threat. However, the executives from both companies worked diligently with the HR staff to integrate employees from both companies into a unified corporate culture that defined the new organization (Baxter Healthcare Corporation). The new hybrid culture helped to facilitate the merger.[31]

Personnel Assessment Systems had ready cash and a highly motivated workforce of people with very limited experience in the expansion areas PAS was considering. While many of its clients were expanding into international markets, PAS had no part in this expansion as a supplier. The "family-oriented" culture could be jeopardized by the need for considerable outside expertise.

These examples provide only a glimpse of the different forces inside and outside the organization that influence HR strategy and how it relates to the overall strategy of the organization. The purpose of SWOT analysis is to *identify* environmental opportunities and threats, *understand* how the mix of these forces interact with each other and the firm's internal strengths and weaknesses, *predict* their future effects, and provide a means to *control* their impact.

It is at this point that HR strategy often turns into HR planning. Such planning may involve a **gap analysis**, for example, which is used to reconcile the forecasts of labor demand and supply. At a minimum, this process identifies potential shortages or surpluses of employees, skills, and jobs based on the organization's competitive strategy. HR planners can juxtapose several environmental forecasts with alternative supply and demand forecasts to determine the firm's preparedness for different business scenarios or competitive strategies. From a problem-solving perspective, gap analysis is used to "pair up" potential opportunities and threats and internal strengths and capabilities in order to evaluate how the firm might attack the future. This decision-making process involves (1) search for alternative solutions, (2) evaluation of alternatives, and (3) choice of solutions. We will discuss labor forecasting and gap analysis in Chapter 5 when we look at HR planning in more detail.

Gap analysis may have revealed a need for employee downsizing for a majority of the *Fortune* 1000 companies in recent years. Approaches to downsizing are many and varied. Some companies adopt a "last in, first out" policy where layoffs are based strictly on employee seniority. Many organizations are constrained by collective bargaining agreements that require such a policy. For example, the 1996 contract between General Motors and the United Auto Workers included specific provisions for methods of reductions-in-force, should they be necessary. Other companies have adopted a policy based strictly on company needs and employee performance. Digital Corporation, for example, imposed such a decision strategy on its managers in its downsizing efforts (the workforce was reduced by over 5,000). Still other companies have offered a variety of options for achieving certain employment levels, including early retirement programs, retraining, and redeployment efforts. IBM, AT&T, Ford, Xerox, and many other of the largest U.S. firms have used various forms of early retirement programs. Since 1984, AT&T has reduced its staff by 150,000 using a variety of programs and working in cooperation with two unions. Each of the 19 operating units had to submit detailed workforce reduction plans, which needed approval at corporate headquarters based on the strategic plan. Both AT&T and Pratt & Whitney conducted redesign studies first based on what they saw as their potential competitive advantages and core competencies, and they then conducted job analysis to determine precisely what skills or competencies were needed in the context of these competitive strategies.

The most effective firms look at downsizing as an opportunity to create or improve the company's competitive advantage through restructuring and overhead reduction. The most effective downsizing efforts are those conducted in the context of some important measurement criterion or benchmark, such as productivity, and not with undue consideration of the stock price for the next quarter. Ford, for example, set a goal of 18 employee hours per vehicle for 1996, a figure superior to GM and Chrysler but still a few hours more than Honda, Nissan, and Toyota. Downsizing was just one of several programs aimed at the employee hour reduction goal. The goal was met in 1996 through these efforts and a 16-hour goal was set for 2000. We will discuss the various approaches to downsizing in more detail in Chapter 5.

Multiple scenarios are likely to be worth considering in meeting the strategic goals of the organization. Environmental scanning and forecasting in the context of the strategic plan identify a range of possible opportunities and threats—some of which are routine, others uncertain, and still others ambiguous. Strategists must exercise their ingenuity to create a range of possible solutions to the opportunities and threats they identify. The extent to which the current HR policies and practices are consistent strategic plans is a critical consideration.

Figure 2.3 presents one framework for evaluating the consistency of HRM activities in the context of a company's strategy. It is an excellent framework for going from a gap analysis to the action programming required to meet strategic objectives.

The choice of any strategy should be made relative to the present and potential organizational capability of the company. The choices should also be driven by what is viewed as actual or potential sources of competitive advantage in the financial, technological, or human capital areas as well. However, since there are likely to be several solutions that are equally viable/desirable, the choice is likely to be heavily influenced by the values of the decision makers (e.g., executives, HR planners, line managers, etc.). Some of these decision makers may differ in their attitudes regarding resource constraints (time and money spent), employee morale, financial performance, customer satisfaction, and so on. These differences may result in a political debate. Ideally, it is advisable to choose a solution that takes advantage of all potential competitive opportunities and that minimizes threats, seizes opportunities, capitalizes on strengths, and ameliorates weaknesses. This approach balances the

FIGURE 2.3
A DIAGNOSTIC FRAMEWORK: INTERNAL AND EXTERNAL CONSISTENCY

1. What is the organization's strategy? What is it doing to distinguish itself from its competitors? What are its intended distinctive competencies and differentiating features?
2. What skills, abilities, attitudes, and behaviors will be required from the workforce at all levels in order for the organization to effectively execute its strategic intent?
3. What are the organization's current or proposed policies and practices with respect to: (*a*) recruitment; (*b*) selection; (*c*) compensation; (*d*) career development; (*e*) training; (*f*) employment security, layoffs, and the firm's obligations to employees; (*g*) the use of temporary employees; (*h*) ownership, including the use of employee stock ownership plans; (*i*) performance appraisal; (*j*) degree of task specialization and division of labor; and (*k*) organization of work, including the use of hierarchy, teams?
4. To what extent are the policies and practices likely to produce the skills, competencies, attitudes, and behaviors necessary to execute the organization's intended strategy?

Source: Reprinted by permission of Harvard Business School Press. From *Competitive Advantage Through People; Unleashing the Power of the Work Force* by Jeffrey Pfeffer, Boston, MA, 1994 pp 226–227.

many and varied demands placed on the organization and HR function and maximizes degrees of freedom for future action. For example, Personnel Assessment Systems had to decide to what extent it would risk its core business in order to embark on a new line of business with much uncertainty.

Most problem solving fails due to lack of action, and most plans fail due to poor implementation. **Action programming** is the final step of HR strategy that takes the adopted solution and lays out a plan for the sequence of events that need to be executed to realize the strategy. As Will Rogers once said, "It does very little good to be on the right track if you are not going anywhere." Any business continually assesses and formulates new strategies in order to meet the needs of its customers in more effective ways. PAS involved its customers in its plan to expand into international staffing. PAS staff members gathered information regarding customers' globalization plans, and a short survey of international staffing objectives was sent to the HR department of each customer.

STRATEGY IMPLEMENTATION. It is important that employees be informed about the organization's strategic mission. For example, at Motorola, employees are kept apprised of their company's strategic plan, goals, and subsequent performance. Employees receive corporate performance data relative to goals and benchmark data on a quarterly basis. PAS developed a reward system for information regarding customer global expansion plans and knowledge of major PAS competitor products and service. All PAS employees were also asked to gather data on the mass-market appeal of the personality test.

HRM practices should be the mechanisms used to focus people's attention on the major strategic issues in the organization. In general, by addressing the choices and issues raised in Figure 2.1, organizations can determine how they should alter their HRM practices to achieve consistency between HRM and strategic goals. For example, if the organization is emphasizing cost or differentiation strategies, several changes in HRM activities can enable those strategies to become a major focus in the organization. A cost-oriented strategy, for example, calls for multiskilled employees; smaller, less experienced staffs; broad and deep delegation and accountability; a focus on performance-based pay with a great emphasis on efficiency and financial impact. A differentiation strategy calls for specialists in product design and development, higher budgets for research and development, rewards for innovative ideas related to quality, a flatter organizational structure, and customer-based performance appraisal. Involving employees and customers in strategy development can facilitate the development of a more effective strategy. J. M. Smucker, the jelly maker, enlisted 140 employees (7 percent of its workforce) in the development of its strategy. As Richard Smucker, president and CEO, put it, "Instead of having just 12 minds working it, we used the team of 140 as ambassadors to solicit input for all 2,000 employees." Several major potential revenue-generating ideas came from the exercise. Hewlett-Packard assembles customers, suppliers, and HP line managers for all business units in strategy sessions aimed at creating new markets.

Unfortunately, many businesses fail to carefully consider the HRM issues described in Figure 2.1 as part of their strategic planning and implementation efforts. These businesses often end up with "strategic plans on top shelf" (SPOTS). These SPOTS are elegantly drafted, documented, and detailed descriptions of what the business strategy should be, but they fail to include the means for accomplishing the strategy.

One organization that successfully conducted HRM strategic planning to meet strategic goals was Borg-Warner. After the LBO at Borg-Warner, the ability to generate cash to cover the large debt was critical. Numerous activities were undertaken to ensure that more cash came into the organization quickly. For example, in one division, the receivables, or the amount due from customers, were averaging payment in 90 days. This meant that for 90 days, customers had use of money due Borg-Warner. In addition, sales commissions were paid on point of sale, so the sales force had no incentive to collect money, only to make sales. Thus, to meet its cash needs, Borg-Warner changed the terms of sale and modified the human resource reward system so that half of the commission was received on point of sale and half on collection of receivables. As a result, receivables were reduced from 90 to 30 days. Clearly, changing the incentive system helped reach the organization's strategic goal of generating cash.

PAS hired a consulting firm to first study the marketing potential of its proposed new product and to then recommend personnel needs if the company decided to launch the new product. It also hired a consultant to study the increased globalization of customers' business and the impact of this trend on PAS's core business. In addition, PAS needed to know more about the impact of the Internet and increased globalization in general on its core business and opportunities for expansion. This approach of hiring consultants was the least aversive to the core business and most compatible with the potential competitive advantages of PAS. While full-time PAS staff members were charged with gathering information, providing the very best in customer service to their primary customers was *the* priority.

HR and the Capacity for Change

In a constantly changing business world, organizations must be able to adapt to changes or risk failure, and yet the first reaction that most people have toward change is one of resistance. Typically, individuals express concern over changing habits, norms, and ways of doing things. In organizations, the capacity for change may be increased by correctly using HRM tools and expertise. For example, organizations interested in becoming more adaptable to environmental pressures and changes should hire people who are more flexible and develop people so they realize that change is an important part of growth. Further, the company should set performance standards for people to encourage flexibility and diversity and should reward employees for being innovative. The J. Walter Thompson ad agency was troubled by the quality and quantity of proposed advertising campaigns. Executives came up with an innovative solution: they let their research and account management departments generate ideas along with the creative department. Executives at JWT credit the new system for winning new accounts with Goodyear Tire and Nuprin. Organizations need to communicate to employees the types of changes that are needed and why they are critical for the company's survival and success.

In an increasingly competitive environment, organizations with a greater capacity for change are more likely to satisfy customers and expand the customer base. We already mentioned the Internet revolution and its potential for retail sales. The projections are $7 billion in sales over the Internet by 2000. Companies that adapt to this new retailing approach will do just fine. Companies that think doing business over your computer is just a passing fad and do nothing to adapt will probably get buried by this revolution in retail.

In the automotive industry, the lead time for new cars was about seven years in the 1970s. That is, it took about seven years to go from new concept to a prototype to production. In the early 1980s, Ford introduced the Taurus/Sable cars in about three and a half years, cutting the lead time by half. This reduced lead time came, in part, from extensive training of all employees involved in the Taurus/Sable project. The lead time was further reduced by creating a product team of suppliers, engineers, manufacturers, distributors, assembly workers, and customers who all worked together offering input into the design and building of the new cars. This novel group effort of involving all important parties, coupled with other HRM changes (e.g., training, staffing, communication, rewards), allowed Ford to increase its capacity for change and significantly reduce its lead time. Consequently, the increased capacity for change had a dramatic impact on Ford's profits and performance. Ford continued to reduce its lead time through 1996.

General Electric initiated a program called "Workout" that focused on attacking bureaucracies, eliminating needless work, and, above all, doing a better job serving customers. Through town-hall meetings, this change process involved employees at all levels.

HR and Strategic Unity

Strategic unity represents the extent to which stakeholders inside (e.g., employees) and outside a business (e.g.,

shareholders, customers) share a core set of values and assumptions about the business. For example, if the stakeholders believe that customer service is of central importance to corporate performance, this core value can be developed and nurtured among employees, suppliers, and customers of the business.

Strategic unity can be more easily realized by focusing HR on deliverables to internal and external customers. As we alluded to in Chapter 1, HR must focus on what HR professionals "deliver."[32] These *deliverables* are the outcomes and results of HR work. The key to strategic unity is the measurement of outcomes or deliverables that are most important for assessing strategic accomplishments. These outcomes should be defined in terms of meeting customer requirements and expanding the customer base.

Nordstrom, a retail chain that started in Seattle and expanded throughout the United States, includes high commitment to customer service as part of its organizational mission. Training programs, incentive programs, and communication programs consistently focus on the importance of customer service. For Nordstrom, internal strategic unity exists since employees at all levels and in all departments share a similar commitment. This commitment is achieved despite the fact that a high percentage of Nordstrom employees are unionized. The internal unity channels employees' attention toward an important organizational goal. Also, the unity helps provide a unique service to customers that cannot easily be copied by competitors. As a result, when customers link Nordstrom with extraordinary service, Nordstrom enhances its competitive position.

At Borg-Warner, organizational capability has been a critical source of sustained competitiveness. Borg-Warner's challenge was to create a new mind-set among managers so they would think like owners. The change in the reward system and the training and communication programs informing employees about the leveraged buyout system were used to build strategic unity among employees. Employee pay was directly linked to paying down the debt, and a monthly communication briefing reported progress toward this strategic goal.

General Electric developed strategic unity by focusing all attention on processes related to six key areas: order fulfillment, new product introduction, quick market intelligence, productivity, globalization, and supplier management. Their change process would be driven by these six areas. Their entire "Workout" effort proceeded in the context of these six areas.

The issue of conflicting stakeholders is one of the most contentious today and underscores the difficulty in attaining strategic unity. Some research suggests that management has become too responsive to stock price and investor demands for a quick return and that some HR decisions are not in the long-term best interests of the organization.

HR professionals can and should play a vital role in

successful organization design efforts that call for downsizing, reengineering, and business expansion for the long-range success of the organization. This approach first calls for a detailed strategic plan with a stipulation of the core competencies necessary to achieve it. The core competencies are then used to construct a performance-based approach to assessing employees as part of the strategic plan. Research shows that this approach to strategy implementation can get a company both short- and long-term gains and that all stakeholders will ultimately benefit.[33]

SKILLS REQUIRED FOR HUMAN RESOURCE MANAGEMENT COMPETITIVENESS

For HRM practices to be used to gain competitive advantage, both general managers and HRM professionals must have a set of skills or competencies that build competitiveness. As noted in Chapter 1, competencies represent an individual's knowledge, skills, abilities, and activities performed. That is, individuals should know the business, keep aware of current HR developments, manage the process of change, and integrate all these roles in the context of the organization's mission and strategy. To refine these broad skills, general managers and HRM professionals must be proficient in oral and written communication, decision making, change processes, leadership, innovative thinking, planning, and organizing. Computer skills are also becoming a must for HRM professionals because more and more products and services related to HR activities are now available as software or through the Internet. Without a working knowledge of software requirements, for example, it is almost impossible to determine whether a given product is right for the organization.

General Manager Skills

General managers have primary responsibility for ensuring that businesses have a competitive advantage. To do this, they must integrate financial, strategic, technological, and organizational capabilities. To strengthen existing organizational capabilities, general managers need to develop at least four broad skills or competencies. These are: creating a need for HRM changes, creating a vision of the importance of HRM practices, generating support for HRM activities, and becoming proficient in the delivery of HRM practices.

COMPETENCY 1: CREATE A NEED FOR HRM CHANGES. Individuals must be convinced that they need to change before they will be committed to any program for change. Until employees feel a need to pay attention to HRM activities, they are unlikely to do so.

Since HRM practices are central to business competitiveness, general managers must encourage employees to be aware of effective HRM practices in the organization and to take them seriously. Some research indicates that technologically oriented managers and supervisors tend to place less value on HR activities such as performance management, staffing procedures, and training in equal employment opportunity. General managers of these individuals have a greater challenge.

One approach to increasing perceived value of HRM is to share outcome data about HRM practices and how they relate to "bottom-line" measures of the success of the company.[34] Effective managers share results of organizational effectiveness criteria (e.g., productivity indexes, customer satisfaction data, absenteeism records, grievances filed, recruiting costs) and their relationship to particular HRM programs (e.g., staffing, training, appraisal). For example, at the Marriott Corporation, data for each facility on turnover and retention rates are shared with employees to indicate how successful the current reward programs or staffing systems are. At Office Depot, store managers receive monthly reports on sales per employee, costs, overtime, and customer satisfaction. The store manager's compensation is tied to customer satisfaction data.

COMPETENCY 2: CREATE A VISION OF THE IMPORTANCE OF HRM PRACTICES. Most successful businesses have identified the direction in which they are headed. This direction reflects not only short-term goals (meeting this quarter's profit plan), but also, more importantly, a longer-term vision (e.g., a 5- or 10-year plan). The long-range vision reflects the organization's strategic goals and core principles and values.

General managers who want to use HRM practices for competitiveness need to relate the company's strategic vision to its HRM practices. That is, general managers must emphasize the important role that employees play in the company's ability to meet its long-term business plans. This was done at the Marriott Corporation when general managers identified the HRM activities that were needed (e.g., staffing, retention, and incentive programs) to assist the corporation in meeting its long-range goal of being the employer of choice.

Similarly, at Borg-Warner, the relationship between the business goals (e.g., generating cash to cover debt) and HRM practices (e.g., rewards, development, performance appraisal, communication practices) were made explicit by general managers.

COMPETENCY 3: GENERATE SUPPORT FOR HRM ACTIVITIES. General managers need to demonstrate their personal support for the effective use of HRM activities. They can do this, for example, by participating in staffing decisions (e.g., selecting managers, succession planning) or serving as trainers or trainees in management development programs. They can also use effective performance management practices (e.g., providing timely feedback to subordinates), encourage their supervisory subordinates to do the same, and hold their subordinates accountable for the extent to which they subscribe to HRM-recommended procedures. General managers also need to build commitment among employees for using HRM practices. They may do this by sharing information throughout the organization about the importance of HRM practices. This may be done through speeches, training programs, orientation programs, newsletters, and slogans. For example, at Marriott Corporation, general managers spoke extensively about the importance of being the employer of choice and used this theme in all the corporation's newsletters, videos, training programs, and annual meetings.

General managers can also enhance commitment to HRM practices by encouraging employees to participate in the various HRM programs. For example, individuals can be appointed to HRM task forces or they can be asked to prepare and deliver presentations on the importance of HRM to employees or external groups. At one computer firm, turnover of high-performing engineers was high (about 20 percent) after three years with the company. To reduce the turnover, the highest-rated engineers were assigned a three-month duty recruiting. As recruiters, the engineers had to present the value of working at the company to college campuses. After three months and many sales pitches for working with the company, the engineers expressed greater personal commitment to the firm and turnover was reduced.

COMPETENCY 4: LEARN AND BECOME PROFICIENT IN THE DELIVERY OF HRM PRACTICES.

General managers who develop competence in HRM practices need to be current on the delivery of alternative and ideal HRM tools. That is, they need to know when to use career development programs, assist in downsizing or reengineering efforts, or adapt staffing systems to address organizational issues. Such proficiency may derive from continued education through attending seminars, reading, or meeting with experts. As discussed in Chapter 3, competence in HRM practices assumes a knowledge of the legal and regulatory implications of HRM activities. As general managers become more knowledgeable about HRM practices, they should make more informed choices about the appropriate activities to use. As a result, the organization's competitive advantage should improve.

Human Resource Management Professional Skills

HRM professionals share responsibility with general managers for using the best HRM practices to build or-

ganizational competitiveness. As HRM professionals link their work with business needs, they become strategic business partners and build competitiveness through HRM practices.[35] As we discussed in Chapter 1, one responsibility is an understanding of the contemporary research on HRM practices so that the choice of practices can be based on the appropriate criteria, such as effects on important outcome measures, rather than some other basis for decision making. Many products and services are marketed to HRM professionals. These professionals must be capable of evaluating the products and services using those criteria most related to the same "bottom-line" criteria that other organizational functions use to evaluate its programs.

HRM professionals must play significant roles as business partners to develop strategic plans for the organization and to design HRM activities that would add value to the business operations. To serve in this partnership role, the HRM professionals must demonstrate mastery of three competencies and must integrate knowledge of these areas. These three competencies are: knowing the business, designing and delivering appropriate HRM programs, and managing the process of change. These are illustrated in Figure 2.4.

FIGURE 2.4
HR COMPETENCIES NEEDED FOR STRATEGIC BUSINESS PARTNERS

BUSINESS COMPETENCIES
- **Financial or economic.** Know the organization's capabilities in finance, strategy, and technology.
- **Strategic or product capabilities.** Know customer requirements and how to measure them.
- **Technological.** Know the most important R&D and technological operations.

HRM DESIGN AND DELIVERY COMPETENCIES
- **Organizational design.**
- **Staffing.**
- **Employee and organizational development.**
- **Performance management.**
- **Reward systems compliance.**
- **Employee relations.**
- **Productivity improvement.**
- **Health and safety.**

MANAGEMENT-OF-CHANGE COMPETENCIES
- **Contracting** to establish relationships with clients, customers, outside experts.
- **Diagnosing** problems from all perspectives.
- **Intervening** as a change agent for implementation.
- **Implementing** changes to facilitate competitive advantage.
- **Evaluating** changes to assess effects and make alterations.
- **Influencing** to make adjustments in interventions.

Source: Reprinted from Tie the Corporate Knot: Gaining Complete Customer Commitment by D. Ulrich, *Sloan Management Review 30*(4) pp. 19–27, by permission of the publisher. Copyright 1989 by Sloan Management Review Association. All rights reserved.

HRM COMPETENCY 1: KNOW THE BUSINESS.
HRM professionals as business partners need to know the business or understand the organization's capabilities in finances, strategy, and technology. Knowing the firm's economic or financial capability means knowing how the firm gains access to capital, how the firm manages cost of capital, how financial systems are used within the firm to measure performance, and how resources are allocated according to financial criteria. Being aware of strategic or product capabilities means understanding customer buying criteria, identifying differentiated product features, and dealing with issues of market segmentation. Knowing the organization's technological capability requires that HRM professionals understand the research and development, engineering, and manufacturing processes of product development. The HR competence encompassed by the phrase *knowledge of the business* is not the ability *to do* all business functions, but the ability to understand them.[36]

Learning about the business requires that HRM professionals spend time with customers, line managers, research and development technicians, and others who are central to business operations. Reading business plans, asking questions about specific technical operations, and subscribing to technical publications exemplify ways to gain this competency.

HRM COMPETENCY 2: DESIGN AND DELIVER HRM PROGRAMS. To design and deliver timely and effective HRM programs, HRM professionals need to be experts in behavioral science. They need to continually update their knowledge and skills in the areas of organizational design, staffing, employee and organizational development, performance management, reward systems, benefits, and labor relations. They can accomplish this by attending conferences, reading current literature, conducting research, and talking with colleagues in companies and professors in academic settings. HRM professionals should also monitor their organizations' HRM programs make any necessary additions and revisions and to ensure that the programs reflect state-of-the-art practices in consonance with the mission and strategic goals of the organization and legal guidelines. As we stated in Chapter 1, HRM professionals often fall short on this competency.

HRM COMPETENCY 3: MANAGE THE PROCESS OF CHANGE. HRM professionals need to be able to manage change processes so that business needs merge with HRM activities. They can do this by contracting relationships with clients, customers, and outside experts; gaining influence within the organization; diagnosing problems; implementing changes; intervening with ideas; and evaluating program results. Merely knowing the contents of a new compensation or performance-appraisal program does not guarantee that the

program will be useful for the organization, even if such programs appear to be consistent with the business strategy. HRM professionals also need to be able to manage the change process by identifying any potential resistance to the changes and by building commitment to the new programs. Knowledge of the key factors related to successful change is required. Figure 2.5 presents seven key factors identified at a recent exercise at General Electric.

There is a perception among many line managers that HR professionals and their various programs actually impede line managers' ability to get the vital work done. One line manager described his HR department as analogous to the federal government interfering with the ability of a small business to do its business. One of the biggest responsibilities on the part of HR managers is convincing line managers that they are working together to meet the strategic goals of the organization. In fact, one study found that *change management* explained more of the effectiveness of HR professionals than either knowledge of the business or knowledge of the practices.[37]

INTEGRATING THE THREE COMPETENCIES.
The ability to integrate business knowledge, HRM design and delivery skills, and change process competencies is essential if HRM practitioners are to be successful. Three cases illustrate the integration of the three competencies.

When Baxter Healthcare and American Hospital Supply merged to form the largest hospital supply firm in the world, HRM professionals at all levels of the organization displayed leadership roles. The greatest challenge to this merger was the ability to integrate diverse cultures, mindsets, and individuals into a commonly focused and rationally organized business that added value to investors and customers. HRM professionals identified a series of processes that would define jobs, identify and create a shared vision, and enable the new company to be competitive in the marketplace. Jobs were redesigned to enhance understanding of customer needs, training programs were established to develop a unified value structure, and performance management and pay for performance systems were installed which directed the focus of operations on increasing perceived customer value.

After the air traffic controller strike, executives at the Federal Aviation Administration realized that they had to improve working conditions and morale throughout the Agency. To begin this implementation effort, the HRM professionals designed training programs for the top 1,000 managers. These programs were designed on the assumption that these managers should use the HRM tools to improve morale within the Agency but in the context of the FAA's objectives. HRM professionals worked as strategic business partners to help create a vision for the Agency and to institute the change process to share the vision. Employee opinion surveys were insti-

FIGURE 2.5
SEVEN KEY FACTORS FOR SUCCESS IN MAKING CHANGE HAPPEN

KEY SUCCESS FACTORS FOR CHANGE	QUESTIONS TO ASSESS AND ACCOMPLISH THE KEY SUCCESS FACTORS FOR CHANGE
Leading change (*who* is responsible)	Do we have a leader . . . who owns and champions the change? who publicly commits to making it happen? who will garner the resources necessary to sustain it? who will put in the personal time and attention needed to follow through?
Creating a shared need (*why* do it)	Do employees . . . see the reason for the change? understand why the change is important? see how it will help them and/or the business in the short- and long-term?
Shaping a vision (*what* will it look like when we are done)	Do employees . . . see the outcomes of the change in behavioral terms (that is, in terms of what they will do differently as a result of the change)? get excited about the results of accomplishing the change? understand how the change will benefit customers and other stakeholders?
Mobilizing commitment (*who else* needs to be involved)	Do the sponsors of the change . . . recognize who else needs to be committed to the change to make it happen? know how to build a coalition of support for the change? have the ability to enlist support of key individuals in the organization? have the ability to build a responsibility matrix to make the change happen?
Modifying systems and structures (*how* will it be institutionalized)	Do the sponsors of the change . . . understand how to link the change to other HR systems, for example, staffing, training, appraisal, rewards, structure, communication, and so on? recognize the systems implications of the change?
Monitoring progress (*how* will it be measured)	Do the sponsors of the change . . . have a means of measuring the success of the change? plan to benchmark progress on both the results of the change and the process of implementing the change?
Making it last (*how* will it get started and last)	Do the sponsors of the change . . . recognize the first steps in getting started? have a short- and long-term plan to keep attention focused on the change? have a plan to adapting the change over time?

Source: Reprinted by permission of Harvard Business School Press. From *Human Resource Champions: The next agenda for adding value and delivering results* by Dave Ulrich. Boston, MA 1997, p. 160.

tuted along with subordinate appraisals of supervisors and managers to assess the extent to which management was helping the controllers do the best possible job.

As the appliance industry became increasingly competitive through mergers within the United States and increased global competition, executives at Whirlpool knew they had to become even more aggressive to remain competitive. Working with the vice president of human resources, the chairperson at Whirlpool established a vision for the company through the year 2000. To institutionalize and build commitment to the vision, a one week executive program was designed for the top 50 officers and managers in the company to discuss the organization's vision and prepare action plans. The program was designed with the business objectives clearly in focus. This executive development program became a major tool for creating unity and making change happen at Whirlpool.

In each of these cases, HRM professionals played a significant role as business partners to develop strategic plans for the organization and to design HRM activities that would add value to the business operations. To serve in this partnership role, the HRM professionals demonstrated mastery in integrating the three broad competencies of knowing the business, designing and delivering appropriate HRM programs, and managing the process of change.

SUMMARY

Competitive advantage has become and will continue to be a major driving force for most businesses. To attain and sustain competitive advantage, businesses need to add value for customers and offer uniqueness. Four capabilities provide a business's uniqueness: financial, physical, human, and organizational. To sustain competitive advantage, organizational capability should be emphasized and, ideally, in the context of the other sources of uniqueness. Organizational capability derives from a business's HRM practices. Optimal organizational capability takes full advantage of the other capabilities of an organization.

HRM practices build competitiveness because they allow for strategic implementation through environmental scanning, creating a capacity for change, and instilling strategic unity. To accomplish these three outcomes, HRM activities from all eight domains need to be used. To use HRM practices for competitiveness, general managers and HRM professionals need to acquire and maintain business competencies, HRM design and delivery competencies, and management of change competencies. The key to effective HRM is a focus on customer value. As Dave Ulrich concluded in *Human Resource Champions,* "When employee-focused HR practices shift to customer-focused HR practices, employees and customers both win. Employees win by seeing their work add value to customers, by enhancing their ability to adapt their work quickly to meet customer needs, and by becoming more intimately involved with satisfying customer expectation. Customers win by dealing with supplier firm employees who are true customer resources, by working with supplies dedicated to their needs, and by reducing the cycle time needed to change how work gets done."[38]

In general, the view of HRM outlined in this chapter provides a foundation for integrating HRM activities with the organization's mission and goals. We have emphasized that HRM professionals should be actively involved in building more competitive organizations through the HRM domains. One critical and necessary competency for both line managers and HRM professionals is an up-to-date knowledge of HRM research and the regulatory environment. Among the most important elements of this competency are the legal implications of HRM activities, particularly the many equal employment opportunity laws and regulations that affect all eight of the HRM domains. As Lado and Wilson put it in an insightful article on strategy and HRM, "We realize that conditions in the firm's external and internal environment may enable or constrain the capacity of HR systems to develop and exploit organization competencies. One of the most pervasive environmental influences on HR systems has been the increasing government legislation and regulation of employment practices."[39] We will explore this critical area in the next chapter.

DISCUSSION QUESTIONS

1. What is meant by the term *competitive advantage*? Why is it important for an organization?

2. How can HRM activities be used to assist organizations in becoming more competitive?

3. To what extent do you consider corporate social responsibility when considering a product or service? Interview five friends to determine if any of them have considered social issues such as the environment or labor policies in their decision to purchase.

4. Provide some recommendations for how general managers and HRM professionals can acquire the skills they need for effectively utilizing HRM programs.

5. Provide two examples of companies you are familiar with that are not using their HRM programs to maintain or create a competitive advantage. What specific suggestions would you offer to them?

6. In the context of a SWOT analysis, evaluate the strategic state of Personnel Assessment Systems. What additional data do you need as a part of your SWOT analysis?

NOTES

1. Ulrich, D. 1997. *Human resource champions.* Boston: Harvard Business School Press; Lake, D. G. (1997). Frameworks for human resource professionals participating in business relationships. *Human Resource Management, 36* (1), 129–134.

2. See Ulrich, note 1; see also, Ulrich, D.; Halbrook, R.; Meder, D.; and Stuchlik, M. (1991). Employee and customer attachment: Synergies for competitive advantage. *Human Resource Planning* (14), 89–104.

3. Porter, M. E. (1980). *Competitive strategy: Techniques for analyzing industries and competitors.* New York: The Free Press; see also, Vesey, J. T. (1991). The new competitors: They think in terms of "speed-to market." *Academy of Management Executive, 5*(2), 23–33; Lawler III, E. E., and Mohrman, S. A. (1997). Transforming the human resource function. *Human Resource Management, 36* (1), 157–162.

4. Porter, M. E. (1985). *Competitive advantage: Creating and sustaining superior performance.* New York: The Free Press; see also, Hitt, M. A.; Hoskisson, R. E.; and Harrison, J. S. (1991). Strategic competitiveness in the 1990s: Challenges and opportunities for U.S. executives. *Academy of Management Executive, 5*(2), 7–22; Eichinger, R. W., and Lombardo, M. M. (1997). HR's role in building competitive edge leaders. *Human Resource Management, 36* (1), 141–146.

5. Hill, C. W. L., and Jones, G. R. (1989). *Strategic management: An integrated approach.* Boston: Houghton Mifflin; see also, Fiol, C. M. (1991). Managing culture as a competitive resource: An identity-based view of sustainable competitive advantage. *Journal of Management, 17*(1), 191–212; Beatty, R. W., and Schneier, C. E. (1997). New HR roles to impact organizational performance: From "partners" to "players." *Human Resource Management, 36* (1), 29–38.

6. Hamel, G., and Prahald, C. K. (1994). *Competing for the future.* Boston: Harvard Business School Press; see also,

Hagan, C. (1996). The core competence organization: Implications for human resource practices. *Human Resource Management Review, 6,* 147–164.

7. Treacy, M., and Wiersema, F. (January–February 1993). Customer intimacy and other value disciplines. *Harvard Business Review,* pp. 84–93, see also, note 5, Beatty and Schneier.

8. Hauser, J. R.; Simester, D. I.; Wernerfelt, B. (August 1996). Internal customers and internal suppliers. *Journal of Marketing Research,* pp. 276–280; Schlesinger, L., and Zornitsky, A. (1991). Job satisfaction, service capability, and customer satisfaction: An examination of linkages and management implications. *Human Resource Planning* (14), 141–150; Schneider, B. (1991). Service quality and profits: Can you have your cake and eat it, too? *Human Resource Planning* (14), 151–158; Wiley, J. (1991). Customer satisfaction and employee opinions: A supportive work environment and its financial cost. *Human Resource Planning* (14), 117–128.

9. Reich, R. (Sept. 18, 1996). Speech at Washington Press Club.

10. Cited in Barasch, D. S. (Dec. 22, 1996). God and toothpaste. *New York Times Magazine,* p. 29.

11. See note 10.

12. Friedman, M. (Sept. 13, 1970). The social responsibility of business is to increase profits. *New York Times Magazine,* p. 98; see also, Dunlap, A. J. (1996). *Mean Business.* New York: Random House.

13. Ulrich, D. (1987). Organizational capability as a competitive advantage: Human resource professionals as strategic partners. *Human Resource Planning, 10*(4): 169–184.

14. Barney, Jay B. (1997). *Gaining and sustaining competitive advantage.* Reading, MA: Addison-Wesley Publishing Co.

15. Prahald, C. K., and Hamel, G. (May–June 1990). The core competence of the organization. *Harvard Business Review,* pp. 79–93; Hagan, C. M. (1996). The core competence organization: Implications for human resource practices. *Human Resource Management Review, 6*(2), 147–164.

16. See note 1.

17. See note 1. See also, Ulrich, D., and Lake, D. (1991). Organizational capability: Creating competitive advantage. *Academy of Management Executive, 5*(1), 77–92.

18. Pfeffer, J. (1994). *Competitive advantage through people.* Boston: Harvard Business School Press, p. 4.

19. Becker, B. E.; Huselid, M. A.; Pickus, P. S.; and Spratt, M. F. (1997). HR as a source of shareholder value: Research and recommendations. *Human Resource Management, 36*(1), 39–48.

20. See note 1.

21. Tichy, N.; Fombrun, C.; and Devanna, M. (February 1982). Strategic human resource management. *Sloan Management Review,* 23–47.

22. Lado, A. A., and Wilson, M. C. (October 1994). Human resource systems and sustained competitive advantage: A competency-based perspective. *Academy of Management Review,* pp. 699–721; Evans, S., and Bahrami, H. (1997).

Human resource leadership in knowledge-based entities: Shaping the context of work. *Human Resource Management, 36*(1) 23–28.

23. Lengnick-Hall, C. A., and Lengnick-Hall, M. L. (1988). Strategic HR management: A review of the literature and a proposed topology. *Academy of Management Review, 13*(3), 454–470; see also, Lado, A. A.; Boyd, N. G.; and Wright, P. (1992). A competency-based model of sustainable competitive advantage. *Journal of Management, 18*(1), 77–91; Bamberger, P., and Fiegenbaum, A. (1996). The role of strategic reference points in explaining the nature and consequence of human resource strategy. *Academy of Management Review, 21,* 926–958; Lengnick-Hall, C. A. (1992). Innovation and competitive advantage: What we know and what we need to learn. *Journal of Management, 18*(2), 399–429.

24. Wright, P., and Snell, S. (1991). Toward an integrative view of strategic human resource management. *Human Resource Management Review, 1,* 203–225; see also, Snell, S. A., and Dean, J. W., Jr. (1992). Integrated manufacturing and human resource management: A human capital perspective. *Academy of Management Journal, 35*(3), 467–504; Wright, P. M. and McMahan, G. C. (1992). Theoretical perspectives for strategic human resource management. *Journal of Management, 18*(2), 295–320.

25. Baytos, L. M., (1984). A "no-frills" approach to human resource planning. *Human Resource Planning, 7,* 39–46; see also, Burack, E. H. (1985). Linking corporate business and human resource planning: Strategic issues and concerns. *Human Resource Planning, 8*(3), 133–145.

26. Brown, M. G. (1996). *Keeping score: Using the right metrics to drive world-class performance.* New York: Quality Resources; see also, Burke, W. W. (1997). What human resource practitioners need to know for the twenty-first century. *Human Resource Management, 36*(1), 71–80; Christenson, R. (1997). Where is HR? *Human Resource Management, 36*(1), 81–84; Ehrlich, C. J. (1997). Human resource management: A changing script for a changing world. *Human Resource Management, 36*(1), 85–90.

27. Cameron, K. 1994. Guest editor's note: Investigating organizational downsizing—Fundamental issues. *Human Resource Management, 33,* 183–188; Ellig, B. R. (1997). Is the human resource function neglecting the employees? *Human Resource Management, 36* (1), 91–96; Kochan, T. A., (1997). Rebalancing the role of human resources. *Human Resource Management, 36* (1), 121–128; Lobel, S. A. (1997). In praise of the "soft" stuff: A vision for human resource leadership. *Human Resource Management, 36* (1), 135–140.

28. Byrne, J. (Aug. 26, 1996). Strategic thinkers. *Business Week,* p. 46; see also, Pucik, V. (1997). Human resources in the future: An obstacle or champion of globalization? *Human Resource Management, 36* (1), 163–168; Schuler, R. S., Dowling, P. J., and De Cieri, H. (1993). An integrative framework of strategic international human resource management. *Journal of Management, 19*(2), 419–459.

29. Ettlie, J. E. (1988). *Taking charge of manufacturing.* San Francisco: Jossey-Bass; see also, Majchrzak, A. (1988). *The human side of factory automation.* San Francisco: Jossey-Bass.

30. Gaines, S. L. (Aug. 31, 1997). Engineering, design jobs, jump on overseas wave of outsourcing. *Chicago Tribune* (cited in *Boca Raton News,* p. 20A).

31. Rucci, A. J.; Lafasto, F. M. J.; and Ulrich, D., (1990). Managing organizational change: A merger case study. Unpublished manuscript; see also, Page, R. C., and Van De Vort, D. M. (1989). Job analysis and HR planning. In W. F. Cascio (ed.), *Human resource planning employment and placement.* ASPA/BNA Series, Washington: Bureau of National Affairs.

32. See note 1, p. viii; see also, Ulrich, D. (1997). HR of the Future: Conclusions and observations. *Human Resource Management, 36* (1), 175–179; Ulrich, D. (1997). Judge me more by my future than by my past. *Human Resource Management, 36* (1), 5–8.

33. Hagan, C. M. (1996). The core competence organization: Implications for human resource practices. *Human Resource Management Review 6*(2), 147–164; see also, Beer, M. (1997). The transformation of the human resource function: Resolving the tension between a traditional administrative and a new strategic role. *Human Resource Management, 36* (1), 49–56; Bowen, D. E., and Siehl, C. (1997). The future of human resource management: March and Simon (1958) revisited. *Human Resource Management, 36* (1), 57–64.

34. See note 19; see also Fitz-enz, J. (1997). The truth about best practices: What they are and how to apply them. *Human Resource Management, 36* (1), 97–104; Rucci, A. J. (1997). Should HR survive? A profession at the crossroads. *Human Resource Management, 36* (1), 169–174; Alvares, K. M. (1997). The business of human resources. *Human Resource Management, 36* (1), 9–16.

35. Eichinger, R. W., and Lombardo, M. M. (1997). HR's role in building competitive edge leaders. *Human Resource Management, 36* (1), 141–146; see also, Anderson, R. W. (1997). The future of human resources: Forging ahead or falling behind? *Human Resource Management, 36* (1), 17–22; Beatty, R. W., and Schneier, C. E. (1997). New HR roles to impact organizational performance: From "partners" to "players." *Human Resource Management, 36* (1), 29–38.

36. See note 1, p. 252; see also, Heskett, J. L., and Schlesinger, L. A. (1997). Leading the high-capability organization: Challenges for the twenty-first century. *Human Resource Management, 36* (1), 105–114; Kerr, S., and Von Glinow, M. A. (1997). The future of HR: Plus ca change, plus c'est la meme chose. *Human Resource Management, 36* (1), 115–120; Evans, S., and Bahrami, H. (1997). Human resource leadership in knowledge-based entities: Shaping the context of work. *Human Resource Management, 36* (1), 23–28.

37. Ulrich, D.; Brockbank, W.; Yeung, A.; and Lake, D. (1995). Human resource competencies: An empirical assessment. *Human Resource Management, 34,* 473–496.

38. See note 1, p. 245; Ryan, A. M.; Schmitt, M. J.; and Johnson, R. (1996). Attitudes and effectiveness: Examining relations at an organizational level. *Personnel Psychology, 49*(4), 853–864; Johnson, J. W. (1996). Linking employee perceptions of service climate to customer satisfaction. *Personnel Psychology 49*(4), 831–842; Paradise-Tornow, C. (1991). Management effectiveness, service quality, and organizational performance in banks. *Human Resource Planning* (14), 129–140; Schlesinger, L., and Zornitsky. (1991). Job satisfaction, service capability, and customer satisfaction: An examination of linkages and management implications. *Human Resource Planning* (14), pp. 141–150; Schneider, B. (1991). Service quality and profits: Can you have your cake and eat it, too? *Human Resource Planning* (14), pp. 151–158; Tornow, W., and Wiley, J. (1991). Service quality and management practices: A look at employee attitudes, customer satisfaction, and bottom-line consequences. *Human Resource Planning* (14), pp. 105–116.

39. See note 22.

C H A P T E R

THE LEGAL ENVIRONMENT OF HRM: EQUAL EMPLOYMENT OPPORTUNITY

OVERVIEW

Chapter 1 summarized the regulatory environment in which HRM is practiced today. Many experts have noted that the legal environment is one of the most important components of the external environment for HRM, and legal considerations are a primary force shaping staffing policy. One recent study of retail managers indicated that knowledge of the legal implications of HRM activities was as important as any other knowledge a general manager must have regarding HRM activities.[1] The same study found that only 32% of managers received training on equal employment opportunity law.

Many federal, state, and local laws and regulations can be the basis of a lawsuit against an employer for actions related to workers' compensation, unemployment compensation, wages, health and safety in the workplace, whistleblower's protection, retirement, employee benefits, rights of privacy, and protection against unjust dismissal. While all these laws are important and will be considered as we address the various HRM activities throughout the book, no other area of the

regulatory environment has had such a profound effect on HRM as equal employment opportunity. More than one in four American workers report they have been victims of racially motivated discrimination in the workforce. Fifty-five percent of African-American federal employees believe minorities are subjected to "flagrant or obviously discriminatory practices." Seventy-seven percent of women surveyed in 1995 indicated that sexual discrimination "remains a serious problem."[2]

These findings, combined with the increasing diversity of the workforce, translate into an increasing rate of legal activity in this area. In fact, litigation under two major pieces of federal legislation, the **Americans with Disabilities Act** of 1990 and the **Civil Rights Act** of 1991, has increased every year since these laws went into effect.[3] As the U.S. workforce continues to age and as employers continue to downsize, claims of discrimination under the **Age Discrimination in Employment Act** are also on the increase.

We will concentrate our discussion in this chapter on EEO issues in order to emphasize the importance of this area and its impact on all eight HRM domains reviewed in Chapters 1 and 2. Every major activity of HRM is affected by the EEO laws and regulations we are about to discuss. The processes by which employers recruit, hire, place, evaluate, train, promote, compensate, monitor, lay off, and terminate employees can fall under the scrutiny of the courts and regulatory agencies based on some form of EEO legislation.

This chapter provides an overview of the legal environment with particular emphasis on equal employment opportunity laws and regulations. We will begin by describing cases that represent some of the hottest issues related to the legal context and then provide descriptions of the most important laws in EEO and the legal interpretations of those laws. We will conclude with a discussion of the implications of these laws for personnel practice.

Our major objective for this chapter is to provide a legal tutorial for general managers practicing HRM in our highly litigious society. *Compliance with these laws and adhering to the guidelines provided by regulatory agencies actually promote better HRM policies and practices.*

OBJECTIVES

After studying this chapter, you should be able to:

1. Understand the legal issues affecting HRM activity and the various laws related to equal employment opportunity and employment discrimination.

2. Identify potential problems in HRM policy and practice as related to equal employment opportunity laws.

3. Understand the importance of judicial interpretation for EEO law.

We have discussed the trend of increasing litigation, which has had an impact on virtually all aspects of HRM. Let's start with some recent cases that represent fairly typical legal actions today.

*   1,500 minority employees sue Texaco claiming racial discrimination in promotions and pay raises.
*   Lockheed Martin Corporation agrees to pay $13 million to settle claims of age discrimination brought by former employees of Martin Marietta.
*   Target Stores is sued for using a psychological test to screen applicants for security guard positions that the plaintiffs regard as an invasion of privacy.
*   A jury finds Circuit City guilty of racial discrimination after plaintiffs' attorneys argued promotion decisions were made under an "excessively subjective" personnel system.
*   A manager fires an employee based on comments the

employee made about him in an E-mail message intended only for the fired employee's friend.
*   Five male professors at Virginia Commonwealth University claim that a university pay policy that attempts to equalize male and female professors' pay is discriminatory against the male professors.
*   A lawyer argues that a New York law firm misrepresented the state of its practice in an effort to lure the attorney from another firm. When she was fired as a part of cutbacks at the firm only a year later, she sued claiming the employer made false and misleading promises.
*   A supervisor gets sued by a former employee who claims the supervisor libeled him in a reference check.
*   Allstate Insurance fires an employee who is later hired by Fireman's Insurance. Allstate's letter of reference claimed the man lost his job in a restructuring. The families of victims of the three people the man murdered claimed he was fired for violent behavior and that Allstate should have warned Fireman's. The families sued Allstate claiming "negligent referral."
*   A victim of a cutback signs a document that waives his right to sue for age discrimination but grants him a more favorable pension settlement. A year later, he claims he was coerced and sues for age discrimination.

What Became of "Employment-at-Will"?

As we discussed in Chapter 1, the rate of litigation related to workplace activity is increasing even though practicing managers should know more about the legal implications of their behavior than managers did 20 or even 10 years ago. One 1996 estimate puts the increase at anywhere from 4 to 10 times as much activity from 1991 to 1995 alone.[4]

One reason for the increase in legal activity is an increase in the legal options and theories available to someone who believes he or she has been treated unfairly in the workplace. One recent review summarized the "piecemeal evolution" of the U.S. employment law system as follows:

> Employees are now statutorily protected from workplace discrimination on the basis of race, color, sex, religion, national origin, age, union status, disability, marital status, and in some places, sexual preference, smoking habits, personal appearance, height and weight, political affiliation, arrest and conviction records, and even the method of birth control they chose. Simultaneously, courts have applied long-standing common law to recognize torts of wrongful discharge, negligent and intentional infliction of emotional distress, breach of contract, invasions of privacy, fraud, defamation, and negligent hiring, retention, training, and supervision. Employment law further affords

employees the right to a minimum wage and to overtime pay, the right to a safe and healthful workplace, and the right to benefits of Social Security, unemployment insurance, worker's compensation, family and medical leave, and proper administration of their pension. Thus, U.S. employment law is a broad patchwork of federal and state statutory rights, common law rights, and administratively created rights that can be implicated by almost any managerial decision that affects employees.[5]

The cases we just listed illustrate this summary. Most Americans work under the **employment-at-will** doctrine that stipulates both employer and employee can terminate a working relationship at any time and for any reason other than those characteristics or situations explicitly covered by law. As illustrated by the summary above, these characteristics and situations are expanding.

There are more and more challenges to the employment-at-will doctrine today and plaintiffs are winning large judgments against employers under creative legal theories related to contract or tort law. For example, courts have ruled that an **implied contract** exists by the actions or statements of the employer. Statements in employment documents and manuals are often used to define the contract. But the use of a theory such as a violation of the implied contract or other exceptions to the employment-at-will doctrine depends on the particular state (the lawyer who claimed false promises won her case in New York, but she may not have prevailed in other states).[6]

The same argument applies to rights of privacy. The legality of the surveillance of employees and the interception of e-mail messages depends to some extent on the jurisdiction of the action. The exact behavior may result in the opposite outcome as a consequence of the particular jurisdiction of the lawsuit.

As the rate of lawsuits related to employment increases, the law gets more confusing to interpret as lawyers attempt different legal theories to support their case and these theories are accepted or rejected by the various jurisdictions. These creative legal theories have been directed at both large and small businesses. Claims of EEO violations are also up significantly for small businesses.[7]

We will discuss the trends in litigation related to specific HR practices when we cover a particular HRM activity. The practice of human resources is a litigious minefield with more mines being planted in the form of new laws or regulations and the judicial acceptance of new legal theories of unfair or injurious employment practice. This expansion of new legal theories combined with the changing demographics of the workforce (an aging, more diverse workforce) strongly support the proposition that the legal "minefield" will be even more heavily mined in the future.

We will first enter perhaps the most contentious of the minefields: equal employment opportunity law. We will bring up other legal issues as they relate to particular HR activities when we discuss those activities throughout the text.

EQUAL EMPLOYMENT OPPORTUNITY LAW

Before the civil rights movement of the early 1960s, employment decisions were often made on the basis of an applicant or worker's race, gender, religion, or other characteristics unrelated to job qualifications or performance. In 1962, for example, nonwhites represented 11 percent of the civilian labor force but 22 percent of the unemployed. Nonwhites were twice as likely as whites to hold semiskilled or unskilled jobs. Median annual income for nonwhite males in 1960 was 60 percent of the median income of white males; nonwhite women earned 50 percent of their white female counterparts' wages.[8] And across racial groups, women earned less than men, even in identical jobs.

The laws we will discuss in this chapter were designed to punish employers that used such criteria as race, gender, disability, or age to exclude certain persons from employment or from certain employment benefits. They were also designed to restore the unfairly treated worker to the position she or he would have held absent the discrimination. Our focus will not be on punishment, however, but on preventing unfair treatment and the potential legal vulnerability of managers under the civil rights laws.

What Is Employment Discrimination?

Employment discrimination occurs in a variety of ways and there are a number of methods for seeking redress through the courts. While the legal definition of **discrimination** differs depending on the specific law, it can be broadly defined as *employment decision making or working conditions that are advantageous (or disadvantageous) to members of one group compared to members of another group.* The discrimination can be *intentional,* such as a decision to *not* promote someone because she is female or *unintentional,* such as the use of a test on which groups score differently. The decision making can apply to personnel selection, admission to training programs, promotions, work assignments, transfers, compensation, layoffs, punishments, and dismissals. The conditions can also pertain to the work atmosphere itself. For example, a common lawsuit today concerns allegations of sexually harassing behaviors at work that place an individual in an offensive or intimidating environment. Over 700 women employed at a Mitsubishi plant in Normal, Illinois, made such a claim in 1996. One secretary for Baker and McKenzie won a $3.5 million judgment for sexual harassment by a partner in the world's largest law firm.

What Are the Major Sources of EEO Redress?

Figure 3.1 lists the possible bases for suits involving allegations of employment discrimination. Of the many sources of redress that are available, the most frequently used sources are **Title VII of the 1964 U.S. Civil Rights Act,** the **Age Discrimination in Employment Act of 1967,** and the **Americans with Disabilities Act of 1990.** Most of the states also have their own fair employment laws. Other laws such as the **Equal Pay Act** and the **Family and Medical Leave Act** are related to discrimination but have particular relevance to compensation and benefits, which we will cover in Chapter 10. Another source of redress is binding arbitration, a process for addressing complaints outside of the court system.

The EEOC typically receives over 95,000 claims of discrimination per year, with about 500 active class action suits brought by groups of people claiming the same or similar forms of discrimination against an organization (check the EEOC's Web site [http://www.eeoc.gov] for current legal activity). The highest percentage of claims of discrimination are for race, gender, age, disability, national origin, and religion (in that order).[9] Unfortunately, claims of discrimination are up for all of these areas. National origin lawsuits increased substantially in 1996; this includes suits from resident aliens. Aliens who are eligible to work in the United States are covered by Title VII. The EEOC has stated that religious discrimination is a priority of investigation for 1997.

The 1991 amendment to Title VII of the Civil Rights Act and the increasing diversity of the workforce have increased the number of lawsuits brought under Title VII. Compensatory and punitive damages are now available for violations of the law, thus creating a greater financial incentive for plaintiffs and plaintiffs' attorneys to pursue these cases. Also, Title VII now covers employees of U.S. companies working abroad.

FIGURE 3.1
BASES AND SOURCES OF REDRESS FOR ALLEGED EMPLOYMENT DISCRIMINATION

SOURCE	PURPOSE	ADMINISTRATION
Fifth Amendment, U.S. Constitution	To protect against federal violation of "due process"	Federal courts
13th Amendment, U.S. Constitution	To abolish slavery	Federal courts
14th Amendment, U.S. Constitution	To protect against state violations of "due process" and to afford equal protection for all	Federal courts
Civil Rights Act, 1866	To establish the right of all citizens to make and enforce contracts	Federal courts
Civil Rights Act, 1871	To make citizens liable for suits	Federal courts
Equal Pay Act, 1963	To prohibit sex discrimination in wages and salary: equal pay for equal work	EEOC and federal courts
Civil Rights Act, 1964 (Title VII), as amended in 1991	In 703(a) and (b), to declare all discriminatory employment practices unlawful	EEOC and federal courts
Age Discrimination in Employment Act (ADEA), 1967, as amended in 1978 and 1986	To prohibit discrimination against persons age 40 and older	EEOC and federal courts
Equal Employment Opportunity Act, 1972	To extend coverage of the 1964 Civil Rights Act to include both public and private sectors, educational institutions, labor organizations, and employment agencies	EEOC and federal courts
Rehabilitation Act, 1973	To protect persons with disabilities against discrimination (public sector)	Department of Labor
Americans with Disabilities Act (ADA), 1990	To prohibit discrimination against persons with disabilities	EEOC and federal courts
Executive Orders 11246 and 11375	To prohibit discrimination by contractors or subcontractors of federal agencies	OFCCP
Executive Order 11478	To prescribe merit as a basis for federal personnel policy, to prohibit discrimination, and to mandate equal opportunity programs	U.S. Office of Personnel Management
Binding arbitration	Hear labor disputes outside of court system	American Arbitration Association
State laws	To prohibit discrimination and to establish fair employment practices commissions	Fair Employment Practices Commissions
Local laws	To prohibit discrimination	Municipal courts

Equal employment laws similar to Title VII exist in 41 states and Washington, D.C., and Puerto Rico. State and local laws vary on the legality of certain personnel practices. For example, 10 states and the District of Columbia and over 80 municipalities have laws prohibiting employment discrimination based on sexual orientation.[10] Several states also provide additional protection beyond the ADA against discrimination against people who are HIV positive, or are victims of AIDS.

What Is the Cost of Violating EEO Laws?

Employers are now well aware of how costly violations of EEO laws can be. In a much publicized case in 1996, Texaco settled a Title VII lawsuit for $176 million. Denny's Restaurant paid out $46 million to African-American employees and customers and an additional $9 million in legal fees in 1994 to settle numerous claims of discrimination. One Ann Arbor, Michigan, clothing store settled a sexual harassment lawsuit for $200,000 in 1996. The store owner had no insurance for harassment and an after-tax profit of only $170,000 for that year. And the $200,000 didn't include the attorney's fees for his defense.

With back-pay awards reaching millions of dollars in some cases and with the possibility of punitive damages, organizations are now much more careful about their personnel practices, using monitoring systems and EEO offices and training programs for personnel decision makers and supervisors. These activities may be paying off as employers are now winning a higher percentage of discrimination cases than they were in the 1980s.[11]

One major component of training programs is simply making personnel decision makers aware of EEO laws. Let us follow this approach by introducing you to the major laws that account for most of the regulation and litigation in EEO. We present these laws in the same order as the frequency with which they are used as a source of redress in employment discrimination claims. Remember also that many other laws affect HRM practice and were the basis of some of the claims we presented at the beginning of the chapter. Those laws will be introduced when we cover the most relevant HRM activity in the text.

TITLE VII OF THE CIVIL RIGHTS ACT OF 1964

The Civil Rights Act was signed by President Johnson in 1964 and was amended by the **Equal Employment Opportunity Act** in 1972 and the **Civil Rights Act** of 1991. *Title VII deals specifically with discrimination in employment and prohibits discrimination based on race, color, religion, sex, or national origin.* Figure 3.2 provides major excerpts from Title VII. The act covers all employers having more than 15 employees except private clubs, religious organizations, and places of employment connected to an Indian reservation.

The **U.S. Equal Employment Opportunity Commission (EEOC),** an agency of the U.S. Department of Labor, was created to monitor and enforce compliance with Title VII. Originally, the major functions of the EEOC were to investigate complaints and to try to resolve the dispute through conciliation. The 1972 amendments increased the authority of the EEOC to bring action against organizations in the courts. For example, the EEOC actually filed Title VII suits against Mitsubishi for sexual harassment and against Texaco for racial discrimination in 1996.

The EEOC also issues interpretive regulations regarding employment practices (you can review these guidelines at www.EEOC.Gov). Among the most important regulatory interpretations issued by the EEOC are the **Uniform Guidelines on Employee Selection Procedures** adopted in 1978, which provide recommendations for employment staffing, and the **Interpretative Guidelines on Sexual Harassment** issued in 1980. While these guidelines are not law, the courts often use them to evaluate whether the behavior violates the law. The EEOC also requires that most organizations submit an annual EEO-1 form, which is illustrated in Figure 3.3. Data from these forms are used to identify possible patterns of discrimination in particular organizations or segments of the workforce. The EEOC may then take legal action against an organization based on these data. Data from these forms prompted the EEOC to file the 1996 lawsuit against Texaco.

What Is Not Prohibited by Title VII?

Title VII does not prohibit discrimination based on seniority systems, veterans' preference rights, national security reasons, or job qualifications based on test scores, backgrounds, or experience, even when the use of such practices may be correlated with race, gender, color, religion, or national origin. Title VII also does not prohibit **bona fide occupational qualifications (BFOQs)** or discriminatory practices whenever these practices are "reasonably necessary to the normal operation of the organization." For example, a BFOQ that excludes one group (e.g., males or females) from an employment opportunity is permissible if the employer can argue that the "essence of the business" requires the exclusion, that is, when business would be significantly affected by not employing members of one group exclusively. Pan American World Airways tried this argument in *Diaz v. Pan American World Airways*.[12] Pan Am presented data that showed a majority of its customers preferred female flight attendants, stating that not hiring males was done for important business reasons. In this case, a federal appellate court ruled that customer preference was not a

FIGURE 3.2
EXCERPTS FROM TITLE VII OF THE CIVIL RIGHTS ACT OF 1964

SECTION 703

(a) It shall be an unlawful practice for an employer
(1) to fail to hire or to discharge any individual, or otherwise to discriminate against any individual with respect to compensation, terms, conditions, or privileges of employment, because of such individual's race, color, religion, sex, or national origin; or (2) to limit, segregate, or classify employees or applicants for employment in any way which would deprive or tend to deprive any individual of employment opportunities or otherwise adversely affect status as an employee, because of such individual's race, color, religion, sex, or national origin.

(e) Notwithstanding any other provision of this title,
(1) it shall not be an unlawful employment practice for an employer to hire and employ those employees . . . on the basis of religion, sex, or national origin in those certain instances where religion, sex, or national origin is a bona fide occupational qualification reasonably necessary to the normal operation of that particular business or enterprise . . .

(h) Notwithstanding any other provision of this title, it shall not be an unlawful employment practice for an employer to apply different standards of compensation, or different terms, conditions, or privileges of employment pursuant to a bona fide seniority or merit system, or a system which measures earnings by quantity or quality of production or to employees who work in different locations, provided that such differences are not the result of an intention to discriminate because of race, color, religion, sex, or national origin, nor shall it be unlawful employment practice for an employer to give and act upon the results of any professionally developed ability test provided that such test, its administration or action upon the results is not designed, intended, or used to discriminate because of race, color, religion, sex, or national origin . . .

(j) Nothing contained in this title shall be interpreted to require any employer . . . to grant preferential treatment to any individual or to any group because of the race, color, religion, sex, or national origin of such individual or group on account of an imbalance which may exist with respect to the total number or percentage of persons of any race, color, religion, sex, or national origin employed by any employer . . . in comparison with the total number or percentage of persons of such race, color, religion, sex, or national origin in any community, State, section, or other ares, or in the available work force in any community, State, section, or other area.

SECTION 704

(a) It shall be an unlawful employment practice for an employer to discriminate against any employees or applicants for employment . . . because the employee or applicant has opposed any practice made an unlawful employment practice by this title, or because he or she has made a charge, testified, assisted, or participated in any matter in an investigation, proceeding, or hearing under this title.

FIGURE 3.3
EEO-1 FORM

Standard Form 100
(Rev. 12-76)
Approved GAO 8-180541 (R0077)
Expires 12-31-78

EQUAL EMPLOYMENT OPPORTUNITY
EMPLOYER INFORMATION REPORT EEO-1

Joint Reporting
Committee
• Equal Employment
Opportunity Commission
• Office of Federal Contract
Compliance Programs

SECTION A—TYPE OF REPORT
Refer to instructions for number and types of reports to be filled

1. Indicate by marking in the appropriate box the type of reporting unit for which this copy of the form is submitted (MARK ONLY ONE BOX)

Multi-establishment Employer
(1) ❏   Single-establishment Employer Report

(2) ❏ Consolidated Report
(3) ❏ Headquarters Unit Report
(4) ❏ Individual Establishment Report (submit one for each establishment with 25 or more employees)
(5) ❏ Special Report

2. Total number of reports being filed by this Company (Answer on Consolidated Report only) _____

Section B—COMPANY IDENTIFICATION (To be answered by all employers)

OFFICE
USE
ONLY

1. Parent Company
   a. Name of parent company (owns or controls establishment in item 2) omit if same as label

a.

Name of receiving office	Address (Number and street)

b.

City or town	County	State	ZIP Code	
			b. Employer Identification No.	

2. Establishment for which this report is filed (Omit if same as label)
   a. Name of establishment

c.

Address (Number and street)	City or town	County	State	ZIP code

d.

b. Employer Identification No. _____   (If same as label skip)

3. Parent company affiliation   (Multi-establishment Employers / Answer on Consolidated Report only)
   a. Name of parent—affiliated company   b. Employer Identification No.

Address (Number and street)	City or town	County	State	ZIP code

---

Section C—EMPLOYERS WHO ARE REQUIRED TO FILE (To be answered by all employers)

❏ Yes   ❏ No   1   Does the entire company have at least 100 employees in the payroll period for which you are reporting?

❏ Yes   ❏ No   2   Is you company affiliated through common ownership and/or centralized management with other entities in an enterprise with a total employment of 100 or more?

❏ Yes   ❏ No   3   Does the company or any of its establishments (a) have 50 or more employees AND (b) is not exempt as provided by 41 CFR 60-1.5. AND either (1) is a prime government contractor or first-tier subcontractor, and has a contract, subcontract, or purchase order amounting to $50,000 or more, or (2) serves as a depository of Government funds in any amount or is a financial institution which is an issuing and paying agent for U.S. Savings Bonds and Savings Notes?

NOTE: If the answer is yes to ANY of these questions, complete the entire form, otherwise skip to Section G.

FIGURE 3.3
(Continued)

Section D—EMPLOYMENT DATA

Employment at the establishment–Report all permanent, temporary, or part-time employees including apprentices and on-the-job trainees unless specifically excluded as set forth in the instruction. Enter the appropriate figures on all lines and in all columns. Blank spaces will be considered as zeros.

JOB CATEGORIES	OVERALL TOTALS (SUM OF COL. B THRU K)	MALE					FEMALE				
		WHITE (NOT OF HISPANIC ORIGIN)	BLACK (NOT OF HISPANIC ORIGIN)	HISPANIC	ASIAN OR PACIFIC ISLANDER	AMERICAN INDIAN OR ALASKAN NATIVE	WHITE (NOT OF HISPANIC ORIGIN)	BLACK (NOT OF HISPANIC ORIGIN)	HISPANIC	ASIAN OR PACIFIC ISLANDER	AMERICAN INDIAN OR ALASKAN NATIVE
	A	B	C	D	E	F	G	H	I	J	K
Officials and Managers											
Professionals											
Technicians											
Sales Workers											
Office and Clerical											
Craft Workers (Skilled)											
Operatives (Semi-Skilled)											
Laborers (Unskilled)											
Service Workers											
TOTAL											
Total employment reported in previous EEO-1 report											

(The trainees below should also be included in the figures for the appropriate occupational categories above)

Formal On-the-job trainees	White											
	Production											

1 NOTE: On consolidated report, skip questions 2–5 and Section E.

2 How was the information as to race or ethnic group in Section D obtained.

    1 ☐ Visual Survey   3 ☐ Other—Specify ....

    2 ☐ Employment Record   ....

3 Dates of payroll period used–

4 Pay period of last report submitted for this establishment

5. Does this establishment employ apprentices?

    This year? 1 ☐ Yes   2 ☐ No

    Last year? 1 ☐ Yes   2 ☐ No

Section E—ESTABLISHMENT INFORMATION

1. Is the location of the establishment the same as that reported last year?	2. Is the major business activity at this establishment the same as that reported last year?	OFFICE USE ONLY
1. ☐ Yes 2. ☐ No 3 ☐ Did not last year 4 ☐ Reported on combined basis	1. ☐ Yes 2. ☐ No 3 ☐ No report last year 4 ☐ Reported on combined	

3. What is the major activity of this establishment? (Be specific, i.e., manufacturing steel castings, retail grocer, wholesale plumbing supplies, title insurance, etc. Include the specific type of product or type of service provided, as well as the principal business or industrial activity.

a.

Section F—REMARKS

Use this item to give any identification data appearing on last report which differs from that given above, explain major changes in composition or reporting units, and other pertinent information.

Section G—CERTIFICATION (See instructions G)

Check one

1. ☐ All reports are accurate and were prepared in accordance with the instructions (check on consolidated only)

2. ☐ This report is accurate and was prepared in accordance with the instructions.

Name of Certifying Official	Title	Signature	Date
Name of person to contact regarding this report (Type or print)	Address (Number and street)		
Title	City and State	ZIP Code	Telephone Area Code Number Extension

All reports and information obtained from individual reports will be kept confidential as required by Section 709 (e) of Title VII

WILLFULLY FALSE STATEMENTS ON THIS REPORT ARE PUNISHABLE BY LAW, U.S. CODE, TITLE 18, SECTION 1001

legally defensible reason for discrimination. Further, the court stated that discrimination based on gender is valid only when the essence of the business would be undermined by not hiring members of one sex exclusively. Gender discrimination has even been disallowed in cases where the company has a legitimate concern for the health and safety of females.[13]

The "essence of the business" issue was quite clear when it came to Pan Am but gets a little murkier when it comes to a restaurant such as Hooters, which employs only females to wait on tables. In a suit filed in 1995 and supported by the EEOC, male plaintiffs maintained they were victims of discrimination because they were denied employment at Hooters. In response, Hooters attorneys have argued that the essence of the business is at least to some extent sex and that the target clientele is young males who would probably prefer young, attractive females waiting on them. This one is obviously a close call, but the EEOC's involvement in the case was subjected to so much derisive newspaper editorializing that it dropped out of the case.[14] The Hooters case settled in 1997.

In general, the position of the courts regarding BFOQs clearly favors judgments about the performance, abilities, or potential of specific individuals rather than discrimination by class or categories. The court has said the BFOQ exception to Title VII is a narrow one, limited to policies that are directly related to a worker's ability to do the job and the essence of the business.

Can an English-only rule be a BFOQ? The short answer to this question is yes, but it depends on the situation. The position of the EEOC is that an organization must present strong evidence of "business necessity" if an English-only rule is to be invoked.

How Do You File a Title VII Lawsuit?

If an individual believes that he or she has been a victim of illegal discrimination and wishes to pursue a claim through the legal system, the complaint must first be filed with an office of the EEOC. Figure 3.4 illustrates this process. This complaint must be filed within six months of the alleged discriminatory practice. The EEOC will investigate the complaint or refer it to a local or state EEO human rights agency (called a "deferral" agency). Through interviews, on-site visits and evaluation of records, the investigating agency will then determine whether there is probable cause to believe there is a violation of Title VII. If the agency determines no probable cause, the complainant is so notified and informed that a private lawsuit may still be filed in federal court. The complainant is given a "right to sue" letter, which signifies that the EEOC no longer has exclusive jurisdiction over the case. A complaining party may obtain a right-to-sue letter before the EEOC has ruled in the case as long as at least 180 days have elapsed since the

individual filed with the EEOC. If probable cause is determined, the EEOC will attempt to settle the matter through a process known as **conciliation.** The objective of conciliation is to gain an agreement by all parties while avoiding litigation. If conciliation fails, the EEOC may file suit in federal district court if the employer is private or refer the case to the U.S. Justice Department if the employer is a public agency.

The EEOC launched a priority system and mediation program in 1995 in an effort to reduce its backlog of cases (about 100,000 cases in 1996). While mediation is nonbinding, early evidence indicates the service has facilitated the resolution of cases.[15]

What Legal Steps Are Followed in a Title VII Case?

The Supreme Court has established the legal steps to be followed in a Title VII action through the federal court system. Although the plaintiff retains the burden of proof, a model is used such that the burden of producing evidence shifts from the plaintiff to the defendant and back to the plaintiff. Initially the complainant, or plaintiff, has the burden to show that a **prima facie** case of discrimination exists. Prima facie means "presumed to be true until proven otherwise"; the plaintiff must show that there is a high likelihood that EEO law has been violated. After the plaintiff produces sufficient evidence to establish a prima facie case, the burden of producing evidence shifts to the employer or defendant, who must provide some proof of a legitimate, nondiscriminatory reason for the employment decision. Finally, the burden of producing evidence shifts back to the plaintiff to either show that the reason given was a pretext for discrimination or that an alternate practice, less discriminatory in its effect, would achieve the employer's purpose equally well. Title VII cases can be brought under one of two theories: **disparate treatment** and **disparate impact.** The steps to follow for each are illustrated in Figure 3.5.

WHAT IS DISPARATE TREATMENT?   Plaintiffs can demonstrate a prima facie case by showing disparate treatment, the most frequently used theory. According to the procedures established in the 1973 *McDonnell Douglas v. Green* Supreme Court case, plaintiffs must show that an employer treats one or more members of a protected group differently.[16] For example, the use of different criteria for promotion depending on the candidate's sex would constitute disparate treatment. Female applicants who were not hired for a firm might show that the employer asked them questions about their marital status or child care arrangements that were not asked of male applicants.

In disparate treatment cases, the Supreme Court established that the burden is on the plaintiff to prove that the employer *intended* to discriminate because of race,

FIGURE 3.4
FLOWCHART:
EEOC CHARGES UNDER TITLE VII

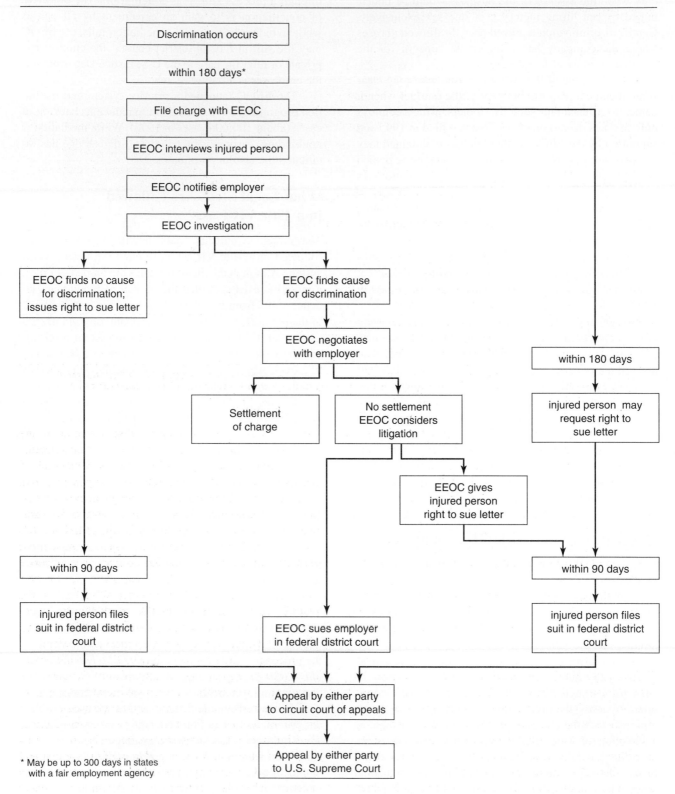

* May be up to 300 days in states
  with a fair employment agency

FIGURE 3.5
EVIDENCE AND PROOF IN TITLE VII CASES

EVIDENCE BURDEN	DISPARATE TREATMENT	DISPARATE IMPACT
Plaintiff's initial burden (prima facie case)	He or she belongs to the discriminated-against group. He or she applied and was qualified. He or she was rejected. The position remained open to applicants with equal or fewer qualifications.	Unequal impact of the practice(s) in question on different groups.
Defendant's rebuttal burden	Articulate a "legitimate nondiscriminatory reason for the rejection."	Demonstrate that the challenged practice is job-related for the position in question and consistent with business necessity.
Plaintiff's burden in response	Show that the stated reason is a pretext by demonstrating, e.g.: • The employer doesn't apply that reason equally to all. • The employer has treated the plaintiff unfairly before. • The employer engages in other unfair employment practices. OR Show the plaintiff's group membership was a factor in the rejection decision.	Show that a less discriminatory alternative practice does exist.
Defendant's burden in response	Show that the decision would have been the same even if it had not taken plaintiff's group membership into account.	

Source: Adapted from *Federal regulation of personnel in human resource management* 2/e by Ledvinka/Scarpello, Copyright © 1992. Wadsworth Publishing. By permission of South-Western College Publishing, a division of International Thompson Publishing, Inc., Cincinnati, Ohio 45227.

sex, color, religion, or national origin. For example, Alice Burdine claimed she was a victim of sex discrimination by the Texas Department of Community Affairs. Her employer was not required, said the U.S. Supreme Court, to prove that it did not discriminate against her but needed only to "articulate some legitimate nondiscriminatory reason" for the negative decision. The court indicated the plaintiff has the ultimate burden of proving that an employer intentionally discriminated against the plaintiff.[17]

One special form of disparate treatment is retaliation. Employers cannot retaliate against employees who file EEO charges or parties who testify on behalf of plaintiffs in such cases.

WHAT IS DISPARATE IMPACT? According to procedures established in the 1971 *Griggs v. Duke Power* case, plaintiffs can show that an employer's practices had a disparate impact on members of a protected group by showing that the employment procedures (e.g., tests, interviews, credentials) had a disproportionately negative effect on members of a protected group.[18] Impact cases are often established as class action cases in which a judge can certify a class of people who make similar claims against a company. For example, the 1,500 plaintiffs in the Texaco case were certified as a class before the rest of the case could be pursued. Such impact is considered *unintentional* but illegal discrimination if the employment practice is not shown to be "job related." For example, if an organization hired 50 whites and 5 blacks from 100 white and 100 black applicants, then disparate impact has occurred. Whether or not the employer had good intentions or didn't mean to discriminate is irrelevant to the courts in this type of lawsuit. After the plaintiff shows evidence of disparate impact, the employer must carry the burden of producing evidence of "business necessity" or "job relatedness" for the employment practice. Finally, the burden shifts back to the plaintiff who must then show that an alternative procedure is available that is equal to or better than the employer's practice and has a less discriminatory effect.

Figure 3.6 lists employment practices having potential disparate impact against minorities or females. The most common examples are employment tests, educational requirements, and physical characteristics (e.g., a height requirement). Whether the use of such practices constitutes illegal discrimination depends on the employment situation. Most experts on EEO law contend that it is easier for employers to defend the use of such practices when the practices can be shown to be closely related to the job.

HOW DO YOU DETERMINE DISPARATE OR ADVERSE IMPACT? The yardstick recommended by

FIGURE 3.6
EMPLOYEE SCREENING DEVICES WITH POTENTIAL DISPARATE IMPACT

Educational requirements	Preferences for relatives of present employees
Tests	Use of walk-in or word-of-mouth recruiting
Experience requirements	
Height and weight requirements	Reference checks
Physical agility tests	Promoting from within
Excluding applicants with arrest-conviction records	Promotion based on supervisor recommendations
Excluding unwed parents	Excluding applicants with less than honorable discharges
Preferences for applicants with honorable discharges	

Source: Bureau of National Affairs. *Fair employment practices manual.* Washington: Bureau of National Affairs, 1983, pp. 401ff., 421.

the EEOC in the Uniform Guidelines and adopted in numerous court cases for determining disparate or adverse impact is the **four-fifths rule.** This rule means that a selection rate (number selected/number applied) for a protected group cannot be less than 80 percent of the rate for the group with the highest selection rate. For example, the city of Columbus, Ohio, used a paper-and-pencil, multiple-choice examination to screen applicants for its firefighter positions. While 84 percent of the whites passed the examination, only 27 percent of the blacks did. Using the four-fifths rule, 80 percent of the highest selection rate (84 percent) is 67 percent. The 27 percent selection rate for the other group (blacks) is less than 67 percent, so the test was determined to have an adverse impact on blacks.

The disparate impact theory has been used in many cases involving "neutral employment practices" such as tests, entrance requirements, particular credentials, or physical requirements. In *Watson v. Fort Worth Bank and Trust,* the Supreme Court extended use of the disparate impact theory in cases involving "subjective" employment practices such as job interviews, performance appraisals, and job recommendations. Thus, statistical data such as the four-fifths rule can be used in a disparate impact case to establish prima facie evidence of discrimination when decisions are based on subjective employment practices.[19] The court also ruled that statistics that can illustrate adverse impact may also be used in disparate treatment cases to support a theory of discrimination.

Despite the court's extension of disparate impact to subjective employment practices, there is little agreement on how a plaintiff can demonstrate disparate impact or how an employer can defend against such a charge with an argument of job relatedness. The Civil Rights Act of 1991 is unclear as to precisely what an employer must demonstrate; it simply says the employer must demonstrate *"that the challenged practice is job related for the position in question and consistent with business necessity."* There is a great deal of litigation over just what both employees and the companies they sue must demonstrate under the CRA of 1991.

How does an employer prove job relatedness? A large body of case law which provides legal definitions of the term *job related.* The first major case in this area is *Griggs v. Duke Power,* in which the Supreme Court struck down the use of an employment test and a high school educational requirement for entry-level personnel selection. Such practices were judged to be discriminatory because they excluded a disproportionate number of blacks from employment and because the employer could not show that the hiring requirements were "job related," or related to performance on the job. As the court noted, if an employment practice cannot be shown to be related to job performance, and that practice operates to exclude a disproportionate number of protected class members, then the practice is prohibited.

Since the Griggs decision was rendered in 1971, many cases have focused on job-relatedness issues. In *Albemarle Paper Company v. Moody,*[20] the Supreme Court clarified the job-relatedness defense, requiring a careful job analysis to identify the specific knowledge, skills, and abilities necessary to perform the job or a study that shows a clear relationship between a test score or particular job requirement and job performance. In *Connecticut v. Teal,* the Supreme Court declared the job-relatedness argument must be applied to *all* steps of a multiple-hurdle selection procedure. Winnie Teal had been denied promotion to a supervisory position because of a low score on a written exam, which was the first hurdle of the promotion process.[21] When the final promotion decisions were made, however, there was no disproportionate impact on blacks. In fact, the bottom line actually favored blacks. Of the 48 black candidates, 22.9 percent were promoted, while of the 259 white candidates, only 13.5 percent were promoted. This outcome didn't help Ms. Teal, who had been eliminated at the first step in the selection process. She claimed a Title VII violation because the written exam had a disproportionate impact against blacks and was not job related. The Supreme Court agreed with Ms. Teal. If one part of the selection procedure has adverse impact against a group covered under Title VII, it must be shown to be job related since it denies an employment opportunity to a disproportionate number of minorities and prevents them from proceeding to the next step in the selection process. This is necessary despite the fact that the bottom-line outcome of the employment decisions may be favorable to the same group.

While proving job relatedness seems like a fairly simple task for an organization, it has proven to be cumbersome in court. Of the cases dealing specifically with job relatedness, after a prima facie case was established, the majority of the cases were lost by the employer. This may have been because some courts have required employers to adhere to the Uniform Guidelines on Employee Selection Procedures. These guidelines describe very specific, difficult procedures for proving job relatedness. Chapter 6 will discuss these requirements in greater detail.

What Constitutes Sexual Harassment under Title VII?

Paula Jones filed a sexual harassment lawsuit against President Clinton for alleged behavior when he was governor of Arkansas. Her claims were not unlike many of the claims made to the EEOC. The rate of claims of sexual harassment has increased every year since 1991. It is estimated that between 50 and 70 percent of the female workforce has been subjected to some form of sexual harassment. Over 15,000 sexual harassment claims were filed with the EEOC in 1997 alone. Over one-third of *Fortune* 500 companies have been sued for sexual harassment. Despite all the training and the increased awareness, the number of complaints is expected to increase. In a publicized case, one San Francisco woman was awarded $3.5 million (reduced by a judge from over $7 million) because of sexual harassment by one partner of Baker and McKenzie, the largest law firm in the world. Obviously, with plaintiffs' attorneys taking an average of 40 percent of the judgment, there is quite an economic incentive for harassment claims.

Under Title VII, sexual harassment, like racial and ethnic harassment, is illegal since it constitutes discrimination with respect to a person's conditions of employment. These conditions can refer to psychological and emotional workplace conditions that are coercive or insulting to an individual. The EEOC has published guidelines for employers dealing with sexual harassment issues. According to the guidelines,

> Unwelcome sexual advances, requests for sexual favors, and other verbal or physical conduct of a sexual nature constitute sexual harassment when (1) submission to such conduct is made either explicitly or implicitly a term or condition of an individual's employment, (2) submission to or rejection of such conduct by an individual is used as the basis for employment decisions affecting such individual, or (3) such conduct has the purpose or effect of unreasonably interfering with an individual's work performance or creating an intimidating, hostile, or offensive working environment.[22]

In 1986, the Supreme Court in *Meritor Savings v. Vinson* stated it was not necessary for the plaintiff to establish a causal relationship between the rejection of sexual advances and a specific personnel action such as a dismissal or a layoff. Rather, it was only necessary for the plaintiff to establish that the harassment created unfavorable or hostile working conditions for him or her.[23] Any workplace conduct that is "sufficiently severe or pervasive to alter the conditions of employment and create an abusive working environment" constitutes illegal sexual harassment. The Supreme Court provided further clarification on this issue in *Harris v. Forklift*.[24] Theresa Harris was asked to remove coins from her boss's front pocket and to go to the Holiday Inn to "negotiate" her raise and was exposed to hundreds of other disgusting suggestions and behaviors. A lower court determined that Harris had not suffered emotionally from the harassment and thus a hostile working environment was not created. The Supreme Court disagreed, stating the psychological effect was unnecessary and that only a "reasonable person" needed to find it hostile or abusive. The court also provided some guidance for the lower courts in determining a hostile working environment. The frequency of the behavior or verbal abuse, its severity, the extent to which it is threatening or humiliating, and whether the abuse interferes with the employee's work performance may all be considered in making the determination of hostile working environment.

Research on the judicial outcomes of sexual harassment claims identified the following correlates of favorable legal outcomes for the claimant: (1) when the harassment involved physical contact of a sexual nature; (2) when sexual propositions were linked to threats or promises of a change in the conditions of employment; (3) when the claimant notified management of the problem before filing charges; (4) when the claims are corroborated; and (5) when the organization had no formal policy toward sexual harassment that had been communicated to its employees.[25] However, under *Meritor,* if the harasser is the victim's supervisor, the harassment need not be reported to the company for the plaintiff to prevail. In some cases, such as *Morris v. American National Can,* when a claimant wins, she or he is entitled to back pay, retroactive seniority, and compensation for workdays missed for trial preparation.[26] The Civil Rights Act of 1991 also provides for compensatory and punitive damages (in addition to back pay) of up to $300,000 for companies with over 500 employees. That's $300,000 per complaint. Remember the 700 claims against Mitsubishi for sexual harassment. You do the math. Also, the price tag for sexual harassment can be even much higher under state laws that have no ceilings on compensatory or punitive damages (this is why the Baker and McKenzie award was so high).

WHAT IS THE EMPLOYER'S LIABILITY IN SEXUAL HARASSMENT CASES? Employers are generally liable for the acts of their supervisors and managers regardless of whether the employer is aware of the acts. Regarding co-workers, if the employer knew or should have known of the harassment and did nothing to stop it, it will be liable. The courts are generally clear that this rule applies to any kind of harassment: racial, ethnic, or religious. Employers may also be liable for behaviors committed by nonemployees, clients, temporary employees, or outside contractors in the workplace if they knew or should have known about the acts and did not take appropriate action. Essentially, the courts have made it clear that an organization is liable for sexual harassment when management is aware of the activity yet does not take immediate and appropriate corrective action.[27]

An employer is not, however, always liable for sexual harassment. For example, a company is less likely to be found liable under the following conditions: (1) There is a specific policy on harassment, which an employee violated; (2) There is a company grievance procedure, which the complainant did not follow; and (3) The grievance procedure allows the complainant to bypass the alleged harasser in filing the violation.

WHAT STEPS SHOULD A COMPANY FOLLOW REGARDING SEXUAL HARASSMENT?

Due to the steady increase in Title VII litigation regarding sexual harassment, the following strategies have been recommended for organizations:

1. Develop a written policy against sexual harassment, including a definition of sexual harassment and a strong statement by the CEO that it will not be tolerated (this is required under Massachusetts state law; some courts have concluded that an employer without a harassment policy is sanctioning a hostile environment).

2. Conduct training to make managers aware of the problem (also required in Massachusetts).

3. Inform employees that they should expect a workplace free from harassment, and what actions they can take under Title VII if their rights are violated.

4. Detail the sanctions for violators and protection for those who make any charges.

5. Establish a grievance procedure for alleged victims of harassment.

6. Investigate claims made by victims.

7. Discipline violators of the policy.

On this last point, companies must be careful. Individuals can claim "unlawful termination" and have prevailed in cases where they show that they were not treated fairly in the investigation or the hearing that led to the dismissal. Judgments have been in the millions of dollars. The person being accused of sexual harassment deserves the same fair treatment afforded the accuser. Miller Brewing executive Jerold MacKenzie was awarded over $26 million after he was fired for "sexually harassing" a female worker by telling her about a *Seinfeld* episode.

Employers should also consider purchasing liability insurance for harassment claims. Although expensive, with the potential employer liability and the increasing number of harassment suits, insurance is probably a good investment (remember the clothing store owner we referred to earlier; he could have gotten harassment insurance for about $135 a month).

What Is the Relationship Between Seniority Systems and Title VII?

Title VII permits bona fide seniority systems if they were established without an intent to discriminate, even if such systems restrict employment opportunities for certain classes of individuals. Thus, a promotional system that awards "points" toward promotion for past service is not illegal under Title VII. Nor is a "last hired, first fired" policy that hurts blacks or females who were recently hired as part of an affirmative action program. For example, the courts state you cannot deny white employees the benefits of their seniority in order to provide remedies for minorities. This rationale has applied to cases involving organizations facing layoffs and operating under consent decrees imposed by the courts for a past history of discrimination such as *Firefighters Local Union No. 1784 v. Stotts.*[28] It has also applied to firms with voluntary affirmative action programs. For example, in *Wygant v. Jackson Board of Education,*[29] the court struck down a Michigan school district plan that sought to protect minority hiring gains by laying off white teachers ahead of blacks with less seniority.

The Supreme Court has mandated retroactive seniority to give the "rightful place" to individuals who were denied employment opportunities because of illegal discrimination under Title VII. For example, in *Franks v. Bowman Transportation Co.,*[30] individuals denied employment opportunities due to illegal discrimination in 1968 would be awarded "retroactive seniority" back to this date to allow them to regain their "rightful place."

AFFIRMATIVE ACTION: EXECUTIVE ORDERS 11246, 11375, SECTION 503 OF THE REHABILITATION ACT

In 1965, President Johnson signed Executive Order 11246, which prohibits discrimination in federal employment on the basis of race, creed, color, and national origin. In 1968, it was amended by Executive Order 11375 to change the word *creed* to *religion* and to add sex discrimination to the other prohibited items. The executive order applies to all federal agencies, contractors, and subcontractors. Contractors and subcontractors with more than $50,000 in government business and 50 or more employees are not only prohibited from discriminating, but also must take affirmative action to ensure that applicants and employees are not treated differently as a function of their sex, religion, race, color, and national origin. Section 503 of the Rehabilitation Act requires federal contractors to take affirmative action to employ and advance qualified people with disabilities.

What Is Affirmative Action?

Although there is no one generally recognized definition, **affirmative action** has to do with the extent to which employers make an effort through their personnel practices to attract, retain, and upgrade members of the protected classes of the 1964 Civil Rights Act or persons with disabilities.

Affirmative action may refer to several strategies including: actively recruiting underrepresented groups in a firm, changing management and employee attitudes about various protected groups, eliminating irrelevant employment practices that bar protected groups from employment, and granting preferential treatment to protected groups.[31] Some argue that *affirmative action* has been replaced with *diversity* programs and policies, but the actual HRM activities defining the old affirmative action programs and the new diversity programs are very similar. The issue of affirmative action and how it is carried out has been identified as the source of more problems between HRM professionals and line managers than any other HR activity.[32] Whether or not preferential treatment can or should be granted based on protected class characteristics is at the heart of the difficulties.

Who Enforces Executive Order 11246 and Section 503?

Executive Order 11246 and Section 503 are enforced by the Department of Labor (DOL) through the Office of Federal Contract Compliance Programs (OFCCP). The OFCCP is charged with processing complaints as well as compliance review. This means that in addition to reviewing complaints, it can visit a company's facilities and review the affirmative action plans for compliance with the law. The OFCCP issued new guidelines in 1996 for Executive Order 11246 compliance that include "targets or goals" to bring the number of minority and female workers up to their percentages in the available labor pool. Such goals are to be "affirmatively pursued."[33] While these goals are not meant to be hard and fast quotas for personnel practices, goals are interpreted as quotas by some OFCCP compliance officers, and pressure and action is taken against federal contractors according to this interpretation (see http://www.dol.gov/esa/public/OFCP_ORG.HTM).

If noncompliance is found, the OFCCP generally first tries to reach a conciliation agreement with the firm through special hiring or recruitment programs, seniority credit, or back pay. For example, Prudential Insurance Company signed a conciliation agreement in which it agreed to provide training to over 8,000 minorities and women who were rejected for jobs over a five-year period. The company also agreed to offer jobs to a percentage of those who were trained. Prudential was never formally charged with discrimination before the company entered into the conciliation agreement. If an agreement cannot be reached, the firm is scheduled to have a hearing with a judge. If an agreement is still not reached during this time, employers may lose their government contracts or have their payments withheld. They may also lose the right to bid on future government contracts or be debarred from all subsequent contract work until "affirmative action" programs are judged to be more effective. Needless to say, contractors and subcontractors pay careful attention to the OFCCP. For example, over 400,000 employers have affirmative action programs reviewed by the OFCCP.

Although Executive Order 11246 applies only to organizations receiving federal funds, many other organizations, both public and private, have implemented voluntary affirmative action or diversity programs, either to redress previous discriminatory employment practices or because they wish to make their workforce more representative of the labor market. There is now a general belief among large employers in particular that AA and diversity programs contribute to the positive image of the organization. As we discussed in Chapter 2, this image can contribute to assessments of "customer value" and assist in recruiting women and minorities.

While there has been considerable political debate over Executive Order 11246, a 1994 study by the Department of Labor found that claims of reverse discrimination based on 11246 policy are very rare. As the DOL report points out, a contractor's only obligation is to make a "good faith effort" to meet affirmative action goals. Hiring unqualified people is not required.[34]

What Is the Legal Status of Affirmative Action?

Federal courts can order involuntary affirmative action programs or organizations can implement voluntary affirmative action without court mandate. The legality of such programs is now more questionable than it was 10 years ago. As part of either a judicial decision or the negotiated settlement of a lawsuit, a court can also order targeted quota hiring. For example, as part of a negotiated settlement with the U.S. Forest Service in 1994, a California federal judge ordered the Forest Service to hire a set number of females over a prescribed time period. The Forest Service had to submit an annual report on compliance with the quota and was subject to punitive action for failure to comply. In an attempt to comply with the numerical mandate, the Forest Service stipulated that, in considering applicants for a field technician's job, "only applicants who do not meet standards will be considered." This was considered code for "we're going to fill this job with a female." Males filed suit against the Forest Service, claiming discrimination against white males. An appeals court agreed. *No consent degree or court order under any executive order requires employers to hire or promote unqualified workers.*

The current status of affirmative action may be different from what is written here because this area is so politically volatile. In 1979, the Supreme Court in *U.S. Steelworkers v. Weber* approved Kaiser Aluminum's voluntary affirmative action plan because it did not "unnecessarily trammel" the interests of majority employees and it was a temporary measure that would cease when blacks reached parity with their representation in the labor market.[35] Lower courts reviewing subsequent challenges to voluntary affirmative action programs have used the *Weber* test to ascertain their legality.

Perhaps the best known affirmative action case is *Bakke v. Regents of the University of California*.[36] Allan Bakke sued the medical school for racial discrimination. UC-Davis had a special minorities-only set-aside program for applicants and, because of this program, some minorities were admitted although their test scores and grades were less than those of Mr. Bakke. In 1978, the court ordered that Mr. Bakke be admitted (he is a doctor today) and that the set-aside program be abolished. The court also allowed, however, that universities could use a person's ethnic classification as a plus factor in admissions decisions.

It has been argued that affirmative action is appropriate only as a remedy for past discrimination against specific individuals. The Supreme Court had clearly opposed this narrow application in early decisions. In the majority opinion in *Wygant v. Jackson Board of Education,* the court stated that "a carefully constructed affirmative action program need not be limited to the remedying of specific instances of identified discrimination." Justice Lewis Powell stated, "In order to remedy the effects of prior discrimination, it may be necessary to take race into account . . . innocent persons may be called upon to bear some of the burden of the remedy."[37]

The 1987 Supreme Court ruling in *Johnson v. Santa Clara Transportation Agency* provided some clarity to the remedies that have been pursued under affirmative action and equal employment opportunity.[38] According to the court, organizations may adopt voluntary programs to hire and promote qualified minorities and women to correct a "manifest imbalance" in their representation in various job categories, even when there is no evidence of past discrimination. This was the first time the Supreme Court explicitly ruled that women as well as blacks and other minorities can receive preferential treatment. The decision also affects the most common employment situation in the United States today: work

situations where it is difficult or impossible to prove past discrimination, but a statistical disparity exists in the number of females and minorities in certain occupations relative to population statistics. Even that decision emphasized that "manifest imbalance" meant substantial, inexplicable differences in workforce representation. The decision also emphasized that preferential treatment may be granted only when job candidates are judged to be "equally qualified."

While the majority of the Supreme Court decisions have favored affirmative action and most forms of preferential treatment, there now appear to be some important qualifiers on their appropriateness. These qualifiers include: (1) affirmative action plans should be "narrowly tailored" to achieve their ends with a timetable for ending the preferential practice; (2) class-based firing or layoff schemes are too harsh on the innocent and inappropriate in most circumstances; and (3) preferential personnel practices of any kind are appropriate only in employment situations where there is a prior history of discrimination. One interpretation is that this last qualifier invalidates Executive Order 11246 because the "goals" required for compliance automatically necessitate preferential hiring and promotion practices by contractors with no such prior history of discrimination. Unfortunately, there is no clear message from the Supreme Court on this interpretation of its latest findings. Also unclear is the literal meaning of *prior discrimination*. In its earlier decision in *U.S. Steelworkers v. Weber,* the Supreme Court said it was acceptable to use affirmative action programs to remedy "manifest racial imbalance" regardless of whether an employer had been guilty of discriminatory job practices in the past. With its latest decisions, it appears preferential treatment for groups covered under Title VII may be more restrictive.

The future of certain voluntary affirmative action programs is in doubt after the court's most recent decisions in related cases. In fact, some experts now believe that judicial commitment to EEO and affirmative action that began with the Griggs case in 1971 may be over and that Congress may be pressured into a more active role on civil rights issues.

Two other cases, *City of Richmond v. J. A. Croson Co* and the 1995 decision in *Adarand Constructions v. Pena,*[39] showed that courts will apply stringent standards to preferential treatment by public agencies. In the first case, the Supreme Court threw out a policy by the city of Richmond to require that 30 percent of the dollar amount of business contracts be given to minority firms. The court stated that the city's plan was not compelling since there was no showing of prior discrimination by the city. This case did not involve employment, so its meaning is unclear for managers. The new civil rights legislation does not change the *Croson* precedent. In *Adarand,* the high court imposed stricter standards for federal programs that favor groups in contract bids. Most experts contend that the stricter standard for most federal preference programs cannot be met and that such programs should be abandoned. The basis for the majority opinion in *Adarand* was the equal protection clause of the U.S. Constitution.

The extent to which these two decisions apply to voluntary affirmative action programs is unclear. In *Hopwood v. Texas* (1996), the Fifth Circuit Court of Appeals barred the University of Texas Law School from considering race in any way for admission to the school. Four white students had sued the university claiming the law school's policy had violated the equal protection clause of the U.S. Constitution (the 14th Amendment). This decision essentially challenged what was regarded as standard practice in the consideration of race for graduate education in public institutions across the United States. The Fifth Circuit Court cited both *Croson* and *Adarand* to justify its decision, stating that public institutions "may not use ethnic diversity simply to achieve racial heterogeneity, even as a part of a number of factors."[40] In 1996, the Supreme Court chose not to hear the appeal of this decision, thus allowing the anti-preferential treatment verdict to stand and contributing to the ambiguity regarding affirmative action programs. The U.S. Department of Justice came out in support of the state of Texas, using an argument that diversity of the student body is an important goal in and of itself and can therefore be offered as an explanation for preferential treatment. (The Fifth Circuit had rejected that argument and the Supreme Court did not disagree with the Fifth Circuit's rejection.) The *New York Times* editorialized that the Fifth Circuit's ruling was "aggressively activist and legally dubious. If the *Bakke* decision is no longer the law, it is for the Supreme Court to say so."[41] But by deciding to not hear the case, the Supreme Court essentially did just that.

What Is Required before a Company Embarks on a Voluntary Affirmative Action Program?

The courts have clarified criteria for *voluntary* affirmative action plans. For voluntary plans, it has been suggested that they:

1. Be designed to eradicate old patterns of discrimination.
2. Not impose an "absolute bar" to white advancement.
3. Be temporary.
4. Not "trammel the interests of white employees."
5. Be designed to eliminate a "manifest racial imbalance."
6. Show preference only from a pool of equally qualified candidates.

For involuntary affirmative action programs, it was suggested that preferential treatment is legal when it

1. Is necessary to remedy "pervasive and egregious discrimination."
2. Is used as a flexible benchmark for court monitoring, rather than as a quota.
3. Is temporary.
4. Does not "unnecessarily trammel the interests of white employees."[42]

Despite the apparent legal protection for voluntary affirmative action plans, managers must tread very carefully to avoid "reverse discrimination" lawsuits. Race- or gender-conscious employment decisions made in the absence of an affirmative action plan may result in a successful claim of reverse discrimination by a rejected majority applicant or employee.[43] Even when OFCCP-approved programs exist, managers must ensure that all individuals meet the stated job requirements and that affirmative action plans are carefully drafted and followed. The most difficult and legally troublesome issue related to affirmative action is when (and if) a protected class characteristic may be considered relative to the qualifications of the job candidates.

How Can You Legally Select from a Pool of "Qualified" Candidates?

The most controversial area of affirmative action is the notion of "qualified" when deciding whom to hire or promote (or fire). Many advocates of affirmative action contend that some standard should be defined for "qualified," that people should be considered on the basis of that standard and then race or gender may be considered from within the pool of "qualified" if there is some form of affirmative action program.

Consider the following: A university requires that the university affirmative action officer sign off on the pool of qualified and unqualified candidates for a faculty position. While there is a large pool of "qualified" candidates, the university can afford to bring only four candidates to the campus for interviews. The affirmative action officer requires, based on his definition of affirmative action, that at least one of the four "qualified" candidates must be either a minority member or a female. All four candidates visit the campus, and after the visits, the faculty deliberate and recommend that the job offer be conveyed to a white male who had been ranked first by the faculty committee. The affirmative action officer then refuses to agree with the recommendation because he believes that affirmative action dictates the offer be conveyed to the minority or female candidate, assuming the department still felt the minority candidate was "qualified" after the interview. The faculty argue that they wish to offer the job to the "most qualified" candidate rather than just from the pool of "qualified" candidates. Who is right here? Does legal affirmative action mean taking race into consideration after you have defined the pool of qualified, or does such an action constitute preferential treatment? Assuming that there was no inherent discrimination in the judgments of relative qualifications, the department is probably on safer legal ground since the *Johnson* decision stipulated that candidates must be "equally qualified." If the department can draw legitimate and job-related distinctions among the applicants (i.e., that one candidate was clearly more qualified than another), it is legal and, of course, effective HR practice to select the very best candidate from the pool of the "qualified."

Is Affirmative Action Still Necessary?

There is an argument that affirmative action is now unnecessary because equal employment opportunity already exists. Women and minorities strongly disagree with this argument. A three-year study conducted by a bipartisan federal commission in 1996 concluded that women and minorities still face barriers to their advancement: the so-called **glass ceiling**.[44] The glass ceiling refers to the lack of women and minorities in top managerial positions. The various AA programs are designed to break down some of these barriers.

Fifty-five percent of African-American federal employees feel that African-Americans have been subjected to "flagrant or obviously discriminatory practices"; only 4 percent of whites believed this statement to be true.[45] A 1996 report by the American Bar Association found that despite a substantial increase in the number of female lawyers, bias against female lawyers "remains entrenched in the legal profession and results in steep inequities of pay, promotion and opportunity."[46] As one reviewer of the study put it, "What it suggests is not a glass ceiling at the end, but a process that begins right off the bat."[47] This conclusion flies in the face of the perception of many male lawyers who believe that females are actually now favored in the profession.

What Is the Future for Affirmative Action?

Changes in the composition of the U.S. Supreme Court may signal a diminution or elimination of judicial support for affirmative action. Three justices who upheld affirmative action in earlier cases have retired and have been replaced by conservative justices. Decisions in the *Croson* and *Adarand* cases, the decision to not hear the *Hopwood* case, and earlier statements by three justices that Title VII prohibits preferential treatment that uses sex or race as a criterion for employment decisions, all suggest that affirmative action as defined by the consideration of race or gender in an employment decision may not be around for the 21st century. Until the Supreme

Court provides clear guidelines on when race or gender may be considered in personnel decisions or college admissions, managers should probably continue to comply with affirmative action plans, particularly if the organization receives federal funds.

One study found that the general public is opposed to "preferential treatment" when it is defined as taking a protected class characteristic such as race or gender into account in making a staffing decision.[48] People tend to favor affirmative action in terms of recruitment, training opportunities, and attention to applicant qualifications. They tend to oppose preferential treatment and any form of quota staffing. The state of California amended its constitution in 1996 when the legislature approved Amendment 209, which explicitly outlaws any preferential treatment for California public agencies. (The language of the amendment is almost identical to Section 703J of the 1964 Civil Rights Act *but* with less ambiguity.) Other states are attempting to adopt similar laws, and the federal government is also considering such a provision (see Critical Thinking Exercise 3.1).

The presence of "identity-conscious" HRM structures (i.e., the consideration of race or gender as one factor in decision making) will result in more favorable outcomes for minorities and women.[49] However, the latest Supreme Court rulings indicate that when "identity conscious" means actually taking a protected class characteristic into account when making a decision, there is now a higher probability that a court may consider such behavior to be illegal. Employers need to be very careful with regard to voluntary programs.

CRITICAL THINKING EXERCISE 3.1

What Are Consequences of the End of Racial Preferences in Higher Education?

Since the *Hopwood v. Texas* decision and the state of California's 1995 decision to ban all consideration of race in higher education, the enrollment of minority students is down in graduate programs of the best schools in those states. As of July 1997, not a single African-American student of the few who had been accepted into the University of Texas Law School had agreed to attend the school in fall 1997. Only one African-American began law school at the University of California Berkeley in fall, 1997. In a June 14, 1997 speech, President Clinton pointed to reports from the University of California system that have found "minority enrollments in law school and other graduate programs are plummeting for the first time in decades. Soon the same will likely happen in undergraduate education . . . we must not resegregate higher education."[1]

Assuming the same sources of data are used to admit students (e.g., test scores, undergraduate GPA) and without a consideration of race in assessing applicants for admission to the most prestigious law schools, medical schools, MBA programs, and other graduate programs, enrollments of African-Americans in these schools will be sharply reduced and have already been reduced in the 5th Circuit and in California. President Clinton favors a determination of those who are "qualified" to be admitted and then the consideration of race only when people are considered "equally qualified."

Assignment

Look into the future and predict what implications these trends will have on American society. Will race relations improve or get worse if all racial preferences are ended? President Clinton asks, "To those who oppose affirmative action, I ask you to come up with an alternative." Do you have any ideas? What is your opinion of President Clinton's position on the use of race to select from the pool of "equally qualified"?

[1] Excerpts from President Clinton's speech on race in America delivered at the University of California at San Diego, June 14, 1997.

THE AGE DISCRIMINATION IN EMPLOYMENT ACT OF 1967, AMENDED IN 1978 AND 1986

The Age Discrimination in Employment Act (ADEA) was designed to prohibit discrimination due to age in employment decisions (e.g., hiring, job retention, compensation, and other terms and conditions). Initially the ADEA was applied to workers aged 40 to 65 years but was amended in 1978 to include workers up to age 70 and in 1986 to include all those over age 39. This means that, with a few exceptions to be discussed below, mandatory or forced retirement for reasons of age is illegal. The ADEA applies to employers with 20 or more employees, unions of 25 or more members, employment agencies, and federal, state, and local governments.

As we discussed in Chapter 1, due to the aging of the workforce, the number of ADEA cases has increased every year since 1978.[50] Many ADEA lawsuits are related to downsizing, where people who were terminated as part of a downsizing or restructuring then claim to be victims of age discrimination. The ADEA provides for a trial by jury, which may be important if jurors are sympathetic to older workers. However, the Supreme Court ruling in *Gilmer v. Interstate/Johnson Lane Corp.*[51] appears to allow mandatory and binding arbitration as a method of settling ADEA disputes instead of a jury trial. Since this ruling, an increasing number of employers have stipulated that labor disputes, including claims of age discrimination, must be handled through this process. The ADEA also permits employees to recover double damages if the employer's conduct is found to have been "willful," which means plaintiffs may win more than simply lost wages if intentional discrimination is proven.

At the beginning of the chapter we mentioned a case about a man who waived his right to sue and then changed his mind. Can he change his mind? The EEOC says he can but under very limited conditions. Under the **Older Workers Benefit Protection Act of 1990,** employees have 45 days to consider such waivers and seven days after signing to revoke the deal.

What Is Required to Establish Prima Facie Evidence of Discrimination?

Requirements for establishing a prima facie case of age discrimination include showing

1. The employee is a member of the protected age group (40 or older).
2. The employee has the ability to perform satisfactorily at some absolute or relative level (e.g., relative to other employees involved in the decision process or at an absolute standard of acceptability).
3. The employee was not hired, promoted, or compensated, or was discharged, laid off, or forced to retire.
4. The position was filled or maintained by a younger person (just younger, not necessarily under age 40).[52]

The second condition is the biggest challenge for the plaintiff and is usually the one where the plaintiff falls short in establishing a prima facie case due to the usual subjectivity in comparing individuals.

Once Prima Facie Evidence Is Established, What Must the Employer Do?

Once a prima facie case has been established based on the evidence presented by the plaintiff, the defendant must then present evidence that "reasonable factors" other than age were the basis of the personnel decision.

One common scenario for litigation under ADEA concerns the termination of an employee due to alleged poor performance. For example, in *Mastie v. Great Lakes Steel Corp.*,[53] the employer maintained that Mr. Mastie had been discharged in reduction-in-force efforts due to his poorer performance relative to other employees. Mr. Mastie presented personnel records reflecting an exemplary performance record and a history of merit-based, salary increases. However, the court found for the employer and said the controlling issue should be whether age was a *determinative* factor in the personnel decision, not the "absolute accuracy" or correctness of the personnel decision. Several other courts have established that it is not the role of the court to "second-guess" employers in their personnel decisions (i.e., did they really discharge the poorest performer or hire the very best person?). The critical question in ADEA litigation is simply whether age was a "determinative factor" in a personnel decision. It is the plaintiff's responsibility to establish this as fact, which makes it very difficult for plaintiffs to win such cases.

Can Employers Claim Age as a Bona Fide Occupational Qualification?

Greyhound Bus Lines survived a court challenge to its rule that it would accept no applicants over 40 years of age to drive its buses. The company successfully contended that age was a bona fide occupational qualification (BFOQ) since it was related to the safe conduct of the bus line.[54] Other cases have supported the use of age as a BFOQ. *In general, if public safety is relevant and the employer must be in good physical condition, the courts have supported the use of age requirements, both in terms of entry-level positions, and, more commonly, mandatory retirement for certain jobs.* Congress specifically exempted public safety personnel in the 1986 amendments, allowing mandatory retirement for police officers and firefighters (usually 55 years of age). The courts have generally recognized these age ceilings as legal BFOQs, but only when the employer can demonstrate that (1) physical fitness, and especially good aerobic fitness, is important to the job; and (2) the employer applies the same physical fitness standards to employees under 40 as well as to older employees. The EEOC provides the following rules for the imposition of BFOQs:

1. The age limit is reasonably necessary for the business.
2. All or almost all individuals over the age are unable to perform adequately.
3. Some people over the age have a disqualifying characteristic (e.g., health) that cannot be determined independent of age.

One managerial implication is to determine if it is in the employer's best interests to impose an age ceiling or mandatory retirement. In the early 1990s, a 54-year-old pilot successfully crash landed a 737, saving hundreds of lives. He celebrated his mandatory retirement only a few weeks later.

Is an Assessment of "Overqualified" a Violation of ADEA?

The downsizing of the past several years has placed a large number of highly qualified and highly trained Americans in the workplace. Can a company reject an applicant on the grounds that he or she is "overqualified"? One appeals court said no, that such an explanation is merely a pretext for age discrimination. While this decision directly affects only one U.S. circuit, telling applicants in other circuits that they are "overqualified" for a position will irritate the applicant at the very least and could lead to a lawsuit. There is also the obvious question as to whether it makes good business sense to reject someone because of a theory that he or she is overqualified.

THE AMERICANS WITH DISABILITIES ACT OF 1990 (ADA)

It is estimated that the government now spends $60 billion a year to support disabled people, including over 8 million who would like to work but cannot find employment. In 1990, Congress passed the Americans with Disabilities Act, which extends the rights and privileges disabled employees of federal contractors have under the **Rehabilitation Act of 1973** to virtually all employees. Figure 3.7 presents excerpts from the ADA. The ADA provides that qualified individuals with disabilities may not be discriminated against by a private-sector organization or a department or agency of a state or local government employing 15 or more employees and employers must provide the disabled with "reasonable accommodations" that don't place an undue hardship on the business. *Reasonable accommodations* are determined on a case-by-case basis and may include reassignment, part-time work, and flexible schedules. They may also include providing readers, interpreters, assistants, or attendants.[55] No accommodation is required if an individual is not otherwise qualified for the position. The EEOC's *Technical Assistance Manual* suggests the following process for assessing reasonable accommodation: (1) Look at the particular job involved; determine its purpose and its essential function; (2) Consult with the individual with the disability to identify potential accommodations; if several accommodations are available, preference should be given to the individual's preferences.

The ADA also specifies requirements for accommodations for public transportation provided by public transit authorities. For example, all new fixed-route buses must have lifts to make them accessible to disabled individuals unless it can be shown that none are available from the manufacturers. In addition, public facilities such as restaurants, doctor's offices, pharmacies, grocery stores, shopping centers, and hotels must be made accessible to the disabled unless undue hardship would occur for the business. It is not clear, however, how organizations will show "undue hardship," although the law suggests that a reviewing court compare the cost of the accommodation with the employer's operating budget.[56]

FIGURE 3.7
EXCERPTS FROM ADA

Discrimination

(a) General Rule. No covered entity shall discriminate against a qualified individual with a disability because of the disability of such individual.

(b) Construction. As used in subsection (a), the term "discrimination" includes:

(1) limiting, segregating, or classifying a job applicant or employee in a way that adversely affects the opportunities or status of such applicant or employee because of . . . disability . . .

(2) participating in a contractual or other arrangement or relationship that has the effect of subjecting a qualified applicant or employee with a disability to the discrimination prohibited by this title . . .

(5) not making reasonable accommodations to the known physical or mental limitations of a qualified individual who is an applicant or employee, unless such covered entity can demonstrate that the accommodation would impose an undue hardship on the operation of the business of such covered entity, and;

(7) using employment tests or other selection criteria that screen out or tend to screen out an individual with a disability or a class of individuals with disabilities unless the test or other selection criteria, as used by the covered entity, is shown to be job related for the position in question and is consistent with business necessity.

(c) Medical Examinations and Inquiries.

(1) In general. The prohibition against discrimination as referred to in subsection (a) shall include medical examinations and inquiries.

Definitions

(2) Disability. The term "disability" means, with respect to an individual:

(A) a physical or mental impairment that substantially limits one or more of the major life activities of such individual;

(B) a record of such an impairment, or;

(C) being regarded as having such an impairment.

Definitions

(7) Qualified Individual with a Disability. The term "qualified individual with a disability" means an individual with a disability who, with or without reasonable accommodation, can perform the essential functions of the employment position that such individual holds or desires.

(8) Reasonable Accommodation. The term "reasonable accommodation" may include:

(A) making existing facilities used by employees readily accessible to and usable by individuals with disabilities, and;

(B) job restructuring, part-time or modified work schedules, reassignment to a vacant position, acquisition or modification of equipment or devices, appropriate adjustment or modifications of examinations, training materials or policies, the provision of qualified readers or interpreters, and other similar accommodations for individuals with disabilities.

(9) (A) In general. The term "undue hardship" means an action requiring significant difficulty or expense.

(B) Determination. In determining whether an accommodation would impose an undue hardship on a covered entity, factors to be considered include:

(i) the overall size of the business;

(ii) the type of operation, and;

(iii) the nature and cost of the accommodation.

Defenses

(b) Qualification Standards. The term "qualification standards" may include a requirement that an individual with a currently contagious disease or infection shall not pose a direct threat to the health or safety of other individuals in the workplace.

Illegal Drugs and Alcohol

(a) Qualified Individual with a Disability. For purposes of this title, the term "qualified individual with a disability" shall not include any employee or applicant who is a current user of illegal drugs . . .

(b) Authority of Covered Entity. A covered entity:

(1) may prohibit the use of alcohol or illegal drugs at the workplace by all employees:

(2) may require that employees shall not be under the influence of alcohol or illegal drugs at the workplace;

(3) may require that employees behave in conformance with the requirements established under "The Drug-Free Workplace Act" (41 U.S.C. 701 et seq.) [See Chapter 14.]

(4) may hold an employee who is a drug user or alcoholic to the same qualification standards for employment or job performance and behavior that such entity holds other employees . . .

(c) Drug Testing.

(1) In general. For purposes of this title, a test to determine the use of illegal drugs shall not be considered a medical examination.

What Is Legal and Illegal under ADA?

The EEOC approved enforcement guidelines on preemployment disability-related inquiries and medical exams under ADA. The guidelines states, "the guiding principle is that while employers may ask applicants about the ability to perform job functions, employers may not ask about disability." Figure 3.8 will give you some idea of the fine line you must walk in making inquiries under ADA.[57] After an employer has made an offer and an ap-

FIGURE 3.8
ADA QUESTIONNAIRE

INDICATE IF THE QUESTION IS PROPER/IMPROPER

_____ 1. Can you perform the functions of this job with or without reasonable accommodation?

_____ 2. Do you have Aids? Do you have Asthma?

_____ 3. How did you become disabled?

_____ 4. Do you have a cold? Have you ever tried Tylenol for fever? How did you break your leg?

_____ 5. Have you ever filed for worker's compensation? Have you ever been injured on the job?

_____ 6. How often did you use illegal drugs in the past?

_____ 7. Can you meet the attendance requirements of this job? How many days did you take leave last year?

_____ 8. Do you illegally use drugs? Have you used illegal drugs in the last two years?

_____ 9. Have you ever been addicted to drugs?

_____ 10. How much alcohol do you drink each week? Have you ever been treated for alcohol problems?

_____ 11. Have you ever been treated for mental health problems?

_____ 12. Do you drink alcohol?

_____ 13. How much do you weigh? How tall are you? Do you regularly eat three meals a day?

_____ 14. Have you even taken **AZT**? What prescription drugs are you currently taking?

See endnote 57.

plicant requests accommodation, the employer may "require documentation of the individual's need for, and entitlement to, reasonable accommodations."

There has been a great deal of litigation under ADA. The EEOC has received over 80,000 charges of ADA discrimination from 1992 to 1997. The two most common areas of disability in the claims are "back impairments," and various "emotional/psychiatric impairments." The most common personnel action has been termination. While some claims of mental duress and headaches are undoubtedly legitimate, some people have taken advantage of the ambiguity in the law to make costly and unwarranted claims.

What Constitutes a Disability under ADA?

Bonnie Cook, a 300-pound Rhode Island woman, was rejected for an attendant's job at a school for the mentally retarded. She sued claiming her obesity was a disability under ADA. The EEOC has taken the position that only severely obese people are covered by ADA (weight in excess of 100 percent of the norm for a particular height) or if their weight can be linked to a medical disorder. The courts have deferred to the EEOC's position on this matter.

The EEOC issued voluminous documents in 1995 and 1997 that attempt to clarify what does and doesn't constitute a disability under ADA. Since almost 13 per-

cent of all complaints filed with the EEOC under ADA from 1993 to 1997 alleged discrimination resulting from emotional or psychiatric impairment, the 1997 guidelines on these impairments were overdue.[58]

PREGNANCY DISCRIMINATION ACT OF 1978

The EEOC receives over 3,500 complaints for pregnancy discrimination each year. The Pregnancy Discrimination Act prohibits employment practices that discriminate on the basis of pregnancy, childbirth, or related medical conditions (e.g., abortion). This means that a woman is protected from being fired or refused a job or promotion simply because she is pregnant or has had an abortion. She also cannot be forced to take a leave of absence as long as she is able to work.

Under the law, women are not guaranteed the same job or, indeed, any job when they return from their pregnancy leave. However, a large percentage of U.S. companies have adopted either a "same job," "comparable job," or "some job" policy for women who wish to return to work.[59] (38 percent, 43 percent, and 6 percent, respectively). The employer must adopt such a policy with consideration to the disparate treatment theory of Title VII, and pregnancy should be treated like any other disability. In other words, if other employees on disability leave are entitled to return to their jobs when they are able to work again, then so should women who have been unable to work due to pregnancy.

The act also requires that employers must provide benefits coverage for pregnancy as fully as for other medical conditions. In other words, a woman unable to work for pregnancy-related reasons is entitled to disability benefits or sick leave on the same basis as other employees unable to work for medical reasons.

The **Pregnancy Discrimination Act** does not prohibit states from requiring additional benefits for pregnant employees. The Supreme Court, for example, upheld a California law that required employees to provide up to four months' unpaid pregnancy disability leave with guaranteed reinstatement, even though disabled males were not entitled to the same benefit.[60] In Chapter 10, we will discuss the Family and Medical Leave Act, which was passed into federal law in 1994. This law provides additional protection related to pregnancy.

EEO AND INTERNATIONAL HRM

Women are oppressed in many parts of the world. In some Middle Eastern countries, for example, women cannot even attain a work visa to enter the country. Female U.S. soldiers stationed in Saudi Arabia are subject to a myriad of discriminatory practices that are the norm in Middle Eastern countries. Sexist legislation is common in many countries, including India, Pakistan, and almost all the Middle Eastern countries. Sexism is endemic to most of Latin America and Japan where women are expected to quit their employment at around age 25 and raise a family.[61] Although this general attitude is slowly changing in Japan, the percentage of women who are managers in Japan is still low. There is also evidence of racism in Japan; Japanese managers would prefer to work with white Americans. In Germany, while things are improving, women face numerous obstacles to managerial careers. As a *New York Times* article put it, "In Germany, the ceiling's not glass, it's concrete."[62]

Given this pervasive sexism and racism, can a company argue "business necessity" when it purposely denies women or minorities the opportunity for certain overseas assignments? Could the company claim a BFOQ, for example, by collecting survey data indicating the host-country nationals preferred white males and use these data as a basis for denying overseas assignments to females and minorities? Probably not. Although there isn't a clear mandate from the courts on this yet, the few related cases seem to indicate, much like *Pan American v. Diaz*, that customer/client preferences do not justify discrimination against classes covered by Title VII. The same principle probably also holds for age and disability discrimination.

Lawrence Abrams was denied a lucrative opportunity to work at a hospital in Saudi Arabia because he was a Jew. The Baylor College of Medicine, which had arranged the three-month assignment, stated that a visa would be very difficult to obtain for him. In fact, Baylor had not even bothered to check on the visa policy. A jury was not persuaded by Baylor's argument and found the college guilty of discrimination under Title VII.[63] But what if Baylor had asked and the Saudi government had refused to grant a work visa? Would this then constitute discrimination?

Could a company use an economic business necessity argument claiming that sending women to Japan, for example, would result in less revenue for the company? If a company made such a claim, it might end up in court trying to explain why the few studies on this subject indicate that the women who do get assignments overseas do just fine. For example, one study in Asia found that 97 percent of the women viewed their assignment as successful and 42 percent said that the fact that they were female actually helped them in their jobs.[64] There is little research supporting the contention that women would be less effective in foreign assignments than males.

Many multinational companies have policies for their expatriates regarding equal employment opportunity. Bechtel's employment manual, for example, states that U.S. citizens are protected by all relevant U.S. federal EEO laws while they are on foreign soil. Many other major multinational U.S. corporations have a similar policy. Expatriates are now covered by federal EEO laws when they are assigned to countries other than the United States, but before passage of the Civil Rights Act of 1991, Americans were not covered when they were assigned overseas.[65]

Many U.S. companies have branches, subsidiaries, or joint-venture partners in Western Europe (and, increasingly, in Eastern Europe as well). Many U.S. multinationals have considerable experience with the various regulatory systems of Western European countries, some of which require national-level collective bargaining and others of which have relatively little labor regulation.

The aim of the 12 member nations of the European Community is to harmonize regulatory systems (in human resources management as well as in other aspects of business) to achieve a single market. Although a more uniform approach to employment relations in these 12 countries might appear to simplify human resource management, changing to a more uniform system has proven to be very difficult. Furthermore, the European Community's agenda provides considerable protection to workers and unions—protection that is contrary to the philosophy of a number of the leaders of multinationals.

The European Community has issued several directives that bind each member nation. For example, three directives require equal treatment by sex, equal pay, and the European version of comparable worth (called "equal value").

These directives are significant because, under the Treaty of Paris (the document that governs the European Community), national courts must reinterpret national laws in light of these directives. This means, for example, that even if the United Kingdom's Parliament does not amend British legislation to conform with European Community law, the British courts are obliged to rewrite British law if an issue arises that must be resolved under European law.

FUTURE TRENDS IN EEO

The issue of affirmative action should be at the forefront of litigation and legislation as we enter the 21st century. More state constitutional amendments or legislation such as Proposition 209 in California are likely along with more high-priced class action lawsuits challenging employers' promotional polices such as the 1997 lawsuit against Home Depot. As one expert put it, the 1996 Texaco case indicates that African-Americans are now gaining enough jobs in corporate America to be able to challenge the so-called glass ceiling. With the plaintiffs' success in publicized cases in the late 90s, an increasing number of class action lawsuits are likely. The number of ADEA cases are also expected to increase due to the aging of the workforce and the increasing proportion of workers who are over 39 and therefore eligible to sue.

The 1996 $13 million settlement of an age case by Lockheed Martin based on decisions made after Lockheed's merger with Martin Marietta could be a typical ADEA case as we enter the 21st century and mergers and acquisitions continue.

Employment practices liability insurance should become much more common in the years ahead. Some policies stipulate how HRM should be practiced as a condition of coverage. Providing training in EEO laws is often one such condition.

Alternative Dispute Resolution: An Employer Reaction to Increased Litigation

One of the strongest trends with regard to management reaction to increased litigation is in the area of **alternative dispute resolution.** A small but growing number of companies have adopted mandatory arbitration to settle all claims related to employment. They cite the provisions of the Civil Rights Act of 1991 which allows alternative dispute resolution as an alternative to litigation.[66] Although mandatory arbitration is controversial, and is opposed by the EEOC, many companies have adopted it as policy. Mandatory arbitration requires employees and job applicants to sign a contract in which they agree to binding arbitration to resolve virtually any dispute related to their employment. Let's say you believe you were a victim of gender discrimination. With the mandatory arbitration policy, the complaint must be submitted to an arbitration association such as the American Arbitration Association for a hearing and binding decision.

Although the research on the effects of such a policy on legal fees and expenses is highly relevant, only one study has addressed the issue in a serious manner. In general, the study showed less cost and faster settlement of claims compared to litigation through the federal courts. The courts in general have supported arbitration as an alternative to litigation in settling employment disputes.[67] Given the likely increases in most forms of EEO litigation, arbitration may prove to be advantageous to all concerned.

SUMMARY

Despite the confusing array of laws and regulations on EEO, the underlying principle is clear. EEO simply means individuals should be given an equal opportunity in employment decisions. EEO does not mean preferential treatment for one individual over another because of race, color, sex, religion, national origin, age, or disability. For instance, white males have won racial and sex discrimination suits against organizations that have violated Title VII for hiring less qualified minorities or women.[68] The EEO laws clearly state that treatment at work and opportunity for work should be unrelated to the race, sex, and other personal characteristics of individual workers. The implications of the most recent Supreme Court rulings related to EEO are still unclear with regard to affirmative action but appear to impose tighter restrictions regarding race- or gender-conscious employment practices.

One Implication of Increased Litigation: Better HRM Practices

While the trend of increasing litigation in general creates competitive problems for U.S. employers in a global economy, many of the regulations and guidelines for HR practice, particularly EEO laws, actually encourage more effective HRM practices. For example, Personnel Assessment Systems (PAS), the privately held company we described in Chapter 2, specializes in assisting companies with their staffing needs in full compliance with all labor laws and regulations. Some of PAS's clients are companies that have lost court decisions because they were using hiring tests judged to be discriminatory because the company either could not prove that test scores were job related or hadn't bothered to try. Perhaps if the organization cannot prove that a test is related to success on the job, it is time to replace the test. PAS is in the business of helping companies use tests that do predict success on the job. So PAS's clients are not only more likely to be in compliance with the law, they are also practicing more effective staffing and making better decisions about people.

One large retailer specified that applicants for a district manager job had to have a minimum of five years' experience as a district manager from some other retailer. This job specification created a disadvantage for women and minorities who may have been denied opportunities throughout the retail industry and thus could not have accumulated the required experience. This illustrates the glass ceiling effect, which refers to invisible barriers for women trying to move up the corporate ladder. In addition, an internal study showed that years of previous experience was unrelated to performance as a district manager. The company was thus vulnerable to a lawsuit and, based on its own study, would have difficulty proving the five-year specification was related to job success. The specification also forced the company to compensate the district manager job at a higher rate and made it much more difficult to recruit. This combination of facts seems to lead to a simple conclusion: Change the job specification and reduce the number of years' experience required to be considered for the job. Many times, EEO laws and regulations and effective HR practices go hand in hand.

The legality of human resource practices is often related to the effectiveness of human resource practices. Organizations would thus do well to evaluate all their HR policies and practices in the context of the laws and case law and adjust those practices accordingly. The result might be more legally defensible and more effective HR policies. The old adage, an ounce of prevention is worth a pound of cure, really applies to the legal issues related to HR.

While the implications of HR-related litigation may be confusing, there can be no question that managers will be on relatively safer ground if they adhere to the following strategy with regard to employment practices: (1) monitor personnel decisions to ensure there is no evidence of disparate treatment or a disproportionate impact caused by particular personnel practices; (2) if there are disparities, determine whether the practices causing the disparity are essential for the business and/or are "job related"; and (3) eliminate the practices if they are not job related or replace them with practices that do not cause such a disparity. Such a strategy will protect managers from EEO claims, and it will also lead to better and more cost-effective personnel decisions.

In general, most would agree that EEO legislation has had positive effects on the occupational status of minorities and females. An additional benefit is that EEO laws and the threat of EEO litigation have forced managers to "clean up their act" with regard to personnel policy and practice. While the paperwork may be voluminous and the compliance requirements may seem ominous, EEO laws and regulations have fostered a fairer system of employment opportunity and a more systematic and valid process for personnel decisions. The efforts of managers are critical to organizational effectiveness and their mistakes can be costly. Personnel practices may be the most heavily regulated area of organizational life today. HR professionals and practicing managers cannot learn too much about this vital area. As we stated earlier, one study indicated that knowledge of the major EEO laws and regulations constitutes essential knowledge for practicing managers.

In the following chapters, we will have much more to say about labor legislation and employment practices. The importance of EEO issues for virtually all HRM activities cannot be overstated. In 1991, after the Civil Rights Act was passed, R. Gaull Silberman, then vice chair of the EEOC, told a convention of HR executives that HR practices will have an impact on corporate bottom lines as "personnel departments become profit and loss centers." Mr. Silberman's remarks were prophetic.[69]

Students should consider the implications of the Civil Rights Act, the ADEA, the ADA, and the many other federal, state, and local laws when we discuss topics such as job analysis and design (Chapter 4), human resource planning and recruitment (Chapter 5), staffing (Chapter 6), training and development (Chapter 7), performance appraisal (Chapter 8), compensation (Chapters 9 and 10), labor relations (Chapter 11), and health and safety (Chapter 14).

As we cover these topics in the pages to follow, we

will test your ability to apply knowledge of EEO and other labor laws to particular HRM activities and actions. Competence in EEO issues is critical for line managers making decisions about people and jobs and for HRM professionals establishing policies and procedures.

The content of this chapter is more likely to go out of date faster than any other area of HRM. In the volatile area of EEO, current, state-of-the-art knowledge is a competitive advantage for the organization. Make sure your knowledge in this area is current.

DISCUSSION QUESTIONS

1. In terms of EEO, how can customer requirements or preferences be used in hiring people?

2. Given the great economic incentives for plaintiffs' attorneys today, why is the EEOC even necessary? Why can't a person simply be allowed to sue without the involvement of the EEOC?

3. Describe the procedures required to file a discrimination lawsuit under the disparate impact and disparate treatment theories. How is adverse impact determined? Provide a scenario illustrating evidence of adverse impact in an employment decision.

4. Based on your reading of the major EEO laws, what information should an employer include in a personnel policies and procedures manual given to all employees?

5. Dave Brooks has a psychiatric disability but works in a warehouse loading boxes. He has no contact with customers. Over six weeks, Dave reports to work looking disheveled and is rude to fellow employees. However, his work has not suffered. The company handbook says employees must be neat and courteous to fellow employees. Dave's boss, Moro Hipple, takes disciplinary action against Dave. If Dave says his appearance deteriorated because of his disability, does he have a lawful claim?

6. What steps would you take to prevent ADEA cases after a major restructuring or reduction in force?

7. Would you be likely to join an organization that required you to agree to binding arbitration regarding labor and EEO disputes and to waive your right to a jury trial?

NOTES

1. Bernardin, H. J.; Hagan, C. H.; Kane, J. S.; and Villanova, P. (1998). Performance management: A customer-focused orientation. In J. Smither (ed.). *Performance management: The state of the art.* San Francisco: Jossey-Bass.

2. Dobrzynski, J. H. (Sept. 12, 1995). Women more pes-

simistic about work. *New York Times,* p. C2; see also, U.S. Merit Systems Protection Board. (1996). *Fair and equitable treatment: A progress report on minority employment in the federal government.* Washington, DC: U.S. Merit Systems Protection Board; see also, Powell, G. and Butterfield, D. A. (1997). Effect of race on promotions to top management in a federal department. *Academy of Management Journal, 40*(1), 112–128.

3. Zigarelli, M. A. (1996). Compulsory arbitration of non-union employment disputes. *Human Resource Management Review, 6,* 183–206.

4. Ferguson, T. W. (Nov. 4, 1996). Boss harassment. *Forbes,* pp. 150–151; see also, Holmes, S. A. (Nov. 17, 1996). Bias suit harbinger. *New York Times,* p. 12; Kahan, S. C.; Brown, B. B.; Zepke, B. E.; and Lanzarone, M. (1984). *Legal guide to human resources.* Boston: Warren, Gorham & Lamont.

5. See note 3.

6. Zigarelli, M. A. (1994). *Can they do that? A Guide to your rights on the job.* New York: Lexington; see also, Block, R. N., and Wolkinson, B. (1996). *Employment law.* Cambridge, MA: Blackwell; LeRoy, M. H., and Schutz, J. M. (1995). The legal context of human resource management: conflict, confusion, and role conversion. In G. R. Ferris, S. D. Rosen, and D. T. Barnum (eds.), *Handbook of human resource management.* Cambridge, MA: Blackwell; pp. 143–158.

7. See note 4, Kahan et al; see also, Boot, M. (February 12, 1997). For plaintiffs' lawyers, there's no place like home depot. *The Wall Street Journal,* A17.

8 Ledvinka, J. and Scarpello, V. (1991) *Federal regulation of personnel and human resource management.* Boston: PWS-Kent; As of 1996, African-Americans comprised 10.9 percent of the workforce but 22 percent of unemployed Americans. While 11 percent of African-Americans were unemployed in 1996, only 4.7 percent of whites were unemployed. Median annual income of African-Americans was 76 percent of whites. Women earned 75 percent of what men made ($22,000 versus $29,000). Male registered nurses earned more than female registered nurses ($38,000 versus $36,000) and female elementary teachers earned 90 percent of male elementary teachers ($34,000 versus $38,000). Black women earned 85 percent of white women ($19,000 versus $22,000). See STP://STATS.BLS.Gov.

9. Equal Employment Opportunity Commission. (1996). *Annual summary of EEO claims.*

10. Day, N. E., and Schoenrade, P. (1997). Staying in the closet versus coming out: Relationships between communication about sexual orientation and work attitudes. *Personnel Psychology, 50,* 147–163; see also Williamson, A. D. (1993). Is this the right time to come out? *Harvard Business Review, 71,* 18–27; Monitor the bill before the U.S. Congress in 1997 to amend the Civil Rights Act to include sexual orientation as a protected class; The 10 states are: CA, CT, HI, MA, MN, NJ, NH, RI, VT and WI. See http://www.NGLTF.ORG.

11. Wolkinson, B. W., and Block, R. N. (1996). *Employment law.* Cambridge, MA: Blackwell.

12. *Diaz v. Pan American Airways* (1971). 422 F.2d 385 (5th Cir.).

13. *International Union, United Automobile Workers v. Johnson Controls, Inc.* (1991). (111 S. Ct. 1196). Johnson Controls, Inc., a car battery manufacturer, excluded women of childbearing years from jobs where there was high exposure to lead and possible harm to the unborn fetus. The company argued that this policy falls within the "BFOQ" exception to Title VII because it is essential to a safe workplace. In its 1991 decision, in *United Automobile Workers v. Johnson Controls,* the Supreme Court disagreed. Such fetal protection policies, used at one time by over a dozen large companies employing over 10,000 workers, are a form of sex discrimination in violation of Title VII. The high court emphasized that the BFOQ exception applies only to a policy that involves the "essence of the business," such as worker or customer safety, not the safety of an unborn fetus. "Women who are as capable of doing their jobs as their male counterparts may not be forced to choose between having a child and having a job," the court said in its majority opinion against Johnson Controls. What should a company do about hazardous situations? First, warnings of potential hazards should be comprehensive and should probably recommend that physicians be consulted on potential reproductive damage. After that, organizations should address the hazard directly to determine if steps could be taken to reduce the hazard. Finally, the Supreme Court also noted that it would be difficult to sue an employer for reproductive damage if employees were informed of the risk before they started working.

14. Bovard, J. (Nov. 17, 1995). The EEOC's war on Hooter's. *The Wall Street Journal,* p. A14. See also, Hooters home page on the World Wide Web (http://www.hooters.com.).

15. Montwieler, N. (March 29, 1996). Commissioners endorse ADR as agency will focus resources through strategic priorities. *Daily Labor Report.*

16. *McDonnell-Douglas v. Green* (1973). 411 U.S. 972 (U.S. Supreme Court).

17. *Texas Department of Community Affairs v. Burdine* (1981). 450 U.S. 248 (U.S. Supreme Court).

18. *Griggs v. Duke Power Company* (1971). 401 U.S. 424 (U.S. Supreme Court).

19. *Watson v. Fort Worth Bank & Trust* (1988). 487 U.S. 977 (5th Cir.); see also, Werner, J. M., and Bolino, M. C. (1997). Explaining U.S. Courts of Appeals decisions involving performance appraisal: Accuracy, fairness, and validation. *Personnel Psychology, 50,* 1–24.

20. *Albemarle Paper Co. v. Moody* (1975). 422 U.S. 405 (U.S. Supreme Court). Open to interpretation, the 1991 CRA's requirement that plaintiffs "demonstrate that each particular challenged employment practice causes a disparate impact, except that if the [plaintiff] can demonstrate to the court that the elements of [an employer's] decision-making process are not capable of separation for analysis, the decision-making process may be analyzed as one employment practice." Since most employers use multiple criteria to make selection, promotion, or

similar decisions, disentangling the contribution of each criteria to the disparate impact will be extremely difficult, if it is possible at all.

21. *Connecticut v. Teal* (1982). 457 U.S. 440 (U.S. Supreme Court).

22. Segal, J. (1996). Sexual harassment: Where are we now? *HRMagazine, 41,* 68–73; see also, Laabs, J. (February 1995). Sexual harassment. *Personnel Journal,* pp. 36–45; Bernardin, L. (1994). Does the reasonable woman standard exist and does she have any place in hostile environment sexual harassment claims under Title VII after Harris? *Florida Law Review, 46,* 291–322; Lengnick-Hall, M. L. (1995). Sexual harassment research: A methodological critique. *Personnel Psychology, 48,* 841–864; Fisher, A. B. (Aug. 23, 1993). Sexual harassment: What to do. *Fortune,* pp. 84–88; Johnson, C. (May 17, 1995). Court cases give firms guidance on sexual harassment. *The Wall Street Journal,* p. B2.

23. Bradshaw, D. S. (1987). Sexual harassment: Confronting the troublesome issues. *Personnel Administrator, 32*(1), 51–53; see also, Hoyman, M., and Robinson, R. (1980). Interpreting the new sexual harassment guidelines. *Personnel Journal, 59*(12), p. 996; *Meritor Savings Bank v. Vinson* (1986). 40 FEP Cases 1822 (U.S. Supreme Court); and Thornton, T. (1986). Sexual harassment: Discouraging it in the work place. *Personnel, 63*(8), 18–26.

24. *Harris v. Forklift Systems* (1993). 114 S. Ct. 367, 370–77. See also, Fitzgerald, L. F., Gelfand, M. J., and Drasgow, F. (1995). Measuring sexual harassment: Theoretical and psychometric advances. *Applied Social Psychology, 17*(4): 425–445; Gutek, B. A. (1995). How subjective is sexual harassment? An examination of rater effects. *Basic & Applied Social Psychology, 17*(4): 447–467; Stockdale, M. S., Vaux, A., and Cashin, F. (1995). Acknowledging sexual harassment: A test of alternative models. *Basic & Applied Social Psychology, 17*(4), 469–496; Tang, T. L., and McCollum, S. L. (1996). Sexual harassment in the workplace. *Public Personnel Management, 25*(1): 53–58.

25. Terpstra, D. E., and Baker, D. D. (1992). Outcomes of federal court decisions on sexual harassment. *Academy of Management Journal, 35,* 181–190; see also, series on harassment in *Applied Social Psychology,* 1995.

26. *Morris v. American National Can* (1989). 52 FEP Cases 210 (USDC, EMo.).

27. Laabs, J. (July 1995). What to do when sexual harassment comes calling. *Personnel Journal,* pp. 42–53; see also, note 22, Lengnick-Hall, M. L. (1995).

28. *Firefighters Local Union No. 1784 v. Stotts* (1984). 34 FEP Cases 1702 (U.S. Supreme Court).

29. *Wygant v. Jackson Board of Education* (1986). 106 U.S. 1842. (U.S. Supreme Court).

30. *Franks v. Bowman Transportation Co.* (1976). 483 U.S. 814 (U.S. Supreme Court).

31. Zelnick, B. (1996). *Backfire: A reporter's look at affirmative action.* Washington, DC: Regnery Publishing. See also, Greenlaw, P. S., and Jensen, S. S. (1996). Race-norming and the Civil Rights Act of 1991. *Public Personnel Management, 25*(1), 13–24; Kravitz, D. A.

(1995). Attitudes toward affirmative action plans directed at Blacks: Effects of plan and individual differences. *Journal of Applied Social Psychology, 25*(24), 2192–2220; Tougas, F., Joly, S., Baton, A. M., and St. Pierre, L. (1996). Reactions of beneficiaries to preferential treatment: A reality check. *Human Relations, 49*(4), 453–464; Nacost, R. W., and Hummels, B. (1994). Affirmative action and the behavior of decision makers. *Journal of Applied Social Psychology, 24*(7), 595–613; Losey, M. R. (1995). Affirmative action is dead! Long live affirmative action! *Managing Office Technology, 40*(6), 28–30.

32. Ruderman, M. N. (1996). Affirmative action: Does it really work? *Academy of Management Executive, 10,* 64–65; see also, Konrad, A. M., and Linnehan, F. (1995). Formalized HRM structures: Coordinating equal employment opportunity or concealing organizational practices? *Academy of Management Journal, 38,* 787–820; Micco, L. (November 1996). Downsizing a challenge to retaining diversity. *HR News,* p. 5.

33. Micco, L. (November 1996). Affirmative action regulator highlights revised rules for federal contractors. *HR News,* p. 6.

34. Brady, R. L. (1995, August) Reverse discrimination: Lawsuits are rare. *HR Focus,* p. 19.

35. *United Steelworkers of America v. Weber* (1979). 443 U.S. 193 (U.S. Supreme Court).

36. *Bakke v. Regents of the University of California* (1978). 17 FEPC 1000.

37. See note 29.

38. *Johnson v. Santa Clara Transportation Agency* (March 26, 1987). *Daily Labor Report,* pp. A1, D1–D19.

39. *City of Richmond v. J. A. Croson Co.* US 109 S. Ct. 706 (1989); *Adarand v. Pena* (US 115 S. Ct. 2097 1995).

40. *Hopwood v. Texas* (5th Circuit, 95–1773 1996).

41. (March 22, 1996). Bad law on affirmative action. *New York Times,* p. A14.

42. See note 37.

43. See note 1.

44. *A solid investment: making full use of the nation's human capital* (1995). Washington, DC: Federal Glass Ceiling Commission. See also, Powell, G., and Butterfield, D. A. (1994). Investigating the "glass ceiling" phenomenon: An empirical study of actual promotions to top management. *Academy of Management Journal, 37,* 68–86.

45. *Fair and equitable treatment: A progress report on minority employment in the federal government* (1996). Washington, DC: U.S. Merit Systems Protection Board; see also, *A question of equity: Women and the glass ceiling in the federal government* (1992). Washington, DC: U.S. Merit Systems Protection Board; *Federal workforce: Continuing need for federal affirmative employment. GAO/GGD-92-27BR* (1991). Washington, DC: U.S. General Accounting Office.

46. Bernstein, N. (Jan. 8, 1996). Equal opportunity recedes for most female lawyers. *New York Times,* p. A12.

47. Donnell, C. Quoted from note 42.

48. Kravitz, D., and Platania, J. (1993). Attitudes and beliefs about affirmative action: Effect of target and respondent

sex and ethnicity. *Journal of Applied Psychology, 78,* 928–938.

49. See note 32, Konrad, A., and Linnehan, F. (1995).

50. Thomas, P. (Aug. 29, 1996). Restructurings generate rash of age bias suits. *The Wall Street Journal,* pp. B1, B13; see also, Finkelstein, L. M., Burke, M. J., and Raju, M. S. (1995). Age discrimination in simulated employment contexts: An integrative analysis. *Journal of Applied Psychology, 80*(6), 652–663; Hassel, B. L., and Perrewe, P. L. (1995). An examination of beliefs about older workers: Do stereotypes still exist? *Journal of Organizational Behavior, 16*(5), 457–468.

51. *Gilmer v. Interstate/Johnson Lane Corp.* (1991). 111 S. Ct. 1647. See also, note 3.

52. *Schwager v. Sun Oil Company of PA* (1979). 591 F.2d. 58 (10th Cir.).

53. *Mastie v. Great Lakes Steel* (1976). 424 F. Supp. 1299 (U.S. District Court, Michigan).

54. *Hodgson v. Greyhound Lines, Inc.* (1975). 419 U.S. 1122.

55. See the special issue on the Americans with Disabilities Act, edited by D. Stone and published by the *Human Resource Management Review* in 1997 (issues 1 and 2); see also, Martinez, M. (November 1990). Creating ways to employ people with disabilities. *HRMagazine,* pp. 40–44, 101; Mullins, M.; Rumrill, J.; and Roesler, D. (February 1994). Use of collaborative approach to reasonable accommodation. *HR Focus,* pp. 110–113; Mello, J. (1995). Employment law and workers with disabilities: Implications for public sector managers and human resource practices. *Public Personnel Management, 24,* 75–88.

56. Lee, B. A. (1996). Legal requirements and employer responses to accommodating employees with disabilities. *Human Resource Management Review, 6*(4), 231–251; The Job Accommodation Network reports that 38 percent of accommodations do not cost anything while 11 percent cost more than $5,000; see also, Cleveland, J. N., Barnes-Farrell, J. L., and Ratz, J. M. (1997). Accommodation in the workplace. *Human Resource Management Review, 7*(1), 77–107.

57. Proper: 1, 4, 7, 8, 12, 13; Improper: 2, 3, 5, 6, 9, 10, 11, 14. See also, Murphy, B.; Barlow, W.; and Hatch, D. (1994). EEOC gives guidance on legal and illegal inquiries under the ADA. *Personnel Journal,* pp. 26–28.

58. Johnson, M. (Aug. 26, 1997). Disabilities Act grows beyond scope. Knight-Ridder Newspapers. Cited in *Boca Raton News,* 2A; see also, Seligman, D. (June 26, 1995). More disability madness. *Fortune,* 176; see also, Lambert, W. (Nov. 12, 1993). Obese workers win on-the-job protection against bias. *The Wall Street Journal,* pp. B1, B7; Pear, R. (April 30, 1997). Employers told to accommodate the mentally ill. *New York Times,* A1; Novack, J. (Dec. 4, 1995). What if the guy shoots somebody? *Forbes,* p. 37; Hayes, T. L., Citera, M., Brady, L. M., and Jenkins, N. M. (1995). Staffing for persons with disabilities: What is "fair" and "job related?" *Public Personnel Management, 24*(4), 413–427; Kim, P. S. (1996). Disability policy: An analysis of the employment of people with disabilities in the American Federal Government. *Personnel Management, 25*(1), 73–88; Riger, S., Foster-Fishman, P., Nelson-Kuna, J., and Curran, B. (1995, October). Insanity, justification, and culpability toward a unifying schema. *Law & Human Behavior, 19*(5), 465–480.

59. *Pregnancy and employment: The complete handbook on discrimination, maternity leave, and health and safety* (1987). Washington, DC: Bureau of National Affairs.

60. *California Federal Savings & Loan Association v. Guerra* (1987). 42 FEP Cases 1073.

61. Tung, R. (1984). *Key to Japan's strength: Human power.* Lexington, MA: Lexington Books.

62. Protzman, F. (Oct. 17, 1993). In Germany, the ceiling's not glass, it's concrete. *New York Times,* p. 16.

63. *Abrams, L. A. v. Baylor College of Medicine* (1990). Civ. A. Nos. H-81-1433, H-82-3253.

64. Adler, N. J. (Summer 1984). Women in international business: Where are they? *California Management Review,* pp. 78–89; see also, Adler, N. J. (1983). Cross cultural management research: The ostrich and the trend. *Academy of Management Review, 8,* 226–232; see also, Kopp, R. (1994). International human resource policies and practices in Japanese, European, and United States multinationals. *Human Resource Management, 33*(4), 581–600.

65. Green, W. E., and Brannigan, M. (Feb. 5, 1990). Appeals court says job-bias law doesn't apply to citizens abroad. *The Wall Street Journal,* p. B4.

66. See note 3.

67. See note 3.

68. See note 1.

69. Holmes, S. A. (Nov. 17, 1996). Bias suit harbinger. *New York Times,* p. 12.

C H A P T E R

JOB ANALYSIS*

OVERVIEW

Job analysis is considered to be the foundation or building block for most HR systems. Corporate restructuring processes, quality improvement programs, human resource planning, job design, recruitment strategies, screening tests, training programs, succession planning, performance appraisal, and compensation are among the systems typically based on information derived from some form of job analysis. Job analysis provides the basic information that leads to specific products used by management to create and sustain **organizational capability.** While sometimes a highly formal system involving trained job analysts and at other times an informal process completed by line management, job analysis is a first step to most functional areas of HR, including redesign or reengineering efforts.[1]

Consider the following scenarios:
• General Cinema is interested in developing a screening test for theater manager positions. It wants to be certain the test is legally defensible, is "job related," and

emphasizes the most important elements of the job. Having read this and the previous chapter on equal employment opportunity, the consultant recommends two methods of job analysis to gather information.
• The state of Virginia passed a law mandating state employee pay be based on performance. However, a new performance appraisal system was needed. The first step in developing the appraisal system was use of the critical incident technique (CIT) to identify the critical outcomes and behaviors for each position to be evaluated.
• Personal Assessment Systems (PAS) decides it will advertise for one or more marketing and management positions to develop a plan for its mass market personality test. It needs to be sure about the kind of person the company wants and the appropriate level of pay.
• PAS has a contract to develop a job-related test to screen applicants for security guard positions. PAS must ensure that the test is in full compliance with all EEO laws and state provisions regarding privacy.
• The Monsanto Corporation has many jobs that stipulate specific physical requirements (e.g., must be able to lift 75 pounds). The company is concerned that some of the requirements are unnecessary and may violate

*Contributed by Peter Villanova.

the Civil Rights Act or the Americans with Disabilities Act.

• A division of Ford Motor Company decided to adopt the Japanese approach to factory work by assigning specific tasks to a team rather than to individuals. The team will divide the work, which is as clearly defined and standardized as in typical American factories, but all team members are expected to be able to perform any of the work tasks. What information will the HR department at Ford need to redesign the jobs into work teams and determine qualifications for team membership?

• The James River Corporation uses a standardized job analysis questionnaire known as the Position Analysis Questionnaire (PAQ) to identify the best written tests to determine admission to its pipefitter and millwright apprenticeship programs. It attempts to establish the "job relatedness" of the tests using the results from the PAQ.

• Pratt & Whitney, the jet engine division of United Technologies, seeks to improve its competitiveness by eliminating activities no longer essential to the business and by improving existing job functions in the context of customer requirements. The modification or elimination of some jobs was anticipated.

• IBM adopted a process management approach to the evaluation and restructuring of each unit. All job tasks and outcomes were assessed in the context of critical internal customers and how their requirements related to the requirements of external customer requirements.

• The state of Maryland asks the consulting firm of Booz, Allen and Hamilton to determine the necessary knowledge, skills, and abilities required to perform certain social work positions for the state. The study leads to the reclassification of many positions stipulating that only a bachelor's degree was required to do the work rather than a master's degree in social work. The reclassification and reduction in salary for the positions saved the state (and taxpayers) millions.

• The city of Fort Lauderdale, Florida, updates all of its job descriptions by identifying the "essential functions" of each job according to the Americans with Disabilities Act and incorporating this language into new job descriptions.

• Columbia Forest Products has transformed its work organization from the traditional job-based approach to a work-team approach. In the future, individuals will be hired as members of process teams rather than to fill a job vacancy. In addition, compensation practices are changing from a job-based approach to one that emphasizes skills and competencies.

• Saudi Arabia has an opening for official executioner. The salary is $36 per month, plus $133 for each head. The job requires "very skilled attention to ensure that the sword does not slip or cut in the wrong place." The incumbent, Saeed Sayyaf (meaning happy swordsman executioner in Arabic), is retiring after 35 years of "looking forward to the opportunity to chop off more heads so

that I can earn more money." A special person is needed to succeed the happy swordsman.

Job analysis information is needed for each of these situations to assist organizations in achieving certain objectives. Job descriptions and job specifications are needed to attract and select qualified (but not overqualified) employees and to evaluate the compensation system and compensation decisions. Job standards and performance criteria are used to evaluate employee performance; job factors are needed to group jobs to assess wage and salary systems; and job duties and context factors are examined to redesign and evaluate jobs, restructure organizations, and develop succession planning. As one expert in HRM put it, "Job analysis may be viewed as the hub of virtually all human resources administration and management activities necessary for the successful functioning of organizations. Hardly a program of interest to human resource specialists and other practitioners whose work pertains to organizational personnel does not depend on or cannot benefit from job analysis results."[2]

This chapter subscribes to this view in describing the importance of job analysis for HRM. Discussion centers on the purposes for job analysis as well as the major approaches for collecting job analysis data. While the world of work may be changing, the basics of job analysis can (and should) be the cornerstone in the more dynamic workplace. As we have said in Chapters 1 and 2, HRM must provide deliverables to management. Good job analysis increases the probability that the deliverables from the HR suppliers will meet the requirements of both internal and external customers. This argument applies whether jobs, positions or projects are becoming more elastic and less static and even if we don't call them jobs anymore.

OBJECTIVES

After studying this chapter, you should be able to:

1. Understand what job analysis is and what its major products are.
2. Explain the purposes and uses for job analysis data.
3. Compare and contrast methods for collecting job analysis data.
4. Describe commonly used and newer methods for conducting a job analysis.
5. Explain how job analysis information is applied to job design efforts.
6. Understand that different job analysis procedures emphasize different kinds of information that may be more or less useful for different HRM functions. And,
7. Explain the objectives of work process maps and

how they may be useful complements to conventional job analysis methods.

WHAT IS JOB ANALYSIS?

Job analysis is a systematic process of gathering information about a job. Conducting a job analysis requires several major steps. Typically, the first step is to determine the major tasks, activities, behaviors, or duties to be performed on the job. This can be done by one or more methods described in a later section. However, to drive a marketing orientation deep within the organizational structure and to give the organization a unity of purpose, we prefer job analysis methods that rely on internal and especially external customers to first identify the critical products or services required of the supplier. This list of carefully defined products and services should then be the frame of reference for the rest of the steps in the job analysis, starting with the major tasks or activities necessary to achieve the required outcomes defined by the customers. The required outcomes as defined by customers are derived from the strategic planning of the organization.[3]

General Cinema, for example, required a cost-effective and job-related test that would help identify persons most likely to be effective theater managers. The product to be delivered by HR was the test and the internal customers were managers who would have to make the hiring decisions. Of course, the main frame of reference of the manager must be the external customer, the ticket buyers.

Once the products are defined and the tasks and activities have been identified, the relative importance, relative frequency, or essentiality with which the various tasks are performed can be assessed. Remember that word *essentiality*. Many job analysis methods now require the determination of essential functions for jobs because of the language of the Americans with Disabilities Act. For example, Personnel Assessment Systems (PAS) uses its own job analysis method, which asks respondents to indicate whether each task, behavior, or job specification is "absolutely essential" for the job, "essential," or "not essential."

Next, the critical **knowledges, abilities, skills,** and **other characteristics** (or **KASOCs**) necessary to perform the tasks must be identified. **Knowledge** refers to an organized body of information, usually of a factual or procedural nature applied directly to the performance of a function. For example, computer programmers may need knowledge of specific languages such as Java. Your instructor in this class should have knowledge of research and practice in human resource management.

An **ability** refers to a demonstrated competence to perform an observable behavior or a behavior that results in an observable product. Police officers, for example, are required to possess the physical ability to apprehend and detain a suspect or the cognitive ability to understand and complete arrest forms.

A **skill** is a competence to perform a learned, psychomotor act and may include a manual, verbal, or mental manipulation of data, people, or things. So, in the case of an officer, she or he must demonstrate an acceptable level of driving skill or skill in operating and maintaining a weapon.

Finally, **other characteristics** include personality factors (attitudes), aptitudes, or physical or mental traits needed to perform the job. Even something as simple as being courteous to civilians plays an important role in determining how well police officers perform their jobs. When officers are unable to empathize with crime victims, are callous in treating witnesses, or impulsive and destroy evidence at a crime scene, they demonstrate some shortcoming in personal characteristics that affect their job performance. Being able to tolerate the belligerence of customers and control one's temper may be critical in certain circumstances. Being able to work in teams is another example of a critical characteristic for many jobs today. A job analysis could conclude, for example, that armed security guards must not have a history of or present conditions indicating psychiatric problems.

As you can tell from these examples, the products of knowledges and skills are typically easier to observe and serve as the basic units of observation for job analysis. For example, the customer of the computer programmer requires a Java program that meets certain specifications. Knowledge of a computer language such as Java can be determined from an interview, responses to a written test, the possession of a certain certification or license or graduation from a certain class, or observing an individual attempt to program. The knowledge required to teach a class in human resource management can be determined based on the possession of certain credentials (e.g., Ph.D. in human resource management or industrial/ organizational psychology) or through an interview or test.

Establishing that someone has the required driving skill to perform a job is somewhat more difficult in that an interview or written test does not afford an opportunity to observe the behaviors that demonstrate the application of this knowledge domain in the job environment. This would seem to require observations of actual motor vehicle operation.

There is considerable confusion as to what distinguishes a skill from an ability. One helpful way to distinguish between them is to think of ability and other characteristics as providing the necessary prerequisites for developing a skill or acquiring knowledge. For example, to develop good driving skills, a person has to have reading ability (to learn from the driver's manual), near and far vision acuity (to safely operate a vehicle), and multi-limb coordination (to physically control its direction and velocity). Ability and Other Characteristics (A&Os) are the basic foundations on which Knowledge and Skills (K&Ss) are built. K&Ss are typically acquired through formal instruction and practice, whereas A&Os are less easily acquired through experience and are also more stable over time. Remember, for example, that Superman had the ability to leap tall buildings in a single bound but he had to learn how to leap as opposed to skip or hurl himself over buildings. This also suggests why screening on ability and other characteristics is so important for many jobs. Because A&Os (such as personality) aren't easy to acquire through formal training, organizations need to be extra careful in identifying job candidates who possess the requisite A&Os for subsequent job training success.

What Are the Major Goals for Job Analysis?

As you've probably gathered by now, much of the success (i.e., validity) of job analysis efforts is a function of the accuracy of the inferences one draws about the job from observations, interviews, and/or questionnaire data gathered through the job analysis. One underlying objective of job analysis is to minimize the inferential leaps required to arrive at a conclusion. The following are offered as goals one should strive for in job analysis:[4]

1. *The objective of job analysis should be the description of observables.* Often the behavior or trait necessary for performing the job or supporting success is not observable but the products or outcomes, kinds of materials or work aids used, and the people included in the decision process can be reported and help substantiate its operation. If a work behavior has no observable component, then it cannot be described in a job analysis.

2. *A job analysis consists of a description of work behavior independent of the personal characteristics of particular people who perform the job.* A job analysis describes how a job is performed and focuses on the position, not the person doing the work. **Performance appraisal** is used to describe how well individuals perform their jobs. The actual performance appraisal instrument may have been developed from a job analysis.

3. *Job analysis data must be verifiable and reliable.* The organization must maintain records of the data, document all decisions that are data based, and be able to justify every job analysis judgment in terms of observable behaviors. The data must be reliable, indicating that different sources agreed on judgments about the work. Recall the importance of job analysis in EEO litigation and, in particular, in establishing job relatedness.

Do We Really Need All the Specificity in Formal Job Analysis?

The stipulations of specific tasks to be performed and specifications for the job are not without critics. In Japan, for example, new employees are typically hired without a job description or specifications. Japan places much greater reliance on in-house training and job rotation to foster versatility in the skills of each new employee. Japanese managers think job descriptions can be harmful to their team-building approach to management. Many experts in job design and organizational restructuring embrace this view and believe job descriptions should be written for units or teams with all team members responsible for (or at least qualified to perform) all unit functions or activities. Individual job descriptions are thought to be detrimental to work group effectiveness. However, particularly in these litigious times, job descriptions are needed and can be written so as to facilitate a team-oriented approach to work processes; this is the intent of the changes occurring at Columbia Forest Products. The basic unit of analysis consists of tasks, but these are then aggregated to the level of the team, reflecting the diversity of skills and competencies required for performance as a member of the team.

Highly detailed job descriptions are very common in Europe where they are frequently required by regulation or collective bargaining agreement. Every employee at the Volvo plant in Sweden, for example, has a detailed job description based on a quantitative job analysis even though the assembly process at Volvo is team-based rather than the traditional assembly line. Daimler-Benz and Siemens, two giant German companies, also use detailed job descriptions for each position, including their U.S. plants.

While job analysis is typically used to derive specific information about particular jobs, as we stated above, the method can be used for organizations. Job analysis data can be aggregated to the unit or function level so that the end products, such as job descriptions or job specifications, are defined at the team level rather than for particular positions. Often this approach to defining the job in terms of team member competencies is coupled with skill-based pay systems where individuals are compensated on their potential to perform multiple tasks as opposed to a limited set of tasks specific to a job. A team member may be expected to perform the tasks of another who is absent, rotate task assignments with others as needed, and provide additional expert opinion on task processes or products. In this way, the team member is cross-trained to perform a number of different tasks, perhaps even all of those involved in a specific work process. No one has a monopoly on a set of tasks as the responsibility for performance of these tasks is shared by team members.

What Is the Legal Significance of Job Analysis?

Interest in job analysis has been strong since passage of the Civil Rights Act in 1964 and subsequent court rulings. In particular, the Supreme Court decisions in *Griggs v. Duke Power* and *Albemarle Paper Company v. Moody* emphasized the importance of demonstrating the job relatedness of employer selection systems. One way to do this is by conducting a thorough job analysis to justify personnel job specifications and other personnel matters such as compensation.

The legal importance of job analysis has not waned since 1964. Many court cases focus on the results of (or the nonexistence of) a job analysis. For example, many women have filed lawsuits contesting the physical ability tests (e.g., push-ups, sit-ups) mandated for entry into police or firefighters' academies. They often claim "adverse impact" because a greater proportion of women than men are disqualified as a result of such tests. A number of lawsuits have also been filed on behalf of older workers who lost their jobs because of a mandatory retirement age. For example, an Indianapolis bus driver used the ADEA to challenge the mandatory retirement age of 55 (he lost). In this case, job analysis data were introduced at trial to support the age limit.

The American Association of Retired Persons has been very active recently in challenging mandatory retirement ages using job analysis data. United Airlines settled a lawsuit brought by female flight attendants contesting weight limits for the position.

As discussed in Chapter 3, statistics can be used to establish prima facie evidence of discrimination under the disparate impact theory of Title VII. The burden of proof then rests with the employer to show that the selection device or job specification (e.g., the test, test score, educational requirement) is "job related" or a "business necessity." In one case involving physical abilities, firefighter candidates in Dallas, Texas, were required to scale a 6-foot-high fence in a prescribed amount of time. Since a higher percentage of women were unable to scale the fence than men, the court asked the city to show how scaling the fence was job related. The city presented job analysis data that demonstrated the average fence in the jurisdiction was six feet in height and that scaling fences was a frequent activity that must be performed by competent firefighters.

Legal challenges to job specifications involving physical attributes (e.g., strength, speed) and mental attributes have increased due to the Americans with Disabilities Act. The ADA specifies that employers must make "reasonable accommodations" that would allow qualified disabled workers to perform the "essential functions" of the job. According to the EEOC, these accommodations may include physical renovations to the job[5] (see the Critical Thinking Exercise 4.1).

| CRITICAL THINKING EXERCISE 4.1 |

Can PAS Defend Its Test in Court?

Personnel Assessment Systems was asked to develop a job-related and valid screening test to hire armed and unarmed security guards for a large corporation. The job analysis method is described below.

REQUIRED ABILITIES AND CHARACTERISTICS RATING FORM

Personnel Assessment Systems is studying security officer jobs in several companies to develop a valid battery of tests for hiring decisions. As part of our research, we are asking you for some information about the kinds of abilities and other characteristics required for effective performance in the entry-level security job with which you are most familiar. In the space below please write in the job title of the security job under study. Then fill in the information requested below on your experience performing and supervising this particular job.

Take a minute to think about the duties performed by security officers in this position and the kinds of abilities and characteristics they should have. On the following pages, we have listed a number of abilities and characteristics that may be necessary for performing as a security officer. Please read each one and decide how important you feel this ability or characteristic is to perform the *essential functions* of the security officer jobs. Use the following scale to make your ratings:

0   Neither useful nor necessary to perform one or more of the essential functions of the job at minimally acceptable level

1   Useful but not necessary to perform one or more of the essential functions of the job at a minimally acceptable level

2   Necessary to perform one or more of the essential functions of the job at a minimally acceptable level

Ability or Characteristic

Color vision: ability to distinguish red, yellow, blue, and green colors

Normal peripheral visual field (150°–180°)

Visual acuity: ability to distinguish small details from a complex background; ability to read indicator numbers from a normal viewing distance

Depth perception

Auditory acuity: ability to hear changes in pitch or loudness of equipment noises; ability to distinguish spoken language from a noisy background

Tactual acuity: ability to feel heat or vibrations in equipment

Sense of smell

Ability to read and comprehend blueprints, schematics, diagrams, or structures

Ability to respond appropriately under stress

Emotional stability

Analytical ability: ability to reason way through problems; detect trends, plan actions in a logical, orderly manner

System comprehension: ability to comprehend entire systems and how they function; ability to foresee system implications of malfunctions or of own actions; ability to *anticipate* required future conditions in numerous interacting systems

Ability to retain and recall information

Attention to detail: ability to perceive and interpret small details

Conscientiousness in checking and caring for equipment

Ability to add, subtract, multiply, and divide whole numbers, decimals, fractions

Ability to comprehend, use, and/or compute logs, powers, trigonometry, scientific notation

Ability to follow complex sequence of activities

Ability to control one's temper

Ability to remain calm in difficult situations

Ability to stay alert for possible unlawful activities

Ability to follow directions carefully

Ability to reason with multiple concepts and operations

Ability to identify clerical errors quickly

Ability to detect rule violations

All of the items above were assessed as "essential functions" (2s) by 75 percent or more of supervisors who were asked to complete the job analysis form. Based on these job analysis results, PAS developed a test, a portion of which is presented below, that would be administered to job applicants. PAS then developed a "suitability" scoring procedure for the test, including the following:

Suitability for *responding to stressful aspects* of the job such as reacting quickly in dangerous situations, always controlling one's temper, remaining emotionally in control under difficult circumstances and dealing with difficult individuals.

The applicant's responses indicate (below average, average, above average) likelihood that the applicant will react appropriately and effectively in stressful situations.

Suitability for *interacting with clients, customers, and others* such as being friendly with customers/clients; always being courteous, treating all people the same regardless of their race, gender, age, na-tional origin or disability, and being able to effectively communicate with different types of clients and customers.

PORTION OF SECURITY OFFICER TEST

Format: Job applicants must indicate whether each statement is TRUE OR FALSE about them:

Most of the time, I feel life has let me down.

I used to steal a lot when I was young.

I'm almost always angry to some extent.

I would like to be a police officer.

People from different races are more different than the same.

I like to jump from job to job.

I have trouble understanding written material.

I often feel things are out of my control.

Almost everyone I know is luckier than I.

I drink liquor or beer almost every day.

At times, I just want to punch someone.

Kids who are bad deserve to be spanked.

I dislike most of the people I know.

Things are out of my control most of the time.

I often lose my self-control.

I have a little problem with alcohol.

Everybody should be allowed to carry a handgun.

I cannot tolerate others' mistakes.

I'm almost always happy.

Stealing from an employer is acceptable if the employer cheats you.

I skipped over 20 days of school in my last year of high school.

I tend to get quite irritable when I'm tired.

I have great difficulty sleeping.

I enjoy watching a good fight.

Police officers deserve respect.

If I got this job, I'd probably keep it for about six months.

I've gotten into more than 15 physical fights in my life.

Success in life is mainly due to luck.

I've been drunk more than five times in my life.

I can tolerate a great deal before I get upset.

If I am hired for this job, I'll almost certainly keep it for over a year.

I almost always reach personal goals I set for myself.

If I am in charge, things have to be done my way or I'll quit.

I tend to get angry when I am criticized in a group.

When a person gets annoyed with me, I quickly get annoyed back.

I get depressed often.

Sometimes I am not in the mood to see anyone.

I get angry often.

I have fewer friends than most people.

Most people think I am too emotional.

I often get angry too quickly with people.

Daring and foolish things are fun to do.

I feel I am an outgoing, social person and fun to be with.

Assignment

Based on your understanding of the ADA and the job analysis results, can the company use this test to screen applicants? What (if any) other information do you need about the job analysis, the test, or anything else to be able to take a definitive position? Do you regard any of these questions as an invasion of privacy?

Not all job analysis methods are equal to the task of providing legal defensibility. And legal defensibility, it seems, is largely a function of whether an impartial observer can place confidence in the inferences arising from a job analysis. When job analysis data are collected from a representative sample of job incumbents and other informed sources (e.g., trained analysts, supervisors or administrators), represent the full breadth of tasks to be completed on a job, are reduced to written form, and specify the level of competency necessary for entry-level work, there is greater likelihood that the subsequent inferences about what KASOCs are needed to perform the job will be received more positively.[6] The argument made in Chapter 1 regarding precision in measurement applies here as well. More precise measures of a job will result in better job analysis products which can contribute to competitive advantage.

What Are the Major Job Analysis Products?

Depending on the particular method of job analysis, numerous products can be derived from job analysis. The most frequent and commonly used products of job analysis include job descriptions and job specifications. **Job descriptions** define the job in terms of its content and scope. Although the format can vary, the job description may include information on job duties and responsibilities, an identification of critical internal and external customers, equipment to be used on the job, working conditions, relationships with co-workers, and the extent of supervision required. Figure 4.1 presents an example of a job description for a compensation manager. You can think of a job description as being a report of the job sit-

uation. Job descriptions are often summarized in classified employment ads and, more recently, available on the Internet through various job placement services (see www.jobsmart.com).

Job specifications consist of the KASOCs needed to carry out the job tasks and duties. Specific educational requirements (e.g., Ph.D., MD, MBA, Ed.D., MSW), certifications or licenses (e.g., CPA, CFP), or other credentials are often listed in job specifications. Cut-off scores on tests are also job specifications. Figure 4.2 presents an example of the job specifications for a compensation manager. A college degree in personnel, human resources, industrial psychology, or a related field is required for the compensation manager job. Job specifications detail the personal requirements for succeeding in the situation as described in the job description. A job analysis should be the basis of this specification.

Job specifications are often contested in court because they may have an adverse impact against groups protected by EEO laws. Job specifications that result in adverse impact against groups covered by EEO legislation should be derived from a thorough job analysis to support the *job relatedness* arguments for the specifications. Data that are available about the relationship between a given job specification and some measure of effectiveness should certainly be used. Analysts should also consider the incremental compensation that may be required by a job specification that may not be essential for performance on the job. Such unnecessary specifications can translate into higher labor costs and thus ultimately higher prices for the customer. The state of Maryland, for example, was concerned about the number of state positions that required a master's degree in social work, a requirement that necessitated a higher starting salary. The consulting firm of Booz-Allen & Hamilton conducted a job analysis of these jobs and determined the extent to which the knowledge acquired by the master's degree was essential for these jobs. In addition, since many positions had some master's-trained occupants and others doing the same work with only a bachelor's degree, Booz-Allen studied whether the more advanced degree was related to better performance on the job (it wasn't). Booz-Allen recommended that the master's in social work job specification be dropped for these positions. The state saved millions of dollars by dropping the higher degree requirement.

Many business schools now stipulate that a Ph.D. is required for any faculty position, although a candidate with an MBA would be less costly and perhaps as (or more) effective as an instructor of undergraduate students. Job specifications such as reading level, formal education requirements, and the like must be established at a level that reflects the minimum necessary for job entry. Establishing specifications at too high a level often results in adverse impact, hindering diversity and affirmative action goals. For this reason, such practices are

FIGURE 4.1
JOB DESCRIPTION FOR A COMPENSATION MANAGER

Job Title: Compensation Manager   DOT Code: 166.167-022

Reports to:

General Summary:

Responsible for the design and administration of employee compensation programs. Insures proper consideration of the relationship of salary to performance of each employee and provides consultation on salary administration to managers and supervisors.

Principal Duties and Responsibilities:

1. Insures the preparation and maintenance of job descriptions for each current and projected position. Prepares all job descriptions, authorizing final drafts. Coordinates periodic review of all job descriptions, making revisions as necessary. Educates employees and supervisors on job description use and their intent by participation in formal training programs and by responding to their questions. Maintains accurate file of all current job descriptions. Distributes revised job descriptions to appropriate individuals.

2. Insures the proper evaluation of job descriptions. Serves as chair of Job Evaluation Committee, coordinating its activities. Resolves disputes over proper evaluation of jobs. Assigns jobs to pay ranges and reevaluates jobs periodically through the Committee process. Conducts initial evaluation of new positions prior to hiring. Insures integrity of job evaluation process.

3. Insures that Company compensation rates are in accordance with the Company philosophy. Maintains current information concerning applicable salary movements taking place in comparable organizations. Obtains or conducts salary surveys as necessary. Conducts analysis of salary changes among competitors and presents recommendations on salary movements on an annual basis.

4. Insures proper consideration of the relationship of salary to the performance of each employee. Inspects all performance appraisals and salary reviews, authorizing all pay adjustments.

5. Develops and administers the performance appraisal program. Develops and updates performance appraisal instruments. Assists in the development of training programs to educate supervisors on using the performance appraisal system. Monitors the use of the performance appraisal instruments to insure the integrity of the system and proper use.

6. Assists in the development and oversees the administration of all bonus payments up through the Officer level.

7. Conducts research and provides recommendations on executive compensation issues.

8. Coordinates the development of an integrated HR information system. Assists in identifying needs; interfaces with the Management Information Systems Department to achieve departmental goals for information needs.

9. Performs related duties as assigned or as the situation dictates.

FIGURE 4.2
JOB SPECIFICATIONS FOR A COMPENSATION MANAGER

Required Knowledges, Skills, and Abilities:

1. Knowledge of compensation and HRM practices and principles.

2. Knowledge of job analysis procedures.

3. Knowledge of survey development and interpretation practices.

4. Knowledge of current performance appraisal issues for designing, implementing, and maintaining systems.

5. Skill in conducting job analysis interviews.

6. Skill in writing job descriptions, memorandums, letters, and proposals.

7. Skill in making group presentations, conducting job analysis interviews, and explaining policies and practices to employees and supervisors.

8. Skill in performing statistical computations including regression, correlation, and basic descriptive statistics.

9. Ability to conduct meetings.

10. Ability to plan and prioritize work.

Education and Experience Requirements:

This position requires the equivalent of a college degree in personnel, human resources, industrial psychology, or a related degree, plus 3-5 years' experience in Personnel, 2-3 of which should include compensation administration experience. An advanced degree in Industrial Psychology, Business Administration, or Personnel Management is preferred.

Work Orientation Factors:

This position may require up to 15% travel.

---

scrutinized by the courts. The so-called glass ceiling in certain industries may to some extent be caused by job specifications that block women from many key positions because they lack certain credentials or experience.

In addition to job description and job specification, job analysis is used for a variety of purposes and products for both the private and the public sector, particularly in larger organizations (see Figure 4.3). Smaller businesses are less likely to use formal approaches for conducting job analyses and may instead rely on less structured methods for writing job descriptions and setting job specifications. In larger organizations, however, such as state and federal government agencies, personnel may be hired, trained, and classified as job analysts. In these positions, their primary duty is to perform job analyses and related activities. Much of their work today concerns legal compliance; in particular, compliance with the ADA. For example, Fort Lauderdale, Florida, developed a new job analysis method that incorporated ADA language such as "essential functions."

Job analysis data have been collected for recruitment and selection purposes in many companies. For example,

General Cinema developed a test and a structured interview using job analysis information derived from the Management Position Description Questionnaire (MPDQ), a standardized job analysis instrument and the **critical incident technique.** Exxon Corporation and AT&T employ a standardized questionnaire to analyze their jobs to develop or identify personnel selection tests for their entry-level employees. The city of New York and the Monsanto Corporation also use a job analysis method to establish very specific job specifications for physical requirements for certain jobs. PAS used a standardized instrument to develop the tests for security guard. The state of Virginia and Palm Beach County, Florida, both used the critical incident technique to derive performance appraisal instruments for their employees.

Job analysis data have also been used for job redesign purposes. Pratt & Whitney, a division of United Technologies, conducted job analyses as a part of a corporatewide restructuring effort. Motorola Corporation and Ford used a standardized, task-based instrument known as the Job Diagnostic Survey to collect the necessary information to develop work teams. Numerous

FIGURE 4.3
PRODUCTS OF JOB ANALYSIS INFORMATION

Job Description. A complete job description should contain job identification information, a job summary, the job duties, accountabilities, and job specification or employment standards information.

Job Classification. Job classification is the arrangement of jobs into classes, groups, or families according to some systematic schema. Traditional classification schemes have been based on organizational lines of authority, technology-based job/task content, and human behavior-based job content.

Job Evaluation. Job evaluation is a procedure for classifying jobs in terms of their relative worth both within an organization and within the related labor market. Job evaluation is used to determine compensation.

Job Design/Restructuring. Job design deals with the allocation and arrangement of organizational work activities and tasks into sets where a singular set of activities constitutes a "job" and is performed by the job incumbent. Job restructuring or redesign consists of reallocation or rearrangement of the work activities into different sets.

Job Specifications. Personnel requirements and specifications for a particular job are the personal knowledge, skills, aptitudes, attributes, and traits that are required for successful performance. Job specifications may be identified as minimum qualifications, as essential characteristics, or as desirable specifications. Cut-off scores on tests are job specifications.

Performance Appraisal. Performance appraisal is a systematic evaluation of employee job performance by their supervisors or others who are familiar with their performance. Job analysis is used to develop the criteria or standards for the appraisal.

Worker Training. Training is a systematic, intentional process

of developing specific skills and influencing behavior of organizational members such that their resultant behavior contributes to organizational effectiveness.

Worker Mobility/Succession Planning. Worker mobility (career development and pathing) is the movement of individuals into and out of positions, jobs, and occupations. From the perspective of the individual, both self-concepts and social situations change, making the process of job/occupational choice continuous due to growth, exploration, establishment, maintenance, and decline.

Efficiency. Improving efficiency in jobs involves the development of optimal work processes and design of equipment and other physical facilities with particular reference to work activities of people, including work procedures, work layout, and work standards.

Safety. Similar to efficiency, improving safety in jobs involves the development of optimal work processes and safe design of equipment and physical facilities. However, the focus is on identifying and eliminating unsafe work behaviors, physical conditions, and environmental conditions.

Human Resource Planning. Human resource planning consists of anticipatory and reactive activities by which an organization ensures that it has and will continue to have the right number and kind of people at the right places, at the right times, performing jobs that maximize both the service objectives and/or profit of the organization. It includes the activities by which an organization enhances the self-actualization and growth needs of its people and allows for the maximum utilization of their skills and talents.

Legal/Quasi-Legal Requirements. Laws, regulations, and guidelines established by government agencies (e.g., EEOC, OFCCP, OSHA) have set forth requirements related to one or more of the job analysis products or purposes listed above.

Source: Adapted from R. A. Ash. Job analysis in the world of work. In S. Gael (ed.), *The job analysis handbook for business, industry, and government.* Vol. I. Copyright © 1988 John Wiley and Sons, Inc. Reprinted by permission of John Wiley and Sons, Inc.

organizations also use job analysis information to develop training curriculum.

Discrepancy between Academic Research and HR Practice

One of the clearest examples of discrepancies between academic research and actual HR practice is in the use of formal job analysis to help in the development or selection of tests used for hiring or promoting personnel. Remember that some case law supports the view that a company is more likely to defend argument of "job relatedness" when a test was selected or developed using job analysis. Numerous scholarly texts and articles support the view that tests should be either developed or selected based on a thorough job analysis. Despite the case law and these academic prescriptions, we found that only 28 percent of surveyed companies using standardized tests for personnel decisions used any form of job analysis. Small businesses were the worst offenders with less than 10 percent doing job analysis before using

tests. With regard to potential lawsuits, a company could do a formal job analysis after a lawsuit was already filed, but the credibility of the results of the job analysis could be called into question because of the timing.

We also found that most job specifications are stipulated without the benefit of a formal job analysis. For example, the specification that a person possess a certain number of years experience or a particular graduate degree is more often than not just based on one person's sometimes costly opinion. The use of a formal system of job analysis such as the PAQ might reduce the likelihood of cronyism or favoritism within an organization where job specifications and job descriptions are simply written to "wire" a job to a particular person rather than to allow for a serious search of candidates for a position.

We also found very little evidence that the setting of cut-off scores for staffing devices such as tests was based on any formal method of job analysis, despite a consensus on this subject in the academic world. For example, the decision to keep only those who scored 75 percent correct in a pool of candidates is rarely determined by a formal job analysis or empirical study based on data available. A common response we received to the question about the source of a particular cut score was "tradition." No academic would support this approach to setting cut-off scores.

What Are the Major Methods of Collecting Job Analysis Information?

A variety of methods can be used to collect information about jobs including observation, performing the job, interviews, critical incidents, diaries, records, customer complaints, and questionnaires. Figure 4.4 presents a list of the various data collection methods available along with some of their relative advantages and disadvantages. An analyst, most often the supervisor for the position under study, can simply observe the job and record his or her observations. The analyst can also perform the job. Many corporations now require high-level managers to spend time performing jobs where there is personal contact with the customer. Blockbuster Video, for example, has its managers work the cash register on weekends, and Xerox Corporation sends its top managers on sales calls. The basic idea is to better understand the customer's perspective on the business. Individual or group interviews can be conducted with incumbents, supervisors, or subordinates for the position under study. Incumbents or observers can be asked to maintain a diary or record critical incidents regarding their performance or behavior on the job. Available records of work activities or other relevant information such as job descriptions, an organizational chart, and policies and procedures manuals can be reviewed by the analyst for background data on the job. Relevant job descriptions listed in the *Dictionary of Occupational Titles* (DOT) can also be reviewed. The DOT includes standardized, comprehensive descriptions of job duties for over *40,000* occupations and is described in a later section[7] (see www.wave.net/upq/immigration/dot_index.html).

Questionnaires or checklists can also be completed by incumbents, supervisors, customers, or subordinates. Respondents can be asked to list the major tasks they perform as well as to rate the importance, frequency, time spent, or "essential" nature of each task. Respondents can also indicate how important a specific knowledge, skill, or ability is for completing the tasks. Methods are available for determining the importance of job tasks. A variety of standardized questionnaires exist for conducting job analyses, and some of the more commonly used ones are described in a later section.

What Are the Dimensions on Which Job Analysis Methods Can Vary?

Job analysis methods can vary along several dimensions including (1) the types of job analysis information pro-

vided; (2) the forms in which job information is illustrated; (3) the standardization of the job analysis content; and (4) the sources of job information. Each of these dimensions is described below.

TYPES OF JOB ANALYSIS INFORMATION. Job analysis methods can solicit a variety of types of information. Some approaches are called task- or job-oriented methods because they indicate the tasks or duties required to perform the job. For example, "performing cardiopulmonary resuscitation" is considered an important task for a nurse. Similarly, "study and evaluate state-of-the-art techniques to remain competitive and/or lead the field" may be considered an essential task for a member of the management information systems (MIS) staff. Task/job-oriented approaches can be distinguished from the other two approaches we will discuss by their identification or at least implication of an end product. That is, task/job-oriented approaches tend to stress "what gets done on the job." These approaches typically produce detailed descriptions of the objectives for each job. As a result, they are very good for fine-grained analysis of jobs but often are too specific to allow for useful comparisons across jobs.

Other methods such as the Position Analysis Questionnaire (PAQ) are considered to be person- or worker-oriented approaches since information is collected on the KASOCs or behaviors (e.g., decision making, communicating) needed to perform the tasks satisfactorily. In the nurse example, a person-oriented job analysis may determine that "knowledge of disorders of the circulatory system" is critical for competent nursing. As for the MIS staff job, "evaluating the potential benefits and costs associated with different operating systems" may be an important worker behavior. Person/worker-oriented approaches are more process as opposed to end-results oriented. They tend to emphasize "how the job gets done." These approaches provide less detailed information than the job/task-oriented approach but tend to provide better information for comparing jobs.

Finally, trait-oriented approaches such as Threshold Traits Analysis focus more on the latent traits (physical and mental abilities and sometimes personality or temperament) or competencies a worker must possess to perform the required behaviors that lead to specific ends. These approaches detail the job specifications necessary for job success. They generate a prototype of the ideal job incumbent who possesses certain traits or competencies. They ask "who can perform these behaviors?" Often several approaches are combined into a systematic job analysis. As you can imagine, it makes little sense to ask "who can perform these behaviors?" without first answering the questions: "What behaviors are performed?" and "For what ends?" In fact, some courts have ruled that detailed task analysis must precede any attempt to identify critical competencies or job specifications if adverse impact is found.[8]

FIGURE 4.4
COMMON JOB ANALYSIS DATA COLLECTION METHODS

COLLECTION METHOD	ADVANTAGES	DISADVANTAGES
Observation: Direct observation of job duties, work sampling or observation of segments of job performance, and indirect recording of activities (e.g., film).	Allows for a deeper understanding of job duties than relying on incumbents' descriptions.	Unable to observe mental aspects of jobs (e.g., decision making of managers, creativity of scientists); may not sample all important aspects of the job, especially important yet infrequently performed activities (e.g., use of weapons by police officers).
Performing the Job: Actual performance of job duties by the analyst.	Analyst receives first-hand experience of contextual factors on the job including physical hazards, social demands, emotional stressors, and mental requirements; useful for jobs that can be easily learned.	May be dangerous for hazardous jobs (e.g., firefighters, patrol officers) or unethical/illegal for jobs requiring licensing or extensive training (e.g., medical doctor, psychologist, pharmacist); analyst may be exposed only to frequently performed activities.
Interviews: Individual and group interviews with job incumbents, supervisors, subordinates, clients, or other knowledgeable sources.	Information on infrequently performed activities, and physical and mental activities can be collected; use of multiple sources instead of one source can provide a more comprehensive, unbiased view of the job.	Value of the data is dependent on the interviewers' skills and may be faulty if they ask ambiguous questions; interviewees may be suspicious about the motives for the job analysis (e.g., fearful it will alter their compensation) and distort the information they provide.
Critical Incidents: Descriptions of behavioral examples of exceptionally poor or good performance, and context and consequences in which they occur.	Since observable and measurable behaviors are described, the information can be readily used for performance appraisal and training purposes; may provide insights into job expectations as defined by incumbents.	Descriptions of average or typical behavior are not collected so the data may be less inclusive of the entire job domain; time-consuming to gather the incidents.
Diaries: Descriptions of daily work activities by incumbents.	Written in terms familiar to incumbents and supervisors so the data may be easier to use (e.g., in developing performance appraisal measures); may provide insights into the reasons for job activities.	Time-consuming to document; may be biased accounts; may not include mental activities (e.g., innovativeness) or a representative account of all activities.
Background Records: Review of relevant materials including: organizational charts, *Dictionary of Occupational Titles* (DOT), company training manuals, organizational policies and procedures manuals, or existing job descriptions.	Provides analyst with preliminary job information that assists in developing interview questions or questionnaires; provides useful contextual information for the job; is relatively easy to collect.	May not provide complete information and generally needs to be supplemented with data collected using other methods; may be outdated materials; usually provides limited information on specific KASOCs required as well as importance ratings of tasks.
Questionnaires: Structured forms and activity checklists (PAQ, FJA, JDS, MPDQ, JCQ) as well as open-ended or unstructured questions.	Generally less expensive and quicker to use than other methods; can reach a large sample of incumbents or sources, which allows for a greater coverage of informed individuals; responses can often be quantified and analyzed in a variety of meaningful ways (e.g., comparisons can be made across jobs or departments for compensation or selection purposes).	Questions may be interpreted incorrectly; difficult to assess how respondents interpreted questions; response rate may be low making the results less generalizable; often expensive and time-consuming to develop, score, or analyze; open-ended questions are difficult to quantify and require content analysis that is time-consuming.

Almost all systematic job analysis methods collect data on the machines, tools, and work aids used. More complete analyses also record contextual factors of the job (e.g., physical working conditions, environmental hazards, contact with co-workers). Some job analysis methods also provide information on work performance standards (e.g., quality and quantity standards, error analysis) and specific customer requirements. These latter pieces of information are essential to support personnel decisions based on performance appraisal such as terminations, assignment to training, or promotion.

Different approaches to job analysis are better suited

to supporting the various HRM functions and providing necessary job analysis products. The wisest strategy is to support one approach through the use of at least a second, somewhat different approach. Figure 4.5 provides a convenient job analysis approach and HRM function matrix to better illustrate this idea. As you can tell from this figure, trait-oriented approaches are well-suited for identifying KASOCs for personnel selection. Also, trait-oriented approaches are useful for identifying skill requirements for skill-based job evaluation plans. Note that job/task-oriented approaches are the best method for job redesign efforts whereas both job/task- and person/worker-oriented approaches are better suited for performance appraisal development than is the trait/competency-based approach. In fact, the trait approach receives a minus for this function as it is uniquely tailored to invite employee grievance, subsequent employer liability for personnel decisions based on trait appraisal, and generally ineffective performance appraisal and management systems (see Chapter 9).

THE FORM OF JOB INFORMATION.   Job analysis information can be presented in qualitative or quantitative form depending on the job analysis method used. Most job analysis methods are **qualitative** in the sense that the job is described in a narrative, nonnumerical manner and the methods result in verbal or narrative descriptions of job information. The critical incident technique (CIT), discussed later, is an example of a qualitative method. Other methods such as the PAQ and the MPDQ are **quantitative** and provide descriptive information in numerical form. Common examples include a listing of tasks and ratings of the relative frequency, essentiality, or importance with which they are performed and descriptions of the production or error rates per time period. In most cases, job analysis approaches include both quantitative and qualitative information.

THE STANDARDIZATION OF THE JOB ANALYSIS CONTENT.   Many HRM professionals have created a uniform or consistent method for obtaining job analysis information. Some job analysis methods, for example, have a set number of questions or items to which responses are required. The job analyst may be asked to write the major objectives of the position, the most important or essential tasks or functions to be performed, what KASOCs an occupant should have for the position, the major work products or outcomes, and who are the critical internal or external customers for the products or services. The quantitative approaches are more standardized. The PAQ, for example, has standard content for all the jobs that are under study. Other methods have a standardized content (listing of tasks) for a group of similar jobs, but another list may be used for a different set of jobs.

Another component of the standardization process is the response format. Many job analysis methods are completed using computer sheets, direct entry through a computer diskette, or, most recently, the Internet. The PAQ, for example, has a variety of response options tailored to the customer's needs (see www.PAQ.com).

Because of the elasticity of work and the speed with which jobs change, we do not recommend too much reliance on a standardized measure since many jobs, their duties, and necessary worker competencies can change dramatically. Who would have envisioned just 15 years ago that clerical jobs would have so much job activity centered on the computer or that automobile assembly plants would require computer competencies to the extent they do today? Think about how the role of human resource assistant has changed from the days when every job in the personnel office was largely clerical and centered around payroll issues.

SOURCES OF JOB INFORMATION.   There are a number of potential sources for information about a job. Cameras can be used to observe tasks and recording devices can be used to assess employees' physiological reactions. For cultural and labor relations reasons, physiological monitoring devices are used more frequently in Sweden and Germany for studying jobs suspected of taxing worker stamina than in the United States. The most

FIGURE 4.5
JOB ANALYSIS APPROACH AND HR FUNCTION MATRIX

JOB ANALYSIS METHOD	HUMAN RESOURCE FUNCTION				
	JOB REDESIGN	PERSONNEL SELECTION	COMPENSATION	TRAINING	PERFORMANCE APPRAISAL
JOB/TASK	+	0	+	+	+
PERSON/WORKER	0	0	+	+	+
TRAIT/COMPETENCY-BASED	0	+	+	0	−

+ = The approach is well-suited for meeting the information requirements of this function.

0 = The approach provides useful information for this function but should not be used in isolation.

− = The approach defeats the aims of this function by providing largely useless information.

common sources for information are job incumbents and supervisors for the job under study. Other possibilities include job analysts or specialists trained to conduct job analyses, outside observers or consultants, subordinates to the job under study, clients or customers, or persons simply in a good position to observe the job as it is performed. Most federal government agencies have job analyst positions with the major responsibility being job analysis of other agency jobs. Obviously, more sources of information will probably more fully capture a job on a project. Again, an eye on the external customer is the ideal perspective for all sources.

WHAT ARE THE MOST USEFUL JOB ANALYSIS METHODS?

Many job analysis approaches are available today. One of the best sources of information on job analysis approaches is the two-volume *Job Analysis Handbook for Business, Industry, and Government.* The handbook describes 18 different job analysis methods in use today.[9] A very readable text for novices is *Everything You Always Wanted to Know About Job Analysis,* written by one of the leading authorities in the field.[10] We will concentrate our discussion on methods that have been used recently to accomplish a specific purpose.

Position Analysis Questionnaire (PAQ)

The **Position Analysis Questionnaire (PAQ)** is a standardized questionnaire that assesses activities using 187 items in six categories.[11] These are:

1. *Information input*—where and how does the worker obtain the information needed to perform the job? (e.g., use of visual or sensory input).

2. *Mental processes*—what reasoning, planning, decision-making, or information-processing activities are necessary to perform the activities?

3. *Work output*—what physical activities are performed, and what tools are used?

4. *Relationships with other people*—what relationships with other people are required to perform the job? (e.g., negotiating, performing supervisory activities).

5. *Job context*—in what physical and social contexts is the work performed? (e.g., hazards, stress).

6. *Other job characteristics*—what other activities or characteristics are relevant to the job (e.g., apparel required, work schedule, salary basis).

Sample items for each of the six PAQ categories are presented in Figure 4.6.

Items on the PAQ are rated using several different scales including importance, amount of time required, extent of use, possibility of occurrence, applicability, and difficulty.[12] The PAQ can be completed in about two-and-one-half hours. The completed questionnaires are then shipped to PAQ services headquarters for computerized scoring. Each job is scored on 32 dimensions, and a profile is constructed for the job. Norms are provided so the job profile can be compared to profiles of benchmark jobs. Usually, a computer printout is prepared for each job that illustrates the job dimension scores and profile, estimates of aptitude test data (e.g., the average scores expected for incumbents on standardized tests), and job evaluation points for compensation purposes. Figure 4.7 presents a printout from a PAQ analysis of a job analyst's job.

The extensive research conducted with the PAQ makes it one of the most useful of the standardized job analysis instruments, particularly for selection and compensation purposes. For example, PAQ results were used to select a particular test to support a successful argument of job relatedness in a Title VII case involving a cognitive ability test that had caused adverse impact at the James River Corporation.[13] The approach is also excellent for small businesses with little or no expertise in human resources.

The data presented in Figure 4.7 was used by a government agency to justify the use of the *Wonderlic Personnel Test* as "job related" and to set a competitive compensation level for a "job analyst" job. PAQ results can help to set a wage for a new job or to reclassify jobs and to identify the valid tests for selecting personnel for the job. Considerable research supports use of the PAQ. However, the PAQ should be completed by trained job analysts rather than incumbents because the language in the questionnaire is difficult and at a fairly high reading level. The instrument also lacks the specificity that can be gained by a questionnaire developed within the company for one or more particular positions. There is also no guarantee that PAQ results alone will successfully support an argument of "job relatedness" after an adverse impact analysis shifts the burden of proof.

Like almost all paper-and-pencil questionnaires, results must be interpreted with caution and with consideration of the "hidden agendas" of the source of the data. The PAQ was once administered to a graphic artist of a specialty mail-order firm. The graphic artist job was part-time and paid about 50 cents per hour above minimum wage. The job entailed creating original stencils for use in casting and dying. The current incumbent had approximately six months' experience at the job and was taking courses part-time at a local community college. PAQ analysis of the job revealed the job required a Ph.D. in art history or related areas and that compensation appropriate for the work approximated $55,000 per year! This result can be explained by a number of factors. First, answers were recorded just as the incumbent pro-

FIGURE 4.6
SAMPLE ITEMS FROM THE PAQ

POSITION ANALYSIS QUESTIONNAIRE (PAQ)

1 INFORMATION INPUT

1.1 Sources of Job Information

Rate each of the following items in terms of the extent to which it is used by the worker as a source of information in performing the job.

Code	Extent of Use (U)
N	Does not apply
1	Nominal very infrequent
2	Occasional
3	Moderate
4	Considerable
5	Very substantial

1.1.1 Visual Sources of Job Information

1 U Written materials (books, reports, office notes, articles, job instructions, signs, etc.)

2 U Quantitative materials (materials which deal with quantities or amounts, such as graphs, accounts, specifications, tables of numbers, etc.)

3 U Pictorial materials (pictures or picturelike materials used as *sources* of information, for example, drawings, blueprints, diagrams, maps, tracings, photographic films, x-ray films, TV pictures, etc.)

2 MENTAL PROCESSES

2.2 Information Processing Activities

In this section are various human operations involving the "processing" of information or data. Rate each of the following items in terms of how *important* the activity is to the completion of the job.

Code	Importance to This Job (I)
N	Does not apply
1	Very minor
2	Low
3	Average
4	High
5	Extreme

39 I Combining information (*combining,* synthesizing, or integrating information or data from two or more sources to establish new facts, hypotheses, theories, or a more complete body of *related* information, for example, an economist using information from various sources to predict future economic conditions, a pilot flying aircraft, a judge trying a case, etc.)

40 I Analyzing information or data (for the purpose of identifying *underlying* principles or facts by *breaking down* information into component parts, for example, interpreting financial reports, diagnosing mechanical disorders or medical symptoms, etc.)

49 S Using mathematics (indicate, using the code below, the highest level of mathematics that the individual must understand as required by the job)

Code Level of Mathematics
N Does not apply.
1 Simple basic (counting, addition and subtraction of 2-digit numbers or less).
2 Basic (addition and subtraction of numbers of 3 digits or more, multiplication, division, etc.)
3 Intermediate (calculations and concepts involving fractions, decimals, percentages, etc.)
4 Advanced (algebraic, geometric, trigonometric, and statistical concepts, techniques, and procedures usually applied in standard practical situations).
5 Very advanced (advanced mathematical and statistical theory, concepts, and techniques, for example, calculus, topology, vector analysis, factor analysis, probability theory, etc.)

3 WORK OUTPUT

3.6 Manipulation/Coordination Activities

Rate the following items in terms of how important the activity is to completion of the job.

Code	Importance to This Job (I)
N	Does not apply
1	Very minor
2	Low
3	Average
4	High
5	Extreme

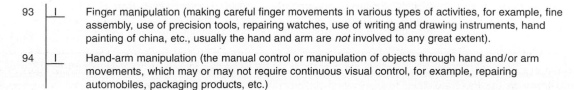

93 I Finger manipulation (making careful finger movements in various types of activities, for example, fine assembly, use of precision tools, repairing watches, use of writing and drawing instruments, hand painting of china, etc., usually the hand and arm are *not* involved to any great extent).

94 I Hand-arm manipulation (the manual control or manipulation of objects through hand and/or arm movements, which may or may not require continuous visual control, for example, repairing automobiles, packaging products, etc.)

FIGURE 4.6
(*Continued*)

RELATIONSHIPS WITH OTHER PERSONS

4 RELATIONSHIPS WITH OTHER PERSONS

This section deals with different aspects of interaction between people involved in various kinds of work.

Code	Importance to This Job (*I*)
N	Does not apply
1	Very minor
2	Low
3	Average
4	High
5	Extreme

4.1 Communications

Rate the following in terms of how *important* the activity is to the completion of the job. Some jobs may involve several or all of the items in this section.

4.1.1 Oral (communicating by speaking)

99 ⌊_I_   Advising (dealing with individuals in order to counsel and/or guide them with regard to problems that may be resolved by legal, financial, scientific, technical, clinical, spiritual, and/or other professional principles).

100 ⌊_I_   Negotiating (dealing with others in order to reach an agreement or solution, for example, labor bargaining, diplomatic relations, etc.)

4.3 Amount of Job-required Personal Contact

112 ⌊_S_   Job-required personal contact (indicate, using the code below, the extent of job-required contact with others, individually or in groups, for example, contact with customers, patients, students, the public, superiors, subordinates, fellow employees, official visitors, etc.; consider *only* personal contact which is definitely *part* of the job).

    Code   Extent of Required Personal Contact

    1   Very infrequent (almost no contact with others is required)
    2   Infrequent (limited contact with others is required)
    3   Occasional (moderate contact with others is required)
    4   Frequent (considerable contact with others is required)
    5   Very frequent (almost continual contact with others is required)

5 JOB CONTEXT

5.1 Physical Working Conditions

This section lists various working conditions. Rate the average amount of time the worker is exposed to each condition during a *typical* work period.

Code	Amount of Time (*T*)
N	Does not apply (or is very incidental)
1	Under 1/10 of the time
2	Between 1/10 and 1/3 of the time
3	Between 1/3 and 2/3 of the time
4	Over 2/3 of the time
5	Almost continually

5.1.1 Outdoor environment

135 ⌊_T_   Out-of-door environment (subject to changing weather conditions).

6 OTHER JOB CHARACTERISTICS

6.4 Job Demands (cont.)

172 ⌊_I_   Following set procedures (need to follow specific set procedures or routines in order to obtain satisfactory outcomes, for example, following check-out lists to inspect equipment or vehicles, following procedures for changing a tire, performing specified laboratory tests, etc.)

173 ⌊_I_   Time pressure of situation (rush hours in a restaurant, urgent time deadlines, rush jobs, etc.)

Source: E. J. McCormick and P. R. Jeanneret, Position Analysis Questionnaire (PAQ). In S. Gael (ed.), *The job analysis handbook for business, industry, and government,* Vol. II. New York: John Wiley & Sons, Inc. Copyright © 1988, pp. 826–827. This material has been reprinted in cooperation with John Wiley & Sons, Inc.

FIGURE 4.7
OPTION 4A: JOB PROFILE—PART 1

IDENTIFICATION INFORMATION

PAQ Number: 002335
Organization: DOTPAQ
Job Title: JOB ANALYST
Dept/Unit: ADMIN SPEC
Analyst(s): AVERAGE/DB
Completed: 01/91
Dot Number: 166267018 N
Dot Coded By: ORGANIZATION
Processed: 08/20/91

Organization Number: 1
Group #: 2335   Record #: 0001
NUMBER OF ANALYSTS / TYPE
Incumbents: Analysts:
Supervisors: Unknown:
WORK FORCE ANALYSIS(optional)
Number of Job Incumbents: 39
% FM: % WH: % BL:
% HS: % TO:

JOB EVALUATION, FLSA EXEMPTION AND JOB PRESTIGE PREDICTIONS

Equation(s) Used to Calculate Job Evaluation Points

(2)
316

Job Evaluation Points:
Reported Median Monthly Compensation:
Probability this job is EXEMPT from the Fair Labor Standards Act: 1.000
Job Prestige Score: 55.1

TEST PREDICTIONS

GATB TESTS	Predicted Score Range Low	Avg	High	Prob. of Use	Pred. Val. Coef.	SIMILAR TESTS	Predicted Score Range Low	Avg	High
G-Intelligence	102	115	128	.93<	.33	Adaptability	17	20	25
						Learning Abilt	37	43	49
						Wonderlic P.T	19	26	33
V-Verbal Aptitude	99	113	127	.37	.27	EAS-Verbal	13	18	22
						PTI-Verbal	24	33	40
						SET-Verbal	24	37	46
						DAT-Verbal Rsn	*	*	*
						DAT-LU Sentenc	*	*	*
						DAT-LU Spelling	*	*	*
N-Numerical Apt.	100	113	127	.60<	.28	Arith Fundmntl	31	36	40
						Arithmtc Index	40	47	53
						EAS-Numerical	25	34	43
						FIT-Arithmetic	28	34	39
						PTI-Numerical	14	20	24
						SET-Numerical	28	40	50
						DAT-Numrcl Abil	*	*	*
S-Spatial Apt.	92	109	126	.16	.18	EAS-Spatial	17	27	34
						FIT-Assembly	8	11	14
						Mn Ppr Frm Brd	42	50	57
						DAT-Space Rltn	*	*	*
P-Form Percept.	94	111	128	.19	.18	None			
Q-Clerical Percept.	101	116	131	.50<	.23	EAS-Visual Spd	83	96	111
						Mn Clrcl-Names	113	136	165
						SET-Clerical	28	34	42
						DAT-Clercl Spd	*	*	*
K-Motor Coord.	95	112	129	.20	.17	None			
F-Finger Dexterity	81	101	120	.01	.15	None			
M-Manual Dexterity	83	104	124	.07	.14	None			

MYERS-BRIGGS TYPE INDICATOR (METI) (est. % of incumbents with high score on):

| Extraversion | 54< | Sensing | 52< | Thinking | 50< | Judgment | 62< |
| Introversion | 46 | Intuitive | 46 | Feeling | 48 | Perception | 38 |

(* Test scores correlated well with GATB scores, but norms were unavailable)

SELECTED PAQ ITEMS

#	NAME	RATING	MEANING
20	Near Visual Acuity	2.9	Moderate Detail
46	Education (Level or Equiv)	3.5	College Degree
47	Job-Related Experience	2.8	1 Year to 3 Years
48	Training (Time to Learn Job)	2.7	6 Months to 1 Year
49	Using Mathematics (Level)	3.2	Intermediate
87	Level of Physical Exertion	1.2	Very Light
134	Supervision Received	2.8	General Direction

PAQ ITEMS WITH HIGHEST PERCENTILE SCORES

#	NAME	RATING	%ILE
46	Education	3.5	88
133	Staff Functions	2.5	88
103	Interviewing	2.9	87
88	Sitting	3.6	77
49	Using Mathematics	3.2	76
107	Writing/Composing	2.8	75
39	Combining Information	2.8	70
134	Supervision received	2.8	67
114	Middle Management/Staff Personnel	2.8	67
132	Coordinates Activities	1.5	65
40	Analyzing Information or Data	2.8	65
117	Semiprofessional Personnel	2.3	64
36	Decision Making	3.2	64
47	Job-Related Experience	2.8	63
41	Compiling	2.9	63
104	Routine Information Exchange	3.1	63
186	Job Structure	3.1	63
150	Strained Personal Contacts	1.7	62
118	Clerical Personnel	2.6	61
37	Reasoning in Problem Solving	3.1	59
12	Behavior	2.2	59
113	Executive/Officials	1.7	58
149	Frustrating Situations	2.2	58
152	Interpersonal conflict Situations	1.5	57
38	Amount of Planning/Scheduling	3.0	57
116	Professional Personnel	1.7	54
99	Advising	2.0	53
112	Job-Required Personal Contact	3.8	53
48	Training	2.7	53
1	Written Materials	3.4	51
153	Non-Job-Required Social Contact	2.6	50
101	Persuading	1.4	48
6	Machines/Equipment	1.4	48
105	Nonroutine Information Exchange	1.5	48
32	Inspecting	2.2	47
106	Public Speaking	0.5	47
102	Instructing	1.7	47
35	Estimating Time	2.1	47

vided them to the analyst despite observations that indicated the incumbent was grossly exaggerating the behavioral requirements of the job. And perhaps more importantly, there had been a rumor in this organization that the job analyses were to be used to revise current compensation practices. The lesson here is that the organizational context can strongly influence the validity of job analysis information provided by sources.

Management Position Description Questionnaire (MPDQ)

Although the PAQ has been used to study managerial positions, the **Management Position Description Questionnaire (MPDQ)** is a standardized instrument designed specifically for use in analyzing managerial jobs.[14] The 274-item questionnaire contains 15 sections, one of which is presented in Figure 4.8.

Two-and-one-half hours are required to complete the entire MPDQ. In most sections, respondents (usually the managers above the position under study) are asked to indicate how significant each item is to the position. For example, they may state that "contact with clerical staff" is of substantial significance to the position. A computer program generates eight reports, including a management position description, a position-tailored performance appraisal form, and a group comparison report.[15] The data provided by this report are particularly valuable for determining areas of emphasis in hiring, training, and staff development. For example, Office Depot relied on the MPDQ results to develop assessment center exercises to be used in hiring its district managers. General Cinema relied on the MPDQ to construct a job-related, behavioral interview and a test for theater managers. Figure 4.8 presents a summary of MPDQ results for the manager of a human resources department and a portion of the questionnaire.

Functional Job Analysis (FJA)

FJA is a worker-oriented job analytic approach that attempts to describe the whole person on the job. This includes the functional, specific, content, and adaptive skills needed by an individual to perform a job satisfactorily.[16] FJA actually emerged as a result of work in the development and extension of the *Dictionary of Occupational Titles (DOT)* in 1939 and 1949.

DOT. The *DOT* classifies jobs based on a nine-digit code. Figure 4.9 presents the *DOT* description for a manager of a personnel department. The first three digits (166) specify the occupational code, the title of the job, and the industry. The next three digits (117) indicate the extent to which the job incumbent has responsibility and judgment over the data (coordinating), people (negotiating), and things (handling). The last three digits (018)

are used to classify the job alphabetically within that occupational group with the same level of complexity. For the middle three digits in the nine-digit DOT code, jobs are classified in a predefined hierarchical order according to their complexity (0 = highest level). These classifications are concerned with the relationships among people, data, and things. The analyst's job is to arrange these relationships by their complexity. An analyst preparing a FJA, for example, would rate *mentoring* in a job as the most complex relationship involving people. Figure 4.10 presents the hierarchy of people, data, and things that must be assessed for each job by the job analyst. The people scale refers to interactions between people, communication, and interpersonal actions. The data scale measures facts, ideas, mental operations, and knowledge of conditions. The things scale assesses interaction with and response to tangibles and images visualized spatially. As you've probably gathered, all these worker function ratings require inference on the part of the analyst. These inferences are largely drawn from the task statements that appear on the Department of Labor Job Analysis Report. For example, the worker function "mentoring" might be inferred from a statement or statements that read something like the following: "Aids in the professional development of apprentices by assigning them to work of increasing complexity and responsibility, evaluating their work, and demonstrating appropriate standards of conduct." Many government agencies, federal, state, and municipal, still use the FJA method to classify and price jobs.

Critical Incident Technique (CIT)

The critical incident method is a qualitative approach for obtaining specific, behaviorally focused descriptions of work or other activities. The technique was originally developed as a training needs assessment and performance appraisal tool.[17] In this regard, individuals recalled and reported specific behavioral examples of incidents that reflected exceptionally good or exceptionally poor performance. A critical incident should possess four characteristics. It should be *specific,* focus on *observable* behaviors that have been exhibited on the job, describe the *context* in which the behavior occurred, and indicate the *consequences,* outcomes, or products of the behavior. A critical incident must also be sufficiently detailed so that knowledgeable people will picture the same incident as it was experienced by the individual.[18] One vivid example of a critical incident characterizing extremely poor performance was provided by a police officer in describing an ex-partner. He wrote "while on duty, this officer went out of his assigned duty area, went into a bar, got drunk, and had his gun stolen."

A critical incident report references actual behavior in a specific situation with no mention of traits or judgmental inferences. The following is an example of a

FIGURE 4.8
SAMPLE PORTION OF MPDQ

MANAGEMENT
POSITION DESCRIPTION

NAME:	B. B. BARKER		ORGANIZATION:	CDBA
EMPLOYEE I.D.:	222		SUPERVISOR:	D.D. DUNCAN
POSITION TITLE:	MANAGER		SUPERVISOR'S TITLE:	MANAGER
FUNCTIONAL AREA:	HUMAN RESOURCES		% OF JOB DESCRIBED:	90%
SUPERVISORY LEVEL:	SUPERVISOR		DATE COMPLETED:	9/11/84

I. GENERAL INFORMATION

A. **HUMAN RESOURCE RESPONSIBILITIES**

– Management responsibility for **7** employees:　　**5 (71%)** Full Time—Salaried Exempt

　　　　　　　　　　　　　　　　　　　　　2 (28%) Part Time—Salaried Nonexempt

– **7** report directly and **0** report on a dotted line basis.

　　　　–Highest direct subordinate: **SR. PROGRAMMER**

– **No** geographically separate facilities managed directly.

B. **FINANCIAL RESPONSIBILITIES**

– No annual operating budget.

– Sales for last fiscal year:	**$　78,000.**
– Sales objective for current fiscal year:	**$　220,000.**
– Revenue for last fiscal year:	**$　275,000.**
– Revenue objective for current fiscal year:	**$　230,000.**

II. POSITION ACTIVITIES

A. **DECISION MAKING**

Decision Making: **5%** of jobholder's time is spent on this function and it is **VERY IMPORTANT** to this position.

– Related activities and their significance:

Significance	Item No.	Activity
CRUCIAL	5	Consider the long-range implications of decisions.
CRUCIAL	8	Make decisions in new/unusual situations without clear guidelines on basis of precedent/experience.
CRUCIAL	11	Make critical decisions under time pressure.
CRUCIAL	18	Process and evaluate a variety of information before making a decision.
CRUCIAL	21	Make decisions that significantly affect customers/clients.
SUBSTANTIAL	4	Make decisions concerning the future direction of operations.
SUBSTANTIAL	7	Consider legal or ethical constraints, as well as company policy or goals, when making decisions.
SUBSTANTIAL	12	Make major product/program/technology/marketing decisions in implementing strategic business plan.
SUBSTANTIAL	14	Make decisions without hesitation when required.
MODERATE	1	Evaluate the costs/benefits of alternative solutions to problems before making decisions.

FIGURE 4.8
(*Continued*)

Significance

The Duties of This Position Require You To:

_____ 1. Define areas of responsibility for supervisory/managerial personnel.

_____ 2. Schedule activities of subordinates on a day-to-day basis to maintain steady work flow.

_____ 3. Interact face-to-face with subordinates on an almost daily basis.

_____ 4. Delegate work and assign responsibility to subordinates.

_____ 5. Facilitate the completion of assignments when subordinates are unable to meet commitments.

_____ 6. Provide detailed instructions to subordinates when making assignments.

_____ 7. Coach subordinates on technical aspects of the job.

_____ 8. Provide on-the-job training for employees.

_____ 9. Frequently review and provide feedback concerning the accuracy and efficiency of subordinates' work.

_____10. Motivate employees through interpersonal interactions rather than through external incentives (e.g., pay, promotion, status, etc.).

_____11. Motivate subordinates to improve performance through a process of goal setting and positive reinforcement (i.e., incentives).

_____12. Work with subordinates to identify and correct weaknesses in performance.

_____13. Conduct formal performance appraisals with subordinates.

_____14. Develop executive-level management talent.

_____15. Establish formal career development plans with employees.

_____16. Implement career development and management succession plans.

_____17. Identify the training needed for employees to acquire the skills/knowledge necessary for advancement and ensure that the appropriate training is obtained.

_____18. Work with employees in highly emotional situations concerning personal or career problems.

_____19. Arbitrate conflicts between supervisors and employees.

_____20. Investigate and/or settle employee grievances/complaints.

_____21. Take necessary action to prevent and/or resolve alleged discriminatory practices.

_____22. Interpret, administer, and enforce personnel policies and practices (e.g., employee benefits, training or education reimbursement, affirmative action).

_____23. Interpret and administer union contract agreements in the supervision of subordinates.

_____24. Interview and hire individuals for approved positions.

Source: The supervising section of the MPDQ. Copyright © 1984 Control Data Business Advisors, Inc. All rights reserved. Reprinted with permission of the Ceridian Corporation.

FIGURE 4.9
DOT DESCRIPTION

MANAGER, PERSONNEL

166.117.018

Plans and carries out policies relating to all phases of personnel activity. Recruits, interviews, and selects employees to fill vacant positions. Plans and conducts new employee orientation to foster positive attitudes toward company goals. Keeps record of insurance coverage, pension plan, and personnel transactions, such as hires, promotions, transfers, and terminations. Investigates accidents and prepares reports for insurance carrier. Conducts wage survey within labor market to determine competitive wage rate. Prepares budget of personnel operations. Meets with shop stewards and supervisors to resolve grievances. Writes separation notices for employees separating with cause and conducts exit interviews to determine reasons behind separations. Prepares reports and recommends procedures to reduce absenteeism and turnover. Contracts with outside suppliers to provide employee services, such as canteen, transportation, or relocation service. May keep records of hired employee characteristics for governmental reporting purposes. May negotiate collective bargaining agreement.

Source: U.S. Department of Labor, *Dictionary of occupational titles,* 4th ed. (1977). Washington, DC: Government Printing Office, p. 98.

FIGURE 4.10
FJA WORKER FUNCTION SCALES

DATA FUNCTION SCALE FOURTH DIGIT	PEOPLE FUNCTION SCALE FIFTH DIGIT	THINGS FUNCTION SCALE SIXTH DIGIT
0 Synthesizing	0 Mentoring	0 Operating/Controlling II
1 Coordinating	1 Negotiating	1 Setting Up
2 Innovating	2 Supervising	2 Precision Working
3 Analyzing	3 Instructing	3 Starting Up
4 Compiling	4 Consulting	4 Driving/Controlling
5 Computing	5 Persuading	5 Operating/Controlling
6 Copying	6 Coaching	6 Manipulating
7 Comparing	7 Exchanging Info.	7 Tending
8 Handling	8 Taking instructions/helping	8 Feeding/Offbearing

Source: Modified from U.S. Department of Labor, *Dictionary of occupational titles,* 4th ed. Washington: Government Printing Office, 1977, p. xviii.

well-written critical incident. "I observed an employee looking through the scrap tub. Shortly later, she came to me stating that someone had thrown a large piece of cast iron piston into the scrap tub. We salvaged this piston and, a short time later, used this piece to make a pulley for a very urgently needed job." The following example does *not* qualify as a well-written critical incident: "The employee completely lacked initiative in getting the job done. While there was plenty of opportunity, I couldn't count on her to deliver." This incident mentions a trait (initiative), does not describe either the situation or the employee's behavior in any detail, and is judgmental.

The critical incident technique has been used to study a variety of jobs such as those of airline pilots, air traffic controllers, research scientists, dentists, industrial foremen, life insurance agents, salesclerks, retail managers, and college professors. One major purpose of the use of CIT is to develop performance appraisal systems. CIT is also an excellent approach for the development of customer satisfaction instruments. Customers provide the examples of effective and ineffective customer service, which are then used to develop a standardized customer service evaluation instrument. Burger King, Office Depot, and Continental Bank used the critical incident method to develop a performance appraisal instrument used by "professional customers" to assess compliance with company regulations regarding customer service. The CIT is also very useful for developing highly detailed selection procedures such as assessment centers or behavioral interviews. Office Depot developed its district manager assessment methods using both MPDQ and critical incident results.

Job Compatibility Questionnaire (JCQ)

The **Job Compatibility Questionnaire (JCQ)** was designed as a job analysis method to be used in developing personnel selection instruments and intervention strategies.[19] Unlike other job analysis methods, the JCQ gathers information on all aspects of a job that are hypothesized to be related to employee performance, absences, turnover, and job satisfaction. Thus, the term *job analysis* is interpreted in the broadest sense to encompass all major factors related to important personal worker outcomes. The underlying assumption of the JCQ is that the greater the compatibility between a job applicant's preferences for job characteristics and the characteristics of a job as perceived by job incumbents, the more likely that the applicant will be effective and stay in the job longer. The goal of the JCQ methodology is to derive perceptions of job characteristics from incumbents' perspectives and to develop selection instruments capable of assessing the extent to which job applicants' preferences are compatible with these perspectives. The selection instrument derived from the JCQ is designed to predict and ultimately increase the level of employee effectiveness. In addition, the instrument can be used to identify job characteristics that can be altered to increase group effectiveness.

The JCQ is a 400-item instrument that measures job factors that have been shown by previous research to be related to one or more effectiveness criteria (e.g., performance, turnover, absenteeism, job satisfaction). Items cover the following job factors: task requirements, physical environment, customer characteristics, co-worker characteristics, leader characteristics, compensation preferences, task variety, job autonomy, physical demands, and work schedule.

The JCQ is administered to job incumbents who are asked to indicate the extent to which each JCQ item is descriptive of the job. An incumbent is asked to indicate on a five-point scale how descriptive each item is of his or her job. A sample list of characteristics is presented below:

> Working alone all day.
>
> Having different projects that challenge the intellect.
>
> Staying physically active all day.
>
> Working at my own pace.
>
> Being able to choose the order of my work tasks.

> Working under the constant threat of danger.
>
> Having to copy or post numerical data all day.
>
> Having to make public speeches.
>
> Working under extreme time pressure.
>
> Having an opportunity to be creative at work.

The average time required to complete the JCQ is 30 minutes and can be reduced by removing items that do not apply to the job (e.g., customer characteristics). There is also a provision for adding important characteristics that are not covered on the JCQ such as those that may characterize organizational culture or climate. Responses are used to derive a selection instrument with a scoring key. The details of this process are discussed in Chapter 6.

Research indicates the test that evolves out of the JCQ does a good job in predicting retention for low-wage jobs such as customer service representatives, theater personnel, security guards, telephone interviewers, and counter personnel.[20] The JCQ is nested within a comprehensive test to select security guards known as the Security Officer Profile, which is designed to adjust the scoring key for the JCQ based on a short, computerized job analysis completed by the hiring supervisor.

The JCQ can also be used to redesign jobs. For example, at Tenneco Corporation, responses to the JCQ indicated strong preferences for a pay-for-performance system and a more reliable work schedule. These work characteristics, shown to be related to employee turnover, were changed at relatively little cost and turnover was reduced by 14 percent.

Job Diagnostic Survey (JDS)

One direct application of job analysis data has been for job design and redesign efforts. This has been particularly true in recent years with the increasing interest in the quality of employees' work life, the team-oriented concept, and the principle of empowerment. In general, most efforts have focused on redesigning jobs by enriching them. Such enrichment entails providing more meaningful work, greater responsibility, a sense of empowerment, and greater worker autonomy.[21] One of the most well-known and researched job enrichment approaches is the **Job Characteristics Model,** which uses the **Job Diagnostic Survey (JDS)** as the job analysis method.[22] Over 200 studies have investigated the validity and utility of this approach.[23] Figure 4.11 presents the job characteristics model.

What Is the Job Characteristics Model?

The Job Characteristics Model emphasizes enhancing the intrinsic aspects of an employee's work to increase satisfaction and performance. The model states that workers will be more motivated and satisfied, produce better qual-

FIGURE 4.11
JOB CHARACTERISTICS MODEL

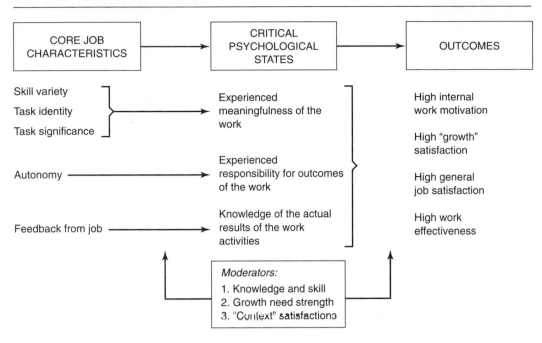

Source: From J. R. Hackman and G. R. Oldham, "Motivation Through the Design of Work: Test of a Theory." *Organizational Behavior and Human Performance* Vol 16, 1996, pp. 250–279. Reprinted by permission of Academic Press and authors.

ity work, and have less absenteeism and turnover to the extent that they experience three psychological states. These states are: (1) the belief that their *work is meaningful,* (2) that they have *responsibility for the outcomes of their work, and (3) that they receive feedback on the results* of their work. These psychological states can be enhanced by building into the job five core dimensions. These consist of skill variety, task identity, task significance, autonomy, and feedback and are defined below.

> **Skill variety** refers to the extent to which a job requires the use of a variety of skills, activities, and abilities to complete the work.
>
> **Task identity** is the extent to which job incumbents can complete a whole and identifiable task (e.g., doing a job from beginning to end with a visible outcome).
>
> **Task significance** is the extent to which the job has a substantial impact on the lives or work of other people.
>
> **Autonomy** is the extent to which the job gives incumbents discretion, independence, and freedom in scheduling and planning work procedures.
>
> **Feedback** from the job itself is the extent to which carrying out the work activities results in incumbents receiving clear and direct knowledge about how well they are performing.

The JDS, a 21-item questionnaire, is used to assess employees' perceptions of the degree to which each of the five core dimensions is present in their job.[24] Figure 4.12 presents some items from the JDS.

The most comprehensive review of the Job Characteristics Model found that it is generally valid and that JDS responses are more highly related to affective worker outcomes such as job satisfaction than to specific work outcomes such as productivity or job turnover.[25]

From Job Analysis to Work Analysis

Many have argued that job analysis is too legalistic and "creates artificial boundaries that interfere with successful adoption of innovative management practices."[26] One proposal is to expand job analysis into "work analysis" to meet the contemporary challenges facing organizations. Figure 4.13 presents a summary of a proposed approach to work analysis which is responsive to these challenges. For example, in the context of enlarged and cross-responsibilities as a trend, work analysis should focus on work flows rather than the traditional job analysis approach of simplified and predetermined job responsibilities. The work analysis would also involve knowledgeable internal and external customers to help develop criteria for multirater, 360 degree performance appraisal system.

The "innovative work analysis" approach is compatible with our prescription for more of a focus on un-

FIGURE 4.12
SAMPLE QUESTIONS FROM THE JDS, AN INSTRUMENT DESIGNED TO MEASURE THE KEY ELEMENTS OF THE JOB CHARACTERISTICS THEORY

1 - - - - - - - - - - 2 - - - - - - - - - - 3 - - - - - - - - - - 4 - - - - - - - - - - 5 - - - - - - - - - - 6 - - - - - - - - - - 7

Very little   Moderately   Very much

1. To what extent do managers or co-workers let you know how well you are doing on your job?
2. In general, how significant or important is your job? That is, are the results of your work likely to significantly affect the lives or well-being of other people?
3. How much autonomy is there in your job?
4. To what extent does your job involve doing a "whole" and identifiable piece of work?
5. How much variety is there in your job? That is, to what extent does the job require you to do many different things at work using a variety of your skills and talents'?
6. To what extent does your job require you to work closely with other people (either clients or people in related jobs in your organization)?
7. To what extent does doing the job itself provide you with information about your work performance? That is, does the actual work itself provide clues about how well you are doing—aside from the feedback co-workers or managers may provide?

Source: J. R. Hackman and G. H. Oldham, The Job Characteristics Survey: An instrument for the diagnosis of jobs and the evaluation of job design projects. *JSAS Catalogue of Selected Documents in Psychology, 4,* Ms. No. 810. Components of Job Characteristics Model. Reprinted by permission of Select Press.

derstanding and meeting customer requirements. While job analysis methods such as the PAQ or FJA are useful for producing certain job analysis products and providing legal protection, without a focus on customer requirements, traditional job analysis results will not be very helpful in meeting the challenges of the 21st century business world. Strategic job analysis and job mapping are examples of this work analysis.

What Is Strategic Job Analysis?

When a job is being created or is changing significantly, job analysis takes on a predictive bent in that the idea is to describe a job through the anticipated tasks that need to be performed to meet organizational goals. This approach has been termed **strategic job analysis** as it intends to forecast what a job may be like in a new environment with new strategic goals, with different work aids (e.g., computers), with increased customer contact, or with expanded duties.[27] Conducting a strategic job analysis involves the following steps:

1. If the job currently exists, a conventional job analysis procedure is used to describe it in detail. If the job isn't in existence yet, then subject matter experts (SMEs) and primary customers of the job's intended services are brought together to identify the tasks that constitute the job based on the new strategic plan. In addition, once the tasks that constitute the job have been identified, sources of standardized job descriptions such as the *DOT* can be consulted to identify any existing jobs that are similar and can further inform job design.

2. Incumbents and/or SMEs discuss how changes to

the job such as new technology or increased contact with external customers will change the tasks making up the job and how the job is performed.

3. Detailed descriptions of the job's tasks and the required KASOCs necessary for successful performance are generated by SMEs and others familiar with the job and the expected changes.

4. The results of the analysis of the projected job are compared to those of the current job to identify differences in tasks and KASOCs.

5. The comparison provides information relevant to performance standards, training content, KASOCs for personnel selection, the need for supervision and management, and the relationship between jobs (internal customers and suppliers).

The utility of this approach depends on how accurately the SMEs and other participants anticipate changes in the job or what a job created from scratch may be like when actually performed. This approach requires widespread involvement from organizational members, often from different functional areas. In addition, when the job change introduces new technology, it may be necessary to involve the hardware or software manufacturer in the analysis of job changes.

What Is Work Process Mapping?

Work processing mapping (WPM) is a tool used with increasing frequency as it has proved to be an important supplement to traditional text-based job descriptions.[28] At Columbia Forest Products, WPM was an important tool of the skill-based, work team approach the company

FIGURE 4.13
TRADITIONAL JOB ANALYSIS, EMERGING BUSINESS TRENDS, AND INNOVATIVE WORK ANALYSIS

TRADITIONAL JA PRINCIPLES	EMERGING BUSINESS TRENDS	INNOVATIVE WORK ANALYSIS	
		PROPOSITIONS	RECOMMENDATIONS
Simplified and Predetermined Job Responsibilities.	Enlarged and Cross-functional Responsibilities.	Use of Work Analysis in Designing Broad Occupations Should Enhance Employee Flexibility.	Analyze Work Activities to Identify Work Flows and Design Occupations Accordingly. Evaluate Task Differences and Interdependencies to Design Meaningful Occupations.
An Adversarial Approach to Labor-Management Relations.	Diffusion of the Management-Labor Distinction.	Use of Work Analysis in Designing Skill-based Pay Systems Should Lead to Improved Management-labor Relations.	Cluster Tasks in Skill Blocks for Which Employees Will Be Rewarded. Use Task-analytic Info to Determine the Relative Importance of Skill Blocks. Use Info on Task-skill Linkages to Design Certification Exams.
Static Job with Stable KASOCs.	Responsibilities and KASOCs in Continuous Flux.	Use of Future-Oriented Work Analysis Should Facilitate Organizational Readiness to Face New Contingencies.	Develop "What-if" Scenarios to Identify Future KASOCs. Identify KASOCs Demanded by Emerging Occupations. Ask SMEs to Describe Their Jobs in the Future Compare and Contrast Present and Future-oriented Work-analytic Ratings.
Scarce Competition and Large Market Share.	Global Competition, Free Trade, and Deregulation.	Use of Work Analysis in Identifying Inimitable Competencies Should Lead to a Competitive Value Advantage.	Form Focus Groups to Study Work-analytic info to Identify Unique KASOCs. Compare Organization's and Applicants' KASOCs to Identify Value-added Employees. Examine Work-analytic Data to Identify Talent for New Ventures.
		Use of Work Analysis in Value Analysis and ABC Accounting Should Lead to a Competitive Cost Advantage.	Rely on Work-analytic Data to Determine Time Allocated to Activities and Their Costs. Study Task-analytic Info to Ascertain Whether Employee Efforts are Distributed According to Importance of Organizational Functions. Revise Work Activity-KASOC Linkages for Needless Worker Specifications.
Isolated Work Stations and Minimum Employee Feedback.	Teamwork and Self-managing Teams.	Use of Work Analysis in Identifying Task Interdependencies and Workflows Should Improve Teamwork.	Include Cooperation Scales in Task Inventories. Study Workflows to Identify "State Changes" of Products or Services and Charge Them to Teams.
Individualistic Approach to Employee Selection.	Selection for Person-Team Strategy Fit.	Use of Work Analysis in Uncovering Strategic KASOCs Should Facilitate Their Inclusion in HR.	Study Work-analytic Info to Identify Key Work Relations and Consequent Strategic KASOCs.
A Hierarchical Approach to Employee Evaluation.	Multiple Constituents Involved in Employee Evaluation.	Use of Work Analysis in Identifying task Interdependencies Should Facilitate the design of 360 Degree Appraisals.	Study Task and Workflow Analysis to Determine the Scope of Performance that Different Constituents Will Evaluate. Involve Knowledgeable Internal and External Customers to Identify and Generate Behaviors That are Critical for Their Satisfaction.

Source: Sanchez, J. I. From documentation to innovation: Reshaping job analysis to meet emerging business needs. *Human Resource Management Review, 4*(1), p. 71. Reprinted with permission.

adopted. Through WPM, the company hopes to better identify coordinated sequences of activities that lend themselves to work team organization and to also assist in identifying skills and competencies needed to staff process teams.

Processes have increasingly been the target of continuous improvement programs as they provide multiple targets of opportunity for improvement including quality, operational efficiency, cost, customer service, and competitive advantage. Processes will become even more important as units of analysis as more organizations adopt work team-based methods of organizing work. Processes lend themselves to coordinated effort and team building because they include a clear terminal goal, multiple skills and competencies to complete, and interdependence among value-added stages of the work.

WPM applies a simplified version of flowcharting to describing work processes. Often it can be performed by incumbents with some modest training. A work process map produces a picture of how people do their work to achieve specific aims. Just as there are many possible paths you may choose to get to school and many landmarks you may pass along the way, there are many paths to getting work done and several features of the path clue you to how far along you are on your work assignment. A work process map illustrates these alternative paths and the key features along the way. WPM involves drawing a map of the work process to illustrate the tasks and decisions (processes) that need to occur to transform inputs to outputs (see Figure 4.14).

The first step in process mapping is to select individuals to serve as the mapping team. They should be knowledgeable about the work and consist of 5 to 10 members. Groups are preferred over an individual because more people can provide more information about alternatives. Second, a process must be selected for mapping. Processes are activities ordered in a sequence of steps that produce value to internal and/or external customers. Processes include activities such as order processing, product development, and shipping. Processes

consist of several activities but culminate in a final product or aim. At each step of the process, each employee receives work, adds value, and directs the work to another worker or group of workers. We'll create an abbreviated map of the job analysis process used in a small toy manufacturing organization.

The next step involves defining the process and includes identifying the output, internal and external customers, customer requirements, positions that allocate resources to sustain the process, suppliers, stakeholders, and process boundaries (starting and ending points of the process).

The fourth step involves mapping the primary process, which represents the primary sequence of work activities necessary to complete the process. Parallel processes may be occurring that also are related to sustaining or speeding up the primary process, such as having a station attendant wipe your windshield while another fills your gas tank or having a clerk bag your groceries while a cashier rings up your purchases. In the case of the job analysis process at our toy manufacturer, the primary process begins with defining the purpose of the job analysis (setting performance standards) as this determines the products that result (appraisal forms and/or production and attendance standards) and the type of job analysis to be performed (task- and/or behavior-based methods). This is followed by identifying job analysis agents, whether in-house or external consultants; the resources necessary to complete the project; the specific methods to be used (interviews and questionnaires to collect task information and collect critical incident data); and the sources of job analysis information such as job incumbents and supervisors. For brevity, we've included the other sequences in the process map shown in Figure 4.15 and now proceed to discuss steps five and six in the mapping effort.

Step five involves mapping alternative paths that may be followed to produce the output. Not everyone does things the same way and there may be occasions where contingencies do not allow the primary process to proceed as intended. In our job analysis situation, it may be that a poor response rate to the task inventory questionnaire requires a second administration or that the poor quality of the critical incidents signals a need for conducting a workshop with information sources to produce data that are more useful. Often these alternative paths are triggered by some quality control decision point, the unavailability of resources, or different customer specifications for a product. At step six, inspection points are mapped and several of these may have already been identified from the mapping of alternative paths.

At step seven, the map is subject to close study and further refinement. At this point, specific performance standards may be included for different subprocesses, such as adopting a questionnaire return rate standard of 50 percent or a standard of 200 usable critical incidents.

FIGURE 4.14
WORK PROCESS MAPPING

Inputs ————	Process ————	Outputs
Purpose	I. Determine purpose	Job descriptions
Agents	II. Define customers and requirements	
Sources	III. Identify agents, sources, methods, and resources	Performance standards
Methods	IV. Develop job analysis protocol	Appraisal format
Resources	V. Collect job information	
	VI. Compile data	
	VII. Analyze and interpret data	
	VIII. Compose report	

FIGURE 4.15
PRIMARY PROCESS FOR JOB ANALYSIS AT NEWCO TOY MANUFACTURING

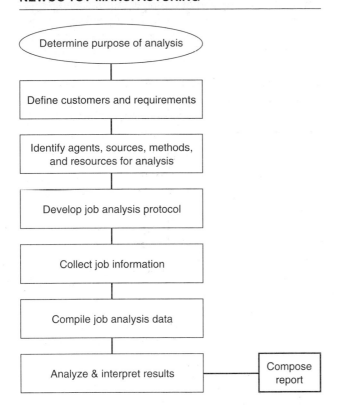

Of course, the standards can also be more precise, such as better defining what *usable* refers to with respect to the critical incident data.

The coupling of strategic job analysis and work mapping can reduce the ambiguity in understanding the work required of new or restructured (reengineered) positions. However, neither is sufficient as a job analysis method; rather, they serve as supplementary tools for conventional job analysis methods. Strategic job analysis is borne out of necessity for specific situations where little information about a job exists or the job is changing radically. Work process mapping is an enabler in that it makes more understandable what is occurring in the course of a work process. Both require careful attention to internal and external customer specifications, include worker participation in the job analysis process, and are relatively novel developments that have become increasingly common in a short time.

IS THERE BIAS IN JOB ANALYSIS DATA?

Considerable research has been conducted on the extent to which job analysis data are subject to some form of bias. Most of this research has focused on potential sex biases in job evaluation for setting pay rates.[29] Job eval-

uation is another product of job analysis that can create considerable trouble for a company *or* result in a rational and reasonable pay system. Research indicates that job analysis data are generally free of gender or racial bias.[30] In other words, the race or gender of the job analyst doesn't seem to matter in terms of results. However, courts have often been critical of the racial/sexual composition of committees responsible for conducting job analysis and deriving job specifications. A job specification stipulated by an all white-male panel of job experts that resulted in adverse impact could be subject to a more problematic legal challenge because of the panel's composition.

Some research also has investigated whether the source of the job information influences the nature of the data collected. In general, the source (e.g., incumbents, supervisors, trained observers) does not appear to greatly influence the type of data collected. There is some evidence, however, that incumbents and supervisors agree more about the tasks performed than they do about the attributes required to perform the job well.[31] Job incumbents and supervisors also tend to inflate job importance ratings relative to professional job analysts. Evidence also shows that those who know more about the job tend to make more reliable and accurate judgments.[32] Naive raters do not seem to provide job analysis information equivalent to the information provided by experts of the job.[33] There is not, however, support for the view that incumbents who are more effective at their jobs provide different information about their jobs than do low performers.[34] Surprisingly, there is no research comparing customer perspectives with those of incumbents or supervisors.

More research is needed to explore possible sources of bias in job analysis data and the processes involved in deriving job analysis data. Such research may reveal better methods for gathering and integrating job analysis data to enhance accuracy and usefulness.

HOW DO YOU CHOOSE THE BEST JOB ANALYSIS METHOD?

A number of studies have examined the relative effectiveness of specific job analysis methods. For example, one study asked experienced job analysts to indicate the extent to which four methods accomplished the various purposes for job analysis.[35] In addition, they were asked to evaluate the amount of training required to use the method, the sample sizes required for deriving reliable results, and the cost to administer and score the job analysis method. The results indicated that, of the methods evaluated, if the purpose is to generate a job description or to do job classification or job design, one of the best job analysis methods is the **FJA. CIT** is not effective for job classification purposes. The best methods for job evaluation are **FJA** and the **PAQ.** The PAQ is also an excellent method for selecting valid tests to use for hiring. If the purpose of the job analysis is to develop a performance-appraisal instrument or to derive training content, the recommended method is **CIT.** No method is ideal in terms of legal compliance, including ADA compliance. For companies needing highly detailed information about a job, developing their own job analysis method is probably preferable to selecting an "off-the-shelf" type such as the **PAQ,** which would not provide the level of detail in describing the job, perhaps a critical issue in developing a training program or in conducting a job mapping or reengineering study.

All experts agree that the choice of job analysis method depends on the purposes to be served by the data and the desired product. There is no one best way to conduct a job analysis. The purposes for the data and the practicality of the various methods for particular organizations must be considered. The most definitive research finding on the relative effectiveness of the various methods is that multiple methods of job analysis should be used whenever possible. For example, a quantitative approach such as the **PAQ** or the **MPDQ** should probably be augmented by a qualitative approach such as the **CIT,** which can provide more specific information about jobs than can typically be derived from the quantitative methods. For most circumstances, the more comprehensive work analysis has greater potential for enhancing *organizational capability.*

SUMMARY

Jobs are important to people because they have surplus meaning beyond just providing a paycheck necessary to sustain their economic survival. Increasingly, people ask a lot of their jobs, certainly more as individuals become better educated and develop rising expectations about what jobs should supply. As a result of technology and the flattening of organizational structures jobs are no longer the static entities they once were thought to be. The entire enterprise of work has become more dynamic, and the lines distinguishing the responsibilities of one job from another continue to blur. Recent research on job performance has shown that some generic dimensions of work behavior apply across a broad spectrum of jobs in the world of work while others are more task-based and are very specific to a limited set of jobs. Generic work behaviors influence the performance of virtually any job.[36] Included among these behaviors are those involving honesty or integrity, attendance, treating co-workers with respect, and maintaining good personal hygiene. As such, the idea of generic work behaviors opens the possibility for more direct comparisons of employee performance regardless of the specific tasks for which they are responsible.

One of the aims of job analysis is to identify differences between jobs so that selection tests, levels of compensation, training and development efforts, and performance standards are demonstrably relevant to job success. An increasing burden on job analysis today is to describe jobs in sufficient detail so that differences between them are recognized and appropriate criteria for personnel decisions result. On the other hand, job analysis should also be flexible enough to be applied to the study of jobs as they change in response to technological demands and organizational strategy.[37]

Despite rhetoric to the contrary, job analysis remains an essential tool for HR professionals despite contemporary changes in the world of work and the new "team" orientation within many companies. The popular press has included much discussion about the "de-jobbing" of organizations.[38] In fact, job analysis may be even more significant in a turbulent work environment. Regardless of the elasticity of the job or projects or tasks, job analysis data can be a starting point in the design of most HR systems including restructuring, human resource planning, reengineering recruitment strategies, selection processes, training and career development programs, performance appraisal systems, customer-based appraisal, job design efforts, compensation plans, and health and safety compliance and improvements.

A job analysis helps to ensure that HR systems will be professionally sound and will comply with legal requirements. As noted in Chapter 3, HR systems that involve personnel decisions such as selection, pay, promotion, and terminations should be based on a determination of the important job duties and KASOCs necessary for successful job performance. Even if the legal mandate did not exist, effective HR practice dictates the linkage between HR practices and job analysis information.

While many contemporary management gurus preach that job descriptions promote individualism to the detriment of unit effectiveness, we believe that job analysis and job descriptions can facilitate more effective group and unit effectiveness. This is done through clearly defining responsibilities, determining the relative importance of tasks and working relationships between positions and individuals, and relating all these to customer requirements. Job descriptions do not usually say that the incumbent will perform only those specific tasks defined on the description regardless of circumstances. The gurus may be right that job descriptions foster an "it's not my job" philosophy of work and a deviation in attention away from customer requirements as related to the work products. The trick is to develop and use job analysis information with customer requirements and expectations as the context and focus for its use. This "trick" also applies to small businesses as well.

Some jobs are changing while the once traditional idea of *the job* is under challenge as more organizations adopt project-based work assignments. Even project-based employment requires hiring, training, compensation, and performance-appraisal functions, and so the need to describe before hiring the work a prospective employee or contractor will perform still requires an inventory of the likely situational demands and worker competencies needed to fulfill even this more broad-banded mission.[39] Therefore, although static unchanging jobs may be on the way out, job analysis or work analysis as a tool for understanding and describing work activities will remain an essential HR competency for the foreseeable future. As we cover the various HR functional areas in the chapters to follow, we will address in more detail how job analysis is used to supply internal and external customers with the very best and most efficient deliverables. The more comprehensive "work analysis" approach is compatible with systematic human resource planning we discuss in the next chapter.

DISCUSSION QUESTIONS

1. How would you go about establishing a BFOQ using job analysis? Do you think you could support the argument?

2. Do you believe having highly detailed job descriptions for every position can interfere with group effectiveness? If so, what can be done?

3. For each of the following HR systems, what information from a job analysis is needed to develop a professional and legally defensible system?
   a. Training program for new employees.
   b. Selection system.
   c. Performance-appraisal system.
   d. Compensation system.
   e. Job design.

4. Describe the advantages and disadvantages to using interviews, observation, and questionnaires for collecting job analysis data.

5. How might you involve customers in the development of job descriptions and job specifications? Are there any constraints on what customers can stipulate in job specifications?

6. The chapter states that a government agency used PAQ results to support an argument of "job relatedness" and to set an appropriate compensation level. Please comment.

NOTES

1. Sanchez, J. I. (1994). From documentation to innovation: Reshaping job analysis to meet emerging business needs. *Human Resource Management Review, 4*(1), 51–74.

2. Gael, S. (ed.) (1988). *The job analysis handbook for business, industry and government,* Vol I. New York: John Wiley & Sons, p. xv. See also, Gael, S., Vol. II.

3. Bernardin, H. J., Hagan, C., Kane, J. S., and Villanova, P. (1998). Effective performance management: Precision in measurement with a focus on customers. In J. Smither (ed.) *Performance appraisal: State-of-the-art methods in practice.* San Francisco: Jossey-Bass.

4. Harvey, R. J. (1991). Job analysis. In M. D. Dunnette and L. M. Hough (eds.), *Handbook of industrial and organizational psychology,* 2nd ed. Palo Alto, CA: Consulting Psychologists Press, 71–163.

5. Mitchell, K. E., Alliger, G. M., and Morfopoulos, R. (1997). Toward an ADA-appropriate job analysis. *Human Resource Management Review, 7*(1), 5–26; see also, Brannick, M. T., Brannick, J. P., and Levine, E. L. (1992). Job analysis, personnel selection, and the ADA. *Human Resource Management Review, 2*(3), 171–182.

6. Arthur, Jr., W.; Doverspike, D.; and Barrett, G. V. (1996). Development of a job analysis-based procedure for weighting and combining content-related tests into a single test battery score. *Personnel Psychology, 49*(4), 971–984.

7. U.S. Department of Labor (1977), *Dictionary of occupational titles* (4th ed). Washington, DC: U.S. Printing Office.

8. *U.S. v. State of New York,* 1979. (Feb. 21, 1986); see also note 5.

9. See note 2, Gael (1988); also see, Spector, P. E., Brannick, M. T., and Coovert, M. D. (1989). Job analysis. In C. L. Cooper and I. T. Robertson (eds.), *International review of industrial and organizational psychology.* New York: John Wiley & Sons, 281–328.

10. Levine, E. L. (1983). *Everything you always wanted to know about job analysis.* Tampa, FL: Mariner Publishing; see also, Arvey, R. D.; Salas, E.; and Gialluca, K. A. (1992). Using task inventories to forecast skills and abilities. *Human Performance, 5,* 171–190.

11. McCormick, E. J., and Jeanneret, P. R. (1988). Position analysis questionnaire. In S. Gael (ed.), *The job analysis handbook for business, industry, and government,* Vol. II. New York: John Wiley & Sons, 825–842.

12. McCormick, E. J.; Jeanneret, P. R.; and Mecham, R. C. (1972). A study of job characteristics and job dimensions as based on the Position Analysis Questionnaire. *Journal of Applied Psychology, 56,* 347–368.

13. *Taylor v. James River Corporation* (Nov. 16, 1989). CA-88-0818-T-C.

14. Page, R. C. (1988). Management position description questionnaire. In S. Gael (ed.), *The job analysis handbook for business, industry, and government,* Vol. II. New York: John Wiley & Sons, 860–879.

15. Tornow, W. W., and Pinto, P. R. (1976). The development of a managerial job taxonomy: A system for describing, classifying, and evaluating executive positions. *Journal of Applied Psychology, 61,* 410–418; McCauley, C. D.; Ruderman, M. N.; Ohlott, P. J.; and Morrow, J. E. (1996). Assessing the developmental components of managerial jobs. *Journal of Applied Psychology, 79*(4), 544; San-

chez, J. I. (1994). An empirical approach to identify job duty-KSA linkages in managerial jobs: A case example. *Journal of Business and Psychology, 8,* 309–325.

16. Fine, A. S. (1988). Functional job analysis. In S. Gael (ed.). *The job analysis handbook for business, industry, and government,* Vol. II. New York: John Wiley & Sons, pp. 1019–1035.

17. Flanagan, J. C. (1954). The critical incident technique. *Psychological Bulletin, 51,* 327–358.

18. Bownas, D., and Bernardin, H. J. (1988). The critical incident method. In S. Gael (ed.), *The job analysis handbook for business, industry and government,* Vol. II, New York: John Wiley & Sons, 1120–1137.

19. Bernardin, H. J. (1989). Innovative approaches to personnel selection and performance appraisal. *Journal of Management Systems, 1,* 25–76; see also, Bernardin, H. J. (1987). Development and validation of a forced-choice scale to measure job-related discomfort among customer service representatives. *Academy of Management Journal, 30,* 162–173.

20. Villanova, P., and Bernardin, H. J. (1990). Work behavior correlates of interviewer job compatibility. *Journal of Business and Psychology, 5,* 179–195; see also, Villanova, P.; Bernardin, H. J.; Johnson, D.; and Dahmus, S. (1994). The validity of a measure of job compatibility in the prediction of job performance and turnover of motion picture theater personnel. *Personnel Psychology, 47,* 73–90; Bernardin, H. J.; Hagan, C.; Schubinski, M.; and Johnson, D. (1997). The development and validation of the security officer profile (SOP) *Security Journal, 8,* 195–200.

21. Hackman, J. R., and Oldham, G. R. (1976). Motivation through the design of work: Test of a theory. *Organizational Behavior and Human Performance, 16,* 250–279; McCann, J. E. III, and Buchner, M. (1994). Redesigning work: Motivation, challenges and practices in 181 companies. *HR Planning, 17,* 23–41.

22. Hackman, J. R., and Oldham, G. R. (1980). *Work redesign.* Reading, MA: Addison-Wesley.

23. Fried, Y., and Ferris, G. R. (1987). The validity of the job characteristics model: A review and meta-analysis. *Personnel Psychology, 40,* 287–322.

24. Hackman, J. R., and Oldham, G. R. (1975). Development of the Job Diagnostic Survey. *Journal of Applied Psychology, 60,* 159–170.

25. See note 23; see also, Munz, D. C., Huelsman, T. J., Konold, T. R., and McKinney, J. J. (1996). Are there methodological and substantive roles for affectivity in job diagnostic survey relationships? *Journal of Applied Psychology, 81,* 795–799.

27. See note 1, Sanchez (1994, p. 52). See also, Schneider,

B., and Konz, A. (1989). Strategic job analysis. *Human Resource Management, 28,* 51–63; Stevens, M. J., and Campion, M. A. (1994). The knowledge, skill, and ability requirements for teamwork: Implications for human resource management. *Journal of Management, 20*(2), 503–530.

28. Galloway, D. (1994). *Mapping work processes.* Milwaukee, WI: ASQC Quality Press.

29. Treiman, D. J., and Hartmann, H. J. (eds.) (1981). *Women, work, and wages: Equal pay for jobs of equal value.* Washington, DC: National Academy Press.

30. See note 4; see also, Schaubroeck, J.; Ganster, D. C.; Sime, W. E.; and Ditman, D. (1996). A field experiment testing supervisory role clarification. *Personnel Psychology, 46*(1), 1–18.

31. Cornelius, E. T. (1988). Practical findings from job analysis research. In S. Gael (ed.), *The job analysis handbook for business, industry, and government,* Vol. I. New York: John Wiley & Sons, 48–68.

32. DeNisi, A. S.; Cornelius, E. T.; and Blencos, A. G. (1987). Further investigation of common knowledge effects on job analysis ratings. *Journal of Applied Psychology, 72,* pp. 262–268; see also, Pine, D. E. (1995). Assessing the validity of job ratings: An empirical study of false reporting in task inventories. *Public Personnel Management, 24*(4), 451–460.

33. Friedman, L., and Harvey, R. J. (1986). Can raters with reduced job descriptive information provide accurate Position Analysis Questionnaire (PAQ) ratings? *Personnel Psychology, 39,* 779–789.

34. Conley, P. R., and Sackett, P. R. (1987). Effects of using high- versus low-performing job incumbents as sources of job analysis information. *Journal of Applied Psychology, 72,* 434–437.

35. Levine, E. L.; Ash, R. A.; Hall, H.; and Sistrunk, F. (1983). Evaluation of job analysis methods by experienced job analysts. *Academy of Management Journal, 26,* pp. 339–348; see also, Clifford, J. P. (1996). Manage work better to better manage human resources: A comparative study of two approaches to job analysis. *Public Personnel Management, 25*(1), 89–102.

36. Hunt, S. T. (1996). Generic work behavior: An investigation into dimensions of entry-level, hourly job performance. *Personnel Psychology, 49,* 51–84.

37. See note 1, Sanchez (1994).

38. Bridges, W. (Sept. 19, 1994). The end of the job. *Fortune.*

39. Ilgen, D. R., and Hollenbeck, J. R. (1991). The structure of work: Job design and roles. In M. D. Dunnette and L. M. Hough (eds.). *Handbook of industrial and organizational psychology.* Vol. 2. Palo Alto, CA: Consulting Psychologists Press, 165–207.

C H A P T E R

HUMAN RESOURCE PLANNING AND RECRUITMENT*

OVERVIEW

Kathryn Connors, the vice president of human resources at Liz Claiborne, described the ideal role for HR in strategic planning. "Human resources is part of the strategic planning process. It's part of policy development, line extension planning and the merger and acquisition process. Little is done in the company that doesn't involve us in the planning, policy or finalization stages of any deal."[1] Unfortunately, the extent of involvement of human resources in strategic planning as practiced by Liz Claiborne is still unusual. While one 1995 study found that most companies surveyed linked HR planning to strategic planning, the linkage was not very strong with much greater emphasis given to functions directly related to the development, production, or sale of the product or service.[2] The more typical practice is for an HRM unit to receive personnel forecasting plans to implement in the context of a strategic decision to reduce overhead by reducing labor costs. One indication that the strategy/ planning process of HRM may not be ideal is the unfortunate announcement of massive layoffs in many of our largest

and most respected organizations. For example, how did AT&T come to be (apparently) overstaffed by 40,000? Did the 1996 Telecommunications Bill have that profound of an effect on the business? And what of IBM's need to cut 100,000 jobs? Maybe there was a breakdown in the strategy/ planning process.

In terms of competitive advantage in the global economy, however, the good news is that most foreign competitors also conduct their HR planning and recruitment in a reactive manner rather than as a fully integrated system. Thus, there is opportunity for competitive advantage in terms of organizational capability for U.S. companies.

Recent survey results from small business and the continuing trend to downsize in large corporations underscore the importance of human resources in strategic planning. The focus of small business in recent years has been on growth and expanding the customer base, while the focus of the largest companies has been on controlling overhead by reducing labor costs and shedding workers. HR planning should be an integral part of either strategy. The most effective approach to staffing, whether adding workers or eliminating them, is to assess staffing needs with a focus on meeting customer require-

---

*Contributed by Scott A. Snell and Monica Favia.

103

ments and, for most products or services, expanding the customer base.

The goal for organizations of all sizes is quite simple: Keep the cost of labor as low as possible while meeting (or exceeding) customer demand and, if this is part of the strategic plan, expanding the customer base. The realization of this goal for HR practice is difficult. This goal can also be applied to the internal customers who require products or services from internal suppliers, including HRM staff. For example, an internal customer could be a district manager in retail who must hire a store manager for a store in the district. One option could be to use an external headhunter group that specializes in retail or perhaps the company relies on internal recruiters to compile a list of qualified candidates. The company is very interested in the cost of the recruiting effort, and the district manager may be particularly interested in filling the position quickly with someone who requires little or no training.

Two of the most important aspects of staffing are HRM planning and recruitment. Planning is the forecasting of HR needs in the context of strategic business planning. As we discussed in Chapter 1, the human resource planning process of the past was typically reactive in nature, with business needs defining personnel needs. However, with major changes in the business environment and increasing uncertainty, many organizations are adopting a longer-term perspective and integrating human resource planning with strategic business planning[3] centered on a consideration of core business competencies.

Recruitment is the process of attracting applicants for the positions needed. This process *should* be fully integrated with the HR planning process and other HR activities, especially the selection process. Most experts maintain that recruitment and other HRM activities are interdependent. For example, recruitment success affects selection success and the use of selection procedures can affect recruitment success.

This chapter provides an overview of the planning and recruitment process. We will discuss the relationship among planning, recruitment, and the other HRM functions; the process of downsizing and reengineering or restructuring; the various sources available for recruiting and their relative effectiveness; the advantages and disadvantages of internal and external recruiting; and the role of equal employment opportunity in the planning and recruitment process.

OBJECTIVES

After studying this chapter, the student should be able to:

1. Understand the importance of human resource planning (HRP) to the organization.

2. Identify the six steps in the HRP process.

3. Identify the methods by which an organization can develop forecasts of anticipated personnel demand and understand labor markets.

4. Understand how an organization can stay apprised of and evaluate its personnel supply and, if necessary, implement a downsizing program.

5. Determine which recruitment methods are best for given situations, including the growing business of automated recruiting through the Internet and other on-line services.

6. Understand the pros and cons of internal versus external recruiting.

7. Know the most important features of recruitment advertising.

8. Know the EEO implications of recruitment and planning.

In 1996, General Motors analyzed its costs relative to its competition and was not pleased with the results. While many areas were related to higher production costs, one of the biggest items was car engineering. GM's analysis revealed 45 percent higher engineering costs per vehicle relative to its domestic competitors. GM first studied the largely independent engineering operations across the various divisions (e.g., Buick, Oldsmobile, Cadillac) and noted the redundancies in design and testing operations. It also noted that the expertise of one division was not fully exploited by the other divisions. For example, the brilliant work of the design engineers at Buick could have been used by Oldsmobile in its engineering operations. Instead, Oldsmobile had its own staff of design engineers who had almost no contact with the Buick people despite obvious opportunities for cooperation and a sharing of expertise. (Remember that all of these folks are GM employees.)

GM decided that having all engineers together in one location would not only eliminate this redundancy but also facilitate the use of effective and efficient engineering (and, ultimately, effective parts exchange). It projected substantial cost savings and efficiencies with the new across-division approach to engineering GM cars. The company began consolidating the engineering operations in 1997. The goal was to reduce the cost of engineering by at least 30 percent in the first year while maintaining the quality of the engineering.

In Chapter 2, we defined *strategy* as "a process through which the basic mission and objectives of the organization are set and a process through which the organization uses its resources to achieve its objectives."[4] One source of competitive advantage for an organization is its organizational capability. The most effective organizations today have fully integrated their

HR planning and recruitment processes with their business strategies.

Recruitment planning should flow directly from the strategic business plan and HR planning. Figure 5.1 presents a model of this relationship.

GM attempted to follow this model. Its strategy was to compete on car price by reducing the relatively excessive overhead, most of which could be attributed to labor costs. HR planning was conducted in the context of this competitive pricing strategy. GM's 1996 HR planning drove the company's negotiations with the UAW, its policy toward outsourcing auto parts, and elimination of duplication across auto divisions, including engineering. Obviously, moving all engineers out of the various GM divisions from all over the country to be relocated in Detroit was no small task. There can be many casualties on the road to greater efficiency.

EFFECTIVE HUMAN RESOURCE PLANNING

We have discussed human resource planning as a problem-solving process conducted in the context of an organization's strategy and policy. Recall our discussion of SWOT analysis in Chapter 2 (strengths, weaknesses, opportunities, and threats). SWOT analysis is critical for the strategic planning and recruitment processes. Effective HRP closes the gap from the current situation to a desired state of affairs in the context of the organization's strategy. The process for determining this match is outlined in Figure 5.2. Effective HRP should involve: (1) environmental scanning, (2) labor/demand forecast, (3) supply forecast, (4) gap analysis, (5) action programming, and (6) control and evaluation. Let us examine each of these on the next page.

FIGURE 5.1
SIMPLIFIED MODEL OF EXTERNAL AND INTERNAL FACTORS THAT INFLUENCE RECRUITMENT

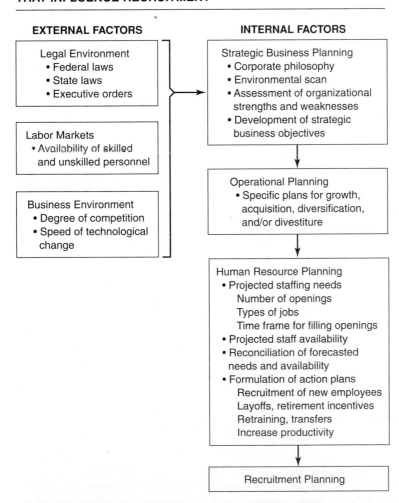

Source: Adapted from *Recruitment: Science and Practice* by James Breaugh. Copyright © 1992 PWS-Kent Publishing. By permission of South-Western College Publishing, a division of International Thomson Publishing Inc., Cincinnati, Ohio 45227.

FIGURE 5.2

1. **Environmental scanning.**   Identify and anticipate sources of threats, and opportunities; scanning the external environment (competitors, regulation) and internal environment (strategy, technology, culture).

2. **Labor demand forecast.**   Project how business needs will affect HR needs, using qualitative methods (e.g., Delphi, nominal) and quantitative methods (trend analysis, simple and multiple linear regression analysis).

3. **Labor supply forecast.**   Project resource availability from internal and external sources.

4. **Gap analysis.**   Reconcile the forecast of labor supply and demand.

5. **Action programming.**   Implement the recommended solution from step 4.

6. **Control and Evaluation.**   Monitor the effects of the HRP by defining and measuring critical criteria (e.g., turnover costs, breakeven costs of new hires, recruitment costs, performance outcomes).

Step One: Environmental Scanning

As we discussed in Chapter 2, environmental scanning helps HR planners identify and anticipate sources of threats, and opportunities and should drive the organization's strategic planning. Scanning provides a better understanding of the context in which HR decisions are or will be made. Both an external and internal environmental scan is critical for effective planning.

GM's analysis of competitors' costs was a part of an environmental scan that clearly identified a problem and a threat. But the best planners are those who can turn a threat into an opportunity. The centralized engineering concept was developed because of the cost problem across divisions. One solution had the potential of turning the problem into an opportunity to improve the engineering of all GM cars. The environmental scan of future markets and competitor positions by GM provided relatively clear opportunities and threats for the future. GM's assessment of its competitive situation was based on its environmental scan of the major competitors with particular emphasis on the cost of labor per car. GM's problem was a labor cost per car that was significantly higher than its domestic or Japanese competitors. This problem was exacerbated by the fact that the extra cost did not translate into any discernible advantage. For example, overall J.D. Power customer satisfaction measures showed Ford, Honda, and Toyota all comfortably ahead of GM.

So the problem of excessive overhead fits into the "routine" threats and opportunities category for GM; it had to reduce costs to compete more effectively. GM's 1996 collective bargaining with the UAW gave it an opportunity to negotiate changes as part of this strategy, and the reengineering of its engineering function focused on reducing the cost of making cars. The ancillary effect could be more effective engineering.

What was uncertain or ambiguous was the effect of the overhead reduction on a number of other critical criteria, most notably, the quality of the cars. Would the centralized engineering reduce costs but also reduce the quality of the engineering? Would GM lose some of the best engineers when they were ordered to relocate to Detroit? GM saw the centralization as an opportunity to improve engineering.

How could GM get the UAW to buy into its strategy of reducing the cost of labor when unions typically attempt to maximize labor costs? These questions were critical in assessing the overall impact of GM's strategic HR plan. Again, GM looked at the 1996 labor negotiations as an opportunity to get more competitive.

An example of the use of environmental scanning to drive strategy and HR planning in a situation of uncertainty is the 1996 reorganization of AT&T after passage of the Federal Telecommunications Bill. The decision by this giant to break into three separate units based on its strategic plan under the new regulations and legislation led to efforts to cut 40,000 jobs by the end of 1996. Some people who were eliminated from one job were rehired for new positions under the new structure.

Personnel Assessment Systems' monitoring of its environment is a good example of scanning that could drive both strategy and planning. The company's major competitors all had developed Web sites and a few were on-line with testing programs through the Internet. While PAS business had not been seriously affected by this trend, there was a belief that the trend would continue and that PAS had to develop alternative forms of testing that included an Internet option. Another potential threat concerned the legislative activity regarding psychological testing. For example, the state of Florida was considering legislation requiring that all forms of psychological screening include a clinical interview by a licensed psychologist. This legislation would be devastating to PAS business in Florida since its main business was low-cost, entry-level screening for unskilled positions such as customer service representatives and security guards. As we discussed in Chapter 4, interpretations of the *Americans with Disabilities Act* concerning mental disabilities also threatened their testing programs.

While there can be (and often are) situations with ambiguous threats and opportunities, the probability of reducing or eliminating the ambiguity is increased by a more thorough environmental scan. The idea is to at least attempt to turn a threat into an opportunity. In general, the greater the amount of relevant information managers have about a threat, the more likely that threat can be turned into an opportunity. Both external and internal environmental scans are critical for this information.

UNDERSTANDING THE LABOR MARKET FOR HR PLANNING. One critical component of environmental scanning for HR planning and recruitment is an understanding of the relevant labor market. Labor market conditions influence HR planning in terms of both the number and types of available employees. In a loose **labor market,** qualified recruits are abundant. However, many labor markets are extremely tight. For example, there are current shortages in cutting-edge technologies (e.g., optics, laser technology, electromagnetics, composites technology), medicine and medical support, computer science and support services, electrical engineering, manufacturing engineering, plastics, languages, and statistics. Tight markets limit the availability of labor, drive up the price of those employees who are selected, and limit the extent to which the organization can be selective in its hiring procedures. For example, many hospitals hesitate to administer valid selection tests to applicants for physical therapist jobs because applicants are in such short supply. Private security guard and trucking companies use psychological tests for screening mainly because of fears of negligent hiring lawsuits. However, because of the level of competition in this area, the demand for services, and the tight labor market for largely unskilled labor, these companies cannot be very selective in hiring people despite what the tests may predict.

There is now a mad scramble among companies to assess the implications of the World Wide Web on strategic plans, positions in the market, and, in general, the threats and opportunities of this fast-paced movement. Experts on the intricacies of all aspects of the Web are in short supply and in great demand.

The relevant labor market for an employer is usually defined by occupation, geography, and employer competition. Obviously, the job and the skills or job specifications play the greatest role in the definition of the relevant labor market and the ease (or difficulty) with which positions can be filled. The labor market for most jobs can also be greatly affected by geography. Bechtel, the giant international construction company, received several million dollars in contracts with Kuwait to rebuild the country after the 1991 war with Iraq. However, the company had difficulty recruiting civil engineers and other specialists to go to Kuwait. Even high wages did not attract the necessary number of qualified professionals. There was such a chronic shortage of qualified teachers for the 1997 school year in Texas, schools were hiring almost anyone with a college degree to fill classes. The state of Michigan, which pays teachers about 30% more to start, had no such shortage.

Competing employers are the third factor defining the labor market. The number and type of employers seeking similarly qualified personnel or offering similar compensation in the same geographical location can also define the labor market.

THE GLOBAL LABOR MARKET. The technological and communications revolution has changed the relationship between geography and labor supply. The world is now the labor market for both skilled and unskilled labor. The chances are very good that the outfit you're wearing now, from your Chicago Bulls hat to your Air Jordans, were all manufactured overseas. The outsourcing of the manufacturing/ assembly process to a foreign location is now common in many industries.

What is also becoming more common is that skilled labor positions are being farmed out to lower-paid, overseas workers. Digital Equipment, Hewlett-Packard, IBM, Texas Instruments, and Compaq Computer all employ skilled workers in Bangalore, India, many of whom write software packages for these companies. The programming costs are estimated to be about half the cost of an American programmer. However, this difference could change rapidly as the demand for Indian programmers grows.

E-mail, fax machines, private satellite links, and the World Wide Web have made workers from all over the world very accessible and have expanded the labor market for U.S. companies. The result is lower labor costs for American companies, and thus greater profits, the shipment of more American jobs overseas, and the continued stagnation of middle-class wages in this country. Sea-Land, a division of CSX Corporation, closed its programming division in Elizabeth, New Jersey, and farmed all the work out to India. M. Clint Eisenhauer, a spokesman for the company, said that to stay competitive, "Any service like this we would shop on a worldwide basis." Experienced programmers in India are paid about $1,500 a month as compared to the $4,000 to 5,000 for programmers in the United States.

Rick Younts, executive vice president for international operations at Motorola, claims more than lower wages as the reason Motorola hires Asian programmers. U.S. programmers can work on a project during the day and then send it through e-mail to Asian counterparts who can work on the project while the U.S.-based programmers are sleeping. Younts estimates a 40 percent reduction in time to completion because of this work schedule.

Companies that do not take advantage of the global labor market for labor will be at a competitive disadvantage as long as consumers do not place a heavy weight on the extent to which a product or service involves American workers. Michael Jordan was paid more money by Nike in 1996 than Nike paid to all the workers who manufactured Nike shoes in Indonesia. As we discussed in Chapter 2, as long as Americans accept this way of doing business, or at least do not consider it in making purchase decisions, Nike and its stockholders will be very happy.

Figure 5.3 presents a summary of the relevant labor market as defined by occupation and geography.

FIGURE 5.3
RELEVANT LABOR MARKETS, BY GEOGRAPHIC AND EMPLOYEE GROUPS

RELEVANT LABOR MARKET		EMPLOYEE GROUPS/OCCUPATIONS					
	GEOGRAPHIC SCOPE	**PRODUCTION**	**OFFICE AND CLERICAL**	**TECHNICIANS**	**SCIENTISTS AND ENGINEERS**	**MANAGERIAL PROFESSIONAL**	**EXECUTIVE**
	Local: Within relatively small areas, such as cities or metropolitan statistical areas— MSAs (e.g., Dallas metropolitan area)	Most likely	Most likely	Most likely	—	—	—
	Regional: Within a particular area of the state or county or several states (e.g., Greater Boston area)	Only if in short supply or critical	Only if in short supply or critical	Most likely	Likely	Likely	—
	National: Across the country	—	—	—	Most likely	Most likely	Most likely
	International: Across several countries	—	—	—	Only for critical skills or those in very short supply	Only for critical skills or those in very short supply	Likely

Source: G. T. Milkovich and J. W. Boudreau. *Human Resource Management,* 6th ed. Homewood, IL: Richard D. Irwin, 1991, p. 36. Reprinted with permission.

Managing the labor market and the cost of labor is a crucial HR activity. Companies usually look at labor first when their corporate performance measures do not meet expectations. Recall our discussion in Chapter 1 about the need to be flexible in this dynamic and more global economy. Compared to European companies, U.S. companies have greater flexibility regarding labor reductions and cost cutting, giving them a competitive advantage regarding price. Employers need to be creative in solving their staffing needs. Radisson Hotels staffed many of its unskilled positions with bilingual employees. To meet growing staffing needs, it began hiring immigrants who could speak only Spanish and installed an English-language course for the new employees. Bechtel paid a substantial per diem rate and above-market salaries to try to fill its engineering needs for Kuwait.

LABOR SHORTAGES IN SERVICES. Companies sometimes have to expand the geographical base for labor because of supply and demand. They may also have to expand the supply of labor by increasing compensation. With heavy competition from cruise ships, fast food restaurants, and shopping malls, the U.S. hotel industry has been forced to add numerous costly employee benefits to attract unskilled labor in their rapidly expanding industry. Many hotels have even expanded the geographical base for unskilled work by providing transportation to and from the hotel.

Bechtel had to increase its compensation package for civil engineers for work in Kuwait after the Persian Gulf War. Bechtel was at a disadvantage not only because of the geographical location of the work, but it was also competing against several other construction companies that also received contracts with Kuwait. Similar problems developed for companies doing business in what was East Germany. Siemens, the German electronics giant, for example, had difficulty hiring engineers and scientists for jobs in its ventures in eastern Germany because a high percentage of these skilled workers had relocated to what was West Germany and to other European countries. Because of the economic conditions and poor living standards in eastern Germany, Russia, and the Republic of Georgia, American companies such as Woolworth, Coca-Cola, and McDonald's report difficulty recruiting expatriates for these overseas assignments. These companies changed their recruiting strategy in favor of nationals for these jobs. Most overseas assignments are now highly valued by U.S. managers and incentives for the expatriate assignments are being reduced.

Companies are also looking at technology and software to replace at least some humans without affecting customer satisfaction. American Airlines is probably the farthest along among airlines in getting you onto a plane with the least interaction with humans. You can book a flight and a seat through the World Wide Web after looking at flight options. You then receive a confirmation code that can be used instead of a ticket to board the plane. Technology has reduced the need for certain categories of employees in numerous industries.

AFFIRMATIVE ACTION/ DIVERSITY PROGRAMS AND THE LAW: A THREAT OR OPPORTUNITY?

As we discussed in Chapter 3, government regulations also influence HR planning and must be considered in any environmental scan. Title VII of the Civil Rights Act, the Age Discrimination in Employment Act, the 1990 Americans with Disabilities Act, and Executive Order 11246 require that companies pay close attention to the manner in which they treat protected class individuals. Section 706 (G) of the Civil Rights Act allows a judge to order an affirmative action program if the employer is found guilty of intentional discrimination.

The most contentious situation, however, is one in which the employer shows some form of preferential treatment toward members of one group when there is no proven history of discrimination, no court mandate, or no consent decree. HR planning often includes very detailed programs directed at increasing the diversity of an organization's workforce. The planning converts to recruiting efforts designed to increase the supply of workers who meet diversity criteria. The ambiguity has been fostered because of the current state of the law regarding the manner in which such diversity is achieved. We return to this issue since diversity goals are an important part of HR planning and recruitment for government and most large U.S. corporations.

Despite the legal confusion, organizations are continuing their efforts to promote diversity in their workforces. Walt Disney Company, for example, has minority hiring targets at every level, according to Marc Pacala, Disney's general manager. Kentucky Fried Chicken maintains separate lists of minority candidates for its executive positions. Xerox continues with its "balanced workforce" program, which has measurable hiring goals for all levels of management. One survey found that 70 percent of *Fortune* 500 companies engage in race-based hiring while only 14 percent said they hired by merit alone.[5] At least one circuit court (the 5th—Texas, Louisiana, and Mississippi) has stated there are no circumstances in which a protected class characteristic can even be considered as part of a voluntary affirmative action program (*Hopwood v. Texas*).

There is little disagreement with organizational diversity goals that entail a concerted effort to recruit females and minorities. An organization may have federal, state, or municipal regulatory pressure to do just that. For example, contracts awarded by the city of Atlanta for the 1996 Olympics stipulated rates of minority hiring as a precondition for the awarding of the contract. We discussed the impact of the OFCCP on federal government contracting in Chapter 3.

Few would argue with the extra expenses incurred when recruitment efforts are targeted to these groups. The OFCCP's Revised Order #4 describes affirmative action activities and several actions an employer may take to "improve recruitment and increase the flow of minority or female applicants." For example, one recommendation is to contact sources such as the Urban League, the Job Corp, and colleges with high minority enrollment. For example, most major U.S. corporations actively recruit at Florida A&M in Tallahassee, Florida, a predominantly African-American college with an excellent business school.

The ambiguity, controversy, and potential illegality occur when preferential treatment is shown toward members of these groups by placing at least some weight on a job candidate's gender or ethnicity. The argument lies in whether such a characteristic should ever be considered and, if so, to what extent.

The safest strategy for an organization today is to meet diversity goals by increasing the recruitment effort to attract women and minorities and, once the pool of candidates is established, by ignoring the gender or ethnicity of members of the pool and concentrating on only the job-related credentials of the candidates. Of course, the issue of diversity and affirmative action often comes up when companies are downsizing. We will return to this issue later.

Step Two: Labor Demand Forecast

In a 1996 survey, 24 percent of small businesses indicated the "lack of qualified workers" posed a serious threat to their survival.[6] Many entrepreneurs in the survey indicated that labor shortages were preventing them from expanding their businesses and that such shortages made any type of planning more difficult. Over half of the respondents who had labor shortages had stepped up recruitment efforts and sought assistance from temporary employment agencies just to meet current demand for products or services. In the same year, over 30 percent of the largest U.S. companies actually reduced the size of their workforce despite a strong economy and, for many companies, record profits.

Nancy Pechloff, managing director of Arthur

Andersen's small-business consulting unit, notes that small companies are growing "but the supply of labor is not there."[7] The companies with sustained growth will be those that have the capability to expand. Meeting staffing needs is critical to this expansion. Fierce price competition and greater demands from investors are driving the restructuring efforts that have cut the workforces of so many profitable companies despite an expanding economy. Staffing decisions to meet customer demands and even expand the customer base can also entail reductions in the cost of labor through reengineering the organization in the context of a new corporate strategy. AT&T's radical moves in 1996 came because of a new strategy driven by technology, new legislation, and deregulation.

A forecast of labor demand derives from a projection of how business needs will affect HR. Each of the environmental forces discussed above is likely to exert pressure on HR demand—both in terms of the number and types of employees required, as well as the number and types of jobs. The HR planner must anticipate these needs, add focus to an otherwise confusing array of possibilities, and set priorities for conflicting goals. Labor demand forecasting methods fall into two categories: qualitative and quantitative. Because each category embraces certain assumptions, a combination of the two is preferred.

QUALITATIVE METHODS.   The simplest method for projecting labor demand is a centralized approach in which the HR department examines the current business situation and determines staffing requirements for the rest of the firm. While this approach is simple, it is generally not accurate. A top-down approach assumes that the central HR office has an accurate understanding of the business as well as the needs of each unit or function. In large complex firms, these assumptions typically do not hold. A more preferred method involves a decentralized process[8] wherein each unit or functional manager subjectively derives his or her own staffing needs. These projections are aggregated to create an overall composite forecast for the company.

At Pratt & Whitney, for example, top management set a goal of 30 percent cost reduction for each functional unit. Unit managers were asked to conduct job analysis of each job under their jurisdiction and, after analysis, to submit proposals for workload reduction and other cost-reduction options. A procedure was established to present the various reduction options including a method for the presentation of a rationale if the manager failed to make the 30 percent target reduction.

Other firms have experimented with formalized problem-solving methods such as the **Delphi technique** to minimize interpersonal and jurisdictional conflicts.[9] The Delphi technique avoids face-to-face group discussion through the use of an intermediary. Experts take turns presenting a forecast statement and assumptions.

The intermediary passes on the forecasts and assumptions to the others. Revisions are then made independently and anonymously by the experts. The intermediary then pools and summarizes the judgments and gives them to the experts. This process is continued until a consensus forecast emerges or until the intermediary concludes that more than one perspective must be presented. The Delphi technique has been shown to produce better one-year forecasts than with linear regression analysis (discussed below), but there can be difficulties in reaching consensus on complex problems.[10]

The full Delphi process can take considerable time. For example, the Gap, a clothing retailer, took over four months to forecast the number of buyers needed for the next year using a Delphi method. The use of networked computers can reduce the time required for Delphi forecasting.

The **nominal group technique** is similar to the Delphi method. However, experts join at a conference table and independently list their ideas in writing.[11] They then share their ideas with the group. As the ideas are presented, a master list of the ideas is compiled so everyone can refer to them. The ideas are discussed and ranked by member vote.

QUANTITATIVE METHODS.   Quantitative methods are based on the assumption that the future is an extrapolation from the past. **Trend analysis** incorporates certain business factors (e.g., units produced, revenues) and a productivity ratio (e.g., employees per units produced). For example, Pratt & Whitney calculated 16 jet engines per factory worker and almost 20 support, marketing, and management personnel for every 100 factory workers. The company's external environmental scanning data indicated more favorable ratios for General Electric, Pratt's chief competitor. By projecting changes in the business factor and/or the productivity ratio, we can forecast changes in the labor demand. There are six steps in trend analysis:

1. Find the appropriate business factor that relates to the size of the workforce.

2. Plot the historical record of that factor in relation to the size of the workforce.

3. Compute the productivity ratio (average output per worker per year).

4. Determine the trend.

5. Make necessary adjustments in the trend, past and future.

6. Project to the target year.[12]

The use of the appropriate business factor is critical to the success of trend analysis.[13] The business factor should be directly related to the essential purpose for the business. Universities typically use student enrollment by discipline, hospitals use patient-days, manufacturers typically use output needs, and retailers use sales adjusted by inventory.

Learning curves predict that the average number of units produced per employee will increase as more units are produced. Such an increase is expected because workers learn to perform their tasks more efficiently over time. Learning curves are evident in virtually all industries. For example, in the automotive industry, learning curves for new models improve by over 50 percent through the life of the model. At Pratt, the learning curve for one particular engine exceeded 60 percent from start-up to the final production year.

Simple linear regression and multiple linear regression are the most commonly used statistical procedures. Simple linear regression uses information from the past relationship between the organization's employment level and some criterion known to be related to employment. For example, most companies can establish a statistical relationship between sales or work output and level of employment. Such a relationship, however, is also influenced by the learning curve. Learning curves can be used to make more accurate projections of future employment levels. More complicated quantitative methods involving multiple regression and linear programming further this process by incorporating operational constraints (e.g., budgets, mix of labor) into the mathematical models. Through this elaboration, it is possible to forecast demand under varying business scenarios. Multiple regression may use several factors that correlate with labor needs. For example, in preparation for its collective bargaining negotiations, General Motors used several different sales figures, gross national product, gross domestic product, capital investments, and other factors to forecast labor needs for the next six years. GM used historical data that statistically related each factor to labor demands. Future demand was then forecasted based on current data on each of the factors.

While our discussion of labor demand may suggest that planners attempt to establish a singular forecast, the outcome of this process is typically a set of potential scenarios. A scenario is a multifaceted portrayal of the mix of business factors in conjunction with the array of HR needs. As such, each scenario/forecast is an elaborate set of "if–then" statements; that is, "if" the business context presents us with scenario A, "then" our labor demand forecast would be B. Ideally, HR planning is as comprehensive as possible to provide leeway for a variety of business activities. Next, we discuss labor supply forecasts that reveal some constraints placed on business planning.

Step Three: Labor Supply Forecast

Whereas the labor demand forecast projects HR needs, the labor supply forecast projects resource availability.

This step of HR planning is vital in that it conveys an inventory of the firm's current and projected competencies. This skill base sets an upper limit on the commitments and challenges the firm can undertake (all else being equal). From a problem-solving perspective, labor supply represents the raw materials available to address threats and opportunities. Supply forecasts are typically broken down into two categories: external supply and internal supply.

INTERNAL SUPPLY. Internal labor supply consists of those individuals and jobs currently available within the firm. Data from personnel/skill inventories are used to make projections for the future based on current trends. These trends include not only the number and kinds of individuals in each job, but also the flow of employees into, through, and out of the organization. Specifically, a skills inventory includes an assessment of the knowledge, skills, abilities, experience, and career aspirations of each worker. This record should be updated at least every two years and should include changes such as new skills, degree completions, and changed job duties. These inventories also aid in the internal recruitment process. If these skills inventories are not updated, present employees may be overlooked for job openings within the organization.[14] This may result in increased search costs in addition to dissatisfaction among employees who were overlooked. Accordingly, internal supply forecasts must consider the company's current practices pertaining to hiring, firing, transfer, promotion, development, and attrition. The performance-appraisal system of the organization should be part of any personnel/ skill inventory.

AT&T applied the skill inventory approach as part of its huge 1996 downsizing. Current employees were asked to prepare résumés indicating job experiences and accomplishments. The résumés were then evaluated for abilities and generic skill factors such as leadership and teamwork. The résumés of AT&T employees who opted out of a generous buyout package were then compared in a roundtable meeting of senior executives in each department. Survivors of this process were then assigned to their jobs. As Adele Ambrose, an AT&T spokesperson, put it, "The idea is that everybody is being asked to step out into the parking lot."

Succession planning and replacement charts are also used by some companies to identify individuals to fill a given slot if an incumbent should leave. These techniques are most useful for individual-level problems with short-term planning time horizons.

More than 300 computerized human resource information systems (HRIS) are now available, many of which include skill inventories. The General Electric Company and Dun & Bradstreet, for example, have used electronic data files on employees for years as an aid for internal promotions and for required EEO reports. Pratt

& Whitney used an HRIS system to project successions, early retirements, future openings, and overstaffing problems. Figure 5.4 presents some sample elements of a skills inventory.

Two of the most important concerns regarding the use of electronic databases for personnel are privacy rights and security problems. The latter issue can be handled with the right systems and software provisions. The privacy issue is much more difficult. Many states and the federal government have privacy laws that may pertain to the use, content, and access of a HRIS.

More complicated transition models such as Markov analysis are used for long-range forecasts in large companies. Markov analysis uses historical information from personnel movements of the internal labor supply to predict what will happen in the future. An estimate is made of the likelihood that persons in a particular job will remain in that job or be transferred, promoted, demoted, terminated, or retired using data collected over a number of years. Probabilities are used to represent the historical flow of personnel through the organization, a "transition matrix" is formed from these probabilities, and future personnel flows are estimated from this matrix.[15] Figure 5.5 presents Markov data from

FIGURE 5.4
SAMPLE ELEMENTS IN SKILLS INVENTORY

Screen 1:   Current employee data

Name:
SS #:
Department:
Position:
Supervisor:
Date in position:
Date of hire:

Screen 2:   Education data

	School Attended	Degree	Major	GPA	Year(s)
High school:					
Undergrad:					
Graduate:					
Doctorate:					

Additional course work:
Certifications/licenses:
Additional training:
Company training:

Additional training recommended:

Screen 3:   Company employment data

	Title	Date in Job	Performance Ratings/Dates
Present position:			
Previous positions:			

Positions in company qualified for:

Screen 4:   Previous employment data

	Company	Title	From	To	Reference Quality
Prev. Empl.					
Prev. Empl.					
Prev. Empl.					
Prev. Empl.					

Screen 5:   Express interests/goals

Areas of company:
Positions:
Additional training/education:

Source: Heneman, H. G., Heneman, R. L. & Judge, T. A. (1997). *Staffing organizations,* Burr Ridge, IL: Irwin, p. 336. Reprinted with permission.

FIGURE 5.5
MARKOV ANALYSIS AT PROGRESSIVE INDUSTRIES

		A	M	F	S	EXIT
Assemblers (A)		.70	.10			.20
Machinists (M)		.05	.80	.10		.05
Foreman (F)			.10	.75	.05	.10
Supervision (S)				.05	.90	.05

	STAFFING LEVELS	A	M	F	S	EXIT
Assemblers (A)	250	175	25			50
Machinists (M)	120	6	96	12		6
Foremen (F)	40		4	30	2	4
Supervision (S)	20			1	18	1
Forecast		181	125	43	20	61

one division of Progressive Industries, one of the largest tool companies serving the domestic automotive industry (Progressive designs and manufactures the tooling for assembly lines). The transition probability matrix presents percentages or probabilities of employee movement through four positions within the division. These data were retrieved from personnel records and averaged over a five-year period. The matrix shows that 70 percent of the assemblers remain in the position after one year with a turnover (quit or fired) rate of 20 percent. The matrix also shows that 80 percent of the more skilled machinist jobs are retained after one year with only a 5 percent turnover rate. These data were used by Progressive to plan its recruiting strategy based on projected contracts. The data indicated a strong need to evaluate the assembler job to determine the causes of the high turnover rate and the need to concentrate recruiting at that level in anticipation of shortages of assemblers in the coming year when contracts were expected to expand.

Both Eaton Corporation[16] and Weyerhaeuser[17] have used Markov analysis successfully in their forecasts. However, two experiences at Corning Glass proved unsuccessful because the transition probabilities were unreliable.[18] A minimum of 50 people in each job of the transition matrix is recommended to ensure adequate reliability in forecasting. At Progressive, for example, projections for oversupplies of foremen were based on small numbers and proved to be relatively inaccurate. More research is needed on Markov analysis to determine the key variables affecting its accuracy. Variables such as unemployment rate, changes in competitor status and business plans, or customer demand that differ significantly from when the probabilities were established will have a profound effect on the usefulness of the Markov projections.

EXTERNAL SUPPLY. External supply consists of those individuals in the labor force who are potential recruits of the firm (including those working for another firm). The skill levels being sought determine the relevant labor market. The entire country (or world) may be the relevant labor market for highly skilled jobs whereas for unskilled jobs, the relevant labor market is usually the local community. Determining the relevant labor market will also determine what type of recruiting approach should be used. Several governmental and industrial reports (e.g., Bureau of Labor Statistics, Public Health Service, Northwestern Endicott Lindquist Report) regularly forecast the supply of labor and estimate available workers in general job and demographic categories. These forecasts are also extrapolations into the future based on current trends.

COMPUTER MODELING. Computers are used in the most sophisticated forecasting approaches. Various mathematical formulas are used in computer models that simultaneously use extrapolation, indexation, survey results, and estimates of employment changes to compute future human resource needs. Over time the computer's formulas are refined with actual changes in human resource demand. Computer modeling for the most part is found only among large organizations with years of experience in human resource planning.[19] Our armed forces probably have the most sophisticated computer modeling approaches to planning and recruitment in employment today. AT&T used computer modeling as part of its HR planning in 1996 to forecast employment needs and develop different scenarios for meeting the needs. The package of incentives for early retirement along with plant closings and other actions were derived from a careful analysis of various options via computer modeling.

Some federal agencies also use computer modeling. The IRS, plagued for years by shortages of auditors and accountants, relies on a computer model to develop college recruiting plans.

Step Four: Gap Analysis

As we discussed in Chapter 2, gap analysis is used to reconcile the forecasts of labor demand and supply. At a minimum, this process identifies potential shortages or surpluses of employees, skills, and jobs. In addition, however, planners can juxtapose several environmental forecasts with alternative supply and demand forecasts to determine the firm's preparedness for different business scenarios. From a problem-solving perspective, gap analysis is used to pair up potential strengths and opportunities with solutions in order to evaluate how the firm might attack the future. This decision-making process involves (1) a search for alternative solutions, (2) an evaluation of alternatives, and (3) a choice of solutions.

IS THERE AN OPTIMAL WAY TO DOWNSIZE?

This type of gap analysis has been used in employee downsizing or reengineering programs for a majority of the *Fortune* 1000 and even some of the most successful and profitable. More than 85 percent of the Fortune 1000 firms downsized their white-collar staff between 1987 and 1996 (more than 30 percent downsized in 1996 alone).[20] The evidence on the effects of downsizing is mixed. However, one of the most recent studies showed that the track records of the 10 largest downsizers between 1990 and 1995 showed a 29 percent reduction in employees while productivity surged by 28 percent. When compared to the 1.5 percent per year productivity improvement for the economy as a whole the 5.6 percent improvement from these 10 companies is impressive. Figure 5.6 presents a summary of the study.

One study of the U.S. auto industry identified the processes used in effective white-collar downsizing.[21] Six general strategies were identified as most predictive of effective downsizing. Figure 5.7 presents a summary of the findings. *Effectiveness* in downsizing in the study was defined as improvements in productivity, product or service quality, and employee morale following the downsizing effort.

Most of the companies had implemented downsizing as a reaction to a loss of market share, increased competition, or lower productivity. Most also looked at downsizing as simply a workforce reduction process rather than a restructuring or reengineering of jobs in the context of corporate strategy or planning. As one CEO put it, "We lost the organization in the process . . . we basically fired people and called it reengineering . . . we jumped on the reengineering bandwagon without under-

FIGURE 5.6
SHRINKING PAYROLLS AND RISING PRODUCTIVITY: TOP 10 CORPORATE JOB CUTTERS

	PERCENT CHANGE 1990 TO 1995	
	IN EMPLOYEES	IN PRODUCTIVITY*
Digital Equipment	−50.2%	+82.0%
McDonnell Douglas	−47.5	+43.2
General Electric	−25.5	+38.0
KMart	−32.4	+37.1
GTE	−31.2	+35.3
IBM	−32.5	+32.5
General Motors	−6.9	+23.4
General Dynamics	−71.7	+5.7
Boeing	−35.1	−6.6
Sears	−40.2	−9.8
10-Company Total	−29.1	+27.9

* Real (inflation-adjusted) sales per employee
Source: Federal Reserve Bank of Dallas

FIGURE 5.7
STRATEGIES FOR EFFECTIVE DOWNSIZING

The most effective downsizing:

1. Was implemented by command from the top-down but initiated and managed from the bottom-up.
2. Was short-term and across-the-board but also long-term and focused.
3. Paid special attention to terminated employees and those who survived.
4. Was targeted inside the firm but also included the external network (e.g., contractors, subcontractors).
5. Resulted in small semi-autonomous units within larger organizations as well as strong centralized functions.
6. Emphasized downsizing as a means to an end but also as the targeted end.

Source: K. S. Cameron, S. J. Freeman, and A. K. Mishra (1991). Best practices in white collar downsizing: Managing contradictions. *Academy of Management Executive, 5,* 57–63. Reprinted with permission.

standing its destination." Another CEO was even more disillusioned with job cutting posing as reengineering. "We cut costs, ruined quality, and eliminated more customers than employees . . . Reengineering has replaced strategic thinking around here."

The most effective reengineering efforts are an opportunity to create or improve the company's competitive advantage through restructuring, overhead reduction, and more effective performance management with constant focus on the core competencies of the organization and the current and/or future customer base. The process can create a frame of mind that can be sustained after the major downsizing is complete. The idea is to create and maintain a "lean and mean" mentality in management that will be sustained long after the specific downsizing goals are met and always in the context of meeting (or exceeding) customer requirements with measurement criteria that best define this customer focus. Reengineering that focuses on the core competencies of the organization and the core business and its customers can help support a clear and compelling organizational strategy. But as strategy expert Darrell Rigby puts it, "Cutting people whose experience is vital to the creation of customer value will never create superior results."

Over 65,000 IBM employees have taken early retirement since the company's first major downsizing in 1988. While the program helped IBM maintain its company policy of never laying off a full-time employee, IBM lost some of its best employees who opted for an attractive termination program. The 1991 downsizing program focused on offering early retirement to only noncritical employees, terminating marginal employees for cause, and offering less attractive transfer options to those who are not needed in their current jobs. One of IBM's biggest problems in achieving its downsizing goals, however, was its performance-appraisal system, which did not provide enough useful data to make performance-based actions.

AT&T "selected" current employees for the new positions based on new job descriptions created by the overhaul of divisions. The skilled-based résumés and the performance appraisals of the "applicants" for the new jobs were assessed in the context of the projected labor demands based on the new corporate strategy. Voluntary buyouts were one option AT&T used to close the gap in its supply and demand for labor.

A 1996 survey of 1,600 chief executives and senior managers by Bain and Company, a Boston-based strategy firm, found that executives viewed customer focus as the framework for downsizing.[22] This focus included increasing an understanding of customer needs, increasing the customer base, and increasing product and service quality. Of course, the relationship between labor costs and pricing is almost always on the top of the list in terms of customer focus. But the list must be longer than just cutting payroll to save money.

Downsizing that is not done in the context of this customer focus will merely exchange old problems for new ones. Many firms that have gone through radical downsizing in recent years have come to realize how important the connection is between customer needs and any form of organizational restructuring, including downsizing.

Pratt & Whitney conducted a strategic job analysis and redesign of its organizational structure, determined labor shortages and excesses, and conducted special performance assessments to identify the most qualified incumbents for the reengineered company after defining its future customer requirements.

In Chapter 2 we discussed GM's successful reengineering goals for 1996. GM's costs were $440 higher per vehicle than Ford and $600 more than Chrysler in 1996. The main reason was that GM purchased fewer car parts from cheaper outside vendors than did its main competitors. As a result of this competitive disadvantage, GM sought (and received) concessions from the United Auto Workers in the 1996 contract. GM also looked at other approaches to reducing labor costs, including reducing the number of engineers involved in car design. Downsizing should always be considered as one option among many in strategic HRM planning.

As indicated in Figure 5.7, some problems associated with downsizing (or rightsizing) can be minimized with good planning and strategy. In addition to examining performance data and redeployment options, such planning may include *outplacement* services for employees who have lost their jobs. Outplacement can involve job coaching, résumé preparation, placement services, and interview training. Every AT&T employee who was not selected for the restructured company was given access to a resource center that provided job counseling and access to job postings within the company and at other companies. Such outplacement services are now available in Europe and even in Japan where Japanese companies are faced with a need to downsize as well. It is generally believed that offering outplacement services to employees who have lost their jobs will reduce the probability of a lawsuit, such as a claim of age discrimination. (There is no definitive study on the subject.)

In 1996, Manpower Inc., the nation's largest temporary employment agency, merged with Drake Beam, the largest outplacement service. The goal is to get terminated employees at least temporary work as soon as possible. The report card so far on this new marriage is positive. Drake Beam reports that outplaced professionals are finding satisfying work faster than before the merger.

WHAT ARE SOME ALTERNATIVE OR ADDITIONAL SOLUTIONS BASED ON THE SWOT ANALYSIS? As discussed above, in HRP there are likely to be multiple scenarios worthy of consideration. Environmental scanning and labor forecasts identify a range of possible options. HR planners must exercise their ingenuity to create a range of possible solutions based on the SWOT analysis. At this stage, the range of possibilities can be increased by seeking input from executives, line managers, employees, customers, and consultants in a "brainstorming" process. A qualitative approach such as Delphi can be used at this point as well.

As part of its HR planning process and after a thorough job analysis, the Upjohn Corporation asks line managers to answer four basic questions:

1. How does each job relate to the strategic plan of the work unit?
2. Are there alternatives to a full-time job that should be considered to accomplish the same objectives (e.g., temporary workers, part-time employees, employee leasing, consultants, contract, overtime)?
3. What are the projected costs of each job?
4. What impact will the job have on critical and clearly defined effectiveness criteria?

WHAT IS THE ROLE OF TEMPORARY EMPLOYMENT? More and more companies have been asking similar questions regarding their workforce and coming up with creative answers. One of the strongest trends in this country is the use of labor that is not full time. Temporary employment, part-time workers, job sharing, and employee leasing are among the most popular solutions to controlling labor costs and responding to fluctuating demand. For example, employee leasing gained popularity with small companies after passage of the Tax Equity and Fiscal Responsibility Act (TEFRA), which formally recognized this employment arrangement. With employee leasing, a leasing company assumes responsibility for the employee, including pay and benefits. Omnistaff, Inc., the largest U.S. leasing company with over 1,500 corporate clients and 16,000 employees, has had a 20 percent growth rate since 1985. The major advantages of employee leasing are a savings in pension benefits, sizable tax breaks, and reduced administrative costs. Employees can benefit as well because the leasing company can offer a better package due to group discounts for insurance. The major disadvantage for the employer is a loss in some control over the employee.[23] This loss of control could affect the effectiveness of employees' performance, which could have a direct impact on the customer. No studies compare the performance, productivity, absence rates, or any other criteria for permanent versus leased employees. In fact, no study even shows the clear cost savings to a leasing program.

More employees are also hiring temporary help, particularly in clerical data processing and industrial jobs. The National Association of Temporary Services reported a growth rate in temporary employment in excess of 30 percent through the 1990s. While employers generally report that temporaries are typically hired for emergencies, an increasing number of companies report considerable cost savings as well with "temps" judged to be as productive as permanent employees.[24]

A more significant trend in creative HR planning is the use of permanent part-time employees.[25] For years, IBM's policy of maintaining a 10 percent part-time workforce enabled the company to maintain a labor pool in line with the business cycle and to preserve its policy of no layoffs. It has now increased the percentage to 20 percent and outsourced many functions, including a large share of the HRM functions. Many other companies, particularly in service, are following suit. Digital Corporation, Federal Express, Ryder Truck, and UPS, are among the major companies now maintaining a sizable percentage of their workforce with part-time status. According to the Bureau of Labor Statistics, 28 percent of the U.S. workforce worked part time in 1996. Two-thirds of this group were women. While working parents consider the part-time employment a good thing, women's groups such as the National Organization for Women decry the trend as fostering a marginal employment policy characterized by low wages and no benefits. Companies that have adopted policies of permanent part-time staff for many job classifications report substantial cost savings and relatively little difficulty in recruiting and retaining a capable staff.

Another alternative to deal with the increasing diversity of the workforce is job sharing. Job sharing divides a single job into two or more workers. American Express has adopted this policy for its customer service

representatives and reduced employee turnover and recruitment costs significantly.

IS THERE A CONFLICT BETWEEN DOWNSIZING AND DIVERSITY GOALS?   One complicated issue regarding a major downsizing is the potential conflict between downsizing efforts and programs aimed at promoting workforce diversity. Ciba-Geigy, the huge pharmaceutical company, had a diversity challenge as part of its retention process. In assessing employee performance, managers were asked to value a diverse organization by "proactively considering diversity in this process." After the initial retention decisions are made, "HR challengers will review retention decisions with respect to diversity . . . and to test for adverse impact." HR compared diversity data after the initial retention decisions to pre-downsizing data. According to documents in a lawsuit, "The result of this analysis may lead to a possible further challenge." Several older Ciba-Geigy employees who were fired maintained that the "diversity challenges" resulted in discrimination against older workers because they were not part of the diversity programs. Given the current state of EEO law regarding preferential treatment, if the plaintiffs could show that race or gender were considered in the retention process and that this consideration affected the status of older workers, would the older workers prevail in an ADEA case? This is a tough call and would probably depend on the process that was followed after the internal audit. If the plaintiff could show that performance ratings were simply changed because of statistical adverse impact and changed in such a way as to avoid the adverse impact and that this process changed the status of some workers over the age of 39, the older workers would probably prevail.

AT&T apparently conducted a similar type of analysis before it made final decisions regarding whom to retain in its 1996 downsizing. After the well-controlled "roundtable" discussions we described earlier and ratings of the job candidates, an analysis of the EEO impact of the "draft" decisions was conducted and legal counsel was sought.

Organizations that undergo downsizing while attempting to maintain any diversity or affirmative action accomplishments should try to avoid showing preferential treatment on the basis of any protected class characteristic. It is possible (and advisable) to evaluate past performance or even potential performance without even considering a protected class characteristic. While conducting adverse impact analysis such as hypothetical violations of the 80 percent rule is recommended, violations of the guidelines should lead to a serious evaluation of the job relatedness of the decision-making system, not the simple adjustment in ratings as a consequence of a protected class characteristic in order to avoid a violation of the 80 percent rule.

Step Five: Action Programming

Action programming is the final step of HRP that lays out the events that need to be executed to realize the HR plan. In the previous four steps of HR planning, the task was to derive a solution that best addresses the SWOTs identified through environmental scanning and labor forecasts. Action programming makes certain that those decisions become reality. In general, there are two aspects of programming: internal and external.

INTERNAL PROGRAMMING. Many of the solutions in HRP rest on actions inside the firm with the current workforce. For routine SWOTs, in particular, bureaucratic adjustments in HR practices can be easily programmed internally (e.g., job design/assignments). GM's action regarding its engineers is one example. In addition, for some uncertain areas identified in the SWOT analysis, adaptive adjustments such as training, career planning, promotions, and compensation design can be made internally. These are the adaptive requirements many companies are now following because of labor shortages in key areas. Taking a closer look at organizational design around changing technologies is one such example.

EXTERNAL PROGRAMMING. Other solutions in HRP require going outside the firm to interact with constituencies in the environment (e.g., labor unions, competitors, etc.). In particular, when HR plans require drastically different skills from what employees currently possess and/or the time frame for change is quite short, the firm will likely need to recruit from the outside labor market. Motorola's experience with the coordinated efforts of U.S. and Asian programmers is one example of reacting to new time frames. GM's negotiation with its unions regarding the outsourcing of certain parts is another example.

Step Six: Control and Evaluation

Control and evaluation monitor the effectiveness of human resource plans over time. Deviations from the plan are identified and actions are taken. The extent to which human resource objectives have been met is provided by the feedback resulting from the outcomes of human resources planning. Essentially it has been suggested that long-range planning activities require the attainment of short-run objectives. Examples include performance or productivity data, turnover costs, workforce reduction effects from early retirement programs, breakeven costs of new hires, and analysis of costs of recruits compared to the training and development costs of existing employees. Obviously, actual staffing levels compared to projected levels should be evaluated for accuracy. Doing evaluations such as cost-benefit analysis make it easier to determine whether long-run planning objectives will be met.

The issue of evaluation in planning can be considered along with the evaluation of recruitment efforts since the criteria used for the evaluation are often the same. We will discuss this vital step to both effective planning and recruitment later in the chapter. The critical consideration here should be identification of the vital measurement criteria that will provide for an assessment of the HR planning implementation in the context of the business strategy.

When HR planning involves adding to the labor force, the organization must rely on the recruitment function to meet its employment needs. The point of the planning exercise is to provide the optimal number and quality of employees to meet internal and external customer requirements. If the gap analysis determines that employees are needed, that is where recruitment comes in. We will deal with this vital HR function next.

THE RECRUITMENT FUNCTION: PUTTING HRP INTO ACTION

Moving from HRP to recruitment is essentially a process of translating broad strategies into operational tasks. The major responsibility for this process typically rests within the HRM department, although most tasks are shared with line managers. While HR managers are responsible for determining recruitment policy, ensuring EEO compliance, and training and evaluating the recruiters, many organizations such as Xerox, IBM, and Procter & Gamble actively involve line managers and employees as recruiters. As mentioned above, conflict between HR and line managers can occur when their priorities diverge. For example, line managers may be more concerned about filling a position quickly (i.e., when the new employee is needed) while HR managers may be more concerned about affirmative action guidelines or complying with EEO regulations. Their goals should be the same: Hiring the most qualified person(s) when needed and without violating any laws or regulations.

Figure 5.8 presents a simplified model of the recruitment process.

Recruitment and Other HR Activities

Recall our earlier statement about the interdependent nature of recruiting and other HR activities. Decisions regarding employee testing, work policies and programs, compensation, and corporate image can all have a profound effect on recruiting. For example, one large retailer required high-level managerial candidates to travel to the company headquarters (for some, over 2,000 miles) to go through a two-day assessment center that was offered only at headquarters. Because of these requirements, many experienced managers who were working for other companies dropped out of the pool of

FIGURE 5.8
A SIMPLIFIED MODEL OF THE RECRUITMENT PROCESS

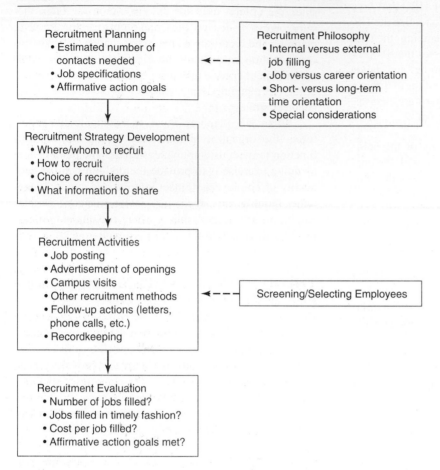

Source: Adapted from *Recruitment: Science and Practice* by James Breaugh. Copyright © 1992 PWS-Kent Publishing. By permission of South-Western College Publishing, a division of International Thomson Publishing Inc., Cincinnati, Ohio 45227.

candidates because they didn't have the time to commit to a two-day assessment center with two additional days of travel. The 2,900 room Opryland Hotel in Nashville had difficulty attracting housekeepers, kitchen helpers, and laundry workers. It instituted seven-day-a-week child care and bus service to transport workers. The two new employee benefits increased the number of applicants by 35 percent.

One university spent over $5,000 advertising for a faculty position and another $4,000 inviting candidates to the campus for one day of interviews. When only two faculty members showed up for one candidate's presentation, the candidate's negative impression of the faculty's collegiality led to her decision to reject the job offer.

A company institutes a comprehensive drug testing program that includes random drug testing with no probable cause for all employees. The company assumes the policy will only have an impact by deterring applicants who would be most likely to use drugs. Another company installs a binding arbitration policy for all employee-employer disputes. A new employee must sign

off on the policy as a condition of employment. Once again, the company does not consider the effect of this new policy on the ability to recruit and retain the most qualified applicants. Another company decides to reduce indirect compensation by reducing health benefits for new employees and increasing the premium. It has no idea what the change in policy will do to its ability to recruit. The company finds out later that recruitment costs have gone up along with the rate of offer rejections. It finally conducts an actual cost-benefit study of the change in policy and discovers the company lost money because of the interactive effect of the policy on staffing and the retention of valuable employees. Recruitment, selection, and personnel policies are indeed interdependent.

Three Essential Steps for Recruitment Planning

Based on the HR plan (more specifically, the gap analysis), the organization has a fairly good idea of its overall recruitment or downsizing needs. However, this information must be operationalized and communicated to others who will be taking the action. Three essential steps for translating future needs into specific operational terms are (1) job analysis, (2) time lapse data, and (3) yield ratio.

JOB ANALYSIS.   Recruiters and HR planners rely on two aspects of job analysis information to identify the critical skills for which they will recruit. First, job descriptions provide an outline of the responsibilities, duties, and tasks to be performed by the potential employee. Second, the job specifications outline the *KASOCs* required of the applicant. In general, the more specific the recruitment design, especially in terms of job specifications, the more efficient and effective it is, assuming the specificity is important for the job. Poorly designed recruiting is more expensive and takes longer.[26]

For example, sometimes job specifications are not essential for the job and are unnecessary and costly. One retailer stipulated five years of experience as a district manager to be eligible for consideration as a district manager for the company. One retail manager made this decision unilaterally based on his "sense" of what was required in the job. The result was a small pool of applicants, higher advertising costs, and fewer females and minorities who were eligible for consideration.

Job analysis information that accurately reflects the requirements needed for the job can have a direct impact on the effectiveness of any recruitment and planning effort. Job analysis information can also be used in a downsizing as jobs are restructured based on the new organizational structure. As we discussed in Chapter 4, specific job analysis strategies are available for writing job descriptions and specifications based on an organization's competitive strategy. AT&T and Pratt & Whitney followed this process as part of their downsizing/cost-reduction methods. The information required on the résumés of all AT&T employees was based on a job analysis that had identified the core competencies AT&T needed for its new organizational structure.

PAS had to write job descriptions for the new positions related to its international expansion interests and the plan to mass market one of its tests. The focus had to be on describing the end product or outcomes for the new positions since PAS was unsure what was entailed in the marketing of its products. The company obviously needed help in the environmental scan to determine whether it should expand into these new areas.

While HRP provides the number of jobs needed and job analysis provides the requirements of the jobs, management must know when to start a recruiting process and how extensive the search should be. This is where time lapse data and yield ratios come in.

TIME LAPSE DATA.   Time lapse data (TLD) provide the average time that elapses between points of decision making in recruiting. For example, if the recruitment plan calls for newspaper advertisements, records may reflect that the job is filled an average of two months after publication of the ad. Thus, the ad should be placed at least two months before the job has to be filled. Data may also be available on the time lapse between interviews and offers and offers and acceptances. When combined with yield ratios, the TLD can provide useful information for planning a recruitment effort.

Time lapse data has been reduced for companies taking advantage of the automated recruiting options available through the World Wide Web. For example, a database known as "Career Taxi" (WWW @ http://www.iquest.net/Career_Taxi/taxi.html) provides on-line services for both job hunters and job employers. Recruiters that use the service report shorter time lapses with no loss in candidate quality. There are now over 20 recruiting Web sites, some of which are narrowly focused on particular jobs or occupations or industries (e.g., nursing, professors, health care, computer technology) to further reduce the time lapse.

Some of the country's largest newspapers now have a job listings service on the Internet. One service is known as CareerPath.com (http://www.careerpath.com) and provides access to the combined classified ads of six papers, which include the *Chicago Tribune,* the *Boston Globe,* the *New York Times,* and the *Washington Post.* This service is particularly valuable for professionals. (See Critical Thinking Exercise 5.1.)

YIELD RATIOS.   A yield ratio for any recruiting step reflects the number of candidates available at a step and the next step. For example, a series of newspaper ads may result in 1,000 applications for employment. Of these 1,000 applications, 100 are judged to meet some minimum qualifications. Thus, the yield ratio at this initial stage is 10 percent. Of the group of 100 candidates, 50 accepted invitations to be interviewed (yield ratio is 50 percent for this stage and 5 percent as the cumulative yield ratio); of the 50, 10 were given job offers (20 percent yield ratio; 1 percent cumulative). Assuming the labor market has not changed dramatically from when the yield ratio was derived and that similar methods of recruiting are to be used (e.g., advertising in the same papers, using a Web site or a headhunter), this ratio can then be used as the basis for planning future recruitment efforts. By going backward from the yield ratio, the recruiter can estimate how many applicants will be necessary to fill a certain number of positions. The recruiter can then adjust the recruiting effort accordingly with more (or less) advertising, more (or fewer) trips to college campuses, and so on.

DISCREPANCY BETWEEN ACADEMIC RESEARCH AND PRACTICE.   The use of time lapse data and yield ratios is another area where there is a wide gap between what academic texts and scholarly research recommend and the extent to which such data drive recruitment planning. While almost every scholar on the subject recommends a recruitment evaluation process to assist decision makers in efficient recruitment planning, few companies actually collect the data as part of recruitment evaluation.

Recruitment is a never-ending process for many jobs where there are critical shortages of highly specialized skills. As we discussed above, there are tight labor markets for many occupations today and strong indications that markets will get even tighter, particularly for knowledge-intensive jobs. Many hospitals recruit for nurses on a continuous basis because they are constantly understaffed. Advertisements for nurses often promise not only high pay, but also more of a say in their jobs and hospital management, bonuses of $3,000 or more for signing up, bonuses for staying on the job a certain length of time, flexible work schedules, child care, and free tuition for advanced courses. Some employers even offer maid service and free housing for nurses who are willing to work at various locations based on demand. Many high-tech manufacturing firms recruit for engineers and computer programmers year round as well.

Some companies have difficulty filling even unskilled positions. Fast food retailers, for example, beset by turnover rates in excess of 300 percent (three incumbents for every job in one year), often advertise and take applications for counter personnel throughout the year for many locations. Many companies have mobile recruiting units that visit high schools and shopping malls to solicit applications. McDonald's cooperates with the American Association of Retired Persons to attract senior citizens for hard-to-fill counter-personnel positions. AMC Theaters also concentrates on senior citizens for its ticket takers and counter personnel. Chemical Bank in New York must interview 50 applicants to find one person who can be successfully trained as a teller. In general, the changing demographics of our workforce and the changing nature of the demands of the work indicate that recruitment will be more challenging in the years to come. As one expert put it, "Until the economy stabilizes, salaries are raised in many areas of health care and education, and our school systems improve, human resource professionals will continue to be faced with the current crisis in employee recruitment."[27] The shortage of unskilled labor may end with the changes to the U.S. welfare system that were instituted in 1997 and 1998.

Internal Recruitment Sources

There are two general sources of recruiting: internal and external. Internal recruiting seeks applicants for positions from among the ranks of those currently employed. With the exception of entry-level positions, most organizations try to fill positions with current employee.[28]

There are three major advantages to internal recruiting. First, it is considerably less costly than external recruiting. Second, organizations typically have a better knowledge of internal applicants' skills and abilities than that which can be acquired of candidates in an external recruiting effort. Through performance appraisal and other sources of information about current personnel, decision makers will typically have much more extensive knowledge of internal candidates and thus make more valid selection decisions. The third advantage to internal recruiting is that an organizational policy of promoting from within can enhance organizational commitment and job satisfaction. These variables have been shown to be correlated with lower employee turnover rates and higher productivity. Ted LeVino, senior vice president at GE, argues that GE's internal recruiting policy has fostered stability and continuity in the managerial ranks. NationsBank has a policy in which newly hired college graduates receive a career planning guide that describes the typical timetable for progression within the company for the best employees.

One advantage of detailed job analysis is that succession planning programs can be developed so that management (and employees) can have a good idea of the sources for internal recruiting. At Ford, for example, associates complete a competency-based job analysis describing their current knowledge and skills required for their present job and what knowledge or skills they would like to acquire. These responses are then linked to vacancies within the company, descriptions of which have already been completed by managers of the vacant positions.

There are disadvantages to internal recruiting as well. Continuity is not always such a good thing. If the organization has decided to change its business strategy, for example, entrenched managers are probably not the "change masters" you want. One theory of internal recruiting is that the approach simply promulgates the old ways of doing things; creative problem solving may be hindered by the lack of new blood or a sort of "managerial in-breeding."

One well-documented managerial blunder is to irrationally stay committed to an initial course of action, particularly if you initiated the action. Irrational commitment, misdirected persistence, and **escalation bias** are much more likely when internal versus external recruiting is emphasized.[29] For example, one U.S. company faced new competition to an established product line from a foreign competitor. The senior managers, all of whom had been at the company for at least 15 years and had great ownership in the product and how it was marketed, agreed to deal with the new competition as they had always dealt with competition, by competing on price. This manner was unfortunately out of step with the upstart competitor's strategy, which included competing on price. The result was a disaster for the U.S.

company with over 30 percent of the workforce laid off because of a loss of market share. A new manager may have been more able to conduct a more rational analysis of the situation.

Entrenched managers sometimes have difficulty understanding that time and money already invested are "sunk costs" and should not be considered in planning. Managers who had something to do with a present course of action seem to have more difficulty in understanding this.

Some organizations complain of unit raiding where divisions may compete for the same people. GM, for example, reported raiding of the best design engineers from one division to another despite an agreement that such recruiting was not in the best interests of the company. Raiding is common in universities for clerical positions where position descriptions can be written in such a way that a secretary can move to another department for a higher salary.

A third possible disadvantage of internal recruiting is that politics probably has a greater impact on internal recruiting and selection than it does on external recruiting. Thus, while more job-related information may be known about internal candidates, personnel decisions involving internal candidates are more likely to be affected by the political agendas of the decision makers. One survey of high-level federal government managers revealed that the easiest way to get rid of a troublesome employee was to evaluate that employee so positively that the employee would be more likely to get an employment opportunity out of the unit (either within or outside the agency). The Peter Principle states that we rise to our level of incompetence. This survey found that once a person reaches his or her level of incompetence, the boss may actually try to get that person moved up a notch to get rid of him or her with the least amount of paperwork. In other words, things may be even worse than the Peter Principle.[30]

As we discussed in Chapter 4, HR managers must constantly monitor very tightly defined job descriptions or job specifications. While this may constitute well-focused recruiting based on precisely what the organization requires, it can also mean a position has been "wired" for an internal candidate. An effective HR manager should be able to make the distinction. The manager writing the job description and job specifications should be required to stipulate why highly specific credentials or areas of expertise are required in the context of the organization's or unit's strategic plan.

Internal recruiting programs must be carefully integrated with other HR functions. Effective HR succession planning, job analysis, personnel selection, and performance appraisal are all important for an effective system that can fill required positions with the most qualified personnel in the shortest time. Administrators of such programs should be knowledgeable of EEO legislation and litigation because numerous lawsuits have been filed related to internal recruiting and placement decisions. There is considerable discussion of the *glass ceiling,* the invisible barrier which prevents women and minorities from advancing to high level positions and even the "glass wall" effect which deprives women of lateral movement into critical positions such as marketing.[31]

While most large companies have formal succession plans at the managerial level, a much lower percentage of small to medium-size firms have formal systems. A job posting system can enhance the effectiveness of internal recruiting. In job posting, announcements of positions are made available to all current employees through company newsletters, bulletin boards, and so on. Surprisingly, only a small percentage of organizations have formal systems of job posting for vacant positions within the organization.[32] When properly implemented, job posting systems can substantially improve the quality of job placements and protect the organization from EEO problems. Figure 5.9 presents guidelines for effective job posting systems.

External Recruitment Sources

External recruiting concerns recruitment from outside the organization. One big advantage of external recruiting is that the approach can facilitate the introduction of new ideas and thinking into corporate decision making. The new blood comes with no ownership of past strategies, which often hinders an objective assessment of future strategy. A major disadvantage of external recruiting is that the introduction of new personnel may have a negative impact on work group cohesion and morale. Also, new personnel from outside the organization typically take longer to learn the ropes. Another possible disadvantage is that external recruiting can be very costly. For example, companies have paid in excess of $75,000 to executive search firms for locating a single, high-level manager. The Employment Management Association estimates that the average cost per hire for external recruiting of managers is now about $16,000.[33]

The Internet is already having a profound impact on the cost and the time involved in recruiting personnel. Most *Fortune* 1000 companies now post available jobs on their Web sites, and more and more skilled employees are applying for these jobs through these sites.

The final disadvantage of external recruiting is that you typically have less reliable performance data on external candidates. There is thus a need for good assessment procedures. Good assessment procedures can be costly, and bad assessment procedures can be deceptive. (Remember the survey of federal managers regarding how to be rid of incompetent employees.) Inflated letters of recommendations or confidential interviews can land a job outside the organization for a troublesome employee. (This is probably the main reason that letters of

FIGURE 5.9

Plan

    Outline details of system

    Involve the employees in planning

Determine Eligibility Requirements

    Tenure with company

    Time in present position

    Allowable number of annual bids

    Allowable number of simultaneous bids

    Lateral transfer

    Status with company

Outline Job Requirements and Content

    Job title and department

    List of specific tasks, duties, responsibilities

    List of job specifications (e.g., training, experience, education)

    Salary ranges

    Application process

    Deadlines

    Work schedule

    Format

    Affirmative action statements

Establish Employee Awareness

    Maximize employee awareness of positions

Establish Time Frames

    Time between posting and application deadline

    Time to notify applicants of hiring decisions

    Time given the superior before his or her subordinate's switching of jobs

Determine Policies for Notifying Present Supervisor

    Informed before bidding?

    Informed only if subordinate seriously considered?

    Informed only if employee selected?

Determine Applicant Review Procedures

Provide Applicant Feedback

    Notification of decision in writing

    If not hired, outline reasons

Establish an Appeals Procedure

Source: L. S. Kleiman and K. J. Clark, Recruitment: An effective job posting system. *Personnel Journal, 63,* 20, 22, 25, February 1984. Reprinted with permission.

reference have almost no validity; there may be an incentive on the part of evaluators to inflate references to move a job candidate out of an organization.)

METHODS OF EXTERNAL RECRUITING. Several methods are available for external recruitment.

Walk-ins and unsolicited applicant files. The most common and least expensive approach for candidates is direct applications where job seekers submit unsolicited material (e.g., a résumé) or simply show up in person seeking employment. Direct applications can also provide a pool of potential employees to meet future needs. While direct applications are particularly effective in filling entry-level and unskilled positions, some organizations, because of their reputations or because of their geographical locations, compile excellent pools of potential employees from direct applications for skilled positions.

We already mentioned Career Taxi on the Internet. E-Span Interactive Employment Network provides a résumé database that is accessible from several on-line service providers. The network is used by most *Fortune* 1000 companies and search firms. And don't forget about the on-line service offered by the newspapers.

The reputation of the company has a great deal to do with the usefulness and size of the pool of unsolicited applicants and résumés. Organizations such as Coca-Cola, Merck, Microsoft, GE, IBM, the *New York Times,* and Harvard University receive thousands of unsolicited applications every year. Many excellent candidates can be found in this pool. One reason companies actively campaign to make one or more of the many top 10 lists of the "best companies to work for" is because the rate of unsolicited résumés is directly related to this honor. For example, Coca-Cola reported a 15 percent increase in unsolicited résumés in 1997, which it attributed to its designation by *Fortune* magazine as America's most admired company.

Not only do unsolicited résumés reduce the cost of recruiting, but they also increase the probability of hiring the best employees. The *New York Times* has led the world in Pulitzer Prize winners for years. The paper spends very little time recruiting the future Pulitzer winners; the best writers just know where to work.

Many companies now scan résumés or applications and then conduct keyword computer searches to quickly get to a reasonable short list of candidates when positions become available. Software now exists to match fairly detailed job specifications with résumé information. The result is usually a much more efficient (and fast) recruiting effort.

Referrals. Some organizations have formal systems of employee referral for occupations with great demand. Pratt & Whitney, for example, pays current employees an $850 bonus if electrical engineers who are referred are ultimately hired and work for the company for at least one year. While formal systems of referral are more effective in attracting interested applicants, some evidence reveals that the quality of the applicants is less than that which results from an informal system of referrals. Microsoft is offering referral incentives to its employees for Internet experts of all shapes and sizes.

The extensive use of employee referrals can cause EEO problems. In *EEOC v. Detroit Edison,* the court concluded: "The practice of relying on referrals by a predominantly white workforce rather than seeking new employees in the marketplace for jobs was discriminatory."[34] Of course, this may not be a problem if the workforce is diverse to begin with, if the organization relies on other methods of recruiting as well, or if the organization offers a referral program that targets minorities and women. Coca-Cola and Disney are among the many large corporations that offer targeted referral programs, another of the recommendations from OFCCP Revised Order #4. Texaco agreed to target African-Americans in recruiting as a part of its 1997 out-of-court settlement for racial discrimination.

Advertising. A third common method for recruiting is advertising. Advertising can range from a simple classified ad to an elaborate media campaign through radio or television to attract applicants. The approach can be quite versatile in its ability to provide information about job opportunities while targeting specific labor markets in particular geographical areas. While the majority of advertising is in newspapers, many organizations go beyond the typical newspaper ads for tight labor markets. Commercials extol the virtues of starting your "career" in our armed forces (Operation Desert Storm has had a positive effect on armed forces recruiting). Xerox, Merrill Lynch, GTE, and Dow Chemical also use television to attract applicants for hard-to-fill positions. One survey found that 88 percent of surveyed companies used newspaper ads to fill positions. Another 40 percent advertised in trade or professional journals.[35]

Employer advertising is common on the World Wide Web. "Career Magazine," for example, includes employer profiles, interactive discussion groups, and a directory of executive recruiters. Employers can place ads for specific jobs right on the Web site (see http://www.careermag.com/careermag/). Another excellent place for advertising professional jobs is "CareerMosaic." This Web site lists jobs by title, duties, and job specifications (see http://www.careermosaic.com).

Most experts agree that advertising through any media (including the Internet) should contain the following information:

1. The job content (primary tasks and responsibilities).
2. A realistic description of working conditions, particularly if they are unusual.
3. The location of the job.
4. The compensation, including the fringe benefits.

5. Job specifications (e.g., education, experience).
6. To whom one applies.[36]

Since advertising can be very expensive, record-keeping on the successes of the various media sources can help to identify the approaches with the biggest potential payoff for future recruiting. Figure 5.10 presents a summary of some of the advantages and disadvantages of the various media options. In general, while advertising or job listings on a Web site are relatively cheap, we don't know how effective they are in attracting qualified applicants.

EEO considerations are also critical for advertising. A men's clothing retailer decided to target younger men with its new fall line. As part of that effort, it advertised for "young, energetic" assistant managers at the same time it was firing a 48-year-old man who had been with the company for 10 years. An ADEA lawsuit resulted in an out-of-court settlement in excess of $100,000. Obviously, a person knowledgeable about EEO laws should review all ad copy for potential legal problems.

There are several excellent outlets for targeted advertising to minorities and women. CareerWeb, on the World Wide Web, includes company profiles, short descriptions of diversity/affirmative action programs, and information on where to apply. Most highly regarded African-American universities have Web sites that post résumés of new graduates. Many universities place their ads in the newspaper *Black Issues* in an effort to attract more minority applicants.

Employment agencies. Employment agencies are used by many companies for identifying potential workers. Publicly funded agencies provide free placement services, and private agencies charge either the employee or the employer for a placement or referral. These agencies increase the pool of possible applicants and do preliminary screening. Private agencies are most effective when: (1) the organization has had difficulty building a pool of qualified applicants, (2) the organization is not equipped to develop a sophisticated recruitment effort, (3) there is a need to fill a position quickly, (4) the organization is explicitly recruiting minorities or females, and (5) the organization is attempting to recruit individuals who are not actively seeking employment.[37]

There are about 2,400 federally funded but state-run employment agencies under the U.S. Training and Employment Service. All persons drawing unemployment compensation must apply through one of these agencies. The most recent approach to job placement under USTES is to attempt a matching of applicants' aptitudes and interests with the requirements of the job. In general, neither employers or employees are satisfied with the service offered.[38]

FIGURE 5.10

TYPE OF MEDIUM	ADVANTAGES	DISADVANTAGES	WHEN TO USE
Newspapers	Short deadlines. Ad size flexibility. Circulation concentrated in specific geographic areas. Classified sections are well organized for easy access by active job seekers.	Easy for prospects to ignore. Considerable competitive clutter. Circulation not specialized; you must pay for great number of unwanted readers. Poor printing quality.	When you want to limit recruiting to a specific area. When sufficient numbers of prospects are clustered in a specific area. When enough prospects are reading help-wanted ads to fill hiring needs.
Magazines	Specialized magazines reach pinpointed occupation categories. Ad size flexibility. High quality printing. Prestigious environment. Long life; prospects keep and reread magazines.	Wide geographic circulation—usually cannot be used to limit recruiting to specific area. Long lead time for ad placement.	When job is specialized. When time and geographic limitations are not of utmost importance. When involved in ongoing recruiting programs.
Directories	Specialized audiences. Long life.	Not timely. Often have competitive clutter.	Appropriate only for ongoing recruiting programs.
Direct mail	Most personal form of advertising. Unlimited number of formats and amount of space. By selecting names by ZIP code, mailing can be pinpointed to precise geographic area.	Difficult to find mailing list of prospects by occupation at home addresses. Cost for reaching each prospect is high.	If the right mailing list can be found, this is potentially the most effective medium; no other medium gives the prospect as much a feeling of being specially selected. Particularly valuable in competitive situations.
Radio and television	Difficult to ignore. Can reach prospects who are not actively looking for a job better than newspapers and magazines. Can be limited to specific geographic areas. Creatively flexible. Can dramatize employment story more effectively than printed ads. Little competitive recruitment clutter.	Only brief, uncomplicated messages are possible. Lack of performance; prospect cannot refer back to ad (Repeated airings are necessary to make an impression.) Creation and production of commercials—particularly TV—can be time-consuming and costly. Lack of special interest selectivity; paying for waste circulation.	In competitive situations when not enough prospects are reading your printed ads. When there are multiple job openings and there are enough prospects in specific geographic area. When a large impact is needed quickly, a "blitz" campaign can saturate an area in 2 weeks or less. Useful to call attention to printed ads.

Source: "Planning for recruitment advertising: Part II," by B. S. Hodes, copyright June 1983. Reprinted with permission of *Personnel Journal*, Costa Mesa, CA.

Search firms.   In selecting a search firm, experts recommend the following criteria:

1. The firm has restricted its recruiting to specific industries.

2. The firm pays its sales personnel based on the completion of an assignment.

3. The firm uses primary data sources rather than secondary sources such as computerized lists of potential candidates and association directories.

4. Firms that also do outplacement services are not recommended (outplacement is professional services for terminated employees, which may include placement in another job).

Many recruiting firms now specialize in targeted recruiting for many jobs. One of the largest firms is DHR International, which for one fee provides a list of candidates whose credentials match job specifications and, for an additional fee, completes the search process. AON Consulting specializes in human resource management practices in Russia, including job recruiting and job placement.

The fees for search firms can be very high, with estimates ranging from 20 to 50 percent of the first-year salaries of the individuals placed. Reviews on the effectiveness of search firms are mixed. According to one review, 50 percent of the fulfilled job searches take twice as long to fill as promised. Less than 50 percent of contracts to fill positions are ever fulfilled.[39] More search firms are now charging a flat rate rather than a percentage of salary. Says one recruiter, "By charging a flat rate, we are able to remain objective in presenting candidates to the client. We do not show only the high-priced candidates; we show the most qualified." Many companies have begun to demand the flat-fee approach because of the tendency of percentage-based recruiters to recommend high-priced candidates.[40]

Campus visits. One major source of recruiting for professional and managerial positions is the college campus. Numerous organizations, in particular the larger organizations, send recruiters to campus once or twice a year to inform graduates and future graduates about career opportunities. One survey found that 62 percent of all managers and professionals with less than three years' experience were hired through college recruiting.[41] There is no question that college recruiting is successful at filling vacancies. There is a question as to the extent to which the vacancies are filled with people most likely to be successful within the organization. Some companies report turnover rates in excess of 50 percent for new college graduates after only one year.

The cost of college recruiting can be enormous. One conservative estimate of the cost is almost $4,000 per hired graduate.[42] Despite this substantial cost, program evaluation is rarely done and little attention is given to recruiting. When evaluation has been done, the criterion for evaluation was simply filled vacancies or number of offers accepted rather than a measure of the quality of those who are recruited or retention rates. Recruiters often receive little guidance on interviewing procedures, despite evidence that the interviewing format is important for the accuracy of predictions.

The recruiting process should commence long before any visits to the campus. Recruiters should be familiar with the university and university personnel before their visit. Job descriptions and specifications should be mailed to the campus before the recruiter arrives. Another good strategy is to set up internship programs through the university.[43] In general, the most effective college recruiting efforts are those that facilitate a long-term relationship with the college through a variety of cooperative programs between the school and the organization. Again, recordkeeping on past experience will be very helpful in planning future campus recruiting. NCR, for example, uses a computer to centralize its college recruiting operation. Résumés are entered or scanned on the computer upon receipt along with applicant preferences for certain job characteristics.

Recruiters can also instantly retrieve extensive information about a particular school and status reports of particular candidates.[44] Due to the expense of college recruiting, reliable yield ratios are even more important. Computerized systems such as NCR's are ideal for planning.

Many companies now employ computer technology to conduct recruiting. Squibb, for example, has an interactive format that allows a job candidate to review virtually all aspects of the job selection process. Other companies use videoconferencing at college campuses. This allows for more cost-effective interviewing than traditional face-to-face interviewing. The extent to which videoconferencing is an effective approach to recruiting is another empirical question. There is now a need to compare the effects (and costs) of campus visits to recruiting (and interviewing) through the Internet. Most college graduates can go on-line and may not be hampered by highly efficient, computerized recruiting and interviewing.

One large recruiter of college graduates is the federal government. Recent research on the government's ability to attract the most qualified graduates is not encouraging. One survey found only 38 percent of graduates were interested in careers with the federal government. The private sector was viewed as offering more prestige and power than the public sector.[45] The research also indicated the government could do a much better job recruiting graduates through more on-campus visits and a concerted effort at changing its negative public image. If anything, the public image has gotten worse in recent years.

Two other sources for recruiting are professional associations and computerized services. College faculty for management departments, for example, are often recruited through the Academy of Management and other academic associations. The Society of Human Resource Management now has a placement service available for jobs in all aspects of HR. The American Compensation Association has a placement service for jobs related to compensation and employee benefits.

ELECTRONIC RECRUITING ON THE WORLD WIDE WEB. Electronic job descriptions and résumés are now retrievable from numerous computerized job listings. Numerous computerized résumé databases are available to employers. Connexions of Cambridge, Massachusetts, for example, charges the employer $500 for an eight paragraph ad and the job applicant $10 to look at the complete listings. Connexion allows a candidate to log on and apply for a job immediately through the computer. Sears fills most of its midlevel technical jobs using a computerized service. One staffing manager concluded that compared to normal advertising, "the computerized database won hands over fist."[46] Intel Corporation often fills jobs through University Pronet, a database of graduates from several universities. Philip Morris uses the services of the Career Placement Registry, which has 125,000 résumés in a database. If an organization is interested in minority hiring, there are several excellent computerized sources of information on minority candidates as well.

Technology has created a "virtual recruiter" where a software program turns résumés into a database that is then searched to fill job openings. Hewlett-Packard, AT&T, Texas Instruments, and Ford are among the companies that routinely screen résumés for particular qualifications. For example, if H-P was looking for an engineer with programming skills, five years' experience, and who can speak Spanish, the software could screen the résumés to identify applicants who meet these specifications. While the efficiency of this approach should be obvious, little problems with the software as it reads the résumés can create errors in the search and eliminate applicants who may have otherwise survived at least the initial screening. For example, if you misspell a keyword, you could be out of luck.

Excellent software tracking is now available. Resumix Inc., for example, contains 10 million terms related to various industries, including terms such as *application design* and *general ledger* for specialized programmer and accounting applications. Some companies report substantial savings in recruiting and advertising due to this type of software tracking system. H-P claims to have over 330,000 résumés in its database, avoiding a paperwork nightmare through the "virtual recruiter" system.

The Restrac system has a monster board (http://www.monster.com) where résumé and job postings are matched over the Internet. Companies can then download a résumé and fold it into their résumé database.

Recruiting in the near future may go something like this for most large companies:

1. A line manager completes a standardized job analysis questionnaire on the Internet identifying employment needs for the unit; the questionnaire may include job location and other details of the job in addition to the critical job specifications.

2. The completed questionnaire is then automatically converted into a job posting on the Internet and matched with a current database of applicants whose credentials are entered using the same terminology as the job analysis.

3. A list of candidates is identified based on the match of job specifications with job credentials.

4. Almost instantaneously, the line manager has a list of interested and qualified candidates with whom he or she can interact.

5. A testing and interview format, in compliance with all EEO guidelines, is derived from the same job analysis information completed at step 1.

6. Using the testing/interview material, additional data are collected on the candidates through e-Mail and/or video and a list of top candidates is compiled.

The Internet has great potential for expediting the recruiting process. The scenario above should be contrasted with the typical methods of recruiting we described earlier. Of course, the Internet approach depends on potential job applicants being aware of this convenient approach and amenable to the process.

What Recruiting Method Is Most Effective?

Few studies have compared the effects of different recruitment methods. The Internet is too new for significant work related to it. The criteria used in the studies that have been done also differ and include: cost per hire, number of résumés, time lapse from recruiting to filling the vacancy, interview/invitation ratio, applicant performance on the job, and job tenure or turnover. A recent emphasis has also been placed on minority hiring patterns as a function of the recruiting effort and relative to population statistics and census data on potential employees. These comparisons may be critical if EEO litigation is pending. (Remember our strong emphasis to conduct internal audits related to EEO.)

Figure 5.11 presents a list of some of the most important criteria that could be used to evaluate different approaches to recruiting.

THE DISCREPANCY BETWEEN RESEARCH AND PRACTICE. Unfortunately, there is very little systematic research on the effects of recruiting options using any of these criteria. Despite numerous calls for systematic research on the effects of various approaches to recruiting, we found little indication there is such a program as a part of recruitment efforts. One study found that only 7 percent of Fortune 1000 companies tracked the performance of employees recruited using different methods. Only 15 percent even kept turnover data on new recruits. Perhaps most incredible was the fact that only 40 percent even maintained records of the costs of the various advertising options.[47] As low as these numbers are, they probably overestimate the extent to which such data are used since they are based on the largest U.S. companies.

A 1997 study revealed little improvement in the extent to which recruiting was systematically evaluated.[48] Figure 5.11 also presents a summary of these results based on surveys of recruiters for *Fortune* 1000 companies. Obviously, the tracking of vital criteria such as those listed in Figure 5.11 is vital in determining the relative effectiveness of the various recruiting options. The study also revealed the limited use of the Internet in job postings and recruiting efforts and strong indication that

FIGURE 5.11
**CRITERIA FOR EVALUATING RECRUITMENT ACTIVITIES AND THE EXTENT
TO WHICH THEY ARE MEASURED BY FORTUNE 1,000 COMPANIES**

GLOBAL CRITERION MEASURES	% MEASURED
Number and/or percentage of	
• Jobs filled	62
• Jobs filled in timely fashion	54
• Jobs filled inexpensively (cost per hire)	45
• Jobs filled with above-average performers	21
• Jobs filled by members of underutilized groups	78
• Jobs filled with people who remain at least one year	16
• Jobs filled with people who are satisfied with their new positions	10

RECRUITER-ORIENTED CRITERION MEASURES	
• Number of interviews conducted	70
• Quality of interviews as rated by interviewees	15
• Number and rated quality of career day presentations	4
• Percentage of people recommended who are hired	29
• Percentage of people recommended who are hired and perform well	15
• Number of minorities and women recruited	68
• Cost per interview	43

RECRUITMENT METHOD-ORIENTED CRITERION MEASURES	
• Number of applications generated	58
• Number of qualified applications generated	32
• Number of applications generated from minorities and women	63
• Cost per application generated	34
• Time required to generate applicants	16
• Cost per hire	31
• Quality of employee hired (performance, turnover, attendance, etc.)	14

the Internet would be used in the future to help fill positions. (See Critical Thinking Exercise 5.1.)

CRITICAL THINKING EXERCISE 5.1

Recruiting on the Internet[1]

An estimated 300 companies used the Internet for recruiting employees in 1995,[2] 1,700 in 1996,[3] and 5,800 in 1997.[4] When the home pages of companies and college recruitment sites are added the figure climbs to 35,000.[5] Although there is little evaluative research regarding comparative costs between recruiting instruments, it is generally agreed that Internet recruiting is less expensive, is longer running, and results in faster hires than the conventional print advertisements.

The latest item to pop up in recruiting sites is "hot jobs." "Hot jobs" are the technical jobs that are high on the demand side. Recruitment firms found it hard to fill the estimated 1.9 million job requests with the 1.2 million résumés that were on-line in 1996.[6]

Cisco Systems, Inc., a software company headquartered in San Jose, California, is one company that aggressively uses its home page to recruit new employees. Cisco's rocketing growth from 250 employees in 1990 to more than 4,000 in 1995 presented an enormous problem to the HR department. To maximize the number of résumés submitted, Cisco's HR department developed a home page touting its "hot jobs." For example, Cisco's (www.cisco.com/job/hotjobs.html) listed 13 "hot jobs" as of June 5, 1997, of which customer service representatives, software engineer, and IT analyst—marketing & business development were featured. Along with the "hot jobs" page, Cisco developed an electronic submission of candidates' résumés. The implementation of these and other recruiting efforts resulted in an almost quadrupling of résumés from 19,500 a year to 75,000 a year after installation of the Web site.[7]

To handle the increase in résumés submitted on-line, companies, such as Cisco are implementing tools to electronically search the résumé database for keywords that match job specifications. Some of these software packages, like the one Cisco uses, *Resumix* (www.resumix.com), and Fidelity's (www.fidelity.com) own résumé database, will automatically generate postcards to the applicant thanking the person for the résumé. "Thank you for your recent inquiry . . . Your résumé is being currently reviewed . . . If we are interested in exploring your candidacy further, you will be contacted . . . your résumé will remain active for one year. It is possible to be considered for job openings *without* sending us your résumé a second time."[8] Another feature is production of the EEOC report indicating the ethnicity and gender of each applicant.

Companies do not have to create their own Web sites to take advantage of Internet recruiting. Many firms will electronically post jobs available and e-mail responses back to the company. For example, E-SPAN (www.espan.com) and On Line Career Center (www.occ.com) post jobs for a company and either keep the résumés that respond for reviewing or instruct the applicant to e-mail the company directly. Some of these recruitment firms will screen applicants and check references of candidates before forwarding them to their clients. The New England (www.tne.com) is one such full-service recruiting firm that specializes in the New England area.

The larger metropolitan newspapers put their classified advertisements on-line, such as the *Boston Globe* (www.boston.com) and the *Miami Herald* (www.miami.com). CareerPath (www.careerpath.com) now has 26 of the leading newpapers on-line for a comprehensive job posting nationwide.

Among the various Internet recruiting resources available in 1997, Internet Business Network chose the top 25 recruiters. Best Jobs in the USA Today (www.bestjobsusa.com), Career Magazine (www.careermag.com), E-SPAN (www.e-span.com), and On Line Career Center (www.occ.com) made the list of the best innovative recruiting sites. Although almost all of these sites offer free résumé posting from applicants, only one of IBN's top picks offer the job posting service for free, ICE (www.softechcorp.com/ice). Companies that have taken advantage of this free service have included Alphatech, American Express, Coca-Cola, Cisco, Digital Equipment Corp., and Marcam.

Those sites that did the best job in networking recruiters, according to IBN, were Contract Employment Weekly, DICE, Entertainment Recruitment Network, Net-Temps, and Recruiters Online Network. The international recruiting sites applauded were Asia-Net (www.asia-net.com), CareerChina (www.globalvillager.com), Computing Japan Magazine (http://cjmagco.ip), Job-Serve (www.jobserve.com), and Recruit Media (www.recruitmedia.co.uk).[9] These sites tout jobs for those people with either a desire or the language skills to work overseas in Korea, China, Japan, and Europe.

Recruiters acknowledge that recruiting diversity requires nonconventional approaches, such as getting the job opening information to organizations that attract minority and women members. Many companies interested in diversity programs are using the Internet sites of those organizations to recruit employees. For example, Cisco,

AT&T, and Microsoft recently posted jobs on the Women in Technology home page (www.witi.com). Others such as Career Mosaic (www.careermosaic.com) have partnered with the National Urban League (www.nul.org) for posting companies' diversity program jobs. Some of the on-line recruiters, such as Career Magazine (www.careermag.com), have their own diversity home page where they offer advice in managing diversity as well as job postings.

How would you conduct a study of the effectiveness of Internet recruiting? What would be the critical "deliverables" from this system? Try one Web site presented in this exercise and be prepared to discuss your reaction. If a company insisted that you first send your résumé through the Internet in a prescribed format, what would be your reaction? Would it affect your interest in this company? Explain your answer.

[1] Contributed by Mary E. Wilson.

[2] Franklin Search Group Online (1995). Interim Report. http://www.2000.ogsm.van...95/interim7.htm, p. 2.

[3] The Internet Business Network (1996). About the electronic recruiting index. *1996 Electronic Recruiting Index*. http://www.interbiznet.com/ibn/abouteri.html, p.1.

[4] The Internet Business Network (1997). 1997 recruiting index. *Electronic Recruiting News*. http://www.interbiznet....rn/archives/970302.html, p. 6.

[5] Michael Frost (Aug. 29, 1996). Attracting employees who surf the Internet. In John Baillie, *People Management, 2*, 46.

[6] The Internet Business Network (1996). About the electronic recruiting index. *1996 Electronic Recruiting Index*. http://www.interbiznet.com/ibn /abouteri.html, p.1.

[7] Gillian Flynn (October 1996). Cisco turns the Internet inside (and) out. *Personnel Journal, 75:* 28–34.

[8] From an actual postcard sent postmarked April 17, 1997, from Fidelity Investments, Human Resources, 82 Devonshire Street A3B, Boston, MA 02109.

[9] Internet Business Network (1997). The 1997 EERI Awards. *Electronic Recruiting News*. http://www.interbiznet....rn/archives/970203.html, pp. 3–9.

In general, the limited comparative studies on recruitment methods suggest that the more informal methods (e.g., walk-ins, referrals) are more likely to lead to longer job tenure than the more formal sources, such as newspaper ads.[49] Newspaper ads typically generate the largest number of applicants for a position compared to the other methods. Another study found that people who had worked for the organization earlier had superior performance records, longer job tenure, and better attendance.[50] There is no good research to date on the relative effectiveness of Internet recruiting, although it is believed that the Internet is an excellent source for recruiting at the high-tech level in particular.

Many recruiting problems may be a consequence of the way recruiters are rewarded. Research shows that those criteria that pertain to direct costs of recruiting to the organization are the ones on which recruiters are typically evaluated.[51] For example, recruiters for a large manufacturing company in the South are compensated in relation to a "cost per hire" measure or what one staff member refers to as the "warm body" phenomenon. This emphasis on cost figures may explain the general lack of systematic research relating recruiting methods to higher level criteria such as work quality. In the context of affirmative action, those persons assigned to meet specific EEO goals or timetables are often evaluated on the extent to which they meet the goals or timetables and not the extent to which the positions have been filled with qualified personnel or whether those individuals are successfully retained. The conflicting incentives of recruiters and line management can cause problems when the time comes to make job offers.

The effectiveness of the various methods of recruiting has also been shown to vary as a function of method characteristics. For example, college recruiting is apparently enhanced when the recruiter is between the ages of 30 and 55, is perceived to have stature in the company (line managers are preferred to professional recruiters), is verbally fluent with good interpersonal skills and an extensive knowledge of the company and the particular job.[52] The success of any recruiting effort, however, is more dependent on the job characteristics themselves. College students, for example, place the greatest weight on pay, fringe benefits, and the type of work. Recruiters often underestimate the importance of such factors relative to others.[53]

Two Philosophies of Recruiting: Flypaper versus Matching

The traditional philosophy of recruiting has been to get as many people as possible to apply for a job. The idea is based on trying to obtain the lowest possible selection ratio given a fixed recruiting cost. A selection ratio (SR) is the proportion of job openings to applicants. An SR of .10 means there are 10 applicants for every job opening. A lower selection ratio is frequently more desirable because it enables the organization to choose a job candidate from a larger pool—thereby increasing selectivity. This assumption holds true as long as the cost of recruiting and subsequent screening is not exorbitant and applicants for the job are at least minimally qualified. In general, selection ratios go down when companies are admired by the working public. For example, the number of job applicants is up for most of *Fortune* magazine's 1997 "most admired" companies (e.g., Coca-Cola, Mirage Resorts, Merck, UPS, and Microsoft) and applicants are down for "least admired" firms that made the list (e.g., TWA, K mart). Of course, the increases in the applicant pool must reflect at least minimally qualified applicants.

In circumstances where "quality" criteria are important, the "matching" philosophy of recruitment may be more efficient.[54] A persuasive argument can be made that matching the needs of the organization to the needs of the applicant will enhance the recruitment process. The result will be a workforce that is more likely to stay with the organization longer and perform at a higher level of effectiveness for a longer time. In the context of this matching philosophy, a process of realistic recruitment is recommended. An important component of realistic recruiting is a **realistic job preview** (RJP). RJPs provide the characteristics of the job to applicants so they can evaluate the compatibility of this realistic presentation of the job with their own work preferences. Applicants for bank teller jobs at Sun Bank are told they will spend most of the workday on their feet, some customers will be rude and demanding, and some work periods will be particularly stressful, and tellers will be expected to work alternate Saturdays. RJPs can result in a self-selection process that screens people most likely to have difficulty on the job. Those applicants who are hired after being exposed to an RJP are also better able to cope because of more realistic expectations about the job.[55] It is said that RJPs "vaccinate" applicants by lowering their unrealistic expectations and bringing them more in line with actual work conditions.

Many companies doing international work provide extensive RJPs for potential expatriates and their families. Bechtel, the giant construction company, provides a 60-minute video of life in Saudi Arabia, which engineers and their spouses view before they commit to a one-year assignment. Research on realistic recruiting shows lower rates of employee turnover for employees recruited with RJPs, particularly for more complex jobs, and higher levels of job satisfaction and performance at the initial stages of employment.[56] RJPs are more beneficial for organizations hiring at the entry level, when there are low selection ratios (i.e., many applicants per position), and under conditions of relatively low unemployment (i.e., where people have more job options). Otherwise, the approach may increase the cost of recruiting by increasing the average time it takes to fill each position. RJPs can be developed using job analysis information. The critical incident technique is particularly effective for developing RJPs. RJPs could also be incorporated in job postings on the Internet to facilitate the self-selection process.

Another staffing approach that fits into the matching philosophy is the use of the Job Compatibility Questionnaire (JCQ) we discussed in Chapter 4 and will illustrate in the next chapter.[57] The JCQ provides a quantitative match between job applicant preferences and the actual characteristics of a job, including compensation system characteristics, benefits, work schedule, and, of course, the characteristics of the actual work to be performed. The JCQ has also been used to construct a realistic job preview. A study of customer service representatives at the *Fort Lauderdale News and Sun Sentinel* found that the combination of JCQ as a selection device plus the RJP after the job offer was conveyed reduced voluntary turnover by 35 percent and increased the job satisfaction of the workforce.[58] An instrument such as the JCQ could also be incorporated into a standardized job analysis method for downloading from the Internet.

Understanding the Recruits

Effective recruiting requires that the organization know what potential applicants are thinking and what their needs and desires are regarding all major characteristics of the job. For example, how important are the various elements of the fringe benefit package? Are applicants interested in special work schedules, child care, particular work locations? Organizations also need to be keenly aware of how candidates search for jobs. What outlets do they rely on for job information? To what extent do they rely on outside referral agencies for job placement? Should recruitment be restricted to specific geographical areas based on the search behavior of potential candidates? At least some answers to these questions can be gathered over time based on the past recruiting successes and failures of the organization. Recruitment is one area of HRM where a computerized system of detailed recordkeeping would be beneficial for recruiting efforts in the future. Unfortunately, most organizations rely on recruiter "hunches" to make decisions and do little to organize their past recruiting efforts in such a way that systematic research could help determine strategies. Research indicates these "hunches" are not particularly accurate.[59] Several computerized data processing systems are now available for maintaining the critical information related to past recruiting efforts.

Human Resource Planning and Recruitment for Multinational Corporations

The majority of *Fortune* 500 companies are now multinational in that some portion of their business and profits are derived from overseas operations. Some of our largest, most prestigious companies (e.g., IBM, Exxon, McDonald's, Coca-Cola) derive close to 50 percent of their revenues from overseas business. With the immense market potential of South America and the Eastern bloc and the level of interest and activity in Russia alone, this figure is likely to go even higher for many U.S. corporations. Approximately 35,000 U.S. firms have offices overseas with over 45 percent of the U.S. business profits from overseas functions. Unfortunately, the relationship between HR planning and strategic planning for international ventures is even weaker than for U.S. operations even though many experts regard human resource issues as even more important to the success of

an overseas operation than they are to domestic operations. Efforts are being made to enhance the recruiting and success of expatriates. As shown in Figure 5.12, some companies are responding by consolidating the external hiring requirements and gaining expertise in overseas staffing needs.

All agree that international HRM is more complicated than domestic HRM. All of the planning and recruitment are more unpredictable because of the volatile environmental and political issues in the host country, which can affect the overseas operations. For example, after considerable success penetrating the Japanese market, Milwaukee-based Harley-Davidson has had to respond to political pressure directed at restricting its growth in Japan. The pressure is affecting forecasts of market penetration in Japan.

Terrorism is taken very seriously with regard to overseas assignments and operations, and it seriously disrupts planning and recruitment. The level and extent of terrorist activity is unpredictable. The implications of the 1992 European Community remain unclear in terms of many HRM activities. With few exceptions (e.g., Poland and Yugoslavia), the current state of the former Eastern bloc nations, including Russia, makes planning and market forecasting for these new potential markets extremely tenuous.

Almost all other HRM activities (e.g., staffing, performance management, reward systems and compliance, and employee development) are more difficult and unpredictable in overseas operations not only because of environmental volatility but also because many of the methods that have proven effective in U.S. settings do not work for international staffing, performance management, and the other domains. The insurance industry, for example, puts considerable weight on biographical information in the selection of insurance agents. The validity of the method for predicting sales success, which we will discuss in Chapter 6, has never been studied for overseas sales and thus may not apply in the hiring of expatriate Americans, in-country nationals, or third-country nationals.

Within the rewards/compliance domain of HRM activities, issues related to family, housing, dependent care and schooling, spouse employment, taxation, and health care all tend to complicate the international HRM function. These issues also make the economic and psychological implications of errors in international HRM relatively greater than for domestic assignments.[60]

One study identified the critical issues affecting planning and recruitment aspects of international HRM.[61] The major challenges were:

1. Identifying top managerial talent early in the process.
2. Identifying criteria for success in overseas assignments.

FIGURE 5.12

INTERNATIONAL PROFESSIONALS

In today's dynamic global environment, there are exceptional opportunities for individuals whose experience and skills equip them to live and work overseas. There are currently positions available to men and women throughout a wide spectrum of professional fields, including the sciences, engineering, information and computer systems, economics/finance, education, marketing, business or management. If you have worked abroad in any of these areas, you have a definite advantage in securing an exciting new overseas career.

These worldwide positions are being offered to people who are already confident and at home in foreign locations. You must be self-reliant and have the integrity to work without direct supervision. Reporting will require excellent verbal and written communications skills, and you must be conversant in at least one foreign language. Advanced degrees are preferred; a bachelor's degree in an appropriate area is a minimum requirement for consideration.

We represent international employers who will pay all fees associated with your selection process. They require that all applicants be U.S. citizens (Legal Permanent Residents also may apply). These positions are open to individuals of all racial and ethnic backgrounds. Compensation and benefits are commensurate with your demonstrated qualifications. For consideration under strict confidentiality, send your resume and a letter describing your credentials. As we are a third party and not an employer, no phone calls from applicants will be accepted. We will respond only to those applicants who are of interest to our clients.

CAREER SYSTEMS INTERNATIONAL
P.O. Box 15788, Dept. 1P-96/27
Philadelphia, PA 19103
Representing equal opportunity employers.

Manager-Expatriate Programs

Philips Electronics North America Corp., a global consumer and electronic business with a significant number of employees on worldwide expatriate assignments, has an excellent career opportunity in Manhattan for a pro-active professional with 5–8 years' human resources expertise to design, develop, implement, and manage the expatriate program. This fundamental position will advise personnel on expatriate and immigration policies/procedures; develop worldwide compensation programs; implementation of program changes; and serve as an international liaison.

To qualify, you must have 4+ years' immigration/expatriate and supervisory experience, plus a B.A. in business, human resources, or related discipline is highly beneficial. Top-notch organizational, technical, business, interpersonal and communication skills are essential.

We offer a competitive salary/benefits package and a stimulating work environment. For confidential consideration, please send resume to:
Human Resources/JM, Philips Electronics North America Corp., 100 East 42nd Street, New York, NY 10017. FAX: 212-850-7314
EOE M/F/D/V. Principals only.

PHILIPS

3. Motivating employees to take overseas assignments.
4. Establishing a stronger connection between the strategic plan of the company and HR planning.

Most experts would agree that these challenges are more onerous for international planning and recruitment. The third challenge, motivating employees to take overseas assignments, is less of a problem than it was in the past. One 1996 survey, for example, found that a majority of managers indicated that a foreign assignment was helpful for one's career.[62]

But repatriation policies are often not adequate to meet the needs of returning expatriates. Lawrence Buckley, personnel manager for GE, for example, says the "reentry process isn't as smooth as we would like it to be." He says GE is making progress in this area but it is "still a problem for us and U.S. industry in general."[63]

Whereas many managers still perceive overseas assignments as a banishment of sorts, corporations now place more weight on overseas experience as a requirement for high-level executive assignments. For example, Honeywell, Allied-Signal, and Rohm & Haas all virtually require overseas assignments before senior management placement. With the increased sophistication of international communications and the growing importance of international operations for corporate strategy, studies showing overseas managers perceiving a loss of visibility at headquarters probably apply less today than only a few years ago.[64]

Underlying all HRM challenges is the strategic position of the multinational corporation regarding the relationship of the overseas operation to the parent company. The recruitment strategy for overseas assignments is directly tied to this strategic position. U.S. companies may recruit and select from one (or more) of three sources: (1) the pool of U.S. personnel who would be expatriated to the foreign assignment; (2) the pool of candidates from the country of the overseas operations; or (3) candidates from all nationalities. Ethnocentrism, the policy of using *only* home-country executives for overseas assignments, really makes sense either financially or strategically only when the company is just starting the operation. Otherwise, the disadvantages of this approach outweigh the advantages. Japanese companies applying this philosophy to U.S. operations have encountered a number of problems, including a proliferation of equal employment opportunity lawsuits and, in particular, age discrimination cases as Japanese companies replace American managers over the age of 40 with sometimes younger and very often Japanese managers. Recall the discussion of the Mitsubishi sexual harassment lawsuit in Chapter 3. The use of nationals in overseas operations can reduce language and cultural problems, the need for expensive training programs, and the tremendous cost of placing expatriates and their families in overseas assignments. This is becoming more and more common for American companies.[65]

Japanese women may be one major pool of highly skilled workers American companies could tap for penetration into Japanese markets. As we discussed in Chapter 3, Japanese females are still subjected to considerable employment discrimination in their own country and are very attracted to U.S. corporations for this reason. The geocentric policy of hiring the best person regardless of nationality is the formal policy of choice for most large U.S. corporations but is certainly not without its problems since such a management team may have more difficulties communicating with each other and understanding the subtle implications of cultural differences.

For corporations maintaining a close strategic relationship to the overseas division (as opposed to a philos-ophy of autonomous operations), the most common strategy for managerial recruitment and job placement for U.S. companies is a balance between expatriates and nationals. Sales and production personnel are typically recruited from the national pool. Companies that have a "hands-off" managerial philosophy to autonomous foreign operations typically use expatriates in coordination with nationals until the parent company is comfortable with the operation and profits of the foreign division are acceptable. Most of the expatriates may then be recalled to reduce overhead. This was the trend in 1996 when one survey found about 160,000 Americans now work abroad, down almost 35 percent from 1989.[66]

SUMMARY

Human resource planning seeks to place the right employees in the right jobs at the right time and at the lowest possible cost, thereby providing the means for the organization to pursue its competitive strategy and fulfill its mission. Planning improves the organization's ability to create and sustain competitive advantage and to cope with problems, threats, and opportunities arising from change—technological, social, political, and environmental. HRP and all its derivatives should always keep the future customer in focus. Reengineering or downsizing programs that lose this focus may ultimately have a negative impact on the organization. HRP systematically attempts to forecast personnel demand, assess supply, and reconcile the two. Personnel demand can be assessed using qualitative methods, such as the Delphi technique, and quantitative methods. Internal supply may be forecast by using human resources information systems (HRIS), replacement charts, and Markov analysis. Internal shortages are resolved through training and/or recruitment. This information is used in action planning to develop human resource strategy. HRP is an ongoing process where control and evaluation procedures are necessary to guide HRP activities. Deviations from the plan and their causes must be identified in order to assess whether the plan should be revised.

Recruitment is the process of finding and attracting applicants who are interested in and qualified for position vacancies. Recruitment should encompass both the attraction and the selection of the most qualified personnel. The ideal recruitment program is one in which a sufficient number of qualified applicants are attracted to and ultimately accept the positions in an efficient manner. Unfortunately, the typical assessment of recruitment policies, programs, and personnel in the past has focused on simply whether positions were filled and the cost and speed of filling positions rather than evaluating the quality of the personnel who were hired and placed. The most recent writing on recruitment, however, has placed a greater emphasis on the quality of the recruiting effort. There is increasing evidence that the various approaches to recruiting result in different outcomes for the organization. The evaluation of recruiting programs in the future is thus more likely to focus on the quality of the people who are hired in addition to the "body count" criteria, which are more typically used. We have emphasized the quality criterion in this chapter and the need to establish a match between job seekers' needs and desires for certain job characteristics and that which the organization can offer. The next chapter continues with this "matching" philosophy.

DISCUSSION QUESTIONS

1. How should HR planning involve a comparison to competitors? What critical data are required?

2. Why is planning an important activity? What are some advantages of effective planning?

3. Some organizations do a thorough job analysis first and then human resource planning as part of a restructuring process. What makes more sense to you?

4. Discuss the possible pros and cons of the two qualitative methods presented for forecasting labor demand.

5. If actual performance of the human resources plan differs from desired performance, what remedial steps might you use?

6. Employee referral is a popular method of recruiting candidates. What are its advantages and disadvantages?

7. What are the advantages and disadvantages of the various external recruitment sources?

8. Can you think of some examples of escalation bias applied to HRM?

9. Suppose a key employee has just resigned and you are the department manager. After you have sent your request to personnel for a replacement, how could you help the recruiter find the best replacement?

10. Discuss the advantages and disadvantages of using the Internet to find a job and to fill a job.

NOTES

1. Lawrence, S. (April 1989). Voice of HR experience. *Personnel Journal*, p. 70.

2. Martell, J., and Carroll, S. (July 1995) *HR Magazine*, pp. 48–52.

3. Jackson, S. E., and Schuler, R. S. (1990). Human resource planning. *American Psychologist*, 78(3), 223–239.

See also, Dyer, L. (ed.) (1986). *Human resource planning: Tested practices in five U.S. and Canadian companies*. New York: Random House; Schuler, R. S., and Jackson, S. E. (1987). Linking human resource practices with competitive strategies. *Academy of Management Executive*, 14(3), 207–218; Cascio, W. F., and Zammuto, R. F. (1989). Societal trends and staffing policies. In W. F. Cascio (ed.). *Human resource planning employment and placement*. ASPA/BNA Series, Washington, DC: Bureau of National Affairs.

4. Tichy, N.; Fombrun, C.; and Devanna, M. (1982). Strategic human resource management. *Sloan Management Review, 23*, p. 47.

5. Cited in Kahlenberg, R. D. (1996). *The remedy*. New York: Basic Books.

6. Bass, D. D. (April 1996). Help wanted desperately. *Nation's Business*, pp. 16–19.

7. See note 6.

8. Golden, K. A., and Ramanujam, V. (1985). Between a dream and a nightmare: On the integration of human resource management and strategic business planning processes. *Human Resource Management, 34*(3), 429–452. Walker, J. W. (1994). Integrating the human resource function with the business *HR Planning, 17*, 59–77.

9. Delbecq, A. L.; Van de Ven, A. H.; and Gustafson, D. H., (1975). *Group techniques for progress planning: A guide to Nominal and Delphi processes*. Glenview, IL: Scott, Foresman.

10. Heneman, H. G., Heneman, R. L., and Judge, T. A. (1997). *Staffing organizations*. Burr Ridge, IL: Irwin.

11. See note 9.

12. Wikstrom, W. S. (1971). *Manpower planning: Evolving systems*. New York: The Conference Board; see also, Piskor, W. G., and Dudding, R. C. (1978). A computer-assisted manpower planning model. In D. T. Bryant and R. J. Niehaus (Eds.), *Manpower planning and organization design*, New York: Plenum Press, pp. 145–154. DeLuca, J. R. (1988). Strategic career management in non-growing volatile business environments. *Human Resource Planning, 11*, 49–62.

13. See note 10.

14. Martinez, M. N. (1997). How do top recruiters snag good grads? *HRMagazine, 42*(8) 61–66; see also, Leicht, K. T., and Marx, J. (1997). The consequences of informal job finding for men and women. *The Academy of Management Journal, 40*(4), 967–988.

15. Heneman, H. G., III, and Sandver, M. G. (October 1977). Markov analysis in human resource administration: Applications and limitations. *Academy of Management Review*, pp. 535–542.

16. Hooper, J. A., and Catelanello, R. E. (1981). Markov analysis applied to forecasting technical personnel, *Human Resource Planning, 4*(2), 41–47.

17. Buller, P. F., and Maki, W. R. (1981). A case history of a manpower planning model, *Human Resource Planning, 4*, 129–138.

18. Dyer, L. (1982). Human resource planning. In K. M. Rowland and G. R. Ferris (eds.), *Personnel Management.* Boston: Allyn and Bacon.

19. Walker, J. W. (1974). Evaluating the practical effectiveness of human resource planning applications. *Human Resource Management, 32,* 21–28. See also, Werther, W. B., Jr., and Davis, K. (1989) *Human resources and personnel management.* New York: McGraw-Hill.

20. Koretz, G. (Feb. 24, 1997). Big payoffs from layoffs. *Business Week,* p. 30; Feldman, D. C.; Doerpinghaus, H. I.; and Turnley, W. H. (Fall 1994). Managing temporary workers: A permanent HRM challenge. *Organizational Dynamics, 23*(2), 49–63; Gordon, D. M. (1996). *Fat and mean: The corporate squeeze of working Americans and the myth of managerial "downsizing."* New York: Martin Kessler Books/The Free Press; and Rigby, D. (July 3, 1996). As a tool, re-engineering is starting to have blunt edges. *The News,* p. 15A.

21. Fowler, E. M. (Dec. 19, 1989). Job help for laid-off employees. *New York Times,* p. 37; and Sherman, S. (Jan. 25, 1993). A brave new Darwinian workplace. *Fortune,* pp. 50–53.

22. Franklin, S. (Oct. 30, 1995). Downsizing realities revealed: American Management Association survey tracks layoff patterns. *The News,* p. 8C.

23. Munchus, G. (1988). Employee leasing: Benefits and threats. *Personnel, 65,* 59–61; Caudron, S. (July 1994). Contingent work force spurs HR planning. *Personnel Journal, 73*(7), 52–60; and Pandya, M. (June 11, 1995). Employee leasing: The risks of swimming in a big pool. *New York Times,* p. 10.

24. Eng. S. (Dec. 11, 1995). Corporate compatibility: Having employer who shares your values is vital to job satisfaction. *The News,* pp. 10C, 11C; Krausz, M.; Brandwein, T.; and Fox, S. (July 1995). Work attitudes and emotional responses of permanent voluntary, and involuntary temporary-help employees: An exploratory study. *Applied Psychology: An International Review, 44*(3), 217–232.

25. Simonetti, J. L.; Nykodym, N.; and Sell, L. M. (1988). Temporary employees: A permanent boom? *Personnel, 65,* 50–56; Hippel, C.; Mangum, S. L.; Greenberger, D. B.; Heneman, R. L., and Skoglind, J. D. (1997). Temporary employment: Can organizations and employees both win? *The Academy of Management Executive, XI*(1), 93–104.

26. Breaugh, J. A. (1992). *Recruitment: Science and practice.* Boston: PWS-Kent; see also, Brocklyn, P. L. (May 1988). Employer recruitment practices. *Personnel,* 63–65.

27. Goltz, S. M., and Giannantonio, C. M. (1995). Recruiter friendliness and attraction to the job: The mediating role of inferences about the organization. *Journal of Vocational Behavior, 46*(1), 109–118; McDowell, E. (July 5, 1996). Hotels are showing the job vacancy sign. *New York Times,* p. C2; and Spina, V. (1995). Boosting your value in the workplace. *HRMagazine, 40*(7), 159–160.

28. See note 26, Breaugh (1992).

29. Bazerman, M. H., and Neale, M. A. (1992). *Negotiating rationally.* New York: The Free Press; see also, Staw, B., Barsade, S. G., and Koput, K. W. (1997). Escalation at the Credit Window: A longitudinal study of bank executives' recognition and write off of problem loans. *Journal of Applied Psychology, 82*(15), 130–142.

30. Kleiman, L. S., and Clark, K. J. (1984). Recruitment: An effective job posting system. *Personnel Journal, 63,* 20, 22, 25. See also, Taylor, M. S., and Schmidt, D. W. (1983). A process oriented investigation of recruitment source effectiveness. *Personnel Psychology, 36,* 343–354; Breaugh, J. A. (1981). Relationships between recruiting sources and employee performance, absenteeism, and work attitudes. *Academy of Management Journal, 24,* 142–147; Rynes, S. L.; Heneman, H. G., III; and Schwab, D. P. (1980). Individual reactions to organizational recruiting: A review. *Personnel Psychology, 33,* 529–542; Rynes, S. L., and Miller, H. E. (1983). Recruiter and job influences on candidates for employment. *Journal of Applied Psychology, 68,* 147–154; Barber, A. E.; Hollenbeck, J. R.; Tower, S. L.; and Phillips, J. M. (1994). The effects of interview focus on recruitment effectiveness: A field experiment. *Journal of Applied Psychology, 79*(6), 886–896; Rosse, J. G.; Miller, J. L.; and Stecher, M. D. (December 1994). A field study of job applicants' reactions to personality and cognitive ability testing. *Journal of Applied Psychology, 79*(6), 987–992; Saks, A. M.; Leck, J. D.; and Saunders, D. M. (September 1995). Effects of application blanks and employment equity on applicant reactions and job pursuit intentions. *Journal of Organizational Behavior, 16*(5), 415–430; Taylor, G. S. (1994). The relationship between sources of new employees and attitudes toward the job. *Journal of Applied Psychology, 134*(1), 99–110.

31. Powell, G. N., and Butterfield, D. A. (1997). Effect of race on promotions to top management in a Federal department. *Academy of Management Journal, 40*(1), 112–128.

32. Meyers, M. (1987). Is your recruitment all it can be? *Personnel Journal, 66,* 56; and Brown, B. K., and Campion, M. A. (1994). Biodata phenomenology: Recruiters' perceptions and use of biographical information in résumé screening. *Journal of Applied Psychology, 79*(6), 897–908.

33. Brocklyn, P. L. (May 1988). Employer recruitment practices. *Personnel,* pp. 63–65; Ashford, S. J., and Black, J. S. (1996). Proactivity during organizational entry: The role of desire for control. *Journal of Applied Psychology, 81*(2), 199–214.

34. *EEOC v. Detroit Edison* (1975). 6th Cir., 515, *F.2nd,* 301. See also, Schenkel-Savitt, S., and Seltzer, S. P. (1987–88). Recruitment as a successful means of affirmative action. *Employee Relations Law Journal, 13*(3), 465–470; Williams, M. L., and Bauer, T. N. (September 1994). The effect of a managing diversity policy on organizational attractiveness. *Human Factors, 36*(2), 315–326.

35. Hodes, B. S. (1982). *The principles and practice of recruitment advertising: A guide for personnel profession-*

als. New York: Frederick Fell; see also, Bucalo, J. P. (1983). Good advertising can be more effective than other recruitment tools. *Personnel Administrator,* 73–79; Caldwell, D. F., and Spivey, W. A. (1983). The relationship between recruiting source and employee success: An analysis by race. *Personnel Psychology, 36,* 67–72; and Decker, P. J., and Cornelius, E. T. (1979). A note on recruiting sources and job survival rates. *Journal of Applied Psychology, 64,* 463–464.

36. See note 35, Bucalo (1983).

37. Rubenfeld, S., and Crino, M. (1981). Are employment agencies jeopardizing your selection process? *Personnel, 58,* p. 71.

38. National Research Council (1989). *Fairness in employment testing.* Washington, DC: National Academy Press.

39. Dee, W. (1983) Evaluating a search firm. *Personnel Administrator, 28,* 41–43, 99–100.

40. Fowler, E. M. (Nov. 14, 1989). Recruiters refocusing techniques. *New York Times,* P. Y35; and Savill, P. A. (June 1995). HR and Inova reengineers recruitment process. *Personnel Journal, 74*(6), 109–114.

41. Lindquist, V. R., and Endicott, F. S. (1997). *Trends in the employment of college and university graduates in business and industry.* Evanston, IL: Northwestern University.

42. Rynes, S. L., and Boudreau, J. W. (1986). College recruiting in large organizations: Practice, evaluation, and research implications. *Personnel Psychology, 39,* 729–757.

43. Hanigan, M. (1987). Campus recruiters upgrade their pitch. *Personnel Administrator, 32,* 56.

44. Lubbock, J. E. (1983). A look at centralized college recruiting. *Personnel Administrator;* Leonard, B. (June 1995). The sell gets tough on college campuses. *HRMagazine, 40*(6), 61–63; and Meredith, R. (April 21, 1996). This hiring spree is rewarding brains, not brawn. *New York Times,* pp. 1, 10.

45. U.S. Merit Systems Protection Board (1988). *Attracting quality graduates to the federal government: A view of college recruiting.* Washington, DC: U.S. Merit Systems Protection Board.

46. Deutsch, C. H. (May 6, 1990). Headhunting from a data base. *New York Times,* p. F25.

47. Rynes, S. L. (1990). Recruitment, organizational entry, and early work adjustment. In M. D. Dunnette (ed.), *Handbook of industrial and organizational psychology,* 2nd ed. Chicago: Rand-McNally; see also, Williams, C. R.; Labig, C. E.; and Stone, T. H. (1993). Recruitment sources and posthire outcomes for job applicants and new hires: A test of two hypotheses. *Journal of Applied Psychology, 78,* 163–172.

48. Bernardin, H. J. (1997). *A survey of recruiting practices and methods of assessment.* Paper presented at Virginia Polytechnic Institute, Blacksburg, VA.

49. Gannon, M. J. (1971). Source of referral and employee turnover. *Journal of Applied Psychology, 55,* 226–228; and Vecchio, R. P. (1995). The impact of referral sources on employee attitudes: Evidence from a national sample. *Journal of Management, 21*(5), 953–965.

50. Rynes, S. L. (1990). Recruitment, organizational entry and early work adjustment. In M. D. Dunnette (ed.). *Handbook of industrial and organizational psychology,* 2nd ed. Chicago: Rand-McNally.

51. See note 48.

52. Bartol, K. M., and Martin, D. C. (1988). *Recruitment source as a resource: The value of pay-related information to part-time job applicants.* Paper presented at the Annual Meeting of the Academy of Management. See also, Taylor, M. S., and Bergmann, T. J. (1987). Organizational recruitment activities and applicants' reactions at different stages of the recruitment process. *Personnel Psychology, 40*(2), 261–285; Taylor, M. S., and Sniezek, J. A. (1984). The college recruitment interview: Topical content and applicant reactions. *Journal of Occupational Psychology, 57;* Irving, P. G., and Meyer, J. P. (1994). Reexamination of the met-expectations hypotheses: A longitudinal analysis. *Journal of Applied Psychology, 79*(6), 937–949.

53. Giles, W. F., and Feild, H. S., Jr. (1982). Accuracy of interviewers' perceptions of the importance of intrinsic and extrinsic job characteristics to male and female applicants. *Academy of Management Journal, 24,* 148–157.

54. Heneman, H. G.; Heneman, R. L.; and Judge, T. A. (1997). *Staffing organizations.* Homewood, IL: Irwin; Wanous, J. P. (1980). *Organizational entry: Recruitment, selection and socialization of newcomers.* Reading, MA: Addison-Wesley.

55. Premack, S. L., and Wanous, J. P. (1985). A meta-analysis of realistic job preview experiments. *Journal of Applied Psychology, 70,* 706–719; see also, Popovich, P., and Wanous, J. P. (1982). The realistic job preview as a persuasive communication. *Academy of Management Review, 7,* 570–579; Dean, R. A., and Wanous, J. P. (1984). The effects of realistic job previews on hiring bank tellers. *Journal of Applied Psychology, 69,* 61–68; and Meglino, B. M.; DeNisi, A. S.; and Ravlin, E. C. (1996). Effects of previous job exposure and subsequent job status on the functioning of realistic job preview. *Personnel Psychology, 46*(4), 803–810.

56. McEvoy, G. M., and Cascio, W. F. (1985). Strategies for reducing employee turnover: a meta-analysis. *Journal of Applied Psychology, 70,* 342–353.

57. Bernardin, H. J. (1989). Innovative approaches to personnel selection and performance appraisal. *Journal of Management Systems, 1,* 25–36.

58. Bernardin, H. J. (1987). The development of a scale of discomfort to predict employee turnover among customer services representatives. *Academy of Management Journal, 30,* 162–173.

59. See note 48.

60. Dowling, P. J.; Schuler, R.; R. S.; and Welch, D. E. (1994). *International dimensions of human resource management.* Boston: PWS-Kent.

61. Dowling, P. J. (1989). Hot issues overseas. *Personnel Administrator, 34,* 68–72.

62. Lublin, J. S. (Jan. 29, 1996). An overseas stint can be a ticket to the top. *The Wall Street Journal,* pp. B1, B5; see also, Moran, R.; Stahl, H.; and Steel, R. (1989). Survey of personnel managers at 56 international companies. Cited in O'Boyle, T. (Dec. 11, 1989). Grappling with the expatriate issue. *The Wall Street Journal,* pp. B1, B4.

63. See note 62, Lublin (1996).

64. Mendenhall, M. E., and Oddou, G. (1995). The overseas assignment: A practical look. In M. E. Mendenhall and G. Oddou (eds.), *Readings and cases in international human resource management.* Cincinnati, OH: South-Western, pp. 206–216.

65. Black, J. S.; Gregersen, H. B.; and Mendenhall, M. E. (1992). *Global Assignments.* San Francisco: Jossey-Bass.

66. Organization Resource Counselors (1996). *The price of expatriates.* Unpublished report. Boston.

C H A P T E R

STAFFING*

OVERVIEW

It sounds simple: Match employees with jobs. Researchers have made this task easier by developing staffing selection methods that successfully predict employee effectiveness. Still, there is a void between what research indicates and how organizations actually carry out staffing. Real-world organizational staffing is replete with examples of methods that have been proven to be ineffective or inferior to other methods.

As you now know, competitive advantage is enhanced by employing those methods with the capacity for high performance. A key to competitive advantage is increasing output (e.g., performance, productivity) with fewer inputs (e.g., recruiting costs, hiring costs, compensation, training costs) with a focus on meeting or exceeding customer requirements and expanding the customer base. We are also interested in selecting employees who will not only be effective, but who also will work for us as long as we want them, and who will not engage in counterproductive behavior such as violence, substance abuse, avoidable accidents, and employee theft.

A multiple-hurdle process involving an application, reference and background checks, various forms of standardized testing, and some form of interview is the typical chronology of events for staffing, particularly for external hiring decisions. Internal decisions, such as promotions, are typically done with less formality. Staffing involves gathering and assessing information about job candidates and ultimately making decisions about personnel. The process applies to both entry-level personnel decisions and decisions regarding promotions, transfers, and even job retention as part of corporate downsizing.

This chapter will introduce you to staffing, describe some of the most popular types of screening procedures, review the research evidence on each, and discuss the social and legal implications of selection methods. We will first provide an overview of staffing and the typical steps employed in the process. We will then introduce you to the various staffing approaches in their usual order of use: First, we will review application and biographical blanks; next, we will review the use of background and reference checks; then we will review the various forms of standardized tests that purport to assess applicants' KASOCs. Finally, the chapter will conclude with a dis-

*Contributed by Michael M. Harris and Barbara K. Brown.

cussion of the use of more sophisticated assessment procedures, such as assessment centers, performance testing and work samples, and drug and medical tests in the pre-employment selection process. Our context for this discussion will be the legal implications of the various personnel practices and areas where there is a clear discrepancy between what happens and what academic research indicates.

OBJECTIVES

After studying this chapter, the student should be able to:

1. Define the various types of staffing methods.
2. Understand the validity evidence for these methods.
3. Discuss approaches to the more effective use for application blanks, reference checks, biographical data, personnel testing and the interview in order to increase the validity and legal defensibility of each.
4. Discuss the approaches available for drug testing.
5. Explain how both individual and situational factors can distort the interview process.
6. Review the validity of different approaches to interviewing.
7. Discuss how the various types of candidate information should be integrated and evaluated.
8. Describe personnel selection issues for overseas assignments.

The Smith Security Company had its share of staffing problems. Although recruitment efforts attracted many applicants for its entry-level security guard positions, profits were sluggish, the rate of new contracts was flat, and customers' complaints about the guards' behavior were increasing. Some customers believed the guards were stealing merchandise. The turnover rate of the guards exceeded 100 percent—meaning, the quit rate in one year exceeded the number of positions. The Smith Security Company was also dissatisfied with the quality of its supervisory personnel.

The company contracted with PAS (Personnel Assessment Systems), the Florida psychological consulting firm that specializes in staffing problems and personnel selection. Smith asked PAS to develop a new personnel selection system for entry-level guards and supervisors. Underlying this request was a need for Smith to improve its competitive position in this highly competitive industry by increasing sales and contracts, decreasing costs, and increasing customer satisfaction.

The company, which already compensated its guards and supervisors more than others in the industry, wanted to avoid an increase in compensation in these areas. The company estimated that the cost of training a

new armed guard was about $1,000. With several hundred guards quitting in less than a year, the company often failed to even recover training costs in sales. Smith needed new staffing methods that could increase the effectiveness of the guards and supervisors and identify guard applicants most likely to stay with the company.

You will recall from Chapter 4 that job analysis should identify the knowledge, abilities, skills, and other characteristics (KASOCs) necessary for successful performance and retention on the job. In this case, the first thing PAS did was to conduct a new job analysis of the various guard jobs to get better information on the KASOCs required for the work. After identifying the critical KASOCs, PAS developed a job-related application blank, screening test, and interview format.

The process of staffing varies substantially from company to company. While Smith initially used only a high school diploma as a job specification, an application blank, a background check, and an interview by someone in personnel, other companies have used more complex methods to select employees. American Protective Services, for example, the company that handled security for the 1996 Olympics, used a battery of psychological and aptitude tests along with a structured interview.

As with the job analysis and the recruitment process, personnel selection should be directly linked to the HR planning function and the strategic objectives of the company. You may recall from our discussion in Chapter 2 that Marriott sought to be the hotel chain of choice by frequent travelers. As part of this strategy, the company developed a selection system designed to identify people who could be particularly attentive to customer demands. Smith also had a major marketing strategy aimed at new contracts for unarmed security guards who were also effective as customer service representatives. It needed a legal selection system that could identify people most likely to perform well in the dual responsibility of security and customer issues.

Figure 6.1 presents a chronology of events in the staffing process and the major options available for personnel selection. Our previous chapters on job analysis, planning, and recruitment have gotten us to the point of selecting job candidates based on information from one or more of the selection methods listed. We will review each of these methods in this chapter.

STAFFING METHODS: ARE THEY EFFECTIVE?

Our review will include a summary of the validity of each approach to staffing and an assessment of relative cost of each method and the applicant's reaction to the method. The most important criterion for a staffing method is validity. **Validity** is the extent to which a staffing method predicts one or more important criterion,

FIGURE 6.1
STEPS IN THE DEVELOPMENT AND EVALUATION OF A SELECTION PROCEDURE

JOB ANALYSIS/HUMAN RESOURCE PLANNING
Identify knowledge, abilities, skills, and other characteristics (KASOCs)

RECRUITMENT STRATEGY: SELECT /DEVELOP SELECTION PROCEDURES
Review options for assessing applicants on each KASOCs:
Standardized tests (cognitive, personality, motivational, psychomotor)
Application blanks, biographical data
Performance tests, assessment centers, interviews

DETERMINE VALIDITY FOR SELECTION METHODS
Criterion-related validation
Expert judgment (content validity)
Validity generalization

DETERMINE WEIGHTING SYSTEM FOR SELECTION METHODS AND RESULTANT DATA

Source: Human Resource Selection by RD Gatewood and H. S. Field. Copyright © 1990 Dryden Press. Reprinted with permission.

such as performance on the job, employee turnover, accidents, and even on-the-job theft. PAS's objective for Smith Security Company was to develop a valid, legally defensible, user-friendly, and inexpensive test that could predict both job performance and long job tenure for security guards. The extent to which the test was able to do this was a measure of the test's validity. The term *validity* is close in meaning but not synonymous with that critical term *job relatedness,* which we discussed in Chapters 3 and 4. **Empirical or criterion-related validity** involves the statistical relationship between performance or scores on some predictor or selection method (e.g., a test or an interview) and performance on some criterion measure such as on-the-job effectiveness (e.g., sales, supervisory ratings, job turnover, employee theft). PAS, for example, conducted a study in which scores on a proposed screening test were correlated with job performance and job tenure. Such a study would strongly support a legal argument of job relatedness.

The statistical relationship is usually reported as a correlation coefficient. This describes the relationship between the predictor and measures of effectiveness (also called criteria). Correlations from -1 to $+1$ show the direction and strength of the relationship. Generally, good correlations showing useful selection methods and job criteria fall between .20 and .60. Assuming the study was conducted properly, such a result could be offered as an argument for job relatedness after adverse impact analysis establishes prima facie evidence of discrimination. Figure 6.2 summarizes the empirical validity evidence for the various selection methods and estimates cost of the method, its legal defensibility, and the job applicant's reaction to it.

The higher the correlation, the more predictive (and valid) the selection method. The correlation can also be used to calculate the financial value of a selection method, using a utility formula, which can convert correlations into dollar savings or profits that can be credited to a particular staffing method.

FIGURE 6.2
THE EFFECTIVENESS OF STAFFING METHODS

METHOD	VALIDITY	COST	LEGAL DEFENSIBILITY	REACTION
Application blank	Low	Low	?	Neutral
Weighted applications	High	High	High	Neutral
Biographical/interest blanks	High	High	High	Negative
Letters of recommendation	Low	Low	?	Positive
Cognitive ability tests	High	Low	Low	Negative
Job knowledge tests	High	High	High	Positive
Performance tests/work samples	High	High	High	Positive
Assessment centers	High	High	High	Positive
Interviews unstructured; one rater	Low	Low	Low	?
Structured behavioral or situational	High	High	High	Positive
PERSONALITY TESTS				
Big-Five Tests	Moderate	Moderate	High	Neutral
MMPI	High	High	Moderate	Negative
Honesty/Integrity	Moderate	Low	High	Negative
Graphology	Low	Moderate	?	?
Miner Sentence Completion	Moderate	Moderate	High	?

Content validity assesses the degree to which the content of a selection method represents (or assesses) the requirements of the job. A knowledge-based test such as the CPA exam could be considered to have content validity for an accounting job. We will have more to say on the subject of content validity in the following pages. Such a study can also be offered as evidence of job relatedness, but the study should follow the directions provided by the Supreme Court in *Albemarle v. Moody* (see Chapter 3) and, just to be safe, comply with the Uniform Guidelines on Employee Selection.

Utility concerns the economic gains derived from using a particular selection method. The basic formula involves estimating the increase in revenue as a function of the use of the selection method after subtracting the cost of the method. A method with extremely high validity that costs little is the ideal. Before contracting with PAS, Smith Security had studied the options and was not impressed with the validity or utility evidence reported by the test publishers, particularly in the context of the $10 to $15 cost per applicant. This was the main reason Smith decided to develop its own methods.

PAS investigated the validity of its proposed new selection systems using both criterion-related and content-validation procedures. This dual approach to validation provides stronger evidence for job relatedness. PAS's study strongly suggested that new methods of personnel selection should be used if the company hoped to increase its sales and decrease the costly employee turnover. The resulting analysis showed substantial financial benefit to the company if it adopted the new methods. The first method PAS considered was the application blank.

APPLICATION BLANKS AND BIOGRAPHICAL DATA

Like most companies, Smith first required a completed application blank requesting standard information about the applicant, such as previous employment history, experience, and education. Often used as an initial screening method, the application blank, when properly used, can provide much more than a first cut. However, HR managers should be cautious about using information on an application blank that disproportionately screens out protected class members, and they must be careful not to ask illegal questions. Passage of the Americans with Disabilities Act (ADA), for example, states that application blanks should not include questions about an applicant's health, disabilities, and worker's compensation history.

Application blanks can obviously yield information relevant to an employment decision. Yet, it is often the weight—or lack of weight—assigned to specific information by particular decision makers that can seriously undermine the usefulness of the application blank. Decision makers often disagree about the relative importance

attached to information on application blanks. For instance, they might disagree about the amount of education or experience required. Smith required a bachelor's degree in business or a related discipline for the supervisory job. This criterion alone, however, should not carry all the weight. Smith's personnel staff made no effort to develop a uniform practice of evaluating the information on the forms. Staff members did not consider other indicators, such as the fact that an applicant lives 20 miles from the workplace. This may indicate that, relative to other responses, the candidate is more likely to when a job closer to home comes along.

A Discrepancy between Research and Practice: The Use of Application and Biographical Data

What companies do to evaluate application blank data and biographical information and what research suggests are worlds apart. Decision makers rarely use a uniform approach to evaluate data. Scholarly research clearly shows, with adequate data available, the best way to use and interpret application blank information is to derive an objective weighting system.[1] The system is based on an empirical research study, resulting in a **weighted application blank (WAB),** with the weights derived from the results of the research. By empirical study, we mean the responses from the application blanks are statistically related to one or more important criteria such that the critical predictive relationships can be identified. For example, PAS was able to show that where a security guard lived relative to his assigned duties was a significant predictor of job turnover. Another useful predictor was the number of jobs held by the applicant during the past three years. Figure 6.3 shows some examples from a WAB.

Statistically weighting the information on an application blank enhances use of the application blank's information and improves the validity of the process. The WAB simply is an application blank that is scored—similar to a paper-and-pencil test. It provides a score for each job candidate and makes it possible to compare the score with that of other candidates.

Biographical information blanks (BIBs) are similar to WABs except the items of a BIB tend to be more personal and experiential—based on personal background and life experiences. Figure 6.3 shows examples of items from a BIB for the U.S. Navy. BIB research has shown the method can be an effective tool in predicting job turnover, job choice, and job performance. In one excellent study conducted for the U.S. Naval Academy, biographical information was derived from life-history essays, reflecting accomplishments that were then written in the form of questions (see Figure 6.3).[2]

WABs and BIBs have been used in a variety of settings for many types of jobs. WABs are used for clerical

FIGURE 6.3
EXAMPLES OF WAB AND BIB

WAB Examples

How many jobs have you held in the last five years?
(a) none (0); (b) 1 (+5) ; (c) 2–3 (+1); (d) 4–5 (–3); (e) over 5 (–5)

What distance must you travel from your home to work?
(a) less than 1 mile (+5); (b) 1–5 miles (+3); (c) 6–10 miles (0); (d) 11–20 miles (–3); and (e) 21 or more miles (–5)

BIB Examples

How often have you made speeches in front of a group of adults?

How often have you set long-term goals or objectives for yourself?

How often have other students come to you for advice?

How often have you had to persuade someone to do what you wanted?

How often have you felt that you were an unimportant member of a group?

How often have you felt awkward about asking for help on something?

How often do you work in "study groups" with other students?

How often have you had difficulties in maintaining your priorities?

How often have you felt "burnt out" after working hard on a task?

How often have you felt pressured to do something when you thought it was wrong?

Source: C. J. Russell, J. Matson, S.E. Devlin, and D. Atwater. Predictive validity of biodata items generated from retrospective life experience essays. *Journal of Applied Psychology, 75* (1990), 569–580. Copyright © 1990 by the American Psychological Association. Reprinted with permission.

and sales jobs and even high-level jobs, such as production supervisors and research scientists. BIBs have been used successfully in the military and the insurance industry. Many insurance companies, for example, use a very lengthy BIB to screen their applicants.

The **accomplishment record** is an approach similar to a BIB. Job candidates are asked to write examples of their accomplishments, illustrating how they had mastered job-related problems or challenges. Obviously, the problems or challenges should be compatible with the problems or challenges facing the institution. The applicant writes these accomplishments for each of the major components of the job. For example, in a search for a new business school dean, applicants were asked to cite a fund-raising project they had successfully organized. HRM evaluates these accomplishments for their predictive value or importance or for the job to be filled. Accomplishment records are particularly effective for managerial and professional jobs.[3]

How Do You Derive WAB or BIB or Accomplished Record Weights?

To derive the weights for WABs or BIBs, you ideally need a large (at least 150) representative sample of ap-

plication or biographical data and criterion data (e.g., job tenure and/or performance) of the employees in the position under study. You can then correlate responses to individual parts of the instrument with the performance data. If effective and ineffective employees responded to an item differently, responses to this item would then be given different weights, depending on the magnitude of the relationship. Weights for the accomplishment record are usually derived by expert judgment for various problems or challenges.

Research supports the use of WABs, BIBs, and the accomplishment record in staffing. Developing the scoring system requires considerable work, but it is work well spent because the resulting decisions are often superior to those typically made based on a subjective interpretation of application blank information. However, since you need a large sample size to validate results, the WAB technique will probably be useful only for jobs with many incumbents.

Even if you can't do the empirical validation study, you might still get better results using a weighted system in which the weights are based on expert judgment. This approach is superior to one in which there is no uniform weighting system and each application blank is evaluated in a more holistic manner.

REFERENCE CHECKS AND BACKGROUND CHECKS

More than 80 percent of companies do some form of reference or background check.[4] The goal is to gain insight about the potential employee from people who have had previous experience with him or her. An important role of the background check is to simply verify the information provided by the applicant regarding previous employment and experience. This is a good practice; research indicates between 20 and 25 percent of job applications include at least one major fabrication.[5] Fear of negligent hiring lawsuits is a related reason employers do reference and background checks. One HMO was sued for $10 million when a patient under the care of a psychologist was committed and it was later revealed that the psychologist was unlicensed and lied about his previous experience.

A second purpose for reference checks is to assess the potential success of the person for the new job. However, HR professionals should be warned: A proliferation of lawsuits has engendered a great reluctance on the part of evaluators to provide anything other than a statement as to when a person was employed and in what capacity. These lawsuits have been directed at previous employers for defamation of character, fraud, and intentional infliction of emotional distress. This legal hurdle has prompted many organizations to stop employees from providing any information about former employees other than dates of employment and jobs. Turnaround is fair play—at least litigiously. Organizations are being sued and held liable if they do not give accurate information about a former employee when another company requests it. The bottom line appears simple: Tell the truth. Several states now have laws that protect employers who provide candid evaluations of previous employees.

Background checks should include police records—particularly convictions—and driving records, if applicable. One Florida exterminator hired a driver with three convictions for drunken driving. While on duty he plowed into an electrician who suffered permanent back injuries. The out-of-court settlement was $750,000. Employers used to retrieve job applicants' worker's compensation records as part of a background check. This is now illegal under ADA.

One problem with letters of reference is that they are almost always very positive. One approach to getting some useful distinctions among applicants is to construct a "letter of reference" or recommendation that is essentially a performance appraisal form.[6] One can construct a rating form and request that the evaluator indicate the extent to which the candidate was effective in performing a list of job tasks. This approach offers the added advantage of deriving comparable data for internal and external job candidates, since the performance appraisal, or reference data, can be completed for both internal and external candidates.

With this approach, both internal and external evaluators must evaluate performances on the tasks that are most important for the position to be filled. An alternative approach asks the evaluator to rate the extent of job-related knowledge, skill, or ability of a candidate. These ratings can then be weighted by experts based on the relative importance of the KASOCs for the position to be filled. This approach makes good sense whenever past performance is a strong predictor of future performance. For example, when selecting a manager from a pool of managers, a candidate's past performance as a manager is important. Performance appraisals or promotability ratings, particularly those provided by peers, are a valid source of information about job candidates.

Employers should do their utmost to obtain accurate reference information despite the difficulties. If for no other reason, a good-faith effort to obtain verification of employment history can make it possible for a company to avoid (or win) negligent hiring lawsuits.

PERSONNEL TESTING

Surveys indicate that between 15 percent and 20 percent of organizations use some form of ability or knowledge testing to make staffing decisions.[7] Many companies now use aptitude or cognitive ability tests to screen ap-

plicants, bolstered by considerable research indicating the tests are valid for virtually all jobs in the U.S. economy. The dilemma facing organizations is this: While mental or cognitive ability tests have been shown to be valid predictors of job performance, they can create legal problems because minorities tend to score lower.

Corporate America is also increasing its use of various forms of personality or motivational testing—in part due to the growing concern over employee theft, the outlawing of the polygraph test, and the potential corporate liability for the behavior of employees. Lawsuits for negligent hiring and negligent retention, for example, attempt to hold an organization responsible for the behavior of employees when there is little or no attempt to assess critical characteristics of those who are hired. Domino's Pizza, for example, settled a lawsuit in which one of its delivery personnel was involved in a fatal accident. The driver had a long and disturbing psychiatric history.

Cognitive ability tests are the most frequently used paper-and-pencil tests in use today. These tests attempt to measure mental, clerical, mechanical, or sensory capabilities in job applicants. You are probably familiar with these cognitive ability tests: the Scholastic Aptitude Test (SAT), the American College Test (ACT), and the General Mental Ability Test (GMAT). Cognitive ability tests, most of which are administered in a paper-and-pencil or computerized format under standardized conditions, are controversial. On the average, African-Americans and Hispanics score lower than whites on virtually all these tests; thus, use of these tests can affect employment and other opportunities for minorities.

We will address the critical issue of test score differences as a function of ethnicity later in the chapter. Let us begin our discussion with a definition of cognitive ability testing and brief descriptions of the most popular tests. Then we will review the validity evidence for these tests. We will conclude with a focus on the legal aspects of cognitive ability testing in the context of the latest research, ethnic score differences, and case law.

What Is a Cognitive Ability Test?

Cognitive ability tests measure one's aptitude or mental capacity to acquire knowledge based on the accumulation of learning from all possible sources. Such tests are often distinguished from **achievement tests,** which attempt to measure the effects of knowledge obtained in a standardized environment (e.g., your final exam in this course could be considered a form of achievement test). Cognitive ability or aptitude tests are typically used to predict future performance. Examples are the SAT and ACT, which were developed to measure ability to master college-level material. In practice, there isn't a clear distinction between these two classes of tests. Achievement tests can be used to predict future behavior, and all tests measure some degree of accumulated knowledge. Knowledge-based tests assess a sample of what is required on the job. If you are hiring a computer programmer, a cognitive ability test score might predict who will learn to be a computer programmer; yet, you would benefit more with an assessment of programming knowledge. Knowledge-based tests are easier to defend in terms of job relatedness and content validity.

Hundreds of mental or cognitive ability tests are available. Some of the most frequently used and highly regarded tests are the Wechsler Adult Intelligence Scale, the Wonderlic Personnel Test, and the Armed Services Vocational Aptitude Battery. In addition, many of the largest U.S. companies have developed their own cognitive ability tests. AT&T evaluates applicants for any of its nonsupervisory positions on the basis of scores on one or more of its 16 mental ability subtests—the weights given to a particular test depend on the particular job and the validation results. Knight-Ridder, the communications giant, has a battery of 10 aptitude tests, some of which are even used to select newspaper carriers.

Let us examine two of the most well-known cognitive ability tests. One of the most widely used mental ability tests is the **Wonderlic Personnel Test.** The publisher of this test, first copyrighted in 1938, has data from more than 2.5 million applicants. The Wonderlic consists of 50 questions, covering a variety of areas including mathematics, vocabulary, spatial relations, perceptual speed, analogies, and miscellaneous topics. Here is an example of a typical mathematics question: "A watch lost 1 minute 18 seconds in 39 days. How many seconds did it lose per day?" A typical vocabulary question might be phrased as follows: "Usual is the opposite of: a. rare b. habitual c. regular d. stanch e. always." An item that assesses ability in spatial relations would require the test taker to choose among five figures to form depicted shapes. Applicants have 12 minutes to complete the 50 items. The Wonderlic will cost an employer from $1.50 to $3.50 per applicant depending on whether the employer scores the test. The Wonderlic is used by the National Football League to provide data for potential draft picks (the average score of draftees is one point below the national population).[8]

You may remember the Wonderlic from our discussion of the Supreme Court ruling in *Griggs v. Duke Power* (discussed in Chapter 3) and *Albemarle v. Moody.* In *Griggs,* scores on the Wonderlic had an adverse impact against African-Americans (a greater proportion of African-Americans failed the test than did whites); and Duke Power did not show that the test was job related. Despite early courtroom setbacks and a decrease in use following the *Griggs* decision, according to the test's publisher, the use of the Wonderlic has increased in recent years.

What Are Tests of Specific Ability?

A variety of tests have also been developed to measure specific abilities, including specific cognitive abilities such as verbal comprehension, numerical reasoning, and verbal fluency, as well as tests assessing mechanical or clerical ability, physical or psychomotor ability, including coordination and sensory skills. The most widely used mechanical ability test is the **Bennett Mechanical Comprehension Test (BMCT).** Developed in the 1940s, the BMCT consists mainly of pictures depicting mechanical situations with questions pertaining to the situations. The respondent describes relationships between physical forces and mechanical issues. The BMCT is particularly effective in predicting success in mechanically oriented jobs.

While several tests are available for the assessment of clerical ability, the most popular is the **Minnesota Clerical Test (MCT).** The MCT requires test takers to quickly compare either names or numbers and to indicate pairs that are the same. The name comparison part of the test has been shown to be related to reading speed and spelling accuracy, while the number comparison is related to arithmetic ability.

Physical, psychomotor, and sensory/perceptual are classifications of ability tests used when the job requires particular abilities. Physical ability tests are designed to assess a candidate's muscular strength, movement quality, and cardiovascular endurance. Scores on physical ability tests have been linked to accidents and injuries. One study found that railroad workers who failed a physical ability test were much more likely to suffer an injury at work. Psychomotor tests assess processes such as eye-hand coordination, arm-hand steadiness, and manual dexterity. Sensory/perceptual tests are designed to assess the extent to which an applicant can detect and recognize differences in environmental stimuli. These tests are ideal for jobs that require workers to edit or enter data at a high rate of speed. For example, NationsBank uses a battery of these tests to screen applicants for checking account data entry jobs.

As we discussed in Chapter 3, the validity of physical ability tests has been under scrutiny lately, particularly with regard to their use for public safety jobs. Many lawsuits have been filed on behalf of female applicants for police and fire jobs who had failed some type of physical ability test, such as push-ups, sit-ups, or chin-ups. In fact, the probability is great for adverse impact against women when a physical ability test is used to make selection decisions.[9] Sensory ability testing concentrates on the measurement of hearing and sight acuity, reaction time, and psychomotor skills, such as eye and hand coordination. Such tests have been shown to be related to quantity and quality of work output and accident rates.

Are There Racial Differences in Test Performance?

Many organizations discontinued the use of cognitive ability tests because of the Supreme Court ruling in *Griggs.* Despite fairly strong evidence that the tests are valid and their increased use by U.S. businesses, the details of the *Griggs* case illustrate the continuing problem with the use of such tests. The Duke Power Company required new employees to have either a high school diploma or to pass the Wonderlic Personnel Test and the Bennett Mechanical Comprehension Test. Fifty-eight percent of whites who took the tests passed, while only 6 percent of African-Americans passed. According to the Supreme Court, the Duke Power Company was unable to provide sufficient evidence to support the job relatedness of the tests or the business necessity for their use. Accordingly, the high court ruled that the company had discriminated against African-Americans under Title VII of the 1964 Civil Rights Act. As we discussed in Chapter 3, the rationale for the Supreme Court's decision gave rise to the theory of disparate impact.

The statistical data presented in the *Griggs* case are not unusual. African-Americans, on average, score significantly lower than whites on cognitive ability tests; Hispanics, on average, fall about midway between average African-American and white scores. Thus, under the disparate impact theory of discrimination, plaintiffs are likely to establish adverse impact based on the proportion of African-Americans versus whites who pass such tests. If the *Griggs* case wasn't enough, the 1975 Supreme Court ruling in *Albemarle Paper Company v. Moody* probably convinced many organizations that the use of cognitive ability tests was too risky. In *Albemarle,* the court applied specific and difficult guidelines to which the defendant had to conform to establish the job relatedness of the particular test. The Uniform Guidelines in Employee Selection Procedures, as issued by the Equal Employment Opportunity Commission, also established rigorous and potentially costly methods to be followed by an organization to support the job relatedness of the test if adverse impact should result. Current interest in cognitive ability tests was spurred by the research on "validity generalization," which strongly supported the validity of these tests for virtually all jobs and projected substantial increases in productivity and cost savings for organizations that use the tests. The average validity of such tests was reported to be .50.[10]

Some major questions still remain regarding the validity generalization results for cognitive ability tests: Are these tests the most valid method of personnel selection across all job situations or are other methods, such as biographical data and personality tests, more valid for some jobs that were not the focus of previous research? Are there procedures that can make more accurate predictions than cognitive ability tests for some job situations? Are cognitive ability tests the best predictors of sales success, for example? (The Unabomber had a Ph.D. in math from the University of Michigan. How would he do in sales?) Another issue is the extent to which validity can be inferred for jobs involving bilingual skills. Would the Wonderlic administered in English have strong validity for a job, such as a customs agent, requiring the worker to speak in two or more languages? Bilingual job specifications are increasing in the United States. Involving the validity generalization argument for this type of job based on research involving only the use of English is somewhat dubious. The validity of such tests for these jobs is probably not as strong.

Another issue concerns the extent to which other measures can enhance predictions beyond what cognitive ability tests can predict. Generally, human performance is thought to be a function of a person's ability, motivation, and personality. The highest estimate of the validity of cognitive ability tests is about .50. This means that 25 percent of the variability in the criterion measure (e.g., performance) can be accounted for by the predictor, or the test. That leaves 75 percent unaccounted for. Industrial psychologists think the answer lies in measures of one's motivation to perform, personality, or the capability of a person's job performance with actual job characteristics.

Would a combination of methods—perhaps a cognitive ability test and a personality or motivational test—result in a significantly better prediction than the cognitive ability test alone? Research indicates that a combination of cognitive and motivational tests may lead to a more comprehensive assessment of an individual.[11] Accordingly, the use of other tests that address the motivational components of human performance, in addition to a cognitive ability test, can help an organization increase its competitive advantage. We will discuss these measures shortly.

Why Do Minorities Score Lower than Whites on Cognitive Ability Tests?

This question has interested researchers for years, yet there appears to be no clear answer. Most HRM experts now generally take the view that these differences are "not created by these tests, but are preexisting, and thus the problem is not a defect or deficiency in the tests." Thus, the issue for HRM experts is not how to modify the test itself, but how to use the test in the most effective way. A panel of the National Academy of Sciences concluded that cognitive ability tests have limited but real ability to predict how well job applicants will perform, and these tests predict minority group performance as well as they predict the future performance of nonminorities. In other words, the tests themselves are not to blame for differences in scores.[12]

How Do Organizations Deal with Race Differences on Ability Tests?

The most effective way to use a valid cognitive ability test would be to select candidates from the top down, using the raw scores. That is, all things being equal, if an organization needed to hire 10 people, the 10 highest scores on the test would be selected. However, as described above, this strategy is likely to result in adverse impact and could create legal problems.

One solution is to set an arbitrary, low cutoff score on the test, ignoring differences above the cutoff score and making hiring decisions on some other basis. Many U.S. cities did this by setting a minimum cutoff score for entrance exams for police and firefighters at the point at which there would be no violation of the 80 percent adverse impact rule. Test score differences above this minimum cut score are not considered in the ultimate selection decision. The major disadvantage of this approach is that there will be a significant decline in the utility of a valid test because people could be hired who are at the lower end of the scoring continuum, making them less qualified than people at the upper end of the continuum who may not be selected. Virtually all the research on cognitive ability test validity indicates the relationship between test scores and job performance is linear; that is, higher test scores go with higher performance and lower scores go with lower performance. Thus, setting a low cutoff score and ignoring score differences above this point can result in the hiring of many people who are only minimally qualified. So, while use of a low cutoff score may enable an organization to comply with the 80 percent adverse impact rule, the test will lose considerable utility.

An alternative approach is called banding. Banding is a procedure where persons scoring within a specified scoring range are considered to have scored at the same level. Thus, candidates for sergeant in the Detroit Police Department who scored between 90 and 100 on the exam were considered to have the same score and ranked equally rather than ranking people based on their raw score. Banding is no different from converting your percentage score in a class to a letter grade using the traditional 90 percent or higher is an A, 80 percent to 89 percent is a B, and so on. The result of banding is reduced levels of adverse impact compared to top-down ranking with relatively small losses in utility for the test.[13]

The use of cognitive ability tests obviously presents a dilemma for organizations. Evidence indicates that such tests are valid predictors of job performance across a wide array of jobs. Employers who use such tests enjoy economic utility with greater productivity and considerable cost savings. However, selection decisions that are based solely on the scores of such tests will result in adverse impact against African-Americans and Hispanics. Such adverse impact could entangle the organization in costly litigation and result in considerable public relations problems. If the organization chooses to avoid adverse impact, the question becomes one of either throwing out a test that has been shown to be useful in predicting job performance or keeping the test and reducing or eliminating the level of adverse impact. Does such a policy leave a company open to reverse discrimination lawsuits by whites who were not selected for employment—their raw scores on the test were higher than scores obtained by some minorities who were hired? Many organizations, particularly in the public sector, have abandoned the use of cognitive ability tests in favor of other methods, such as interviews or performance tests, which result in less adverse impact and are more defensible in court.

What Is Personality/Motivational Testing?

While research supports the use of cognitive ability tests for personnel selection, virtually all HRM professionals regard performance as a function of both ability and motivation. Scores on ability tests say little or nothing about a person's motivation to do the job. We can all think of examples of very intelligent individuals who were unsuccessful in many situations (we're back to the Unabomber!). Most of us can remember a classmate who was very bright, but received poor grades due to low motivation. The general validity of cognitive ability tests for predicting sales success is rather low and much could be done to improve prediction.

Most personnel selection programs attempt an informal or formal assessment of an applicant's motivation through psychological testing or a job interview. Some of these assessments are based on scores from standardized tests, performance testing such as job simulations or assessment centers. Others are more informal, derived from an interviewer's gut reaction or intuition. This section will review the abundant literature on the measurement and prediction of motivation and personality using various forms of testing.

There is an increased use of various types and formats for personality or motivational testings, including paper-and-pencil types, video and telephone testing, and, most recently, on-line testing.[14] Some organizations place great weight on personality testing for employment decisions. PAS, the company working with Smith Security, does psychological screening for hundreds of companies using specialized reports from the Big-Five Test. Sears, Roebuck and Company, Standard Oil of New Jersey, and AT&T have used personality tests for years to select, place, and even promote employees. More companies today use some form of personality test to screen applicants for risk factors related to possible counterproductive behavior.

We will begin this section with a definition of personality and provide brief descriptions of some of the more popular personality tests. We will review the validity of these tests and provide an overview of relevant legal and ethical issues. We will conclude with a description of four relatively new personality tests that have shown potential as selection and placement devices.

WHAT IS PERSONALITY? While personality has been defined in many ways, the most widely accepted definition is that **personality** refers to an individual's consistent pattern of behavior. This consistent pattern is comprised of psychological traits. One review notes that an "impressive body of literature has accumulated which provides compelling evidence for the robustness of the five-factor model" of personality.[15] These five factors are as follows:

1. Introversion/extraversion (outgoing, sociable).
2. Emotional stability.
3. Agreeableness/likability (friendly, cooperative).
4. Conscientious (dependable, careful).
5. Openness (imaginative, curious, experimenting).

Several tests measure the so-called "big five" factors.

Some psychologists prefer a "situationist" perspective, maintaining that behavior is inconsistent—particularly across situations and measurement methods. A popular approach today is the "interactionist" perspective, which maintains that behavior is a function of personality, the situation, and the interaction between the two.[16]

While most measures of personal characteristics have adopted the pure trait approach, some of the more recent efforts have attempted to enhance prediction with this interactionist approach. Trait-based personality tests have been developed to predict behavior in a variety of contexts, including the workplace. Thousands of personality tests are available that purport to measure hundreds of different traits or characteristics. We will review the basic categories of personality testing next. Figure 6.4 presents a summary of some of the most popular tests.

HOW DO WE MEASURE PERSONALITY? Personality tests can be sorted into two broad categories: projective tests and self-report inventories. We can also use the interview and data from other sources such as performance appraisals as a means for assessing personality as well. **Projective tests** have many common characteristics, the most significant of which is that the purpose and scoring procedure of the test is disguised from the test taker. Among the most famous projective tests is the **Rorschach Inkblot Test,** which presents a series of inkblots to respondents who must then record what they see in each one.

While numerous projective tests exist, the **Miner Sentence Completion Scale (MSCS)** is one of the few specifically designed for use in the employment setting. Its aim is to measure managers' motivation to manage others.[17] And the test appears to work well! The test consists of 40 incomplete sentences, such as "My family doctor . . . ," "Playing golf . . . ," and "Dictating letters . . ." The test taker is instructed to complete each sentence. According to the developer of these tests, the way in which an applicant completes the sentences reflects his or her motivation along seven areas. These areas are: capacity to deal with authority figures, conduct in competitive games, handling of competitive situations, assertiveness, motivation to direct others, motivation to stand out in a group, and desire to perform day-to-day administrative tasks.

Another projective test that has been used occasionally for employment purposes is the **Thematic Apperception Test (TAT),** a test that typically consists of a series of pictures that depict one or more persons in different situations. Test takers are asked to describe who the people are and what is happening in the situation, which is somewhat ambiguous and open to interpretation. The test taker then determines the outcome of the situation. Although a variety of scoring systems have been developed for interpreting a test taker's responses, one of the most popular approaches involves rating the responses with regard to the test taker's need for power (i.e., the need to control and influence others), achievement (i.e., need to be successful), and affiliation (i.e., the need for emotional relationships). Like the MSCS, the TAT has been used primarily for managerial selection and has been shown to have some validity as a predictor of managerial and entrepreneurial success.

One form of projective test that has received considerable attention recently is **graphology,** or handwrit-

FIGURE 6.4
EXAMPLES OF PERSONALITY/MOTIVATIONAL TESTS

Projective Techniques	Self-Report Inventories
Thematic Apperception Test	The Big-Five Tests (e.g., NEO-PR)
Miner Sentence Completion Scale	Gordon Personal Profile Inventory
Graphology	Myers-Briggs Type Indicator
Rorschach	Minnesota Multiphasic Personality Inventory
	California Personality Inventory
	Sixteen Personality Factors Questionnaire
	Job Compatibility Questionnaire

ing analysis. With this approach, a sample of your handwriting is mailed to a graphologist who (for anywhere from $10 to $50) assesses your intelligence, creativity, emotional stability, negotiation skills, problem-solving skills, and numerous other personal attributes. According to some writers, graphology is used extensively in Europe as a hiring tool. *The Wall Street Journal* and *Inc.* magazine reported an increase in the use of the method in the United States since 1989. As described in *The Wall Street Journal,* "With the government pulling the plug on the polygraph, and employers clamming up on job references and liabilities from negligent hiring, it is one alternative managers are exploring in an effort to know whom they are hiring." While the use of the method may be increasing, there is no compelling evidence that the method does anything but provide an assessment of penmanship. The only published studies on the validity of graphology have found no validity for the approach.[18]

SELF-REPORT PERSONALITY INVENTORIES

Self-report inventories, which purport to measure personality or motivation with the respondent knowing the purpose and/or the scoring procedure of the test, are more popular today than projective techniques. Some instruments screen applicants for aberrant or deviant behavior (e.g., the MMPI, the 16 Personality Factors), others attempt to identify potentially high performers, and others, particularly more recently developed tests, are directed at specific criteria such as employee theft, job tenure/turnover, accident proneness, or customer orientation.[19]

Self-report inventories typically consist of a series of short statements concerning one's behavior, thoughts, emotions, attitudes, past experiences, preferences, or characteristics. The test taker responds to each statement using a standardized rating scale. During the testing, respondents may be asked to indicate the extent to which they are "happy" or "sad," "like to work in groups," "prefer working alone," and so on.

One of the most respected personality tests is the **Minnesota Multiphasic Personality Inventory (MMPI),** used extensively for jobs that concern the public safety or welfare, including positions in law enforcement, security, and nuclear power plants. The MMPI is designed to identify pathological problems in respondents, not to predict job effectiveness.

The revised version of the MMPI consists of more than 566 statements: "I am fearful of going crazy." "I am shy." "Sometimes evil spirits control my actions." "In walking, I am very careful to step over sidewalk cracks." "Much of the time, my head seems to hurt all over." Respondents indicate whether the statement is true, false, or cannot say. The MMPI reveals scores on 10 clinical scales, including depression, hysteria, paranoia, schizophrenia, as well as four "validity" scales, which enable the interpreter to assess the credibility or truthfulness of the answers. Millions of people, from at least 46 countries, from psychotics to Soviet cosmonauts, have struggled through the strange questions. Litigation related to negligent hiring often focuses on whether an organization properly screened job applicants. Failure to use the MMPI in filling sensitive jobs has been cited in legal arguments as an indication of negligent hiring—although not always persuasively. Unfortunately, some companies are damned if they do and damned if they don't. Target stores negotiated an out-of-court settlement based on a claim of invasion of privacy made by a California job candidate who objected to a few questions on a version of the MMPI. Had one of the armed guards who was hired used his or her weapon inappropriately, Target could have been slapped with a negligent hiring lawsuit (see the Critical Thinking Exercise 6.1).

CRITICAL THINKING EXERCISE 6.1

What Privacy Do We Have in the Workplace?[1]

Currently debated privacy issues have included drug testing, medical information kept on employees and family members, and certain questions on personality tests. Employers have maintained records on employees since the employer/employee relationship was first established. Research on personnel recordkeeping has revealed that as the employer/employee relationship changed the level and amount of information collected on employees also changed. Employers had personal knowledge of employees in the 1800s, could vouch for the employees' integrity, and could observe the personal patterns of behaviors (going to church, etc.). The amount of information kept in files was not as important because of the face-to-face interaction.[2] Companies and cities have grown to such proportions since that time that face-to-face interactions are not possible. In order to hire the right person, limit negligent hiring claims and provide employee benefits, companies need (and are required) to keep extensive dossiers on employees. The management (sharing and disclosing) of those dossiers were the subject of the 1977 report by the U.S. Privacy Protection Commission investigation established by the Privacy Act of 1974. The Survey Research Laboratory at the University of Illinois provided follow-up surveys in 1979, 1989, and 1996.[3]

The Commission recommended the following as fair information practices:

- Acquire only relevant information.
- Consider pretext interviews unacceptable methods of gathering information.
- Use no polygraph or lie detector tests in employment.

- Allow and encourage employees to see and copy records pertaining to them.
- Keep no secret records.
- Establish a procedure for challenging and correcting erroneous reports.
- Use information only for the purpose for which it was originally acquired.
- Transfer no information without the subjects' authorization or knowledge.
- Destroy data after its purpose had been served.[4]

The results of the follow-up surveys revealed the majority of companies do not have formal policies that follow the Commission's guidelines in regards to disclosure and access. Informing and evaluating the record-keeping system are being done by most companies. However, many *Fortune* 500 companies surveyed are still shy of following the Commission's recommendations. The survey results are listed below:

Policy to inform employees of routine disclosure?	49%
Personal access to records?	28%
Policy of evaluating record system?	58%
Inform employees on types of records maintained?	62%
Inform employees of how information is used?	56%
Inform individual of collecting information?	51%[5]

Based on the information provided by the Commission and subsequent surveys as well as information from Chapter 3 on job relatedness evaluate and justify your reaction to the following questions:

You have just come from a job interview in which you were asked the following questions in a personality screening test for a store security officer position. The company has assured you that your answers will be strictly confidential and that emotional stability (which this test proports to test) is essential for the job. You realize that this position is a high stress and safety sensitive job yet it seems that some of these questions are not job relevant.

1. I enjoy social gatherings just to be with people.
2. The only interesting part of the newspaper is the "funnies."
3. Our thinking would be a lot better off if we would just forget about words like "probably," "approximately," and "perhaps."
4. I usually go to the movies more than once a week.
5. I looked up to my father as an ideal man.
6. I liked *Alice in Wonderland* by Lewis Carroll.
7. When a person "pads" his income tax report so as to get out of some of his taxes, it is just as bad as stealing money from the government.
8. Women should not be allowed to drink in cocktail bars.
9. I think Lincoln was greater than Washington.
10. I feel sure there is only one true religion.
11. I am embarrassed by dirty stories.
12. Maybe some minorities get rough treatment, but it is no business of mine.
13. I fall in and out of love rather easily.
14. I wish I were not bothered by thoughts about sex.
15. My home life was always happy.
16. Only a fool would ever vote to increase his own taxes.
17. When a man is with a woman, he is usually thinking about things related to her sex.
18. I hardly ever feel pain in the back of my neck.
19. I have no difficulty starting or holding my urine.
20. My sex life is satisfactory.
21. I am very strongly attracted by members of my own sex.
22. I used to like drop-the-handkerchief.
23. I've often wished I were a girl (or if you are a girl) I've never been sorry that I'm a girl.
24. I go to church almost every week.
25. I believe in the second coming of Christ.
26. I believe in life hereafter.
27. I've never indulged in any unusual sex practices.
28. I believe my sins are unpardonable.[6]

Assignment

Should the company be allowed to ask such questions? Think of all issues which you considered in taking a position *or,* if you aren't sure what your position is, what additional information do you need?

[1] Contributed by Mary E. Wilson

[2] Linowes, D. F., and Spencer, R. C. (1996). Privacy in the workplace in perspective. *Human Resource Management Review 6* (3), 165–182.

[3] Ibid., p. 173.

[4] Ibid., pp. 177–178.

[5] Ibid.

[6] Taken from Psychscreen, a screening tool used by Target stores based on the Minnesota Multiphasic Personality Inventory (MMPI) and the California Personality Inventory (CPI) source Alderman, E., and Kennedy, C. (1995). *The Right to Privacy.* Alfred A. Knopf, New York.

One instrument we mentioned earlier that has been used extensively for personnel selection is the 16 Personality Factors (16PF), which also provides scores on the so-called big five factors plus others. The test is also used to screen applicants for counterproductive behavior, such as potential substance abuse or employee theft. AMC Theaters, C & S Corporation of Georgia, and Kelly Girls are among the companies that use the 16PF to screen most employees. The weights for the 16 factors assessed on the test are determined by a job analysis. Another very popular self-report inventory is the **Myers-Briggs Type Indicator (MBTI),** which also provides for assessments on the big five factors along with other characteristics. While effective as a career counseling instrument, the MBTI is not a good tool for personnel decisions.[20]

What Is the Validity of Personality Tests?

Potentially useful personality tests exist among a great number of bad ones, making it difficult to derive general comments regarding their validity. Some instruments have shown adequate validity while others show no validity at all. A review of 26 studies involving the MSCS found an average validity coefficient of .35.[21] A 1991 review found an average validity of .38, when the relevant big five factors were first identified and weighted in a formal job analysis.[22] However, a much wider variance in validities was found among personality tests than among cognitive ability tests. The conscientiousness factor of the big five appears to be a valid predictor of performance across all jobs studied. In general, the validity of the other four factors depends on the circumstances of the job. One recent study found high conscientiousness combined with low agreeableness was the best combination in a managerial situation involving a difficult union–management problem while the ability to perform effectively in a team-based work situation was a function of high agreeableness, high emotional stability, and high conscientiousness.[23]

Why do personality tests have low validity? Experts have given a number of explanations for the low validity of personality tests in the employment context. First, applicants can fake personality tests so their personality is reflected on the tests as compatible with the requirement of the job. Second, some proponents of personality testing have asserted that most of the validity studies involving personality tests are poorly designed with very small sample sizes. These experts contend that more carefully designed research would demonstrate higher validity for personality tests. Several studies support this view.

Another possible explanation is that behavior is to a great extent determined situationally, making stable personality traits unpredictable for criteria such as job performance or employee turnover. Most items in personality tests are not specific to the workplace; in fact, most of them are quite general. Research in other areas has found that behavior is very dependent on the situation. A person who is friendly in outside work might be less sociable in the work setting. To enhance predictability, per-

sonality assessment should involve more than one method (e.g., tests, interviews by clinical psychologists). It should also be more specific to the workplace and target particular measures of interest, such as employee theft, honesty or integrity, or job capability. Let us examine these newer approaches next.

Approaches to the Prediction of Particular Criteria

Some newer forms of personality or motivation assessment attempt to focus on either particular problems or criteria characteristic of the workplace. Examples are honesty and integrity tests, which attempt to predict the growing problem of employee theft. Another new test attempts to measure job capability in order to predict turnover. Other new instruments are designed for particular employment situations and problems, such as customer service, violence, or accident proneness.

HONESTY/INTEGRITY TESTS. It is estimated that more than 5 million job applicants took some form of honesty test in 1996.[24] These tests are commonly used for jobs in which workers have access to money, such as retail stores, fast food chains, and banks. Honesty tests have become more popular since the polygraph, or lie detector, test was banned in 1988 by the Employee Polygraph Protection Act. This federal law outlawed the use of the polygraph for selection and greatly restricts the use of the test for other employment situations. There are some employment exemptions to the law, such as those involving security services, businesses involving controlled substances, and government employers.

Most honesty tests contain items concerning an applicant's attitude toward theft. Sample items typically cover beliefs about the amount of theft that occurs, asking test takers questions such as the following: "What percentage of people take more than $1.00 per week from their employer?" The test also questions punitiveness toward theft: "Should a person be fired if caught stealing $5.00?" The test takers answer questions reflecting their thoughts about stealing: "Have you ever thought about taking company merchandise without actually taking any?" Other honesty tests include items that have been found to correlate with theft: "You freely admit your mistakes." "You like to do things that shock people." "You have had a lot of disagreements with your parents." Many banks and retail establishments use honesty tests for employee screening.

The validity evidence for honesty tests is fairly strong, with no adverse impact. Still, critics point to a number of problems with the validity studies. First, most of the validity studies have been conducted by the test publishers themselves; there have been few independent validation studies. Second, very few of the criteria-related validity studies use employee theft as the criterion.

A report by the American Psychological Association concluded that the evidence, albeit limited, supports the validity of some of the most carefully developed and validated honesty tests. The most recent studies on honesty tests support their use.[25]

THE PREDICTION OF ACCIDENT PRONENESS. Accidents are a major problem in the workplace, causing deaths, injuries, and expense. Some companies have turned to preemployment testing in an effort to lower accident rates. We have already discussed the railroad study involving the validity of physical ability testing. Another test developed to predict (and prevent) accidents is the Safety Locus of Control (SLC), which is a paper-and-pencil test containing 17 items assessing attitudes toward safety.[26] A sample item is as follows: "Avoiding accidents is a matter of luck." Although the SLC is a rather new measure, initial validity studies have been encouraging. The studies have been conducted in several different industries, including transportation, hotel, and manufacturing. In addition, these investigations indicate no adverse impact against minorities and women.

CUSTOMER SERVICE ORIENTATION. The Service Orientation Index (SOI) was initially developed to predict the helpfulness of nurses' aides in large, inner-city hospitals.[27] The test items were selected from three main dimensions: patient service, assisting other personnel, and communication. Here are some examples of SOI items: "I always notice when people are upset," and "I never resent it when I don't get my way." Several other studies of the SOI involving clerical employees and truck drivers have reported positive results as well.

THE PREDICTION OF JOB COMPATIBILITY. We discussed the Job Compatibility Questionnaire (JCQ) in Chapters 4 and 5. The JCQ was developed to determine whether an applicant's preferences for work characteristics match the characteristics of the job.[28] One theory is that the compatibility of preference with the job will predict job tenure and performance. Test takers are presented groups of items and are instructed to indicate which item is most desirable and which is least desirable. As we discussed in Chapter 4, the items are grouped based on a job analysis that identifies those characteristics that are common to the job(s) to be filled. Here is an example of a sample group: (*a*) being able to choose the order of my work tasks; (*b*) having different and challenging projects; (*c*) staying physically active on the job; (*d*) clearly seeing the effects of my hard work. The items are grouped together in such a way that the scoring key is hidden from the respondent, reducing the chance for faking.

Studies involving customer service representatives, security guards, and theater personnel indicate that the JCQ can successfully predict employee turnover for low-skilled jobs. In addition, no evidence of adverse impact has been found. PAS used the JCQ in its study of security guards for Smith Security.

How Do You Establish a Testing Program?

Establishing a psychological testing program is a difficult undertaking—one that should involve the advice of an industrial psychologist. HR professionals should follow these guidelines before using psychological tests:

1. Most reputable publishers provide a test manual. Study the manual carefully, particularly the adverse impact and validity evidence. Has the test been shown to predict success in jobs similar to the jobs you're trying to fill? Have adverse impact studies been performed? What are the findings? Are there positive, independent research studies in scholarly journals? Have qualified experts with advanced degrees in psychology or related fields been involved in the research?

2. Check to see if the test has been reviewed in *Mental Measurements Yearbook (MMY)*, which is available in most libraries. The *MMY* publishes scholarly reviews by qualified academics who have no vested interest in the tests they are reviewing.

3. Ask the test publishers for the names of several companies that have used the test. Call a sample of them and determine if they have conducted any adverse impact and validity studies. Determine if legal actions have been taken related to the test; if so, what are the implications for your situation?

4. Obtain a copy of the test from the publisher and carefully examine all the test items. Consider each item in the context of ethical, legal, and privacy ramifications. Organizations have lost court cases because of specific items on a test.

Proceed cautiously in the selection and adoption of psychological tests. Don't be wowed by a slick test brochure; take a step back and evaluate the product in the same manner you would evaluate any product before buying it. Be particularly critical of vendors' claims and remember that you might be able to assess personality and motivation by other means. If you decide to adopt a test, maintain the data so that you can quickly evaluate whether the test is working. In general, it is always advisable to contact someone who can give you an objective, expert appraisal.

DRUG TESTING

Drug abuse is one of the most serious problems in the United States today, with productivity costs in the billions and on the rise. Drug abuse in the workplace has also been linked to employee theft, accidents, absences, use of sick time, and other counterproductive behavior. To combat this growing problem, many organizations are turning to drug testing for job applicants and incumbents. One survey found 87 percent of major U.S. corporations now use some form of drug testing.[29]

While some of the tests are in the form of paper-and-pencil examinations, the vast majority of tests conducted are clinical tests of urine or hair samples. Ninety-six percent of firms refuse to hire applicants who test positive for illegal drug use (they are not as tough on applicants who test positive for alcohol). While the most common practice is to test job applicants, drug testing of job incumbents, either through a randomized procedure or based on probable cause, is also on the increase.

The most common form of urinalysis testing is the immunoassay test, which applies an enzyme solution to a urine sample and measures change in the density of the sample. The drawback of the $20 (per applicant) immunoassay test is that it is sensitive to some legal drugs as well as illegal drugs. Because of this, it is recommended that a positive immunoassay test be followed by a more reliable confirmatory test, such as gas chromatography. The only errors in testing that can occur with the confirmatory tests are due to two causes: passive inhalation, a rare event (caused by involuntarily inhaling marijuana), and laboratory blunders (e.g., mixing urine samples). Hair analysis is a more expensive but also more reliable and less invasive form of drug testing.

Positive test results say little regarding one's ability to perform the job, and most testing gives little or no information about the amount of the drug used, when it was used, how frequently it was used, and whether the applicant or candidate will be (or is) less effective on the job.

The legal implications of drug testing may have changed significantly since this chapter was written. Currently, drug testing is legal in all 50 states for preemployment screening and on-the-job assessment; however, employees in some states have successfully challenged dismissals based solely on a random drug test. For those employment situations in which a collective bargaining agreement has allowed drug testing, the punitive action based on the results is subject to arbitration. One study found that the majority of dismissals based on drug tests were overturned by arbitrators.[30] Among the arguments against drug testing are that it is an invasion of privacy, it is an unreasonable search and seizure, and it violates the rights of due process. Most experts agree that all three of these arguments may apply to public employers, such as governments, but do not apply to private industry. State law is relevant here since some drug testing programs have been challenged under privacy provisions of state institutions. With regard to public employment, the Supreme Court has ruled that drug testing is legal when the public safety could be at risk, as is the case in transportation. We will explore the matter of drug testing in more detail in Chapter 14.

Is Testing an Invasion of Privacy?

Some have critiqued the widespread use of employment tests on the grounds that these procedures may be an invasion of an individual's privacy, produce information that will affect an individual's employment opportunities, and compel an individual to falsify information. Some types of employment tests seem particularly prone to these concerns.[31] Among the devices we have reviewed in this chapter that seem most likely to face these problems are drug tests, reference checks/applications blanks, background checks, honesty/integrity tests, and personality tests. One survey revealed that more than 60 percent of respondents felt that questions regarding arrest records, memberships in community organizations, and the like were inappropriate (see Critical Thinking Exercise 6.1).

Experts in employment testing who support the use of these selection procedures have responded to the challenges in a number of ways. First, various professional standards and guidelines have been devised to protect the confidentiality of test results. Second, almost any interpersonal interaction, whether it be an interview or an informal discussion with an employer over lunch, involves the exchange of information. Thus, advocates of employment testing contend that every selection procedure comprises some invasion of the applicant's privacy. Finally, in the interests of high productivity and staying within the law, organizations may need to violate an individual's privacy to a certain degree. Companies with government contracts are among those obliged to maintain a safe work environment and may need to require drug testing of employees.

There are those who will continue to voice concern over the confidentiality and ethics of employment testing, particularly as computer-based databases expand in scope and availability to organizations. It also is likely that there will be increasing calls for more legislation at federal, state, and local levels to restrict company access to and use of employment-related information.

PERFORMANCE TESTING*

Despite making valuable contributions to employee selection, paper-and-pencil tests have their problems and limitations. The validity of cognitive ability tests is clear; unfortunately, considerable potential legal implications stem from their use. As we discussed, the validity of paper-and-pencil measures of applicant motivation or personality is not nearly as impressive. Many experts sug-

---

*This section contributed by Joan E. Pynes.

gest that the prediction of job performance can be enhanced through performance or situational testing that involves samples of actual or simulated job tasks and/or behaviors. Performance testing is usually more complex than paper-and-pencil testing in that behavioral responses are required by test takers that are similar to the responses required on the job.[32] A work sample consists of tasks representing the type, complexity, and difficulty level of the activities that are required on the job. Applicants must demonstrate that they possess the necessary competencies or skills needed for successful job performance. The most obvious example of a work sample is a word processing test for clerical personnel. More complex examples attempt to simulate what managers must do on the job. **Assessment centers,** for example, often entail several work samples or simulations of on-the-job behaviors typically exhibited by managers.

The objective of performance testing is to assess candidates' ability to do the job. Thus, applicants for clerical positions may be required to exhibit word processing (typing) skills or demonstrate proficiency in shorthand or filing. These exercises are work samples because word processing, shorthand, and filing are representative of the tasks a clerical worker might be asked to perform, and applicants are expected to possess these skills at the time of the interview. But requesting that clerical applicants demonstrate shorthand skills is effective only if shorthand skills are required for the position. To ensure that performance tests are tailored to match the important activities of the job, HR professionals should develop the performance test from the tasks, behaviors, and responsibilities identified in a job analysis (see Chapter 4).

The performance testing process should be as standardized as possible with consistent and precise instructions, testing material, conditions, and equipment. All the candidates must have the same time allotment to complete tests, and there must be a specific standard of performance by which to compare the applicants' efforts. For example, a minimum passing score for a typing exam might be set at 40 words a minute with two errors. This standard would apply to all applicants. Today, performance tests are available through the Internet. One large retailer had candidates for its district manager position complete an in-basket test over a Web site. Once responses are made through the Web site, trained assessors conduct interviews that focus on the candidates' responses. Recent research shows this approach is more efficient than assessment centers and reveals highly similar results.

What Is an Assessment Center?

An assessment center generally offers a "standardized evaluation of behavior on multiple inputs."[33] These centers use trained observers and a variety of techniques to make judgments about behavior, in part, from specially developed assessment simulations. Assessors typically test job candidates with a collection of performance tests that simulate the work environment. Some centers also use paper-and-pencil tests as part of the assessment process. At the Center for Creative Leadership in Greensboro, North Carolina, high-level managers complete an extensive battery of cognitive and personality tests and receive subordinate and peer assessments before their participation in the weeklong assessment center.

Private-sector organizations, educational institutions, military organizations, public safety and other governmental agencies have used the assessment center method to identify candidates for selection, placement, and promotion. Organizations in private and public sectors often use assessment centers for supervisory or managerial positions. The method has also been used for nonadministrative positions such as sales personnel, vocational rehabilitation counselors, planning analysts, social workers, personnel specialists, research analysts, firefighters, and police officers. One advantage of this approach for managerial selection is that internal and external candidates can go through the center for direct comparisons.

Among the numerous organizations that use the assessment center method for selection are AT&T, IBM, Ford, Office Depot, Xerox, Procter & Gamble, the Department of Defense, the CIA, and the Federal Aviation Administration. Assessment centers are expensive; costs range from a low of about $125 for each candidate to as much as $3,000 for upper-level managerial selection.

With the typical assessment center method, information about an employee's strengths and weaknesses is provided through a combination of **performance tests,** which are designed to simulate the type of work to which the candidate will be exposed. Trained assessors observe and evaluate performance in the situational exercises. The assessors compile and integrate their judgments on each exercise to form a summary rating for each candidate.

Individual assessment centers operate differently from one another. Assessment center programs tend to vary in purpose and use, such as selection, promotion, training, and development; length of the assessment process—one day to one week; the ratio of assessors to those being assessed; the extent of assessor training; and the number and type of assessment instruments and exercises used.[34]

All assessment centers call for an assessment of job dimensions. United Technology evaluates managers on the following dimensions: oral presentation, initiative, leadership, planning and organization, written communication, decision making, and interpersonal skills. **Dimensions** are clusters of behaviors that are specific, observable, verifiable, and that can be reliably and logically classified together. The dimension "written communication" was defined by United Technology as the following: "clear expression of ideas in writing and in good grammatical form." United Technology breaks down behavioral examples of written communication as: "Exchanges information/reports with superior regarding the day's activities. Completes all written reports and required forms in a manner that ensures the inclusion of all data necessary to meet the needs of the personnel using the information. Uses appropriate vocabulary and avoids excessive technical jargon in required correspondence." Figure 6.5 presents a set of dimensions and their definitions as used in an assessment center for selecting supervisors.

FIGURE 6.5
ASSESSMENT CENTER DIMENSIONS

Leadership: To direct, coordinate, and guide the activities of others; to monitor, instruct, and motivate others in the performance of their tasks: to assign duties and responsibilities and to follow up on assignments; to utilize available human and technical resources in accomplishing tasks and in achieving solutions to problems; to follow through within organizational guidelines.

Interpersonal: To be sensitive to the needs and feelings of others; to respond empathetically; to consistently display courtesy in interpersonal contacts; to develop rapport with others; to be cognizant of and respect the need in others for self-esteem.

Organizing and Planning: To create strategies for self and others to accomplish specific results; to utilize prescribed strategies; to fix schedules and priorities so as to meet objectives; to coordinate personnel and other resources; to establish and utilize follow-up procedures.

Perception and Analysis: To identify, assimilate, and comprehend the critical elements of a situation; to identify alternative courses of action; to be aware of situational or data discrepancies; to evaluate salient factors and elements essential to resolution of problems.

Decision Making: To use logical and sound judgment in use of resources; to adequately assess a situation and make a sound and logical determination of an appropriate course of action based on the facts available, including established procedures and guidelines; to select solutions to problems by weighing the ramifications of alternative courses of action.

Oral and Nonverbal Communication: To present information to others concisely and without ambiguity; to articulate clearly; to use appropriate voice inflection, grammar, and vocabulary; to maintain appropriate eye contact; to display congruent nonverbal behavior.

Adaptability: To modify courses of action to accommodate situational changes; to vary behavior in accordance with changes in human and interpersonal factors; to withstand stress.

Decisiveness: To make frequent decisions; to make decisions spanning many different areas; to render judgments, take action, make commitments; to react quickly to situational changes; to make determinations based on available evidence; to defend actions when challenged by others.

Written Communications: To present and express information in writing, employing unambiguous, concise, and effective language. To use correct grammar, punctuation, and sentence structure; to adjust writing style to the demands of the communication.

Assessors develop the assessment dimensions and exercises from the results of a job analysis. The exercises allow assessors to observe, record, classify, and evaluate relevant job behaviors. Some of the most common assessment exercises are in-baskets, leaderless group discussions, oral presentations, and role plays. We will review each of these next.

IN-BASKET. The in-basket consists of a variety of materials of varying importance and priority that would typically be handled by an incumbent. Candidates are asked to imagine that they are placed in an administrative position and must deal with a number of memos and items accumulated in their in-baskets in a limited amount of time. Assessors give them background information about the unit they are managing. After writing their responses to the memos, the candidates are interviewed by trained assessors who review the "out-basket" and question the actions taken. In-baskets are typically designed to measure oral and written communication skills, planning, decisiveness, initiative, and organization skills.

LEADERLESS GROUP DISCUSSION. Candidates assemble in groups of three to six people after individually considering an issue or problem and making specific recommendations. While a leader is not designated for the group, one usually emerges during the group interaction. Two or more assessors observe the interaction as the group attempts to reach consensus on the issue. Assessors use the leaderless group discussion to determine oral communication, stress tolerance, adaptability, leadership, and persuasiveness. Some graduate schools now use the leaderless group discussion to select doctoral students for their business and other graduate programs.

ORAL PRESENTATION. In the brief time allowed, candidates plan, organize, and prepare a presentation on an assigned topic. An assessment center developed by IBM requires candidates for sales management positions to prepare and deliver a five-minute oral presentation in which they present one of their hypothetical staff members for promotion and then defend the staff member n a group discussion. IBM uses this exercise to evaluate aggressiveness, selling ability, self-confidence, resistance, and interpersonal contact.[35]

ROLE-PLAYING. For this common assessment center exercise, candidates assume the role of the incumbent and must deal with a subordinate about a performance problem. The subordinate is a trained role-player. Another example is to have candidates interact with clients or individuals external to the organization, requiring them to obtain information or alleviate a problem. Vocational rehabilitation counselor candidates who apply for jobs with the Massachusetts Rehabilitation Commission assume the role of a counselor who is meeting a client for the first time. The candidate has the responsibility of gaining information about the client's case and establishing rapport with the client. Figure 6.6 presents summary descriptions of four exercises used in an assessment center to select first-line supervisors for high-tech organizations.

How Are Assessments Done?

Assessors who have received extensive training on assessment center methodology evaluate all the candidates in an assessment center—usually 6 to 12 people—as they perform the same tasks. Assessors are trained to rec-

FIGURE 6.6
DESCRIPTION OF
ASSESSMENT CENTER EXERCISES

Customer situation: A large equipment user (a select national account) has been experiencing recent problems involving a particular piece of equipment, culminating in a systems down situation. Problems with the equipment could include software, and parts received to fix the equipment are damaged.

The participant will be required to review information about the problem for 30 minutes and generate potential courses of action. Participants will then meet in groups to devise a consensus strategy for dealing with the problem. Assessors should expect a plan of action from the participants and may probe the participants for additional contingency plans. The participants will have 45 minutes to discuss the customer problem and develop a strategy.

Employee discussion: In this exercise the participant must develop a strategy for counseling a subordinate (a senior customer service engineer) who has been experiencing recent performance problems. The participant will have 30 minutes to review information regarding the technician's declining performance over the last few months.

The participant will then have 15 minutes to prepare a brief report on the individual with recommendations for submission to the district manager. The participant will then meet with two assessors to discuss the strategy.

In-basket: In this exercise, the participant will assume the role of a newly transferred branch manager. The participant will have 90 minutes to review information related to various issues (technical developments, equipment maintenance specifications, customer information, etc.). The participant will be instructed to spend this time identifying priorities and grouping related issues, as well as indicating courses of action to be taken.

The participant will then take part in a 15-minute interview with an assessor to clarify the actions taken and logic behind decisions made.

Problem analysis: In this exercise the participant will be required to review information on three candidates and recommend which of the three should be promoted to a branch manager position. The participant will have 90 minutes to review information and prepare a written recommendation.

The participants will then meet in groups to derive a consensus recommendation for the district manager.

ognize designated behaviors, which are clearly defined before each assessment.

Assessors are often representatives from the organization who are at higher levels than the candidates being assessed. This is done to diminish the potential for contamination, which may result from an assessor allowing prior association with a candidate to interfere with making an objective evaluation. Some assessment centers use outside consultants and psychologists as assessors.

Different assessors observe assessment center candidates in each exercise. The assessors are responsible for observing the actual behavior of the candidate during each exercise and documenting how each candidate performed. Figure 6.7 presents an example of an assessor rating form for the "leadership" dimension at an assessment center for the selection of supervisors at the Bendix Corporation.

After the participants complete all the exercises, the assessors typically assemble at a team meeting to pool their impressions, arrive at an overall consensus rating for each candidate on each dimension, and derive an overall assessment rating. Recent evidence reveals that assessment centers can be broken down to make them more efficient. Research shows that you probably do not have to assemble candidates together; performance tests and follow-up interviews by trained assessors reveal essentially the same results as centers.

What Is the Validity and Adverse Impact of Assessment Centers and Other Performance Tests?

There is a scarcity of well-done, criterion-related validity studies on assessment centers. With a few exceptions, assessment center validity studies focus on administrative positions such as managers and supervisors.[36] The method has also proved to be valid for law enforcement personnel.[37] One review of this literature found that assessment centers correlated .53 with promotion within the organization.[38]

The validity evidence of work samples and performance testing is also strong. One review found an average validity of .54 for work samples.[39] While the validities reported for assessment centers are generally no higher than those reported for most cognitive ability tests, decisions made from assessment centers appear to be substantially more defensible in court and result in less adverse impact than cognitive ability tests. The method is ideal when a company has both internal and external candidates. Most companies use assessment centers as one of the last steps in a selection process considering both internal and external candidates. People who are assessed by the assessment center method or performance tests perceive the procedure to be fair and job related, making them less likely to take legal action.

FIGURE 6.7
EXAMPLE OF ASSESSOR RATING FORM

Leadership Rating _____

To direct, coordinate and guide the activities of others; to monitor, instruct, and motivate others in the performance of their tasks; to assign duties and responsibilities, and to follow up on assignments; to utilize available human and technical resources in accomplishing tasks and in achieving solutions to problems; to follow through within organizational guidelines.

*Key points**

- Requested technical support when necessary.
- Provided specific guidance to others through written means.
- Took initiative to reallocate Branch I workforce personnel.
- Assigned tasks to others.

POSITIVE	NEGATIVE

* These are general points; specific behaviors need to be listed by the assessor.

INTERVIEWS*

While the use of paper-and-pencil tests and performance tests has increased, the employment interview continues to be the most common personnel selection tool. Primarily due to its expense, the interview is typically one of the last selection hurdles used after other methods have reduced the number of potential candidates. The manner in which interviews are conducted is not typically conducive to high validity for the method. As one review of the research concluded, "The typical unstructured selection interview is invalid. The interviewer operates as a poor information processor; he/she collects unsystematic and incomplete data and weighs it according to an invalid stereotype; then, combines it into an often invalid prediction."[40]

One of the great discrepancies between HRM research and practice is in the area of interviewing. Research provides clear prescriptions for interviewing the right way. Figure 6.8 presents the most important discrepancies between research and practice. Even academic institutions, from which the vast majority of this research is derived, do not usually practice what they preach when it comes to selecting a new faculty member or administrator.

---

*This section contributed by Diana Dendrick.

Almost every student will eventually take part in a job interview. Nearly 100 percent of organizations use the employment interview as one basis for the personnel selection. Even some universities now use interviews to select students for graduate programs. Dartmouth, Carnegie-Mellon, and the Wharton School at the University of Pennsylvania routinely interview applicants for their prestigious MBA programs. Many companies now provide extensive training programs and specific guidelines for interviewers. As Tom Newman, director of training at S.C. Johnson & Son, said, interviewing is now "much more of a science." This "science" clearly pays off as research shows greater validity for more systematic interviewing. Mobil Oil, Radisson Hotels International, the Marriott Corporation, and Sun Bank are among many of the companies with extensive programs to prepare their interviewers.

What Factors Affect the Validity of Interviews?

A variety of factors influence the interviewing process, yet they can be categorized under three general headings of **influence factors,** or cues affecting the job interview.

1. Attributes of the applicant: the intensity, motives, and physical characteristics of the job applicant.

FIGURE 6.8
DISCREPANCIES BETWEEN RESEARCH AND PRACTICE FOR STAFFING METHODS

WHAT DOES RESEARCH SAY?	WHAT IS THE PRACTICE?
Use a WAB or BIB	Less than 2% of companies use validated WAB or BIB
Monitor methods for adverse impact	Less than 10% of companies do
Validate cognitive ability tests	Less than 26% do
Graphology is invalid	Use is on the increase
Weight personality factors based on job analysis	Less than 5% do
Use structured, situational, or behavioral interview	Only 28% do
Use formal interview rating system	Only 16% do
Use more than one interviewer	Only 41% do
Use statistical model to combine data	Less than 5% use actuarial model

2. Attributes of the interviewer(s): the motives, previous learning, personality, and physical characteristics of the interviewer(s).

3. Attributes of the situation: the environmental conditions such as time, noise, light, heat.

In the context of the interview, the attributes of the applicant refer to characteristics that influence an interviewer's attention and impression of the applicant. Voice modulation, body language, posture, and visible characteristics such as sex, weight, ethnicity, and physical attractiveness are among the factors that might influence the interviewer's judgments about a job applicant.[41] A common phenomenon here is stereotyping, in which an impression about an individual is formed due to his or her group membership rather than any individual attributes. **Stereotyping** involves categorizing groups according to general traits and then attributing those traits to a particular individual once the group membership is known. Although stereotypes are a common and convenient means of efficiently processing information, they can be a source of bias when people attribute traits they believe to be true for an entire group to one member — without considering that person as an individual. Figure 6.9 lists some of the more common applicant attributes that have been shown to cause rating bias.[42]

The attributes of the interviewer refer to the interviewer's personal characteristics, which might influence his or her ability to make decisions. Personal values and previously learned associations between certain information cues and decision responses might influence one's decision-making process. One type of perceptual influence due to the interviewer's personal characteristics is a "similar-to-me" attribution, meaning the interviewer forms an impression due to his or her perceived similarity between an applicant and himself or herself. This perceived similarity might be based on the interviewer's attitudes, interests, or group membership, causing certain information, or individuals, to be placed in a more favorable light than others. The danger is that these judgments of similarity can cause rating errors; they might not be relevant to the particular job for which the

FIGURE 6.9
APPLICANT ATTRIBUTES THAT CAUSE RATING BIAS

FACTORS	EXAMPLES OF RESEARCH FINDINGS
Gender bias	Both male and female interviewers gave lower evaluations to female candidates, yet this effect was moderated by type of job (role-congruent jobs) and competence. Female interviewers gave higher ratings than male interviewers.
First impression effect	Early impressions were more important than factual information for interviewer judgments. Hire decisions were related to the interviewer's causal interpretation (attribution) of an applicant's past outcomes.
Contrast effect	Interviewers' evaluations of job candidates were influenced by the quality and characteristics of the previous candidates.
Nonverbal communication	Applicants who looked straight ahead, as opposed to downward, were rated as being more alert, assertive, dependable; they were also more likely to be hired. Applicants that demonstrated a greater amount of eye contact, head moving, and smiling received higher evaluations.
Physical attractiveness	More attractive applicants receive higher evaluations.

interview is being conducted. Figure 6.10 lists interviewer attributes that have been shown to distort the interview process

Factors such as stress, background noise, interruptions, time pressures, decision accountability, and other conditions surrounding the interview can influence interviewers' attention to information. An important factor is the amount of information the interviewer has prior to the actual interview session. Little background information about the job may cause distortion in the decision-making process because of resulting irrelevant or erroneous assumptions about job requirements. This lack of job information causes the interviewer to rely on his or her assumptions about what the job requires. These assumptions can be inconsistent among different interviewers or across different interview sessions. Rating errors occur because interviewers collect non-job-related information and use the information to make decisions. Figure 6.11 contains a list of some of the situation attributes that have been found to distort the interview process.[43]

Applicant, interviewer, and situation attributes can potentially bias decision making and result in erroneous evaluations during the interview. In response to the problems of interviewer bias and the high cost of face-to-face interviews, many companies conduct computer interviews to screen applicants. Telecomputing Interviewing Services in San Francisco lists more than 1,000 clients that conduct computer interviews for mostly entry-level jobs. Bloomingdale's hired all the personnel for its Miami store using computer interviewing, which questions applicants about work attitudes, substance abuse, and employee theft. As Ellen Pollin, personnel manager at Bloomingdale's, puts it, "The machine never forgets to ask a question and asks each question in the same way." Other companies are using videoconferencing to interview employees, particularly managerial prospects.

Merrill Lynch and Texas Instruments claim considerable cost savings with no loss in validity using videoconferences.

Citizens Bank of Maryland has sharply reduced interviewer involvement by combining a short, structured interview with a video developed especially for tellers and customer service representatives. The video provides a realistic job preview that describes the positive and negative features of the job and then tests applicants on job-related verbal, quantitative, and interpersonal skills. The test is completed on a computer and is scored for $27. Citizens Bank reports a significant drop in turnover with this method compared to turnover rates when hiring decisions were based on an unstructured interview (i.e., in which interviewers have no formal set of questions to ask).

What Is the Validity of Employment Interviews?

The information obtained from the interview provides a basis for subsequent selection and placement decisions. The importance lies in the overall quality of those employment decisions based on interviews: How reliable is the interview information? How valid is that information for predictive purposes? That is, to what extent do interview judgments predict subsequent job performance?

The validity of the employment interview has often been hampered by perceptual factors such as first impressions, stereotypes, and lack of adequate job information. The influences listed in Figures 6.9 to 6.11 help explain these findings. The interview procedure's validity has also been impaired by factors such as different information utilization, different questioning content, and lack of interviewer knowledge regarding the requirements of the job to be filled.

FIGURE 6.10
INTERVIEWER ATTRIBUTES THAT CAUSE RATING BIAS

FACTORS	EXAMPLES OF RESEARCH FINDINGS
Similarity effect	Interviewers gave more positive ratings to applicants perceived to be similar to themselves. Interviewers resisted using additional information to evaluate applicants once they perceived the applicants to be similar to themselves.
Likability	Interviewers gave more positive ratings to candidates they liked. Interpersonal attraction was found to influence interviewers' perceptions of applicant qualifications.
Ideal stereotype	Interviewers judged applicants against their own stereotype of an ideal job candidate. These stereotypes may be unique to each interviewer, or they may be a common stereotype shared by a group of raters.
Information favorability	Interviewers weighed negative information more heavily than positive information. Interviewers spent more time talking when they had already formed a favorable decision.
Information utilization	Interviewers placed different importance (weights) on the information content of the interview resulting in idiosyncratic information-weighing strategies. Discrepancies often arise between interviewers' intended (nominal) information weights and the actual information weights they used to arrive at a decision.

FIGURE 6.11
SITUATIONAL ATTRIBUTES THAT CAUSE RATING BIAS

FACTORS	EXAMPLES OF RESEARCH FINDINGS
Job information	Interviewers who received more information about the job used it for evaluation decisions.
	Increased job information reduced the effect of irrelevant attributes and increased inter-rater reliability.
Applicant information	Interviewers' pre-interview impressions of applicant qualifications had a strong influence on post-interview impressions and recommendations to hire.
	Interviewers with a favorable pre-interview impression of applicants evaluated those applicants as having done a better job answering the interview questions.
Decision time	Interviewers reached a final decision during the interview; some studies have indicated the decision is made after an average of 4 minutes.
	Hire decisions were made sooner than no-hire decision.

However, recent efforts to improve interview effectiveness indicate that certain types of interviews are more reliable and valid than the typical unstructured format. For instance, interview questions that are based on a job analysis (see Chapter 4), as opposed to psychological or trait information, increase the validity of the interview procedure. **Structured interviews,** which represent a standardized approach to systematically collecting and rating applicant information, have yielded substantially higher reliability and validity results than unstructured interviews. These recent research findings suggest that the effectiveness of interview decisions can be improved by carefully defining what information is to be evaluated and by systematically evaluating that information using consistent rating standards. The most recent review on the subject concluded that structured interviews are more valid than unstructured interviews; in general, the structured interview has at least modest validity. Specifically, overall validity for structured interviews was about .30 versus .14 for unstructured interviews.[44]

With the potential bias affecting employment interviews comes potential litigation. Many cases have involved the questions asked at the interviews. The employment interview is in essence a "test" and is thus subject to the same laws and guidelines prohibiting discrimination on the basis of age, race, sex, religion, national origin, or disability. Furthermore, the interview process is similar to the subjective nature of the performance appraisal process; hence, many of the court decisions concerning the use of performance appraisals also apply to the interview. The courts have not been kind to employers using vague, inadequate hiring standards; subjective, idiosyncratic interview evaluation criteria; or biased questions unrelated to the job. The courts have also criticized employers for inadequate interviewer training and irrelevant interview questions. In general, the courts have focused on two basic issues for determining interview discrimination: the content of the interview and the impact of those decisions.

The first issue involves discriminatory intent: Do certain questions convey an impression of underlying discriminatory attitudes? Discrimination is most likely to occur when interviewers ask non-job-related questions of only one protected group of job candidates and not of others. Women applying for work as truck drivers at Spokane Concrete Products were questioned about child care options and other issues not asked of male applicants. The court found disparate treatment against females and a violation of Title VII. An interviewer extensively questioned a female applicant of a bank about what she would do if her six-year-old got sick. The same interviewer did not ask that question of the male applicants. The woman didn't get the job but did get a lawyer. The court concluded that this line of questioning constitutes sex discrimination.

The second issue pertains to discriminatory impact: Does the interview inquiry result in a differential, or adverse, impact on protected groups? If so, are the interview questions valid and job related? Discriminatory impact occurs when the questions asked of all job candidates implicitly screen out a majority of protected group members. For example, questions about arrests can have a discriminating impact on minorities. The Detroit Edison Company provided no training, job analysis information, or specific questions for its all-white staff of interviewers. The process could not be defended in light of the adverse impact that resulted from interview decisions.

In summary, the inherent bias in the interview and the relatively poor validity reported for unstructured interview decisions make this selection tool vulnerable to charges of discrimination. Employers need to quantify, standardize, and document interview judgments. Furthermore, employers should train interviewers, continuously evaluate the reliability and validity of interview decisions, and monitor interviewer decisions for any discriminatory effects. As we discussed earlier, many companies such as S.C. Johnson, Radisson Hotels, and Mobil Oil now have extensive training programs for interviewers. This training covers interviewing procedures, potential discriminatory areas, rating procedures, and role plays.

The research evidence regarding the discriminatory effects of the interview is based on the stereotyping processes that affect female and minority job applicants. In the paragraphs that follow, we summarize the evidence, which is generally inconclusive.

SEX DISCRIMINATION. Although early research studies indicated that female applicants generally receive lower interview evaluations than male applicants, more detailed analyses suggest that this effect largely depends on the type of job in question, the amount of job information available to the interviewer, and the qualifications of the candidate. In fact, recent research suggests that females typically do not receive lower ratings in the selection interview; in some studies, females scored higher ratings than male applicants.

RACE DISCRIMINATION. There is mixed evidence about racial bias in interviewer evaluations. Positive and negative results have been reported in the relatively few studies that have investigated race discrimination. There is some indication that African-American interviewers rate African-American applicants more favorably while white interviewers rate white applicants more favorably.

AGE DISCRIMINATION. Although the research indicates that older applicants generally receive lower evaluations than younger applicants, this effect is influenced by the type of job in question, interviewer characteristics, and the content of the interview questions (i.e., traits versus qualifications). The evidence for age bias is mixed and suggests that, as in sex bias, age bias might be largely determined by the type of job under study.

DISABILITY DISCRIMINATION. Few studies have examined bias against disabled applicants. The evidence that exists suggests that some disabled applicants receive lower hiring evaluations but higher attribute ratings for personal factors such as motivation. Before any conclusions about disability bias can be made, more research needs to be conducted that examines the nature of the disability and the impact of situational factors, such as the nature of the job. (See Chapter 3 for discussion of the ADA.)

Overall, the research evidence on discriminatory bias is insufficient to draw any firm conclusions. Employers should, however, examine their interview process for discriminatory bias, train interviewers about ways to prevent biased inquiries, provide interviewers with thorough job specifications, structure the interview around a complete and up-to-date job analysis, and monitor the activities and assessments of individual interviewers. Some interviewers, no dou[bt,] or more of the discriminatory biase[s]

How Do We Improve the Validity of Interviews?

Many multinational corporations use successful overseas managers to develop and conduct interviews for the selection of managers for distant assignments. These people tend to understand the major requirements of these jobs better than managers who have no overseas experience. Many U.S. companies, including Ford, Procter & Gamble, Texaco, and Philip Morris, credit improvements in their expatriate placements to their interviewing processes, which involve successful expatriates who have had experience in the same jobs to be filled.

The physical environment for the interviews should be maintained consistently by providing a standardized setting for the interviews. The conditions surrounding the interview might influence the decision-making process; therefore, extraneous factors such as noise, temperature, and interruptions should be controlled. Some companies use computer interviewing to standardize the interview process and reduce costs. Bloomingdale's is among the companies that use either a computerized voice system or a keyboard format to question applicants about work attitudes, employee theft, and other issues.

There is a great need for interviewer training. Our previous discussion about the decision-making process indicates that interviewers need to be trained regarding how to evaluate job candidates, the criteria to be used in the evaluation, how to use evaluation instruments, and how to avoid common biases and potentially illegal questions.

S.C. Johnson Wax found that most interviewers had made their decisions about applicants after only five minutes. The company trained its interviewers to withhold judgment and gather information free of the first-impression bias. Companies should use workshops and group discussions to train interviewers how to do the following:

1. Use job information: understand job requirements and relate these requirements to their questioning content and strategy.

2. Reduce rating bias: practice interviewing and provide feedback and group discussion about rating errors.

3. Communicate effectively: develop a rapport with applicants, "actively listen," and recognize differences in semantics.

This training should focus on the following:

1. Use of interview guides and outlines that structure the interview content and quantitatively rate applicant responses.

xchange of information that stresses relevant applicant information and provides applicants with adequate and timely information about the job and company.

The content of the interview determines what specific factors are to be evaluated by the interviewers. The following are general suggestions based on legal and practical concerns; more specific content guidelines should be based on the organization and the relevant state and local laws.

1. Exclude traits that can be measured by more valid employment tests; for example, intelligence, job aptitude or ability, job skills, or knowledge.

2. Include motivational and interpersonal factors that are required for effective job performance. These two areas seem to have the most potential for both overall and interviewer validity. Interviewers should assess only those factors that are specifically exhibited in the behavior of the applicant during the interview and are critical for performance in the job to be filled.

3. Match interview questions (content areas) with the job analysis data of the job to be filled and the strategic goals of the organization.

4. Avoid biased language, jokes that may detract from the formality of the interview, and inquiries that are not relevant to the job in question.

5. Limit the amount of pre-interview information to complete information about the applicants' qualifications and clear up any ambiguous data. While knowledge of test results, letters of reference, and other sources of information can bias an interview, it is a good strategy to seek additional information relevant to applicants' levels of KASOCs.

The format suggestions deal with how the interview content is structured and evaluated. These suggestions describe different types of interview procedures and rating forms for standardizing and documenting interviewer evaluations.

Interview questions are intended to elicit evaluation information; therefore, rating forms are recommended to provide a systematic scoring system for interpreting and evaluating information obtained from applicants. Based on the job analysis, the specified content of the interview, and the degree of structure for the procedure, ratings forms should be constructed with the following features. First, the ratings should be behaviorally specific and based on possible applicant responses exhibited during the interview. Second, the ratings should reflect the relevant dimensions of job success and provide a focused evaluation of only the factors required for job performance. Third, the ratings should be based on quantitative rating scales that provide a continuum of possible responses. These anchors provide examples of good, av-

erage, and poor applicant responses for each interview question. The use of anchored rating forms reduces rater error and increases rater accuracy. This approach, using specific, multiple ratings for each content area of the interview, is preferred to using an overall, subjective suitability rating that is not explicitly related to the job. Figure 6.12 presents an example of an actual rating form.

What Are Major Types of Interviews?

A variety of interview formats are used today. While this lack of standardization has contributed to poor reliability and validity of both overall interview decisions and the decisions of individual interviewers, improvements in the effectiveness of the procedure have been made based on the following types of interview formats.

Structured interviews range from highly structured procedures to semistructured inquiries. In a highly structured interview, interviewers ask the same questions of all candidates in the same order. The questions are based on a job analysis and are reviewed for relevance, accuracy, completion, ambiguity, and bias. A semistructured interview provides general guidelines, such as an outline of either mandatory or suggested questions, and recording forms for notes and summary ratings. In contrast, the traditional, unstructured interview is typically characterized by open-ended questions that are not nec-

FIGURE 6.12
SAMPLE SITUATIONAL INTERVIEW QUESTIONS

1. A customer comes into the store to pick up a watch he had left for repair. The repair was supposed to have been completed a week ago, but the watch is not back yet from the repair shop. The customer is very angry. How would you handle the situation?

   1 (low) Tell the customer the watch is not back yet and ask him to check back with you later.

   3 (average) Apologize, tell the customer that you will check into the problem and call him or her back later.

   5 (high) Put the customer at ease and call the repair shop while the customer waits.*

2. For the past week you have been consistently getting the jobs that are the most time-consuming (e.g., poor handwriting, complex statistical work). You know it's nobody's fault because you have been taking the jobs in priority order. You have just picked your fourth job of the day and it's another "loser." What would you do?

   1 (low) Thumb through the pile and take another job.

   2 (average) Complain to the coordinator, but do the job.

   3 (high) Take the job without complaining and do it.†

* Jeff A. Weekley and Joseph A. Gier, Reliability and validity of the situational interview for a sales position. *Journal of Applied Psychology*, 3 (1987), 484–487.

† Gary P. Latham and Lise M. Saari, Do people do what they say? Further studies on the situational interview. *Journal of Applied Psychology*, 4 (1984), 569–573.

essarily based on or related to the job to be filled. Interviewers who use either of the structured interview procedures standardize the content and process of the interview, thus improving the reliability and validity of the subsequent judgments.

Group/panel interviews consist of multiple interviewers who independently record and rate applicant responses during the interview session. The panel typically includes the job supervisor and a personnel representative or other job expert who helped develop the interview questions. As part of the interview process, the panel reviews job specifications, interview guides, and ways to avoid rating errors before each applicant. Procter & Gamble uses a minimum of four interviews for each applicant. The CIA uses a minimum of three interviews for each job candidate. Use of a panel interview reduces the impact of idiosyncratic biases that single interviewers might introduce, and the approach appears to increase interview reliability and validity. Many team-based production operations, such as GM's new Saturn Plant in Spring Hill, Tennessee, use team interviews to add new members and select team leaders. In general, there is greater validity in interviews that involve more than one interviewer for each job applicant.

Situational or behavioral interviews require applicants to describe how they would behave in specific situations. The interview questions are based on the critical incident method of job analysis, which calls for examples of unusually effective or ineffective job behaviors for a particular job (see Chapter 4). These incidents are converted into interview questions and require job applicants to describe how they would handle a given situation. Each question is accompanied with a rating scale, and interviewers evaluate applicants according to the effectiveness or ineffectiveness of their responses. The Palm Beach County, Florida, school board asked the following question of all applicants for the job of high school principal: "Members of the PTA have complained about what they regard as overly harsh punishment imposed by one teacher regarding cheating on an exam. How would you handle the entire matter?" Another question had to do with a teacher who was not complying with regulations for administering standardized tests. The job candidate was asked to provide a sequence of actions to be taken regarding the situation. The situational approach may be highly structured and may include an interview panel. In the case of Palm Beach County, three principals trained in situational interviewing listened to applicants' responses, asked questions, and then independently evaluated each response. The underlying assumption is that applicants' responses to the hypothetical job situations are predictive of what they would actually do on the job. This technique improves interviewer reliability and validity.

Behavioral interviewing may involve probing beyond the initial answer. At GM's new Saturn plant, employees are first asked to describe a project in which they participated as group or team members. Probing may involve work assignments, examples of good and bad teamwork, difficulties in completing the project, and other related projects. While hypothetical interview questions are valid, asking candidates to describe actual experiences with important job-related situations are slightly more valid.[45]

COMBINING DATA FROM VARIOUS STAFFING METHODS

We have proposed a number of selection procedures in this chapter, and PAS recommended that Smith Security use more than one approach. PAS recommended an accomplishment record, which could be completed on the World Wide Web, for the supervisory job. Applicants could also complete an in-basket on the Internet. The next step involved videoconference interviews between assessors and candidates followed by a detailed structured and behavioral interview.

But how should the data from the different tests be combined so that a final decision can be made? One way is to weigh scores from each approach equally after standardizing the data (convert scores to a common scoring key). Each applicant would receive a standard score on each predictor, the standard scores would be summed, and candidates would then be ranked according to the summed scores. Another approach is to weigh scores based on their empirical validity; that is, the extent to which each is correlated with the criterion of interest, including sales, performance, and turnover. A third approach is to rely on expert judgment regarding the weight that should be given to each source. Experts could review the content and procedures of each of the methods and give each a relative predictive weight, which is then applied to applicant scores.

PAS conducted an empirical validity study and derived weights based on the validity of each of the data sources. Structured, behavioral interviewing for only the top candidates was recommended based on the number of positions Smith Security had to fill. This multiple-step process saved time and money. Most companies that use a variety of different instruments follow a similar procedure by initially using the least expensive procedure (e.g., paper-and-pencil tests, biodata) and then using a set of procedures, such as performance tests, for those who do well in the first round. These companies conduct interviews only with the top scorers from the second phase of testing. The CIA, the FBI, numerous insurance companies, and a number of the most prestigious graduate business schools follow a similar procedure. The Wharton School at the University of Pennsylvania initially screens on the basis of the GMAT and undergraduate performance. The school then requests answers to lengthy essay questions. If the student survives this hurdle, several faculty members conduct interviews with the student.

Interviewing, especially in this context, is perhaps the most important of the selection options for assessing the "person–organization" fit. Sun Microsystems, the fastest growing U.S. company during the last five years, interviews job applicants several times by as many as 20 interviewers. The interview data are considered in the context of the results of an extensive battery of psychological tests. Toyota (USA) conducts a formal interview for its Georgetown, Kentucky, factory jobs. The interview results are combined with assessment center data, a work sample, and an aptitude test. The most effective selection systems integrate the data from the interview with other sources and weigh the information using the person–organizational fit model.[46]

What are the legal implications of this multiple-step process? In the *Connecticut v. Teal* case (Chapter 3), Ms. Teal was eliminated from further consideration at the first step of a multiple-step selection process and claimed she was a victim of Title VII discrimination. The Supreme Court said that even if the company actually hired a disproportionately greater number of minorities after the entire selection process, the job relatedness of that first step must be determined because this was where Ms. Teal was eliminated.

Another issue is where you set the cutoff score in a multiple cutoff system such as that recommended by PAS. Where, for example, do you set the cutoff score for the paper-and-pencil tests in order to identify those eligible for further testing? Unfortunately, there is no clear answer to this important question. If data are available, cutoff scores for any step in the process should generally be set to ensure a minimum predicted standard of job performance is met. If data are not available, cutoff scores should be set based on a consideration of the cost of subsequent selection procedures per candidate, the legal defensibility of each step in the process (i.e., job relatedness), and the adverse impact of possible scores at each step.

PERSONNEL SELECTION FOR OVERSEAS ASSIGNMENTS

One expert on expatriate assignments tells the story of a major U.S. food manufacturer who selected the new head of the marketing division in Japan. The assumption made in the selection process was that the management skills required for successful performance in the United States were identical to the requirements for an overseas assignment. The new director was selected primarily because of his superior marketing skills. Within 18 months, his company lost 89 percent of its existing market share.[47]

What went wrong? The problem may have been the criteria used in the selection process. The selection criteria used to hire a manager for an overseas position must focus on more facets of a manager than the selection of someone for a domestic position. The weight given to the various criteria may also be different for overseas assignments. Besides succeeding in a job, an effective expatriate must adjust to a variety of factors: differing job responsibilities even though the same job title is used, language and cultural barriers that make the training of local personnel difficult, family matters such as spouse employment and family readjustment, simple routine activities that are frustrating in the new culture, and the lack of traditional support systems, such as religious institutions or social clubs. The marketing head in Japan, for example, spent considerable time during the first six months of his assignment simply trying to deal with family problems and adjusting to the new environment. This experience is hardly unique. One survey of 80 U.S. multinational corporations found that over 50 percent of the companies had expatriate failure rates of 20 percent or more.[48] The reasons cited for the high failure rate were as follows (presented in order of importance):

1. Inability of the manager's spouse to adjust to the new environment.
2. The manager's inability to adapt to a new culture and environment.
3. The manager's personality or emotional immaturity.
4. The manager's inability to cope with new overseas responsibilities.
5. The manager's lack of technical competence.
6. The manager's lack of motivation to work overseas.

Obviously, some of these problems have to do with training and career issues.

Several of the factors listed above concern the selection of personnel for such assignments. The food manufacturer placed almost all the decision weight on the technical competence of the individual, apparently figuring that he and his family could adjust or adapt to almost anything. In fact, adjustment can be predicted to some extent, and staffing systems should emphasize adaptability along with the ability to interact well with a diverse group of clients, customers, and business associates. Surprisingly, few organizations emphasize so-called relational abilities in the selection of expatriates. In fact, one review of expatriate selection cites the "domestic equals overseas performance equation" as one of the major problems in expatriate selection. The result is an overemphasis on technical skills and previous accomplishments in a domestic setting.[49] The study concluded that the selection of expatriates should focus on four key dimensions: (1) self-orientation, (2) other-directedness, (3) perceptual factors, and (4) cultural toughness. The self-orientation dimension is concerned with activities that enhance self-esteem through reinforcement substitution, stress reduction, and technical competence. Stress levels can be measured with personality instruments. The other-directed dimension addresses the ability to interact with host-country nationals. The perceptual dimension reflects an ability to understand how foreigners behave and can also be measured with standardized personality instruments. The cultural toughness dimension has to do with the extent to which the culture and environment of the host country are different from those in the United States. If the difference is great, more weight should be given to the other three dimensions.

Of course, the company must first address whether it would be better off hiring someone from within the host country. Figure 6.13 presents a decision model that addresses this option. If the answer to this question is no, the model provides a chronology of the questions to be answered in the selection of an expatriate. If the answer is yes, the decision makers must be aware of any applicable host laws regarding personnel selection. In Poland and Sweden, for example, prospective employees must have prior knowledge of any testing and can prohibit the release of testing data to the company. Many European countries require union participation in all selection decisions for host nationals. Thus, companies may find that hiring host nationals is more problematic than going the expatriate route. Assuming that the host option is rejected, what steps should be followed to make better staffing decisions about expatriates? Let us examine some organizations that select large numbers of expatriates successfully.

The Peace Corps has only a 12 percent turnover rate (i.e., people who prematurely end their assignments). Of the 12 percent, only 3 to 4 percent are attributed to selection errors. The Peace Corps receives an average of 5,000 applications per month. The selection process begins with an elaborate application and biographical data form that provides information on background, education, vocational preferences, and volunteer activity in the past. Second, the applicant must take a placement test to assess general intelligence and language aptitude. Third, college or high school transcripts are used for placement rather than screening. The fourth step requires up to 15 references from a variety of sources. Although the general tendency among references is to provide positive views of candidates, one study found that for sensitive positions such as the Peace Corps volunteer, references often provide candid comments about applicants. The final step is an interview with several Peace Corp representatives. During the interview process, the candidate is asked about preferred site locations and specific skills as well as how he or she would deal with hypothetical overseas problems. An ideal candidate must be flexible and tolerant of others and must indicate a capacity to get work done under adverse conditions. The interviews also provide Peace Corps staff with details concerning the

candidate's background and preferences so that appropriate work assignments may be determined.

Based on these four sources of information, the screeners assess a candidate using the following questions: (1) Does the applicant have a skill that is needed overseas or a background that indicates he or she may be able to develop such a skill within a three-month training period? This question is designed to match the candidate with a job required by a foreign government, such as botanist, small business consultant, or medical worker. (2) Is the applicant personally suited for the assignment? This question focuses on personality traits such as flexibility, conscientiousness, and emotional stability.

Another expert on expatriate selection suggests focusing the process on environmental, task, and individual factors.[50] Environmental factors concern the specific national setting to which an expatriate may be assigned. Task factors deal with the specific job to be performed. Individual factors concern the makeup and situation of the person being considered for the assignment. Candidates should be selected on the basis of all these dimensions rather than solely on job competence.

The weight to be given to these factors differs as a function of the position to be filled. For example, a position that has an operational element requiring an individual to perform in a preexisting structure does not require strong interpersonal skills. However, a "structure reproducer"—an individual who builds a unit or department—does need strong interpersonal skills. Thus, the selection system should focus on the cultural environment, job elements, and individual talents. The weights given to the various criteria should be determined by the individual job. A job analysis would be helpful in this regard. This system is exemplified by Texas Instruments (TI), a manufacturer of electronics and high-technology equipment based in Dallas. In seeking expatriates for start-up ventures, the company focuses on such issues as an individual's familiarity with the region and culture (environment), specific job knowledge for the venture (job elements), knowledge of the language spoken in the region, and interpersonal skills. TI uses several methods to make assessments on these dimensions, including paper-and-pencil personality tests.

Many companies emphasize the "manager as ambassador" approach since the expatriate may act as the sole representative of the home office. IBM and GE, for example, select people who best symbolize the esprit de corps of the company and who recognize the importance of overseas assignments for the company.

Our review of the most successful systems for selecting expatriates provides a set of recommendations for a selection system. First, potential expatriates are identified through posted announcements, peer and/or superior nominations, or performance-appraisal data. Second, promising candidates are contacted and presented with an overview of the work assignment. A real-

FIGURE 6.13
MODEL OF THE SELECTION PROCESS FOR OVERSEAS ASSIGNMENTS

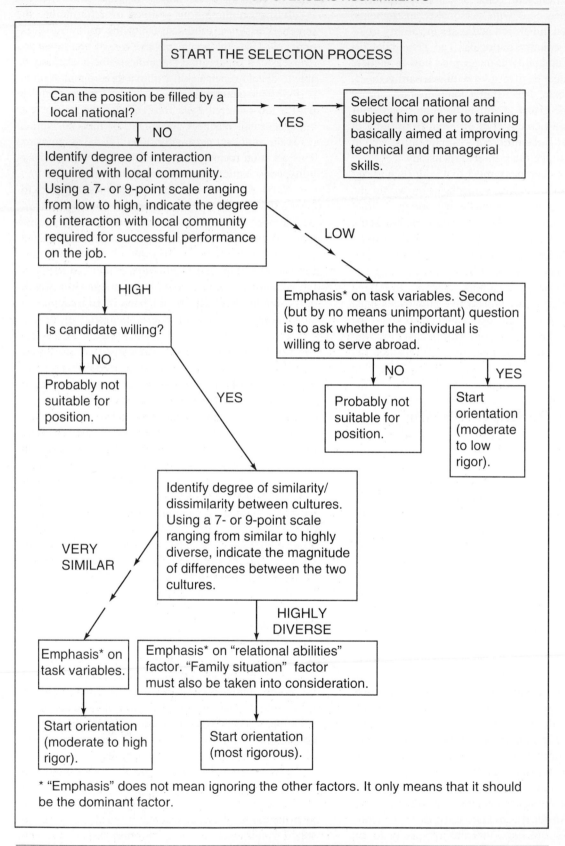

Source: R. L. Tung, Selection and training for overseas assignments. *Columbia Journal of World Business, 16,* 68–78, 1981.
Reprinted with the permission of the Columbia Journal of World Business, copyright 1981.

istic job preview would be ideal at this stage. Third, applicants are examined using a number of selection methods, including paper-and-pencil tests and performance tests. A growing number of companies now use standardized instruments to assess personality traits. The 16PF, for example, has been used for years to select overseas personnel for the U.S. Department of State and is now used by some U.S. companies and executive search companies that specialize in expatriate assignments. Although relational ability is considered to be a major predictor of expatriate success, the one available survey on the subject found that only 5 percent of companies were assessing this ability through a formal process (e.g., paper-and-pencil tests, performance appraisals).

After a small pool of qualified candidates is identified, candidates are interviewed and the best matches are selected for the assignment. Successful expatriates are ideal as interviewers. Our coverage of employment interviews provides recommendations for enhancing the validity of these interview decisions. Do the more rigorous selection systems result in a higher rate of expatriate success? One study found a strong relationship between the rigor of the selection process and the success of the expatriate.[51]

STAFFING IN OTHER COUNTRIES

The use of employment tests in other countries of the world varies considerably as do the government regulations regarding the use of tests. Among Asian countries, Korean employers use employment tests extensively; one survey indicated that more than 85 percent of Korea's largest conglomerates selected new employees solely on the basis of tests.[52] These tests tend to be written examinations covering English-language skills, common sense, and knowledge of specific disciplines. A much smaller percentage of Japanese companies use employment tests. Some Japanese companies use the Foreign Assignment Selection Test (FAST) to identify Japanese who are more likely to be successful expatriates in the United States. The FAST assesses cultural flexibility, sociability, conflict-resolution style, and leadership style. Within Japan, however, most people are hired directly from the universities, and the prestige of the university attended is a major criterion for selection purposes. A survey of companies in Hong Kong and Singapore revealed little use of employment tests. Aside from some use of clerical and office tests (e.g., typing), only two companies from these countries indicated use of any personality, cognitive ability, or related tests. China also uses little employment testing; this is not surprising given that employees are usually assigned to companies rather than chosen by the organization.[53]

European countries have more controls than the United States does on the use of tests for staffing, but there is considerable variability in usage. The power of unions in most European countries restricts the use of tests for employment decisions. Although systematic reports on the use of tests in these countries are generally not available, some general conclusions can be made.[54] A wide variety of employment tests appear to be used in Switzerland, including graphology and astrology, but in Italy selection tests are illegal! In Holland, Sweden, and Poland, job applicants have access to all psychological test results and can choose to not allow the results to be divulged to an employer.[55]

Several surveys have given us clues about selection methods in England. One survey found that more than 80 percent of companies in England do some type of reference check and another found almost 40 percent had used personality tests and 25 percent had used cognitive ability tests to assess managers.[56] Interestingly, compared to the United States, the use of graphology was relatively high—about 8 percent of the surveyed firms in England reported using this procedure occasionally.

In general, there is wide variation in the use of employment tests outside the United States. While some countries have outlawed the use of tests (e.g., Italy), their use appears to be far more extensive in others (e.g., Korea). The United States and England appear to be major centers for research and development of employment tests. Japanese companies make extensive use of testing for their U.S. plants as well as for their expatriates.[57] The Japanese-owned Nissan plant in Tennessee relies on team assessment using a structured interview and a battery of cognitive ability tests to select new team members. U.S. HRM specialists considering the use of tests outside the United States to hire employees must be very familiar with laws and regulations within the country where the testing is being considered. These laws, regulations, and collective bargaining issues are very different across countries.

SUMMARY

Employment testing and assessment continues to be a critical part of HRM. We have reviewed a number of commonly used staffing procedures which vary in terms of their validity and legal implications. While cognitive ability tests are among the most valid measures, they also frequently result in adverse impact against minority groups. Conversely, many personality tests are safe from legal problems because they typically have no adverse impact, yet they are less valid. Many companies have also begun to use preemployment drug tests. These tests are generally legal, but there are differences from state to state. There is recent evidence that drug tests will screen out less effective employees. Reference checks may not be a particularly valid selection devices; still, court decisions regarding negligent hiring lawsuits indicate that employers should do their best to check applicants' references. Today, paper-and-pencil honesty tests are being used by a growing number of companies because of the restrictions on polygraph testing. Research on these tests seems to support their use.

Assessment center and performance testing are valid, job related, more legally defensible, but certainly more expensive than other selection techniques, including the employment interview. There is evidence, however, that structured, behavioral interviewing conducted by more than one interviewer can increase the validity of interviews.

Most companies use a variety of selection procedures, proceeding through the process in the order described in the model in Figure 6.1. Some organizations combine the information using a statistical or expert model, which enhances the accuracy of decision making. Unfortunately, most companies gather information from several sources (e.g., application blanks, cognitive and personality tests) and apply a subjective and unreliable weighting system to determine the rank of candidates. Almost all companies use an employment interview at some point in the selection process. These companies also tend to place too much weight on the results of an unstructured, often invalid, interview.

The accuracy of interview decisions is limited by the information processing capabilities of interviewers. Factors such as the characteristics of the applicant, the interviewer, and the situation can influence and distort the decision-making process, resulting in less-than-optimal interview decisions. Because employment interviews entail complex decision-making activities, interviewers often try to simplify that process and, in doing so, bias their decisions. This inherent bias poses both legal and practical implications for management. Overall organization performance can be affected because interviewer bias reduces the probability of selecting the highest performing candidates.

The administrative guidelines described in this chapter help ensure that the validity of the interview is maximized while interviewer bias is minimized. In turn, the procedural guidelines define both the content and the method of the interview inquiry, providing a means of improving the overall effectiveness of the interview procedure.

A final dilemma facing organizations that use the interview as a selection tool continues to be the issue of "functional utility": What is the unique contribution of the interview in the employment decision? This is a practical assessment of the usefulness of the interview based on a determination of which information is best collected through the interview process, and whether interviewer decisions based on that information are consistent and accurate. To achieve any functional utility from the interview, organizations must evaluate their overall selection procedures and determine: (1) what factors are best and most consistently evaluated during the interview; and (2) whether other selection procedures can measure those identified factors as well as or better than the interview. Organizations should also focus on the purpose of the selection interview. Interviews that attempt to assess candidate "fit" while simultaneously recruiting the candidate usually fail at both.

The most effective staffing systems emphasize the interaction of the person and the organization in the prediction of effectiveness. The "matching" model we presented in Chapter 5, for example, calls for an assessment of the applicant in the context of both job and organizational characteristics and a realistic assessment of the organization and the job by the applicant. This matching model is particularly effective in "high-involvement organizations" where employees have considerably more latitude in the workplace.

The "matching" model would not be complete without a discussion of training and development. While testing and assessment are vital for the matching process, employees almost always need some training and development to enhance this match. We turn to this HRM activity next.

DISCUSSION QUESTIONS

1. Are cognitive ability tests more trouble than they are worth? Given that minorities are more likely to score lower on such tests, would it be advisable to find some other method for predicting job success?

2. Should personality tests be regulated with restrictions on what can and cannot be asked?

3. Under what circumstances would mental ability tests be appropriate for promotion decisions? Are there other methods that might be more valid?

4. If you were given a personality test as part of an employment application process, would you answer the questions honestly or would you attempt to answer the questions based on your image of the "correct" way to answer? What implications does your response have for the validity of personality testing?

5. Discuss the advantages and disadvantages of banding. Under what circumstances would such a practice be most appropriate?

6. Given that the validity of assessment centers and work samples is not significantly greater than that reported for mental ability tests, why would an organization choose the far more costly approach?

7. It has been proposed that students be assessed with work simulations similar to those used in managerial assessment centers. Assessments are then made on a student's competencies in decision

making, leadership, oral communication, planning and organizing, written communication, and self-objectivity. What other methods could be used to assess student competencies in these areas?

8. What is stereotyping? Give examples of legal and illegal stereotypes. Are stereotypes ever valid?

9. Describe how an organization might improve the reliability and validity of the interview.

10. Contrast an unstructured interview with a situational or behavioral interview.

11. "The most efficient solution to the problem of interview validity is to do away with the interview and substitute paper-and-pencil measures." Do you agree or disagree? Explain.

NOTES

1. Heneman, H. H.; Heneman, R. L.; and Judge, T. A. (1997). *Staffing organizations.* Homewood, IL: Irwin.

2. Russell, C. J.; Mattson, J.; Devlin, S. E.; and Atwater, D. (1990). Predictive validity of biodata items generated from retrospective life experience essays. *Journal of Applied Psychology, 75,* 569–580. See also, Kluger, A.; Reilly, R. R.; and Russell, C. J. (1991). Faking biodata tests: Are option-keyed instruments more resistant? *Journal of Applied Psychology, 76,* 889–896; Mael, F. A. (1991). A conceptual rationale for the domain and attributes of biodata items. *Personnel Psychology, 44,* 763–792; and Mael, F. A.; Connerley, M.; and Morath, R. A. (1996). None of your business: Parameters of biodata invasiveness. *Personnel Psychology, 49*(4), 613–622.

3. Hough, L. M.; Keyes, M. A.; and Dunnette, M. D. (1983). An evaluation of three alternative selection procedures. *Personnel Psychology, 36,* 261–276.

4. Click, J. (July 1995). SHRM survey highlights dilemmas of reference checks. *HR News,* p. 13.

5. LoPresto, R.; Micham, D. E.; and Ripley, D. E. (1986). *Reference checking handbook.* Alexandria, VA: American Society of Personnel Administration; Bartram, D.; Lindley, P. A.; Marshall, L.; and Foster, J. (1995). The recruitment and selection of young people by small businesses. *Journal of Occupational & Organizational Psychology, 68*(4), 339–358.

6. Bernardin, H. J., and Beatty, R. W. (1984). *Performance appraisal: Assessing human behavior at work.* Boston: Kent-PWS.

7. Judge, T.; Blancero, D.; Cable, D. M.; Johnson, D. E. (1995). Effects of selection systems on job search decisions. *Paper presented at the annual meeting of the Society of Industrial Organizational Society,* Orlando, FL.

8. Plaschke, B., and Alomond, E. (April 21, 1995). Has the NFL draft become a thinking man's game? *Los Angeles Times.*

9. See note 1 for reviews.

10. Hunter, J. E., and Schmidt, F. L. (1990). *Methods of meta-analysis.* Beverly Hills, CA: Sage; Hanisch, K. A., and Julin, C. L. (1994). Two-stage sequential selection procedures using ability and training performance: Incremental validity of behavioral consistency measures. *Personnel Psychology, 47,* 767–785; Latham, G. P., and Whyte, G. (1994). The futility of utility analysis. *Personnel Psychology, 47,* 31–46; and Russell, C. J.; Colella, A.; and Bobko, P. (1993). Expanding the context of utility: The strategic impact of personnel selection. *Personnel Psychology, 46,* 781–801.

11. Goffin, R. D.; Rothstein, M. G.; and Johnston, N. G. (1996). Personality testing and the assessment center: Incremental validity for managerial selection. *Journal of Applied Psychology, 81*(6), 746–756.

12. Hartigan, J. A., and Wigdor, A. K., eds. (1989). *Fairness in employment testing.* Washington, DC: National Academy Press; Chan, D. (1997). Racial subgroup differences in predictive validity perceptions on personality and cognitive ability tests. *Journal of Applied Psychology, 82*(2), 311–320; see also, Chan, D.; Schmitt, N.; DeShon, R. P.; Clause, C.S.; and Delbridge, K. (1997). Reactions to cognitive ability tests: The relationships between race, test performance, face validity perceptions, and test-taking motivation. *Journal of Applied Psychology, 82*(2), 300–310; Smither, J. W.; Reilly, R. R.; Millsap, R. E.; Perlman, K.; and Stoffey, R. (1993). Applicant reactions to selection procedures. *Personnel Psychology, 46,* 49–76.

13. Sackett, P. R., and Wilk, S. L. (1994). Within-group norming and other forms of score adjustment in preemployment testing. *American Psychologist, 49,* 929–954; Schmidt, F. L., and Hunter, J. E. (1995). The fatal internal contradiction in banding: its statistical rationale is logically inconsistent with its operational procedures. *Human Performance, 8,* 203–214.

14. Potosky, D., and Bobko, P. (1997). Computer versus paper-and-pencil administration mode and response distortion in noncognitive selection tests. *Journal of Applied Psychology, 82*(2), 293–299; Computer-aided interviewing helps to overcome first impressions (March 1995). *Personnel Journal, Product News Supplement,* pp. 11–16; and Burke, M. J. (1993). Computerized psychological testing impacts on measuring predictor constructs and future job behavior. In N. Schmitt, W. C. Borman, and associates (eds), *Personnel Selection in Organizations.* San Francisco: Jossey-Bass, pp. 203–239.

15. Digman, J. M. (1990). Personality structure: Emergence of the five-factor model. *Annual Review of Psychology, 41,* 417–440. See also, Cortina, J. M.; Doherty, M. L.; and Schmitt, N. (1992). The "big-five" personality factor in the IPI and MMPI: Predictors of police performance. *Personnel Psychology, 45,* 119–140; Barrick, M. R., and Mount, M. K. (1991). The big five personality dimensions and job performance: A meta-analysis. *Personnel Psychology, 44,* 1–26; Cellar, D. F.; Miller, M. L.; Doverspike, D. D.; and Klawsky, J. D. (1996). Comparison of factor structures and criterion-related validity coefficients for two measures of personality based on the five factor model. *Journal of Applied Psychology, 81*(6), 694–704; Bernardin, H. J.; Cooke, D.; Villanova, P.; and Gagne, J. (May 1997). The big-five as predictors of rat-

ing leniency. *Paper presented at the annual meeting of the American Psychological Science Association,* Washington, DC; Block, J. (March 1995a). A contrarian view of the five-factor approach to personality description. *Psychological Bulletin, 117*(2), 187–215; and Block, J. (March 1995b). Going beyond the five factors given: Rejoinder to Costa and McCrae (1995) and Goldberg and Saucier (1995). *Psychological Bulletin, 117*(2), 226–229.

16. Patsfall, M. R., and Feimer, N. (1985). The role of person-environment fit in job performance and satisfaction. In H. J. Bernardin, and D. Bownas (eds.), *Personality assessment in organizations.* New York: Praeger, pp. 53–81. See also, Trevino, L. K. (1986). Ethical decision making in organizations: A person-situation interactionist model. *Academy of Management Review, 11,* 601–617; and O'Reilly, C. A. III; Chatman, J.; and Caldwell, D. F. (1991). People and organizational culture: A profile comparison approach to assessing person-organization fit. *The Academy of Management Review, 34,* 487–516.

17. Miner, J. B. (1985). Sentence completion measures in personnel research: The development and validation of the Miner Sentence Completion Scales. In H. J. Bernardin and D. Bownas (eds.), *Personality assessment in organizations.* New York: Praeger, pp. 145–176. See also, Miner, J. B.; Chen, C. C.; and Yu, K. C. (1991). Testing theory under adverse conditions: Motivation to manage in the People's Republic of China. *Journal of Applied Psychology, 76,* 343–349.

18. Driver, R. W.; Buckley, M. R.; and Frink, D. D. (1996). Should we write off graphology? *International Journal of Selection and Assessment, 4*(2), 78–87. See also, McCarthy, M. J. (Aug. 25, 1988). Handwriting analysis as a personnel tool. *The Wall Street Journal,* p. B1.

19. Bernardin, H. J., and Bownas, D. (1985). *Personality assessment in organizations.* New York: Praeger; see also; Ones, D. S.; Viswesvaran, C.; and Reiss, A. D. (1996). Role of social desirability in personality testing for personnel selection: The red herring. *Journal of Applied Psychology, 81*(6), 660–679.

20. Gardner, W. L.; and Martinko, M. J. (1996). Using the Myers-Briggs type indicator to study managers: A literature review and research agenda. *Journal of Management, 22*(1), 45–83.

21. Miner, J. B. (1985). Sentence completion measures in personnel research: The development and validation of the Miner Sentence Completion Scales. In H. J. Bernardin and D. Bownas (eds.), *Personality testing in organizations.* New York: Praeger, pp. 145–176. See also, Miner, J. B.; Chen, C. C.; and Yu, K. C. (1991). Testing theory under adverse conditions: Motivation to manage in the People's Republic of China, *Journal of Applied Psychology, 76,* 343–349.

20. Tett, R. P.; Jackson, D. N.; and Rothstein, M. (1991). Personality measures as predictors of job performance: A meta-analytic review. *Personnel Psychology, 44,* 703–742. See also, Hough, L. M.; Eaton, N. K.; Dunnette, M. D.; Kamp, J. D.; and McCloy, R. A. (1990). Criterion related validities of personality constructs and the effect of response distortion on those validities. *Journal of Applied Psychology, 75,* 581–595.

23. Bernardin et al. (1997). The big-five as predictors of managerial effectiveness. Paper presented at the annual meeting of the American Psychological Society, Washington, DC; see also, Salgado, J. F. (1997). The five factor model of personality and job performance in the European community. *Journal of Applied Psychology, 82*(1), 30–43; and Stewart, J. L. (1996). Reward structure as a moderator of the relationship between extraversion and sales performance. *Journal of Applied Psychology, 81*(6), 619–617.

24. Sackett, P. R., and Wanek, J. E. (1996). New developments in the use of measures of honesty, integrity, conscientiousness, dependability, trustworthiness, and reliability for personnel selection. *Personnel Psychology, 49*(4), 787–795; Ones, D. S.; Viswesvaran, C. and Schmidt, F. L. (1993). Comprehensive meta-analysis of integrity test validities: Findings and implications for personal selection and theories of job performance. *Journal of Applied Psychology, 78* (monograph), 531–537; and Goldberg, L. R.; Grenier, J. R.; Guion, R. M.; Sechrest, L. B.; and Wing, H. (1991). *Questionnaires Used in the Prediction of Trustworthiness in Pre-Employment Selection Decisions: An APA Task Force Report.* Washington, DC: American Psychological Association.

25. See note 23; see also, Bernardin, H. J., and Cooke, D. (1993). The validity of honesty tests in the prediction of employee theft. *Academy of Management Journal;* and Sackett, P. R. (1994). Integrity testing for personnel selection. *Current Directions in Psychological Science, 3,* 73–76.

26. Bernardin, H. J. (1989). Innovative approaches to personnel selection and performance appraisal. *Journal of Management Systems, 1,* 25–36.

27. Hogan, J.; Hogan, R.; and Busch, C. M. (1984). How to measure service orientation. *Journal of Applied Psychology, 69,* 167–173.

28. Bernardin, H. J. (1989). Innovative approaches to personnel selection and performance Appraisal. *Journal of Management Systems, 1,* 25–36.

29. Zigarelli, M. A. (1995). Drug testing litigation: Trends and outcomes. *Human Resource Management Review, 5,* 267–288.

30. Geidt, T. (1985). Drug and alcohol abuse in the work place: Balancing employer and employee rights. *Employer Relations Law Journal, 11,* 181–205. See also, Faley, R. H.; Kleiman, L. S.; and Wall, J. (1988). Drug testing in public and private-sector workplace: Technical and legal issues. *Journal of Business and Psychology, 3,* 154–186; Murphy, K. R.; Thornton, G. C. III; and Reynolds, D. H. (1990). College students' attitudes toward employee drug testing programs. *Personnel Psychology, 43,* 615–632; Crant, J. M., and Bateman, T. S. (1990). An experimental test of the impact of drug testing programs on potential job applicants' attitudes and intentions. *Journal of Applied Psychology, 75,* 127–131; and Zigarelli, M. A. (1995). Drug testing litigation:

Trends and Outcomes. *Human Resource Management Review, 5*(4), 267–288.

31. Linowes, D. F., and Spencer, R. C. (1996). Privacy in the workplace in perspective. *Human Resource Management Review, 6*(3), 165–182.

32. Wernimont, P. F., and Campbell, J. P. (1968). Signs, samples, and criteria. *Journal of Applied Psychology, 52,* 372–376. See also, Chan, D., and Schmitt, N. (1997). Video-based versus paper-and-pencil method of assessment in situational judgment tests: Subgroup differences in test performance and face validity perceptions. *Journal of Applied Psychology, 82*(1), 143–159.

33. Task Force Assessment Center Standards (1980). Standards and ethical considerations for assessment center operations. *Personnel Administrator, 25,* 35–38.

34. Thornton, G. C., III, and Byham, W. C. (1982). *Assessment centers and managerial performance.* New York: Academic Press. See also, Fitzgerald, L. F., and Quaintance, M. K. (1982). Survey of assessment center in state and local government. *Journal of Assessment Center Technology, 5,* 9–19; Schneider, J. R., and Schmitt, N. (1992). An exercise design approach to understanding assessment center dimension and exercise constructs. *Journal of Applied Psychology, 77,* 32–41; Schmitt, N.; Schneider, J. R.; and Cohen, S. A. (1990). Factors affecting validity of a regionally administered assessment center. *Personnel Psychology, 43,* 1–12; Gaugler, B. B., and Rudolph, A. S. (1992). The influence of assessee performance variation on assessors' judgements. *Personnel Psychology, 45,* 77–98; Reilly, R. R.; Henry, S.; and Smither, J. W. (1990). An examination of the effects of using behavior checklists on the construct validity of assessment center dimensions. *Personnel Psychology, 43,* 71–84.

35. Kraut, A. I., and Scott, G. J. (1972). Validity of an operational management assessment program. *Journal of Applied Psychology, 56,* 124–129.

36. Bray, D. W., and Campbell, R. J. (1968). Selection of salesmen by means of an assessment center. *Journal of Applied Psychology, 52,* 36–41. See also, McEvoy, G. M.; Beatty, R. W.; and Bernardin, H. J. (1987). Unanswered questions in assessment center research. *Journal of Business and Psychology, 2,* 97–111.

37. Pynes, J. E., and Bernardin, H. J. (1989). Predictive validity of an entry-level police officer assessment center. *Journal of Applied Psychology, 74,* 831–833.

38. Gaugler, B. B.; Rosenthal, D. B.; Thornton, G. C., III; and Benton, C. (1987). Meta-analysis of assessment center validity. *Journal of Applied Psychology, 72,* 493–511; and Schippmann, J. S.; Prien, E. P.; and Katz, J. A. (1990). Reliability and validity of in-basket performance measures. *Personnel Psychology, 43,* 837–860.

39. Hunter, J. E., and Hunter, R. F. (1984). Validity and utility of alternative predictors of job performance. *Psychological Bulletin, 96,* 72–98.

40. Porter, L.; Lawler, E.; and Hackman, J. R. (1975). *Behavior in organizations.* New York: McGraw-Hill, p. 145.

41. Gatewood, R. D., and Feild, H. S. (1996). *Human resource selection.* Chicago: Dryden. See also, Pulakos, E. D.; Schmitt, N.; Whitney, D.; and Smith, M. (1996). Individual differences in interviewer ratings: The impact of standardization, consensus discussion, and sampling error on the validity of a structured interview. *Personnel Psychology, 49*(4), 85–98.

42. See note 1. See also, Douglas, J. A.; Feld, D. E.; and Asquith, N. (1989). *Employment testing manual.* Boston: Warren, Gorham, Lamont.

43. Bobocel, D. R., and Farrell, A. C. (1996). Sex-based promotion decisions and interactional fairness: Investigating the influence of managerial accounts. *Journal of Applied Psychology, 81*(1), 22–35. See also, Howard, J. L., and Ferris, G. R. (1996). The employment interview context: Social and situational influences on interviewer decisions. *Journal of Applied Social Psychology, 25*(2), 111–136; Marlowe, C. M.; Schneider, S. L.; and Nelson, C. E. (1996). Gender and attractiveness biases in hiring decisions: Are more experienced managers less biased? *Applied Psychology, 81*(1), 11–21; and Prewett-Livingston, A. J.; Feild, H. S.; Veres, J. G., III; and Lewis, P. M. (1996). Effects of race on interview ratings in a situational panel interview. *Journal of Applied Psychology, 81*(2), 178–186.

44. McDaniel, M. A.; Whetzel, D. L.; Schmidt, F.; and Maurer, S. (1994). The validity of employment interviews: A comprehensive review and meta-analysis. *Journal of Applied Psychology, 79,* 599–616.

45. Pulakos, E., and Schmitt, N. (1995). Experience-based and situation interview questions: Studies of validity. *Personnel Psychology, 48,* 289–308.

46. Arthur, W., Jr.; Doverspike, D.; and Barrett, G. V. (1996). Development of a job analysis-based procedure for weighting and combining content-related tests into a single test battery score. *Personnel Psychology, 49*(4): 971–984.

47. Tung, R. L. (May 1987). Expatriate assignments: Enhancing success and minimizing failure. *The Academy of Management Executive,* pp. 118–125; see also, Sprietzer, G. M.; McCall, M. W., Jr.; and Mahoney, J. D. (1977). Early identification of international executive potential. *Journal of Applied Psychology, 82*(1), 6–29.

48. Mendenhall, M., and Oddou, G. (1985). The dimensions of expatriate acculturation: A review. *Academy of Management Review, 19,* 39–47.

49. Henry, E. R. (1951). What business can learn from Peace Corps selection and training. *Personnel, 42,* 17–25. See also, Dowling, P. J., and Schuler, R. S. (1990). *International dimensions of human resource management.* Boston: PWS-Kent.

50. Jenkins, L. (Summer, 1995). Overseas assignments: Sending the right people. *International HR Journal,* pp. 41–43; see also, Black, J. S.; Gregersen, H. B.; Mendenhall, M. E. (1992). *Global assignments.* San Francisco: Jossey-Bass; and Hays, R. D. (1971). Ascribed behavioral determinants of success-failure among U.S. expatriate managers. *Journal of International Business Studies, 2,* 40–46.

51. Tung, R. L. (1981). Selection and training of personnel for overseas assignments. *Columbia Journal of World Business, 16,* 68–78; and Love, K. G.; Bishop, R. C.; Heinisch, D. A.; and Montei, M. S. (1994). Selection across two cultures: Adapting the selection of American assemblers to meet Japanese performance dimensions. *Personnel Psychology, 47,* 837–846.

52. Von Glinow, M. A., and Chung, B. J. (1990). Comparative human resource management practices in the United States, Japan, Korea, and the People's Republic of China. In A. Nedd, G. R. Ferris, and K. M. Rowland (eds.), *Research in personnel and human resources management: International human resources management.* Greenwich, CT: JAI Press (suppl. 1), pp. 153–171.

53. Latham, G. P., and Napier, N. K. (1990). Chinese human resource management practices in Hong Kong and Singapore: An exploratory study. In A. Nedd, G. R. Ferris, and K. M. Rowland (eds.), *Research in personnel and human resources management: International human resources management.* Greenwich, CT: JAI Press (Suppl. 1), pp. 173–199.

54. Levy-Leboyer, C. (1994). Selection and assessment in Europe. In M. Dunnette and L. Hough (eds.), *Handbook of Industrial and Organizational Psychology.* Palo Alto, CA: Consulting Psychologists Press, pp. 173–190; see also, Cascio, W. F. and Bailey, E. (1995). International HRM: The state of research and practice. In O. Shenkar (ed.), *Global perspectives of human resources management.* Englewood Cliffs, NJ: Prentice-Hall, pp. 15–36.

55. Shimmin, S. (1989). Selection in a European context. In P. Harriot (ed.), *Assessment and selection in organizations.* Chichester, England: John Wiley & Sons, pp. 109–118.

56. See note 55.

57. Shackleton, V. J., and Newell, S. (1989). Selection procedures in practice. In P. Herriot (ed.), *Assessment and selection in organizations.* Chichester, England: John Wiley & Sons, pp. 257–271.

C H A P T E R

ORGANIZATIONAL TRAINING*

OVERVIEW

The staffing methods discussed in Chapter 6 attempt to assess the match between an applicant's ability and the requirements of the job. Some of the methods (e.g., cognitive ability tests) are clearly designed to predict ability to learn the job requirements through some form of training program while other methods (e.g., performance testing) attempt to measure knowledge, skills, or abilities that are a necessary condition for acceptable performance at the outset of employment. While some of these methods have proved to be reasonably good predictors of performance, there remains a great deal of performance variability that is not explained by what the person brings to the workplace. That's where training comes in.

As we discussed in Chapters 1 and 2, U.S. firms face greater challenges than ever and should constantly monitor their competitive positions. In addition to more valid staffing methods, companies can seek competitive advantage through the training and retraining of workers.

Given the more intense pressures to compete, improve quality and customer service, and lower costs, leading American companies have come to view training as a key to organizational survival and success.

Some HR directors view the skill level of their workforce as the top priority for planning. They worry that increasing technology is "de-skilling" 75 percent of the population. Their suggestion is continual training for employees. As Chuck Nielson, vice president of HR at Texas Instruments, notes, "Our challenge is creating an environment in which people love to learn." The company mandates a minimum of 40 hours of training per year. Peter Drucker, well-known management author, says the fastest growing industry in the United States will be the continuing education and training of adults because things are changing so fast in every field and occupation. Stanford professor Jeffrey Pfeffer cites training as a major source of sustained advantage. He concludes that "worker autonomy, self-managed teams, and even a high-wage strategy depend on having people who not only are empowered to make changes and improvements in products and processes but also have the necessary skills to do so."[1]

*Contributed by Philip J. Decker and Joyce E. A. Russell.

While companies such as GE, Motorola, Corning Glass Works, IBM, Ford Motor Company, Saturn Corporation, and Johnson & Johnson have moved training to the top of their corporate agenda (IBM spends over $1 billion yearly on employee education), most research concludes that companies "have been slow to make a strong commitment to training the workers they do hire."[2] About 30 percent of what U.S. companies spend annually for training goes to outsourcing strategies (e.g., forming alliances with colleges and universities, forming partnerships with vendors to share resources, pooling training resources across companies).

This chapter provides an overview of employee training. We will discuss the importance of training in the context of the organization's competitive strategy and the need to link training needs with the mission and goals of the organization. You will learn how to design and evaluate a training program and to tailor the training to particular situations.

OBJECTIVES

After studying this chapter, you should be able to:

1. Define what is meant by training, and describe why it is a critical function for corporations today.

2. Explain how to conduct a needs assessment, including performing organizational, task, and person analyses and deriving instructional objectives for a training program.

3. Know how to design a training program to facilitate learning, particularly among adult learners.

4. Identify the critical elements related to transfer of training.

5. Compare and contrast the various techniques available for training, including their relative advantages and disadvantages.

6. Identify and distinguish between the four types of evaluation criteria.

7. Compare and contrast the different experimental designs available for evaluating training programs.

8. Understand some of the components of training programs for employee orientation, teamwork, creativity training, and international assignments.

Chapter 1 discussed some of the strongest trends and challenges affecting American business today. Increased competition, rapid changes in technology, the growing diversity of the workforce, and occupational obsolescence are among the most important challenges for the next decades. Training is one of the most important responses to these challenges.

DEFINING TRAINING AND DEVELOPMENT

Training is defined as any attempt to improve employee performance on a currently held job or one related to it. This usually means changes in specific knowledges, skills, attitudes, or behaviors. To be effective, training should involve a learning experience, be a planned organizational activity, and be designed in response to identified needs. Ideally, training should also be designed to meet the goals of the organization while simultaneously meeting the goals of individual employees. The term *training* is often confused with the term *development*. **Development** refers to learning opportunities designed to help employees grow. Such opportunities do not have to be limited to improving employees' performance on their current jobs. At Ford, for example, a new systems analyst is required to take a course on Ford standards for user manuals. The content of this training is needed to perform the systems analyst job at Ford. The systems analyst may also, however, enroll in a course titled "Self-Awareness," the content of which is not required on the current job. This situation illustrates the difference between "training" and "development."[3] The focus of development is on the long term to help employees prepare for future work demands or career goals, while training focuses on the immediate period to help fix any current deficits in employees' skills (see Chapter 8).

The most effective companies look at training and career development as an integral part of a "human resources development" (HRD) program carefully aligned with corporate business strategies. Figure 7.1 illustrates this changing mind-set.[4]

POPULARITY OF TRAINING

While training and development are popular, this functional area of HR is one in which discrepancies between actual practice and academic findings may be the greatest. For example, while 70 percent of companies provide training in sexual harassment, only 24 percent of these programs comply with the prescriptions for effective training we are about to describe.[5] In 1995, it was estimated that U.S. organizations with more than 100 employees spent $52.2 billion on formal training for their employees.[6] This is a 3.2 percent increase from 1994 ($50.6 billion), and since 1990 the total spent on formal training has increased by 15 percent in noninflation-adjusted dollars. Most of the expenses reported in 1995 were for the internal training budget such as training staff salaries (72 percent) and facilities and overhead (8 percent). The other 20 percent is spent on outside expenditures such as seminars and conferences (6 percent), hardware (5 percent), off-the-shelf materials (4 percent), custom materials (3 percent), and outside services (2 percent).[7]

Virtually all organizations with more than 1,000 employees train their managers. Further, it is expected that in most industries, particularly finance, insurance, banking, and other business services, training budgets will continue to increase. Generally, the transportation, communications, and utilities companies spend the most on training, followed closely by manufacturing organizations.[8]

The companies that spend the most on training typically average about 3.2 percent of payroll on training and provide employees with an average of 3.4 days of training per year.[9] For example, Mercedes-Benz built a $30 million training center, called the Mercedes-Benz Institute, in its new $300 million plant in Alabama. The 100,000-square-foot center houses labs for teaching basic skills in welding, hydraulics, pneumatics, computer-aided design, measurement, and robotics. In addition, the firm set aside $60 million to send new workers to Germany for training.[10] Clearly, training activities are big business in terms of the amount of money spent and the number of employees involved.

While top managers recognize the value of training to help their firms gain a competitive edge, so too do employees. Employees understand that opportunities for training enable them to grow and advance in their careers. In the recent review of the 100 best sales companies to work for, training was rated by job candidates as the most important variable to consider in job selection. Twenty-nine companies in the "best 100" were given perfect ratings for their training for sales employees. Among the most highly rated for training were Aetna Life & Casualty, AT&T, Black & Decker, Eastman Kodak Company, GE, IBM, Procter & Gamble, Westinghouse Electric Corp., and Eli Lilly & Co.[11]

The jobs most likely to receive training in corporations include: management (executives, senior managers, middle managers, first-line supervisors), professionals, administrative employees, and office/clerical staff. For example, in 1995 it was reported that about 27 percent of all formal training was dedicated to managers, 27 percent to professionals, 14 percent to salespeople, and the remaining 32 percent to all other employees (production workers, service workers, administrative staff). Primarily because of changes in technology and lack of skills at the entry level, there has also been an increase in the training provided for customer service employees, salespeople, and production workers.[12] Corporations are offering a variety of training programs to meet their organizational needs. Figure 7.2 lists some common training programs and the percentage of firms who reported using them in 1988 and in 1997. A greater percentage of firms in 1997 reported using training than did in 1988. Note also that some topics listed in 1997 were not even listed in 1988, including: training on sexual harassment, diversity, marketing, and reengineering.

While some part of these percentages reflect the latest "fads" in training, these topics also reflect the need for employees to work more effectively with the changing demographics of the workplace and the need for firms to be able to effectively structure themselves (reengineering) given all of the downsizings and to better understand their customers' needs (marketing). The recent trend toward teams is also reflected in the greater use of training for topics such as listening, team building, problem solving, decision making, and conducting meetings. In addition, as firms continue to become more competitive, greater demands have been felt for training on managing change, creativity, and quality improvements. In fact, a growing number of companies have recently initiated productivity and quality improvement

FIGURE 7.1
HRD IN THE UNITED STATES: CHANGING MIND-SETS

TRADITIONAL CORPORATE PERSPECTIVE	THE NEW CORPORATE REALITIES
1. HRD, HRM, and organizational development actions are loosely connected to both each other and corporate business strategies.	1. Strategic HRD actions must be aligned with corporate business strategies.
2. HRD demonstrates reactive, quick fixes with modest organizational impact.	2. HRD must assume a proactive leadership role in responding to business and training needs.
3. Isolated, labor-intensive, and often ineffective activities drive HRD practices.	3. Systems and technology approaches are required to integrate HRD in the workplace.
4. HRD's credibility and responsiveness and the significant value they bring to the organization are often perceived as inconsistent and questionable.	4. The value and impact of HRD services need to be measured and demonstrated.
5. Moderate and fluent changes in HRD functions will meet organizational needs.	5. Bold, creative, comprehensive strategies are required with the new corporate agenda.

Source: D. Shandler, *Reengineering the training function: How to align training with the new corporate agenda.* Delray Beach, FL: St. Lucie Press, 1996, p. 33.

FIGURE 7.2
COMMONLY USED TRAINING PROGRAMS

TYPES OF TRAINING	PERCENTAGE PROVIDING	
	1988*	1997†
New-employee orientation	81	92
Performance appraisals	66	79
Leadership	62	75
Personal computer applications	43	78
Sexual harassment	—	74
Team building	51	75
Safety	51	69
Hiring/selection process	60	71
New equipment operation	61	71
Train-the-trainer	53	71
Listening skills	52	64
Decision making	43	64
Product knowledge	57	66
Time management	63	62
Conducting meetings	38	66
Delegation skills	47	66
Quality/control improvement	34	63
Problem solving	48	61
Managing change	40	63
Goal setting	45	65
Motivation	49	60
Stress management	55	54
Computer programming	41	58
Diversity	—	52
MIS/data processing	40	60
Public speaking/presentation	45	61
Planning	42	54
Strategic planning	34	53
Writing skills	41	54
Negotiating skills	36	51
Finance	28	57
Marketing	—	43
Substance abuse	35	39
Ethics	20	46
Creativity	22	48
Outplacement/retirement planning	24	39
Purchasing	25	40
Smoking cessation	34	32
Reading skills/business literacy	19	40
Reengineering	—	30
Foreign language	11	22
Other (topics not listed)	5	4

*Of organizations with 100 or more employees. Source: J. Gordon, Who is being trained to do what? Reprinted with permission from the October 1988 issue of *Training* magazine. Copyright 1988, Lakewood Publications, Inc., Minneapolis, MN. All rights reserved.

†Of organizations with 100 or more employees. Based on 803 responses.

Source: Vital statistics: 1997 Industry Report, *Training,* October 1997. Reprinted with permission from the October 1997 issue of *Training* magazine. Copyright 1997, Lakewood Publications, Minneapolis, MN. All rights reserved. Not for resale.

programs. For example, Lantech, a machine manufacturer, provided training to its 300 plus employees on total quality management (TQM) issues.[13]

The importance of training is likely to continue given recent trends in the workforce. As the United States shifts from manufacturing to service jobs, increasingly more workers are needed in service-based industries.[14] In addition, increasing technology demands that current employees enhance their skills and technical sophistication. For example, U.S. Steel (USX) invested money in training for workers so that they would be able to use the new technology implemented in production processes.[15] Similarly, Xerox spent about $7 million on its training center to assist its sales staff in gaining additional training to better meet customers' needs for handling documents.[16] Employees at RJR Nabisco who have been confronted with new technology in their jobs are given the option of receiving retraining or early retirement.[17]

The greater diversity of employees in the workplace indicates that more training will be needed for different racial and ethnic groups, immigrants, older workers, women, and people with disabilities as well as other employees who may need training in appreciating the diversity of the workforce (e.g., diversity awareness training). For instance, Prudential Insurance Company's western home office has provided training for AIDS awareness since 1987.[18] In addition, Herman Miller Company provides training in diversity awareness to help employees better understand and appreciate employees of various ethnic groups. In its 1997 out-of-court settlement with the EEOC, Texaco agreed to provide "diversity" training for all its managers. Companies such as McDonald's, Home Shopping Network, AT&T, Texas Refinery Corporation, and Good Samaritan Hospital have spent considerable effort recruiting and training older workers.[19] As firms continue to become more global, more international training will also be needed. In addition, as the structures of organizations change and continue to flatten and move toward using teams, more team-based training will be needed to prepare employees for working in groups. In addition, training for shift workers and part-time employees and contractors will be needed.[20] Finally, with the past decade of downsizings, more and more workers have been sent for retraining and retooling. A continuation of this trend will necessitate more retraining programs for employees.

A SYSTEMS VIEW OF TRAINING

Whatever training activities are planned, the basic process of training remains the same. Figure 7.3 illustrates this process by showing the three major steps involved in training efforts. This systematic process includes assessment, development, and evaluation. Briefly,

FIGURE 7.3
A SYSTEMS MODEL OF TRAINING

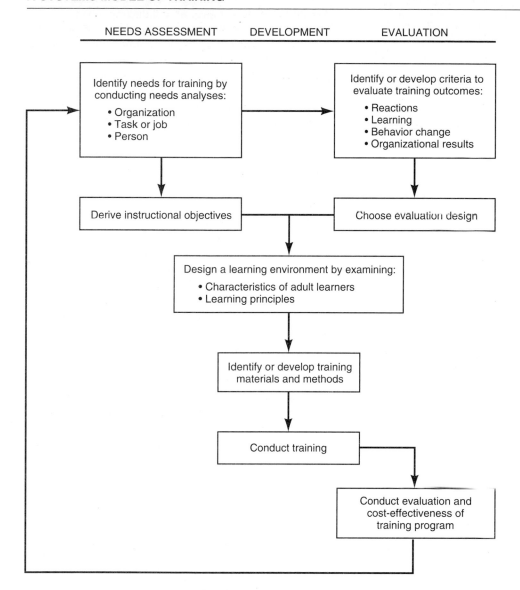

the goal of the *assessment* phase is to collect information to determine if training is needed in the organization. If it is needed, it is then important to determine where in the organization it is needed, what kind of training is needed, and what specific knowledges, abilities, skills, or other characteristics (KASOCs) should be taught. This information is collected by conducting three types of analyses—at the organizational, job, and individual level. After the information is compiled, objectives for the training program can be derived.

The goal of the *development* phase of training is to design the training environment necessary to achieve the objectives. This means human resource (HR) professionals must review relevant learning issues, including characteristics of adult learners and learning principles as they apply to the particular training and potential

trainees under consideration. Also, HR professionals must identify or develop training materials and techniques to use in the program. Finally, after the appropriate learning environment is designed or selected, the training is conducted.

The goal of the *evaluation* phase is to examine whether the training program has been effective in meeting the stated objectives. The evaluation phase requires the identification and development of criteria, which should include participants' reactions to the training, assessments of what they learned in the training program, measures of their behavior after the training, and indicators of organizational results (e.g., changes in productivity data, sales figures, employee turnover, accident rates). The evaluation phase necessitates choosing an experimental evaluation design to assess the effectiveness of training. The choice of the criteria and the design are both made *before* training is conducted to ensure that training will be properly evaluated. After the training is completed, the program is then evaluated using the criteria and design selected.

Discrepancies between Research and Practice

A recent survey of training processes used in corporate America revealed some disturbing discrepancies between the academic recommendations regarding training program development and evaluation and the current state of the practice.[21] While larger companies were more likely to have done formal needs assessment, written specific instructional objectives, and evaluated the training with something other than a simple, post-training reaction questionnaire, the majority of all classes of respondents did none of these things. Small businesses rarely did any of these things as part of their training.

Over 50 percent of all surveyed companies, regardless of company size, relied only on trainee reactions to assess the training, taken upon completion of the training, and had no systematic follow-up to further evaluate the training. Less than 20 percent of companies used any form of control group to evaluate the effects of the training (see Figure 7.3).

Over 50 percent of companies admitted that managerial training programs were first tried because some other company had been using them. As one training director put it, "A lot of companies buy off-the-shelf training programs just because they had heard or knew that a competitor was using the same training. Shouldn't we expect more data to determine training need?"

NEEDS ASSESSMENT

The first step in training is to determine that a need for training actually exists. An organization should commit its resources to a training activity only if the training can be expected to achieve some organizational goal. The decision to conduct training must be based on the best available data, which are collected by conducting a needs assessment. This needs analysis should ideally be conducted in the context of a human resource planning (HRP) program and the strategic objectives of the organization. Companies that implement training programs without conducting a needs assessment may be making errors or spending money unnecessarily. For example, a needs assessment might reveal that less costly interventions (e.g., personnel selection, a new compensation system, job redesign) could be used in lieu of training. The regional automation manager for the Internal Revenue Service conducted his needs assessment not only to determine the training needed by employees but also to be able to record the training history of each employee.[22] Despite the importance of conducting needs assessments, few employers conduct such an analysis in the context of their strategic plans or any form of strength, weakness, opportunity, or threat analysis.[23] In another survey, the vast majority of organizations (81 percent) revealed that they identified training needs by either reacting to issues that arose or because of requests made by supervisors.[24]

A **needs assessment** is a systematic, objective determination of training needs that involves conducting three primary types of analyses. These analyses are used to derive objectives for the training program. The three analyses consist of an organizational analysis, a job analysis, and a person analysis.[25] After compiling the results from these analyses, the HR professional is ready to derive objectives for the training program.

Many trainers suggest that a training need is any discrepancy between what is desired and what exists. Thus, one goal of the needs assessment is to note any discrepancies. For example, the World Bank recently determined through a needs assessment that many of its constituents from Eastern Europe required training in transforming state-owned businesses into self-sustaining businesses. The organization contracted with a number of universities to develop and provide the necessary training. Some argue that needs assessment should be done before an organization pursues diversity training (see Critical Thinking Exercise 7.1 for a consideration of the issues related to diversity training).

CRITICAL THINKING EXERCISE 7.1

Workplace Diversity Training[1]

What is workplace diversity? The answer to this question may be the first step in initiating diversity training in the workplace. Whether to include only the protected groups under Title VII or to broaden the definition to include the "invisible" minorities, such as individuals with mental disabilities, substance abuse conditions, or various sexual orientations, may be a factor specific to the organization or the company's location.

Once diversity has been defined, the next question to address is: what is it about workplace diversity that is important for the organization? Some organizations that have looked to diversity training to "sensitize" employees to the differences of cultures and biases have been greeted with multimillion-dollar settlements from the "sensitizing." Lucky Stores supermarket chain in California was ordered to pay $90 million in damages to about 20,000 women in 1988 after airing sex and racial stereotypes in a workshop designed to increase sensitivity.[2] Jeffrey Mello asserts that a "best practice" workplace diversity initiative relates that program with the overall strategy of the organization, "such as meeting the changing needs of customers and/or expanding markets both domestically and abroad."[3] A strong argument is made that a "solid business case increases the likelihood of obtaining the leadership commitment and resources needed to successfully implement diversity initiatives."[4]

Third, what is to be trained? The damages in court cases are awarded based on behavior and instances of illegal conduct. San Diego Gas & Electric Company and Wal-Mart were ordered to pay $3 million in 1994 and $5 million recently, respectively, to employees who were subjected to illegal conduct. At the power company, a black former employee had been called "nigger," "coon," and "boy" and was threatened by a coworker in the presence of a manager to "beat his black ass." He also had racial and sexual graffiti written about him on the men's room walls. SDG & E did not stop or discipline the transgressions. A woman stockroom clerk was subject to comments concerning her anatomy and unwelcome attempts to kiss her by her supervisor at Wal-Mart. Wal-Mart was ordered to pay even though the company has a strong sexual harassment policy because the store manager did nothing to stop the harassment after the employee complained.[5]

How is the training going to be done? Careful planning and designing will prevent problems such as poor attendance and nonownership of diversity management. A division executive of a major insurance firm declined to send his managers to the company's diversity training. His response was a blunt "if there's a problem, just tell us what you want us to do. Don't waste our time with this diversity stuff."[6]

Finally, how will the diversity training be evaluated? Accounting for the benefits, which may include increased productivity due to incident-free workdays (much like accident-free workdays promoted by OSHA), enhanced public opinion about the organization, or recruitment and retention of valued diverse employees, is crucial to an effective workplace diversity program.

Assignment

You have been asked to design a diversity training program for incoming freshmen at your school. Try to answer the questions presented above in this context.

[1] Contributed by Mary E. Wilson.

[2] Murray, K. (Aug. 1, 1993). The unfortunate side effects of 'diversity training.' *New York Times*, p. F5.

[3] Mello, J. A. (1996). The strategic management of workplace diversity initiatives: Public sector implications. *International Journal of Public Administration, 19*(3), 425–447.

[4] Robinson, G., and Dechart, K. (1997). Building a business case for diversity. *Academy of Management Executive, 11*, 21–31.

[5] Paskoff, S. A. (August 1996). Ending the workplace diversity wars. *Training, 33*(8), 42–47.

[6] Ibid., p. 43.

Comparisons between the expected level of performance specified (from the job analysis) and the current level of performance exhibited (evident in the person analysis) may indicate performance discrepancies. The Sheraton Corporation, for example, specified that all hotel managers must be familiar with the implications of the 1990 Americans with Disabilities Act (ADA) for hotel operations (see Chapter 3). A test of the law was administered, and scores on the test were used to identify those managers who needed training on the implications of the law. Performance discrepancies should not, however, be automatically interpreted as a need for training.[26] The analyst must determine whether the discrepancy is a skill or knowledge deficiency, thus requiring training. If, however, the required skill is present and performance is still lacking, then the problem may be motivational and thus require some other type of organizational intervention (e.g., pay for performance, discipline). Let us next examine the three levels of analysis in more detail.

Organizational Analysis

An organizational analysis tries to answer the question of *where* the training emphasis should be placed in the company and what factors may affect training. To do this, the HR professional should examine organizational goals, personnel inventories, and climate and efficiency indexes. This examination should ideally be conducted in the context of the labor supply forecast and gap analysis, discussed in Chapter 5, as a part of the HRP effort. Organization system constraints that may hamper the training process should also be explored. Many companies rely on very detailed surveys of the workforce to determine training needs as part of the planning effort. Motorola and IBM, for example, conduct annual surveys that assess particular training needs in the context of the company's short- and long-term goals.

The review of short- and long-term goals of the organization and any trends that may affect these goals is done to channel the training toward specific issues of importance to the firm (e.g., international expansion, improved customer satisfaction or employee quality of work life, increased productivity). For example, after Merrill Lynch pleaded guilty to a number of fraudulent business practices, the new CEO ordered training in business ethics for all employees. To reduce layoffs, IBM retrained hundreds of employees to be sales representatives. Not only was IBM able to minimize layoffs, but the larger sales staff was able to attack another corporate goal—to improve customer satisfaction. When Personnel Assessment Systems (PAS) decided to test Germany as a new market for its tests, it first surveyed the workforce to determine expertise in Germany.

As we discussed in Chapter 5, an HRs inventory can reveal projected employee mobility, retirements, and turnover. The more sophisticated personnel inventories can also indicate the number of employees in each knowledge and skill group, which can then be compared to the skills needed based on the gap analysis of the HR planning process. For example, the Ford Manufacturing Systems Division decided to change to a new programming language for future support work. The first step it took was to determine the extent to which current staff was sufficiently skilled in the new language. A computerized personnel inventory quickly revealed how many of the staff had at least basic knowledge of and experience with the new language. PAS's survey found two employees who were fluent in German.

A review of climate, job satisfaction, and efficiency indexes is important to identify problems that could be alleviated with training.[27] Climate indexes are quality-of-work-life indicators and include records on turnover, grievances, absenteeism, productivity, accidents, attitude surveys, employee suggestions, and labor–management data (e.g., strikes, lockouts). Job satisfaction indexes derive data on employee attitudes toward the work itself, supervision, and coworkers. Efficiency indexes consist of costs of labor, materials, and distribution, the quality of the product, downtime, waste, late deliveries, repairs, and equipment utilization. These data are examined to find any discrepancies between desired and actual indexes. The U.S. military now relies on attitude data from female recruits to determine where training is needed in sexual harassment and gender discrimination.

It is also important to identify any organization system constraints on training efforts. For example, if the benefits of training are not clear to top executives, they may not plan and budget appropriately for training. Consequently, the training program may not be properly designed or implemented. Omni Hotels requires senior executives to attend training programs to ensure that they are supportive of the training that lower-level managers receive. In addition, HR staff make sure that the training is tailored to Omni so that trainees can more readily see the value of the training.[28]

Job Analysis

A job analysis tries to answer the question of *what* should be taught so the trainee can perform the job satisfactorily. As we discussed in Chapter 4, a job analysis should document the tasks or duties involved in the job as well as the KASOCs needed to carry out the duties. When conducting a job analysis to determine training needs, both a worker-oriented approach, which focuses

on identifying behaviors and KASOCs, and a task-oriented approach, which describes the work activities performed, should be used. The critical incident technique (CIT), is particularly valuable because it provides considerable detail on the job and the consequences of specific work behaviors. A task-oriented approach is beneficial in identifying very specific training objectives, which are then used in curriculum development and program evaluation. As discussed in Chapter 4, ideally more than one method of job analysis should be used to determine training needs. If interviews or questionnaires are used and discrepancies exist between what a supervisor says is an important job duty and what an employee states, these discrepancies should be resolved before any training programs are designed.[29]

Person Analysis

A **person analysis** attempts to answer the question of *who* needs training in the firm and the specific type of training these people need. To do this, the performance of individuals, groups, or units on major job duties (taken from the performance appraisal data) is compared to expected performance standards (as identified in the job analysis). Given these data, one should be able to determine which job incumbents (or groups of incumbents) are successful at completing the tasks required. Many companies use self-assessments in this process. For example, Ford determined the training needs for a new computer language based on a self-assessment questionnaire distributed to the staff. At the managerial level, many organizations (e.g, IBM, AT&T, Federal Express, the World Bank, and the Federal Aviation Administration) use peers and subordinates to provide performance information about their managers. Knight-Ridder uses 360-degree appraisal to determine training needs. Managers receive "competency" ratings from customers, subordinates, peers, and their managers. At Ford, each supervisor is responsible for completing an individual training plan for each subordinate. The plan is developed jointly by the supervisor and the subordinate. The two decide on the courses that should be taken and the time frame for completion. The goal is for each employee to reach a certain level of proficiency considered necessary for current and future tasks. Many organizations in the service sector rely on customers for information about sales personnel. Bloomingdale's, for example, uses "paid" customers to assess the sales techniques of probationary employees. The data are then used to determine the appropriate managerial intervention to take with the employee (e.g., training, discipline, new compensation). We will discuss some of these interventions in greater detail in Chapter 9.

Performance discrepancies are used to indicate areas needing attention. It is important to determine whether any discrepancies are due to a lack of KASOCs, which KASOCs are lacking, and whether they can be developed in employees through training. Individuals may lack the necessary skills or perceive themselves as lacking the skills (i.e., they may lack confidence in their abilities). In these cases, training may be needed. In other situations, employees may have the skills yet lack the needed motivation to perform, and other action may be necessary (e.g., changes in the reward system, discipline). Employees can also be tested on the desired behaviors (or knowledge) using a performance test such as those discussed in Chapter 6. If they can perform the duties satisfactorily, the organization will know that skills training is not required. The U.S. Navy, for example, uses miniature training and testing to determine skill level before comprehensive training. Pratt & Whitney and Office Depot are among the many companies that use an assessment center to measure supervisory skills judged to be critical based on its goals.

Many companies skip the person analysis and instead institute required training for whole work units "whether they need it or not." This approach can be inefficient, particularly if some workers have no need for the training and, as one trainee put it, "plenty of *actual* work on my table."

Techniques for Collecting Needs Assessment Data

A variety of techniques have been suggested for conducting a needs assessment and for collecting data to use in the organizational, job, and person analyses. Figure 7.4. lists these techniques. Some techniques (e.g., work sampling) can be used for more than one type of analysis. Thus, efforts to coordinate and integrate results are recommended.

Deriving Instructional Objectives

After completing the three types of analyses in the needs assessment, the HR professional should begin to develop instructional or learning objectives for the performance discrepancies identified. Instructional objectives describe the performance you want trainees to exhibit. Well-written learning objectives should contain observable actions (e.g., time on target, error rate for things that can be identified, ordered, or charted), measurable criteria (e.g., percentage correct), and the conditions of performance (e.g., specification as to when the behavior should occur).[30] Figure 7.5 provides examples of the effective characteristics of learning objectives.

ADVANTAGES TO LEARNING OBJECTIVES. Although training programs can be developed without deriving learning objectives, there are several advantages to developing them. First, the process of defining learning objectives helps the HR professional identify criteria for **evaluating** training programs. For example, specifying an instructional objective of a 20 percent reduction in waste reveals that measures of waste may be important indicators of program effectiveness. Second, learning objectives direct trainers to the specific issues and content to focus on. This ensures that trainers are addressing important topics that have been identified through strategic HR planning. Also, learning objectives guide trainees by specifying what is expected of them at the end of training. Finally, specifying objectives makes the HR department more accountable and more clearly linked to HR planning and other HR activities, which may make the training program easier to sell to line managers. Unfortunately, a minority of training programs have explicit training objectives for contemporary issues such as sexual harassment and diversity.[31]

FIGURE 7.4
DATA SOURCES USED IN TRAINING NEEDS ASSESSMENT

ORGANIZATIONAL ANALYSIS	JOB/TASK ANALYSIS	PERSON ANALYSIS
Organizational goals and objectives	Job descriptions	Performance appraisal data
		Work sampling
Personnel inventories	Job specifications	Interviews
Skills inventories	Performance standards	Questionnaires
Organizational climate indexes	Performing the job	Tests (KASOCs)
Efficiency indexes	Work sampling	Attitude surveys
Changes in systems or subsystems (e.g., equipment)	Reviewing literature on the job	
		Training progress
Management requests	Asking questions about the job	Assessment centers
Exit interviews	Training committees	Critical incidents
Management-by-objectives or work planning systems	Analysis of operating problems	

Source: Modified from M. L. Moore and P. Dutton, Training needs analysis: Review and Critique. *Academy of Management Review, 3,* 1978, pp. 534–535, 537–538. Used with permission.

FIGURE 7.5
STANDARDS FOR LEARNING (BEHAVIORAL) OBJECTIVES

	THE OBSERVABLE ACTION MAY BE EXPRESSED AS:		MEASURABLE CRITERIA ANSWER QUESTIONS AS:	CONDITIONS OF PERFORMANCE	
	VERB OR ACTION	OBJECT	HOW OFTEN? HOW WELL? HOW MANY? HOW MUCH? HOW WILL WE KNOW IT IS OKAY?	WHAT'S GIVEN?	WHAT ARE THE VARIABLES?
After training, the worker will be able to	add	6% sales tax	exactly 6% on *all* sales	by checking a chart on the cash register.	
	identify	corporate officers	18 of the top 20	by looking at a photo or by hearing the title.	
	activate	the turn signal	for *all* turns	by using the automatic signal in the car.	
After training, drivers will	1. raise 2. extend 3. give	left arm right arm proper signal	upward at elbow for straight left for ⅛ mile before turning *or* ¼ block before turning	right turn left turn when driving when driving	if no automatic signal. in the country. in the city.
After training, the worker will be able to	smile		at *all* customers	even when exhausted or ill	unless customer is irate.
	express	concern about the fact that the customer is unhappy	with *all* irate people by brief (fewer than 10 words) apology only after customer has stopped talking		no matter how upset, or abusive, or profane the customer becomes.
	ask	open questions	which cannot be answered *yes* or *no* or with *facts*	whenever probing for feelings.	
	relieve	tension in subordinates	by asking open questions	when employee seems angry, frustrated, confused, or tense.	

Source: D. Laird, *Approaches to training and development,* 2nd ed. Reading, MA: Addison-Wesley, 1985, p. 106. Used with permission.

DEVELOPMENT OF THE TRAINING PROGRAM

After a needs analysis has been conducted and the HR professional is confident that training is needed to address the performance problem or to advance the firm's mission, the training program is developed. This can be done by an in-house training staff or by outside consultants. Many firms now even design and manage their own corporate training centers. Some of them include Ford, Disney, GE, Union Carbide, IBM, Home Depot, Xerox, Motorola, Black & Decker, Aetna Life & Casualty, Kodak, and Goodyear Tire & Rubber. To develop the program, the HR professional should design a training environment conducive to learning. This can be done by setting up preconditions for learning and arranging the training environment to ensure learning. Following this, the HR professional should examine various training methods and techniques to choose the combination most beneficial for accomplishing of the instructional objectives of the training program.

Designing a Learning Environment for Training

To design a training program in which learning will be facilitated, HR professionals should review the basic principles of how individuals learn. This is done in order to set up effective preconditions for learning so trainees will be prepared for the training program.[32] Learning principles should be reviewed and integrated into the design of the training program and materials. Also, issues of how to maximize transfer of new behaviors back to the job should be addressed. Finally, trainers should design their programs to meet the needs of adults as learners, which means understanding how adults best learn.

Preconditions of Learning

Trainees must be ready to learn before they are placed in any training program. To ensure this, HR professionals should determine whether trainees are **trainable** (i.e., whether they have the ability to learn and are motivated to learn). In addition, HR professionals should try to gain the support of trainees and their supervisors before implementing the program. This is particularly important for training in sensitive areas such as diversity and gender discrimination. Yet, only 9 percent of companies measure such preconditions.[33]

TRAINABILITY. Before the learner can benefit from any formal training, he or she must be trainable or ready to learn. This means the trainee must have both the ability and the motivation to learn. To have the ability, the trainee must possess the skills and knowledge prerequisite to mastery of the material. One way to determine this is to give trainees a work sample (i.e., an example of the types of skills to be performed on the job) and measure how quickly they are able to learn the material or how well they are able to perform the skills. Assessing trainees' ability to learn is of increasing concern to corporate America. The CEO of Johnson & Johnson describes the need for readiness as "the American dream turned nightmare" simply because individuals do not have the ability to learn.[34] In view of the increasing technological knowledge required in most jobs, many Americans are not being educated at a level compatible with the requirements of most entry-level jobs. The chair of the board of BellSouth stated, "Fewer than 10 percent of employment candidates met our skill and ability requirements for sales, services, and technical jobs."[35] This situation appears to be getting worse in the United States since the entry-level jobs of the future are being "upskilled" while the pool of qualified workers is shrinking.

Some firms spend money training employees so that they have the basic skills needed before learning the specific job-related skills. One report indicated that 22 percent of employers offer basic education in reading, writing, mathematics, and English as a second language.[36] For example, Planters Nuts in Suffolk, Virginia, spent $40,000 to improve the reading and writing skills of 48 employees. Hewlett-Packard spent $22,000 to teach high school mathematics to 30 production supervisors in its Spokane, Washington, plant. Polaroid spent $700,000 to teach basic English and mathematics to 1,000 new and veteran employees in its Cambridge, Massachusetts, location.[37] Mirage Resorts, rated in 1997 as one of the most admired companies, spends major dollars on employee education programs. For example, since many of its workers are recent immigrants, Mirage offers an opportunity for them to earn a high school equivalency degree on the premises.[38]

It has been estimated that over 30 million workers in the United States are functionally illiterate, meaning they cannot read or write well enough to perform their job duties. Sun Oil, Campbell Soup, and Digital Equipment work with state and local governments in partnership programs to help address literacy issues among the workforce.[39]

It's not enough that trainees have the ability to learn the skills; they must also have the desire or motivation to learn. One way to assess motivation to learn is to examine how involved they are in their own jobs and career planning. The assumption is that those individuals who are more highly involved will have higher motivation to learn.[40] Some companies also link successful completion of training programs and acquired skills with compensation (see Chapter 10). At Ford, for example, employees must select 40 hours of training from a list of options. An employee must fulfill the 40 hours to qualify for merit pay.

GAINING THE SUPPORT OF TRAINEES AND OTHERS. If trainees do not see the value of training, they will be unlikely to learn new behaviors or use them on their jobs. Trainees should be informed in advance about the benefits that will result from training. If they see some incentives for training, it may strengthen their motivation to learn the behaviors, practice them, and remember them.[41] To gain the support of trainees for the training program, the trainer must point out the intrinsic (e.g., personal growth) and extrinsic (e.g., promotion) benefits of attending training. At Saturn, employees are strongly encouraged to receive skills training. In fact, 5 percent of their yearly compensation is based on the amount of training they receive.

In addition to garnering the support of trainees for training, the support of their supervisors, coworkers, and subordinates should be sought. For example, if the trainees' supervisors are not supportive of training, then they may not facilitate the learning process (e.g., allow employees time off for training, reward them for using new skills). Likewise, if their peers or subordinates ridicule them for attending training, they may not be motivated to attend training programs or to learn in them. HR professionals can improve the likelihood of acquiring others' support for training by getting their opinions on the content of training, the location, and the times. For example, a training program conducted during a department's slow times might meet with greater acceptance than the same program offered during the busiest times.

Conditions of the Learning Environment

After ensuring that the preconditions for learning are met, trainers should build a training environment in which learning is maximized. To do this, trainers need to decide how to best arrange the training environment.

That is, should they use whole versus part learning? Massed versus spaced practice? Overlearning? Should they provide knowledge of results or feedback? They also need to determine how to maximize attention and retention. Learning principles should be built into the training environment as well as into the training materials used. Each of these issues is briefly described below.

WHOLE VERSUS PART LEARNING. Research has shown that when a complex task is to be learned, it should be broken down into its parts. Trainees should learn each part separately, starting with the simplest and going on to the most difficult. However, part learning should be combined with whole learning; that is, trainees should be shown the whole performance so they know what their final goal is. The training content should be broken down into integrated parts, and each part should be learned until it can be performed accurately. Then a trainee should be allowed to put all the parts together and practice the whole task.

MASSED VERSUS SPACED PRACTICE. Practice is important for trainees to learn a new skill or behavior. Trainers can also observe the practice sessions and provide feedback to the trainees so they can correct their mistakes. It has been shown that spaced practice (i.e., practicing the new behavior and taking rest periods in between) is more effective than massed practice (practicing the new behavior without breaks), especially for motor skills. For example, it would be easier for you to learn how to play golf by having a lesson on putting and then going out to practice putting, rather than learning how to do all the possible golf shots (e.g., putting, chipping, pitching, driving, etc.) and then going out to play. If a learner has to concentrate for long periods without some rest, learning and retention may suffer. It's a little like cramming for an examination: rapid forgetting sets in very soon. Consequently, spaced practice seems to be more productive for long-term retention and for transfer of learning to the work setting.

OVERLEARNING. Overlearning (i.e., practicing beyond the point of first accurate recall) can be critical in both acquisition and transfer of knowledge and skills. Generally, overlearning increases retention over time, makes the behavior or skill more automatic, increases the quality of the performance during stress, and helps trainees transfer what they have learned back to the job setting.[42] Overlearning is desirable in a program when the task to be learned is not likely to be immediately practiced in the work situation and when performance must be maintained during periods of emergency and stress. For example, **overlearning skills** for driving or flying may be important so that in a crisis the individual will be able to quickly remember what actions should be taken. Pat Head Summit, rated as one of the best coaches for collegiate basketball, has her nationally ranked team, the Tennessee Lady Volunteers, practice free throw shots over and over in preparation for critical games.

GOAL SETTING. Goal setting can help employees improve their performance by directing their attention to specific behaviors that need to be changed. If employees set specific, challenging goals, they can reach higher levels of performance. For example, research has shown that goal setting has led to 16 percent to 27 percent performance improvements with an average increase of 19 percent.[43] Goal setting improves performance because it affects four mechanisms: (*a*) it directs and focuses a person's behavior, (*b*) it increases an individual's effort toward attaining the goal, (*c*) it encourages an individual to persist on the goal or work harder and faster to attain it, and (*d*) it enables an individual to set specific strategies for attaining the goal.[44] Training programs should include specific, yet challenging goals so trainees can reach higher levels of performance or greater mastery of the training material.

KNOWLEDGE OF RESULTS. For trainees to improve training performance, they need to receive timely and specific feedback or knowledge of results.[45] Feedback serves informational and motivational purposes. It tells trainees how discrepant their performance is from the desired performance and what particular skills or behaviors they need to correct. Also, it can motivate them to meet their performance goals once they see that they are coming close to accomplishing them. Trainers should build into the training environment opportunities for providing feedback to trainees. For example, the trainer could give pop quizzes to trainees during the session and call out the correct answers. Trainees could quickly score their work to see how well they are doing in the session and what they need additional learning or practice in.

ATTENTION. Trainers should try to design training programs and materials to ensure that trainees devote attention to them. They can do this by choosing a training environment that is comfortable to trainees (e.g., that has good temperature, lighting, seats, plenty of room, snacks) and free from distractions (e.g., phone calls, interruptions from colleagues). No matter how motivated trainees are, if the environment is not comfortable, trainees will have difficulty learning. For example, in one training session with sales employees, 30 trainees were forced to sit in a room that only had enough space for 20 comfortably. Without enough chairs and tables, some trainees really could not focus on the session. In another session with 40 managers, the training was conducted in a hotel conference room that was right next to a choir show. As much as they tried to concentrate, they could hardly hear what the trainers had to say. In both cases, the training environment was not conducive to effective learning. Also, trainers should make sure that trainees are familiar with and have accepted the instructional objectives. They can do this by asking trainees to describe how accomplishing the objectives will resolve problems on the job. If trainees are able to translate learning objectives into relevant job issues, they may pay more attention to the training sessions.

RETENTION. The ability to retain what is learned is obviously relevant to the effectiveness of a training program. Many factors have been found to increase retention. If the material presented is meaningful to trainees, they should have an easier time understanding and remembering it. Trainers can make the content meaningful by: (1) presenting trainees with an overview of what is to be learned so they will be able to see the overall picture; (2) using examples, concepts, and terms familiar to the trainees (e.g., use medical terms and examples when training doctors and nurses); and (3) by organizing the material from simple to complex (e.g., teach someone how to serve before you teach them strategies in tennis). Retention can also be enhanced by rehearsal or requiring trainees to periodically recall what they have learned (e.g., by testing them).

Using Learning Principles to Develop Training Materials

The learning principles described above should be considered not only when designing the training environment, but also when developing training materials. Any materials used with trainees should be able to stimulate them into learning and remembering the information. To ensure that this occurs, trainers need to make sure the learning principles are built into their training materials. For example, the materials should provide illustrations and relevant examples to stimulate trainees. In addition, the objectives of the material should be clearly stated and a summary should be provided.[46]

Transfer of Training

The ultimate goal of any organizational training program is that the learning that occurs during training be transferred back to the job. To maximize transfer, the following suggestions have been offered.[47] These include ideas for the training session itself as well as for the employee once he or she has returned to the job:

1. Maximize the similarity between the training context and the job context. That is, the training should resemble the job as closely as possible. At GE, for example, the "action-learning" process focuses on real business problems.

2. Require practice of the new behaviors and even overlearning in training.

3. Encourage trainees to practice skills on their jobs between training sessions. For example, The University of Tennessee's Management Development Center offers a four-week Executive Development Program (EDP) in which executives come for one week for each of four months. In between their attendance, they complete "homework assignments" such as customer value projects, organizational systems projects, and individual leadership development plans (LDP). The assignments encourage trainees to apply their new skills in the workplace, using an **action learning model.**[48]

4. Include a variety of stimulus situations in the practice so trainees will learn to generalize their knowledge and skills.

5. Label or identify the important features of the content to be learned to distinguish the major steps involved.

6. Develop, and have available on the job, job aids to remind employees of the key action steps necessary on the job. For example, ALCOA uses job aids in many of its manufacturing jobs.

7. Make sure the general principles underlying the specific content are understood in training.

8. Ensure that there is a supportive climate for learning and for transferring new behaviors. This can be done by building managerial support (emotional and financial) for training, providing trainees with the freedom to set personal performance goals, and encouraging risk-taking among trainees. One study used 505 supermarket managers from 52 stores and found that the work environment, measured by training climate and learning culture, was directly related to the transfer of trained behaviors.[49]

9. Build the trainee's self-efficacy for learning and using the new skills. Self-efficacy is a feeling of control and accomplishment; that you can control your own destiny. Self-efficacy has been shown to be related to learning using a sample of Navy warfare officers in mid-level managerial positions.[50] In addition, encourage trainees to develop an action plan including specific measurable goals.[51]

10. Once back on the job, employees should be given opportunities to demonstrate that they can use the new skills. For example, one study of plane mechanics from the Air Force found that after training they were given opportunities to perform only about half the tasks they learned in training.[52] Likewise, in a study of university employees, it was found that situational constraints (e.g., adequate resources, time) limited the amount of train-

ing skills that trainees could transfer to the work environment.[53]

11. Encourage continual learning by employees. They should realize that onetime training in an area is not sufficient to maintain effective skills. Retraining may also be needed to update skills.

RELAPSE PREVENTION. Sometimes despite trainers' best efforts to get individuals to transfer what they have learned back to the job, it is difficult for trainees to maintain new behaviors or skills over a long period. They may revert back to their old habits. **Relapse prevention** is needed to assist trainees.[54] A model of the relapse prevention process used to increase the long-term maintenance of newly acquired behaviors is presented in Figure 7.6. It emphasizes the learning of a set of self-control and coping strategies.[55]

Employees should be made aware of the relapse process itself by informing them there are some situa-

tions that make it difficult for trainees to use their new behaviors. For example, they may be faced with peers or supervisors who are not supportive of their new skills.[56] They should learn to identify and anticipate high-risk situations. Also, they should be instructed on how to use coping strategies to avoid such situations. Teaching these issues should increase trainees' self-efficacy or perception that they have control over the situation and can effectively use their new behaviors.

Choosing Methods for the Training Program

Training methods can be divided into two categories: (1) methods that are primarily informational or transmittal in nature; that is, they use primarily one-way communication in which information is transmitted to the learners; and (2) methods that are experiential in nature; that is, the learner interacts with either the instructor, a com-

FIGURE 7.6
A MODEL OF THE RELAPSE PREVENTION PROCESS

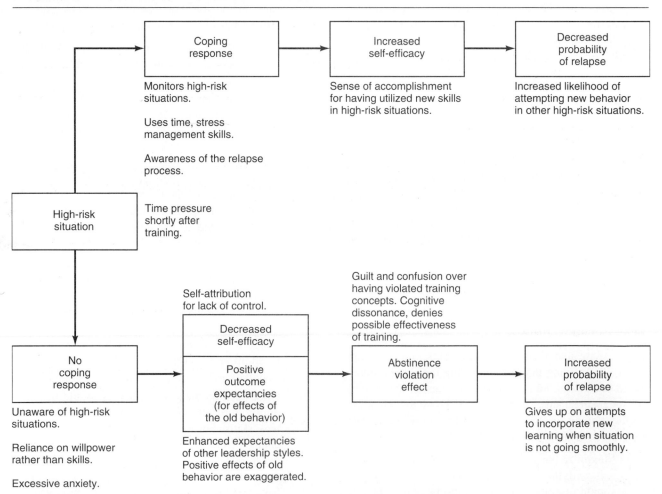

Source: R. D. Marx, Relapse prevention for managerial training: A model for maintenance of behavioral change. *Academy of Management Review, 7,* 1982, 434. Used with permission.

puter/simulator, customers, or other trainees to practice the skill.[57] Some of the major methods including their uses, benefits, and limitations are described below and in Figures 7.7 and 7.8.

Most training programs use several training techniques since no one approach is best suited for every purpose. For example, IBM's international sales training program includes both classroom and on-the-job training (OJT) which is given over one year.[58] AMC Theatres uses videotapes, detailed training manuals, and OJT programs to train ushers and concession personnel. To determine which combination of methods to select for a particular training program, a developer should first clearly define the purpose of and the audience for the training. In addition, an assessment of the resources available to conduct the training is necessary. This will mean examining the staff, materials, and budget capable of handling the training demands.

At a minimum, the training methods selected should (1) motivate the trainee to learn the new skill; (2) illustrate the desired skills to be learned; (3) be consistent with the content (e.g., use an interactive approach to teach interpersonal skills); (4) allow for active participa-

tion by the trainees to fit with the adult learning model; (5) provide opportunities for practice and overlearning; (6) provide feedback on performance during training; (7) be structured from simple to complex; (8) encourage positive transfer from the training to the job; and (9) be cost-effective.[59] In many cases, trainers will use several different techniques. For example, teaching supervisors how to give performance feedback may first begin with a lecture or overview of the performance appraisal process, followed by small-group discussions or videotapes depicting effective coaching, and then role-plays to have supervisors practice their feedback skills.

Informational Methods

Informational methods are used primarily to teach factual material, skills, or attitudes. Generally, they do not require the trainee to actually experience or practice the material taught during the training session.[60] Some of the more commonly used informational techniques include lectures, audiovisual presentations, and self-directed learning (SDL) methods (e.g., independent study and programmed instruction).

FIGURE 7.7
INFORMATIONAL TRAINING METHODS

USES	BENEFITS	LIMITATIONS
	LECTURE	
Gaining new knowledge	Equally as good as programmed instruction and television	Learners are passive
To present introductory material		Poor transfer
	Low cost	Depends on the lecturer's ability
	Reaches a large audience at one time	Is not tailored to individual trainees
	Audience is often comfortable with it	
	AUDIOVISUALS	
Gaining new knowledge	Can reach a large audience at one time	Is not tailored to individual trainees
Gaining attention	Allows for replays	Must be updated
	Versatility	Passive learners
	INDEPENDENT STUDY	
Gaining new knowledge	Allows trainees to go at their own pace	Expensive to develop a library of materials
Completing degree requirements	Minimizes trainers' time	
Continuous education	Minimizes costs of development	Materials must be designed to adjust to varying reading levels
		Performance depends on trainee's motivation
		Is not applicable for all jobs
	PROGRAMMED INSTRUCTION	
Gaining new knowledge	Allows trainees to go at their own pace	Expensive to develop
Pretraining preparation to ensure that all trainees have similar backgrounds	Can guarantee mastery at a specified level	Is not applicable for all tasks (e.g., cognitive tasks)
	Encourages active trainee involvement	Does not lead to higher performance than lectures
	Provides immediate feedback to trainees	

FIGURE 7.8
EXPERIENTIAL TRAINING METHODS

USES	BENEFITS	LIMITATIONS
ON-THE-JOB TRAINING		
Learning job skills	Good transfer	Depends on the trainer's skills and willingness
Apprenticeship training	Limited trainer costs	May be costly due to lost production and mistakes
Job rotation	High trainee motivation since training is relevant	May have frequent interruptions due to job demands
		Often is haphazardly done
		Trainees may learn bad habits
COMPUTER-ASSISTED INSTRUCTION (CAI)		
Gaining new knowledge	Self-paced	Costly
Drill & practice	Standardization of training over time	Trainees may have difficulties using computers
Individualized training	Feedback given	Limited opportunities for trainee interaction
	Good retention	Less useful for training interpersonal skills
EQUIPMENT SIMULATORS		
To reproduce real-world conditions	Effective for learning and transfer	Costly to develop
For physical and cognitive skills	Can practice most of the job skills	Sickness can occur
For team training		Requires good fidelity
GAMES AND SIMULATIONS		
Decision-making skills	Resembles the job tasks	Highly competitive
Management training	Provides feedback	Time-consuming
Interpersonal skills	Presents realistic challenges	May stifle creativity
CASE STUDY OR ANALYSIS		
Decision-making skills	Decision-making practice	Must be updated
Analytical skills	Real-world training materials	Criticized as being unable to teach general management skills
Communication skills	Active learning	Trainers often dominate discussions
To illustrate diversity of solutions	Good for developing problem-solving skills	
ROLE-PLAYING		
For changing attitudes	Gain experience of other roles	Initial resistance of trainees
To practice skills	Active learning	Trainees may not take it seriously
To analyze interpersonal problems	Close to reality	
BEHAVIORAL MODELING		
To teach interpersonal skills	Allows practice	Time-consuming
To teach cognitive skills	Provides feedback	May be costly to develop
	Retention is improved	
SENSITIVITY TRAINING		
To enhance self-awareness	Can improve self-concept	May be threatening
To allow trainees o see how others see them	Can reduce prejudice	May have limited generalizability to job situations
	Can change interpersonal behaviors	

LECTURES. The lecture method is the most commonly used technique for training employees and teaching students. In a 1995 survey of organizations with 100 or more employees, 90 percent indicated they used lectures for employee training.[61] The method is often supplemented with audiovisual aids, motion pictures, or television. The approach can also vary in the degree to which discussion is permitted, since some lectures involve all one-way communication, while others may allow trainees to participate by asking questions or providing comments. Many companies employ motivational speakers who provide lectures to employees on product and service quality, competitive advantage, and higher productivity. Among the most popular speakers are Pat Riley, head coach of the Miami Heat basketball team, and Phil Jackson, head coach of the Chicago Bulls.

AUDIOVISUALS. A variety of audiovisuals are available to trainers including films, videos, slides, overheads, audiotapes, flip charts, and chalkboards.[62] Audiovisuals are typically used to supplement other training techniques, including lectures and self-directed learning methods. They can address a variety of topics such as motivational techniques, performance-appraisal interviews, leadership skills, and teamwork. Generally, many of these aids are inexpensive. They are also useful because of their versatility, and they typically allow for replays to help trainees grasp difficult points. For instance, IBM used multiple training techniques, including several videos of effective and ineffective performance, when conducting training to improve telephone skills. At Morse Bros. Inc. of Tangent, Oregon, a ready-mix construction company, videotapes are used to teach drivers a variety of costly learning points such as how to avoid excessive idling of trucks or rollovers and how to make cold weather preparations for their trucks. After watching the video, truck drivers hold discussions and communicate their views on the safety procedures.[63] The U.S. State Department requires that employees assigned to a particular embassy be shown (and tested on) a videotape describing the country and its people.

SELF-DIRECTED LEARNING (SDL) METHODS. Several informational methods for training are considered to be SDL approaches because the trainee takes responsibility for learning the necessary knowledge and skills at his or her own pace. A wide range of decisions can be given to the trainee, including the topic of study, objectives, resources, schedule, learning strategy, type and sequence of activities, and media.[64] In most cases, trainees work without direct supervision, set their own pace, and are allowed to choose their own activities, resources, and learning environments. Generally, the training department's role is to provide assistance by establishing learning centers with available materials and by having trained facilitators on hand for questions. Larger companies such as Motorola, Sunoco, and Office Depot have been successful in setting up such centers and encouraging self-directed learning by employees.[65] In these centers, trainees can be given self-assessment tools or instruments. In fact, 49 percent of firms surveyed in 1995 indicated they used self-assessment tools, while 33 percent indicated they used noncomputerized self-study programs. Andersen Consulting devised a 15-module, self-study, multimedia program that its trainees can complete in their own offices. As a result,

the company has been able to save about $4 million each year in transportation and lodging expenses alone since trainees do not have to travel to corporate headquarters for training.[66]

The advantages of SDL include: (1) reduced training time, as compared to more conventional methods (e.g., lecture); (2) more favorable attitudes by trainees as compared to conventional techniques; (3) minimal reliance on instructors or trainers; (4) mobility (i.e., a variety of places can be used for training); (5) flexibility (i.e., trainees can learn at their own pace); (6) consistency of the information taught to all trainees; and (7) cost savings. There are also several disadvantages, including: (1) high developmental time for course materials and extensive planning requirements; (2) difficulties in revising and updating materials; and (3) limited interactions with peers and trainers.[67]

Research indicates that employees with high levels of readiness for SDL as measured by the Self-Directed Learning Readiness Scale (SDLRS) were more likely to be higher-level managers,[68] to be satisfactory or outstanding performers,[69] to possess greater creativity,[70] and to have a higher degree of life satisfaction.[71] Also, employees who were outstanding performers in jobs requiring high levels of creativity or problem solving or involving high levels of change were likely to have high SDLRS scores. In addition, employees with higher SDLRS scores were successful in relatively unstructured learning situations in which more responsibility rests on the learners.[72]

A variety of SDL approaches are available. Two of the more commonly used techniques include independent study and PI. **Independent study** requires a trainee to read, synthesize, and remember the contents of written material, audio or videotapes, or other sources of information. The training or personnel department can develop a library of materials for trainees to use in teaching themselves at their own pace about various skills or knowledge. Companies such as Coors, Digital Equipment Corporation, Kraft, and U.S. Gypsum utilize extensive self-study materials for their sales employees.[73] Trainees can also design their own training curriculum by opting for correspondence courses or enrolling in independent study courses at local schools. Generally, in these programs, trainees are required to master the content on their own without direct supervision.

Programmed instruction (PI) is an individualized learning method that allows self-paced study of books and written materials on a variety of technical and nontechnical topics. For example, Dean Witter uses a three-month PI program to train new stockbrokers. Most PI programs build in the important learning principles by (1) specifying what is to be learned (i.e., the behavioral objectives); (2) breaking down the learning topic into small, discrete steps; (3) presenting each step to the trainee and requiring him or her to respond to each step of the learning process (i.e., by reading each part); (4) testing the trainees' learning at each step (i.e., by responding to questions); (5) providing immediate feedback to the trainee on whether his or her response was correct or incorrect; and (6) testing the level of skill or knowledge acquired at the end of the training module.[74]

Experiential Methods

Experiential methods are used primarily to teach physical and cognitive skills and abilities. These techniques include OJT, computer-based training (CBT), equipment simulations, games and other simulations, case analyses, role-playing, behavior modeling, and sensitivity training. We will briefly review each of these techniques.

ON-THE-JOB TRAINING. Approximately 90 percent of all industrial training is conducted on the job.[75] OJT is conducted at the work site and in the context of the job. Often, it is informal as when an experienced worker shows a trainee how to perform the job tasks. The trainer may watch over the trainee to provide guidance during practice or learning. For example, sales employees use coaching calls where a senior sales person coaches a new sales employee. Five steps are utilized:

1. Observation of the new employee.
2. Feedback obtained by the new employee.
3. Consensus (i.e., the coach and the new employee arrived at an agreement as to the positives and negatives for the sales call).
4. Rehearsal of a new sales call.
5. Review of the employee's performance.[76]

Although OJT is often associated with the development of new employees, it can also be used to update or broaden the skills of existing employees when new procedures or work methods are introduced.[77] In some OJT cases, the trainer may be a retired employee. For instance, at Corning Glass Works, new employees are paired with retirees for a brief on-the-job introduction regarding the company culture and market data. After this, they are exposed to formal classroom and field training.[78] Many companies combine OJT with formal classroom training. At McDonald's, after a three-hour induction, new employees are partnered with a buddy who is a member of the training squad.[79] Dow Chemical alternates sales employees between classroom training at corporate headquarters and OJT experiences in the field for a year. Similarly, Wang Laboratories spends up to nine months alternating salespeople from company headquarters and field offices.[80] At HM Customs & Excise, classroom training and OJT are interdependent. At Liford, new employees have a work-based trainer allocated to them for up to three months.[81] The Federal National Mortgage Association hired entry-level workers and

places them in a 16-week full-time training program called Business Systems Training. They receive training in programming, data structures, logic, database concepts, and case studies, with an emphasis on client/server and object-oriented programming. Following this, the trainees move on to two years of OJT.[82] In its new plant in Alabama, Mercedes-Benz utilizes training circles as a visual record to reveal who is learning what jobs and how quickly their learning is progressing. These are detailed drawings and descriptions of the steps necessary to execute tasks at each workstation. Pie-sized charts are used to indicate the progress of each team member in learning the steps for each task and at what proficiency level.[83]

OJT is best used when: one-on-one training is necessary, only a small number (usually fewer than five) employees need to be trained, classroom instruction is not appropriate, work in progress cannot be interrupted, a certain level of proficiency on a task is needed for certification, and equipment or safety restrictions make other training techniques inappropriate. The training should emphasize equipment or instruments that are to be used, as well as safety issues or dangerous processes.[84]

Apprenticeship programs are often considered OJT programs because they involve a substantial amount of OJT, even though they do consist of some off-the-job training. Typically, the trainee follows a prescribed order of coursework and hands-on experience. The Department of Labor regulates apprenticeship programs, and many require a minimum of 144 hours of classroom instruction each year, as well as OJT with a skilled employee.[85] Many professions (e.g., medicine) or trades require some type of apprenticeship program, which may last anywhere from two to five years, although typically four years. Some of the most common occupations to offer apprenticeship programs include: electricians, carpenters, plumbers, pipe fitters, sheet-metal workers, machinists, tool-and-die makers, roofers, firefighters, bricklayers, cooks, structural-steel workers, painters, operating engineers, correction officers, and mechanics.[86] A large part of these programs involves OJT in addition to formal coursework. In Europe, apprenticeships are still one of the most likely ways for individuals to gain entry into skilled jobs. Germany is known for its apprenticeship program. But in the United States only 2 percent of high school graduates enter apprenticeship programs.[87] This is a problem for the U.S. workforce since the pool of qualified skilled labor for future jobs has been shrinking.

Another commonly used technique for OJT training is **job rotation,** which involves moving employees from one job to another to broaden their experience. Japanese companies are among the best in the world for providing job rotation. Once employees join a firm, the Japanese company spends an enormous amount of money and time training them and exposing them to various job functions. The training is "just-in-time" so that employees are taught skills and then apply their learning within a short period.[88] Many U.S. companies are showing greater interest in having their employees be able to perform several job functions so that their workforce is more flexible and interchangeable. For example, in the automobile industry today, it is fairly common to see employees being trained on two or more tasks (e.g., painting and welding). This is done at GM's Saturn plant in order to relieve employees' boredom as well as to make the company less dependent on specialized workers. GE requires all managerial trainees to participate in an extensive job rotation program in which the trainees must perform all jobs they will eventually supervise. This helps managers develop a broader background required for future managerial positions. We will discuss job rotation in more detail in Chapter 12.

COMPUTER-BASED TRAINING. Use of computers to train employees is becoming increasingly more common among organizations, especially for training technical skills. As of 1997, it was estimated that 40 percent of U.S. organizations with more than 100 employees indicated they used computer-based training (CBT).[89] One leading provider of CBT software, CBT Group, has deals with Cisco Systems, IBM, Informix, Microsoft, Netscape Communications, Novell, Oracle, PeopleSoft, SAP, and Sybase, among others.[90] Training experts believe that by the year 2000, CBT will be the predominant education method for insurance industry employees. For example, Massachusetts Mutual Life Insurance Company uses CBT to train employees and agents.[91]

Chunking refers to chopping computer-based training into its smallest parts and sending them through a network so that learners receive just the instruction they need when they need it. Spring Corporation chunks CBT on the corporate intranet and is one of the leaders in using training over the intranet.[92] The most popular word processing software packages (e.g., Microsoft Word, Word Perfect) use CBT to introduce learners to the use of the software. The U.S. Armed Forces use CBT extensively for training many of their technicians. Electronic Data Systems Corporation (EDS) requires computer-based courses for many of its employees.[93] In some CBT programs, trainees interact directly with computers to actually learn and practice new skills. This is done similarly to the PI system and is called computer-assisted instruction (CAI). For example, Dialect Interactive Lectures (DIALECT) are university lectures that have been converted into multimedia-based digital learning material. DIALECT uses animation, computer simulations, and hyperlink facilities to guide students through lectures.[94]

CBT systems can have computers on hand for trainees to use periodically to solve problems. In most cases, computers are used to teach computer skills such as programming, word processing, data processing, and how to use applications software (e.g., Lotus Notes, Microsoft Excel). However, computer software is available in many other areas as well. For example, a program titled "Keep your hands to yourself" simulates a sexual harassment scenario. At Ameritech, the midwestern regional Bell company, Yello is a simulation used to teach account representatives how to sell Yellow Pages advertising. Sales reps have to relate to customers on the simulation, and this helps them learn how to deal with different types of customers (e.g., selling an ad to a florist may be different from selling to a lawyer). In 1995, McDonald's altered its training budget from primarily technical skills training courses to leadership and project management skills. The learning manager convinced management to deliver computer-based training courses over the company's network.[95]

Despite the relatively high cost of CBT, it has the advantage of being self-paced, standardized, self-sufficient, easily available, and flexible. This is particularly important in today's fast-paced environment, where organizations cannot afford for employees to be away from the job for large amounts of time. In fact, many trainers see CBT as the most innovative training method ever created. Others view it as a proven way to save time and money while delivering consistent content. For example, CONDUIT (Cooperative Network for Dual-Use Information Technologies) developed new and efficient training techniques based on advanced computer technologies such as simulation, multimedia, and the Internet. The training was for new manufacturing employees and experienced workers who needed to expand their skills. The firm was able to provide more accessible training at a lower cost at local schools and on company PCs.[96]

The latest round of CBT-oriented software offers revolutionary ways in which interactive training is developed and delivered. For example, many CBT systems support links to the Internet and to corporate intranets. Internet-based training emerged in early 1997 as a cost- and time-efficient way to address many companies' training needs. Global Knowledge Network is working with the Canadian government and Microsoft to deliver on-line technical training. Many universities have also begun to offer on-line education (e.g., Indiana University, Penn State University) or virtual classrooms (The University of Tennessee). Offering training over the Internet enables employees that travel frequently or live in remote areas to be able to access high-quality education at their own pace.[97]

EQUIPMENT SIMULATIONS. Some training may involve machines or equipment systems designed to reproduce physiological and psychological conditions of the real world that are necessary for learning and transfer to occur. For example, driving simulators or flight simulators are often used to train employees in driving or flying skills. Another example of a simulation is the FireArms Training System (FATS), which is used by more than 300 law enforcement agencies in the United States.[98] In this simulation, officers are confronted with a number of everyday work situations (e.g., fleeing felons) on a video screen. The military uses virtual reality simulators for training of war game demonstrations. One exercise, called the Synthetic Theater of War, links tactics, techniques, and processes of modern systems to illustrate battles.[99] Equipment simulators are also relied on to a great deal in training for space missions (e.g., astronaut training). While many of these simulations are costly, some have become more affordable. In addition, using simulators for training is only a fraction of the cost of using the real equipment to train employees.

GAMES AND OTHER SIMULATIONS. Many training programs rely on the use of a variety of games or nonequipment simulations. In fact, simulation games appear to be gaining in popularity with hundreds of different types of games available for teaching technical, managerial, professional, or other business-related skills. Some of the more common games include in-baskets and business games. A 1995 survey indicated that games and simulations were used for training by 63 percent of firms.

Generally, most games are used to teach skills such as decision making as well as analytical, strategic, or interpersonal skills. Business games typically require trainees to assume various roles in a company (e.g., president, marketing vice president) where they are given several years' worth of information on the company's products, technology, and HRs and asked to deal with the information in a compressed time period (several weeks or months). They make decisions regarding production volumes, inventory levels, and prices in an environment in which other trainees are running competitor companies. "Looking Glass" is an example of one managerial business game developed by the Center for Creative Leadership to train managers. "The Marketplace Simulation" is another internationally known computer simulation used in training executives, employees, and business students in all business areas, especially marketing, strategic planning, leadership, and team-building skills.[100] The most successful business games keep the focus on specific corporate objectives or problems such as profits, customer service, or labor costs.[101]

In-baskets are used to train managerial candidates in decision-making skills by requiring them to act on a variety of memos, reports, and other correspondence that are typically found in a manager's in-basket. As we discussed in Chapter 6, participants must prioritize items and respond to them in a limited time period. In-baskets are often included in assessment centers. For example, the method is used as one component of the weeklong executive development program at the Center for Creative Leadership.

CASE ANALYSES. Most business students are very familiar with case analysis, a training method often used in management training to improve analytical skills. Trainees are asked to read a case report that describes the organizational, social, and technical aspects of some organizational problem (e.g., poor leadership, intergroup conflict). Each trainee prepares a report in which he or she describes the problems and offers solutions (including potential risks and benefits). Working in a group, trainees may then be asked to justify the problems they have identified and their recommendations. The trainer's role is to facilitate the group's learning and to help the trainees see the underlying management concepts in the case.

ROLE-PLAYING. In a role-playing exercise, trainees act out roles and attempt to perform the behaviors required in those roles. Role-plays are commonly used in training, and a recent study indicated that 49 percent of the firms reported using role-plays for employee training.[102] This method is often used to teach skills such as oral communication, interpersonal styles, leadership styles, performance feedback reviews, and interviewing techniques. At the *Chicago Tribune,* trainees are assigned the role of supervisor giving performance-appraisal feedback to a subordinate, while other trainees play the role of the subordinate. Banks use role-plays among other techniques (videos, team exercises) to teach new employees about commercial lending, consumer lending, deposit operations, real estate lending, and consumer loan account servicing.[103] Xerox uses role-plays in some of its training programs to teach managers how to develop a culturally diverse workforce. At Digital Equipment Corporation, two training center employees act out a scene in which a woman fails to express her displeasure with the sexual advances of a colleague. The trainees analyze the role-play and recommend an appropriate response. Role-plays are very common components of sexual harassment training programs.[104] Role-playing as a training technique has become so popular that Roleplay UK provides professional role-players directly to client companies or to training consultants.[105]

BEHAVIOR MODELING. Behavior modeling is quickly growing as a technique for training managers on interpersonal and communication skills.[106] Many large companies such as Exxon, Westinghouse, and Union Carbide use this approach.[107] Based on Bandura's theory of social learning,[108] the method consists of four consecutive components: (1) *attention* (watching someone perform a behavior usually through videotapes); (2) *retention* (processes to help the trainee retain what was observed); (3) *motor reproduction* or behavioral rehearsal (using role-plays to practice new behaviors); and (4) *motivation* or feedback/reinforcement (receiving feedback on the behaviors performed). The success of this approach to training is based on the notion that many of us learn by observing others. For example, suppose you have just taken a job as a sales representative. You may spend some time watching the techniques used by other reps to get ideas for how to perform the job. If you practice the behaviors you have observed and get feedback from the "models" or others, your learning should be enhanced. Generally, trainees should observe predominantly positive examples of the behaviors if the goal is to get them to reproduce the behaviors. Behavioral modeling has been used successfully at the U.S. Naval Construction Battalion at Gulfport, Mississippi. The use of behavior modeling resulted in superior retention of knowledge, transfer of learning, and end-user satisfaction.[109]

SENSITIVITY OR LABORATORY TRAINING. In this training method, which was very popular for management training in previous decades, a small group of about 8 to 14 individuals work together to develop interpersonal or team-building skills. In an unstructured setting, trainees focus on the "here and now" to describe issues of interest or concern to them. The trainer generally does not structure the discussion, yet may intercede if the comments become harmful to participants. In the discussions, trainees provide feedback to one another about interpersonal styles or skills in order to help each other grow as individuals. The purposes may be to help trainees develop as individuals, to improve listening skills, to gain insights into why individuals behave as they do, or to practice new ways of behaving in an environment where feedback and practice are allowed.

EVALUATION*

Evaluation involves the collection of information on whether trainees were satisfied with the program, learned the material, and were able to apply the skills learned. It may be important to determine whether trainees are capable of exhibiting the appropriate level of a skill (e.g., do new supervisors know all the organization's policies and procedures). Also, it may be important to know whether trainees have changed their behavior and if the change was due to training (e.g., do supervisors complete the necessary paperwork for disciplining an employee more so after the training than before it was conducted). Further, it may be critical to

___
*Contributed by Joyce E. A. Russell, Phillip J. Decker, and Barry R. Nathan.

know whether a new group of supervisors in the same training program will also improve learning or behaviors. Evaluation efforts can be designed to answer these questions or issues.[110]

Evaluation ensures that programs are accountable and are meeting the needs of employees in a cost-effective manner. This is especially important today, as organizations attempt to cut costs and improve quality. Without evaluation, it is very difficult to show that training was the reason for any improvements. As a result, management may reduce training budgets or staffs in times of financial hardship. For example, 10 percent of respondents to a training survey indicated budget reductions in 1988 after the stock market crash.[111]

While most companies recognize the importance of evaluation, few actually evaluate their training programs.[112] A review of *Fortune* 500 companies found that only a small number conduct sound evaluations of their programs.[113] Another study found that less than 12 percent of 285 companies evaluated their supervisory training programs.[114] Evaluations are conducted routinely by companies such as Motorola, Xerox, Merck, and Federal Express. These firms recognize that training programs must be evaluated in order to ensure that employees are being prepared for the future and possible skill obsolescence. A study of more than 40 organizations identified IBM, Motorola University, Arthur Andersen, Florida Power & Light's Nuclear Division, and the AT&T School of Business as the companies with the best training evaluation practices.[115]

Most training evaluations primarily assess the reactions of participants. One survey found that 84 percent of 982 companies collected reaction data, 69 percent collected learning data, 60 percent measured changes in trainees' behaviors, and 43 percent measured changes in business results.[116] However, a more recent survey found that many respondents claiming to have measured changes in behavior were merely collecting follow-up reaction data from trainees with questions such as "were you able to use the material taught in the training program?"[117]

For an evaluation to be complete, several types of criteria should be collected. In addition, an experimental design should be utilized to be able to show that any changes detected in trainees' performance before and after training were due to the training program and not some other factor (e.g., change in top management, equipment, or compensation packages).

Types of Criteria

HR professionals should try to collect four types of data when evaluating training programs: measures of reactions, learning, behavior change, and organizational results. These criteria, based on Kirkpatrick's model, are widely used to evaluate corporate training programs.[118]

REACTIONS. Reaction measures are designed to assess trainees' opinions regarding the training program. Using a questionnaire, trainees are asked at the end of training to indicate the degree they were satisfied with the trainer, subject matter and content, the materials (books, pamphlets, handouts), and the environment (room, breaks, meals, temperature). Also, they may be asked to indicate the aspects of the program they considered to be most valuable and least useful to them. You have undoubtedly been asked to complete a course evaluation instrument for some of your classes. This is a reaction measure.

Favorable reactions to a program do not guarantee that learning has occurred nor that appropriate behaviors have been adopted. However, it is important to collect reaction data for several reasons: (1) to find out how satisfied trainees were with the program; (2) to make any needed revisions in the program; and (3) and to ensure that other trainees will be receptive to attending the program. Trainees should be given ample time at the end of the session to complete the reaction form. Also, HR professionals should assess trainees' reactions several months after the program to determine how relevant trainees felt the training was to their jobs. An example of a reaction form is presented in Figure 7.9.

LEARNING. Learning measures assess the degree to which trainees have mastered the concepts, knowledges, and skills of the training. Typically, learning is measured by paper-and-pencil tests (e.g., essay-type questions, multiple choice), performance tests, and simulation exercises.[119] These measures should be designed to sample the content of the training program. Trainees should be tested on their level of understanding before and after training to determine the effect of training on their knowledge. Figure 7.10 presents two examples of performance tests used to assess learning. Figure 7.11 presents a more commonly used type of learning measure.

BEHAVIORS. Behaviors of trainees before and after training should be compared to assess the degree to which training has changed their performance. This is important because one goal of training is to modify the on-the-job behavior or performance of trainees. Behaviors can be measured by relying on the performance evaluation system to collect ratings of trainees both before and after training. For example, trainees of the Federal Aviation Administration must submit subordinate evaluations of their supervisory behavior before attending the national training center in Florida. Subordinates also submit evaluations of the same supervisors' behavior six months after the training. To determine whether or not the supervisors' skills have improved due to training, the performance evaluations they received from their subordinates before and after completion of train-

ing are compared. A variety of performance-appraisal measures can be used to assess behavioral changes of trainees. These are described in more detail in Chapter 9. Figure 7.12 presents a sample behavioral measure.

ORGANIZATIONAL RESULTS. The purpose of collecting organizational results is to examine the impact of training on the work group or entire company. Data may be collected before and after training on criteria such as productivity, turnover, absenteeism, accidents, grievances, quality improvements, scrap, sales, and customer satisfaction. The HR professional will try to show that the training program was responsible for any changes noted in these criteria. This may be difficult to do without a careful design and data collection strategy, since many other factors could explain the changes detected. For example, changes in dollar sales could be due to a new pay system rather than to a sales training program. Some of the experimental designs that can help to evaluate the effects of the training are described below.

Designs for Evaluating Training

After determining the criteria to use in evaluating the training program, the HR professional should choose an experimental design. The design is used to answer two primary questions: (1) whether or not a change has occurred in the criteria (e.g., learning, behavior, organizational results); and (2) whether or not the change can be attributed to the training program.[120]

Designs employ two possible strategies to answer these questions. The first is to compare the trainee's performance before and after participation in training. This is done to see what changes may have occurred in learning, behavior, or organizational results. While this is important for answering the question of whether change has taken place, it is deficient in answering the question of whether the change can be attributed to the training program since the criteria may have changed for a number of reasons. Answering the second question requires a design comparing the changes that occurred in the trainees with change that occurred in another group of employees who did not receive the training (e.g., a control group), yet are similar to the training group in important ways (e.g., similar job titles, rank, geographical location). The most effective experimental designs use both strategies (i.e., before-after measures and a control group) and are better able to answer both questions.[121] Some of the more commonly used designs for training evaluation are described below.[122]

ONE-SHOT POSTTEST-ONLY DESIGN. In many organizations, training is designed and conducted without prior thought given to evaluation. For example, a plant manager may decide to put all his or her personnel through a course on "Using Total Quality Techniques."

FIGURE 7.9
AN EXAMPLE OF A TRAINEE REACTION QUESTIONNAIRE

Evaluation Questionnaire

(Please return this form *unsigned* to the Training and Development Group)

1. Considering everything, how would you rate this program? (Check one)

   Unsatisfactory _____ Satisfactory _____ Good _____ Outstanding _____

   Please explain briefly the reasons for this rating you have given:

2. Were your expectations: exceeded _____ matched _____ fallen below _____? (Check one)

3. Are you going to recommend this training program to other members of your department?

   Yes _____ No _____ If you checked "yes," please describe the job titles held by the people to whom you would recommend this program.

   _____

4. Please rate the relative value (1 = very valuable; 2 = worthwhile; 3 = negligible) of the following components of the training program to you:

   Videocassettes _____   Role-playing exercises _____
   Workbooks _____   Small group discussions _____
   Small group discussions _____ Lectures _____
   Cases _____   Readings, articles _____

5. Please rate the main lecturer's presentation (1 = not effective; 2 = somewhat effective; 3 = very effective) in terms of:

   Ability to communicate _____
   Emphasis on key points _____
   Visual aids _____
   Handout materials _____

6. Please rate the following cases, readings, and videocassettes by placing a checkmark in the appropriate column:

	Excell.	Good	Fair	Poor
Overcoming Resistance to Change				
Reviewing Performance Goals				
Setting Performance Goals				
Handling Employee Complaints				
Improving Employee Performance				
Slade Co.				
Superior Slate Quarry				
McGregor's Theory X and Y				
Henry Manufacturing				
First Federal Savings				
Claremont Industries				

7. Was the ratio of lectures to cases (check one): High _____ OK _____ Low _____?

8. Were the videocassettes pertinent to your work? (check one)

   To most of my work? _____
   To some of my work? _____
   To none of my work? _____

9. To help the training director and the staff provide further improvements in future programs, please give us your frank opinion of each case discussion leader's contribution to your learning. (Place your checkmarks in the appropriate boxes.)

	Excellent	Above Average	Average	Below Average	Poor
DAVIS					
GLEASON					
LAIRD					
MARTIN					
PONTELLO					
SHALL					
SOMMERS					
WILSON					
ZIMMER					

10. How would you evaluate your participation in the program? (check)

Overall workload:	Too heavy _____	Just right _____	Too light _____
Case preparation:	Too heavy _____	Just right _____	Too light _____
Homework assignments:	Too heavy _____	Just right _____	Too light _____

11. What suggestions do you have for improving the program?

    _____
    _____
    _____

Source: K. N. Wexley and G. P. Latham, *Developing and training human resources in organizations.* Glenview, IL: Scott, Foresman, 1991, pp. 110–111. Reprinted with permission.

FIGURE 7.10
EXAMPLES OF LEARNING PERFORMANCE TESTS

MECHANICS

"You have in front of you a gear reducer, a line shaft, bearings, and coupling. I want you to assemble and adjust the proper alignment so that the finished assembly is a right-hand (or left-hand) driven assembly. Set the coupling gap ⅛ inch apart. You do not have to put the grind member in place or fasten the coupling covers. After you are finished, I will ask you where and how the grid member should go in. You will have 45 minutes to complete this job."

PAINTERS

"I want you to boost yourself up about 10 feet off the floor using this boatsman chair, and then tie yourself off so that you don't fall. After that, I would like you to hook this spraygun to the air supply, set the regulator to the correct pressure, and then spray this wall."

Source: K. N. Wexley and G. P. Latham, *Developing and training human resources in organizations,* 2nd ed. Glenview, IL: Scott, Foresman, 1991, p. 117. Reprinted with permission.

After the course is completed the manager decides to evaluate it. At this point, the design would look like the one below:

$$\text{TRAINING} \longleftarrow\text{-------}\longrightarrow \text{MEASURE}$$

Any of the four types of criteria (e.g., reactions, learning, behavior, organizational results) could be used as the "after" measures. It would be difficult, however, to know what, if any, changes occurred because no "before" measure (e.g., pretest) was made. In addition, because the results may not be compared with those of another group who did not receive training, it would not be possible to say whether any change was due to the training. As a result, this design is not recommended.

ONE-GROUP PRETEST-POSTTEST DESIGN. Another design for evaluating the training group on the criteria is to measure the group before and after the training. This design is as follows:

$$\text{MEASURE} \longleftarrow\text{-}\longrightarrow \text{TRAINING} \longleftarrow\text{-}\longrightarrow \text{MEASURE}$$

This design can assess whether a change has occurred for the training group in the criteria (e.g., learning, behavior). Unfortunately, it is not able to tell whether or not the change is due to training, since there is no control group. A change that is detected could have been caused by the introduction of new equipment or a new manager or by any number of other reasons. Thus, this design is not extremely useful and is not recommended.

POSTTEST-ONLY CONTROL GROUP DESIGN. A much stronger design for assessing the effectiveness of a training program is shown here:

FIGURE 7.11
LEARNING MEASURE

SAMPLE ITEMS FROM A MGIC TEST TO EVALUATE SUPERVISOR KNOWLEDGE

1. T or F When preparing a truth-in-lending disclosure with a financed single premium, mortgage insurance should always be disclosed for the life of the loan.

2. T or F GE and MGIC have the same refund policy for refundable single premiums.

3. T or F MGIC, GE, and PMI are the only mortgage insurers offering a nonrefundable single premium.

4. _____ Which one of the following is not a category in the loan progress reports?
   a. Loans approved
   b. Loans-in-suspense
   c. Loans denied
   d. Loans received

5. _____ Which of the following do not affect the MGIC Plus buying decision?
   a. Consumer
   b. Realtor
   c. MGIC underwriter
   d. Secondary market manager
   e. Servicing manager

6. _____ The new risk-based capital regulations for savings and loans have caused many of them to:
   a. Convert whole loans into securities
   b. Begin originating home equity loans
   c. Put MI on their uninsured 90s

Source: D. L. Kirkpatrick, *Evaluating training programs: The four levels.* San Francisco: Berrett-Koehler Publishers, 1996, p. 48.

GROUP 1: R: TRAINING $\longleftarrow\text{-}\text{-}\longrightarrow$ **MEASURE**
GROUP 1: R: NO TRAINING $\longleftarrow\text{-}\text{-}\longrightarrow$ **MEASURE**

In this design, two groups are used and individuals are randomly assigned (R) to either group (i.e., an individual has an equal chance of being put in either group 1, the training group, or group 2, the control group). The use of random assignment helps to initially equalize the two groups. This is important to ensure that any differences between the two groups after training are not simply caused by differences in ability, motivation, or experience. The posttest-only control group design is useful when it is difficult to collect criteria measures on individuals before offering them the training. For example, the HR professional may believe that giving individuals a pretest, such as a learning test, may overly influence their scores on the posttest, which might be the same learning measure. Another HR professional may not have time to give tests. Individuals are randomly assigned to the two groups, and their scores on the posttest are compared. Any differences on the posttest can be attributed to the training program since we can assume the two groups were somewhat equal before training. From the organization's standpoint, it would be beneficial to

FIGURE 7.12
SAMPLE SURVEY BEHAVIORAL MEASURE

Instructions: The purpose of this questionnaire is to determine the extent to which those who attended the recent leadership program have applied the principles and techniques that they learned back on the job. The survey results will help us to assess the effectiveness of the program. Please circle the appropriate response for each question.

| 5 = Much more | 4 = Some more | 3 = The same |
| 2 = Some less | 1 = Much less | |

Time and energy spent after the program compared to time and energy spent before the program

Understanding and Motivating

1. Getting to know my employees	5	4	3	2	1
2. Listening to my subordinates	5	4	3	2	1
3. Praising good work	5	4	3	2	1
4. Talking with employees about their families and interests	5	4	3	2	1
5. Asking subordinates for their ideas	5	4	3	2	1
6. Managing by walking around	5	4	3	2	1

Orienting and Training

7. Asking new employees about their past experiences, etc.	5	4	3	2	1
8. Taking new employees on a tour of the department and facilities	5	4	3	2	1
9. Introducing new employees to their coworkers	5	4	3	2	1
10. Being patient with employees	5	4	3	2	1

Source: D. L. Kirkpatrick. *Evaluating training programs: The four levels.* San Francisco: Berrett-Koehler Publishers, 1996, p. 59.

make sure the employees from the control group are placed in a training program later.

PRETEST-POSTTEST CONTROL-GROUP DESIGN. Another powerful design that is recommended for use in training evaluation is as follows:

GROUP 1: R:
MEASURE $\leftarrow$ - $\rightarrow$ TRAINING $\leftarrow$ - $\rightarrow$ MEASURE

GROUP 2: R:
MEASURE $\leftarrow$ - $\rightarrow$ NO TRAINING $\leftarrow$ - $\rightarrow$ MEASURE

Individuals are randomly assigned to the two groups. Criteria measures are collected on both groups before and after the training program is offered, yet only one group actually receives the training. Comparisons are made of the changes detected in both groups. If the change in group one is significantly different from the change in group two, we can be somewhat certain that it was caused by the training. Since many organizations will want all of the employees in both groups to receive

the training, the training can be offered to group two later.

MULTIPLE TIME-SERIES DESIGN. Another design recommended for use in training evaluation is shown below:

GROUP 1: R:
MEASURE $\leftarrow$ - $\rightarrow$ MEASURE $\leftarrow$ - $\rightarrow$
MEASURE $\leftarrow$ - $\rightarrow$ TRAINING $\leftarrow$ - $\rightarrow$
MEASURE $\leftarrow$ - $\rightarrow$ MEASURE $\leftarrow$ - $\rightarrow$ MEASURE

GROUP 2: R:
MEASURE $\leftarrow$ - $\rightarrow$ MEASURE $\leftarrow$ - $\rightarrow$
MEASURE $\leftarrow$ - $\rightarrow$ NO TRAINING $\leftarrow$ - $\rightarrow$
MEASURE $\leftarrow$ - $\rightarrow$ MEASURE $\leftarrow$ - $\rightarrow$ MEASURE

In this design, individuals are randomly assigned to either of two groups, and the criteria measures are collected at several times before and after the training has been offered. This design allows the HR professional to observe any changes between the two groups over time. If the effects of training held up over several months, this design would offer stronger support for the program.

Assessing the Costs and Benefits of Training

To conduct a thorough evaluation of a training program, training departments can benchmark their practices against the best in the industry.[123] Also, they should assess the costs and benefits associated with their programs. This is difficult but may be important for showing top management the value of training for the organization. For example, in one case, the net return of a training program for bank supervisors was calculated to be $148,400 over a five-year period. At Ford, all training programs are evaluated against the criterion of product line profitability. A tracking system shows costs and revenue for training facilities and individual courses.[124]

Generally, a utility model would be used to estimate the value of training (benefits minus costs). See Chapter 6 for a discussion of the estimation of utility. Some costs that should be measured for a training program include needs assessment costs, salaries of training designers, purchase of equipment (computers, videos, handouts), program development costs, evaluation costs, trainers' costs (e.g., salaries, travel, lodging, meals), facilities rental, trainee wages during training, and other trainee costs (e.g., travel, lodging, meals).[125]

It is also important to compare the benefits of the training program with its costs. One benefit that should be estimated is the dollar payback associated with the improvement in trainees' performance after receiving training. Since the results of the experimental design will indicate any differences in behavior between those trained versus those untrained, the HR professional can then estimate for that particular group of employees (e.g., managers, engineers) what this difference is worth in terms of the salaries of those employees. Another factor that should be considered when estimating the benefits of training is the duration of the training's impact; that is, the length of time during which the improved performance will be maintained. While probably no programs will show benefits forever, those that incur longer-term improved performance will have greater value to the organization.

Recent research indicates that companies with sophisticated training systems look to training to support corporate strategy and change much more often than they look for measuring financial returns on training investment. At successful companies such as Frizzell Financial Services, ICI, Royal Mail's Anglia Division, and Yamazaki Machinery UK, the firms focused on *pay-for-ward,* a term used to describe the benefits from training in terms of the company's capacity to learn and change. This differs from *pay-back,* which refers to a straight financial return from the training.[126]

SPECIAL TRAINING PROGRAMS

Employee Orientation Programs

At least 80 percent of U.S. firms with more than 50 employees provide some type of orientation.[127] In this type of training, new employees are informed about their roles and responsibilities (i.e., what is expected of them) in an effort to ease their transition to the company. The trend seems to be continuing as more firms have been placing their new employees in orientation programs to familiarize them with their supervisors and coworkers, the company policies and procedures, the requirements of their jobs, and the organizational culture. Unfortunately, most of these programs are not properly planned, implemented, or evaluated. All too often new employees are given a brief introduction to the company and are then left to learn the ropes by themselves. Often this leads to feelings of confusion, frustration, stress, and uncertainty among new employees.[128] If employee dissatisfaction leads to turnover, this can be quite costly for the firm. For example, at Merck & Company, turnover cost has been estimated to range from 1.5 to 2.5 times the annual salary paid for a job.[129]

Generally, the objectives of an employee orientation program are threefold: (1) to assist the new employee in adjusting to the organization and feeling comfortable and positive about the new job; (2) to clarify the job requirements, demands, and performance expectations; and (3) to get the employee to understand the organization's culture and quickly adopt the organization's goals, values, and behaviors.[130] A Realistic Orientation Program for new Employee Stress (ROPES) has been suggested as the model.[131] Employees would be given realistic information about the job and the organization, given general support and reassurance from managers, and helped to identify and cope with the stresses of the job. This should reduce turnover of new employees, resulting in savings for the company.[132] Corning Glass Works developed an orientation program for all its new employees to help them make the transition to the company, their specific jobs, and the community. Corning reduced voluntary turnover among new hires by 69 percent after two years.[133] Texas Instruments also developed an orientation program to help employees cope with possible stressors in the workplace.[134]

Most orientation programs consist of three stages: (1) a general introduction to the organization, often given by the HR department; (2) a specific orientation to the department and the job typically given by the employee's immediate supervisor; and (3) a follow-up meeting to verify that the important issues have been addressed and employee questions have been answered.[135] This follow-up meeting usually takes place between a new employee and his or her supervisor a week or so after the employee has begun working. A follow-up meeting is very important because often new employees may feel uncomfortable seeking out a supervisor regarding any questions they face. A supervisor or an HR representative should meet with the employee to be sure that he or she is effectively "learning the ropes" of the organization.

The orientation program used by Disney for employees of Walt Disney World in Orlando, Florida, follows this multiple-stage format in most respects. Individuals begin their employment by attending a one-day program, Disney Traditions II, which describes the history of the organization and the values of the culture. On this first day, employees are also taken on a tour of the facilities. On the second day, they are provided with descriptions of the policies and procedures. The third day, OJT begins with an assigned buddy who is an experienced coworker. Buddies spend anywhere from two days to two weeks showing new employees their job duties and providing feedback as they attempt to perform the tasks. As a result of participating in the orientation program, employees express less confusion with their new jobs.[136]

The HR department should be actively involved in planning, conducting, and evaluating orientation programs. They should also enlist the support of senior employees to serve as mentors to new employees. Also, supervisors should be called on to help orient new employees to the workforce and should receive training on how to do this. In the follow-up meeting, supervisors should be required to complete a checklist, indicating that they have discussed with new employees the major issues of concern. Employees should sign the checklist to confirm that they have received the orientation information. Evaluation of the orientation program is the responsibility of the HR department. To assess the effectiveness of the program, HR professionals should examine whether the program is appropriate, easy to understand, interesting, flexible for diverse types of employees, and economical or cost-effective.[137]

Training for Teams

Training techniques can be chosen for individual level training or for training that is conducted for work teams. With the increasing popularity of teams in organizations,[138] it is common for employers to send their teams to training sessions. For example, Hewlett-Packard started its team members on a two-week training and orientation program to familiarize everyone with the existing processes and the needs of the business.[139] Likewise, Allied Signal sent its maintenance teams from the Garrett Engine Division to a two-day course in team building. Motorola also provides training for its employee work teams.[140] Cummins Engine Company places improvement teams through a five-day training program, which is based on an action learning model (classroom and OJT training).[141] GE sends entire teams to participate in business games, all of which deal with real GE strengths, weaknesses, opportunities, and threats (SWOTs).

Team training often focuses on teaching members how to work more effectively or efficiently in teams. Some topics include: team building, problem solving, running effective meetings, managing stress, managing productivity, appraising team members' performance, and managing conflict. Trust building is also an important component of the training.[142] According to one survey, employers were most likely to offer the following types of training to self-directed work teams: problem solving (83 percent of companies offered this training), meeting skills (65 percent), communication skills (62 percent), handling conflict (61 percent), roles and responsibilities (58 percent), quality tools and concepts (56 percent), and evaluating team performance (39 percent).[143] In general, trainers will probably use a variety of training techniques when conducting team training (e.g., experiential exercises as well as group discussions). In some cases, "ropes" courses or "outward bound" activities are used to build stronger, more cohesive teams.[144]

Often, teams are formed with individuals from various functional areas (e.g., marketing, finance, sales, production). These **cross-functional teams** may require training in other disciplines to help them understand what is involved in other functional areas (called multiskilling or cross-training). Generally, job rotation may be used or individuals may receive training from their peers on other disciplines. For example, peer trainers have been used at T.J. Maxx, a national retail chain.[145] The benefits of cross-training are that it may provide employees with more skill variety or interesting tasks, allow for more flexibility in getting the work done when teammates are absent, and help workers to better understand the entire work process.[146]

Creativity Training

As organizations attempt to become more competitive in today's global marketplace, they have recognized the need for employees to become more innovative. They have tried to instill a spirit of risk taking and innovativeness among employees by providing them with creativity training. By 1990, the number of organizations with 100 or more employees who offered creativity training was about 32 percent.[147] Using experiential exercises and brainstorming techniques, trainers try to get trainees to think "outside-the-box." In some cases, the training has been shown to be effective. For example, Frito-Lay indicated that creative problem-solving training saved the firm more than $500 million from 1983 through 1987.[148] 3M tries to provide a supportive culture and safe environment for risk-taking entrepreneurship. The company seems to be successful since it has achieved its goal of consistently getting 30 percent of sales from products less than four years old. New employees are pushed to learn about the "nourishing and ruthless environment" by taking a class in risk taking. They attend with their supervisors yet are taught that they need to be willing to go against their supervisors.[149]

Another way to maximize creativity and innovativeness is by fully utilizing the potential of all employees in the firm. Some companies deliver diversity training programs to ensure that the ideas of all employees, regardless of their background characteristics (e.g., race, gender, age, ability) or personalities, are encouraged. Employees attend diversity awareness programs to learn how to better communicate and relate to employees who may be different from them. As noted earlier in Figure 7.2, diversity training has gained in popularity.

Training for International Assignments

As one expert puts it, "The key to successfully competing in the global marketplace may be staffing key expatriate positions with accomplished/skilled leaders.[150] Thus, U.S. firms have begun to realize that to be successful in their overseas projects, they need to better prepare individuals to work in international assignments. As we discussed in Chapter 6, studies document the high rate of expatriate failures ranging from 25 percent to 50 percent.[151] These early returns can be costly for firms with respect to goodwill, reputation, and finances.[152] In fact, costs have been estimated between $55,000 and $150,000 per expatriate failure, and some companies have determined that costs are as much as $750,000, for a total of about $2 billion a year.[153] In many cases, the difficulties encountered by expatriates have been blamed on inadequate training programs. For example, Honeywell surveyed 347 managers who lived abroad or traveled regularly and found that increased training was cited as critical for executives and employees assigned overseas.

Training and orientation for international assignments is now common. A 1985 survey revealed that less than 25 percent of U.S. companies offered any type of training for international assignees, and those that did offer training provided only brief introductory training.[154] In 1990, it was reported that 30 percent of American companies operating abroad provide formal cross-cultural training (CCT) programs for employees.[155] By 1997, it was estimated that 50 percent of companies who sent employees overseas were doing pretraining and orientation.[156] Other countries, such as Japan, are more committed to the importance of training for international assignments. This may explain the low (less than 10 percent) failure rate cited for most of Japan's multinational corporations. In Japanese firms, overseas training is typically conducted over a one-year period where international assignees are taught about the culture, customs, and business techniques of the host country.[157]

A growing number of U.S. firms have shown a strong commitment to international training, and orientation.[158] Federal Express sends future expatriates and their families on "familiarization" trips, which also serve as "realistic job previews." Over 70 percent of companies now pay for similar trips. Gillette is a leader in this area with international assignments as a part of its junior trainee program. The objective of the program is to build careers with a global perspective.[159] American Express provides U.S. business school students summer jobs in a foreign location. Colgate-Palmolive trains recent graduates for multiple overseas assignments. Many large international companies have also established health care policies for traveling executives.

SKILLS NEEDED BY INTERNATIONAL ASSIGNEES. To design effective training programs to better prepare U.S. managers and employees for assignments overseas, it is important to understand the kinds of skills they will need for international assignments. As we discussed in Chapter 6, in addition to good technical skills, individuals who will be working overseas need skills in languages and an understanding of social customs, cultural values, codes of conduct, and motivation and reward systems in the host country. For Middle Eastern assignments, for example, Bechtel emphasizes the importance of religion in the culture. Also, expatriates need assistance in the practical aspects of foreign assignments (e.g., housing, schools, currency, health issues). Visits to the country can aid in reassuring employees and their families about their home, hospitals, dentists, doctors, and schools. Training programs should

include expatriates and their families, particularly in cultures where women are excluded culturally from doing a variety of things during the day. For instance, in Saudi Arabia women have many restrictions about dress and proper behaviors.

Before presenting several specific examples of cross-cultural training programs, it is useful to discuss how cultural training differs from traditional training. Cultural training focuses on several goals:

1. Communication—Expatriates will need to understand and communicate directly and through nonverbal means in order to listen to the concerns and motives of others.

2. Decision making—They will have to develop conclusions and take actions on the basis of inadequate, unreliable, and conflicting information, and to trust their feelings, impressions, and facts.

3. Commitment—They will need to become involved in relationships and inspire confidence in others.

4. Ideals—They will have to value the causes and objectives of others from a radically different social environment.

5. Problem solving—They will have to make decisions needed to achieve common goals.

Understanding cultural influences at the individual level is the key to understanding cultural influences in the workplace. Cultural self-knowledge is critical for this understanding.[160]

There are several examples of cross-cultural training programs used by organizations. For instance, ARAMCO, a Saudi Arabian corporation, uses an extensive orientation program for employees and their families. The program includes practical housekeeping information such as local transportation, shopping, day-to-day finances, and comparisons of the beliefs and customs of the Saudi and American people. The International Development Agency's predeparture program for overseas volunteers has several objectives, including the following: communicate respect, be nonjudgmental, display empathy, practice role flexibility, and tolerate ambiguity. Research on cross-cultural training indicates expatriates perform better and are more satisfied with their assignments after such training.[161]

TRAINING TECHNIQUES. To acquire the skills necessary to be successful in an international assignment, a variety of training techniques can be used. Procter & Gamble uses several methods to refine language skills and to improve intercultural awareness among international assignees.[162] Its "P&G College" for new and midlevel managers emphasizes globalization issues. In any program developed, it is recommended that the international assignee and his or her family be actively involved in the training to ease the transition and build a supportive environment. It is further suggested that the training should be led by people who have served in the specific country, and that the training should begin a year before the employee's move to that country. This is often not done, however; many companies try to squeeze the training into the last six weeks.[163]

To teach employees about area studies or the host country's environment (e.g., geography, climate, political system, customs, religion, labor force, economy, etc.) and the company's international operations, *informational* approaches such as lectures, reading material, videotapes, and movies can be effectively used. One technique, the cultural assimilator, was designed as a programmed learning technique to test trainees' knowledge of cultural differences and their understanding of these issues for effective functioning in a foreign culture.[164] To teach trainees about the host country's norms, values, and interpersonal styles so that they will be able to effectively understand and negotiate with host individuals, *experiential* approaches may be beneficial. These might include role-playing and simulations (simulations specific to the culture). Using both a cognitive approach to training (e.g., cultural assimilator) and an experiential approach (e.g., behavior modeling) together has been tried for cross-cultural training. With U.S. government managers, it was discovered that using both techniques together resulted in higher performance than using either technique alone.[165]

Field experiences are recommended to provide a more in-depth view of the host country's customs, values, and behaviors. These experiences can take a variety of forms including: (1) short family trips to the host country; (2) informal meetings with other American families who have lived in the host country; (3) minicultures (i.e., the family visits a multicultural environment in the United States such as an ethnic neighborhood); and (4) host-family surrogates (i.e., a U.S. family from a background similar to the host country has the expatriate family stay with them so they can observe the customs). Finally, *language skill* classes and cassettes are recommended for use in developing skills in interpersonal communication and the day-to-day dealings that the family will encounter in the host country.

TRAINING FOR INPATRIATES. In addition to providing training for expatriates, U.S. firms are increasingly providing training for foreign nationals who are coming to the United States to work. For example, S.C. Johnson Wax has been bringing employees into the United States for the past 10 years. Chrysler Corporation brings in about 15 to 20 people at any one time, generally from its subsidiary in Mexico. Eli Lilly and Company brings in about 20 people a year typically in the fields of science, finances, and marketing. Their training needs are very similar to those of expatriates. To help them adjust, the following tips are offered:[166]

1. Make sure the spouse and children are content with the new location.

2. Make the necessary arrangements to process Social Security numbers in order to help them get a driver's license, bank account, and credit cards.

3. Provide training with U.S. managers on dealing with people from the other culture.

4. Help them establish credit in the new country.

5. Use relocation counselors to help them with real estate, schools, stores, community activities, and other information to help them get settled.

6. Provide assistance to accompanying spouses (e.g., jobs, educational reimbursements, career guidance, etc).

7. Provide cross-cultural training to inpatriates and U.S. employees.

8. Offer competitive compensation.

9. Provide language training for employees and their spouses and children.

SUMMARY

Over the years, training has become increasingly popular as an HR tool for increasing employee and managerial performance in organizations. It has been estimated that the majority of organizations provide some type of formal training and spend millions of dollars doing so. The U.S. government spends over $500 million each year to train new employees and to retrain current employees.[167]

Successful training in organizations depends on a systematic approach that involves a careful needs assessment, solid program design, and thorough evaluation of results. Training programs should not be designed as quick fixes for every organizational problem, nor should they rely on faddish techniques. Instead, training should be designed to meet the particular needs of the organization and its employees. It should be viewed as a *continuous learning* endeavor by employees and managers to stay current and to anticipate future needs. As greater demands are placed on organizations to remain competitive, firms must ensure that their workforces are motivated and able to take on these challenges.

An emphasis on continual training and development is one way this can be done. For example, it has been predicted that by the year 2000, managers in the United States will spend 82 hours per year on educational activities.[168] Employees who receive training will not only be more valuable to their firms, but will also earn 30 percent more than those who don't receive such training.[169] Some training departments (e.g., Motorola University, Disney University, Intel University, Sprint's University of Excellence, Tennessee Valley Authority's University) are using the "Corporate Quality University" model for conveying the corporate value of perpetual learning.

This model is a guiding philosophy that argues for involving all employees as well as primary customers and suppliers in continuous learning to improve overall productivity. Other goals associated with this philosophy are to link training to the strategic direction of the company, to provide an infrastructure for the organization's training initiatives that minimizes duplication, and to form collaborative alliances with employees, suppliers, customers, and academic institutions.[170]

Most successful training programs are those that have strong support from top management. Managers make a commitment to invest the necessary resources to provide sufficient money and time for training. For example, training is considered a part of the corporate culture. This is true at Saturn and at Motorola where employees are all assigned to some continual training each year. Likewise, Xerox spends about 2.5 percent of its revenue on training annually, which means about $2,500 per employee per year, and Hewlett-Packard spends about 5 percent of its revenues to train its workers. Training should also be tied to the company's business strategy and objectives and linked to bottom-line results.[171]

Technological change, worker displacement, and new markets are among the reasons training and development is so critical for competitive advantage. Former Labor Secretary Robert Reich put it best: "If we have an adequately educated and trained workforce and a state-of-the-art infrastructure linking them together with the rest of the world, then global capital will come here to create jobs. If we don't, the only way global capital will be invested here is if we promise low wages."[172] Needless to say, America (thankfully) would have great difficulty competing for low wage jobs.

Many of the most successful U.S. companies have integrated their training programs with their employee career development programs. In the past, training programs and departments have emphasized employer needs for training in the context of the firm's strategic plan. Career development programs tend to emphasize the employee's perspective. Ideally, training and career planning should be well integrated into an HRM system with a focus on the strategic plan of the organization and customer requirements. For example, when Eastman Chemical, headquartered in Kingsport, Tennessee, reorganized its 18,000 employees, it made sure that all training and career programs were consistent with the organization's mission and core competencies. The CEO informed employees about how the training was linked to the restructuring effort and to the firm's vision.[173] Chapter 8 elaborates on these issues.

DISCUSSION QUESTIONS

1. What would be the major features of a training program designed to make workers aware of sexual harassment in the workplace? Who would you select to attend such a training program and how would you evaluate the effects of the training? Would such training be effective? Explain your answer.

2. Suppose that you are instructed to determine whether a training curriculum is needed to address literacy issues in the workplace. How would you conduct the needs assessment?

3. Describe several characteristics of adult learners. Why is it important to consider these factors when designing training for employees?

4. Suppose you are the professor for this class. Write several instructional objectives for the class. Why is it important to prepare objectives *before* developing and conducting training?

5. Suppose you were going to design a training program for newly hired first-line sales managers. Results from the needs assessment indicated they would need training on company policies and procedures, handling customer complaints, and motivating sales personnel. What learning principles would you build into the program? What training methods would you choose for your training program? Explain your choices.

6. Describe what you would say to convince top management of the importance of *evaluating* a company training program. Explain what criteria you would use, and what design you would recommend. Provide a rationale. What if the executives say they want to be able to show the bottom-line impact that the training has had. How would you do this?

7. A large sales firm in your area has decided to use teams for selling to customers. Previously, all the reps have worked as individual salespeople, having very little interactions with the other reps. Offer some ideas for the type of training the reps would need to work effectively in teams. Suppose the first-line supervisors will now become team leaders. What type of training should they receive to take on this new role?

8. What ideas do you have for training employees who are coming back to an organization after an international assignment? What issues would you discuss and what techniques would you recommend?

NOTES

1. Pfeffer, J. (1994). *Competitive advantage through people*. Boston: Harvard Business School Press, p. 45; see also, Rosenberg, M. J. (1990). Performance technology: Working the system. *Training, 27*(2), 43–48; Forward, G. E.; Beach, D. E.; Gray, D. A.; and Quick, J. C. (1991). Mentofacturing: A vision for American industrial excellence. *Academy of Management Executive, 5*(3), 32–44; Tannenbaum, S. I., and Yukl, G. A. (1992).

Training and development in work organizations. *Annual Review of Psychology, 43,* 399–441; Noe, R. A., and Ford, J. K. (1992). Emerging issues and new directions for training research. In G. R. Ferris and K. M. Rowland (eds.), *Research in personnel and human resource management,* vol. 10, Greenwich, CT: JAI Press, pp. 345–384; Laabs, J. J. (January 1996). Eyeing future HR concerns. *Personnel Journal,* pp. 28–30, 32, 34–37.

2. Fuchsberg, G. (July 20, 1990). Many businesses responding too slowly to rapid workforce shifts, study says. *The Wall Street Journal,* p. B1; see also, Schaaf, D. (January 1990). Lessons from the '100 best.' *Training,* 18–20; Cox, T. (1991). The multicultural organization. *Academy of Management Executive, 5*(2), 34–47; Goldstein, I. L. (1993). *Training in organizations,* 3rd ed. Pacific Grove, CA: Brooks/Cole; and Milkovich, G. T., and Boudreau, J. W. (1991). *Human resource management.* Homewood, IL: Irwin; See note 1, Laabs (1996).

3. Nadler, L. (1984). Human resource development. In L. Nadler (ed.), *The handbook of human resource development.* New York: John Wiley & Sons, pp.1–47; see also, Cox, T., and Blake, S. (1991). Managing cultural diversity: Implications for organizational competitiveness. *Academy of Management Executive, 5*(3), 45–56.

4. Shandler, D. (1996). *Reengineering the training function: How to align training with the new corporate agenda.* Delray Beach, FL: St. Lucie Press; see also Goldstein, I. L., and Gilliam, P. (1990). Training system issues in the year 2000. *American Psychologist, 45,* 134–143.

5. Bernardin, H. J., and McKinney, N. (1998). *An assessment of training programs in sexual harassment: Discrepancies between research and practice.* Under review.

6. 1995 Industry Report. (October 1995). *Training,* pp. 41–48, 55–57, 60–62, 64, 66, 69–74; see also, Who's learning what? (October 1994). *Training,* pp. 45–55; and Training budgets edge upwards. (October 1994). *Training,* pp. 35–42.

7. Filipczak, B. (June 1993). Frick teaches Frack. *Training,* pp. 30–34; see also, Filipczak, B. (October 1993). Training budgets boom. *Training,* pp. 37–44; see note 6, *Training* (1995).

8. See note 6, *Training* (1995). Gordon, J. (1986a). Training magazine's industry report 1986. *Training, 23*(10), 26–28; and Goldstein, I. L., and Gilliam, P. (1990). Training system issues in the year 2000. *American Psychologist, 45,* 134–143.

9. Kimmerling, G. (September 1993). Gathering best practices. *Training & Development Journal,* pp. 28–36; see also, Saari, L. M., Johnson, T. R., McLaughlin, S. D., and Zimmerle, D. M. (1988). A survey of management training and education practices in U.S. companies. *Personnel Psychology, 18*(4), 731–743.

10. Stamps, D. (March 1997). Mercedes-Benz sows a learning field. *Training,* 26–32; see also, Brody, M. (June 8, 1987). Helping workers to work smarter, *Fortune,* pp. 86–88.

11. See note 2.

12. See note 6, *Training* (1995). See also, Gordon, J. (October, 1986). Where the training goes. *Training,* 49–50, 52–54, 57–60, 62–63.

13. Galagan, P. A. (October 1992). How to get your TQM training on track. *Nation's Business,* pp. 24–28.

14. The perplexing case of the plummeting payrolls (Sept. 20, 1993). *Business Week,* p. 27.

15. Gomez-Mejia, L. R.; Balkin, D. B.; and Cardy, R. L. (1995). *Managing human resources.* Englewood Cliffs, NJ: Prentice Hall.

16. Thornburg, L. (August 1992). Training in a changing world. *HR Magazine,* pp. 44–47.

17. Overman, S. (October 1993). Retraining our work force. *HR Magazine,* pp. 40–44.

18. Breuer, N. L. (January 1992). AIDS issues haven't gone away. *Personnel Journal,* pp. 47–49.

19. Johnson, R. (April 1992). Integral steps for bridging race, language, gender gaps. *Training Director's Forum Newsletter,* pp. 1–3; see also, Solomon, C. M. (October 1995). Unlock the potential of older workers. *Personnel Journal,* pp. 56–58, 60, 62, 64–66.

20. See note 8, Goldstein and Gilliam (1990). See also, Training for shift workers (1997). *Training, 34*(6), 14.

21. Bernardin, H. J., and McKinney, N. (1997). *An assessment of the processes in training program development and evaluation.* Manuscript under review.

22. Rossett, A. (1990). Overcoming obstacles to needs assessment. *Training, 27*(3), 36, 38–41; see also, Harp, C. (August 1995). Link training to corporate mission. *HR Magazine,* pp. 65–68.

23. See note 3.

24. Digman, L. A. (Winter 1980). Determining management development needs. *Human Resource Management,* pp. 12–17; see also, Fisher, C. D.; Schoenfeldt, L. F.; and Shaw, J. B. (1996). *Human resource management,* 3rd ed. Boston: Houghton Mifflin; Rummler, G. (April 1996). In search of the holy performance grail. *Training and Development,* pp. 26–32.

25. Moore, M. L., and Dutton, P. (1978). Training needs analysis: Review and critique. *Academy of Management Review, 3,* 532–545; see also, McAfee, R. B., and Champagne, P. J. (1988). Employee development: Discovering who needs what. *Personnel Administrator, 33*(2), 92–98; see note 22, Harp (1995).

26. Mager, R. F., and Pipe, P. (1984). *Analyzing performance problems or "You really oughta wanna,"* 2nd ed. Belmont, CA: David Lake Publishing. See note 2.

27. See note 3.

28. Salinger, R. D. (1973). *Disincentives to effective employee training and development.* Washington, DC: U.S. Civil Service Commission Bureau of Training; see also, Joinson, C. (May 1995). Make your training stick. *HR Magazine,* pp. 55–60.

29. See note 2, Goldstein (1993).

30. Laird, D. (1985). *Approaches to training and development,* 2nd ed. Reading, MA: Addison-Wesley.

31. See note 21.

32. See note 5.

33. See note 30.

34. Fiske, E. B. (Sept. 25, 1989). Impending U.S. jobs 'disaster': Work forces unqualified to work. *New York Times,* pp. 1, 12. See note 10.

35. See note 34, p. 12.

36. See note 6.

37. The literacy gap (Dec. 19, 1988). *Time,* pp. 56–57. See also note 21.

38. See note 24, Fisher, Schoenfeldt, and Shaw (1996); see also, Smith, T. L. (July 1995). Job-related materials reinforce basic skills. *HR Magazine,* pp. 84–86, 89–90.

39. Lund, L., and McGuire, E. P. (1990). *Literacy in the workforce.* New York: The Conference Board; see also, Rosow, J. M., and Zager, R. (1992). *Job-linked literacy: Innovative strategies at work: Part II. Meeting the challenges of change: Basic skills for a competitive workforce.* Scottsdale, NY: Work in America Institute.

40. Noe, R. A., and Schmitt, N. (1986). The influence of trainee attitudes on training effectiveness: Test of a model. *Personnel Psychology, 39,* 497–523; see also, Baldwin, T. T., Magjuka, R. J., and Loher, B. T. (1991). The perils of participation: Effects of choice of training on trainee motivation and learning. *Personnel Psychology, 44* (1), 51–66.

41. Facteau, J. D.; Dobbins, G. H.; Russell, J. E. A.; Ladd, R. T.; and Kudisch, J. D. (1995). The influence of general perceptions of the training environment on pretraining motivation and perceived training transfer. *Journal of Management, 21*(1), 1–25.

42. Driskell, J. E.; Willis, R. P.; and Copper, C. (1992). Effect of overlearning on retention. *Journal of Applied Psychology, 77,* 615–622.

43. Locke, E. A., and Latham, G. P. (1984). *Goal setting: A motivational technique that works.* Englewood Cliffs, NJ: Prentice Hall. See also, Mento, A. J.; Steel, R.; and Karren, R. (1987). A meta-analytical study of the effects of goal setting on task performance: 1966–1984. *Organizational Behavior and Human Decision Processes, 39,* 52–83; and Mealiea, L. W., and Latham, G. P. (1996). *Skills for managerial success: Theory, experience, and practice.* Chicago: Irwin.

44. Latham, G. P., and Locke, E. A. (1991). Self-regulation through goal-setting. *Organizational Behavior and Human Decision Processes, 50,* 212–247.

45. London, M. (1997). *Job Feedback.* Mahwah, NJ: Erlbaum.

46. Silber, K. H., and Stelnicki, M. B. (1987). Writing training materials. In R. L. Craig (ed.), *Training and development handbook,* 3rd ed. New York: McGraw-Hill, pp. 263–285.

47. Ellis, H. C. (1965). *The transfer of learning.* New York: Macmillan; see also, Stark, C. (1986). Ensuring skills transfer: A sensitive approach. *Training and Development Journal, 10*(3), 50–51; Rouiller, J. Z., and Goldstein, I. L. (1993). The relationship between organizational transfer climate and positive transfer of training. *Human Resource Development Quarterly, 4,* 377–390; Baldwin, T. T., and Ford, J. K. (1988). Transfer of training: A review and directions for future research. *Personnel Psychology, 41,* 63–105; Baldwin, T. T., and Magjuka, R. J. (1991). Organizational training and signals of importance: Linking pretraining perceptions to intentions to transfer. *Human Resource Development Quarterly, 2,* 25–36; Garavaglia, P. L. (October 1993). How to ensure transfer of training. *Training and Development Journal,* pp. 63–68; Gist, M. E., Bavetta, A. G., and Stevens, C. K. (1990). Transfer training method: Its influence on skill generalization, skill repetition, and performance level. *Personnel Psychology, 22*(3), 501–523.

48. See note 24, Fisher, Schoenfeldt, and Shaw (1996).

49. Tracey, J. B.; Tannenbaum, S. I.; and Kavanagh, M. J. (1995). Applying trained skills on the job: The importance of the work environment. *Journal of Applied Psychology, 80,* 239–252.

50. Morrison, R. F., and Branter, T. M. (1992). What enhances or inhibits a new job? A basic career issue. *Journal of Applied Psychology, 77,* 926–940.

51. Gist, M. E. (1991). Effects of self-efficacy and posttraining intervention on the acquisition and maintenance of complex interpersonal skills. *Personnel Psychology, 44,* 837–861.

52. Ford, J. K., Quinones, M. A., Sego, D., and Sorra, J. (1992). Factors affecting the opportunity to perform trained tasks on the job. *Personnel Psychology, 45,* 511–527.

53. Mathieu, J. E.; Tannenbaum, S. I.; and Salas, E. (1992). Influences of individual and situational characteristics on measures of training effectiveness. *Academy of Management Journal, 35,* 828–847.

54. Marx, R. D. (1982). Relapse prevention for managerial training: A model for maintenance of behavior change. *Academy of Management Review, 7,* 433–441.

55. See note 54.

56. See note 41.

57. Shandler, D. (1996). *Reengineering the training function: How to align training with the new corporate agenda.* Delray Beach, FL: St. Lucie Press.

58. See note 2, Schaaf (1990).

59. See notes 21 and 24. See also, Carroll, S. J., Jr.; Paine, F. T.; and Ivancevich, J. M. (1972). The relative effectiveness of training methods: Expert opinion and research. *Personnel Psychology, 25,* 495–510.

60. Simon, S. J., and Werner, J. M. (1996). Computer training through behavior modeling, self-paced, and instructional approaches: A field experiment. *Journal of Applied Psychology, 81*(6), 648–659.

61. See note 6.

62. See note 6.

63. See note 15; see also, Skylar, T. (March 1996). When training collides with a 35-ton truck. *Training,* 32–34, 36, 38.

64. Budd, M. L. (1987). Self-instruction. In R. L. Craig (ed.), *Training and development handbook: A guide to human resource development,* 3rd ed. New York: McGraw-Hill, pp. 488–499.

65. Guglielmino, L. M., and Guglielmino, P. J. (1987).

Self-directed learning in business and industry: An information age imperative. In H. Long and associates (eds.), *Adult self-directed learning: Application and theory.* Athens: Adult Education Office, University of Georgia.

66. See note 6. See also, Rao, S. S. (August 1995). Putting fun back into learning. *Training,* 44–45, 47–48.

67. See note 64.

68. Roberts, D. G. (1986). *A study of the use of the self-directed learning readiness scale as related to selected organization variables.* Doctoral dissertation. Washington, DC: George Washington University.

69. Guglielmino, L. M., and Guglielmino, P. J. (1991). *Expanding your readiness for self-directed learning.* King of Prussia, PA: Organizational Design and Development. See also note 68.

70. Torrance, E. P., and Mourad, S. (1978). Some creativity and style of learning and thinking correlates of Guglielmino's Self-Directed Learning Readiness Scale. *Psychological Reports, 43,* 1167–1171.

71. Sabbaghian, Z. (1979). *Adult self-directedness and self-concept: An exploration of relationship.* Doctoral dissertation. Ames: Iowa State University.

72. Savoie, M. (1979). *Continuing education for nurses: Predictors of success courses requiring a degree of learner self-direction.* Doctoral dissertation. Toronto, Canada: University of Toronto. See also note 65. Durr, R. E. (1992). *An examination of readiness for self-directed learning and selected personnel variables at a large midwestern electronics development and manufacturing corporation.* Unpublished doctoral dissertation. Boca Raton, FL: Florida Atlantic University.

73. See note 2, Schaaf (1990).

74. Campbell, J. P.; Dunnette, M. D.; Lawler, E. E.; and Weick, K. E. (1970). *Managerial behavior, performance, and effectiveness.* New York: McGraw-Hill.

75. Barron, J. M.; Berger, M. C.; and Black, D. A. (1997). *On-the-job training.* Kalamazoo, MI: Upjohn Institute; Bureau of National Affairs (1990). Training facts and figures. *Bulletin to Management.* Washington, DC: Bureau of National Affairs; see also, Phipps, P. A. (1996). On-the-job training and employee productivity. *Monthly Labor Review, 119*(3), 33.

76. Monoky, J. F. (1996). Master the coaching call. *Industrial Distribution, 85*(6), p. 112.

77. Cannell, M. (1997). Practice makes perfect. *People Management, 3*(5), 26–33.

78. See note 2, Schaaf (1990).

79. See note 77.

80. See note 2, Schaaf (1990). See also, Mayor, T. (Jan. 15, 1996). Doing equals learning. *CIO, 9*(7), 52–59.

81. See note 77.

82. Alexander, S. (1996). Training you can build on. *Computerworld, 30*(3), 77.

83. See note 10.

84. Mullaney, C. A., and Trask, L. D. (October 1992). Show them the ropes. *Technical and Skills Training,* pp. 8–11; see also, Filipczak, B. (1996). Who owns your OJT? *Training, 33*(12), 44–49.

85. Reynolds, L. (July 1993). Apprenticeship program raises many questions. *HR Focus,* pp. 1, 4; see also, Gitter, R. J. (April 1994). Apprenticeship-trained workers: United States and Great Britain, *Monthly Labor Review,* pp. 38–43.

86. Apprenticeship (Winter 1991–1992). *Occupational Outlook Quarterly,* p. 29.

87. McKenna, J. F. (Jan. 20, 1992). Apprenticeships: Something old, something new, something needed. *Industry Week,* pp. 14–20. See also note 85.

88. Mondy, R. W., and Noe, R. M. (1990). *Human resource management,* 4th ed. Boston: Allyn & Bacon; see also, Overman, S. (January 1995). Japan shares ways to improve job training, *HR Magazine,* pp. 60, 62, 64.

89. Gordon, J., and Hequet, M. (November 1997). Live and in person. *Training,* 24–31. See also, notes 6, 12; Filipczak, B. (November 1997). The tug-of-war over computer training. *Training,* 35–40; Madlin, N. (1987). Computer-based training comes of age. *Personnel, 64*(11), 64–65; Turnage, J. J. (1990). The challenge of new workplace technology for psychology. *American Psychologist, 45,* 171–178; Webster, J., and Martocchio, J. J. (1993). Turning work into play: Implications for microcomputer software training. *Journal of Management, 19,* 127–146.

90. Computer-based training enters the mainstream—CBT Group shows strong growth as it makes impact with big companies (Jan. 27, 1997). *Informationweek,* p. 140.

91. Allen, M. (1996). Training via computer on the rise. *National Underwriter Property and Casualty Risks and Benefits Management, 100*(42), 9, 28.

92. Filipczak, B. (February 1996). Chunking CBT. *Training,* 28–34.

93. Swoboda, F. (Oct. 29, 1989). When you promise to pay training costs. *Washington Post,* pp. H3, H4. See also, Schwade, S. (February 1985). Is it time to consider computer-based training? *Personnel Administrator,* pp. 25–35.

94. See note 12. See also, Apostolopoulos, N.; Albert, G.; and Zimmerman, S. (1996). DIALECT—Network-based digital interactive lectures. *Computer Networks and ISDN Systems, 28*(14), 1873–1886.

95. How McDonald's Corporation brought training to the desktop (1997). *Training, 34*(3), p. 55; see also, Beating "I can't learn that way" syndrome (1997). *Training, 34*(3), 55; see note 66, Rao (1995); Lee, C., and Zemke, R. (November 1995). No time to train. *Training,* 29–37; Granger, R. E. (1989). Computer-based training improves job performance. *Personnel Journal, 68,* 116–123; Rakow, J. (September 1991). Training computer users on a limited budget. *Small Business Reports,* pp. 45–49.

96. Wiley, J. (1997). CBT evolves. *Air Transport World, 34*(4), 81–83. See also, Aronson, R. B. (1996). Curtain call for CONDUIT. *Manufacturing-Engineering, 117*(3), 70–72.

97. Hefner, D. (1996). The CBT (r)evolution and the authoring engines that drive it. *CD ROM Professional, 9*(10), 46–65. See also, Hefner, D. (1996). Two trends: The internet and the suite. *CD ROM Professional,*

9(10), 54–56; Crenshaw, D. (1997). 'Net training. *Infoworld, 19*(9), 61–62; Teas, D. (1996). The Internet means opportunity. *Life Association News, 91*(3), 135–138; and Advice on authoring CBT—Learn the basics and you can build anything (1997). *Training, 34*(3), 51, 53.

98. Geber, B. (May 1990). Simulating reality. *Training,* 41–46.

99. Agres, T. (1997). VR for war games and for real. *R-and-D, 39*(2), 45–46.

100. See note 6. See also, Cadotte, E. R., and Bruce, H. J. (eds.) (1997). *The management of strategy in the marketplace.* Knoxville, TN: The College of Business Administration, The University of Tennessee.

101. Robinson, G., and Dechart, K. (1997). Building a business case for diversity. *Academy of Management Executive, 11,* 21–31.

102. See note 6.

103. Performance-based compliance training programs (1996). *ABA-Bank Compliance, 17*(3), 28.

104. Hoult, S. L., and Cellar, D. F. (April 1997). *An application of the elaboration likelihood model to sexual harassment training.* Paper presented at the annual meeting of the Society of Industrial and Organizational Psychologist, St. Louis.

105. Cotton, G. (1996). Roleplay set to boom in 1996. *Management Services, 40*(6), 24–25; see also, Hough, R. (1997). A make or break proposition. *Canadian Business, 70*(2), 18.

106. Mayer, S. J., and Russell, J. S. (1987). Behavior modeling training in organizations: Concerns and conclusions. *Journal of Management, 9,* 21–40.

107. See note 88; see also, Baldwin, T. T. (1992). Effects of alternative modeling strategies on outcomes of interpersonal skill training. *Journal of Applied Psychology, 77*(2), 147–154; Pescuric, A., and Byham, W. C. (1996). The new look of behavior modeling. *Training and Development, 50*(7), 24–30.

108. Bandura, A. (1986). *Social foundations of thought and action: A social cognitive theory.* Englewood Cliffs, NJ: Prentice Hall; see also, Goldstein, I. L., and Sorcher, M. (1974). *Changing supervisor behavior.* New York: Pergamon Press; Jentsch, F., and others (April 1997). *What determines whether observers recognize targeted behaviors in modeling displays.* Paper presented at the annual meeting of the Society of Industrial and Organizational Psychologists, St. Louis.

109. See note 107, Baldwin (1992). See also, Simon, S. J., and Werner, J. M. (1996). Computer training through behavior modeling, self-paced, and instructional approaches: A field experiment. *Journal of Applied Psychology, 81*(6), 648–659; Byham, W. C., and Pescuric, A. (1996). Behavior modeling at the teachable moment. *Training, 33*(12), 50–56; Pescuric, A., and Byham, W. C. (1996). The new look of behavior modeling. *Training and Development, 50*(7), 24–30; Simon, S. J.; Grover-Varun, T.; Teng, J. T. C.; and Whitcomb, K. (1996). The relationship of information system training methods and cognitive ability to end-user satisfaction,

comprehension, and skill transfer: A longitudinal field study. *Information Systems Research, 7*(4), 466–490.

110. Sackett, P. R., and Mullen, E. J. (1993). Beyond formal experimental design: Towards an expanded view of the training evaluation process. *Personnel Psychology, 46,* 613–627.

111. Gordon, J. (June 1988). Who is being trained to do what? *Training,* 51–60.

112. Dionne, P. (1996). The evaluation of training activities: A complex issue involving different stakes. *Human Resource Development Quarterly, 7*(3), 279–281; see also, Latham, G. P. (1988). Human resource training and development. *Annual Review of Psychology, 39,* 545–582.

113. Clegg, W. H. (1987). Management training evaluation: An update. *Training and Development Journal, 41*(2), 65–71.

114. Smeltzer, L. R. (August 1979). Do you really evaluate, or just talk about it? *Training,* 6–8.

115. Dixon, N. M. (1996). New routes to evaluation. *Training and Development Journal, 50*(5), 82–85; see also, Bushnell, D. S. (1990). Input, process, output: A model for evaluating training. *Training and Development Journal, 44*(4), 41–43; and note 21.

116. See note 6. See also, Catalanello, R. L., and Kirkpatrick, D. L. (1968). Evaluating training programs: The state of the art. *Training and Development Journal, 22*(5), 2–9; and Arvey, R. D., Maxwell, S. E., and Salas, E. (1992). The relative power of training evaluation designs under different cost configurations. *Journal of Applied Psychology, 77*(2), 155–160.

117. See note 5.

118. Kirkpatrick, D. (1983). Four steps to measuring training effectiveness. *Personnel Administrator, 28*(11), 19–25; see also, Trost, A. (1985). "They may love it but will they use it?" *Training and Development Journal, 39*(1), 66–68; Alliger, G. M., and Janak, E. A. (1989). Kirkpatrick's levels of training criteria: Thirty years later. *Personnel Psychology, 42,* 331–342; Kirkpatrick, D. L. (1996). *Evaluating training programs: The four levels.* San Francisco: Berrett-Koehler Publishers; Oberman, G. (1996). An approach for measuring safety training effectiveness. *Occupational Health and Safety, 65*(12), 48, 58; and Kirkpatrick, D. (1996). Great ideas revisited: Revisiting Kirkpatrick's four-level model. *Training and Development, 50*(1), 54–57.

119. Phillips, J. J. (1983). *Handbook of training evaluation and measurement methods.* San Diego, CA: University Associates. See also note 110; and Brookshaw, C., and Seoane, D. (1996). Training effectiveness. *InfoWorld, 18*(42), 76–80.

120. See note 24.

121. See note 24.

122. Campbell, D. T., and Stanley, J. C. (1963). *Experimental and quasi-experimental designs for research.* Boston: Houghton Mifflin.

123. Ford, D. J. (June 1993). Benchmarking HRD. *Training and Development Journal,* pp. 36–41; see also, Industry Report 1996 (1996). *Training, 33*(10), 36–39.

124. Mathieu, J. E., and Leonard, R. L. (1987). Applying utility concepts to a training program in supervisory skills: A time-based approach. *Academy of Management Journal, 30,* 316–335; see note 1, Laabs (1996).

125. See note 24; see also, Yang, H.; Sackett, P. R.; and Arvey, R. D. (1996). Statistical power and cost in training evaluation: Some new considerations. *Personnel Psychology, 49*(3), 651–668.

126. Lee. R. (1996). The 'pay-forward' view of training. *People Management, 2*(3), 30–32; see also note 1.

127. See note 12.

128. Feldman, D. C., and Brett, J. M. (1983). Coping with new jobs: A comparative study of new hires and job changers. *Academy of Management Journal, 26,* 258–272; see also, Fisher, C. D. (1986). Organizational socialization: An integrative review. In K. M. Rowland and G. R. Ferris (eds.), *Research in personnel and human resources management, 4,* 101–145.

129. Solomon, J. (Dec. 29, 1988). Companies try measuring cost savings from new types of corporate benefits. *The Wall Street Journal*, p. B1.

130. See note 24; see also; Cook, M. F. (ed.) (1992). *The AMA handbook for employee recruitment and retention.* New York: AMACOM.

131. Wanous, J. P. (1992). *Organizational entry,* 2nd ed. Reading, MA: Addison-Wesley.

132. See note 131.

133. See note 21; see also, McGarrell, E. J. (1984). An orientation system that builds productivity. *Personnel Administrator, 29*(10), 75–85.

134. See note 15.

135. Reed-Mendenhall, D., and Millard, C. W. (1980). Orientation: A training and development tool. *Personnel Administrator, 25*(8), 42–44.

136. London, M. (1989). *Managing the training enterprise: High-quality, cost-effective employee training in organizations.* San Francisco: Jossey-Bass; see also, Caffarella, R. S. (1985). A checklist for planning successful training programs. *Training and Development Journal, 39*(3), 81–83.

137. See note 21.

138. Russell, J. E. A., and DeMatteo, J. S. (1997). Group dynamics, processes, and teamwork. In E. J. Cadotte and H. J. Bruce (eds.). *The management of strategy in the marketplace.* Knoxville, TN: The College of Business Administration, The University of Tennessee; see also, Wellins, R., and George, J. (April 1991). The key to self-directed teams. *Training and Development Journal,* pp. 26–31.

139. Sherman, S. (March 18, 1996). Secrets of HP's "muddled team." *Fortune,* pp. 116–118, 120.

140. See note 15.

141. Taylor, D. L., and Ramsey, R. K. (May 1993). Empowering employees to "just do it." *Training and Development Journal,* pp. 71–76. See also note 24.

142. Banker, R. D.; Field, J. M.; Schroeder, G.; Sinha, K. K. (1996). Impact of work teams on manufacturing performance: A longitudinal study. *Academy of Management Journal, 39,* 867–890.

143. See note 138, Wellins and George (1991).

144. Ames, L. (July 21, 1991). An obstacle course, lessons in teamwork. *The New York Times,* p. WC 2; see also, Kezman, S. W., and Connors, E. K. (May 1993). Avoid legal pitfalls in nontraditional training. *HR Magazine,* pp. 71–74.

145. See note 7; see also, Messmer, M. (1992). Cross-discipline training: A strategic model to do more with less. *Management Review, 81,* 26–28; Santora, J. E. (June 1992). Keep up production through cross-training. *Personnel Journal, 45,* 21–24; and Rickett, D. (February 1993). Peer training: Not just a low-budget answer. *Training,* 70–72.

146. Kaeter, M. (March 1993). Cross-training: The tactical view. *Training,* 35–39. See also note 24.

147. Hequet, M. (February 1992). Creativity training gets creative. *Training,* 41–46; see also, Solomon, C. M. (1990). Creativity training. *Personnel Journal, 69,* 65–71.

148. Wise, R. (1991). The boom in creativity training. *Across the Board, 28,* 38–42.

149. Stewart, T. A. (February 5, 1996). 3M fights back, *Fortune,* pp. 94–99.

150. Harvey, H. G. (1996). Developing leaders rather than managers for the global marketplace. *Human Resource Management Review, 6,* 279.

151. Hogan, G. W., and Goodson, J. R. (1990). The key to expatriate success. *Training and Development Journal, 44*(1), 50, 52; see also, McEnery, J., and DesHarnais, G. (1990). Culture shock. *Training and Development Journal, 44*(4), 43–47; and Dowling, P. J., and Schuler, R. S. (1990). *International dimensions of human resource management.* Boston: PWS-Kent.

152. Ronen, S. (1989). Training the international assignee. In I. L. Goldstein and Associates (eds.), *Training and development in organizations.* San Francisco: Jossey-Bass, pp. 417–453.

153. See note 151, McEnery and DesHarnais (1990); see also, McCrea, J. (July 1997). Rx for expatriates. *World Traveler,* pp. 18–20, 22, 25–27.

154. See note 151, Hogan and Goodson (1990).

155. See note 153; see also, Black, J. S. and Mendenhall, M. (1990). Cross-cultural training effectiveness: A review and theoretical framework for future research. *Academy of Management Review, 15*(1), 113–136.

156. See note 154.

157. French, W. (1990). *Human resources management,* 2nd ed. Boston: Houghton Mifflin.

158. Odds and ends. (November 11, 1992). *The Wall Street Journal,* p. B1; see also, Copeland, L. (November 1985). Cross-cultural training: The competitive edge. *Training,* 49–53; and Lubin, J. S. (March 31, 1992). Younger managers learn global skills. *The Wall Street Journal,* p. B1.

159. Lubin, J. S. (January 29, 1996). An overseas stint can be a ticket to the top. *The Wall Street Journal,* pp. B1; B5.

160. Earley, P. C., and Erez, M. (1997). *The transplanted executive.* New York: Oxford University Press.

161. See note 155, Black & Mendenhall (1990).

162. Copeland, M. J. (1987). International training. In R. L. Craig (ed.), *Training and development handbook.* New York: McGraw-Hill, pp. 717–725; see also note 152; and McCaffery, J. A. (1986). Independent effectiveness: A reconsideration of cross-cultural orientation and training. *International Journal of Intercultural Relations, 10,* 159–178.

163. See note 153, McCrea (1997).

164. Fiedler, F. E.; Mitchell, T.; and Triandis, H. C. (1971). The culture assimilator: An approach to cross-cultural training. *Journal of Applied Psychology, 55,* 95–102.

165. Harrison, J. K. (1992). Individual and combined effects of behavior modeling and the cultural assimilator in cross-cultural management training. *Journal of Applied Psychology, 77,* 952–962.

166. Solomon, C. M. (November 1995). HR's helping hand pulls global inpatriates onboard. *Personnel Journal,* pp. 40–46, 49.

167. See note 2, Goldstein (1993).

168. Fulmer, R. M. (1986). Educating managers for the future. *Personnel, 18*(2), 70–73; see also, The new shape of global business. (July 31, 1989). *Fortune,* pp. 280–323.

169. Galagan, P., and Wulf, K. (February 1996). Signs of the times. *Training and Development,* pp. 32–36.

170. Myers, S. (1997). *The role of person, outcome, environmental, and learning variables in training effectiveness.* An unpublished dissertation. Knoxville, TN: The University of Tennessee.

171. Sirota, A., and Pfau, Inc. (1989). *Report to respondents: Survey of views toward corporate education and training practices.* New York: Author.

172. Reich, R. (Feb. 9, 1992). In Greenhouse, S. Attention America! Snap out of it! *New York Times,* pp. 1F, 8F.

173. Keith, J. D., and Payton, E. S. (1995). The new face of training. *Training and Development,* February, pp. 49–51; see also note 22, Harp (1995).

CAREER DEVELOPMENT

OVERVIEW

The business environment is highly turbulent and complex, resulting in terribly ambiguous and contradictory career signals. Individuals, perhaps in self-defense, are becoming correspondingly ambivalent about their desires and plans for career development. The traditional psychological contract in which an employee entered a firm, worked hard, performed well, was loyal and committed, and thus received ever-greater rewards and job security, has been replaced by a new contract based on continuous learning and identity change . . . In short, the organizational career is dead, while the protean career is alive and flourishing.[1]

The sentiments expressed above reflect the fact that the workplace has changed, and that individuals are altering some of their career-related attitudes and behaviors. Not long ago, individuals believed that there was *only one* occupation for which each person was best suited, that the best career decision would be made when a person was *young,* and that once a field was chosen the choice was *irreversible.* They also believed that *interests* were more important in determining career choices than were skills and aptitudes, and that individuals who were

successful in a career only moved *upwards.*[2] Today, fewer people subscribe to these assumptions about careers.

> The career as we once knew it—as a series of upward moves, with steadily increasing income, power, status, and security—has died. Nevertheless, people will always have work lives that unfold over time, offering challenge, growth, and learning. So, if we think of the career as a series of lifelong work-related experiences and personal learnings, it will never die.[3]

The career of the 21st century is measured by continuous learning and identity changes rather than by chronological age and life stages.[4] In addition, employees used to believe there was a covenant of employment between the employer and employee. But with the increase in downsizings, delayerings, rightsizings, restructurings, and layoffs, the covenant seems null. As Jack Welch, CEO of General Electric, noted: There is a one-day contract between employer and employee, in which all that counts is the current value that each party contributes to the relationship.[5] Some argue that the focus today should be on an individual's *employability.* Individuals should not worry about holding onto a specific job, but rather they should make sure they have developed the competitive skills needed in the marketplace.[6]

Now more than ever, individuals must develop new and better personal skills of self-assessment and career planning, especially because organizations do not have the resources to completely plan individuals' careers.[7] The protean career is one that is driven by the person, not the organization. It can be reinvented by the person from time to time as the person and the environment change. Pursuing the protean career requires a high level of self-awareness and personal responsibility. This new career will be a continuous learning process and necessitates that the individual develops self-knowledge and adaptability. These are considered meta-skills because they are the skills required for learning how to learn.[8]

Some organizations have become more active in implementing career development programs. Companies are designing career programs to increase employee productivity, prevent job burnout and obsolescence, and improve the quality of employees' work lives.[9] Human resource departments of some large companies have taken a greater interest in career development, and the human resource manager has never before faced so many challenges in meeting the needs of individual employees and organizations in designing career systems.[10] To cope in today's turbulent times, it has become increasingly important for both organizations and employees to better address career needs. It is the employee's responsibility to manage his or her own career, yet it is the employer's responsibility to provide employees with the tools and opportunities to enhance their skills. The end result should be a career-resilient workforce, one that has self-reliant workers who are capable of reinventing themselves to keep up with the fast pace of organizational changes.[11] In 1997, a number of organizations such as Chevron, CIGNA, Sears Information Services, Texaco, Turner Broadcasting, Internal Revenue Service, and Marriott International participated in a conference to share their strategies for creating a career-resilient workforce.[12]

This chapter describes some career-related issues relevant to human resource professionals and practicing managers. We will begin by defining some key career concepts and models and then describe some of the issues involved in designing career development systems in organizations. We will also describe the various components of career systems and how career systems can be coordinated with other HR programs.

OBJECTIVES

After studying this chapter, you should:

1. Understand the important definitions of organizational career development, and the reasons for understanding career development.

2. Understand the importance of integrating career development programs with other organizational HR systems.

3. Be able to identify the steps involved in designing career development systems.

4. Be able to describe the components of career development systems.

DEFINITIONS

While most people think the term **career** means "advancement" in an organization, a broader view of career defines it as an "individually perceived sequence of attitudes and behaviors associated with work-related activities and experiences over the span of a person's life."[13] In other words, the term *career* has an *internal* focus and refers to the way an individual views his or her career and it has an *external* or objective focus and refers to the actual series of job positions held by the individual.[14] Understanding career development in an organization requires an examination of two processes: how individuals plan and implement their own career goals (career planning), and how organizations design and implement their career development programs (career management). These processes are illustrated in Figure 8.1. As noted, **career planning** is a deliberate attempt by an individual to become more aware of his or her own skills, interests, values, opportunities, constraints, choices, and consequences. It involves identifying career-related goals and establishing plans for achieving those goals.[15] **Career management** is considered to be an organizational process that involves preparing, implementing, and monitoring career plans undertaken by an individual alone or within the organization's career systems.[16]

A **career development system** is a formal, organized, planned effort to achieve a balance between individual career needs and organizational workforce requirements.[17] For example, the organization has certain needs for staffing and employees have needs to effectively utilize their personal skills.[18] It is a mechanism for meeting the present and future human resource needs of the organization. Stanford professor Pfeffer looks at formal systems of career development as a key to competitive advantage. Says Pfeffer, "Career systems that emphasize promotions from within not only promote advantages in terms of managing the employment relationship but also make it more likely that strategies for achieving competitive advantage through people will be understood and pursued."[19] A career planning system coordinated with HR planning will foster a well-integrated HRM system. Figure 8.2 illustrates this relationship. For instance, Coca-Cola implemented a career development system so it would be better able to develop its own em-

FIGURE 8.1
A MODEL OF ORGANIZATIONAL CAREER DEVELOPMENT

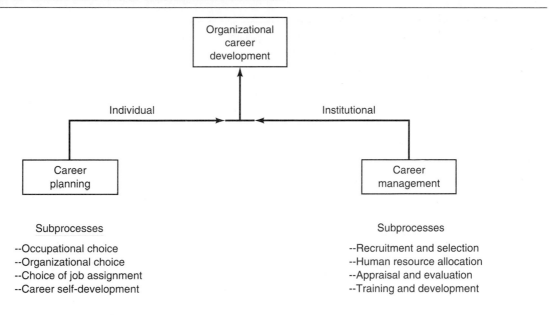

Career: The sequence of a person's work-related activities and behaviors and associated attitudes, values, and aspirations over the span of one's life.

Organizational career development: The outcomes emanating from the interaction of individual career planning and institutional career management processes.

Career planning: A deliberate process for (1) becoming aware of self, opportunities, constraints, choices, and consequences, (2) identifying career-related goals, and (3) programming of work, education, and related developmental experiences to provide the direction, timing, and sequence of steps to attain a specific career goal.

Career management: An ongoing process of preparing, implementing, and monitoring career plans undertaken by the individual alone or in concert with the organization's career system.

Source: T. G. Gutteridge, Organizational career development systems: The state of the practice. In D. T. Hall and associates, *Career development in organizations*. San Francisco: Jossey-Bass, 1986, p. 54. Used with permission.

ployees to meet future staffing needs and to be able to promote employees internally.[20]

Basically, career development practices are designed to enhance the career satisfaction of employees and to improve organizational effectiveness.[21] It may, however, be difficult to completely integrate individual and organizational career efforts because the rate at which an individual grows and develops may not parallel an organization's needs. For example, many of the baby boomers in the workforce are interested in advancing in their present positions, yet they are finding those positions to be more scarce given the thinning of management jobs through downsizings.[22] A recent survey conducted by Tenneco Oil found that 48 percent of surveyed employees felt ready to assume supervisory responsibilities. Unfortunately, the company was in a downsizing mode and had no plans to promote anyone in the next two years.[23] With all the recent changes in orga-

nizations (e.g., downsizings, mergers, divestitures) it has become even more important to try to integrate the needs of employers with those of employees.

This chapter emphasizes the importance of understanding career development in organizations by examining the interaction of individual and organizational career processes. Of particular value is an understanding of career processes within an HR system and the role that managers must play to design career development systems. One model focuses on a dynamic interaction of the individual and the organization over time through the "matching" process we described in Chapters 5 and 6. If the matching process works well, the organization and the individual will benefit. The organization may experience increased productivity and higher organizational commitment and long-range effectiveness, and the employee may have greater satisfaction, security, and personal development.[24]

FIGURE 8.2
RELATIONSHIP BETWEEN CAREER PLANNING AND HR PLANNING

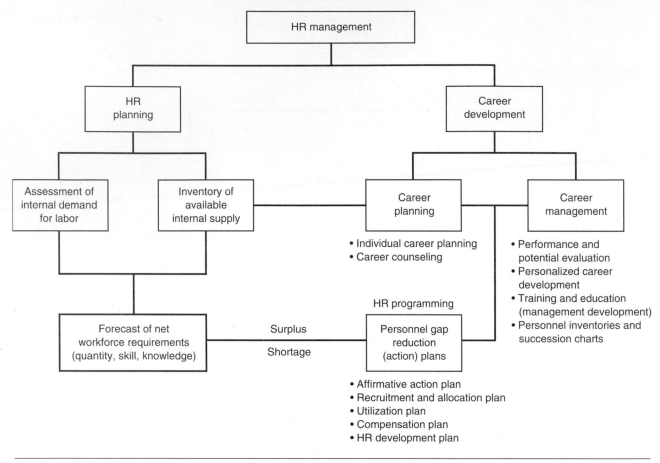

Source: T. G. Gutteridge, Organizational career development systems: The state of the practice. In D. T. Hall and associates, *Career development in organizations.* San Francisco: Jossey-Bass, 1986, p. 57. Used with permission.

IMPORTANCE OF UNDERSTANDING CAREER DEVELOPMENT

Today's competitive business environment has forced organizations to restructure and downsize, resulting in fewer hierarchical levels and traditional promotional opportunities for employees.[25] At the same time, there is increased pressure to improve productivity or risk falling prey to larger corporations. The creation of new technologies has required that individuals update their skills or else they will become outdated. One internal study at Ford, for example, found that there was only a 19 percent overlap between the knowledge acquired to earn a computer science degree in 1980 and the knowledge required to be a practicing computer scientist in 1990. The gap will be just as big between 1990 and 2000.

A number of organizational change initiatives could have unintended and undesired consequences for individuals. These include the following:

• **Downsizing**—jobs are cut from the organization.
• **Delayering**—jobs are reclassified more broadly, yet

old reporting lines exist to maintain managerial control.

• **Decentralizing**—responsibilities are reassigned from the corporate centralized function to functions in each location or at lower levels.

• **Reorganizations**—company may be refocusing around core competencies.

• **Cost-reduction strategies**—the same work is done with fewer resources.

• **IT innovations**—how the work is done is altered due to advances in information technology.

• **Competency measurement**—skill sets required of employees are redefined or measured in different ways.

• **Performance-related pay**—pay is linked to performance and used as a motivator.

Figure 8.3 depicts some organizational change initiatives, their effects on jobs and careers, their psychological impact on individuals, and the necessary strategies to remedy or mitigate the negative effects.[26]

FIGURE 8.3
ORGANIZATIONAL CHANGE INITIATIVES AND THEIR EFFECTS ON CAREERS AND INDIVIDUALS

ORGANIZATIONAL CHANGE FORM	EFFECTS ON JOBS AND CAREERS	PSYCHOLOGICAL IMPACT ON INDIVIDUALS	REMEDIAL AND MITIGATING STRATEGIES
Downsizing	Job security	Anxiety	Openness and involvement
Delayering	Plateauing	Lowered self-esteem	Delegation and self-management
Decentralization	Segmentation and fragmentation	Competitive behaviors	Team building and mobility
Reorganization	Displacement	Frustration	Self-appraisal and pathfinding
Cost-reduction	Work intensification	Stress	Time and task management
IT innovation	Deskilling	Lowered self-efficacy	Re-skilling
Competency measurement	Obsolescence	Self-defense	Coaching and mentoring
Performance-related pay	Individualism and politics	Low trust behaviors	Team-based objectives and feedback

Source: N. Nicholson, Career systems in crisis: Change and opportunity in the information age. *Academy of Management Executive, 10*(4), 1996, p. 43.

Understanding career development is also important today because of changing workforce characteristics. Current labor force changes include a greater proportion of older workers, working mothers, and members of the baby-boom generation who are competing for a limited number of jobs. As we discussed in Chapter 1, employees have changed their values such that now they want more self-fulfillment in work and to be in charge of managing their own career planning. They want opportunities for growth in their careers and to expand their knowledge and skills.[27] They also demand well-balanced lives in which comparable value is placed on work, family, and leisure.[28] Generation X employees have different values. They seem less interested in climbing the corporate ladder, acquiring fancy titles, or spending their careers in one type of work or job. Rather, they want to explore and do different kinds of jobs where they can express their own individual values.[29]

Social changes have included increased societal pressures on organizations to be more responsible. For example, corporations are now more likely to offer child care programs, flexible work scheduling, and parental leave. In addition, as discussed in Chapter 3, the increasing rate of litigation concerning employment opportunity through laws such as the Age Discrimination Act in Employment, Americans with Disabilities Act, the Civil Rights Act, and the Equal Pay Act has placed more responsibility on companies to avoid discrimination in their career development programs.[30]

A greater emphasis will be now placed on designing and implementing relevant career systems in organizations. Organizations will have to find more creative ways for people to develop because employees will not be able to rely on organizational growth to provide career opportunities (e.g., promotions). The line manager may experience greater pressure to provide career counseling to employees, and the HR department may be called on to offer training for managers in career coaching skills.[31] For example, the Coca-Cola and Ford career systems require training for all managers in how to conduct career development discussions with employees in the context of performance appraisal. The intent is to make managers more accountable for the development of their employees.[32]

DESIGNING CAREER DEVELOPMENT SYSTEMS

An effective career development system attempts to integrate a series of individual career planning and organizational career management activities that involve the employee, management, and the organization. For example, most corporations with career programs (e.g., Lincoln Electric, Wal-Mart, IBM, Bell Atlantic, Xerox) involve career assessment by the employee with the manager serving as a facilitator and the organization providing a supportive environment. To determine if your organization has a culture that supports career development, complete the 20 questions listed in Figure 8.4.

Benefits of Career Development Systems

Some of the benefits of a career development system for employees, managers, and the organization are presented in Figure 8.5. As shown, managers can benefit from career development programs by being better able to communicate with and develop their staff. For example, the Federal National Mortgage Association reduced turnover of its sales force by 50 percent after instituting a supervisory training program on career planning. Employees may also benefit from a career development system by acquiring a deepened appreciation for their own skills and career possibilities and assuming a greater responsi-

FIGURE 8.4
TWENTY QUESTIONS: A CAREER DEVELOPMENT CULTURE INDEX

Instructions: If your answer is yes to a question, make a check mark in the space to the left of the number of that item. See scoring instructions at the end of the exercise.

_____ 1. Does senior management use work assignments and work relationships to develop employees?

_____ 2. Do they do it consciously or intentionally for developing people (as opposed to doing it only for business purposes)?

_____ 3. Are these career development activities part of the business plan for the employee's unit?

_____ 4. Is the organization's purpose expressed in human terms with which employees can identify?

_____ 5. Does top management value employee development?

_____ 6. Is career development owned by senior line management (as opposed to being seen as owned by HR)?

_____ 7. Is diversity actively promoted by senior line management?

_____ 8. Is employee development done by senior line management for the explicit purpose of supporting the business strategy?

_____ 9. Are new forms of employee mobility being used (such as cross-functional, cross-business teams)?

_____ 10. Is personal development or self-knowledge (for example, 360-degree feedback) promoted?

_____ 11. Is career development part of the overall corporate strategy?

_____ 12. Is there a strong succession planning process, which puts emphasis on development as well as identification?

_____ 13. Do employees have significant input to plans for their future development and assignments?

_____ 14. Does career development include opportunities for risk and learning (adaptability)?

_____ 15. Does career development include personal (identity) learning as well as task learning?

_____ 16. Do most people here believe that career development should also take family and personal balance needs into account?

_____ 17. Is there general agreement in management about whether historical career development approaches are appropriate for the future?

_____ 18. Is it relatively easy for employees to access information about other job opportunities in the company?

_____ 19. Are employees encouraged to be empowered and self-directed in their careers?

_____ 20. (The acid test): Are individual employees aware of your organization's career development activities?

Scoring:

Add up the number of checks (symbolizing "yes" to the item).

Key: 17 or more checks . . . . Outstanding

 10–16 . . . . Good

 6–9 . . . . Fair

 < 5 . . . . Work needed!

Source: D. T. Hall and P. H. Mirvis, The new protean career: Psychological success and the path with a heart. In D. T. Hall and associates (eds.), *The career is dead: Long live the career: A relational approach to careers.* San Francisco: Jossey-Bass, 1996, pp. 39–40.

FIGURE 8.5
BENEFITS OF A CAREER DEVELOPMENT SYSTEM

MANAGERS/SUPERVISORS	EMPLOYEES	ORGANIZATION
Increased skill in managing own careers	Helpful assistance with career decisions	Better use of employee skills
Greater retention of valued employees	Enrichment of present job and increased job satisfaction	Dissemination of information at all organization levels
Better communication between manager and employee	Better communication between employee and manager	Better communication within the organization as a whole
More realistic staff and development planning	More realistic goals and expectations	Greater retention of valued employees
Productive performance-appraisal discussions	Better feedback on performance	Expanded public image as a people developer
Greater understanding of the organization	Current information on the firm and the future	Increased effectiveness of personnel systems
Enhanced reputation as a people developer	Greater personal responsibility for career	Clarification of goals of the organization

Source: Z. B. Leibowitz, C. Farren, and B. L. Kaye, *Designing career development systems,* San Francisco: Jossey-Bass, 1986, p. 7. Used with permission.

bility for managing their own careers. The organization may gain from a career development system by increased employee loyalty, improved communication throughout the organization, and strengthened HR systems.

To maintain the career development program, it is essential to integrate the career program into the organization's ongoing employee training and development strategy. The program should also be evaluated to determine revisions and to win the continued support of top management. Figure 8.6 illustrates some criteria that may be used to evaluate the program or indicate success. As noted, success can be measured by individual and organizational goal attainment, the actions that are completed (e.g., use of career tools), and any changes in performance measures and attitudes.

Research on the effectiveness of career development programs is sparse, yet promising. One study found that 44 percent of administrators of career development programs for *Fortune* 500 companies regarded them as "very helpful."[33] IBM evaluated the effectiveness of its

career development workshop and found improvements in the participants' abilities and responsibilities for their own career planning. IBM also discovered that employee perceptions of better job opportunities (defined as opportunities to use new and different skills) had increased substantially.[34] DuPont found that after participating in a career program, employees had clearer career objectives, were more familiar with possible career options, and felt that management had shown a greater concern for career development.[35] Pratt & Whitney also reported that its turnover rate for new engineers had decreased by 25 percent after instituting a career development program.

Of course, measures of program success may vary depending on *who* you are asking in the organization. Employees, managers, organizations, and the HR staff may differ in the specific factors they view as indicative of program success. For example, employees may say that a career program is effective if it organizes a way for them to plan and manage their career interests or offers

FIGURE 8.6
INDICATORS OF CAREER PROGRAM EFFECTIVENESS

Goal Attainment

Achievement of prespecified individual and organizational objectives on qualitative as well as quantitative dimensions

INDIVIDUAL	ORGANIZATIONAL
Exercise greater self-determination	Improve career communications between employees and supervisors
Achieve greater self-awareness	Improve individual/organizational career match
Acquire necessary organizational career information	Enhance organization's image
Enhance personal growth and development	Respond to EEO and affirmative action pressures
Improve goal-setting capability	Identify pool of management talent

Actions or Events Completed

1. Employee use of career tools (participation in career workshops, enrollment in training courses)
2. Career decisions conducted
3. Employee career plans implemented
4. Career actions taken (promotions, cross-functional moves)
5. Management successors identified

Changes in Performance Indexes

1. Reduced turnover rates
2. Lower employee absenteeism
3. Improved employee morale
4. Improved employee performance ratings
5. Reduced time to fill job openings
6. Increased promotion from within

Attitudes/Perceptions

1. Evaluation of career tools and practices (participant's reaction to career workshop, supervisor's evaluation of job-posting system)
2. Perceived benefits of career system
3. Employees express career feelings (responses to career attitude survey)
4. Evaluation of employee career planning skills
5. Adequacy of organizational career information

Source: T. G. Gutteridge, Organizational career development systems: The state of the practice, In D. T. Hall and associates. *Career development in organizations.* San Francisco: Jossey-Bass, 1986, p. 76. Used with permission.

them opportunities to discuss their career decisions with their supervisors. Managers may view a career program as successful if it offers them staffing flexibility or helps them to identify pools of qualified employees to meet forecasted openings. Organizations may find a program to be useful if it increases the attractiveness of the organization to potential employees (recruits) or raises the motivation and productivity of current employees. Finally, the HR staff may determine that a program is successful if it has credibility or enhances the reputation of the HR department with line managers.[36]

COMPONENTS OF CAREER DEVELOPMENT SYSTEMS

A variety of career components (i.e., activities and tools) exist for use in organizations. HR managers should be familiar with these components because the managers often serve as internal consultants responsible for designing the career development system. Some of the activities described are individual career planning tools and others are commonly used for organizational career management.[37] In general, the most effective career development programs will use both types of activities.

A variety of career development activities are available for use. Some of the more popular ones include: (1) self-assessment tools (e.g., career planning workshops, career workbooks); (2) individual counseling; (3) information services (e.g., job posting systems, skills inventories, career ladders or career paths, career resource centers and other communication formats); (4) initial employment programs (e.g., anticipatory socialization programs, realistic recruitment, employee orientation programs); (5) organizational assessment programs (e.g., assessment centers, psychological testing, promotability forecasts, succession planning); and (6) developmental programs (e.g., assessment centers, job rotation programs, in-house training, tuition-refund plans, mentoring). No matter what tools are used for career development, it is important that employees develop an individualized career development plan. For example, Raychem requires every person to have a learning or development plan.[38] Figure 8.7 reveals the prevalence of many of the career development tools. This is based on a survey of 182 of the *Fortune* 500 firms. These programs were cited as having the greatest positive impact on employees' job satisfaction, communication, retention, work motivation, and their views or image of the company as well as their commitment to the firm.[39]

Self-Assessment Tools

Self-assessments are usually among the first techniques implemented by organizations in their career development efforts.[40] Thus, it is important for managers to be-

**FIGURE 8.7
PREVALENCE OF ORGANIZATIONAL CAREER DEVELOPMENT INTERVENTIONS**

Self-assessment tools	
Career planning workshops	36%
Career workbooks	35%
Individual counseling	75%
Information services	
Job posting systems	83%
Skills inventories	53%
Career ladders and paths	47%
Career resource centers	25%
Organizational assessment programs	
Assessment centers	16%
Psychological testing	29%
Promotability forecasts	50%
Succession planning	77%
Developmental programs	
Assessment centers	12%
Job rotation programs	53%
Tuition refund plans	98%
Internal training programs	91%
External training seminars	98%
Formal mentoring programs	21%
Career programs for special target groups	
Fast-track or high-potential employees	48%
Terminated employees (outplacement programs)	79%
Supervisors and managers	58%
Senior-level executives	58%
Professional employees	43%
Technical employees	42%
Women	26%
Minorities	26%
Employees with disabilities	13%
New employees (early-career issues)	
Employee orientation programs	89%
Anticipatory socialization programs	43%
Realistic recruitment	60%
Middle-career and older-career issues	
Programs to combat obsolescence or plateauing	23%
Workshops on older worker issues	10%
Preretirement programs	63%
Incentives for early retirement	40%
Programs to assist employed spouses and parents	
Policies on hiring couples	37%
Work–family programs	36%
Part-time work	76%
Job-sharing programs	36%
Relaxed policies on transfers and travel	24%
Flexible work arrangements	56%
Paid maternity/paternity leave	74%
Child care services	41%
Adoption benefits	24%

Note: Based on 182 U.S. *Fortune* 500 companies surveyed.

Source: J. E. A. Russell and L. B. Curtis. *Career development practices and perceived effectiveness in Fortune 500 firms.* Paper presented at the annual meeting of the Society of Industrial and Organizational Psychology, San Francisco, April 1993.

come familiar with the different self-assessment and career exploration instruments available. Typically, individuals completing self-assessment exercises for career planning think through their life roles, interests, skills, and work attitudes and preferences. They try to plan their short- and long-term goals, develop action plans to meet those goals, and identify any obstacles and opportunities that might be associated with them.[41] Hewlett-Packard employees at the Colorado Springs Division complete a variety of self-assessment exercises including a written self-assessment, vocational interest tests (e.g., Strong Interest Inventory), and 24-hour diaries before meeting with their managers for career counseling.[42] Six months after the course, 40 percent of the participants had planned internal career moves and 37 percent had already advanced to new positions in the firm. Of those, 74 percent stated that the career development program played a critical part in their job change. Two tools often used to assist individuals in their self-assessments include career planning workshops and career workbooks.

CAREER PLANNING WORKSHOPS. After individuals complete their self-assessments, they may share their findings with other individuals in career workshops. For example, General Electric provides career training to its engineering staff followed by periodic meetings to share results.[43] In general, most workshops use experiential exercises in a structured, participative group format to educate individuals on how to prepare and follow through on their career strategies. A group format allows participants to receive feedback from others so they can check the reality of their plans and consider other alternatives. In addition, workshops are beneficial in helping employees gain greater self-awareness and insight and learn more about career opportunities in the organization. TVA offered career planning workshops to many of its employees, and employees found them to be helpful in understanding their career needs and insights.[44] Sprint, the third-largest long-distance telephone service provider, used a different type of career workshop to recruit people for a new sales center in Portland, Oregon. It had Matt Weinstein, author of *Managing to Have Fun,* lead a career fair/workshop, and over 100 people showed up, of which Sprint was able to hire 25.[45] At NASA Goddard Space Flight Center, the HR director and his staff have been conducting career awareness workshops to educate employees about alternative career paths and to provide counseling. Eli Lilly and Company in Indianapolis uses workshops with executives and managers to give them feedback on their own career concepts and motives, as well as advice on how to provide career counseling to their subordinates.[46]

CAREER WORKBOOKS. Career workbooks consist of questions and exercises designed to guide individuals to figure out their strengths and weaknesses, job and career opportunities, and necessary steps for reaching their goals. One popular example of a generic career workbook is the annual book *What Color Is Your Parachute?*[47] Individuals use this manual to learn about their career possibilities since it provides suggestions for job hunting and making career changes. Many workbooks are tailor-made for a particular company and can be completed in several sessions. If "homegrown" workbooks are used, they should contain a statement of the organization's career policy and a description of the relevant career options in the organization and the strategies available for obtaining career information. The workbooks should also illustrate the organization's structure, career paths, and job qualifications for jobs along the career ladders.[48]

Individual Counseling

One common career development activity is career counseling. Individual career counseling helps employees discuss their career goals in one-on-one counseling sessions using workbooks and other self-assessment exercises. Discussions of the employees' interests, goals, current job activities and performance, and career objectives often occur. Because the counseling sessions are often conducted on a one-on-one basis they may be very time-consuming and not as cost-effective as other career development methods.

Generally, career counseling is provided by the HR department, although some organizations (e.g., Disney, Coca-Cola) hire professional counselors, and others use line managers as career counselors.[49] If supervisors are used in career counseling sessions, they should be given clearly defined roles and training in career issues, performance appraisal, listening, and communication skills. In addition, they should be required to meet with their subordinates on a consistent basis to review career goals and plans and to assist employees in developing their career objectives. Supervisors should also be instructed that part of their job is to help employees develop. In addition, they should be rewarded for their efforts as career coaches to encourage them to devote the necessary time to this role. For example, at Federal National Mortgage Association and Baxter Health Care Corporation, managers' bonuses are directly linked to the career development programs for women and minorities. Both companies identify key females and minorities early in their careers and develop specific plans for them to acquire the necessary skills for advancement. In general, supervisors can be valuable sources of career information for employees. Some tips for helping managers be more effective as coaches include those below:[50]

- Practice active listening and paraphrasing to make sure you truly understand what the employee is saying.
- Support the employee's learning by asking him or her

about the actions he or she has taken and how successful they were.

- Help the employee to work on easier career goals first, then more difficult ones.

- Help the employee write out scripts and role-play possible scenarios (e.g., interviewing for jobs).

- Provide positive feedback as employees take relevant career actions (e.g., attending career workshops).

Information Services

Internal communication systems are often used by organizations to alert employees to employment opportunities at all levels including upward, downward, and lateral moves. They may also be used to keep ongoing records of employees' skills, knowledges, and work experiences and preferences. These records are valuable for pointing out possible candidates for job openings. Several systems commonly used for compiling and communicating career-related information include job posting systems, skills inventories, career ladders and paths, and career resource centers.

JOB POSTING SYSTEMS As discussed in Chapter 5, job posting systems are commonly used by companies (e.g., 3M, TVA, IBM) to inform employees about openings in the organization using bulletin boards, newsletters, computer systems (e-mail), and other company publications. While they serve an informational purpose, postings may also be useful as a motivational tool. They imply that the organization is more interested in selecting employees from within the company than outside the organization. Guidelines for effective job posting systems include:

- Posting all permanent promotion and transfer opportunities for at least one week before recruiting outside the organization.

- Outlining minimum requirements for the position (including specific training courses).

- Describing decision rules that will be used.

- Making application forms available.

- Informing all applicants how the job was filled.

It is also important that all employees have access to the job postings. At Ford, a training matrix is available for each job family in which specific courses are linked as optional or recommended for a particular job classification. Raychem has created an internal network, called Internal Information Interview Network, of more than 360 people within the firm who are willing to talk with any employee who wants to learn more about their job.[51]

SKILLS INVENTORIES. Skills inventories are company files of data on employees' skills, abilities, experiences, and education that are often computerized.

They may contain comprehensive records of employees' work histories, qualifications, education degrees and major fields of study, accomplishments, training completed, skill and knowledge ratings, career objectives, geographical preferences, and anticipated retirement dates.[52] Skills inventories are created to help organizations know the characteristics of their workforce so they can effectively utilize employees' skills. They also reveal shortages of critical skills, which is useful for indicating training needs. Skills inventories can also help employees review their skill set relative to other employees.

CAREER LADDERS AND CAREER PATHS. Organizations usually map out steps (job positions) that employees might follow over time. These steps are used to document possible patterns of job movement including vertical or upward moves and lateral or cross-functional moves. Illustrations of career paths and ladders are helpful for answering employees' questions about career progression and future job opportunities in the organization. For example, General Motors groups jobs by job families such as HR, engineering, clerical, systems professional, and so on, to show employees the career possibilities in each of the various job fields.[53] ARCO (Atlantic Richfield Company) has a lot of lateral movement for positions. It makes special arrangements for employees who want to shift career paths.[54]

Typically, the description of a career path or ladder illustrates a career plan complete with the final goal, intermediate steps, and timetables for reaching the goal. In addition, the qualifications necessary to proceed to the next position are specified as is any minimum time required before advancing. For example, in an academic position, the path may look like: Instructor → Assistant Professor → Associate Professor → Professor. A faculty member may be required to spend a minimum amount of time in each level before moving to the next higher level.

Common in many organizations is the development of career paths for "fast-track" employees that outline the series of career moves that will prepare them for upper management. In recent years, many companies have developed multiple or dual career paths.[55] This is becoming more common in firms hiring professional employees (e.g., scientists, engineers). Previously, if an engineer wanted to advance in a firm, he or she had to eventually move into a management position to move up the corporate ladder. Today, many organizations offer dual career ladders so that engineers or other professionals can advance either through a management track or a scientist track. This enables them to remain in a technical, professional field yet still be able to advance in the firm to a higher status and higher paying position.[56]

CAREER RESOURCE CENTER AND OTHER COMMUNICATION FORMATS. One of the least expensive approaches for providing career information is setting up a career resource center. A center consists of a small library in the organization set up to distribute career development materials such as reference books, learning guides, and self-study tapes. Kodak, for example, has three internal career services "Kodak Career Services" which consist of a career library of tapes, books, and career counselors.[57] Other methods for communicating organizational career information and programs may include the use of flyers, brochures, newsletters, and manuals. Sun Microsystems, Apple Computers, and Raychem have centers set up with career specialists where employees can work on self-assessments, receive counseling, check on internal and external job openings, and attend seminars on networking or interviewing. Their centers are highly visible and easily accessible, which conveys to employees that the firms want their career centers to be used. Other companies have formed partnerships to enable their employees to receive career assistance. For instance, several firms located in the Silicon Valley, including, 3Com, Quantum, Aspect Telecommunications, Novell, Octel Communications, Silicon Graphics, Claris, and ESL, have formed a consortium to provide career services for their employees.[58]

Initial Employment Programs in Organizations

As discussed in Chapter 5, when an employee first starts working in a company, he or she generally has been exposed to some type of recruitment effort and company orientation. Or if the employee has worked part-time for a company or served in an internship program, he or she has been socialized regarding the unique characteristics of the job and organization. These initial employment programs may be valuable mechanisms to familiarize the employee with the career policies and procedures of the organization.

ANTICIPATORY SOCIALIZATION PROGRAMS. Socialization programs (e.g., internships, cooperative education programs) are beneficial for individuals to develop accurate, realistic expectations about their chosen career field and about the world of work. By working for an organization part-time or for several months, individuals may learn how well they are suited to the particular job or organization. This knowledge may help them gain a better sense of responsibility, maturity, and self-confidence about work. Andersen Consulting, Frito-Lay, IBM, Procter & Gamble, and Saturn are some of the many companies that hire interns and then make permanent offers if those internships are successful.

REALISTIC RECRUITMENT. As discussed in Chapter 5, when job applicants are given a realistic, balanced, accurate view of the organization and the job (i.e.,

provided with positive and negative information), they experience less reality shock, dissatisfaction, and turnover.[59] This is true for new employees as well as current employees who are transferring to new jobs in the organization. To meet career development needs, job applicants should be informed in realistic job previews about the skills required of various positions in the organizations and their own readiness and aptitude for those positions. This information should assist them in developing their career goals and action plans.

EMPLOYEE ORIENTATION PROGRAMS. As stated in Chapter 7, orientation programs for new employees help reduce anxieties because they provide information on organizational policies, procedures, rules, work requirements, and sources of information. Orientation programs may also be used to educate employees about any career programs, career paths, and opportunities for advancement. For example, Texas Instruments has developed an orientation program to address the unique concerns of new employees regarding career options.[60] The program includes a realistic job preview, an introduction to the formal mentoring program, a bibliography of readings relevant to career planning, and a guideline for career planning based on a study of Texas Instrument employees.

Organizational Assessment Programs

Assessment programs consist of methods for evaluating employees' potential for growth and development in the organization. For example, Johnson & Johnson has used career assessment to facilitate the staffing and development of special "tiger teams," which are formed to speed up the development of high-priority, new products.[61] Some of the more popular assessment programs include assessment centers, psychological testing, promotability forecasts, and succession planning.

ASSESSMENT CENTERS. In addition to their use as decision-making tools, assessment centers are popular as developmental tools. One survey of 256 U.S. firms found that 43 percent used assessment centers as part of their career development programs.[62] AT&T; JCPenney; Sears, Roebuck & Co.; IBM; GE; TVA; Bendix; and Pratt & Whitney are among the companies using assessment centers for development as well as employee decision making. As described in Chapter 6, participants of an assessment center engage in a variety of situational exercises, including tests, interviews, in-baskets, leaderless group discussions, and business games. Their performance on these exercises is evaluated by a panel of trained raters (usually middle- to upper-level managers), and they are given in-depth developmental feedback on their strengths and weaknesses. This feedback is often very useful for improving their own insights about their skills and for helping them outline realistic career goals and plans.

PSYCHOLOGICAL TESTING. Diagnostic tests, such as the "big five," and other inventories may be used for self-assessment or with career counseling. They consist of written tests that help individuals determine their vocational interests, personality types, work attitudes, and other personal characteristics that may reveal their career needs and preferences. Among the useful tests, in addition to the "big five," are the Strong Vocational Interest Inventory, the Kuder Preference Schedule, both of which assess preferences for certain jobs and job characteristics. (PAS, you will recall, wanted to mass market its "BIG FIVE" test for vocational guidance.)

PROMOTABILITY FORECASTS. Forecasts are used by the organization to identify the individuals who have exceptionally high career potential. Once individuals are identified, they are given relevant developmental experiences (e.g., attending conferences, training) to groom them for higher positions. Several companies now have such programs for women and minorities in an effort to get greater female and minority representation at higher managerial levels. Others, such as AT&T, track the progress of high-potential managers and provide them with developmental assignments.[63]

SUCCESSION PLANNING. Succession planning involves having senior executives periodically review their top executives and those in the next-lower level to determine several backups for each senior position. This is important because it often takes years of grooming to develop effective senior managers.[64] Succession planning is usually restricted to senior-level management positions and can be informal or formal. For informal succession planning, the individual manager identifies and grooms his or her own replacement. This is more prevalent in smaller firms. In fact, a survey of 800 small-business owners found that only 25 percent have a succession plan and that only 50 percent of them have even written it down.[65]

Formal succession planning involves an examination of strategic (long-range) plans and HR forecasts and a review of the data on all potential candidates. The objective is to identify employees with potential and increase managerial depth as well as promoting from within the company. In addition, it includes determining and clarifying the requirements of the managerial position and developing plans for how future managerial requirements will be met. In one study of *Fortune* 500 firms with succession plans, components used in the plans included: identification of high-potential employees, updated lists of possible replacements, performance appraisals of all employees, and individual development plans and management development programs. Addi-

tionally, the factors rated as most important in selecting specific candidates for grooming included: past job performance, past positions or prior employment, perceived credibility, area of expertise and career path, and values and attitudes.[66]

There are many benefits of having a formal succession planning system. In a survey of Fortune 500 firms, succession planning programs were perceived to have a positive impact on an organization's profitability, organizational culture, and organizational efficiency. Some general benefits of a succession planning program are illustrated in Figure 8.8.

Regardless of what type of succession planning program is used (formal or informal), most successful programs obtain the support and commitment of top man-

FIGURE 8.8
BENEFITS OF FORMAL SUCCESSION PLANNING

- Provides a specific connection to business and strategic planning.
- Provides a more systematic basis to judge the risks of making particular succession and development moves.
- Assists in developing systematized succession plans that fit with a distinct trend to codify, wherever possible, more general and comprehensive corporate planning actions.
- Reduces randomness of managerial development movements.
- Helps to anticipate problems before they get started—and thereby avoids awkward or dysfunctional situations.
- Increases managerial depth, which can be called on as needed.
- Provides a logical approach for locking succession planning into the process of human resource planning—connecting formats (data, timing) with process (judgments, discussions, analyses).
- Facilitates integration of the many components of human resource planning after having done many of these separately in the past.
- Improves the identification of high-potential and future leaders.
- Exploits the use of computer power or capabilities to improve succession planning formats and processes further.
- Broadens the use of cross-functional development techniques to improve competencies and quality of decision making.
- Stimulates inquiry into the fit of succession planning with the philosophy of the organization.
- Improves internal promotion opportunities.
- Overcomes the limitations of reactive management approaches and goes to planned management of managerial positions.
- Establishes a logical basis for choices among qualified candidates.
- Improves fulfillment of EEO objectives.
- Makes informal but critical criteria (e.g., "fit") more explicit.

Source: E. H. Burack, *Creative human resource planning and applications: A strategic approach.* Englewood Cliffs, NJ: Prentice Hall, 1988, p. 167. Used with permission.

agers. Usually, committees of top managers work together to identify high-potential candidates and then outline developmental activities for them.[67] They may also include a formal assessment of the performance and potential of candidates and written individual developmental plans for candidates.[68] Of course, with the current turbulent times in organizations (i.e., with downsizings, layoffs, mergers), some argue that it is foolish to spend a lot of time on succession planning efforts or identifying candidates for jobs that may not even exist in the future. In addition, the firm's strategic goals may change, making some candidates, previously groomed for top positions, no longer the right choice.[69] It is clear that each organization has to weigh the pros and cons of providing a succession planning system. In general, in most organizations, a succession planning system seems to be highly beneficial.

Developmental Programs

Developmental programs consist of skills assessment and training programs that organizations may use to develop their employees for future positions. Development programs can be internal and run by the human resource staff or be offered externally in the form of seminars and workshops. DuPont offers in-house seminars on various job functions and hands out a list of employee contacts that individuals can use to find out more about various job functions.[70] Other corporations have three- to four-year training programs at lower levels to groom employees for subsequent managerial positions.[71] One survey of 12 leading companies found that they agreed on the criteria for a successful executive development process: (1) extensive CEO involvement, (2) a clearly stated development policy, (3) CEO development linked to the business strategy, (4) an annual succession planning process and on-the-job developmental assignments, and (5) line management responsibility for the program.[72]

Some commonly used programs for development include assessment centers, job rotation programs, in-house training programs, and tuition-refund or assistance plans. Xerox and 3M use many of these programs to develop their employees.[73] In some cases, organizations (e.g., Pacific Bell) provide college credit to an employee when he or she has completed courses offered by the firm (e.g., training or human resource courses).[74] Assessment centers are useful for helping employees better understand their strengths and weaknesses for managerial jobs, although they can be expensive, with costs ranging from $125 to over $3,000 per candidate. Some research indicates that their effectiveness as interventions is limited.[75] Many companies use job rotation programs that enable employees to develop a broader base of skills (cross-functional training) as part of the managerial training program. Apple Computer lets people sample jobs by filling in for employees who are on sabbaticals.[76]

Some firms, such as Xerox, American Express, and Wells Fargo & Co., use sabbaticals to enable employees to get paid while working for charitable organizations. In this way, employees come back to their jobs refreshed and possessing new skills. Most Fortune 500 companies cover expenses for job-related and career-oriented courses taken at colleges. They also offer internal programs on a variety of topics including technical training and interpersonal skills.

MENTORING. Another developmental program gaining in popularity is mentoring.[77] Mentoring consists of establishing formal relationships between junior and senior colleagues or peers that contribute to career functions (e.g., sponsorship, coaching, and protection of the colleague, exposure to important contacts and resources, assignment of challenging work) and to psychosocial functions (e.g., role modeling, counseling, acceptance and confirmation of the colleague, friendship).[78] Having a mentor is an important aid in the development of an employee and may also be valuable for improving the job involvement and satisfaction of the mentor.[79] Some of the companies with formal mentoring programs include Federal Express, Merrill Lynch, and The Jewel Companies.[80] Bank of America's program uses "quad squads" that consist of a mentor and three new hires (a male, female, and a racial minority group member). Coopers & Lybrand has a program called the C&L 100 mentoring initiative where each one of the hundred top partners has assumed personal responsibility as a mentor for one female or minority manager. The goal is to retain the managers and to help them achieve partnership status.[81]

Formal mentoring systems are still new. Large law firms and consulting firms are not as effective at mentoring and often don't even designate a partner to help new associates prioritize the work heaped on them by several partners.

CAREER PROGRAMS FOR SPECIAL GROUPS

Career development programs are often instituted to meet the unique needs of particular employees. Although many different groups and issues may be targeted for career development, some of the more common programs are those that focus on work–family issues, outplacement, entrenched employees, late-career employees and preretirement, disadvantaged employees, fast-track employees, and supervisors.

Work–Family Programs

In recent years, organizations have been much more interested in developing family-responsive policies. Even presidential administrations have joined the push for family-friendly practices. For example, in 1996, the White House sponsored the first conference on corporate citizenship. One conference goal was to showcase companies that, as President Clinton noted, "do the right thing" by their employees, by offering benefits such as on-site child care, flexible work hours, and parental leave.[82] A month later, Vice President Al Gore led another conference to examine how work and family lives affect each other. By the end of 1996, several organizational trends in these practices were noted:[83]

- Increasing use of flexible work schedules and training for managers in implementing the schedules.
- More openings of on-site child care centers.
- A greater number of companies (e.g., Xerox, Motorola) setting aside monies that employees can use for paying child care costs or buying a first home.
- Greater use of paid leaves for fathers and adoptive parents.
- More programs that set goals for advancing women into senior management positions, and increasing number of companies holding managers accountable for meeting these goals.
- Continued support and funding for American Business Collaboration for Quality Dependent Care, which is a $100 million, six-year commitment that participating companies have made to improve and expand child and elder care in their communities.

As noted, society has seen increasing numbers of working mothers and two-income households. For example, in 1993, it was reported that 67 percent of mothers with preschool aged children were employed at some time during the year.[84] With the passage in 1993 of the Family and Medical Leave Act, employers with more than 50 employees are required to allow 12 weeks of unpaid leave from work for either parent following the birth, adoption, or severe illness of a child.

Despite these advances, some unresolved issues and obstacles facing pregnant employees still exist. With pressures at work, they may be rushed by their bosses through maternity leave or denied comparable jobs or promotions when they return to their jobs. Job pressures also bear great risks for pregnant women. One study found that women lawyers who worked more than 45 hours a week were three times more likely to experience a miscarriage in the first trimester of pregnancy than were women who worked less than 35 hours a week. Pregnant employees may also face stereotypes from their colleagues who believe they will lose interest in their jobs or quit. But a study of 140 bank employees found that their performance actually increased during pregnancy. In addition, it has been noted that 80 percent of women return to work after maternity leave. Cigna HealthCare in Hartford, Connecticut, developed a train-

ing program to debunk stereotypes about pregnant women and to help managers be supportive in dealing with pregnant employees. A few tips from the program follow:[85]

- Discuss and reach agreement with a pregnant employee on how her work will be covered during her leave.
- Discuss with co-workers worries they have about covering for a woman on leave. Make sure the work is distributed fairly.
- Be patient with new mothers' efforts to balance their expanded responsibilities.
- Weigh short-term scheduling hassles against the long-term benefits of retaining an employee.

In recent years, organizations have become more interested in helping individuals face demands from their work and family roles. Employers are beginning to realize that these individuals may experience role conflict and difficulties dealing with travel, child care, household tasks, job transfers, and relocations, and they may have trouble determining priorities for their various roles and responsibilities.[86] This may be especially true for dual-career couples since each partner has a high level of commitment to his or her career. In fact, it was recently reported that couples before having children and couples without children reported having the happiest marriages.[87] Couples with children reported the least contentment when their children were teenagers.

Family-responsive HR policies adopted by organizations may include: flexible work scheduling (part-time work, job sharing, and variable starting and quitting times), family-leave policies allowing periods away from work for employees to take care of family matters, and child care assistance (e.g., referral service, on-site or off-site day care centers).[88] In addition, some companies (e.g., Ford Motor Company) have full-time work–family managers to help employees with these issues.[89] Some of the most common policies are described below.

RELOCATION ASSISTANCE AND HIRING PRACTICES. Many employees, particularly members of dual-career couples, have expressed less willingness to accept relocation offers from their employers. In a large-scale study of U.S. firms, spouse willingness to relocate was shown to be the most important factor related to employee willingness to relocate.[90] It is not surprising then that some organizations have begun offering relocation assistance to the spouses of their employees.[91] Companies, however, vary in the amount and type of assistance provided to spouses and employees considering relocations. It ranges from no assistance to locating jobs for spouses. One study found that 50 percent of U.S. firms provide job-related assistance to a "trailing spouse." For example, Unisys pays up to $500 to a spouse to help with résumé writing and job hunting.[92] Johnson & Johnson offers personal counseling and job search information to relocating families. Compaq Computer Corporation has a relocation resource center with information for employees to assist their trailing spouses.[93]

Some firms have altered their policy on nepotism to allow hiring both spouses. They may still, however, keep the rule that an employee cannot work under the direct supervision of his or her spouse. The benefits of hiring both spouses include lower recruiting and relocation costs for the employer, and it encourages employees to remain with the firm or to accept intraorganizational moves or transfers. It also helps employers who are trying to hire for branches in a remote geographical area. Of course, one downside is that if one spouse wants to leave the firm, the other may also leave.

WORK–FAMILY SEMINARS AND FLEXIBLE HR PRACTICES. Organizations are becoming more involved in designing programs to help employees manage their work–family role conflict by providing a place and procedure for discussing conflicts and coping strategies. Organizations are also changing their practices for recruitment, travel, transfers, promotions, scheduling hours, and benefits to meet the needs of the larger numbers of dual-career couples. For example, General Electric and Procter & Gamble require fewer geographic moves in order to advance.[94]

DuPont has been very active in providing assistance to its more than 3,500 dual-career couples and has developed more flexible employment plans to accommodate the family demands of both male and female employees. DuPont also trains its supervisors to be more sensitive to family issues, allows longer parental leave for fathers and mothers, and has instituted adjustable work schedules. Mobil Oil provides flexible work schedules, a proposed part-time option, childbirth and other leaves, and a national network of child care information.

FLEXIBLE WORK SCHEDULES. Employers have been adopting a number of flexible work arrangements. These include flextime, job sharing, part-time work, compressed workweeks, temporary work, and work at home (telecommuting). These programs enable employees to address their work and family concerns and reduce their potential stress or conflict between their various life roles. Of the 100 companies rated the best for working mothers, 54 have established training programs to educate managers on how to implement alternative work arrangements. Some of these companies include Aetna, TRW, Texas Instruments, SAS Institute, Sara Lee Corporation, and Prudential.[95]

McDonald's tries to recruit part-time employees, including women with young children and retirees. On the job application form it notes that McDonald's is an ideal employer for people who want flexible hours in order to spend more time with their children or their leisure pursuits.[96] Andersen Consulting has instituted a "7 to 7" travel policy, which stipulates that no one has to leave home before 7 A.M. Monday and everyone is encouraged to return home by 7 P.M. Friday.[97] In 1993, First Tennessee Bank enabled workers to establish flexible schedules, allowed full-time workers to switch to part-time status without giving up benefits, and offered mandatory training in work–family conflict resolution for managers. Productivity surged, as did customer satisfaction. The bank saved more than $3 million in turnover costs alone. Total savings in replacements costs were $5,000 to $10,000 for each nonmanagerial employee and $30,000 to $50,000 for each executive. In addition, performance ratings for managers have increased and the bank has one of the highest customer retention rates of any U.S. bank.[98] Procter & Gamble reduced its workweek for employees, without forfeiting their benefits, to care for a young child. More popular now (e.g., Price Waterhouse LLP, Amoco, Dow Chemical, TRW, Patagonia) are compressed workweeks, which call for 80 hours of work over nine days, allowing for a long weekend every other week. Job sharing has also gained in popularity among firms such as Lotus Development Corporation, Life Technologies, KPMG Peat Marwick LLP, Lancaster Laboratories, Glaxo Wellcome, and John Hancock Financial Service. Quaker Oats has experimented with having "part-time brand managers" so the manager can better balance his or her work–family issues (e.g., caring for a new child at home). Hemmings Motor News, an old-car magazine publisher, offers flexible scheduling, dependent care assistance, and benefits for part-time employees.

Telecommuting has become very popular. An estimated 9 million U.S. workers are telecommuters. In fact, at least two-thirds of Fortune 500 companies currently employ telecommuters.[99] Home-based work is used primarily by firms in industries such as education, professional work, business, repair, and social-service occupations. Gandalf Technologies, a computer networking company, allows employees to telecommute from home several days a week. AT&T lets many of its employees telecommute at least part of the week from home via computer. Some difficulties with telecommuting are communication problems with other employees, limited access to necessary supplies and equipment, and family interruptions. In come cases (e.g., Hewlett-Packard) employees have to purchase their own computers and fax machines. Some companies explicitly state they do not want managers telecommuting. Travelers Insurance Company encourages telecommuting in jobs where the need to manage is minimal.[100]

There are a number of benefits to telecommuting. For instance, IBM has saved considerable money on office space by going mobile through telecommuting, "hoteling" (being assigned to a desk via a reservations system), and "hot desking" (several people using the same desk at different times). About 10,000 employees share offices with four people on average. Many studies show that people's strategic planning skills go up when they telecommute because they have uninterrupted time to think clearly. It has been estimated that people who work at home are 5 percent to 20 percent more productive because they have fewer distractions. It may be important to provide orientation or training to educate employees and managers on the rules of telecommuting. Travelers Insurance Company gives orientation programs for telecommuters, their managers, and their nontelecommuting coworkers.

CHILD AND ELDER CARE. Today, employees must concern themselves with child care while they are at work. In addition, many are discovering that they need to care for their parents or older members of their families. Elder care may be of great concern to employees, particularly if their parents suffer from health problems (e.g., Alzheimer's disease, heart conditions, depression). Firms providing elder care as a benefit to employees include Gannett Co., First Union Corporation, General Motors Corporation, Eddie Bauer, The Dupont Merck Pharmaceutical Company, Corning, and Deloitte & Touche LLP.[101]

Child care assistance is still not prevalent despite the increased need. As of 1993, one survey noted that only 7 percent of U.S. workplaces with 50 or more employees provided on- or near-site child care.[102] In 1995, another survey indicated that 40 percent of large employers offered child care resource and referral programs. seventy-seven percent of them also provided information on elder care.[103] The rates of child care services are much higher for more progressive companies. Of the 100 best companies for working mothers rated in 1996, 75 percent of them support at least one on- or near-site child care center. In addition, at least 12 of the top 100 companies had three centers (Allstate Insurance, Barnett Banks, Motorola, Johnson & Johnson, MBNA America Bank, N.A.).[104]

By 1996, more companies were offering financial aid for adoption. Two-thirds of the top rated 100 companies for working mothers provided this benefit (e.g., Eli Lilly offers up to $10,000). In addition, 23 of the top 100 companies offered paternity leave for fathers, including firms such as Calvert Group, BE&K, Ben & Jerry's Homemade, MBNA America Bank, and NationsBank Corporation. Some companies provide support for infertility treatments to employees.[105]

Employers who do provide some type of child care assistance either offer information to employees about the available assistance, provide financial assistance at nearby centers, or provide actual on- or near-site facilities. Ridgeview Hosiery, a sock and hosiery maker in

North Carolina, offers subsidized on-site day care and brings school counselors into the plant every two months to talk to parents on company time.[106] Generally, employers find it beneficial to provide child care assistance to employees. They may find greater morale, easier recruitment of parents, lower turnover, and tax savings.[107]

By assisting employees with child care or elder care concerns, these employees did not have to use company time to make phone calls, visit doctors, and so on. DuPont reported savings of $6.78 for every dollar spent on resource and referral, and Aetna reported $3.59 in savings per dollar spent.[108] Marriott reported savings in reduced turnover with its "Associate Resource Line," a toll-free hot line with bilingual social workers who provide advice on child care and elder care issues among other things. Marriott estimates that since 1994, for every dollar spent it has saved $5 through reduced turnover, absenteeism, and lateness. Lancaster Laboratories in Pennsylvania opened a child care center in 1986 and found that the organization saves at least twice as much as the $50,000 it spends annually on the center because women are more likely to return to work after childbirth, thereby reducing replacements costs for employees. Lost Arrow, a clothing firm in Ventura, California, spent $360,000 in 1995 to operate its on-site child care center, and it received savings of $660,000 in reduced turnover, federal income taxes, state tax credit, and state income taxes for operating the center.[109]

Some employers (e.g., Bankers Trust New York Corporation, Merrill Lynch & Co.) have opened backup centers to help employees who run into problems with their child care arrangements.[110] First Tennessee Bank opened a center for mildly sick children to cut down on employee absences when parents had to stay home with sick children. The center has saved the company considerable money.

Other companies have sponsored public schools at their work sites. American Bankers Insurance Group spent $2.4 million to build a satellite public school on its 84-acre corporate campus. The company paid $146,000 in 1996 toward the school's operation. Currently, 225 children of American Bankers employees attend the school. Parents can visit their children at lunchtime and after school. The company believes it has seen some payback; the turnover rate has been reduced from 13 percent to 5 percent for employees with children in the school.[111]

OTHER SERVICES. Today, companies have implemented a number of new programs or policies to help their employees better manage their time and deal with pressing demands from their work and personal lives. For example, Andersen Consulting in Chicago offers an on-site concierge service. Employees can use the service for picking up laundry, house sitting, making dinner reservations, sending someone to pick up the car at the shop, and so on.[112] Wilton Connor Packaging in Charlotte, North Carolina, enables employees to take their laundry to work and have it washed, dried, and folded courtesy of the company. It also has a handyman on staff who does free minor household repairs for employees while they are at work (e.g., fixing plumbing). Wilton Connor has reported virtually no turnover or quality problems with employees and few supervisors. Similarly, PepsiCo offers its 700 employees in its Purchase, New York headquarters an on-site dry cleaning drop-off as well as financial counseling for $20 per month.

EFFECTIVENESS OF PROGRAMS. Businesses that offer flexible schedules, part-time or alternative work options, work–family conflict seminars, and telecommuting are not just being nice to their employees. These programs have an impact on the bottom line. They have been shown to increase employees' loyalty, thereby reducing turnover and absenteeism and increasing organizational productivity.[113] A 1987 survey of 2,376 pregnant women in 80 communities across the United States found that those in the most accommodating companies in terms of health insurance, sick days, job-protected leave, flexible scheduling, and supervisor understanding were more satisfied with their jobs, took fewer sick days, worked more on their own time, worked later into their pregnancies, and were more likely to return to work.[114] Similarly, a 1991 survey of 745 randomly selected employees in the United States found that family-responsive HR policies such as parental leave, flexible schedules, and child care assistance were related to greater organizational commitment by employees and a lower intention to leave their jobs, regardless of the extent to which the employees might personally benefit from the policies.

A 1994 survey of 75 large corporations found that 20 percent formally evaluated the savings from their programs. They reported increased commitment to the job, higher morale, higher productivity, superior job performance, and reduced absenteeism.[115] Interestingly, programs such as flextime, job sharing, and part-time work seem to be the most effective and least costly in terms of keeping employees and increasing productivity. NationsBank of Charlotte, North Carolina, introduced a child care subsidy for lower-income workers in 1989 and found that absenteeism and turnover were lowered. Neuville Industries, a 575-employee sock manufacturer in North Carolina, found that with its work–family programs (on-site day care center, flextime, emergency backup child care) turnover was half (45 percent a year) the industry average (80 to 100 percent at other plants). At Aetna Health Plans, telecommuting has increased productivity of claims processed by 29 percent. The firm is also saving $12,000 per year in office space. Deloitte & Touche, one of the large accounting firms, allowed re-

duced hours for partners and the opportunity for employees to be made partner while working part time, and this has decreased turnover 8 percent between 1993 and 1995. Also, more women were made partners. In 1995, 21 percent of the women were admitted to partners, up from the 8 percent reported in 1991. Organizations have learned, however, that it isn't enough to have work–family programs in place. Managers must also be supportive. For example, Johnson & Johnson found that employees who had supportive bosses had stronger feelings toward the company than those who had only used specific work–family programs.[116]

Outplacement Programs

Downsizing has become the norm in corporate America and in the federal government.[117] One half of U.S. business organizations eliminated jobs in 1995, displacing 415,000 employees. One survey noted that over 40 percent of the managerial labor force is extremely concerned about work security.[118] As employers continue to downsize and reduce their workforces, they have attempted to assist affected employees.[119] Outplacement programs have been instituted to assist terminated employees, particularly those laid off by reduction-in-force efforts (RIFs), in making the transition to new employment. Generally, outplacement programs involve individual counseling sessions with external or internal counselors where individuals are able to share their feelings about being let go. The programs may also contain financial counseling. In addition, workshops may be used to show individuals how to become successful job seekers by teaching them how to identify their skills and abilities, develop résumés, and interview with prospective employers. For example, when Tennessee Valley Authority had to reduce its workforce, the HR department provided counseling and helped former employees find jobs with other firms. Similarly, General Motors, AT&T, and Boeing used a variety of activities including workshops, skills assessments, practice in interviewing and networking, and seminars on financial planning, stress management, and managing layoffs.[120]

Outplacement programs stressing the importance of self-confidence and individual career planning may be particularly beneficial for middle or late-career employees who have been laid off. This is because many older people are forced into involuntary retirement, often with insufficient skills and financial assets.[121] The programs should help laid-off employees deal with their anger, depression, stress, grief, or loss of self-esteem associated with the job loss. Many terminated employees suffer changes in their mental health. The programs should also encourage them to develop support networks.[122] If an organization is going to use downsizing to reduce employee numbers, the following recommendations can make it less traumatic and more fair:[123]

- Be fair in implementing layoffs; spread them throughout the organizational ranks, not just among lower-level employees.
- Allow employees to leave with dignity; if possible, allow them to leave of their own accord.
- Help those displaced find new jobs.
- Avoid belittling laid-off employees.
- Be cautious when hiring outside executives; educate them on the internal morale.
- Keep employees informed about the company's goals and expectations.
- Set realistic expectations.
- Use ceremonies to reduce anger and confusion and convey to employees what is going on.

Outplacement programs have been shown to benefit employees by helping them cope with the shock and stress associated with losing a job and by helping them find jobs faster than they could on their own. This may also lower the likelihood that they will sue the firm for laying them off.[124] In addition, a firm that offers outplacement programs may be viewed more positively by the "survivors," which could help improve their morale and reduce fears of job insecurity.

In some cases (e.g., Motorola), employees have been given the option of "job sharing" or reduced workweeks. This enables employees to keep their jobs, although with fewer hours and less pay. The organization also benefits because it reduces labor costs and overtime as well as retains valuable expertise and knowledge about the company. AT&T developed an innovative program, called Resource Link, that consists of an internal contingent of displaced managers and professionals who can be assigned to temporary projects of 3 to 12 months' duration. This gives project managers the assistance they need without hiring permanent staff. The program has been so popular that some employees have volunteered to be assigned to the unit to gain exposure to different parts of the business.[125] Chevron Corporation used severance packages and outplacement programs even though it was not undergoing a downsizing. The company moved employees around from one unit to another to provide them with a variety of marketable skills.[126]

It is also important to provide some assistance to survivors. Their attitudes will be influenced by how fairly they thought the layoffs were done. Often the morale of those remaining hits an all-time low, confidence is shaken, and communication and trust are fragmented. In addition, in many cases, survivors will have increased workloads and job responsibilities due to the loss of personnel. They may experience work overload and stress and could benefit from counseling and realistic information about the firm's future and their future role with the company.[127] It is critical that a firm address the needs of the remaining employees if it is to be competitive.

A number of recommendations have been offered for fostering the successful redeployment of displaced workers due to restructurings and downsizings. Figure 8.9 lists some of these suggestions.

FIGURE 8.9
ROLES FOR EXECUTIVES AND MANAGERS TO FOSTER THE SUCCESSFUL REDEPLOYMENT OF DISPLACED WORKERS

To Build Career Resilience
- Enhance and maintain value of current employees (continuous learning environment)
- Foster a culture of entrepreneurship internal to the organization by rewarding creative new ideas and self-management
- Assign people to teams and work processes rather than to single, unifunctional jobs
- Adopt continuous improvement programs based on employee participation
- Partner with regional universities and colleges and government and community agencies to develop support systems for displaced workers
- Train people in areas that create or add value through problem solving and support
- Form new initiatives and joint ventures

To Build Career Insight
- Offer assessment and feedback processes to help people better understand their strengths and weaknesses
- Provide problem-focused (in addition to symptom-focused) training to teach the unemployed job search skills, entrepreneurship, and realistic expectations
- Conduct human resource forecasting to inform and direct organizational initiatives. This entails conducting job analyses for positions that do not yet exist and communicating the results as input to individual and organizational planning. Moreover, scenarios of likely environmental trends and organizational strategies can be constructed as ways to envision different sorts of change and its implications
- Assist federal and state programs for reemployment and coping that recognize individual (e.g., age, profession, malleability) and regional economic factors

To Build Career Identity
- Fund and implement outside redeployment efforts stemming from restructuring (outplacement)
- Support the professional development of all functional specialities; develop job families and career paths within speciality areas
- Train employees in multiple skills and use these different skills in role assignments
- Join with other organizations and agencies in the community to create new economic opportunities (e.g., participate in job fairs)

Source: M. London, Redeployment and continuous learning in the 21st century: Hard lessons and positive examples from the downsizing era. *Academy of Management Executive, 10*(4), 1996, p. 76.

Entrenched Employees

Because of the large number of organizational restructurings and downsizings, many employees stay with their organizations to keep their jobs, but they do not stay as committed or attached to them as their employers would like. In fact, Gallup reported that one of every three workers would choose a different career if given the chance to start over. These employees have become entrenched in their careers. They stay in the job because of their investments, psychological preservation, and a perception that there are few career opportunities. To eliminate the potentially adverse consequences of entrenchment, organizations can take some of the following steps:[128]

- Offer generous severance pay packages to fund employees' explorations into new careers.
- Encourage portability of benefits such as pension funds, accrued time-off.
- Provide ongoing career counseling and outplacement assistance to attend classes while still employed.
- Offer tuition reimbursement and time off for employees to attend classes.
- Implement staged retirement programs.
- Give employees time to rotate to other positions in the organization to explore other career options.
- Allow employees to phase out jobs and not automatically eliminate them.
- Emphasize the importance of learning and development throughout the organization.
- Encourage employees to think about career planning issues.
- Extend portability of medical coverage and other insurances for 18 to 24 months.

Late-Career Employee Programs and Preretirement Workshops

In recent years, the number of older workers has increased because of the aging of the baby-boom generation. By the year 2000, over 22 percent of the U.S. population will be over 65 years of age. With the increasing corporate restructurings, many of these older employees have lost their jobs. Generally, firms have opted to use early retirement for their older employees rather than retraining and redeploying them. And more employees have been choosing early retirement. As a result, late-career and retirement issues have become increasingly important to organizations.[129]

Some organizations offer programs to help supervisors increase their awareness of issues facing late-career employees. It is critical that employers handle retirement issues effectively because they affect not only the retirees but also the morale of the remaining staff. Generally, supervisors are instructed on the changing demographics of the workforce, laws regarding older employees, stereotypes and realities of the aging process, and strategies for dealing with the loss of older employees who retire (i.e., the loss in their departments of expertise and skills). Supervisors may also be taught to develop action plans for enhancing the performance of their older workers. These plans may consist of giving older workers more concrete feedback, allowing them to serve as mentors, and providing them with training and cross-training opportunities. It is also important that managers help their older employees make the transition into retirement. Many companies have instituted retirement planning programs.[130]

The focus of preretirement workshops is to help preretirees understand the life and career concerns they may face as they prepare for retirement. Topics that may be discussed include health, finances, making the transition from work to retirement status, safety, housing and location, legal affairs, time utilization, Social Security, second careers, use of leisure time, and problems of aging. Often, individual counseling and group workshops are used, and efforts are made to tailor the programs to the needs of the participants and their spouses. Another type of assistance given to preretirees may be for education, such as the Retirement Education Assistance Plan available to potential retirees at IBM.

It is also important to offer flexible work schedules for late-career employees. Some do not want to quit their jobs, but want to cut back the number of hours they work so they can enjoy their hobbies, go back to school, or spend more time with their families. Polaroid gave its older employees the option to share jobs rather than be laid off. Many companies, such as McDonald's, Home Shopping Network, Aetna, Prudential, GEICO, and Monsanto, have hired older employees to work part time or for temporary jobs. This has been beneficial since there are fewer young people to employ in many part-time jobs. In fact, in a 1992 study by the Society for Human Resource Management, over 80 percent of firms that aggressively recruited and hired older employees found them to be more amenable than younger individuals for working part time.[131] As employees continue to age, it will be imperative for organizations in the United States and in other parts of the world to make good use of the expertise and talent residing in their older employees if they are to remain competitive.

Special Programs for Women, Minorities, and Employees with Disabilities

With the increasing number of women and minorities and people with disabilities entering the workplace, employers have recognized the importance of assisting these employees with their career needs.[132] In addition, to adhere to EEO or affirmative action guidelines, some organizations are supporting minority recruitment, selection, and training efforts. They are also beginning to provide additional feedback, educational opportunities, counseling, and career management seminars to meet the unique needs of these groups. These practices are designed to help these employees compete for management positions.[133] For example, top managers at Xerox encourage the development of networks and support groups for women and minority groups (e.g., African-Americans, Hispanics). Avon, unlike the majority of *Fortune* 500 companies, has no glass ceiling because women are groomed for top jobs. Four of the top eight officers are women and 4 of the 11-member board are women. In addition, more than 40 percent of its global managers are women.[134]

Some firms (e.g., Corning, Merck, Texaco, Gannett Company) tie managers' bonuses to their success at meeting EEO or upward mobility goals for women's progress.[135] Similarly, Tenneco established a women's advisory council to help identify the barriers that keep women from advancing into management. As a result, more women were able to move in to Tenneco's upper management. Other companies, including Dow Chemical, Honeywell, and Polaroid, have also solicited assistance and advice from women's groups in the recruitment, mentoring, and advancement of women.[136] Catalyst is an organization designed to enable women in business and professions to achieve their maximum potential and to help employers capitalize on the talents of their female employees.[137]

Some firms have focused on trying to retain their female employees. Some have tried to do this by showing a commitment to the health of their female employees. In 1996, *Working Woman* magazine rated the 10 healthiest companies for women—Fannie Mae, First Chicago, Merck & Co., Pacific Bell, Southern California Edison, Unum America, Ben & Jerry's, Champion International, Wells Fargo, and Marriott International headquarters. Practices they have implemented include increasing insurance coverage to help women affected by depression and by providing employee assistance services; prenatal services; health resource centers; work-exercise programs; in vitro treatments; screenings for blood pressure, cholesterol, breast cancer, and osteoporosis; medical libraries; stress prevention programs; and counseling. The companies have lowered their insurance costs because they prevented more serious illnesses from developing.[138]

DIVERSITY AWARENESS PROGRAMS. At Merck and Mead Corporation, male executives participate in workshops designed to change their attitudes toward women and to sensitize supervisors to the need for balancing work and family. Some firms have developed programs to help break the glass ceiling. When Texaco settled a race discrimination lawsuit, it agreed to put its 29,000 employees through a two-day workshop on race, gender, and culture. Texaco has tripled the number of workshops it offered each month and hired an additional 27 consultants. The workshops focus on four broad areas: creating a diverse workforce, managing a diverse workforce, creating an environment that values a diverse workforce, and leveraging diversity into a competitive business advantage.[139] AT&T boasts one of the nation's most progressive diversity programs.[140] Chase offers a comprehensive diversity program for all its employees that includes awareness training and skill building. Similarly, Mobil has a training program, called Internal Resource Education, that is an intense team-based course conducted in three one-week segments.

Diversity awareness programs seem to be particularly needed because the progress of women and minorities into upper management has been slow.[141] U.S. West, for example, found that 1 in 21 white males reached middle management or higher positions at the Denver-based communications company, but only 1 in 138 white women and 1 in 289 nonwhite women attained this status. The company started a leadership development program for women. Over one-half of the female participants were ultimately promoted. Likewise, Fannie Mae's training and development programs to support the professional development of its employees resulted in an upper management that is now over 50 percent women and minority.[142]

Diversity programs must start at the top with the support of top management. American Express formed a high-level diversity council to guide and drive the company's diversity efforts. Likewise, at Hewlett-Packard, the diversity initiatives are driven by the Diversity Leadership Council, which is comprised of senior executives. The chair, president, and CEO of Chrysler Corporation, Robert J. Eaton, signed a statement detailing the company's two diversity goals: (1) to assure that Chrysler's workforce is reflective of the global communities it serves, and (2) to create a culture that uses diversity to its competitive advantage. The chair and CEO of Coopers & Lybrand, Nicholas Moore, chaired its Diversity Advisory Group, stating that "attracting and retaining the highest intellectual capital are critical objectives of C&L."

To assist in the placement and advancement of employees with disabilities, the EEOC has written material and a video on hiring and developing individuals with disabilities. In recent years, researchers have offered suggestions for assisting employees with disabilities to become more effectively socialized in organizations.[143] Some firms (e.g., Xerox, American Express, Disney) have begun offering diversity training programs to reduce discrimination due to disability, race, gender, and age. The intent is to teach employees, particularly managers, to value diversity. One factor shown to be highly related to the adoption and perceived success of diversity training programs has been top management support.[144] In addition, whether or not a company adopts a diversity training program has been shown to be related to large organizational size, high strategic priority of diversity relative to other competing objectives, presence of a diversity manager, and the existence of a large number of other diversity-supportive policies. The perceived success of the diversity training programs were related to mandatory attendance for all managers, long-term evaluation of training results, managerial rewards for increasing diversity, and a broad definition of diversity in the organization.[145]

Fast-Track Employees

Organizations often identify "stars" or individuals with high career potential and place them on a fast track for upward moves in the company. AT&T, for example, uses assessment centers for the early identification of managerial talent. These specially recruited and selected employees are given rapid and intensive developmental opportunities in the company.[146] The identification and development of these employees requires organizations to exert extra recruitment efforts and to monitor career progress of these employees frequently. Organizations must provide considerable feedback, training, and counseling to these employees as well as offer quicker job changes and more challenging job assignments, particularly during the employees' first few years on the job. Southland Corporation, for example, has a computerized career development program for fast-track employees that helps them establish their career plans.[147]

Managers who are responsible for identifying and developing fast-track employees should be recognized for their efforts if they are to take their responsibilities seriously. For example, Baxter Health Care links managers' bonuses to the early identification and development of promising female employees. At Eli Lilly, managers assess their employees make decisions about their career potential and offer them opportunities for development. Similarly, Northern Telecom has a program that identifies fast trackers and helps them to develop a variety of skills that go beyond their own technical expertise.[148]

Supervisors

Supervisors serve four roles with their subordinates: coach, advisor, performance appraiser, and referral agent. As such, they should be taught how to help subordinates develop and implement their career plans in one-on-one counseling sessions and should be instructed on how to integrate counseling into their performance-appraisal and selection activities. AT&T has one such program in place for training supervisors in career counseling, performance-appraisal skills, and mutual goal setting with subordinates.

Career Development Issues with Teams

More and more U.S. firms are using teams as the unit of work.[149] Consequently, much discussion has centered on the human resource practices that are needed with teams (e.g., selection systems, training programs, performance-appraisal systems, rewards). Much less attention, however, has been devoted to the career development issues relevant to teams. Teams can, however, be quite important to the career development and progress of members. Members can serve as role models for one another and teach each other new skills and competencies. This would lead to greater staffing flexibility for the organization. Similarly, teams can identify training needs for members. For instance, at Cadillac, each plant and staff unit has a training needs analysis that specifies the KSAs needed to meet quality goals.[150] In addition, rotating assignments among members enables individuals to gain a diverse set of skills. Further, by evaluating team member performance, developmental plans can be established for each member. Teams can serve as a powerful way in which individuals enhance their career-related skills.

Repatriates*

As we discussed in Chapter 7, increasingly more organizations have been offering training for expatriates to prepare them for their overseas assignments. While this is important, it is also critical to offer developmental opportunities for repatriates to prepare them for their return back to the firm after an overseas assignment. While common in Japanese and European firms, this is often not done in most American firms. One survey revealed that only 31 percent of American companies reported any type of repatriation program for managers reentering the domestic organization.[151] This may explain why American managers who are repatriates have more difficulties adjusting than their Japanese and European counterparts.[152]

Often the difficulties associated with reentry are not anticipated by an employee, his or her family, or the organization. Most American repatriates experience considerable adjustment problems and "reentry shock" upon their return to their firm. They report having difficulty getting back to high levels of productivity. If they have been abroad for a long time, they may be technologically obsolete.[153] Problems often occur because the organization may simply be insensitive to the fact that the repatriate may need some assistance in readapting to work-related and nonwork-related routines.

Because the person is coming "home," issues such as reverse culture shock are often not addressed.[154] The foreign experience may have changed the employee's at-

---

*Contributed by Sabine Maetzke and Joyce E. A. Russell.

titudes and beliefs in a profound way. The changes may have occurred so subtly that the employee does not initially recognize these internal changes. Repatriates are often not given enough time to become reacclimated to life in the United States. Some experts state that it may take as long as 18 months for them to readjust.[155] Repatriates often report feeling disoriented with their communities and coworkers.

Also, they report frustration with their organizations' limited attempts to place them back in permanent assignments.[156] In fact, many of them complain that they are penalized for taking international assignments because they are placed in lower-level positions than their peers when they return. They may find that they have been passed over for promotion opportunities. In one survey of 56 U.S.-based multinational firms, 56 percent said a foreign assignment was detrimental or immaterial to one's career, 47 percent said the repatriates are not guaranteed jobs with the organization upon completion of the assignment, and 65 percent reported that the foreign assignment was not integrated into their overall career planning. In addition, only 20 percent considered the organization's repatriation policies adequate to meet the needs of the repatriates.[157] Further, most organizations do not fully utilize the new skills and experiences that repatriates bring back to their firms. Managers often are not sure how to establish career paths or ladders for those taking an international assignment.[158] As a result, many of the current international assignments are not being utilized as cost-effectively as they could be.

Repatriates often face problems within their companies as noted below:[159]

- Feeling out of place in the corporate culture of the home office.

- Receiving little, if any, guidance regarding the career opportunities available on their return.

- Being passed over for promotions that go to coworkers who did not go abroad.

- Receiving lower salaries than while they were on the international assignment.

- Not being able to effectively use the new skills that were acquired while abroad; not receiving support for using those skills.

- Not receiving recognition for the work that was completed during the international assignment.

- Losing the social status that was obtained while being a key employee at the foreign office.

It has been estimated that 10 to 25 percent of repatriates leave the company within one year of their return.[160] Many organizations find themselves losing valuable, highly skilled employees simply because the repatriation process was handled poorly.

For a repatriation program to be effective, it must be part of an overall organizational philosophy that values continued productive employment of international employees. The organization must be committed to addressing all phases of repatriation, beginning with a pretraining program to prepare employees before they leave on their assignments. The HR professional must be willing to take on the role of a "repatriation advocate" to help the company and the employees. The HR department can also keep records of the international assignments and reasons employees leave assignments early or leave the company early. In addition, many companies have set up permanent offices in other countries. Information should be collected that can address cultural, communication, and job-related issues faced by most employees in that region of the world. Linkages between the type of assignment held and the difficulties experienced with returning to the home office should be documented. By using this information, the HR department can more accurately determine the specific career needs of repatriates.

For a repatriate transition to be successful, several career development practices are recommended.[161] Once back to the firm, repatriates should be given opportunities to use the experiences and skills they gained from the international assignments. They should be given definite assignments, and these assignments should be clearly linked to their career paths. Mentors should be provided to repatriates to help them cope with their transition. If necessary, retraining and reorientation should be provided to help them learn of any new changes in their job, department, or the organization. Finally, assistance in housing and compensation should be provided to ease their transition. Taken together, these practices should reduce the amount of stress and disorientation experienced by repatriates as well as improve the quality and quantity of their performance. Additionally, repatriates may become more committed to the firm and opt to remain there.

SUMMARY

Career development programs must be integrated with and supported by the existing HR programs if they are to be successful. Career programs and HR programs are linked to the degree they help each other meet individual and organizational needs. While career development and HR planning systems are not identical, they are related to the degree that they use some of the same techniques to meet individuals' growth needs and organizations' staffing needs. The linkage with training and development programs is most critical.

Career development programs should be supported by other HR systems in addition to HR planning and training. For example, 3M has established a career resources department to better integrate its career programs, performance-appraisal process, and HR planning systems. Similarly, Boeing developed a program called CAREERS, which is linked with its other HR programs.[162] Individuals should refer to performance-appraisal information and illustrations of organizational career paths to help them in career planning. This information may help employees evaluate their strengths and weaknesses and set goals based on possible career alternatives. Supervisors should also be able to use performance-appraisal data to assist employees in developing realistic career plans. In Coca-Cola's career program, managers are given training to provide such guidance.[163] We will discuss the performance-appraisal process in the next chapter.

Career or job changes by employees should be based on an understanding of organizations' job descriptions, job posting systems, and selection policies. The continued development of employees and rewards for their performances should be founded on organizational training and development systems and compensation plans. Finally, organizational career information and planning systems should be developed to be consistent with the organization's strategic plans and existing forecasting systems, skills inventories, and succession plans.

Coordinated, integrated efforts of the HR staff, employees, managers, and organizations are the key to success in career development. Career development programs must be concerned with organizational and individual effectiveness over the short and long run. It is the responsibility of the HR staff to work with management to ensure that career programs are integrated with the HR functions and are routinely evaluated. It is, however, the responsibility of management to view career development as necessary to an effective HR system. Managers must be willing to work with HR professionals to formulate new strategies for career development and to provide support to them as they design and implement new career development programs.[164] Finally, it is the responsibility of the individual to create his or her own career opportunities. The following quote provides some advice for individuals as they attempt to navigate their way through their careers.

> Careers in today's world are what you make them. The apparent boundaries in a department are also your platforms for further opportunity. Organize your employment around your professional and social networks . . . Don't wait for formal training, but make sure the colleagues you surround yourself with sustain new learning for you, and try to reciprocate for them. Look after yourself, but don't be afraid to trust and to build trust around you. Remember that who you are and what you achieve will always be embedded in your relationships with others.[165]

DISCUSSION QUESTIONS

1. Can corporations afford to have formal career development policies and programs, given the need to be flexible in terms of staffing?

2. What is the role of EEO in career development? What should be the role of the HR staff in designing and implementing career development programs?

3. Recently, the role of managers has changed and today more are being called to be career "coaches" for their employees. What suggestions would you give to a manager about what that new role involves?

4. Describe several kinds of career development programs that are available for career planning and career management.

5. What is the value of self-assessment for individual career planning and organizational career management? Why should employees seek feedback from others regarding their job performance and career plans? How could performance-appraisal information (360-degree appraisal) be used to assist individuals in career development? (Refer to Chapter 9.)

6. Why is it important to integrate career development programs with other HR programs (e.g., performance appraisal, training, selection, compensation)? Offer some suggestions for how this can be done.

7. Should organizations make special efforts to deal with career–family issues through part-time work, job sharing, flextime, relocation assistance, and other programs?

8. With the increasing number of organizations experiencing downsizings and layoffs, it has become critical that they have career programs to assist outplaced employees. What suggestions would you offer for the types of assistance that are needed in outplacement programs?

NOTES

1. Hall, D. T. (1996). Protean careers of the 21st century. *Academy of Management Executive, 10*(4), 8–16; see also, Hall, D. T., and Mirvis, P. H. (1995). Careers as lifelong learning. In A. Howard (eds.), *The changing nature of work.* San Francisco: Jossey-Bass, pp. 323–361; Deigh, R.; Rachlin, J.; and Saltzman, A. (April 25, 1988). How to keep from getting mired. *U.S. News & World Report,* pp. 76–77, 79–80; Rachlin, J. (April 25, 1988). Best jobs for the future. *U.S. News & World Report,* pp. 60–62; London, M., and Stumpf, S. A. (1986). Individual and organizational career development in changing times. In D. T. Hall and associates (eds.), *Career development in organizations.* San Francisco: Jossey-Bass, pp. 21–49; London, M. (1994) (ed.). *Employees, careers, and job creation.* San Francisco: Jossey-Bass; and Cascio, W. F. (1995). Whither industrial and organizational psychology in a changing world of work? *American Psychologist, 50,* 928–939.

2. Osipow, S. H. (1986). Career issues through the life span. In M. S. Pallak and R. Perloff (eds.), *Psychology*

and work: Productivity, change, and employment. Washington, DC: American Psychological Association, pp. 137–168; see also, Dalton, G. W., and Thompson, P. H. (1985). *Novations: Strategies for career management.* Glenview, IL: Scott, Foresman; Mirabile, R. J. (1987). New directions for career development. *Training and Development Journal, 41*(12), 30–33; Fox, D. (March 1996). Career insurance for today's world. *Training & Development,* pp. 61–64; and O'Herron, P., and Simonsen, P. (May 1995). Career development gets a charge at Sears Credit. *Personnel Journal,* pp. 103–106.

3. Hall, D. T., and associates (eds.) (1996). *The career is dead—Long live the career.* San Francisco: Jossey-Bass, p. 1.

4. See note 1, Hall (1996). See also, Miles, R., and Snow, C. (1996). Twenty-first century careers. In M. Arthur and D. Rousseau (eds.), *The boundaryless career: A new employment principle for a new organizational era.* New York: Oxford University Press, pp. 261–307.

5. See note 3, Hall (1996), p. 5; see also, Allred, B. B.; Snow, C. C.; and Miles, R. E. (1996). Characteristics of managerial careers in the 21st century. *Academy of Management Executive, 10*(4), 17–27.

6. Waterman, R. H.; Waterman, J. A.; and Collard, B. A. (1994). Toward a career-resilient workforce. *Harvard Business Review, 72*(4), 87–95; see also, Arthur, M. B. (1994). The boundaryless career: A new perspective of organizational inquiry. *Journal of Organization Behavior, 15,* 295–309; Mirvis, P. H., and Hall, D. T. (1994). Psychological success and the boundaryless career. *Journal of Organization Behavior, 15,* 365–380; and Special Report, Managing your career. (Jan. 15, 1995). *Fortune,* 34–78.

7. Brousseau, K. R.; Driver, M. J.; Eneroth, K.; and Larsson, R. (1996). Career pandemonium: Realigning organizations and individuals. *Academy of Management Executive, 10*(4), 52–66; see also, Hall, D. T. (1987). Careers and socialization. *Journal of Management, 13,* 301–321; Slaney, R. B., and Russell, J. E. A. (1987). Perspectives on vocational behavior, 1986: A review. *Journal of Vocational Behavior, 31,* 111–173; Fierman, J. (September 1993). Beating the midlife crisis. *Fortune,* pp. 52–60; and Dennis, H., and Axel, H. (1991). *Encouraging employee self-management in financial and career planning.* New York: The Conference Board, Report No. 976.

8. See note 1, Hall (1996).

9. Leibowitz, Z. B., and Schlossberg, N. (1981). Designing career development programs in organizations. In D. H. Montross and C. J. Shinkman (eds.), *Career development in the 1980's: Theory and practice.* Springfield, IL: Charles C. Thomas, pp. 277–291. See also Brown, D., Brooks, L., and associates (1984). *Career choice and development: Applying contemporary theories to practice.* San Francisco: Jossey-Bass; Von Glinow, M. A.; Driver, M. J.; Brousseau, K.; and Prince, J. B. (1983). The design of a career oriented human resource system. *Academy of Management Journal, 8,* 23–32. Mirabile, R. J. (1988). Using action research to design career development programs. *Personnel, 65*(11), 4, 6, 10–11; Otte, F. L., and Hutcheson, P. G. (1992). *Helping employees manage careers.* Englewood Cliffs, NJ: Prentice Hall; Montgomery, C. E. (January 1996). Organizational fits is key to job success. *HR Magazine,* pp. 94–96; and Quinn, J. B.; Anderson, P.; and Finkelstein, S. (March–April 1996). Managing professional intellect: Making the most of the best. *Harvard Business Review,* pp. 71–80.

10. Walker, J. W., and Gutteridge, T. G. (1979). *Career planning practices: An AMA survey report.* New York: AMACOM.

11. See note 6, Waterman et al. (1994), p. 88.

12. *Linking career development with the new corporate agenda: Strategies for creating a career-resilient workforce* (February 1997). Conference sponsored by the National Career Development Association, Atlanta.

13. Hall, D. T. (1976). *Careers in organizations.* Glenview, IL: Scott, Foresman; see also, Arthur, M. B., and Rousseau, D. M. (1996). A career lexicon for the 21st century. *Academy of Management Executive, 10*(4), 28–39.

14. See note 7.

15. Hall, D. T. (1986). Dilemmas in linking succession planning to individual executive learning. *Human Resource Management, 25,* 235–265; see also, Carnazza, J. (1982). *Succession/replacement planning: Programs and practices.* New York: Center for Research in Career Development, Columbia University Graduate School of Business.

16. See note 15.

17. Leibowitz, Z. B.; Farren, C.; and Kaye, B. L. (1986). *Designing career development systems.* San Francisco: Jossey-Bass; see also, Farren, C., and Kaye, B. (1984). The principles of program design: A successful career development model. *Personnel Administrator, 29,* 109–118, and Granrose, C. S., and Portwood, J. D. (1987). Matching individual career plans and organizational career management. *Academy of Management Journal, 30,* 699–720.

18. Gutteridge, T. G., Leibowitz, Z. B., and Shore, J. E. (1993). *Organizational career development: Benchmarks for building a world-class workforce.* San Francisco: Jossey-Bass.

19. Pfeffer, J. (1994). *Competitive advantage through people.* Boston: Harvard Business School Press, p. 200; see also, Bolyard, C. W. (1981). Career development: Who's responsible in the organization. In D. H. Montross and C. J. Shinkman (eds.), *Career development in the 1980s: Theory and practice.* Springfield, IL: Charles C. Thomas, pp. 292–299, and Moses, B. M., and Chakins, B. J. (July 1989). The manager as career counselor. *Training and Development Journal,* 60–65.

20. Slavenski, L. (May 1987) Career development: A systems approach. *Training and Development Journal,* 56–60.

21. Pazy, A. (1987). Sex differences in responsiveness to organizational career management. *Human Resource Management, 26,* 243–256.

22. Byrne, J. A. (1993). Belt-tightening the smart way. *Business Week,* Special 1993 Bonus Issue: Enterprise, pp. 34–38.

23. See note 9, Leibowitz and Schlossberg (1981); see also, Feldman, D. C. (1988). *Managing careers in organizations.* Glenview, IL: Scott, Foresman.

24. Schein, E. H. (1978). *Career dynamics: Matching individual and organizational needs.* Reading, MA: Addison-Wesley.

25. Tichy, N.; Fombrun, C.; and Devanna, M. (1984). Strategic human resources management. In J. A. Sonnenfeld (ed.), *Managing career systems: Channeling the flow of executive careers.* Homewood, IL: Irwin, pp. 303–318.

26. Nicholson, N. (1996). Career systems in crisis: Change and opportunity in the information age. *Academy of Management Executive, 10*(4), 40–51.

27. Gooding, G. J. (1988). Career moves—for the employee, for the organization. *Personnel, 65*(4), 112, 114, 116.

28. London, M., and Mone, E. M. (1987). *Career management and survival in the workplace.* San Francisco: Jossey-Bass; see also, Derr, C. B. (1986). *Managing the new careerists.* San Francisco: Jossey-Bass.

29. See note 7, Brousseau et al. (1996); see also, Sellars, P. (Dec. 12, 1994). Don't call me a slacker. *Fortune,* pp. 181–196.

30. Minor, F. J. (1986). Computer applications in career development planning. In D. T. Hall and associates (eds.), *Career development in organizations.* San Francisco: Jossey-Bass, pp. 202–235.

31. Hall, D. T., and Goodale, J. G. (1986). *Human resource management: Strategy, design, and implementation.* Glenview, IL: Scott, Foresman; see also, note 3 and Souerwine, A. H. (1981). The manager as career counselor: Some issues and approaches. In D. H. Montross and C. J. Shinkman (eds.), *Career development in the 1980's: Theory and practice.* Springfield, IL: Charles C. Thomas, pp. 363–378.

32. See note 20.

33. Keller, J., and Piotrowski, C. (1987). Career development programs in Fortune 500 firms. *Psychological Reports, 61*(3), 920–922.

34. Bardsley, C. A. (1987). Improving employee awareness of opportunity at IBM. *Personnel, 64*(4), 58–63.

35. See note 23, Feldman (1988).

36. See note 17, Leibowitz, Farren, and Kaye (1986).

37. Russell, J. E. A. (1991). Career development interventions in organizations. *Journal of Vocational Behavior, 38,* 237–287; see also, Gutteridge, T. G. (1986). Organizational career development systems: The state of the practice. In D. T. Hall and associates (eds.) *Career development in organizations.* San Francisco, CA: Jossey-Bass, pp. 50–94, and Meier, S. T. (1991). Vocational behavior 1988–1990: Vocational choice, decision-making, career development interventions, and assessment. *Journal of Vocational Behavior, 39,* 131–181.

38. See note 6, Waterman et al.

39. Russell, J. E. A., and Curtis, L. B. (April 1993). *Career development practices and perceived effectiveness in Fortune 500 firms.* Paper presented at the annual meeting of the Society of Industrial & Organizational Psychology, San Francisco.

40. Gutteridge, T. G., and Otte, F. L. (1983). *Organizational career development: State of the practice.* Washington, DC: ASTD Press.

41. Martin, J. (Jan. 13, 1997). Job surfing: Move on to move. *Fortune,* pp. 50–54. See also, Greenhaus, J. H., and Callanan, G. A. (1994). Career management (2nd edition), New York: Dryden Press.

42. Wilhelm, W. R. (1983). Helping workers to self-manage their careers. *Personnel Administrator, 28*(8), 83–89.

43. Jackson, T., and Vitberg, A. (1987). Career development, part 2: Challenges for the organization. *Personnel, 64*(3), 68–72.

44. Curtis, L. B. (1996). *An examination of factors related to the effectiveness of a career development workshop.* Unpublished dissertation. Knoxville, TN: The University of Tennessee.

45. Dolan, K. A. (Nov. 18, 1996). When money isn't enough. *Forbes,* pp. 164–170.

46. See note 7, Brousseau et al. (1996).

47. Bolles, R. N. (1997). *What color is your parachute?* Berkeley, CA: Ten Speed Press.

48. Burack, E. H., and Mathys, N. J. (1980). *Career management in organizations: A practical human resource planning approach.* Lake Forest, IL: Brace-Park.

49. See note 37, Gutteridge (1986).

50. Waldroop, J., and Butler, T. (1996). The executive as coach. *Harvard Business Review, 74*(6), 111–117, and Peters, H. (March 1996). Peer coaching for executives. *Training & Development,* pp. 39–41.

51. See note 6, Waterman et al.

52. See note 37, Russell (1991).

53. Sherman, A. W., Bohlander, G. W., and Chruden, H. J. (1988). *Managing human resources.* Cincinnati, OH: South-Western Publishing; see also, note 108.

54. See note 7, Brousseau et al. (1996).

55. Leibowitz, Z. B.; Kaye, B. L.; and Farren, C. (October 1992). Multiple career paths. *Training and Development Journal,* pp. 31–35.

56. Dewhirst, H. D. (1991). Career patterns: Mobility, specialization, and related career issues. In Morrison, R. F., and Adams, J. (eds.), *Contemporary career development issues.* Hillsdale, NJ: Lawrence Erlbaum, 73–107.

57. See note 18.

58. See note 6, Waterman et al.

59. Wanous, J. P. (1980). *Organizational entry: Recruitment, selection, and socialization of newcomers.* Reading, MA: Addison-Wesley. See also, Adkins, C. L. (1995). Previous work experience and organizational socialization: A longitudinal examination. *Academy of Management Journal, 38,* 839–862, and Major, D. A.; Kozlowski, S. W.; Chao, G. T.; and Gardner, P. D. (1995). A longitudinal investigation of newcomer ex-

pectations, early socialization outcomes, and the moderating effects of role development factors. *Journal of Applied Psychology, 80,* 418–431.

60. See note 23, Feldman (1988).

61. See note 7, Brousseau et al. (1996).

62. See note 18.

63. Rocco, J. (August 1991). Computers track high-potential managers. *HR Magazine,* pp. 66–68.

64. Lieber, R. B. (Aug. 4, 1997). Even CEOs don't live forever. *Fortune,* p. 230.

65. Garrett, E. M. (April 1994). Going the distance. *Small Business Reports,* pp. 22–30.

66. Curtis, L. B., and Russell, J. E. A. (April 1993). *A study of succession planning programs in Fortune 500 firms.* Paper presented at the annual meeting of the Society of Industrial & Organizational Psychology, San Francisco.

67. Kramer, D. (1990). Executive succession and development systems: A practical approach. In M. London, E. S. Bassman, and J. P. Fernandez (eds.), *Human Resource Forecasting and Strategy Development.* New York: Quorum, pp. 99–112.

68. Wellington, J. K. (1981). Management succession at Arizona Public Service. *Human Resource Planning, 4,* 157–167. See also notes 64, 67.

69. Borwick, C. (May 1993). Eight ways to assess succession plans. *HR Magazine,* pp. 109–114. See also, Kets de Vries, M. F. R. (1995). *Life and death in the executive fast lane.* San Francisco: Jossey-Bass, and notes 64, 67, 68.

70. Nusbaum, H. J. (1986). The career development program at DuPont's Pioneering Research Laboratory. *Personnel, 63*(9), 68–75.

71. Gaertner, K. N. (1988). Managers' careers and organizational change. *Academy of Management Executive, 11,* 311–318.

72. Fenwick-Magrath, J. A. (1988). Executive development: Key factors for success. *Personnel, 65*(7), 68–72. See also, Friedman, S. D. (1986). Succession systems in large corporations: Characteristics and correlates of performance. *Human Resource Management, 25,* 191–213; Mahler, W. R. (1987). Executive development. In R. L. Craig (ed.), *Training and development handbook: A guide to human resource development,* 3rd ed. New York: McGraw-Hill, pp. 564–579; and Mahler, W. R., and Gaines, F. (1983). *Succession planning in leading companies.* Midland Park, NJ: Mahler Publishing.

73. Lesly, E. (Nov. 29, 1993). Sticking it out at Xerox by sticking together. *Business Week,* p. 77, and Georgemiller, D. (Winter 1992). Making the grades: The ABCs of educational reimbursement. *The Human Resource Professional,* pp. 16–19.

74. Kurschner, D. (1996). Getting credit. *Training, 34*(6), 52–53.

75. Jones, R. G., and Whitmore, M. D. (1995). Evaluating developmental assessment centers as interventions. *Personnel Psychology, 48*(2), 377–388.

76. See note 6, Waterman et al.

77. Russell, J. E. A., and Adams, D. M. (1997). The changing nature of mentoring in organizations: An introduction to the special issue on mentoring in organizations. *Journal of Vocational Behavior, 51*(1), 1–14. See also, McManus, S. E., and Russell, J. E. A. (1997). New directions for mentoring research: An examination of related constructs. *Journal of Vocational Behavior, 51*(1), 145–161.

78. Kram, K. E. (1986). Mentoring in the workplace. In D. T. Hall (ed.), *Career development in organizations.* San Francisco, CA: Jossey-Bass, pp. 160–201. See also, Kram, K. E. (1985). Mentoring at work. Glenview, IL: Scott, Foresman; Kram, K. E., and Isabella, L. (1985). Mentoring alternatives: The role of peer relationships in career development. *Academy of Management Journal, 28,* 110–132; Rothman, H. (April 1993). The boss as mentor. *Nation's Business,* pp. 66–67; Bell, C. R. (1996). *Managers as mentors: Building partnerships for learning.* San Francisco: Berrett-Koehler Publishers; and Kaye, B., and Jacobson, B. (April 1995). Mentoring: A group guide. *Training & Development,* pp. 23–27.

79. See note 7, Hall (1987). See also, Turbin, D. B., and Dougherty, T. W. (1994). Role of protege personality in receipt of mentoring and career success. *Academy of Management Journal, 37*(3), 688–702; Gaskill, L. R. (1993). A conceptual framework for the development, implementation, and evaluation of formal mentoring programs. *Journal of Career Development, 20*(2), 147–160; Chao, G. T. (1997). Mentoring phases and outcomes. *Journal of Vocational Behavior, 51*(1), 15–28; Allen, T. D.; Poteet, M. L.; and Burroughs, S. M. (1997). The mentor's perspective: A qualitative inquiry and future research agenda. *Journal of Vocational Behavior, 51*(1), 70–89; and Burke, R. J., and McKeen, C. A. (1997). Benefits of mentoring relationships among managerial and professional women: A cautionary tale. *Journal of Vocational Behavior, 51*(1), 43–57.

80. Odiorne, G. S. (1985). Mentoring—An American management innovation. *Personnel Administrator, 30*(5), 63–70. See also, Rigdon, J. E. (Dec, 1, 1993). You're not all alone if there's a mentor just a keyboard away. *The Wall Street Journal,* p. B1; Allen, T. D.; Poteet, M. L.; Russell, J. E. A.; and Dobbins, G. H. (1997). Factors related to supervisors' willingness to mentor others. *Journal of Vocational Behavior, 50,* 1–22; Gunn, E. (August 1995). Mentoring: The democratic version. *Training,* pp. 64–67; Skylar, T. (March 1996). When training collides with a 35-ton truck. *Training,* pp. 32–34, 36, 38; and Eby, L. T. (1997). Alternative forms of mentoring in changing organizational environments: A conceptual extension of the mentoring literature. *Journal of Vocational Behavior, 51*(1), 125–144.

81. Diversity: America's strength. (June 23, 1997). *Fortune.*

82. Moskowitz, M. (October 1996). 100 best companies for working mothers. *Working Mother Magazine,* pp. 10–13, 15–16, 18, 20, 24, 26, 28, 30–34, 36–38, 40–42, 44, 46, 50, 52–54, 56, 58, 60, 62, 64–66, 68, 70.

83. See note 82, p. 10.

84. Hayghe, H. V., and Bianchi, S. M. (June 1994). Married mothers' work patterns: The job-family compromise. *Monthly Labor Review,* pp. 24–30; Read, C. M., and Bruce, W. A. (Summer 1993). Dual-career couples in the public sector: A survey of personnel policies and practices. *Public Personnel Management,* pp. 187–199. Smith, C. R. (Summer 1992). Dual careers, dual loyalties: Management implications of the work/home interface. *Asia Pacific Journal of Human Resources,* pp. 19–29; and Shellenbarger, S. (June 21, 1993). So much talk, so little action. *The Wall Street Journal,* pp. R1, R4.

85. Shellenbarger, S. (June 11, 1997). Employees, managers need to plan ahead for maternity leaves. *The Wall Street Journal,* p. B1.

86. See note 41, Greenhaus, and Callanan (1994). See also, Brooks, J. L., and Seers, A. (1991). Predictors of organizational commitment: Variations across career stages. *Journal of Vocational Behavior, 38,* 53–64. Lobel, S. A. (1991). Allocation of investment in work and family roles: Alternative theories and implications for research. *Academy of Management Review, 16*(3), 507–521; and Allen, T. D.; Russell, J. E. A.; and Rush, M. C. (1994). The effects of gender and leave of absence on attributions for performance, perceived organizational commitment, and allocation of organizational rewards. *Sex Roles, 31*(7/8), 443–451; and Allen, T. D.; McManus, S. E.; Russell, J. E. A.; and Reiniger, A. (1995). An examination of the impact of peer mentoring on socialization and stress. *Proceedings of the Southern Management Association,* Valdosta, GA: Valdosta State University.

87. Elias, M. (Aug. 12, 1997). Couples in pre-kid, no-kid marriages happiest. *USA Today,* p. D1.

88. Rynes, S., and Rosen, B. (1995). A field survey of factors affecting the adoption and perceived success of diversity training. *Personnel Psychology, 48*(2), 247–270.

89. See note 82.

90. Eby, L. T. (1996). *Intra-organizational mobility: An examination of factors related to employees' willingness to relocate.* Unpublished dissertation. Knoxville, TN: The University of Tennessee.

91. Eby, L. T.; DeMatteo, J. S.; and Russell, J. E. A. (1997). Employment assistance needs of accompanying spouses following relocation. *Journal of Vocational Behavior, 50,* 291–307.

92. Lublin, J. S. (April 13, 1993). Husbands in limbo. *The Wall Street Journal,* pp. A1, A8. See also, Labor Letter (April 11, 1989). *The Wall Street Journal,* p. A1; Work and Family (June 28, 1993). *Business Week,* pp. 80–88; Owen-Cooper, T. (Oct. 1, 1990). Job sharing slowly gaining in appeal. *Denver Post,* p. 1C, 5C; Sunoo, B. P. (April 1996). From Santa to CEO—Temps play all roles. *Personnel Journal,* pp. 34–35, 37, 39–44; Solomon, C. M. (September 1994). Job sharing: One job, double headache. *Personnel Journal,* pp. 88–96; Brotherton, P. (December 1995). Staff to suit. *HR Magazine,* pp. 50–55.

93. Relocating dual career couples. (Oct. 4, 1990). *Bulletin to Management,* p. 320.

94. Mathis, R. L., and Jackson, J. H. (1996). *Personnel/human resource management.* St. Paul, MN: West Publishing.

95. See note 82.

96. McDonald's Corporation, 1995. Mini-application form.

97. See note 45.

98. Lawlor, J. (July/August 1996). The bottom line on work-family programs. *Working Woman Magazine,* pp. 54–56, 58, 74, 76.

99. Warner, M. (March 3, 1997). Working at home—The right way to be a star in your bunny slippers. *Fortune,* p. 165.

100. See note 99. See also, Morris, B. (March 17, 1997). Home-office heaven and hell. *Fortune,* p. 82.

101. See note 82.

102. See note 85, Shellenbarger.

103. See note 98.

104. See note 82.

105. See note 82.

106. Kerr, J. (July 1, 1993). The best small companies to work for in America. *INC,* p. 57.

107. Kossek, E. E., and Nichol, V. (1992). The effects of on-site child care on employee attitudes and performance. *Personnel Psychology, 45,* 485–509; see also, Goff, S. J.; Mount, M. K.; and Jamison, R. L. (1990). Employee supported child care, work/family conflict, and absenteeism: A field study. *Personnel Psychology, 43,* 793–810.

109. See note 98.

110. See note 82.

111. See note 45.

112. See note 45; see also, Caudron, S. (September 1995). Andersen is at employees' service. *Personnel Journal,* pp. 88, 90, 92, 94, 96.

113. See note 98; see also, Bureau of National Affairs (1993). Measuring results: Cost-benefit analyses of work and family programs. *Employee Relations Weekly.* Washington, DC: Bureau of National Affairs.

114. See note 88.

115. See note 98.

116. See note 98.

117. Balutis, A. P. (1996). Getting thin the healthy way. *Government Executive, 28*(2), 45–48.

118. Carson, K. D., and Carson, P. P. (1997). Career entrenchment: A quiet march toward occupational death? *Academy of Management Executive, 11*(1), 62–75.

119. Rockefellar, D. (Nov. 1, 1996). America after downsizing: Maximizing society's profits. *Vital Speeches of the Day, 63*(2), 40–43; see also, Tang, T., and Fuller, R. M. (1995). Corporate downsizing: What managers can do to lessen the negative effects of layoffs. *SAM Advanced Management Journal, 60*(4), 12–15, 31; and Richman, L. S. (Sept. 20, 1993). When will the layoffs end? *Fortune,* pp. 54–56.

120. Feldman, D., and Leanna, C. (1994). Better practices in managing layoffs. *Human Resource Management,*

33(2), 239–260; Cole, J. (Nov. 7, 1995). Boeing teaches employees how to run small business. *The Wall Street Journal,* pp. B1, B2; Keller, J. J. (March 18, 1996). AT&T tries to put new spin on big job cuts. *The Wall Street Journal,* pp. B1, B6; and Allen, T. D.; Russell, J. E. A.; Poteet, M. L.; and Dobbins, G. H. (1994). Attitudes of state government managers who are "more or less" career plateaued. In M. Schnake (ed.), *Proceedings of the Southern Management Association.* Valdosta, GA: Valdosta State University, pp. 199–202.

121. London, M. (1996). Redeployment and continuous learning in the 21st century: Hard lessons and positive examples from the downsizing era. *Academy of Management Executive, 10*(4), 67–79.

122. Kozlowski, S. W.; Chao, G. T.; Smith, E. M.; and Hedlund, J. (1993). Organizational downsizing: Strategies, interventions, and research implications. *International Review of Industrial and Organizational Psychology, 8,* 263–332; Allen, T. D.; Freeman, D. M.; Russell, J. E. A.; Reizenstein, R. C.; and Rentz, J. O. (1995). Just another transition? Examining survivors' attitudes over time. In D. P. Moore (ed.), *Academy of Management Association Best Paper Proceedings,* Charleston, SC: The Citadel, pp. 78–82; The higher the pay, the longer the job hunt (Dec. 15, 1989). *The Wall Street Journal,* p. B1; and Collarelli, S. M., and Beehr, T. A. (1993). Selection out: Firings, layoffs, and retirement. In N. Schmitt, and W. C. Borman (eds.), *Personnel selection in organizations.* San Francisco: Jossey-Bass, pp. 341–384.

123. See note 119, Tang and Fuller.

124. Dawson, K., and Dawson, S. (1994). Immediate outplacement can help everyone through the transition. *HR Focus, 71*(2), p. 4; Nobile, R. J. (1991). Outplacement counseling: Minimizing legal liability. *Personnel, 68*(10), p. 10. Cowden, P. (September 1992). Outplacement services assessment. *HR Magazine,* pp. 69–70; and Hill, J. C., and Fannin, W. R. (1991). Developing an effective outplacement program. *Business Forum, 16*(1), 14–17.

125. See note 121.

126. Flynn, G. (1996). New skills equal new opportunities. *Personnel Journal, 75*(6), 77–79.

127. Brockner, J.; Konovsky, M.; Cooper-Schneider, R.; Folger, R.; Martin, C.; and Bies, R. J. (1994). Interactive effects of procedural justice and outcome negativity on victims and survivors of job loss. *Academy of Management Journal, 37,* 397–409, and O'Neill, H. M., and Lenn, D. J. (1995). Voices of survivors: Words that downsizing CEOs should hear. *Academy of Management Executive, 9,* 23–34.

128. See note 118, p. 73.

129. Mirvis, P. H. (ed.) (1993). *Building a competitive workforce: Investing in human capital for corporate success.* New York: John Wiley & Sons. See also, Mirvis, P. H., and Hall, D. T. (1996). Career development for the older worker. In D. T. Hall and associates (eds.), *The career is dead—Long live the career: A relational approach to careers.* San Francisco: Jossey-Bass, pp. 278–296.

130. Bowman, W. (August 1992). 10 steps to retirement. *HR Magazine,* pp. 86–87.

131. American Association of Retired Persons (1993). *The older workforce: Recruitment and retention.* Washington, DC: Author.

132. Johnson, R. S. (Aug. 4, 1997). The new black power. *Fortune,* pp. 46–82; see also, Walker, B. A. (1996). The value of diversity in career self-development. In D. T. Hall and Associates (eds.), *The career is dead—Long live the career: A relational approach to careers.* San Francisco: Jossey-Bass.

133. See notes 6, 13, 16. See also, Ragins, B. R. (1997). Antecedents of diversified mentoring relationships. *Journal of Vocational Behavior, 51*(1), 90–109; Swanson, J. L., and Tokar, D. M. (1991). Development and validation of the career barriers inventory. *Journal of Vocational Behavior, 39,* 344–361; Advancing women in the workplace (September 1993). *Training and Development Journal,* pp. 9–10; and Kalish, B. B. (March 1992). Dismantling the glass ceiling. *Management Review,* p. 64.

134. Morris, B. (July 21, 1997). If women ran the world. *Fortune,* pp. 74–79.

135. Trost, D. (Nov. 22, 1989). New approach forced by shifts in population. *The Wall Street Journal,* pp. B1, B4. See also, Pave, I. (June 23, 1986). A woman's place is at GE, Federal Express, P&G . . . *Business Week,* pp. 75–76; Jacobs, J. A. (ed.) (1994). *Gender inequity at work.* Newbury Park, CA: Sage Publications; note 34, Russell (1994). Schwartz, F. N. (1989). Management women and the new facts of life. *Harvard Business Review, 67*(1), 65–76; Taylor, A. (Aug. 18, 1986). Why women managers are bailing out. *Fortune,* pp. 16–23; Zeitz, B., and Dusky, L. (1988). *The best companies for women.* New York: Simon & Schuster; Williams, M. J. (Sept. 12, 1988). Women beat the corporate game. *Fortune,* pp. 128–138; and Deutsch, C. H. (Jan. 28, 1990). Saying no to the mommy track. *New York Times,* p. F29.

136. Deutsch, C. H. (Dec. 16, 1990). Putting women on the fast track. *New York Times,* p. F25.

137. Advancement of women study initiated by CEO (1997). *Women in Management Newsletter, 7*(4), 1–2.

138. Chambliss, L. (June 1996). The 10 healthiest companies for women. *Working Women,* pp. 61–63, 73.

139. Mirabella, L. (June 15, 1997). Helping staff be aware of diversity. *Baltimore Sun,* p. D1; see also, Gadsden, E. N. (June 15, 1997). Teaching diversity awareness in workplace, *Baltimore Sun,* pp. D1, D3.

140. Swisher, K. (July/August 1996). Coming out in corporate America. *Working Woman Magazine,* pp. 50–53, 78, 80.

141. See note 7, Hall (1987); see also Cox, T. H., and Harquail, C. V. (1991). Career paths and career success in the early career stages of male and female MBAs. *Journal of Vocational Behavior, 39,* 54–75; Russell, J. E. A., and Eby, L. T. (1993). Career assessment strategies for women in management. *Journal of Career assessment, 1,* 267–293; and Colombo, J. (June 12, 1997). A law

school's diversity checklist, *The Wall Street Journal,* p. A18.

142. See note 81.

143. Stone, D. L., and Colella, A. (1996). A model of factors affecting the treatment of disabled individuals in organizations. *Academy of Management Review, 21*(2), 352–401; Putney, D. M.; Russell, J. E. A.; and Colvin, C. (November 1996). *Factors related to the effective socialization of people with disabilities.* Paper presented at the annual meeting of the Southern Management Association, New Orleans, LA; and Veves, J. G., and Simms, R. R. (eds.) (1995). *Human resource management and the Americans with Disabilities Act.* Westport, CT: Quorum Books.

144. Russell, J. E. A., Atchley, K. P., Eby, L. T., and Fausz, A. T. (1994). Attitudes of white employees and managers towards diversity issues. In M. Schnake (ed.), *Proceedings of the Southern Management Association,* Valdosta, GA: Valdosta State University, pp. 466–471; Jackson, S. E., and Ruderman, M. N. (eds.) (1995). *Diversity in work teams: Research paradigms for a changing workplace.* Washington, DC: American Psychological Association; Milliken, F. J., and Martins, L. L. (1996). Searching for common threads: Understanding the multiple effects of diversity in organizational groups. *Academy of Management Review, 21*(2), 402–433; Nemetz, P. L., and Christensen, S. L. (1996). The challenge of cultural diversity: Harnessing a diversity of views to understand multiculturalism. *Academy of Management Review, 21*(2), 434–462; and Larkey, L. K. (1996). Toward a theory of communicative interactions in culturally diverse workgroups. *Academy of Management Review, 21*(2), 463–491.

145. See note 88. See also, Fine, M. G. (1995). *Building successful multicultural organizations: Challenges and opportunities.* Westport, CT: Quorum, Books; Herriot, P., and Pemberton, C. (1995). *Competitive advantage through diversity: Organizational learning from difference.* London: Sage; Chemers, M. M., Oskamp, S., Costanzo, M. A. (eds.) (1995). *Diversity in organizations.* Newbury Park, CA: Sage; Kossek, E. E., and Lobel, S. A. (eds.) (1996). *Human resource strategies for managing diversity.* Oxford, England: Basil Blackwell; Gallos, J. V., and Ramsey, V. J. (eds.) (1996). *Listening to the soul and speaking from the heart: The joys and complexities of teaching about workplace diversity.* San Francisco: Jossey-Bass; and Prasad, P., Mills, A. J., Elmes, M., and Prasad, A. (eds.) (1996). *Managing the organizational melting pot: Dilemmas for workplace diversity.* London: Sage.

146. Thompson, P., Kirkham, K., and Dixon, J. (1985). Warning: The fast track may be hazardous to organizational health. *Organizational Dynamics, 13,* 21–33; Kimeldorf, M. (1994). *Serious play: A leisure wellness guidebook.* Berkeley, CA: Ten Speed Press; and Magid, R. Y., and Codkind, M. M. (1995). *Work and personal life: Managing the issues.* Menlo Park, CA: Crisp Publications.

147. See note 23, Feldman (1988).

148. See note 7, Brousseau et al.

149. Cianni, M., and Wnuck, D. (1997). Individual growth and team enhancement: Moving toward a new model of career development. *Academy of Management Executive, 11*(1), 105–115; see also, Applebaum, E., and Batt, R. (1994). *The new American workplace: Transforming work systems in the United States.* Ithaca, NY: ILR Press.

150. See note 149; see also, Dumaine, B. (June 17, 1991). The bureaucracy busters. *Fortune,* pp. 36–44.

151. Harvey, M. G. (1989). Repatriation of corporate executives: An empirical study. *Journal of International Business Studies, 20,* 131–144.

152. Tung, R. L. (1988). *The new expatriate.* Cambridge, MA: Ballinger; see also, Murray, F. T., and Murray, A. H. (1986). SMR Forum: Global managers for global businesses. *Sloan Management Review, 27,* 75–80.

153. Engen, J. R. (March 1995). Coming home. *Training,* pp. 37–40.

154. Black, J. S.; Gregersen, H. B.; and Mendenhall, M. (1992). *Global assignments: Successfully expatriating and repatriating international managers.* San Francisco: Jossey-Bass; see also, Solomon, C. M. (May 1995). Navigating your search for global talent. *Personnel Journal,* pp. 94–95, 99, 101.

155. Feldman, D. C. (1991). Repatriate moves as career transitions. *Human Resource Management Review, 1*(3), 163–178.

156. Views on the expatriate (Dec. 11, 1989). *The Wall Street Journal,* p. B1.

157. Napier, N., and Patterson, R. (1991). Expatriate reentry: What do expatriates have to say? *Human Resource Planning, 14*(1), 18–28.

158. Solomon, C. M. (January 1995). Repatriation: Up, down, or out? *Personnel Journal,* pp. 28–35.

159. *Global Relocation Trends Survey Report* (January 1995). National Foreign Trade Council and Windham International, and Finney, M. I. (April 1996). Global success rides on keeping top talent. *HR Magazine,* pp. 69–72.

160. See note 151.

161. See note 155; see also, Gregersen, H. B. (1992). Commitments to a parent company and a local work unit during repatriation. *Personnel Psychology, 45*(1), 29–54.

162. See note 41, Greenhaus and Callanan (1994).

163. See note 20.

164. See note 7, Hall (1987); see also, note 13, Hall (1986); Colby, A. G. (June 1995). Making the new career development model work. *HR Magazine,* pp. 150, 152; Bennis, W. (January 1996). What lies ahead. *Training & Development,* pp. 75–79; Thornburg, L. (May 1995). HR in the year 2010. *HR Magazine,* pp. 63–70; Jones, F. F.; Morris, M. H.; Rockmore, W. (May 1995). HR practices that promote entrepreneurship. *HR Magazine,* pp. 86–88, 90–91; and Cherrington, D. J., and Middle-

ton, L. Z. (June 1995). An introduction to global business issues. *HR Magazine,* pp. 124–126, 128, 130.

165. Arthur, M. B., and Rousseau, D. (1996). A new career lexicon for the 21st century. *Academy of Management Executive, 10*(4), 28–39; see also, Jones, C., and DeFillippi, R. J. (1996). Back to the future in film: Combining industry and self-knowledge to meet the career challenges of the 21st century. *Academy of Management Executive, 10*(4), 89–103, and Fisher, A. (Jan. 13, 1997). Six ways to supercharge your career. *Fortune,* pp. 46–48.

C H A P T E R

PERFORMANCE APPRAISAL AND MANAGEMENT*

OVERVIEW

As one recent review concluded, "The appraisal of performance appraisal is not good."[1] *The Wall Street Journal* recently reported, "In almost every major survey, most employees who get . . . evaluations and most supervisors who give them rate the process a resounding failure."[2] While over 95 percent of organizations report the use of formal systems of appraisal, the majority of those involved in this activity express considerable dissatisfaction with it. The Society of Human Resource Management concluded that over 90 percent of appraisal systems are unsuccessful, and a 1993 survey by Development Dimensions International found that most employers expressed "overwhelming" dissatisfaction with their performance management (PM) systems. Other surveys have reported similar negative results.[3]

Those doing the rating, those being rated, and administrators have expressed dissatisfaction with their appraisal systems. As one manager from Digital Corporation put it while attending a training session on appraisal,

"I'd rather kick bricks with my bare feet than do appraisals!" Appraisal systems are rarely able to deliver all of their intended benefits to employers or employees.[4] In fact, several surveys have revealed widespread dissatisfaction in *Fortune* 500 companies, which presumably have the resources to acquire the best appraisal technology available.[5]

All the attention paid to performance appraisal in general is testimony to its potentially pivotal role in influencing organizational performance and effectiveness. Thus, it is unfortunate that neither concern about nor passion for a subject matter can be directly translated into operational recommendations that are guaranteed to succeed. Central to our perspective is the view that the most effective PM systems recognize that appraisal is not an end in itself; rather it is a critical component of a much broader set of human resource practices that should be clearly linked to business performance, personal and organizational development, corporate strategy, and culture.[6] Many organizations have reported that their appraisal systems offer little or no value to their organizations, and 64 percent cited plans to redesign their process.[7] Surveys of small and medium-sized companies report even more dissatisfaction.

*Contributed by Jeffrey S. Kane, Joyce E. A. Russell, and John Bernardin.

Organizations are constantly searching for better ways to appraise performance. Lyndel Petrochemical was so dissatisfied with its appraisal system that it abolished ratings and separated the performance evaluation system from its pay system.[8] Pratt & Whitney, the jet engine division of United Technologies, made significant changes in its appraisal system in two consecutive years only to abandon the system for a different approach the very next year. Blockbuster Video revised its appraisal system for three consecutive years. IBM installed a new system as part of a major downsizing effort because the old, highly regarded performance-appraisal system resulted in such lenient ratings that few performance distinctions could be made among the workers and little evidence indicated there were any unproductive workers.

In addition to the potential value of performance appraisal as a source of competitive advantage, as we discussed in Chapter 3, performance appraisal is the most heavily litigated personnel practice today.[9] Because the legal grounds for challenging appraisal systems are expanding, litigation can be expected to increase. The Civil Rights Act of 1991, the Age Discrimination in Employment Act (ADEA), and the 1990 Americans with Disabilities Act are but three examples of federal laws that have generated a plethora of litigation related to performance appraisal.

The growing diversity of the workforce also increases the probability of legal and work-related difficulties. With greater proportions of women, members of minority groups, people of varying sexual orientation, employees with disabilities, and older workers comprising the labor force, unfairness and biases already present in appraisal systems, either real or perceived, may be magnified by greater diversity and differences between those doing the rating and those being rated. Consequently, organizations will need to be increasingly scrupulous in encouraging fairness and objectivity in appraisal practices and personnel decisions.[10]

This chapter provides recommendations for improving the effectiveness of performance appraisals. We believe research provides guidance for improving this critical HRM function. We also believe that there are major discrepancies between the way in which appraisal is *practiced* and the way in which experts say it should be done. We will emphasize these discrepancies throughout the chapter.

OBJECTIVES

After reading this chapter, you should be able to:

1. Understand the value and uses of performance appraisals in organizations and the prescriptions for effective appraisal.

2. Describe legal issues associated with performance appraisals.

3. Describe the decisions necessary when designing an appraisal system (e.g., content, process, raters, ratees, administrative issues).

4. Explain the steps to follow when developing an appraisal system.

5. Describe the necessary steps for implementing an appraisal system.

6. Understand how to evaluate the effectiveness of an appraisal system.

7. Describe performance appraisal systems in quality-driven organizations.

Is there any hope for performance appraisal? We think so. A recent review of research, practice, and litigation related to performance appraisal led to the proposal that some things can be done to improve the effectiveness of appraisal systems.[11] The effects of appraisal and performance management systems will be more positive if and when certain prescriptions are followed that have generally *not* been heeded by practitioners. These prescriptions are: (1) Precision in the definition and measurement of performance is a key element of effective appraisal; (2) the content and measurement of performance should derive from internal and external customers, and (3) the PM system should incorporate a formal process for investigating and correcting for the effects of situational constraints on performance. Figure 9.1 presents these prescriptions.

Recent research shows that performance management, when done correctly, can affect corporate performance and the bottom line.[12] In Chapters 6 and 7, we discussed the role of performance measurement in the

FIGURE 9.1
PRESCRIPTIONS FOR EFFECTIVE PERFORMANCE MANAGEMENT

1. Strive for as much precision in defining and measuring performance dimensions as is feasible.
   - Define performance with a focus on valued outcomes.
   - Outcome measures can be defined in terms of relative frequencies of behavior.
   - Define performance dimensions by combining functions with aspects of value (e.g., quantity, quality, timeliness).
2. Link performance dimensions to meeting internal and external customer requirements.
   - Internal customer definitions of performance should be linked to external customer satisfaction.
3. Incorporate the measurement of situational constraints.
   - Focus attention on perceived constraints on performance.

Source: Adapted from Bernardin, H. J., Hagan, C., Kane, J. S., and Villanova, P. Effective performance management: Precision in measurement with a focus on customers and situational constraints. In J. Smither (ed.) *Performance Appraisal: State-of-the-Art Methods for Performance Management.* Jossey-Bass, San Francisco, 1998.

evaluation and improvement of personnel selection systems and training and development programs. The identification and measurement of critical performance criteria are vital for improving an organization's competitive advantage through better products and services and greater responsiveness to customer requirements.

HOW DO WE DEFINE PERFORMANCE?

Despite the importance of performance appraisal, few organizations clearly define what it is they are trying to measure. To design a system for appraising performance, it is important to first define what is meant by the term **work performance.** Although a person's job performance depends on some combination of ability, effort, and opportunity, it can be measured in terms of outcomes or results produced. Performance is defined as the *record of outcomes* produced on a *specified job function* or *activity* during a *specified time period*.[13] For example, a trainer working for the World Bank was evaluated on her "organization of presentations," which was defined as "the presentation of training material in a logical and methodical order." The extent to which she was able to make such "orderly" presentations would be one measure of outcomes related to that function. A sales representative would have some measure of sales as an outcome for a primary function of that job. Customer service would have very different outcome measures for defining performance. College professors are typically evaluated on three general work functions: teaching, research, and service. Performance in each of these three areas is defined with different outcome measures.

Performance on the job as a whole would be equal to the sum (or average) of performance on the job functions or activities. For example, the World Bank identified eight job functions for its trainers (e.g., use of relevant examples, participant involvement, evaluation procedures). The functions have to do with the work that is performed and *not* the characteristics of the person performing. Unfortunately, many performance-appraisal systems confuse measures of performance with measures of the person. The definition of performance refers to a set of outcomes produced during a certain time period; it does not refer to the traits, personal characteristics, or "competencies" of the performer (see the Critical Thinking Exercise 9.1).[14]

| CRITICAL THINKING EXERCISE 9.1 |

Should We Measure Competencies in Performance Appraisal?

One strong trend in performance appraisal is the assessment of so-called competencies. Competencies have been defined as bundles of knowledges, skills, or abilities. Many of these "competencies" look a lot like the old traits that have been condemned in a plethora of articles on appraisal. As an illustration, the managerial competencies used by the American Management Association include self-confidence, positive regard, self-control, spontaneity, stamina, and adaptability.[1]

Some argue that performance appraisal should focus on *the record of outcomes* that the person (or persons) actually achieved on the job. There is nothing wrong with assessing what qualities a person possesses, but that should not be confused with measuring performance. We can assess the extent to which a person possesses certain technical skills through ratings by those familiar with a person's skills (although it would probably be better to use some form of test). It is the manifestation of those skills on the job in the form of outcomes that constitutes performance. We can assess L.A. Laker Shaquille O'Neal's psychomotor skills, his height, and his weight, all of which may be predictors or correlates of his performance. But his foul shooting in 1996 was 46 percent and that is one element of his performance.

Many companies use a software program that gives ratings on a competency labeled "integrity." Some appraisal experts would suggest that an elimination of such "competency" labels would help focus the managers' attention on actual behavior and the outcomes that result from the behaviors. Another popular software package calls for evaluations of managers on their "personal maturity." Needless to say, store managers often disagree with ratings indicating they need work on their "personal maturity."

Assignment

When is it appropriate to measure competencies? Describe an appraisal system in which the purposes for the appraisal system were accomplished when the system called for assessments of personal competencies as opposed to a record of performance outcomes. Can these two views be reconciled? How?

1 S. B. Parry, The quest for competencies. Training, July 1996, pp. 48–53.

Uses for Performance Appraisal

The information collected from performance appraisals is most widely used for compensation, performance improvement or management, and documentation. As we discussed in previous chapters, appraisal data are also used for staffing decisions (e.g., promotion, transfer, discharge, layoffs), training needs analysis, employee development, and research and evaluation. Several of these uses are described below.

PERFORMANCE MANAGEMENT AND COMPENSATION. Performance-appraisal information may be used by supervisors to manage the performance of their employees. Appraisal data can reveal employees' performance weaknesses, which managers can refer to when setting goals or target levels for improvements. Performance management programs may be focused at one or more of the following organizational levels: individual performers, work groups or organizational subunits, or at the entire organization. Data on performance should be collected at the appropriate level and over time to indicate trends.[15]

To motivate employees to improve their performance and achieve their target goals, supervisors can use incentives such as pay-for-performance programs (e.g., merit pay, incentives, bonus awards). One strong trend in this country is toward some form of pay-for-performance (PFP) system. When employees have the opportunity to be rewarded for good performance in an equitable way, they can be highly motivated and perform better. **Expectancy theory** states that your motivation is a consequence of the perceptions you have about the connection between your level of effort and your performance and then the perceived connection between that level of performance and desirable outcomes. The outcomes also vary on their level of desirability, or what psychologists called **valence.** So if an employee believes that a higher level of effort will lead to greater performance and greater performance will lead to more (or better) desired outcomes, the motivation will be stronger and the employee will try harder.[16] Obviously, effective performance measurement is critical for PFP systems to work. In general, when the performer and the observer of performance disagree on the level of performance achieved, the two probabilities that go into expectancy theory will be lower and lower levels of motivation will follow.

INTERNAL STAFFING. Performance-appraisal information is also used to make staffing decisions. These decisions involve finding employees to fill positions in the organization or reducing the number of employees that exist in certain positions. Many organizations rely on performance-appraisal data to decide which employees to promote to fill openings and which employees to retain in a downsizing.

One problem with relying on performance-appraisal information to make decisions about job movements is that employee performance is measured only for the current job. If the job at the higher, lateral, or lower level is different from the employee's current job, then it may be difficult to estimate how the employee will perform on the new job. Consequently, organizations have resorted to using assessment procedures in addition to appraisal data to make staffing decisions. These assessment methods include those described in Chapter 6 such as assessment centers, work samples, and structured interviews. Unfortunately, assessment methods indicate only how employees will perform when peak performance is de-

manded and not how they will perform on a typical basis.[17] As we discussed in Chapter 5, most companies focus on internal recruiting to fill supervisory/managerial jobs. Despite problems, performance appraisal still plays a major role in moving people through the organization.

Many companies use performance-appraisal data to make decisions about reducing the workforce. In most private-sector firms, appraisal information along with job needs are the only data used to determine which employees to lay off or terminate, while in unionized companies, seniority is the primary basis for making reduction in force decisions. In agencies of the federal government, reduction in force measures must be made by applying equal weight to performance and length of employment (i.e., seniority).

At least 23 states now have provisions that may require terminations to be based on "just cause."[18] In such states, if an appraisal system can be shown to be biased, unreliable, or inaccurate, force reduction decisions based on it may not be defensible. Moreover, when force reductions are based on comparisons of appraisal scores for people in different jobs, the organization must be prepared to defend the comparability of scores across jobs.

Training Needs Analysis

In one survey, nearly 90 percent of respondents indicated their firms use appraisal data to determine employees' needs for training and development. For example, Northern Telecom uses appraisal data with exempt employees to determine training needs and career paths for individual employees.[19] Hundreds of companies, including Digital, IBM, and Merck, now use subordinates to evaluate their supervisors or managers. The results are revealed to each manager with suggestions for specific remedial action (if needed). Honeywell, for example, has specific training modules based on appraisal ratings for several job functions. Carnival Cruise Lines monitors customer service representative calls to determine specific training needs related to customer requirements.

Research and Evaluation

Appraisal data can also be used to determine whether various human resource programs (e.g., selection, training) are effective. For example, when Weyerhaueser wanted to assess the effects of its managerial training program, it gathered on-the-job performance data on the specific areas that had been the objectives of the training. When Toledo, Ohio, wanted to know whether its police officer selection test was valid, it collected performance-appraisal data on officers who had taken the test when they were hired so that test scores could be correlated with job performance. When London House, the

Chicago-based test publisher, attempted to establish the validity of its employee integrity test, it developed a specially designed appraisal form to assess counterproductive behavior.

LEGAL ISSUES ASSOCIATED WITH PERFORMANCE APPRAISALS

Since performance-appraisal data are used to make many important personnel decisions (e.g., pay, promotion, selection, termination), it is a major target of legal disputes involving employee charges of unfairness and bias.[20] A person may pursue several legal avenues to obtain relief from discriminatory performance appraisals. As discussed in Chapter 3, the most widely used federal laws are Title VII of the Civil Rights Act and the Age Discrimination in Employment Act. Exceptions to the **employment at will** doctrine often involve performance appraisals as well. One theory accepted in some states as an exception to the employment at will doctrine is known as "implied covenant of good faith." This theory essentially states that termination for cause only is required after the employee has established a long record of acceptable (or better) performance with an organization. Betty Benninger worked for the AAA Motor Club for over 15 years, all of which were judged to be at a very high level of performance. After she was dismissed, she filed a wrongful discharge suit, espousing the "implied covenant of good faith" theory. In the state of Michigan, this theory was accepted and Ms. Benninger prevailed. Obviously, performance-appraisal data played a vital role in this litigation. Ms. Benninger could probably not prevail in most states. Florida, for example, does not accept the "implied covenant of good faith" exception.

Termination for cause only is the most common policy on the international scene. All of Europe, for example, operates on this doctrine. Thus, decisions to terminate employees who either have overseas assignments or who are from the host country or another country must usually be based on performance and not "at will." This termination for cause only policy puts even greater pressure on multinational corporations to have effective performance-appraisal systems.

There are several recommendations to assist employers in conducting fair performance appraisals and avoiding legal suits. Gleaned from case law, these recommendations are intended as prescriptive measures that employers should take to develop fair and legally defensible performance-appraisal systems.[21] Since case law and court rulings are continually updated, this is not a guaranteed "defense-proof" listing, but rather constitutes sound personnel practices that protect the rights of both employers and employees and increases the likelihood that an employer would prevail in a legal action.

1. Legally defensible appraisal *procedures:*
   - Personnel decisions should be based on a formal, standardized performance-appraisal system.
   - Performance-appraisal processes should be uniform for all employees within a job group, and decisions based on those performance appraisals should be monitored for differences according to the race, sex, national origin, religion, or age of employees. While obtained differences as a function of any of these variables are not necessarily illegal, an organization will have more difficulty defending an appraisal system with ratings related to these variables.
   - Specific performance standards should be formally communicated to employees.
   - Employees should be able to review their appraisal results.
   - There should be a formal appeal process for ratees to rebut rater judgments.
   - Raters should be provided with written instructions and training on how to conduct appraisals properly to facilitate systematic, unbiased appraisals.
   - Personnel decision makers should be informed of anti-discrimination laws and made aware of legal and illegal activity regarding decisions based on appraisals.

2. Legally defensible appraisal *content:*
   - Performance appraisal content should be based on a job analysis.
   - Appraisals based on ratee traits should be avoided.
   - Objective, verifiable performance data (e.g., sales, productivity, not ratings) should be used whenever possible.
   - Constraints on employee performance that are beyond the employee's control should be prevented from contaminating the appraisal to ensure that employees have equal opportunities to achieve any given performance level.
   - Specific job-related performance dimensions should be used rather than global measures or single overall measures.
   - Performance dimensions should be assigned weights to reflect their relative importance in calculating the composite performance score.

3. Legally defensible *documentation* of appraisal results:
   - A thorough written record of evidence leading to termination decisions should be maintained (e.g., performance appraisals and performance counseling to advise employees of performance

deficits and to assist poor performers in making needed improvements).

- Written documentation (e.g., specific behavioral examples) for extreme ratings should be required and must be consistent with the numerical ratings.
- Documentation requirements should be consistent among raters.

4. Legally defensible *raters:*
   - Raters should be trained in how to use the appraisal system.
   - Raters must have the opportunity to observe the ratee firsthand or to review important ratee performance products.
   - Use of more than one rater is desirable in order to lessen the amount of influence of any one rater and to reduce the effects of biases. Peers, subordinates, customers, and clients are possible sources.

DESIGNING AN APPRAISAL SYSTEM

The process of designing an appraisal system should involve managers, employees, HR professionals, and both internal and external customers[22] in making decisions about each of the following issues:

- Measurement content.
- Measurement process.
- Defining the rater (i.e., who should rate performance).
- Defining the ratee (i.e., the level of performance to rate).
- Administrative characteristics.

It is a challenge to make the correct decisions because no single set of choices is optimal in all situations. The starting point should be the strategic plan and objectives of the organization. The details of the plan should be reviewed to design an appraisal system consistent with the overall goals of the firm. For example, Key Bank designed a performance management system to meet specific corporate, department, and individual strategies and goals.[23] National Car Rental developed a new appraisal system that would be directly compatible with the objectives of the organization. One of those objectives was to increase repeat corporate business. Thus, greater weight was placed on behaviors and results related to this objective.

The approach advocated here is to systematically assess the factors of a situation, which we call a *contingency model for appraisal system design.* In the rest of this section we shall examine the choices that must be made for each issue.

Measurement Content

In designing an appraisal system, three choices that concern the content on which performance is to be measured:

- The focus of the appraisal.
- Aspects of value.
- Performance-level anchors.

THE FOCUS OF THE APPRAISAL.   Appraisal can be either person-oriented (focusing on the person who performed the behavior) or work-oriented (focusing on the *record of outcomes* that the person achieved on the job). Effective performance appraisal focuses on the record of outcomes, in particular outcomes directly linked to an organization's mission and objectives. Some Sheraton Hotels offer 25-minute room service or the meal is free. Sheraton employees who are directly related to room service are appraised on the record of outcomes specifically related to this service guarantee. Lenscrafters guarantees most new glasses in 60 minutes or they're free. Individual and unit performance is measured by the average time taken to get the new glasses in the customer's hands. These are outcomes. In general, personal traits (e.g., dependability, integrity, perseverance, loyalty) should not be used when evaluating performance because they tend to foster stereotyping and other biases and are difficult to defend should litigation result. In addition, people who are evaluated on such traits perceive little value in the feedback and are often less motivated to perform well after the appraisal than before.[24]

ASPECTS OF VALUE.   Most conventional appraisal systems require raters to make a single overall judgment of performance on each project or job function. For example, determining an overall rating for a manager's performance on "Planning & Organizing" would be characteristic of this approach. Making an overall rating of the extent to which your instructor presented "organized lectures" is another example. There are, however, at least six criteria by which the value of performance in any work activity may be assessed.[25] For example, raters could evaluate the "timeliness" of the manager's "Planning & Organizing" performance or they could rate the "quality" of his or her "Planning & Organizing." You could assess the "quantity" of "organized lectures" or the "quality" of these lectures. These six criteria are listed and defined in Figure 9.2. Although all these criteria may not be relevant to every job activity, some of them will be. It is also important for organizations to recognize the relationships among the criteria. For example, sometimes managers encourage employees to push for quantity, without recognizing that quality may suffer. Likewise, they may focus on quality without

FIGURE 9.2
THE SIX PRIMARY CRITERIA ON WHICH THE VALUE OF PERFORMANCE MAY BE ASSESSED

1. *Quality:* The degree to which the process or result of carrying out an activity approaches perfection, in terms of either conforming to some ideal way of performing the activity or fulfilling the activity's intended purpose.

2. *Quantity:* The amount produced, expressed in such terms as dollar value, number of units, or number of completed activity cycles.

3. *Timeliness:* The degree to which an activity is completed, or a result produced, at the earliest time desirable from the standpoints of both coordinating with the outputs of others and maximizing the time available for other activities.

4. *Cost-effectiveness:* The degree to which the use of the organization's resources (e.g., human, monetary, technological, material) is maximized in the sense of getting the highest gain or reduction in loss from each unit or instance of use of a resource.

5. *Need for supervision:* The degree to which a performer can carry out a job function without either having to request supervisory assistance or requiring supervisory intervention to prevent an adverse outcome.

6. *Interpersonal impact:* The degree to which a performer promotes feelings of self-esteem, goodwill, and cooperativeness among coworkers and subordinates.

emphasizing timeliness; thereby resulting in missed delivery dates.

The HR professional must determine whether raters should assess employees' performance on each job function as a whole (i.e., considering all relevant criteria simultaneously) or whether raters should assess each relevant criterion of performance for each job activity separately. For example, a very common appraisal form is the narrative or essay in which the rater simply writes an unstructured evaluation of the employee, which may or may not break the evaluation down in terms of specific work functions or criteria. The overall rating approach is faster than making assessments on separate criteria but has the major drawback of requiring raters to simultaneously consider as many as six different aspects of value and to mentally compute their average. The probable result of all this subjective reasoning may be less accurate ratings than those done on each relevant criterion for each job activity and less specific feedback to the performer. In general, the greater the specificity in the content of the appraisal, the more effective the appraisal system. Internal and external customers should play a critical role in determining the content that is the basis for the appraisals of the "supplier."[26] If their assessments are to be sought as inputs to the appraisal, then they should also be involved in determining the content of the appraisal form.

PERFORMANCE-LEVEL ANCHORS. Work-oriented appraisal systems typically require raters to compare performance on each job function against a set of benchmarks. These benchmarks are brief descriptions of levels of performance, and are referred to as "anchors" or **performance-level anchors.** Performance anchors may take three different forms: adjectives or adjective phrases, behavioral descriptions or critical incidents, and outcomes or results produced by performing.

Adjectival benchmarks (e.g., "satisfactory," "very low," "below standard," "rarely," etc.) are highly subjective because their interpretation can mean different things to different raters. For example, one manager's definition of "below standard" may be quite different from another manager's definition.

Behavioral anchors consist of descriptions of the actions or behaviors taken by the person being appraised. For example, if the job function is "scheduling meetings," the behavioral anchors may look like "sends notices about meetings," "visits employees to remind them about meetings," and "posts notices about meetings in key locations." Behavioral anchors are very useful for developmental purposes since raters are able to give specific behavioral feedback to employees (e.g., identifying skill areas that need improvement). Results-oriented anchors are based on outcomes produced and may look like the "number of customer complaints," "number of units produced," the "number of units rejected by quality control," or the "number of days absent." Generally, results-oriented anchors are preferable to either adjectival or behavioral anchors when performance outcomes are important and identifiable and when the person's contribution to the results can be clearly distinguished. Behavioral anchors should be used if outcomes cannot be linked to a particular person or group of persons. At Sheraton, for example, the "timeliness" of room service was assessed by work unit (i.e., all persons related to room service for specified work shifts). At Blockbuster Video, paid "customers" evaluate the quality of service they receive from particular stores and individual employees.

Measurement Process

The second set of issues to be considered when designing an appraisal system is the system's measurement process. Among the choices are the type of measurement scale, types of rating instruments, control of rating errors, accounting for situational constraints on performance, and the overall score computation method.

TYPE OF MEASUREMENT SCALE. Certain types of personnel decisions need higher levels of precision than others. For example, if the organization wants to be able to single out the highest (or lowest) performers in a group for some special recognition (discipline), then measurements at the ordinal level will suffice. That is, employees need to be ranked only from best to worst. Other personnel decisions (e.g., selection decisions and identification of developmental needs) require the use of a more precise measurement scale (e.g., interval level). For example, at Digital Equipment Corporation, managers determine promotions based on appraisal data across units. The extent to which one employee is judged to be superior to another is thus needed. An interval level scale will be able to indicate this because it reveals the ranking of employees' performance as well as the actual difference in their scores (i.e., how much better one employee is compared to others). An appraisal system must be designed using a measurement scale at the needed level of precision.

TYPES OF RATING INSTRUMENTS. There are three basic ways in which raters can make performance assessments: (1) they can make comparisons among ratees' performances, (2) they can make comparisons among anchors or performance-level anchors and select one most descriptive of the person being appraised, and (3) they can make comparisons of individuals *to* anchors. These are shown in simplified form in Figure 9.3. Some of the most popular rating instruments representing each of these three ways are described in the next section. The essay or narrative method we discussed above does not fit into any of these categories because this approach has no measurement process itself and, if numbers must be derived, the numbering system would then fit into one of these three categories.

Rating instruments: Comparisons among ratees' performances. Paired comparisons, straight ranking, and forced distribution are appraisal systems that require raters to make comparisons among ratees according to some measure of effectiveness. *Paired comparisons* require the rater to compare all possible pairs of ratees on "overall performance" or some other, usually vaguely defined standard. This task can become cumbersome for the rater as the number of employees increases and more comparisons are needed. The formula for the number of possible pairs of employees is n(n–1)/2, where n = the number of employees. *Straight ranking* or rank ordering asks the rater to simply identify the "best" employee, the "second best," and so on, until the rater has identified the worst employee. For example, the NCAA rankings in football and basketball are based on a rank ordering of the teams by coaches and the press. When Safeway Foods had to downsize its workforce, it required managers to derive a rank ordering of all line supervisors within their unit for purposes of terminating the lowest ranked 30 percent.

Forced distribution usually presents the rater with a limited number of categories (usually five to seven) and requires (or "forces") the rater to place a designated por-

FIGURE 9.3
RATING FORMAT OPTIONS

COMPARISONS AMONG PERFORMANCES

Compare the performances of all ratees to each anchor for each job activity, function, or overall performance. Rater judgments may be made in one of the following ways:

- Indicate which ratee in each possible pair of ratees performed closest to the performance level described by the anchor or attained the highest level or overall performance. (Illustrative method: paired comparison)
- Indicate how the ratees ranked in terms of closeness to the performance level described by the anchor. (Illustrative method: straight ranking)
- Indicate what percentage of the ratees performed in a manner closest to the performance level described by the anchor. (Note: the percentages have to add up to 100% for all the anchors within each job activity/function.) (Illustrative method: forced distribution)

COMPARISONS AMONG ANCHORS

Compare all the anchors for each job activity or function and select the one (or more) that best describes the ratee's performance level. Rater judgments are made in the following way:

- Indicate which of the anchors fit the ratee's performance best (and/or worst). (Illustrative method: forced choice)

COMPARISONS TO ANCHORS

Compare each ratee's performance to each anchor for each job activity or function. Rater judgments are made in one of the following ways:

- Whether or not the ratee's performance matches the anchor. (Illustrative methods: graphic rating scales such as BARS; MBO)
- The degree to which the ratee's performance matches the anchor. (Illustrative methods: all summated rating scales such as BOS and PDA methods)
- Whether the ratee's performance was better than, equal to, or worse than that described by the anchor. (Illustrative method: Mixed standard scales)

---

tion of the ratees into each category. A forced distribution usually places the majority of employees in the middle category (i.e., with average ratings or raises) while fewer employees are placed in higher and lower categories. Some organizations use forced distributions to assign pay increases while others use them to assign performance ratings to ensure that raters do not assign all their employees the most extreme (e.g., highest) possible ratings. Forced distributions have been used by Merck & Company by requiring divisions to place employees in one of five performance categories ranked relative to their peers. They are to place 5 percent of employees in the top category "exceptional," 15 percent in the next highest "with distinction," 70 percent in the middle "high Merck standard," 8 percent in the next lowest "room for improvement," and 2 percent in the lowest performance category, "not acceptable."[27] Merck began using the system when it found that its previous rating scale was unable to distinguish among employees for merit purposes (almost everyone was rated at the highest level). Figure 9.4 presents an example of a general forced distribution rating format.

Rating instruments: Comparisons among performance-level anchors. The *forced choice* technique is a rating method that requires the rater to make comparisons among anchors given for a job activity. The method is designed to reduce (or eliminate) intentional rating bias where the rater deliberately attempts to rate individuals high (or low) irrespective of their performance. The rationale underlying the approach is that statements are grouped in such a way that the scoring key is not known to the rater (i.e., the way to rate higher or lower is not apparent). The most common format is a group of four statements from which the rater must select two as "most descriptive" of the person being rated. The rater is unaware of which statements (if selected) will result in higher (or lower) ratings for the ratee because all four statements appear equally desirable or undesirable. There are usually a minimum of 20 of these groups of four statements. For example, if you were asked to select the two statements that are most descriptive of your instructor for this class, which two would you select?

1. Is patient with slow learners.
2. Lectures with confidence.
3. Keeps the interest and attention of the class.

4. Acquaints classes with objectives for each lesson in advance.

The statements are chosen to be equal in desirability to make it more difficult for the rater to pick out those that can give the ratee the highest or lowest ratings. However, only two of the items are characteristic of highly effective performers. Items 1 and 3 have been shown to discriminate between the most effective and the least effective professors. Items 2 and 4 did not generally discriminate between effective and ineffective performers. If you selected statements 1 and 3 as most descriptive of your instructor, then he or she would be awarded two points. This procedure would be used with each of the groups of statements to determine the total score for each ratee. Raters are not given the scoring scheme so they are unable to intentionally give performers high or low ratings.

Rating instruments: Comparisons to performance-level anchors. Methods that require the rater to compare the employee's performance to specified anchors include: graphic rating scales, behaviorally anchored rating scales (BARS), management by objectives (MBO), summated scales (e.g., behavioral observation scales (BOS), and mixed standard scales (MSS), and performance distribution assessment (PDA). *Graphic rating scales* are the most widely used type of rating format. In fact, a recent survey of organizations reported that they were used in 57 percent of the firms surveyed.[28] Figure 9.5 presents some examples of graphic scales.

FIGURE 9.4
A FORCED DISTRIBUTION SCALE

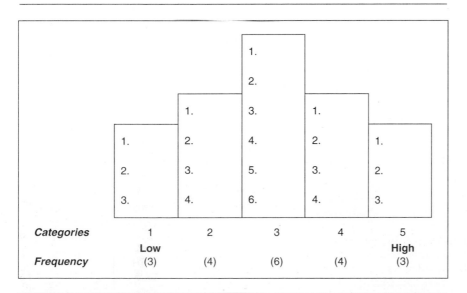

Note: In this example, 20 persons must be rated in five categories based on their overall performance. The numbers in parentheses indicate the number of persons who must be placed in each category. Rank orderings within categories are not usually required.

Source: H. J. Bernardin and R. W. Beatty, *Performance appraisal: Assessing human behavior at work.* Boston: PWS-Kent, 1984, p. 112. Reprinted with permission.

FIGURE 9.5
EXAMPLES OF GRAPHIC RATING SCALES

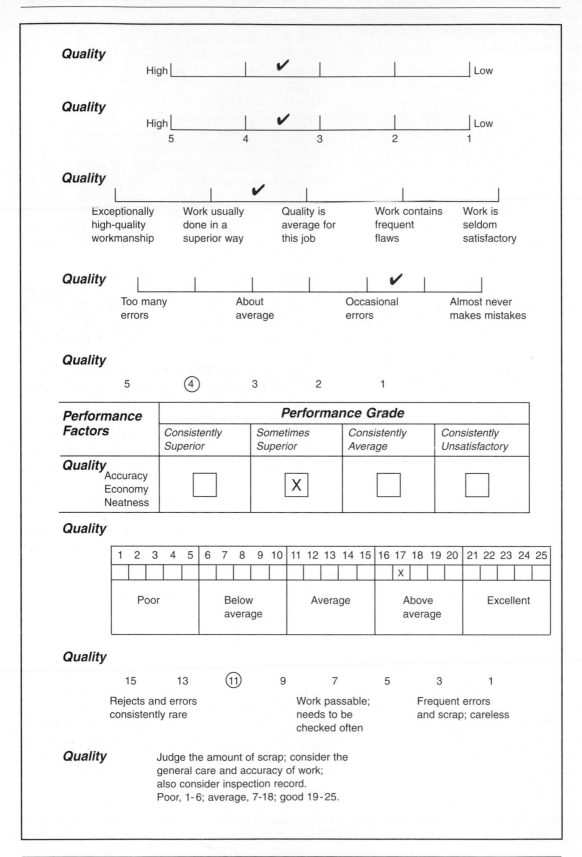

Source: R. M. Guion, *Personnel Testing.* New York: McGraw-Hill, 1984, p. 98. Reprinted with permission.

Generally, graphic rating scales use adjectives or numbers as anchors. The system used at Textron requires ratings of "problem areas," "meets expectation," "significant strength," or "not applicable" for functions such as meeting deadlines, team building, and safety effectiveness.[29]

One of the most heavily researched types of graphic scales is the *behaviorally anchored rating scales (BARS).* As shown in Figure 9.6, BARS are graphic scales with specific behavioral descriptions defining various points along the scale for each dimension. One rating method for BARS asks raters to record specific observations of the employee's performance relevant to the dimension on the scale. For example, in Figure 9.6, the rater has written in "Stuck to the course outline . . ." between points 9 and 10 on the left side of the scale. The rater would then select the point along the right side of the scale that best represents the ratee's performance on that function. That point is selected by comparing the ratee's actual observed performance to the behavioral expectations that are provided as "anchors" on the scale. The rationale behind writing in observations on the scale before selecting an anchor is to ensure that raters are basing their ratings on actual performance observations. In addition, the observations can be given to ratees as feedback. Research shows this form of feedback is effective at improving performance.[30]

The method of *summated scales* is one of the oldest formats and remains one of the most popular for performance appraisal. Two of the most recent versions of summated scales are behavioral observation scales (or BOS) and performance distribution assessment (or PDA). An example of a summated scale is presented in Figure 9.7. For this scale, the rater is asked to indicate how frequently the ratee has performed each of the listed behaviors.

Mixed standard scales represent rating instruments that, like the forced choice measure, attempt to control deliberate response bias by raters. Mixed standard scales usually consist of sets of three statements that describe high, medium, and low levels of performance on a job activity or dimension. For example, in its validation study, the Toledo Ohio Police Department developed a dimension called "Crime prevention" for their patrol officers. The high performance item for crime prevention was "takes numerous steps both to prevent and to control crime." The average performance item was "makes some effort to emphasize crime prevention," and the low performance item was "has very little or no contact with citizens to inform them of crime prevention methods." Statements are then randomized on the rating form and the rater is asked to indicate whether the ratee's performance is "better than," "as good as," or "worse than" the behavior described in the statement.

Management by objectives (MBO) calls for a comparison between specific, quantifiable target goals and the actual results achieved by an employee. The measurable, quantitative goals are usually mutually agreed upon by the employee and supervisor at the beginning of an appraisal period. During the review period, progress toward the goals is monitored. At the end of the review period, the employee and supervisor meet to evaluate whether the goals were achieved and to decide on new goals. The goals or objectives are usually set for individual employees or units and usually differ across employees (or units) depending on the circumstances of the job. For this reason, MBO has been shown to be useful for defining "individual" or unit performance in the context of strategic plans. As a motivational technique, the goals or objectives set are specific in nature and perceived by the performer as attainable while still being difficult, MBO is an effective approach to improving performance and motivating employees. MBO is not recommended for comparing people or units unless the objectives can be judged to be equally attainable in the context of potential situational constraints on performance, which we discuss in the next section. While MBO has not been used in organizations as frequently as graphic rating scales, its use is very common at the managerial level.

Rating instrumentation and rating accuracy. Generally, the choice of a rating instrument seems to have little effect on rating accuracy,[31] with the critical exception being that the greater the precision in the definition of *performance,* the more effective the appraisal for any of the purposes we described above. Thus, the main basis for selecting a rating instrument should be based on other factors such as how well it fits with the level of precision needed and the purposes to be served by the data. If only ordinal levels of measurement are needed, formats using comparisons among ratee performance (e.g., ranking) are adequate if performance is carefully defined as the basis for the comparisons. At the higher levels of precision (e.g., interval level), the rating instruments based on "comparison to anchors" offer the most direct approaches to eliciting the needed responses. Ease of use and acceptability to raters and ratees should also be considered when choosing a rating instrument.

Some organizations use a combination of rating instruments. For example, state employees in the Colorado Governor's Job Training Office use a system that combines the attributes of management by objectives, an essay appraisal, and forced choice component.[32] Amoco uses essay, forced distribution, and graphic scales to evaluate managers. Pratt & Whitney used a ranking and a BARS format to conduct a special appraisal as part of its downsizing program.

Sixty percent of organizations surveyed use different appraisal systems for different levels of employees. For example, at Electro-Biology, nonexempt employees are rated on simple graphic rating scales and exempt employees are rated on a combination of MBO objectives

FIGURE 9.6
AN EXAMPLE OF A BEHAVIORALLY ANCHORED RATING SCALE

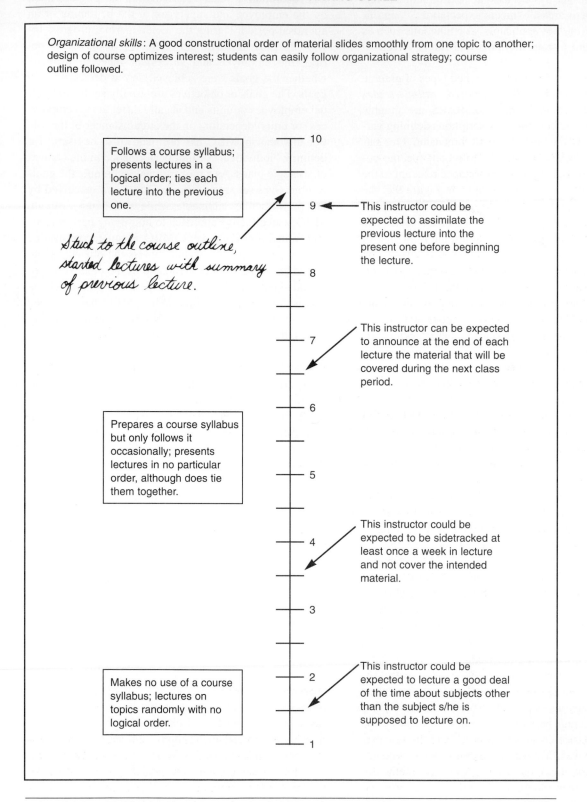

Organizational skills: A good constructional order of material slides smoothly from one topic to another; design of course optimizes interest; students can easily follow organizational strategy; course outline followed.

Follows a course syllabus; presents lectures in a logical order; ties each lecture into the previous one.

Stuck to the course outline, started lectures with summary of previous lecture.

10

9 — This instructor could be expected to assimilate the previous lecture into the present one before beginning the lecture.

8

7 — This instructor can be expected to announce at the end of each lecture the material that will be covered during the next class period.

6

Prepares a course syllabus but only follows it occasionally; presents lectures in no particular order, although does tie them together.

5

4 — This instructor could be expected to be sidetracked at least once a week in lecture and not cover the intended material.

3

Makes no use of a course syllabus; lectures on topics randomly with no logical order.

2 — This instructor could be expected to lecture a good deal of the time about subjects other than the subject s/he is supposed to lecture on.

1

Source: H. J. Bernardin and R. W. Beatty, *Performance appraisal: Assessing human behavior at work.* Boston: PWS-Kent, 1984, p. 84. Reprinted with permission.

FIGURE 9.7
A SUMMATED RATING SCALE

Directions: Rate your manager on the way he or she has conducted performance appraisal
interviews. Use the following scale to make your ratings:

1 = Always

2 = Often

3 = Occasionally

4 = Seldom

5 = Never

1. Effectively used information about the subordinate in the discussion.
2. Skillfully guided the discussion through the problem areas.
3. Maintained control over the interview.
4. Appeared to be prepared for the interview.
5. Let the subordinate control the interview.
6. Adhered to a discussion about the subordinate's problems.
7. Seemed concerned about the subordinate's perspective of the problems.
8. Probed deeply into sensitive areas in order to gain sufficient knowledge.
9. Made the subordinate feel comfortable during discussions of sensitive topics.
9. Projected sincerity during the interview.
11. Maintained the appropriate climate for an appraisal interview.
12. Displayed insensitivity to the subordinate's problems.
13. Displayed an organized approach to the interview.
14. Asked the appropriate questions.
15. Failed to follow up with questions when they appeared to be necessary.
16. Asked general questions about the subordinate's problems.
17. Asked only superficial questions that failed to confront the issues.
18. Displayed considerable interest in the subordinate's professional growth.
19. Provided general suggestions to aid in the subordinate's professional growth.
20. Provided poor advice regarding the subordinate's growth.
21. Made specific suggestions for helping the subordinate develop professionally.
22. Remained calm during the subordinate's outbursts.
23. Responded to the subordinate's outbursts in a rational manner.
24. Appeared to be defensive in reaction to the subordinate's complaints.
25. Backed down inappropriately when confronted.
26. Made realistic commitments to help the subordinate get along better with others.
27. Seemed unconcerned about the subordinate's problems.
28. Provided poor advice about the subordinate's relationships with others.
29. Provided good advice about resolving conflict.
30. When discussing the subordinate's future with the company, encouraged him/her to stay on.
31. Used appropriate compliments regarding the subordinate's technical expertise.
32. Motivated the subordinate to perform the job well.
33. Seemed to ignore the subordinate's excellent performance record.
34. Made inappropriate ultimatums to the subordinate about improving performance.

---

and forced distribution ranking.[33] Digital Equipment uses both MBO and summated scales to evaluate managers while using a graphic approach for nonmanagerial personnel.

CONTROL OF RATING ERRORS. Performance ratings are subject to a wide variety of inaccuracies and biases referred to as rating errors. These errors occur in rater judgment and information processing[34] and can se-

riously affect performance-appraisal results. For example, one employee at Southern California Edison remarked, "Basically, everyone gets the same rating, so why all the fuss about this stuff?" HR staff noted a number of problems with the appraisal process, particularly rater errors, and totally redesigned the system.[35] Unfortunately, many of these errors cannot be eradicated easily. The most commonly cited rating errors are the following:

Leniency. Ratings for employees are generally at the high end of the scale regardless of the actual performance of employees. Surveys have identified leniency as the most serious problem with appraisals whenever they are linked to important decisions such as compensation or promotions.[36]

Central tendency. Ratings for employees tend to be toward the center of the scale regardless of the employees' actual performance.

Halo effect. The rater allows a rating on one dimension (or an overall impression) to influence the ratings he or she assigns to other dimensions for that employee. That is, the rater inappropriately assesses performance similarly across different job functions, projects, or performance dimensions. Despite the name (halo), this error also applies to a sort of "horns" effect when someone is rated low on all functions.

In addition to these common measurement errors, there are six major cognitive errors that often occur in performance appraisal. We will suggest some methods for dealing with each of them. They underscore the difficulties of making valid performance appraisals (we'll deal with intentional bias later).

1. Fundamental attribution errors. This error refers to the tendency to attribute observed behaviors to the disposition of the person being observed and to thereby underestimate the causal role of environmental influences. This phenomenon has been found to be particularly potent where the behavior observed connotes failure or negative social effects. This error seems to occur in reverse when people observe others exhibiting successful performances and other positive behaviors. The observers tend to overestimate the causal influence of the situation and minimize the role of the person observed. This is known as actor-observer bias. This error tends to result in people being given insufficient credit for their successes and excessive blame for failures. It is particularly pernicious from the standpoint of ratee acceptance of appraisal results because people tend to make the exact opposite attributions for their *own* behavior. They tend to attribute their successes to their own competence and their failures to the influence of external factors beyond their control.

Several things can be done to minimize this error's effect on performance appraisals. First, employees should be counseled to bring any mitigating circumstances surrounding their less effective performances to the immediate attention of their supervisors or others who will be involved in their appraisals. Second, those who are responsible for appraising others should take special care to look for such circumstances that may mitigate less effective performances. They should also ask

themselves whether anyone else could have achieved the successes recorded by the person being observed or whether, in fact, this particular person's competence really made a difference. Finally, it is extremely desirable for a rater to meet with each ratee just before rendering appraisal judgments and attempt to reach a consensus on the extent to which performance on each rating factor was constrained by factors beyond the ratee's control.

2. Representativeness. Representativeness refers to the tendency to make judgments about people (or their performance) on the basis of their similarity to people who exhibited prominent or memorable levels on the attribute being judged, even though the similarity may have no causal connection to the attribute. For example, popular stereotypes may have given the rater the image that people who use intimidation to resolve disputes tend to be men of Italian heritage with New York accents who wear gold necklaces and flashy clothes. When rating someone on factors relating to their interpersonal effectiveness, the rater will tend to rate in accordance with his or her preconceptions rather than in accordance with observations. Such a rater would be ignoring the fact that the vast majority of such men do not engage in such interpersonal intimidation. The same error can work to inflate ratings when a ratee possesses a number of characteristics that the rater associates with effective performance. This type of thinking ignores the fact that although some prominent examples of people who performed at the upper or lower extremes of effectiveness may have possessed a certain constellation of traits, most of the people who possess such traits do not perform at the extremes.

This is a difficult tendency to overcome. Perhaps the best means of suppressing it is to use rating scales that are anchored with detailed descriptions of behaviors or outcomes. Raters should focus on the relative incidence of the behaviors or outcomes that occurred rather than on finding the level on each rating factor that is consistent with the other nonperformance information known about the ratee.

3. Availability. This is a rule of thumb that some people use in judging the relative incidence of events. Specifically, people tend to mistake the ease with which a category of events can be recalled as an indication of its frequency of occurrence relative to other events. The relevance to performance-appraisal judgments should be obvious: Because more extreme events tend to be more memorable, raters will tend to attribute greater frequency to them than was the case. This results in such events being given excessive weight in the formation of appraisal judgments. Negative events—instances of ineffective performance—seem to have the greatest availability in memory. As a consequence, such events exert an undue influence on appraisal judgments. Unfortunately, even negative events in which a performer is ultimately absolved of all responsibility can have a negative impact on the performer's reputation.

There is no easy solution to the availability problem. The act of making raters aware of their proneness to this type of error, as this description of the problem is intended to do, may cause them to make efforts to compensate for this tendency. However, there is no research to substantiate this possibility. About the only strategy that the research suggests may be effective is to have raters estimate the actual frequencies at which they observed behaviors/outcomes to have occurred. These numbers can then be transformed into overall ratings on each scale.

4. Cognitive distortion. It has been conclusively established that people develop theories about "what goes with what" in virtually all areas of human activity. These theories have been given the name of cognitive **schemata.** When asked to recall how people behaved, subjects tend to make their ratings on the different attributes conform to their theories or schemata of how such attributes relate to each other. Thus, a person rated low on sociability may also tend to be rated as being devious, paranoid, low in self-confidence, and cynical even if none of these latter characterizations is true. The factors on which people are appraised invite the formation of cognitive schemata that specify how such factors interrelate. It is likely, therefore, that raters will strive to ensure that their ratings on a set of appraisal factors will conform to their schemata for such factors. Halo effect is probably caused by this cognitive error.

To the extent that raters are forced to recall the actual behaviors or outcomes that occurred rather than allowed to focus on the overall meaning of each factor, they are less likely to rely on their schemata as the basis for their ratings. This can be accomplished by using scales anchored by specific descriptions of behaviors or outcomes and, ideally, by eliciting ratings in the form of the estimated frequencies of the behaviors or outcomes anchoring each scale level.

5. Insufficient adjustment from anchors. This error, which is also known as conservatism (not to be confused with the political variety), refers to the tendency to insufficiently alter one's judgment away from one's starting point when new information is received. Most of us start with some initial impression of any situation we encounter, or we form one very quickly after our initial immersion in a situation. This is very true of observations of other people's performances. Either from past experience, stereotyping, interpersonal affect, or reputation, we generally start any period of observing another's performance with some initial impression or we form one very quickly. And once an initial starting point, or anchor, is selected, we tend to resist being moved from this point

by subsequent information that warrants movement. As a consequence, our final appraisal judgments will be much nearer to our starting points than they should be. This is an obvious source of unfairness in appraisals. A person's reputation or even his or her past performance, much less our initial impression, should not be a factor in how his or her performance during the period under consideration is judged. This error is quite potent. For example, if a person regarded as unreliable and untrustworthy told the rater that your performance was terrible, the rater would be affected by that person's opinion in evaluating you even though he or she had other sources of highly credible information.

The origin of this problem again seems to be the holistic consideration of a person's performance on each rating factor rather than attending to the specific behaviors or outcomes that were exhibited. If rating scales are used that don't call for an overall judgment but rather elicit estimates of the frequencies with which the behaviors or outcomes anchoring each level occurred, it seems we could overcome the problem of insufficiently responsive judgments. In other words, if we don't ask raters to make judgments per se, we should be able to avoid this problem. Short of implementing such scales, raters should consider the relative incidence of each scale level and try to estimate the average level at which the ratee performed. This is in contrast to simply going down a scale and finding the one category that fits best.

6. Egocentric attribution. This is the tendency to assume that anyone who behaves in a manner different from oneself is deviant and inferior. In the context of performance appraisal, this translates into the tendency to see the performance of someone who carries out higher job functions in a different way than the rater would perform them as being inferior. Where there is one best way of carrying out a particular job function, this may be a legitimate judgment. However, most job functions do not fit this description. There are usually equally acceptable ways of arriving at the same desired outcome, and this becomes progressively more true at higher occupational levels. Giving low ratings to people because their methods of achieving successful outcomes are different from those the rater would choose is not only unfair but also counterproductive. It tends to force ratees to adopt behaviors or methods they may not be able to use as effectively, resulting in lower performance.

The solution to this problem is for raters to focus their attention on the outcomes achieved rather than on the behaviors or methods used to achieve them. To assist raters in this effort, rating scales should, to the maximum extent possible, employ outcomes rather than behaviors as the anchors for their various levels. In cases where behaviors must be used, the anchors should include descriptions of *all* the behaviors that qualify for their respective levels.

All these errors can arise in two different ways: as the result of *unintentional* errors in the way people observe, store, recall, and report events, or as the result of *intentional* efforts to assign inaccurate ratings.[37] If rating errors are unintentional, raters may commit them because they do not have the necessary skills to make accurate ratings or the content of the appraisal is not carefully defined. Attempts to control unconscious, unintentional errors most often focus on rater training. Training to improve the rater's observational and categorization skills (called **frame-of-reference training**) has been shown to increase rater accuracy and consistency.[38] This training consists of creating a common frame of reference among raters. Raters are familiarized with the rating scales and are given opportunities to practice making ratings. Following this, they are given feedback on their practice ratings. They are also given descriptions of critical incidents of performance that illustrate outstanding, average, and unsatisfactory levels of performance on each dimension. This is done so they will know what behaviors or outcomes to consider when making their ratings. Frame of reference training is usually combined with descriptions, discussions, and illustrations of the common rating errors. For example, all supervisors at the Tribune Company receive a case and discussion of the rating errors we just covered.

Another strategy to control unintentional rating errors is to reduce the amount of obvious performance judgments a rater is required to make. For example, a rating instrument using this strategy might pose rating questions that require objective responses such as, "On what percent of all the times that Sue organized a meeting did she fail to contact everyone to attend the meeting?" or "On what percent of all the times that Sue organized a meeting did it begin and end on time?" The responses to these questions would be mathematically converted into appraisal scores. **PDA** is one such rating instrument.

Raters may commit rating errors intentionally for political reasons or to provide certain outcomes to their employees or themselves.[39] For example, one common intentional rating error is leniency. Managers may assign higher ratings than deserved to avoid a confrontation with the employee, to protect an employee suffering from personal problems, to acquire more recognition for the department or themselves, or to be able to reward the employee with a bonus or promotion. Although less common, managers may also intentionally assign more severe ratings than an employee deserves to motivate him or her to work harder, to teach the employee a lesson, or to build a case for firing the employee. Attempts to control intentional rating errors include making ratings observable and provable, hiding scoring keys by using certain rating instruments (e.g., forced choice, mixed standard scales), requiring checks or reviews of ratings

by other people, training raters on how to provide negative evaluation, and reducing the rater's motivation to assign inaccurate ratings. For example, the state of Virginia reduced rater motivation to rate leniently by rewarding raters for the extent to which they carefully define *performance* for their employees and conform to the regulations of the rating system regarding documentation for extreme ratings.[40] In general, the more managers are held responsible for the appraisal process itself, the more effective the appraisal system will ultimately be.

ACCOUNTING FOR SITUATIONAL CONSTRAINTS ON PERFORMANCE. Attribution bias, and particularly the actor-observer bias, is a major cause of inaccurate and unfair performance appraisals.[41] Any student who has been graded on a group project may have experienced this problem. Many conditions can hold a person back from performing as well as he or she could. These constraints include inadequate tools, lack of supplies, not enough money, too little time, lack of information, breakdowns in equipment, and not enough help from others. For example, truck inspectors may be limited in the number of trucks they can check for defects if they spend a considerable portion of their workday in court presenting testimony against offenders. They may, however, still be held accountable for inspecting a certain number of trucks despite these other job duties. If in a group project, one of your team members fails to retrieve vital information, the constraint could hamper your ability to do your tasks. Situational factors that hinder an employee's job performance are called situational constraints and are described in Figure 9.8.[42] An appraisal system design should consider the effects of situational constraints so ratees are not unfairly downgraded for these uncontrollable factors. Rater training programs should also focus on making raters aware of potential constraints on employee performances and the tendency to commit this attributional error. Research shows that this approach to training results in more effective appraisals and, more importantly, higher unit performance.[43] Legitimate constraints on performance are the responsibility of management.

OVERALL SCORE COMPUTATION. Once performance has been assessed on each of the job's important activities or functions, it is usually necessary to produce an overall score reflecting the level of performance on the job as a whole. There are two primary ways of producing an overall score:

- *Judgmental:* The rater forms a subjective judgment of overall performance, usually after completing the performance ratings on each of the job's separate activities or functions (e.g., oral communication, negotiation).

FIGURE 9.8
POSSIBLE SITUATIONAL CONSTRAINTS ON PERFORMANCE

1. Absenteeism or turnover of key personnel.
2. Slowness of procedures for action approval.
3. Inadequate clerical support.
4. Shortages of supplies and/or raw materials.
5. Excessive restrictions on operating expenses.
6. Inadequate physical working conditions.
7. Inability to hire needed staff.
8. Inadequate performance of coworkers or personnel in other units on whom an individual's work depends.
9. Inadequate performance of subordinates.
10. Inadequate performance of managers.
11. Inefficient or unclear organizational structure or reporting relationships.
12. Excessive reporting requirements and administrative paperwork.
13. Unpredictable workloads.
14. Excessive workloads.
15. Changes in administrative policies, procedures, and/or regulations.
16. Pressures from coworkers to limit an individual's performance.
17. Unpredictable changes or additions to the types of work assigned.
18. Lack of proper equipment.
19. Inadequate communication within the organization.
20. The quality of raw materials.
21. Economic conditions (e.g., interest rates, labor availability, and costs of basic goods and services).
22. Inadequate training.

- *Mathematic:* The rater or some other scorer mathematically computes the weighted or unweighted mean of the performance ratings on each of the job's activities or functions.

The judgmental approach to determining an overall score is commonly used by many organizations, although it can easily lead to overall performance ratings that bear little relation to performance on each part of the job. The mathematic approach is more likely to accurately reflect overall performance based on all job activities or functions. The question for the rater using the mathematic approach is whether to compute the overall score by equally weighing the ratings on each of the various job activities or functions or by assigning them different weights based on their relative importance. Assuming you can derive reliable measures of importance, the latter approach is superior, particularly when the importance weights are derived in the context of the unit or organization's strategic goals.

Defining the Rater

Ratings can be provided by ratees, supervisors, peers, clients or customers, or high-level managers. While most companies still give the supervisor the sole responsibility for the employee's appraisal, formal multirater systems are becoming common.[44] A growing number of companies also use formal self-assessments.[45] The purpose is to encourage employees to take an active role in their own development.[46] In general, however, formal self-appraisals are still rare. One survey found that only 6.7 percent of firms allow for a formal self-appraisal, even though employees want to add their input to the appraisal process.[47] Upward appraisals (ratings by subordinates) are also on the increase. A 1992 study showed that subordinates were critiquing their supervisors and peers in 12 percent of the 397 U.S. companies surveyed. By 1993, the figure was up to 26 percent.[48]

With increasing frequency, organizations are concluding that multiple rater types benefit their appraisal systems. Ratings collected from several raters are thought to be more accurate, have fewer biases, are perceived to be more fair, and are less often the targets of lawsuits.[49] Also, many of the rater types used (e.g., customers, peers) have direct and unique knowledge of at least some aspects of the ratee's job performance and provide reliable and valid performance information on some job activities. In fact, the use of raters who represent all critical internal and external customers contributes to the accuracy and relevance of these so-called 360-degree systems.[50]

Many organizations have found that it is not difficult to set up a system using more than one source for ratings.[51] IBM, for example, has been using a multiple rating system for its managers since 1964. Subordinate appraisal plays a critical role in the process. In addition, in many organizations (e.g., Xerox, IBM, Motorola), with the advent of team-based structures, project teams, and leaderless work groups, multiple rater types are being used because there is no longer a traditional supervisor or the supervisor is no longer directly observing the employees' performance. For example, in high-technology firms (IBM, Texas Instruments, Intel Corporation) or think tanks (Lawrence Livermore Laboratories, GA Technologies), employees work on tasks and projects apart from their supervisor's direct guidance.[52] A growing number of firms, including (Federal Express, Tennessee Valley Authority, Domino's Pizza) use multiple rater types (e.g., subordinates, customers, supervisors) to determine how effectively managers are meeting goals for improved quality of services.[53] Many organizations use self-, subordinate, peer, and superior ratings as a comprehensive appraisal before a training program. The FAA, for example, provides feedback from superiors, subordinates, and peers to each participant before the start of the mandatory supervisory training program. The data are contrasted with the participant's self-appraisal on the same performance factors. The Center for Creative Leadership in Greensboro, North Carolina, requires all participants in its one-week assessment center to first submit evaluations from superiors, peers, and subordinates. These data are tabulated by the Center, and the feedback is reported to participants on the first day of the assessment center program. Participants consider this feedback to be among the most valuable they receive. Of course, it is important for any 360-degree system that individuals believe that the feedback they receive is from raters who have observed the relevant aspects of their performance.[54] The Powertrain Division of GM uses peers, subordinates, and superiors to evaluate its managers. A recent company survey found that 90 percent of managers prefer the new system to the old ranking system.

Many companies now use external customers as an important source of information about employee performance. At Avis Rent a Car, for example, customers can evaluate employees on customer-care balance sheets. The Britannia Building Society in the United Kingdom has developed criteria for assessing both internal and external customer service for purposes of individual appraisal. The Marriott Corporation places considerable weight on its customer survey data in the evaluation of each hotel as well as work units within the hotels. In addition to Blockbuster Video, which we mentioned earlier, Burger King, McDonald's, Domino's Pizza, and Taco Bell are among the companies that hire professional "customers" or "mystery shoppers" to visit specific installations to provide detailed appraisals of several performance functions (see the Critical Thinking exercise 9.2).

CRITICAL THINKING EXERCISE 9.2

The Role of Mystery Shoppers in Performance Appraisal[1]

The retail industry has made noteworthy efforts in soliciting customer feedback through its use of mystery shopping. Typically, this involves contracting with an organization to provide anonymous individuals who periodically shop the store, evaluating and reporting about the experience from a customer's viewpoint. Mystery shoppers usually review a predetermined menu of variables for each store they shop, based on criteria established by the retail organization. At the Limited and the Gap, for example, mystery shoppers follow a script to test the extent to which store employees adhere to their training regarding customer interactions.

The use of mystery shopping has become so popular that, in 1994, one contractor reported a professional

shopping staff of 8,800 and a business that was growing at the rate of 50 percent per year.[2] Other organizations, including Burger King, Neiman Marcus, Hyatt Hotels, Hertz Auto Rentals, Barney's New York, and Revco Drug Stores have had extensive experience using mystery shoppers to obtain customer-based information.

Office Depot converts its mystery shopping data into a customer satisfaction index, which also includes customer complaints. The index is reported to each store manager once a month. The data, aggregated across the year, become a key determinant of each manager's annual appraisal, bonus, base salary increase, and objectives for the next appraisal cycle.

Our literature search turned up no systematic study of the validity and reliability of mystery shopping, nor has the effect of mystery shopping on business performance been rigorously examined. Since efficiency data are easiest to identify and contract out, mystery shoppers may be focusing on issues such as determining the length of time it takes an associate to approach them, or how long they await final service delivery, or the number of times the telephone rings before it is answered, or the number of different individuals that become involved when a customer request strays from the norm. These measures are effective customer measures *only* when they capture information that real customers value highly. In other words, if an organization's source of competitive advantage is price, or convenience, or uniqueness of service features, or value in relation to competitors, then the above efficiency measures may create an inaccurate, or a mixed, signal to employees about the performance efforts that are really valued.

Assignment

Pick a job in which "mystery shoppers" might provide helpful and unique data. Describe how you would develop the system and incorporate data from this system into the performance-appraisal system. Also, could your university use "mystery shoppers"? If you think it could, should it and what would the "shoppers" look for?

[1] Contributed by Christine M. Hagan.

[2] K. Helliker, Smile: That cranky shopper may be a store spy. *The Wall Street Journal,* Nov. 30, 1994, p. B1.

The number of rater types that should be used in rating the performance of an employee depends on the number of rater types that can furnish unique perspectives on the performance of the ratee. By *unique perspective* we mean people in a position to furnish not only different information but also information processed through less severe biases. To decide how many rater types should be used, cost-benefit ratings and logistic feasibility should be considered. For example, do the payoffs of multiple rater types offset the costs entailed (e.g., for development of additional forms, rater training, allocation of additional time to administrative activity)? Also, can ratings by multiple raters be coordinated to ensure the timely completion of all ratings without disrupting regular operations?

Another consideration is the symbolic significance of participation in the appraisal process. Do Marriott customers perceive better customer service simply because they have been asked to participate? Are subordinates more satisfied with their jobs or with management in general because they participated in the evaluation of their managers?

Conceptualizing all possible raters as all possible customers (internal and external) is a good approach to setting up a multiple rater system. The approach is also consistent with the recent emphasis on total quality management, which is discussed in Chapter 12. If only a supervisor or manager is to be used, that rater should seek performance information from all critical internal and external customers. To the extent that ratees look at the evaluator (e.g., the supervisor or manager) as their only important customer, the system can easily operate to the detriment of the organization. The focus for both raters and ratees should be on actual internal and external customer requirements. Just as the measurement of the performance dimensions should have this focus, so should the identification of the sources of rating.

WHAT IS 360-DEGREE APPRAISAL?*   The most comprehensive form of multirater feedback that has gained popularity recently is **360-degree appraisal** and often involves an employee's supervisor, other higher-level managers, peers, internal and external customers, suppliers, recipients of reports or presentations, subordinates, and the individual employee (self-rating). Such appraisal seeks to evaluate all sides and facets of an employee's performance to gain the maximum amount of information available from sources who observe that person in action. The objective is to provide as complete a picture of the employee's behavior as possible in order to provide an assessment that is both informative and developmental.

A number of companies have initiated 360-degree appraisal processes. A recent survey noted that of the 756 companies surveyed, 13 percent stated they used a 360-degree system (evaluations by supervisors, direct reports, peers) and another 9 percent reported that they used a partial 360 system (ratings by supervisors and peers or supervisors and direct reports).[55] These companies saw their systems as having a superior impact on workplace behavior compared to the traditional "super-

visors only" system that had been in place. In addition, 90 percent of the firms used the 360-degree information for personnel decisions such as merit increases and promotions.[56] Another survey of 45 organizations using 360-degree feedback systems found that employees welcomed and supported the process, although there was some initial opposition. In addition, it was considered a success in 65 percent of the companies that have used it, and 78 percent of the firms were planning on extending its use.[57]

Some firms have used 360-degree systems only for developmental purposes to give employees candid information about their work-related strengths. Others use 360-degree feedback as an information tool to help supervisors assess and reward their employees. Both sides agree that feedback from a variety of sources provides a more accurate picture of employees' day-to-day performance.[58] One tool by Performance Support Systems, called 20/20 Insight, allows employees to learn how their work behavior is perceived by supervisors, peers, customers, and direct reports.[59]

Federal Express uses a 360-degree system as the foundation of objective goal setting. By receiving information from internal and external customers, an individual gains feedback as to what areas are seen as superior and what areas are seen as deficient. This feedback is then used in a management by objective (MBO) system to define the goals for that individual according to the needs of his or her customers. These new goals help to focus the employee on what is required to improve performance *and* achieve customer satisfaction at the same time. Digital Equipment Corporation found that 360-degree evaluation provides more opportunity for an employee to develop. By providing information from customers and peers, performance dimensions that a manager might not see regularly are given weight, and an individual can learn to be cognizant of these factors in addition to those that were traditionally part of the performance appraisal. Digital also found that employees perceive the 360 appraisal process as more fair, because they receive feedback from all environments in which they perform.[60] Hasbro uses a 360-degree appraisal system in its employee development process to avoid over-relying on line managers' judgments.[61]

In 1994, the Diagnostics Division of Abbott Laboratories implemented an assessment-based development program with its sales managers in the United States. The process became known as stakeholder or 360-degree feedback. Each sales manager receives an individual profile that is comprised of detailed feedback from his or her sales representatives. By 1996, the system had become a regular part of the development planning process.[62] Other firms that have used a 360 system with sales reps have included Bell Atlantic, Chrysler, and G.D. Searle.[63] Other organizations that have implemented 360-degree evaluation systems include Alcoa,

_____
*Contributed by Joseph G. Clark, Jr., and Joyce E. A. Russell.

DuPont, Levi Strauss, the Tennessee Valley Authority, Saint Francis Medical Center, PhotoDisc, and United Parcel Service.[64]

There are a variety of advantages to using the 360-degree evaluation process. The first and foremost of these is that receiving feedback from so many diverse sources allows the manager to gain information about instances and levels of behavior that he or she might not be privy to. For example, a manager who coordinates sales representatives in a large region may have sales information and firsthand knowledge of an employee's behavior. However, with a 360-degree feedback system, that same manager may receive feedback from peers in the same sales team, customers, distributors, and other regional personnel who have observed the same employee in different settings and situations. This provides the manager with a bigger picture of the individual's behavior and performance. The same employee who seemed absentminded and aloof to the manager might shine in front of the customers.

Another advantage to using other sources to rate an employee is that, with organizations becoming flatter and more streamlined, one manager may be in charge of an increasing number of employees. Receiving information from other sources takes some of the pressure off the manager to gather information. The approach is also compatible with the trend to drive a marketing orientation deep within the company by having external and internal customers evaluate the supplier's performance.[65] The 360-degree appraisal is also seen by recipients as more fair, the material is perceived as more job relevant, and the feedback has more potential for developmental and goal-setting applications (as with FedEx and Digital). At the WH Smith Group, a 360 system was implemented to improve individual development, support teamwork, determine pay increases, and change the organization's culture. The head of personnel believes that the 360 system provides a more accurate assessment of an employee's strengths and weaknesses than was previously available, while reducing the time spent in meetings.[66]

Critics of the 360-degree appraisal system cite a number of potential flaws in the mechanism.[67] The first is rater error. Each source of feedback suffers from varying sources of potential rater error (e.g., halo error, leniency or severity, attribution errors). Using all these differing sources of information means dealing with all the different potential avenues for rater error to seep into the evaluation.

The second criticism is cost and confusion. It can often be very costly and tedious to implement a 360-degree program. The multiple sources of feedback are difficult to coordinate, may contradict each other, and are often confusing to sort out and process effectively. This puts the burden on the manager to filter through the material provided and refine it into a coherent evaluation.

Critics also fear a negative attitude in 360-degree appraisal. The added sources of information may be used by a manager to bolster negative appraisals with a "see, I told you so" approach. Finally, employees alike worry about confidentiality. With so many sources of feedback about a single individual floating around, it is feared that both rater and ratee may lose their rights to confidentiality. In particular, peers worry about retribution resulting from negative feedback, as do subordinates who are evaluating their supervisors.[68] Instead of changing their behavior, managers receiving feedback from others may become defensive and vindictive or they may simply ignore the feedback and go back to business as usual. They may also be nervous initially about receiving the feedback from others.[69]

But steps can be taken to lessen the severity of potential problems with the 360-degree appraisal system. Computer appraisal software makes dealing with the glut of incoming information easier to handle. This software can also present the wealth of available data in a simple format to give to or discuss with the employee. Rater training and orientation in 360-degree appraisal programs is becoming increasingly popular. This training introduces employees to the concept of multiple-source feedback, and it makes them aware of rater error and methods to diminish it. Rating formats that focus on *the frequency of specific behaviors* can also help to limit sources of error.[70] To give the feedback more objectivity (and help avoid dwelling on negatives), a third party may be used. For example, AT&T managers send all the received feedback to a consultant, who analyzes the data for content and explains the results to the manager before the appraisal interview. This method also takes the organizational burden off the manager and assures the confidentiality of the sources of feedback.[71] Other suggestions for assuring confidentiality include sending appraisals in sealed packets, using scannable forms (not handwritten), including a return mailing address directly to the manager (or consultant), and preventing the recipient of the evaluation from having any access to individual responses.[72] These recommendations along with others are listed in Figure 9.9.[73]

Overall, 360-degree appraisal systems provide a wealth of information about an employee's behavior that might be unavailable in traditional manager evaluation formats. Customers (both internal and external), peers, subordinates, and others may all have access to unique performance data that can provide a truer picture of the individual's performance. This method of evaluation can also provide information on the state of the company's goals and needs. For example, Digital executives use the feedback from external customers to determine if the strategic plan they laid out is filtering down to employees. The customer data also allow them to adjust strategy and employee guidelines to better meet the customer's needs (if, for example, employees are failing to meet a

FIGURE 9.9
RECOMMENDATIONS FOR IMPLEMENTING A 360-DEGREE APPRAISAL SYSTEM

INSTRUMENT ISSUES

- Items should be directly linked to effectiveness on the job.
- Items should focus on specific, observable behaviors (not traits, competencies).
- Items should be worded in positive terms, rather than negative terms. Ratees, particularly employees, may be less likely to respond honestly to negative items about their boss.
- Raters should be asked only about issues for which they have firsthand knowledge (i.e., ask subordinates about whether the boss delegates work to them; don't ask peers since they may not know).

ADMINISTRATION ISSUES

- Select raters carefully by using a representative sample of people most critical to the ratee and who have had the greatest opportunity to observe his or her performance.
- Use an adequate number of raters to ensure adequate sampling and to protect the confidentiality of respondents (at least three per source).
- Instruct respondents in how the data will be used and ensure confidentiality.
- To maintain confidentiality, raters should not indicate their names or other identifying characteristics and surveys should be mailed back directly to the analyst in a sealed envelope.
- Alert and train raters regarding rater errors (e.g., halo, leniency, severity, attributional bias).

FEEDBACK REPORT

- Separate the results from the various sources. The ratee should see the average, aggregated results from peers, subordinates, higher-level managers, customers, or other sources that may be used.
- Show the ratee's self-ratings as compared to ratings by others. This enables the ratee to see how his or her self-perceptions are similar or different from others' perceptions.
- Compare the ratee's ratings with other norm groups. For example, a manager's ratings can be compared to other managers (as a group) in the firm.
- Provide feedback on items as well as scales so ratees can see how to improve.

FEEDBACK SESSION

- Use a trained facilitator to provide feedback to ratees.
- Involve the ratee in interpreting his or her own results.
- Provide an overview of the individual's strengths and areas for improvement.
- Provide feedback on recommendations and help him or her to develop an action plan.

FOLLOW-UP ACTIVITIES

- Provide opportunities for skill training in how to improve his or her behaviors.
- Provide support and coaching to help him or her apply what has been learned.
- Over time, evaluate the degree to which the ratee has changed behaviors.

Source: Modified from G. Yukl and R. Lepsinger, 360° feedback. *Training,* December 1995, pp. 45–48, 50.

perceived need of the customer).[74] A 360-degree evaluation process, because of its complexity and relative difficulty to properly organize, requires a strong commitment from management and much planning and forethought. It is probably a good idea to pilot test the program before attempting to replace the current performance-appraisal format. It is also important to address any legal and administrative issues if the system will be used for administrative purposes in addition to developmental purposes.[75] With planning, sound evaluation instruments, assurances of anonymity, and adequate orientation and rater training, 360-degree performance appraisal can provide a clearer picture of employee performance.

Defining the "Ratee"

Many people assume that appraisals always focus on an *individual* level of performance. But alternatives to using the individual as the ratee are becoming more common as more firms (e.g., General Foods Corporation, Rohm & Haas, General Motors, Saturn, Westinghouse) use more self-managing teams, autonomous work groups, teamwork (e.g., Exxon), and participative management (e.g., Motorola).[76] Specifically, the ratee may be defined at the individual, work group, division, or organizationwide level. It is also possible to define the ratee at multiple levels. For example, under some conditions it may be desirable to appraise performance at the work group level for merit pay purposes and at the individual level to identify developmental needs. Burger King, for example, awards cash bonuses to branch stores based on a customer-based evaluation process while maintaining an individual appraisal system within each store. Delta Air Lines assesses customer service at the unit level only, while other job activities are assessed at the individual employee level. Sheraton derives a unit-level evaluation for "room service" while evaluating other functions at the individual level.

Two conditions that make it desirable to assess performance at a higher aggregation level than the individual level are high work group cohesiveness and difficulty in identifying individual contributions. *High work group cohesiveness* refers to the shared feeling among work group members that they form a team. Such an orientation promotes cooperation among group members for highly interdependent tasks.[77] Appraisals focused on individual performance may undermine the cooperative orientation needed to maintain this cohesiveness and tend to promote individualistic or even competitive orientations. *The difficulty in identifying individual contributions* is also important to consider. In some cases, workers are so interdependent, or their individual performance is so difficult to observe, that there is no choice but to focus appraisals on the performance of the higher aggregate of which they are a part. For example, team members at the Saturn plant have received cross training and may engage in all aspects of the job. In most cases, their individual performance is difficult to separate from that of the team's. This was also the case with regard to Delta Air Lines. To the extent that the two conditions exist, it is advisable to consider using a higher level than the individual when evaluating performance. Evaluations, instead, could be made of the group's performance, the department's, or the organization's as a whole.

Administrative Characteristics

In any appraisal system, a variety of administrative decisions must be made. These decisions include the frequency and timing of appraisals, rating medium, and method of feedback.

FREQUENCY AND TIMING OF APPRAISALS. This refers to the number of times per year each employee is to be formally appraised and the time period (e.g., months) between formal appraisals. Usually, appraisals are conducted once or twice per year, with equal intervals between them (e.g., every 12 months or 6 months). For example, 69 percent of firms surveyed reported that appraisals were conducted annually, 22 percent reported they were done semiannually, and 9 percent stated they were done at varying intervals.[78] In another survey, 90 percent of the respondents indicated that appraisals were conducted annually.[79] In some organizations (e.g., Minnesota Department of Transportation) employees reported that appraisals conducted once a year "were enough."[80] Other organizations are finding that it may be desirable to have more frequent (e.g., quarterly) formal appraisals if blocks of work regularly get completed or adequate samples of behaviors/outcomes can be obtained by the end of each quarter. This may be especially helpful for poorer performers so they receive more feedback to make improvements.[81] In addition, at Southern California Edison, three milestones are observed: a performance plan at the beginning of the year, a midyear review, and a final evaluation at the end of the year.[82]

Many organizations conduct appraisals as frequently as every 30 or 60 days during the first six months to one year of employment in order to monitor new employees during their probationary or orientation period.[83] These firms find that more frequent appraisals are desirable because they provide more feedback to employees about their performance. Also, they help avoid the surprises that employees report about their ratings during annual performance reviews.[84] They also find that one formal appraisal a year cannot provide enough timely or specific feedback to accomplish significant improvements in performance.[85]

Intervals between appraisals may be fixed (e.g., every six months, anniversary date, during the last month of fiscal year, and so on). For example, one survey found that half of the respondents used anniversary dates and half used a common review date.[86] Intervals may also be variable and may be based on such factors as the occurrence of very poor or very high performance, consideration for a promotion, and project completion dates. College instructors, for example, are typically evaluated at the completion of each semester with ratings from all classes averaged to derive a semester or academic year score. Many organizations use both types of intervals: fixed for regularly occurring personnel decisions (e.g., merit pay) and variable for appraisals triggered by unusual events (e.g., needs for reduction in force). Pratt & Whitney, for example, conducted annual appraisals at the end of the year but developed and used a new appraisal system for a major downsizing. This approach can cause problems, however. A class action suit was brought by terminated employees over the age of 39 under the Age Discrimination in Employment Act. The plaintiffs maintained that their performance was judged to be superior to many of the younger employees under the annual appraisal system but dropped substantially with the special appraisal in the context of managers who were faced with the need to reduce overhead by 40 percent.

RATING/DATA COLLECTION MEDIUM. The widespread use of desktop personal computers in the workplace has made viable the option of having raters record performance-appraisal ratings directly on computers and using the computer to record performance data. There are several advantages to using the computer as a rating medium. The results can immediately be integrated into the computerized central personnel record systems that most organizations are now using, thereby eliminating the need for clerks to enter the data. The amount of paper that has to be generated, distributed, and filed is drastically reduced. Many computer programs are now available, some of which can monitor rater responses for logic and completeness during the rating process. The choice of a medium depends, however, on the sophistication of the raters and the availability of computers in the workplace. If computers or terminals are readily available, computerized systems make sense.

The computer and other high-tech tools are now used routinely to monitor employee performance. Workers in customer service, telecommunications, and travel are routinely monitored via the computer. Supervisors also surreptitiously monitor calls with customers. Employers using these monitoring methods claim that performance has increased as a direct consequence of these systems. Employee advocacy groups argue that such monitoring creates great stress and that turnover rates and even productivity ultimately suffer. The Association of Working Women, for example, reports thousands of complaints about this electronic eavesdropping since the organization established a hotline. As a result of the controversy, federal legislation is pending that would curb the practice. Among the provisions of the bill is a restriction on the use of computer-generated data as the sole means of performance appraisal.[87]

METHOD OF FEEDBACK. Raters should communicate appraisal results to ratees through a formal feedback meeting held between the supervisor and the employee. Feedback serves an important role both for motivational and informational purposes and for improved rater–ratee communications.[88] For example, supportive feedback can lead to greater motivation, and feedback discussions about pay and advancement can lead to greater employee satisfaction with the process.[89] Specific feedback is recommended instead of general feedback because it is more likely to increase an individual's performance.[90]

The biggest hazard for the rater in providing performance feedback may be ratee reactions to the feedback. Generally, ratees believe they have performed at higher levels than observers of their performance believe.[91] This is especially true at the lower performance levels where there is more room for disagreement and a greater motive among ratees to engage in ego-defensive behavior. It is no wonder that raters are often hesitant about confronting poor performers with negative appraisal feedback and may be lenient when they do.[92] Although pressure on managers to give accurate feedback may override their reluctance to give negative feedback,[93] the pressure doesn't make the experience any more pleasant nor any less likely to evoke a leniency bias. Feedback to inform poor performers of deficiencies and to encourage improvement doesn't always lead to performance improvements.[94] Many employees view their supervisors less favorably after the feedback and felt less motivated after the appraisal.[95] The fear or discomfort experienced in providing negative feedback tends to differ across managers. One survey, known as the Performance Appraisal Discomfort Scale (PADS), showed that the level of discomfort felt by a rater was correlated with leniency. Rater training to reduce the level of discomfort is available.[96]

Steps should be taken to create a supportive atmosphere for the feedback meeting between the employee and supervisor. The rater should remove distractions, avoid being disturbed, and take sufficient time in the meeting. Raters seem to have trouble adhering to these guidelines. For example, employees of the Minnesota Department of Transportation reported that their supervisors generally spent less than 15 minutes in feedback meetings, which is substantially less than the 60 minutes typically recommended.[97] Raters should keep notes on effective and ineffective behavior as it occurs so that they will have some notes to refer to when conducting

the feedback session.[98] Raters should be informal and relaxed and allow the employee the opportunity to share his or her insights. Topics that should be addressed include praise for special assignments; the employee's own assessment of his or her performance; the supervisor's response to the employee's assessment; action plans to improve the subordinate's performance; perceived constraints on performance that require subordinate or supervisory attention; and employee career aspirations, ambitions, and developmental goals.[99] Nuffield Hospitals incorporates many of these ideas in its appraisal feedback meetings. In sum, raters should provide feedback which is clear, descriptive, job related, constructive, frequent, timely, and realistic.[100]

DEVELOPING AN APPRAISAL SYSTEM

After deciding on the design of an appraisal system by making decisions about the measurement content and process, determining who should rate performance and at what level, and making necessary administrative decisions, it is time to actually develop the appraisal system. In some organizations, employees are directly involved in developing their own appraisal system. For example, a task force of 20 employees and supervisors at Southern California Edison threw out the current system and redesigned and developed a new appraisal system that they called "performance enhancement process" or PEP.[101] To develop an effective appraisal system, the seven steps described below should be followed:

1. *Start with a job analysis.* Any effort to develop an appraisal system must begin with complete information about the jobs to be appraised. This information is generated through a job analysis that describes the job requirements (e.g., KASOCs), job content (e.g., major tasks, activities, or duties), and job context features (e.g., responsibilities, physical surroundings).[102] Reading & Bates recognized the importance of relying on job descriptions as the basis for the development of the appraisal context. This approach enabled supervisors to focus on employee behaviors and outcome rather than traits and have better documentation for making administrative decisions.[103] (See Chapter 4 for a more thorough discussion of the importance of conducting a job analysis for performance-appraisal purposes.) As we discussed in Chapter 4, the critical incident method is ideal for the development of highly detailed appraisal content.

2. *Specify performance dimensions and develop performance-level anchors.* Using as much involvement by incumbents, supervisors, and any other critical constituents as possible, specify the job functions and the criteria (e.g., quality, quantity, timeliness; see Figure 9.2) relevant to each function on which employee performance is to be appraised. These job activity or function-by-criterion combinations will make up the system's performance dimensions. Then compose the necessary number of performance-level anchors for each performance dimension. These anchors should be defined as specifically as possible and in the context of the unit or organization's strategic goals. Wherever possible, these anchors should include countable results or outcomes that are important for the strategic goals of the unit or organization. Even in the case of a ranking or forced distribution, one anchor per dimension should be used (usually called a "ranking factor") that describes the standard or ideal performance on the basis of which employees are compared or ranked. Avoid trait labels if you possibly can.

3. *Scale the anchors.* This is the process of determining the values to attach to each anchor. At this time you can also have raters determine the weights to be assigned to each performance dimension when computing an overall performance score. For example, raters may decide that answering phones makes up 30 percent of a clerical person's job. This factor would be assigned a weight of .30. The necessary information to compute scale values and weights is typically collected through a scaling survey questionnaire administered to both incumbents and supervisors. The survey asks for opinions about the value of anchors and the relative value of the functions.

4. *Develop rating form or program.* The actual device to collect ratings or reports of performance usually is a form to be completed by the rater. Figure 9.10 presents a typical, but not particularly good format for rating. A growing number of organizations now use personal computers to record and maintain ratings. A goal to strive for in developing either manual forms or computer-based systems is ease of use. That is, the process should be easy to understand and the rating of each performance dimension should require no more than a minute or two.

5. *Develop scoring procedure.* In more simplistic systems, the score on each performance dimension is simply the rating that was entered and the overall score is just the average of the dimension scores. More sophisticated systems require a more involved process of hand or computer scoring. These may require development of scoring formulas, scoring sheets, procedures to submit raw ratings for scoring, and procedures to record the scores and to prepare score reports for the rater and ratee.

6. *Develop appeal process.* In one survey, 79 percent of respondents indicated that their appraisal systems allow employees an opportunity to provide comments on appraisal forms, and in 32 percent of the firms, formal appeal or grievance systems existed to enable employees to appeal "unfair" appraisals.[104] Another survey reported that 94 percent of the firms gave ratees the opportunity to rebut ratings.[105] Recall our discussion of the importance of appeal processes with regard to litigation about appraisal. Generally, specific appeal procedures should be developed for dealing with disputed appraisal results. Disputed appraisal results may include cases of ratees disagreeing with their appraisals and cases where appraisals are challenged by the higher-level manager reviewing the ratings. For any appeal, procedures should be specified for the number of appeal stages, the composition of any arbitration panel(s), the rules of evidence, and the criteria for reaching judgments.

7. *Develop rater and ratee training program and manuals.* Every appraisal system needs to clearly describe the duties of the raters and ratees. These may be described in written instructions on the appraisal forms or in training manuals for the rater and ratee. The rater duties refer to observing performance (i.e., by providing a frame of reference); preparing for the appraisal; and considering possible constraints on performance, the rating procedure, the scoring procedure, what to do with the completed set of ratings, and how to best provide the results to ratees. The degree to which the rater's ratings will be reviewed by higher-level management should also be covered; in 74 percent of firms surveyed, appraisals are reviewed by higher-level managers.[106] Finally, the appeal and adjudication process should be fully described. All this information is necessary to ensure that the appraisal system is effectively used and legally defensible; one prescription for a legally defensible system is that raters are given instructions and training on the system. Generally, most organizations do provide written instructions for raters (82 percent of firms surveyed) or rater training (60 percent of firms surveyed).[107]

Ratees should be made fully aware of the appraisal process through publication of a ratee manual, training, or some other communication. They should be given a description of how the appraisal system was developed, how ratees can get copies of the standards they will be appraised against, how to interpret the feedback report, what the ratings will be used for in the organization, how to appeal their appraisal scores and the standards by which their appeal will be evaluated and finally judged, and the protection they have against retaliation for challenging their appraisals. The FAA has all of this plus a guideline for specific remedial steps the ratee can take if ratings are not at an optimal level for certain performance dimensions.

IMPLEMENTING AN APPRAISAL SYSTEM

After an appraisal system has been designed and developed, it must be implemented. Actually putting the system into operation requires the following steps: training, integration with the organization's human resource information system (HRIS), and a pilot test.

FIGURE 9.10
A TYPICAL PERFORMANCE APPRAISAL FORM

1. Employee's Name—Last, First, Middle	2. Department	3. Division or Agency
Brown, Mary Eloise	Institutions	State Home and Training School

4. Social Security No.	5. Class Title, Grade, and Step	6. Period of Report From: To:	7. Reason for Report
123-45-6789	Personnel Officer	2/1/97 2/1/98	Annual

8. **GENERAL INSTRUCTIONS**

THIS FORM IS TO BE COMPLETED IN DUPLICATE, AND ALL ENTRIES SHOULD BE TYPE-WRITTEN OR PRINTED IN INK. AFTER THE EMPLOYEE'S PERFORMANCE HAS BEEN EVALUATED BY THE SUPERVISOR AND REVIEWED BY HIGHER-LEVEL SUPERVISION, THE EMPLOYEE WILL BE COUNSELED CONCERNING HIS OR HER PERFORMANCE AND WILL SIGN ALL COPIES OF THIS FORM. THE EMPLOYEE'S SIGNATURE INDICATES THAT PERFORMANCE HAS BEEN REVIEWED AND DISCUSSED. EMPLOYEES WHO DO NOT CONCUR WITH THE EVALUATION MAY INDICATE THEIR DISAGREEMENT NEXT TO THEIR SIGNATURE. THE ORIGINAL WILL BE FILED IN THE INDIVIDUAL'S DEPARTMENT PERSONNEL FOLDER. THE SECOND COPY WILL BE GIVEN TO THE EMPLOYEE AT THE TIME OF THE EVALUATION. IF THE RATING IS "OUTSTANDING", "BELOW STANDARD", OR "UNSATISFACTORY", A THIRD COPY SHOULD BE COMPLETED AND FORWARDED WITH SUPPORTING NARRATIVE TO THE DEPARTMENT OF PERSONNEL. DETAILED INFORMATION ON HOW TO FILL OUT THIS FORM CAN BE FOUND IN THE "SUPERVISOR'S PERFORMANCE PLANNING AND REVIEW MANUAL."

9. Overall Employee Evaluation:

Total of Performance Values __28.0__

☐ Outstanding*　　☐ Below Standard*

☒ Above Standard　　☐ Unsatisfactory*

☐ Standard

Refer to the "Supervisor's Performance Planning and Review Manual" to determine overall evaluation.

* Attach narrative explanation describing specific areas of Outstanding, Below Standard, or Unsatisfactory performance.

10. _Sherman L. Studley_   _Feb 8, 1998_
　　 Supervisor's Signature　　　　　　　Date

11. _Betty Lincoln_   _Feb 10, 1998_
　　 Higher-Level Supervisor's Signature　　Date

12. _____　　_____
　　 *Principal Department Head's Signature　　Date

　　 *Required for Outstanding, Below Standard, or Unsatisfactory Reviews.

13. The performance plan and review have been discussed with my supervisor.

Mary Eloise Brown   _Feb. 15, 1998_
Employee's Signature　　　　　　　　Date

FIGURE 9.10
(Continued)

PERFORMANCE VALUE DEFINITIONS

4 CONSISTENTLY EXCEEDS WHAT IS EXPECTED	3 FREQUENTLY EXCEEDS WHAT IS EXPECTED	2 CONSISTENTLY ACHIEVES WHAT IS EXPECTED	1 OCCASIONALLY FAILS TO ACHIEVE WHAT IS EXPECTED	0 CONSISTENTLY FAILS TO ACHIEVE WHAT IS EXPECTED

Performance Factors	Performance Values				
	4	3	2	1	0
1. Quality of Work `4.2` Consider the extent to which completed work is accurate, neat, well-organized, thorough, and applicable					
Researches and compiles data for reports. Takes dictation, transcribes, and types correspondence, reports, and minutes of meetings. Prepares and maintains monthly reports of training activities.					
2. Quantity of Work `2.5` Consider the extent to which the amount of work completed compares to quantity standards for the job or compares to quantity produced by other employees.					
Maintains internal records system to ensure replies to correspondence within 4 working days. Reduces processing time of applications within the unit by 2 weeks.					
3. Taking Action Independently Consider the extent to which the employee shows initiative in making work improvements, identifies and corrects errors, develops new work tasks, or solves problems.					
4. Relationship with People Consider the extent to which the employee works cooperatively with others, recognizes the needs and desires of other people, treats others with respect and courtesy, `1.3` and inspires their respect and confidence.					
Answers phone, makes appointments and reservations for division chief. Answers routine inquiries by visitors to the division. The department will receive no more than 1 complaint because of discourteous service.					
5. Work Habits `2.0` Consider how well the employee organizes and uses work tools and time, cares for equipment, is reliable and punctual, and observes established safety standards.					
Prepares and maintains monthly report in accordance with established procedures. Ensures that clerical equipment is in good operating condition. Cleans and covers each piece of equipment daily per established procedures.					
6. Effectiveness of Supervision Consider how well the supervisor leads, directs, and utilizes subordinates; conducts performance reviews and employee development reviews on schedule; and administers personnel policies and procedures effectively and fairly among subordinates.					
7. Pertinent Performance Factors Not Shown Above					
Sub-total					
Grand Total					

Training

This is the most important component of a system's implementation. In many cases, raters are given only superficial training in filling out the rating form or avoiding rating errors. Separate training sessions should be held for at least three groups: raters, ratees, and all decision makers and analysts. The training should focus on a clarification of the information provided in the manuals for raters and ratees and should "sell" the benefits of the program to all system users including top management. For example, at Reading & Bates, half-day workshops for rater training are provided to all supervisors and top management support is generated for the appraisal system. In Nuffield Hospitals, no hospital is allowed to use the appraisal system until all involved parties receive formal training. The training is in interviewing techniques, performance coaching, and mentoring and uses videos, role-plays, and other exercises. Likewise, at Westinghouse, all raters in a new appraisal system are required to receive training in coaching and counseling, documentation, and conducting formal appraisals. Employees are also taught to document performance observations and the details of performance review sessions.[108] We also strongly recommend training in the "cognitive errors" we discussed earlier. The Tribune Company developed special cases to illustrate these errors.

Often, raters are not given any training in how to conduct feedback sessions.[109] To prepare raters for the feedback session, they should receive training that uses case studies for discussion and role-playing to practice dealing with difficult situations. Training should also address legal issues and "what if" questions about ratings or compensation that may arise during the review session.[110]

Integration with HRIS

The results of every appraisal (whether manual or computer-based) of every employee should ideally be entered into a computerized database. This is necessary to handle the data administration and scoring and to evaluate ratings for errors (e.g., leniency, halo, central tendency).[111] For example, at Hilton International, appraisal data are entered into an HRIS computer database, which is combined with other information about individuals, work units, and specific hotels.[112] The appraisal system at E-Systems, Inc., is computerized and is tied to a mainframe and linked with the personnel and payroll systems. Using graphics software, the distribution of appraisal ratings is analyzed to show the types of rating errors that may exist in the entire organization and in specific departments.[113] At the Defense Communications Agency, a division of the Department of Defense, all appraisal data are linked with the career ladders program as an important component of the succession planning system. Wells Fargo Bank and Continental Bank integrated their managerial appraisal systems with their employee survey to provide more comprehensive information to managers about the quality of worklife of their employees.[114]

In addition to linking the appraisal results to the organization's other HR systems, it is important to make sure the appraisal system is easy for raters to use and the results can be computerized or tabulated in some way. Recently, a number of software packages have been developed to help raters in compiling and drafting their initial ratings. Four new systems include, *Review Writer, Employee Appraiser, Performance Now!, and WorkWise Evaluations*. In most cases, the packages can be customized to the firm's evaluation format, comments can be included, and a legal language scanner can be used to ensure that the language is not discriminatory or harassing. In addition, password protection is included for confidentiality purposes, and most contain an advice feature for coaching evaluations.[115] Many companies now use computerized performance monitoring systems which record performance data automatically.[116]

Pilot Test

A final, critical step in the implementation process is a tryout of the system, or a pilot test. Given all the details involved in the design, development, and implementation of an appraisal system, it is unrealistic to expect that everything is going to run smoothly the first time the system is used. The system will have problems that can't be foreseen, and the only way to find and solve them without suffering minor or major disasters is to try out the system. The pilot should be made as realistic as possible, even down to having employees file mock appeals. Questionnaires should be distributed to raters and ratees after the process to get their reactions and to identify trouble spots. It is vital that a new appraisal system get off on the right foot. If it doesn't leave people with a favorable impression the first time it is used, it may lose the cooperation necessary to make it work effectively. The FAA and U.S. Postal Service conducted extensive pilot testing for their subordinate appraisal system of managers. Several important changes were made based on the results of the pilot studies. For example, the FAA needed to better coordinate its subordinate appraisal system with its annual employee opinion survey so that contradictory information would not flow to management. (The pilot data had indicated that managers reported confusion over the seemingly contradictory results from the two sources of information.)

EVALUATING APPRAISAL SYSTEM EFFECTIVENESS

After an appraisal system is implemented, it should be evaluated to ensure that it meets its intended purposes. For example, when Marriott installed its new appraisal system, it was part of its renewed emphasis on customer service. The critical measure of the appraisal system's effectiveness was thus the extent to which it improved customer service. Few organizations evaluate appraisal systems at this level, however. As with many HR systems (e.g., training), evaluations are often not conducted at all. A comprehensive evaluation of a performance-appraisal system requires the collection of several types of data, including user reactions, inferential validity, discriminating power, and possible adverse impact. Let us review each of these measures of effectiveness next.

User Reactions

It is vital to learn the attitudes and reactions of raters and ratees to an appraisal system because any system ultimately depends on them for its effectiveness. Attitudes of employees can be assessed before implementation of a new system to see how receptive they may be. A survey of state government employees found that employees who believed that their supervisors could rate them fairly and thought that they could measure quality were more receptive and less resistant to a pending appraisal system. Reactions should also be assessed after implementing a new system. No matter how sophisticated an appraisal system may be, if employees and managers resist using it, the appraisal system will not be effective. At Westinghouse, both raters and ratees are asked to evaluate the appraisal system in terms of the coaching and counseling sessions, the practicality of the forms, and the quality of performance standards. A task force works with the HR staff each year to formally review the appraisal system to ensure that it is working.[117] Employees at the Minnesota Department of Transportation are surveyed to assess their opinions regarding the frequency of appraisals, use of informal appraisal methods, and the opportunity for self-appraisals.[118] At American Cyanamid Company, pre and post surveys were administered to managers to compare reactions to a new system with the current system. They found that those using a system that did not require forced distribution ratings were more likely to report that the system was fair, showed logical links between the appraisals and pay and promotions, and was based on the major aspects of the job.[119]

Raters' reactions are important to assess whether they perceive the system to be easy to use and the content representative of the important job content.[120] Also, raters should be asked whether they feel they have been adequately trained to use the system or have been given enough time to complete appraisals. Furthermore, they should be asked to indicate their commitment to making the system work. One survey that assesses the extent to which raters perceive other raters are using the system fairly and successfully predicts rating bias in the system.[121]

Ratee reactions to an appraisal system are important to collect because they exert powerful influences on the tendency of raters to appraise accurately. If ratees feel unfairly appraised and resent raters, they will probably react in a defensive or hostile fashion to raters. The raters may then assign more lenient ratings to the employees for the next appraisal session in order to avoid conflict and confrontations. This inflation will damage the accuracy of the appraisals. Generally, ratees want a system that they perceive as being fair, informative, useful, and free of bias. Their opinions on these issues should be assessed after the system has been implemented. One study found that ratees perceived a system that incorporated possible constraints on employee performance as fairer than another system.[122]

Inferential Validity

When considering how effectively an appraisal system operates, the issue of its validity refers to accuracy; that is, the extent to which its scores correspond to the *true* levels and standings of the performances being appraised (e.g., to what degree an employee who is rated as "average" really is exhibiting "average" performance). But often we have no idea of what the "true" level of performance is.[123] We can only rely on subjective ratings or records of performance. If we had the means of assessing true performance, we would be using it as our appraisal measure.

In the absence of any way to assess a system's internal validity directly, the best approach seems to infer validity by determining whether the appraisal system is reliable, free from bias, relevant, and has discriminant validity.[124] The most important measure of appraisal reliability is the extent to which independent raters agree on an evaluation. Freedom from bias is the degree to which the scores are free from evidence of errors (e.g., leniency, central tendency, halo, sexual stereotyping). Discriminant validity, related to halo effect, is the degree to which ratees are ordered differently on each performance dimension; in other words, whether the ratings on one dimension are unrelated to ratings on other dimensions. This is desirable so that each performance dimension is measuring a separate work function. Relevance is the degree to which the appraisal system encompasses all of a job's critical functions and their applicable criteria and excludes irrelevant activities or functions. Appraisals that are relevant also weight the functions in proportion to their relative importance to effective performance and, more importantly, the static goals of the organization or unit.

Discriminating Power

If an appraisal system is successful at differentiating performances, then it is said to have discriminating power. The difficulty in assessing appraisal systems on this criterion is in defining what constitutes success at differentiating. How much differentiation is optimal? Can we expect the distribution of ratees' scores to form a normal curve over the possible range of scores? In many cases, this may be unreasonable to expect if employees are carefully recruited, selected, and trained. The question of how much differentiation is desirable must be answered before a system's discriminating power can be evaluated. One organization recently installed a pay-for-performance system and the first round of appraisals under the new system found that 98 percent of rated employees were eligible for the highest merit raise. Management concluded that this was insufficient discriminating power and contracted with the consulting firm of Booz-Allen & Hamilton to gain more discrimination in the appraisal system. IBM had the same problem with its appraisal system and instituted a ranking method because of the lack of differentiation

Adverse/Disparate Impact

This criterion focuses on the question of whether the appraisal scores of members of groups protected by laws (e.g., race, sex, age, disabilities, veterans) are significantly different from others. For example, if the performance of minority employees is evaluated significantly lower than the performance of white employees, then adverse or disparate impact may be evident (see the related discussion in Chapter 3).

If adverse impact is found, the organization will need to check the appraisal system. For example, the organization should determine if the group of employees adversely affected was more likely to be given assignments that were more difficult, aversive, or subject to more extraneous constraints or whether they received lower appraisals than they deserved based on other data. If so, then it would be unwise to continue to use the appraisal system. Pratt & Whitney had difficulty defending the fact that many older workers received lower ratings than younger employees doing the same work only after the company embarked on a substantial cost-cutting program in which managers were evaluated on the extent to which they could achieve a 40 percent reduction in overhead. Pratt opted to settle the lawsuit.

If no problems are found with the appraisal system, then it can be used even if differences are found in appraisal results as a function of race, sex, age, or disabilities. In general, however, personnel decisions based on appraisal systems that result in adverse impact are difficult to defend, particularly if the prescriptions we presented in the first part of this chapter are not part of the system.

PERFORMANCE APPRAISAL SYSTEMS IN QUALITY-DRIVEN ORGANIZATIONS

Many organizations today are trying to improve customer focus and quality (see Chapter 12). To do so, they need effective performance management systems. Yet, as noted earlier, Deming and others in the quality movement have identified a number of problems with performance-appraisal systems in organizations.[125] Specifically, they have argued that appraisal systems are generally not designed to be consistent with a firm's emphasis on total quality management. Some of the charges they have leveled against appraisal systems are noted below.

1. Workers are often held accountable for errors that may be the result of faults within the system. For example, poor equipment, computer problems, or training deficiencies may be responsible for performance problems yet employees are held accountable as if the problems were solely due to them.

2. Appraisal systems often promote worker behaviors that compromise quality. For example, by emphasizing outputs in an MBO system, employees may push to meet their quotas while sacrificing the quality of their work. One sales organization encouraged sales employees to find customers but did not penalize them for losing customers. As a result, reps brought in many new customers, yet subsequently lost them because the reps did not devote any time to maintaining the "old" customer accounts.

3. Many appraisal systems use relative rankings, rather than absolute scales, which discourage employees who are told they are below average. This is problematic when the employee's performance actually meets the standards and expectations in an absolute sense. The appraisal systems rob workers of their pride in workmanship by getting them to focus on reaching average output.

To address these concerns, an appraisal system must be consistent with the tenets of the quality movement. Several suggestions are offered below for developing an appraisal system in a quality-driven organization.[126]

1. Make the primary purpose of the appraisal system to help employees improve their performance. In one state agency, all employees and managers were told that the primary goal of the new appraisal system would be to improve communication between em-

ployees and their supervisors, rather than choose employees for salary increases or promotions.

2. Involve all employees in the design of the appraisal system. At Southern California Edison, all employees were given opportunities to design the new system. As a result, their commitment and acceptance of the system was extremely high.[127]

3. Evaluate the existing appraisal system using quality tools (e.g., process flowcharts, cause and effect diagrams, pareto diagrams; see Chapter 12). The focus is to identify opportunities to improve the system.[128]

SUMMARY

Performance appraisals have become an increasingly important tool for organizations to manage and improve the performance of employees, to make more timely and accurate staffing decisions, and to enhance the overall quality of the firm's services and products.[129] The design, development, and implementation of appraisal systems are not endeavors which can be effectively handled by following the latest fad or even by copying other organizations' systems. Instead, a new appraisal system must be considered a major organizational change effort which should be pursued in the context of improving the organization's competitive advantage. This means, like any such change effort, there will be vested interests in preserving the status quo which will be resistant to change, no matter how beneficial it may be for the organization. These sources of resistance to the change have to be identified and managed to build incentives for using a new appraisal system.

We have offered prescriptions for developing and sustaining effective and legally defensible performance appraisal and management systems which should provide a closer link between performance measurement and customers.[130] The term "customers" is used here to refer to both the internal and external consumers of an employee's record of outcomes. We advocate multirater PM systems that include as one of the key sources of input the perspectives of the internal and external consumers of employee and group work products.[131]

We believe that measurement precision is a worthwhile goal to strive for. Much like the research on greater precision in employment interviews, recent research indicates that precision in performance appraisal also translates into more effective systems.[132]

We further believe that the attributional errors that can be so troublesome can be reduced with improved precision in measurement.[133] Raters and ratees are more likely to agree on the level of performance as a function of the precision in the measurement tools. Greater appraisal agreement also implies greater attributional agreement. Precision in measurement should also help identify legitimate constraints on performance which need the attention of management. Such an orientation in PM systems is compatible with TQM processes seeking to reduce system variance.[134]

We also recognize that performance appraisals are widely used to achieve political purposes rather than to accurately report a record of performance outcomes.[135] This is largely due to the fact that existing PM systems, including the plethora of competency-based systems being marketed today, are so readily amenable to such distortion, as well as to the prevalence of organizational cultures which tacitly approve of it. We believe that such manipulation of appraisals leads not to enhanced organizational effectiveness but rather to the opposite effect. Organizations should strive to make accurate performance assessments the basis for all of its selection and reward decisions. Only in this way can aggregated gains in individual effectiveness lead to overall gains in organizational effectiveness. The recent research with High Performance Work Systems (HPWS) identified effective pay for performance compensation systems as a correlate of corporate performance outcomes.[136]

Effective compensation systems rely on accurate measures of performance which are tied into corporate strategy. In fact, the various forms of pay-for-performance systems, which are so popular today, are completely dependent on accurate and relevant performance measurement.

At a recent seminar for a *Fortune* 200 company, one of the authors spent two hours introducing the newly designed performance management system which was modelled after the prescriptions presented in this chapter. The first eight questions from the employees after the presentation all concerned the connection between the performance management system and pay. Most people get very concerned about performance appraisal when it has an impact on their paychecks. We turn to compensation next.

DISCUSSION QUESTIONS

1. Why has performance appraisal taken on increased significance in recent years?

2. As the workforce becomes more diverse, why does performance appraisal become more difficult?

3. How would you determine whether an organization's appraisal system was legally defensible?

4. Many managers describe performance appraisal as the responsibility they like the least. Why is this so? What could be done to improve the situation?

5. Should a professor's pay be directly linked to student evaluations?

6. What steps would you take if your performance-appraisal system resulted in disparate or adverse impact?

7. Under what circumstances would you use customer or client evaluation as a basis for appraising employees?

8. Some companies use 360-degree appraisal systems as strictly developmental tools. The appraisal data only goes to the *ratee,* not the ratee's supervisor. What is your view on this policy?

9. Why should managers provide ongoing and frequent feedback to employees about their performance?

10. Some leaders of the total quality movement such as Deming say performance appraisal is counterproductive. Do you agree or disagree? Why?

NOTES

1. Bernardin, H. J., Hagan, C., Kane, J. S., and Villanova, P. Effective performance management: Precision in measurement with a focus on customers and situational constraints. In J. Smither (ed.), *Performance Appraisal: State-of-the-Art Methods for Performance Management.* Jossey-Bass, San Francisco, 1998. See also, Wigdor, A. K., and Green, B. F. (eds.) (1992). *Performance assessment for the workplace, vols. I and II: The technical issues.* Washington, DC: National Academy Press; Moravec, M.; Juliff, R.; and Hesler, K. (January 1995). Partnerships help a company manage performance. *Personnel Journal,* pp. 105–108; Cardy, R. L., and Dobbins, G. H. (1994). *Performance appraisal: Alternative perspectives.* Cincinnati, OH: South-Western Publishing Co.

2. The Wall Street Journal. Cited in *Palm Beach Post* (Dec. 15, 1996), p. 3F; see also, Smith, B., Hornsby, J. S., and Shirmeyer, R. (Summer 1996). Current trends in performance appraisal: An examination of managerial practice. *SAM Advanced Management Journal,* pp. 10–15; and Antonioni, D. (1994). Improve the performance management process before discontinuing performance appraisals. *Compensation & Benefits Review, 26*(3), 29–32.

3. Bretz, R. D., Jr., Milkovich, G. T., and Read, W. (1992). The current state of performance appraisal research and practice: Concerns, directions, and implications. *Journal of Management, 18,* 321–352; Vinson, M. N. (1996). The pros and cons of 360-degree feedback: Making it work. *Training and Development, 50*(4), 11–12.

4. Lwumeyer, J., and Beebe, T. (1988). Employees and their appraisal: How do workers feel about the company grading scale? *Personnel Administrator, 33*(12), 76–80.

5. Kane, J. S., and Kane, K. F. (1988). *A survey of performance appraisal effectiveness in Fortune 500 firms: A report of the findings.* Unpublished report. See also, Laud, R. L. (1984). Performance appraisal practices in the *Fortune 300.* In C. J. Fombrun, N. M. Tichy, and M. A. Devanna (eds.), *Strategic human resource management.* New York: John Wiley & Sons, pp. 111–126.

6. Ulrich, D., Halbrook, R., Meder, D., and Stuchlik, M. (1991). Employee and customer attachment: Synergies for competitive advantage. *Human Resource Planning, 14,* pp. 89–104; McNerney, D. J. (1995). Improved performance appraisals: Process of elimination, *HR Focus, 72*(7), 1, 4–5; and Flynn, G. (1995). Employee evaluations get so-so grades. *Personnel Journal, 62,* 21–23.

7. See note 6, McNerney (1995).

8. See note 6, McNerney (1995).

9. Austin, J. T., Villanova, P., and Hindman, H. D. (1995). Legal requirements and technical guidelines involved in implementing performance appraisal systems. In G. R. Ferris and M. R. Buckley (eds.), *Human resources management: Perspectives, context, functions, and outcomes,* 3rd ed. Englewood Cliffs, NJ: Prentice Hall; see also, Bernardin, H. J.; Hennessey, H. W.; and Peyrefitte, J. (1995). Age, racial, and gender bias as a function of criterion specificity: A test of expert testimony. *Human Resource Management Review, 5,* 63–77.

10. Taylor, M. S., Tracey, K. B., Renard, M. K., Harrison, J. K., and Carroll, S. J. (1997). Due process in performance appraisal: A quasi-experiment in procedural justice. *Administrative Science Quarterly, 18*(5), 792–815.

11. See note 1; Bernardin et al (1998); see also, Kane, J., and Kane, K. (1992). The analytic framework: The most promising approach for the advancement of performance appraisal. *Human Resource Management Review, 2,* 37–70.

12. Becker, B. E., Huselid, M. A., Pickus, P. S., and Spratt, M. F. (1997). HR as a source of shareholder value: Research and recommendations. *Human Resource Management, 36,* 39–48; see also, Lawler, E. E., III (1987). Paying for performance: Future directions. In D. B. Balkin; and L. R. Gomez-Mejia (eds.), *New perspectives on compensation.* Englewood Cliffs, NJ: Prentice Hall; McDonald, D., and Smith, A. (1995). A proven connection: Performance management and business results. *Compensation & Benefits Review, 27*(1), 59–64.

13. Bernardin, H. J., and Beatty, R. W. (1984). *Performance appraisal: Assessing human behavior at work.* Boston: PWS.

14. Romanoff, K. E. (1989). The ten commandments of performance management. *Personnel, 66*(1), 24–28.

15. Ricciardi, P. (March 1996). Simplify your approach to performance measurement. *HR Magazine,* pp. 98–100, 102, 104, 106.

16. Vroom, V. (1964). *Work motivation.* New York: John Wiley & Sons.

17. Kane, J. S. (1986). Performance distribution assessment. In R. A. Berk (ed.), *Performance assessment: Methods and applications.* Baltimore: Johns Hopkins University Press, pp. 237–273. See also, Sackett, P. R.; Zedeck, S.; and Fogli, L. (1988). Relations between measures of typical and maximum job performance. *Journal of Applied Psychology, 73,* 482–486.

18. Buckley, M. R., and Weitzel, W. (1988). Employing at will. *Personnel Administrator, 33*(8), 78–80; see also, Holley, W. H., and Walters, R. S. (1987). An employ-

ment at will vulnerability audit. *Personnel Journal, 66*(4), 130–139; Krueger, A. B. (1991). The evolution of unjust-dismissal legislation in the United States. *Industrial and Labor Relations Review, 44,* 644–660.

19. Levine, H. Z. (1986). Performance appraisals at work. *Personnel Journal, 6,* 63–71.

20. See note 9, Bernardin et al; see also, note 1, and Koys, D. J., Briggs, S., and Grenig, J. (1987). State court disparity on employment-at-will. *Personnel Psychology, 40,* 565–577; Mineham, M. (August 1997). Employment litigation on ongoing concern. *HRMagazine,* p. 144.

21. See note 1, see also, Rosen, D. I. (November 1992). Appraisals can make—or break—your court case. *Personnel Journal,* pp. 113–116.

22. Bernardin, H. J. (1992). The "analytic" framework for customer-based performance content. *Human Resource Management Review, 2,* 81–102.

23. Adams, H. L., and Embley, K. (1988). Performance management systems: From strategic planning to employee productivity. *Personnel, 65*(4), 55–60.

24. See note 22.

25. See note 17, Kane, J. S.

26. Villanova, P. (1992). A customer-based model for developing job performance criteria. *Human Resource Management Review, 2*(1), 103–114; see also, Borman, W. C. (1991). Job behavior, performance, and effectiveness. In M. D. Dunnette and L. M. Hough (eds.), *Handbook of industrial and organizational psychology,* 2nd ed., Vol. 2. Palo Alto, CA: Consulting Psychologists' Press, pp. 271–326.

27. Wagel, W. H. (1987). Performance appraisal with a difference. *Personnel, 64*(2), 4–6.

28. See note 13.

29. Levy, M. (1989). Almost-perfect performance appraisals. *Personnel Journal, 68*(4), 76, 78, 80, 83.

30. See note 13; see also, Kane, J. S., and Kane, K. F. (1992). The analytic framework: The most promising approach for the advancement of performance appraisal. *Human Resource Management Review, 2*(1), 37–40.

31. Bernardin, H. J. (1992). An "analytic" framework for customer-based performance content development and appraisal. *Human Resource Management Review, 2*(1), 81–102; Tubbs, M. (1986). Goal setting: A meta-analytic examination of the empirical evidence. *Journal of Applied Psychology, 71,* 474–483; Bobko, P., and Colella, A. (1994). Employee reactions to performance standards: A review and research proposition. *Personnel Psychology, 47,* 1–36. See also, Landy, F. J., and Farr, J. (1983). *The measurement of work performance.* New York: Academic Press.

32. Hall, T. C. (1987). Starting over. *Training and Development Journal, 41*(12), 60–62.

33. See note 19.

34. Sanchez, T. I., and De La Torre, P. (1996). A second look at the relationship between rating and behavioral accuracy. *Journal of Applied Psychology, 81*(1), 3–10;

see also, Feldman, J. (1992). The case for nonanalytic performance appraisal. *Human Resource Management Review, 2*(1). See also, Feldman, J. M. (1981). Beyond attribution theory: Cognitive processes in performance ratings. *Journal of Applied Psychology, 66,* 127–148; and Murphy, K. R., and Cleveland, J. N. (1991). *Performance appraisal: An organizational perspective.* Boston: Allyn & Bacon.

35. See note 1, Moravec, Juliff, and Hesler (1995).

36. Milkovich, G. T., and Wigdor, A. K. (1991). *Pay for performance: Evaluating performance appraisal and merit pay.* Washington, DC: National Research Council; see also, Harris, M. M.; Smith, D. E.; and Champagne, D. (1995). A field study of performance appraisal purpose: Research- versus administrative-based ratings. *Personnel Psychology, 48,* 151–160.

37. Banks, C. G., and Murphy, K. R. (1985). Toward narrowing the research-practice gap in performance appraisal. *Personnel Psychology, 38*(2), 335–345. See also, Hogan, E. A. (1987). Effects of prior expectations on performance ratings: A longitudinal study. *Academy of Management Journal, 30,* 354–368; Kane, J. S., and Lawler, E. E., III (1979). Performance appraisal effectiveness: Its assessment and determinants. In B. Staw (ed.), *Research in organizational behavior,* Vol. 1. Greenwich, CT: JAI Press; and note 34, Murphy and Cleveland (1991).

38. Athey, T. R., and McIntyre, R. M. (1987). Effect of rater training on rater accuracy: Level-of-processing theory and social facilitation theory perspectives. *Journal of Applied Psychology, 72,* 239–244. See also, Bernardin, H. J., and Buckley, M. R. (1981). A consideration of strategies in rater training. *Academy of Management Review, 6,* 205–212; Bernardin, H. J., and Pence, E. C. (1980). Rater training: Creating new response sets and decreasing accuracy. *Journal of Applied Psychology, 65,* 60–66; McIntyre, R. M.; Smith, D. E.; and Hassett, C. E. (1984). Accuracy of performance ratings as affected by rater training and perceived purpose of rating. *Journal of Applied Psychology, 69,* 147–156; Pulakos, E. D. (1984). A comparison of rater training programs: Error training and accuracy training. *Journal of Applied Psychology, 69,* 581–588; Pulakos, E. D. (1986). The development of training programs to increase accuracy with different rating tasks. *Organizational Behavior and Human Decision Processes, 38,* 76–91; and Sulsky, L. M., and Day, D. V. (1994). Effects of frame-of-reference training on rater accuracy under alternative time delays. *Journal of Applied Psychology, 79*(4), 535–543.

39. Longenecker, C. O.; Gioia, D. A.; and Sims, H. P., Jr. (1987). Behind the mask: The politics of employee appraisal. *The Academy of Management Executive, 1,* 183–193. See also, note 34, Murphy and Cleveland (1991); Wilson, M. C. (1990). *Factors related to distortion of performance appraisal ratings.* Unpublished doctoral dissertation. Knoxville: The University of Tennessee; Harris, M. M. (1994). Rater motivation in the performance appraisal context: A theoretical framework. *Journal of Management, 20*(4), 737–756.

40. Fox, S., and Dinur, Y. (1988). Validity of self-assess-

ment: A field evaluation. *Personnel Psychology, 41,* 581–592. Farh, J. L., and Werbel, J. D. (1986). Effects of purpose of the appraisal and expectations of validation on self-appraisal leniency. *Journal of Applied Psychology, 71,* 527–529; note 17, Kane (1986); note 37, Kane and Lawler (1979); and note 34, Murphy and Cleveland (1991).

41. Bernardin, H. J., and Villanova, P. J. (1986). Performance appraisal. In E. A. Locke (ed.), *Generalizing from laboratory to field settings:* Lexington, MA: Lexington Books, pp. 43–62.

42. Peters, L. H., and O'Connor, E. J. (1980). Situational constraints and work outcomes: The influence of a frequently overlooked construct. *Academy of Management Review, 5,* 391–397; Dobbins, G. H., Cardy, R. L., Facteau, J. D., and Miller, J. S. (1993). Implications of situational constraints on performance evaluation and performance management. *Human Resource Management Review, 3,* 105–128; and Villanova, P., and Roman, M. A. (1993). A meta-analytic review of situational constraints and work-related outcomes: Alternative approaches to conceptualization. *Human Resource Management Review, 3,* 147–175.

43. See note 1, Bernardin et al. (1998); and Bernardin, H. J. (1989). Increasing the accuracy of performance measurement: A proposed solution to erroneous attributions. *Human Resource Planning, 12,* 239–250.

44. Johnson, J. W.; Olson, A. M.; and Courtney, C. L. (1996). Implementing multiple perspective feedback: An integrated framework. *Human Resource Management Review, 6,* 253–277.

45. Collins, R. L. (1996). For better or worse: The impact of upward social comparison on self evaluations. *Psychological Bulletin, 119*(1), 51–69.

46. Wilson, J., and Cole, G. (1990). A healthy approach to performance appraisal. *Personnel Management, 22*(6), 46–49.

47. Farh, J., Dobbins, G. H., and Cheng, B. (1991). Cultural relativity in action: A comparison of self-ratings made by Chinese and U.S. workers. *Personnel Psychology, 44*(1), 129–148; London, M., and Wohlers, A. J. (1991). Agreement between subordinate and self-ratings in upward feedback. *Personnel Psychology, 44*(2), 375–390; Smither, J. W., London, M., Vasilopoulos, N. L., Reilly, R. R., Millsap, R. E., and Salvemini, N. (1995). An examination of the effects of an upward feedback program over time. *Personnel Psychology, 48,* 1–34; and Atwater, L., Roush, P., and Fischthal, A. (1995). The influence of upward feedback on self- and follower ratings of leadership. *Personnel Psychology, 48,* 35–60.

48. London, M., and Smither, J. W. (1995). Can multisource feedback change perceptions of goal accomplishment, self-evaluations, and performance-related outcomes? Theory-based applications and directions for research. *Personnel Psychology, 48,* 803–839.

49. Bernardin, H. J. (1986). Subordinate appraisal: A valuable source of information about managers. *Human Resource Management, 25,* 421–439. See also, Harris, M. M., and Schaubroeck, J. (1988). A meta-analysis of self-supervisor, self-peer, and peer-supervisor ratings.

Personnel Psychology, 41, 43–62.; Tsui, A. S., and Barry, B. (1986). Interpersonal affect and rating errors. *Academy of Management Journal, 29,* 586–598; and Wohlers, A. J., and London, M. (1989). Ratings of managerial characteristics: Evaluation difficulty, co-worker agreement, and self-awareness. *Personnel Psychology, 42,* 235–261.

50. See note 22; see also, Bernardin, H. J., and Beatty, R. W. (1984). *Performance appraisal: Assessing human behavior at work.* Boston: Kent Publishing Co; Mabe, P. A., III, and West, S. G. (1982). Validity of self-evaluation of ability: A review and meta-analysis. *Journal of Applied Psychology, 67,* 280 296; and Borman, W. C., White, L. A., and Dorsey, D. W. (1995). Effects of ratee task performance and interpersonal factors on supervisor and peer performance ratings. *Journal of Applied Psychology, 80*(1), 168–177.

51. Edwards, M. R., and Ewen, A. J. (1996). *360-degree feedback: The powerful new model for employee assessment and performance improvement.* New York: AMACOM. See also, Edwards, M. R. (1990). Implementation strategies for multiple rater systems. *Personnel Journal, 69*(9), 130, 132, 134, 137, 139.

52. Edwards, M. R. (1990). A joint effort leads to accurate appraisals. *Personnel Journal, 69*(6), 122, 124, 126, 128.

53. See note 51.

54. Maurer, T., and Tarulli, B. A. (1996). Acceptance of peer/upward performance appraisal systems: Role of work context factors and beliefs about managers' development capability. *Human Resource Management, 35*(2), 217–241.

55. Bohl, D. L. (1996). Minisurvey: 360-degree appraisals yield superior results, survey shows. *Compensation and Benefits Review, 28*(5), 16–19; Gruner, S. (February 1997). Feedback from everyone. *Inc.,* pp. 102–103.

56. See note 55, Bohl (1996).

57. Employees welcome 360 degree feedback (October 1996). *IRS-Employment Review, 618,* 2.

58. Brotherton, P. (1996). Candid feedback spurs changes in culture. *HR Magazine, 41*(5), 47–50.

59. Dalessio, A. T. (1996). 20/20 Insight. *Personnel Psychology, 49*(4), 1050–1056.

60. Milliman, J. F., Zawacki, R. A., Schulz, B., Wiggins, S., and Norman, C. A. (1995). Customer service drives 360-degree goal setting. *Personnel Journal, 6,* 136–141.

61. See note 51.

62. Stoffel, G. (1996). Assessment-driven development: A case study. *Human Resources Professional, 9*(3), 25–27.

63. Snader, J. (Feb. 17, 1997). How sales reps make 360-degree turnaround. *Marketing News, 31*(4), 11.

64. Hirsch, M. S. (August 1994). 360-degrees of evaluation. *Working Woman,* pp. 20–21; see also, note 58 and note 55, Gruner (1997).

65. Hauser, J. R., Simester, D. I., Wernerfelt, B. (1996). Internal customers and internal suppliers. *Journal of Marketing Research,* 276–280; see also, Antonioni, D.

(1996). Designing an effective 360-degree appraisal feedback process. *Organizational Dynamics, 25*(2), 24–38.

66. Thatcher, M. (1996). Allowing everyone to have their say. *People Management, 2*(6), 28–30, see also, Welch, D. (1996). The positives of performance reviews. *Network World, 13*(51), 46.

67. Filipczak, B., Hequet, M., Lee, C., Picard, M., and Stamps, D. (1996). 360-degree feedback: Will the circle be broken? *Training, 33*(10), 24–25; see also, Serven, L. (Sept. 1, 1996). Full-circle scrutiny. *CIO, 9*(20), 30–32.

68. Ward, P. (1995). A 360-degree turn for the better. *People Management, 2*, 20–22.

69. Yukl, G., and Lepsinger, R. (December 1995). How to get the most out of 360 degree feedback. *Training,* pp. 45–49, and Molvig, D. (1996). Tell me what you think. *Credit Union Management, 19*(1), 14–16.

70. Church, A. H. (1995). First-rate multirater feedback. *Training & Development, 8,* 42–43; see also, note 1, Bernardin et al., 1998.

71. Carey, R. (1995). Coming around to 360-degree feedback. *Performance, 3,* 56–60.

72. Nowack, K. M. (1993). 360-degree feedback: The whole story. *Training & Development, 1,* 69–72; see also, Fisher, A. (March 3, 1997). Ask Annie. *Fortune,* pp. 177–178.

73. See note 69.

74. Hoffman, R. (1995). Ten reasons you should be using 360-degree feedback. *HRMagazine, 4,* 82–85.

75. See note 70. See also, Edwards, M. R., and Ewen, A. J. (1996). How to manage performance and pay with 360-degree feedback. *Compensation and Benefits Review, 28*(3), 41–46.

76. See note 52; see also, Gabor, A. (Jan. 26, 1992). Take this job and love it. *New York Times,* pp. F1, F6.

77. Lanza, P. (1985). Team appraisals. *Personnel Journal, 64*(3), 47–51.

78. See note 14.

79. See note 19.

80. See note 4.

81. See note 66, Welch (1996).

82. See note 1, Morevac, Juliff, and Hesler (1995).

83. See note 4.

84. See note 1.

85. Lawrie, J. W. (1989). Your performance: Appraise it yourself. *Personnel, 66* (1), 21–23.

86. See note 19.

87. Allen, M. (Sept. 24, 1991). Legislation could restrict bosses from snooping on their workers. *The Wall Street Journal,* pp. B1, B7.

88. Ashford, S. J., and Cummings, L. L. (1983). Feedback as an individual resource: Personal strategies of creating information. *Organizational Behavior and Human Performance, 32,* 370–398; see also, Locke, E. A., Cartledge, N., and Koeppel, J. (1968). Motivational effects of knowledge of results: A goal-setting phenom-

enon. *Psychological Bulletin, 70,* 474–485; see note 34, Murphy and Cleveland (1991); and Northcraft, G. B., and Earley, P. C. (1989). Technology, credibility and feedback use. *Organizational Behavior and Human Decision Processes, 44,* 83–96.

89. Dorfman, P. W.; Stephan, W. G.; and Loveland, J. (1986). Performance appraisal behaviors: Supervisor perceptions and subordinate reactions. *Personnel Psychology, 39,* 579–597. See also, note 47, Farh, Dobbins, and Cheng (1991); note 47, London and Wohlers (1991); and Nathan, B. R.; Mohrman, A. M., Jr.; and Milliman, J. (1991). Interpersonal relations as a context for the effects of appraisal interviews on performance and satisfaction: A longitudinal study. *Academy of Management Journal, 34,* 352–369.

90. Kluger, A. N., and DeNisi, A. (1996). Effects of feedback intervention on performance: A historical review, a meta-analysis, and a preliminary feedback intervention theory. *Psychological Bulletin, 119*(2), 254–284; see also, Earley, P. C. (1988). Computer-generated performance feedback in the magazine-subscription industry. *Organizational Behavior and Human Decision Processes, 41,* 50–64.

91. See note 1, Bernardin et al., 1998; see also, Fiske, S. T., and Taylor, S. E. (1984). *Social cognition.* Reading, MA: Addison-Wesley Publishing Co.; Jones, E. E., and Davis, K. E. (1965). From acts to dispositions: The attribution process in person perception. In L. Berkowitz (ed.), *Advances in experimental social psychology,* Vol. 2. New York: Academic Press, pp. 220–266, and Ross, L. (1977). The intuitive psychologist and his shortcomings: Distortions in the attribution process. In L. Berkowitz (ed.), *Advances in experimental social psychology,* vol. 9. New York: Academic Press, pp. 174–226.

92. Fisher, C. D. (1979). Transmission of positive and negative feedback to subordinates: A laboratory investigation. *Journal of Applied Psychology, 64,* 533–540; see also, Ilgen, D. R., and Knowlton, W. A. (1980). Performance attributional effects on feedback from superiors. *Organizational Behavior and Human Performance, 25,* 441–456.

93. Larson, J. R. (1986). Supervisors' performance feedback to subordinates: The impact of subordinate performance valence and outcome dependence. *Organizational Behavior and Human Decision Processes, 37,* 391–408.

94. See note 78.

95. Becker, T. E., and Klimoski, R. J. (1989). A field study of the relationship between the organizational feedback environment and performance. *Personnel Psychology, 42,* 343–358.

96. Villanova, P., Bernardin, H. J., Dahmus, S., and Sims, R. (1993). Rater leniency and performance appraisal discomfort. *Educational and Psychological Measurement, 53,* 789–799.

97. Kirkpatrick, D. L. (1986). Performance appraisals: Your questions answered. *Training & Development Journal, 40*(5), 68–71.

98. See note 66, Welch (1996).

99. See note 1; see also, Meyer, H. H. (1991). A solution to the performance appraisal feedback enigma. *Academy of Management Executive, 5*(1), 68–76.

100. Day, D. (1989). Performance management year-round. *Personnel, 66*(8), 43–45; see also, note 14 Romanoff.

101. See note 1, Morevac, Juliff, and Hesler (1995).

102. Bemis, S. E.; Belenky, A. H.; and Soder, D. A. (1983). *Job analysis: An effective management tool.* Washington, DC: The Bureau of National Affairs.

103. Woods, J. G., and Dillion, T. (1985). The performance review approach to improving productivity. *Personnel, 62*(3), 20–27.

104. See note 13.

105. See note 19.

106. See note 13.

107. See note 13.

108. See note 14.

109. See note 13.

110. Hubbartt, W. S. (May 1995). Bring performance appraisal training to life. *HR Magazine,* pp. 166, 168, see also, Austin, J. T., Villanova, P., and Hindman, H. D. (1995). Legal requirements and technical guidelines involved in implementing performance appraisal systems. In G. R. Ferris and M. R. Buckley (eds), *Human resources management: Perspectives, context functions, and outcomes* (3rd ed.) Englewood Cliffs, NJ: Prentice Hall.

111. See note 51.

112. See note 19.

113. See note 27.

114. See note 49, Bernardin (1986).

115. Adams, J. T. (May 1995). Four performance packages add ease and speed to evaluations. *HR Magazine,* pp. 151–155.

116. Bates, R. A., and Holton, E. F. (1995). Computerized performance monitoring: A review of human resource issues. *Human Resource Management Review, 5*(4), 267–288.

117. Rush, M. C., Facteau, J. D., Russell, J. E. A., and Dobbins, G. H. (April 1991). *Contextual factors related to perceptions of a pending appraisal system.* Paper presented at the annual meeting of the Society for Industrial and Organizational Psychology, St. Louis.

118. See note 4.

119. Gellerman, S. W., and Hodgson, W. G. (1988). Cyanamid's new take on performance appraisal. *Harvard Business Review, 66,* 36–37, 40–41.

120. See note 19.

121. Bernardin, H. J., and Orban, J. A. (1990). Leniency effects as a function of rating format purpose for appraisal, and rater individual differences. *Journal of Business and Psychology, 5,* 197–211; Ferris, G. R.; Judge, T.; Rowland, K. M.; and Fitzgibbons, D. E. (1994). Subordinate influence and the performance evaluation process: Test of a model. *Organizational behavior and Human Decision Processes, 58,* 101–135.

122. See note 1, Bernardin et al., 1998.

123. Sulsky, L. M., and Balzer, W. K. (1988). Meaning and measurement of performance rating accuracy: Some methodological and theoretical concerns. *Journal of Applied Psychology, 73*(3), 497–506.

124. See note 37, Kane and Lawler (1979).

125. Deming, W. E. (1986). *Out of the crisis.* Cambridge, MA: Center for Advanced Engineering Study, Massachusetts Institute of Technology. See also, Juran, J. M. (1989). *Juran on planning for quality.* New York: The Free Press; Scholtes, P. R. (1987). *An elaboration on Deming's teachings on performance appraisal.* Madison, WI: Joiner Associates; Scholtes, P. R. (Summer 1992). Total quality or performance appraisal: Choose one. *National Productivity Review,* pp. 93–103; Waldman, D. A. (1994). The contributions of total quality management to a theory of work performance. *Academy of Management Review, 19,* 510–536; and Waldman, D. A. (1994). Designing performance management systems for total quality implementation. *Journal of Organizational Change Management, 7*(2), 31–44.

126. Ghorpade, J., and Chen, M. M. (1995). Creating quality-driven performance appraisal systems. *Academy of Management Executive, 9*(1), 32–39; see also, Masterson, S. S., and Taylor, M. S. (1996). Total quality management and performance appraisal. *Journal of Quality Management, 1,* 67–89; Villanova, P. (1992). A customer-based model for developing job performance criteria. *Human Resource Management Review, 2*(1), 103–114.

127. See note 1, Moravec, Juliff, and Hesler (1995).

128. See note 6, McNerney (1995).

129. Murphy, K. R., and Cleveland, J. N. (1995). *Understanding Performance Appraisal: Social, Organizational, and Goal-Based Perspectives.* Thousand Oaks, CA: Sage.

130. See note 9, Bernardin et al. (1995). Age, racial, and gender bias as a function of criterion specificity: A test of expert testimony. *Human Resource Management Review, 5,* 63–77.

131. Johnson, J. W., Olson, A. M., and Courtney, C. L. (1996). Implementing multiple perspective feedback: An integrated framework. *Human Resource Management Review, 6,* 253–277; Podsakoff, P. M., Ahearne, M. and MacKenzie, S. B. (1997). Organizational citizenship behavior and the quantity and quality of work group performance. *Journal of Applied Psychology, 82*(2), 262–270.

132. See note 1 (Bernardin et al. (1988)); see also, Schrader, B. W., and Steiner, D. D. (1996). Common comparison standards: An approach to improving agreement between self and supervisory performance ratings. *Journal of Applied Psychology, 81*(6), 813–820; Visweswaran, C., Ones, D. S., and Schmidt, F. L. (1996). Comparative analysis of the reliability of job performance ratings. *Journal of Applied Psychology, 81,* 557–574; Wright, P. M., and Kacmar, K. M. (1994). Goal specificity as a determinant of goal commitment

and goal change. *Organizational Behavior and Human Decision Processes, 59,* 242–260.

133. Villanova, P. (1996). Predictive validity of situational constraints in general versus specific performance domains. *Journal of Applied Psychology, 81,* 532–547.

134. Waldman, D. A. (1994). The contributions of total quality management to a theory of work performance. *Academy of Management Review, 19,* 510–536.

135. Ferris, G. R., Judge, T., Rowland, K. M., and Fitzgibbons, D. E. (1994). Subordinate influence and the performance evaluation process: Test of a model. *Organizational Behavior and Human Decision Processes, 58,* 101–135.

136. Becker, B. E., Huselid, M. A., Pickus, P. S., and Spratt, M. F. (1997). HR as a source of shareholder value: Research and recommendations. *Human Resource Management, 36,* 39–48; see also, McDonald, D., and Smith, A. (1995). A proven connection: Performance management and business results. *Compensation & Benefits Review, 27*(1), 59–64.

C H A P T E R

DIRECT AND INDIRECT COMPENSATION*

OVERVIEW

The Tribune Company recently developed a new performance management system, closely following the prescriptions provided in Chapter 9. At an orientation session in which the new system was introduced to management, the first several questions had to do with the relationship between the new system and pay. With the possible exception of the pope and, of course, the authors of this text, most of us go to work as opposed to the golf course or beach because we're getting paid (or, as Bernadette Peters once said, "I don't care about the money, I just want the stuff"). Unfortunately, we need money to buy the stuff.

The term *compensation* refers to all forms of financial returns and tangible benefits that employees receive as part of an employment relationship. Beyond this pure economic exchange model, compensation may also be viewed as (*a*) a system of rewards that motivates employees to perform; (*b*) a critical communications device through which organizations convey and reinforce the

values, culture, and the behaviors they require; and (*c*) an important mechanism that enables organizations to achieve their business objectives.

As the business environment becomes increasingly complex and global, the challenge to create and maintain effective compensation programs, given cost constraints, also requires greater professional expertise, organizational understanding, creativity, and vision than ever before.

Compensation practices have important implications for organizations, for individuals, and for society as a whole. Harvard professor Rosabeth Moss Kanter considers compensation a key to competitive advantage (or disadvantage). She asserts, "Innovations in compensation are necessary to succeed at the doing-more-with-less balancing act: simultaneously reducing obligations and stretching capacities, lowering fixed costs and encouraging new ideas. In the postentrepreneurial corporation, pay must more nearly match contribution."[1]

From the organization's perspective, compensation represents a major investment. In labor-intensive organizations, labor costs typically constitute the single largest proportion of the organization's operating budget. In some organizations, employee remuneration costs may be 70 to 80 percent of operating budget.

---

*Contributed by Christine M. Hagan.

Organizations that have higher labor costs than their main competitors might have to charge higher prices to make up the difference, and price is a major source of competitive advantage (or disadvantage). But these organizations may also be competing against each other in the labor market for scarce skills. Microsoft has been able to recruit the very best computer engineers to some extent because of its superior compensation packages. Thus, while labor costs may be higher, at least for certain jobs, Microsoft takes the position that winning in the labor market is worth it. If higher labor costs translate into higher productivity, new products, and higher quality, the cost may be worth it. Effective compensation systems should constantly monitor the trade-off between labor costs and personnel requirements.

Many downsizing/reengineering efforts are directed at shrinking payrolls and reducing the cost of labor. Companies are vigilant about controlling or reducing labor costs to stay competitive. Some experts maintain that this recent vigilance has paid off in the form of higher productivity, higher profits, and the late 90s exuberance of the U.S. stock market. Indeed, according to Commerce Department figures from 1997, for every $100 in new production in the United States, almost $10 was going into profits, the highest percentage since 1968. At the same time, wages and benefits had declined as a percentage of output to their lowest level in over 10 years.

The vigilance comes in many forms. As we discussed in Chapter 5, outsourcing, the use of temporary and part-time employees, and the expansion of labor markets into lower wage countries have all contributed to the control of employee wages (except at the executive level—see the Critical Thinking Exercise on CEO pay). With the increased globalization of the world economy, fostered by improvements in technology, communications, logistics, and distribution, even the service sector of the U.S. economy is taking advantage of lower wages in other countries to get work done. The high-tech industry, for example, now routinely contracts with operations in India for computer programming previously done by U.S. workers. The result is a substantial reduction in labor costs.

Other countries now look outside their borders to produce products and services. Mercedes-Benz and BMW cars are now built in the United States instead of in Germany, partly because of reduced labor costs (German workers have the highest pay and the shortest working hours in the world). But why didn't BMW build a plant in Mexico (instead of South Carolina) to reduce labor costs even further? The cost of labor can be assessed only in the context of other variables such as access to markets, distribution, and workforce quality. As we discussed in Chapter 5, labor costs must always be assessed in context with a focus on corporate strategy, corporate performance, and the critical relationship between what

a company pays and its ability to attract and retain valuable employees.

The recent trend among multinationals toward hiring host-country managers instead of expatriates (U.S. citizens assigned to overseas duty) is mainly related to labor costs; expatriates are much more expensive. The result can be difficult at times, particularly when people performing the same work, sometimes in close communication, are being paid substantially less or more depending on their geographical status. It is little wonder that the job of international compensation and benefits specialist is high paying and in great demand today (try www.hrjobs.com for a sample of such jobs). The notion of equity becomes very complicated when we think and employ globally.

With the decreased influence of unions in the U.S. economy, U.S. companies now have more flexibility to reduce labor costs. For example, according to the Bureau of Labor statistics, unit labor costs decreased for the United States for 1995–1996 while net increases were reported for most of its major competitors. Even the collective bargaining agreements negotiated in the United States allow for more flexibility than do European contracts. For example, Seattle-based Boeing has been outperforming Airbus, the state-owned European competitor, at least to some extent because of the flexibility of Boeing's labor contracts, which allow more outsourcing and the use of part-time workers.

The 1997 Teamsters strike against United Parcel Service (UPS) was another example of a corporation's attempt to maintain flexibility. UPS was struck mainly to force the company to hire more full-time employees. Since 1994, under the old collective bargaining agreement, over 80 percent of the new hires at UPS were part-timers who were hired at about $8 per hour. These part-timers cost the company about one-third of what a full-time employee costs the company for the same number of hours worked (when you include indirect compensation). UPS argued that its high profits were a direct function of its policies of employing so many lower cost part-timers and proposed a profit-sharing plan in which the full- and part-time workers would get 41 percent of the 1996 profits. The agreement hammered out results in a plan for UPS to hire 10,000 full-time workers.

Compensation practices are a key factor that influences the type and level of talent an organization can attract and retain. They also represent an important opportunity to align, focus, and direct workers' attention to critical projects and priorities. Thus, compensation practices can directly influence an organization's survival, profitability, long-term growth potential, and competitive advantage.

From the individual perspective, compensation plays a major role in influencing one's lifestyle, status, and self-esteem. Compensation affects where people live, how much disposable income they have, how they spend vacations, and where their children will be educated. Compensation influences people's choices of which jobs to accept, how long they will stay, and the degree of effort they will apply. From a societal viewpoint, the general compensation practices of organizations have long been viewed as a platform for social change. Legislation such as the Fair Labor Standards Act, the Walsh-Healey Act, the Employee Retirement Income Security Act (ERISA), the Equal Pay Act, the Pregnancy Discrimination Act, and the Consolidated Omnibus Budget Reconciliation Act (COBRA) directly regulate compensation practices within the employer–employee relationship in a direction that society believes to be desirable. Some argue that excessive compensation practices are the principal reason the United States has trouble competing globally in certain industries. Some assert that industry setbacks can be traced to product price increases necessitated by the unreasonable wage and benefits demands of its workers.

OBJECTIVES

After studying this chapter, you should be able to:

1. Understand the traditional model for compensation systems.
2. Know the basic approaches to job evaluation.
3. Know the contemporary trends in compensation.
4. Know the role of government in compensation.
5. Understand the various forms of indirect compensation, including government-mandated programs.
6. Understand the different types of pension plans.
7. Understand the complexities of international compensation.

Compensation is typically divided into direct and indirect components. The term **direct compensation** is used to describe financial remuneration, usually cash, and includes such elements as base salary, overtime pay, shift differentials, bonuses, sales commissions, and so on. **Indirect compensation** refers to the general category of employee benefits, including mandated protection programs; health, life, and other insurance; holiday, vacation, and sick leaves; executive perquisites, and so forth. Direct compensation is further divided into two components: (1) the wage and salary program (base salary, overtime pay, shift differential, etc.) and (2) pay that is contingent on performance (merit increases, bonuses, gainsharing pay, commissions, etc.). This chapter covers wage and salary programs and employee benefits. Pay for performance (PFP) will be covered in Chapter 11. It is interesting to note that writers on this subject invariably refer to the topics covered in Chapter

11 as "pay for performance" and that PFP represents a small percentage of the total compensation package. If this is so, what is the other part of the compensation package for if not for performance. Harvard's Kanter and many others argue that corporations need more PFP systems to sustain the economy.

An effective compensation system typically has the following characteristics:

1. It enables an organization to attract and retain qualified (and necessary) workers.
2. It complies with government regulations.
3. It motivates employees, fosters a feeling of equity, and provides direction to their efforts.
4. It communicates and reinforces an organization's culture, values, and competitive strategy.
5. Its cost structure reflects the organization's ability to pay.

Traditional approaches to compensation management focus primarily on enabling an organization to attract and retain qualified workers, while complying with government mandates concerning pay. "Status, not contribution, was the traditional basis for the numbers on people's paychecks . . . pay was cemented to hierarchical position, regardless of performance," says professor Kanter. Newer pay models attempt to balance the traditional objectives with increased attention to motivating employee performance and aligning pay with key organizational performance objectives. Says Kanter, "America is . . . well on its way to transforming the meaning of a paycheck, and some argue that it is none too soon if we are to remain competitive in world markets."[2] We explore this transformation below.

DIRECT COMPENSATION: WAGE AND SALARY PROGRAMS

The traditional model for structuring wage and salary programs has existed in its relatively unchanged form for more than 40 years. The traditional salary administration model is a product of the same complex web of economic, social, and political forces that shaped the structure of the 20th century U.S. corporation.[3] In the 1800s most business owners knew their employees, their performance, and their financial needs, and pay was established on that basis. With the rapid growth of business organizations, bureaucracies were created to provide structure, organization, and direction. Professional managers replaced business owners, while rapidly growing hierarchies distanced them from workers. Organizational systems and structured approaches replaced firsthand knowledge, as efficiency and effectiveness became the primary objectives. In the late 1800s, Frederick Taylor designed a formal, systematic way of assigning pay to jobs while helping a steel company identify methods for improving productivity. His methodology came to be called "job evaluation."

In the following sections, we will describe the traditional approach to salary administration, examine some recent trends in pay program design, and discuss the government's role in shaping employer practices in the direct compensation area. Figure 10.1 depicts and summarizes the steps involved in creating and installing a traditional compensation plan.

THE TRADITIONAL APPROACH TO COMPENSATION

What Is Job Evaluation?

Traditional compensation programs use job evaluation to establish **internal equity** among jobs. Internal equity means that employees perceive a fair input-output balance relative to others within an organization (usually but not always people doing the same kind of work—see

FIGURE 10.1
THE TRADITIONAL APPROACH TO COMPENSATION

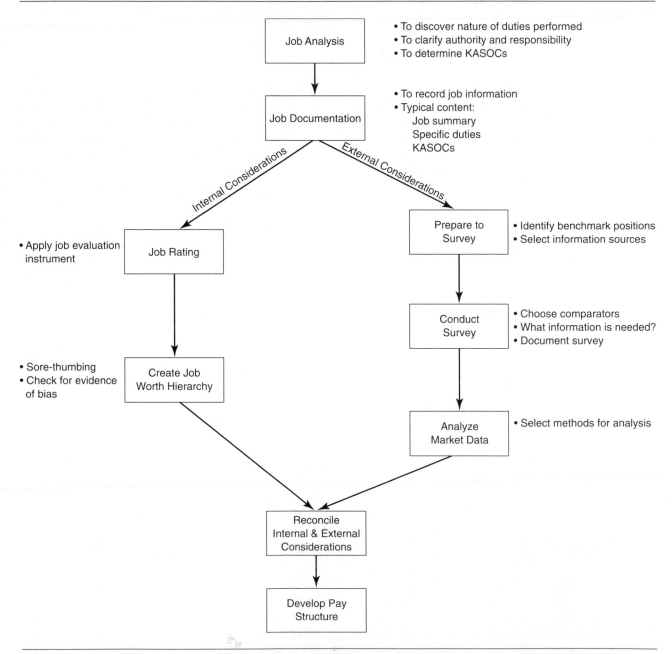

the Critical Thinking Exercise on CEO pay). Feelings of inequity, particularly perceptions of underpayment, can lead to job dissatisfaction, lower performance, and higher turnover. **Job evaluation** is defined as the systematic process of assessing the value of each job in relation to other jobs in an organization. It is intended to provide a rational, orderly hierarchy of jobs based on their worth to the company by analyzing the difficulty of the work performed and the importance of the work to the organization.[4] The factors used to assess a job's worth are identified, defined, and weighted in the company's job evaluation plan.

The focus of job evaluation is typically on the duties and responsibilities assigned to a job, not on the credentials or characteristics of the person who occupies the job, nor the quality or quantity of the incumbent's performance. This approach assumes that a true sense of a job's elements and demands can be ascertained, measured, and valued only through separating jobs from incumbent employees.[5] Traditional job evaluation is described as an objective, fact-finding, scientific approach that seeks to measure and quantify the relative complexity, the degree of responsibility, and the degree of effort demanded by the duties assigned to a position. The outcome is a hierarchy of jobs, or a "top-down" list, ranked in order of their assigned responsibilities, or their relative worth. While this is how job evaluation is described, some critics argue that the job evaluation process is discriminatory and at least partially responsible for the differences in pay between male- and female-dominated jobs.

Job evaluation, typically, involves four steps: (1) job analysis; (2) job documentation; (3) job rating using the organization's job evaluation plan; and (4) creating the job hierarchy.[6]

Step 1: Job Analysis

You will recall from the discussion in Chapter 4 that job analysis is the process of collecting and evaluating relevant information about jobs. The data collected should clarify the nature of the work being performed (principal tasks, duties, and responsibilities) as well as the level of the work being performed. Information should include the types and extent of knowledge, skill, mental and physical efforts required, as well as the conditions under which the work is typically performed. Chapter 4 summarizes the numerous options available for job analysis.[7]

Step 2: Job Documentation

Job documentation is the process of recording job content information, usually in the form of a written job description, one of the most important products of job analysis. Most job descriptions contain a summary of the position, a detailed description of the duties, examples of work typically performed, and a statement identifying the knowledges, abilities, skills, and other characteristics (KASOCs) that are required to satisfactorily perform the duties. The ideal job description for compensation reflects not just information concerning "what" a job does, but also the "how" and "why" of the duties.[8]

Step 3: Rating the Job

In the third step, a job's assigned duties are assessed using the job evaluation plan, or instrument, selected by the organization. Discussions about job evaluation approaches focus attention on three basic models: job ranking, job classification, and point factor plans. Each of these methods is described and explained below. A summary of the approaches is provided in Figure 10.2.

JOB RANKING.   The oldest, fastest, and simplest method of job evaluation, **job ranking** involves ordering jobs from highest to lowest based on some definition of value or contribution. The job that evaluators believe to be the most valuable is placed first; the job that evaluators believe to be the least valuable is placed last and

FIGURE 10.2
SUMMARY OF THREE TRADITIONAL JOB EVALUATION METHODS

METHOD	PROCEDURE	ADVANTAGES	DISADVANTAGES
Ranking (paired comparison)	Rank order whole jobs for worth or compare pairs of jobs.	Simplest method; inexpensive, easily understandable.	Only general rating of "worth"—not very reliable; doesn't measure differences between jobs.
Classification	Compare job descriptions to grade descriptions.	Simple, easy to use for large number of jobs; one rating scale.	Ambiguous, overlapping grade descriptions.
Point factor	Reduce general factors to subfactors: give each factor weights and points; use points to determine grades.	More specific and larger number of factors; off-the-shelf plans available (e.g., Hay plan); more precise measurements.	Time-consuming process; more difficult to understand; greater opportunity to disagree.

other jobs are ranked in a similar fashion in between, producing a hierarchy. This method typically looks at whole jobs, rather than their component parts, and gives little attention to the particular collection of tasks that comprise any single job. In addition, the basis for comparison is limited to the other jobs in the organization. No attempt is made to consider the universe of possible work that exists outside the organization.

Two approaches to this method are most common: (1) alternation ranking; and (2) paired comparison.[9] Alternation ranking involves ordering the positions alternately at each extreme. For example, beginning with a list of 15 jobs, evaluators try to agree on which job is the most valuable among the collection of jobs, then which job is the least valuable. In the next round, evaluators will try to agree on which of the remaining 13 jobs is the most valuable, then which is the least valuable. This alternating process continues until all jobs have been ranked and a hierarchy of jobs has been developed.

In the paired comparison approach, each job is evaluated by comparing it with every other job (one at a time). For each two-position comparison, the more valuable job is given a score of 1. When all the possible comparisons have been made, the hierarchy of jobs is developed by counting the number of times that a job was awarded a 1.

Although it is the simplest method, ranking is seldom the recommended approach.[10] The ranking criteria are usually inadequately defined so that the resultant hierarchy is difficult to explain to employees. In addition, since the approach focuses on the total job, often the highest level duty becomes the basis for the evaluation. Finally, the ranking approach yields limited information concerning *how much* more valuable one job is over another, or how the KASOCs of one job relate to those of another. This could be a key drawback for an organization that is committed to employee development and promotability or to creating cross-training opportunities and career ladders.

JOB CLASSIFICATION. This method was originally developed, and continues to be used, by the federal government. Within this approach, each job is measured against a preexisting set of job classes that have been designed to cover the full range of possible positions that would be employed by the federal government. Broad descriptions, or specifications, are designed in advance to delineate the characteristics of the jobs that would be placed within that category. Within this method, job evaluation involves comparing a position with these generic descriptors and deciding where it fits best; that is, which job level, or class, best reflects the types of duties and level of responsibility assigned to the job under review. Figure 10.3 presents the generic descriptors for two job levels within the federal job classification system.

The **classification system** is relatively inexpensive

**FIGURE 10.3
GRADE DESCRIPTIONS FOR FEDERAL JOB CLASSIFICATION SYSTEM—SERVING AS A YARDSTICK IN JOB RATING**

Grade GS-1. Includes all classes of positions the duties of which are to perform, under immediate supervision, with little or no latitude for the exercise of independent judgment, the following: (1) the simplest routine work in office, business, or fiscal operations or (2) elementary work of a subordinate technical character in a professional, scientific, or technical field.

Grade GS-18. Includes all classes of positions the duties of which are: (1) To serve as the head of a bureau. This position, considering the kind and extent of the authorities and responsibilities vested in it, and the scope, complexity and degree of difficulty of the activities carried on, is exceptional and outstanding among the whole group of positions of heads of bureaus. (2) To plan and direct, or to plan and execute, new or innovative projects.

and easy to administer.[11] But as the number and diversity of positions grow, it is increasingly difficult to write level descriptors in advance that will cover the full range of jobs. Without this specificity, the classification method becomes ambiguous and difficult to communicate to workers. In addition, like the ranking method, it is difficult to know how much difference exists between job levels. Finally, in any whole job rating system, one must be cautious about the same type of rater errors that can creep into performance appraisal (see Chapter 9). For example, a halo-type error might be committed when a rater is overwhelmed by one particular component of a position such that he or she assigns the entire job to a grade level that might not be warranted, particularly if the job involves considerable work of a routine nature.

POINT FACTOR METHOD. Under a point factor plan, various factors are the basis for determining relative worth. Factors are the specific characteristics of jobs that will be measured. In choosing factors, the organization decides: "What particular job components do we value? What job characteristics will we pay for?"[12] Mental effort, responsibility, complexity of work, physical demands, skill required, and working conditions are the most common factors.[13] Factors chosen by a company for use in a job evaluation plan should have four characteristics. First, as already suggested, they should represent the job characteristics for which the company is willing to pay. Second, they should be present to varying extent in the jobs to be evaluated. Unless they vary across the population of jobs, there is no point in viewing them as distinguishing features of jobs. Third, they should represent factors that comply with the Equal Pay Act's skill, effort, responsibility, and working conditions framework. Finally, the factors should be business re-

FIGURE 10.4
MAJOR FACTORS OF THE HAY PLAN

KNOW-HOW	PROBLEM SOLVING	ACCOUNTABILITY
Sum total of every kind of skill, however acquired, required for acceptable job performance. Know-how has three subfactors:	Original, "self-starting" thinking required by the job for analyzing, evaluating, creating, reasoning. Problem solving has two subfactors:	Answerability for action and for the consequences of the action; the measured effect of the job. Accountability has three subfactors:
(1) Practical procedures, specialized techniques.	(1) The thinking environment in which problems are solved.	(1) Freedom to act (personal control).
(2) Ability to integrate and harmonize the diversified functions of management.	(2) The thinking challenge of the problem.	(2) The impact of the job on end results (direct, indirect).
(3) Interpersonal skills.		(3) Magnitude—general dollar size of areas most affected by the job.

lated; that is, they should support the organization's culture and values, its chosen strategy and direction.[14] Figure 10.4 presents a summary of the three major factors within the **Hay plan,** which is the most popular point factor plan.

Once the factors are identified and described, they should be weighted because all factors are not equally important to an organization. Typically, factors such as responsibility, decision making, and mental effort are more heavily weighted than physical effort or working conditions.[15] Next, factor scales must be constructed. Factor scales are statements of the degree to which the factor is present in any given job. Factor scales are sometimes referred to as degree statements. Figure 10.5 illustrates a typical degree statement for the factor "Physical Requirements." Higher degree ratings translate into a greater number of job evaluation points in a point factor plan.

FIGURE 10.5
EXAMPLE OF DEGREE STATEMENTS FOR THE FACTOR "PHYSICAL REQUIREMENTS"

FACTOR: PHYSICAL REQUIREMENTS

This factor appraises the physical effort required by a job, including its intensity and degree of continuity. Analysis of this factor may be incorrect unless a sufficiently broad view of the work is considered.

DEGREE

1. Light work involving a minimum of physical effort. Requires only intermittent sitting, standing, and walking.

2. Repetitive work of a mechanical nature. Small amount of lifting and carrying. Occasional difficult working positions. Almost continuous sitting or considerable moving around.

3. Continuous standing or walking, or difficult working positions. Working with average-weight or heavy materials and supplies. Fast manipulative skill in almost continuous use of machine or office equipment on paced work.

A higher degree rating for a job translates into a greater number of job evaluation points.

Some organizations that are attempting to develop a more quantitative approach to setting wage rates and to establish internal equity use a statistical method known as **policy capturing** to derive the weights for the job factors rated in a point factor system. Policy capturing calls for job experts to rate each job on the job factors and then correlate these ratings with the actual pay for these jobs. Through this type of regression analysis, the "policy" weights that were used in the past to "capture" pay rates, or the ability of the factor ratings to predict the wages of the jobs under study, provides the statistical formula that can be used to price jobs in the future. For example, a statistical weight can be derived for each factor such as skill, education level, working conditions, and responsibility. Ratings on these factors can be made and the ratings can be plugged into the regression formula to predict the wage level of the job rated. The approach can also be used to test for any problems in the pay system such as discrimination or wage setting that cannot be justified based on actual job content or work performed.

How does the point factor method differ from ranking or classification? Unlike job ranking, point factor plans do not rank jobs in an organization purely based on a comparison of one against another, and they do not rely on a rater's perception of the whole job. Instead, each job is examined concerning the degree to which each factor is present. In this way, the point factor plan is similar to the classification approach in that it uses an external standard, evaluating each job in relation to that standard. Unlike the classification system, however, the point factor approach breaks jobs down into component parts and assigns point values for various characteristics. In a point factor plan, a job's relative worth is the sum of the numerical values for each degree within each factor. A job hierarchy is derived by ranking jobs by their total point score.

Point factor plans have a number of advantages.[16] The written evaluation enables an organization to trace, analyze, and document differences among jobs. Such differences can be the foundation for training, development, and career progression initiatives that can benefit the organization in the long run. The fact that jobs are broken down into parts and evaluated using the same criteria over and over again limits the opportunity for rater bias to enter the process. Finally, when explaining job evaluation to employees, point factor plans appear to have a high level of integrity. On the other hand, point factor plans are expensive to design or buy and they are time-consuming to install and maintain. Some consultants assert that point factor plans should be administered by an evaluation committee consisting of line operating managers.[17] The time and cost of such commitments must be considered.

In summary, an organization chooses a job evaluation approach that it believes will best meet its needs and systematically evaluates each job within or against that standard. In addition, many organizations combine elements from each of these approaches to create a hybrid, or combination, approach.[18] Regardless of the method used, job evaluation ratings are typically done by a committee of persons knowledgeable about the jobs under study, with different committees charged with the evaluation of different **job families.**

What is a job family?   A job family is a cluster of jobs that fits together as a profession. The clerical family, for example, clusters various types of secretaries and word processors. The technical family clusters mechanics, electricians, and other skilled tradespeople.

Step 4: Creating the Job Hierarchy

As indicated earlier, the result of a job evaluation plan is a hierarchical ordering of jobs in terms of their relative worth to the organization. Whether this hierarchy is determined using job ranking or whether it is created by totaling the points assigned to each position, the resulting top-down list should reflect an ordering of positions that makes sense to and is meaningful for a particular organization. Before finalizing this hierarchical list, it is important that the evaluations be studied carefully in relation to one another. Consider this something of a "sore thumbing" process that looks at the final results of the job evaluation and identifies positions that don't appear to fit best where the job evaluation plan has placed them.

The purpose of a compensation plan is not only to create an internally equitable program, but also one that is externally competitive. The next step is to consider marketplace pay practices so that the organization may effectively compete for workers.

What Is External Equity?

If an organization expects to recruit and retain workers, it needs to establish a pay strategy that considers pay practices in the marketplace (see the Critical Thinking Exercise 10.1). This process of pricing jobs is concerned with identifying the market rates or **external equity** of the jobs under study. When we concern ourselves with external equity, we shift our focus from an administrative value system to an economic one. Thus, one should not expect absolute correspondence between the results of job surveying and the results of job evaluation.[19]

Some small companies, in fact, bypass the time and expense of establishing relative internal worth and go straight to the marketplace to find the wage information they need to set pay do just that. This is called a market pricing approach. Some authors say the use of this approach is one of the fastest growing trends in U.S. industry today.[20] Others assert that it is not an effective method for two reasons. First, most companies have many jobs that are unique to the organization and cannot be effectively priced using a pure labor market comparison. In these cases, pay information is best obtained for other positions within the job evaluation structure that most closely resemble the position in terms of its relative worth to the company. Second, the importance of a job can differ from organization to organization, such that the pure market value may be misleading or irrelevant. A scientist's role in a research and development organization where she is one of many experts, who enjoys a noteworthy structure of colleagues with whom to collaborate and solve problems, may not be the same as a scientist's role in a manufacturing organization where she is the one and only expert, serving as the reference point for all technical problems and decision making.

Surveys provide information about the pay trends in the area; but organizations must still make judgments concerning what the information means and how it applies to their own situation. An internal job hierarchy will help surface key differences in the way the market views certain jobs and the importance of a particular job within a single organizational environment.

A well-trained HR professional understands the importance of these issues and recognizes the need to relate the organization's pay practices to those that exist in its marketplace(s). Salary surveying is used for accomplishing this.

CRITICAL THINKING EXERCISE 10.1

Are U.S. CEOs Overpaid?[1]

According to Graef Crystal, named America's "foremost authority on executive compensation" by *Fortune* magazine, "The modern American CEO is a cross between an ancient pharaoh and Louis XIV—an imperial personage who almost never sees what the little people do, who is served by bootlicking lackeys, who rules from posh offices, who travels in the modern day equivalent of Cleopatra's barge, the corporate jet, and who is paid so much more than the ordinary worker that he hasn't the slightest clue as to how the other 99.9 percent of the country lives."

Crystal's 1991 book, *In Search of Excess,* outlines the processes that led to the 400 percent increase in U.S. CEO pay over the last 20 years while worker pay has been stagnant. CEOs in other countries get nowhere near U.S. CEO pay and they pay higher taxes. Japanese CEOs, for example, earn approximately 16 times the average Japanese worker while German CEOs earn about 21 times as much as the average German worker. CEOs in the United States now earn over 200 times as much as the average American worker. Bob Nelson, author of *1001 Ways to Reward Employees,* believes that we should take a closer look at the Japanese CEO compensation system. "When Japanese companies decide to cut pay, the cutting starts at the top . . . Executives are expected to make sacrifices before they ask employees to do so."

While Coca-Cola was rated as America's most admired company in 1997, did Roberto Goizueta, the CEO, really deserve an annual salary of over $100 million? (He also has in excess of $1 billion in tax deferred accounts.) What exactly did Mr. Goizueta do to earn this level of compensation? *Fortune* says Coca-Cola has been particularly successful in opening new markets all over the world. What a brilliant concept! Did the late Coca-Cola CEO think this up all by himself? As Aubrey Daniels asks in her book *Bringing Out the Best in People,* "What do you have to do to get $50 million?!" Not unlike many others, Daniels cannot comprehend the great disparity between CEO pay and employee pay.

What makes CEOs' performance so superior to warrant these astronomical salaries? David Hofrichter, vice president of the Hay Group, suggests that not only do CEOs shoulder the welfare of entire organizations, but they also can bring vast sums of money into the company that their underlings cannot. Daniels argues that CEO pay is "way out of line in terms of what the organization gets for what it pays." Robert Allen, AT&T's former CEO who had been at the helm of numerous AT&T blunders, including the disastrous purchase of computer maker NCR (a $6 billion write-off for AT&T), had to "shoulder the welfare" of AT&T on a meager $20 million in 1995 while he fired employees to cut payroll and downsized the company. Here's the breakdown of Mr. Allen's 1995 pay: salary, $1.5 million; bonus, $1.5 million; miscellaneous, $581,000; free stock, $1.8 million; and stock options, $11 to $15 million (a 10-fold increase). He earned this money while AT&T was hiring more consultants than any other company. The consultants recommended cutting the pay of workers retained and reducing the workforce. Many AT&T employees took big pay cuts to retain their positions.

Crystal conducted one study in which he compared the pay of 16 American CEOs with British CEOs heading the same size companies. He found the Americans' pay was 3.2 times more. Since CEOs love to explain plant closings and other downsizing efforts in terms of the doctrine of comparative advantage, he asks, "Why don't we bring all the Brits over to run the American companies; because we can get them for a third the price and they speak better English than we do!"

The response of the defenders of CEO pay is that their pay is not unreasonable when compared to Michael Jordan, Tiger Woods, Greg Maddux, Barry Sanders, and other super athletes and entertainers such as Sly Stallone and Tom Hanks.

While a 1993 law designed to control CEO pay has been virtually worthless, a political movement has evolved in the United States to curb the rising inflation in CEO pay. Should the government do anything about CEO pay and, if so, what should be done? Do the defenders have a point regarding CEO pay relative to sports and entertainment superstars? To what extent do American CEOs deserve credit for the success of the American economy in the late 90s? Mr. Allen defends his pay package by claiming that AT&T's board, like other public companies, determines his pay. He further states that he "will not debate what a front-line worker gets and what the president of a company gets."

Assignment

What's your view? Do we need more or less regulation of CEO pay? Should the entire CEO pay package, no matter how high, be fully deductible from the corporation's taxes?

[1] Contributed by Lauren J. Lispi.

Source: Bob Filipczak, Can't buy me love. *Training,* January 1996, p. 30; G. Crystal, *In Search of Excess.* New York: Norton, 1991; J. S. Lublin, The great divide. *The Wall Street Journal,* April 11, 1996, p. R1; *Business Week.* Gross compensation? pp. 32, 33; Johnstown, D.C. (September 2, 1997). Executive pay increases at a much faster rate than corporate revenues and profits. *The New York Times,* p. C4.

HOW DO YOU COMPILE MARKET DATA?   Before an organization compiles labor market salary data, a few decisions must be made. First, the positions that will be surveyed must be chosen. Typically, an organization surveys **benchmark** positions. Benchmarks are well known jobs, with many incumbents, which are structured in such a way that one would expect to find them in the general marketplace. Typically organizations do not survey unusual or unique positions, nor do they survey positions that they use in fundamentally different ways from the rest of the marketplace.

Next, the organization should decide what sources it

will use to gather market data. There are several options in this regard, each with fundamentally different cost and information quality ramifications. Some entrepreneurs, who don't want to spend the time or money conducting or reviewing formal surveys, use the classified ads in the area newspaper or speak to employment agency personnel to get an idea of what the market demands in terms of pay. The least expensive and the quickest approach is to obtain data from public sources, such as local chambers of commerce, the U.S. Department of Labor, and some state agencies. A second alternative is to purchase a survey from a consulting firm. These are more expensive than local or government surveys, but they are usually of better quality both in terms of participants and quality and completeness of information. Third, an organization can conduct its own survey or can contract with an outside firm to conduct such a survey on its behalf. This is the most expensive of the three options, but it affords the greatest amount of control in terms of the organizations that will be invited to participate, the depth of the information that will be gathered, and the choice of which jobs to include.

WHAT IF THE ORGANIZATION CHOOSES TO CONDUCT ITS OWN SURVEY? If the organization chooses to conduct its own survey, it will first need to decide which companies to include. To do this, the organization must define the relevant labor marketplace based on its current collection of jobs.[21] An organization may tap different labor markets for different positions, including: (1) similar organizations in the local market; (2) all employers in the local market; (3) similar organizations in the regional or national markets; (4) all employers in the regional or national markets, or even international markets. Identification of the relevant market is based on the answer to the key question, "With whom do we compete when we want to hire a (*job title*)?" For example, if the position is a customer service assistant and the organization typically finds qualified candidates in the local market, regional or national trends are irrelevant.

Sometimes markets are defined using multiple dimensions, including areas of interest and particular types of employers. When an organization is interested in finding research scientists, its market may be the national market for high-technology research and development organizations. In addition, it may seek graduating scientists each year that it will develop over time to fulfill some of its future needs. In this case, depending on the caliber of talent the organization desires, the market may be master's degree science graduates from the top 25 schools in the United States or the world. These issues should be given careful consideration during the planning stage. In some cases, the overall effectiveness of the emergent compensation program hinges on the appropriate identification of comparator organizations. As we discussed in Chapter 5, the geographical pool is expanding for many jobs. Improved technologies, logistics, and communications now make it possible to consider international labor markets to control labor costs, even for highly skilled work (see the Critical Thinking Exercise on Compensation abroad).

Equally important is ensuring that compensation surveys are performed on the basis of job descriptions rather than job titles. Different organizations title jobs differently. What one company calls a senior accountant may be an accountant elsewhere. A well-conducted survey provides a job description for the purpose of job matching. In fact, it might improve the art of surveying considerably if surveying organizations dispensed with the use of job titles and focused solely on job content, labeling the positions under review Job A, Job B, Job C, and so on.

A surveying organization must also decide what information it needs concerning each position. As mentioned above, a well-designed survey typically requests information about the elements of direct compensation: base salary, additional pay (e.g., overtime earnings, shift differential pay), plus incentive compensation opportunities (e.g., bonuses, gainsharing, incentive profit sharing, commissions, overrides, etc.). Most surveys request actual pay averages (the means), medians, and sometimes first and third quartiles. Organizations with formal pay structures are asked to report the current salary range, job rate, and their current hiring salary. Typically, it is useful to know the number of persons employed in a particular job by a participating company, because large employers have greater capacity to influence the market value of work than small organizations. Additionally, it is good practice to know the general benefits (e.g., medical, life, day care) and perquisites (e.g., club membership, company car). Employees do not always value these at their true dollar value, but a surveying company should consider the types of direct and indirect compensation differences that exist across employers. The Society of Human Resource Management publishes a report annually titled "Innovative Benefits Survey" that explores the more innovative approaches to attracting and retaining personnel (call 1-800-638-8094 for information). Finally, a surveying organization must also decide how the survey will be conducted: (1) written questionnaires that are mailed; (2) telephone interviews; (3) a meeting of all participating organizations to discuss the survey in general and job matches in particular; (4) personal visit to the companies being surveyed; or (5) some combination of the above. The above options are listed from low to high in terms of potential information richness.[22]

HOW DO YOU ANALYZE MARKET DATA? There are almost as many ways to analyze market data as there are ways to conduct labor market surveys.[23] Some organizations look across competitors only very generally, using average salaries, or median starting salaries, or some other index that it believes to be meaningful, and make decisions about pay policy. Other organizations spend considerable time and effort with such statistics as least squares regression analysis to aggregate data across jobs and across companies. Certainly different approaches to analyzing data will yield different outcomes. An organization should choose the type and the depth of the analysis based on its own individual needs, the complexity of the market with which it is concerned, the amount of time the organization can afford to allocate to this project, the professional expertise that is available within the organization, and the resources that it is able and willing to spend for outside advice and assistance.[24]

Generally, organizations tie their pay practices for most positions to the market average, although there are situations when organizations choose to pay above or below average based on their strategy or goals. For example, Merck, the highly successful pharmaceutical company, allows its research and development division to go above market for researchers with particular specialties compatible with its objectives for product markets.

HOW DO YOU DEVELOP THE FINAL STRUC-TURE?   How an organization structures its base salary program is primarily a matter of organizational philosophy, although marketplace practices are often important to consider in highly competitive situations. In deciding on the form of the structure, two key questions that must be answered are, "What will be the format of our salary structure?" and "On what basis will we actually pay our employees?"

Several structural options are available. First, an organization can use a single rate structure in which all employees performing the same work receive the same pay rate. Second, an organization can use a time-progression structure in which employees receive pay increases as they reach important tenure milestones. Third, some organizations use a combination of a time progression and a merit component. In other words, employees begin at a fixed rate, progress to higher rates solely based on time in job, then reach a point beyond which they cannot proceed except based on merit. Yet a fourth option would be a pay system based on productivity. An individual paid only a sales commission is an example of this. A fifth and increasingly popular option could be some form of base pay with an incentive opportunity, either based on individual, team, unit, or company performance. Finally, many organizations combine various elements of these approaches to create their own. The most common traditional pay structure involves a salary range, with a minimum, midpoint, and maximum.[25] Pay ranges, as opposed to pay rates, provide increased flexibility to allow organizations to consider the particular job-related characteristics of individual employees. Typically, employees move through such ranges based on a combination of experience, tenure, and merit.

In response to the question, "On what basis will we actually pay our employees?" several alternatives are common. First, an organization can focus primarily on job content. Under this approach, employees may receive pay increases from time to time, but the principal way of building one's salary is by seeking opportunities to assume greater responsibilities, either through promotions or other forms of developmental assignments. Second, an organization can pay for job seniority, or organizational tenure, by advancing the salaries of loyal employees who stay with the company. Third, an organization can choose to pay primarily for performance. In other words, once employees are hired, their pay progresses to the degree that they contribute directly and in a meaningful way to company performance. This latter approach typically requires that a formal performance management system be in place to assess contribution. Pay for performance is the subject of the next chapter; performance management and appraisal were covered in Chapter 9. Still a fourth option is to pay primarily for the credentials, or the knowledges and skills, that an individual brings to the particular task. Fifth, it is not unusual for organizations to pay for cost of living, particularly when it is on the rise and their employees risk losing economic ground unless their pay keeps pace. Most companies, in fact, use some combination of the above factors to determine the pay of an individual.

Assessing the Traditional Approach

The traditional model of compensation focuses on internal equity (through job evaluation), external equity (through market surveying), and some reconciliation of these to arrive at a final pay structure that is aligned with the organization's philosophy concerning pay and enables the organization to attract and retain qualified employees. As stated above, this general approach has dominated compensation practice for the past 50 years. Recent developments have triggered a reconsideration of whether this traditional approach continues to be the most effective framework for developing pay plans. Several new approaches to pay have developed in the last several years, and many of them represent a break from tradition. Before describing these trends, it is useful to look at why new approaches are being sought.[26]

First, the basic nature of work is changing as a result of globalization, the turbulent business environment, and the shift from a manufacturing to a service economy. TQM thinking has strongly influenced philosophies about where work responsibility, accountability, and control are really housed. Critics of the traditional approach assert that job evaluation and market surveys are no longer appropriate tools with which to measure and value work. "Job description" types of jobs are no longer the prescribed method for organizing work. Typically, they are characteristic of bureaucratic, hierarchical organizational structures in which managers or supervisors decide what authority to retain and what responsibility to delegate. Such thinking assumes that jobs are composed of discreet, describable elements that remain stable for long periods. Today, jobs are more fluid and more broadly defined. Traditional job description tasks are being replaced by the concept of worker roles that call for worker empowerment, team-based activities, and a coaching style of supervision. Traditional job evaluation plans place value on the size and scope of areas managed, encouraging an empire-building mind-set that is not aligned with the downsized, leaner, flat organizations of today.

Second, the traditional approach may lose effectiveness as organizations increase their focus on customers and quality. Job evaluation is the product of the scientific management era that valued effectiveness and efficiency above all. Today, successful companies are seeking competitive advantage by being fundamentally different from other organizations. Traditional market surveys rely on the assumption that paying competitively is the primary objective. It has been suggested that this concern with what others are doing is not applicable given today's business context.

Third, critics argue that traditional plans support "incremental" thinking and entitlement mind-sets on the part of employees. Annual base salary increases and similar scale adjustments create an expectation that pay only moves in one (upward) direction. Organizations in highly competitive situations may not be able to absorb continuous increases in fixed costs.

One strength of the traditional approach was that it conveyed a sense of orderliness, rationality, fairness, and objectivity. Job evaluation plans identify—explicitly or implicitly—the job factors that an organization values. Salary surveys are based on the compiling and analysis of specific competitor practices for comparative purposes. Despite this systematic foundation, the traditional compensation process provides numerous opportunities for bias, rater errors, and other forms of distortion and controversy.[27] Many have argued, for example, that traditional compensation programs have been biased against jobs traditionally held by women.

Referred to as the comparable worth dilemma, traditional plans have been criticized for measuring internal job worth and then relying on market survey information to establish wages or salaries within job families. The net result is that some jobs could be rated quite high in terms of their job content using a job evaluation plan but paid comparatively low if the market undervalues their contribution. Comparable worth supporters argue that this occurs frequently because the marketplace is discriminatory. The prestigious National Academy of Science drew this conclusion in 1981.[28] We will discuss the comparable worth/pay equity issue in the section on government compliance below. Proponents of comparable worth legislation argue that waiting for an economic market adjustment is too slow and that it ignores a basic inequity in our society. They point to countries where women are much closer to equity.[29]

Finally, critics of the traditional compensation approach argue that such programs do not provide a sense of pay equity among employees. Equity theory is based on a highly subjective determination made at the individual level about his or her perception of inputs and outcomes compared with those of others. They argue that even the fairest, most equitable program cannot avoid the probability that the perception of many employees may be subjective, personal, and incorrect.

In summary, there are a variety of reasons the traditional internal equity/external competitive approach to compensation has been called into question. Over the last several years there has been an increase in the number and type of alternative approaches that are being designed and implemented with an eye toward overcoming many of these disadvantages and creating approaches that are more effectively built around today's work and organizational structures. In the next section, we will review and evaluate some of the noteworthy efforts in this direction. Figure 10.6 illustrates the characteristics of three contemporary pay approaches that are described and discussed below.

Current Trends in Salary Administration

BROADBANDING. Broadbanding is an approach to base pay that is receiving considerable attention in the business press.[30] Broadbanding is the redefinition of an organization's job hierarchy using less precise concepts and measures than are typically found in traditional job evaluation plans. The result is that the traditional narrow, structured pay grades are replaced by fewer and wider bands. The broadbanding approach gives management much greater flexibility in setting and adjusting pay rates. Where a typical pay grade may contain a 50 percent spread in pay between the minimum and maximum (e.g., $30,000 to $45,000), job bands may have a 200 to 300 percent spread (e.g., $25,000 to $75,000). Northern Telecom clustered more than 34 pay grades into 10 bands and replaced 19,000 job titles with approximately 200 more generic job titles. General Electric collapsed 30 pay grades covering administrative, executive, and professional employees into five broad bands. A banded approach is also thought to be more consistent with the broader, downsized, flatter organizations that exist today.

Hewitt Associates studied the experience of 106 organizations that replaced traditional pay grades with broad bands by conducting focus groups that included

FIGURE 10.6
A COMPARISON OF THREE CONTEMPORARY APPROACHES TO PAY

APPROACH	DESCRIPTION	ADVANTAGES	DISADVANTAGES
Broadbanding	Replaces traditional narrow salary ranges (40–60% spread) to fewer, wider bands (200–300% spread)	More consistent with downsized, flatter organizational structures Breaks down previous structural pay barriers among jobs to facilitate empowerment, teamwork, etc. Greater flexibility; more useful managerial tool	Traditional cost control in pay structure is lost Job pricing more difficult May be more difficult to communicate to employees
Pay for Knowledge	Employees paid on basis of either: (1) degree of specific knowledge they possess or (2) an inventory of skills	Encourages workforce flexibility and enhanced competence Fewer supervisors needed as employees improve knowledge and skill Fosters sense of individual empowerment about pay	Pay costs may get out of control Unused skills may get rusty Creating and maintaining skill and competency menus take time and efforts Do we pay for inputs or outcomes?
Team Pay	Any form of compensation contingent on group membership or team results	Reinforces concepts of teams, empowerment May better communicate and support organization's culture and goals	May demotivate top individual performers Few existing plans; beginning to emerge

affected employees, the managers responsible for administering the new plans, and top organizational executives.[31] Employee groups asserted that broadbanding encourages developmental and lateral career moves and facilitates cross-functional teams because differences in titles, levels, and salaries are minimized. Managers agreed with these observations and added that they liked the greater flexibility the approach provided in setting and managing pay. Executives viewed bands as a mechanism that could be molded to support a business's organizational style, strategy, and vision. An American Compensation Association study of broadband organizations found that 78 percent considered the approach to be effective.[32] Bob Stonaker, a 1997 winner of the Society of Human Resource Management "innovative practice" award, reduced 20 pay levels at MetLife into five career bands: administrative, management, technical, leadership, and professional. Each of the bands has equal value at MetLife and none has either a salary minimum or maximum. As proposed, MetLife's banding approach eliminates promotions and career ladders and emphasizes skill or knowledge acquisition and pay for performance.

Insufficient research has been conducted to date to indicate whether broadbanding is a long-term, effective pay model for future pay programs. Some experts argue that broadbanding could have some noteworthy drawbacks.[33] Traditionally, narrow ranges limited potential earnings. It is not known to what degree an organization's payroll costs may increase without corresponding increases in worker productivity. Some argue that broadbanding is appropriate for higher level positions only.

PAY FOR KNOWLEDGE, CAPABILITY, OR COMPETENCE. In these types of plans, employees are paid on the basis of either the degree of specific, technical knowledge they hold or an inventory of knowledge and/or skills, that they possess. These plans are based on the assumption that knowledge, skill, or competence will be translated into improved employee performance and, ultimately, superior organizational effectiveness. Advocates assert that such plans can increase worker productivity and product quality, while decreasing absenteeism, turnover, and accident rates. One estimate of the popularity of the approach is that as many as 40 percent of large organizations use this approach, but only for a very small percentage of their workforce.[34]

Paying for knowledge has long been a viable pay strategy in scientific, technical, and professional disciplines in which expertise and innovation were sources of competitive, albeit intangible, advantage. Business schools, for example, typically pay considerably more for an "assistant professor" with a Ph.D. than for an instructor with an MBA. These plans are based on the assumption that professional competence increases with longevity in one's profession. Similarly, unionized professions, such as teachers and nurses, have strongly favored pay based on education and experience. As technology continues to move forward at its rapid pace, such plans are increasing in popularity.

The most modern application of this thinking can be found in organizations designing and implementing skills-based pay. Originally found in new, nonunion manufacturing organizations, interest in this approach has grown considerably. Although it is not used as

publicity might indicate (only 5 percent of
izations are believed to have implemented
on of the approach), its influence has been felt
ndustries, such as pharmaceuticals and telecommunications.

In a typical skills-based pay plan, the array of
knowledges or skills that the organization values becomes the pay menu. Employees begin at an entry-level
rate. Incremental pay increases are awarded as employees demonstrate knowledge, or mastery, of specific, additional skills. Three types of potentially useful skills enhancements have been identified: (1) Skill depth is
increased when employees learn more about specialized
areas, moving along a career track to becoming an expert, or master; (2) skill breadth is improved when employees learn more and more tasks in the organization;
(3) self-management skills—the abilities of employees
to schedule work and to perform similar administrative
roles—may benefit an organization in a variety of ways.

Supporters argue its merits: (1) the cross-training
and acquisition of knowledge can create a flexible, empowered workforce whose competence extends well
beyond the boundaries envisioned in traditional "job description" jobs; (2) fewer supervisors are needed, providing support in a downsized, delayered organization;
(3) programs foster in employees a sense of power over
and responsibility for their own development and their
own compensation.

Opponents assert that potentially higher individual
pay costs may be uneconomical unless they are offset by
higher worker productivity. Second, unless skills are
used or knowledges are applied, they become rusty, although the pay may continue indefinitely. Third, depending on the growth and direction of the organization,
employees can still reach the top of the pay scale, resulting in the same frustration that these plans are designed
to remedy. Fourth, the process of reviewing, attaching
monetary values to, and certifying skills can create the
same type of bureaucratic structure and recordkeeping
requirement that these plans are created to eliminate. Finally, one very controversial issue is whether organizations should pay for inputs or outcomes. Skills-based
pay represents paying for input. In contrast, some organizations believe that the best response to rising costs in
uncertain environments is to put increasing amounts of
pay at risk, that is, paying for outcomes, for the attainment of concrete individual, group, or organizational
goals. Paying for knowledge, competence, skills, or abilities suggests that these qualities hold potential performance value. But it is up to the organization to make
certain that its culture, work rules, and other control systems ensure that such inputs are transformed into improved work products.

TEAM PAY PLANS.   With the wide growth in the use
of teams within organizations has come discussion con-

cerning how team members should be compensated.
There appears to be a general consensus that a team organizational model requires an alternative compensation
approach, but there currently appears to be more questions than answers.[35] In a 1995 study of 230 large U.S.
organizations, Hay Associates reported that 80 percent
were satisfied with their use of teams, but that only 40
percent were pleased with the compensation approach in
use to reward their teams.

One group of experts argues that it is important to
distinguish between behaviors that a company values (as
in teamwork) versus a true organizational form (as in
teams). In addition, at least five types of teams have been
identified—management teams, work teams, quality circles, virtual teams, and problem-solving teams. In sorting
through the types and uses of teams, three criteria have
been suggested as a basis for determining whether a team
is a candidate for some kind of customized form of pay:
(1) the team is a dedicated one, that is, the primary work
organizational model that is in use; (2) the work is truly
interdependent; and (3) the team is empowered to make
the majority of decisions concerning its work and such
decision making is shared across team members.

Some experts recommend that team organizations
use broadbanding in combination with incentive profit-
sharing plans based on team results. Depending on the
environment, a division and/or organizational component may be added to the incentive plan as well. Some
have used pay for knowledge systems, particularly
skills-based pay, as a compensation approach for teams.

Government Influence on Compensation Issues

In Chapter 3, you read about equal employment opportunity regulations that were enacted by the federal government to positively influence social change. The government also provides a legal framework concerning
direct compensation within which organizations must
operate. These rules ensure that minimum operating
standards of fairness and humanity are applied to compensation matters in the employer–employee relationship.[36] Figure 10.7 summarizes the principal provisions
of the most important federal regulations governing pay.
Of course, like most HRM activities, the reader should
be aware that state, county, and local laws may also regulate pay policies.

THE FAIR LABOR STANDARDS ACT.   The broadest, most comprehensive legislation that affects direct
compensation is the Fair Labor Standards Act of 1938.
This law regulates the employment relationship in several areas:

1.   Minimum wage.

2.   Hours of work (including overtime provisions).

**FIGURE 10.7
SUMMARY OF FEDERAL LAWS
AFFECTING COMPETITION**

PROVISIONS	LAW
Fair Labor Standards Act (FLSA) of 1938	Sets minimum wage ($5.15 per hour in 1998, overtime, child-labor conditions).
Equal Pay Act (EPA) of 1963	Equal pay for equal work (amended FLSA).
Davis-Bacon Act of 1931	Workers in construction industry must be paid at prevailing local rate for government contracts.
Walsh-Healey Act of 1936	Workers in goods must be paid at prevailing industry rates.
Services Contract Act of 1936	Workers in services must be paid at prevailing industry rates.

3. Child labor.
4. Equal pay.
5. Recordkeeping requirements.

The minimum wage provision establishes a lower limit on what an employer may pay. When the law was enacted, the minimum wage was $.25. As of January 1998, it is $5.15 per hour. Most states also have an established minimum wage, although in the majority of cases, the state minimum stipulated is lower than the federal minimum.

There has been much discussion about whether the notion of a minimum wage represents too much government intrusion into the private sector and whether a minimum wage is healthy for an economy.[37] Those in favor of the regulation argue that the minimum wage is necessary to ensure that employers do not take unfair advantage of workers. Opponents argue that the law actually puts people out of work because employers tend to eliminate jobs as the cost of doing business rises.

The **Fair Labor Standards Act** establishes 40 hours as the standard workweek and stipulates that employers must pay workers at least 1½ times their regular rate for all work in excess of 40 hours in any workweek (hence the expression, time-and-one-half). The act also stipulates certain exceptions to these overtime regulations and provides extensive regulations concerning the nature of the positions that can be considered as exempt from these rules. In general, administrative, executive, and professional positions are excluded from the overtime payment requirements along with certain types of "outside salespeople." The act provides detailed tests that such positions must meet to qualify for exemption, however. Various elements of these provisions can be complicated.

The act also restricts the employment of children by

organizations. Employees must be at least 18 years old to perform any kind of hazardous work; at least 16 years old to work in manufacturing, mining, and transportation positions; and at least 14 years old to perform work in most other jobs.

The FLSA was amended in 1963 to include the Equal Pay Act (EPA). This provision requires that men and women be paid the same when they work within an organization in jobs that require equal skill, effort, and responsibility and are performed under the same working conditions. The EPA covers jobs that are substantially equal, or identical. It also provides for a few exceptions. When pay differences are traceable to differences in job tenure, quality of job performance, or individual differences in education or experience—provided that the pay system operates to explicitly recognize and reward these factors—pay differences between men and women are permitted. The filing of a claim under the EPA does not preclude pursuing a claim under Title VII. This can be important because the Civil Rights Act contains no provision stipulating job similarity. Plaintiffs who can establish that they have been paid a lower rate due to gender, race, religion, or national origin are eligible for judicial relief under Title VII, regardless of the job's similarity to other work. For example, Home Depot was sued for Title VII gender discrimination in 1997 when the plaintiffs maintained that the pay system discriminated against women. As part of the settlement, Home Depot agreed to redo their pay system.

PREVAILING WAGE LAWS. Several federal laws have been designed to make certain that workers employed on government contracts receive fair wages relative to other local workers. The three pieces of legislation—the **Davis Bacon Act of 1931,** the **Walsh-Healey Act of 1936,** and the **Services Contract Act of 1936**—cover federal contracts for construction, goods, and services, respectively.

Typically, prevailing wage levels have been equal to union wage levels, which, in effect, creates a higher minimum wage for federally funded projects. At the same time, these regulations ensure that large federal projects, awarded on the basis of competitive bids, do not create a decline in an area's wage rates.

Pay Equity/or Comparable Worth Policy

One contemporary pay topic concerns the policy of comparable worth or pay equity we introduced above. First enunciated in 1934 and adopted as policy in 1951 by over 100 nations (not the United States), a comparable worth or pay equity policy requires a pay structure that is strictly based on an internal assessment of job worth. It has been proposed as a means of eliminating gender and racial discrimination in the wage-setting process.

Pay equity assumes that the traditional method of

achieving equity within, *but not between,* job families is inherently unfair. The theory of "within but not between" assumes, for example, that clerical jobs are compared to each other, that skilled trades jobs are compared to each other, and that professional jobs are compared to each other. The critical assumption of "within but not between" is that jobs in different families are *not* compared (and cannot be compared) with each other. Thus, a skilled trade job evaluated at 400 points on a point factor plan might be paid 20 percent higher than a clerical job receiving the same number of points. The external market is used to set rates within the various job families. Advocates of comparable worth maintain that the labor market undervalues the importance of jobs performed predominantly by women.

Traditionally, the lower paid job families include many women's jobs. For a number of reasons, the families with a large proportion of "female-dominated" jobs (defined in most comparable worth studies as jobs where more than 70 percent of the incumbents are women) have been compensated at a lower rate than have families with many "male-dominated" jobs. In Washington state, for example, the average wages of women were 20 percent lower than men for jobs found to have the same number of job evaluation points. Thus, jobs in the clerical families were found to have internally inequitably lower salaries when compared to predominantly male jobs such as skilled trades. Over 60 percent of working women still hold clerical, sales, or service jobs.

Pay equity proponents such as the National Committee on Pay Equity in Washington, D.C., maintain that job evaluation can be used to derive an internally equitable pay system and that the external market should not be used because it is discriminatory. They refer to a 1981 study conducted by the National Academy of Science that concluded gender discrimination accounts for a significant portion of the difference between male and female wages (the wage "gap" was 29 percent in 1997). Comparable worth studies are designed to identify and alleviate problems of pay inequity. The focus of the study is on pay inequities between female-dominated and male-dominated jobs.

Opponents to comparable worth pay policies present four arguments against the issue. First, they assert that there is no legal mandate to pay comparable worth salaries. The Equal Pay Act requires only that jobs with "substantially equal" (or identical) responsibilities be paid the same. Second, they argue that a comparable worth approach would mean inflating salaries and that most companies could not afford to do this and stay in business. In the state of Washington, for example, it was estimated in 1986 that providing a pay plan based on comparable worth carried an annual cost of $400 million. Third, opponents argue that if women really want to advance in terms of salary, they can do so by preparing themselves to enter traditionally male-dominated jobs

where they will enjoy the same pay—a right that is protected legally. This argument relies on an assumption that, over time, as women migrate away from lower paid jobs because they can obtain more lucrative pay in other careers, the pay for such traditionally female work will rise to reflect the worker shortage. Indeed, advocates of this market approach point to figures indicating that the wage gap between men and women is narrowing. According to the Center for National Policy, in 1983, women on average earned 58 cents for every dollar earned by men. In 1997, women earned 71 cents compared to the man's dollar. The fourth argument, related to migration, is that such policies can be justified from an economic point of view only if data such as turnover, productivity, or job satisfaction indicate a problem with the pay of certain job families. For example, the pay of international compensation specialists has gone up substantially in recent years because of the growing globalization of multinational workforces and the turnover driven by the demand for such skills. Microsoft is one of several companies that has had to increase the pay for this HR specialization in an effort to attract and retain these individuals.

Most pay equity/comparable worth studies have been conducted in the public sector. Several states and municipalities have some form of pay equity policy in place. In 1997, Connecticut adopted the policy of paying state employees at the same rate when the job has the same number of job evaluation points.

Although there is still considerable political activity on the subject, there is no federal mandate for a comparable worth pay policy. Many collective bargaining agreements have proposed comparable worth pay adjustments. The American Federation of State, County and Municipal Employees (AFSCME), one of the fastest growing American unions, has been most successful in negotiating such agreements.

The Equal Pay Act requires only that identical or highly similar jobs are paid equally; it does not require comparable pay for dissimilar jobs. However, in *Gunther v. County of Washington,* the Supreme Court held that claims of sex discrimination in compensation were not restricted to identical jobs under Title VII of the Civil Rights Act. However, the courts have yet to decide a case in favor of comparable worth as a pay policy under Title VII.

Washington state provided one of the biggest tests of the effects of comparable worth when, in 1986, new pay rates were set for 62,000 workers based on a comparable worth study. Many of the adjusted pay levels differed sharply from external market rates. Wages for female-dominated state jobs have increased over twice as much as for male-dominated jobs and the gap between the wages of men and women has been reduced to 5 percent. For example, based on the point factor job evaluation, secretaries, nurses, and teachers' aides were granted substantial comparable worth adjustments while other jobs (e.g., prison guard, truck driver) were given no adjustment. Unfortunately, to defray the $400 million price tag for the comparable worth adjustments, the state was forced to cut cost-of-living adjustments for many other state jobs resulting in differences in excess of 30 percent between what the state and the private sector pay some male-dominated jobs.

Some concerns about the ramifications of a comparable worth policy are now being echoed in Ontario, Canada, where comparable worth is required for all jobs, public and private. For example, disagreement has developed in the retail food industry over the weights to be assigned to each of the point factors. Some organizations (e.g., Warner-Lambert, T. Eaton) report few difficulties in implementing the plan but lament over the cost for pay adjustments. On balance, however, the cost has been low and the effect has been successful in moving female-dominated jobs closer to "equity." In Minnesota, for example, 30,000 state workers received raises due to a pay equity policy for state employees at a cost of 3.7 percent of the state's payroll budget. Pay equity was achieved in Washington state at a cost of 2.6 percent of the state's payroll costs over eight years.

There can be no question that differences between male and female wages will be reduced under a comparable worth policy. Women in Sweden, for example, earn 92 percent of what men earn under a long-standing pay equity program. Other examples of reductions in the wage gap since the implementation of a pay equity program are found the United Kingdom, Ireland, Switzerland, and Australia. No country in the world pays women as much as men. (Sri Lanka, just southeast of India, pays women at 96 percent of what men earn to lead the world in this comparison.)

The Fair Pay Act, mandating a comparable worth policy for federal employees, was introduced in Congress in 1997. While passage of such legislation in the United States is highly unlikely, the influence of unions and the successes at the state and local level to legislate and bargain for the policy is likely to continue. As of 1997, according to the National Committee on Pay Equity, 20 states have some form of pay equity policy for segments of the workforce. Seven states have comprehensive pay equity policies for all or almost all state workers.

Other Compliance Issues

Governments sometimes implement some form of wage and/or price controls. Typically, such controls are invoked to maintain low inflation when unemployment is also low.[38] Usually the controls limit pay raises and price increases. Most recently, wage-price controls were implemented during the latter part of President Carter's administration (1978–1980).

Many states and localities have their own regulations that cover workers in addition to the federal legislation. Human resource professionals must stay educated on these matters and be prepared to ensure that their organization complies with such laws. Often legislation covers areas with which business management would rather not concern itself. Such issues as maintaining records that document compliance with the overtime provisions of the FLSA or documenting the basis for a particular position's exemption from coverage under the overtime provisions of FLSA are not issues that are foremost in the minds of most CEOs. However, the cost of noncompliance can be extremely high and can include back pay awards, penalties, and interest. One method that has been recommended to assist HR professionals in ensuring organizational compliance has been the compliance audit.[39] This consists of an analysis of employee records and organizational policies and communications to ensure that both the letter and the spirit of the laws are being observed. This audit is an abbreviated form of the audit that would be conducted by a federal compliance officer if the organization were under review. The audit pinpoints problem areas so they can be proactively addressed.

In this section, we have examined the general methods and processes used by organizations to establish pay programs. We discussed the traditional approach, which may still be very effective in some organizations, and we noted some recent trends. In addition, we briefly looked at the way the government involves itself in direct compensation issues. In the next section, we shift our emphasis away from wage and salary payments to the area of employee benefits.

INDIRECT COMPENSATION: EMPLOYEE BENEFITS

Employee benefits are indirect forms of compensation that are intended to maintain or improve the quality of life for employees. Three benefits programs are federally mandated: unemployment insurance, social security, and workers' compensation. Like direct compensation, the major objective for most organizational indirect compensation programs is to attract, retain, and motivate employees.

The rise in the popularity of employee benefits programs during the past few decades is attributable to a variety of forces. During World War II, the War Labor Board (WLB) excluded employee benefit improvements from wage stabilization controls because such benefits were "on the fringe of wages," so increases in this area were not expected to be inflationary. Since then, benefits have grown largely due to favorable federal tax policies.[40] Provided that they comply with certain rules, employers are allowed current-year tax deductions for expenditures related to the pension and welfare programs it provides to its employees. In addition, employees receive the benefit plans, as well as most plan payouts, on a tax-free basis. In other words, when an employer offers a health care plan, three things typically occur: (1) the organization deducts the cost of the plan from its earnings for tax purposes; (2) an employee is not taxed on the cost of the plan that is borne on his behalf by the organization; (3) an employee is not taxed on the reimbursement he receives under the terms of the plan for covered services. Particularly when individual tax rates are rising significantly, these tax advantages make employee benefits programs attractive alternatives to direct compensation for many employees.

However, beginning with the Employee Retirement Income Security Act of 1974 (ERISA), increasing restrictions have been placed on employee benefits plans if they are to continue to qualify for favorable tax treatment. For the most part, these restrictions involve ensuring that such programs benefit all employees, not just the highly compensated employees; plan assets are adequately safeguarded; and future benefit promises are financed responsibly. The net result has become an increasingly complex set of regulations that has increased the administrative burden, as well as the cost, of developing and maintaining employee benefits plans.[41] There is every reason to believe that state and federal legislative interests in this area will continue. Particularly in light of the federal deficit, employee benefits could be a lucrative source of extra tax revenue.

In 1943, when the federal War Labor Board excluded fringe benefits from wage stabilization controls, benefits averaged less than 5 percent of pay.[42] According to surveys conducted by the U.S. Chamber of Commerce, the U.S. Department of Commerce, and the Bureau of Labor Statistics (BLS), employer costs for employee benefits averaged 40.7 percent of payroll costs in 1994, up from 40.2 percent in 1992.[43] Recent evidence suggests that this upward trend may be slowing, perhaps even reversing largely due to a decline in health care costs.[44]

While employee benefit programs were at one time quite uniform, there is now considerable variance. Benefit programs vary as a consequence of the organization's human resource philosophy, its size, location, the type of business, and the type of job that an individual holds.[45] Some companies such as Stride Rite, Arthur Andersen, and Johnson & Johnson have a strong pro-family orientation to their benefit package with options such as family care leave, child and elder care support, dependent care accounts, adoption benefits, alternative work schedules, and on-site day care. In general, larger companies offer a wider array of benefits.[46] Across large, medium, and small organizations, benefits programs for professional and technical employees tend to be the most comprehensive (in terms of types of coverages) and generous (in terms of plan provisions), followed by clerical

and sales employees, and then blue-collar and service employees.[47]

Research supports the importance of the benefits package in applicants' job selection process.[48] Recent research, for example, shows that women are particularly attracted to a company with a strong pro-family indirect compensation package. These packages become relatively more important when the unemployment rate is low and the competition for low-supply/high-demand jobs is high. However, employees tend to grossly underestimate the cost of benefits to the organization. For example, one study found that current employees estimated the cost of benefits to the organization was 12 percent when the actual cost was 31 percent.[49] Another study found that 7 percent of employees surveyed estimated the cost to the employer to be zero.[50] Organizations are now working harder to better explain the cost of the benefit package to employees.

Due to their enormous costs, benefits planning is a critical component of human resource planning. Benefits managers typically begin with a general policy statement and develop a three- to five-year strategic plan in the context of a number of internal and external factors. The most important of these factors are general and specific business objectives for the future, cost factors, the organization's compensation strategy, employee preferences, collective bargaining issues, benefit programs of competitive employers, taxation/legal/regulatory implications and changes, the human resource management philosophy of the organization, and other organizational issues relevant to the delivery of products and services. The list of variables becomes even more complex for multinational corporations. Experts agree that benefits programs should be closely coordinated with direct compensation for the entire compensation program to be most effective.

Five Categories of Employee Benefits

Employee benefits may be classified into five general categories: (1) government-mandated programs, including social security, unemployment insurance, workers' compensation, and certain state-mandated disability programs; (2) employee welfare plans, including all forms of health care plans, survivor benefits, and disability programs; (3) pension plans and other long-term capital accumulation programs, including 401(k) plans, profit-sharing plans, and other thrift and savings plans; (4) time-off programs (whether paid or unpaid), such as vacation, personal days, sabbaticals, and family leave; and (5) employee services, which include tuition reimbursement plans, child/family care, housing and relocation services, employee assistance programs, and employee recognition programs. In the sections that follow, each of these general benefits categories is reviewed and discussed.

MAJOR GOVERNMENT-MANDATED PROGRAMS. Social security. The U.S. Chamber of Commerce reports that many employers—particularly small organizations and those in the manufacturing segment of the economy—spend more in Federal Insurance Contribution Act (FICA) payments for social security coverage than for any other employee benefit.[51] Under the social security program, eligible individuals are covered by a comprehensive program of retirement, survivor, disability, and health benefits. Individuals are eligible for full social security retirement benefits in the form of monthly payments when they reach age 65, or for reduced benefits at the age of 62, provided that they fulfill the requisite number of quarters of coverage by working for an employer who pays FICA taxes.

Disability social security benefits are comparable to retirement benefits and are often integrated with disability payments from private, insured disability plans. Health care benefits are Medicare Part A (covering primarily hospital costs) and Part B (medical expenses). Medicare Part B coverage is voluntary and partially funded by participant payments. Individuals are eligible for Medicare upon reaching age 65 (regardless of whether or not they are eligible for social security retirement benefits) or after they have been receiving social security disability payments for 24 months.

In 1998, the retirement, survivor, and disability portion of the social security program was 12.4 percent of the first $68,400 earned by an employee. Half this amount (6.2 percent) was paid by the employer; the other half was paid by the employee through payroll deduction. In 1997, the Medicare portion of the social security program cost 2.9 percent (with the same employer–employee split) but, since 1994, all compensation paid to an employee has been subject to the Medicare tax. The total tax rate then that was shared between the employer and employee in 1997 was 15.3 percent for the first $65,400 of base pay and 2.9 percent on all pay above that.

Unemployment insurance. The basic unemployment compensation system in the United States is jointly enforced by the federal government and the states. It promotes the financial security of American workers by encouraging employers to stabilize their workforces and by providing emergency income for workers during joblessness.[52] The dual, federal–state nature of the unemployment compensation system is unique among the employment tax withholding laws. With respect to the federal portion of the system, employers must (1) determine whether their employees are included within the program (note: certain types of domestic and agricultural workers, as well as certain family members and student workers, are examples of exclusions); (2) remit taxes on wages; and (3) file an annual return. In 1997, federal unemployment tax was .8 percent on the first $7,000 of wages.

The state laws are more complex, particularly for employers who operate in more than one state. Professional HR members should remain up-to-date concerning the applicable provisions governing their operating areas.

In most places, employees who are covered under FUTA (the Federal Unemployment Tax Act) and whose employment is terminated are eligible for unemployment compensation for up to 26 weeks. A 1991 bill extended these benefits for up to an additional 20 weeks. Eligible employees must apply for the insurance through a state employment agency, which will attempt to locate suitable alternative employment. To be eligible for the insurance, the worker must have been employed previously in an occupation covered by the insurance, must have been dismissed by the organization but not for misconduct, must be available for work and actively seeking employment, and (in all states but Rhode Island and New York) may not be unemployed due to a labor dispute.

The amount of the benefit varies by state and is determined by the employee's previous wage level up to a maximum amount. The average is about $175 per week. An unemployed worker's benefits are charged to the company; the insurance rates vary as a function of the amount charged to each.

Supplemental unemployment benefit (SUB) programs are also common in some industries (e.g., auto, steel, rubber). Typically negotiated through collective bargaining, these programs augment unemployment compensation and can provide weekly benefits in the event that employees' workweeks are reduced or they are terminated. Through the efforts of the United Automobile Workers, union employees who are laid off in the auto industry can receive over 80 percent of their after-tax pay because of unemployment insurance and the negotiated supplemental programs.[53]

Only about 8 percent of employees of medium to large firms are covered by some form of SUB at the present time, but many employees are covered by severance pay if they are terminated for reasons other than misconduct.[54] Professionals and managers are generally granted higher severance allowances because it usually takes longer for them to obtain comparable employment.[55]

Workers' compensation insurance. Unlike unemployment compensation insurance, workers' compensation (WC) programs have been initiated and are administered by the states with no direct federal involvement or mandatory standards. Typically, workers' compensation provides for medical expenses and pay due to lost work time in cases where the illness or injury is work related. The primary purpose of workers' compensation programs is to provide for benefits to injured or ill workers on a no-fault basis and thus to eliminate the costly lawsuits that would otherwise clog the legal system and disrupt employer–employee relations.[56]

The first laws for handling occupational disabilities and death were enacted in 1910, and they have existed in all states since 1948. Employers are fully responsible for the cost of the coverage, and they may not require any employee contributions. To facilitate the consideration of claims, most states have established workers' compensation boards or commissions. Employers, generally, are free to select their own carriers to insure the risk, investigate claims, and process payments with the exception of six states that maintain monopolistic insurance funds (Nevada, North Dakota, Ohio, Washington, West Virginia, and Wyoming). Also, all states except North Dakota, Texas, and Wyoming permit employers to self-insure workers' compensation benefits.

State-mandated disability insurance plans. Five states (California, Hawaii, New Jersey, New York, and Rhode Island) and Puerto Rico have laws requiring short-term disability income protection. The goal of these plans is to protect workers from lost income in the event of sickness or accidents that are not job related. In general, the plans are designed to replace a portion of an employee's wages during a fixed duration of disability. The plans typically impose a short waiting period before payments begin. Payments are based on a formula—either a percentage of earnings or a fixed dollar amount paid weekly. Typically, benefits are paid for up to six months. These plans are one means of protecting workers from lost income as a result of a short-term illness or injury. Another form of protection is employer-sponsored sick leave plans, which typically provide full pay to disabled employees.[57]

EMPLOYEE WELFARE PROGRAMS. The benefits of greatest concern to both employees and employers in this category are health care plans. Also included in this category are survivor benefits, which include all types of life insurance.

Health care plans. The vast majority of employers in the United States provide health insurance for employees. The 1993 BLS survey of employee benefits in medium and large private establishments (i.e., 100 or more employees) found that 82 percent of workers were covered under some form of medical plan.[58] In addition, 62 percent of full-time employees participate in a dental care plan and 26 percent have vision coverage.[59] BLS's 1994 survey of employee benefits in small, private establishments (i.e., fewer than 100 employees) found that 66 percent of the workers were covered under medical plans.[60] Coverage in small businesses varies considerably among occupational groups with professionals more likely to be covered compared to blue-collar and service workers.[61] Recent surveys suggest a stabilization

of health care costs.[62] At least some of the difference is due to the increased cost sharing that has characterized most employer-sponsored plans over the past 10 years.

Health care management tools. Four other health care management tools are increasingly popular: (1) wellness programs, (2) personal responsibility clauses, (3) periodic health care plan audits, and (4) managed care plans. Wellness programs are not a new idea, but they are becoming more common and more pivotal in the strategic management of benefits.[63] Trying to move beyond the "feel good" approach, today's wellness plans are aimed at basic lifestyle issues. Typically, they are used in two ways: to educate employees to make informed decisions about their lifestyles and their health care, and to challenge employees' entitlement attitude (e.g., the belief that employers are responsible for their health and for paying all their medical care costs). One survey found that 76 percent of respondents had health promotion initiatives, or wellness plans, in place.[64]

Personal responsibility clauses are based on the principle that if employees or their dependents take personal risks, then they should bear additional responsibility for the costs arising from resulting injuries. The two most targeted behaviors for plan incentive or disincentive strategies are smoking and seat belt use.

Health care plan audits are also not a new idea, but they are being directed at more strategically reviewing whether an organization's health care spending is effective.[65] Typical plan audits are directed at six areas:

1. Cost and efficiency (e.g., examining claims on a regional basis and using such information as a negotiating tool for creating preferred provider networks).

2. Quality of care (e.g., comparing outcomes on the basis of types of health care providers).

3. Access (e.g., reviewing the degree to which distance to providers influences outcomes).

4. Employee satisfaction (e.g., the degree to which employees value the benefits).

5. Operational excellence of the program's administration (e.g., whether claims are paid correctly and in a timely manner, or whether coordination of benefits with other plans is performed correctly).

6. Overall employee health status (e.g., which risk factors most significantly affect the organization's absenteeism and productivity).

Managed care continues to grow. Popular approaches include **health maintenance organizations (HMOs)** and **preferred provider organizations (PPOs).** HMOs are organizations comprised of health care professionals who provide services on a prepaid basis. PPOs are usually hospitals that offer reduced rates based on a contractual arrangement with the organization. Many larger organizations have realized considerable savings since implementing HMO or PPO programs. General Motors, for example, experienced the first reduction in health care costs in over 25 years since it contracted for HMO and PPO services.[66] One survey found that 52 percent of corporate respondents indicated that HMOs saved them money.[67] A few big employers have made HMOs mandatory for new employees, thus restricting their options in the selection of medical services. Employees at GM's Saturn plant, the Lockheed Corporation, and Rockwell International, for example, are given health benefits only through HMOs. Lockheed's evaluation of this program found that employees were generally satisfied.

Recent studies, however, call these cost-saving statistics into question.[68] At least one expert asserts that HMOs specifically recruit healthy patients. A study by the federal government reports that, when favorable patient selection is taken into account, HMO costs are 6 percent higher than costs under traditional fee-for-service plans.

In addition, there is recent evidence that managed care may increase an employer's legal liability. The danger lies in whether the employer is drawn into an increasingly influential role in health care decisions made when the employer has been very involved in negotiating specific plan terms within a managed care program. Recent court decisions have chipped away at employers' long-standing protection against costly negligence suits for health care decisions.[69]

Health Care Programs have been considerably influenced by legislation. Employer-sponsored health care plans are subject to certain ERISA requirements. Under ERISA, health care plans must be set forth in written documents that clearly describe the terms of the plan.[70]

Under the Age Discrimination in Employment Act (ADEA), employer health plans must offer the same benefits to employees aged 65 and older (and their spouses, if applicable) as the plan provides to younger employees. The Pregnancy Discrimination Act of 1978 requires that pregnancy and pregnancy-related disabilities be treated the same as other illnesses or disabilities. Employers who offer health care plans, temporary disability plans, and sick leave are now legally required to include pregnancy as a covered condition. A 1990 study found that 84 percent of companies provide medical coverage to retirees. However, 53 percent of the respondents also indicated that they have reduced the benefit in some way in the last two years.[71] The Retirees Health Benefits Bankruptcy Protection Act of 1988 is designed to protect retirees in situations where the employer cuts retirement benefits after filing for bankruptcy.

The Consolidated Omnibus Budget Reconciliation Act (COBRA, 1986 amended in 1988) requires employers with 20 or more employees to continue offering employees health care benefits at no more than 102 percent of the premium cost for as long as 18 months after the employee leaves. Divorced or surviving spouses are allowed up to 36 months of coverage.

Life insurance. One of the oldest and most common forms of employee benefit is group life insurance. According to the BLS, life insurance protection is available to 91 percent of full-time employees in medium and large organizations and to 61 percent of full-time employees in small organizations.[72] Group life insurance typically provides coverage to all employees of an organization without physical examinations, with premiums typically based on the group characteristics. The most common level of life insurance is twice the salary level of the employee.[73] Many companies now offer additional life insurance along with dependent term insurance and other survivor benefits.[74]

PENSION PLANS AND OTHER LONG-TERM CAPITAL ACCUMULATION PLANS. A pension is a payment to a retired employee based on the extent and level of employment with the organization. The term *long-term capital accumulation plan* is the generic name for any program that seeks to systematically set aside money during one's working lifetime, primarily for use during one's retirement. This category includes not only pensions, but also 401(k) programs, thrift and other savings arrangements, traditional profit-sharing plans, and a large variety of similar arrangements.

Surveys of large, successful companies[75] indicate that at least 85 percent offer pension plans and that an estimated 80 percent offer both a defined benefit and a defined contribution plan (these terms are explained below). On the other hand, according to surveys conducted by the federal government, only 50 percent of workers are covered by employer-sponsored plans. According to the Economic Policy Institute, a union-sponsored research group, corporate spending on retirement plans has fallen from 84 cents for every hour worked in 1977 to 53 cents in 1996.[76]

As mentioned earlier, tax advantages are available to employers who offer a "qualified" plan to their employees. A long-term capital accumulation plan, including a pension plan, is said to be a qualified plan if it meets a set of criteria set forth by the federal government (see the discussion of ERISA below).[77]

The major pension plans. There are two types of plans: defined benefit plans and defined contribution plans. A defined benefit plan guarantees a specific retirement payment based on a percentage of preretirement income. Typically, the amount is based on years of service, average earnings during a specified time period (e.g., last five years), and age at time of retirement. The typical target benefit in a defined benefit plan is to replace approximately 50 percent of an individual's final average pay.[78] A small but growing percentage of defined benefit plans (approximately 5 percent) are indexed to adjust pensions for inflation.[79] In a defined benefit plan, the employer funds an employee's pension over her working lifetime. An employer's commitment to an employee is for a particular payout, at a particular time, based on a formula specified by the plan.[80]

In a defined contribution plan, an employer provides a specific amount of money (typically a percent of base salary) that is paid into an individual's account each period. In defined contribution plans, employees choose among investment options and, typically, may take the vested portion of the account with them if they leave employment. The vested amount is the portion of the plan to which an individual is legally entitled. In defined contribution plans, the employer makes no promise relating to a pension amount. An individual's pension is the account balance at the time of retirement. As a result, administrative costs are typically lower than under-defined benefit plans, and plan communication is simplified. Defined benefit plans have been the more extensively used type, but recent trends have been away from these complex, usually more expensive plans, toward defined contribution plans. The percentage of American workers with defined contribution plans was 33 percent in 1997.[81]

Government role in capital accumulation plans. Most government regulation of capital accumulation plans have had two principal objectives. First, there has been a philosophical concern that qualified plans must be created and managed for the direct benefit of all employees, not just the most highly compensated employees. For example, a plan that covered only employees who earned over $100,000 per year would probably not comply and would not qualify for favored tax treatment.[82] Second, more recent regulations have aimed at significantly curtailing the benefits available to the highly compensated in general, regardless of whether the plan benefited lower paid employees. This second agenda is probably attributable to the sizable federal deficit and the philosophical question of exactly which individuals and how much money should be permitted to accumulate on a tax-exempt or tax-deferred basis.

The **Employee Retirement Income Security Act (ERISA, 1974)** is the most comprehensive piece of employee benefits legislation ever enacted in the United States. Described as "a massive and exceedingly complex piece of legislation,"[83] the law was enacted because many retiring workers were not getting the benefits that had been promised to them. ERISA provisions may be broken down into six general categories, including extensive recordkeeping, fiduciary responsibilities, and eligibility requirements.[84] In addition, the PBGC was established by ERISA, and all defined benefit pension plans were required to purchase insurance through this organization. Since establishment of the agency, more than 1,500 pension plans have resorted to the PBGC to

meet their pension commitments.[85] Statutes enacted since ERISA have been frequent and have generally made the requirements for plan qualification more stringent.[86]

Other nonbenefits legislation has significantly influenced pension plan provisions. The Civil Rights Act of 1964 and subsequent amendments, which prohibit discrimination on the basis of gender, outlawed pension differences between men and women even if such distinctions were due to life expectancy differences. Today, most plans use unisex tables that combine the life expectancies of men and women.[87] Amendments to the Age Discrimination in Employment Act (ADEA) outlawed mandatory retirement ages and forbade any differences in treatment for individuals who were above a plan's "normal" retirement age.[88]

Trends in pension benefits. Two trends in benefits are particularly noteworthy. First, there is every reason to believe the current trend of seeking sources of tax revenue to pay down the federal deficit will continue. The benefits of highly paid employees are likely targets. This means that organizations may need to find ways to make up the after-tax reduction in benefits where such benefits were promised to employees. Supplemental executive retirement plans (SERPs) have been growing.[89] These nonqualified plans, funded with after-tax dollars (corporate and/or individual), are important if an organization wishes to attract and retain competent executive management. Second, there is growing concern that the retirement resources of today's middle-aged workers will be considerably below those of their parents due to four trends. First, social security is projected to be bankrupt by 2030.[90] Second, private savings are at an all-time low.[91] Third, the percentage of private-sector employees with defined benefit pensions will continue to fall. Finally, despite the broad coverage of employer capital accumulation plans, a growing percentage of 401(k) participants have outstanding loans on their account balances.[92] (See the Critical Thinking Exercise 10.2, "How Will Baby Boomers Afford Retirement?" for more discussion on this subject.)

CRITICAL THINKING EXERCISE 10.2

How Will Baby Boomers Afford Retirement?

Even though favorable tax treatment facilitated the growth and popularity of long-term capital accumulation plans, other societal characteristics made pension plans an attractive employee benefit from an organizational viewpoint.[1] First, pensions grew in the late 1940s when the United States was a growing economy coping with

15 years of a population "birth dearth" due to the Great Depression and World War II. Pensions became a "sweetener"—over and above pay—that an organization could use to lure competent workers. The favorable treatment of benefits by the War Labor Board made these plans even more attractive.

Second, based on the same demographics, organizations foresaw difficulties in retaining top talent past middle age. Without today's technology, learning curves were slower and longer. The most valuable employee was the 15-to-25-year individual whose sense of organizational history and expertise was an important asset to an organization. The problem was made even more acute by the expanding U.S. economy. New or expanding businesses sought to hire "middle-agers" away from older, more experienced organizations. Preventing such turnover was a major objective of established organizations, and pension plans were a primary tool in this effort. Third, the society of the 1940s was a security-conscious society. Memories of the Great Depression lingered, and the government was focusing attention on assembling a safety net of help and benefits to provide for the welfare of society's disadvantaged. Add to this the fact that members of this "birth dearth" generation were having a record number of children (who would later be tagged "baby boomers"), with relatively little sense of how they would provide for their long-term needs.

Thus, pensions and other forms of long-term financial planning held particular appeal to this generation of workers. In addition, the money that was being accumulated in these pension plans was used to indirectly support America's growing free enterprise system. Typically, organizations invested pension funds in corporate stocks, which, in turn, fueled society's economic growth. Thus, the growth of pension plans was seen by society as an opportunity to provide for employees as well as to contribute to the growth and health of the national economy.

As stated earlier in this chapter, recent legislation has taken aim at significantly curtailing the tax-favored pension benefits that are being accumulated for highly compensated individuals. The Tax Reduction Act (TRA, 1986) placed a $200,000 cap, or limit, on the amount of salary that could be considered in calculating tax-advantaged pension benefits or contributions. This meant that employees who earned more than $200,000 were treated as though they earned $200,000. Indexed to inflation, this cap grew to $235,840 by 1993. In searching for sources of tax revenue, the 1993 Congress passed the Omnibus Budget Reconciliation Act (OBRA), which reduced this limit to $150,000 and restricted how it would be indexed to inflation in the future. This means that any retirement savings done for individuals that would consider salary in excess of $150,000 must be done using after-tax dollars.

This same trend is evident at the individual level. From 1975 to 1985, individual retirement accounts (IRAs) permitted people to save up to $2,000 per year on a pre-tax basis. In addition, the interest earned on these accounts was deferred until the money was withdrawn. By the late 1980s, however, this favorable tax treatment had been seriously limited. Today, individuals may save $2,000 per year on a pre-tax basis in an IRA only if they earn less than a stipulated amount and are not covered under an employer-sponsored plan. However, the tax deferral of interest earned on an IRA is still available, even when the IRA is funded with after-tax contributions.

Most experts agree that balancing the need for Americans to save for their retirement with the need to identify additional sources of tax revenue is a major challenge facing legislators today. Traditionally, when people retire, they rely on three major sources of income (called the "three-legged stool"): social security benefits, pension plans, and individual savings. Employers play a major role in all three of these sources. They pay half of all social security taxes, sponsor pension plans, and provide for a variety of individual savings incentives through 401(k) plans, thrift and savings plans, and other capital accumulation programs. Based on a study of 9.5 million couples and 14 million singles (aged 65 and older), the U.S. Department of Health and Human Services reported the following breakdown of the income sources of today's retirees:[2]

Social security—40 percent.

Pensions—20 percent.

Asset income—21 percent.

Earnings—17 percent.

Other—3 percent.

However, this three-legged stool has become wobbly and projections are that it will get much worse. First, the social security system is projected to incur major shortfalls in the near future. Based on current projections, Medicare Part A, the current hospital insurance, will be bankrupt by the year 2002. In 2011, social security will begin cashing in its government bonds to make up the shortfall between its intake (through payroll taxes) and its outgo (through retirement benefits payouts). By 2030, the system is projected to be bankrupt. If the system were to remain solvent at its current level, it has been estimated that the social security tax would need to have been increased from its current 15.3 percent level to 20.84 percent, effective in 1996.[3] These shortfalls are primarily due to the system's "pay as you go" financing.[4] As baby boomers age, the number of people paying in relation to those drawing benefits diminishes. In 1950, there were 16 workers paying in for each of the relatively few individuals drawing benefits. Today, there are about 3 payers per beneficiary. By 2030, when the last baby boomers are retiring, there will be 2.

In addition, reports indicate that Americans are not saving enough for retirement on their own. The average worker puts aside a scant 4.1 percent of his earnings for retirement. In general, the U.S. savings rate is at an all-time low, when viewed as a percent of gross domestic product (GDP).[5] Considering the composite savings rate of business, government, and individuals, savings dropped below 1 percent of GDP in 1993. In contrast, between 1951 and 1980, savings were stable at 7 percent. Two other factors complicate matters. First, baby boomers have high demands and more expensive tastes than their parents did. Such items as VCRs, CDs, and PCs require a certain level of discretionary income. Second, real estate, on which the previous generation made immense amounts of money, is questionable as a fruitful investment in today's environment.

Finally, despite the broad coverage of long-term capital accumulation funds, 21 percent of 401(k) plan participants have outstanding loans on their account balances.[6]

These three trends have led at least one expert to project that baby boomers, despite their plans, will either work longer than they expect to work or they will retire with substantially reduced standards of living.[7]

Assignment

What do you think should be done about this problem? Do company-sponsored pension plans make sense, given today's business realities? Should we settle the deficit by reducing the tax-favorable treatment of pension plans? Should we create programs that encourage private savings? What should we do about social security? Keep in mind that tax-favored programs will prolong the deficit, possibly make it worse. What trade-offs do you suggest in order to achieve the "optimum solution" from a societal point of view?

[1] R. C. Ochsner, Beyond pensions: How should business define new objectives for the private retirement system? *Compensation & Benefits Review,* January–February 1996, pp. 8–13.

[2] Cited in G. Cole and M. N. Taylor, Caught between demographics and the deficit: How can retirement plans meet the challenges ahead? *Compensation & Benefits Review,* January–February 1996, pp. 32–39.

[3] Ibid.

[4] L. Stern, Can we save social security?" *Modern Maturity,* January–February 1997, pp. 28–36.

[5] N. C. Pratt, The road to retirement. *Compensation & Benefits Review,* January–February 1996, pp. 14–19.

[6] Ibid.

[7] Cole and Taylor, Caught between demographics and the deficit.

TIME-OFF PROGRAMS.   The cost of paid time off represents one of the highest benefit costs for employers today.[93] While a high-cost item in the United States, the cost to employers in many other industrialized nations is even higher. Of course, multinationals must comply with the laws of the host country for its citizens. In small, private organizations, vacations are the most prevalent type of paid time-off benefit.[94] In these same organizations, approximately 57 percent of employees are covered by an employer-sponsored paid sick leave program.[95]

Long-term disability (LTD) coverage typically provides for the replacement of at least some income in the event that an individual contracts a long-term illness or sustains an injury that prevents him from working. In small organizations, 20 percent of full-time workers are covered by such plans. In medium and large organizations, 41 percent of full-time workers are covered under LTD programs. Among organizations offering such benefits, the majority provide 60 percent of predisability income with a monthly benefit cap that averages between $6,000 and $7,000.[96] In addition, most small, medium, and large organizations offer other types of paid time off. The most common include funeral (or bereavement) leave, personal days, military leave, and jury duty.[97]

Government regulation of leave.   The most significant federal legislation related to leave is the **Family and Medical Leave Act (FMLA, 1993).** This legislation requires that employers with 50 or more workers provide eligible employees with up to 12 weeks of unpaid, job-protected leave each year to care for a newborn, a newly placed adopted or foster child, or an ill family member (child, spouse, or parent). An employee is eligible for family or medical leave if he or she has been employed for at least 12 months and has worked at least 1,250 hours of service during the 12 months immediately preceding the start of the leave. The law requires that employers provide an employer with reasonable notification (i.e., at least 30 days) of their intent to take family leave. Employers are counseled, however, to be flexible concerning such notification, particularly if the event that triggers a family leave request involves an emergency or some other type of unforeseeable event. Upon return from family leave, employees must be reinstated to their former position or a position equivalent in pay, benefits, and other terms and conditions of employment. Generally, while seniority and benefits do not accrue during a period of unpaid family leave, any benefits accumulated before the leave must be restored on an individual's return to work. Health benefits must be maintained while an employee is on leave. Many states and most collective bargaining agreements have leave policies and regulations that are as stringent as or more stringent than the FMLA. Also, the FMLA is far less of a burden to employers than European laws, regulations, and collective bargaining agreements.[98]

As stated earlier, the **Pregnancy Discrimination Act (1978)** requires that pregnant employees be treated in the same manner as other employees in determining ability to work. Thus, sick or disability leave must be available to pregnant employees on the same basis that it is available to employees with other illnesses or injuries.

EMPLOYEE SERVICES.   Although there are a variety of programs, the most common employee services are education programs, financial services such as credit unions, employee assistance programs, housing and relocation services, employee recognition programs, and child care. We will briefly discuss each of these below.

Education programs.   Many organizations have educational programs for their employees that range from tuition refunds for college to literacy training. Some companies are helping their workers cope with educating their kids. Aluminum Co. of America, for example, hands out over 200 scholarships a year to employees' children. According to the Bureau of Labor Statistics, 86 percent of full-time employees of medium to large U.S. firms are covered by some form of tuition aid plan. While the principle objective of these programs is to keep employees up to date in their fields of expertise, some programs are designed to prepare employees for other opportunities within the organization. Surprisingly, despite the wide availability of educational assistance through American employers, only about 5 percent of employees take advantage of this benefit. Most employers do a poor job of communicating the availability of the assistance and the connection between education and career mobility.

Financial services.   Through a variety of programs, some organizations provide assistance to employees on financial matters. Payroll savings plans, credit unions, and various thrift plans are three of the most common. Payroll savings plans often provide company matching funds for employee savings. Credit unions provide convenient savings options and often offer competitive loans to employees. There are over 17,000 credit unions active today with assets in excess of $125 billion and over 52 million members.[99] Many employers also offer extensive financial counseling to executives.

Employee assistance programs and mental health care.   Employee Assistance Programs (EAPs) typically provide counseling, diagnosis, and treatment for substance abuse, family and marital problems, depression, and financial and other personal difficulties. EAPs are used by about 70 percent of Fortune 500 companies with about one-third of U.S. employees having access to the programs. Other companies simply cover treatment for mental disorders. One survey found a 27 percent increase in costs associated with EAPs and other mental health care in one recent year. EAPs tend to be cheaper and more effective than simple reimbursement.[100] We will discuss wellness programs and EAPS in more detail in Chapter 14.

Housing and relocation.   It is estimated that U.S. companies spend over $14 billion annually to relocate employees. One survey found that the average cost of a domestic relocation is over $40,000. Of course, international relocation is substantially higher.[101] Most companies also offer assistance in selling homes in a relocation and in search expenses for locating a new home. Special loan programs are sometimes available for purchasing the new home. Some companies provide spouse placement services as well.

Employee recognition programs.   A growing number of organizations offer awards to employees for extended service, work-related achievements, and suggestions for improving organizational effectiveness. Awards are often in the form of gifts and travel rather than cash. Suggestion systems offer incentives to employees who submit ideas that result in greater efficiency or profitability for the company. According to the National Association of Suggestions Systems, employees were awarded almost $128 million for suggestions in one year.

Child care.   A growing number of companies are also offering various forms of child care benefits. There is evidence that this benefit can reduce employee absences, improve recruitment, and help retain valuable employees.[102] Barnett Bank in Florida, for example, reported a substantial increase in job applications as a direct function of its child care program. Dominion Bankshares in Roanoke, Virginia, reported decreased absences among its 950 employees since its on-site day care center was established. A small but growing number of companies offer on-site centers. With a variety of government financial incentives now available, and considerable political activity on the subject, there is every reason to believe that child care will become quite common as an employee benefit in years to come. Child care assistance is usually included in a cafeteria-style benefit program, which is discussed below.

There is a growing recognition that illness among employees' children can be costly to the company in terms of absenteeism, tardiness, and work stress. AT&T invested in sick bays through hospitals and child care centers. Hoffman-LaRoche and Hughes Aircraft offer sick care to employees' children through convenient medical centers. The 3M Company covers up to 78 percent of the fees for home health care for kids.

CAFETERIA-STYLE BENEFIT PLANS.   A growing number of U.S. companies now offer flexible, or cafeteria-style, benefit plans.[103] With the increased diversity of the workforce, employees tend to prefer the flexible plans and employers can realize cost savings.

Cafeteria plans enable the employee to select a benefit package from a list of available options. The benefit program can thus provide a closer match between the individual employee's needs and what is offered. Organizations typically assess employee preferences for various benefit options through a survey. Cafeteria plans are particularly advantageous to the two-earner family because all redundant coverage can be eliminated and savings can be realized.

The simplest and most common form of cafeteria plan is the reimbursement account, which allows employees to pay for certain benefits through a tax-free account. The Educational Testing Service, for example, allocates either 3 percent or 6 percent of employees' salaries for the selection of the optional component of the benefit package, the difference depending on length of service. Other models prescribe a core benefit package plus optional add-ons or a modular approach which has a set number of plans from which the employee selects one.

With the increased sophistication in user-friendly computer software and consulting firms that specialize in such plans, there is likely to be a steady increase in the use of cafeteria-style benefit plans. One variation of the cafeteria plan is a reimbursement account where employees set aside an amount from their salary that is used to pay for child care, health care, and other benefits. The advantage of these accounts is that the money is deducted from employee paychecks before taxes. The disadvantage is that any money not spent reverts to the company.

COMMUNICATING THE BENEFITS PROGRAM

Most employees have little understanding of the costs involved in a benefits program. According to one expert, employee communication is the "keystone of the program . . . without effective communication, a benefit program remains incomplete and the considerable effort and expense consumed in planning, designing, and administering plans becomes largely unproductive."[104] While distributing benefit summaries pursuant to ERISA requirements provides a cursory understanding of major components of the benefit package, the effectiveness of the package is undermined unless employees appreciate the advantages and superiority of the program relative to competitors. ERISA simply requires that "Summary Plan Descriptions" be "written in a manner calculated to be understood by the average plan participant." Employees must be aware of and understand the benefits that are available to them in order for the employer to fully realize the objectives for which the benefits were established.

The goal in benefit communication should be to present the worth of the benefit package to current and future employees. To that end, many employers now provide

counseling for employees to enhance their understanding of the benefit program. Among the other methods used to explain benefits are paycheck inserts, employee publications, posters, and audio/video recorded messages. At Citicorp, for example, 56,000 employees are exposed to software, videos, seminars, and several other teaching tools that explain their new flexible benefit program. Each Citicorp employee receives a printout of benefits compared to the previous year, a computer disk, and a workbook that explains how to determine the tax and "out-of-pocket" implications of the benefit options.

Benefit programs that require some employee contribution are not only more efficient but also tend to enhance employee understanding of the benefit and its cost to the employer. Also, with the growth in cafeteria-style plans, employees should be more informed about the costs of the various benefit options.

INTERNATIONAL COMPENSATION*

With over 100,000 U.S. companies now involved in some type of global venture, it is estimated that over 60 million workers are employed overseas. Included in this growing number are expatriates (U.S. citizens working abroad) and host nationals (citizens of another country). McDonald's now has over 10,000 restaurants in over 100 countries and the vast majority of the employees are nationals. The expansion of retail giants such as Wal-Mart, Home Depot, and Office Depot into foreign markets has followed this same pattern. More than 75 percent of the employees of Gillette work outside the United States and more than 70 percent of profits come from overseas sales. Coca-Cola and Pepsi products are sold worldwide.

To fully realize their growth potential, U.S. companies must staff their international operations with personnel who are both technically competent, culturally proficient, and cost-effective. In almost all cases, it is cheaper to employ host-country nationals than to send American expatriates. AT&T, like so many other American companies, has seen its overseas business increasing, but it has reduced the number of expatriates in favor of host-country nationals. AT&T estimates that expatriate managers cost three times as much as host-country nationals. GM spends close to $1 million for a three-year assignment for an executive expatriate and her family, over twice as much as for a host-country executive. In addition, the failure rate of expatriates is also high relative to host-country nationals.[105] While job aid for the "trailing" spouse is becoming more popular for executive expatriates, finding suitable employment for the spouse in a foreign country is a major challenge.

There has been little research on compensation

---

*Contributed by Thomas Becker.

strategies in the global environment. In general, multinationals have been standardizing their pay policies and strategies on a global basis. This does not mean they pay everyone who does the same work the same pay regardless of the host-country compensation environment. Burger King, for example, uses a standardized job evaluation instrument (translated into eight languages) and a standard pay structure for its restaurants. However, personnel performing essentially the same work are paid differently as a function of market surveys conducted within each country. While this is not a problem for Burger King counter personnel around the world, what about an IBM computer programmer in India who discovers while collaborating with an American on a program that his pay is one-third that of the American? This has become a common problem for international consulting firms such as Booz-Allen & Hamilton and Andersen where consultants living in different countries collaborate on a project for another country.

While the discussion below will focus on executive and professional compensation for multinational corporations, there is no question that labor costs (both direct and indirect compensation) play a major role in corporate decisions regarding plant and operations openings, closings, and locations. Virtually no teddy bears are made on U.S. soil today because they can be produced at a fraction of the cost in a developing country such as Haiti or Honduras. The costs of direct and indirect compensation plus ancillary regulation are the main reasons manufacturing and even some service organizations have moved from the United States.

As we discussed in Chapter 5, the world is now the labor market for even highly skilled workers, particularly engineers, computer programmers, and other computer technicians. One of the hottest (and highest paying) jobs in compensation today is international benefits analysts who conduct research on benefits and provide data for financial, regulatory, and tax analysis. Many consulting firms now specialize in providing cost comparisons for various employment and compensation strategies for U.S. companies doing business overseas.

The type and amount of compensation necessary to attract technically and culturally qualified international executives and technical professionals vary widely according to the nationality category from which employees are chosen. Three nationality categories are commonly recognized in shaping international compensation policies:

1. **Parent-country nationals (PCNs).** PCNs are employees whose nationality is the same as that of the country in which the parent company is based. Thus, an American manager of a General Motors leasing subsidiary in the United Kingdom would be a PCN, as would an Italian manager of an Olivetti distribution facility in the United States.

2. **Third-country nationals (TCNs).** TCNs are professionals whose nationality is neither that of the parent-company country nor that of the host country where the parent company's affiliate (and the TCN's job) is located. A German working for a Dow Chemical experimental laboratory in Mexico would be an example of a TCN.

3. **Host-country nationals (HCNs).** HCNs are nationals of the country in which the foreign affiliate is located. A Frenchman managing the French sales subsidiary of 3M or an American managing a Mitsubishi plant in Illinois would be classified as HCNs.

The compensation package structured for the expatriate (i.e., PCN or TCN) is ordinarily more complex and expensive than that for the HCN. Because of that greater complexity and cost, we will discuss first, and in somewhat greater detail, those compensation issues affecting the expatriate. The more frequent, but less exacting and more comfortably budgeted, situation of compensating HCN professionals is addressed subsequently.

Developing an Expatriate Compensation Package

Although many of a TCN's compensation features may vary markedly from those included in a PCN's package, the fact that each is an expatriate compels us to treat the TCN as a special case of the PCN in this discussion.

The salary and fringe benefits paid to a PCN are intended to ensure that U.S. professionals do not suffer any material loss due to working abroad. By using a balance-sheet approach to compensation, U.S. companies attempt to keep overseas professionals on at least a financial par with their domestic colleagues.[106] Maintaining such purchase power equality typically proves to be very expensive. The total cost to the employer of maintaining an American manager overseas is estimated to be between three and six times the cost of a manager in a comparable position at home.[107]

The high cost of the compensation package required to induce a U.S. professional to move to, and perform well in, a foreign country is a function of three factors comprising the assignment profile: (1) the position, (2) the locale, and (3) the individual. The primary roles that these factors play in matching a compensation package to an assignment profile are shown in Figure 10.8.

The compensation needs shown in the figure are described below.

THE MAJOR POSITION FACTORS. Every position has a unique set of characteristics that occasion a corresponding set of compensation needs. Such position-specific compensation needs are summarized below. In

FIGURE 10.8
MATCHING A COMPENSATION PACKAGE TO AN ASSIGNMENT PROFILE

		THESE ASSIGNMENT VARIABLES	OCCASION THESE COMPENSATION NEEDS	
	Position factors	Responsibilities and duties	Base salary	
		Operating performance	Incentive bonus	
		Assignment duration	Periodic salary adjustments	
		Status and prestige	Representation allowance	
		Travel requirements	Official travel allowance	
	Locale factors	Remoteness	Rest and relaxation	
		Physical or cultural adversity	Hardship and home leave	
		Sanitation	Medical care	
		Physical security	Hazardous duty or security allowance, ransom insurance	
Assignment profile		Housing cost	Housing allowance	Compensation package
		Housing availability	Temporary quarters allowance	
		Transfer incidentals	Relocation allowance	
		School availability	Education allowance	
		Economic security	Retirement benefits	
		Income taxes	Tax equalization	
		Purchasing power	Currency of payment	
	Individual factors	Reluctance to move	Foreign service premium	
		Family income	Spousal employment	
		Asset exposure	Home and auto protection	
		Number of dependents	Dependent costs	

general, the length of an overseas assignment is critical for determining a compensation policy. When assignments are for less than a year, major changes are typically not made.[108]

Base salary.   A PCN's base salary must be competitive with the amount that an employee with similar responsibilities and duties would receive at home; it is *not* geared to what a similar job would pay in the host-country labor market. TCN salaries are typically priced according to that particular country's going rates.

Incentive bonus.   Because of variables such as exchange-rate changes, transfer prices, and inflation over which a PCN manager may have little or no control, a majority of U.S. companies base PCNs' incentive bonuses on local-currency budget compared to actual operating performance.

Periodic salary adjustment.   Some research suggests the possibility that the longer a PCN remains in an overseas position, the greater is the risk that her job skills will have obsolesced and her career prospects will have ebbed upon her eventual return to headquarters.[109] To soften the effect of such an unwelcome contingency, and to compensate for normal seniority-based pay incre-

ments, periodic salary increases are often included in compensation negotiations.

Representation allowance.   Middle-level American managers working abroad may find that their duties entail dealing with high-level individuals such as CEOs of major local corporations or cabinet ministers in the host country. Because authority tends to be more visible in many countries than it is in the United States, it is often essential that PCN professionals, especially country managers, learn to display the accoutrements of rank. Such "power signals" may include club memberships, chauffeured vehicles, sumptuous offices, and prestigious home addresses.

Travel allowances.   Foreign assignments often require more travel—both local and international—than domestic positions. It is common to compensate official travel by reimbursing the transportation component against receipts, and the lodging, meals, and incidentals component on a per diem basis.

THE MAJOR LOCALE FACTORS.   Because the cost of living varies widely from locale to locale (even within the same country), cost-of-living allowances (COLAs) should be designed to enable the PCN or TCN to enjoy a standard of living abroad that is comparable to what she would enjoy at home. Some of the compensation elements often negotiated as COLAs are described below.

Rest and relaxation (R&R).   Living in a remote, culturally unfamiliar, or climatically harsh locale extracts its toll and may impair job performance if PCNs (and occasionally TCNs) are not allowed to "recharge their batteries" in more pleasant or comfortable surroundings. While R&R time is generally charged against the employee's vacation leave balance, the related travel and per diem expenses for the employee and accompanying dependents are reimbursed by the employer.

Hardship allowance and home leave.   Locales qualifying for R&R frequently also qualify the PCN for hardship payment granted as a percentage of base salary. The U.S. Department of State established a hardship list in 1996. (Kabul, Afghanistan led the hardship list in 1997.) In addition to this payment, the hardship allowance may also include fees for family membership in a social or recreational club and home leave. A typical home leave policy may grant the PCN professional, on a biannual basis, one month of salaried vacation time in the United States with round-trip transportation to her U.S. home of record and per diem expenses paid by the employer. Most companies discourage taking home leave closely in conjunction with the beginning or the end of an overseas assignment or with R&R leave. It is common to take advantage of the PCN's presence in the United States and accompany home leave with training and consultation at headquarters.

Medical care.   Sanitary and security conditions in some foreign locales may compel a company to provide PCN professionals with additional life, health, or dental insurance coverage. In some locales, the employee and dependents may need to travel to another country to receive care comparable to that given in the United States.

Hazardous duty allowance.   Terrorism, political instability, kidnapping, and criminal violence in places such as Colombia, Brazil, Beirut, and Peru expose PCNs to a higher personal risk than they would experience at home. To compensate for these potential dangers, the employee may be provided with hazardous duty allowance (computed as a percentage of base salary), bodyguards, home and office security systems, training (frequently for the entire family) in self-defense and evasive driving techniques, and ransom insurance. Interestingly (and for obvious reasons), ransom insurance is one of the few employee benefits of which neither the company boasts publicly nor the employee is briefed in detail.

Housing allowance.   Duplicating the amenities of a typical American home in a foreign environment is often a tall order and may entail substantial additional costs. The costs of leasing a home, round-trip shipment of certain of the PCN's personal and household effects, and storage in the United States of other PCN effects (e.g., boats, classic cars, valuable jewelry or collections, and artwork) should be included in calculating housing allowance. Most U.S. companies consult the *U.S. Department of State Indexes of Living Costs Abroad, Quarters Allowances, and Hardships Differentials.* Figure 10.9 presents an example of data provided by the Department of State.

Temporary quarters allowance.   Housing closely equivalent to U.S. standards is not always readily available. As a consequence, the U.S. professional and her family may have to reside in a hotel or other interim furnished lodging until they can move into "permanent" housing. On one occasion, an American professional assigned to a South American country resided with his family in a hotel for three months while awaiting promised construction to be finished on the house he had agreed to lease. Losing patience, he opted to move into the house prematurely—and for the next three years was forced to enter and exit his second-floor bedroom by an outside wooden ladder and use his not-too-nearby landlord's home for occasional hot-water showers. Universities in Singapore, eager to recruit U.S. professors, often offer a substantial housing allowance because the cost of suitable housing in Singapore is so much higher than in the United States.

Relocation allowance.   This allowance helps ease the transition into living abroad by compensating for related additional expenses such as clothing appropriate to severe climates, electricity converters, and a local driver's license.

Education allowance.   Local public and private schooling for the expatriate's children may be inadequate or expensive. In some cases, children may have to attend a boarding school in the United States or a third country. Allowances for local or foreign education of PCN or TCN children may include transportation (typically one round trip per year if the school and job assignment locations are widely separated), room and board, tuition, books and supplies, and uniforms.

Retirement benefits.   Most U.S. PCNs stay under the home company's benefit program. TCNs are typically not covered. They further state that because "in some countries PCNs cannot opt out of local social security programs . . . the multinational corporation normally pays for these additional costs."[110]

FIGURE 10.9
QUARTERS ALLOWANCES, JANUARY 1996

COUNTRY: CITY	SURVEY DATE	FOREIGN UNIT	NO. OF FOREIGN UNITS PER U.S. $	FAMILY STATUS	ANNUAL INCOME		
					LESS THAN $31,000	$31,000 TO $55,000	$55,000 & OVER
Australia: Melbourne	Jan. 1995	Dollar	1.34	Family	$14,100	$15,400	$16,400
				Single	$12,900	$14,700	$15,400
Belgium: Brussels	Nov. 1994	Franc	29.60	Family	$27,500	$28,800	$32,600
				Single	$23,700	$27,500	$28,800
France: Paris	Dec. 1994	Franc	4.85	Family	$29,300	$35,100	$35,100
				Single	$26,500	$31,300	$31,300
Germany: Berlin	May 1995	Mark	1.41	Family	$24,800	$29,700	$30,500
				Single	$22,700	$24,800	$30,500
Italy: Rome	July 1995	Lira	1,571.00	Family	$21,400	$24,800	$35,900
				Single	$20,000	$22,400	$35,900
Japan: Tokyo	Feb. 1995	Yen	102.00	Family	$65,600	$81,000	$81,000
				Single	$60,200	$76,400	$78,000
Thailand: Bangkok	May 1994	Baht	24.70	Family	$17,400	$21,000	$21,900
				Single	$15,900	$17,400	$19,600
England: London	Mar. 1995	Pound	0.63	Family	$26,300	$29,100	$31,400
				Single	$23,100	$28,900	$30,000
Netherlands: The Hague	Mar. 1995	Guilder	1.61	Family	$30,000	$32,800	$36,500
				Single	$26,500	$29,600	$31,100

Source: U.S. Department of State, *The U.S. Department of State indexes of living costs abroad, quarters allowances, and hardship differentials—January 1996,* Department of State Publication 10197 (Washington, DC: U.S. Government Printing Office, 1996).

Tax equalization. Because a U.S. PCN must pay U.S. income tax as well as host-country income tax, most U.S. companies will make up the difference if the latter tax liability exceeds the former. It is important to note that the U.S. Tax Reform Act of 1986 allows a U.S. citizen to exempt the first $70,000 of qualifying foreign-earned income from federal income tax. This provision significantly reduces a PCN's U.S. tax liability and, as a consequence, increases the amount that the PCN's employer would have to pay to close the gap between the U.S. and host-country tax liabilities. For this reason, employers will often calculate the tax equalization payment as if the PCN were earning the taxable income in the United States.

Currency of payment. The thrust of practice is to pay U.S. expatriate salaries partly in dollars and partly in host-country currency. Being paid in U.S. dollars may enable PCN professionals to save in dollars (if host-country currency exchange controls are in effect), to forgo paying host-country income taxes on the dollar portion of income received, and to enjoy full local purchasing power (if host-country inflation is outpacing devaluation of its currency). U.S. companies, on the other hand, would often prefer to make all compensation payments in host-country currency to avoid saddling the lo-

cal subsidiary with a hard-currency liability, a particularly onerous burden if exchange controls or remittance limits exist.

INDIVIDUALIZED COMPENSATION PACKAGES. We have seen that a variety of position- and locale-related factors play a central role in shaping a compensation package to fit a particular assignment profile. In the final analysis, however, the compensation package is designed to fit the individual professional who, after all, is the pivotal factor in determining the ultimate success or failure of the assignment. Some compensation elements devised to meet the widely variant responses of individual professionals to a foreign job assignment are discussed below.

Foreign service premium. Individuals respond differently to the prospect of a foreign assignment. Leaving familiar surroundings, adjusting to a new culture and job challenges, and exposing oneself to possible career-path disruptions upon repatriation may be an exciting adventure for some or an onerous sentencing for others. To ease the discomfort of these adjustments, companies often negotiate a foreign service premium to induce reluctant professionals to accept an overseas position.

Spousal employment. A spouse's employment income may make an important contribution to the total income of the professional's family. Often the expatriate's working spouse is unable to find appropriate employment or to receive a work permit in the foreign country. All or a portion of the resulting relinquished income may have to be indemnified by the company.[111]

Home and automobile protection. The ownership of a home or car by a U.S. expatriate being assigned abroad may raise questions about what to do with these possessions before transfer. If the professional is concerned about suffering monetary losses due to being forced to rent or sell these assets under adverse conditions, the company may have to indemnify all or a portion of such losses.

Dependent costs. As the number of the professional's dependents increases, so will the company's cost of covering many of the COLAs and perhaps even the foreign service premium. In the case of particularly prolific professionals, companies may find that the associated dependent-driven escalations in compensation expense make overseas assignments prohibitively costly.

HCN Compensation

Not long ago, it was traditional for U.S. affiliates to staff their overseas affiliates with U.S. professionals. This practice stemmed partially from a lack of qualified HCN managerial candidates and partially from the conviction that only an experienced U.S. manager could represent the "company way" of doing business. These rationales for favoring the use of U.S. PCNs in key overseas positions have become increasingly difficult to defend in recent years, particularly with the number of HCNs who have been educated in the United States. Indeed, there now is a heightened general awareness of the cost-effective contributions HCNs can make to subsidiary performance. As a result, U.S. companies today largely employ HCN managers in their subsidiaries abroad.

Because the compensation standard of expatriates is competitive with their home salaries and benefits, expatriate compensation will generally be at a higher level than that of local nationals. (See Critical Thinking Exercise 10.3, "Compensation Abroad: Local Employees, Local Pay.") While the resulting gap between expatriate and HCN compensation does not go unnoticed in the subsidiary, it is generally accepted that the expatriate possesses special expertise—even if it is only nationality—that justifies the disparity in compensation levels. To eliminate the compensation gap between expatriates and HCNs by raising HCN compensation would eliminate one compensation disparity while creating another—that between MNC HCNs and local company HCNs—and would set in motion a salary cost spiral that

would benefit no one in the long run. To avoid that contingency, the "best practice" is to use the local compensation packages as the major guidelines when developing HCN compensation policies.[112]

CRITICAL THINKING EXERCISE 10.3

Compensation Abroad: Local Employees, Local Pay?[1]

William O'Dell, vice president for human resources at LeBert Graphics (LG), a fast-growing software development firm headquartered in Boston's Route 128 technology belt, was visiting the firm's first overseas subsidiary, LeBert Graphics Bangalore, Ltd. (LGB). The visit had been going well, but a recent lunch with his good friend Ashok Rao had left him troubled. Rao was one of many Indian expatriates who had migrated to the United States in the 1980s. He had been with LG for a number of years and had recently accepted an assignment to return to his hometown to head the firm's new development lab. O'Dell was thankful to have him there—not just because of his development skills, but because he hoped Rao would serve as a cultural broker between headquarters and local employees.

During lunch, Rao noted how the city had changed. Rao had first decided not to return to Bangalore after college in the United States because of the lack of opportunities. Now the city was booming, and computer software was the driving force. Neighbors in the technology park where LG had located included Siemens Components and Hitachi Asia.[2] The nature of the industry had changed too. Initially, foreign firms had employed Indian workers for basic programming. Although cheap, these employees did not always have the training or skill levels seen in their American counterparts. No longer. There were still large pools of these competent, but not exceptional employees. However, while recruiting for the new operations, he found many of the applicants had technical skills that would equal those of any of the Boston staff.[3] These were the employees they needed for the software development operations.

The market had changed in other ways too. Today, the best of these software engineers had more options. Because of a worldwide shortage, a host of firms were looking for skilled engineers. An engineer could work for the local operations of a foreign firm, on temporary assignment basis in the United States or Europe, or in one of the many local, start-up firms.[4] Some had great success starting their own software firms in the United States. While the same range of opportunities might not exist for those with more basic skills, the growth in foreign investment and start-ups in Bangalore also gave these employees many attractive options locally.

At first, the conversation appeared casual, the reminiscences of an old friend. However, Rao had also mentioned a conversation he had overheard in which one of the brightest engineers in the development unit had complained to a co-worker that although he was a principal engineer on a joint Boston-Bangalore project, his American counterpart was receiving over four times his salary. On reflection, O'Dell was convinced that Rao had been attempting to draw his attention to an issue that was important to some of the Indian staff.

O'Dell's initial reaction had been, "Of course, that's why we located in Bangalore in the first place." Technology skills were abundant, and pay rates for software engineers were a fraction of those in Boston. Moreover, the pay levels reflected the fact that productivity in the programming unit was not always up to U.S. standards. On reflection, he realized that the issue was much more complex.

On one hand were the economics. Cost savings not achieved now might be lost forever. Manufacturing firms that had moved operations to low-cost, off-shore sites had often found that the benefits were partly illusory. Wages were low, but at times so was productivity. Employees were often motivated, and with appropriate training, supervision, and equipment, productivity levels would rise. However, as these employees became more productive, they also become more attractive to other employers. Moreover, as the economy in these regions developed, there was often a shift in the exchange rate. Salaries rose locally, but because of exchange rate effects they rose even more in U.S. dollars. Firms using contractors might shift to another, lower-cost site. Such shifts could be disruptive, however, and more difficult when the firm had invested directly in the overseas location.

It would be simpler, O'Dell thought, if the firm were in Bangalore for the short-term. LG's interests in Bangalore had changed dramatically over the past year, however. LG had been using an Indian subcontractor to outsource basic programming for years. Individual pay levels had not concerned them directly. The Indian firm handled all issues related to recruitment, performance evaluation, and compensation. Recently, LG had decided both to bring the programming in-house (by acquiring the Indian firm) and to open a software development lab.

The decision to move the operation in-house reflected a desire for greater control. It would allow greater emphasis on quality, especially after the programmers were trained to more closely meet the company's special needs. The decision to open the software development lab represented an even more dramatic shift. The new lab operation could take advantage of the rapidly developing skills of the Indian engineers, particularly in "hot jobs" for which there was a worldwide shortage. Moreover, the fast-growing Asian markets held real potential for LG. This required the development of programs that met the special needs of their Asian customers. At first the technology would originate in Boston, but substantial local adaptation was required. Later, the lab should stand alone in developing programs for the region and possibly the world market. These efforts required day-to-day interaction and teamwork between engineers at both locations. Soon the projects would require short-term transfers of personnel between facilities.

The discussion reminded him of a project he had left on his desk before the trip—developing a compensation plan for the revamped India operations. The project had not focused on compensation levels, but it had raised related questions. What type of compensation package was appropriate? Should they follow local custom as to vacations and leave? Should the generous stock option and pension plans, available to employees in Boston, be extended to these operations?

Custom and government regulation varied substantially from one nation to the next. In some nations, pensions were part of a government social security system; in others they were provided by firms. In some nations they were not required at all. Even something as simple as "monthly pay" differed; in Singapore a typical compensation package paid the employee by the month for 13, instead of 12 months.[5] These were just a few of the differences O'Dell had run across in research for the project. The list could go on and on. No wonder compensation systems, like other aspects of human resource management, traditionally had been one of the most "local" aspects of a multinational's operations. Local wages scales were used, and the firms tended to follow local custom regarding vacations, pensions, and other aspects of the compensation package. But with engineers of similar skill levels working together on a daily basis, how long would these distinctions be possible? Some of these engineers might be hired in the United States. Would LG offer different packages based on the facility they were assigned to? How would that affect recruiting? And what about the engineers transferred to Boston for six months? Should they receive a different package while on tour? For the programmers doing more routine work the issues might not be as complex, but were still important. Considering the cost of the training planned for the Bangalore staff, it was vital to keep these employees on board and motivated despite the many opportunities open to them.

While the focus was on India for now, the firm had also considered opening subsidiary operations in Russia and Brazil. His project was the first step in an effort to decide the extent to which the firm's performance review and compensation plans should be integrated globally. The issue did not just concern the employees abroad. At home, some concern had been expressed about the long-term outlook. Software engineers were hot now, but in 10 years would the salaries reflect a lower global scale? And would all the jobs be overseas? The opportunities abroad were exciting, but had brought their share of headaches.

Assignment

What would be the advantages and disadvantages of using the existing LG compensation package in India? How might it differ from a more typical Indian package? What additional information would O'Dell need to make this decision? What other human resource issues might O'Dell need to be concerned about? How do these issues relate to compensation? How do these compensation issues relate to the strategic choices that the firm has made? Does the analogy to a manufacturing firm seem appropriate? What are the societal effects of the outsourcing of jobs, both in India and at home?

[1] Contributed by Brenda E. Richey, assistant professor, Florida Atlantic University.

[2] Robert Ristelhueber, Bangalore builds a high-tech future. *Electronic Business Today,* April 1997, p. 20.

[3] John Stremlau, Bangalore: India's Silicon City. *Monthly Labor Review,* November 1996, pp. 50–51.

[4] James Leung, Brains fuel technology: Boom town. *Asian Business,* June 1996, pp. 28–34.

[5] Learning to manage host-country nationals. *Personnel Journal,* March 1995, pp. 60–67.

When designing compensation policies for HCNs, it is essential to adjust for differences in compensation practices among different countries. The examples below illustrate some of the reasons it is important to adapt HCN salaries and benefits to local practices:

- High severance-pay consequences in Latin America may incline a company to relegate aging but highly paid local professionals to secondary management positions so that more dynamic, younger managers may be promoted to positions of high responsibility.

- High personal income tax rates in the United Kingdom may argue in favor of keeping down taxable salaries for HCNs there and raising their nontaxable perquisites accordingly.

- Strong group cohesiveness in Japan may dictate against compensation policies that, in rewarding individual performance, may broaden differences in intragroup salaries and benefits.

SUMMARY

Because of the importance that compensation holds for their lifestyle and self-esteem, individuals are very concerned that they be paid a fair and competitive wage. Organizations are concerned with pay, not only because of its importance as a cost of doing business but also because it motivates important decisions of employees about taking a job, leaving a job, and working on the job.

When designing direct compensation plans, it is important that an organization choose an approach that is in alignment with its organizational philosophy and that supports its organizational goals. In some cases, the traditional approach to pay still provides the best answer. This approach rests on the use of a job evaluation plan (to measure internal job worth and foster internal equity), the review of market salary data (to identify externally competitive practices), and the reconciliation of these two in the form of a final pay structure. Due to the basic changes in organizations today and the new global challenges and opportunities, there is a growing search for new direct compensation approaches in the hope that they will better focus employees on achieving organizational goals. Such new approaches to pay include broadbanding, pay for knowledge (or skills-based pay), and team pay plans. To date, however, the relative effectiveness of these new approaches remains to be tested.

Employee benefits programs continue to grow and expand, although there are considerable differences in the benefits that are offered by different types and sizes of employers. Benefits mainly have been directed at assisting employees in maintaining a particular lifestyle and providing for their long-term welfare and security. At the same time, however, the federal government is increasing its scrutiny of the existing tax advantages of most indirect compensation plans. The resulting legislation has raised administrative costs of many plans and has chipped away at the ability of some organizations to meet previous benefits commitments.

The government's goal concerning its regulation of pay and benefits is to ensure that discrimination does not exist and that certain minimum levels of fairness are maintained in compensation programs. A number of federal, state, and local laws regulate compensation. In addition, regulation is aimed at managing the delicate balance between tax revenue maximization and maintaining the positive social forces that tax-favored employee benefit plans have contributed to society.

Direct and indirect compensation programs must be assessed for the extent to which they attract, retain, and motivate the workforce required relative to major competitors. The cost of labor is critical to corporate performance and must be constantly monitored to determine whether costs can be reduced with no loss in the products or services necessary for fulfilling the organizational strategy. The bottom line is that if the company is not doing it, its competitors may be doing it and a competitive advantage is not far behind. The use of part-time employees and outsourcing and the relocation of operations, including overseas operations, are all part of a strategy to reduce the cost of labor. By the same token, when required skills for competitive advantage are in great demand, companies that do not respond with competitive pay packages will lose out and end up cutting their labor costs at the expense of organizational capability. While America's most admired companies such as

Coca-Cola, Mirage Resorts, Merck, United Parcel Service, and Microsoft all take steps to control and (at times) reduce their labor costs, they also make certain that their compensation packages attract and retain the key personnel they require to maintain their admirable status.

Regardless of which particular compensation program is chosen, organizations need the capacity to measure individual or group results so that such performance may be reflected in pay. In the next chapter, we consider the methods that are used to reward employees for their individual (or group) contributions to an organization. As we shall see, these decisions are by no means easy, but when combined with other components of direct and indirect compensation, an effective pay-for-performance program can be a powerful tool with which to attract, retain, and motivate a competent workforce. Almost all the companies named in *Fortune*'s 1997 rating of America's most admired companies have compensation systems with relatively more pay at risk in the form of stock awards for its key employees. We will discuss this growing component of American compensation next.

NOTES

1. Kanter, R. M. (1989). *When giants learn to dance*. New York: Simon & Schuster, p. 230; For detailed discussion of organization, individual, and societal implications of pay, see Wallace, M. J., and Fay, C. H. (1988). *Compensation theory and practice,* Boston: PWS-Kent; see also, Gordon, G. G. (1991). Cultural and psychological implications for compensation. In M. L. Rock and L. A. Berger (eds.), *The compensation handbook: A state of the art guide to compensation strategy and design.* New York: McGraw-Hill, pp. 579–591; Milkovich, G. T., and Newman, J. M. (1996). *Compensation.* Plano, TX: Business Publications; DeLuca, M. J. (1993). *Handbook of compensation management.* Englewood Cliffs, NJ: Prentice Hall; Berg, J. G. (1976). *Managing compensation.* New York: AMACOM; Lawler, E. E. (1990). *Strategic pay: Aligning organizational strategies and pay systems.* San Francisco: Jossey-Bass. Sibson, R. E. (1990). *Compensation.* New York: AMACOM; and Bureau of National Affairs (1996). *Compensation.* Washington, DC: BNA.

2. See note 1, Kanter (1989). For full discussion of characteristics of effective compensation programs, see Gubman, E. L. (1995). Aligning people strategies with customer value. *Compensation & Benefits Review, 27*(1), 15–22. See also, Abosch, K. S. (1995). The promise of broadbanding, *Compensation & Benefits Review, 27*(1), 54–58; Gross, S. E., and Blair, J. (1995). Reinforcing team effectiveness through pay. *Compensation & Benefits Review, 27*(5), 34–38; Morgenstern, M. L. (1995). The board's perspective: Compensation and the new employment relationship. *Compensation & Benefits Review, 26*(2), 37–44; Turnasella, T. (1994).

Aligning pay with business strategies and cultural values. *Compensation & Benefits Review, 26*(5), 65–72; Dolmat-Connell, J. (1994). A new paradigm for compensation and benefits competitiveness. *Compensation & Benefits Review, 26*(5), 51–64. Trillet, A. A. (1991). Cost Containment. In M. L. Rock and L. A. Berger (eds.), *The compensation handbook: A state of the art guide to compensation strategy and design.* New York: McGraw Hill, pp. 122–144; Dewey, B. J., and Hawk, E. J. (1996). Economic value: A better approach to people management. *Compensation & Benefits Review, 28*(3), 30–36; Haslett, S. (1995). Broadbanding: A strategic tool for organizational change. *Compensation & Benefits Review, 27*(6), 40–46; LeBlanc, P. V. (1994). Pay for work: Reviving an old idea for the new customer focus. *Compensation & Benefits Review, 26*(4), 5–14; and note 1, Sibson (1990), DeLuca (1993), and Berg (1976).

3. For full discussion concerning the history of compensation in organizations, see Rock, M. L. (1991). Looking back on forty years of compensation programs. In M. L. Rock and L. A. Berger (eds.), *The compensation handbook: A state of the art guide to compensation strategy and design.* New York: McGraw Hill, pp. 3–11. See also note 1, Wallace and Fay (1988), and DeLuca (1993).

4. See note 1, Berg (1976).

5. See note 1, Berg (1976), and DeLuca (1993).

6. American Compensation Association (1988). *Elements of soundbase pay administration.* Scottsdale, AZ: American Compensation Association.

7. See note 6. See also note 1, DeLuca (1993). Review the discussion on the Position Analysis Questionnaire in Chapter 4. The PAQ provides job evaluation points with no further steps.

8. Lange, N. R. (1991). Job analysis and documentation. In M. L. Rock and L. A. Berger (eds.), *The compensation handbook: A state of the art guide to compensation strategy and design.* New York: McGraw Hill, pp. 49–71.

9. Martocchio, J. J. (1998). *Strategic Compensation.* Upper Saddle River, NJ: Prentice-Hall.

10. For full discussion of the advantages and disadvantages of job ranking, see note 1, Sibson (1990), Berg (1976), and the Bureau of National Affairs (1996).

11. For full discussion of the advantages and disadvantages of job classification, see note 1, Sibson (1990), Berg (1976), and the Bureau of National Affairs (1996).

12. Hewitt Associates (1991). *Total compensation management: Reward management strategies for the 1990s.* Cambridge, MA: Basil Blackwell. See also note 1, Milkovich and Newman (1996), and Sibson (1990).

13. See note 1, Wallace and Fay (1988).

14. See note 1, Sibson (1990), and Milkovich and Newman (1996). See also note 12, Hewitt Associates (1991).

15. See note 1, Sibson (1990). See also note 6.

16. For full discussion of advantages and disadvantages of point factor plans, see note 1, Sibson (1990), and DeLuca (1993).

17. Kanin-Lovers, J. (1991). Job evaluation technology. In M. L. Rock and L. A. Berger (eds.), *The compensation handbook: A state of the art guide to compensation strategy and design.* New York: McGraw Hill, pp. 72–86. See also note 1, DeLuca (1993).

18. See note 1, Sibson (1990).

19. Dolmat-Connell, J. (1994). Labor market definition and salary survey selection: A new look at the foundation of compensation program design. *Compensation & Benefits Review, 26*(2), 38–46. See also Lichty, D. T. (1991). Compensation surveys. In M. L. Rock and L. A. Berger (eds.), *The compensation handbook: A state of the art guide to compensation strategy and design.* New York: McGraw-Hill, pp. 87–103. For full discussion of the economic forces in the labor market (both supply and demand sides) see note 1, Wallace and Fay (1988).

20. For full discussion concerning advantages and disadvantages of market pricing, see Gomez-Mejia, L. R.; Balkin, D. B.; and Cardy, R. L. (1995). *Managing human resources.* Englewood Cliffs, NJ: Prentice Hall. See also Brennan, J. P., and McKee, B. (1995). Structureless salary management: A successful application of a modest approach. *Compensation & Benefits Review, 27*(2), 56–62, and note 1, Sibson (1990).

21. For full discussion of defining relevant labor markets, see note 19, Dolmat-Connell (1994). See also note 1, Sibson (1990).

22. See note 6, and note 1, Sibson (1990).

23. See note 1, Milkovich and Newman (1996).

24. See note 19, Lichty (1991), and note 1, Sibson (1990).

25. See note 1, DeLuca (1993).

26. For full discussion concerning theoretical support for new compensation approaches, see Lissy, W. E., and Morgenstern, M. L. (1994). Currents in compensation and benefits. *Compensation & Benefits Review, 26*(5), 10–18. See also, Schuster, J. R., and Zingheim, P. K. (1992). *The new pay: Linking employee and organizational performance.* New York: Lexington Books; Bergel, G. I. (1994). Choosing the right pay delivery system to fit banding. *Compensation & Benefits Review, 26*(4), 34–38; see also, note 2, Abosch (1995), Gross and Blair (1995), Dewey and Hawk (1996), Haslett (1995), LeBlanc (1994), and Dolmat-Connell (1994), note 20, Brennan and McKee (1995); and note 1, DeLuca (1993), and Lawler (1990).

27. For full discussion of bias in compensation programs, see Arvey, R. D. (1987). Potential problems in job evaluation methods and processes. In D. B. Balkin and L. R. Gomez-Mejia (eds.), *New perspectives on compensation.* Englewood Cliffs, NJ: Prentice-Hall, pp. 20–30. See also, Cook, F. W. (1994). Compensation surveys are biased. *Compensation & Benefits Review, 26*(5), 19–22, and note 1, Berg (1976), and the Bureau of National Affairs (1996).

28. Treiman, D. J., and Hartmann, H. (eds.) (1981). *Women, work and wages: Equal pay for jobs of equal value.* Washington, DC: National Academy Press.

29. Acker, J. (1989) *Doing comparable worth.* Philadelphia, PA: Temple University Press. For information on pay equity, write the National Committee on Pay Equity, 1126 16th St., Washington, DC 20036 (202-331-7343).

30. For full discussion of broadbanding, see LeBlanc, P. V., and McInerney, M. (1994). Need a change? Jump on the banding wagon. *Personnel Journal, 73*(1), 72–82. See also, Donnelly, K.; LeBlanc, P. V.; Torrence, R. D.; and Lyon, M.A. (1992). Career banding. *Human Resource Management, 31*(1–2), 35–43; note 26, Lissy and Morgenstern (1994), and Bergel (1994), note 2, Haslett (1995), and note 20, Brennan and McKee (1995).

31. Hewitt study cited in Abosch (1995), see note 2.

32. ACA study cited in Lissy and Morgenstern (1994), see note 26. Write the ACA at www.ahrm.org/aca/aca.htm or call at 602-922-2020.

33. For discussion of broadbanding disadvantages, see Sibson, R. E. (1990). *New compensation plans: A consultant's report.* Vero Beach, FL: Sibson. See also Reissman, L. (1995). Nine common myths about broadbands. *HRMagazine, 40*(8), 79–88; note 2, Abosch (1995), and note 30, LeBlanc and McInerney (1994).

34. For full discussion of pay-for-knowledge programs, including advantages and disadvantages, see Bennett, L. (1996). The C&BR board comments on compensation fads, custom pay plans, and team pay. *Compensation & Benefits Review, 28*(2), 67–75. See also Vogeley, E. G., and Schaeffer, L. J. (1995). Link employee pay to competencies and objectives. *HRMagazine, 40*(10), 75–81; Parent, K. J., and Weber, C. L. (1994). Case study: Does pay for knowledge pay off? *Compensation & Benefits Review, 26*(5), 44–50; note 1, Lawler (1990); note 33, Sibson (1990), note 26, Bergel (1994), and note 20, Gomez-Mejia, Balkin, and Cardy (1995).

35. For full discussion of teams and team-related pay, see Zingheim, P. K., and Schuster, J. R. (1995). First findings: The team pay research study. *Compensation & Benefits Review, 27*(6), 6–14. See also, Cauldron, S. (1994). Tie individual pay to team success, *Personnel Journal, 73*(10), 40–47; Gross, S. E. (1995). *Compensation for teams: How to design and implement team-based reward programs.* New York: AMACOM; Dumaine, B. (Sept. 15, 1994). The trouble with teams. *Fortune,* pp. 86–92; note 26, Lissy and Morgenstern (1994), and Bergel (1994), note 2, Morgenstern (1995) and Gross and Blair (1995); and note 34, Bennett (1996).

36. See note 1, Wallace and Faye (1988).

37. For full discussion concerning minimum wage, see Dunham, S. R. (July 26, 1996). We interrupt this revolution to hike the minimum wage. *Business Week,* p. 47. See also, Norton, R. (May 27, 1996). The minimum wage is unfair. *Fortune,* p. 53; Prasch, R. E. (1996). In defense of the minimum wage. *Journal of Economic Issues, 30*(2), 391–397; Laabs, J. J. (1996). Maximum debate over minimum wage hike—again, *Personnel Journal, 75*(6), 12; and Bernstein, A. (May 20, 1996). Commentary: A minimum wage argument you haven't heard before, *Business Week,* p. 42.

38. See note 1, Wallace and Fay (1988).

39. For detailed instruction on the way to conduct a compliance audit, see note 6.

40. McCaffery, R. M. (1988). *Employee benefit programs: A total compensation perspective.* Boston: PWS-Kent. See also, Steinberg, A. T. (1995). Beyond the tax code: How employee needs are driving employee benefits design. *Compensation & Benefits Review, 27*(1), 29–32, and Bureau of Labor Statistics (September 1992). *Employee Benefits in a Changing Economy: A BLS Chartbook.* Washington, DC: U.S. Government Printing Office.

41, Snarr, B. B. (1994). The 1993 Tax Act and the $150,000 cap: Ramifications for retirement plans. *Compensation & Benefits Review, 26*(1), 5–6. See also Price, S. C., and Rader, E. P. (1994). OBRA '93 puts the squeeze on retirement plans. *Compensation & Benefits Review, 26*(1), 65–68, and Klein, J. S. (1996). Contingent workers: Weighing the legal considerations. *Compensation & Benefits Review, 28(4)* 52–59. Klein argues that an employer who intentionally prevents a part-time employee from becoming full-time to avoid covering that employee under the benefits plan may violate Section 510 of ERISA.

42. U.S. Chamber of Commerce (1986). *Employee Benefits.* Washington, DC: U.S. Chamber of Commerce. See also note 40, McCaffery (1988).

43. Morgenstern, M. L. (1995). Currents in compensation and benefits. *Compensation & Benefits Review, 27*(3), 14–19. See also, Bureau of Labor Statistics (April 1996). *Employee Benefits in Small, Private Establishments, 1994.* Washington, DC: U.S. Government Printing Office; Bureau of Labor Statistics (November 1994). *Employee Benefits in Medium and Large Establishments, 1993.* Washington, DC: U.S. Government Printing Office; and U.S. Chamber of Commerce (1994). *Employee Benefits.* Washington, DC: U.S. Chamber of Commerce.

44. Cited in Morgenstern (1995), see note 43.

45. Morgenstern, M. L. (1996). Currents in compensation and benefits. *Compensation & Benefits Review, 28*(3), 10–15.

46. See note 43, Bureau of Labor Statistics (1994 and 1996).

47. See note 43, Bureau of Labor Statistics (1994 and 1996).

48. For full discussion of the role of benefits in job selection, see note 40, McCaffery (1988). See also, Dreher, G. F.; Ash, R. A., and Bretz, R. D. (1988). Benefit coverage and employee cost: Critical factors in explaining compensation satisfaction. *Personnel Psychology, 41,* 237–254, and Barber, A. E.; Dunham, R. B.; and Formisano, R. A. (1992). The importance of flexible benefits on employee satisfaction: A field study. *Personnel Psychology, 45,* 55–76.

49. Bernardin, H. J. (1989). *A survey of state employee attitudes toward benefits.* Unpublished report to the Florida legislature.

50. See note 40, McCaffery (1988).

51. See note 42, U.S. Chamber of Commerce (1986). For a videotape on social security benefits, call 1-800-941-0435 or on the Internet at http://www.fedworld.gov/pft.

52. Bureau of National Affairs (1994). *Compensation.* Washington, DC: BNA.

53. See note 40, McCaffery (1988).

54. See note 40, McCaffery (1988).

55. See note 40, McCaffery (1988).

56. Rosenbloom, J. S., and Hallman, G. V. (1986). *Employee benefit planning.* Englewood Cliffs, NJ: Prentice Hall.

57. Thompson, J. (July 1993). Incidence and type of disability insurance benefits, 1958–1990. *Monthly Labor Review,* pp. 57–62.

58. See note 43, Bureau of Labor Statistics (1994).

59. See note 43, Bureau of Labor Statistics (1994).

60. See note 43, Bureau of Labor Statistics (1996).

61. See note 43, Bureau of Labor Statistics (1994 and 1996).

62. See note 43, Bureau of Labor Statistics (1994 and 1996).

63. For full discussion of wellness programs, see Haltom, C. (1995). Shifting the focus from sickness to wellness. *Compensation & Benefits Review, 27*(1), 47–53. See also, Povall, J. (1994). Wellness strategies: How to choose a health risk assessment appraisal. *Compensation & Benefits Review, 27*(1), 47–53.

64. Study cited in Haltom (1995), see note 63.

65. For discussion of health plan audits, see Reace, D. (1995). The collapse of health care reform—What now? *Compensation & Benefits Review, 27*(2), 69–74. Also see note 63, Poval (1994).

66. Bureau of National Affairs (April 3, 1986). *Bulletin to Management,* p. 115.

67. Labor Letter (Jan. 30, 1990). *The Wall Street Journal.*

68. For full discussion of HMO real costs, see Gibson, W. S. (1996). Beyond rationing: Resolving the healthcare dilemma needs a coordinated approach. *Compensation & Benefits Review, 28*(2), 55–57. See also, Snarr, B. B. (1995). Managed care: Recent cases increase employers' liability risk. *Compensation & Benefits Review, 27*(6), 36–39; Burke, G. (1996). Rationing health care: A societal imperative. *Compensation & Benefits Review, 28*(2), 54–59.

69. *Dukes v. U.S. Healthcare, Inc.* (U.S. 3rd Circuit Court of Appeals), *Pacificare of Oklahoma v. Burrage* (U.S. 10th Circuit Court of Appeals), and *Rice v. Panchal* (U.S. 10th Circuit Court of Appeals). All three cases have been returned to state courts for hearing and disposition. See also note 68.

70. For full discussion of ERISA provisions, see Bureau of National Affairs (1995). *Compensation.* Washington, DC: BNA.

71. Solomon, J. (May 17, 1990). Retirees, companies head for showdown over moves to reduce health coverage. *The Wall Street Journal,* pp. B1, B10.

72. See note 43, Bureau of Labor Statistics (1994 and 1996).

73. See note 43, Bureau of Labor Statistics (1994 and 1996).

74. See note 43, Bureau of Labor Statistics (1994 and 1996).

75. Studies cited in Pratt, N. C. (1996). The road to retirement. *Compensation & Benefits Review, 28*(1), 14–19. See also, Scheiber, S. J. (1996). The sleeping giant awakens: U.S. retirement policy in the 21st century. *Compensation & Benefits Review, 28*(1), 20–31.

76. Cole, G., and Taylor, M. N. (1996). Caught between demographics and the deficit: How can retirement plans meet the challenges ahead. *Compensation & Benefits Review, 28*(1), 32–39. See also note 43, Bureau of Labor Statistics (1994 and 1996).

77. For full description of plan qualification, consult Bureau of National Affairs (1993). *Compensation.* Washington, DC: BNA.

78. See note 52, Bureau of National Affairs (1994).

79. See note 52, Bureau of National Affairs (1994).

80. See note 52, Bureau of National Affairs (1994). This gives rise to three important characteristics of defined benefit plans. First, the employer assumes all investment risk. This means that any shortfalls due to adverse investment results must be made up for by the employer, since its liability is for a specific plan payout. Second, defined benefit plans are typically not portable, that is, they cannot be transferred, or "rolled over," to other plans in the event that an employee leaves an organization. If such a terminating employee has a right to a pension under a defined benefit plan, typically, he waits until he qualifies for a payout under the provisions of the plan and then receives his benefit directly from his previous employer. Third, administrative expenses of defined benefit plans tend to be high. To ensure that adequate funding is maintained to meet the future pension liabilities, extensive actuarial services are needed and the plan is required to purchase insurance from the federal Pension Benefit Guaranty Corporation (PBGC—see discussion of ERISA). In addition, defined benefit plans typically require considerable consulting advice since the communication of pension plan terms and features must be translated into projected payouts to individuals, if the plan is to have meaning or value to its participants

81. Johnston, D. C. (Aug. 10, 1997). Pensions concerns move to the picket line. *New York Times,* p. F11. See note 40, McCaffery (1988).

82. See note 52, Bureau of National Affairs (1994).

83. McGill, D. M., and Grubbs, D. S. (1989). *Fundamentals of Private Pensions.* Philadelphia, PA: University of Pennsylvania Press, p. 54.

84. See note 52, Bureau of National Affairs (1994). ERISA requirements are: First, reporting and disclosure rules require that employees and beneficiaries must be informed in writing and in understandable language about their rights and entitlements under the plan. Second, fiduciary provisions establish standards governing the safety and security of investment decisions concerning plan assets. Third, plan participation rules establish a floor of eligibility stipulations that plans must observe. Included here is the establishment of the 1,000-hour rule, which is considered to constitute a year of service for plan purposes. This rule swept many part-time and seasonal workers into pension plans if they worked at least 1,000 hours per year. The law also defines a "break in service" as a year in which an individual fails to work at least 500 hours. Employees absent due to pregnancy, childbirth, and adoption must be credited with at least 501 hours of service for that year, thus protecting these absences from disrupting an individual's service under a qualified pension plan. Fourth, vesting guidelines were standardized. Vesting is the term that applies to the guarantee that an employee, having satisfactorily met certain requirements, will retain a right to the benefits he or she has accumulated, or some portion of them. ERISA permitted the use of one of three calculations for vesting. Under all options, an employee was vested for at least 50 percent of an employer-provided benefit after 10 years of service and 100 percent after 15 years of service (note: individuals are always fully vested for their own contributions). For defined benefit plans, ERISA established funding rules that regulated the approach that must be taken to finance future benefits. Similar regulations were not applied to defined contribution plans, since the retirement benefit typically equals the account balance at any point in time. Finally, defined benefit plans were required to purchase insurance through the Pension Benefit Guaranty Corporation, which ERISA established. Operating in a way similar to the FDIC, this insurance guarantees a level of pension benefits to employees in covered organizations if the organization becomes unable to fulfill its pension obligation.

85. See note 52, Bureau of National Affairs (1994).

86. Such legislation includes the Tax Reform Act of 1976, the Social Security Amendments of 1977, the Revenue Act of 1978, the Multiemployer Pension Plans Amendment Act of 1980, the Economic Recovery Tax Act of 1981 (ERTA), the Tax Equity and Fiscal Responsibility Act of 1982 (TEFRA), the 1983 Social Security Amendments, the Deficit Reduction Act of 1984 (DEFRA), the Retirement Equity Act of 1985 (REACT), the Tax Reform Act of 1986 (TRA), the Single Employer Pension Plan Amendments of 1986, the Consolidated Omnibus Budget Reconciliation Act of 1986, superseded and amended in 1988 (COBRA), the Omnibus Budget Reconciliation Act of 1987 (OBRA-87), and the Omnibus Budget Reconciliation Act of 1993 (OBRA-93).

87. See note 52, Bureau of National Affairs (1994).

88. See note 52, Bureau of National Affairs (1994).

89. For full discussion of SERPs and their importance in attracting/retaining executive talent, see note 41, Price and Rader (1994).

90. Cole, G., and Taylor, M. N. (1996). Caught between demographics and the deficit: How can retirement plans

meet the challenges ahead. *Compensation & Benefits Review, 28*(1), 32–39.

91. See note 75, Pratt (1996).

92. See note 75, Pratt (1996).

93. See note 40, McCaffery (1988).

94. See note 43, Bureau of Labor Statistics (1994 and 1996). Paid vacation, provided to 88 percent of full-time employees in small establishments, average 8 vacation days after 1 year of service, 13 days after 10 years, and 15 days after 25 years. Eighty-two percent of full-time workers in small companies average 4 paid holidays per year. In medium and large organizations, virtually all full-time workers are entitled to paid vacation averaging 9.4 days after 1 year of service, 16.6 days after 10 years of service, and 21.6 days after 25 years of service. In addition, virtually all full-time workers are entitled to an average of 10 paid holidays per year.

95. See note 43, Bureau of Labor Statistics (1994 and 1996). Survey data on paid sick leave indicate that 80 percent of workers covered under employer-sponsored plans are allowed a fixed number of paid sick days per year, with the average being 8 days after 1 year of service, 10 days after 5 years of service, 12 days after 15 years of service, and 13 days after 25 years of service. In medium and large organizations, an estimated 75 percent of employees are eligible for employer-sponsored paid sick leave, although professional and technical workers are more likely to have such protection than blue-collar workers. Survey data indicate that most workers are entitled to a fixed number of paid sick days per year averaging 12 days after 1 year of service, 16.9 days after 5 years, 21.8 days after 15 years, and 24.5 days after 25 years.

96. See note 43, Bureau of Labor Statistics (1994 and 1996).

97. See note 43, Bureau of Labor Statistics (1994 and 1996).

98. See note 52, Bureau of National Affairs (1994).

99. Credit Union National Association (March 1986). *Economic Report.* Madison, WI: Credit Union National Association,

100. Winslow, R. (Dec. 13, 1989). Spending to cut mental health costs. *The Wall Street Journal,* p. B1.

101. Johnson, A. A. (April 1984). Relocation: Getting more for the dollars you spend. *Personnel Administrator,* pp. 29–37.

102. Densford, L. E. (May/June 1987). Make room for baby: The employer's role in solving the day care dilemma. *Employee Benefits News,* pp. 19–37.

103. Labor Letter (March 27, 1990). *The Wall Street Journal,* p. 1.

104. See note 40, McCaffery (1988).

105. Martocchio, J. J. (1998), *Strategic compensation.* Upper Saddle River, N.J.: Prentice-Hall; see also, Earley, C. (ed.) (1998). *International industrial-organizational psychology.* New York: John Wiley & Sons; Swaak, R. A. (1995). Expatriate management: The search for best practices. *Compensation & Benefits Review,* 27(2) pp. 21–29.

106. Harvey, M. (1993). Designing a global compensation system: The logic and a model. *The Columbia Journal of World Business, 28,* 56–72. See also; Kates, S. M. and Speilman, C. (1995). Reducing the cost of sending employees overseas. *The Practical Accountant, 28,* 50–55; O'Reilly, M. (1988). Total Remuneration: The international view. *Compensation & Benefits Review, 20*(2), 46–55; Capdeveille, P. (June, 1989). International comparisons of hourly compensation costs. *Monthly Labor Review,* 112, 10–12. Drucker. P. F. (March 16, 1988). Low wages no longer give competitive edge. *Wall Street Journal,* p. 32. Freeman, R. B., and Weitzman, M. L. (1987). Bonuses and employment in Japan. *Journal of the Japanese and International Economics,* 1, 168–194. Hashimoto, H. (1990). Employment and wage systems in Japan and their implications for productivity. In A. S. Blinder (ed.), *Paying for Productivity,* Washington, DC: The Brooking Institute, pp. 245–294.

107. Harvey, M. (1993). Empirical evidence of recurring international compensation problems. *Journal of International Business Studies, 19,* 785–799.

108. Wederspahn, T. M. (1992). Costing failure in expatriate human resource management. *Human Resource Planning, 15,* 27–35.

109. See note 106, Kates and Spielman, 1995.

110. McKay, J. (December 1994). International benefits policy: A U.S. multinational perspective. *Employee Benefits Journal,* 22–25. See also; Horn, M. E. (1992). *International employee benefits: An overview.* Brookfield, WI: International Foundation of Employee Benefit Plans.

111. Swaak, R. A. (1995). Today's expatriate family: Dual careers and other obstacles. *Compensation and Benefits Review,* 27(1), 21–26. See also; Lublin, J. (Jan. 26, 1984). More spouses receive help in job searches when executives take positions overseas. *The Wall Street Journal,* p. 35. Eby, L. T., DeMatteo, J. S., and Russell, J. E. A. (1997). Employment assistance needs of accompanying spouses following relocation. *Journal of Vocational Behavior, 50,* 291–307.

112. See note 105, Swaak (1995).

C H A P T E R

PAY FOR PERFORMANCE*

OVERVIEW

As Harvard professor Rosabeth Moss Kanter put it,

> America is . . . already well on its way to transforming the meaning of the paycheck, and some argue that it is none too soon if we are to remain competitive in world markets. Although popular attention has focused on comparable worth . . . the most important trend in pay determination has actually been the loosening relationship between job assignment and pay level.[1]

Professor Kanter's remarks were prophetic for the 1990s. As we discussed in Chapters 9 and 10, in addition to broadbanding, a strong trend in compensation administration over the past 10 years is the installation of various forms of pay-for-performance (PFP) systems. The term *pay-for-performance* is a little misleading because many incentive systems now award something other than pay for desired performance. We will use the PFP term but you should understand that company stock, vacation trips, and golf outings are also used to recognize and reward desired performance. In general, these PFP systems put more employee pay at risk and loosen the relationship between assignments and pay levels. This loosening at least theoretically provides more flexibility for organizations.

Controlling labor costs and increasing productivity through the establishment of clearer linkages between pay and performance is considered to be a key human resource management component for competitive advantage. In addition, increased concerns over productivity and meeting customer requirements have prompted renewed interest in methods designed to motivate employees to be more focused on meeting (or exceeding) customer requirements and increasing productivity. What better way to do this than by establishing a closer connection between meeting such requirements and compensation. Stanford's Pfeffer and Michigan's Ulrich both emphasize the importance of incentive-based compensation systems for the successful companies on which they focus in their popular books on HRM practices. Recent research has labeled PFP systems as one characteristic of "high performance work systems" (HPWS) and linked PFP to firm performance, particularly when the PFP system is closely aligned with the company's strategic objectives.[2]

*Contributed by C. Brian Peach and M. Ronald Buckley.

311

But many firms jump on the PFP bandwagon without thoroughly understanding the potential difficulties and limitations of PFP systems. Research has clearly established that there are preferred methods for installing PFP systems,[3] and that failure to follow these guidelines can doom a PFP system.[4] And there are many classic failures. Harvard professor Kevin Murphy summarized the research on PFP nicely: "Business history is littered with firms that got what they paid for."[5] Sears had a very clear PFP system in which mechanics were paid bonuses as a percentage of repair receipts. Receivables went up, mechanics got higher pay, and 41 states indicted Sears for fraud. Columbia Hospitals has found that when you increase your profits by "gaming" a government entitlement system like Medicare, the government just might think the "gaming" constitutes fraud. Needless to say, organizations need to be very careful about setting up the performance measures used for the PFP system.

Many of our most successful companies have endeavored to establish a stronger connection between employee pay and strategic goals. Federal Express, for example, won the prestigious Baldrige Award in 1990 and was cited for the clear linkage it established between worker pay and customer satisfaction data. Stanford professor Pfeffer, whose research we discussed in Chapters 1 and 2, identified a successful PFP system as a key to the success of some of the most profitable companies in the United States.[6] As so many other writers on PFP have done, Pfeffer attributes Lincoln Electric's success to its PFP system. But he also emphasizes that Lincoln's PFP system could be pulled off only in the context of a particular management system and philosophy, a system based on great trust between workers and management.

A recent survey of *Fortune* 1000 companies found that 44 percent of companies have PFP systems that cover all employees in the organization.[7] Among the many companies that have implemented some form of PFP system for nonmanagerial employees in the last 10 years are General Motors, the Tribune Company, Blockbuster Video, Coca-Cola, Burger King, Office Depot, Merck, Mirage Resorts, United Parcel Service (UPS), Federal Express, Merrill Lynch, Grumman, and Wal-Mart. GM, for example, put more than 26,000 workers on a merit pay system after abandoning across-the-board increases. Wendy's and Office Depot even have bonus systems based on assessments conducted by "mystery shoppers" (see Chapter 9).

PFP systems are very common for executives and great deal more rewarding for the recipients. A 1996 study by Graef Crystal found that while chief executive officer pay is generally tracking with corporate performance, there are many examples of exorbitant pay for CEOs.[8] According to Crystal, CEO pay has increased by 400 percent since 1976 with CEOs now earning 200 times what the average American worker earns. Most of the increase in CEO pay is due to the PFP components of the pay package.

This chapter reviews the major types of PFP systems and discusses their relative advantages and disadvantages. The determinants of effective PFP systems are described first, followed by an exploration of questions of fairness and practicality regarding PFP. Next, the major problems associated with PFP will be reviewed. The second part of the chapter reviews the major types of PFP and the problems with measuring performance.

OBJECTIVES

After studying this chapter, you should be able to:

1. Understand the determinants of effective PFP systems.

2. Identify the critical variables related to the selection of the most appropriate PFP systems.

3. Review the evidence on the effectiveness of different PFP systems.

4. Describe issues related to executive pay plans.

PFP systems come in all shapes and sizes. One of the most important considerations is the level-of-performance measurement. The most common type of PFP is to tie pay to individual performance in a merit pay system. However, in an effort to promote teamwork, a growing number of companies now tie pay to unit or group performance, and others tie pay to organizational or company performance. Within each of these three general categories, however, there are numerous approaches. As we discussed in Chapter 9, the accurate measurement of performance and the linkage of the performance measures to the strategic goals of the organization are the keys to successful PFP efforts.

DOES PFP WORK?

The Wall Street Journal described the research evidence as "skimpy,"[9] and a review from 1990 concluded, "The evidence is insufficient to determine conclusively whether merit pay can enhance individual performance."[10] More recent research is also disappointing for some types of PFP systems but much more positive for certain types of systems.[11] A recent study of "high performance work systems" found certain types of PFP systems were correlated with stronger firm performance.[12] Many firms have developed new forms of incentive programs in the past few years despite arguments published in the *Harvard Business Review* that "incentive plans cannot work."[13] (See Critical Thinking Exercise 11.1.)

CRITICAL THINKING EXERCISE 11.1

The Case For and Against Pay-for-Performance Systems[1]

If you want employees to perform at a higher level, you can motivate them to excel by tying their compensation to a particular performance index. After all, the way to influence employees is through the wallet. Right? According to Alfie Kohn, author of four books and professional business lecturer, this is not the case.[2] Drawing from Frederick Herzberg's motivation theory, Kohn claims that financial incentives cannot motivate employees to improve their performance; however, the absence of financial incentives can create employee dissatisfaction or demotivation. For example, if your salary was cut you would become frustrated and might seek another source of employment, but if you received a raise, you wouldn't improve your performance over the long haul. Sure, you might become exceptionally productive right before your evaluation for your yearly bonus or right after you received a raise, but not when looking at the big picture. At best, pay-for-performance (PFP) incentives motivate employees to *temporarily* alter their behavior; they do not encourage any lasting changed behavior. In fact, once the reward is taken away, employees will revert back to their old patterns of behavior.

So, according to this argument, PFP incentives are generally ineffective, temporary employee bribes. "Jump through these hoops and you'll get this" is the inevitable philosophy behind reward systems. Employees are reduced to mere objects controlled by the wiles of manipulative bosses. Surprisingly enough, a rewarding system is not much different from a punishing system; not receiving a reward has a similar effect to being punished. For every employee that "wins" (receives an award), there is an employee who "loses" (does not receive an award). With increased emphasis on self-managed work teams and quality work circles (see Chapter 12), competition and hostility among workers over who secured the largest reward is the last thing a U.S. firm needs. Employees will abandon risk taking, innovation, and creativity—the key ingredients for competitive advantage—in an attempt to minimize challenges and maximize their personal wealth. In the worst case scenario, employees will engage in unethical or illegal behavior just to finesse a greater payoff. Therefore, the emphasis shifts from employees excelling at their jobs to excelling at the incentive-winning game. Examples from 1997 may include Columbia Hospitals and the Internal Revenue Service. PFP incentives, Kohn argues, do not motivate employees to improve their performance, "they motivate [them] to get rewards."

Charles M. Cummings, senior compensation consultant at William M. Mercer, Inc., has refuted Kohn's "blanket condemnation of incentive plans," citing that properly constructed pay-for-performance systems can be successful.[3] Cummings finds fault with Kohn's premise that PFP systems reduce employees to simple objects trying to take a bite off the golden carrot dangling in front of their noses. Such manipulative and highly ineffective systems are found only in "hierarchical, tradition organizations" and are not representative of the way PFP systems should be designed nor of the way these systems are now being built. Furthermore, in such a traditional organization, employees are largely performing specialized tasks that do not directly effect the firm's bottom line. Rather, they have to rely on their supervisors to integrate their tasks into a meaningful, profitable whole. Without a feeling of worth to the organization, it is little wonder that employees will lack **intrinsic** (inner) motivation and have to be "bribed" by their bosses to perform their meaningless jobs. Cummings suggests that more firms today are shifting to **team-based PFP plans** (e.g., profit sharing, gain sharing) rather than **individualistic plans** (e.g., the ill-fated merit pay), which Kohn describes in his argument. Team-based PFP plans not only help employees comprehend their significance to the organization as a whole but also provide the intrinsic motivation necessary for optimum job performance. (Participants in quality work circles, self-managed work teams, and the like will experience this intrinsic motivation because they can see the fruits of their labors with results that hit the bottom line.)

Contrary to Alfie Kohn's assumption, Cummings believes that "most people have a need to have their achievements acknowledged by others." Because employees are being respected for their accomplishments with a properly designed and implemented PFP system, they will generate "goodwill and commitment" towards the organization. These feelings are much different from the feelings of ill will that Kohn describes. A proper PFP system can be very successful in an organization and can attain a competitive advantage through loyal and motivated workers.

Assignment

Consider the arguments above and take a position. Do you agree with Kohn or Cummings? Are there situations in which the opposing position would ever apply? Think of a real-life example to support the position you have taken.

[1] Contributed by Lauren J. Lispi

[2] Kohn, A. (September–October). Why incentive plans cannot work. *Harvard Business Review*, pp. 54–63.

[3] Cummings, C. M. (May–June, 1994). Incentives that really do motivate. *Compensation and Benefits Review*, pp. 38–40.

The bottom line on the effects of PFP systems is that they can be very effective if they are tailored to particular work situations and contribute to high probability estimates by employees concerning their effort and their performance and their performance and desired outcomes. Expectancy theory, particularly when combined with goal-setting, has a great deal of predictive power in understanding the value of PFP systems.

Domino's Pizza claimed an increase in sales in excess of 20 percent after implementing a complicated PFP system. IBM reported a 200 percent productivity increase over 10 years in the manufacturing of typewriters—an increase that IBM attributes to its PFP system. Ford Motor Company credits its PFP system with "improved worker morale and quality of work."[14] One survey reported improved output from two out of three companies using some form of PFP when incentives are provided for meeting specific performance targets.[15]

DETERMINANTS OF EFFECTIVE PFP SYSTEMS

Although pay is generally regarded as a motivator, organizations are often confronted with unique sets of issues and problems related to PFP and must develop strategies to deal with them. The most important determinants of effective PFP are summarized in Figure 11.1.

You may recall our discussion of **expectancy theory** in Chapter 9. Motivation is a function of the perception a worker has about the likelihood that more effort will lead to higher performance and that higher performance will lead to valued outcomes. Of course, performance is also a function of a worker's (or student's) knowledge, skills, and abilities. A worker's perception of the critical effort-to-performance relationship is to some extent a consequence of that worker's self-assessment of his or her KASOCs as related to the work. In addition, if workers believe that situational constraints beyond their

FIGURE 11.1
DETERMINANTS OF EFFECTIVE PFP SYSTEMS

1. Worker values outcomes (money, prizes).
2. Outcome is valued relative to other rewards.
3. Desired performance must be measurable.
4. Worker must be able to control rate of output.
5. Worker must be capable of increasing output.
6. Worker must believe that capability to increase exists.
7. Worker must believe that increased output will result in receiving a reward.
8. Size of reward must be sufficient to stimulate increased effort.
9. Performance measures must be compatible with strategic goals for short and long term.

control have more to do with performance than their own effort or KASOCs, their perception of the likelihood that effort will lead to higher performance will be very low (see points 4 to 6 in Figure 11.1). While the determinants presented in Figure 11.1 can increase the likelihood of an effective PFP system, all are not required for an effective PFP system.

Increases in pay as a reward for increases in performance must be valued by the specific employee or work unit for which the PFP plan is intended—and must be valued highly relative to other rewards. Occasionally, group norms or cultural values deemphasize money or at least differential rewards for differential outputs. Unions, for example, have traditionally opposed pay systems based on individual or unit-level output, such as piece-rate incentive systems. A major reason for this is doubt by workers that increased productivity will result in increased pay. Some unions (e.g., the United Auto Workers, the Communications Workers of America, and the Teamsters) have become more receptive to PFP systems in recent years when trust is established between the union and management. Ford's profit-sharing plan resulted in each of the over 125,000 eligible Ford employees receiving an average of $2,650 in 1995. The Teamsters supported a profit-sharing plan for UPS workers in its 1997 collective bargaining agreement. At GM's new Saturn plant, UAW members work for a salary (about $35,000 per year), with 20 percent of the amount fluctuating up or down because it is tied to assessments of car quality, productivity, and profits. These examples are exceptions rather than the rule. In general, unions favor only organizationwide PFP systems and not individual PFP systems, which the unions maintain will inevitably pit worker against worker. When the state of Florida mandated an individual merit pay system for teachers, the American Federation of Teachers (AFT) worked to promote regulations regarding the merit pay, which ultimately led to the demise of the system. Within two years, the state had rescinded the individual PFP program.

Some companies regard individual PFP systems as contrary to their team-oriented philosophy of management and organizational culture. United Technologies espouses this view. Its PFP reward system uses only aggregated methods of rewards in which unit and companywide performance measures are the basis of the awards.

The organization must identify those measures of performance (e.g., outputs, products, services, behaviors, cost reductions) that are related to their strategic plans. For example, increased output may be desirable only when there is customer demand for more product. The organization should tie pay only to those aspects of value that are critical for the organization. You may recall from Chapter 9 that we distinguished among six aspects of value in the measurement of performance.

While most organizations place equal weight on the quality and quantity of a worker's performance, some companies have a clear preference for one of these aspects over the other.

The PFP system should establish a reward system for those aspects of value that are compatible with the strategic goals of the company. For example, retailers often offer incentives for the sale of overstocked merchandise. Inventory control and sales projections drive the time for the incentive system. The Marriott's strategic goal was to be the "hotel of choice" for business travelers. It conducted a telephone survey of patrons' experiences and then tied the customer satisfaction data to bonuses. Home Depot outsources all its installations, but it does a follow-up survey to customers of the recommended installers to determine whether the customer was pleased with the service. A favorable review gets the vendor a small bonus, while an unfavorable review could jeopardize the priority rank of the outsourcing company. Therefore, its PFP system placed significant weight on the measurement and rewarding of performance in this area.

Perhaps encouraged by the Valdez oil spill in Alaska and Exxon's woeful response, Conoco made environmental issues a major strategic priority. Environmental criteria became a component of its incentive system for top managers. Xerox Corporation emphasizes customer service and now uses customer survey data as a criterion in its bonus system. According to Xerox's president, an executive of a profitable unit would not get a bonus if the customer survey data indicated poor performance. The Aluminum Company of America now emphasizes improvements in safety records as part of its managerial bonus system.

Merrill Lynch was concerned about the loss of new brokers who had recently completed the expensive 17-week training program. The company installed a straight salary system with deferred commission contingent on two years of service. All commission was lost if the brokers quit in less than two years. The new incentive system also included a $100,000 bonus for brokers who stayed with the company for 10 years. Workers at a Monsanto Corporation chemical plant in Louisiana can earn bonuses for meeting goals that include reducing injuries and preventing emissions from escaping into the environment. Texaco placed considerable weight on diversity issues in its 1996 PFP plan for executives as a partial response to a class-action racial discrimination lawsuit. Executives were evaluated and paid based on their ability to keep and develop minorities and women.

Successful PFP systems recognize that all the determinants presented in Figure 11.1 are intimately related as well as necessary. For example, to determine the nature of a reward that should be offered for an increased level of effort, a firm must know the relative importance of money to its typical worker, the increased value to the

firm of any given performance increase, the worker's perception of the increased effort required, and the likelihood of receiving the reward. Money also fails to motivate if the required level of extra effort results in unacceptable fatigue to the worker or prevents the worker from enjoying a valued social life.

PROBLEMS WITH PFP PROGRAMS

There are many potential problems with PFP systems.[16] Figure 11.2 presents a summary of the problems judged by experts to be most responsible for the failure of such systems. PFP systems can be expensive to develop and maintain. In addition to the initial cost of establishing standards and rates, changes in procedures, equipment, and product may require revision of any existing standards and reward structures. In many cases a revision of the compensation system will be viewed with suspicion. Historically, some shortsighted firms have taken advantage of changes in the production process to reduce the amount of reward for any given level of effort. General Motors established what it thought were challenging production targets at its Hamtramck, Michigan, plant and let workers go home when the targets were achieved, but GM later increased the targets when it found workers were able to go home after lunch. Such actions can have a long-term negative effect on worker responses to PFP systems.

Many problems can arise in a PFP system that relies on performance appraisals. One frequent problem is that workers do not feel that their rewards are closely linked to their performance, a critical component of expectancy theory. This low probability often occurs when employees believe that the performance measure does not accurately assess their performance. As we discussed in Chapter 9, employees often have inflated ideas about their performance levels, which translate into unrealistic expectations about rewards. One study found that the

FIGURE 11.2
REASONS FOR THE FAILURES OF PFP SYSTEMS

1. Poor perceived connection between performance and pay.
2. The level of performance-based pay is too low relative to base pay. The cost of more highly motivating programs may be prohibitive.
3. Lack of objective, countable results for most jobs, requiring the use of performance ratings.
4. Faulty performance appraisal systems, with poor cooperation from managers, leniency bias in the appraisals, and resistance to change.
5. Union resistance to such systems and to change in general.
6. Poor connection between PFP outcomes and corporate performance measures.

majority of workers who were rated even slightly less than the highest level (e.g., eight on a nine-point scale) were more dissatisfied than satisfied with the rating. Those with even larger discrepancies between their self-assessments and their supervisor's ratings were more dissatisfied with their merit pay increase.[17] Given these beliefs, a large portion of the workforce may receive performance ratings below their expectations, and rewards will likely fall short of expectations.

As discussed in Chapter 9, there can be a perception of bias in the process even if such bias does not exist. If workers perceive that the performance measurement component of the PFP system is biased or invalid, the perceived connection between pay and performance will be undermined and the PFP system will be less effective. This is a common problem when performance is measured by ratings. Some PFP experts say that if performance must be measured by ratings, PFP is not worth the trouble. One such expert concluded that when ratings must be used, "The approach is so flawed that it is hard to imagine a set of conditions which would make it effective."[18] While this conclusion may be overly pessimistic, there is no denying that PFP systems based on performance ratings can be problematic. Many of the largest class-action lawsuits brought in 1996, the Texaco case included, concerned possible discrimination in pay increases based on the PFP system.

Many PFP plans have failed because the performance measure that was rewarded was not related to the performance objectives of the entire organization and to those aspects of performance that were most important to the organization. For example, a PFP system may put inordinate emphasis on the quantity of output when the organizational emphasis is on quality improvement or cost-effectiveness.[19] The organization must constantly ensure that the aspects of value emphasized in the appraisal and PFP system are the priority of the organization. Recall from our discussion of performance appraisal in Chapter 9 that it is possible to weight performance dimensions (which are combinations of job functions with aspects of value: quantity, quality, timeliness, need for supervision, effects on constituents, and cost). This weighting process should reflect the strategic plan of the unit and the organization. Unfortunately, the typical measurement process for PFP systems is far more haphazard than this. One survey found that the majority of workers who were paid on a PFP system had little understanding of the criteria for performance measurement.[20]

The organization should also ensure that workers are capable of increasing their performance. You may recall the discussion in Chapter 10 regarding constraints on performance. An employee working on an assembly line or operating a machine with a preset speed may not have the opportunity to increase the quantity of performance. For higher pay to result in higher performance, workers must believe in and be capable of higher levels of performance. When workers believe that performance standards exceed their capabilities, they will not expend extra effort.

One common problem with PFP systems is that an insufficient amount of money is available for meritorious performance. There is some indication that this situation may be improving. While a 1990 survey of 459 firms found that the most effective workers received 8 percent increases, while lower-rated workers received around 5 percent, a more recent study found that more money was available for PFP.[21] At one company, the most effective computer programmers received $17 a month more than satisfactory workers on annual salaries of about $40,000. Says one expert on the subject, this difference is "hardly enough to push someone to excel."[22] While experts differ on the subject, the lowest level recommended is between 10 and 15 percent of base salary for the money to be considered significant and for the PFP system to be effective.[23] Digital Equipment Corporation has a range of 0 to 30 percent, and Westinghouse has a range of 0 to 19 percent, but most companies are at lower levels. At Continental Bank, for example, an employee earning $3,000 per month who achieved the very highest performance appraisal was eligible for the highest PFP award of 5 percent, which increased earnings $150 per month (before taxes). Most employees who were surveyed on the PFP system didn't think the amount of money involved in the PFP system was worth the extra effort.

LEGAL IMPLICATIONS OF PFP

As we discussed in Chapter 10, all decisions regarding compensation, including those derived from PFP systems, are subject to complaints using the same sources of redress we have discussed throughout the book. PFP systems have been challenged for more subtle forms of alleged discrimination. For example, as we discussed in Chapter 9, situational constraints on performance can affect the basic fairness and equity of the PFP system. They have also been the basis of Title VII actions. An office furniture retailer terminated a female employee for failure to meet a sales quota in a difficult territory. She argued that her opportunity to meet the quota was severely restricted by situational constraints that were beyond her control and that men were not so constrained. She also argued that constraints such as not providing sample products, which were made available to the male sales personnel, were deliberately denied her. Her complaint resulted in a large out-of-court settlement.

SELECTING A PFP SYSTEM

In designing a PFP system, three major questions should be asked: (1) Who should be included in the PFP system? (2) How will performance be measured? and (3) Which incentives will be used? The process for developing the characteristics of a performance-appraisal system apply to the first two questions, which were discussed in Chapter 10.

Who Should Be Included in a PFP System?

In general, all groups should be included in a PFP system, with one critical condition: The PFP system should be developed with specific groups and conditions in mind. Production workers, middle management, salespeople, engineers, professionals, senior executives, and top management should probably have different systems. Many companies use very different PFP systems for different jobs. For example, McDonald's has eight PFP systems for various classes of employees. IBM has six systems. Many companies have different PFP systems as a function of their organizational and unit-level strategies, with some form of market share measurement for a start-up product or service and cost-cutting for a more established product or service line. Some companies use a variety of PFP systems for the same job families. For example, Amoco has an individual merit pay system, a unit-level PFP measurement, and an employee stock ownership program (ESOP) for the same employees.

Other companies have reward systems that are compatible with an egalitarian culture that attempts to minimize the distance between people at different levels in the organizational hierarchy. Digital Equipment Corporation, for example, has only one reward system for all employees. In general, however, American workers prefer individual PFP systems where they can control their own destinies. Great deference should be given to this preference unless a compelling argument can be made that individual PFP systems will foster a competition among employees that will interfere with meeting company or unit-level strategic objectives. You should try to involve as many workers in a PFP system as possible but each system should be tailored to particular work situations. Organizations should avoid PFP systems that promote individual competition among workers that interferes with meeting major corporate or unit-level objectives.

What Are the Rewards in a PFP System?

Cash payments, percentage increases in base pay, and numerous noncash prizes are still the most common rewards for performance. While these incentives are flexible and well suited to short-run objectives, stock options are an excellent approach for meeting long-run objectives. Stock options are becoming more common for lower-level employees and are a bigger percentage of the raise for lower-level managers. In addition to quarterly bonuses based on "mystery shopper" data, Wendy's also awards stock to employees for performance and time on the job.

Options are typically additions to upper-management pay, which also includes a cash bonus. Over 90 percent of U.S. *Fortune* 500 companies offer some form of stock option for executives. Although there are several types of stock options, the most popular today are incentive options, which give an executive the right to purchase stock at a specified price within a designated time period. The price is lower than the market price. If the company does well and the stock price goes up, everyone is happy. Many highly successful companies offer options to low-level employees. For example, some experts argue that Federal Express has low turnover among its drivers and maintains a union-free environment to some extent because these employees own part of the company. Stock options are especially appealing to executives and corporations because of tax benefits relative to other compensation options.[24]

Should Merit Pay Be Tied into Base Pay?

With regard to actual *pay* for performance, another strong trend today is a PFP system in which the performance-based pay is not permanently tied to an employee's base pay.[25] In fact, experts have been recommending this approach for years, mainly because the size of the bonus can be greater and the cost to the organization in the long run is far less (a bonus that goes in your base salary is in your base salary forever).[26]

Compensation experts maintain that base pay should be tied to expected levels of work and that PFP should be tied to performance that exceeds that level. Workers are more likely to exceed that level if the performance–outcome connection is strong. This connection is typically stronger with bonus-based systems.

GM, Ford, and Coca-Cola are among the many companies that pay lump sums based on corporate profits, and the lump sum does not increase an employee's base salary. As we mentioned above, the Saturn plant operates on a 20 percent rate of "risk" for all salaried workers, with no tie-in to the base salary. Champion International pays managers based on growth in earnings per share of stock relative to the stock of 15 major competitors. The bonus awarded to the 12 senior managers is not tied to the managers' base pay. Federal Express managers have "small spot" awards of $100, which are available for unusual achievement. For example, one "small spot" award was given to a driver who went well beyond the call of duty to deliver a package when the weather would have been a justifiable excuse. Home Depot has a holiday, bonus-based system available to all employees and awards deep discounts on Home Depot products.

The long-term costs of PFP systems that are tied into base pay can be enormous. For example, one state awarded $5,000 increases to the base pay of 797 faculty based on the quality and quantity of undergraduate teaching they had performed up to three years earlier. The conservative amortized cost of the 797 $5,000 awards was $148.2 million over 20 years if all professors stayed on the payroll. Remember this was for work already performed. In addition, recipients were not eligible for the award for three years. No evidence was ever presented that the program actually increased either the quality or the quantity of undergraduate teaching.

Should You Use Individual, Group, or Company-Level PFP?

As we discussed in Chapter 9, the major issues are the extent to which output is controlled at the group or individual level, whether individual contributions can be measured, and the extent to which teamwork among unit members would be affected by the PFP system.

At Champion, for example, earnings are compared only to the company's major competitors so as to control for factors beyond the influence of the managers, such as inflation, interest rates, and general state of the economy. Managers perceive this relative comparison to be fairer than comparisons to absolute earnings, which are more susceptible to changes in the general state of the economy. (Recall our discussion of constraints on performance and the importance of perceived constraints on the critical probability statements in expectancy theory; if you believe factors beyond your control have more to do with performance outcomes than your own effort, your motivation to try harder will diminish.) In general, PFP systems are more effective when specific worker contributions can be clearly measured. If individual contributions cannot be measured reliably, then the smallest number of workers whose performance is determined to be important (e.g., related to strategic objectives) and measurable would constitute the incentive group.

An organization may choose to use a group plan even when it is possible to measure output on an individual basis. Individual PFP plans can increase competition between workers and may reduce cooperation and teamwork. As two experts put it, "When companies change the dynamics of work from structure driven—organized around individual role and functions—to process driven—often organized around teams—they should change the reward system to support those new dynamics."[27] Workers will be less likely to assist their coworkers if such an effort will hurt their own production rate or potential rewards. If teamwork and cooperation are important but team members are competing for a set number or amount of awards, a group or unit-based system is preferable.

For example, at the GM Saturn plant in Tennessee, while individual measurement was possible on a number of important outcome measures, an individual PFP system was thought to be contrary to the company's team-oriented approach to production. Thus, Saturn's UAW-endorsed PFP system is based strictly on unit-level and companywide measures of performance. One health care products manufacturer designed work teams around project teams for its 50 product development employees. But it maintained the old compensation system with job classes, individual performance appraisal, and merit pay. The compensation system turned out to be dysfunctional for the new project-based job structure.

When Should Team-Based PFP Be Used?

A growing number of organizations now use some form of team bonus. One survey of *Fortune* 1000 companies found that 70 percent of companies now use some form of team bonus, with 17 percent of these organizations applying bonuses to at least 40 percent of their employees.[28] Team-based PFP is a useful approach when it is part of a comprehensive team-based model of HRM and compensation—the focus of the pay structure in general is on objectives and results *of the team*. For example, the job evaluation process should place more emphasis on the work products of the team with less emphasis on individual job descriptions. The performance-appraisal and career development systems should also focus on team performance and contributing to team performance by new skill acquisition. However, the performance-appraisal system usually includes peer assessment and great weight is given to the extent to which employees contribute to team performance. These individual assessments, however, are usually only used as developmental tools and are not directly tied to pay. All other forms of reward and recognition programs should also emphasize the team. Companywide recognition programs, for example, should also focus on team performance and team contribution to the company's strategic goals. Reactions to team-based approaches depend on individual team member characteristics. For example, one study found that people who are more collectivist in their orientation (high on Factor A of the "Big Five," for example) tend to prefer team-based rewards.[29]

There are many examples of individually based PFP systems even where teamwork is critical. Michael Jordan would probably go elsewhere if the Chicago Bulls paid him the same as the other starters, basing everyone's pay on team performance because teamwork is so critical to the Bulls' success. Remember, the critical issues regarding the level of aggregation of the performance measures (individual, group, organization) are identifying and measuring performance criteria that the organization seeks to increase or improve in its strategic plan and then linking pay to performance on those measurements. When the pool of award or merit money is not fixed or set among team members, combining individual and group systems may be the most motivating.

Now that we've introduced the major factors that

should be considered in designing a PFP system, let's look at the individual, group, and company-based systems in some detail.

INDIVIDUAL PFP PLANS: MERIT PAY AND INCENTIVE SYSTEMS

Individual PFP systems can be divided into merit pay systems and incentive systems specifically tied to production rates. **Merit pay plans** are the most common and perhaps the most troublesome of PFP systems because performance is typically measured by ratings done by supervisors. **Incentive plans** rely on some countable result or results to be used as a basis for setting the PFP rate. These are also known as piece-rate systems. **Sales incentive plans** set certain commissions for sales of specified products or services. We will examine each of these methods next.

Merit Pay Plans

Merit pay plans call for a distribution of pay based on an appraisal of a worker's performance. The merit pay is usually folded into the base pay of the recipient and is usually granted as a percentage of a worker's base pay. At the Tribune Company, for example, 4 percent merit money was distributed to individual units (e.g., TV and radio stations and newspapers owned by the Tribune). Unit heads then distributed the money to department heads who had a total pool of 4 percent of their payroll to distribute among the workers. Obviously, the bigger the pool of meritorious workers, the smaller the average percentage that could be granted.

Surveys indicate that workers prefer merit pay plans that link individual performance with desired outcomes over straight pay with no tie-in to performance. Workers generally prefer merit pay plans even after they've been granted what they regarded as less than satisfactory raises based on the plan. But studies have found little relationship between merit pay plans that rely on performance appraisals by supervisors and important organizational outcomes, such as productivity increases or cost reductions.[30]

Many of the reasons listed in Figure 11.2 for the failure of PFP systems are characteristic of merit pay systems. The most serious problem is the failure to create a clear linkage between employee performance and pay. The performance-appraisal system and the evaluators of performance are mainly responsible for this problem. Several factors related to the appraisal system contribute to this breakdown in the linkage between pay and performance. The fundamental problem is with measuring performance, a problem compounded in service industries in which individual performance is difficult to measure. Another cause of the measurement problem is the lack of skill of those who do the appraisals. As we discussed in Chapter 9, this lack of skill is often manifested in leniency bias in the ratings. Leniency causes ratings to be bunched at the high end of the rating scale so that little distinction can be made between superior and other performances. The result is twofold: (1) a merit pay system in which the amount of the merit pay is relatively trivial because so many individuals are judged to be eligible and (2) a system in which the best performers perceive their merit pay as a gross inequity because the system is supposed to be based on merit.

Although we discussed leniency in Chapter 9, the discussion of methods designed to reduce leniency bias bears repeating because leniency is so critical to the effectiveness of any merit pay system based on performance appraisal. One approach is to impose a forced distribution rating, forced choice, or ranking system in which the number of people rated at the highest level is controlled (recall the discussion of IBM's new system in Chapter 9). Raters tend to dislike these approaches. Another approach is to train managers who are most susceptible to this error. (See Critical Thinking Exercise 11.2.) We could also select managers on the basis of this tendency.

CRITICAL THINKING EXERCISE 11.2

The Performance Appraisal Discomfort Scale (PADS)[1]

Research indicates that the people who commit leniency bias tend to commit it across rating situations (e.g., no matter whom they are rating).[2] In essence, some people feel relatively more discomfort in giving negative feedback than others. The PADS is an instrument that assesses the level of discomfort in giving feedback. Because of the anticipated discomfort, raters are more likely to take steps to avoid the discomfort if they can do so. Thus, as supervisors, they are more likely to rate with leniency in order to avoid the discomfort that may result from giving a more accurate but more critical review.[3] Complete the PADS below and score it as directed. Your instructor will provide the interpretation of the score.

THE PADS[4]

Indicate the degree of discomfort you would feel in the following situations. Answer as candidly as possible for what is true for you. Use the following scale to write in one number in the blank to the left of each item: 5 = high discomfort; 4 = some discomfort; 3 = a little discomfort; 2 = very little discomfort; 1 = no discomfort at all.

_____ 1. Telling an employee who is also a friend that he or she must stop coming into work late.

_____ 2. Telling an employee that his or her work is only satisfactory, when you know that he or she expects an above satisfactory rating.

_____ 3. Conducting a formal performance appraisal interview with an ineffective employee.

_____ 4. Telling an employee who has problems in dealing with other employees that he or she should do something about it (take a course, read a book, etc.).

_____ 5. Telling a male subordinate that his performance must improve.

_____ 6. Having to terminate someone for poor performance.

_____ 7. Being challenged to justify an evaluation in the middle of an appraisal interview.

_____ 8. Being accused of playing favorites in the rating of your staff.

_____ 9. Recommending that an employee be discharged.

_____10. Telling an employee that his or her performance can be improved.

_____11. Warning an ineffective employee that unless performance improves, he or she will be discharged.

_____12. Telling a female employee that her performance must improve.

To score

Add up your ratings on the 12 items. The maximum score is 60; minimum score is 12.

Assignment

To what extent do you agree with the interpretation of your score that has been provided? Do you see any practical value in the PADS? Could a company use PADS scores for any type of personnel decision making?

[1] Contributed by Jarold Abbott

[2] Kane, J. S., Bernardin, H. J., Villanova, P., and Peyrefitte, J. (1995). The stability of rater leniency: Three studies. _Academy of Management Journal, 38,_ 1036–1051.

[3] Villanova, P., Bernardin, H. J., Dahmus, S., and Sims, R. (1993). Rater leniency and performance appraisal discomfort. _Educational and Psychological Measurement, 53,_ 789–799.

[4] Adapted from: Abbott, J., and Bernardin, H. J. (1983). _The development of a scale of self-efficacy for giving performance feedback._ Unpublished manuscript. Florida Atlantic University, Boca Raton, FL 33431.

Many quality improvement experts maintain that pay should not be linked to performance, particularly at the individual level. Deming, the most highly regarded of the quality gurus before he died in 1995, believed that performance appraisal fosters competition among individual workers and diverts attention away from systems related to the quality of the product or service. We will discuss this issue more thoroughly in Chapter 12.

Despite Deming's comments, most individuals prefer to be paid on the basis of some measure of their own performance. The problem is creating the linkage when the criteria are ambiguous. The merit pay principle is easy when criteria are available that are countable (e.g., not rated by supervisors) and important (linked to the strategic plan of the organization or unit or to specific customer requirements). Although most jobs do not easily provide objective criteria, and firms thus rely on ratings, alternatives to ratings are available. As we discussed in Chapter 9, ratings by internal and external customers on the extent to which their expectations are met could be a preferable alternative to supervisory ratings. Studies have found that including some measure of customer satisfaction as one of the outcome measures has a positive effect on sales, profits, and customer satisfaction.[32] Federal Express conducts customer-related performance reviews every six months.

Although they have problems, merit pay systems are still widely used. In addition to the recommendations presented in Chapter 9 for sound performance-appraisal systems, Figure 11.3 presents a set of recommendations for the use of individual merit pay systems.

Incentive Pay Plans

Incentive pay is based on units produced and provides the closest connection between individual effort or per-

---

FIGURE 11.3
RECOMMENDATIONS FOR MERIT PAY PLANS

1. Use a bonus system in which merit pay is not tied to the base salary.

2. Maintain a bonus range from 0 to 20 percent for lower pay levels and from 0 to 40 percent for higher levels.

3. Pay attention to the process issues of the merit pay plan. Involve workers in decision making and maintain an open communication policy.

4. Take performance appraisal seriously. Hold raters accountable for their appraisals, and provide training.

5. Focus on key organizational factors that affect the pay system. Information systems and job designs must be compatible with the performance measurement system.

6. Include group and team performance in evaluation. Evaluate team performance where appropriate, and base part of individual merit pay on the team evaluation.

7. Consider special awards separately from an annual merit allocation that recognizes major accomplishments.

Source: Adapted from E. E. Lawler, _Strategic pay._ San Francisco: Jossey-Bass, 1990. Reprinted with permission.

formance and individual pay. There are two types of individual incentive systems based on nonrated output: the piece-rate system and the standard hourly rate.

PIECE-RATE SYSTEMS. Many variations of piece work have been used over the years, but most share common characteristics. A firm using the piece-rate system will determine an appropriate amount of work to be accomplished in a set time period (e.g., an hour) and then define this as the standard. (Recall from our discussion in Chapter 4 that job analysis methods can be used to establish work standards.) Then, using either internal or external measures, a fair rate is set for this time period. The piece rate is then calculated by dividing the base wage by the standard. Today, to comply with regulations such as the minimum wage, piece-rate plans usually include an hourly wage and a piece-rate incentive.

The basic piece rate is the oldest and most common wage incentive plan. The earliest approach, popular in textile and apparel mills, was called straight piece work. In this approach, a worker was paid per unit of production. Used in early American times when work was done at home on the piece-rate system, the piece-rate approach is still popular today, particularly with the increased use of electronic monitoring of performance. Data processing personnel, customer service representatives, and some clerks, for example, are paid based on a specific formula tied to the finished product or the number of customers served or processed.

The piece-rate pay method is also very common in factories around the world, particularly in textile factories where (typically) young women are paid by the piece of clothing produced. Nike, Ralph Lauren, Liz Claiborne, and Tommy Hilfiger maintain that the hourly rate they pay with the piece-rate system complies with the minimum wage laws of the country. For example, in 1997 Nike paid the following wages in *full compliance with the minimum wage requirements of the respective countries:* 20 cents an hour in Vietnam; 30 cents an hour in Haiti; and 48 cents an hour in Indonesia. While Michael Eisner was earning over $200 million for a single year of work, Disney was contracting with factories in Haiti paying workers 20 cents an hour to make stuffed animals (and none of the Haitian workers had anything to do with hiring David Orvitz!) According to Medea Benjamin of Global Exchange, a San Francisco-based world labor watchdog group, these hourly rates do not even get the employees three decent meals a day. Nike, Liz Claiborne, Reebok, and numerous other companies signed a "Code of Conduct" in 1997 that put some controls on the pay and treatment of international workers. With regard to wages, however, compliance with the minimum wage laws of the country is all that is stipulated.

The basic piece rate provides a production incentive based on paying only for what is actually produced. A simple piece-rate approach often results in production variability that can disrupt the flow of product to customers. **Production variability** occurs because employees may be willing to forgo extra effort on some days when they are tired, bored, or ill, but will work especially hard on other days when they need some extra money. Frederick Taylor developed the **differential rate** as a response to the variation potential in piece-rate systems.[33] Taylor's differential rate had two piece rates: one for performing below standard and a higher rate for meeting or exceeding the standard, thus encouraging workers to at least meet the standard.

One major advantage of piece-rate systems is that they are easy to understand. They are useful in labor-intensive industries such as textiles or agriculture, where individual production can be reliably measured. Migrant workers who harvest fruit and vegetables are often paid by unit of production.

Lincoln Electric, a *Fortune* 500 company based in Ohio, is cited as *the* success story regarding piece-rate pay. Stanford's Jeff Pfeffer considers Lincoln to be one of corporate America's greatest success stories, citing Lincoln's piece-rate system as a primary reason for its success. (See the Critical Thinking Exercise 11.3 for more on Lincoln Electric.)

CRITICAL THINKING EXERCISE 11.3

Can We (and Should We) Apply the Lincoln Electric Method?[1]

The sign on the front door at Lincoln Electric in Cleveland, Ohio, says it all: "No admittance prior to 30 minutes before the start of work." That's right. Lincoln Electric, a highly successful maker of welding machinery, has to keep workers from starting early! How does it motivate workers?

Although some unionists compare it to "sweatshops," this *Fortune* 500 company pays its 3,000 employees according to the piece-rate system. Workers are simply paid for what they produce. Except for a two-week vacation and a pension, workers earn only what they produce according to a piece-rate formula. According to CEO Don Hastings, the average Lincoln worker earns over $50,000 based on the piece-rate system, a rate he claims is the highest salary for a factory worker in the world.

Some other company policies are also unusual. First, Lincoln still maintains a lifetime employment policy. It has never laid off a worker, even during recessionary times when it had a 40 percent reduction in sales volume. Second, it distributes substantial bonuses to workers based on company performance; some workers earned over $40,000 in bonuses in 1996. Third, the base pay of the CEO is only about seven times that of the average annual wage of a factory worker (CEO Hastings argues that trust is critical for this process to work and that obscene executive salaries ruin trust). His bonus is a direct function of company profits and fluctuates just like the workers' bonuses do. Hastings credits this trust with the incredible cooperation Lincoln got from its Cleveland plant when international ventures turned sour in the early 90s. Workers stepped up production and exceeded all targets during difficult times with factories in Brazil and Germany.

Although Hastings has called the Lincoln method "barbaric," the workers seem to love the company or at least the money. But according to the late Dan Lacey, who was editor of *Work Place Trends,* a pro-union newsletter, using the piece-rate method to improve American productivity is like saying we "have to improve transportation in America so let's whip the horses a little harder."

Chapter 9 discussed different aspects of value in performance. If the piece rate pays a worker for a quantity produced, what happens to quality? At Lincoln, workers are paid only for pieces that meet carefully defined specifications. If there is a quality problem with a piece, workers are responsible for the correction. And what about teamwork? Lincoln also uses performance appraisals that reveal a letter grade for each worker's dependability, quality, output, and cooperation. The straight A workers get the highest bonuses.

The executives and factory workers at Lincoln agree that management is overhead. Their philosophy is "every worker must be a manager, and every manager must be a worker . . . in self-management is found the true meaning of efficiency, because nothing increases overhead as quickly and nonproductively as extra layers of management."[2] The workers are also heavy stockholders; over 80 percent of the workers own stock and the stock is closely held by the Lincoln family, the workers, and several foundations. The year-end profit sharing probably breaks the record for distribution. An average of over 40 percent of Lincoln's pre-tax income goes to the employees.[3]

Assignment

Does the Lincoln system generalize to many work situations? Think of one work setting in which you think the piece-rate method might work. Generate a list of the key contingencies that may be related to the success of a piece-rate system in that setting.

Also, in addition to the piece-rate method, to what extent are the other characteristics of the Lincoln compensation and management systems critical for Lincoln's success? (As of 1997, Lincoln had still maintained its lifetime employment record.) Do you think a CEO's pay relative to that of the producers of the goods and services

is critical for establishing and maintaining employee trust? Do you think trust is important? Expectancy theory says nothing about trust. Or does it? Also, is this a work setting for Type A personalities or so-called workaholics only?

[1] Contributed by John Bernardin

[2] H. C. Handlin, (1992). The company built upon the Golden Rule: Lincoln Electric. In B. L. Hopkins, and T. C. Mawhinney (eds.), *Pay for performance: History, controversy, and evidence.* New York: Haworth Press, 1992, p. 156.

[3] K. W. Chilton, Lincoln Electric's incentive system: A reservoir of trust. *Compensation & Benefits Review,* November/December 1994, pp. 29–34.

Except for some industries such as textiles, individual piece-rate systems are less popular now than they were 20 years ago because a growing number of jobs are team-based or are in areas such as the service sector, which often precludes establishment of a clear standard for determining the rate of production and the piece rate. Piece-rate incentive systems in their various forms tend to work better when the situation is repetitive, the pace is under the direct control of individual workers, little or no interaction or cooperation is required among workers, and the results can be easily measured.

But even for companies in which incentive systems would seem to work, there is often trouble. The major problem with incentive systems is that an adversarial relationship usually develops between workers and management. Workers make every effort to maximize their financial gains by attempting to manipulate the system of setting rates, setting informal production norms, and filing grievances regarding rate adjustments. Lincoln, for example, had great difficulty implementing this system in some of its international plants when it expanded in the early 90s. Plants in Germany and Brazil were ultimately shut down. The highly acclaimed management system apparently does not automatically transfer around the world.

There are numerous examples of worker attempts to sabotage piece-rate incentive systems. One expert on pay systems tells the story of how a sales force selling baby food in south Florida kept secret their highly successful efforts at selling the food to senior citizens because they feared their method would be rejected by management.[34]

Unfortunately, most jobs outside of sales and straight assembly work do not have a reliable measure of production or performance. Another problem with piece-rate systems is that adjustments in the standard are required whenever there is a significant change in the machinery or production methods. Finally, work group norms can develop that will restrict the productivity of any one individual. Employees may worry that high earnings under the PFP system will result in an adjustment of the standard. Also, some workers may worry that high productivity may ultimately translate into layoffs or terminations if inventories get too large.

Some banks have piece-rate systems for data entry jobs in which individuals entering check amounts have virtually no interaction with coworkers: workers control the rate of data entry, and the computer tallies the rate of production. One bank reported a 30 percent increase in production after installing a piece-rate system for data entry personnel.[35] Many telephone reservationists, whose performance is closely monitored by computer, are also paid by piece rate. Many of the reservation services left the United States because lower rates can be set on foreign soil. When you call American Airlines, for example, you may be talking to an agent working in the Bahamas.

The adversarial relationship that quickly develops between workers and management can be reduced or eliminated if workers participate in the rate-setting process through task forces. Says one expert, "If they do not involve employees, there is a good chance that the employees will find a way to get involved—for example, by organizing a union."[36]

STANDARD HOURLY RATES. Standard hourly rates differ from piece-rate systems in that the production standard is expressed in time units. Using job analysis, the standard time for a given task is established and the organization then sets a fair hourly wage rate. The standard rate for any task is the wage rate times the standard. For example, if the standard time for a task is four hours and the fair hourly wage is $10, the standard rate is $40. The worker receives the $40 standard rate of pay regardless of the length of time it takes to complete the task. A common example is auto body repair. A customer is given an estimate based on a standards book listing the time required to repair various parts of a car and the hourly wage rate. Insurance companies use a similar book to check the accuracy of the estimate.

In some standard hourly plans, the rate varies with output. For example, the **Halsey plan**,[37] developed in 1891 by Frederick Halsey, divided between employer and worker the savings realized from performing a task in less than the standard time. Halsey believed that sharing the rewards with management would reduce the likelihood that management would increase the standard as worker output increased. Although Halsey proposed a one-third worker and two-thirds organization split, today his plan is more commonly known as the **Halsey 50-50 plan,** because savings are equally divided.

DECLINE TO CONTINUE. When managers are considering an incentive system, they must take into account the firm's organizational strategy, culture, and position in the marketplace. Incentive plans in manufacturing are advisable if there are (1) high labor costs, (2) a high level of cost competition in the marketplace, (3) relatively slow advances in technology, and (4) a high level of trust and cooperation between labor and management.[38]

The loss of jobs conducive to individual incentive systems, particularly the manufacturing sector, combined with the trend toward more team-based work systems indicate that the decline in individual incentive systems based on rates of production will continue.

Sales Incentive Plans

Performance-based incentive plans have been found to increase sales over time.[39] Sales incentive plans share many of the characteristics of individual incentive plans, but there are also unique requirements. Both the determinants of employee control over output and the measurability of performance have added dimensions for sales. Because an output measure can be easily established as the level of sales, in dollars or units, a common assumption is that salespeople are paid strictly on the volume of product sold. In many cases, however, employers expect salespeople to perform duties beyond strictly sales. Like any PFP system for a job with many important performance dimensions, if sales duties include customer training, market analysis, and credit checks, then the PFP system should involve complex measures of performance that include these dimensions along with sales data. Thus, a critical first step for a sales incentive program, as for all other incentive programs, is to determine what aspects of performance are most important to the firm. The next step is to decide on the methods of measurement and the appropriate levels of compensation. To motivate employees to increase customer satisfaction, many companies now incorporate client- or customer-based survey results into their sales compensation systems to underscore the need for nurturing customer relations as well as selling products and services.[40]

Approximately 75 percent of salespeople are on an incentive plan.[41] **Commission plans** pay the salesperson directly on sales data. Although simple in concept, commissions can become complex. Ordinarily, commissions are a percentage of the dollar value of sales. However, the percentage can increase, decrease, or be constant in relation to changes in sales volume, depending on the nature of the product and its market. Commissions should provide sufficient incentive to the salesperson without adding too much to product cost.

Because commissions can be highly variable over time, some firms protect salespeople from low sales periods by using a **draw-plus commission system.** At JCPenney, for example, a salesperson can draw against an account up to a predetermined limit during slack periods. During periods of higher commissions, the draw account is repaid from commissions in excess of the draw limit. A draw is essentially an interest-free loan to the salesperson, repayable when commissions exceed the draw limit.

Another common sales incentive plan uses commissions in conjunction with a salary. The base salary serves as a guaranteed minimum wage, and the commissions are an incentive to sell. Inclusion of salary as part of compensation is useful when the firm requires the salesperson to perform activities other than sales.

Many variations of sales compensation exist. Bonuses for a specific product and bonuses for sales levels are common. In each case, the reward should be tied to a specific performance that is of value to the firm and that justifies the additional expense.

Sales incentive programs may have equity problems that differ from a manufacturing situation. Operators of similar machines face the same workplace challenge, but salespeople with different territories may experience different levels of opportunity and challenge. Most companies now have databases that enable them to establish and sustain a fair sales incentive program through the maintenance of the sales history of particular territories. For example, Steelcase offers greater incentives for new business in low-volume territories where analysis indicates greater competition.

Many companies now offer rewards other than money as recognition for sales performance. Trips and prizes, which can be purchased by the company at a price considerably less than the cost of cash-only incentive programs, are common as a form of sales commission today, particularly in insurance, real estate, and the tourism industry.

GROUP INCENTIVE PLANS

There are three major types of group-based incentive plans: **profit sharing, gain sharing,** and **employee stock ownership plans (ESOPs).** Profit sharing distributes a portion of corporate profits among designated employees. Gain sharing divides a portion of cost reductions or productivity increases between groups covered by the plan. ESOPs distribute stocks and stock options to employees based on corporate performance measures such as return on equity.

All three types are designed to establish a link between pay and performance, but performance is measured at the group, unit, or company level. Many PFP systems combine individual PFP systems with some form of group incentives. Recall the discussion of Lincoln Electric, which combines the piece-rate method with profit sharing for all employees. In general, as expectancy theory would predict, group-based systems are at least theoretically less motivating because individual employees typically do not perceive a strong connection between their efforts and performance.

All three of the group plans have increased in the past few years, and the majority of gainsharing plans in the United States were introduced in the past 15 years. Changes in the federal tax code have made ESOPs more attractive since the 1970s. Manufacturing organizations are more likely to adopt group plans than are service-oriented firms. Group plans are generally preferable to individual plans under the increasingly popular team-based approaches to production or service we discuss in Chapter 12, although this depends principally on the ability to sort out individual contributions to important outcomes.

Successful group incentive plans require the same determinants as individual plans. The measures differ in that a group plan must be based on a measure of group performance or productivity. The use of group plans is particularly effective when cooperation and teamwork are essential and when a goal of the system is to enhance the feeling of participation. Group plans are most useful when tasks are so interrelated that it is difficult (or impossible) to identify a measure of individual output. The size of the group can range from two people to plantwide or companywide. The smaller the group, the more a worker will identify individual effort as affecting group performance.

Group PFP plans require special considerations. First, there is potential for conflict when all group members receive the same reward regardless of individual input. Second, strong group norms that control output can inhibit group efforts. Third, the variable compensation distribution formula must meet the Fair Labor Standards Act requirements for calculating overtime pay.[42] However, there is increasing evidence that group incentives increase productivity.[43]

Profit Sharing

Profit sharing is designed to motivate cost savings by allowing workers to share in increased profits. As we discussed in Chapter 10, retirement income for employees is frequently linked to a profit-sharing plan. Rewards can be periodic cash disbursements or deposits to an employee account. Either a predetermined percentage of profit or a percentage above a certain threshold is allocated to a pool (e.g., 10 to 25 percent). This pool is disbursed to employees on the basis of some ratio, usually related to their wage. Most companies now have options from which the employee may select a particular profit-sharing plan compatible with his or her long-range plans.[44]

Profit sharing has been criticized as being remote and perceptually unrelated to individual performance, but research indicates that it produces generally positive results.[45] Many firms also use profit sharing as a tool to control employee turnover. At Johnson & Johnson, the allocation is distributed in equal increments over a period of years, and an employee sacrifices remaining distributions by leaving the firm before the period is up. Obviously, some of the incentive value of profit sharing for higher performance is lost when it is used in this fashion. In general, profit sharing works best as an incentive when the group size is small enough that employees believe they have some impact on group profitability.

While employees generally approve of profit sharing, they get testy when their base pay is affected in a negative way by profit-sharing provisions. When DuPont Corporation announced there would be 4 percent cuts in the base pay of all its 20,000 employees due to poor sales in the fibers division, worker dissatisfaction was so high that the profit-sharing plan was scrapped. If the company was profitable, workers would have earned an additional 12 percent above their base pay under the plan. The major reason for the dissatisfaction with the system was the lack of perceived connection between worker performance and company profits. UAW workers at Caterpillar struck the company partially because they wanted an increase in base salary and a decrease in the risk of the profit-sharing plan. One UAW contract for the 4,700 Saturn workers scaled back the profit-sharing component of the innovative wage accord. Poor sales at Saturn had a great deal to do with the union's position.

Gain Sharing

As team performance becomes increasingly important in our society, gain sharing is becoming a popular approach to motivate higher levels of group productivity. While there are subtle differences among various PFP programs classified as gain sharing, all of them essentially deal with worker involvement and the process of sharing in the financial benefits of reducing costs or increasing productivity. One survey found that gain sharing is the second most important topic among human resource managers.[46] More gain sharing plans were instituted in the mid-1980s than in the previous 50 years,[47] and almost 40 percent of *Fortune* 1000 firms rely on some form of gain sharing.[48]

Gain sharing plans either try to reduce the amount of labor required for a given level of output (cost saving) or increase the output for a given amount of labor (productivity increase). The method for determining the standard production rate and the incentive rate must be clearly defined. Gain sharing plans generally are based on the assumption that better cooperation among workers and between workers and managers will result in greater effectiveness. Successful plans require an organizational climate characterized by trust across organizational levels, worker participation, and cooperative unions. An organized employee suggestion system is also characteristic of almost all gain sharing plans. To maximize cost saving and productivity increases, there must be employee involvement in the plan development and execution. A successful gain sharing plan requires workers and management to work toward a common goal. Gain sharing encounters difficulty when management downgrades employee input or unions adopt a strong adversarial position.

Gain sharing plans can get complicated. Measures of productivity can be (and often are) adapted to particular situations. For example, one firm uses both the labor/sales ratio and the cost-of-quality/sales ratio as financial measures. Another firm uses savings on warranty costs as a measure for its engineers and designers. As one expert puts it, "The financial measures of performance have great educational value in spurring employee understanding of business fundamentals . . . financial measures tend to closely parallel overall firm performance."[49]

All types of gain sharing plans use a productivity ratio to capture labor's contribution to value added. The differences among them tie in how labor's cost is calculated for the numerator and how organizational output is measured for the denominator.

Gain sharing plans are different from profit sharing in two major ways: (1) Gain sharing is based on a measure of productivity, not profit, and (2) Gain sharing rewards are given out frequently, whereas profit sharing is annual and usually tied to a retirement plan as deferred payment.

FOUR APPROACHES TO GAIN SHARING. There are four basic approaches to gain sharing, although there is considerable variation within these categories. The four approaches are the Scanlon plan, the Rucker plan, the improshare plan, and Winsharing. In addition to the productivity ratio, other issues influence the selection of a gainsharing plan. The most important aspect of a PFP system, strength of reinforcement, is roughly equal for the four methods. A summary of the issues to be considered in selecting a plan is provided in Figure 11.4.

The **Scanlon plan,** the most common gain sharing plan, measures the relationship between the sales value of production and labor costs. Like all gain sharing options, employee participation is an important component of this approach. Screening committees are used to evaluate cost-saving suggestions from employees with labor cost savings serving as the incentive. Savings are measured by a monthly calculation of the ratio of payroll to sales value of production compared to baseline data.

The Scanlon plan is the oldest form of gain sharing.[50] Developed by Joseph Scanlon, a steelworker, a union official, and later a professor at the Massachusetts Institute of Technology, the plan was originally devised to keep the La Pointe Steel Company from going bankrupt. The plan received wide public attention because of a *Life* magazine article published in 1946. At the time, its unique aspects were: (1) rewarding the group for suggestions by individuals in the group; (2) joint

FIGURE 11.4
FACTORS TO CONSIDER IN DESIGNING A GAIN SHARING PROGRAM

1. **Performance and financial measures.** The bonus formula must be perceived as reasonable, accurate, and equitable.

2. **Plant or facility size.** Plants with fewer than 500 employees are ideally suited to gain sharing, while plants with over 2,000 employees are not.

3. **Types of production.** Plants with highly mixed types of production will find it difficult to introduce gain sharing because the measurement process is so complicated.

4. **Workforce interdependence.** Highly integrated work units are ideal for gain sharing.

5. **Workforce composition.** Some workforces may not be as motivated by financial incentives.

6. **Potential to absorb additional output.** Initial increase in productivity must be useful to the organization and must not entail negative consequences for the workforce (e.g., layoffs).

7. **Potential for employee efforts.** Can employee efforts actually affect productivity to a significant extent, or does automation (or other factors) impede worker effects?

8. **Present organizational climate.** An initial level of trust is required.

9. **Union-management relations.** Union should be an active partner in program development.

10. **Capital investment plans.** Don't install gain sharing if large capital investments are planned.

Source: Adapted from M. Schuster, Gain sharing: Do it right the first time. *Sloan Management Review,* Winter 1987, pp. 17–25.

labor–management committees designed to propose and evaluate labor-saving suggestions; and (3) a worker reward share based on reduced costs, not increased profits.

Scanlon plans require a considerable commitment by workers and management to cooperate in the development and maintenance of the program. While the track record for Scanlon plans is mixed, there are some great success stories. One paint manufacturer in Texas reported a 78 percent increase in production over its 17-year history of using a Scanlon plan.[51] The key seems to be employee trust, understanding, and contributions to improvements. For example, a Levi Strauss executive from the Blue Ridge, Georgia, plant described its highly successful Scanlon plan this way: "a formal method for having all organizational members contribute ingenuity and brainpower to the improvement of organizational performance . . . and improvement of relations across functional groups and levels of the organizational hierarchy."[52]

The **Rucker plan** is another successful group incentive system. While similar to Scanlon, the Rucker formula includes the value of all supplies, materials, and services. The result is a bonus formula based on the value added to the product per labor dollar. Thus, an incentive is created to save on all inputs, including materials and supplies. The advantage of Rucker over Scanlon is the linkage of rewards to savings other than labor savings, plus greater flexibility. The disadvantage is that concepts such as value added and the adjustments for inflation make the Rucker plan more difficult to understand and explain compared to the Scanlon plan.

A third category of gain sharing is **improshare,** which stands for "improved productivity through sharing."[53] Improshare is similar to Scanlon except that the improshare ratio uses standard hours rather than labor costs. Engineering studies or past performance data are used to specify the standard number of hours required to produce a base production level. Savings in hours result in reward allocation to workers. Improshare "rewards all covered employees equally whenever the actual number of labor hours used to produce output in the current week or month is less than the estimated number it would have taken to produce the current level of output in the base period."[54]

Winsharing combines gain sharing with profit sharing.[55] Winsharing is based on the rational proposition that if the PFP system results in more product being produced than can be sold, the PFP system needs some alterations. Winsharing considers market demand. Winsharing payouts are based on whether group performance is achieved relative to business goals. Financial performance in excess of the goals is split evenly between workers and the company. Winsharing differs from profit sharing because group performance measures are used that are independent of profit measures. Whirlpool in Benton Harbor, Michigan, has been operating on a winsharing program since 1988 with a productivity gain of 19 percent since it began using the system.[56]

THE BOTTOM LINE ON GAIN SHARING. Research has found numerous benefits from gain sharing plans, including improved productivity and quality.[57] Kendall-Futuro, a health care products company, improved both TQM and JIT performance with gain sharing. The Volvo-GM plant at Orrville, Ohio, completed its fifth year of TQM implementation through gain sharing in 1997.[58] It reports strong success so far. Other major companies offering gain sharing plans include Georgia Pacific, Huffy Bicycle, Inland Container, Eaton Corp., TRW, and General Electric.[59] Gain sharing is evolving from a simple productivity concept into a family of measures all designed to improve performance.[60] Whirlpool instituted such a family, which featured gain sharing. The board of directors receives stock options when targets are met. Senior managers can receive up to 100 percent of base salary as annual stock options. Whirlpool eliminated profit sharing and instituted at the plant level a winsharing plan that increased worker performance as well as knowledge about shareholder value.[61]

Success of gain sharing plans in general depends on significant involvement and support by high-level management, actual employee participation, and realistic employee and (if applicable) union expectations.[62] Companies that are reluctant to involve unions in strategic planning will also have difficulty with gain sharing programs.[63]

Employee Stock Ownership Plans

Whether it is to provide incentives for productivity reasons, to generate sources of cash, to ward off corporate raiders, or to reduce tax liability, employee stock ownership plans (ESOPs) are becoming more common. Like numerous European companies, many of our nation's largest companies have ESOPs (e.g., Anheuser-Busch, Lockheed, JCPenney, Texaco, Procter & Gamble, Avis, Polaroid).[64] By 1996 another 2,000 firms had added stock plans.[65] Since Congress passed the first ESOP bills in the 1970s, over 20,000 companies with more than 10 million workers have established ESOPs.

In principle, ESOPs sound like a terrific idea: companies sell stock to workers to give them a financial stake in the company. Stock allocations are made to the employee's account based on relative base pay. Constant revision of the tax code has led to other names for ESOPs, such as TRASOPs from the Tax Revision Act of 1976 and PAYSOPs from the Economic Recovery Act of 1981.[66]

Research results on the effects of ESOPs are ambiguous. A recent review concluded that "few of the studies have found strong and significant effects."[67] However, ESOPs tend to work better when combined with extensive employee involvement and problem solving. A popular method designed to replace fixed compensation costs with variable wages and benefits, ESOPs give the organization greater flexibility in response to a competitive environment. Santa Fe Railway reduced employee pay in 1990 for the first time in the company's 122-year history. The pay cuts were replaced with stock options, which resulted in bonus checks for all 2,400 salaried employees in 1992. Some employees received checks in excess of $100,000. Needless to say, Santa Fe Railway employees are now very happy with the new incentive system. Behlen Manufacturing has had great success in using a blend of base pay, gain sharing, profit sharing, and ESOPs to support its organizational goals.[68] There are also some sad stories indicating ESOPs are no panacea. At Burlington Industries, employees bought out the company only to watch the stock plummet to less than half its purchase value.

MANAGERIAL AND EXECUTIVE INCENTIVE PAY

As we discussed in Chapter 10, executive pay, particularly for CEOs, keeps going up and up.[69] Correlational research generally supports the use of long-term reward systems for executives that are directly tied to the long-term strategic goals of the firm. Incentives for managers and executives can have a significant impact on the fortunes of an organization.[70] In general, executive incentive plans are linked either to net income, some measure of return on investment, or total dividends paid. These incentives are paid in the form of bonuses not permanently tied to base pay. CEOs often receive almost 50 percent of their compensation from this type of plan. But while corporate revenues and profits have soared in recent years, CEO pay actually increased at a much faster rate. Tax-deductible pay for senior executives rose 182 percent from 1980 to 1995 while corporate revenues rose 129 percent and profits rose 127 percent.[71]

Incentive plans can raise total pay to astronomical levels. In 1996, average CEO pay and bonuses rose 21 percent from 1995 to $1,923,500, clearly above the 15 percent gain in corporate profits.[72] Adding long-term options, however, raised average pay to $3,746,392—a whopping 30 percent increase. Between 1990 and 1995, CEO pay has increased 92 percent; profits, 75 percent; and worker pay, 16 percent—while worker layoffs increased 39 percent. Another disturbing fact: CEOs of the 20 firms with the highest number of layoffs averaged 25 percent pay increases. (Other than hiring consultants to recommend a certain level of downsizing, what do these executives do to earn such compensation?)

According to one 1996 survey, among the executives with the highest pay, including salary, bonuses, and long-term payouts, were Lawrence Coss of Green Tree Financial ($65 million) and Sanford Weill of Travelers Group ($50 million). Sanford Weill received $67 million in 1992 as CEO of Primerica.[73] Roberto Goizueta of Coca-Cola received over $2 million in base pay and has earned over $100 million since 1990. He has also accumulated $400 million in stock options; receiving another $25 million worth in 1995 alone. In 1993, Michael Eisner executed options on 5.4 million shares of Disney stock for a take-home prize of $202.3 million. We could fill this chapter with other illustrations of what could be termed the megalomania that is executive pay.

CEOs in Canada, Europe, and Japan earn less than half of what U.S. CEOs make. U.S. CEO pay seems to be primarily driven by what other U.S. CEOs make, no matter how absurd. While there has been much political discussion of the absurdity of CEO pay and the U.S. Congress passed a bill in 1993 to require certain conditions in order to make the CEO pay package tax deductible, the legislation and political discourse have done little to curtail this disturbing trend, which is almost impossible to reconcile with the constant concern over international competition.[74] While CEOs obviously deserve some credit (and pay) for the improvement in the U.S. economy in the late 90s, to take such a large slice of the pie while preaching global competition and the need for austerity invites cynicism and political reaction.

Consequences of Widening Pay Dispersion

While there has been considerable writing about the negative consequences of the widening gap between CEO pay and the pay of others, no research has shown any relationship between this dispersion and subsequent performance decrements or higher turnover among employees.

The problem of pay dispersion may be most acute in more technologically intensive industries where executives are encouraged to be entrepreneurially aggressive and they are often compensated very well based on their performance. However, intensive teamwork and coordination is often required in the development of high-tech products or services, indicating the need for a PFP system with a team or corporate-level orientation. A 1997 study found that pay dispersion in high-tech firms is predictive of subsequent performance decrements.[75] Pay dispersion tends to diminish communication, increase status gaps, and foster aggressive competition for advancement to lucrative top posts within a company. The same effect was found for low-technology firms but the effect was not as profound. We believe this is the first evidence to clearly document the deleterious effects of exorbitant CEO pay.

Short- or Long-Term Measures of Performance

A principal distinction between managerial and executive incentives is the time horizon of the performance measure that is the basis of the incentive. Although more lower-level managers are being awarded stock options, they typically have incentives based on short-term measures. Top executives have both short- and long-term performance incentives.

Managers and executives have a wider area of discretion in making decisions that affect the firm. As a consequence, the PFP system is designed to reinforce a sense of commitment to the organization. Most managers receive bonuses related to profit. The amount is usually awarded as a percentage of their base pay, although there is a trend toward awarding lump sums not tied to the base pay. As higher profitability thresholds are attained, the manager receives bigger bonuses. The bonus structure for any given manager often depends on the relative contributions of all managers, with the assessment of relative contribution made at a higher level. This method suffers from the drawbacks discussed previously regarding profit sharing for individuals. Many managers might feel that they have a negligible impact on organization profits. As the link between performance and pay becomes weaker, the reward loses incentive value. The link can be strengthened by clearly defining performance standards, while basing the amount of the reward on corporate profitability.

Executives and their boards should be concerned with the long-term viability of the firm. There are many situations in which a decision can have a conflicting impact on a firm's short- and long-run profitability. Investing in research and development will depress short-term profit but should lead to maintenance of a long-run competitive position. Cutting back on services provided may add to short-run profits but damage market share in the long run.

Long-term rewards focus on future profitability. The most popular approach is based on appreciation of stock value using various stock purchase plans.[76] Almost 100 percent of the 500 largest industrials had stock option plans in 1995, up from 52 percent in 1974.[77] A stock option plan gives an executive the right to purchase a stock, over a specified period, at a fixed price. The theory is that if the executive is prudent and hardworking, the stock price will go up. If the stock price does increase, the executive can purchase it at the lower fixed price, effectively receiving as a bonus the difference between the fixed purchase price and the higher market price. Congress periodically revises legislation controlling the awarding of stock options. These limitations have typically affected only options exceeding $100,000 per year.

There are many variations on stock options. *Stock appreciation rights* (SARs), for example, do not involve buying stock. Having been awarded rights to a stock at a fixed price for a specified period, the executive can call the option and receive the difference between the fixed and market prices in cash. *Restricted stock plans* give shares as a bonus, but with restrictions.[78] The restrictions may be that the executive cannot leave the company or sell the stock for a specified time. *Performance share plans* award units based on both short- and long-term measures. These units are later translated into stock awards. Other incentive stock option plans are part of executive retirement packages. These may include profit-sharing and stock bonus plans. In both cases, employers pay into a retirement fund based on corporate profits. Recent evidence suggests that stock incentives may not be effective.[79]

In addition to stock awards, executive incentives of the future are likely to be tied to long-term corporate performance, which may involve qualitative assessment of performance along with corporate financial performance. New products and service lines, environmental impact assessments, and new territorial penetration are some of the long-range measures that may be used to assess executive performance. For example, McDonald's, Burger King, and General Electric place considerable weight on their long-term growth in the European sector as a basis for compensating senior management. The trend in executive compensation is against heavy reliance on stock prices as a basis for compensating executives because such reliance would promote short-term perspectives to the detriment of the long-term strategic plan of the organization.

Paying the Board of Directors

What about the corporate boardroom? How should directors be paid? Sunbeam's Al Dunlap calls corporate boards "America's last dirty little secret."[80] They have very lucrative and comprehensive compensation packages that are rarely linked to corporate performance. Dunlap says directors should be paid *only* in stock in the companies on whose boards they sit. "If they are unwilling to own stock, what message does that send to the shareholders?" At Sunbeam, board members had to first buy 1,000 shares in the first year and then were awarded 1,000 shares on an annual basis. They received no base salary and no fancy perks. Dunlap's recommendations are supported by research. One study found companies with outside directors who owned substantial stock holdings were less likely to overpay the CEO and, more importantly, reported superior corporate performance.[81]

KEEPING ENTREPRENEURS AND PROMOTING INTRAPRENEURS

With the current competitive pressures and the opportunities for launching new businesses, many companies are attempting to retain entrepreneurial mavericks within the corporate umbrella and promote intrapreneurial thinking.[82] For example, many high-tech firms are funding employee ventures through innovative compensation schemes. At IBM, employees can submit business plans for IBM risk capital. Employees can negotiate a share of the profits from an idea that they may have otherwise pursued on the outside.[83] When Personnel Assessment Systems (PAS), a small psychological testing company, decided to launch its personality test to the mass market, it developed special entrepreneurial pay packages for a psychologist who knew the most about vocational testing and a marketing specialist with expertise in direct marketing. The pay package provided a 20 percent commission on all future profits from the business that could be developed as part of the normal work assignment.

The basic principle of entrepreneurial pay is that the employee places a major portion of salary at risk, with the percentage of employee ownership of the venture determined by the portion of salary at risk. For example, at PAS, the psychologist's base pay was reduced by 20 percent in exchange for his potential profit from the new venture.

The potential for large returns replaces many of the standard perks expected by employees. Payoffs may have a variety of bases, from profits produced by the venture to increases in parent company stock value. Although such payoffs may be less than if the venture were truly independent, the risk for the venture employee is also more limited. In addition, the parent can provide support and expertise. AT&T, for example, wanted to increase the risk its people were willing to take in entrepreneurial efforts. Three venture approaches were offered, corresponding to the levels of risk the venture employee was willing to take.

Many companies have adopted special award programs for major accomplishments. Microsoft, IBM, Amoco, Xerox, and Bell South, for example, have programs in which the awards can exceed $100,000 for R&D discoveries. American Express has $5,000 awards for "exceptional performers." These special programs are independent of any other PFP systems within the company.

MANAGERIAL IMPLICATIONS OF PFP PROGRAMS

A well-designed PFP system should lead to lower costs, higher profits, and a higher degree of individual or group motivation, which thus requires less supervision. Introduction of a well-designed PFP system can provide a more accurate estimate of labor costs as well as prompt workers to make more effective use of their time, supplies, and equipment. Using a mix of plans often has the best results. These same general principles apply to both large and small businesses.

PFP systems are more complicated than lock-step, straight compensation. Numerous challenges must be met. Emphasizing one measure can lead to reduced performance levels in other measures. A strong focus on output or quantity can reduce quality, which could lead to increased costs in quality control. In addition, a focus on output could jeopardize safety. A PFP system should reward all important dimensions of performance. An overemphasis on one dimension or one aspect of value, such as quantity, will result in a deemphasis on other aspects, such as quality.

A second challenge is the increased overhead expense of installing and maintaining the PFP system. Unless the production process is very stable, maintenance costs for PFP systems can be substantial and PFP consultants are very expensive. A third challenge is the difficulty in setting standards that accurately reflect task requirements and are perceived as fair. This problem can be greater when a system adds new processes or equipment because workers will be suspicious of new standards. A fourth challenge is that there will be resistance to any change involving employee compensation, particularly when base pay is affected. Unions have been born out of attempts to radically alter compensation systems. In addition to the typical fear of anything new, workers may oppose change to avoid being victimized by new rates and standards. The final challenge is that PFP systems are more likely than straight compensation plans to be subject to legal actions for possible discrimination.

Management may resist change because of the expense of revising the pay system, the time required to do more valid performance appraisals, and the difficulties that develop in defending PFP decisions. Finally, variations in pay due to performance differences may lead to conflict, a big potential problem in a team- or process-oriented work setting focused on the external customer. When measures are explicit and objective, some conflict will occur. When methods are subjective or ambiguous, as with the typical performance-appraisal system, significant reward differences may not be perceived as justified, resulting in even greater conflict.

SUMMARY

The PFP system must support the competitive strategy and values of the organization. If the strategy emphasizes entrepreneurial activity and independent effort, individual PFP systems become increasingly important and effective. Incentive systems must be compatible with organizational values. Closed, secretive cultures do not mix well with performance incentives. Openness and trust is necessary if employees are to accept the standards and believe in the equity of the rewards. Lincoln Electric's much touted piece-rate system would probably not be successful without the other elements of Lincoln management, a system based on mutual trust and a fair distribution of the products of hard work. Organizational culture clearly affects the nature of incentives selected and, in the end, the effectiveness of the system. Individual PFP plans are preferable when individuals contribute important criteria that can be clearly measured and teamwork is not seriously undermined by individual performance measurement and rewards. Highly interdependent jobs or groups will dictate group or organizational-based PFP plans.

As one expert on the subject has put it, "Paying for performance will not solve all of the motivational problems associated with the new workforce and strong national competition. However, it can be an important part of a total performance management system that is designed to create a highly motivating work environment."[84] Following the measurement principles we presented in Chapter 9 for defining performance is a critical step in linking performance appraisal, performance management, and pay for performance.

The bottom line remains that for any PFP system to work, rewards valued by the worker must be clearly linked to outcomes valued by internal and, most important, external customers.[85] Virtually all of the "best practices" literature supports the view that proper PFP systems can help to create and sustain a competitive advantage. The evidence supports the value of carefully designed PFP systems. When the focus is on organizations that follow academic guidelines for development and maintenance, PFP systems look like a winner.

Chapter 12 will turn to other HRM systems and HRM interventions that can contribute to the productivity and the competitive advantage of the organization.

DISCUSSION QUESTIONS

1. Deming and others think PFP is a bad idea. What do you think?

2. Why is trust so important for PFP systems?

3. When is a group-based PFP system better than an individual system?

4. Al Dunlap believes that a corporation's board of directors should be paid only with stock options. What do you think?

5. How would you combine individual and group-based PFP systems?

6. Some experts believe that if you have to use performance appraisals as the main source of data for a PFP system, you shouldn't bother with the PFP system. What do you think?

NOTES

1. Kanter, Rosabeth Moss (1989). *When giants learn to dance.* New York: Simon & Schuster, p. 232; see also, Heneman, R. (1992). *Merit pay.* Reading, MA: Addison-Wesley; Martocchio, J. J. (1998). *Strategic compensation.* Upper Saddle River, NJ: Prentice-Hall.

2. Becker, B. E.; Huselid, M. A.; Pickus, P. S.; and Spratt, M. F. (1997). HR as a source of shareholder value: Research and recommendations. *Human Resource Management, 36,* 39–47; see also, McDonald, D., and Smith, A. (January/February 1995). A proven connection: Performance management and business results. *Compensation and Benefits Review,* pp. 59–64.

3. Cummings, C. M. (May–June 1994) Incentives that really do motivate. *Compensation and Benefits Review,* pp. 38–40. See also, Rubino, J. A. (January–February 1995). Achieving true "pay for performance": A comprehensive approach. *Journal of Compensation and Benefits, 10*(4), 38–43; Schmid, R. O. (July 1994). Structuring gain sharing for success. *Industrial Engineering, 26*(7), 62–66; Schuster, M. H.; Schuster, J. M.; Montague, M. K. (1992). Excellence in gain sharing: From start to renewal. *Journal for Quality and Participation, 17*(3), 18–26; and McGrath, T. C. (May 1994). Tapping the groove in human productivity. *Industrial Engineering, 26*(5), 16–19.

4. Collins, D. (Summer 1995). Death of a gain sharing plan: power politics and participatory management. *Organizational Dynamics, 24*(1), 23–38. See also, Lawler, E. E., III, and Cohen, S. G. (1992). Designing a pay system for teams. *American Compensation Association Journal, 1*(1), 6–19.

5. Murphy, K. (June 13, 1994). Quoted in Fierman, J. The perilous new world of fair pay. *Fortune*, p. 58.

6. Pfeffer, J. (1994). *HR for competitive advantage*. Boston: Harvard Business Press; see also, Lawler, E. E. (1990). *Strategic pay*. San Francisco: Jossey-Bass.

7. Hay and Associates (1996). Annual survey of pay policy in Fortune 1000 companies.

8. Crystal, G. (1996). *Annual report of CEO pay*. San Diego, CA: G. Crystal and Associates; Labor Letter (Sept. 24, 1991). *The Wall Street Journal*, p. 1; see also, The Conference Board (1990). *Variable pay: New performance rewards*. Research Bulletin No. 246. New York: The Conference Board.

9. See note 3.

10. Milkovich, G. T., and Wigdor, A. K. (1991). *Pay for performance*. Washington: National Academy Press, p. 4; see also, Heneman, R. L. (1992). *Merit pay*. Boston: Addison-Wesley.

11. Heneman, R. L. (May–June 1995). Survey of merit pay systems. *Compensation and Benefits Review*, pp. 41–44.

12. See note 2; see also, Gerhart, B., and Milkovich, G. T. (1992). Employee compensation: Research and practice. In M. D. Dunnette and L. M. Hough (eds.), *Handbook of Industrial and Organizational Psychology*, 2nd ed., vol. 3. Palo Alto, CA: Consulting Psychologists Press, pp. 481–496.

13. Kahn, A. (September–October 1993). Why incentive plans cannot work. *Harvard Business Review*, pp. 54–63; see also, Bassett, G. (January/February 1996). Merit pay increases are a mistake. *Compensation and Benefits Review*, pp. 20–22.

14. See note 5.

15. Labor Letter (Dec. 5, 1989). *The Wall Street Journal*, p. 1. See also, Wright, P. (May–June 1994). Goal setting and monetary incentives: Motivational tools that can work too well. *Compensation and Benefits Review*, pp. 41–49.

16. Geis, A. A. (January 1987). Making merit pay work. *Personnel*, pp. 52–60. See also, Heneman, R. L. (1990). Merit pay research. *Research in Personnel and Human Resource Management*, 8, 203–263; Heneman, R. L.; Greenberger, D. B.; and Strasser, S. (1988). The relationship between pay-for-performance perceptions and pay satisfaction. *Personnel Psychology*, 41, 745–759; Markham, S. E. (1988). Pay-for-performance dilemma revisited: Empirical example of the importance of group effects. *Journal of Applied Psychology*, 73, 172–180; Schwab, D. P., and Olson, C. A. (1990). Merit pay practices: Implications for pay-performance relationships. *Industrial and Labor Relations Review*, 43, 237–255; and Scott, W. E., Jr.; Farh, J.; and Podsakoff, P. M. (1988). The effects of intrinsic and extrinsic reinforcement contingencies on task behavior. *Organization Behavior and Human Decision Processes*, 41, 405–425.

17. Bernardin, H. J. (1992). An 'analytic' framework for customer-based performance content development and appraisal. *Human Resource Management Review*, 2, 81–102.

18. Lawler, E. E. (1984). *Pay for performance: A motivational analysis*. University of Southern California Report, G84-9(57), p. 12. See also, Wagner, J. A., III; Rubin, P.; and Callahan, T. J. (1988). Incentive payment and non-managerial productivity: An interrupted time series analysis of magnitude and trend. *Organizational Behavior and Human Decision Processes*, 42, 47–74.

19. See note 1, Martocchio (1998).

20. Bernardin, H. J., and Villanova, P. J. (1986). Performance appraisal. In E. Locke (ed.), *Generalizing from laboratory to field research*. Boston: D. C. Heath.

21. Tully, S. (Nov. 1, 1993). Your paychecks gets exciting. *Fortune*, p. 83.

22. Kay, I. (Aug. 9, 1990). Quoted in Labor Letter, *The Wall Street Journal*, p. 1.

23. Kanter, R. M. (January 1987). From status to contribution implications of the changing basis for pay. *Personnel*, pp. 12–24. See also, Konrad, A. M., and Pfeffer, J. (1990). Do you get what you deserve? Factors affecting the relationship between productivity and pay. *Administrative Science Quarterly*, 35, 258–285.

24. See note 1, Martocchio (1998)

25. See note 1, Martocchio (1998). See also, Folger, R., and Konovsky, M. A. (1989). Effects of procedural and distributive justice on reactions to pay raise decisions. *Academy of Management Journal*, 30, 115–130.

26. See note 1 (Heneman, 1992).

27. Sauner, A. M., and Hawk, E. J. (July–August 1994). Realizing the potential of teams through team-based rewards. *Compensation and Benefits*, pp. 24–33; see also, Wageman, R. (March 1995). Interdependence and group effectiveness. *Administrative Science Quarterly*, 40(1), 145–180; Wright, P. M. (May/June 1994). Goal setting and monetary incentives: Motivational tools that can work too well. *Compensation & Benefits Review*, pp. 41–49; Zingheim, P. K., and Schuster, J. R. (November/December 1995). First findings: The team pay research study. *Compensation and Benefits Review*, pp. 6–32.

28. Ledford, G. E.; Lawler, E. E.; and Mohrman, S. A. (January–February 1995). Reward innovations in Fortune 1000 companies. *Compensation and Benefits Review*, 27, 76–80; see also, DeMatteo, J. S., and Eby, L. T. (August 1997). Who likes team rewards? An examination of individual difference variables related to satisfaction with team-based rewards. *Best papers proceedings*. Boston: Academy of Management, pp. 134–138.

29. See note 28, DeMatteo and Eby (1997).

30. See note 1, Heneman (1992); see also, Kahn, L. M., and Sherer, P. D. (1990). Contingent pay and managerial performance. *Industrial and Labor Relations Review*, 43, 107S–120S, and Pearce, J. L.; Stevenson, W. B.; and Perry, J. L. (1985). Managerial compensation based on organization performance: A time series analysis of the effects of merit pay. *Academy of Management Journal*, 28, 261–278.

31. Kane, J. S.; Bernardin, H. J.; Villanova, P.; and Peyrefitte, J. (1995). The stability of leniency: Three studies. *Academy of Management Journal*, 38, 1036–1051; see also,

Bernardin, H. J.; Cooke, D.; Villanova, P.; and Gagne, J. (April 1997). *The big-five as predictors of rating leniency.* Paper presented at the annual meeting of the American Psychological Society, Washington, DC.

32. Banker, R. D.; Lee, S.; Potter, G.; and Srinivasan, D. (1996). Contextual analysis of performance impacts of outcome-based incentive compensation. *Academy of Management Journal, 39*(4), 920–948.

33. Taylor, F. W. (1967). *Principles of Scientific Management.* New York: Norton.

34. Peck, C. (1993). *Variable pay: Nontraditional programs for motivation and reward.* New York: The Conference Board.

35. See note 4.

36. See note 4.

37. Halsey, F. A. (1891). The premium plan of paying for labor. *Transactions, American Society of Mechanical Engineers, 12,* 755–764.

38. Schwinger, P. (1975). *Wage incentive systems.* New York: Halsted.

39. Banker, R. D.; Lee, S.; and Potter, G. (1996). A field study of the impact of a performance-based incentive plan. *Journal of Accounting and Economics, 21*(2), 195–226; see also, note 20.

40. Hauser, J. R.; Simester, D.; and Wernerfelt, B. (1994). Customer satisfaction incentives. *Journal of Marketing, 13*(4), 327–350. See also, notes 20 and 27. Bivins, J. (1989). Focus on compensation. *Stores, 71*(9), 25–30; Burns, K. C. (1992). A bonus plan that promotes customer service: Star performance—bonus plan of Aetna Life and Casualty Co. *Compensation and Benefits Review, 24*(5), 15–20; Coopers & Lybrand (1993). *Compensation planning for 1993.* New York: Coopers & Lybrand; Hills instills employee incentives to lure repeat business. (1993). *Discount Store News, 32*(9), 61; Kanter, R. M. (July–August 1989). The new managerial work. *Harvard Business Review,* pp. 85–92; Levy and Olive Garden restaurants introduce incentive plans to improve customer service (November 1992). *Restaurants and Institutions;* and Schlesinger, L. A., and Heskett, J. L. (May–June 1991). The service driven service company. *Harvard Business Review,* 71–81.

41. Henderson, R. I. (1995). *Compensation Management,* 6th ed. Englewood Cliffs, NJ: Prentice Hall.

42. Mercile, K., and Lund, J. (August 1995). Variable compensation plans, overtime calculations and the *Fair Labor Standards Act. Labor Law Journal, 46*(8), 492–503.

43. Pritchard, R. D.; Jones, S. D.; Roth, P. L.; Stuebing, K. K.; and Ekeberg, S. E. (1988). Effects of group feedback, goal setting, and incentives on organizational productivity. *Journal of Applied Psychology, 73*(2), 337–358.

44. See note 33.

45. See note 4. See also, Stenhouse, Thomasina R. (February 1995). The long and short of gain sharing. *The Academy of Management Executive, 9*(1), 77–78, and Imberman, Woodruff. (January–February 1996). *Gain sharing: A lemon or lemonade. Business Horizons, 39*(1), 36–41.

46. Alexander Consulting Group (1992). Health care costs, quality top lists of human resource concerns. *Employee Benefit Plan Review, 47*(3), 38–39; see also, Welbourne, T. M.; Balkin, D. B.; and Gomez-Mejia, L. R. (June 1995). Gain sharing and mutual monitoring: A combined agency-organizational justice interpretation. *Academy of Management Journal, 38*(3), 881–899; and Belcher, J. G., Jr. (May/June 1994). Gain sharing and variable pay: The state of the art. *Compensation and Benefits Review,* pp. 50–60.

47. Welbourne, T. M., and Gomez-Mejia, L. R. (July/August 1988). Gain sharing revisited. *Compensation and Benefits Review,* pp. 19–28.

48. Lawler, E. E., III, and Cohen, S. G. (1992). Designing a pay system for teams. *American Compensation Association Journal, 1*(1), 6–19.

49. Schuster, M. (Winter 1987). Gain sharing. Do it right the first time. *Sloan Management Review,* p. 23. See also, Bullock, R. J., and Lawler, E. E. (1984). Gain sharing: A few questions, and fewer answers. *Human Resource Management, 23*(l), 23–40; Hatcher, L., and Ross, T. L. (1991). From individual incentives to an organization-wide gainsharing plan: Effects on teamwork and product quality. *Journal of Organizational Behavior, 12,* 169–183; and Rollins, T. (May/June 1989). Productivity-based group incentive plans: Powerful, but use with caution. *Compensation and Benefits Review,* pp. 39–50.

50. Lesieur, F. (1958). *The Scanlon plan: A frontier in labor management relations.* New York: John Wiley & Sons.

51. Graham-Moore, B. (1990). 17 years of experience with the Scanlon plan: Desota revisited. In B. Graham-Moore and T. L. Ross (eds.), *Gain sharing.* Washington, DC: Bureau of National Affairs, pp. 139–173. See also, Graham-Moore, B., and Ross, T. L. (1990). *Gain sharing.* Washington, DC: Bureau of National Affairs.

52. Thigpen, P. (1994). Quoted in Pfeffer, J. *Competitive advantage through people.* Boston: Harvard Business Press, p. 62.

53. Fein, M. (1980). *An alternative to traditional managing.* Hillsdale, NJ: Mitchell Fein.

54. Kaufman, R. (1992). The effects of IMPROSHARE on productivity. *Industrial and Labor Relations Review, 45,* 312.

55. Schuster, J. R., and Zingheim, P. K. (1992). *The new pay: Linking employee and organizational performance.* New York: Lexington Books.

56. Wartzman, R. (May 4, 1992). A Whirlpool factory raises productivity—and pay of workers. *The Wall Street Journal,* pp. A1, A4.

57. Scontrino, P. (July–August 1995). An effective productivity and quality tool. *Journal for Quality and Participation, 18*(4), 90–93. See also, Sharing the gains of improved performance (March 1994). *Personnel Review, 23*(2), 47–49.

58. McAninch, L. (November 1995). Gain sharing creates an environment that supports TQM. *Management Accounting, 77*(5), 38–39.

59. Imberman, W. (November 1995). Is gain sharing the

wave of the future? *Management Accounting, 77*(5), 35–38.

60. Belcher, J. G., Jr. (May/June 1994). Gain sharing and variable pay: The state of the art. *Compensation and Benefits Review,* pp. 50–60.

61. Hewitt Associates (January/February 1995). Case studies: Whirlpool, Nike, Salomon and PSEG. *Compensation and Benefits Review,* pp. 71–76.

62. Kim, D. (April 1996). Factors influencing organizational performance in gain sharing programs. *Industrial Relations, 35*(2), 227–244.

63. See note 41. Sec also, Collins, D. (March/April 1996). Case study: 15 lessons learned from the death of a gain sharing plan: How power struggles and political gamesmanship killed one company's gainsharing plan. *Compensation and Benefits Review,* pp. 31–41.

64. Farrell, C., and Hoerr, J. (May 1989). ESOPS: Are they good for you? *Business Week,* pp. 116–123. See also, Chelius, J., and Smith, R. S. (1990). Profit sharing and employment stability. *Industrial and Labor Relations Review, 43,* 256–273; Cone, M. A., and Svejnar, J. (1990). The performance effects of employee ownership plans. In A. S. Blinder (ed.), *Paying for productivity,* Washington, DC: The Brookings Institution, pp. 245–294; and Coates, E. M., III (April 1991). Profit sharing today: Plans and provisions, *Monthly Labor Review,* pp. 19–25.

65. Capell, K. (July 22, 1996). Options for everyone. *Business Week,* pp. 80–84.

66. See note 48.

67. Blasi, J.; Conte, M.; and Kruse, D. (1996). Employee stock ownership and corporate performance among public companies. *Industrial and Labor Relations Review, 50,* p. 63; see also, Blasi, J. (1985). *Employee ownership: Revolution not ripoff.* New York: John Wilcy & Sons; Florkowski, G. W. (1991). Profit sharing and public policy: Insights for the United States. *Industrial Relations, 30,* 96–115; Florkowski, G. W. (1987). The organizational impact of profit sharing. *Academy of Management Review, 12,* 622–636; Hammer, T. H. (1988). New developments in profit sharing, gain sharing, and employee ownership. In J. P. Campbell, R. J. Campbell, and associates (eds.), *Productivity in Organizations.* San Francisco: Jossey-Bass; Klein, K. J. (1987). Employee stock ownership and employee attitudes: A test of three models. *Journal of Applied Psychology [monograph], 72,* 319–332; Kruse, D. L. (1991). Profit-sharing and employment variability: Microeconomic evidence on the Weitzman theory. *Industrial and Labor Relations Review, 44,* 437–453; and Pierce, J. L.; Rubenfeld, S.; and Morgan, S. (1991). Employee ownership: A conceptual model of process and effects. *Academy of Management Review, 16,* 121–144.

68. McNerney, D. J. (September 1994). Team compensation: Simple, variable and profitable. *HR Focus, 71*(9), 9–10.

69. Johnston, D. C. (September 2, 1997). Executive pay in-

creases at a much faster rate than corporate revenues and profits. *The New York Times,* p. C4.

70. Crystal, G. S. (1984). Pay for performance: It's not dead after all. *Compensation Review, 3,* 24–25.

71. See note 69.

72. Byrne, J. A. (April 22, 1996). How high can CEO pay go? *Business Week,* pp. 100–122.

73. Peach, E. B. (1996). CEO pay: Problems and concerns. In G. R. Ferris, and M. R. Buckley (eds.), *Human Resources Management: Perspectives and Issues,* 3rd ed., Boston: Allyn & Bacon, pp. 436–446.

74. See note 69; see also, Lublin, J. (June 4, 1991). Are chief executives paid too much? *The Wall Street Journal,* p. Bl.

75. Hambrick, D. C., and Siegel, P. A. (1997). Pay dispersion within top management groups: Harmful effects on performance of high-technology firms. *Best paper proceedings.* Boston: Academy of Management, pp. 26–28.

76. Thompson, J. H.; Smith, L. M.; and Murray, A. F. (September/October 1986). Management performance incentives: Three critical issues. *Compensation and Benefits Review,* pp. 41–47.

77. See note 69.

78. Edelstein, C. M. (1981). Long term incentives for management, Part 4: Restricted stock. *Compensation Review,* pp. 31–40. See also, Kerr, J., and Bettis, R. A. (1987). Board of directors, top management compensation, and shareholder returns. *Academy of Management Journal, 30,* 645–665.

79. See note 69; see also, Castro, J. (April 15, 1991). CEOs: No pain, just gain. *Time,* pp. 40–41; and Puffer, S. M., and Weinrop, J. P. (1991). Corporate performance and CEO turnover: The role of performance expectations. *Administrative Science Quarterly, 36,* 1–19.

80. Dunlap, A. (Aug. 10, 1997). Final front in crusade for corporate reform. *New York Times,* p. F13.

81. See note 75. Research by Professor Charles Elson of Stetson Law School.

82. Balkin, D. B., and Logan, J. W. (January/February 1988). Reward policies that support entrepreneurship. *Compensation and Benefits Review,* pp. 19–32; see also, Kahn, L. M., and Sherer, P. D. (1990). Contingent pay and managerial performance. *Industrial and Labor Relations Review, 43,* 107S–120S.

83. See note 4. See also, Kerr, J., and Slocum, J. W., Jr. (1987). Managing corporate culture through reward systems. *Academy of Management Executive, 1*(2), 99–108, and Lawler, E. E., III (1989). Pay for performance: A strategic analysis. In L. R. Gomez-Mejia (ed.), *Compensation and Benefits.* Washington, DC.

84. See note 4, Collins (1995).

85. Gomez-Mejia, L. R., and Balkin, D. B. (1992). *Compensation, organizational strategy, and firm performance.* Cincinnati, OH: South-Western.

C H A P T E R

STRATEGIES FOR IMPROVING COMPETITIVENESS: QUALITY, PRODUCTIVITY, AND QUALITY OF WORK LIFE

OVERVIEW

A recurring theme of this book is that competitive advantage can be created and sustained by enhancing organizational capability in the form of more effective HRM programs. We have described the most effective approaches to HR planning and job analysis, recruitment strategies, staffing methods, training and development programs, performance management, and compensation systems that can create the competitive advantage. Many firms have also turned to interventions designed to enhance product and service quality, productivity, and quality of work life. As we discussed in Chapter 11, pay for performance is one such intervention for improving productivity and quality. Other quality and productivity programs are the focus of this chapter.

Each year, thousands of companies request applications for the government-sponsored Baldrige award or at-

tempt to meet ISO 9000 certification. These models of quality and productivity improvement have had a major impact on the intervention and organizational change strategies of both large and small U.S. corporations. Even companies that have not formally applied for the award or certification are implementing quality improvement programs based on the Baldrige or ISO 9000 criteria. HRM activities are a critical component of both of these awards. We will explore these activities in this chapter.

OBJECTIVES

After studying this chapter, you should be able to:

1. Understand the importance of strategies for enhancing U.S. productivity, quality, and quality of work life.

2. Describe ways to redesign the work environment to improve organizational capability and increase competitive advantage.

3. Describe several strategies for enhancing employee participation and involvement, and explain what is involved in the total quality management (TQM) movement.

4. Describe the Baldrige criteria for quality and the relationship of these criteria to improvement programs.

5. Describe what is meant by reengineering.

6. Understand the relative effectiveness of various interventions for enhancing quality, productivity, and quality of work life (QWL).

DEFINING PRODUCTIVITY

The definition of productivity varies as a function of the type of firm and industry. Generally, productivity refers to a ratio of output to input. Inputs may include labor hours or costs, production costs, and equipment costs. Outputs may consist of sales, earnings, market share, and mistakes made. Many firms now assume or have shown that productivity is affected by employee knowledge, skills, abilities, attitudes, motivation and behaviors. The improvement programs start with this assumption and proceed with different intervention strategies.[1]

DEFINING QUALITY

Quality can be assessed by looking at performance, reliability, conformance to standards, durability, serviceability, aesthetics, and complying with customer requirements.[2] Three of the leading experts on quality—Philip Crosby, Joseph Juran, and W. Edwards Deming—have offered their opinions on it.[3] Crosby defines quality as "conformance to the requirements . . . and doing what you said you were going to do." Quality refers to "freedom from waste, freedom from trouble, and freedom from failure." Juran says quality involves "those features of what's being produced that respond to the customer's needs and that create the income." Deming defines quality as "meeting and exceeding the customer's needs and expectations—and then continuing to improve."

Regardless of the specific definition, most experts agree that quality must be defined by the particular firm with major input from internal and external customers. Quality cannot, however, simply refer to customer satisfaction. The customer must be satisfied, but at a low enough cost to enable the organization to be competitive with other firms. Virtually anyone can have high quality with an infinite supply of expense. The idea is to achieve high quality with the lowest possible cost.

Quality and price are considered to be the two most important determinants of a company's reputation. Customer service, responsiveness to complaints, and the behavior of employees to customers rank right behind them.[4] A good example of a firm very successful at providing customer service at low cost is Southwest Airlines. It has been rated at the top in customer service, which includes baggage handling, on-time performance, and customer complaints. At the same time, it has been the driving force behind the steady decline of ticket prices since airline deregulation. In addition, Southwest has one of the most productive workforces in the industry with low turnover and no layoffs. Between 1990 and 1994, with the industry showing a $12.8 billion loss, Southwest was profitable each year, continuing to expand and demonstrating outstanding stock performance.[5] The airline delights its customers by making and keeping a promise to be cheap and fast, and it seizes every opportunity to let passengers know this. Southwest is featured in Jeff Pfeffer's book *Competitive Advantage through People,* which lists the airline among the top five best performing firms.[6]

Companies have different ways of defining quality. Motorola, a quality leader in the United States, established the goal of "Six Sigma." This is a level of quality achieved by only a few U.S. companies to date (e.g., Motorola, Texas Instruments, Hewlett-Packard). It involves producing virtually defect-free products, services, and transactions. The Six Sigma process involves four steps: (1) measuring every process and transaction, (2) analyzing each process, (3) improving each process, and (4) controlling each process for consistency.[7]

General Electric has taken on the goal of becoming a Six Sigma quality company by the year 2000. To do this, it is training all 222,000 GE employees in Six Sigma methodology and has weighted 40 percent of bonus compensation for managers on their progress. By the end of 1996, GE had committed $200 million toward the goal. The company wants to reduce defects to save the $7 to $10 billion spent on mistakes. To reach the Six Sigma rate, GE will need to go from 35,000 defects per million to fewer than 4. Jack Welch, chairman and CEO of GE, believes that achieving Six Sigma will not only help the firm financially due to increased sales, but will also lead to greater pride, job satisfaction, and job security among GE employees.[8] Similarly, at Deere & Company, quality is currently measured in parts per million and soon will be measured in parts per billion. The goal is 100 percent customer satisfaction, which means no defects.[9]

As we discussed in Chapter 9, organizations need to measure and strive for both high quality and high productivity. One without the other is usually not acceptable. For example, a focus on quality alone may generate great products, but also unacceptable lead times, missed delivery dates, and increased costs. Similarly, an emphasis on productivity alone may lead to a large quantity of products, but accompanied with errors and defects. Recall our definition of performance from Chapter 9. Performance is a *record of outcomes* with criteria which may include quantity, quality and cost. Obviously the cost of labor is a critical part of the productivity ratio, particularly in the global environment where many companies seek out the lowest labor costs.

ASSESSING THE NEEDS FOR QUALITY AND PRODUCTIVITY IMPROVEMENT

Since a variety of different measures can be used to estimate productivity and quality, each organization will need to determine its own measures with a focus on its business and strategic initiatives. For example, one firm may decide to focus on improving market share, while another firm may be more interested in decreasing the rate of defects. Certainly, multiple measures should be used to gauge organizational improvements. For example, at Northern Telecom, a design engineering team may develop anywhere from three to seven performance ratios, including reworked drawings as a percentage of total drawings, overdue drawings as a percentage of total drawings, and overtime hours as a percentage of total hours.

Diagnosing the Problem(s)

Reliable measurements of the key quality and production criteria are a necessary condition for measuring improvement. Productivity/quality interventions should not begin without reliable and valid measures of the key criteria. In Chapters 9 and 11, we discussed the need for valid measurements of individual or unit performance in the context of customer requirements in order to diagnose problems and award exemplary performance. Of course, a variety of variables could account for poor productivity or quality. We discussed constraints on performance such as low employee ability or effort, outdated equipment, unpredictable workloads, inefficient work flow, inappropriate job design, and poor or inadequate training as examples of HRM activities that can be very costly. In Chapter 9 we listed 22 possible constraints on individual and group performance that were beyond the control of the worker or work unit, all variables that may account for low productivity or quality of work.

Intervention strategies should be planned and implemented in the context of these possible constraints, the probability of changing them with some intervention strategy, and the extent to which the change is important in terms of customer requirements and business initiatives. Most intervention strategies assume the major

causes of productivity or quality problems are employee abilities and motivation. However, leaders of the total quality management movement suggest that at least 80 to 85 percent of productivity and quality problems are due to system factors, not people factors.

The total quality management (TQM) gurus such as Deming suggest defective materials, poor product design, management errors, and outdated or poorly maintained equipment account for the vast majority of problems.[10] They contend the emphasis should be on improving these system factors, and less on "people" factors. TQM enthusiasts insist, however, that workers are a great source of information about how to reduce or eliminate these problems. Interestingly, Japanese supervisors are likely to see system factors as the causes of poor quality rather than workforce problems.[11] The issue of how much poor productivity and quality is due to person or system factors is under debate. Most experts would agree, however, that what is important is diagnosing the reasons for the performance problem before implementing any improvement strategies. All would agree that employees and customers are in great positions to identify problems and suggest improvements.

The strategies chosen to address the problems should be tailored to the specific problems. Many different approaches are being marketed as productivity- and quality-enhancing programs. For example, a plethora of consulting firms use the Baldrige criteria as their intervention model. Organizations need to be careful to avoid the latest fad and to choose the program that will be best able to meet their specific needs in terms of customer requirements. The interventions they select may focus on changing the work environment or adopting a participative culture to enhance productivity or motivation. Some of the more popular programs are described in a later section.

Benchmarking

Many organizations today have started using benchmarking to determine the specific types of quality or productivity improvements they should be making. Xerox Corporation popularized benchmarking in the early 1980s and defined it as the continuous process of measuring one's own products, services, systems, and practices against the world's toughest competitors to identify areas for improvement.[12] Benchmarking has been recommended to focus attention where attention is needed. Benchmarking is the process of gauging the internal practices and activities within a firm to an external reference or standard. It is considered more than a onetime measurement; benchmarking is a tool for creating a learning organization.[13] Figure 12.1 illustrates a model of the phases involved in benchmarking.

An estimated 70 percent of the *Fortune* 500 companies use benchmarking on a regular basis.[14] For example,

FIGURE 12.1
A MODEL OF BENCHMARKING

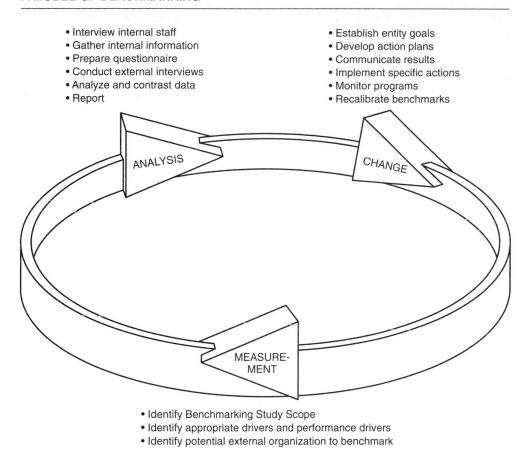

- Interview internal staff
- Gather internal information
- Prepare questionnaire
- Conduct external interviews
- Analyze and contrast data
- Report

- Establish entity goals
- Develop action plans
- Communicate results
- Implement specific actions
- Monitor programs
- Recalibrate benchmarks

ANALYSIS

CHANGE

MEASURE-MENT

- Identify Benchmarking Study Scope
- Identify appropriate drivers and performance drivers
- Identify potential external organization to benchmark

Source: C. J. McNair and K. H. J. Leibfried, *Benchmarking: A tool for continuous improvement.* New York: Harper Collins, 1992.

Ford Motor Company benchmarked its accounts payable function against Mazda Motor Corporation. Ford found that it had about five times as many employees as it needed. The automaker redesigned the system for tracking orders, deliveries, and invoices and thereby helped employees to perform the same tasks more efficiently. As a result, Ford was able to simplify the process, reduce the number of employees, and reduce errors.[15] Goodyear Tire and Rubber changed its compensation practices by benchmarking what several *Fortune* 100 firms were doing in compensation. It developed a system to link employee performance to the firm's financial gains.[16] Avon Products used internal benchmarking to improve all of its customer service branch offices. Janssen Pharmaceutical used external benchmarking to examine administrative overhead and was able to eliminate nonvalue-added overhead throughout the organization. Exxon Chemical used external benchmarking to make its information systems applications more efficient. AT&T examined the role of chief financial officers to redesign the job duties and functions of the CFO to be more in line with what world-class CFOs were doing.[17] Many motor carrier companies also use benchmarking of their quality improvement programs and practices.[18]

Recent studies on the effectiveness of benchmarking have found that it is critical to have top management support and commitment to the project. In addition, in the best-performing companies, benchmarking produced positive results on bottom-line variables. When it results in setting moderately difficult goals that employees believe are attainable, it seems to work. But when poorer performing companies receive benchmarking data that their practices are significantly different from the "best practices," and their managers set radical, unrealistically high goals, employees have difficulty embracing the changes and may resist them.[19] As a result, performance may actually decline. These findings should not discourage managers from benchmarking their practices. Instead, managers should be alerted to the types of goals they should set after receiving benchmarking data. Perhaps setting more realistic goals and gradually increasing the difficulty of the goals would encourage employees.[20] This is known as shaping, which is a behavioral change technique that promotes gradual improvement from a known, initial behavior to a desired goal, or in this case, the benchmark.[21] For example, if an organization wants to meet the best practice of having 1 percent defects in its industry, and their initial performance is at 20 percent defects, the company may need to first use 15 percent defects as a goal. Once workers master that goal and are reinforced (or rewarded), then the company can change the goal to 10 percent defects. In this way, the company is continually moving toward the benchmark goal and employees are less resistant than if they were initially assigned the goal of 1 percent defects, which they may have felt was unattainable. To use shaping effectively in benchmarking practices, the following tips are offered:[22]

1. Identify what is to be benchmarked (a process, product, service, etc.).

2. Identify comparable companies.

3. Collect data to precisely define the target goal (benchmark).

4. Collect data to determine the organization's current performance level against the benchmark.

5. Reduce the target to discrete, measurable, smaller steps or goals.

6. Train, as needed, any employees so that they can meet the smaller goals (subgoals).

7. Periodically provide feedback and use appropriate, valued reinforcers for meeting the subgoals.

8. Increase the subgoals so that they are getting closer to the target goal.

9. Recalibrate benchmarks periodically.

The recalibration is important so that the organization continually monitors the benchmark or target goal because it may change. Successes by companies may lead to new standards. Benchmarking practices support continual improvement and reengineering efforts by organizations. Reengineering is described in a later section. One recent review put the effects of benchmarking in a proper context.

> "Benchmarking can provide a useful source of ideas; however while becoming 'best in class' may be a necessary condition for ultimately improving firm performance, it is not a sufficient condition. The more crucial strategic decision is how the total HRM system is designed such that it supports key business priorities."[23]

DEFINING QUALITY OF WORK LIFE

Quality of work life (QWL) refers to the level of satisfaction, motivation, involvement, and commitment individuals experience with respect to their lives at work. QWL is the degree to which individuals are able to satisfy their important personal needs while employed by the firm. Companies interested in enhancing employees'

QWL generally try to instill in employees the feelings of security, equity, pride, family democracy, ownership, autonomy, responsibility, and flexibility. They try to treat employees in a fair and supportive manner, open communication channels at all levels, offer employees opportunities to participate in decisions affecting them, and empower them to carry through on assignments. Many companies pursue QWL initiatives through the guidelines of the Malcolm Baldrige Award.

Malcolm Baldrige Award

The most significant award for quality and for assessing QWL initiatives in the United States is the **Malcolm Baldrige National Quality Award,** established by the U.S. Congress in 1987. Named for the late commerce secretary, the Baldrige is administered by the National Institute of Standards and Technology of the Department of Commerce. The president personally presents these prestigious awards in a ceremony in Washington, D.C. As President Bill Clinton remarked, "The Malcolm Baldrige National Quality Award is helping U.S. companies satisfy customers and improve overall company performance and capabilities."[24]

The purpose of the Baldrige award is to promote national awareness of the importance of total quality management and to recognize U.S. firms for quality achievements. As Mickey Kantor, secretary of commerce, stated, "the award has had a profound impact on increasing U.S. competitiveness and heightening awareness to the challenges faced in a global economy."[25]

Seven categories are used to assess quality management and improvement. These are in order of points: business results (450), leadership (110), human resource development and management (100), process management (100), strategic planning (80), customer and market focus (80), and information and analysis (80). Figure 12.2 briefly defines each of these categories. The total number of points that can be obtained is 1,000. The seven categories are based on a set of core values and concepts, including the importance of customer-driven quality, leadership, continuous improvement and learning, employee participation and development, fast response, design quality and prevention, long-range view of the future, management by fact or data, partnership development, company responsibility and citizenship, and results focus.

The Baldrige award allows any publicly or privately owned business in the United States to apply, with the stipulation that only one division or subunit of a company can apply for the same award category in the same year. Not eligible are local, state, and national government agencies; not-for-profit organizations; trade associations; and professional societies. Two awards may be given annually in each of three categories: manufacturing companies, service companies, and small businesses.

FIGURE 12.2
1997 MALCOLM BALDRIGE NATIONAL QUALITY AWARD CRITERIA

A total of 1,000 points are possible among the seven categories:

1. Leadership (110 points)

1.1 Leadership System 80
1.2 Company Responsibility and Citizenship 30

This category examines senior leaders' personal leadership and involvement in creating and sustaining values, company directions, performance expectations, customer focus, and a leadership system that promotes performance excellence. Also examined is how the values and expectations are integrated into the company's leadership system, including how the company continuously learns and improves, and addresses its societal responsibilities and community involvement.

2. Strategic Planning (80 points)

2.1 Strategy Development Process 40
2.2 Company Strategy. 40

This category examines how the company sets strategic directions and how it determines key action plans. Also examined is how the plans are translated into an effective performance management system.

3. Customer and Market Focus (80 points)

3.1 Customer and Market Knowledge 40
3.2 Customer Satisfaction and Relationship Enhancement. 40

This category examines how the company determines requirements and expectations of customers and markets. Also examined is how the company enhances relationships with customers and determines their satisfaction.

4. Information and Analysis (80 points)

4.1 Selection and Use of Information and Data 25
4.2 Selection and Use of Comparative Information and Data 15
4.3 Analysis and Review of Company Performance 40

This category examines the management and effectiveness of the use of data and information to support key company processes and the company's performance management system.

5. Human Resource Development and Management (100 points)

5.1 Work Systems. 40
5.2 Employee Education, Training, and Development. 30
5.3 Employee Well-Being and Satisfaction 30

This category examines how the workforce is enabled to develop and utilize its full potential, aligned with the company's objectives. Also examined are the company's efforts to build and maintain an environment conducive to performance excellence, full participation, and personal and organizational growth.

6. Process Management (100 points)

6.1 Management of Product and Service Processes 60
6.2 Management of Support Processes 20
6.3 Management of Supplier and Partnering Processes. 20

This category examines the key aspects of process management, including customer-focused design, product and service delivery processes, and supplier and partnering processes involving all work units. The category examines how key processes are designed, effectively managed, and improved to achieve better performance.

7. Business Results (450 points)

7.1 Customer Satisfaction Results 130
7.2 Financial and Market Results 130
7.3 Human Resource Results 35
7.4 Supplier and Partner Results 25
7.5 Company-Specific Results 130

This category examines the company's performance and improvement in key business areas—customer satisfaction, financial and marketplace performance, human resource, supplier and partner performance, and operational performance. Also examined are performance levels relative to competitors.

Source: 1997 Malcolm Baldrige National Quality Award Criteria for Performance Excellence, United States Department of Commerce, Technology Administration, National Institute of Standards and Technology, Rt. 270 and Quince Orchard Rd., Administration Bldg., Room A 537, Gaithersburg, MD 20899-0001.

Applications for the Baldrige award require submission of up to 75 pages for a completed application form.

Some companies that have won the Baldrige award since its inception in 1988 are: Motorola, Xerox, Cadillac, IBM, Federal Express, and Ritz Carlton Hotels.[26] Winners are expected to share information about their successful performance strategies with other U.S. organizations. The Baldrige award has spawned a consulting industry specializing in preparing companies for a Baldrige application and suggesting major interventions in the way the company does business and deals with its employees. Most U.S. companies requesting the application materials are simply using them to evaluate their own programs and make changes. Many of the largest U.S. corporations have used the Baldrige criteria as a model for instituting major organizational change processes. IBM, Eastman Chemical, and Ford are three notable examples.[27]

Figure 12.3 presents details on the criteria in the HR Development and Management category.

Internal Quality Awards

In addition to the national awards like the Baldrige many firms have established their own quality awards or standards. Ford Motor Company introduced the Q1 Preferred Quality Award in 1981 and by 1988 made it a standard by stating that suppliers would have to meet it if they wanted to continue selling to Ford.[28] Westinghouse created the George Westinghouse Quality Award program as its own competition for quality. All divisions are eligible for two awards—"most improved" and "best." The winners receive a trophy and a $200,000 check to spend any way they want within the firm's code of conduct.[29] Motorola, Xerox, IBM, and Mayflower Moving also have internal quality award programs. Haggar Clothing Company awards an Excellence in Education Award, which was given in 1996 to a senior vice president of manufacturing for his improvement of Haggar's human resources, particularly his efforts with quality improvement teams.[30]

ISO Certification

In 1946, the International Organization of Standardization (ISO) was founded to develop a common set of standards in manufacturing, trade, and communications. Today, ISO certification (e.g., ISO 9000) is used by many companies as a marketing tool (i.e., to say they have met the standards of ISO 9000) and as a quality management and continuous improvement tool.[31]

The ISO is headquartered in Geneva, Switzerland, and is composed of the national standards institutes of 97 countries, including the American National Standards Institute (ANSI).[32] ISO 9000 is a set of quality systems standards that are used on an international scale for quality management and assurance. The objective of ISO 9000 is to provide standard language that can be used to document the degree to which a company is meeting quality procedures. Currently, it is the national standard for over 60 countries,[33] including the United States, Japan, Canada, France, Germany, Russia, China, and Mexico. This means customers or buyers in those countries are requiring ISO 9000 of their suppliers. The ISO sponsors and publishes standards, but leaves the enforcement of those standards to the nations and organizations that adopt the standards.

The ISO 9000 Standards Series on quality management and assurance was published in 1987 and updated in 1994. It has five subsections described below:

- ISO 9000—*Quality Management and Quality Assurance Standards—Guidelines for Selection and Use.* This contains guidelines to be used with the other four standards in the series.

- ISO 9001—*Quality Systems—Model for Quality Assurance in Design/Development, Production, Installation, and Servicing.* This is the most comprehensive standard and is used by organizations that want to show competencies in all areas from design and manufacturing to distribution and packaging.

- ISO 9002—*Quality Systems—Model for Quality Assurance in Production and Installation.* This standard is typically adopted by manufacturing firms and is less stringent than ISO 9001.

- ISO 9003—*Quality Systems—Model for Quality Assurance in Final Inspection and Test.* This is used in firms that want to document their inspection and testing policies and procedures. It is the most narrowly focused and is the least used.

- ISO 9004—*Quality Management and Quality System Elements—Guidelines.* This provides ideas for which elements to include in a quality system and what the system's expected structure should be.

Generally, a firm tries to meet a particular standard by following guidelines from a quality manual and by implementing an internal audit system. A quality system registrar certifies the organization's quality system by performing an on-site audit.[34] The certification requires documentation and keeping operational records. With certified quality systems and higher product quality, firms that become ISO 9000 certified have a competitive advantage because they are better able to satisfy their customers and attract new ones. Other reported benefits of ISO 9000, according to 250 midsize U.S. manufacturing companies with annual sales ranging from $10 million to $500 million, include: spurring internal competitiveness, signaling a commitment to quality, and giving a strategic advantage over noncertified competitors.[35] ISO 9000 also plays a pivotal role in the future of world trade as more and more countries and trading blocs (e.g.,

FIGURE 12.3
MALCOLM BALDRIGE CRITERIA FOR "HR DEVELOPMENT AND MANAGEMENT"

5.0 Human Resource Development and Management (100 points)

5.1 Work Systems   (40 points)

Describe how the company's work and job design and its compensation and recognition approaches enable and encourage all employees to contribute effectively to achieving the company's performance and learning objectives.

a. Work and Job Design[1]

How work and jobs, including those of managers at all levels in the company, are designed, organized, and managed to ensure:

1. Opportunities for individual initiative and self-directed responsibility in designing, managing, and improving company work processes.

2. Flexibility, cooperation, rapid response, and learning in addressing current and changing customer and operational requirements.

3. Effective communications, and knowledge and skill sharing across work functions, units, and locations.

b. Compensation and Recognition[2]

How the company's compensation and recognition approaches for individuals and groups, including managers at all levels in the company, reinforce the overall work systems, performance, and learning objectives.

5.2 Employee Education, Training, and Development (30 points)

Describes how the company's education and training address key company plans and needs, including building knowledge and capabilities, and contributing to improved employee performance and development.

a. Employee Education, Training, and Development[3]

Describe:

1. How education and training address the company's key performance plans and needs, including longer-term employee development objectives.

2. How education and training are designed to support the company's approach to work and jobs. Include how the company seeks input from employees and their managers in education and training design.

3. How education and training, including orientation of new employees, are delivered.[4]

4. How knowledge and skills are reinforced on the job.

5. How education and training are evaluated and improved, taking into account company performance, employee development objectives, and costs of education and training.

5.3 Employee Well-Being and Satisfaction   (30 points)

Describe how the company maintains a work environment and work climate that support the well-being, satisfaction, and motivation of employees.

a. Work Environment

How the company maintains a safe and healthful work environment. Include how employee well-being factors such as health, safety, and ergonomics are included in improvement activities. Briefly describe key measures and targets for each important factor. Note significant differences, if any, based upon different health and safety factors in the work environments of employee groups or work units.

b. Employee Support Services[5]

How the company supports the well-being, satisfaction, and motivation of employees via services, facilities, activities, and opportunities.

c. Employee Satisfaction[6]

How the company determines employee well-being, satisfaction, and motivation. Include:

1. A brief description of formal and informal methods used. Outline how the company determines the key factors that affect employee well-being, satisfaction, and motivation and assesses its work climate. Note important differences in methods, factors, or measures for different categories or types of employees, as appropriate.[7]

2. How the company relates employee well-being, satisfaction, and motivation results to key business results and/or objectives to identify improvement activities.

---

[1] Work design refers to how employees are organized and/or organize themselves in formal and informal, temporary, or longer-term units. This includes work teams, problem-solving teams, functional units, cross-functional teams, and departments—self-managed or managed by supervisors. Job design refers to responsibilities, authorities, and tasks assigned to individuals.

[2] Compensation and recognition refer to all aspects of pay and reward, including promotions and bonuses. This includes monetary and nonmonetary, formal and informal, and individual and group compensation and recognition.

[3] Education and training address knowledge and skills employees need to meet their overall work and development objectives.

[4] Education and training delivery might occur inside or outside the company and involve on-the-job, classroom, computer-based, or other types of delivery.

[5] Services, facilities, activities, and opportunities might include: counseling, career development and employability services; recreational or cultural activities; non-work-related education; day care; special leave for family responsibilities and/or community service; safety off the job; flexible work hours; outplacement; and retiree benefits, including extended health care.

[6] Specific factors that might affect satisfaction, well-being, and motivation include: effective employee problem or grievance resolution; safety; employee views of management; employee development and career opportunities; employee preparation for changes in technology or work organization; work environment; workload; cooperation and teamwork; recognition; benefits; communications; job security; compensation; equality of opportunity; and capability to provide required services to customers.

[7] Measures and/or indicators of well-being, satisfaction and motivation might include safety, absenteeism, turnover, turnover rate for customer-contact employees, grievances, strikes, and worker compensation, as well as results of surveys. Results relative to such measures and/or indicators should be reported in Item 7.3.

Source: 1997 Malcolm Baldrige National Quality Award Criteria for Performance Excellence, United States Department of Commerce, Technology Administration, National Institute of Standards and Technology, Rt. 270 and Quince Orchard Rd., Administration Bldg., Room A 537, Gaithersburg, MD 20899-0001, pp. 12–14.

European Community (EC), NAFTA, and an eastern Asia bloc) require it of their suppliers.

The ISO standards have been applied to many different kinds of organizations, including manufacturers, distribution services, consulting services, software developers, public utilities, and financial and educational institutions. Among 250 U.S. manufacturing firms surveyed, 7 percent said they were already certified, 15 percent were pursuing certification, and 41 percent noted they were going to pursue certification in the next two years.[36] By 1995, registered sites around the world exceeded 95,000, and registered sites in the United States passed 8,100.[37] A number of companies and agencies have facilities registered to ISO 9000 standards, including DuPont, Union Carbide, Pitney-Bowes, General Electric, Eastman Kodak, Hewlett-Packard, 3M, AL-COA, Allen-Bradley, Caterpillar, John Deere, Exxon, Federal Express, Georgia Pacific, IBM, Motorola, NCR, Texas Instruments, Unisys, Xerox, Dow Corning, AT&T, U.S. Department of Defense, and NASA. In 1994, the big three auto dealers (Ford, GM, and Chrysler) announced QS9000. This embeds ISO 9001 along with requirements that address specific auto industry concerns. By early 1996, both Chrysler and General Motors instituted mandatory 1997 deadlines on third-party audits of all parts suppliers.

If a company is interested in seeking certification in one of its functions (manufacturing or engineering design), several suggestions are offered:

1. Secure support from top management. A high-level manager should be devoted to the project to ensure that it gets accomplished and that someone in a position of power can get others to devote the time and energy to complete the necessary steps.

2. Establish a cross-functional task team to be involved in reviewing the company's practices to see what needs to be done to meet certification. The team should be trained in ISO standards.

3. Make sure consultants, if used, understand the company's business and practices.

4. Provide the necessary resources (time, training budget) so the team can devote the time to examining procedures and can offer training to employees on the new procedures.

5. Make sure to train employees in any new procedures that are developed (e.g., new rules to follow in manufacturing).

6. Make sure an internal or pre-audit is conducted before the final, external audit so the organization can gauge how much work needs to be done to get the procedures written appropriately.

7. Seek certification in one area first since the process is a time-consuming one (e.g., manufacturing vs. design).

ISO certification has been criticized for requiring so much paperwork and recordkeeping, yet this is critical to cost-effective auditing. If management did not generate documents and records, it would take an auditor much longer to evaluate the systems.

PROGRAMS FOR ENHANCING QUALITY, PRODUCTIVITY, AND QUALITY OF WORK LIFE

A variety of programs exist for improving quality, productivity, and the QWL experienced by employees. The following sections describe those that emphasize redesigning work environments and those that focus on enhancing employee participation. You will note that all fit within the Baldrige framework for quality improvement as well.

Redesigning Work Environments

Productivity and quality may be influenced by factors associated with the work environment. Unpredictable or excessive workloads, last-minute changes to the assigned work, lack of proper equipment, and inefficient work flow can severely inhibit the productivity of even the best employee. Thus, it is important to ensure that the work is designed to maximize productivity and quality. Several strategies exist for designing the work environment to meet the organization's goals for high quality and productivity. They include work site design/ergonomics, robotics, computers/office automation, job design (job enrichment, job rotation), and alternative work arrangements (flexible work arrangements, permanent part-time work, job sharing, compressed workweek). All these interventions have implications for HRM activities.

WORK SITE DESIGN OR ERGONOMICS. Ergonomics is a science concerned with designing jobs and equipment to fit the physical abilities of individuals (e.g., their senses, movement patterns, physical limitations). Research illustrates that the physical aspects of the workplace influence employee productivity and morale. For example, limited office privacy and work space have been shown to be related to lower employee job satisfaction.[38]

Strategies for work redesign. Some ways the work site can be redesigned are as follows:

- Improve the work flow.
- Reduce repetitive physical motions (e.g., hand movements).
- Adjust the lighting.
- Allow employees to personalize the work area (e.g., with pictures, plants).

- Use pleasing colors in the office.
- Create private offices and work spaces.
- Supply lounges for rest breaks.
- Rearrange, adjust, or replace equipment, parts, and work spaces.
- Place team members close together so they can interact easily.
- Provide adjustable office furniture to fit varying body physiques and particular work activities.

Popularity and benefits of ergonomics.   For years, an ergonomic approach has been used to design jobs in such firms as Armco, Days Inn, Martin Marietta, and Hanes Corporation.[39] Recently it has become even more popular as employees stay in the workforce longer and jobs are altered to meet their changing physical needs (e.g., better lighting for older workers). In addition, with the passage of the Americans with Disabilities Act (ADA) in 1990, the ergonomic approach has become increasingly popular to redesign jobs to accommodate individuals with disabilities (e.g., hearing impaired, loss of mobility in the limbs). The Occupational Safety and Health Administration (OSHA) is considering specific guidelines on ergonomics in an effort to improve worker safety.

Redesigning jobs according to principles of ergonomics is valuable because it helps accommodate individuals to jobs, breaks down physical barriers, and makes jobs more accessible to individuals. For example, the hotel chain Days Inn has created opportunities for individuals with physical handicaps to serve as reservationists. Without the use of their hands to type in reservations, employees are able to make reservations with special equipment built into their head and chin set.

The passage of the ADA mandates that organizations make reasonable accommodations for individuals with disabilities. In many cases, this will necessitate redesigning jobs.[40] While costly in some cases, it is believed that the benefits will far outweigh the costs in terms of enhanced organizational productivity and increases in the potential labor pool.

ROBOTICS.   U.S. firms have increasingly turned to robotics and other forms of automation to enhance organizational productivity and quality. Robots have become more prevalent in manufacturing companies such as General Motors, Ford Motor Company, Whirlpool, and Chrysler.[41] One interesting trend is the way U.S. firms have shifted their use of automation. In addition to adopting new technologies to reduce labor costs, companies are now implementing robotics to cut lead times, increase quality, and decrease inventories.[42]

Advantages of robots.   Robots are capable of performing a variety of tasks such as moving parts, tools, and equipment; cutting; welding; painting; detecting errors; sewing; sorting parts; product testing; and quality control. In addition, they can make and communicate decisions with minimal human supervision. Relative to humans, robots are very cost-effective. While an assembly-line worker may cost a firm up to $40 an hour, including benefits, a robot can be operated for far less. Since one robot does the work of up to six employees, this can ultimately lead to tremendous cost savings.[43]

Robots work more efficiently than humans (i.e., their uptime is 95 percent compared to 75 percent for blue-collar workers). They don't require benefits (sick leave, vacations, health insurance, retirement, pension, child care), or have absenteeism problems. They can work multiple shifts; perform dirty, hazardous, or dangerous jobs; be exposed to toxic substances; detect defects; and perform operations to the same level of quality each time. Also, with robots, ethical counterproductivity problems such as theft and espionage and labor difficulties (e.g., discrimination) are not a problem.

Cautions with using robots.   There are some cautions associated with using robots in the workplace. Start-up costs may preclude their development or adaptation, especially in smaller firms. Also, organizations can't just adopt the latest technologies as a quick fix. They need to be able to make compatible changes in management practices as well and show that the costs of automation are worth it to the firm.

Plans to bring robots into the workplace may be met by employee concerns about job security, job changes, management attitudes toward workers, and the value of robots. Generally, lower-skilled employees fear losing their jobs or having to relearn their jobs. On the other hand, higher-skilled employees report more positive attitudes toward robots and see them as providing them with opportunities to expand their skills.[44] In part, employee fears about job security are justified. Generally, each robot replaces several workers (from two to six). It is estimated that by the year 2000 robots will replace almost 3 million manufacturing employees, and only 2 percent to 5 percent of the U.S. workforce will be employed in manufacturing, down from 22 percent in 1979. Not everyone, however, agrees that robots will displace large numbers of employees.[45]

COMPUTERS AND OFFICE AUTOMATION.   Office automation and computers have been increasingly used by staff, managers, and professionals. The equipment includes word and image processors, audiovisual conferences, graphics preparation, personal computers, electronic mail, and software specifically designed for HRM activities. Computers are now used routinely to analyze the quality of a product while it is still on the computer screen. More user-friendly HRM and managerial software becomes available every year and more companies are adopting the methodology for HRM practices and quality improvement. HRM software is available for HR planning, EEO compliance, job analysis, personnel selection, and performance management. Automated office tools and software could save American businesses up to $300 billion through the 1990s.[46]

With the increased automation of HRM and managerial practices come potential problems. Now that individuals communicate through fax machines and electronic mail, they may have fewer opportunities to refine their social and interpersonal skills. This could be detrimental for jobs where social skills are critical (e.g., sales, public relations). Having information that is readily accessible makes concerns over privacy, secrecy, and espionage greater. Also, employees may resist using computers. They may be fearful of being unable to master the new technology or worried that they will be replaced once the computers are implemented. Additionally, they may be concerned (and justifiably so) that management will be able to better monitor their work output (e.g., examining their computer usage). As we discussed in Chapter 9, performance monitoring via the computer is much more common today and the subject of pending federal legislation to control it.

Dealing with employee concerns about robots, computers, and automation. To reduce the resistance employees may have regarding robots and automation, several suggestions are offered:[47]

- Involve employees in the decision to automate or implement robots.
- Communicate implementation issues to all employees (i.e., when the robots or computers will be brought on, what jobs they will perform).
- Inform employees about the benefits of automation.
- Provide employees with training to use the automated equipment and evaluate the effects of the training.
- Allow employees time to practice and experiment with the new equipment.
- Get line management support for the new equipment.
- Address problems of displaced workers.
- Have training staff on hand who can readily answer ongoing questions.
- Have maintenance staff readily available to fix equipment failures.
- Upgrade the equipment in a timely fashion.

JOB DESIGN APPROACHES. **Job enrichment.** Job enrichment is one approach to enhance employees' motivation, satisfaction, and performance on the job. The Job Characteristics Model was described in Chapter 4 as a popular enrichment model and process. Based on this model, the job is redesigned by building in the five core job characteristics of skill variety, task identity, task significance, autonomy, and feedback. **Skill variety** refers to the degree to which tasks are performed that require different abilities and skills. **Task identity** means completing a whole identifiable piece of work having a visible outcome, such as preparing a budget report or assembling an entire radio. **Task significance** refers to the degree to which the job has substantial importance or meaning. **Autonomy** refers to the degree of freedom and discretion allowed in scheduling work and work procedures (e.g., scheduling breaks, time to work on projects). **Feedback** refers to the amount of direct information received from the job about performance effectiveness. As we discussed in Chapter 4, the extent to which a job is perceived to have these characteristics is measured by the Job Diagnostic Survey (JDS), sample items of which can be found in Figure 4.12. In many ways, the JDS is like an employee attitude survey that is used to assess worker perspectives on major issues related to the workplace.

If the five core characteristics are built into the job, employees should experience several critical psychological states including finding the work *meaningful,* feeling *responsible* for work outcomes, and having *knowledge of the actual results* of work activities. The extent to which the employee experiences these psychological states should be related to important personal and work-related outcomes such as higher motivation and job satisfaction and, to a lesser extent, lower absenteeism and turnover.[48]

Job rotation. **Job rotation** is a job "redesign" technique only in the sense that individuals are given the opportunity to move from one job to another to learn and experience a variety of tasks. One benefit of job rotation is that it increases the variety of employees' skills and thus the number of employees who can perform any one type of job. This gives an employer more flexibility in staffing. Research on job rotation is not as impressive as that on job enrichment.[49]

Using job design approaches. Regardless of the job redesign approach used, employees' reactions will vary. Some are interested in receiving more challenge, autonomy, and responsibility in their jobs, and others prefer routine and predictable jobs. In addition, jobs vary in the degree to which they can easily be redesigned. Many employees and union representatives look at redesign efforts as an attempt to get more work out of them and, when not combined with adjustments in compensation, as just another form of "exploitation."

ALTERNATIVE WORK ARRANGEMENTS. In recent years, many organizations have begun using a variety of new work arrangements. One recent survey of 521 of the nation's largest firms indicated that more than 90 percent offered alternative work schedules ranging from flextime to job sharing to summers off.[50] These programs are designed to help employees balance their work and nonwork lives (e.g., families, leisure, community activities).[51] Some of the more popular programs include flexible working arrangements (e.g., flextime, permanent part-time work, job sharing, and compressed workweeks).

Flexible working arrangements. Nearly 30 percent of U.S. firms now offer some version of flextime. **Flextime** means that the employee has flexible starting and stopping hours. Generally, most employees are required to be at work during the middle (core) of the day (i.e., between 10 A.M. and 2 P.M.). About 15 percent of employers make 9 A.M. to 3 P.M. their core period, while another 28 percent make 9 A.M. to 4 P.M. their core period.

Flextime has been shown to be effective in relieving work–family conflict among private-sector employees.[52] In addition, the federal government's survey of 325,000 employees who participated in a flextime program discovered that 90 percent of them believed the program was at least somewhat important for resolving their work–family problems.[53] Flextime has been related to less tardiness, absenteeism, and sick leave taken by employees and increases in productivity and quality of work.[54]

One disadvantage associated with flextime is the difficulty in scheduling meetings and trying to locate employees. Also, it may require the use of time clocks, which are often perceived by employees as a managerial control mechanism. Flextime may not be appropriate for all jobs. Where tasks are highly interdependent (e.g., assembly line), it may be more difficult to administer.

Today, some firms are expanding on the idea behind flextime. For instance, Barrios Technology offers flexible work hours and flexible workplaces (**flexplace**). Flexplace offers employees the option of working at home or in a satellite office closer to home. At Pacific Bell, 70 percent of the employees working at home reported higher job satisfaction.[55] **Telecommuting** is another option that enables employees to work at home using computers, video displays, and phones to transmit letters and completed work back to the office.

Permanent part-time work. A recent work arrangement is the use of permanent part-time work. While part-time work has always been available on a temporary basis for some jobs, it has only recently been applied on a permanent basis to professional jobs. Among the companies offering permanent part-time work are: AT&T, Barrios Technology, Digital Equipment Corporation, DuPont, UPS, Arthur Andersen, and Herman Miller. While little research is available on the effectiveness of these changes, research in some firms shows that part-timers were more productive than full-timers and had lower absenteeism.[56]

Job sharing. Job sharing refers to a situation where two people divide the responsibilities for a regular, full-time job. For example, one person may work mornings, while the other person works in the evenings. Aetna Life & Casualty Insurance Company has 125 job-sharing teams.[57] DuPont has used the approach to avoid lay-offs.

Job sharing provides the organization with more staffing flexibility and enables the firm to attract and keep good employees. In addition, one early study found that each person does closer to 80 percent of the work of a full-time employee, rather than the expected 50 percent.[58] Employees also favor job-sharing programs because it allows them to reduce their work hours while still keeping their professional skills up-to-date.[59]

Compressed workweeks. One innovative arrangement allows employees to work fewer days during the week, with longer hours per day worked. For example, employees could work four 10-hour days instead of five 8-hour days. This type of work schedule has been an option for years in some occupations such as firefighters, police officers, nurses, hair stylists, and technicians. Today, it is being used in other occupations and firms including tellers at Citibank and operators at US Sprint.[60] Using compressed workweeks has shown a number of benefits for employers. This arrangement allows employees to better accommodate their other life demands (e.g., parental roles) so they are not forced to leave the firm. In addition, the organization can make better use of its equipment and resources. Employee morale and productivity is higher, and tardiness and absenteeism are lower.[61] There are some drawbacks. Understaffing, scheduling meetings, and coordinating team projects are three common problems. One of the most serious concerns is the increased employee fatigue brought on by working longer hours in a given day.

Participative Interventions

Participative programs for enhancing QWL have been in existence for years. They have become even more popular in recent years due to the perceived importance of the Baldrige award and the growing recognition that such programs work. The Wallace Company, a Houston-based industrial pipe, valve, and fittings distributor, instituted a quality program at the recommendation of one of its major customers in order to improve on-time delivery and invoice accuracy, and so keep the customer's business. Numerous other companies have adopted participative, employee involvement (EI) programs in recent years; among them are Bell South, First Union Bank, Procter & Gamble, and Upjohn.

Generally, it is believed that involving employees in decision making will result in improved job attitudes and cooperation and reduced turnover, absenteeism, and grievances. These effects are, however, contingent on whether there is sufficient time to involve employees in decision making and whether employees have the ability and interest to be participative.

Three approaches to employee involvement have been identified: parallel suggestion involvement systems, job involvement systems, and high involvement work systems.[62]

In **parallel suggestion involvement systems,** job design, organizational structures, and managerial roles are not altered. Employees are allowed to participate in problem identification, problem solving, and decision making through such vehicles as quality circles, task forces, opinion surveys, and suggestion systems. In these forms of involvement, participation is something that occurs outside of one's regular job assignments. Lincoln Electric uses all these methods to promote quality and increase productivity.

Job involvement approaches may be individual (e.g., job enrichment) or group-based (e.g., autonomous work groups or self-managing teams). In job enrichment, jobs are changed so that individual workers are allowed more variety, autonomy, feedback, and personal growth. In group-based strategies, work is organized around teams, and work groups are allowed to take over certain "management" functions. In job involvement systems, the job design is altered, however, the organizational structure and managerial roles are not changed.

High involvement work systems combine job involvement and a team-oriented work design with changes in organizational structure and managerial roles. These systems typically have fewer layers of management than traditional work systems. Such systems can operate very efficiently and with high flexibility.

The three EI approaches can be useful in different situations. However, the EI approach must match the current operating system and practices of the organization. Sometimes EI is implemented in direct contradiction to current organizational systems. When this happens, EI is more likely to fail than it is to change the organization.[63] Let us now turn to various components of the three EI approaches.

SURVEY SYSTEMS.* A major component of the scoring system for the Baldrige award involves accounting for the state of the human organization through participative programs. In addition, a growing body of research shows that participative programs are effective in increasing productivity and product and service quality. As a result, greater attention is being paid to developing tools for analysis and control of both the human resources management function and the human organization. These tools may be used for measuring the performance of the human resource system, evaluating that performance, and initiating corrective action when

---

*Contributed by Fred E. Schuster.

needed to bring performance in line with organizational objectives. The measurements reflect the attitudes, motivations, and satisfaction levels that characterize the human organization. A number of leading firms including IBM, Xerox, General Electric, Texas Instruments, and Motorola have pioneered the development of survey systems that facilitate these measurements. Based on the winners of past Baldrige awards, it is obvious that Baldrige judges place considerable weight on formal survey feedback systems.

Survey results reveal an organization's strengths and weaknesses and provide a means for comparing results against norms established by data from other organizations as well as against internal norms established in other departments. An example of a typical employee survey and definitions of the factors that are assessed are shown in Figures 12.4 and 12.5.

In addition to their measurement function, employee surveys may also be used to facilitate planned organization change and team building based on feedback and discussion of the survey data.[64] Companies often begin the review of survey data by comparing the organization's data against outside or internal norms to establish an initial benchmark. If the same survey is repeated in subsequent years, it becomes especially valuable to compare data in a given year for the organization as a whole and for various subdivisions (such as departments or divisions) with the data from previous years. Analyzing the trend of data over several years is a particularly powerful tool for understanding what is going on in the organization. Many companies combine attitude surveys with 360 degree appraisals for a more comprehensive perspective.

Many organizations also find it useful to compare the data (and trends) for different units across the organization to pinpoint specific parts of the organization where particular issues or concerns may be arising. This approach facilitates the development of action strategies specific to individual parts of the organization as well as other action strategies relevant for the entire organization. Survey data also promote the early identification of difficulties and permit timely response before minor concerns become major issues.

Along with opinion surveys, a variety of participative interventions exist ranging from informal suggestion systems to formalized job involvement programs or autonomous work teams. Some of the more popular programs are described in a later section.

THE RELATIONSHIP BETWEEN PARTICIPATIVE PROGRAMS AND THE UNION. The U.S. Department of Labor estimates that at least one-third of all major companies have some form of employee participation program.[65] In designing participative interventions, employers must be sure that the programs are not directly related to union activities. Committees should

FIGURE 12.4
EXAMPLE OF AN EMPLOYEE OPINION SURVEY

HUMAN RESOURCES INDEX

The objective of this survey is to determine how members of this organization feel about the effectiveness with which the organization's human resources are managed. The survey provides you an opportunity to express your opinions in a way that is constructive. Your views will be valuable in assisting the organization to evaluate and improve its performance.

The survey is to be done anonymously. Please **do not put your name** on the response sheet or identify your response in any way. Responses can in no way be traced to any individual. The frank and free expression of your own opinions will be most helpful to the organization.

Listed below are a series of statements. After you have read each statement, please decide the extent to which the statement describes your own situation and your own feelings, using the following scale:

A) almost never
B) not often
C) sometimes (i.e., about half the time)
D) often
E) almost always

Then, using a No. 2 pencil darken the appropriate box on the response sheet. For example, if you believe that the statement is true "sometimes" darken block C on the answer sheet next to the number corresponding to the indicated statement.

Questions 65 and 66 should be answered in **pencil** on the back of the **response sheet.**

When you have completed the survey, please return the response sheet and this survey form in accordance with the directions in the cover letter.

IN THIS ORGANIZATION:

1. There is sufficient communication and sharing of information between groups.

2. The skills and abilities of employees are fully and effectively utilized.

3. Objectives of the total organization and my work unit are valid and challenging.

4. The activities of my job are satisfying and rewarding.

5. I have received the amount and kind of training which I need and desire to do my job well.

6. Leadership in this organization is achieved through ability.

7. Rewards are fairly and equitably distributed.

8. First-level supervision is of a high quality.

9. Management has a high concern for production and effectively communicates this concern.

10. My job provides ample opportunity for a sense of individual responsibility.

11. There is a sense of loyalty and belonging among members of this organization.

-
-
-

63. By and large, most members of this organization are sensitive, perceptive, and helpful to one another.

64. In general, complete and accurate information is available for making organizational decisions.

- -

65. The things I like best about this organization are: _____

66. The things I would most like to change are: _____

**FIGURE 12.5
FACTOR DEFINITIONS
FROM AN EMPLOYEE SURVEY**

1. **Reward system** (RWD): compensation, benefits, perquisites, and other (tangible and intangible) rewards.
2. **Communication** (COM): flow of information downward, upward, and across the organization.
3. **Organization effectiveness** (OE): level of confidence in the overall abilities and success of the organization; how well the organization achieves its objectives.
4. **Concern for people** (PLP): the degree to which the organization is perceived of as caring for the individuals who work for it.
5. **Organization objectives** (OO): the extent to which individuals perceive the organization to have objectives that they can understand, feel proud of, and identify with.
6. **Cooperation** (COP): the ability of people throughout the organization to work effectively together to achieve shared goals.
7. **Intrinsic satisfaction** (IS): rewards that people receive from the work itself (sense of achievement, pride in a job well done, growth and development, feeling of competence).
8. **Structure** (STC): rules and regulations, operating policies and procedures, management practices and systems, the formal organization structure and reporting relationships.
9. **Relationships** (REL): feelings that people have about others in the organization.
10. **Climate** (CLM): the atmosphere of the organization, the extent to which people see it as a comfortable, supportive, pleasant place to work.
11. **Participation** (PAR): opportunity to contribute one's ideas, to be consulted, to be informed, and to play a part in decision making.
12. **Work group** (WG): feelings about the immediate group of people with whom one works on a daily basis.
13. **Intergroup competence** (ITG): the ability of separate work groups to work smoothly and effectively together to accomplish shared objectives.
14. **First-level supervision** (FLM): confidence that members of the organization have in the competence and integrity of first-line supervisors.
15. **Quality of management** (QM): confidence that members of the organization have in the competence and integrity of middle and higher management.

Source: Fred E. Schuster, Professor of Management, Florida Atlantic University, Boca Raton, FL 33431. Copyright 1979. Reprinted with permission.

not serve as a bargaining unit for employees nor be connected to a union-organizing drive. In addition, the committees should be comprised primarily of volunteer employee representatives, more than management members. We will discuss this issue at greater length in Chapter 13.

QUALITY CIRCLES. A **quality circle** (QC) is a small group of employees (usually 7 to 10) who volunteer to meet several hours each week to address produc-tivity and quality problems. The members identify, analyze, and make recommendations about problems in their work area. Usually, the employees are members of a work unit from the same department. Often, their supervisor serves as the circle leader, while a staff member is a facilitator who helps guide the circle through the problem-solving process. The primary topic of discussion of most circles is quality issues, although they do consider other topics such as cost, safety, and efficiency.

For the QC to be effective, several suggestions are offered:[66]

1. *Introduce the basics.* In the first group meeting, present an overview and give members a chance to ask questions and express concerns.
2. *Find the real cause of the problem.* The group should list all possible causes and then evaluate them to determine which are minor or major causes.
3. *Brainstorm solutions.* Evaluate solutions based on how feasible they will be to implement.
4. *Develop an implementation plan.* Determine who will be affected and whether the necessary resources are available.
5. *Present the plan to management.*

Developing a QC program. Most QC programs in U.S. firms are similarly developed, although there are some differences in how they are tailored to particular firms. Generally, most QCs exist for several years, usually until their members run out of problems to address or lose interest in the activity.[67]

QC programs can be used in a variety of ways including: (1) collecting ideas for work improvements from those closest to the work itself (i.e., the work group), (2) providing opportunities for problem solving, (3) dealing with special projects on a temporary basis, (4) enhancing personal and professional growth of QC members, (5) team building, and (6) helping the organization make the transition toward a more participative culture. Regarding the last use, some organizations implement QC programs to get employees adjusted to the idea of being more involved. They have QC members work on identifying and solving problems. Following this, they change the voluntary circle meetings to on-the-job staff meetings, provide training for QC members, and form semiautonomous work groups.

A variety of suggestions have been given for ensuring that QCs are used effectively in organizations. They include:[68]

- Obtain managerial support and involvement for the program.
- Start quality groups with problems that are persistent yet relatively easy to solve.
- Use the right mix of staff so that they have the abilities to solve the problems.

- Identify goals for the program and criteria to evaluate it on.
- Do not expect the QC program to solve all problems in the organization.
- Make sure managers realize that any changes will take time.
- Inform all employees about the philosophy and goals of the program.
- Keep the program voluntary.
- Select group members based on their technical expertise and their support of the program's goals.
- Prepare individuals for their new roles in a participative culture.
- Provide ongoing training for participants in the techniques to be used.
- Provide training for managers as coordinators.
- Provide training for support staff who will serve as facilitators. For example, Polaroid trains its HR staff to be facilitators. The best facilitators are people who volunteer for the job, have strong interpersonal skills, and have a strong commitment to excellence.
- Start with a pilot test of the program in a supportive department.
- Implement the suggestions made by employees.
- Provide recognition for the employees' efforts.

Research is mixed about the effects of QC programs. Some studies indicate positive effects on productivity, quality, absenteeism, and job attitudes, and other studies indicate no changes or less positive results.[69] As a result, many firms are combining QCs with other job involvement programs.

AUTONOMOUS WORK GROUPS (AWG) OR SELF-MANAGING TEAMS.

Autonomous work groups (also known as self-managing work teams) are employee groups given a high degree of decision-making responsibility and behavioral control for completing their work. Usually, the team is empowered or given the responsibility for producing the entire product or service. A team essentially replaces the boss by taking over responsibilities for scheduling, hiring, ordering, and firing. Digital Equipment Corporation, Mercedes-Benz, Rubbermaid, and Corning are examples of major manufacturing facilities with work teams, but the approach is catching on in the services sector. At the team-based Chrysler plant in New Castle, Indiana, team members communicate with customers and do all the hiring.[70] At the new Mercedes-Benz plant in Alabama, managers are considered team members. They occupy a second-story office area at the very center of the plant with windows overlooking the factory floor. Cubicles are not used so there can be open communication among all team members. In addition, workers are trained so that if they dis-

cover a problem with a vehicle, they can follow it for several stations to try to correct the problem.[71]

AWGs have some similarities to QCs because they are based on employee participation, but they also have some differences. For example, AWGs usually elect an internal leader who also serves as a full-time member. Management may appoint an external leader or coordinator. The external leader serves primarily as a facilitator rather than as a supervisor. He or she may assist the group members in receiving feedback on the quality and quantity of their performance as well as make any structural changes in the work design. The coordinator is also responsible for helping the team acquire needed resources (e.g., equipment) and technical assistance.[72]

Activities of AWGs or self-managing work teams. Self-managing teams are involved in a number of different activities including:[73]

- Recording quality control statistics.
- Making scheduling assignments.
- Solving technical problems.
- Setting group or team goals.
- Resolving internal conflicts.
- Assessing group or team performance.
- Making task assignments to group or team members.
- Preparing a budget.
- Training team members.
- Selecting new members.
- Allocating pay raises for members.

Suggestions for using AWGs or self-managing work teams. For AWGs or self-managing work teams to be effective, several conditions are necessary. Training is necessary for team members on a variety of human relations skills, such as problem solving, group dynamics, conflict resolution, cooperation, and participation, and technical skills, such as statistical quality control and budget preparation. The training should be updated to keep individuals current and focused on the goals of the team. Training is also necessary for managers on their new role as facilitator, especially since their new role requires a very different relationship with their subordinates. In addition to training, AWGs and teams need to receive current information and resources to carry out their work assignments, as well as time and space to engage in team activities.

The effectiveness of AWGs or self-managing work teams. Some managers believe that self-managing work teams or AWGs help increase productivity anywhere from 20 to 50 percent and reduce scrap, lost time, and poor-quality products. Chrysler, for example, reports reduced production costs, defects, and employee absenteeism. At the Procter & Gamble plant in Lima, Ohio, which makes Liquid Tide, Downy fabric softener, and Biz bleach, teams are responsible for their own safety, production targets, quality goals, and their needs to improve customer service. Team meetings occur at every shift change, and the teams reorganize themselves as they deem necessary. Based on the way in which the plant was reorganized into only three levels (one plant manager, 10 managers, and about 350 technicians working in teams), the plant was considered to be at least 30 percent more productive.[74] At Pacific Bell, employees on craft, clerical, and engineering self-managed teams reported higher productivity and performance and satisfaction with their jobs, work units, and growth potential as compared to similar traditional work groups.[75]

In other cases, results have been mixed regarding the effect of AWGs on productivity.[76] Teams are being used even in service industries. At one of the most successful retailers in the United States, Katherine Barchetti's clothing stores, sales associates work in teams. One greets the customer, another pulls up the customer's record in the database, and a third may come over with a pair of shoes and a belt. They do not work on individual commission, consequently, employees are more willing to help one another.[77] In the hotel industry, service quality-improvement teams have been implemented. Using a service quality audit, managers and quality-improvement teams identify errors and determine their frequency, assign costs of fixing (or not fixing) the errors, and identify steps to prevent them. For example, the audit of a hotel found that the most common error at the front desk was not posting late charges on a guest's bill, which cost the hotel an estimated $250,000 per year. By addressing this and other errors, the hotel's management was able to control costs and improve the guest's hotel experience.[78] In some organizations, "green teams" have been formed to serve as quality-improvement teams to address environmental issues (e.g., how the organization can identify and eliminate waste).[79]

Employees report that team membership provides them with more autonomy, flexibility, skill variety, training opportunities, and financial benefits (e.g., group-based bonuses). It is not surprising then that firms have found members of AWGs experience higher job satisfaction and morale.[80] However, it often takes up to two years for some of the positive effects of AWGs to materialize. Managers need to be patient in expecting results and should guarantee job security to enable employees to feel comfortable taking risks and being creative and innovative.

TOTAL QUALITY MANAGEMENT (TQM). Total quality management is a participative intervention involving every employee and manager in the organization. Today, TQM conveys a total, companywide effort that includes all employees, suppliers, and customers and that seeks continuously to improve the quality of products and processes to meet the needs and expectations of customers. The basic attributes are (1) customer focus, (2) strategic planning and leadership, (3) continuous improvement, and (4) empowerment and teamwork.[81] It involves significant changes in an organization's culture including the goals, mission, philosophy, and procedures. The major emphasis of the TQM movement is to make every employee and manager responsible for making continuous improvements in the quality of their services and products in order to satisfy customers' needs.[82]

A "customer" includes anyone who is the recipient of some product or service, whether inside or outside the firm. For example, a receptionist's customers could include the boss who gave the receptionist a report to be typed, employees in other departments who exchange files and information with the receptionist, and individuals who phone in with their requests regarding the firm. At Federal Express and American Express, employees are responsible for developing formal contracts with their customers that outline what is expected of them. Performance criteria are defined by customers, not by supervisors.[83]

Guiding principles of TQM. Many of the major principles of TQM are based on the ideas of two Americans, W. Edwards Deming and Joseph M. Juran, who are experts on statistical process control and quality management. Their ideas have been embraced by Japan since the 1950s. Some of their ideas are described below:

- Meet the customer's requirements on time, the first time, and 100 percent of the time. This involves identifying who the customers are and clarifying what their requirements or expectations are. For example, at Pittsburgh-based Katherine Barchetti's high-fashion clothing stores, sales associates emphasize knowing their customers' needs, desires, styles, and shopping habits. This has enabled the stores to be rated as "the best retailer in more than 80 cities."[84]

- Strive to have 0 percent defects and to do error-free work. For example, at Motorola, employees have achieved a goal called Six Sigma which means no more than 3.4 defects per million Motorola products and services.[85]

- Manage by prevention. Defects and errors can occur at any part of the process from design of a product to completion. Don't wait until after the product is completed to look for defects. Make sure defects are not built into any phase. Trace all errors to their sources and correct them.

- Use statistical process control (SPC) methods. SPC gauges the performance of the manufacturing process by monitoring changes in whatever is being produced. The intent is to detect potential problems before they lead to poor-quality products, determine the reason for the deviation, and adjust the process to make it more stable.

- Measure the cost of quality. Illustrate the difference in the costs incurred for preventing errors *before* products are produced versus detecting and correcting them *after* they have been produced.

Deming's 14 principles. Many organizations (e.g., Cadillac, American Express, Johnson & Johnson) have profited from seminars on Deming's philosophy of quality improvement. He outlined 14 points that should be followed.[86] These are:

1. Create constancy of purpose for improvement of product and service.
2. Adopt the new philosophy.
3. Cease dependence on mass inspection.
4. End the practice of awarding business on the basis of price tag alone. Instead, minimize total cost by working with fewer suppliers.
5. Improve constantly and forever every process for planning, production, and service.
6. Institute modern methods of training, using statistics.
7. Adopt and institute leadership. Focus supervision on helping people to do a better job.
8. Drive out fear. Encourage two-way communication.
9. Break down barriers between staff areas. Encourage problem solving through teamwork.
10. Eliminate slogans, exhortations, and targets for the workforce.
11. Eliminate numerical quotas for the workforce and numerical goals for people in management.
12. Remove barriers that rob people of pride of workmanship.
13. Encourage education and self-improvement for everyone.
14. Take action to accomplish the transformation.

Suggestions for TQM programs. Once a TQM program is designed and ready to be implemented, there are a variety of suggestions for enhancing the TQM experience. These are:

- Make the program organizationwide.
- Have the support of managers at all levels.
- Prioritize problem areas and start work on only a few critical problems.
- Provide ongoing training for employees in the importance of quality, statistical control methods, analytical skills, and strategies for solving quality problems. Allow employees opportunities to use their new skills on the job.

- Encourage and facilitate collaboration between divisions in the firm (i.e., across cross-functional boundaries).
- Provide training in TQM to suppliers and don't accept poor quality from them. Motorola drops suppliers who do not state intentions for applying for the Baldrige award.
- Use reward systems to support the participative culture. Make rewards congruent with the work design (i.e., use group-based rewards if the intent is to foster a collaborative environment).
- Have supervisors provide recognition to employees.
- Use natural work units for the teams.
- Recognize that the focus is on *continuous* improvements (i.e., that improvements are never completed).
- Give employees the tools and resources they will need to analyze and solve problems.
- Follow up on the suggestions made by employees.
- Keep quality improvements cost-effective.

TQM requires some changes in the fundamental assumptions about people in organizations as well as the values, goals, and assumptions about organizations. (See Figure 12.6.)

Popularity of TQM. In the past decade, TQM programs have become extremely popular in a variety of private and public organizations, including manufacturing firms, service industries, and government agencies. Textile, steel, automobile, and major appliance industries have become committed to TQM principles after suffering severe market share losses due to poor quality. Organizations that have implemented TQM include AT&T, DuPont, Hewlett-Packard, Kodak, Cadillac, Federal Express, L.L. Bean, Toyota, Xerox, Motorola, Baxter Health Care, Corning Glass Works, IBM, General Motors, McCormick Spice, Westinghouse, Tennessee Valley Authority, Wallace Company, M&M Mars, Florida Power & Light, Procter & Gamble, Alcoa, and Ford Motor Company.[87] One reason for the popularity of TQM is its effectiveness in Japan. For example, TQM programs have been attributed with having a large role in making the Japanese world leaders in quality.[88] While some organizations have shown successes with TQM (e.g., Motorola, Xerox), others have experienced false starts or failures.[89]

Many TQM efforts have been specifically developed and implemented in the context of the Baldrige award. Figure 12.7 presents a TQM model developed in the context of the seven Baldrige categories. This framework has three basic elements, from top to bottom. These include the strategy and action plans, the system, and information and analysis. The strategy and action plans are the set of company-level requirements, derived from short- and long-term strategic planning. These

FIGURE 12.6
TRADITIONAL ORGANIZATION VERSUS TQM ORGANIZATION: VALUES, GOALS, AND ASSUMPTIONS

	TRADITIONAL ORGANIZATION	TQM ORGANIZATION
Values, goals, and assumptions about the organization	Efficiency	Create value
	Specialization	Continuous improvement of processes
	Monetary incentives	Organizational learning
	Control over worker	Team-based structure
	Division of labor	Utilize worker insights to creatively improve processes
	Emphasis on short results	Emphasis on long-term survival and renewal
	Groups foster inefficiency	System is self-nourishing
Assumptions about people	Individuals dislike work	Work is as natural as play
	Individuals must be directed	Individual commitment is necessary
	Individuals cannot be trusted	Individuals want responsibility
	Individuals have little ambition	Individuals can solve problems
	Individuals avoid responsibility	Work is an important source of rewards
	Individuals must be monitored	Individuals can exercise self-control
	Individuals want to avoid work	Individuals have the capacity to be creative

Source: D. L. Stone and E. R. Eddy, A model of individual and organizational factors affecting quality-related outcomes. *Journal of Quality Management,* 1(1) 1996, 21–48.

plans guide the overall resource decisions and drive the alignment of measures for all work units to ensure customer satisfaction and market success. The system is comprised of the six Baldrige categories that define the organization, its operations, and its results. Information and analysis (category 4) are essential to the effective management and improved competitiveness of the firm.

Effectiveness of TQM.   Although few empirical studies have been conducted, both Juran and Deming both reported numerous case examples to illustrate that TQM is a cost-effective strategy. Juran stated that in a typical firm with $1 billion in revenues, the average savings per TQM project exceeds $100,000 a year. With the training costs ranging from $5,000 to 20,000, the average firm will see a 5 to 20 times payback in the first year, with improved productivity, market share, and profitability over the long term.[90] Other evidence suggests that TQM programs are effective at improving quality and reducing the costs of rework, as well as improving job satisfaction, internal communications, and work procedures.[91]

In many firms using TQM, the numbers speak for themselves. TQM practices resulted in a 38 percent decrease in customer complaints at Xerox and an 80 percent reduction in defects at Motorola. At IBM, revenue per employee increased 35 percent from 1986 to 1989, and the time to develop a new midrange computer was reduced in half. Cadillac, a 1990 Baldrige winner, applied Deming's process model for quality improvement and found reductions of up to 71 percent in reliability problems since 1986. It also found a 16 percent increase in customer satisfaction from 1985 to 1989.[92]

Most of the reports of the positive effects of TQM and statistical process control emanate from manufactur-

ing and not service, although increasingly more service industries are applying TQM principles. For example, decreased turnaround time for refunds was reported in the state of Wisconsin and substantial cost savings were reported at the University of Michigan hospital.[93] Much greater attention is being given to quality management in U.S. corporations, particularly in the context of the Baldrige award and ISO 9000. In addition, increasingly more research attention is being devoted to TQM as it relates to HR practices.[94] One finding has shown that it is critical that quality-improvement programs be headed by full-time coordinators. If the coordinator is already handling other firefighting or routine problems, then that person may not have enough time to devote to the quality-improvement efforts.[95]

Recent results on TQM effectiveness.   Results from the 1990s have not been as positive as those from the 1980s regarding the effectiveness of TQM programs. A survey of 500 executives in U.S. manufacturing and service firms found that only one-third felt that TQM made them more competitive.[96] In addition, winners of previous quality awards (e.g., Florida Power and Light; Wallace Company) had cut their staffs or filed for bankruptcy. These findings may be due to the following: programs being used that are really not TQM programs, managers being oversold and thereby having unrealistic expectations about what TQM can really do, and varying views by top managers about the goals and practice of TQM.

Top managers' views on TQM.   It has often been acknowledged that for TQM to be effective, top managers must support it. Few studies have examined the views of

FIGURE 12.7
MODEL OF TQM IN THE CONTEXT OF THE BALDRIGE AWARD CRITERIA

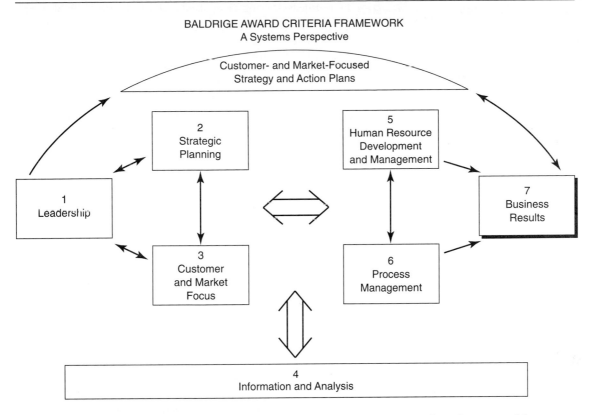

BALDRIGE AWARD CRITERIA FRAMEWORK
A Systems Perspective

Source: 1997 Malcolm Baldrige National Quality Award Criteria for Performance Excellence, United States Department of Commerce, Technology Administration, National Institute of Standards and Technology, Rt. 270 and Quince Orchard Rd., Administration Bldg., Room A 537, Gaithersburg, MD 20899-0001, p. 42.

top managers toward TQM. One notable exception is a recent study that explored the views of top managers toward TQM programs and found notable differences in their views. Some managers had a *developmental orientation* whereby they viewed TQM as an essential tool to grow the company's business or transform the firm into one of the best in the business. They focused on the future and viewed customers as a partner. In these firms, numerous TQM practices were employed. Other executives had a *tactical orientation,* meaning they believed the customer always came first. They focused on the present and concentrated on identifying and managing responses to customers' immediate needs. The customer was seen as a demanding buyer. They used TQM as a tool for reducing rejection rates and improving customer satisfaction, but not as a mechanism for future growth. Finally, others had a *defensive orientation,* meaning that they saw their role as one of surviving in a hostile world. They focused on the past and saw the customer as an opponent. They did not see any value to TQM techniques for the firm and felt forced to use them to meet customers' needs. These managers had no commitment to TQM and adopted the principles in a superficial way.[97] These differing views among top managers help to explain why in some cases TQM is successful, yet in other cases it is not.

REENGINEERING

Reengineering, or business process improvement, is a set of practices for periodically examining and improving the business processes in an organization.[98] It is defined as "the fundamental rethinking and radical redesign of business processes to achieve dramatic improvements in critical, contemporary measures of performance such as cost, quality, service, and speed."[99] The intent is to streamline an operation and adapt it to existing market realities.[100] More recently, it has been defined as "a coordinated, continuous improvement approach required to rethink, redesign, retool, and reinvent new processes that will perform better than existing ones."[101] The internal processes include: billing, distribution, order entry, procurement, and materials management.

Reengineering has five goals:[102]

1. *Increase productivity* by creating innovative processes.

2. *Optimize value to shareholders* including employees, customers, stockholders, and so on.

3. *Achieve quantum results* in productivity, inventory reductions, cycle-time improvements, indirect-cost improvements, and head-count redeployments.

4. *Consolidate functions* and create a leaner, flatter, and faster organization.

5. *Eliminate unnecessary levels and work* (nonvalue-added activities).

In the 1990s, reengineering became very popular as companies tried to become increasingly more productive and to realize substantial gains in cost, time, or service. It has been used in a number of companies (e.g., IBM) that have adopted other quality-improvement approaches, such as TQM, participative interventions, work redesign. For example, AT&T Global Information Systems used it because of changes in the computer and information systems market. It had a major reengineering effort known as Quote to Cash. Promus Hotels combined a reengineered work process with on-line, just-in-time learning support to eliminate the need for formal training at a central-site classroom.[103] Reengineering has been so popular in recent years that it has been estimated to be a $4.7 billion industry for consultants.[104]

Generally, when reengineering or business process improvements are conducted, a manager leads a cross-functional team to examine a process and determine

ways to improve it. For example, GTE Service Corporation's Management Education and Training Process Reengineering Team used a task force made up of members from the groups of directories, spacenet, communications, corporate training, information services, and TELOPS training to determine their needs for process redesign.[105] GTE is the largest U.S.-based local telephone company and the second largest cellular service provider in the United States. The reengineering team came up with recommendations for a total savings of $4.7 million in 1993.[106]

Often, various statistical techniques may be used to determine the types of problems that exist and the causes of the problems. The team may make some changes to see the effect on the process and then continue to monitor the process, making additional changes and improvements. One model that illustrates the various systems involved in reengineering is presented in Figure 12.8. This model considers four primary systems for reengineering or organizational transformation. The *management system* provides the vision and strategies; the *social system* provides the cultural support to implement new ideas; the *technical system* provides the tools to achieve outstanding service or products; and the *behavioral system* provides the human side of the reengineering process. Another way of conceptualizing the approach is given with the six Rs in Figure 12.9. It starts with *realizing* the extent of the problem, identifying the *requirements* of

**FIGURE 12.8
A MODEL OF ORGANIZATIONAL TRANSFORMATION
AND REENGINEERING**

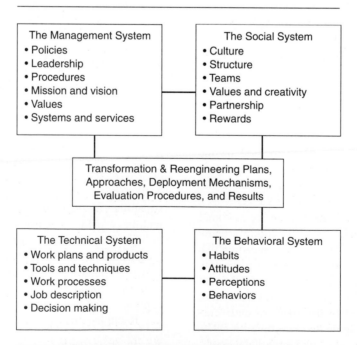

Source: J. A. Edosomwan, *Organizational Transformation and Process Engineering.* Delray Beach, FL: St. Lucie Press, 1996.

FIGURE 12.9
THE SIX R'S OF TRANSFORMATION AND REENGINEERING

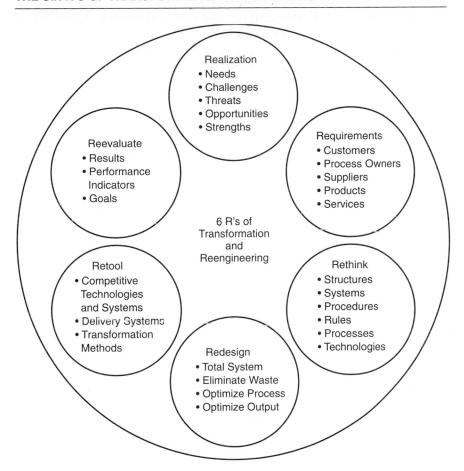

Source: J. A. Edosomwan, *Organizational transformation and process engineering.* Delray Beach, FL: St. Lucie Press, 1996.

the internal and external customers, *rethinking* the current practices, *redesigning* the processes, *retooling* or adopting new technologies and tools, and *reevaluating* the entire process.

One outcome of reengineering may be that very specialized jobs are combined into larger, more enriched jobs. If management levels are reduced, this may lead to greater responsibilities for employees. For example, IBM used reengineering in its credit corporation to cut down on the amount of time taken to complete credit checks. As a result, IBM was able to combine several jobs that allowed workers to make more decisions.[107] Managers may also gain larger spans of control if the organizational structure is flattened. For example, Computer Associates, the third largest independent software company after Microsoft and Oracle, uses just four management levels to separate the 2,500 sales employees from the top executives.[108]

Some companies use the Japanese word *Kaizen* to talk about their process improvements; this word refers to the process of continuous, incremental improvements. Since total quality is a never-ending process, organiza-

tions should always be looking for ways to make improvements. Toyota Motor Manufacturing, USA uses its workers to help improve their systems. Toyota selects employees who have a high commitment to improve quality and look for innovative ways to improve their systems.[109]

Recently, some critiques have stated that reengineering has led to many companies immediately laying off workers, particularly middle-level managers, some argue reengineering is really just a concept for laying off workers or outsizing, downsizing, or rightsizing.[110] For example, AT&T's recent layoffs were called a "force management program" designed to reduce "an imbalance of forces or skills."[111]

Although this is how some critics have viewed the reengineering movement, reengineering was never meant to simply mean restructuring or downsizing, delayering or flattening an organization, software reengineering, or total quality management.[112] It was never meant to be a mechanism for outplacing employees under the guise of improvement or a onetime radical strategy or quick fix.[113]

As we discussed in Chapter 5, for **rightsizing** to be effective, American companies should develop a strategy of rightsizing that is tailored to business and strategic objectives. Several strategies are recommended.[114]

- Consider cost-cutting options other than employment reductions (e.g., pay cuts, unpaid holidays, reduced workweeks, job sharing). If reductions are necessary, then managers should provide assistance and outplacement programs.

- Build support by full disclosure of information and communication with employees. Illustrate the firm's concern by explaining the measures the company is taking to minimize layoffs and by describing the assistance that will be provided to those laid off.

- Redesign work based on positions not people. Remaining workers should receive higher-value-added tasks, not simply higher workloads.

- Use a system of reviews and appeals to make sure the redeployment process is perceived to be fair and equitable.

- Retain employees with key organizational knowledge as possible consultants.

- Provide generous outplacement assistance and benefits to those who have been laid off. Use available government resources.

- Plan for and provide leadership for organizational recovery, morale, and performance improvement.

The HR department should play a pivotal role in ensuring that the organizational systems support the reengineering effort. For example, the recruitment and selection systems should encourage the hiring of workers who believe in making continuous improvements on the job. In addition, employees may need training in working collaboratively in teams and in performing more job responsibilities. For example, Ford rebuilt its competitiveness by adopting Japanese lean manufacturing systems and by reinventing teamwork and worker–management collaboration.[115] Compensation systems may also need to be changed if job activities are altered and if the organization wants to promote a team-based culture. As noted in a later section, any organizational improvement plans require the support of the firm's HR systems.

Benefits of reengineering that are relevant to the HR mission of the firm, especially the continuous learning emphasis, include the following:[116]

- Meeting job and skill demands for the new economy.

- Positioning HR programs as a way to bring the organization into the future.

- Presenting learning as a performance tool.

- Utilizing HR programs, particularly training and career development, as tools for dealing with change.

- Deploying a strategy for maximizing success at the employee level.

- Providing an opportunity to develop organizational learners and leaders.

- Capitalizing on the potential to leverage the human capital investment.

- Increasing the value of HR, particularly training, to the organization.

In many cases, reengineering has been quite successful and has led to productivity improvements of 25 to 100 percent, head-count redeployments of 25 to 50 percent, and inventory reductions of 40 to 50 percent. In addition there have been reports of cycle-time improvements of 50 to 300 percent and indirect-cost improvements of 25 to 50 percent.[117] Bell Atlantic reduced personnel costs from $88 million to $6 million in its Carrier Access Service Area dealing with long-distance access and hook-up when it used self-managed work teams.[118]

A COMPARISON OF THE LEADING CHANGE APPROACHES

In recent years, with the advent of the TQM and reengineering approaches, there has been some confusion about their similarities and differences. Some similarities have been identified: (1) they both require a strategic decision that involves major financial and resource investment and commitment; (2) they focus on the entire system; (3) they follow both a customer and an improvement focus; (4) organizational learning is an integral component of the change process; and (5) they require transformation and modification of the organization's culture. In terms of differences: (1) their espoused objectives vary since reengineering focuses on radical changes of key processes and TQM focuses on continuous quality improvement of products, processes, and services; (2) they follow different change processes and phases: reengineering change processes follow clearly defined inductive-based phases, while TQM seems to have broadly defined deductive phases; (3) they incorporate the technological subsystem differently: reengineering is concerned with implementing new technology, particularly information technology, while TQM focuses on the improvements of processes in general; and (4) the measurements differ such that outcomes are to be realized in TQM over the long term, but more quickly with reengineering. Figure 12.10 illustrates what it might look like if the basic tenets of the two approaches were combined. Such an approach is based on a systems view of the firm, involves the development of individual competencies and the learning organization, and addresses both short- and long-run challenges for the firm.[119]

**FIGURE 12.10
AN ECLECTIC APPROACH TO ORGANIZATIONAL
CHANGE**

Phase 1: Project Initiation
- Define scope and purpose
- Secure management commitment
- Establish organizational awareness of the need for radical changes
- Create a parallel learning mechanism and educate organizational members

Phase 2: Mapping Customers' Key Processes
- Identify customers' requirements, needs, and potential
- Determine the key processes

Phase 3: The Inquiry Process
- Establish benchmarks
- Conduct business analysis based on sociotechnical systems framework:
  —Verify key processes
  —Uncover system pathologies
- Revise company vision based on analysis, strategic opportunities, and enabling technology (i.e., information technology)
- Identify potential improvements to the existing processes

Phase 4: Design/Redesign in order to Modify Existing Processes and Organizational Structure
- Formulate specific alternative sociotechnical-based design solutions (e.g., includes the optimal integration of key organizational elements such as rewards, control, structure, information, people, and technology)
- Explore potential impact of proposed solutions
- Develop joint optimization of key processes
- Establish learning processes for continuous improvements

Phase 5: Implementation and Reconstruction of the Key Processes and Organization
- Foster climate that is conducive to change
- Create the implementation and support mechanisms
- Develop training programs
- Establish learning loops as an integral part of continuous improvement

Source: A. B. Shani and Y. Mitki, Reengineering, total quality management and sociotechnical systems approaches to organizational change: Towards an eclectic approach? *Journal of Quality Management,* 1(1), (1996), 131–145.

THE ROLE OF THE HR DEPARTMENT IN ORGANIZATIONAL IMPROVEMENTS

According to the criteria for the Baldrige award, human resource management and development is considered one of the most important issues for companies to emphasize. This includes specific training programs in quality, general training and development programs, communication systems, suggestions systems, performance-appraisal systems, and opinion surveys.[120]

In most firms, HR professionals are in the best position to address these issues. They understand the organization's mission and can develop improvement programs to be consistent with the firm's goals. In addition, they are familiar with the various personnel systems in the organization (e.g., training, compensation, motivation) and can make sure new programs are designed to fit with the existing systems. Also, HR professionals generally have more training than managers and employees in human relations skills and can train others in management participation and employee involvement.

While the HR department should be actively involved in organizational efforts to improve productivity and quality, this often does not occur. In fact, HR professionals are often the targets of major downsizing efforts.[121] Even in progressive companies, HR professionals are so busy with "putting out fires" that they have difficulty finding the time for new programs.

There are, however, many cases where the HR staff is actively involved in designing, implementing, and evaluating improvement interventions.[122] At the Tennessee Valley Authority, for instance, some HR staff members have been reassigned to work more closely with top managers in the organizationwide TQM initiative. At IBM, all TQM training was developed, implemented, and evaluated through the HR function working closely with line management.

Roles in Designing Programs

HR professionals need to involve employees, managers, and the union when designing improvement programs. This can be done by establishing a task force comprised of representatives from every group who work together to define the problems and offer recommendations. This level of teamwork and joint planning is necessary to ensure that the final programs will be accepted and used by all organizational members. It is especially important to solicit the ideas and suggestions of middle-level managers and supervisors because these individuals are in a position to greatly influence how others view the new interventions. Their opinions can be collected by interviews, survey methods, or less formal means.

When they are designing improvement programs, HR professionals often conduct a needs assessment to determine the systems that are working well and those that are not. To do this, they may gather data by conducting individual or group interviews, observing work practices, administering surveys, or leading employee focus groups. Focus groups consist of employees who usually volunteer to meet to try to identify and discuss organizational concerns related to productivity or quality.

After conducting a needs assessment, the HR professional must be able to work with the organizational representatives to establish priorities for initiating improvements. The HR professional should keep everyone informed and be prepared to revise the design. Changes may be necessary to fine-tune the new program or to adjust it according to new philosophies articulated by top managers. The HR staff should review the reward system to be sure the new programs are compatible with any compensation or incentive systems.

Roles in Implementing and Evaluating Programs

When programs are being implemented, HR professionals are usually responsible for training managers and employees in the new systems. They are also often responsible for convincing others in the organization of the importance of the new programs. Thus, they have to deal with any potential resistance to change and sell individuals on the benefits of the proposed programs. While some organizational members may support the new programs, others (e.g., managers) may be concerned about costs, time off from work for employee participation, and the potential usefulness of the interventions. HR professionals should try to gain managerial participation early in the process to build support and lessen later resistance. Using pilot projects may aid in checking out the program and fostering positive attitudes about the intervention.

To evaluate the programs, HR professionals should provide a baseline for measuring and tracking results. They should also be prepared to describe the potential cost-effectiveness of the proposed programs and collect data to show actual dollar value.

THE EFFECTIVENESS OF IMPROVEMENT PROGRAMS

Organizational improvement programs are generally effective in improving employee quality, productivity, and quality of work life. In a review of 207 published studies, the 11 interventions examined increased employee productivity in 87 percent of the studies. The programs that were most effective included pay-for-performance, training, goal setting, participative management, and sociotechnical systems (e.g., AWGs, alternative working arrangements). Also, favorable attitudes toward work resulted from the programs, indicating that productivity and QWL could be improved at the same time.[123]

Criteria and Designs for Measuring Effectiveness

As noted throughout this chapter, interventions may be implemented to meet a variety of purposes. The primary purposes are to enhance productivity, quality of services and products, and employee quality of work life. To assess whether programs are working, the firm needs to examine changes in the relevant criteria described earlier in this chapter.

Research designs should be used so that the organization is in a position to assess changes as a result of the new programs. Refer to Chapter 7 to review these designs. Essentially, measurements on the important criteria should be taken both before and after the program is implemented to determine whether the program affected the criteria of interest (e.g., productivity, absenteeism). Reactions can also be collected from employees after implementing the programs to see if they had favorable opinions about the program. Longitudinal designs should be used because organizationwide improvement programs often take years to show any effects. For example, with TQM, many firms realize that it takes anywhere from 1 to 10 years just to implement the system.

Factors Affecting the Effectiveness of Programs

COMMITMENT.   In the United States, quality programs are not typically tied to the rest of the organizational systems (e.g., appraisal, rewards). Quality teams work on company time by taking individuals out of their normal work activities, and team members have to report their findings and recommendations back to the organization. In addition, most U.S. manufacturing firms do not determine defect rates by statistical methods, although these approaches are gaining in popularity.[124]

According to a survey conducted by the American Society for Quality Control, 20 percent of the respondents said their companies do not have quality improvement programs. In firms having quality programs, few employees actually participate. A variety of reasons are given including: they aren't given opportunities to participate in the process, they don't believe that quality programs have any effect, or they were too busy. Employees also stated that their firms talked about quality, but did not seem committed to it. In other words, firms rarely followed through on the action plans developed. Twenty-five percent of the respondents expressed dissatisfaction with their firms' rate of quality improvement, although an equal number were highly satisfied.[125]

It appears that if improvement programs are to be effective in the United States, employees and managers will need to increase their level of commitment to enhancing quality and productivity. As Juran noted, Americans have the tendency to focus on short-term goals (e.g., "take the money and run") rather than be concerned about meeting customers' long-term needs and requirements.[126] Top managers need to illustrate that they are serious about improvements. Lower-level managers need to give employees greater opportunities to participate in the process and the autonomy to implement their ideas. Creating a stronger connection between quality improvements and the reward system is certainly a constructive step.

For any organizational change program to be effective, commitment is critical. In addition, there are eight stages that can be followed:[127]

1. **Establish a sense of urgency.** Examine the market and competition and identify crises or major opportunities.
2. **Create a guiding coalition.** Put together a group of people who have the power to lead the change and can work together as a team.
3. **Develop a vision and strategy** to direct the change effort.
4. **Communicate the change vision.**
5. **Empower broad-based action.** Eliminate obstacles or systems that undermine the vision or discourage employees from taking risks.
6. **Generate short-term wins.** Visibly reward people who make wins possible.
7. **Consolidate gains and produce more change.** Continue to reinvigorate the process with new change agents and projects.
8. **Institutionalize new approaches to the culture.** Create the means to continue focusing on customers and more effective management.

TRAINING. Training will have to become an integral part of any improvement program. This has been true for firms that have won the prestigious Baldrige award. For example, at Federal Express, all employees are required to complete two formal training programs. TQA, The Quality Advantage, teaches employees how to write contracts with their customers, while QAT, Quality Action Teams, emphasizes developing problem-solving skills.

Not only is it important to provide training for employees, but they also must be given the opportunities to use the new skills. In addition, evaluations of the effectiveness of the training programs are becoming increasingly more important. In fact, conducting evaluations of programs is one area that clearly distinguishes the Baldrige award winners from the applicants.

COMPATIBILITY WITH OTHER SYSTEMS. It is critical that improvement programs be developed to be compatible with other systems in the firm. For example, employees will need to be thoroughly trained in the skills they will need and should be rewarded for using those skills.[128]

Relative Effectiveness of Programs

One review found that participative interventions and job enrichment were able to increase productivity (i.e., reported productivity gains of 0.5 and 17 percent, re-

spectively). These gains, however, were lower than those acquired through the use of financial incentives (money) and goal-setting techniques (gains of 30 and 16 percent, respectively).[129]

Another study found that the use of job enrichment, sociotechnical approaches (e.g., AWGs), and alternative work arrangements (e.g., flextime) were related to increased productivity, but not to the same degree as the gains from financial incentives and training programs. Interestingly, work rescheduling methods were related to less employee turnover while other programs were not. The effects of improvement programs varied as a function of organization size, organization type, and type of worker. The impact of intervention programs was greater in small firms and government agencies and with managerial, professional, and sales employees. Finally, it was suggested that firms should use multiple, well-integrated interventions to improve productivity.[130]

SUMMARY

Quality, productivity, and QWL may be popular buzzwords, but the basic concerns are here to stay.[131] Many experts argue that these are critical issues as American firms try to gain market share in major industries such as computers, motor vehicles, metals, electronics, and aerospace.[132] U.S. organizations must integrate into their entire firms the tenets of quality and productivity improvement with a focus on meeting or exceeding customer requirements.[133] In addition, continuous improvements on all domains are needed if U.S. firms are going to remain competitive. The criteria for the Baldrige award or ISO certification are excellent models for organizational change in this area.

Fortunately, a number of interventions offer U.S. firms the opportunity to improve employees' QWL. Improvement programs include interventions to redesign the work environment and participative approaches. Work redesign interventions include ergonomics, robotics, computers/office automation, job design (e.g., job enrichment, job rotation), and alternative work arrangements (e.g., flexible work arrangements, part-time work, job sharing, compressed workweeks). Participative programs include quality circles, opinion surveys, autonomous work groups or self-managing teams, and TQM.

Many U.S. firms now use these programs with positive results. By making investments in people, product design, and process improvement they have improved quality, productivity, and QWL for their employees.[134] A recent survey of over 400 American-based corporations (including manufacturing, financial services, and other service industries) found that the most successful companies were those that combined downsizing with restructuring, reengineering, employee involvement programs, and team-based work redesign. As "human resource leaders," they retrained and redeployed twice as many workers as "human resource laggards." They put most of their training money into technical skill development and management training. They sponsored private-public partnerships with schools and offered paid leaves of absence for their employees who volunteered at schools. They also gave more money and equipment to local schools. They offered employees flexible work arrangements such as job sharing, telecommuting, executive sabbaticals, and part-time work options for managers and professionals. Further, HR leaders sponsored diversity training for managers and employees and mentoring programs for women and minorities.[135] Essentially, the firms that were HR leaders were more innovative than the followers or laggards in every aspect of HR practices.

For companies to be HR leaders, top managers must be attentive to HR practices and employee needs, middle managers must be supportive, and employees and unions cannot place obstacles in the way of improvements.[136] Fortunately, unions have been more receptive recently to the productivity programs we describe here and the pay-for-performance systems we discussed in Chapter 11. For example, the successful Chrysler assembly plant in Indiana was designed and developed with full cooperation from the United Auto Workers. Rubbermaid's Wooster, Ohio, plant is team-based, a manufacturing process endorsed by the union. There are numerous other examples where unions have cooperated in improvement programs.[137] Managers must be fully aware of union issues as they contemplate such programs. We will examine labor relations and collective bargaining in Chapter 13.

DISCUSSION QUESTIONS

1. How could HRM activities be coordinated with the Baldrige criteria?

2. What are the benefits of using benchmarking?

3. Do you agree that variability in individual or group performance is primarily due to factors beyond the individual's or group's control (e.g., poor resources, inadequate training, weak management, inefficient work flow)? Explain your response.

4. What are the individual and organizational benefits of improving employees' quality of work life?

5. Describe a situation in which redesigning the work environment could enhance productivity or quality.

6. Describe the steps you would take to change an organization from an autocratic state to one where there is a high degree of employee involvement and participation.

7. What impact has the total quality movement had on enhancing organizational effectiveness (i.e., quality and productivity)?

8. Offer some suggestions for how various HR systems in organizations (e.g., performance appraisal, training, career development) can be designed to reflect the tenets of the total quality movement.

9. Which organizational improvement strategies are most likely to encounter employee resistance? Why? What recommendations would you offer to management to manage the resistance?

10. Could you use TQM at a university? How would you do it?

11. How would you convince workers or unions that productivity improvement programs are not simply attempts to exploit workers?

12. How could you ensure that reengineering efforts are not simply ways to downsize and lay off workers? How could you get employees involved in reengineering efforts if they were worried that the organization was going to lay off workers?

13. Should TQM be combined with pay for performance? How? Explain your response.

NOTES

1. Ulrich, D. (1997). *Human resource champions*. Boston: Harvard Business School, p. viii; see also, Beer, M. (1997). The transformation of the human resource function: Resolving the tension between a traditional administrative and a new strategic role. *Human Resource Management, 36*(1), 49–56.

2. Garvin, D. A. (1987). Competing on the eight dimensions of quality. *Harvard Business Review, 65*(6), 101–109.

3. Schaaf, D. (1991). Beating the drum for quality. *Training, 28*(3), 5–12; see also, Forker, L. B. (1991). Quality: American, Japanese, and Soviet perspectives. *Academy of Management Executive, 5*(4), 63–74; Deming, W. E. (1986). *Out of the crisis*. Cambridge, MA: Massachusetts Institute of Technology, Center for Advanced Engineering Study; Deming, W. E. (1994). *The new economics,* 2nd ed. Cambridge, MA: Massachusetts Institute of Technology, Center for Advanced Engineering Study; Juran, J. M. (1992). *Juran on quality by design*. New York: The Free Press; and Crosby, P. B. (1989). *Let's talk quality*. New York: McGraw-Hill.

4. Stewart, T. A. (July 21, 1997). A satisfied customer isn't enough. *Fortune,* pp. 112–113.

5. Freiberg, K., and Freiberg, J. (1996). *Nuts! Southwest Airline's crazy recipe for business and personal success*. Austin, TX: Bard Press.

6. Pfeffer, J. (1994). *Competitive advantage through people*. Boston: Harvard Business School.

7. Welch, J. F., Jr. (1996). Quality 2000. *Executive Excellence, 13*(9), 4–5.

8. See note 7.

9. Lawson, J. K. (1996). Workplace 2000. *Executive Excellence, 13*(9), 15.

10. Bluestone, M. (June 8, 1987). The push for quality. *Business Week,* pp. 130–135; see also, Garvin, D. A. (1988). Quality problems, policies, and attitudes in the United States and Japan: An exploratory study. *Academy of Management Journal, 29*(4), 653–673.

11. See note 10, Garvin (1988).

12. Shandler, D. (1996). *Reengineering the training function: How to align training with the new corporate agenda.* Delray Beach, FL: St. Lucie Press; see also, Camp, R. C. (1989). *Benchmarking: The search for industry best practices that lead to superior performance.* Milwaukee, WI: American Society for Quality Control (ASQC) Quality Press; Ford, D. J. (June 1993). Benchmarking HRD. *Training and Development,* pp. 37–41; Bemowski, K. (January 1991). The benchmarking bandwagon. *Quality Progress,* pp. 19–24; Spendolini, M. J. (1992). *The benchmarking book.* New York: AMACOM; and Glanz, E. F., and Dailey, L. K. (1992). Benchmarking. *Human Resource Management, 31,* 9–20.

13. McNair, C. J., and Leibfried, K. H. J. (1992). *Benchmarking: A tool for continuous improvement.* Essex Junction, VT: Oliver Wright Publications.

14. Greengard, S. (November 1995). Discover best practices through benchmarking. *Personnel Journal,* pp. 62–73; see also, Schneier, C. E., and Johnson, C. (Spring/Summer 1993). Benchmarking: A tool for improving performance management and reward systems. *American Compensation Association Journal,* pp. 14–31.

15. Hammer, M. (July–August 1990). Reengineering work: Don't automate, obliterate. *Harvard Business Review,* pp. 104–112; see also, Fisher, C. D.; Schoenfeldt, L. F.; and Shaw, J. B. (1996). *Human resource management,* 3rd ed. Boston: Houghton Mifflin Company.

16. Noe, R. A.; Hollenbeck, J. R.; Gerhart, B.; and Wright, P. M. (1997). *Human resource management,* 2nd ed. Chicago: Richard D. Irwin.

17. See note 12, Shandler (1996).

18. Wisner, J. D., and Lewis, I. A. (1996). Quality improvement programs in the motor carrier industry. *Transportation Journal, 36*(2), 26–34; see also, Dant, B., and Kensinger, S. (1997). Re-engineering engineering: Methods or madness? *Computer-aided Engineering, 16*(2), 56–60.

19. American Quality Foundation (1992). *International quality study.* New York: Author; see also, Reger, R. K.; Gustafson, L. T.; DeMarie, S. M.; and Mullane, J. V. (1994). Reframing the organization: Why implementing total quality is easier said than done. *Academy of Management Review, 19,* 565–584, and American Productivity & Quality Center (1993). *The benchmarking management guide.* Portland, OR: Productivity Press.

20. London, M. (1997). *Job feedback.* Mahwah, N.J.: Erlbaum; see also, Locke, E. A., and Latham, G. P. (1990). *A theory of goal setting and task performance.* Englewood Cliffs, NJ: Prentice Hall; Osgood, C. E., and Tannenbaum, P. H. (1955). The principle of congruity in the prediction of attitude change. *Psychological Review, 62,* 42–55.

21. Grant, L., and Evans, E. (1994). *Principles of behavior analysis.* New York: Harper Collins.

22. See note 14, Greengard (1995); see also, Von Bergen, C. W., and Soper, B. (1995). A problem with benchmarking: Using shaping as a solution. *SAM Advanced Management Journal, 60*(4),16–19.

23. Becker, B. E., Huselid, M. A., Pickus, P. A., and Spratt, M. F. (1997). HR as a source of shareholder value: Research and recommendations. *Human Resource Management, 36*(1), p. 41.

24. *Malcolm Baldrige National Quality Award* (1997). U.S. Department of Commerce. Technology Administration. National Institute of Standards and Technology. Gaithersburg, MD 20899.

25. See note 24.

26. Segalla, E. (1989). All for quality and quality for all. *Training and Development Journal, 43*(9), 36–45; see also, Hill, R. C., and Freedman, S. M. (1992). Managing the quality process: Lessons from a Baldrige award winner: A conversation with CEO John W. Wallace. *Academy of Management Executive, 6*(1), 76–88.

27. Kurschner, D. (1997). Getting credit. *Training, 34*(6), 52–54.

28. Uzumeri, M. V. (1997). ISO 9000 and other metastandards: Principles for management practice. *Academy of Management Executive, 11*(1), 21–36.

29. Sellers, P. (Aug. 4, 1997). Pepsi's eateries go it alone. *Fortune,* pp. 27, 30.

30. DesMarteau, K. (December 1996). Rawls rallies Haggar associates to continually improve. *Bobbin, 38*(4), 44–46.

31. Hormozi, A. M. (1995). Understanding and implementing ISO 9000: A manager's guide. *SAM Advanced Management Journal, 60*(4), 4–11.

32. See note 31. See also, *Competing in the Global Marketplace* (1994). Fifth Annual Grant Thornton Survey of American Manufacturers; Lutman, W. (Second Quarter 1994). ISO 9000: Can America demonstrate a commitment to quality? *Production and Inventory Management Journal,* pp. 81–85, and Quality System Requirements QS-9000 (August 1994). Chrysler Corporation/Ford Motor Company/General Motors Corporation Supplier Quality Requirements Task Force.

33. Breitenberg, M. (April 1993). *ISO 9000-NISTIR 4721 and NISTIR 5122,* U.S. Department of Commerce, National Institute of Standards and Technology.

34. Brewer, P. C., and Mills, T. Y. (February 1994). ISO 9000 Standards: An emerging CPA service area. *Journal of Accountancy,* pp. 63–67; see also, Potts, L. (1993). *What is ISO 9000 and why should I care?* Houston: ABS Quality Evaluations, Inc.

35. Brecka, J. (November 1994). ISO 9000 is not dead! Study says U.S. manufacturers are pursuing ISO 9000 registration. *Quality Progress,* p. 23.

36. See note 35; see also, Swamidass, P. M. (December 1994) *Technology on the factory floor II: Benchmarking manufacturing technology use in the United States.* Washington, DC: The Manufacturing Institute.

37. See note 28.

38. Oldham, G. R., and Fried, Y. (1987). Employee reactions to work space. *Journal of Applied Psychology, 72*(1), 75–80.

39. Micco, L. (December 1996). California releases ergonomics regulations. *HR News,* p. 5.

40. Mitchell, K. E., Alliger, G. M., Morfopoulos, R. (1997). Toward an ADA-appropriate job analysis. *Human Resource Management Review, 7*(1), 5–26.

41. Schonberger, R. J. (1996). *World class manufacturing: The next decade.* New York: Free Press.

42. Pennar, K. (June 6, 1988). The productivity paradox. *Business Week,* pp. 100–102; see also, Orr, J. E. (1996). *Talking about machines: An ethnography of a modern job.* Ithaca, NY: Cornell University Press.

43. See note 41; see also, Mitchell, R.; Brandt, R.; Schiller, Z.; and Ellis, J. (Dec. 22, 1986). Boldly going where no robot has gone before. *Business Week,* p. 45; Snell, S. A., Pedigo, P. R., and Krawiec (1995). Managing the impact of information technology on human resource management. In G. R. Ferris, S. D. Rosen, and D. T. Barnum (eds.) *Handbook of human resource management.* Cambridge, Mass: Blackwell Business (159–174).

44. Chao, G. T., and Kozlowski, S. W. (1986). Employee perceptions on the implementation of robotic manufacturing technology. *Journal of Applied Psychology, 71*(1), 70–76.

45. See note 41; see also, Shenkar, O. (1988). Robotics: A challenge for occupational psychology. *Journal of Occupational Psychology, 61*(1), 103–112.

46. See note 43, Snell et al. (1995); see also, Parthasarthy, R., and Sethi, S. P. (1992). The impact of flexible automation on business strategy and organizational structure. *Academy of Management Review, 17,* 86–111.

47. See note 41; see also, Bates, R. A., and Holton, E. F. III, (1995). Computerized performance monitoring: A review of human resource issues. *Human Resource Management Review 5*(4), 267–288; Stanton, J. M., and Barnes-Farrell, J. L. (1996). Effects of electronic performance monitoring on personal control, task satisfaction. *Journal of Applied Psychology 81*(6), 738–745.

48. Hackman, J. R., and Oldham, G. R. (1980). *Work redesign.* Reading, MA: Addison-Wesley.

49. See note 48; see also, Hazzard, L.; Mautz, J.; and Wrightsman, D. (1992). Job rotation cuts cumulative trauma cases. *Personnel Journal, 71,* 29–33.

50. Holcomb, B. (July 1991). Time off: The benefit of the hour. *Working Mother,* pp. 31–35.

51. Russell, J. E. A. (1991). Career development interventions in organizations. *Journal of Vocational Behavior, 38,* 237–287; see also, Loscocco, K. A., and Roschelle, A. R. (1991). Influences on the quality of work and nonwork life: Two decades in review. *Journal of Vocational Behavior, 39,* 182–225.

52. Greenhaus, J. H., and Beutell, N. J. (1985). Sources of conflict between work and family roles. *Academy of Management Review, 10,* 76–88; see also, Kush, K., and Stroh, L. (September–October 1994). Flextime: Myth or reality? *Business Horizons,* pp. 51–55, and Bureau of National Affairs (Sept. 3, 1992). Flexible work schedules. *Bulletin to Management,* pp. 276–277.

53. Fernandez, J. P. (1986). *Child care and corporate productivity: Resolving family/work conflicts.* Lexington, MA: D. C. Heath & Co.

54. Sheppard, E. M., Clifton, T. J., and Kruse, D. (1996). Flexible work hours and productivity: Some evidence from the pharmaceutical industry. *Industrial Relations, 35,* 123–129; see also, Nollen, S. (1977). Does flexitime improve productivity? *Harvard Business Review, 56*(9/10), 12–22.

55. See note 50.

56. See note 53.

57. See note 50.

58. Closson, M. (Oct. 25, 1976). Company couples flourish. *Business Week,* p. 112.

59. Solomon, C. M. (September 1994). Job sharing: One job, double headache? *Personnel Journal,* pp. 88–96.

60. Pierce, J., and Dunham, R. (1992). The 12-hour work day: A 48-hour, eight-day week. *Academy of Management Journal, 42*(3), 1086–1098.

61. See note 50; see also, Solomon, C. M. (August 1991). 24-hour employees. *Personnel Journal,* p. 56.

62. Lawler, E. E. (1986). *High-involvement management: Participative strategies for improving organizational performance.* San Francisco: Jossey-Bass. See also, Atchison, T. (1991). The employment relationship: Untied or re-tied? *Academy of Management Executive, 5*(4), 52–62, and Magjuka, R. J., and Baldwin, T. T. (1991). Team-based employee involvement programs: Effects of design and administration. *Personnel Psychology, 44*(4), 793–812.

63. See note 23.

64. Schuster, F. E. (1986). *The Schuster report: The proven connection between people and profits.* New York: John Wiley & Sons; see also, The Red Cross learns to listen and earns employee commitment (1991). *Personnel, 68*(4), 12.

65. Keller, R. T. (1997). Job involvement and organizational commitment as longitudinal predictors of job performance: A study of scientists and engineers. *Journal of Applied Psychology, 82*(4), 539–545; see also, Griffin, R. W. (1988). Consequences of quality circles in an industrial setting: A longitudinal assessment. *Academy of Management Journal, 31*(2), 338–358; Ingle, S. (1982). How to avoid quality circle failure in your company. *Training and Development Journal, 36*(6), 54–59; Lawler, E. E., III, and Mohrman, S. A. (1987). Quality circles: After the honeymoon. *Organizational Dynamics, 15*(4), 42–54; see note 96.

66. Anonymous (February 1994). When is a team not a team? *Management Review Form.* New York: American Management Association; see also, Bailey, K., and Leland, K. (1996). Quality groups. *Executive Excellence, 13*(9), 17.

67. Lawler, E. E., III, and Mohrman, S. A. (1985). Quality circles after the fad. *Harvard Business Review, 63*(1), 64–71.

68. See note 65.

69. Brown, S. P. (1996). A meta-analysis and review of organizational research on job involvement. *Psychological Bulletin, 120,* 235–255; Steininger, D. J. (1994). Why quality initiatives are failing: The need to address the foundation of human motivation. *Human Resource Management, 33*(4), 601–606; see also, Adam, E. E. (1991). Quality circle performance. *Journal of Management, 17*(11), 25–39; Barrick, M. R., and Alexander, R. A. (1987). A review of quality circle efficacy and the existence of positive-findings bias. *Personnel Psychology, 40*(3), 579–592.

70. Sims, H. P., and Dean, J. W., Jr. (1985). Beyond quality circles: Self-managing teams. *Personnel, 62*(1), 25–32; see also, Lublin, J. S. (Feb. 13, 1992). Trying to increase worker productivity, more employers alter management style. *The Wall Street Journal,* pp. B1, B3.

71. Stamps, D. (1997). Mercedes-Benz sows a learning field. *Training, 34*(6), 26–32.

72. Lawler, E. E., Mohrman, S. A., and Ledford, G. E. (1992). *Employment involvement and total quality management.* San Francisco: Jossey-Bass; see also, Kirkman, B. L., and Shapiro, D. L. (1997). The impact of cultural values on employee resistance to teams: Toward a model of globalized self-managing work team effectiveness. *Academy of Management Review, 22*(3), 730–757.

73. Bettenhausen, K. I. (1991). Five years of groups research: What we've learned and what needs to be addressed. *Journal of Management, 17*(2), 345–382; Recardo, R., and Jolly, J. (1997). Organizational culture and teams. *SAM Advanced Management Journal, 62* (2), 4–7.

74. Waterman, R. H., Jr. (September 1996). A model of learning. *Executive Excellence, 13*(9), 3–4.

75. Cohen, S. G., and Ledford, G. E. (1994). The effectiveness of self-managing teams: A quasi-experiment. *Human Relations, 47*(1), 13–43; see also, Fisher, K. (1993). *Landing self-directed work teams.* New York: McGraw-Hill; Katzenbach, J. K., and Smith, D. K (1993). *The wisdom of teams: Creating the high performance organization.* Cambridge, MA: Harvard Business School Press; Ray, D., and Bronstein, H. (1995). *Teaming up.* New York: McGraw-Hill; and Rummler, G. A., and Brache, P. P. *Improving performance.* San Francisco: Jossey-Bass.

76. Barry, B., and Stewart, G. L. (1997). Composition, process, and performance in self-managed groups: The role of personality. *Journal of Applied Psychology, 82*(1), 62–78.

77. Peters, T. (September 1996). Excellence in service quality. *Executive Excellence, 13*(9), 9–10.

78. Luchars, J. Y., and Hinkin, T. R. (1996). The service quality audit: A hotel case study. *Cornell Hotel and Restaurant Administration Quarterly, 37*(1), 34–41.

79. Hitchcock, D. (1996). Being green isn't so hard. *Journal for Quality and Participation, 19*(5), 86–89.

80. See note 70. See also, Schilder, J. (1992). Work teams boost productivity. *Personnel Journal, 71,* 67–86, and Cordery, J. I.; Mueller, W. S.; and Smith, I. M. (1991). Attitudinal and behavioral effects of autonomous group working: A longitudinal field study. *Academy of Management Journal, 34*(2), 464–476.

81. Dean, J. W., Jr., and Evans, J. R. (1994). *Total quality: Management, organization and strategy.* St. Paul, MN: West Publishing, p. 12.

82. Walton, M. (1990). *Deming management at work.* New York: G.P. Putnam's Sons. See also, Cardy, R. L., and Dobbins, G. H. (1996). Human resource management in a total quality organizational environment: Shifting from a traditional to a TQHRM approach. *Journal of Quality Management, 1*(1), 5–20.

83. Bernardin, H. J. (1992). An 'analytic' framework for customer-based performance content development and appraisal. *Human Resources Management Review, 2,* 81–102.

84. See note 77.

85. See note 26.

86. See note 3, Deming (1986).

87. See note 10, Bluestone (1987); see also, Stone, D. L., and Eddy, E. R. (1996). A model of individual and organizational factors affecting quality-related outcomes. *Journal of Quality Management, 1*(1), 21–48; and Quality at Xerox (Nov. 9, 1989). *New York Times,* p. D1.

88. Nemoto, M. (1987). *Total quality control for management.* Englewood Cliffs, NJ: Prentice Hall.

89. Greising, D. (Aug. 8, 1994). Quality: How to make it pay. *Business Week,* pp. 54–59; see also, Puffer, S. M., and McCarthy, D. J. (1996). A framework for leadership in a TQM context. *Journal of Quality Management, 1*(1), 109–130.

90. Cocheu, T. (1989). Training for quality improvement. *Training and Development Journal, 43*(1), 56–62.

91. See note 15, Fisher, Schoenfeldt, and Shaw (1996). See also, Quality is as quality does (1991). *Personnel, 68*(1), p. 16; Munroe-Faure, L., and Munroe-Faure, M. (1992). *Implementing total quality management.* London: Pittman; Hebert, F. J.; Dellana, S. A.; and Bass, K. E. (1995). Total quality management in the business school: The faculty viewpoint. *SAM Advanced Management Journal, 60*(4), 20–22, 27–31; and Lawler, E. E.; Mohrman, S. A.; and Ledford, G. E. (1992). *Employee involvement and total quality management: Practices and results in Fortune 1000 companies.* San Francisco: Jossey-Bass.

92. See note 87, Stone and Eddy (1996). See also, Grant, R. M.; Shani, R.; and Krishnan, R. (Winter 1994). TQM's challenge to management theory and practice. *Sloan Management Review,* pp. 25–35; Caudron, S. (August 1993). How HR drives TQM. *Personnel Journal,* p. 48B; Jacob, R. (Oct. 18, 1993). TQM: More than a dying fad? *Fortune,* pp. 66–72; and Henkoff, R. (April 18, 1994). Keeping Motorola on a roll. *Fortune,* pp. 67–78.

93. See note 87, Stone and Eddy (1996).

94. See note 82, Cardy and Dobbins (1996). See also, Hod-

getts, R. M.; Luthans, F.; and Lee, S. M. (Winter 1994). New paradigm organizations: From total quality to learning to world-class. *Organizational Dynamics*, pp. 4–19; Feigenbaum, A. V. (September 1994). Quality education and America's competitiveness. *Quality Progress*, 27(9), 83–84; Dean, J. W., Jr., and Bowen, D. E. (July 1994). Management theory and total quality: Improving research and practice through theory development. *Academy of Management Review*, 19(3), 392–418; Spencer, B. A. (July 1994). Models of organization and total quality management: A comparison and critical evaluation. *Academy of Management Review*, 19(3), 446–471; and Waldman, D. A. (1994). The contributions of total quality management to a theory of work performance. *Academy of Management Review*, 19(3), 510–536.

95. Anand, K. N. (1997). Give success a chance. *Quality Progress*, 30(3), 63–64; see also, Prewitt, E. (1996). Fusion is the best policy. *Harvard Business Review*, 74(3), 9–10.

96. Choi, T. Y., and Behling, O. C. (1997). Top managers and TQM success: One more look after all these years. *Academy of Management Executive*, 11(1), 37–47.

97. Davenport, T. H. (1995). Business process reengineering: Where it's been, where it's going. In V. Grover and W. J. Kettinger (eds.), *Business process change: Concepts, methods, and technologies*. Harrisburg, PA: Idea Group Publishing, pp. 1–13.

98. Hammer, M., and Champy, J. (1993). *Reengineering the corporation: A manifesto for business revolution*. New York: Harper Collins; see also, Horney, N. F., and Koonce, R. (September 1996). Competency alignment. *Executive Excellence*, 13(9), p. 19; Hunt, V. D. (1993). *Reengineering*. Essex Junction, VT: Oliver Wright Publications; Allen, D., and Nafius, R. (March/April 1993). Dreaming and doing: Reengineering GTE Telephone Operations. *Planning Review*, pp. 28–31; and Champy, J. (1995). *Reengineering management: The mandate for new leadership*. New York: Harper Business.

99. See note 98, Hammer and Champy (1993). See also, Morris, D., and Brandon, J. (1993). *Reengineering your business*. New York: McGraw-Hill. Harrington, H. J. (1989). *The quality/profit connection*. Milwaukee, WI: ASQC Quality Press; Kinni, T. B. (January 1994). A reengineering primer. *Quality Digest*, pp. 26–30; Reengineering is helping health of hospitals and its patients (February 1994). *Total Quality Newsletter*, p. 5; and Recardo, R. (June 1994). Process reengineering in a finance division. *Journal for Quality and Participation*, pp. 70–73.

100. Smith, B. (January 1994). Business process reengineering: More than a buzzword. *HR Focus*, pp. 17–19; see also, Harrison, D. B., and Pratt, M. (March/April 1993). A methodology for reengineering businesses. *Planning Review*, pp. 6–11.

101. Edosomwan, J. A. (1996). *Organizational transformation and process reengineering*. Delray Beach, FL: St. Lucie Press.

102. Bennis, W., and Mische, M. (September 1996). 21st century organization. *Executive Excellence*, 13(9), 7–8.

103. See note 12, Shandler (1996).

104. Thomas, L. (Dec. 3, 1996). Re-engineering is new term for describing when workers get shaft. *Knoxville News Sentinel*, p. C1.

105. See note 12, Shandler (1996).

106. See note 12, Shandler (1996); see also note 102.

107. See note 98, Hammer and Champy (1993).

108. Teitelbaum, R. (July 21, 1997). Tough guys finish first. *Fortune*, pp. 82–84.

109. Ishikawa, K. (1994). What is total quality control? The Japanese way. In H. Costin (ed.), *Readings in Total Quality Management*. Fort Worth: The Dryden Press, pp. 155–166.

110. Willmott, H. (1994). Business process reengineering and human resource management. *Personnel Review*, 3(3), 34; see also, Greengard, S. (July 1994). New technology is HR's route to reengineering. *Personnel Journal*, pp. 32c–32o; Why more looks like less (April 27, 1995). *The Economist*; (April 20, 1996). Fire and forget? *The Economist*; Reengineering vs. tradition (Sept. 5, 1996). *Industry Week*; and America's recipe for industrial extinction (May 14, 1996). *Financial Times*.

111. See note 104; Cascio, W. F. (1993). Downsizing: What do we know? What have we learned? *Academy of Management Executive*, 7(1), 95–104.

112. See note 98, Hammer and Champy (1993).

113. See note 12, Shandler (1996); see also, Adams, C., and Peck, T. (September 1996). Process redesign. *Executive Excellence*, 13(9), 14–15.

114. Mroczkowski, T., and Hanaoka, M. (1997). Effective rightsizing strategies in Japan and America: Is there convergence of employment practices? *Academy of Management Executive*, 11(2), 57–67.

115. See note 114.

116. See note 12, Shandler (1996), pp. 129–130.

117. See note 102.

118. See note 98, Hammer and Champy (1993).

119. Shani, A. B., and Mitki, Y. (1996). Reengineering, total quality management, and sociotechnical systems approaches to organizational change: Towards an eclectic approach? *Journal of Quality Management*, 1(1), 131–145.

120. See note 1.

121. Cameron, K. S. (1994). Strategies for successful organizational downsizing. *Human Resource Management*, 33(2), 189–212; see also, Whetten, D. A., Keiser, J. D., and Urban, T. (1995). Implications of organizational downsizing for the human resource management function. In G. R. Ferris, S. D. Rosen, and D. T. Barnum (eds.), *Handbook of human resource management*. Cambridge, Mass: Blackwell Business (282–296).

122. See note 1.

123. Katzell, R. A., and Guzzo, R. A. (1983). Psychological approaches to productivity improvement. *American Psychologist*, 38(4), 468–472; see also, Hyatt, D. E., and Ruddy, T. H. (1997). An examination of the relationship between work group characteristics and perfor-

mance: Once more into the breach. *Personnel Psychology, 50*(3), 553–586.

124. See note 119.

125. See note 91, *Personnel* (1991).

126. Dumas, R. A.; Cushing, N.; and Laughlin, C. (1987). Making quality control theories workable. *Training and Development Journal, 41*(2), 30–33.

127. Kotter, J. (September 1996). Transforming organizations. *Executive Excellence, 13*(9), 13–14; see also, Hamel, G. (June 23, 1997). Killer strategies that make shareholders rich. *Fortune*, pp. 70–84.

128. See note 23.

129. Locke, E. A.; Feren, D. B.; McCaleb, V. M.; Shaw, K. N.; and Denny, A. T. (1980). The relative effectiveness of four methods of motivating employee performance. In K. D. Duncan and M. M. Wallis (eds.), *Changes in working life*. New York: John Wiley & Sons; see also, Liden, R. C., and Tewksbury, T. W. (1995). Empowerment and work teams. In G. R. Ferris, S. D. Rosen, and D. T. Barnum (eds.), *Handbook of human resource management*. Cambridge, MA: Blackwell Business, 386–404.

130. Guzzo, R. A.; Jette, R. D.; and Katzell, R. A. (1985). The effects of psychologically based intervention programs on worker productivity: A meta-analysis. *Personnel Psychology, 38*(2), 275–291.

131. Schaaf, D. (1991). Beating the drum for quality. *Training, 28*(3), 5–12.

132. Taylor, A. (March 17, 1997). Danger: Rough road ahead. *Fortune*, pp. 114–118.

133. Johnson, J. W. (1996). Linking employee perceptions of service climate to customer satisfaction. *Personnel Psychology 49*(4), 831–844; see also, Ulrich, D. Halbrook, R., Meder, D., and Stuchik, M. (1991). Employee and customer attachment: Synergies for competitive advantage. *Human Resource Planning 14*(1), 89–194.

134. Beer, M. (1997). The transformation of the human resource function: Resolving the tension between a traditional administrative and a new strategic role. *Human Resource Management, 36* (1), 49–56.

135. Mirvis, P. (1997). Human resource management: Leaders, laggards, and followers. *Academy of Management Executive, 11*(2), 43–56; see also, Alvares, K. M. (1997). The business of human resources. *Human Resource Management, 36*(1), 9–16; Beatty, R. W., and Schneier, C. E. (1997). New HR roles to impact organizational performance: From "partners" to "players." *Human Resource Management, 36* (1), 29–38.

136. Ulrich, D. (1997). Judge me more by my future than by my past. *Human Resource Management, 36* (1), 5–8; see also, Lawler, E. E., and Mohrman, S. A. (1997). Transforming the human resource function. *Human Resource Management, 36* (1), 157–162.

137. Ellig, B. R. (1997). Is the human resource function neglecting the employees? *Human Resource Management, 36* (1), 91–96; see also, Kochan, T. A. (1997). Rebalancing the role of human resources. *Human Resource Management, 36* (1), 121–128.

C H A P T E R

LABOR RELATIONS
AND COLLECTIVE BARGAINING*

OVERVIEW

The previous two chapters covered increasing productivity and performance through pay or other HRM interventions. Unions generally oppose such efforts and prefer greater stability and equality in workers' paychecks. This opposition may have something to do with the negative attitudes business students have toward unions, and it certainly contributes to the antipathy that management has toward organized labor.

But there is some evidence that student attitudes toward unions may be changing. The majority of Americans supported the Teamsters members in their 1997 strike against UPS. This support may have had a lot to do with UPS settling the strike in 15 days, giving the union almost everything it demanded. There is also evidence that unions are getting more supportive of innovative pay-for-performance systems and productivity enhance-

ment programs such as quality circles and work team designs.

Management students today often learn the "ideal" way to manage firms' human resources, making it difficult for them to comprehend the adverse working environments that led to unionization. People in the early part of the century often worked under conditions many of us cannot fathom—"dark, satanic mills," with workweeks of at least 60 hours and with no provisions for safety, illness, vacations, or retirement.[1] Thus, the union's role in improving these conditions was clear. While the goal of unions today in the United States is still to improve working conditions and increase workers' economic status, the need and effects are far more subtle than they were during the early years of unions.

The United States has legislation governing wages and hours, equal employment opportunity (EEO), family and medical leave, pensions, mergers, social security, and health and safety. Research shows that there is little to be gained from worker exploitation in this country. Further, the relatively clean service industry, not the harsh factories, provides for a substantial proportion of

*Contributed by Nancy Brown Johnson, Roger L. Cole, and Joseph G. Clark, Jr.

present-day employment. Most workers today face mental rather than physical strains, which makes the need for union intervention less clear-cut.

Union membership in the United States has declined over the years. For example, membership in the United Farm Workers of America (UFW) has fallen from a high of 80,000 in 1970 to 21,000 in 1994, which is only a fraction of the nation's 2.8 million farmworkers. However, with new leadership, the UFW has become the fastest growing union in the country since 1994 by devoting more of its budget to organizing. One current fight, supported by John Sweeney, president of the AFL-CIO, is the strawberry campaign. Pickers perform stoop labor for up to 10 hours a day, rarely get health insurance despite chronic back injuries, and earn an average of only $8,500 for a seven-month season. Despite these issues, not all workers are interested in joining the union and fights break out between union supporters and anti-union workers.[2]

Union membership in the United States has dropped substantially, to less than 15 percent of the nonfarm U.S. workforce. Unions are nonetheless an important influence on workers and firms—both union and nonunion. There are still over 70,000 local unions and 173 national unions. Of these, 110 belong to the influential AFL-CIO (http://www.aflcio.org/), which represents about 80 percent of all unionized employees in the United States. In union firms, HR decisions such as compensation, promotion, demotion, and termination require union involvement. In general, management must handle personnel matters with the union rather than with each individual employee. As we discussed in Chapters 10 and 11, unions have a great influence over pay structure and the compensation system in general. Nonunion firms also concern themselves with union activities because they usually desire to maintain their nonunion status. To do so, these firms must be aware of unions and their history, their goals, their influences on firms, and the legal issues binding both sides. Obviously, the working conditions, wages, and terms of employment of unionized firms affect the way in which nonunion employers manage their HR to maintain nonunion status. For example, the Nissan automobile plant in Smyrna, Tennessee, provides favorable benefits to its employees and, despite considerable effort on the part of union organizers, the employees have voted to stay nonunionized. As we discussed in Chapter 12, unions are also very much involved in productivity improvement programs.

This chapter begins with a brief history of the labor movement in the United States. We will review the major legislation affecting the labor movement and management today. The factors and procedures related to union organizing will also be covered. We then discuss collective bargaining and the methods that unions and organizations employ to achieve their goals. The chapter closes with a discussion of the contemporary labor movement and its future, as well as international issues.

OBJECTIVES

After studying this chapter, you should be able to:

1. Be familiar with the development and effects of labor unions.
2. Understand the basic elements of labor law and the major laws.
3. Understand why people join unions.
4. Understand collective bargaining as a tool for labor negotiation.
5. Identify the bases of power in collective bargaining related to both unions and management.
6. Describe current trends and issues in labor relations.
7. Understand the state of labor relations in other countries.

Today, many Americans hold a negative view about unions and their leaders. At the end of 1996, only 16 percent of Americans surveyed said they thought union leaders had "high" or "very high" honesty or ethical standards. This was up from 1985, however, when the number was 13 percent. Views on the level of honesty and ethics of business executives also declined over this same period. In 1985, 23 percent thought business leaders were honest and ethical; this dropped to 17 percent by 1996.[3]

Most business students today hold a negative view of the American labor movement. Many view unions as antimanagement, striving to control or even reduce productivity while demanding higher wages and ironclad protection for workers regardless of their performance. This extreme view may derive to some extent from a lack of historical perspective on labor relations in this country. We begin this chapter by providing this perspective.

THE LIFE CYCLE OF THE AMERICAN LABOR MOVEMENT

Most organizations go through relatively uniform and progressive life cycles that are not easily reversed.[4] The labor movement is no exception. Labor unions in the United States have developed in a predictable pattern, evolving from the unique circumstances facing labor. This life cycle approach yields a useful framework for exploring and interpreting the historical development of the U.S. labor movement. Figure 13.1 summarizes the life cycle of the U.S. labor movement.

FIGURE 13.1
LIFE CYCLE OF THE U.S. LABOR MOVEMENT

STAGE	PERIOD	CHARACTERISTICS
Entrepreneurial	Colonial–1885	Experimentation; anticapitalist; Knights of Labor; *Philadelphia Cordwainers* case; mixed assemblies
Collectivity	1886–1930	Rise of AFL—basic structure for U.S. labor; AFL accepted capitalism; exclusive jurisdiction; skilled trades only; temporary injunction; yellow-dog contracts; open shop movement
Formalization, control, and elaboration	1931–1954	CIO formed; NLRA passed (1935); decentralization of movement; changing legal environment; *yellow-dog contracts* unenforceable
Decline	1955–1979	AFL-CIO merger membership down; increased management opposition; Landrum-Griffin Act (1959)
Late decline	1980–1996	Significant drop in membership; increasing international competition; deregulation of labor movement
Renewal	1997–present	More aggressive organizing; UPS strike; organized U.S. Airways

Entrepreneurial Stage: Colonial Times to 1885

In the entrepreneurial stage, organizations experiment with alternative philosophies and structures before settling on the form they will eventually take. Little planning and coordination occur within these organizations. Yet, at the same time, they attempt to develop a niche. Early labor movements that failed in the 1800s experimented with various ideas and beliefs, providing useful lessons for the founders of the existing labor movement. Early labor endeavors included the workingmen's political parties that used the political system to elect candidates and obtain legislation. Further, they believed in bringing the means of production under the direct control of the workers through direct action such as strikes. These movements served as early experiments in dealing with the adverse conditions facing workers of the 1800s and the early 1900s. All these movements advocated dramatic reform to the existing capitalistic system, which was a major factor in their downfall. In contrast, a few successful skilled trade unions, arising during the Civil War period, accepted capitalism and focused on basic economic issues such as raising wages and improving working conditions. Several of these unions still exist today. In general, however, the early 1800s served as a time of trial and error for labor movements.

The Knights of Labor provided particularly salient lessons for the founders of today's labor movement. The Knights took a peaceful, reformist approach, supporting education and workers' cooperatives for improving workers' societal positions. The leadership did not advocate the use of the strike, although the members did strike against Jay Gould, a well-known railroad financier. This strike brought them notoriety and additional members, yet also illustrated the inconsistencies between beliefs and actions, which contributed to their later downfall. In addition, their structure, known as "mixed assemblies," allowed virtually all workers to become members. Because these workers had little in common, limited attachment to the Knights resulted.[5] In particular, frustration developed among the craft workers. They held more bargaining power than unskilled workers due to the difficulty in replacing them during a strike; therefore, they felt that they supported the entire organization. The strike's success and the mixed assemblies' failure supplied lessons for the American Federation of Labor (AFL).

During the entrepreneurial stage, management also experimented with legal weapons to fight labor unions. No legislation governed unions at this time; therefore, common-law principles took precedence. The 1794 *Philadelphia Cordwainers's* case originated the criminal conspiracy doctrine. The court found the cordwainers (shoemakers) guilty of a conspiracy because of restraint of trade across state lines. In 1842, *Commonwealth vs. Hunt* later overturned the criminal conspiracy doctrine by stating that actions designed to convince nonmembers of the Boston Journeymen Bootmakers' Society to join were no longer seen as criminal. This case established the ends-means test, in which a strike's legality depended on the legality of the end sought and means used. The courts judged the legality of the ends and means, and they tended to sympathize with business.

Collectivity Stage: The Rise of the AFL

In the collectivity stage, the basic organizational model is formed. Informal structures, high commitment, and a sense of mission characterize this stage—and the AFL's early days. In 1894, Samuel Gompers, founder and long-term president of the AFL, stated, "It was the crusading spirit that sustained many of us in those early days. We placed the cause of labor before everything else—personal advancement, family, comfort, or anything."[6] The AFL formed the basic structure and principles for the U.S. labor movement.

In contrast to earlier movements, the AFL accepted capitalism. Pragmatically oriented and working within the existing economic system, the AFL established a primary goal of improving workers' economic position by advocating avoidance of long-run reformist goals, collective bargaining buttressed by the strike, and no government intervention. In addition, it restricted membership to skilled trades because of the bargaining power of these trades. It also advocated "exclusive jurisdiction," in which a group of employees could be represented by only one union. The existing U.S. labor movement differs little in principle from the model formally established in 1886.[7]

With labor's growing successes, management began to develop new legal tactics for resisting labor unions. The temporary injunction, one of these tactics, is a court order originally intended to prevent irreversible financial or property damage by barring labor's actions (e.g., strikes) until the court ruled formally on the actions' legality. In the case of strikes, the courts issued frequent injunctions, which served as effective strike breakers. The yellow-dog contract is an agreement stating that joining a union will result in termination. This tactic also effectively thwarted unions because employers required workers to sign such contracts as a condition of employment. Although workers could be fired "at will" anyway, the yellow-dog contract remained a useful strategy for obtaining court injunctions to defeat union organizing attempts.

The turn of the century brought relatively steady growth in labor union membership. Union membership, as a percent of the total labor force, climbed steadily from about 6.5 percent in 1900 to 17.6 percent of the nonagricultural labor force in 1920. The government, for the first time, recognized the labor movement's viability and partially contributed to this growth. To reduce strikes during World War I, the government created the tripartite National War Labor Board, with members from labor, management, and the public. In exchange for unions giving up the right to strike, employers agreed to recognize labor's right to organize and bargain collectively.

But the 1920s brought declining union membership. With the advent of the human relations school of management, employers began to provide workers with better wages and working conditions. Thus, workers had less reason to unionize. Further, some firms established company unions, which were controlled by the company and deterred legitimate unions. Employers also joined forces to frustrate unions through the open shop movement and the American Plan. For example, the Chamber of Commerce created the open shop movement, advocating union-free shops by mounting an antiunion publicity campaign. In contrast to the chamber's openness, employers secretly established the American Plan to associate the labor movement with foreign subversives. These factors, combined with the relative prosperity during the 1920s, contributed to the decline of unions.[8]

Formalization, Control, and Elaboration of Structure: The Statutory Period

In the formalization and control stage, organizations rely heavily on rules, maintenance, and efficiency. Procedures become institutionalized and the leadership becomes conservative, and so organizations resist change. The AFL leadership actively opposed change in the 1930s by resisting industrial unionists and strictly adhering to craft unionism. By the 1930s, major industries such as automobiles, steel, and rubber had expanded. Yet the AFL believed that organizing the "unskilled" workers of these industries would weaken the labor movement because they lacked bargaining power. The issue came to a head at the 1935 AFL convention when the industrial unionists formed the Committee for Industrial Organization against the craft unionists' will. The committee's explicit purpose was to organize industrial workers. The committee was expelled by the AFL and renamed itself the Congress of Industrial Organization (CIO).

Domain expansion, adaptation, renewal, and decentralization characterize organizations in this stage. Consistent with domain expansion, the CIO began an extensive drive to organize industries such as steel, rubber, meatpacking, and automobiles in the late 1930s and early 1940s. The AFL began adapting to CIO competition through a renewed organization effort. These endeavors contributed to tremendous membership gains for the entire labor movement, despite the movement's decentralization into two separate entities. Figure 13.2 illustrates trends in union membership beginning in 1930. Figures for 1995 indicate that less than 15 percent of all U.S. wage and salary workers are members of unions, and by 1997 this figure was 14 percent.[9]

The changing legal environment also fostered growth in union membership during the 1930s. Figure 13.3 highlights the provisions of key legislation affecting the labor movement. In 1926, the Railway Labor Act, the first significant piece of labor legislation, encouraged collective bargaining for handling railroad disputes. Labor's large legal inroads occurred during the Depression. During this time, sympathies began changing from supporting big business to backing labor. Many believed that labor unions provided a "countervailing power" to aid in controlling business interests. Thus, in 1932 Congress passed the Norris-LaGuardia Act, which restricted the use of the injunction and made yellow-dog contracts unenforceable. Considered to be neutral, the act was intended to restore a balance of power between labor and management.

Congress enacted the 1935 National Labor Relations Act (NLRA) as a pro-labor bill; it is also known as the Wagner Act. The NLRA formally recognized workers' rights to organize and bargain collectively with representatives of their own choosing. To enforce that right, the bill described what constituted unfair labor

FIGURE 13.2
TRENDS IN THE U.S. LABOR MARKET

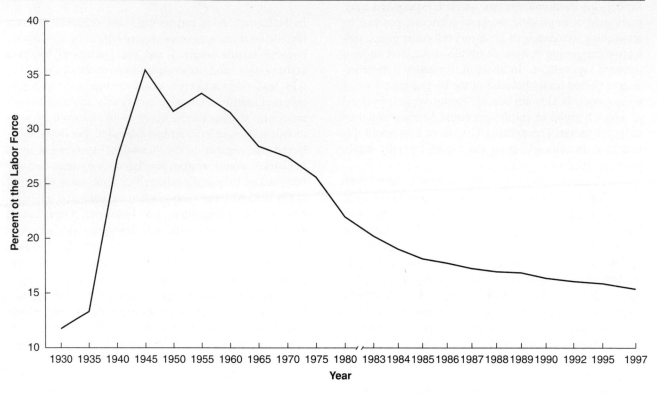

Source: Bureau of Labor Statistics, Department of Labor, 1997.

FIGURE 13.3
SUMMARY OF MAJOR U.S. LABOR LEGISLATION

YEAR ENACTED	LEGISLATION	KEY PROVISIONS
1926	Railway Labor Act	Recognized the right of railroad employees (later amended to include airline employees) to join unions and bargain collectively. Specified procedures for resolution of disputes over negotiation and interpretation of the contract.
1932	Norris-LaGuardia Act	Restricted the use of injunctions against labor and made yellow-dog contracts unenforceable.
1935	National Labor Relations Act (NLRA) (Wagner Act)	Recognized employees' rights to organize and bargain collectively, described employer unfair labor practices to enforce employees' rights, provided for union certification elections, and created the National Labor Relations Board (NLRB) to conduct elections and investigate unfair labor practices.
1947	Labor-Management Relations Act (Taft-Hartley Act)	Described union unfair labor practices, including secondary boycotts, established the Federal Mediation and Conciliation Service (FMCS) to aid in dispute resolution, provided for emergency procedures, and enable states to pass right-to-work laws.
1959	Labor-Management Reporting and Disclosure Act (Landrum-Griffin Act)	Established employee "bill of rights," required unions to file annual financial reports, and regulated trusteeships. Union members have the right to: (1) nominate candidates for union office, (2) vote in union elections, and (3) attend union meetings.
1978	Civil Service Reform Act	Established right of federal employees to have union representation. Created the Federal Labor Relations Authority to monitor federal labor relations. Forbade wage negotiations and prohibited strikes.

practices by employers. Prohibited activities included: (1) interfering with employee representation and collective bargaining rights; (2) dominating or interfering with the affairs of unions; (3) discriminating in regard to hiring, retention, or any employment condition against workers who engage in union activity or who file unfair labor practice charges; and (4) not bargaining in good faith with employee representatives. Further, the bill established the National Labor Relations Board (NLRB at http://www.nlrb/gov) to enforce the Wagner Act and to conduct representation elections. Essentially, the goal of the NLRA was to regulate the *processes* of organizing and collective bargaining, not necessarily the *outcomes.*

World War II inspired the creation of another board, this one called the War Labor Board, which requested no-strike pledges and wage–price controls from labor. At the end of the war, the strike rate skyrocketed because of labors' attempts to regain wages forgone during the war. Public sentiment quickly turned against the labor movement and ultimately led to the passage of the 1947 Taft-Hartley Act. Taft-Hartley drafters intended to restore a balance between labor and management by regulating labor activities. Labor, however, called it the "slave labor bill." The bill amended the NLRA by describing what constituted unfair labor practices by unions including: (1) restricting the usage of the strike, including granting the president of the United States the power to issue an injunction against a strike; (2) restricting unions from interfering with workers' right to organize; and (3) prohibiting union discrimination against workers who did not want to participate in union activities, including strikes.

The Taft-Hartley Act provided states with the option of enacting right-to-work legislation. Right-to-work laws declare that union security agreements that require membership as a condition of employment are illegal. Twenty-one states have enacted right-to-work laws. To aid in the peaceful settlement of contractual disputes, Congress created the Federal Mediation and Conciliation Service (FMCS) and provided emergency dispute provisions for the settlement of strikes affecting national health and safety. Thus, the Taft-Hartley Act further restricted union activity. Unfair labor practices by management were also reaffirmed under the Taft-Hartley Act. Figure 13.4 summarizes the implications of the NLRA and the Taft-Hartley Act.

A recent study quantified the impact of the Taft-

FIGURE 13.4
MAJOR IMPLICATIONS OF NLRA AND TAFT-HARTLEY ACT

BY MANAGEMENT (WAGNER ACT)	BY UNION (TAFT-HARTLEY ACT)
Interfere with, restrain, or coerce employees in the exercise of their rights to organize, bargain collectively, and engage in other activities for their mutual aid or protection (e.g. threaten employees with the loss of a job if they vote for the union).	Restrain or coerce employees in the exercise of their right to join or not join a union.
Dominate or interfere with the formation or administration of any labor organization or contribute financial or other support to it.	Restrain or coerce an employer in the selection of his or her bargaining or grievance representative.
Encourage or discourage membership in any labor organization by discrimination with regard to hiring or tenure or conditions of employment, subject to an exception for valid union-security agreements.	Cause or attempt to cause an employer to discriminate against an employee due to membership or nonmembership in a union, subject to an exception for valid union-shop agreements.
Discharge or otherwise discriminate against an employee because he or she has filed charges or given testimony under the Wagner Act.	Refuse to bargain collectively (in good faith) with an employer if the union has been designated as a bargaining agent by a majority of the employees.
Refuse to bargain collectively with representatives of the employees; that is, bargain in good faith.	Induce or encourage employees to stop work in order to force an employer or self-employed person to join a union or to force an employer or other person to stop doing business with any other person (secondary boycott).
	Induce or encourage employees to stop work in order to force an employer to recognize and bargain with the union where another union has been certified as a bargaining agent (strike against a certification).
	Induce or encourage employees to stop work in order to force an employer to assign particular work to members of the union instead of to members of another union (jurisdictional strike).
	Charge an excessive or discriminatory membership fee as a condition to becoming a member of the union.
	Cause or attempt to cause an employer to pay for services that are not performed or not to be performed (featherbedding).

Source: Adapted with permission from J. J. Kenny and L. G. Kahn, *Primer of labor relations.* Washington, DC: Bureau of National Affairs, 1989, pp. 1–3.

Hartley Act on the balance of power in labor relations by examining the change in stock prices (profits) associated with the act's passage. When shareholder returns were investigated, it was noted that all the firms studied had higher stock prices than they would have had without the act.[10]

Decline: 1955–1980

A glance at Figure 13.2 illustrates that union membership began a decline in 1955 and has been declining ever since. In particular, union density dropped significantly in the 1980s; as of 1996, less than 15 percent of the U.S. workforce is unionized. Conflict, bureaucracy, rigidity, and conservatism differentiate organizational decline. Similar criticism has been leveled against organized labor and may partially account for the drop in membership. Targets of criticism include a lack of effective leadership, more time spent on worker representation rather than on organization, and membership apathy. Yet organizational decline need not be inevitable, and the elaboration of the structure stage can lead to organizational renewal. Nonetheless, since the mid-1950s the labor movement has decreased for several reasons.[11] The structural hypothesis contends that unions have less success in organizing *growing* sectors of the economy as compared to *declining* economic sectors. For example, the labor movement experiences more success in organizing goods-producing industries than service industries, and northern industries relative to southern industries.

New technology represents another force that affects industrial relations. For example, Caterpillar's plant modernization precipitated a prolonged strike that swept the company in late 1991 and 1992. The company demanded concessions in the form of reduced job classifications and less strict work rules to increase workforce flexibility to adapt to changes in manufacturing processes.

Another hypothesis for union membership declines suggests that management opposition has increased and has become more sophisticated. For example, many consulting firms today specialize in union prevention. In addition, management can indirectly oppose unions through positive personnel policies, offering nonunion workers wages and benefits comparable to those of union workers. These policies may make unions relatively less attractive into the 21st century. Further, management can directly oppose unions by fighting them through legal or illegal organizing campaigns.

Union membership declines may also result from public policy changes, such as right-to-work laws that have imperiled union growth. Additionally, protective labor legislation (e.g., the Civil Rights Act of 1991, antitakeover laws, plant-closing legislation, state restrictions on employment-at-will, and pension reform) provides many services that are comparable to union representa-

tion, reducing the attractiveness of unions. Finally, some people believe that unions have shifted their emphasis from organizing new workers to representing existing workers, thus naturally leading to lower levels of unionization.[12]

The decline of unions has also been partially attributed to the fact that Congress has not supported favorable labor legislation. In the late 1950s, the U.S. Senate held hearings investigating and exposing union corruption that ultimately resulted in the 1959 Landrum-Griffin Act. Designed to protect workers from their unions, the act provided for the employee "bill of rights," union filing of annual financial statements with the Department of Labor, and the requirement that unions hold national and local officer elections every five years and three years, respectively. Some unions had been using trusteeships to control dissident local unions, placing the local union under the national's control. The Landrum-Griffin Act began regulating trusteeships to ensure that they were used for legitimate purposes. After the act was passed, the labor unions made two failed attempts to pass favorable private-sector labor legislation in the 1970s. Unions have, however, successfully supported an extension of unemployment benefits and general social legislation, including the 1990 Americans with Disabilities Act (ADA) and the 1991 Civil Rights Act (see Chapter 3). At the state level, the labor movement has also been successful in supporting family leave laws and merger and acquisition regulation. All this legislation, however, may lead to the decline of union membership as individual workers perceive enough protection being offered from government legislation.

Late Decline: 1980s

Between 1980 and 1996 union membership declined by 5.6 percentage points.[13] Some have argued that this dramatic drop in membership has come about because of growing environmental pressures, and that it reflects a significant transformation in industrial relations.[14] For example, increased international competition and deregulation affect union membership rates. International competition in industries such as automobiles, rubber, and steel greatly affected industrial relations issues for these industries. In the late 1960s, for instance, the United Auto Workers (UAW) organized unions in the "big three" automakers, which accounted for virtually all the U.S. market. This level of organization was combined with pattern bargaining (in which a settlement reached with the first company serves as a model for the remaining negotiations and settlements), which meant all automakers had comparable labor costs that could be passed on to the consumer. With the Japanese entry into the U.S. automotive market, U.S. consumers could choose between Japanese or American cars. This led to U.S. autoworkers' wages being brought into competition with Japanese workers' wages, since industry survival depends partially on wage, benefit, and work-rule concessions. During this same time, many other American industries suffered similar pressures from international competition.

Deregulation of industries such as airlines and trucking played a critical role in shaping the current industrial relations environment. In the late 1970s, Congress deregulated airlines and trucking. The regulatory effect apparently caused wages to be above competitive levels. This wage effect resulted from regulators setting prices based on costs (of which wages were a portion) and from regulators' creating entry barriers to prevent nonunion competitors from entering the industry and competing on the basis of wages.

Deregulation introduced new competitive pressures in both industries. In trucking, because of nonunion industry entrants, unionization declined from about 50 percent in 1974 to less than 25 percent in 1988.[15] In the airline industry, financial barriers to entry restricted the number of new entrants, so concession bargaining became the norm. In 1986, 70 percent of the airline collective bargaining agreements had two-tier wage scales, in which new employees' wages were below those of existing workers on the same job.[16] For example, the two-tier pay system negotiated with American Airlines in 1983 resulted in new pilots getting up to 50 percent less pay than current employees. However, deregulation has apparently not led to lower wages for employees overall and the trend was moving away from two-tier agreements.[17] For example, the 1997 agreement to end the transit strike in the San Francisco Bay area did away with the two-tier system that had been part of the collective bargaining agreement.

Reorganization: Into the 21st Century

Union leaders have been trumpeting the victory of the Teamsters over UPS in 1997 as a "watershed" event. One 1997 review of the state of unions concluded, "The labor movement is in its strongest position in nearly a generation and is poised to increase its membership after a two-decade decline."[18] The AFL-CIO is spending $20 million a year organizing new members (compared to $2.5 million in the early 90s). In late 1997, there were major organizing efforts to unionize 16,000 teachers in Dallas, 20,000 strawberry workers in California, 55,000 apple workers in Washington, 70,000 home health care workers in California, and over 25,000 nursing home workers in the Southeast.

Downsizing in many organizations has put pressure on keeping jobs rather than on simply increasing wages or benefits. Unions have recognized that an unemployed member causes the union to lose money. Unions have begun to focus more on security and retirement/pension issues than ever before.

A 1993 model of contracts to be negotiated by the United Steelworkers is a prime example of the refocusing of union objectives. The new model stresses labor involvement at all levels of the organization, guarantees of no layoffs, plant modernization, a guarantee to maintain pensions and insurance of at least current levels for current and retired workers, and a desire to push for public policy that is seen as mutually beneficial to both parties. Wage and benefit issues are still of great import on union dockets; however, the past uncertainties seem to have pushed the unions to seek stability wherever they can find it. Another example of this new philosophy is the contract negotiated by diesel workers at Cummins Engine. The union signed an 11-year contract that guaranteed a minimum number of employment hours per year. Why? Because when the contract expires, all the represented employees will be eligible for retirement; this contract assured present security and retirement security for all employees.[19] Recently other unions have been placing a greater emphasis on job security for employees. Union members of local 27 of the United Food and Commercial Workers International Union negotiated with Giant Food Stores (45 stores involved) to provide greater job security for its 6,000 Giant employees in the event the company is sold.[20] Job security is also a bargaining issue in other countries. In South Korea, the largest strike ever occurred in 1997. Workers were not fighting for higher wages; instead, they were protesting a new labor law that allows companies to lay off workers more easily.[21]

Another facet of the changing union focus has been a more cooperative environment with management. A 1994 study showed that 61 percent of employees surveyed preferred cooperative employee–management relationships for problem solving over the use of collective bargaining.[22] Unions are trying to appeal to this preference by approaching negotiations with an attitude of open-mindedness and strategic concession. An example of this is the relationship at Whirlpool. The union signed a five-year contract (as opposed to the traditional three-year deal) in return for commitments to funding growth opportunities (i.e., product development and modernization) by the company. By helping to promote the growth of the company, the union hopes to maintain job security for its employees and to gain new members as the company expands. This represents the approach that many unions are taking—working *with* management rather than against it to help both parties in the long run. In the 1980s, the UAW entered into a cooperative relationship with Ford Motor Company that is still in effect today.[23] In general, it is uncertain whether this new bargaining focus and approach to management will curb the declining numbers in unions; however, it has allowed the union movement to readjust to a new corporate environment that includes greater international competition, deregulation of additional industries, downsizing, and empowerment.[24]

At the same time that some unions have become more cooperative, there are hints that the labor movement is taking a stronger stance against aggressive management tactics. For example, the "Justice for Janitors" campaign initiated by the Service Employees International Union in the last decade has been successful at unionizing over 33,500 building service workers.[25] The success emanated from the union targeting major corporations that contract with nonunion cleaning companies. The election of John Sweeney as president of the AFL-CIO also signaled a change for the U.S. labor when he pledged to revitalize the labor movement.[26] Contrary to recent AFL-CIO leadership, Sweeney believes the AFL-CIO should play a direct and creative role in union organizing.[27] Sweeney has argued against the "one size-fits-all pattern of unionism" and is experimenting with the other organizational structures that the labor movement might use to address workers' needs.[28]

The new and more aggressive approach was bolstered by a 1995 Supreme Court ruling that went against Town & Country Electric.[29] The nonunion electrical contractor refused to hire or even interview 10 job applicants who were known union organizers. The court ruled that all job applicants and employed workers are protected by the NLRA. Because of this ruling, several major unions now have paid organizers who seek employment in nonunion companies for the purpose of organizing.

The AFL-CIO also committed millions of dollars to electing political candidates in the 1996 elections. Although the election results did not return control of Congress to the Democrats, union efforts helped reelect President Clinton and defeated several Republicans. Further, the campaign contributions may have also sent a signal to Congress that labor was becoming more active politically than it had been in recent years.

Certain economic factors also point to this being a good time for the revitalization of the labor movement. Certainly, the strength of the economy gives labor an edge in strikes when workers become difficult to replace. Secondly, the widening wage gap also suggests that workers on the lower rung of the economic ladder feel more inequity and may be willing to risk jobs for economic gain. Contingent workers may also feel a sense of inequity relative to those in more standardized work arrangements with whom they are working side by side. These factors suggest that workers may be more receptive to unions than when working conditions were more favorable and equitable.

PUBLIC-SECTOR UNION MEMBERSHIP

While private-sector union membership dropped to under 15 percent of wage and salary earners by 1995, the public sector suffered a much less substantial decline to 37.7 percent of their workforce. Despite the currently high level of representation rates for government workers, public-sector unions appear to be following the same growth and development stages as private-sector unions—albeit at a lagged pace.[30] Public-sector growth and development can be characterized in three phases: little organization (before 1960), rapid increase in bargaining and membership (between 1960 and 1975), and leveling off (from 1975 to the present). Several reasons are offered for this trend. Limited union organization occurred before 1960 partly because private-sector labor legislation did not cover public-sector employees and public-sector laws did not begin emerging until after 1960. Second, public-sector employment remained relatively stable compared to that of the private sector, giving public-sector workers a sense of security. Finally, the public-sector strike prohibition combined with no protective labor legislation left unions with little bargaining power. These factors combined to give public-sector workers before 1960 little reason to organize.

After 1960, however, environmental changes created more incentives for public-sector unionization. Factors such as relatively low wages eroded by inflation provided some impetus for public-sector workers to organize. Further, many government workers, such as teachers, were already members of organizations that could, and did, become bargaining agents. Today, university faculty members face threats to their economic well-being, professional status, and academic freedom similar to the problems they faced in the 1970s. Universities have to cope with increasing governmental pressure to do more with less funding, and faculty issues such as tenure and academic freedom are under attack. Faculty are working longer hours at a lower real wage than in 1972; hence many faculty are rejoining unions.[31]

The relative lack of sophistication of public-sector employers in organizing anti-union campaigns fostered unionization efforts. This lack of sophistication often meant the employers did not strongly resist unionization. The first state legislation and federal executive orders providing for public-sector collective bargaining were also enacted during this period. While prohibiting strikes, the 1978 Civil Service Reform Act established the right of federal employees to have union representation. Now federal regulations make it easier for unions to try to organize large sections of the public workforce, such as the 3 million employees of public hospitals. These factors have all contributed to the rise in public-sector labor union growth. However, public-sector structural changes such as the tax reform movement of the 1980s, along with increased management resistance, may have led to a flattening of public-sector unionization growth in the most recent years.[32]

Public-sector employees generally have less bargaining power than private-sector employees because unions often have to negotiate or bargain with several government agencies rather than just one employer. Also, many U.S. governmental agencies restrict or forbid their employees to strike. For example, if city firefighters went on strike there may not be anyone available to handle emergency situations. With less power, public-sector unions have developed alternative ways to negotiate, such as mediation and mandatory arbitration.[33] These are described in a later section. In a study of attitudes toward collective bargaining and compulsory arbitration among fire, health care, and government employees in Ontario, Canada, it was discovered that most union and management officials were neutral or dissatisfied with arbitration. Most agreed that arbitration inhibited genuine collective bargaining.[34]

WHY WORKERS JOIN UNIONS

Psychological research indicates three general reasons workers join unions: (1) perceptions of the work environment, (2) desires to participate in or influence employment conditions, and (3) employee beliefs about the effects of unions. Figure 13.5 presents a model of these determinants.

Workers' dissatisfaction with their wages, benefits, and supervision are most related to the tendency to vote for a union.[35] For example, one study of over 87,000 workers in retail found that attitudes toward supervision, wages, and benefits measured 3 to 15 months before a

formal union organizing effort were strong predictors of the subsequent vote for unionization. A study within the Federal Aviation Administration (FAA) found similar results before a certification vote to reunionize air traffic controllers. The union vote varied across regions of the FAA and correlated significantly with attitudes toward supervision, pay, and perceived work stress. One surprising finding from the research on why people vote for unions is that the work itself does not seem to be strongly related to union voting. The best predictors in several studies are attitudes toward pay and working conditions, rather than the work itself. In 1995, even fashion models were organizing and attempting to build a new labor union to address their benefits and long hours. Fashion agencies do not provide models with health insurance, dental insurance, pensions, life insurance, or workers' compensation. In addition, most models make between $30,000 and $70,000 in a year and have difficulty affording health insurance. The Models Guild was founded for models, although photographers and makeup artists were also invited to join. The Models Guild has also been adopted by the 130,000-member Office and Professional Employees' International union, which has more money and power.[36]

A second general reason for joining unions is a belief that there are no other options for either gaining more influence in the workplace or finding employment elsewhere. In general, if employees have mechanisms to voice their concerns about HRM policy, there is less tendency to favor unionization. A formal grievance proce-

FIGURE 13.5
DETERMINANTS OF PROPENSITY TO JOIN UNIONS

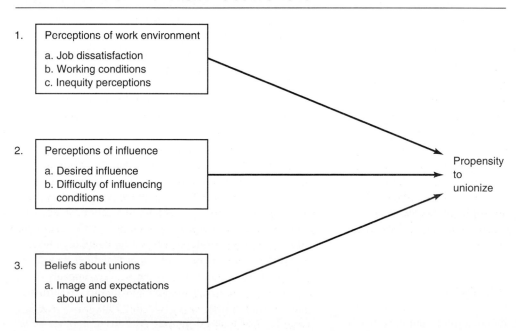

Source: T. Kochan, *Collective bargaining and industrial relations.* Homewood, IL: Richard D. Irwin, 1980, p. 144. Reprinted with permission.

dure, for example, which has been used successfully by employees, would deter union activity because workers perceive that there are alternatives to unions for correcting problems at work.

The third critical reason for joining unions is that employees believe unions can actually improve conditions and, in particular, can have an impact at their own workplace.[37] Companies attempt to influence employees' beliefs in this regard. Campaign tactics by management include written communications, meetings, threats, and actions against union supporters. These can negatively affect workers' votes for unionization. Japanese firms with U.S. operations have been particularly adept at launching anti-union campaigns and quite successful in winning certification elections. Companies often use consultants who specialize in refuting the claims of union organizers and presenting horrendous scenarios if the union should prevail. It is estimated there are over 1,000 such firms and an additional 1,500 private consultants in the union prevention or "busting" business.[38]

Union tactics, although less often examined, also influence workers' willingness to join unions. A recent study found that unions that conducted a rank-and-file organizing strategy were more likely to win certification.[39] Such a strategy involves reliance on a slow underground person-to-person campaign that involves using the employees to organize the campaign. Further, a union with a strong commitment to organizing also increases the probability that the union will win the election.

While many Americans believe unions can improve things at work, many are generally hostile to unions. They think unions protect ineffective workers, abuse their power through strikes, are corrupt, and impede productivity improvement programs. One study found that knowing an employee's general opinion about unions in these areas was a strong predictor of how an employee would vote for union representation.[40] Critical Thinking Exercise 13.1 illustrates this point.

CRITICAL THINKING EXERCISE 13.1

Unionizing FedEx[1]

In a world of more competition and higher profits and shareholders' return on investment, unionizing does not seem to make sense. Or does it? Employees at Federal Express have been trying to unionize since 1991.[2] The pilots were finally successful in 1993.[3] The ground employees have sought unionization at various sites for the six years it took for the National Labor Relations Board to rule that Federal Express continues to be covered under the Railway Labor Act. This prevented the local sites from unionizing because the election to unionize has to be conducted at all sites within a given job category simultaneously.

The Federal Express employees have not given up. They are using newsletters, union literature, e-mails, and Web pages to get the reasons they seek to unionize to the rest of their colleagues who are not yet convinced. A trip to either the Teamsters Web site (http://www.teamster.org/fedex.html) or the FedUp home page (http://ourworld.compuserve.com/homepages/kevin_osiowy/homepage.htm) or its mirror site (http://www.megsinet.com/kevinosiowy/) show how serious this effort is.

Now, with the United Parcel Service's 1997 negotiated contract, Federal Express employees are even more motivated to contract with their employer. Before the UPS strike, UPS delivery drivers made $19.86 per hour plus incentive program payouts. Federal Express delivery drivers made about $15.98 with fewer incentives than their counterparts at UPS. With the new contract in place, the wage differential exceeds approximately $6 per hour. One of the "biggest beefs" the FedEx employees have is the fact that CEO Fred Smith announced in 1996 that wages were not going to increase, but his own benefit package and that of his executives increased by an average of over 6 percent. Employees believe that the threat of unionization changed Smith's mind. He then announced a 3 percent increase for employees starting April 1997. This increased the top-of-the-range courier from the $15.51 per hour to $15.98 per hour.[4]

Wages, however, are not the only issue. Part-time and subcontract work are cited by Federal Express employee literature (see above mentioned Web sites) as grievances against Smith's PSP (People–Service–Profits) labor behavior. FedEx currently has 32 percent of its workforce as part-time employees and subcontracts 23 percent of its business. This business, argue employees, should be done by full-timers. The Teamsters union agrees. The Teamsters negotiation of the August 1997 UPS contract included "no shift of package delivery work to part-timers" and "no subcontracting of feeder work except during peak season, and then only if local union agrees."[5]

FedEx officials have argued that their PSP philosophy mitigates the need for unionization. And with laws on occupational safety, working hours, and minimum wage, unions are not needed like they were "40, 50, 60 years ago."[6] Grievances at FedEx are settled by a "guaranteed fair treatment" program. This program is one reason some employees have signed a card indicating their intention to vote for a union should a national election be scheduled. These employees include Joe Coleman, who after 18 years of service was fired for allegedly changing an airbill. His manager "felt" that Coleman had altered the airbill. Coleman lost two out of three appeals for reinstatement even with his spotless record. His third appeal, at the highest level, reinstated his position due to the efforts of union organizer Al Ferrier, another FedEx employee. Ferrier coached Coleman for his hearing and stressed to other employees that this could happen to them.[7] This would not happen if FedEx employees had their own union. For example, a UPS employee cannot be discharged with one reprimand in his file. It takes three, of the same complaint. And the UPS reprimands are not admissible after nine months. At FedEx they stay in the file indefinitely and managers can go back 18 months for reprimands.[8]

Fear tactics are the most widely used by management against unionizing. In March 1997, Fred Smith issued a memo titled "From the Chief Executive Officer: People-Service-Profit Philosophy vs. The Competition." In it Smith uses the fear of FedEx's existence. "A third party, with no history of association with this company, and no true stake in its future, could, through an inflexible negotiating strategy, undercut the ability of FedEx to provide consistently superior service at reasonable rates to its customer base." Yet both UPS and Airborne, which have similar express delivery services, were not shut down because of their union contracts. In fact, they have experienced substantial growth rates since unionizing.

Assignment

You are a newly hired FedEx employee. Based on what you know now about FedEx and its competitors, would you sign a card to certify a union at FedEx? If yes, explain what information weighed the heaviest in your decision. If no, is there additional information you need to help you make your decision? Compile a list of questions you believe to be vital for your decision? If no and you request no further information, explain what information weighed the heaviest in that decision.

[1] Contributed by Mary E. Wilson.

[2] Duvoisin, M. (May 7, 1995). Nice work if you can keep it: FedEx employees love their company. *Philadelphia Inquirer,* p. 16.

[3] Chevan, H. (April 1993). Mailers wary of new FedEx union. *Catalog Age 10*(4), 34.

[4] Beckman, P. (1997). Payday! In K. Osiowy, (http://ourworld. compuserve.com/homepages/kevin_osiowy/payday.htm).

[5] Teamsters (1997). What we won by striking. *Ups_whatwon_ p1 JPG.* (http://teamster.org/ups_whatwon_p1.html).

[6] Duvoisin, M., *Philadelphia Inquirer,* p. 16.

[7] Ibid.

[8] Osiowy, K. (1997). Why we need a union at FedEx. *FedEx Sum97 p2.* (http://www.teamster.org/fedex_sum97_p2).

THE EFFECTS OF UNIONS

Workers join unions to improve their wages, working conditions, and job security. This section presents opinions regarding whether or not unions actually do provide these improvements and what these effects mean for firm performance. Two perspectives dominate the literature on the effects of labor unions: monopoly and collective voice.[41] Economists traditionally believe labor unions behave as labor market monopolies. They primarily see unions as raising wages, which results in economic inefficiencies and adverse effects for workers and firms. The collective voice perspective views unions more positively by concentrating on their beneficial economic and political aspects. These two perspectives are described below.

Monopoly Effects

The monopoly view of unions starts with the premise that unions raise wages above competitive levels. How much unions raise wages varies across labor markets, industries, occupations, and demographic groups, as well as data and estimation procedures. Overall, estimates of union and nonunion wage differentials are around 15 percent.[42] Unions also apparently have a large positive fringe benefit effect. These estimates, however, vary by demographic group. This variation partially results from a union philosophy that workers doing the same job should receive the same pay. Thus, those who are usually paid the least tend to benefit the most from unionization. Studies show that younger workers, nonwhites, people living in the South and the West, and blue-collar workers seem to gain the most from unionization. Interestingly, little apparent difference exists between the wage gains from unionization for males and females. Research on public-sector unions shows a plus 5 percent pay differential for public-sector employees represented by unions versus public-sector employees not represented.[43]

Variations in union wage effects across industries partially occur due to the union's ability to take "wages out of competition." Wages can be taken out of competition in several ways. Primarily, labor demand may be relatively insensitive to wage changes (inelastic). That is, consumers will absorb the increased labor costs without offsetting employment effects. Factors that contribute to labor demand inelasticity include labor costs being a small proportion of total costs; insensitivity of product demand to changes in prices; and an inability to substitute labor for capital, either through technology or through markets.[44]

The extent of union organization in a particular market can also affect union monopoly power. More unionized markets have greater union/nonunion wage differentials because of less nonunion wage competition. The extent of bargaining coverage further augments this effect. This coverage can take several forms. For example, one union may bargain for the entire market—so that all union firms in the industry have virtually identical contracts. In the auto industry, the UAW bargains with one of the big three automakers and then uses this contract as a pattern for the remaining settlements. However, since the internationalization of the industry, the big three automakers are no longer the majority of the labor market. A union negotiating simultaneously with numerous employers, as occurred in steel and coal, provides another example of extensive industry coverage. A union that bargains at the plant level has much less monopoly power than those that negotiate on a broader basis.

Some economists condemn unions because they believe the union wage effect leads to inefficient firm responses such as substituting labor for capital. They argue that society suffers due to resource misallocation between the union and nonunion sectors. However, unions strongly believe in equal pay for equal work. This union policy reduces the amount of wage dispersion within firms, within the union sector, and between blue-collar workers and white-collar workers. These equalizing effects, estimates show, outweigh the inequality produced by the union/nonunion wage differential by almost 3 percent, although these findings are somewhat controversial.[45]

Collective Voice Effects

Workers have several choices when they feel dissatisfied with their jobs: They can do nothing, they can quit, or they can complain and try to improve the conditions around them (i.e., voice their concerns). In work settings, the voice of one employee is rarely effective at bringing about change. In addition, many workers fear termination for revealing their true feelings to management. Most workers find it easier to fight for work improvements when in a union. Banding together and creating a "collective voice" offers protection from the fear of raising concerns to management.

Union advocates maintain that the collective voice reduces worker quit rates, thereby leading to retention of experienced workers, lowering a firm's training costs, and raising its productivity.[46] Another side benefit is that management is forced to become more efficient when faced with the necessity of providing higher wages to unionized employees.

Union Effects on Firm Performance: Productivity, Profits, and Stock Price

The collective voice mechanism suggests that unions may actually have positive effects on management. If so, why does management strenuously resist unions? Are executives behaving rationally? Or do they resist unions only because unions threaten their decision-making autonomy?

Two theories exist regarding unions' effects on firms' productivity.[47] On one hand, productivity is predicted to decrease in unionized firms because unions create resource misallocation and demand restrictive work rules. In contrast, the collective voice view predicts that productivity gains may occur because the union wage ef-

fect causes firms to manage better, employ better-quality labor, substitute capital for labor, and reduce voluntary turnover, leading to the development of a more experienced and better-trained labor force. Others attribute any productivity gains more to organizational survival than to collective voice effects.[48] To remain competitive, management *must* improve productivity.

The evidence is mixed regarding the effects of unions on organizational productivity. Unions tend to have a negative effect on productivity when there is relatively greater conflict between the union and management. Stanford professor Pfeffer summed up the confusing evidence on unions and productivity this way: "The effects of unions depend very much on what management does."[49] Positive productivity effects generally tend to be found in competitive industries with higher union wage effects (i.e., where firm survival apparently depends on offsetting the higher wage costs with increased productivity). One review of the research concluded that, in general, productivity remains higher in union establishments than in nonunion establishments. This conclusion is controversial and the subject of much debate.[50] The researchers concluded that when unions and management are working for a "bigger pie" as well as fighting over their relative share, the result is higher productivity. Under conditions of poor labor–management relations, where the focus is on taking a bigger share of the same size pie, the result is usually lower productivity.

What of the argument that unions raise wages to noncompetitive levels and have thus seriously affected the ability of some U.S. industries to compete? One surprising study of 134 industries concluded that "heavily unionized industries are not found to have lost any more to imports nor gained any more in exports than comparable U.S. industries . . . industrial concentration appears to be a significant disadvantage."[51] This means that U.S. industries facing a more globally competitive environment after less domestic competition tended to have more difficulty competing *regardless of union status.*

If unions do improve productivity, how can management behave rationally by resisting unions? Apparently union productivity effects do not sufficiently outweigh the negative impact of unions on accounting profits and stock prices or shareholder wealth. For example, shareholder wealth decreases during union organizing campaigns and strikes and increases during concession bargaining.[52] In addition, unions do not seem to change the overall firm value, but they do redistribute the firm's economic profits from the stockholders to the workers.

In other countries, concessions by unions have resulted in greater profits for employers. For example, at Gustav Selter Ltd., a knitting-needle maker near Dortmund, Germany, workers agreed to flexible working hours and pay cuts totaling 16 percent since 1994. In return, they receive a share of the profits. Results indicated that sales were growing 15 percent a year versus 5 percent before the concessions were implemented, and profits were expected to jump 50 percent in 1997. Agreements such as these are contributing to a productivity boom in Germany. After accounting for inflation, productivity jumped by 4.6 percent in 1996. As sales increase, so do corporate earnings, and for the 30 companies represented in the DAX stock index, profits jumped an average 45 percent in 1996.[53]

Unions and Quality of Work Life Issues

As we discussed in Chapter 12, quality of work life (QWL) issues came to the forefront in the 1980s and play an important role in the labor–management relationship. Some QWL programs such as job redesign, upward communication, team-based work configurations, and quality circles (QCs) have elicited a variety of union responses.[54] Overt hostility and resistance characterize some unions' reactions to QWL programs. A significant faction of the UAW membership at the Saturn plant, for example, strongly opposes the negotiated worker involvement programs. These members fear that management intends to use these programs to circumvent the union and the collective bargaining relationship. Other members cautiously indicate they prefer the collective bargaining process to QWL programs but will support QWL programs if there is no attempt to bust the union or interfere with the collective bargaining process. Many have argued that union support remains critical for successful implementation of QWL programs. One study cited management neglect in inviting union participation early enough, or not at all, as a contributing factor to many failures of QWL programs.[55] Generally, in union settings, management is seen to be more careful in evaluating the decision to implement a QWL program than in firms where a union is not present.[56]

Recently, the UAW noted that the goods that workers manufacture and the services they provide must succeed in the marketplace (with good quality) to ensure long-term job and income security for workers. The union further noted that UAW workers have everything to gain by demanding that employees work to achieve the highest possible product and service quality. This means that QWL programs can be quite important in addition to training, up-to-date equipment, and quality materials and resources. These will enable employees to achieve first-rate quality in goods and services and better guarantee their own future employment.[57]

There is limited research on the effects of QWL efforts in union settings. Two studies found that QWL programs did not have any effect on firms' economic performance.[58] However, more recent research states that unionized firms had more gains from employee participation than did nonunion firms.[59] Additionally, recall the positive results reported in Chapter 12 at Chrysler's New Castle, Indiana, assembly plant. The UAW-endorsed, work team approach has reduced car defects and decreased absenteeism and grievances.

Other research has shown that QWL programs can improve the firm's industrial relations.[60] Some early research has, however, elicited evidence that QWL programs may negatively influence perceptions of unions. One study found that participants in employee involvement programs thought these were better at resolving differences than collective bargaining. Similar individuals not in those programs maintained preference toward collective bargaining.[61] In addition, nonunion companies that encourage communication and participation programs have apparently been successful in maintaining nonunion status.[62] However, firms must be cautious in their implementation of nonunion work teams because of legal concerns regarding violations of the Wagner Act's prohibition regarding company unions. The act states that it is unlawful for an employer "to dominate or interfere with the formation or administration of any labor organization or contribute financial or other support to it." In the 1994 *Electromation* case, the U.S. Court of Appeals upheld the National Labor Relations Board's ruling that management committees addressing employee dissatisfaction with absenteeism and attendance bonuses represented illegal employer domination.[63] However, the facts of this case suggest that management had established these committees to avoid unionization. Because of the *Electromation* decision, Congress considered the *Teamwork for Employees and Management Act* (TEAM) which would amend the Wagner Act and allow employers to establish worker involvement committees.[64] As of 1997, the TEAM had not become law.

Union Effects on Worker Satisfaction

Better wages, benefits, and improved working conditions would seem to predict that union workers would be more satisfied than nonunion workers. Early evidence points to the contrary. Supervision, coworkers, and job content create more dissatisfaction for union workers than for nonunion workers. Only pay provides more union satisfaction.[65] The exit/voice hypothesis suggests that this results from unions encouraging members to voice their dissatisfaction rather than to quit. Voluntary turnover rates are substantially lower under unions. Alternatively, union workers may feel compelled to stay because of the "golden handcuffs" of better wages, health insurance, and working conditions: they may feel that they cannot afford to quit when they are dissatisfied. The most recent research indicates that union membership has no effect on either job satisfaction or intention to quit.[66]

COLLECTIVE BARGAINING

Collective bargaining occurs when representatives of a labor union meet with management representatives to determine employees' wages and benefits, to create or revise work rules, and to resolve disputes or violations of the labor contract. For over 16 million workers, collective bargaining represents the primary process for determining their wages, benefits, and working conditions. Despite the decline in unions and their membership in recent years, it is unlikely that either unions or collective bargaining will ever disappear. This means that both organizations and unions will need to maintain knowledge of bargaining strategies and guidelines to successfully represent their interests.

For those in the field of human resource management, a knowledge of labor relations and collective bargaining is important. It is often difficult to separate labor relations as a human resource function from the many other HR functions. For example, labor relations is closely tied to HR planning because the labor contract generally stipulates policies and procedures related to promotions, transfers, job security, and layoffs. Recruiting and selection are also tied to the labor contract because, in a union shop, those hired must eventually join the union. Finally, the area of HR where a knowledge of collective bargaining is probably most critical is compensation and benefits, since almost all aspects of wages and benefits are subject to negotiation.

Collective bargaining should be viewed by both the union and management as a two-way street. This means the basic interests of management must be protected as well as the rights of employees. Both sides have a responsibility to each other. For example, unions should not expect management to concede to issues that would ultimately impair the company's ability to stay in business. Likewise, management must recognize the rights of employees to form unions to argue for improved wages and working conditions.

The Labor Contract

A labor contract is a formal agreement between a union and management that specifies the conditions of employment and the union–management relationship over a mutually agreed on period of time (typically two to three years but more recently five years). The labor contract specifies what the two parties have agreed on regarding issues such as wages, benefits, and working conditions. The process involved in reaching this agreement is a complex and difficult job requiring a willingness from both sides to reconcile their differences and compromise their interests. This process is also bound to certain "good-faith" guidelines that must be upheld by both parties.

The Taft-Hartley Act of 1947 (section 8d) states: "to bargain collectively is [to recognize] . . . the mutual obligation of the employer and representative of the employees to meet at reasonable times and confer in good faith with respect to wages, hours, and other terms and conditions of employment, . . . or the negotiation of an agreement, or any question arising thereunder, and the execution of a written contract incorporating any agreement reached if requested by either party, . . . such obligation does not compel either party to agree to a proposal or require the making of a concession."[67] Thus, the law requires that the employer negotiate with the union once the union has been recognized as the employees' representative. In good-faith bargaining:

- Meetings for negotiating the contract are scheduled and conducted with the union at reasonable times and places.
- Realistic proposals are submitted.
- Reasonable counterproposals are offered.
- Each party signs the agreement once it has been completed.

Good-faith bargaining does not mean that either party is required to agree to a final proposal or to make concessions.

The National Labor Relations Board further defines the "duty to bargain" as covering bargaining on all matters concerning rates of pay, wages, hours of employment, and other conditions of employment.[68] "Mandatory" issues for bargaining include wages, benefits, hours of work, incentive pay, overtime, seniority, safety, layoff and recall procedures, grievance procedures, and job security. "Permissive" or "nonmandatory" issues have no direct relationship to wages, hours, or working conditions. These might include changes in benefits for retired employees, performance bonds for unions or management, and union input into prices of the firm's products. Permissive issues can be introduced into the discussion by either party; however, neither party is obligated to discuss them or include them in the labor contract.

The Major Issues in Collective Bargaining

The major issues discussed in collective bargaining fall under the following four categories:[69]

1. *Wage-related issues* such as basic wage rates, cost-of-living adjustments (COLAs), wage differentials, overtime rates, wage adjustments, and two-tier wage systems.

2. *Supplementary economic benefits,* which include pension plans, paid vacations, paid holidays, health insurance plans, dismissal pay, reporting pay, and supplementary unemployment benefits (SUB).

3. *Institutional issues* such as the rights and duties of employers, employees, and unions, including union

security (i.e., union membership as a condition of employment), employee stock ownership plans (ESOPs), and quality of work life (QWL) programs.

4. *Administrative issues* such as seniority, employee discipline and discharge procedures, employee health and safety, technological changes, work rules, job security, worker privacy issues, and training.

The wage and benefit issues receive the greatest amount of attention at the bargaining table. In recent years, however, issues of job security and employee benefits have become increasingly important as bargaining items.[70] In addition, the unions have adapted to a variety of workplace changes and have played an important role in defining public policies. For example, they have been active in negotiating family-friendly contract provisions such as child care, elder care, domestic partnership benefits, and paternity leaves. They have also been involved in promoting health and safety protections for their members.[71]

PREPARING FOR NEGOTIATIONS. Successful negotiations are contingent on each side remaining flexible. It is hoped that the end result will be a "package" representing the maximum and minimum levels acceptable to each party. If neither the union nor management is willing to change its demands enough to bring them within a theoretical "bargaining zone," or if neither is willing to extend the limits to accommodate the other's demands, then negotiations reach a impasse.

The union team is first to present its initial proposals. Usually, the original union proposal demands more than it expects to end up with (i.e., excessive demands in terms of changes in, additions to, and deletions from the previous contract), which will allow leverage for trading off for management concessions. The management negotiating team then states the management case, often presenting unrealistic counterproposals and data supporting the view that union workers are treated well. For example, in the 1992 negotiations between the National Hockey League (NHL) and the NHL Players Association, the president of the NHL asked early on why the union would "reject an offer when $9 out of every $10 a fan spends on a game ticket goes to NHL players, and the proposed system would raise wages to an average of at least $420,000?" The union countered with average salary data from the National Basketball Association and Major League Baseball. The early meetings are often characterized by both parties remaining far apart on the issues; however, as negotiations proceed, there is generally movement toward agreement. As topics are discussed and considered, mutual concessions are offered, counterproposals are made, and eventually a tentative agreement is reached.

When a tentative agreement is reached, in most cases, the union members vote on the contract. If it is approved, the contract is ratified; if it is voted down, more negotiating occurs. The next step involves the actual drafting of a formal document, attempting to keep it in simple, clear, and concise terms. In fact, however, most contracts are difficult to read and some sections are virtually incomprehensible for the rank and file (e.g., most often sections on seniority and grievance procedures). The last step is the actual signing of the agreement by the representatives of the union and management. The typical labor agreement defines the responsibilities and authority of unions and management and stipulates what management activities are not subject to union authority (e.g., purchasing and hiring).

RESOLVING BARGAINING DEADLOCKS AND IMPASSE RESOLUTION. If neither the organization nor the union is willing to remain flexible and make concessions, then negotiations reach a deadlock or impasse, which can eventually result in a strike on the part of the union or a lockout on the part of management. How can these breakdowns in negotiations be avoided? One way is to delay consideration of the more difficult issues until the latter stages of bargaining and, for the time being, to simply agree to disagree on the tougher decisions. The easier questions can be considered in the beginning, giving both sides a feeling of progress. Another way to avoid breakdowns in negotiations is for each side to be prepared to offer propositions and to accept alternative solutions to some of the more controversial issues.

If the two parties are unable to compromise and resolve a deadlock, then they have the option of calling in a **mediator,** a neutral third party who reviews the dispute between the two parties and attempts to open up communication channels by suggesting compromise solutions and concessions. Mediation is based on the principle of voluntary acceptance. This means mediators act as go-betweens to help clarify the issues, but they have no conclusive power or authority to impose or recommend a solution. In fact, either party may accept or reject the mediator's recommendations. The Federal Mediation and Conciliation Service (FMCS) was established by the Taft-Hartley Act; 199 mediators perform their services for free and mediate about 15,000 labor disagreements a year.[72]

Sometimes government intervention is necessary to resolve deadlocks. This is generally in cases where a work stoppage would threaten national security or the public welfare. For example, the Taft-Hartley Act includes a national emergency strike provision that gives the president of the United States the power to stop a strike if it imperils national health or safety.[73] In most cases the government will call upon the services of the FMCS to resolve such bargaining deadlocks. In the 1997 UPS strike, a survey of Americans found that 75 percent believed that UPS and the workers should settle the dispute themselves, and only 21 percent favored federal intervention.[74]

The Union's Economic Power in Collective Bargaining

The basis for the union's power in collective bargaining is economic and generally takes one of three forms: striking the employer, picketing the employer, or boycotting the employer.

STRIKING THE EMPLOYER. One tool a labor union can use to motivate an employer to reach an agreement is to call a strike. A strike is simply a refusal on the part of employees to perform their jobs.[75] Strikes occur when the union is unable to obtain an offer from management that is acceptable to its members. Strikes are rare. There were only 37 large-scale strikes in 1996.

While strikes tend to receive a lot of attention from the media, they represent less than 1 percent of total workdays lost each year. In addition, strike activity has been steadily declining since the 1970s. Around 1974, there were more than 400 work stoppages and over 2 million workers involved. By 1980, there were less than 200 work stoppages involving less than 1 million employees, and by 1995 there were fewer than 50 work stoppages and around 250,000 workers involved. By mid-1997, the number of work stoppages was running slightly higher than in the past, yet the pace was still below the 1995 level and much less than the 1990 level.[76] Two very successful strikes from the unions' perspective may encourage more aggressive tactics. The pilots strike against American Airlines and the Teamsters strike against UPS are considered by most experts to be major union successes.

Before a union goes on strike, it must first assess the consequences of a strike and its members' willingness to make the sacrifices and endure the hardships (e.g., lost pay) that are part of striking. Even when the union perceives the strike as necessary, employees may not be willing to strike. Factors such as loyalty to the organization and commitment to the job have been shown to differentiate workers who are willing to strike and those who are not.[77] Another part of this assessment also involves determining whether the employer can continue operating by using supervisory personnel, nonstriking employees, or replacement workers. Automated firms such as AT&T and the baby Bells have fully developed strike plans that enable the companies to operate at near 100 percent capacity.

A number of risks to the union and its members are attached to striking. For one, replacement workers can be hired and then vote the union out in an NLRB-conducted decertification election. Also, a strike can result in a loss of union members. The public may also

withdraw its support from union members and often does. Most Americans sided with the 1997 Teamsters fight to win more higher-paying, full-time jobs. One study found that 55 percent of Americans surveyed supported the Teamsters union while only 27 percent backed UPS. This high level of support existed despite the fact that 31 percent of those surveyed stated that they disapprove of unions.[78] These findings reflect a big change from strikes of several decades ago (e.g., Caterpillar, Inc., and McDonnell Douglas Corp.) when union members felt the country was against them. In the UPS case, it seemed that the public supported the union's case that its part-timers need to work full time if they are to earn a decent living and get adequate benefits. UPS full-time employees earn on average $20 an hour and get full benefits, while part-timers get $11 an hour with reduced benefits. It may also be that many Americans actually know their UPS delivery person, who is also a Teamster. The support was also surprising in that many Americans were inconvenienced by the strike, especially small-business owners who have fewer shipping alternatives.

The power of the strike to pressure management has been seriously diminished during the past decades. Automation, recent court rulings, and a growing number of unemployed workers willing to serve as replacements have helped management. After Congress passed the Wagner Act in 1935, workers' rights to organize and to strike were guaranteed. However, in 1938 a court decision weakened this right by permitting the permanent replacement of economic strikers by management.[79] The use of replacement workers seriously undermines the economic pressure strikes once had. Even though this court decision was made in 1938, it was not until the 1980s that the ruling was frequently applied. Many workers who went on strike in the last decade have found that their jobs were not waiting for them when the strike ended.[80] Since President Reagan hired nonunion workers to replace air traffic controllers in 1981, management's hiring of nonunion members has been a regular and successful strikebreaking weapon. The actions of Caterpillar and the *Detroit News/Free Press* are two recent examples of the use of replacement workers as a strike weapon. Nonetheless, it appears that in some industries strikes lessen the value of struck firms but enhance the value of their competitors.[81]

PICKETING THE EMPLOYER. Another basis for union power is the picket. The picket is used by employees on strike to advertise their dispute with management and to discourage others from entering or leaving the premises. Picketing usually takes place at the plant or company entrances. It can result in severe financial losses for a firm and can eventually lead to a shutdown of the plant if enough employees refuse to cross the picket line. For example, the machinists of Eastern Airlines picketed the company in 1989. When pilots and flight attendants honored the picket lines of the machinists, the airline faced severe difficulty with operations.[82] Picket lines can become very emotional at times, especially when employees or replacements attempt to cross them. These people may become the target of verbal insults and sometimes even physical violence. Companies now hire security firms to protect nonstriking and replacement workers. For example, Dannon, the yogurt maker, maintained operations during a strike with the Teamsters union with replacement workers and 100 guards who escorted Dannon trucks. All the guards were "armed" with video cameras. Similarly, Vance International, a protective service firm, took over 60,000 photographs and shot thousands of hours of videotape during a coal strike. This evidence resulted in the assessment of over $64 million in fines levied against the mineworkers' union by the courts.[83]

BOYCOTTING THE EMPLOYER. Boycotting involves refusing to patronize an employer—in other words, refusing to buy or use the employer's products or services. As an incentive to employees to honor the boycott, heavy fines may be levied against union members if they are caught patronizing an employer who is the subject of a union boycott. The union hopes that the general public will also join the boycott to put additional pressure on the employer. For example, in 1997 the United Farm Workers (UFW) called for the boycott of California strawberries. The Teamsters, in collaboration with the UFW, ran television ads in Washington state regarding the treatment of apple pickers and were close to ordering a boycott on this product as well.

The Employer's Power in Collective Bargaining

Employers may come to the bargaining table with their own base of power. Foremost is their ability to determine how to use capital within the organization. This enables them to decide whether and when to close the company, the plant, or certain operations within the plant; to transfer operations to another location; or to subcontract out certain jobs. All these decisions must be made in accordance with the law. This means management must be sure its actions are not interpreted by the National Labor Relations Board as attempting to avoid bargaining with the union.[84]

Today, employers are more able to endure strikes than they were in the past. The permanent hiring of replacements has greatly weakened the power of the strike. Research finds that the use of replacement workers usually prolongs strikes.[85] The NFL used mainly replacement players during the 1987 strike with the players union. The owners realized higher profits during the strike although attendance was down. The players had no

strike fund and negotiated a settlement to management's liking in only three weeks. In general, union members now are less willing to support a strike, and without strike unity, the power of the strike is negligible. Also, technological advances have increased some employers' ability to operate during a strike with a substantially reduced staff. Strikes in the public sector are illegal in most states, although walkouts have occurred in some states where strikes are illegal. Federal employees cannot strike because of the 1978 Civil Service Reform Act.

Federal legislation was introduced in 1997 to severely restrict the use of replacement workers; this legislation was supported by President Clinton. However, the legislation was not likely to pass a Republican-controlled Congress. (See Critical Thinking Exercise 13.2 on strike-replacement legislation.)

CRITICAL THINKING EXERCISE 13.2

Do You Support Striker Replacement Legislation?

The labor movement first started to suffer major setbacks in the 1980s when management started hiring replacement workers with the intent of disarming organized labor while continuing to remain productive. In actuality, the hiring of new permanent workers to replace striking employees was sanctioned by the Supreme Court in 1935. However, this policy was not widely practiced until the federal air traffic controllers strike in 1981. President Reagan's firing and replacement of 12,000 union workers was certainly one impetus for this practice becoming widely used and accepted. Also cited as a factor in this widespread practice of hiring permanent replacement workers was the wave of corporate mergers and leveraged buyouts. As a result of these financial megadeals, some argue that management no longer placed high value on a long term workforce with stable community roots.

Congress has proposed legislation to prohibit employers from hiring permanent replacement workers during a strike. As part of this legislative package there is also a section prohibiting management from giving employment preference to employees willing to cross the picket line in order to return to work. President Clinton supports this legislation.

The **Workplace Fairness Act** was designed to protect the interests of those employed under collective bargaining agreements. The law would amend the National Labor Relations Act and make it an unfair labor practice to offer or grant the status of permanent replacement employee to an individual for performing bargaining unit work for the employer during a labor dispute between the employer and the labor organization that is acting as the collective bargaining representative involved in the dispute.

It would also be an unfair labor practice to offer or grant an individual any other employment preference based on the fact that such an individual performed bargaining unit work, or indicated a willingness to perform such work during a labor dispute, over an individual who was an employee at the commencement of the dispute, who in connection with such dispute has exercised the right to join, to assist, or to engage in other concerted activities for the purpose of collective bargaining.

Assignment

Choose one of the following two positions and be prepared to justify it.

Pro Position

In general, supporters of the new law believe that legislation is necessary to rebalance the relationship between labor and management in contract disputes. Supporters further contend that this imbalance leans heavily toward management thus enabling unfair practices through this power. Reflection of this belief is manifested in the declining rates of unionization, decreasing strike activity, inadequate contract settlements, and a new propensity of employers actively hiring permanent replacement workers. These effects, they maintain, send a message to employees that if they strike they will lose their jobs.

Con Position

The essence of the opponent's argument is that by empowering striking employees with the right to displace their permanent replacements would guarantee that there would never be labor/management balance. They feel this act would place unequal power in the union's hands in the context of bargaining over contract terms. Furthermore, opponents of the law contend that prohibiting the hiring of permanent replacements would force many small businesses to close down operations because attracting temporary replacement employees can be extremely difficult (especially in rural areas).

The lockout is another source of power for the employer. A **lockout** is basically a shutting down of operations, usually in anticipation of a strike. The lockout can also be used to fight union slowdowns, damage to property, or violence within the plants. For example, owners of Major League Baseball teams used the lockout in 1990 and 1995 as a response to strikes by the players.[86] Generally, lockouts are not used very often because they lead to financial revenue losses for the firm. In 1997,

Navistar International Corp. stated it would close an Indianapolis factory after the UAW local turned down a contract that would have frozen wages.[87] Many states allow employees to draw unemployment benefits, thus weakening the power of the lockout.

In an unusual type of lockout, the *Detroit Free Press* and *News* agreed to take back striking workers only when jobs opened up. They had endured a 19-month strike in which the newspapers had hired replacement workers and some union workers who crossed the picket lines. Hence, the firms were locking out striking workers from getting their jobs back once the strike was over unless job openings surfaced. As a result, the six unions involved went to federal court to get an injunction to order the companies to hire back the strikers.[88] The NLRB recently ruled in the unions' favor and found that the newspaper had not bargained in good faith.

Administration of the Labor Contract

Despite the incredible amount of time and effort that goes into negotiating and carefully writing the contract, most are written in such broad, ambiguous terms that a great deal of interpretation is required to put the contract to work. Most union workers do not clearly understand the labor contract.

Most problems associated with the interpretation or application of the labor contract are resolved at the lower levels of the **grievance** procedure (i.e., between the supervisor and the union steward). Grievance procedures and the time limits associated with them are generally spelled out in the contract so that quick, fair, and equitable solutions to contract problems are reached. Unresolved grievances proceed progressively to higher and higher levels of management and union representation. If the grievance procedure fails (i.e., the grievance reaches a deadlock or stalemate), most contracts stipulate that the final step will be binding **arbitration.** Arbitration involves bringing in a third party, an impartial outsider mutually agreed on by both parties, to decide the controversy. The following section reviews both the grievance procedure and the arbitration process. Figure 13.6 illustrates what these processes look like.

GRIEVANCE PROCEDURE. When an employee believes the labor agreement has been violated, the employee files a grievance. A grievance is a formal complaint regarding the event, action, or practice that violated the contract. The grievance procedure serves a number of purposes.[89] The primary purpose is to determine whether the labor contract has been violated. Also, the grievance procedure is designed to settle alleged contract violations in a friendly and orderly fashion, before they become major issues. Other purposes of the grievance procedure include preventing future grievances from arising, improving communication and cooperation

**FIGURE 13.6
A GRIEVANCE PROCEDURE**

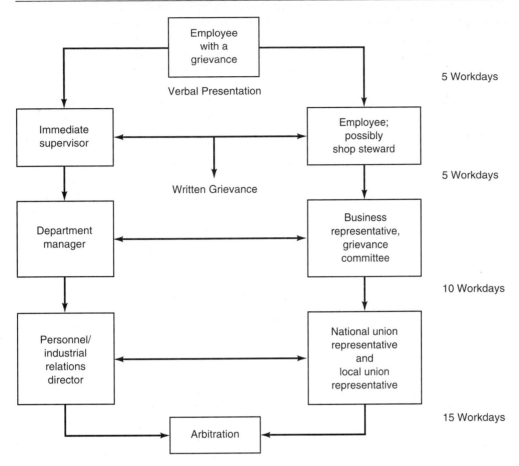

Source: R. E. Allen and T. J. Keaveny, *Contemporary labor relations,* 2nd ed. Reading, MA: Addison-Wesley, 1988, p. 530. Reprinted with permission.

between labor and management, and helping to obtain a better climate of labor relations. The grievance procedure also helps to clarify what often is not clear in the contract (e.g., defining lawful or unlawful conduct).

Grievance procedures generally establish the following: (1) how the grievance will be initiated, (2) the number of steps in the process, (3) who will represent each party, and (4) the specified number of working days within which the grievance must be taken to the next step in the hearing. Failure to comply with time limits may result in forfeiture of the grievance.[90]

RESOLUTION OF GRIEVANCES. In most cases the labor contract stipulates that the employee's grievance be expressed orally or in writing to the employee's immediate supervisor. One advantage of expressing the grievance in written form is that it reduces the chance that differing versions of the grievance will be circulated. It also forces the employee to approach the grievance in a comparatively rational manner, thus helping to eliminate or reduce the likelihood of trivial com-

plaints or feelings of hostility. Generally, the grievance is processed through the union steward, who will discuss it with the employee's supervisor.

When a grievance does not get settled in the first or second step, it goes to a higher level, often to company representatives (e.g., a general superintendent) and union representatives (e.g., a grievance committee). These representatives meet to further discuss the grievance and try to reach a solution agreeable to all. In most cases, the burden of proof in a grievance proceeding is on the union.

Sometimes a mediator will be brought in to help resolve the grievance. The mediator's role in a grievance resolution is much the same as in contract mediation (i.e., to get the two parties to communicate and to offer compromise solutions). The mediator's role is not to establish which side is right or wrong. His or her recommendations and suggestions can be accepted or rejected by either party. The role of the mediator, as will be seen later, is much different from that played by the arbitrator, whose decisions are final and binding.[91]

NONUNION GRIEVANCE PROCEDURES. Grievance procedures are found not only in companies where a labor contract exists but are also increasingly common in nonunion companies. Almost two-thirds of nonunion firms have developed some form of formal grievance system.[92] Like union grievance procedures, the immediate supervisor plays a key role. Often, a "roundtable" is established that consists of employee and management representatives. This group generally meets on a regular basis to resolve grievances.

ARBITRATION PROCESS. While no law forces parties to include arbitration in their labor agreements (either party can refuse to incorporate arbitration provisions), almost all labor agreements in the United States do provide for arbitration as the final step in the grievance procedure. In the majority of grievances filed, arbitration is not necessary because resolutions are usually made during lower-level discussions. Arbitration should be the last resort after all other options have failed. Because both parties share the cost of arbitration, there is a financial disincentive to rely on it. Arbitration involves bringing in an impartial third party (referred to as the arbitrator or adjudicator), who is mutually agreed on by both parties to break the deadlock between the union and management. Unlike the mediator's role of providing *recommended* solutions, the arbitrator's role is to make a ruling that is "final and binding upon both parties."

As we discussed in earlier chapters, a requirement that new hires and even current employees sign on to a binding arbitration agreement is becoming more common in nonunion settings.[93] At LensCrafters, for example, job applicants agree to submit any employment dispute to binding arbitration administered by the American Arbitration Association. Thus, if a LensCrafter employee thinks she has been a victim of gender discrimination, she must submit her complaint to the binding arbitration process. So far, the courts have allowed this job requirement and precluded the employee from filing a subsequent claim in federal court. (See Critical Thinking Exercise 13.3 on binding arbitration as a company policy.)

CRITICAL THINKING EXERCISE 13.3

Binding Arbitration as a Corporate Policy[1]

You have just been hired as the special projects coordinator for the human resource department in a company that has over 500 employees. Your boss hands you your first project. You have been instructed to put together a report on binding arbitration with a recommendation on whether the company should adopt one. Management is anxious about this subject especially since the com-

pany's main competitor just settled an employee grievance lawsuit totaling several million dollars due to compensatory and punitive damages.

You contact the legal department for the proposed arbitration agreement and get an earful at the same time. The company's counsel gives you the reasons why a mandatory binding arbitration agreement is necessary. The attorney articulates four reasons. The first reason cited is that arbitration reduces costs and reduces the time it takes to reach resolution. The savings in employment related arbitration can be up to 50 percent when you add in the depositions, discovery time, and preparation time it would take to get to trial versus the two day process under the supervisory arbitration.[2]

The second justification is that binding arbitration is final. With a trial the appeals process can lengthen an incredibly long litigation battle. The finality is one employers are willing to accept even if the risk is one of an aberrant award.[3]

The idea that an arbitrator will be less emotional and therefore more objective is the third reason given in favor of a binding arbitration agreement. Companies see arbitrators as informed decision makers with less bias than a jury. The awards upon which arbitrators decide will better reflect the merits of the cases given by both parties.[4]

Finally, much to your relief, the corporate lawyer finishes by telling you that the reduction in psychological damage is another reason why you should recommend a binding arbitration policy. The totality of litigation becomes an obsession of both the plaintiff and the defendant. Arbitration because of its speedy process will free up both parties so that life can resume.[5]

You thank the legal department for the advice but say you are unclear why it should be a mandatory arbitration and not voluntary. The answer given is that by requiring a blanket (covering all employees, new and existing) mandatory agreement it would be less messy, less tracking as to who signed on what date, and less convincing to go to mandatory later.

You ask how the arbitrator will be selected, and the answer is a list of acceptable private arbitrator services from which an arbitrator will be selected is in the proposed agreement. You return to your office with all this information ready to begin your report.

You call a friend, a corporate attorney, who recently voted against a binding arbitration at her place of employment. She tells you that management should be consistent in its treatment of all employees and base all decisions on good cause. Thus, there is no need for a binding arbitration agreement. She states that it seems the companies that use binding arbitration agreements are those that do not have good human resource management practices.[6] So, you ask, what do you do when there is a grievance?

Mediate, she says. Mediation with an impartial party acceptable to both parties assists in a mutual settlement of the dispute. The mediator has no authority to render the agreement binding. Although both sides are heard separately as well as jointly, the final agreement is based on consensus. The mediator's job is to persuade and define the issues. He or she also explains to each side the strengths and weaknesses of their case. Because of the mutually accepted resolution, both sides are winners. Mediation seems to be less expensive and less divisive than arbitration. And, mediation does not give up the right to trial if resolution cannot be reached.[7]

You thank her for her input and get back to drafting your report. You realize you will need to look at the other ways of grievance resolution to round out your report. You cite an internal grievance program similar to the FedEx grievance program. You also mention a peer review system where employees and management select one or more representatives of equal numbers for a grievance panel to which each side presents their case. After solutions are given by each party, a vote is taken and the majority vote sets the solution.

Assignment

Based on the above information, write your recommendation to management on whether the company should adopt a binding arbitration agreement. If you were applying for a job, would a company's binding arbitration agreement have an impact on your job choice? What additional information do you require regarding this policy?

[1] Contributed by Mary E. Wilson.

[2] Mathiason, G. G. (Spring 1994). Achieving workplace justice through binding arbitration. Legal Report of the Society for Human Resource Management, 1–4.

[3] Ibid, p. 3.

[4] Ibid.

[5] Ibid.

[6] Fitzpatrick, R. B. (Spring 1994). The war in the workplace must end, but arbitration is not the answer. Legal Report for the Society for Human Resource Management, 5–8.

[7] Ibid, p. 7.

Major League Baseball uses binding arbitration in salary determination. In this form of negotiation, the player and the team each put in an offer for what they consider to be an acceptable salary. If no agreement is reached, the arbitrator hears arguments from both sides and chooses one of the figures. The decision reached then becomes binding to both the player and the team.

Arbitration is generally not used for breaking a deadlock in negotiating a new labor contract in the private sector. Both labor and management would prefer to make their own decisions regarding conditions of employment rather than have these decisions made by a third party (i.e., the arbitrator). However, because most public-sector workers do not have the right to strike, arbitration is often used as a substitute for the strike.

A fair decision and award under union arbitration must be based strictly on the contract if relevant contract language exists. Also, decisions should be based on an accurate assessment and interpretation of the contractual clauses of the labor agreement. The contract is the final authority. That is why the contract language is so important; it should be as clear-cut and precise as possible. Unfortunately, contractual language usually is unclear and ambiguous. When contract language is silent, such factors as past practice, negotiation history, and other relevant laws play an important role in the arbitrator's decision. In nonunion arbitration procedures, arbitrators are supposed to stick to the law.

In reaching a decision, an arbitrator must decide if the employee was accorded due process. The arbitrator must also determine whether the employer had just cause for any actions taken against the complainant.

CRITICISMS OF THE ARBITRATION PROCESS. The major criticisms about arbitration relate to costs and arbitrator fairness. Arbitration can be both expensive and time-consuming. However, supporters of arbitration counter that argument with the fact that the costs associated with strikes and lockouts are even greater. The average fee for an arbitrator now typically exceeds $2,000 per day, plus expenses. These costs include all the arbitrator's expenses such as hotel, travel, and meals; his or her time to analyze and write up the case and opinion; and other miscellaneous costs such as those associated with lawyers and stenographers. In nonunion arbitration cases, the costs of arbitration are lower for both parties and the complaint is handled much more quickly.

Some employers try to reduce arbitration time and costs by using a form of expedited arbitration sometimes referred to as miniarbitration. Miniarbitration requires that a hearing be held within 10 days after an appeal is made. Also, arbitration hearings are completed in one day, the arbitrator's decision must be made within 48 hours after the close of the hearing, there are no transcripts or briefs, and the fee is paid for only the hearing day. Miniarbitration is not always appropriate, but it generally works well with simple, routine cases. Another alternative is a process called grievance mediation, which combines aspects of both mediation and arbitration. It is much less formal than arbitrations, with no briefs or cross-examinations of witnesses.

CURRENT AND FUTURE U.S. TRENDS IN LABOR RELATIONS

Union Membership

The future of unions in the United States is unclear. The numbers indicate that overall membership remains flat, showing no conclusive gains. However, at a meeting of the AFL-CIO's executive council in early 1997, union leaders asserted that organized labor was on the rebound.[94] Another group of experts predicts that the decline in unionization will level off, and that a minimum level of unionization will keep nonunion employers from slipping back into past abuses of employees. Other experts predict that the union movement will resume its growth.[95] This group believes that more workers will desire unionization as workers in the white-collar and service sector become increasingly frustrated. For example, even private practice physicians have been discussing unionizing so that they can bargain collectively with payers (insurers). However, they are running into obstacles with antitrust laws.[96]

Unions are gaining support from women, minorities, gays, and lesbians, groups that have often been neglected by organizations. Because the rate of women and minorities entering the workforce is higher than the rate for white males, this represents a bright spot for the future of unions. In fact, the one highlight for unions in the 1980s was the great increase in the number of women who joined unions.

Due to the growing public acceptance of replacement workers (striking unionists call them scabs), strikes are losing their effectiveness. The five-month strike by UAW workers at Caterpillar ended abruptly in 1992 when the company began hiring workers to replace the 12,000 strikers. The number of strikes decreased through the 1980s and continued to fall well into the 90s, along with the number of workdays lost to labor activity.[97] The NLRB decision that allows employers to hire temporary workers during a union-endorsed work slowdown was also a major blow.[98] A report by the Economic Policy Institute, a liberal research group, concluded that walkouts lasted almost a year longer when permanent employee substitutes were hired, almost six times the average duration of a strike when temporary or no replacements are used. Unions want Congress to ban "permanent replacements" because some employers are now provoking a strike to replace union members with low-wage, low-benefit workers. (See the Critical Thinking Exercise on striker replacement legislation.) In response to union complaints, Executive Order 12954 was enacted in 1995 to penalize federal contractors for hiring permanent replacements during labor strikes. These penalties could include contract termination and barring of future government contracts.[99] However, the number of NLRB cases in this domain continue to rise.

The failure to organize the Nissan plant in Tennessee illustrates some fundamental obstacles to the labor movement today. The UAW spent 18 months recruiting the 2,400 workers of the plant, only to lose the election by over a 2-to-1 margin. Nissan's antiunionization effort was very sophisticated, using strategies by outside consultants, videotapes, and closed-circuit television (CCTV) programs about the problems with unions. Communications focused on the cost of union dues, strike possibilities, and the loss of employee control to national union leadership. It was an uphill battle for the union. The company even selected the plant site in Tennessee and the individual workers based on their attitudes toward unions and collective bargaining. Further, the company used a number of legal maneuvers to delay the certification vote. Similarly, the union spent considerable energy trying to organize a Wisconsin outlet of Wal-Mart Stores Inc., which has no unions in its U.S. stores, and failed by a 2-to-1 margin.

Today, employers are resisting unionization efforts with greater skill, and the results have been successful. As we discussed in Chapter 12, many companies use annual employee opinion surveys to assess the attitudinal pulse of the workforce. Significant changes in attitudes toward pay, benefits, supervision, hours, or workload are red flags signaling potential trouble. The Tenneco Corporation, for example, will use a labor relations specialist to intervene in any region of the United States on the basis of changes in employee attitudes as reflected in a nationwide survey. This quick response has been highly successful in deterring organizing efforts.

Some labor leaders have called for a more militant position and greater solidarity across unions. When John J. Sweeney became president of the AFL-CIO in 1995, he vowed to revive labor's organizing efforts. There are major strategy disagreements even within major unions. Within the UAW, for example, some factions strongly oppose the "jointness" agreements between the automotive industry and the UAW. *Jointness* refers to the Japanese style of labor–management cooperation within the plant. Militants maintain that this cooperative spirit amounts to nothing more than a sellout to management at a time of major concessions by unions.

Unions continue to challenge worker involvement programs as violations of the NLRA. Republicans in Congress will press for passage of the TEAM Act to reverse the *Electromation* decision.[100]

These rulings make the environment unclear as to the continued formation of employee committees and have left many organizations wary of testing empowerment programs in a union environment. Of course, quality circles are still legal if first agreed to as part of a collective bargaining contract; however, these and other challenges to employee empowerment represent a major success for the more militant factions within the unions.[101]

A 1989 report by the AFL-CIO recommended a strategy for the 1990s and beyond.[102] Along with the call for associate, or partial, memberships, the report recommends a focus on the growing service sector of the labor force. The most sophisticated (and successful) of the service-sector unions has been the American Federation of State, County, and Municipal Employees (AFSCME), which emphasizes workplace dignity and safety, pay equity programs (comparable worth), resistance to performance monitoring, and career development. AFSCME claimed an addition of 50,000 workers in 1997. Most experts predict that if union representation is to increase by the end of the century, organizing must focus on clerical workers, data processors, salespersons, nurses, auditors, financial services, computer technicians, and other major occupations of the service sector. In many of these jobs, women represent the majority of workers. Interestingly, while total union membership declined in the 1990s, the number of women who belong to unions increased in the 90s relative to the 80s. Women now represent 39 percent of the total number of union members. By 1988, in the services and financial industries, fewer than 8 percent of employees belonged to unions. The number in 1997 was 13 percent. From the perspective of union organizers, this signifies improvement and expansion, but there is still a long way to go. A prime and successful target has been nursing home employees who toil at very difficult and physically taxing jobs at slightly more than the minimum wage.

Labor leaders are also looking for members among "workfare" recipients. They state that these individuals may be subject to lower pay, poor working conditions, and other forms of mistreatment since they are required to work for their keep under new federal laws.[103]

Many have felt that the balance of power has been on the side of management for the past two decades. The average working person has had to deal with stagnant pay (despite solid economic growth), downsizing, outsourcing, and an increase in the number of part-time and temporary workers. The fact that wages have not increased more has been attributed to a weakened labor movement. Federal Reserve Chairman Alan Greenspan stated he believed that the "subdued wage gains" were "the consequence . . . of job insecurity."[104] Recently, however, there have been a few significant wins for labor. In 1997, the International Union of Electronics Workers and other unions won a 13 percent pay gain over three years from General Electric Co. In early 1997, the Hotel Employees and Restaurant Employees Union local 100 in New York was embroiled in a bitter contract negotiation with a large New York City restaurateur, the Riese Organization. The union's head-on attack of Riese was indicative to many of the renewed power of the U.S. labor movement.[105] The goal of the union, which represents over 350 workers at 18 unionized Riese restaurants in New York City, was to stop Riese from closing union restaurants and then reopening them under different names as nonunion shops.[106]

In the 1997 strike by UPS workers, Teamster President Ron Carey stated that the pact between workers and management signified a "historic turning point for working people in the country" (i.e., that the balance of power had shifted from management to labor). Involving 185,000 workers and one of the largest strikes in years, labor received many of its demands in a relatively short time frame (several weeks). Full-time workers will receive 3 percent annual pay increases for five years, and part-timers get a 7 percent pay increase. Others felt that the UPS strike was at best a bottoming out, and that it would take much more to shift the power to labor. They believe that the UPS strike does not indicate any meaningful trend. In fact, for some, the direct economic impact of organized labor has been so minimal in recent years, that the Bureau of Labor Statistics stopped keeping track of collective bargaining data in 1996.

Mergers and Acquisitions

A common occurrence in the 1980s, and one that has continued through the 1990s, is for a new company to buy a failing (or failed) business. What are the legal obligations of the new company with regard to active collective bargaining agreements? Federal labor law addresses the duties of the new employer to recognize and bargain with the predecessor's union. In the 1987 *Fall River Dyeing v. the NLRB,* the U.S. Supreme Court established that when (1) a successor employer shows "substantial continuity" in business operations, (2) the bargaining unit is appropriate (performing essentially the same jobs under the same working conditions), and (3) the predecessor employed a majority of the new employer's workers, then the successor employer is required to recognize and bargain with the predecessor union.[107] However, there is no duty imposed on the successor employer to hire the predecessor's workers unless the failure to hire them was based on their union status. Also, the successor is not legally required to adopt an old collective bargaining agreement that was made with the predecessor.

Union lobbyists have been successful in pushing legislation regulating mergers and acquisitions. According to the Investor Responsibility Research Center, 39 states now have some form of antitakeover statute. This legislation typically requires a lengthy waiting period for completion of a takeover or the approval by the corporation's board of directors. Legislation enacted in Massachusetts is considered the most favorable for unions. Hostile takeovers in Massachusetts require approval by the board of directors, and a long waiting period is stipulated for the takeover. Workers laid off within two years of the takeover get severance pay, and new management must recognize all existing collective bargaining agreements.

Retraining Provisions

Mergers and acquisitions, downsizing, and deregulation have all imposed great threats to job security, particularly for union workers. Unions have begun to deal with this threat through retraining provisions in collective bargaining agreements. For example, job security has become a prime concern of unions in the deregulated and technologically changing telephone industry. The Communication Workers of America (CWA) responded to this security threat in 1992 by negotiating an elaborate system of job posting and retraining provisions that help prepare workers through education to move into new positions as old ones are being phased out. The agreement proved invaluable to AT&T workers, as the company eliminated 6,000 jobs with computerized voice recognition systems. The recent contracts negotiated between the UAW and the big three U.S. automakers also include several job security provisions. The most recent Saturn contract offered by the UAW enables workers to earn bonus money if they undergo additional training.

Some unions have cooperated with management to enhance employee development in order to limit downsizings and maintain jobs. Model programs have been initiated in the past decade by the United Auto Workers with Ford and GM and the Communications Workers of America with AT&T. These programs were jointly funded by management and the union. They were designed to help employees prepare for reemployment in the face of layoffs or to help workers gain more marketable skills that could be used within or outside the firm.[108]

Employee Benefits

With declining membership and the need to attract women, unions have emphasized health care and family-oriented benefits in recent years.[109] Generally, women represent a majority of the membership in most of the unions that are taking an active role in child care and family leave. Unions such as the American Federation of Teachers (AFT), the Amalgamated Clothing and Textile Workers Union, International Ladies Garment Workers Union, the Communication Workers of America, and the National Union of Hospital and Health Care Employees were instrumental in the passage of the Family and Medical Leave Act.

International Issues

There are considerable regulatory differences between the United States and most industrialized countries. The United States has more of an "at-will" employment policy than most industrialized nations, and indirect compensation such as health insurance is required in most European countries and discretionary for U.S. firms, giving the United States some competitive advantage.

But the United States is at a competitive disadvantage to some countries where there is little in the way of labor law or worker safety. This is the main reason unions have strongly opposed free trade agreements such as NAFTA. Improvements in technology, communications, and logistics are making it easier for American companies to relocate plants in the United States and open plants in other countries where the cost of labor is lower. In 1997, Guess Jeans, facing stiff competition from Calvin Klein, Tommy Hilfiger, and Ralph Lauren, shifted 40 percent of its manufacturing to Mexico and South America. Only three years earlier, Guess had been making 97 percent of its garments in the United States. Union leaders reacted by filing charges with the NLRB stating that they believed Guess was moving abroad to keep workers from organizing. Guess prevailed.

The U.S. labor relations system differs from systems in most other countries in several ways.[110] Among the most significant are the following:

1. In the United States, unions have exclusive representation (i.e., there is representation by only one union for any given job in the United States). In Europe, more than one union, often with religious and political affiliations, may represent the same workers.

2. In the United States, the government plays a passive role in labor relations and dispute resolution, characterized by regulating the process not the outcomes. In Western and Eastern European countries, Australia, Canada, and Latin America, the role of the government is much more active.

3. In the United States, there is generally an adversarial relationship between the union and management, while in most other countries the relationship is much more conciliatory and cooperative.

4. Collective bargaining in the United States is more decentralized (i.e., agreements are negotiated primarily at the local level). Unions in Europe, Japan, and Canada rely primarily on macro-negotiation by industry.

5. In the United States, unions emphasize economic issues such as wages, benefits, and job security, while in other countries (e.g., France), the unions emphasize political issues to a greater degree. Swedish unions emphasize both economic and political issues.[111] For example, the Swedish model is considered more humane because one goal is to replace unemployment benefits by a guarantee of work or training for long-term unemployed people.[112]

In several countries, trade unions influence firms' economic and financial decisions by including worker representatives as members of supervisory boards. In

Germany, workers are represented at the plant level in work councils and at the corporate level through codetermination. Work councils are committees that have representatives from both employees and managers. They have responsibility for the governance of the workplace, including hiring and firing workers, training issues, and overtime.[113] **Codetermination** is usually associated with Germany, which established a full-parity system in the steel and coal industry. Labor and management are equally represented on the supervisory or corporate boards of these companies. Some form of codetermination can also be found in other industries in Germany. Since 1976, German law has required companies with over 2,000 employees to have the same number of management and worker representatives on the supervisory board (usually comprised of 11 members including the chair, who is chosen by the other 10 members). The decisive vote is cast by the "neutral" chair in tie situations. AEG-Telefunken, a German appliance and machinery company, provides a good example of the codetermination principle. AEG (today a division of Daimler-Benz) was in deep financial trouble in the early 1980s. Surprisingly, the chair cast the deciding vote in favor of the labor representatives' proposal to persuade the government to provide more aid.[114]

When making union comparisons across countries it is important to recognize that even within a country, there may be marked differences among unions. In Germany today, two of the biggest unions are IG Metall with 2.7 million members representing cars and electronics and IG Chemie with 1.35 million members representing chemicals. Their approaches to union issues are quite different even though both were established in the 1890s. The main goal of IG Metall is to fight for better benefits, wages, and hours even if it means losing members as companies lay off workers. On the other hand, IG Chemie recently signed an agreement that allows employers who are in trouble to cut wages up to 10 percent in return for job security. IG Metall has a similar agreement in the former East Germany, but so far has not been willing to allow a similar system in western Germany.[115]

The head of the works council at the Hamburg factory of Daimler-Benz Aerospace (DASA), Hans-Gunter Eidtner, persuaded the IG Metall union to eliminate overtime pay so that employees would not lose their jobs. German workers seem more eager to compromise given the large number of people out of work (4.3 million). In fact, as in the United States, employers are increasingly making deals with workers that improve productivity and flexibility. Most companies negotiate concessions with the works councils at individual factories then gain approval (often reluctantly) from national unions. Companies in eastern Germany have an easier time making deals and cutting labor costs because the unions are less powerful than in western Germany. Some recent agreements reached in Germany are similar to those reached in the United States where employees are expected to make some concessions to help struggling companies.[116]

A lack of understanding of European union structure and the underlying social dimension is often cited as a major cause of difficulties for expatriate American managers of multinational corporations. While American managers tend to have an antiunion orientation in their management style, unions carry considerably more clout in other countries. This attitude can often result in serious (and quick) trouble. For example, Johnson & Johnson's joint venture with a German pharmaceutical company ran into difficulties at the start because Johnson & Johnson managers apparently did not recognize the importance of the work councils at German plants and the practical implications of **codetermination** for the manufacturing process.

Codetermination also stipulates that a labor director be treated as a manager who is charged with attending to worker concerns. Labor directors have great influence in Germany and often participate in corporate strategic planning. The management board is elected by the supervisory board and must include a labor director who is approved by labor representatives. Johnson & Johnson's expatriate managers did not recognize the significance of the labor director in the daily operation of the joint-venture plants. Consequently, the firm experienced problems on matters related to work rules, productivity measures, and job responsibilities.

Similar cases of difficulties for expatriate managers have been noted in Japan, where joint consultation systems are very common yet very alien to American managers. Over 75 percent of Japan's largest employers have a joint consultation system in which employee groups meet monthly with management to discuss policy, production, personnel issues, and even financial matters. Although not as common as in large companies, consultation systems and participative management systems are becoming more common for small and medium-sized Japanese companies as well. Japan has **enterprise unions** in which most firms have a single union with virtually all job families in the same union. For instance, in large firms such as Toyota, Toshiba, and Hitachi, workers in each company are organized into a union. This ensures that the union's loyalty will not be divided among different companies.[117] There is no clear distinction between labor and management. In fact, many Japanese executives started their careers as union members, were promoted to leadership positions in the union, and then moved into management jobs in the same company. Thus, they have an appreciation for the perspective of labor and management. There is considerable trust between labor and management. Bargaining is done by the central organization during the "spring offensive" with details negotiated at the individual company.

Union membership is lower in the United States

than in most industrialized countries. For example, union participation is highest among Sweden (95 percent), Denmark (88 percent), and Italy (61 percent). Union membership is also higher than in the United States in Canada (36 percent), Australia (43 percent), Japan (25 percent), the Netherlands (28 percent), Switzerland (31 percent), and the United Kingdom (51 percent).[118] While many Central and South American countries have a higher percentage of workforce union membership (e.g., Mexico, Argentina, Brazil), there is no guaranteed right to collective bargaining. Unions in Central and South America are generally very political but not particularly effective for the labor force.

Union membership is decreasing in many European countries. In Great Britain, for example, membership has dropped about 15 percent in the past 15 years. Unions there are closely tied to the Labour Party and are quite militant. Wildcat strikes, for example, which are illegal in the United States, have replaced the grievance process as the means of labor protest.[119]

Many unions are crossing international boundaries. For example, union officials from the Hotel Employees and Restaurant Employees (HERE) local 11 recently traveled to Tokyo where they staged a demonstration and met with representatives of the Japanese Trade Union Confederation-Rengo, which pledged support of the local 11's organizing drive and its boycott of the New Otani hotel in Los Angeles, a Japanese-owned hotel.[120]

Labor unions influence multinational corporation (MNC) decisions in several ways:[121] (1) by manipulating wage levels to the point where cost structures may become noncompetitive, (2) by restricting the ability to vary employment levels at will, and (3) by objecting to global integration of MNC operations. Perhaps the most serious labor relations difficulty for MNCs in other countries is the inability to vary employment levels at will, which is so common in the United States. For example, when Ford's sales plummeted during the 1991 Gulf War, several U.S. plants closed almost immediately to control inventory. Ford plants in Germany, however, could be closed only after an extended period of consultation with affected parties. Many European countries impose stiff fines for terminating employees, even if the layoffs are temporary. Dismissals are usually the last resort, because of the large social impact of firing.

There are two types of agreements that are usually made between companies and employees on the subject of dismissal. The first is made in advance and states the conditions for layoffs, if and when warranted. The second type stipulates the treatment of employees after termination. Reactions to both of these agreements vary. In the United Kingdom, for example, advance provisions for dismissal tend to be viewed by both employers and trade unions with some objections. Employers perceive reduced options and a lack of flexibility. Trade unions feel that agreements in advance imply acceptance of dis-

missals, which contradicts union policy. French unions view prior agreements as opportunities to organize the opposition, while French employers think that prior agreements provide a framework that keeps them from being forced into post-termination concessions under stress. In Germany, advance agreements on dismissals are not mandatory, and some companies prefer to avoid them. Experience has shown that the work councils use the framework agreement only as a basis for negotiation of better financial compensation due to job losses.

Another problem for MNCs is the inability to integrate optimal manufacturing operations across borders because powerful labor unions exert strong political pressure. The result of this suboptimization is higher manufacturing costs. The influence of the German Metal Workers union on GM operations is often cited as a case in point.

As the former Soviet Union countries move to a free market, substantial changes in labor relations are ongoing. If the countries continue to follow the trend toward democracy, trade union power will probably rise, as it has in Poland through the Solidarity Union.

The pro-labor Organization for Economic Cooperation and Development in Paris has issued "Guidelines for MNCs" that attempt to guarantee the same basic social and labor relations rights for all workers. However, union attempts to develop uniform standards for MNCs have not proved very fruitful. As noted earlier, the National Labor Relations Act enacted in the United States in 1935 was designed to enable workers to exert pressure on companies to achieve fair wages and address poor working conditions. The NLRA has not been extended to U.S. firms located in other countries, even though some argue that this would be advantageous for employers and unions. Some possible benefits would include providing some stability for corporations and unions dealing in the global labor market, discouraging multinational firms from establishing facilities in foreign countries that have poor working conditions and weak labor standards, and allowing unions to use legal means to exert pressure on firms without worrying about whether the firms will flee to underdeveloped countries.[122]

The National Labor Committee, a coalition formed in 1983 of 25 of the 96 member unions of the AFL-CIO to monitor conditions in Central America, has alleged that some companies have contracted with offshore manufacturers that use child labor, maintain sweatshops, and severely underpay their employees. It also contends that U.S. firms have a duty to monitor their offshore contractors to ensure they are not acting unethically or illegally. This means U.S. firms should perform self-checks, adopt a code of conduct for their offshore operations, communicate the code and monitor compliance with it, and train managers to ensure that they understand the code and enforce it.[123]

What should be clear from this brief discussion of

international labor relations is that we can make very few generalizations about labor relations across borders. The role of government, social agendas, religious affiliation, and underlying political and economic issues must be understood before one can thoroughly understand the diversity of international labor relations.

SUMMARY

As a result of the changes occurring in the size and composition of the workforce, the advances in technology, and the increased competition from foreign businesses, the future of unions and the collective bargaining system is uncertain. Some have predicted that the days of unions are over unless they incorporate these changes into their collective bargaining strategies. There is little doubt that unions must be willing to be flexible and to adapt to the changes.[124] What worked in the 1800s and even through the 1950s will probably not work in the 21st century. Unions must find a way to attract the new entrants into the labor force such as women, minorities, and immigrants—if they are to survive.

What does the future hold for unions and collective bargaining? As we move closer to the 21st century, will we continue to use our current methods of bargaining to reach a contract settlement? Some critics of conventional collective bargaining say the current system cannot survive because it is inefficient, ineffective, excessively time-consuming, and characterized by exaggerated opening demands and inflated counterproposals.

During the 1980s and 1990s, a number of changes occurred in the labor relations environment. The massive layoffs caused by recessions and foreign competition caused both union and management to reexamine their bargaining goals and tactics. Unions had always believed they had the right to challenge the way management ran the business. While they still expect this to some degree, there has been a movement away from the adversarial bargaining relationship beset by conflict and toward a relationship characterized more by accommodation. For example, cooperation and collaboration were evident in the labor negotiations between the National Basketball Association and the players' association, when the union agreed to keep the unwanted salary cap, with a schedule of minimum annual increases.[125] U.S. Steel managers and union officials now have regular meetings to discuss quality, customer service, retraining, and health care costs. Ten years ago, management and the union discussed such issues only at the bargaining table.

A great example of cooperation comes from the Xerox agreement with the 6,000 members of the Amalgamated Labor and Textile Workers Union.[126] The union participated on study teams to reduce costs and increase quality in order to keep plants open in the United States.

Without the cooperation between labor and management and the mutual trust, Xerox would have had to close U.S. plants to compete with the lower labor costs of their global competition.

Cooperation and *collaboration* are the words being used to describe contract negotiations today. This is true in the United States and in other countries. For example, in the United Kingdom, banking unions UNIFI and BIFU have signed a joint working agreement that ends decades of divided staff representation at Barclays and breaks new ground in the U.K. finance sector.[127] Collaboration can take many forms. For example, management can create committees on which employees are represented (e.g., shop committees, department committees, quality circles) providing the Wagner Act is not violated. Also, there has been a movement toward greater cooperation in handling disciplinary problems and resolving grievances.

Unions and collective bargaining will continue to play an important role in the lives of American workers as long as they are able to help workers overcome dissatisfaction with management and to meet their economic needs. Greater cooperation between labor and management is needed to make organizations more effective and competitive. In some industries, that cooperation may be necessary to survive. Stanford's Pfeffer believes management's attitude toward workers and unions has a great deal to do with the level of cooperation between labor and management and the extent to which unions will help or hinder organizational capability. Management practices compatible with effective HRM increase the probability that a union can be avoided or, if there is a union, that unions will cooperate with productivity enhancement efforts.[128]

Time will tell whether the 1997 UPS strike was *the* event that turned things around for organized labor. Other recent events don't support the optimism. Under the first full year of the aggressive John Sweeney's leadership, the AFL-CIO still lost 92,000 workers. Retirements, plant closings, and downsizings are still taking their toll. There have also been major defeats in 1996 and 1997, such as for the Fieldcrest Cannon textile workers in North Carolina. Unions won only 47 percent of elections in 1996, the lowest figure since 1992 (1997 figures will probably be better).

The political landscape in the U.S. is volatile. While unions strongly oppose trade agreements, Democrats, and especially the Clinton administration, have generally pressed for more free trade agreements in cooperation with Republicans. In addition to the TEAM Act, Republicans also proposed the *Worker Right to Know Act* to allow unions to collect dues only for collective bargaining, contract administration, and grievance adjustment. One goal is to reduce the amount of union funds used in political campaigns. While the bill did not pass, it signifies that legislation regarding unions and their influence will continue to be a subject of debate in the U.S. Congress.[129] The worker replacement legislation unions support so strongly will probably go nowhere with Republicans in control of Congress.

But many are still predicting a resurgence of union activity with new, aggressive leadership and a more sympathetic ear from middle-class workers. The widening gap between executive pay and the average worker is contributing to this renewed sympathy and greater receptivity to union arguments.[130] In addition, unions have emphasized that corporate profits have rebounded while employee compensation has languished. These two themes were used by the Communications Workers of America in their successful organization of 10,000 reservation and ticket takers at U.S. Airways in 1997. Cornell University labor professor Kate Bronfenbrenner calls this labor victory "very significant . . . it's the kind of workers that people questioned whether the labor movement could organize. These are white-collar workers in an industry where unions have really been struggling."[131] There is no question that 1997 ended on a more promising note for unions.

DISCUSSION QUESTIONS

1. Should public employees be allowed to strike?
2. What are the major effects of unions on wages? What other effects do unions have on management and the organization?
3. How do you explain the fact that unions sometimes have a positive impact on productivity?
4. If unions are to survive, what do you think they will have to do to attract and maintain members?
5. Should companies be allowed to hire workers based on their attitudes toward unions?
6. Why is it advantageous for both the union and management to remain flexible during collective bargaining negotiations?
7. When is a work team or work group illegal under the Wagner Act?
8. Describe how union and management might prepare for labor negotiations. How are their preparations similar and different?
9. Should the federal government be allowed to intervene in strikes that are not a threat to national security or public welfare in order to expedite their resolution? Why or why not?
10. How might a multinational corporation better prepare itself for dealing with the differing union environments in other countries?
11. Compare and contrast unions in the United States, Germany, and Japan. How are they similar and different? What can they learn from one another?
12. Do you think employers should be allowed to require binding arbitration agreements as a condition of employment? Should a company be allowed to change its policy and require current employees to sign such a document?

NOTES

1. Schrank, R. (February 1979). Are unions an anachronism? *Harvard Business Review, 57,* 107–115; see also, Flynn, G. (1997). How HR has weathered the changing legal climate. *Workforce, 76*(1), 159, 162.
2. Hornblower, M. (Nov. 25, 1996). Picking a new fight. *Time,* pp. 64–65.
3. Duff, C. (Aug. 14, 1997). We are so attached to our UPS man, we feel for him. *The Wall Street Journal,* pp. A1, A6.
4. Quinn, R. E., and Cameron, K. (1983). Organizational life cycles and shifting criteria of effectiveness: Some preliminary evidence. *Management Science, 29,* 33–51.
5. Perlman, S. (1929). *History of trade unionism in the United States.* New York: MacMillan.
6. Gompers, S. (1919). Labor and the Common Welfare. Freeport, N.Y.: Books for Libraries Press, p. 20.
7. Strauss, G. (1988). Australian labor relations through American eyes. *Industrial Relations, 27,* 131–148.
8. Cameron, K. S.; Kim, M. U.; and Whetten, D. (1987). Organizational effects on decline and turbulence. *Administrative Science Quarterly, 32,* 222–240.
9. Schlesinger, J. M., and Wysocki, B. (Aug. 20, 1997). UPS pact fails to shift balance of power toward U.S. workers. *The Wall Street Journal,* pp. A1, A6.
10. Abraham, S. E. (1996). The impact of the Taft-Hartley Act on the balance of power in industrial relations. *American Business Law Journal, 33*(3), 341–371.
11. Moore, W. J., and Newman, R. J. (1988). A cross-section analysis of the postwar decline in American trade union membership. *Journal of Labor Research, 9,* 111–112.
12. Northrup, H. R. (1996). The Dunlop Commission report: Philosophy and overview. *Journal of Labor Research, XVII*(1), 1–8.
13. See http://Stats.BLS.Gov:80/newsrels.htm; see also, Freeman, R. B., and Medoff, J. L. (1984). *What do unions do?* New York: Basic Books.
14. Kochan, T. A.; Katz, H. C.; and McKersie, R. B. (1986). *The transformation of American industrial relations.* New York: Basic Books. See also, Holley, W. H., and Jennings, K. M. (1991). *The labor relations process.* Hinsdale, IL: Dryden Press, and Strauss, G., Gallagher, D. G., and Fiorito, J. (1991). *The state of the unions.* Madison, WI: Industrial Relations Research Association, University of Wisconsin.
15. Hendricks, W. (1994). Deregulation and labor earnings. *Journal of Labor Research, 15*(3), 207–234.
16. Thomas, S. L., and Kleiner, M. M. (1992). The effect of

two-tier collective bargaining agreements on shareholder equity. *Industrial and Labor Relations Review, 45*(2), 339–351.

17. See notes 15 and 16; see also, Johnson, N. B. (1991). Airline worker's earnings and union expenditures under deregulation. *Industrial and Labor Relations Review, 45*(1), 154–165.

18. Greenhouse, S. (Sept. 1, 1997). Gains put unions at turning point, many experts say. *New York Times,* pp. A1, A11.

19. Caudron, S. (August 1995). The changing union agenda. *Personnel Journal,* pp. 42–49.

20. Giant Stores to close for union vote today (July 16, 1996). *Baltimore Sun,* p. C1.

21. Kim, C. T. (February 1997). Strike three? *Business Korea, 14*(2), 16–17.

22. See note 19.

23. Corman, L. (1996). Ford had vision to bring to the labor talks. *World Business, 2*(6), 16.

24. See note 19; see also, Brothers in alms (1996). *Economist, 340*(7984), 61–62.

25. Http://www.seiu.org/j4j.

26. Hiatt, J. P., and Jackson, L. W. (1997). Union survival strategies for the twenty-first century. *Journal of Labor Research, 18*(4), 487–501.

27. Cobble, D. S. (1997). Lost ways of organizing: Reviving the AFL's direct affiliate strategy. *Industrial Relations, 36*(3), 278–301.

28. Sweeney, J. J. (1996). *America needs a raise: Fighting for economic security and social justice.* Boston: Houghton-Mifflin.

29. Barlow, W.; Hatch, D.; and Murphy, B. (February 1996). Paid union organizers have "employee" rights. *Personnel Journal,* p. 86.

30. Steel, B. S., and Lovrich, N. P. (1996). Public personnel management in county government. *Review of Public Personnel Administration, 16*(2), 32–56; see also, Burton, J. F., and Thomason, T. (1988). The extent of collective bargaining in the public sector. In B. Aaron, J. M. Najita, and J. L. Stern (eds.), *Public sector bargaining.* Madison, WI: Industrial Relations Research Association, pp. 1–51.

31. Villa, J., and Blum, A. A. (1996). Collective bargaining in higher education: Prospects for faculty unions. *Journal of Collective Negotiations in the Public Sector, 25*(2), 157–169.

32. Coleman, C. J. (1989). Federal sector labor relations: A reevaluation of the policies. *Journal of Collective Negotiations in the Public Sector, 16*(1), 121–124; see also, Ball, C. (1996). Is labor-management cooperation possible in the public sector without a change in law? *Journal of Collective Negotiations in the Public Sector, 25*(1), 23–30.

33. Overman, S. (June 1991). The union pitch has changed. *HR Magazine,* pp. 44–46.

34. Rose, J. B., and Manuel, C. (1996). Attitudes toward collective bargaining and compulsory arbitration. *Journal of Collective Negotiations in the Public Sector, 25*(4), 287–310; see also, Rose, J. B., and Piczak, M. (1996). Settlement rates and settlement stages in compulsory interest arbitration. *Industrial Relations Quebec, 51*(4), 643–664.

35. Feared, J., and Greyer, C. R. (1982). Determinants of U.S. unionism: Past research and future needs. *Industrial Relations, 21,* 1–32; see also, Heneman, H. G., III, and Sandver, M. H. (1983). Predicting the outcome of union certification elections: A review of the literature. *Industrial and Labor Relations Review, 36,* 537–560; Curme, M. A., Hirsch, B. T., and Macpherson, D. M. (1990). Union membership and contract coverage in the United States, 1983–1988. *Industrial and Labor Relations Review, 44,* 5–33; and Newton, L. A., and Shore, L. M. (1992). A model of union membership: Instrumentality, commitment, and opposition. *Academy of Management Review, 17,* 275–298.

36. Greenhouse, S. (Nov. 20, 1995). Models joining together to make the union movement a thing of beauty. *The New York Times,* p. A9.

37. Deshpande, S. P., and Fiorito, J. (1989). Specific and general beliefs in union voting models. *Academy of Management Journal, 32,* 883–897; see also, Feared, J., Lowman, C., and Nelson, F. D. (1987). The impact of human resource policies on union organizing. *Industrial Relations, 26,* 113–126, and Newton, L. A., and Shore, L. M. (1992). A model of union membership: Instrumentality, commitment, and opposition. *Academy of Management Review, 17,* 275–298.

38. Getman, J. G., Goldberg, S. B., and Herman, J. B. (1976). *Union representation elections: Law and reality.* New York: Russell Sage Foundation; see also, Ivancevich, J. M. (1992). *Human Resource Management.* Homewood, IL: Richard D. Irwin.

39. Bronfenbrenner, K. (1997). The role of union strategies in NLRB certification elections. *Industrial and Labor Relations Review, 50*(2), 195–212.

40. Brett, J. M. (1980). Why employees want unions. *Organizational Dynamics, 8,* pp. 47–59.

41. Freeman, R. B., and Medoff, J. L. (1984). *What do unions do?* New York: Basic Books.

42. Lewis, H. G. (1986). *Union relative wage effects.* Chicago: University of Chicago Press.

43. See note 41.

44. Marshall, A. (1929). *Principles of Economics.* New York: MacMillan.

45. See note 41.

46. See note 41.

47. Hirsch, B. T., and Addison, J. T. (1986). *The economic analysis of unions: New approaches and evidence.* Boston: Allen & Unwin.

48. Bemmels, B. (1987). How unions affect productivity in manufacturing plants. *Industrial and Labor Relations Review, 40,* 241–253.

49. Pfeffer, J. (1994). *Competitive advantage through people.* Boston: Harvard Business School Press, p. 163; see also Hirsch, B. T. (1991). Union coverage and prof-

itability among U.S. firms. *Review of Economics and Statistics, 73,* 69–77.

50. Burton, J. F. (ed.) (1985). Review symposium: *What do unions do? Industrial and Labor Relations Review, 38,* 244–263; see also, Kramer, J. K., and Vasconcellos, G. M. (1996). The economic effect of strikes on the shareholders of nonstruck competitors. *Industrial and Labor Relations Review, 49*(2), 213–222; Beaumont, P. B., and Harris, R. I. D. (1996). Good industrial relations, joint problem solving, and HRM. *Industrial Relations Quebec, 51*(2), 391–406; GM local labor dispute spins out of control (March 13, 1996). *The Wall Street Journal,* pp. B1, B3. In 1996, GM found that it was having difficulty becoming more productive in its plants and more cost-efficient in its corporate structure without clashing with labor. The UAW's Dayton local with 3,000 hourly workers went on strike and crippled the company because the Dayton plants produced 90 percent of the brake systems used in GM. As a result, 21 of the 29 North American vehicle-assembly plants had idled and 30 parts plants were either partially or totally shut down. A total of 72,000 workers could not work, costing GM nearly $45 million a day.

51. Karier, T. (1991). Unions and the U.S. comparative advantage. *Industrial Relations, 30,* p. 1.

52. Becker, B. E., and Olsen, C. A., (1987). Labor relations and firm performance. In M. M. Kleiner, R. N. Block, M. Roomkin, and S. W. Salsburg (eds.), *Human resources and performance of the firm.* Madison, WI: Industrial Relations Research Association, pp. 43–86; see also, Cutcher-Gershenfeld, J. (1991). The impact of economic performance on a transformation in workplace relations. *Industrial and Labor Relations Review, 44,* 241–260.

53. Woodruff, D. (July 28, 1997). The German worker is making a sacrifice. *Business Week,* 46–47.

54. Gershenfeld, W. J. (1987). Employee participation in firm decisions. In M. M. Kleiner, R. N. Block, M. Roomkin, and S. W. Salsburg (eds.), *Human resources and performance of the firm.* Madison, WI: Industrial Relations Research Association, pp. 123–158; see also, Ferman, L. A., Hoyman, M., Cutcher-Gershenfeld, J., and Savoie, E. J. (eds.) (1991). *Joint training programs: A union-management approach to preparing workers for the future.* Ithaca, NY: ILR Press, School of Industrial and Labor Relations, Cornell University, and Hammer, T. H., Curall, S. C., and Stern, R. N. (1991). Worker representation on board of directors: A study of competing roles. *Industrial and Labor Relations Review, 44,* 661–680.

55. Gold, C. (1986). *Labor management committees: Confrontation, cooptation, or cooperation?* Ithaca, NY: ILR Press.

56. Goll, I., and Hochner, A. (1987). Labor-management practices as a function of environmental pressures and corporate ideology in union and nonunion settings. *Proceedings of the Fortieth Annual Meeting of the Industrial Relations Research Association,* pp. 516–524. See also, Miller, R. L. (1996). Employee participation

contemporary labor law in the U.S. *Industrial Relations Journal, 27*(2), 166–174.

57. The UAW continues its efforts to improve quality (1996). *Quality Progress, 29*(7), 62–63.

58. Katz, H. C., Kochan, T. A., and Gobeille, K. R. (1984). Industrial relations performance, economic performance, and QWL programs: An interplant analysis. *Industrial and Labor Relations Review, 37,* 3–17; see also, Katz, H. C., Kochan, T. A., and Weber, M. C. (1985). Assessing the effects of industrial relations systems and efforts to improve the quality of working life on organizational effectiveness. *Academy of Management Review, 28,* 509–526.

59. Cooke, W. N. (1994). Employee participation program, group-based incentives and company performance: A union-nonunion comparison. *Industrial and Labor Relations Review, 47*(4), 594–609.

60. Steel, R. P.; Jennings, K. R.; Mento, A. J.; and Hendricks, W. H. (August, 1988). *Effects of institutional employee participation on industrial labor relations.* Paper presented at the meeting of the Academy of Management, Anaheim, CA.

61. Leana, C. R., Ahlbrandt, R. S., and Murrell, A. J. (1992). The effects of employee involvement programs on unionized workers' attitudes, perceptions, and preferences in decision making. *Academy of Management Journal, 35*(4), 861–873.

62. Feared, J.; Lowman, C.; and Nelson, F. D. (1987). The impact of human resource policies on union organizing. *Industrial Relations, 26,* 113–126.

63. *Electromation, Inc. v. NLRB,* CA 7, No. 92-4129, 9/15/94; 63 LW 1041 (9-27-94).

64. Flynn, G. (February 1996). TEAM Act: What is it and what it can do for you. *Personnel Journal,* 85–87.

65. Schwochau, S. (1987). Union effects on job attitudes. *Industrial and Labor Relations Review, 40,* 219–220.

66. Gordon, M. E., and DeNisi, A. S. (1995). A re-examination of the relationship between union membership and job satisfaction. *Industrial Relations Review, 48,* 222–236.

67. Lawyer, J. E. (1947). The United States Labor-Management Relations Act of 1947. *International Labor Review, 56*(2), 125–166.

68. McCulloch, F. W., and Bornstein, T. (1974). *The National Labor Relations Board.* New York: Praeger.

69. Sloan, A. A., and Witney, F. (1997). *Labor relations.* Upper Saddle River, NJ: Prentice Hall. See also, Extejt, M. M., and Lynn, M. P. (1996). Trends in computer use in collective bargaining. *Information and Management, 30*(3), 111–117; Issacharoff, S. (1996). Contracting for employment: The limited return of the common law. *Texas Law Review, 74*(7), 1783–1812; Korman, R. (May 6, 1996). Court upholds job targeting. *ENR, 236*(18), 14; Lissy, W. E., and Morgenstern, M. L. (1996). Labor. *Compensation and Benefits Review, 28*(2), 14–15; and Berreth, C. A. (Jan/Feb. 1996). Workers' compensation laws enacted in 1995. *Monthly Labor Review, 119,* 59–72.

70. Blumenfeld, S. B., and Partridge, M. D. (Winter 1996). The long-run and short-run impacts of global competition on U.S. union wages. *Journal of Labor Research, 17*(1), 149–171.

71. Pynes, J. E. (1996). The two faces of unions. *Journal of Collective Negotiations in the Public Sector, 25*(1), 31–43.

72. Sunoo, B. P. (February 1995). Managing strikes, minimizing loss. *Personnel Journal*, pp. 50–60; see also, Barlow, W. E.; Hatch, D. D.; and Murphy, B. (1996). Recent legal decisions affect you. *Personnel Journal*, 100.

73. Morse, B. (1974). *How to negotiate the labor agreement.* Detroit: Trands.

74. Field, D. (Aug. 15–17, 1997). Poll: 55% support strikers at UPS. *USA Today*, p. A1.

75. Imberman, W. (August 1983). Who strikes—and why? *Harvard Business Review, 61*, 18–28.

76. See note 9.

77. Tivendell, J., and Watson, C. (1995). Attitudes towards unions as predictors of actual strike behavior. *Ergonomics, 38*(3), 534–538.

78. See note 74.

79. *AFL-CIO Committee for Workplace Fairness* (1990). Washington, DC: AFL-CIO. See also, Budd, J. W. (1996). Canadian strike replacement legislation and collective bargaining: Lessons for the U.S. *Industrial Relations, 35*(2), 245–260.

80. See note 79.

81. DeFusco, R. A., and Fuess, J. R. (1991). The effects of airline strikes on struck and nonstruck carriers. *Industrial and Labor Relations Review, 44*(2), 324–333.

82. Associated Press (March 6, 1989). Eastern pleads with its pilots, plan to picket railroads dropped. *Knoxville News-Sentinel*, p. A1.

83. See note 72.

84. Hornblower, M. (Jan. 27, 1997). Guess gets out. *Time*, p. 48. See also: Stein, L. W. (1996). Preserving unionized employees' individual employment rights: An argument against section 301 preemption. *Berkeley Journal of Employment and Labor Law, 17*(1), 1–61.

85. Schnell, J. F., and Gramm, C. L. (1994). The empirical relations between employers' striker replacement strategies and strike duration. *Industrial and Labor Relations Review, 47*(2), 189–206.

86. Chass, M. (March 15, 1990). Negotiators led to water but don't drink. *The New York Times*, p. B12.

87. See note 9.

88. Fitzgerald, M., and Garneau, G. (Feb. 22, 1997). Strike ends in Detroit. *Editor and Publisher, 130* (8), 6–7.

89. Dastmalchian, A., and Ng, I. (1990). Industrial relations climate and grievance outcomes. *Industrial Relations, 45*, 311–324. See also Salipante, P. F., and Bouwen, R. (1990). Behavioral analysis of grievances: Conflict sources, complexity and transformation. *Employee Relations, 12*, 17–22.

90. See note 69, Sloan and Witney (1997).

91. See note 89, Salipante and Bouwen (1990).

92. Diaz, E. D., Minton, J. W., and Saunders, D. M. (April, 1987). A fair nonunion grievance procedure. *Personnel Journal*, 13–18; see also, Feuille, P., and Hildebrand, R. L. (1995). Grievance procedures and dispute resolution. In Ferris, G. R., Rosen, S. D., and Barnum, D. T. *Handbook of human resource management.* pp. 340–369. Cambridge, MA: Blackwell.

93. Zigarelli, M. A. (1996). Compulsory arbitration of nonunion employment disputes. *Human Resource Management Review, 6*(3), 183–206; see also, Holmes, S. A. (March 18, 1994). Some employees lose right to sue for bias at work. *The New York Times*, pp. A1, B6.

94. Not striking (Feb. 22, 1997). *Economist, 342*(8005), 73.

95. Heckschier, C. S. (1988). *The new unionism.* New York: Basic Books.

96. Meyer, H. (Dec. 5, 1996). Look for the union label. *Time*, 69–70.

97. Capelli, P. (1990). Collective bargaining. In J. A. Fossum (ed.), *Employee and labor relations.* Washington, DC: Bureau of National Affairs, pp. 4–180 to 4–217. See also, Kotlowitz, A. (Feb. 28, 1987). Labor's turn. *The Wall Street Journal*, pp. 1, 14.

98. Kotlowitz, A. (April 12, 1987). Labor's shift: Finding strikes harder to win, more unions turn to slowdowns. *The Wall Street Journal*, pp. 1, 7.

99. Final rules on striker replacement order written (August 1995). *HRMagazine*, p. 4.

100. Putting a damper on the old team spirit (May 4, 1992). *Business Week*, p. 60; see also, note 64.

101. Hanson, R.; Porterfield, R. I.; and Ames, K. (1995). Employee empowerment at risk: Effects of recent NLRB rulings. *Academy of Management Executive, 9*(2), 45–54.

102. Brown, C., and Reich, M. (1989). When does union-management cooperation work? A look at NUMMI and GM-Van Nuys. *California Management Review, 31*, pp. 26–41; see also, Cooke, W. N. (1990). Factors influencing the effect of joint union-management programs on employee-supervisor relations. *Industrial and Labor Relations Review, 43*, 587–603.

103. The new slavery? (Oct 5, 1996). *Economist*, pp. 33–34.

104. See note 9.

105. McLaughlin, J. (Feb. 15, 1997). Fighting mad. *Restaurant Business, 96*(4), 23–24.

106. Zuber, A. (Feb. 10, 1997). NYC union protests Riese Organization policies. *Nation's Restaurant News, 31*(6), 3, 64.

107. Mace, R. F. (1921). The Supreme Court's labor law successorship doctrine after *Fall River Dyeing. Labor Law Journal, 39*, 102–109.

108. London, M. (1996). Redeployment and continuous learning in the 21st century: Hard lessons and positive examples from the downsizing era. *Academy of Management Executive, 10*(4), 67–79.

109. Auerbach, J. D. (1988). *In the business of child care.* New York: Praeger.

110. Dunlop, J. T. (May 1988). Have the 1980s changed U.S. industrial relations? *Monthly Labor Review*, pp. 29–34; see also, The changing face of collective bargaining (May 1996). *European Industrial Relations Review, 268*, p. 1.

111. Ofori-Dankwa, J. (1993). Murray and Reshef revisited: Toward a typology/theory of paradigms of national trade union movements. *Academy of Management Review, 18*, 269–292.

112. Layard, R. (February 1997). Sweden's road back to full employment. *Economic and Industrial Democracy, 18*(1), 99–118.

113. Mills, D. Q. (1989). *Labor-Management Relations*. New York: McGraw-Hill.

114. A Business International Research Report (1982). *Managing Manpower in Europe*. Business International Corporation. See also, Hoerr, J. (February 1991). What should unions do? *Harvard Business Review*, pp. 30–45.

115. Steinmetz, G. (June 12, 1997). One union accepts reality, breaking with inflexible past. *The Wall Street Journal*, p. A14; see also, Steinmetz, G. (June 12, 1997). Germans falter in struggle to regain competitive edge. *The Wall Street Journal*, p. A14.

116. See note 53.

117. Gomez-Mejia, L. R.; Balkin, D. B.; and Cardy, R. L. (1995). *Managing Human Resources*. Englewood Cliffs, NJ: Simon & Schuster Co; see also, Marsland, S. E., and Beer, M. (1985). Note on Japanese management and employment systems. In M. Beer and B. Spector (eds.), *Readings in Human Resource Management*. New York: The Free Press.

118. Chang, C., and Sorrention, C. (1991). Union membership statistics in 12 countries. *Monthly Labor Review, 48;* see also, Deyo, F. C. (Feb. 24, 1997). Labor and post-Fordist industrial restructuring in East and Southeast Asia. *Work and Occupations*, 97–118.

119. Consultation on new strike restrictions (December 1996). *IRS Employment Review*, pp. 5515–5516.

120. Seal, K. (March 3, 1997). Unions cross international boundaries. *Hotel and Motel Management, 212*(4), 3, 38.

121. Dowling, P. J., and Schuler, R. S. (1994). *International dimensions of human resource management*. Boston: PWS-Kent. See also, Sasaki, N. (1990). *Management and industrial structure in Japan*. Oxford: Pergamont Press; Adams, R. J. (1989). North American industrial relations: Divergent trends in Canada and the U.S. *International Labor Review, 128*, 47–64; Okubayashi, K. (1989). The Japanese industrial relations system. *Journal of General Management, 14*, 67–88; and Stevenson, Y. A. (Jan/Feb. 1996). Unions and contracts. *China Business Review, 23*(1), 12.

122. Hammock, B. T. (1996). The extraterritorial application of the national Labor Relations Act: A union perspective. *Syracuse Journal of International Law and Commerce, 22*, 127–154.

123. Rolnick, A. L. (Feb. 3, 1997). Muzzling the offshore watchdogs. *Bobbin, 8*(6), 72–73.

124. Pfeffer, J. (1994). *Competitive advantage through people*. Boston: Harvard Business School Press; see also, Rosenbaum, M. (1989). Partners in productivity: An emerging consensus in labor-management relations. *Productivity Review, 8*, 357–364, and Drucker, P. J. (April 1990). Peter Drucker asks: Will unions ever again be useful organs of society? *Industry Week*, 16–22.

125. NBA and union in accord (April 27, 1988). *The New York Times*, p. B17.

126. Stuart, P. (August 1993). Labor unions become business partners. *Personnel Journal*, pp. 54–63.

127. Joint working at Barclays (January 1997). *IRS Employment Review*, p. ET4; see also, Abbey, A. (1996). Labor-management programs: Fostering bilateral cooperation. *Industrial Management, 38*(5), 21–23.

128. See note 49.

129. Kelly, N. E. (1997). Are union dues due for a change? *Iron Age New Steel, 13(*1), 80; see also, note 64.

130. Johnston, D. C. (Sept. 2, 1997). Executive pay increases at a much faster rate than corporate revenues and profits. *The New York Times*, p. C4.

131. Greenhouse, S. (Sept. 30, 1997). Workers vote to join union at U.S. Airways. *The New York Times*, p. A1.

C H A P T E R

EMPLOYEE HEALTH AND SAFETY*

OVERVIEW

Employers, unions, and employees have a great and growing interest in health and safety issues related to the workplace. With the number of work-related injuries, illnesses, and deaths, it is no surprise! In any given year, 1 out of every 10 employees is killed or injured on the job. Based on the most current data available, there were 6.8 million incidents of occupational injury or illness in just one year! Approximately 25 percent of Americans with disabilities have those disabilities because of work-related accidents or illnesses. In 1994, 514,000 new cases of nonfatal occupational illness and injury were reported.[1] More than 10,000 occupational deaths occur each year, and almost 5 million accidents are reported, resulting in over 90 million days of productive time lost. Studies indicate that reported accidents represent only about half of all accidents. In addition, research indicates that of the total employer costs related to occupational accidents and illness, ill health now accounts for 93 percent.[2]

The National Safety Council estimated that workplace injuries cost the U.S. economy over $119 billion in 1995. Examples of the costs to individual employers are immense as well. General Motors (GM) was fined $1.94 million for safety violations by the Occupational Safety and Health Administration (OSHA) in 1994. One of the largest meatpackers, John Morrell and Co. of Sioux Falls, South Dakota, was cited by OSHA in 1988 and assessed a $4.33 million fine for safety violations. According to the federal agency, more than 800 of the 2,000 employees at the plant sustained "serious and sometimes disabling injuries." The rate of injuries at the plant was 652 times more than the rate of injuries for businesses in general. USX, the giant steel company, was fined $7.3 million for numerous violations of safety, health, and recordkeeping, including 58 "willful" hazards.

Criminal charges and convictions against management for willful neglect of worker health and safety are now quite common. In 1997, health and safety officials investigated allegations that employees at CoSteel Sheerness were pressured to return to work swiftly after suffering injuries. Documents alleged that the firm's management (1) routinely requested staff to take days

*Contributed by Susan M. Burroughs and Harriette S. McCaul.

lost through sickness or injury as annual leave, (2) penalized workers financially for lost-time accidents, and (3) pressured sick employees to return to light duties at the plant.[3] In addition, fines are being levied against companies that violate the 1991 government regulation mandating the protection of workers against AIDS and other viruses.

This chapter will review the costs of employee injuries, illnesses, deaths, and the regulatory environment that seeks to improve work safety and health. HR professionals should understand these issues so they can take a proactive stance in managing employee health and safety. Considerable attention will be given to the role of the Occupational Safety and Health Administration Act of 1970 and the federal regulations that have been issued regarding this law. OSHA is responsible for establishing and enforcing occupational health and safety standards and for inspecting and issuing citations to organizations that violate these standards. OSHA is without question one of the greatest legislative accomplishments of organized labor, and research on its effectiveness will be reviewed in this chapter. The final portion of the chapter will cover contemporary issues related to employee health and safety and will discuss some of the controversial steps organizations are taking to improve their employee health, safety, and performance records (e.g., drug testing, anti-smoking policies, threat management teams, employee assistance and wellness programs).

OBJECTIVES

After studying this chapter, you should be able to:

1. Describe the extent and costs of employee accidents, illnesses, and deaths on the job.

2. Discuss the role of workers' compensation programs for job-related injuries and illnesses.

3. Describe legal issues related to health and safety.

4. Explain the functions of OSHA and review research on the effectiveness of this act and related regulation.

5. Discuss recent approaches that have been used to improve workplace safety and health.

6. Review contemporary issues and programs that seek to improve worker health and safety, including drug testing, anti-smoking policies, threat management teams, stress management interventions, employee assistance programs and employee wellness programs.

There is an increasing awareness of management failures to pay greater attention to the health and safety of employees. This awareness has translated into criminal charges and financial devastation for some companies. OSHA levied fines against companies in excess of $90 million in 1995. Many deaths, injuries, and illnesses occur because of safety violations, poor equipment design, or negligence. The Union Carbide accident in Bhopal, India, for example, which killed over 4,000 people in 1984, was considered by most experts to be a result of equipment design flaws that could have been avoided. More than 40 lawsuits worth billions of dollars were filed against the company. Phillips Petroleum was fined $5.7 million for willful safety breaches after 23 workers were killed in an explosion at a Texas petrochemical plant. Two USX plants reported 17 deaths related to employer safety violations. A meatpacker, the Iowa Beef Packers, agreed to redesign jobs to curtail crippling muscle and nerve ailments after a horrible record of injuries.

State prosecutors have argued successfully for criminal prosecution of managers who cause injury or illness to employees.[4] For example, three senior managers of Film Recovery Systems in Illinois received 25-year sentences for recklessly exposing their employees to toxic cyanide fumes. Five senior executives of Chicago Magnet Wire Company were prosecuted for causing illnesses by allowing workers to be exposed to hazardous chemicals. A supervisor at Jackson Enterprises in Michigan was convicted of involuntary manslaughter for an employee's death.[5] The list goes on.

The death and accident figures presented above vary substantially as a function of the industry, occupation, and organization size. Moderate-sized organizations (50 to 100 employees) have higher accident rates than smaller or larger companies. This may be because moderate firms cannot offer extensive safety programs or cannot closely supervise their employees. According to the Bureau of Labor Statistics (BLS), the industries with the highest number of fatalities in 1995 included construction; transportation and public utilities; agriculture, forestry, and fishing; services; and the retail trade. Among the industries that have the highest number of reported injuries and illnesses are meatpacking; automobile manufacturing; shipbuilding; iron foundries; and mobile home manufacturers. Meatpacking showed the highest increase in accidents in 1995, with four times as many employee injuries as the national average.

While the current statistics are disturbing, they do not compare to the early days of industrial growth in the United States. The Industrial Revolution was born with little concern for employee health or safety. Working conditions were often so unbearable and serious injuries were so pervasive that employees began to demand that management implement safeguards. Union activity emphasized improving employee working conditions. Today, many older Americans suffer because of the conditions to which they were exposed at work decades ago. For example, 49 workers from a foundry in Michigan got tuberculosis because of their exposure to silica at the foundry in the 1940s (silica is a glassy material found in sand). There are thousands of other examples.

Despite the work-related injuries, illnesses, and deaths that occur each year in this country, U.S. health and safety standards are superior to those in many developing parts of the world. In most other countries that maintain reliable data on the subject, injury and illness figures are even more alarming than those in the United States. Most developing countries have very basic safety laws and few resources for safety enforcement. In addition, they have antiquated equipment and limited training available to employees about safety issues. These developing countries are often so in need of economic development that they accept any industry, even those that have the potential for significant harm. This presents serious ethical questions for firms operating in the developing nations. However, in many European countries with strong national unions, safety law enforcement mechanisms are often ranked higher than those in the United States. The rankings are as follows: Sweden, former East Germany, Finland, former West Germany, United Kingdom, and the United States. In countries such as the Netherlands, France, Belgium, Denmark, and Luxembourg, legally mandated employee safety committees give workers more control over workplace safety issues.[6]

Without question, the American workplace is safer today than it was 50 years ago, but there is still considerable room for improvement. More than 30 million workers are potentially exposed to one or more chemical hazards per year. There are an estimated 650,000 existing hazardous chemical products, and hundreds of new ones are introduced annually. Most have never been tested for toxicity, and no regulatory restraints affect their use. New materials, composed of exotic combinations of plastics, carbons, and other substances, are introduced into the workplace at an alarming rate, with little knowledge of their interactive effects on worker health.

Another growing problem is **repetitive stress injury** (RSI), the so-called disease of the 90s. RSI is an occupational injury that occurs from continuous and repetitive physical movements, such as assembly-line work or data entry. The most frequently hit area with this disorder is in the wrist and is called carpal tunnel syndrome. The Labor Department reported that this disorder accounted for 65 percent of the 514,000 job-related injuries in 1994 (up 30,000 cases from 1993). Since 1990, cases of RSI have increased by 80 percent. OSHA is collecting a database on repetitive motion injuries for the purpose of creating definitive standards.

Workers today also suffer more subtle forms of health problems at work. Research concludes that workplace stress, for example, has reached epidemic proportions due to company restructuring, increased work demands, layoffs, downsizing, conflicts with family obligations, and so on.[7] Chronic and long-term stress is commonly referred to as burnout. Worker burnout is

costing U.S. industry billions of dollars. One estimate revealed that almost $90 billion is lost each year due to burnout and its related implications. Prolonged stress, along with fatigue, drugs, exposure to harmful chemicals, and disorders can result in worker errors that are the cause of most workplace accidents.[8]

In addition to the obvious effects of pain, suffering, and quality of life, the impact of injuries and illnesses on productivity is enormous. Over 125 million workdays were lost to work-related illness or injury in 1995, an increase of 1 percent from the previous year. In that same year, wage and productivity losses, medical expenses, and administrative expenses amounted to $105 billion, with 2.3 percent of payroll used for disability payments through workers' compensation. Indirect costs to the employer, including the monetary value of time lost by workers, replacing workers, damage to company equipment or property, and the cost of time required to investigate incidents (i.e., written reports), amounted to $11 billion.[9] The bottom line work-injury cost is in excess of $119 billion per year. A recent study reported that employees who had suffered accidents were unsatisfied with their jobs and had higher levels of job tension and lower organizational commitment and faith in management.[10] Given these facts, the growing interest in health and safety issues by employees, employers, and government agencies is understandable.

COMMON WORKPLACE INJURIES AND DISEASES

Employees are subjected to a number of on-the-job injuries each day. The most common parts of the body injured in work-related accidents are listed in Figure 14.1. As noted, back injuries are the most common of the compensation claims reported in 1994. Generally, injuries are caused by overexertion such as picking up heavy objects, falling, being struck by objects, or hyperextending a limb.

Figure 14.1 also depicts common occupational diseases that may occur as a result of work. Long-term exposure to a variety of substances (e.g., asbestos, radiation) can result in a number of diseases as shown in Figure 14.1. Often, it is difficult for employers to detect the cause of certain diseases. For example, an individual may suffer a hearing loss due to working in a plant with an extremely high noise level or for other reasons not related to the workplace. In fact, more and more supervisors are beginning to worry about the effects of noise on employee health, morale, and productivity. Some adverse effects caused by persistent loud noise include constriction of blood vessels to the brain and other key organs, damage to the nervous system, and triggering seizures among epileptics. OSHA's prescribed standard for acceptable noise levels in the workplace is 85 deci-

FIGURE 14.1
WORKPLACE INJURIES AND DISEASES

BODY PART INJURED	PERCENTAGE OF WORKPLACE ACCIDENTS*	BODY PART INJURED	PERCENTAGE OF WORKPLACE ACCIDENTS
Back	24%	Eyes	4.5%
Legs	13	Feet	4
Arms	12	Head	4
Fingers	11	Body systems	3
Trunk	11	Neck	2
Multiple injuries	10	Toes	1
Hands	5		

OCCUPATIONAL DISEASES†	CAUSES
Lung cancer	Coke oven emissions, asbestos, passive cigarette smoke
White lung disease	Asbestos
Black lung disease	Coal dust
Brown lung disease	Cotton dust
Leukemia	Benzene, radiation
Cancer of other organs	Asbestos, radiation, vinyl chloride, coke oven emissions
Sterility/reproductive problems	Radiation
Deteriorating eyesight	Chemical fumes, office equipment
Hearing loss	High noise levels

* *Accident Facts* (1994). National Safety Council, p. 38.
† A. Trafford, Is your job dangerous to your health? *U.S. News & World Report,* September 14, 1979, pp. 39–42.

bels. Unfortunately, many work settings today have daily noise levels well over the OSHA standard. Workers who are most at risk of noise pollution include factory workers, jack hammer operators, and printing press operators. For effective noise management, supervisors should take worker complaints about noise seriously and act on them and rotate workers so that no one worker has lengthy exposure to loud noises. In addition, to avoid litigation, employers must introduce and enforce safety regulations in the workplace.

Many employee illnesses are caused by food poisoning. A likely source of infections is the plant or office lunchroom, where improperly handled food can contaminate tabletops and work surfaces. Another threat is from food that employees bring from home. In the workplace, it is important to provide employees with refrigerated food storage and disposable utensils, plus a sink and paper towels for cleanup. Housekeeping personnel should make sure to use germicides or disinfectants rather than liquid soap.[11]

LEGAL ISSUES RELATED TO HEALTH AND SAFETY

Many laws are designed to protect workers from illness and injury. The Michigan foundry referred to earlier now must abide by strict OSHA standards regarding silica emissions. As evidenced by the fines against GM, John Morrell and Company, USX, and others discussed above, penalties are imposed for violating these laws and regulations. In the past, Chrysler was cited for safety abuses and, in particular, for failure to notify workers that they may be exposed to harmful chemicals. Under OSHA rules, employees now have a "right to know" about hazards to which they may be exposed at work. Companies are now required to issue a "hazard communication" to their workers when they may be exposed to certain hazardous chemicals. (We will discuss this and other OSHA regulations below.) Under OSHA, employees can refuse to work and be supported by the law when certain unsafe conditions exist. Employers need to keep equipment, machinery, and the workplace in good, safe working order.[12]

In some states, if a fatality occurs from a willful violation of safety rules, company officials can serve time in prison and pay substantial fines. In addition, as one state attorney general said, "The workplace offers no refuge from criminal laws."[13] Prosecutors are now charging employers and supervisory personnel with involuntary manslaughter for negligence regarding workplace safety. This type of criminal prosecution can involve much heavier penalties.

In addition to this legal pressure, many employers

seek a safe working environment because they wish to foster a high quality of work life (QWL) for their employees. Other employers recognize the costliness of accidents, illnesses, and injuries and endeavor to reduce these costs as much as possible through a variety of health and safety programs.

The major legislation related to health and safety, the steps that organizations have taken to reduce accidents and injuries, and the major contemporary issues that affect employee health and safety are reviewed below. Following this, the major controversies of the day such as AIDS policies, drug testing, anti-smoking positions, and responses to workplace violence are examined.

Workers' Compensation

As we discussed in Chapter 10, **workers' compensation** is a federally mandated insurance program developed on the theory that work-related accidents and illnesses are costs of doing business that should be paid for by the employer and passed on to the consumer. About $43 billion was paid out in 1993. Workers' compensation is based on the concept of **liability without fault,** which provides that workers who are victims of work-related injury or illness are granted benefits regardless of who is responsible for the accident, injury, or illness. This means that if an organization participates in the workers' compensation system, a worker may not sue the employer for negligence, even if the injury was clearly the employer's fault. On the other hand, even careless or accident-prone workers are generally covered by workers' compensation, and injuries that are the result of co-workers' negligence are also covered. Some state laws, however, deny benefits if the worker was under the influence of alcohol or controlled substances (illegal drugs) when the injury occurred.

The policy and provisions of workers' compensation vary across states, and not all jobs are covered. Workers' compensation provides for death, medical, and wage benefits derived from premiums paid by employers. To encourage safety, the size of the premium paid by employers is partially determined by the health and safety record of the particular industry and the particular employer (i.e., premiums are lower for industries with better safety records). There is great variability in payouts for injuries; even today, injuries to body parts are worth different amounts in different states.

When a worker is injured on the job or develops a disabling occupational disease, the worker must file a claim, either with the company or its insurance carrier (or in some states, with a state agency), to request workers' compensation benefits. In most states, benefits begin after a short waiting period (two to five days), include a wage replacement payment (a percentage of the worker's salary), and a reimbursement of medical costs.

The employer (or its insurance carrier) may require the injured worker to be treated by a doctor selected by the company.

Employers may contest a worker's compensation claim if they believe (1) the injury (or illness) is not a result of the work; (2) the employee is capable of performing the job despite the injury or illness; or (3) the employee has made a fraudulent claim. Other issues that may involve a challenge to a worker's compensation claim include heart attacks, strokes, or other stress-related problems. In some states, the law places the burden on the employee to prove that the disabling condition was a result of work effort or work-related stress and would not have occurred otherwise.

Some employees are challenging the no-fault assumptions of the workers' compensation system, arguing that an employer who knowingly exposes workers to hazardous substances or dangerous working conditions should not be protected from negligence lawsuits. In most instances, the courts have ruled that all employer conduct short of an "intentional wrong" will fall under the rubric of workers' compensation. However, there are some exceptions to this general rule. One state court ruled that a company that withholds information from employees regarding the development of a serious occupational disease could be sued for negligence and fraud.[14]

The fact that a company may have violated an OSHA standard will not necessarily remove the protection of workers' compensation. The no-fault provisions of the system (with the above noted exception) make irrelevant the issue of whether the employer or the worker was to blame. The worker gets medical treatment and a portion of his or her wages; the employer is insulated from litigation in return for paying the workers' compensation benefits.

If a worker becomes disabled due to a job-related accident or illness, the employer is then obligated under the 1990 Americans with Disabilities Act (ADA) to provide "reasonable accommodations" for that worker. This might include job restructuring or reassignment.

While provisions of workers' compensation laws, such as the premium imposed, encouraged employers' efforts to improve their health and safety records, the effects of such provisions were not very impressive. Many states took matters into their own hands to do more in this area. Between 1911 and 1948 each state passed a workers' compensation law. This created a myriad of rules and regulations, which resulted in a lack of uniformity in policies and regulations across the states. This prompted political pressure from numerous constituencies, particularly unions, for a federal law aimed primarily at the reduction and prevention of occupational fatalities, injuries, and illness. The result of the pressure was passage of the Occupational Safety and Health Act in 1970.

The Occupational Safety and Health Administration Act (http://www.osha.gov/)

The **Occupational Safety and Health Administration (OSHA)** was created in 1970 within the U.S. Department of Labor. It was designed to reduce occupational diseases and on-the-job injuries. Specifically, the purpose of OSHA is to accomplish the following:

1. Encourage employers and employees to reduce workplace hazards and to implement new or improve existing safety and health programs.

2. Provide for research in occupational safety and health to develop innovative ways of dealing with occupational safety and health problems.

3. Establish "separate but dependent responsibilities and rights" for employers and employees to achieve better safety and health conditions.

4. Maintain a reporting and recordkeeping system to monitor job-related injuries and illnesses.

5. Establish training programs to increase the number and competence of occupational safety and health personnel.

6. Develop mandatory job safety and health standards and enforce them effectively.

7. Provide for the development, analysis, evaluation, and approval of state occupational safety and health programs.

Coverage of the OSHA Act of 1970, which includes virtually all employers and their employees in the United States, is provided either directly by federal OSHA or through an OSHA-approved state program. Federal OSHA covers about 56 million employees at 3.6 million workplaces, and 25 state programs cover 50 million employees at 2.9 million workplaces. In states with OSHA-approved plans, employer and employee rights and responsibilities comparable to those under the federal OSHA program are enforced by the states under their own laws and regulations.

STANDARDS. OSHA is responsible for developing enforceable safety standards. It is the employers' responsibility to become familiar with the standards applicable to their establishments and to ensure that employees have and use personal protective gear and equipment when required for safety. Where OSHA has not promulgated specific standards, employers are responsible for following the act's general duty clause.

The general duty clause states that each employer "shall furnish . . . a place of employment which is free from recognized hazards that are causing or are likely to cause death or serious physical harm to his [or her] employees." This means that if a workplace situation involves foreseeable danger of potential injury, the employer is required to eliminate or reduce that danger through redesign, new equipment, or training workers about safety.

In 1989, OSHA greatly expanded its role in protecting workers from hazardous materials. Maximum exposure limits were set for 164 substances, and limits were tightened for 212 others. The limits cover the maximum amount of time a worker can be exposed to specific substances during an eight-hour workday. Among the substances regulated for the first time were cotton dust, wood dust, grain dust, gasoline, acrylic acid, tungsten, and welding fumes. OSHA also cut maximum exposure limits for carbon monoxide, chloroform, and hydrogen. In addition to exposure to hazardous materials, it is also important to examine the protective clothing worn by employees. Choosing the appropriate protection level and material of personal protective apparel is critical.[15]

Employers may ask for a temporary (up to one year) variance from a standard when they cannot comply with a new standard by its effective date. OSHA may grant a permanent variance from a standard when an employer can demonstrate that it has alternatives in place that protect employees as effectively as compliance with the standard would.

RECORDKEEPING AND REPORTING. Before OSHA became effective, no centralized and systematic method existed for monitoring occupational safety and health problems. Statistics on job injuries and illnesses were collected by some states and by some private organizations. With OSHA came the first basis for consistent, nationwide procedures—a vital requirement for gauging safety problems and solving them.

Employers with 11 or more employees must maintain records of occupational injuries and illnesses as they occur. The records permit the Bureau of Labor Statistics to compile data, to help define high hazard industries, and to inform employees of the status of their employers' record. OSHA provides a free 24-hour hot line for reporting workplace safety or health emergencies.

Recordkeeping forms must be maintained for five years at the establishment and must be available for inspection by representatives of OSHA. Only two forms are needed for recordkeeping. Figures 14.2 and 14.3 present copies of OSHA forms 200 and 101.

Keeping records of accidents is important not only to meet compliance issues, but also for identifying ergonomic problems in the workplace. Records should be kept not only for visible traumas, but also for musculoskeletal injuries such as strained backs and pulled necks. Analyzing these records can identify areas where poor manual handling or ergonomics cause work-related injuries. Statistics on absences are also valuable and enable organizations to draw comparisons between their firm and others. Unfortunately, many firms do not keep very detailed absence records, if they keep any.[16]

FIGURE 14.2
OSHA FORM 200

Bureau of Labor Statistics
Log and Summary of Occupational
Injuries and Illnesses

U.S. Department of Labor

NOTE: This form is required by Public Law 91-506 and must be kept in the establishment for 5 years. Failure to maintain and post can result in the issuance of citations and assessment of penalties.

RECORDABLE CASES: You are required to record information about every occupational death; every nonfatal occupational illness; and those nonfatal occupational injuries which involve one or more of the following: loss of consciousness, restriction of work or motion, transfer to another job, or medical treatment (other than first aid).

For Calendar Year 19 _____   Page _____ of _____

Form Approved
O.M.B. No. 1220 -0029

Company Name

Establishment Name

Establishment Address

Case or File Number

Enter a nonduplicating number which will facilitate comparisons with supplementary records.

(A)

Date of Injury or Onset of Illness

Enter Mo./day.

(B)

Employee's Name

Enter first name or initial, middle initial, last name.

(C)

Occupation

Enter regular job title, not activity employee was performing when injured or at onset of illness. In the absence of a formal title, enter a brief description of the employee's duties.

(D)

Department

Enter department in which the employee is regularly employed or a description of normal workplace to which employee is assigned, even though temporarily working in another department at the time of injury or illness.

(E)

Description of Injury or Illness

Enter a brief description of the injury or illness and indicate the part or parts of body affected.

Typical entries for this column might be: Amputation of 1st joint right forefinger; Strain of lower back; Contact dermatitis on both hands; Electrocution—body.

(F)

PREVIOUS PAGE TOTALS

Extent of and Outcome of INJURY

Fatalities — Injury Related

Enter DATE of death. Mo./day/yr.

(1)

Nonfatal Injuries — Injuries With Lost Workdays

(2) Enter a CHECK if injury involves days away from work, or days of restricted work activity, or both.

(3) Enter a CHECK if injury involves days away from work.

(4) Enter number of DAYS away from work.

(5) Enter number of DAYS of restricted work activity.

Injuries Without Lost Workdays

(6) Enter a CHECK if no entry was made in columns 1 or 2 but the injury is recordable as defined above.

Type, Extent of, and Outcome of ILLNESS

Type of Illness — CHECK Only One Column for Each Illness

(a) Occupational skin diseases or disorders
(b) Dust diseases of the lungs.
(c) Respiratory conditions due to toxic agents
(c) Poisoning (systemic effects of toxic materials)
(d) Disorders due to physical agents
(f) Disorders associated with repeated trauma
(g) All other occupational illnesses

(7)

Fatalities — Illness Related

Enter DATE of death. Mo./day/yr.

(8)

Nonfatal Illnesses — Illnesses With Lost Workdays

(9) Enter a CHECK if illness involves days away from work, or days of restricted work activity, or both.

(10) Enter a CHECK if illness involves days away from work.

(11) Enter number of DAYS away from work.

(12) Enter number of DAYS of restricted work activity.

Illnesses Without Lost Workdays

(13) Enter a CHECK if no entry was made in columns 8 or 9.

TOTALS (Instructions on other side of form.)

Certification of Annual Summary Totals By _____   Title _____   Date _____

POST ONLY THIS PORTION OF THE LAST PAGE NO LATER THAN FEBRUARY 1.

OSHA No. 200

INJURIES

ILLNESSES

FOLD

FIGURE 14.3
OSHA FORM 101

U.S. Department of Labor

Bureau of Labor Statistics
Supplementary Record of
Occupational Injuries and Illnesses

This form is required by Public Law 91-596 and must be kept in the establishment for *5 years.* Failure to maintain can result in the issuance of citations and assessment of penalties.	Case or File No.	Form Approved C.M.B. No. 1220-0029

Employer

1. Name

2. Mail address (*No. and street, city or town, State, and zip code*)

3. Location, if different from mail address

Injured or Ill Employee

4. Name (*First, middle, and last*)   Social Security No.

5. Home address (*No. and street, city or town, State, and zip code*)

6. Age

7. Sex: (Check one)   Male ☐   Female ☐

8. Occupation (*Enter regular job title, not the specific activity (s)he was performing at time of injury.*)

9. Department (*Enter name of department or division in which the injured person is regularly employed, even though (s)he may have been temporarily working in another department at the time of injury.*)

The Accident or Exposure to Occupational Illness

If accident or exposure occurred on employer's premises, give address of plant or establishment in which it occurred. Do not indicate department or division within the plant or establishment. If accident occurred outside employer's premises at an identifiable address, give that address. If it occurred on a public highway or at any other place which cannot be identified by number and street, please provide place references locating the place of injury as accurately as possible.

10. Place of accident or exposure (*No. and street, city or town, State, and zip code*)

11. Was place of accident or exposure on employer's premises?   Yes ☐   No ☐

12. What was the employee doing when injured? (*Be specific. If (s)he was using tools or equipment or handling material, name them and tell what (s)he was doing with them.*)

13. How did the accident occur? (*Describe fully the events which resulted in the injury or occupational illness. Tell what happened and how it happened. Name any objects or substances involved and tell how they were involved. Give full details on all factors which led or contributed to the accident. Use separate sheet for additional space.*)

Occupational Injury or Occupational Illness

14. Describe the injury or illness in detail and indicate the part of body affected. (*E.g., amputation of right index finger at second joint; fracture of ribs; lead poisoning; dermatitis of left hand, etc.*)

15. Name the object or substance which directly injured the employee. (*For example, the machine or thing he struck against or which struck him (her); the vapor or poison (s)he inhaled or swallowed; the chemical or radiation which irritated his (her) skin; or in cases of strains, hernias, etc., the thing (s)he was lifting, pulling, etc.*)

16. Date of injury or initial diagnosis of occupational illness

17. Did employee die? (Check one)   Yes ☐   No ☐

Other

18. Name and address of physician

19. If hospitalized, name and address of hospital

Date of report	Prepared by	Official position

OSHA No. 101 (Feb. 1981)

DEFINING OCCUPATIONAL INJURY OR ILLNESS. An **occupational injury** is any injury, such as a cut, fracture, sprain, or amputation, that results from a work-related accident or from exposure involving a single incident in the work environment. An occupational illness is any abnormal condition or disorder, other than one resulting from an occupational injury, caused by exposure to environmental factors associated with employment. Included are acute and chronic illnesses or diseases that may be caused by inhalation, absorption, or ingestion of or direct contact with toxic substances or harmful agents. Alcoholism has even been considered an occupational illness in a case involving an employee who developed an alcohol-related problem as a result of the socializing responsibilities associated with his job.

All occupational illnesses must be recorded, regardless of severity. All occupational injuries must be recorded if they result in the following:

- Death (must be recorded regardless of the length of time between the injury and death).
- One or more lost workdays.
- Restriction of work or motion.
- Loss of consciousness.
- Transfer to another job.
- Medical treatment (other than first aid).

WORKPLACE INSPECTION. To enforce its standards, OSHA is authorized under the act to conduct workplace inspections. Every establishment covered by the act is subject to inspection by OSHA compliance safety and health officers (COSHOs), who are chosen for their knowledge and experience in the occupational safety and health field, and who are trained in OSHA standards and in recognition of safety and health hazards.

Under the act, "upon presenting appropriate credentials to the owner, operator, or agent in charge," a COSHO is authorized to carry out the following:

- "Enter without delay and at reasonable times any factory, plant, establishment, construction site or other areas, workplace, or environment where work is performed by an employee of an employer.
- "Inspect and investigate during regular working hours, and at other reasonable times, and within reasonable limits and in a reasonable manner, any such place of employment and all pertinent conditions, structures, machines, apparatus, devices, equipment and materials therein, and to question privately any such employer, owner, operator, agent, or employee."

OSHA's highest priorities for inspections are to first go to imminent danger situations and actual fatal accident sites. Next, it inspects workplaces with valid employee complaints or target industries (those with high rates of accidents). Finally, it performs random inspections and reinspections of various work sites.[17]

With very few exceptions, inspections are conducted without advance notice. In fact, alerting an employer in advance of an OSHA inspection can bring a fine of up to $1,000 and/or a six-month jail term. If an employer refuses to grant admittance to the COSHO, or if an employer attempts to interfere with the inspection, the act permits appropriate legal action.

Based on a 1978 U.S. Supreme Court ruling in *Marshall v. Barlow's Inc.*,[18] OSHA may not conduct warrantless inspections without an employer's consent. It may, however, inspect after acquiring a judicially authorized search warrant based on administrative probable cause or on evidence of a violation.

If employees are represented by a recognized bargaining representative, the union ordinarily will designate an employee representative to accompany the compliance officer. Similarly, if there is a plant safety committee, the employee members of that committee will designate the employee representative.

Inspection tour. After an opening conference, the COSHO and accompanying representatives proceed through the establishment and inspect work areas for compliance with OSHA standards. The route and duration of the inspection are determined by the compliance officer. While talking with employees, the compliance officer makes every effort to minimize work interruptions. The compliance officer observes conditions, consults with employees, may take photos (for recordkeeping), takes instrument readings, and examines records.

Employees are consulted during the inspection tour. The compliance officer may stop and question workers, in private if necessary, about safety and health conditions and practices in their workplaces. All employees are protected, under the act, from discrimination from their employer for exercising their safety and health rights.

Posting and recordkeeping are checked. The compliance officer inspects records of injuries, illnesses, and deaths that the employer is required to keep. He or she checks to see that a copy of the totals from the last page of OSHA Form 200 have been posted.

Closing conference. After the inspection tour, a closing conference is held between the compliance officer and the employer or the employer's representative. This is the time for free discussion of problems and needs—a time for frank questions and answers.

The compliance officer discusses with the employer all unsafe conditions observed on the inspection and indicates all apparent violations for which a citation may be issued or recommended: (1) a description of the violation; (2) the proposed financial penalty, if any; and (3) the date by which the hazard must be corrected. The employer is then informed of appeal rights.

The compliance officer explains that OSHA area offices are full-service resource centers that provide a number of services such as training speakers and technical materials on safety and health matters. The compliance officer also explains the requirements of the *Hazard Communications Standard,* which requires employers to establish a written, comprehensive hazard communication program that includes provisions for container labeling, material safety data sheets, and an employee training program. (Employers have been cited for over 50,000 violations of the Hazard Communication Standard since 1985.) As of 1997, employers are required to certify to OSHA that they have corrected workplace hazards cited by the agency.[19]

SERVICES AVAILABLE.   Consultation assistance.
Free consultation assistance is available to employers who want help establishing and maintaining a safe and healthful workplace. Largely funded by OSHA, the service is provided at no cost to the employer. As part of this service, no citations are issued nor are penalties imposed and information is kept confidential. Besides helping employers to identify and correct specific hazards, consultation can include assistance in developing and implementing effective workplace safety and health programs with emphasis on the prevention of worker injuries and illnesses. Training and education services can also be provided.

Voluntary protection programs.   Voluntary protection programs (VPPs) represent one component of OSHA's effort to extend worker protection beyond the minimum required by OSHA standards. When combined with an effective enforcement program, VPPs, expanded on-site consultation services, and full-service area offices can expand worker protection to help meet the goals of the OSHA.

The two VPPs, Star and Merit, are designed to perform the following functions:

- Recognize outstanding achievement of those who have successfully incorporated comprehensive safety and health programs into their total management systems.

- Motivate other companies to achieve excellent safety and health results in the same outstanding way.

- Establish a relationship between employers, employees, and OSHA that is based on cooperation rather than coercion.

The **Star program,** OSHA's most demanding and the most prestigious VPP, is open to an employer in any industry who has successfully managed a comprehensive safety and health program to reduce injury rates below the industry's national average. Specific requirements for the program include systems for management commitment and responsibility; hazard assessment and control; and safety planning, rules, work procedures, and training that are in place and operating effectively. Among the 1996 "Stars" were Midas International in Hartford, Wisconsin; Lucent Technologies in Norcross, Georgia; General Electric in Worthington, Ohio; and Springfield Remanufacturing in Springfield, Missouri.[20]

The **Merit program,** also open to any industry, is primarily a stepping-stone to Star program participation. A company with a basic safety and health program that is committed to improvement and has the resources to do so within a specified time period may work with OSHA to meet merit qualifications. Among the 1996 Merit winners were Texaco ENP in Maysville, Oklahoma; Flexcon in Spencer, Massachusetts; Alumax Aluminum Corporation in Magnolia, Arkansas; Wakefern Food Corporation in Jamesburg, New Jersey; and Westpoint Stevens in Opelika, Alabama.[21]

Training and education.   OSHA's 85 area offices are full-service centers offering a variety of informational services such as speakers, publications, audiovisual aids on workplace hazards, and technical advice. The OSHA Training Institute in Des Plaines, Illinois, provides basic and advanced training and education in safety and health for federal and state compliance officers; state consultants; other federal agency personnel; and private-sector employers, employees, and their representatives. Institute courses are also offered to the public and cover areas such as electrical hazards, machine guarding, ventilation, and ergonomics.

RESPONSIBILITIES UNDER OSHA.   As an employer, you must abide by these OSHA guidelines:

- Meet your general duty responsibility to provide a workplace free from recognized hazards that are causing or are likely to cause death or serious physical harm to employees and comply with standards, rules, and regulations issued under the act.

- Familiarize yourself and employees with mandatory OSHA standards and make copies available to employees for review upon request.

- Examine workplace conditions to ensure they conform to applicable standards.

- Minimize or reduce safety and health hazards.

- Ensure that employees have and use safe tools and equipment (including appropriate personal protective equipment) and that such equipment is properly maintained.

- Employ color codes, posters, labels, or signs in several languages to warn employees of potential hazards.

- Establish or update operating procedures and communicate them so that employees follow safety and health requirements.
- Provide medical examinations when required by OSHA standards.
- Report to the nearest OSHA office within 48 hours of any fatal accident or one that results in the hospitalization of five or more employees.
- Keep OSHA-required records of work-related injuries and illnesses and post a copy of the totals from the last page of OSHA Form 200 during the entire month of February each year.
- Post, at a prominent location within the workplace, the OSHA poster (OSHA 2203) informing employees of their rights and responsibilities.
- Provide employees, former employees, and their representatives access to the Log and Summary of Occupational Injuries and Illnesses (OSHA Form 200) at a reasonable time and in a reasonable manner.
- Cooperate with the OSHA compliance officer by furnishing names of authorized employee representatives who may be asked to accompany the compliance officer during an inspection.
- Refrain from discriminating against employees who properly exercise their rights under the act.
- Post OSHA citations at or near the work site involved. Each citation, or citation copy thereof, must remain posted until the violation has been abated or for three working days, whichever is longer.

Although OSHA does not cite employees for violations of their responsibilities, each employee "shall comply with all occupational safety and health standards and rules, regulations, and orders issued under the act" that are applicable.

RIGHTS FOR EMPLOYEES. Employees have a right to seek a safe workplace without fear of punishment. That right is spelled out in Section 11(c) of the act.

The law says employers shall not punish or discriminate against workers for exercising the following rights:

- Complaining to an employer, union, OSHA, or any other government agency about job safety and health hazards.
- Filing safety or health grievances.
- Participating on a workplace safety and health committee or in union activities concerning job safety and health.
- Participating in OSHA inspections, conferences, hearings, or other OSHA-related activities.

If an employee is exercising these or other OSHA rights, the employer is not allowed to discriminate against that worker in any way, such as through firing, demotion, transferring the worker to an undesirable job or shift, or threatening or harassing the worker.

In *Whirlpool v. Marshall,* the Supreme Court ruled in 1981 that although there is no specific language in the law about walking off a job, employees who have a reasonable apprehension of death or serious injury may refuse to work until that safety hazard is corrected. The employer may not discipline or discharge a worker who exercises this right, although the employer is not required to pay the worker for the hours not worked.[22]

Workers believing they have been punished for exercising safety and health rights must contact the nearest OSHA office within 30 days of the time they learn of the alleged discrimination. A union representative can file the complaint for the worker. The worker does not have to complete any form. Any OSHA staff member will complete the forms after asking what happened and who was involved.

Following a complaint, OSHA investigates the organization. If an employee has been illegally punished for exercising safety and health rights, OSHA asks the employer to restore that worker's job earnings and benefits. If necessary, and if it can prove discrimination, OSHA takes the employer to court. In such cases, the worker does not pay any legal fees. If a state agency has an OSHA-approved state program, employees may file their complaint with either federal OSHA or the state agency under its laws.

Employees also have these additional rights under OSHA:

- Review copies of appropriate OSHA standards, rules, regulations, and requirements that the employer should have available at the workplace.
- Request information from your employer on safety and health hazards in the area, on precautions that may be taken, and on procedures to be followed if an employee is involved in an accident or is exposed to toxic substances.
- Request the OSHA area director to conduct an inspection if you believe hazardous conditions or violations of standards exist in your workplace.
- Have your name withheld from your employer, upon request to OSHA, if you file a written and signed complaint.
- Learn about OSHA actions regarding your complaint and have an informal review, if requested, of any decision not to inspect or to issue a citation.
- Have your authorized employee representative accompany the OSHA compliance officer during the inspection tour.
- Respond to questions from the OSHA compliance officer, particularly if there is no authorized employee representative accompanying the compliance officer.

- Observe any monitoring or measuring of hazardous materials and have the right to see these records, as specified under the act.

- Have your authorized representative, or yourself, review the Log and Summary of Occupational Injuries (OSHA Form 200) at a reasonable time and in a reasonable manner.

- Request a closing discussion with the compliance officer following an inspection.

- Submit a written request to the National Institute for Occupational Safety and Health (NIOSH) for information on whether any substance in your workplace has potentially toxic effects in the concentration being used, and have your name withheld from your employer, if you so request.

- Receive notification from your employer if he or she applies for a variance from an OSHA standard, testify at a variance hearing, and appeal the final decision.

- Submit information or comment to OSHA on the issuance, modification, or revocation of OSHA standards and request a public hearing.

THE EFFECTS OF OSHA. OSHA has had a profound impact on employer actions regarding health and safety issues. The establishment of formal safety committees, improved equipment and machinery, improved medical facilities and staff, and, in general, greater emphasis on safety and prevention are among the major changes that are the direct result of OSHA. Of course, many employers and legislators consider some of the standards to be unacceptable, arbitrary, trivial, and unattainable and many of the regulations to be excessively detailed and costly (see Figure 14.4). One study puts the figure at $25 billion over the first 10 years of the law.[23] OSHA has come under fire from safety experts for trivial fines—at times, only in the hundreds of dollars. Two months before the horrendous Phillips Petroleum explosion in 1989, OSHA neglected to conduct a complete inspection of the plant after an accident killed one worker. OSHA does have some power to ask the Justice Department to prosecute employers who intentionally or negligently injure their employees, but critics of OSHA have maintained that state prosecutions are necessary because few employers have been charged under federal law.

FIGURE 14.4
THE COWBOY AFTER OSHA

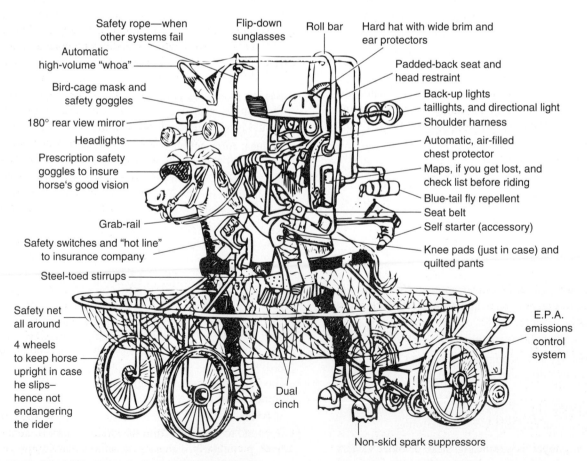

Source: Copyright © 1972 by Devin. Reprinted with permission.

There is renewed vigor at OSHA, however. Enforcement and fines have increased sharply since former President Ronald Reagan cut back OSHA activity during his first presidential term. Fines for health and safety violations exceeded $90 million in 1995, and OSHA has requested an increase in fine limits and criminal penalties for willful violations.[24] OSHA is now using its subpoena powers to have employees testify under oath about safety violations. Business executives now face jail terms for their behavior and policies regarding the health and safety of their workers. State Supreme Courts in New York, Illinois, and Michigan have already ruled that employers can face criminal charges and prison. The renewed zeal has created a fearful perspective among employers. As one expert put it, "For the first time, the cost of ignoring OSHA has become greater than the cost of complying."[25] An increase in enforcement of significant cases in 1997 reflects improved targeting of inspections by OSHA. Initiatives such as special emphasis programs on silica and nursing homes has enabled OSHA to do a better job of getting to the most hazardous workplaces. Figures from the first half of fiscal 1997 (October 1, 1996 to March 31, 1997) indicated that OSHA conducted 83 significant cases, compared to 45 in fiscal 1996 and 63 in fiscal 1995. Significant cases are those in which initial penalties exceed $100,000 or are deemed significant due to the nature or number of violations. The agency's enforcement staff is fully operational, and the total number of inspections in 1997 was higher than in 1996.[26]

The key question, however, is whether having OSHA in place has reduced workplace deaths, accidents, or injuries. The data regarding fatalities is clear. Workplace deaths went from 21 per 100,000 in 1912 to only 2 per 100,000 in 1994.[27] There has been an increase in injuries and illnesses since 1984, mainly due to reports of RSI.[28] Nearly two-thirds of all workplace injuries are some form of RSI with over 332,000 cases reported in 1994.

OSHA is focused almost exclusively on unsafe working conditions and managerial responsibility; however, virtually no attention is given to employee behavior and responsibility. Because of this lack of attention, most experts agree that the impact of OSHA on accident rates will be moderate. Experts generally agree that more attention must be paid to behaviors and attitudes.[29] GM, for example, reported that in 1976 it was spending $15 per car to comply with OSHA regulations, but there had been no positive impact on accident rates as a function of the regulations.[30] Other experts maintain that the long-term impact of OSHA will be overwhelmingly positive because of the increased knowledge of hazardous substances discovered through OSHA activities. For example, critical information about a great number of carcinogens such as PCBs, cotton dust, asbestos, and vinyl chloride can be directly linked to OSHA research. The banning of asbestos in 1989 would probably not have occurred had it not been for OSHA research.

The **right-to-know** provisions of OSHA should also have a positive impact on company health and safety records. These provisions specify the employees' right to know if they are working with unsafe substances, how to work with them safely, and how to administer first aid if workers come in contact with toxic chemicals. These provisions also require that a "material safety data sheet" be provided with each chemical used. This form provides all necessary information about the substance, what precautions to take, and how to treat any injury associated with its use.

Unions take a much more positive position on the effects of OSHA and have been at the forefront in advocating many of the preventative provisions of OSHA. For example, over 20,000 workers are trained annually in the recognition and control of work hazards. Still, unions favor more aggressive enforcement that is more uniform across the country and a faster process for the development of new standards. Unions have worked very hard for the development of national ergonomic standards to control RSI.[31]

PROGRAMS TO REDUCE ACCIDENTS AT WORK

Organizations have tried a variety of strategies directed at reducing or eliminating unsafe behaviors at work. These programs can be classified into four general areas: personnel selection, employee training, incentive programs, and safety rules and regulations. Figure 14.5 summarizes key principles to a Total Safety Culture. Health and safety guru E. Scott Geller has 50 key principles to a Total Safety Culture, a subset of which is presented in Figure 14.5. All four general areas are covered by these principles.[32] Views by top management toward safety are very important and vary across cultures. In general, plants are safer in the United States, Japan, and the European Union.[33]

Good communication is vital to successful safety and health programs and to business in general. Employee participation and involvement in safety issues and programs is critical for successful programs.[34] In addition, research has shown that management's demonstration of concern after an employee's injury creates a "halo effect" that can aid the worker's recovery and speed return to work. Also, workers who experienced the halo effect expressed more satisfaction with their treatment from the firm and were less likely to seek a lawyer.[35]

Recently, OSHA took the position that people employed to work at home for an employer should generally be accorded the same rights as any other employee regarding health and safety. The 1992 Management of

FIGURE 14.5
SOME KEY PRINCIPLES OF A TOTAL
SAFETY CULTURE

1. Safety should be internally, not externally, driven.
2. Culture changes require people to understand the principles and how to use them.
3. A total safety culture requires continuous attention to factors in three domains: environment, behavior, and person.
4. Don't count on common sense for safety improvement.
5. Safety incentive programs should focus on process rather than outcomes.
6. People view behavior as correct to the degree they see others doing it.
7. On-the-job observation and interpersonal feedback are key to Total Safety Culture.
8. Behavior is directed by activators and motivated by consequences.
9. People compensate for increases in perceived safety by taking more risks.
10. Stressors lead to positive stress or negative distress, depending on appraisal of personal control.
11. When people feel empowered, their safe behavior spreads to other situations.
12. Numbers from program evaluations should be meaningful to all participants.

Source: Adapted from Geller, E. S. (1996). *Working safe: How to help people actively care for health and safety.* Radnor, PA: Chilton Book Company. (Dr. Geller has 50 principles.)

Health and Safety at Work Regulations require that employers carry out a risk assessment of home workers.[36]

Personnel Selection

We describe as "accident-prone" people who inadvertently hurt themselves or destroy something at work. Is it possible to predict accident proneness? If so, we might change our personnel decisions to select those people who are less likely to be in accidents. Organizations such as Domino's Pizza, Greyhound, and every police department in the nation would love to be able to avoid employing individuals with a knack for traffic mishaps. Unfortunately, while there have been numerous attempts to identify careless, accident-prone people, the evidence really boils down to only two general findings: (1) older employees are safer than younger ones (regardless of job tenure); and (2) physical characteristics, such as hearing and vision, are related to accident rates when they are critical aspects of a job. Chapter 6 describes some tests which have potential for the prediction and prevention of employee accidents. Related tests should identify applicants who don't use drugs and are honest, value-driven, customer-oriented, respectful, and responsive to authority—in short, "safe" employees.[37] Further research is needed in this area.

Safety Training

One survey indicated that most manufacturing plants have only informal safety training procedures. Typically, a new employee is given a brief orientation to company policy, including safety issues; spends a day or two with the first-line supervisor or lead person; and is then expected to work safely at a reasonable level of productivity. Research indicates that a formal system of safety training is much more effective. In addition, because safety programs are so costly, it is important to be able to show that the programs save the firm money.[38] Interactive approaches to training may be the best way to get employees to really understand safety issues. At True-Time Inc., the safety staff gives a brief review of the company's safety procedures to the employees each year at the company meeting. Each employee is then given a custom, randomly generated quiz. Employees have to seek answers to the questions by checking source materials and glossaries, studying the policies, and examining reports. This encourages employees to take an active learning approach to learning about the firm's safety procedures.[39]

OSHA has issued "voluntary training guidelines" for employers that provide a framework for the development, administration, and evaluation of training programs. These guidelines are especially helpful for organizations that have no expertise in formal training development and evaluation. One study supported the use of accident simulations as a training method.[40] In addition, providing training sessions in several languages increases the chance of compliance by the 32 million workers for which English is a second language. The message on safe work practices and job hazards needs to get through to everyone.

A 1997 OSHA standard requires training for employees who operate powered industrial trucks. The training rule covers nearly 1.2 million employees who drive trucks in general industry and for maritime employers. There are about 823,000 powered industrial trucks operating in the workplace. As of 1997, statistics indicate that about 85 workers are killed each year in incidents related to industrial truck operations and nearly 35,000 suffer injuries that result in lost workdays. Approximately 20 to 25 percent of those incidents are partly due to inadequate training. The cost for employers to comply with the rule would be approximately $34.9 million in the first year and $19.4 million annually each year thereafter. It is believed that the rule will prevent between 17 and 22 worker deaths each year, as well as 10,898 to 14,118 injuries resulting in lost workdays. In addition, compliance will ultimately save employers between $8 million and $42 million annually in property damage and $770,000 paid as a result of lawsuits involving workers injured in forklift accidents that could be attributed to deficiencies in training.[41]

Training programs are typical in industries with serious accident problems. For example, the construction industry employs only 5 percent of the workforce yet has the highest lost-time injury rate of any major industry (it accounts for 20 percent of all occupational fatalities). As a result, some contractors include the cost of supplying safety equipment and employee training in their bids.[42] Training programs also exist in public safety arenas. For example, in the restaurant industry, training is used to educate restaurant employees about food illnesses. This is critical because as many as 9,000 people die annually in the United States and an estimated 9 million become sick from illnesses transmitted by restaurant food.[43]

Most training programs generally focus on hazards at work, safety rules and regulations, and safe and unsafe work behaviors. For example, one study describes a bakery which developed a detailed behavior observation code of safe and unsafe behaviors.[44] Participants in the safety program were then shown slides of the unsafe and safe behaviors. Goals were set for increasing the percentage of safe behaviors, and a feedback chart was set up for monitoring group performance. Supervisors were also trained in giving positive reinforcement for safe work behaviors. The training and monitoring increased the percentage of safe behaviors more than 20 percent.

Today, when developing training programs, HR professionals should recognize the aging of the workforce and be sure that training addresses changes in workers' strength, size, flexibility, and stamina. The National Institute on Aging's Gerontology Research Center recommends that employers use routine medical checkups to determine employee health initially and then track positive or negative changes in work ability.[45] Training should be adjusted to fit the needs of the aging workforce. In addition, with the increasing number of downsizings, it is important to be sure that a core set of employees (who will be with the company for some time) are trained in safety procedures. In high turnover facilities, long-term training for all employees is impractical. However, it is possible to find long-term employees who are interested in worker safety and health. These employees can be the core group who are able to train new employees as they enter the organization.[46]

Many manufacturers use a peer review process to improve safety records. The objective is to shape behavior with immediate and constant feedback and positive reinforcement. At Alcoa, all workers must submit safety suggestions and are rewarded for good ones. Production-line workers can stop the line at any time if they spot a safety problem. Other companies employ industrial psychologists and engineers to study the worker–machine interface. At DuPont Corporation, engineers observe workers and then redesign valves and install key locks to reduce accidents. At Monsanto's Pensacola, Florida, plant psychologists used the critical incident technique (CIT) of job analysis. Experts drew "cause trees" to identify the root causes of the less-than-obvious problems. If a worker slipped on oil, for example, the root cause was not oil but the failure of maintenance to attend to an oil leak. A safety scorecard was also prepared, and workers reviewed processes to check for "shortcuts and deviations," which ultimately predict trouble. Safe workers win recognition at weekly safety meetings, and free lunches and promotions have been tied to safety records. As a result of this comprehensive approach to safety, Monsanto's record improved from 6.5 to 1.6 lost-time injuries per hundred workers in the five years of the program.

Safety training is not only important for employees, but also for supervisors. Workplace health and safety efforts cannot succeed without the support and efforts of supervisors. In general, supervisors must know (1) about any hazards in their area of supervision and any hazards that may affect their subordinates when traveling outside their area of supervision; (2) what safety procedures and devices are needed to safely carry out the jobs in their departments, (3) about safety rules, policies, procedures, and programs that have been developed, and (4) what is required under all applicable occupational health and safety legislation.[47] Supervisors should also be aware of safety rules associated with contractors. For example, companies that hire contractors who fall short on safety procedures may find themselves jointly liable when workers are injured. A key factor in determining contractor status and employer liability is who supervises outside employees working under a specific contract. Management should assume that the company can have some liability for anything that occurs on the property. Thus, a firm would be wise to make a contractor's health and safety record a factor in the selection process when contractors are hired.[48]

Incentive Systems

Today, safety incentives are a hotly competitive and growing segment of the highly profitable corporate incentive industry. Even small incentives can change employees' attitudes.[49] As we discussed in Chapter 11, many employers use safety contests where company units compete with one another for cash or prizes. Other contests are set up so that each unit competes with its own safety record. If a lower number of accidents occurs over a period of time, an award is given. At DuPont, directors give safety awards and workers win cash prizes if their units remain accident-free for six months. These prizes are only one part of their safety philosophy. As part of an overall safety management that focuses on injury prevention and a goal of zero accidents and injuries, DuPont has used many forms of recognition to increase awareness of safety excellence.[50] At Kodak, volunteer observers take turns supervising peers and providing token awards (e.g., free soft drinks). Summer construction workers at Colorado State University started driving more safely when the city began offering the incentive of small coolers for carrying meals.[51] At Hunter Industries, a sprinkler manufacturer, the safety and health coordinator created a three-level safety incentive program. Level one involves mandatory safety activities; level two includes wellness and self-enrichment activities; and level three includes community involvement. Based on the program, the company has met total regulatory compliance for the past three years and has reported improved work habits and cost savings.[52]

There has been little systematic research on incentive systems for accident reduction. Some research, however, suggests that safety programs help offset the high cost of health insurance benefits, worker compensation claims, and lost-time injuries.[53] Bulova Corporation of Woodside, New York, has a guide for setting up a successful safety incentive program.[54]

When awards are substantial, failure to report accidents is a possibility. For example, offering safety prizes of significant worth (e.g., new car, tropical vacation) may provide employees with an incentive not to report injuries.[55] To decrease occupational accidents, safety programs must be run and promoted effectively. First, it is necessary to determine what types of behaviors are to be controlled. Next, the HR professional must prioritize the behaviors and then develop a plan and the appropriate rewards. For example, one common program used by many firms is safety bingo. Monthly drawings and quarterly drawings are also popular, as are special contests.[56]

Safety Rules

Most companies now publish employee handbooks with formal rules and regulations that stipulate what employees can and cannot do in the workplace. Unfortunately, many of these rules and regulations are too general to be effective. The most effective employee safety handbooks are those that carefully describe the steps to be taken on the job to ensure maximum safety. For each step, potential dangers are identified to alert the worker. In addition to specificity in the rules, it is also critical to get workers to read and comprehend safety handbooks. Some companies require that employees pass a test about safety-related issues before they begin work.

No matter how thorough the training, safety rules will be meaningless if they are not enforced. There are, unfortunately, numerous cases where a worker ignored a safety rule and was injured, or when a supervisor ordered workers to ignore a safety rule. Consistent enforcement of safety rules, with discipline for infractions, will benefit management in several ways. First, it will send a clear message to employees that the company takes safety seriously. Second, it should reduce injuries. Third, a company may be able to avoid an OSHA citation if it can demonstrate that it complied with relevant OSHA stan-

dards (or the general duty clause), that it trained its workers properly, and that the injury was the result of a worker's intentional refusal to adhere to work rules. Documentation of consistent discipline for work rule violations would be necessary for a company to avoid OSHA liability. Safety committees comprised of management and nonmanagement employees can be used to enforce safety rules. Committee members can identify safety hazards and devise solutions to safety problems. In addition, they can organize safety training courses or workshops to increase employees' awareness of safety issues.

CONTEMPORARY ISSUES RELATED TO HEALTH AND SAFETY

AIDS and the Workplace

As human immunodeficiency virus (HIV) and acquired immune deficiency syndrome (AIDS) continue to plague millions of Americans, numerous organizations are becoming more vulnerable to the tremendous loss exposure associated with the increasing presence of these diseases in the workplace.[57] According to the Centers for Disease Control (CDC), two or three employees in all U.S. companies with a workforce of at least 300 people suffer from AIDS or have dependents, spouses, significant others, or friends with the disease. AIDS is now the leading cause of death for people between the ages of 25 and 44, with the majority of the U.S. workforce in this age group. The CDC reported that 319,849 Americans died of the disease from June 1981 through December 1995. The virus is expected to spread to around 40 million people worldwide by the year 2000, with most of those people in their prime working years. AIDS has become a critical health care issue for employers and employees alike, with corporations incurring increasing costs related to the growing number of AIDS cases. Overall, AIDS-related corporate expenses include the patient's health insurance, disability benefits, employee life insurance, and pension costs. They also include the costs of hiring and training replacements and the costs of any lawsuits. The cumulative costs of treating AIDS exceeded $15 billion in 1995. The estimated losses in productivity were over $65 billion in 1993.

AIDS victims are now protected by a variety of state and local laws that prohibit discrimination against disabled people. As discussed in Chapter 3, AIDS has typically been defined as a legal disability under the Rehabilitation Act of 1973, which prohibits discrimination against the disabled by federal contractors, and is covered by the 1990 Americans with Disabilities Act (ADA). The ADA protects the jobs of people with AIDS-related disabilities and helps keep them in the workforce. Few jobs exist where having HIV or AIDS prohibits an employee from performing essential job functions. However, should such a situation occur, employers must make reasonable accommodations for the employee under the ADA (e.g., equipment changes, workstation modifications, flexible work schedules). With appropriate and reasonable accommodations, there is no reason people with HIV and AIDS cannot continue to work for many years. Businesses also must be careful to abide by the ADA when hiring. They cannot ask job candidates about their HIV or AIDS status, nor can they require HIV testing on a pre-employment or pre-offer basis. Upon the extension of an offer, however, employers may require an HIV test or pose questions concerning the prospective employee's HIV status, as long as all applicants in a particular job category are treated similarly. Of course, test results must be treated confidentially. A positive HIV test result cannot prompt a job revocation unless the employer can demonstrate that the individual poses a direct health threat to coworkers or customers that cannot be eliminated through reasonable accommodations.

Managers and HR professionals should understand the legal implications of HIV and AIDS in the workplace; in 1966, over 50,000 claims of AIDS-related discrimination cases were filed. For example, the Florida Commission of Human Relations ruled that a teacher who was fired because he had AIDS was a victim of disability discrimination. The teacher was awarded almost $200,000. Another example was when an HIV-positive physician sued Philadelphia's Mercy Health Corporation for discrimination when he was barred from performing invasive medical procedures unless his patients signed a consent form that disclosed his HIV status. The doctor sued under Section I of the ADA, which prohibits discrimination in employment, and Section III, which prohibits public facilities from discriminating against people with disabilities.

In July 1992, OSHA passed its Bloodborne Pathogen Standards, which state that all workplaces with employees that could be "reasonably anticipated" to contact blood or body fluids must comply. Under these guidelines, OSHA takes the position that there is no such thing as a risk-free population. According to these OSHA standards, employers must write an "exposure control plan," which details the procedure for identifying individuals at risk and how the organization will comply with the standards; "universal precautions," which detail how blood and body fluids are handled; and "cleaning protocols," which detail the location of cleaning supplies and the handling of cleaning wastes. Furthermore, employers must provide "personal protective equipment" such as gloves, masks, mouth guards, and smocks for workers who might come in contact with blood and other bodily fluids; "communicate the presence of hazards," which places warning labels and signs for restricted areas; educate and train employees of OSHA standards; and keep records as evidence that companies are complying. Employers who violate the regulations are subject to OSHA penalties. OSHA made 1,175 citations against nonhealth care entities for violations of its Bloodborne Pathogens Standards and issued $821,690 in fines in Region V (Midwestern states) in 1993 and 1994.

The ADA mandates that businesses have a comprehensive HIV/AIDS policy and communicate the plan throughout the workplace. A recent survey found that only one-third of large and mid-size companies have formal HIV/AIDS policies.[58] The CDC AIDS Clearinghouse provides businesses with information on policy formation, employee education, manager and supervisor training, volunteerism, and family education in a kit titled "Business Response to AIDS." This kit helps companies develop specific policies and programs to deal with AIDS-related work issues. Most major companies take the position that AIDS-afflicted employees should be treated the same as other employees as long as they can perform their jobs. The Bank of America allows coworkers to transfer from departments where there are AIDS victims, but there has not been a single request to date. This is undoubtedly because the bank has provided a great deal of information about the disease to its employees and about the very low risk of transmission in the workplace. Through 1995, the CDC has not found a single case of AIDS transmission based on casual contact at work. The CDC believes that AIDS-afflicted employees do not have to be isolated or restricted from any work area, although there is much debate about possible restrictions in hospitals, food service, and dental settings. Caution is suggested for health care workers and patients or clients who may be exposed to blood, mucous membranes, or lesions.

Levi Strauss and IBM have been at the forefront in the development of a comprehensive AIDS-awareness program. The educational component of the Levi Strauss program includes informative brochures, a manager's guide to treating AIDS-afflicted employees, a policy manual, and a guidebook for policy makers. The company also provides an opportunity for employees to meet with medical professionals to discuss HIV/AIDS issues in more detail.[59] Since the enactment of the program, Levi Strauss has not incurred any lawsuits, employees refusing to work with AIDS-afflicted employees, or requests for reassignment. The IBM policy is to encourage AIDS-afflicted employees to work as long as they are capable and to ensure their privacy.

Drugs in the Workplace

It is not necessary to remind students that the abuse of controlled substances is a serious social problem—one that plagues employers as well as law enforcement agencies. The Substance Abuse and Mental Health Services Administration estimated that drug abuse costs U.S. businesses $102 billion annually in lost productivity, accidents, absenteeism, turnover, medical claims, and thefts.[60] Other reported consequences of drug abuse include increased on-the-job violence, workforce irritability, fistfights on assembly lines, and job mistakes. Employees using drugs are 3.6 times more likely to be involved in on-the-job accidents than other employees, and more liability-insurance-covered accidents are caused by drug-impaired employees. This may be because today's drug users are relying more on amphetamines (e.g., crystal methodine), which accelerates their systems, turning them from "recreational users" into "volatile abusers." Previously, employees had relied more on depressants such as alcohol and marijuana.[61] Of course, alcohol abuse still leads to a number of workplace symptoms including unexcused and frequent absences, tardiness and early departures, fights with employees, on-the-job accidents, and poor judgments.

As we discussed in Chapter 6, many companies have responded to the drug crisis with a drug testing program. In one such company, personal injuries reportedly dropped from 15.5 per year before random urine testing to 5.8 per year five years after initiating the program. The Drug Free Workplace Act of 1988 requires federal contractors to provide a drug-free workplace. Under the law, employers must educate employees about the risks of drug use and establish penalties for substance abuse. Furthermore, organizations must have specific policies on substance abuse, establish awareness programs, and notify employees and applicants that a drug-free state is a condition of employment. In response, U.S. companies have increasingly turned to drug testing both as a screening device for job applicants and as a means of evaluating current employees.

A 1996 American Management Association (AMA) survey found that 78 percent of all companies test at least some employees and applicants for drug abuse.[62] The firms that participated in the survey stated the rise in drug testing was due to the following factors:

- Department of Transportation (DOT) and Department of Defense (DOD) regulations that, with local and state legislation, mandated testing in certain job categories.
- The practical effects of the Drug Free Workplace Act of 1988.
- Court decisions that recognize an employer's right to test both employees and job applicants in the private sector.
- Action by insurance carriers to reduce accident liability and control health costs.
- Corporate requirements that vendors and contractors certify that theirs is a drug-free workplace.

According to the AMA survey, over 70 percent of companies conduct random drug testing of current employees. Motorola, for example, recently ordered all of its U.S. employees to undergo random drug testing at least once every three years, with more frequent testing for employees with positive test results. Recently, a Kansas City manufacturer of food processing equipment used a private undercover drug agent to monitor drug use. In a drug "sweep," she found that two dozen workers were either using or dealing drugs. The icing on the cake was the internal theft of a $16,000 piece of equipment. The agent found that an employee had sold it for $800 to buy drugs. Investigators are doing the same thing at a number of other companies that are suffering financial and behavioral consequences from employee drug abuse.[63]

Before a company initiates drug testing, the following questions should be addressed: Why do we want this program? Do we have a problem with drugs in our company? What will we do with the results of drug tests? Can our current discipline policy handle violations of this policy? How much will the program cost? Can we afford it? Will it affect morale? Should it be a punitive or rehabilitative program? Only after these questions are answered satisfactorily should a company consider implementing drug testing.

Companies use five approaches to drug testing: preemployment screening, random testing of current employees, "reasonable cause" testing in response to performance problems, return-to-duty testing after drug treatment or suspension, and postaccident testing. Science makes it possible to ascertain if a person has ingested a controlled substance, and more and more companies are joining the ranks of those who at least test applicants for the presence of drugs. The AMA survey found that 77 percent of the companies that responded test all new hires for drugs in preemployment physical examinations. Surprisingly, workers are quite tolerant of testing. The aforementioned survey found 60 percent of those questioned supported random drug testing of current employees with no probable cause.[64]

Two questions that science has not yet been able to answer, however, are exactly how much of a controlled substance an individual must ingest to be impaired and just what *impaired* means. For example, most states have set a 0.10 percent blood alcohol level to establish impairment by alcohol; a similar standard does not exist for controlled substances. While some employers declare that a drug test result showing *any* amount of a controlled substance will be grounds for rejecting an applicant or discharging a worker, other employers have set some level as the threshold for an assumption that the employee is impaired. Computerized tests are now available to help employers determine whether workers in safety-related jobs are impaired. One test operates like a videogame and takes less than a minute to determine eye–hand coordination and reaction time. Old Town Trolley Tours of San Diego, California, uses the test to assess drivers.

Because of the lack of a standard for impairment, combined with the manner in which the presence of drugs is usually ascertained (generally, a urine test), many employment decisions made on the basis of positive drug test results have been legally challenged. Some experts maintain that hair analysis, a reliable but more costly alternative to urinalysis, is a less invasive technique that may not be as legally troublesome. A hair analysis screens a strand of hair to detect the metabolics of illegal substances that remain in a person's system for up to several months. Charles Carroll, president of ASET Corporation, which specializes in undercover drug detection, recommends that companies substitute hair analysis for urinalysis. Carroll points out that drug users have learned how to beat preemployment urine tests, but "hair follicles, on the other hand, are permanent recorders of what is in a person's system."[65]

Although there are no federal laws regulating drug testing, drug testing programs have been challenged using a number of legal theories. Private-sector employers have generally been able to successfully defend their drug testing programs in court, but there are a number of exceptions. In California, for example, the court ruled that Southern Pacific wrongfully fired a computer programmer when she refused to provide a random-test urine specimen. Another California court ruled that Kerr-McGee Chemical Corporation violated a worker's privacy by requiring her to submit to a drug test. However, other California decisions have supported drug testing. Lower courts in Michigan and Texas have sided with employers on random urinalysis, while a court in New Jersey found for the plaintiff. In the words of one labor attorney, employee drug testing is a "legal minefield . . . a quagmire of legal problems."[66] Utah is the only state that clearly permits drug testing of employees and applicants and authorizes firing employees who refuse to be tested. Maine explicitly allows testing for "probable cause," but limits random testing to safety-sensitive jobs.

Public employers are bound by the Fourth Amendment of the U.S. Constitution, which forbids "unreasonable" searches and seizures. However, even characterizing a urine test as either a search (of the urine) or a seizure (of body fluids) has not legally established that drug testing by public employers is unconstitutional. Supreme Court decisions now permit public employers to use drug testing for employees engaged in jobs where public safety is an issue, such as railroad engineers, U.S. Customs agents, and nuclear power plant workers. Private-sector employers, however, are not bound by the Fourth Amendment, and challenges must be based on contract claims or "public policy" grounds.

This does not mean, however, that a company should establish a drug testing program without concern for potential legal consequences. Unionized employers must bargain with the union about the procedures to be used, according to the National Labor Relations Board

(NLRB). Nonunionized employers must consider that not all positive drug results indicate that the employee is presently impaired or has even ingested a controlled substance, as the ingestion of innocuous substances (poppy seeds, quinine water) may result in a positive test result. At a minimum, the company should make sure its program includes the following components:

- Notice to employees (or applicants) that drug testing will be conducted and the procedures to be used.
- An opportunity for the individual to disclose which prescription or over-the-counter drugs he or she is currently taking as well as other information that might skew the test results.
- A careful chain of custody to ensure that samples are not lost, mixed up, or switched.
- A dignified but secure method of collecting samples.
- Confirmation of all positive drug results with more sensitive tests.
- The opportunity for the individual to have the sample retested at his or her own expense.
- Confidentiality of test results.

In developing a drug testing policy, a company must determine what, if any, substances are permissible. For example, will a positive reading for marijuana be treated the same way as a positive reading for heroin? If testing is performed on current employees, will it be done only "for cause" (for example, after an accident or if a supervisor determines that an employee appears impaired) or randomly without cause?

Potential legal claims to drug testing in the public sector include Fourth Amendment challenges to the testing. This occurs if there was no reasonable cause to conclude that the employee had ingested controlled substances or if the drug testing represented a violation of the employee's constitutional due process rights. This may occur if the employee is discharged without being given an opportunity to challenge the test results. All employers may face charges of defamation (if test results become known to anyone but those who need the information); contract claims (for currently employed workers); and claims of discrimination against workers with disabilities (e.g., if the employee is a recovering drug abuser).

HR managers are well advised to consult with legal counsel before developing a drug testing program. Model programs that have withstood litigation are available, and an attorney can advise managers of any state laws that may affect the way the program is designed or administered.

Smoking in the Workplace

One of the most volatile issues for HR professionals today is a company's position on smoking. Growing information about the adverse effects of secondhand smoke have led some people to call for a ban on smoking in the workplace. The U.S. Environmental Protection Agency reported that secondhand smoke causes 3,800 lung cancer deaths per year and classified it as a "class A" life-threatening carcinogen, a rating used only for substances (i.e., asbestos, radon, benzene) proven to cause cancer in humans. The Centers for Disease Control estimates that cigarette smoking costs the national economy at least $50 billion a year in direct medical expenses. This number does not include costs due to increased absenteeism or decreased productivity.[67] The American Heart Association reported that passive smoking is the third greatest preventable cause of death in the United States.

The current trend of nonsmoking employees is to file workers' compensation and disability claims and legal suits against companies where smoking is not restricted. For example, the Wisconsin Labor and Industry Review Commission awarded an employee $23,400 in workers' compensation benefits because her eight-year exposure to secondhand smoke resulted in a permanent disability. The California Compensation Insurance Fund paid $85,000 in damages to an employee who suffered a heart attack from her exposure to smoke at work. In addition, a federal hearings examiner awarded a widower $21,500 a year for life to compensate for his wife's death due to lung cancer believed to be caused by her job as a Veterans Administration nurse on a hospital ward where heavy smoking was common.

The U.S. Environmental Protection Agency "Guide to Workplace Smoking Policies" recommends that employers create ventilated smoking lounges to separate smokers from nonsmokers. A growing number have developed restrictive policies ranging from the use of designated smoking areas to banning smoking in the workplace to requiring nonsmoking as a condition of employment. A 1994 study found that smokers in a nonsmoking organization reduced the number of cigarettes smoked per work shift and decreased levels of nicotine and carbon monoxide. Thus, work-site smoking restrictions may promote meaningful reductions in tobacco exposure and consequent health risks. However, there are no laws that prohibit employers either from banning smoking at work or from taking action against employees who violate such bans.

OSHA is trying to issue regulations regarding smoking in the workplace. Section 654(a) of OSHA states that the "general duty" of employers is to provide places of employment "free of recognized hazards that are causing or likely to cause death or serious physical harm to his/her employees." OSHA currently has a proposal under review regarding indoor air quality, including environmental tobacco smoke. The proposal would require that employers write and implement indoor air quality compliance plans including inspection and maintenance of current building systems to ensure they are functioning as designed. This may require some building owners

and employers to install new ventilation systems. In buildings where smoking is not prohibited by employers or local requirements, the proposal would require designated smoking areas that are separate, enclosed rooms exhausted directly to the outside. If passed, this proposal will be very costly to organizations. Recently, Texas Instruments found the cost for constructing these rooms averaged $70,000 each. Yet, given that the surgeon general's report now documents the effects of sidestream smoke and the EPA places tobacco smoke in the top tier of known carcinogens, the OSHA obligation seems obvious.

While the approval of new federal laws is under review, 28 state laws have been put into effect.[68] A New Jersey state law, for example, prohibits discrimination in hiring, pay, and working conditions against smokers "unless the employer has a rationale basis for doing so." Unfortunately, it is now up to employers to determine what constitutes a "rational basis." Are higher health care costs a rational basis?

Growing evidence that health care costs more for smokers than nonsmokers is prompting some companies to levy additional charges on smokers and offer incentives for quitting. Provident Indemnity Life Insurance Co. offers nonsmokers 33 percent discounts on health and life insurance. At Mahoning Culvert in Youngstown, Ohio, smokers who are attempting to quit contribute 50 cents a day to a pool that accumulates for one year. To that pool of $182.50, the company adds $817.50 to reward each smoker who manages to quit for a year. An additional $500 is given the second year. Other companies have drawings for prizes and other incentives to encourage employees to quit smoking. Some companies have taken the punitive route. Lutheran Heath Systems, a Fargo, North Dakota, hospital and nursing home chain, charges smokers a 10 percent premium on their health insurance. U-Haul International deducts $5 every other week from the paychecks of smokers. Several fire departments have imposed deadlines by which smoking firefighters must quit or be terminated. Particularly in hazardous work environments where the risks of cancer are great (e.g., daily exposure to chemical fumes), companies are more likely to impose no-smoking rules. While insurance premiums and increased health care costs are major reasons for employers' move toward a smoke-free workplace, pressure by nonsmokers has also contributed to the development of formal no-smoking policies at many organizations. In fact, as of 1994, 85 percent of organizations surveyed indicated they had prohibited or restricted workplace smoking.[69]

A seven-step plan has been proposed for the development of a smoking policy:[70]

1. Top management should make a commitment to the development of a smoking policy.

2. Pertinent state and local laws should be reviewed.

3. Unions should be involved (if applicable).

4. The smoking policy should be tailored to particular work situations or stations.

5. A committee of smokers and nonsmokers from a cross-section of the workforce should be formed.

6. The workforce should be surveyed to determine attitudes toward smoking and toward possible smoking policies.

7. A proposed policy should be circulated throughout the workplace. Enforcement of policy violations on a consistent basis will encourage employee compliance.

Violence in the Workplace

Violence has infiltrated all aspects of American life: home, community, school, and work. The workplace appears to be no safe haven from the threat or reality of violence, and research suggests that both the frequency and severity of work-related violence are increasing. Workplace violence, often perpetrated by disgruntled employees, has reached epidemic proportions. Estimates indicate that more than 1.9 million violent workplace crimes occur each year with half of these infractions caused by employees or former employees. About 10 percent of these violent workplace crimes involve offenders armed with handguns. An estimated 7 percent of all rapes, 8 percent of all robberies, and 16 percent of all assaults occur at work, according to data collected from 1987 through 1992 by the National Crime Victimization Survey of U.S. households.[71] A 1994 American Management Association survey of 311 organizations found that almost 25 percent indicated at least one employee had been attacked or killed on the job since 1990. A 1996 Society for Human Resource Management (SHRM) survey found that of more than 1,000 employers, 48 percent had experienced at least one violent incident in the workplace since the start of 1994, compared with one-third of employers in 1993.[72]

The National Institute for Occupational Safety and Health (NIOSH) reported that over 7,000 homicides occur annually in the workplace, placing homicides third among leading causes of workplace death in the United States—surpassed only by motor vehicle crashes and machine-related fatalities.[73] Criminologists call the trend in workplace homicide the fastest growing form of murder in America. The statistics on extreme cases of workplace violence (e.g., murder, rape) are staggering. OSHA indicates that the trend may get worse because now 40 states have legalized the possession of concealed weapons.[74] Employers can, however, ban concealed weapons in the workplace. They should have a written policy that is communicated to all employees and is contained in an employee handbook or in the policies and procedures manual.

The European Commission's definition of workplace violence includes "incidents where persons are abused, threatened, or assaulted in circumstances relating to their work, involving an explicit challenge to their safety, well-being, or health." The Manufacturing, Science, and Finance Union is currently drafting a private member's bill to outlaw workplace bullying. According to the bill, if an employer fails to adequately address a complaint from an employee about bullying, the employer could be subject to civil proceedings. In general, as awareness of the problem increases, employers are installing various security systems and training employees to avoid or diffuse incidents.[75]

HR professionals must also be aware of the many forms of less severe violence (see Figure 14.6) that is occurring and must be taken seriously.[76] Although no method exists that can perfectly predict a violent employee, the growing number of workplace homicides has made it possible to construct a profile of the typical perpetrator (see Figure 14.7). While violent employees may not have all the profile characteristics, most have a majority of them.

OSHA issued the first federal guidelines regarding workplace violence on March 14, 1996. The guidelines, which are not mandatory, recommend that social service and health care employees carefully assess security issues that may result in workplace violence. About 66 percent of all those assaulted in the workplace are health care and social service employees. While OSHA's initial guidelines focus on these industries, another set of guidelines is being prepared to protect workers in the night retail industry, which also is disproportionately victimized by violence. In general, OSHA's guidelines

FIGURE 14.6
LEVELS OF WORKPLACE VIOLENCE

MODERATELY INJURIOUS

- Property damage, vandalism
- Sabotage
- Pushing, fistfights
- Major violations of company policy
- Frequent arguments with customers, coworkers, or supervisors
- Theft

HIGHLY INJURIOUS

- Physical attacks and assaults
- Psychological trauma
- Anger-related accidents
- Rape
- Arson
- Murder

Source: S. M. Burroughs and J. W. Jones. Managing violence: Looking out for trouble. *Occupational Health and Safety,* April 1995, pp. 34–37.

**FIGURE 14.7
VIOLENT EMPLOYEE PROFILE**

PRIMARY CHARACTERISTICS

- White middle-aged male
- Holds a white- or blue-collar position, possibly as department head, manager, or supervisor
- History of violence towards others
- Abuses illicit drugs
- Weapon owner and/or served in the military
- Extremely withdrawn, a "loner"
- Few interests outside of work
- Constantly disgruntled, a "troublemaker"
- Perceives unfairness, injustice, or malice in others

SECONDARY CHARACTERISTICS

- Overreacts to corporate changes
- Suffers from interpersonal conflict
- Recently fired or laid off, or perceives soon will be
- Argumentative/uncooperative
- Extremist opinions and attitudes
- Makes sexual comments or threats of physical assault
- Disobeys company policies and procedures/has difficulty accepting authority
- May sabotage equipment and/or property
- Steals

Note: Most individuals prone to violence will possess a majority of these traits.

Source: S. M. Burroughs and J. W. Jones, Managing violence: Looking out for trouble. *Occupational Health and Safety,* April 1995, *pp. 34-37.*

state that a workplace violence prevention program should include the elements of any good safety and health program, which are management commitment, employee involvement, work-site analysis, hazard prevention and control, and training and education.[77]

CONSEQUENCES. Although there are many opinions about why it is happening, it is clear that employee violence costs companies dearly. There is the immediate cost of human suffering, pain, and possibly the precious loss of life. The effect of workplace violence on traumatized employees, families of employees, and coworkers is difficult to put into exact financial terms. Beyond human losses, the organization itself becomes a victim of workplace violence. The National Safe Workplace Institute estimates that workplace violence cost employers $4.2 billion in 1992.[78] Rising health care costs, higher workers' compensation fees, and increased legal expenditures are a few of the significant consequences. For example, in 1994, insurers paid $12 million to settle lawsuits by parents of four teenage girls who were murdered during a robbery at an Austin, Texas, I Can't Believe It's Yogurt store where the girls worked. In the aftermath of a violent incident, the organization usually pays for medical and post-trauma stress treatments, lost wages due to

increased absences (1.75 million lost workdays in 1995), increased security and property damage, and investigations, which may include the use of outside experts such as management consultants. Another cost component is the loss of employee productivity. Revenue losses from disruption in work progress, turnover, and the diminished public image of the organization may result in reduced sales potential and lower stock value.

VIOLENCE PREVENTION PROGRAMS. Taking specific actions to prevent workplace violence can create a security-conscious organizational culture, thereby potentially reducing a company's exposure to violent employee crime. These prevention programs involve screening potential employees, communicating your company's commitment to nonviolence through policies and procedures, training and educating supervisors and workers, employee assistance programs building a threat management team, and implementing security measures.

Preemployment screening. Human resource professionals can reduce the potential for violent incidents and negligent hiring claims by using comprehensive preemployment screening procedures. Such procedures can usually detect service-oriented employees with strong interpersonal skills, as opposed to excessively violent and aggressive workers. Scientifically based paper-and-pencil tests can serve as a baseline assessment for measuring future changes in an employee's behavior. To obtain credible information about a high-risk applicant, a valid measure of violence potential that complies with professional guidelines should be chosen. One such test, the Personnel Selection Inventory (PSI), published by Rosemont, Illinois-based London House, measures the likelihood that an applicant is not prone to abusive, argumentative, or hostile workplace behavior. Research shows that well-validated instruments like the PSI can detect applicants who possess a history of violent behavior who, once hired, may become counterproductive employees.

The optimum preemployment screening program will combine testing with employment verification (if there's a gap in work history, find out why), reference checks, criminal record checks, drug testing, and structured interviews. Interviewers should be educated to ask questions that may elicit responses indicating a candidate's likelihood for future violent outbursts. It is useful to design a standard assessment form to ensure candidates are compared consistently. Examples of structured interview questions include the following:

- Tell me about a time at work when you were so angry that you yelled at a supervisor or fellow employee.
- Were you ever angered to the point where you felt like yelling at someone, even though you didn't?
- Did you ever actually push or hit someone who made you really angry?

- Did you ever yell at or hit an obnoxious customer?
- Would any of your past supervisors or co-workers remember a situation where you yelled at or hit anybody?

To avoid potential litigation, have the preemployment screening process, including structured interview questions, reviewed by an expert in human rights legislation. This will ensure that the department keeps within any legal restrictions. Furthermore, such processes may provide necessary information about the candidate should that person become violent after being hired and file a discrimination suit under the Americans with Disabilities Act (ADA), which protects people with mental impairments. There is a strong overlap between violent behavior and mental illness. The evidence gathered about the individual at the front end may help the charged organization to show that it tried to avert preventable violence to maintain a safe work environment. One or two hours of legal advice in advance could make the world of difference. A small employer could easily spend $100,000 on litigation, related to claims of negligent hiring.

Policies and procedures. By sending a strong message about the company's commitment to workplace safety, employees will feel more secure about reporting statements or behaviors that they perceive as threatening. One way to encourage such reports is to require employees to read and sign a "Zero Tolerance for Violence Policy" prohibiting the use of weapons, harassment, and verbal or physical threats on the job. Under this policy, employees will feel obligated to notify the human resource or security department regarding threats or violent encounters. A 1994 survey report by the Society for Human Resource Management (SHRM) revealed that 73 percent of the survey respondents said their organizations have a written policy addressing rules and regulations about weapons in the workplace, 59 percent said they have a written policy addressing violent acts in the workplace, and 39 percent do not have a written policy. Some companies offer a confidential hot line through which reports can be made. A zero-tolerance policy will be effective only if the HR or security departments have the reputation for promptly handling matters seriously and with concern for all employees involved. As part of this policy, security procedures (e.g., visitors should wear ID badges) and planned escape routes should be identified, and emergency phone numbers should be published. This way employees can refer to these important policies and procedures to know exactly what is expected of them.

Training and education. Most employees do not become violent without displaying some early warning signs or symptoms. Therefore, employees and supervisors should learn to recognize and respond to highly stressed individuals and violent incidents and use nonconfrontational response techniques to defuse potential problems. Supervisors must learn to recognize workers who display signs of extreme stress and whose work deteriorates significantly. Employees who begin to display irresponsible and inappropriate behaviors such as chronic absenteeism and lateness, grievances and complaints, and overt anger and resentment also should be monitored. Too many tragic situations occur because warning signs go unnoticed, suspicious acts never get reported, or reported information is ignored. It is in these cases that a situation explodes and workers shake their heads and wonder how they could have missed such obvious signs.

Management can help ease a frustrating work environment by giving employees an outlet to air their grievances without fear of reprisal. When possible, managers should take action to resolve the complaints. Establishing trust, cooperation, creativity, and internal teamwork will encourage mutual respect and allow for the development of team problem-solving skills. Basic interpersonal skills such as listening, giving positive encouragement, and learning to be prepared for change should be part of any program.

Employee assistance programs (EAPs) provide specific programs designed to help employees with personal problems. EAPs are a resource to intervene with violent employees, but they are only one way in which human resource departments can help. Training and education programs should incorporate stress management, active coping techniques, and drug abuse awareness. Employers can make educational materials available to employees and their families to help them identify and handle harassment, domestic abuse, substance abuse, and other emotional problems. Companies can even provide voluntary self-defense training and classes in personal safety and security to teach employees how to reduce their chances of being victimized.

Companies where violence has previously occurred need to be especially aware of situations that could lead to employee anger or frustration because that workplace is already perceived by employees as unsafe. Workplace violence should be an ongoing topic of company meetings, workshops, newsletters, and new-hire orientation classes.

Handling layoffs and terminations is a highly sensitive area that requires special training because certain employees may become hostile after a dismissal. A person charged with this responsibility needs to remain neutral when disciplining or terminating employees. In return, employees should have the opportunity to submit written grievances or appeals about their termination or any other pertinent issues. Consideration should be made as to how the dismissal is conducted. Some managers recommend using only one room during the process. The affected individual should remain in the room while meeting with the manager, HR representative, and outplacement counselor. This prevents the person from moving around the building and possibly causing a scene.

After a dismissal, confidential psychological counseling should be offered as well as outplacement services such as vocational counseling and job search or résumé-writing assistance. It is critical that keys, identification badges, and access cards are collected. Following up with an employee after termination is a good idea because violent acts typically occur within one week after an ex-employee has threatened to retaliate. This follow-up may be in the form of a structured exit interview where the former employee can vent his or her feelings or a simple phone call to find out how the person is doing.

Threat management teams.   Most experts agree that in addition to formal policies and procedures, companies need to form a threat management team. A **threat management team** is responsible for translating workplace violence policies into action, with particular emphasis on prevention. Typically this team is staffed with individuals from both inside and outside the company including an HR professional, psychologist, lawyer, security guard, and a key front-line manager who is capable of supervising a tense situation. A strong negotiator can also be part of the team.

The first task of the team is to conduct an initial risk assessment to determine if a threat is serious enough to justify deployment of the team and its resources. Risk assessment involves collecting personnel data to identify past and present problems with the employee posing the threat. Based on such assessment, the team then develops an initial action plan. This phase involves mobilizing the resources needed to intervene in the situation and planning additional steps.

The team should outline the scope of activities and operations that it will cover and set criteria for convening and reporting incidents to law enforcement and the media. Before extreme violence hits, the team must establish a relationship with local police and designate a spokesperson to deal with press reports. A formal procedure for investigating threats must also be defined. Some companies bring in an expert to evaluate the threat objectively and to guide action after the investigation.

Threat management teams also plan escape routes, coordinate medical and psychological care of injured victims, train employees to administer emergency aid to victims, and organize transportation for employees who are in no condition to drive following an incident. Employees and their families must be kept informed during the crisis and immediately thereafter. Therefore, a team member will be responsible for telephoning families to provide updates of victims' conditions, answer payroll or

use of sick leave questions, and other necessary matters. Primary and refresher training criteria should be set for all team members. It is recommended that a company develop crisis scenarios against which the threat management team can practice its response. The team can also prepare news releases and potential question-and-answer lists before a crisis occurs.

Security.   Workplace violence can be prevented in some cases by employing security measures. Often these are used to protect employees and employers from violent people outside the organization (e.g., former employees). In this area, much can be accomplished at little cost. For example, a threat management team member can arrange regular police checkups and rearrange offices and furniture to provide escape routes that are accessible to employees who, because of their positions, may be obvious targets of disgruntled persons. Limited and controlled access, security awareness briefings, surveillance cameras, and silent alarms can all help reduce employee vulnerability. Making high-risk areas visible to more people and installing good external lighting are two more strategies. In short, the company should make it difficult for anyone to engage in violence.

As stated earlier, the goal of the U.S. Occupational Safety and Health Act of 1970 is "to ensure, so far as possible, every working man and woman in the nation safe and healthful working conditions." By law it is every organization's responsibility to prevent workplace violence from occurring and to be prepared to handle it should a situation arise. If a violent incident occurs on a company's premises, and inquiries show an absence of reasonable preventive efforts, the company could be held liable. While it is unrealistic to believe that a company can eliminate the threat of workplace violence, proper precautions can increase employee protection.

Video Display Terminals

Over 30 million Americans now work with video display terminals (VDTs). Many workers who spend considerable time in front of VDTs complain of eye fatigue and irritation, blurred vision, headaches, dizziness, and various muscular and wrist problems. Some VDT users have reported complicated or failed pregnancies. While one California study found that pregnant women who worked at VDTs for 20 hours or more a week had twice the risk of miscarriage as other clerical workers, a larger, more recent study sponsored by the federal government found no relationship between long exposure to VDTs and miscarriage.[79] Unions such as the American Federation of State and Municipal Employees (AFSME) are now demanding that pregnant women be allowed to switch to jobs not involving VDTs. Although there is no denying that electric and magnetic fields can influence biological processes, the critical question related to

VDTs is the extent to which exposure is harmful. More research is urgently needed on this topic.

Repetitive Stress Injuries (RSI)

It is estimated that over 300,000 people are afflicted by ergonomic injuries each year at an annual cost of $20 billion in workers' compensation claims. Repetitive stress injuries (RSIs) such as carpel tunnel syndrome are now a very common workers' compensation claim in jobs involving essentially the same movements over and over again. Digital Equipment lost a large class action lawsuit in 1996 for RSI injuries a jury concluded had been caused by the design of their VDT keyboards. Similar lawsuits against several manufacturers are now pending.

Ergonomics is the science of designing work space and equipment to be as compatible as possible with the physical and psychological limits of people. Although the Clinton Administration has called for ergonomic regulations, there is great political resistance to any further workplace regulations from OSHA.

As of 1997, OSHA can now cite employers for hazards which may cause RSIs. Although a specific OSHA rule may never be implemented, OSHA can use the general duty clause of the law. Pepperidge Farm has been fined $310,000 based on an inspection of a Pennsylvania plant. In the appeal of the fine, a judge ruled that OSHA could use the general duty clause for the reported RSI.

In 1997, California became the first (and only) state in the nation to adopt safety standards designed to protect workers from repetitive motion injuries such as carpel tunnel syndrome. Applied to all California employers with 9 or more employees, the regulation require improved working conditions if employees suffer nerve, muscle or joint injuries as a consequence of repetitive motion. Workers can also demand that employers at least consider wrist guards, adjustable tables, increased breaks, and job rotation as ways of combating the injuries. The standards give the California OSHA broad authority to cite employers for noncompliance.

Employees should be properly trained in using ergonomic work methods and equipment to reduce the visual and muscular problems associated with VDTs. Visual problems can be minimized by correcting seat levels and angles, by using monitors that control contrast and brightness or have antiglare screens, and by lowering light levels in places where VDTs are used. Muscular and wrist problems can be reduced by using adjustable chairs, keyboard support equipment, and physical therapy for the eyes, hands, wrists, shoulders, and back. The World Health Organization (WHO) has adopted a standard that states workers should sit at least three feet away from the back of a terminal (where the radiation is generated).

While evidence on the physical effects of VDTs is questionable, the psychological stress related to work with VDTs is now well documented, because workers are concerned that increased usage could affect their health or offspring. It seems that the speed with which technology has evolved has not been matched by the dissemination of knowledge about health and safety issues related to its use.[80]

Occupational Stress

The shock of seeing a highly regarded National League umpire collapse and die on the field at Cincinnati's Riverfront Stadium on opening day of the 1996 baseball season turned the sports world's attention to questions about wellness and stress on the job. An autopsy established that Jerry McSherry, 51, died of severe coronary artery disease. He had an enlarged heart and a reoccurring weight problem. Richie Phillips, the head of the umpires' union, reported that Jerry brought "a lot of stress onto himself."

The description sounds both familiar and universal. Sky-high and rising stress levels have been blamed on work stressors such as the information age, widespread layoffs, global competition, NAFTA, as well as violent crime, immigration, or any other modern threat Americans zero in on.[81] Stress is making workers sick, increasing the potential for violence at work, and affecting productivity and accident rates. Job stress can also lead to alcohol and drug use and is a frequently cited problem in workers' compensation claims. Problem drinkers file five times more compensation claims and use three times more accident benefits than nonabusers.[82] Job stress costs corporate America an estimated $200 billion annually in absenteeism, lost productivity, accidents, and medical insurance. Worse, stress is contributing to the deaths of hundreds of workers every year. The Bureau of Labor Statistics' Census of Fatal Occupational Injuries shows that heart attacks were responsible for 2,631 occupational deaths in 1991–1993, or 67 percent of the 3,926 fatal occupational illnesses reported during that period. Ninety-four percent of the 2,631 were men. The highest concentration of deaths occurred among operators, fabricators, laborers, and service workers. The most common day of the week when fatal heart attacks occur, not surprisingly, is Monday.

Job stress has been defined as a "situation wherein job-related factors interact with a worker to change his or her psychological and/or physiological condition such that the person is forced to deviate from normal functioning."[83] Stress is considered to be a major problem for workers in today's turbulent and highly competitive environment, with its emphasis on cost control, reduced labor expense, and higher productivity. Stress should be distinguished from a **stressor,** which is the object or event that causes the stress. For example, the speculation that work with VDTs may be hazardous could be considered a stressor that may cause stress in some employees. Exposure to secondhand smoke, that may cause cancer, now serves as a stressor for many nonsmoking workers. Figure 14.8 presents a model of the antecedents, outcomes, and consequences of stress. Stressors can be found in the physical environment due to lighting or noise problems, temperature, or polluted air. We know that these potential stressors can have an interactive effect such that, for example, temperature combined with a noisy environment may cause even greater stress than the two sources independently.

Prolonged exposure to certain job demands has been linked to several measures of mental and physical stress as well as productivity problems and absenteeism. **Job demands** have been defined as psychological stressors, such as working too hard or too fast, having too much to do (role overload), or having conflicting demands from several sources (role conflict).[84] An individual may perceive role conflict when pressures from two or more sources are exerted such that complying with one source creates greater problems regarding another source. For example, workers may try to maintain a high quality standard while simultaneously trying to meet a very difficult quantity standard, or managers may attempt to hit a quota for production while reducing labor costs. Also, employees in matrix organizational structures may expe-

FIGURE 14.8
A MODEL FOR ORGANIZATIONAL STRESS RESEARCH

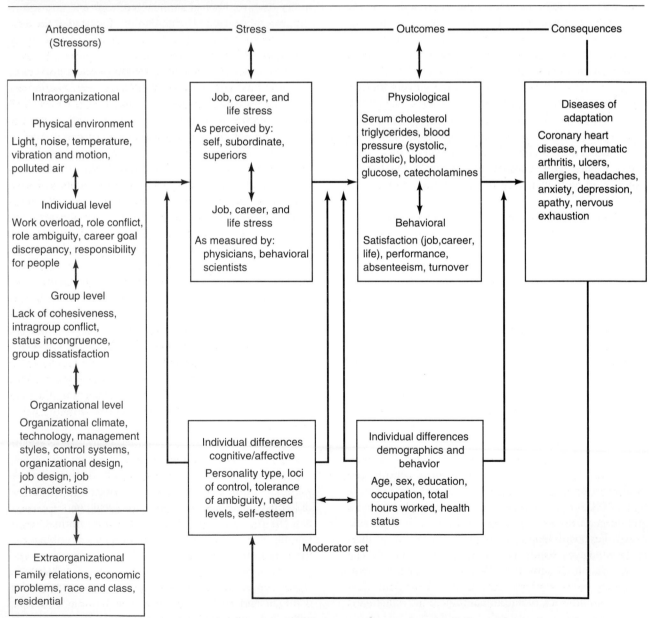

Source: J. M. Ivancevich and M. T. Matteson, Stress and work: A managerial perspective. Glenview, IL: Foresman, 1980. Reprinted with permission.

rience role conflict if they have two bosses; one in charge of their "line" job and one in charge of the "project" job or team they have been assigned to. Another source of stress is **role ambiguity,** in which workers simply do not understand what is expected on the job or where what is expected is contrary to what they think should be done. An example of role ambiguity occurs when a boss is vague about an employee's responsibilities or the time frame in which the employee has to complete specific tasks. Research on role ambiguity and conflict is plentiful. As in other areas related to stress, the reactions to the stressors tend to vary widely depending on an individual's characteristics. For example, people with Type A personalities suffer more stress and experience a greater number of health problems than do Type B people. Type A people tend to do just about everything quickly (walk, talk, eat) and have little tolerance for people who go at a more moderate pace.[85]

Other sources of individual stress include conflicts between job obligations and family obligations. Women in particular tend to experience this conflict. "Family responsibilities can place tremendous pressure on women. When both husband and wife have careers, the wife is often expected to keep her housekeeping role in addition to her work role . . . More and more Superwomen are now questioning their multiple roles. With this uncertainty comes more conflict and stress."[86] Dual-career couples, in particular, face increasing time pressures as they try to balance work and family responsibilities. As we discussed in Chapter 8, many corporations are aware of this extra burden on women and are providing employment options designed to reduce this source of stress. Companies such as DuPont, Merck, and General Mills offer family leave, flexible work schedules, and on-site day care. A 1991 Conference Board review of 80 studies found reduced turnover, absenteeism, and increased productivity in companies that help employees balance work with family obligations.[87] For example, Xerox, Tandem Computers, and Corning Inc. enabled their employees working in teams to develop their own schedules that would meet their personal needs while addressing their work demands. They found a decrease in absenteeism, and the teams became more effective, self-directed, and independent.[88]

The work group, unit, or organization can be a stressor as well, aside from the issues of role ambiguity and conflict. Particularly in this era of downsizing or "rightsizing," many U.S. corporations are feeling the competitive crunch by making hard decisions to reduce overhead costs. Supervisors and managers are being asked to make hard personnel decisions regarding employee cutbacks. As a result, employees worry more now that their jobs may be on the line. Survey data from IBM since 1988, for example, reflect the downturn in the company's fortunes and managers' pressures to make substantial labor cutbacks through unfavorable reassignments and terminations. Jobs affected by recent major changes are generally stressful. If a company was purchased, has gone through a layoff or downsizing, imposed mandatory overtime, or has undergone a major reorganization, the employees, regardless of rank, are likely to have high levels of stress.

Some jobs are more likely to cause stress than others. Air traffic controllers, for example, report higher rates of ulcers, chest pains, and headaches than other workers and after only three years of work! While high-level executives lament their stressful responsibilities, the evidence regarding stress-related illnesses does not support the belief that higher-level management jobs are more stressful than other jobs. In fact, one large-scale study found that rates of coronary heart disease were greater at lower management levels.[89] Researchers hypothesize that stress is a function of high job demands in combination with low control at work. So when an individual has little authority to make decisions in a highly demanding job, the most negative aspects of stress should be expected.[90] Since executives often have more control over their work demands than employees, they may experience relatively less stress. Of course, with all the recent firings of CEOs and downsizings of middle-level managers, their stress levels may have increased.

Because stress and fatigue cannot be measured by biochemical testing, some employers have turned to testing an employee's ability to perform a safety-sensitive job. These job performance exams are generally computer-based and check an employee's visual acuity, coordination, and reaction time. Even though such exams were developed nearly 30 years ago by NASA to check the performance skills of astronauts, the technology was first made available to the general public just a few years ago. An example of a test is one that measures responses while the test subject tries to keep a diamond-shaped cursor aligned with the center of the computer screen. The cursor moves randomly and quickly, so the subject's responses must be fast and accurate. This test takes 30 seconds to complete and employees have eight chances to match or beat their baseline score. If they fail, then the employer can reassign them for the day or request that they take the day off.

A relatively new term for one type of stress is **burnout,** which reflects an emotional reaction in people who often work in human services and work closely with people. Burnout is common among police officers, teachers, social workers, and nurses. People experiencing burnout may develop cynical attitudes toward their jobs and clients and may feel emotional exhaustion, depersonalization, and a sense of low personal accomplishment or control.[91] But burnout is not inevitable in these jobs. A stress reduction program for public school teachers found that the effects of burnout could be reduced using positive feedback about teacher competencies.[92]

To address stress-related issues and other employee concerns in the United Kingdom, the Working Time Directive became effective in November 1996. This directive contains specific rules relating to all workers, additional rules for those working at night, and general rules on health and safety. The time that an employee spends at work is restricted to 48 hours a week, averaged over a period of up to four months.[93]

As noted in Figure 14.8, there are psychological, physiological, and behavioral consequences of stress. However, reactions to the same stressors vary greatly with the individual. Although individual reactions are difficult to predict, it is known that some people can handle tremendous amounts of stressors without any manifest stressful reactions. Other people fall apart, become violent, or turn to drugs or alcohol. Psychological stress may be manifested in anxiety, depression, irritability, and hostility and may also have physiological consequences such as high blood pressure, numbness, fatigue, and heart problems. Of course, the stress may also affect work performance, work attendance, and accident rates. These consequences can have profound (and costly) organizational consequences, including union organizing, workers' compensation, poor work products, and legal problems. In 1991, for example, McDonald's Corporation was held liable for a fatal crash caused by a 19-year-old who had worked a double shift. More recently, a social worker was paid damages after a legal battle to prove that his job caused him to have two nervous breakdowns, brought on by stress and his "impossible workload."

Figure 14.9 provides a framework of specific intervention programs and the stress outcomes that they may be directed toward. The three intervention targets in the figure correspond to (1) changing the degree of stress potential in a situation by reducing the intensity or number of stressors present, (2) helping employees to modify their appraisal of potentially stressful situations, and (3) helping employees to cope more effectively with the consequences of stress. Stress management and reduction programs are common in industry today. At Motorola, for example, programs emphasize exercise, nutrition, relaxation techniques, time management, and self-awareness. Cigna Corporation provides employees with breaks during which they can relax with new age music, meditation, and stretches or increase their energy level by listening to a tape of empowering thoughts or getting up and moving to upbeat music. Cigna even has a massage therapist who will come to an employee's desk to soothe tense neck muscles. Other organizations have attempted to reduce physical stressors by redesigning the workplace. Role ambiguity and role conflict can often be reduced by interventions following a job analysis and survey research. Studies point to immediate supervisors as a primary source of stress among workers. Survey data may help to pinpoint unit-level problems be-fore they result in serious organizational difficulties such as termination, absences, and disabilities.

Many organizations incorporate their stress reduction programs into comprehensive employment assistance programs. We will examine these programs next.

Employee Assistance Programs

As we discussed in Chapter 10, EAPs are a growing form of employee benefit that provide help to over 26 million U.S. employees for a variety of problems. For example, executives at Banc One Financial Services receive in-office counseling.[94] Lucent Technologies also set up its own internal counseling divisions to coach difficult workers. In San Francisco, companies pay Noon-Time University $8,000 for six three-hour lunchtime training sessions for 20 to 24 employees.[95] There are over 10,000 organizations with formal EAPs treating job stress, alcoholism, and other forms of drug abuse, marital and emotional difficulties, and financial problems. In 1991 over 36 percent of American workers had access to EAPs, and more than 75 percent of all *Fortune* 500 companies offered EAPs for their employees.[96] A recent poll of *Employee Benefit Plan Review* subscribers revealed that 32 percent of employees turned to EAPs because of corporate restructurings and downsizings. The number of EAPs has increased because the thousands of companies with federal contracts must adopt formal antidrug policies under the provision of the 1988 Drug Free Workplace Act. Many EAPs are also equipped to handle problems related to AIDS and workplace violence. In addition, EAPs can be designed to provide physical help with controlling blood pressure, weight, and smoking.

The general goal of an EAP is to provide treatment for employees who are having problems so they can return to normal, productive functioning on the job. While the vast majority of EAPs are in large organizations, even small businesses are getting involved with EAPs through consortiums with other small businesses. Most EAP referrals are based on an assessment of job performance and referrals by supervisors, although many employees also volunteer to attend EAPs. EAP staff often provide training for managers and supervisors on making "constructive confrontations" with their employees regarding work-related deficiencies. Supervisors are thus exempted from trying to diagnose the causes of a problem. Getting at the cause of the performance problem is left to professionals (e.g., people with graduate degrees in psychology and social work), who are trained to make such diagnoses and treat people accordingly. Most EAPs are based on the principle of voluntary participation. Labor unions generally support drug counseling and EAPs but oppose coercion to participate in such programs as a condition of employment, as well as opposing drug testing of any kind.[97]

An EAP is typically run by an outside health service

FIGURE 14.9
STRESS MANAGEMENT INTERVENTIONS: TARGETS, TYPES, AND OUTCOMES

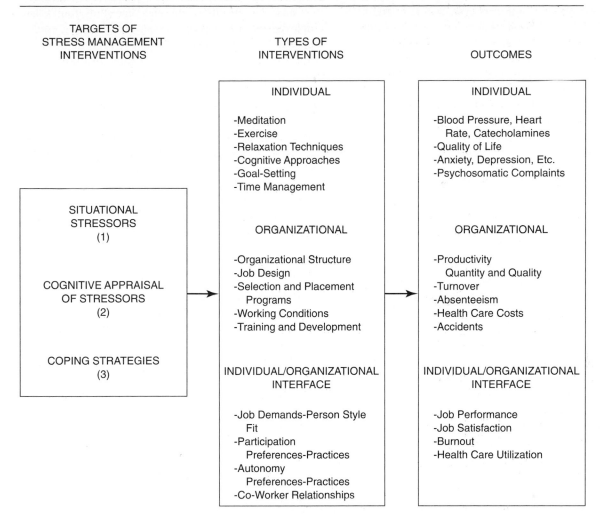

Source: J. M. Ivancevich, M. T. Matteson, S. M. Freedman, and J. S. Phillips, Worksite stress management interventions. *American Psychologist,* February 1990, pp. 252–261.

organization, with an average cost of about $35 per employee per year. It is estimated that U.S. companies spend almost $1 billion each year on EAPs. The limited data on the effects of EAPs are quite positive. Adolph Coors Company reported savings of $6 for every $1 spent on the EAP. AT&T reported a savings of almost $600,000 as a result of its EAP activities. In one study of 110 employees, 85 percent of poor performers were judged to be no longer poor after the EAP. The rate of improvement for all participants was 86 percent. There was a significant decrease in the number of accidents in which these individuals were involved. Absenteeism also went down as did visits to the medical department. In short, at least for this sample of AT&T workers, the EAP was a great success.[98] United Airlines estimates that for every $1 spent for its EAP, it realizes savings of $16.35 through reduction in employee absences.[99]

GM reports that about 10 percent of its 600,000-employee workforce is experiencing alcohol or other drug-related problems, so GM emphasizes substance abuse in its EAP programs. As we stated earlier, many other organizations have responded to problems of substance abuse by implementing drug testing programs, which may involve entry-level screening for drug usage as well as random drug testing of current employees. Such policies are controversial but, in most circumstances, legal. Under the doctrine of employment at will, employers may dismiss employees for any reason other than those covered by statute (e.g., race, sex, religion, age, national origin, disability). Firing a non-union employee who fails a drug test is legal in almost every state and has been done thousands of times. However, most HRM experts take the position that termination should be a last resort after an attempt at intervention through an EAP, which should be prompted by unacceptable performance.

Employee Wellness or Fitness Programs

Due to the staggering health care costs we described in Chapter 10, many companies have set up wellness, fitness, or health management programs for employees. Unions have also been increasingly involved in promoting health and safety protections for their members.[100] **Wellness** is defined as a "freely chosen lifestyle aimed at achieving and maintaining an individual's good health."[101] Companies have discovered that the best way to reduce health care costs is to keep employees healthy. In general, healthy employees are more productive than unhealthy ones. Research shows that employees who set specific, obtainable goals related to improving their health often increase their perceived control and confidence to overcome barriers to performing healthy behaviors.[102] As long as goals are reasonable and employees experience success in their first few attempts at reaching their goals, a motivational change is brought about by this mastery. This motivational change involves increasingly higher levels of control and confidence, especially over work-related barriers (i.e., work piling up while the employee uses release time to exercise).

A majority of U.S. corporations now offer some form of formal wellness programs involving health assessment, exercise planning, counseling or support groups, stress management, weight control, and smoking cessation. Some insurance companies offer reduced rates for organizations with organized wellness programs.[103]

At New York Telephone, the wellness program focuses on the following major areas of health: smoking cessation, cholesterol reduction, alcohol abuse control, fitness training, stress management, and cancer screening. New York Telephone reported a savings of almost $3 million in reduced absences and medical treatment because of its wellness program. Kimberly-Clark offers a variety of health-related programs, including an exercise routine available at the fitness center on the premises, weight control consultation, blood pressure analysis and treatment, and nutritional advice. These programs are available to the company's entire workforce, and 88 percent of employees are enrolled in one or more of the programs. While the cost is high (about $435 per employee per year), the director of the program is certain the bottom line will support its effectiveness. There are many other success stories. IBM, Johnson & Johnson, Tenneco, Campbell Soup, and Xerox all report success with their fitness and wellness programs. One Xerox work location provides a soccer field, an Olympic-size pool, two gyms, tennis courts, a weight room, and over 2,000 acres of running space. Johnson & Johnson reports savings of $378 per employee as a result of its comprehensive wellness program, which it now also administers for 60 other companies. The goals of the program are basic: stop smoking, eat fruit and fewer fatty foods, get some exercise, and buckle up.[104]

The effectiveness of Pacific Bell's FitWorks health promotion program was assessed in four of its construction sites. The results of the one-year study found that employees who had access to physical training equipment had lower heart rates after step tests, greater lower-body muscular endurance, and greater flexibility than those who did not work out.[105] John Alden Financial has found that corporate wellness programs boost productivity, lower health care costs, and help firms attract and retain top-quality employees.[106] This organization's wellness activities include a health fair, an employee-published cookbook of nutritious recipes, numerous sports clubs, substance abuse prevention campaigns, an in-house fitness center, and many health-related seminars and workshops. Provided below are some tips for launching wellness programs based on the experience of John Alden Financial and other corporate members.[107]

- Start small: Launch simple programs such as blood pressure and cholesterol screening or distribute information about nutrition to employees.
- Delegate responsibility: Let employees plan and implement activities and conduct a survey to assess employees' health and recreational interests.
- Schedule activities around the workday: Schedule events before work, during lunch, or after work so the activities do not take employees away from their regular duties.
- Learn from other companies: Find out what other firms in the area or industry have done and learn from their experiences.
- Take advantage of community services: Many local health agencies and nonprofit organizations provide health screenings and information for free.

SUMMARY

Top management is taking a more active role in improving the health and safety of workers. Figure 14.10 summarizes the managerial steps for improving the work environment as recommended by one expert.[108]

The first step (affirming management commitment) means that management must make resources available for health and safety issues. Research shows that plants with superior health and safety records spend more money on health and safety. In addition to management commitment to safety, it is also crucial to have employee participation. This can be done by empowering employees to take ownership in the safety of the organization.[109] The second step for improving the work environment calls for a clearly established policy and results-oriented set of objectives for health and safety. Third, managers should perform planned and unplanned inspections of work sites to assess compliance. Fourth, as the safety manager at DuPont states, "When plant managers begin

FIGURE 14.10
EIGHT ESSENTIAL STEPS IN IMPROVING THE WORK ENVIRONMENT

1. Affirm management's commitment to a safe and healthy environment.
2. Review current safety objectives and policies.
3. Conduct periodic evaluations and inspections of the workplace.
4. Identify potential and existing work hazards in the areas of safety and health.
5. Identify the employees at risk.
6. Make the necessary improvements in the workplace.
7. Prepare and conduct preventive programs.
8. Monitor the feedback results and evaluate costs.

Source: S. Greenfeld, *Management's safety and health imperative: Eight essential steps to improving the work environment.* Minerva Occasional Paper Series (2.9). Cincinnati, OH: Xavier University, 1989.

to audit people and their actions, dramatic changes occur . . . Audits foster fewer unsafe acts." Managers should also establish an atmosphere in which employees feel comfortable reporting unsafe working conditions so that all potential hazards can be identified. Managers must form a partnership designed to maximize employee safety and health and acknowledge that a trained, safe workforce is the most productive workforce an employer can have.[110] The fifth step is to identify particular employees at risk so that appropriate training and policies can be developed. The development of an employee database or the use of a comprehensive personnel inventory (see Chapter 5) could assist with this effort. The sixth step for enhancing managerial attention is to make corrections in the work environment based on the research and employee data analysis. This may include a number of preventive measures. With the proliferation of complaints regarding carpal tunnel syndrome and related stress symptoms, this step may include ergonomics or work station redesign. Where the job situation contributes to an unsafe environment, management should take the appropriate action. The seventh step calls on management to prepare and conduct preventive programs. Aggressive antidrug policies, EAPs, threat management teams, and wellness programs are examples. The final step is for management to evaluate actions and feed the results back to employees. An assessment of the monetary value of health and safety programs is one necessary component of this step. Many companies report considerable savings from such programs.

Gillette saved over $1.2 million from its health and safety programs. Procter & Gamble reported direct cost savings in excess of $1.5 million. A. M. Castle & Company in Franklin Park, Illinois, started a safety program in 1980. Since then it has reported fewer injuries and reduced lost time, as well as significant cost savings for the

company. In addition, employees are involved in the program, which covers a wide range of health and safety issues, including alcohol and drug abuse, fleet safety, and equipment maintenance.[111] Exeter Healthcare, Inc., implemented a program called PEPS—Patient/Resident, Employee, Plant Safety. It took place in four phases: program development, implementation, outcome analysis, and program enhancements. Within the first eight months of the program, patient/resident falls were reduced 40 percent in one quarter with further reductions in following quarters. Exeter's work-related costs were far below what was ever anticipated, and work injuries and related costs showed an 85 percent drop in one year.[112] Milliken & Company's emphasis on employee participation in safety has elevated the textile firm to unrivaled status in American industry. Of Milliken's 55 U.S. facilities, 30 have been judged good enough for inclusion in OSHA's elite voluntary protection program. The basic belief of the programs is that all incidents can be prevented. Star status is awarded to those sites that excel in these areas: management commitment and planning, hazard assessment, hazard correction and control, safety and health training, association awareness/ownership participation, and safety and health process assessments. One of the most recent Star designees is Milliken's New Holland Plant in Gainesville, Georgia.[113]

A more aggressive OSHA, new regulations, the threat of heavy fines and possible criminal prosecution, staggering health insurance costs, and research that shows healthy employees are more productive have all contributed to the attention to health and safety issues in the workplace. New legislation shifting the burden of proof for violations of work practices are being drafted.[114] More companies are developing formal health and safety policies, and management is now more likely to be held accountable for accident rates and other health-related measures. In the next century, even greater interest in the subject and more programs that focus on employee behavior are likely. Drug testing, antismoking programs, threat management teams, EAPs, and wellness programs hold promise as methods that can contribute to a more productive and healthy workforce.

Employee health and safety are not simply issues of importance in the United States. Most other countries have some policies on these issues, and their rules are changing to reflect greater concerns among employees for injuries and illnesses. For example, in Ireland, in 1989 the Safety, Health, and Welfare Work Act was enacted. This set out provisions for establishment of the National Authority for Occupational Safety and Health to promote, encourage, and foster the prevention of accidents and injury to health at work. Under the act, the employer's duties are to provide: (1) a safe place at work, (2) safe equipment, and (3) personal protective equipment. These efforts initially cost the companies money, but over the long term have reduced premiums, absenteeism, and claims against the firms.[115] In Britain, an important case occurred in 1994; *Walker v. Northumberland County Council* extended the common law duty of an employer to provide a safe system of work for employees in terms of mental as well as physical health.[116] In Canada, the city of Toronto recently began a new program for its workforce of approximately 7,000. The goal of the new initiative is the successful return to work for employees with psychological disabilities (e.g., suffering from work-related stress). Toronto now provides a wide range of rehabilitation services for injured and ill employees.[117]

For U.S. HR professionals, a key element of HRM in a foreign country is employee morale. Companies operating in harsh and high-threat locations can maintain good morale and prevent unnecessary turnover by providing safe working and living conditions as well as basic comforts. HR professionals can prepare their employees if they have analyzed the working conditions in the other country and have developed plans to deal with potential illnesses or injuries.[118]

DISCUSSION QUESTIONS

1. Why is a 20-year-old with three years of experience more likely to be involved in an accident than a 30-year-old with three years of experience? After you develop your theory for this fact, explain how companies can intervene to reduce (or wipe out) the effect.

2. How could you as a manager develop a strategy for increasing employees' motivation to work more safely?

3. Devise a training program and a policy directed at increasing the physical fitness of your employees. Take a position on smoking, alcohol use, and other health-related matters, and state whether you would make the programs mandatory.

4. Do you think managers should be held criminally liable for health and safety violations? Should they go to jail for such violations? If so, under what conditions? If not, why not?

5. Do you support a policy of random drug testing for all employees? Explain.

6. Should a company be allowed to prohibit smoking or drinking alcohol on or off the job for its employees? Explain your answer.

7. Given the accumulated evidence on the effects of smoking, why hasn't OSHA taken steps to regulate smoking and second-hand smoke in the workplace?

8. What kinds of work-related factors affect employees' stress levels? What recommendations would you offer a company to manage the stress of its employees?

9. Compare and contrast employee assistance and wellness programs. What is the value of each for an organization?

10. Why has violence in the workplace become a larger problem for organizations? What recommendations would you offer to a company to ensure that it does not experience any violence? Be specific.

NOTES

1. Bureau of Labor Statistics (1995). *Statistics-occupational injuries and illnesses.* Washington, DC: Department of Labor; see also, DeWitt, K. (May 7, 1992). Senate panel hears of human tolls in workplace. *The New York Times,* p. C20, and *Accident Facts* (1994 edition). Chicago: National Safety Council, pp. 34–53.

2. Health concerns dominate construction lecture (1997). *Occupational Safety, 15*(1), 37.

3. Overell, S. (1997). CoSteel faces health and safety inquiry, *People Management, 3*(4), 7–8.

4. Garland, S. B. (Feb. 20, 1989). This safety ruling could be hazardous to employer's health. *Business Week,* p. 34.

5. See note 4; see also, Bureau of National Affairs (July 24, 1989). Michigan Supreme Court rules OSH Act does not preempt state proceedings. *BNA's Employee Relations Weekly, 7,* 945.

6. *52nd Yearbook of Labor Statistics* (1993). Geneva: International Labour Organization, pp. 1091–1108. See also, Elling, R. H. (1986). The struggle for workers' health: A study of six industrialized countries. Farmingdale, NY: Baywood Publishing, and Fisher, C. D.; Schoenfeldt, L. F., and Shaw, J. B. (1996). *Human Resource Management,* Boston: Houghton Mifflin Company.

7. Bureau of Labor Statistics (1991). *Survey of work-related health.* Washington, DC: Department of Labor.

8. Leonard, B. (February 1996). Performance testing can add an extra margin of safety. *HR Magazine,* pp. 61–64.

9. National Safety Council (1996). *Accident Facts;* see also, Hoskin, A. F. (May 1995). 1994 work-related deaths decline. *Safety and Health, 151*(5), 70–71; Labor Letter. (June 13, 1991). *The Wall Street Journal,* p. 1; and Karr, A. R. (May 2, 1990). White House backs raising penalties levied by OSHA. *The Wall Street Journal,* p. A8.

10. Colburn, L. E. (1995). Defending against workers' compensation fraud. *Industrial Management, 37,* 1–2.

11. Elsberry, R. B. (1996). Food for thought on plan sanitation. *Electrical Apparatus, 49*(12), 42–43.

12. Atkinson, L. (1996). Avoiding safety walkouts. *HR Focus, 73*(10), 20.

13. Vlasic, B. (July 23, 1989). Death in the workplace. *Detroit News,* p. 1.

14. Verespej, M. A. (May 21, 1990). OSHA goes to court.

Industry Week, pp. 91–92; see also, Redeker, J. R., and Tang, D. J. (April 1988). Criminal accountability for workplace safety. *Management Review,* pp. 32–36; and Glaberson, W. (Oct. 17, 1990). Court upholds prosecution of employer for job hazard. *New York Times,* p. A16.

15. Johnson, L. F. (1996). Selecting personal protective apparel. *Occupational Health and Safety, 65*(5), 67–76' see also, How to comply with OSHA PPE regs (1997). *BNAC Communicator, 15*(3) 10, and Balden, A. R. (1996). Hazard assessment and PPE selection. *Occupational Health and Safety, 65*(10), 154–160.

16. Jones, B. (1996). Health audits: The way to protect a major investment. *Works Management, 49*(6). 53–55.

17. See note 6, Fisher, Schoenfeldt, and Shaw (1996). See also, U.S. Department of Labor (June 1975). *OSHA Inspections.* Programs and Policy Series, OSHA.

18. *Marshall v. Barlow's, Inc.* (1978). *1978 OSH D., Sn. 22, 735.* Chicago: Commerce Clearing House.

19. OSHA issues final rule requiring employers to certify hazard corrections (1997). *BNAC Communicator, 15*(3), 10.

20. Occupational Safety and Health Administration (1996). *Voluntary Protection Programs,* Washington, DC.

21. See note 20.

22. *Whirlpool Corp. v. Marshall* (Feb. 26, 1981). *Daily Labor Report,* Washington, DC: Bureau of National Affairs.

23. *Accident Facts* (1983). Chicago: National Safety Council.

24. Occupational Safety and Health Administration (1996). Washington, DC.

25. See note 14, Verespej, (1990). See also, Brooks, J. (1977). *Failure to meet commitments in the Occupational Safety and Health Act.* Washington, DC: U.S. Congress, Committee on Government Operations, and Uzumeri, M. V. (1997). ISO9000 and other metastandards: Principles for management practice? *Academy of Management Executive, 11*(1), 21–36.

26. OSHA doing better job of finding most hazardous workplaces, acting administrator says (1997). *BNAC Communicator, 15*(3), 29.

27. National Safety Council (1994). *Accident Facts, 1994 Edition.* Itasca, IL: National Safety Council; Kilborn, P. (Nov. 6, 1989). Rise in worker injuries is laid to computer. *New York Times,* p. B1; see also, Swoboda, F. (Jan. 12, 1990). OSHA targets repetitive motion injuries. *Washington Post,* p. A10; Tuscano, G., and Windau, J. (1995). National census of fatal occupational injuries, 1994. *Job Safety & Health Quarterly, 6,* 28–34.

28. See note 1.

29. Geller, E. S. (1996). *The psychology of safety: How to improve behaviors and attitudes on the job.* Radnor, PA: Chilton Book Company; Geller, E. S. (1996). *Working safe.* Radnor, PA: Chilton Book Company; Geller, E. S. (1994). Ten principles for achieving a total safety culture. *Professional Safety, 39*(9), 18–24; Guastello, S. J. (1993). Do we really know how well

our occupational accident prevention programs work? *Safety Science, 16,* 445–463.

30. Ashford, N. A. (1977). Crisis in the workplace: Occupational disease and injury. *A Report to the Ford Foundation.* Cambridge, MA: MIT Press.

31. Schwartz, R. G., and Weinstein, S. M. (1996). Getting a handle on cumulative trauma disorders. *Patient Care, 30,* 118–120; Gangemi, R. A. (July 1996). Ergonomics: Reducing workplace injuries. *Inc.,* 92.

32. See note 20.

33. Taylor, A. (1997). Danger: Rough road ahead. *Fortune,* pp. 114–118.

34. Pierce, F. D. (1996). 10 rules for better communication. *Occupational Hazards, 58*(5), 78–80.

35. (June 12, 1997). It pays to be nice. *Wall Street Journal,* p. A1.

36. How to get management and employees on board (1996). *Occupational Health and Safety, 65*(1), 27.

37. Rogers, B. (February 1995). Creating a culture of safety. *HR Magazine,* pp. 85–88.

38. HSE does its homework for the first time (1996). *IRS Employment Review, 615,* S3.

39. VonderPorten, M. (1996). An interactive approach to safety training. *Occupational Health and Safety, 65*(6), 32–33; see also, Stewart, W. H.; Ledgerwood, D. W.; and May, R. C. (1996). Educating business schools about safety and health is no accident. *Journal of Business Ethics, 15*(8), 919–926.

40. Dunbar, R. (June 1975). Manager's influence on subordinate's thinking about safety. *Academy of Management Journal, 18,* 364–369.

41. OSHA rule requiring forklift training becomes final in September '97 (1997). *BNAC Communicator, 15*(3), 1, 28.

42. Nwaelele, D. D. (1996). Prudent owners take proactive approach. *Professional Safety, 41*(4), 27–29.

43. Van Houten, B. (1997). In the trenches. *Restaurant Business, 96*(5), 25–30.

44. Komaki, J.; Barwick, K. D.; and Scott, L. R. (1978) A behavioral approach to occupational safety: Pinpointing and reinforcing safe performance in a food manufacturing plant. *Journal of Applied Psychology, 63,* 434–445; see also, Dehaas, D. (1996). The problem with training. *OH and S Canada, 12*(6), 4.

45. LeBar, G. (1996). The age(ing) of ergonomics. *Occupational hazards, 58*(4), 32–33.

46. Breeding, D. C. (1996). Worker empowerment: A useful tool for effective safety management. *Occupational Health and Safety, 65*(9), 16–17.

47. Strahlendorf, P. (1996). What supervisors need to know? *OH and S Canada, 12*(1), 38–40.

48. Roughton, J. E. (1996). When contractors fall short. *Security Management, 40*(3), 68–71; see also, note 29.

49. Laws, J. (1996). The power of incentives. *Occupational Health and Safety, 65*(1), 24–28.

50. Wilson, J. C. (1996). Employee well-being is the real

prize. *Occupational Health and Safety, 65*(10), 168–169.

51. See note 49.

52. Minter, S. G. (1996). Putting incentives to work. *Occupational Hazards, 58*(6), S7–S9.

53. Case study in safety (1996). *Incentive, 170*(10), P22–P23.

54. See note 53.

55. See note 50.

56. Swearingen, M. H. (1996). Do safety incentive programs really help? *Occupational Health and Safety, 65*(10), 164–165.

57. Oswald, E. M. (1996). No employer is immune: AIDS in the workplace. *Risk Management, 43,* 18–21.

58. Smith, J. M. (March 1993). How to develop and implement an AIDS workplace policy. *HR Focus,* p. 15.

59. Feuer, D. (June 1987). AIDS at work: Fighting the fear. *Training,* pp. 61–71; see also, Elliott, R. H., and Wilson, T. M. (1987). AIDS in the workplace: Public personnel management and the law. *Public Personnel Management,* pp. 209–219; Breuer, N. L. (January 1992). AIDS issues haven't gone away. *Personnel Journal, 71,* 47–49; Elkiss, H. (1991). Reasonable accommodation and unreasonable fears: An AIDS policy guide for human resource personnel. *Human Resource Planning, 14,* 183–190; and Brown, D. R., and Gray, G. R. (Summer 1991). Designing an appropriate AIDS policy. *Employment Relations Today, 18,* pp. 149–155.

60. Kedjidjian, C. B. (December 1995). Say no to booze and drugs in your workplace. *Safety and Health, 152*(6), 38–41; see also, Labaton, S. (Dec. 5, 1989). The cost of drug abuse: $60 billion a year. *New York Times,* pp. B1, B30; Zigarelli, M. A. (1995). Drug testing litigation: Trends and outcomes. *Human Resource Management Review 5*(4), 267–288. Like, S. K. (Winter 1990–1991). Employee drug testing. *Small Business Reports, 16*(3), 347–358; and Lehman, W. E., and Simpson, D. D. (1992). Employee substance use and on-the-job behaviors. *Journal of Applied Psychology, 77,* 309–321.

61. Drug use on the job being probed (July 5, 1996). *Baltimore Sun,* pp. 9c, 11c.

62. American Management Association (1997). *The AMA handbook for developing employee assistance and counseling programs.* Washington, DC: AMA. See also, Cunningham, G. (1994). *Effective employee assistance programs.* Palo Alto, CA: Sage Publications, and Carroll, M. (1996). *Workplace Counseling.* Palo Alto, CA: Sage Publications.

63. See note 61.

64. See note 62.

65. See note 61; see also, Kirk, M. O. (Jan. 21, 1996). At work, a different test for drugs. *The New York Times,* F11.

66. See note 60, Zigarelli (1995); see also, Green, W. (Nov. 21, 1984). Drug-testing becomes corporate mine field. *The Wall Street Journal,* p. B1; Flynn, G. (April 1996).

Will drug testing pass or fail in court? *Personnel Journal,* 141–144.

67. deLisser, E. (July 8, 1994). U.S. health costs tied to smoking total $50 billion a year, CDC says. *The Wall Street Journal,* p. B3.

68. Litvan, L. M. (1994). A smoke-free workplace? *Nation's Business, 82,* 65; see also, Winslow, R. (March 6, 1990). Will firms shift costs to smokers? *The Wall Street Journal,* pp. B1, B4; Rundle, R. L. (Jan. 14, 1990). U-Haul puts high price on vices of its workers. *The Wall Street Journal,* pp. 1, B10; and Beck, J. (February 1994). Helping workers breathe free. *Journal of Commerce and Commercial, 399*(28163), 8A.

69. Yandrick, R. M. (July 1994). More employers prohibit smoking. *HR Magazine,* pp. 68–71.

70. Smith, L. (August 9, 1993). Can smoking or bungee jumping get you canned? *Fortune, 128*(3), 92; see also, Karr, A. R., and Gutfeld, R. (Jan. 16, 1992). OSHA inches toward limiting smoking. *The Wall Street Journal,* pp. B1, B7, and Bureau of National Affairs (1991). *Employment Guide.* Washington, DC: The Bureau of National Affairs.

71. National Crime Victimization Survey (March 1992). *Criminal victimization in the United States,* NCJ-145125.

72. Epstein, B. D. (1996). Preventing workplace violence. *Provider, 22,* 71–72; see also, Bureau of National Affairs. (April 26, 1993). Preventing workplace violence: Legal imperatives can clash. *Employee Relations Weekly, 11*(17), 451–452.

73. *National Institute for Occupational Safety and Health* (1992). Washington, DC: Government Printing Office.

74. Flynn, G. (1996). What can you do about weapons in the workplace? *Personnel Journal, 75*(3), 122–125.

75. Davies, E. (1996). How violence at work can hit employees hard. *People Management, 2*(18), 50–53.

76. Burroughs, S. M., and Jones, J. W. (April 1995). Managing violence: Looking out for trouble. *Occupational Health and Safety,* pp. 34–37.

77. Stage, J. K. (1997). Attack on violence. *Industry Week, 246*(4), 15–18.

78. Kinney, J. A., and Johnson, D. L. (1993). *Breaking point: The workplace violence epidemic and what to do about it.* Chicago: National Safe Workplace Institute.

79. Stevens, W. K. (March 14, 1991). Study backs safety of video terminals. *New York Times,* p. C21. See also, Sullivan, J. F. (Nov. 29, 1989). New Jersey acts on video terminals. *New York Times,* p. Y13; Gettings, L., and Maddox, E. N. (1989). Overview: When health means wealth. *The Human Resources Yearbook.* Englewood Cliffs, NJ: Prentice Hall, pp. 6.1–6.4.

80. Fine, B. (1997). Coping with computers. *Safety and Health Practitioner, 15*(3), 42–43.

81. See note 7. See also, Breo, D. L. (March 1986). *Living with stress. Chicago,* pp. 121–127, and Everly, M. (1996). Hire and fire culture causing high stress at work. *Safety and Health Practitioner, 14*(11), 12.

82. Madonia, J. F. (June 1984). Managerial responses to alcohol and drug abuse among employees. *Personnel Administrator,* pp. 134–139.

83. Beehr, T. A., and Newman, J. E. (1990). Job stress, employee health, and organizational effectiveness: A facet analysis, model and literature review. *Personnel Psychology, 31,* 665–699. See also, Ivancevich, J. M., and Ganster, D. C. (1987). *Job stress: From theory to suggestion.* New York: Haworth, and Schaubroeck, J.; Ganster, D. C.; and Fox, M. L. (1992). Dispositional affect and work-related stress. *Journal of Applied Psychology, 77,* 322–335.

84. Bruening, J. C. (1996). The ergonomics of the mind. Psychosocial issues in the office. *Managing Office Technology, 41*(4), 35–36.

85. Matteson, M. T.; Ivancevich, J. M.; and Smith, S. V. (1984). Relation of Type A behavior to performance and satisfaction among sales personnel. *Journal of Vocational Behavior, 25,* 203–214.

86. Loerch, K. J.; Russell, J. E. A.; and Rush, M. C. (1989). The relationship among family domain variables and work-family conflict for men and women. *Journal of Vocational Behavior, 35,* 288–308. See also, Allen, T. D.; Russell, J. E. A.; and Rush, M. C. (1994). The effects of gender and leave of absence on attributions for high performance, perceived organizational commitment, and allocation of organizational rewards. *Sex Roles, 31*(7/8), 443–464; Chusmir, L., and Durand, D. (May 1987). Stress and the working woman. *Personnel,* pp. 38–43.

87. Conference Board (1991). *Work schedules and productivity.* Atlanta: The Conference Board.

88. Azar, B. (1997). Quelling today's conflict between home and work. *APA Monitor, 28*(7), 1, 16.

89. Modic, S. (Feb. 20, 1989). Surviving burnout: The malady of our age. *Industry Week,* pp. 28–34; see also, Ganster, D. C., and Schaubroeck, J. (1991). Work stress and employee health. *Journal of Management, 17,* 235–271; and Cartwright, S., and Cooper, C. L. (1997). *Managing workplace stress.* Palo Alto, CA: Sage Publications.

90. Ganster, D. C., and Fusilier, M. R. (1989). Control in the workplace. In C. L. Cooper and I. T. Robertson (eds.), *International Review of Industrial and Organizational Psychology.* Chichester, England: Wiley, pp. 235–280.

91. Gordes, C. L., and Dougherty, T. (1993). A review and integration of research on burnout. *Academy of Management Journal, 18,* 621–656.

92. Russell, D. W.; Altmaier, E.; and Velzen, D. V. (1987). Job-related stress, social support, and burnout among classroom teachers. *Journal of Applied Psychology, 72,* 269–274. See also, Cherniss, C. (1992). Long-term consequences of burnout: An exploratory study. *Journal of Organizational Behavior, 13,* pp. 1–11, and McKeown, S. (1996). Stress: No quack cures just sensible management. *Works Management, 49*(9), 60–63.

93. Arkin, O. (1997). Time to take account of work, rest, and play. *People Management, 3*(2), 47–48.

94. Buskin, J. (July/August 1997). Executive Prozac. *Working Women,* p. 22.

95. See note 94.

96. Feldman, S. (February 1991). Today's EAPs make the grade. *Personnel, 68,* 3; see also, Spangler, J. (June 29, 1992). Assistance available for those under stress. *Amoco Torch,* pp. 1–2.

97. Leonard, B. (July 1993). The tough decision to use confidential information. *HR Magazine,* pp. 72–75; see also, Schultz, E. E. (May 26, 1994). If you use firm's counselors, remember your secrets could be used against you. *The Wall Street Journal,* p. C1.

98. Gaeta, E.; Lynn, R.; and Grey, L. (May–June 1982). AT&T looks at program evaluation. *EAP Digest,* pp. 22–31; see also, Freudenheim, M. (Nov. 13, 1989). More aid for addicts on the job. *New York Times,* pp. 27, 39.

99. See note 79.

100. Pynes, J. E. (1996). The two faces of unions. *Journal of Collective Negotiations in the Public Sector, 25*(1), 31–43.

101. Health Insurance Association of America (1983). *Your guide to wellness at the worksite.* Washington, DC: Health Insurance Association of America, p. 3.

102. Harrison, D. A., and Liska, L. Z. (1994). Promoting regular exercise in organizational fitness programs: Health-related differences in motivational building blocks. *Personnel Psychology, 47,* 47–71.

103. Wolfe, R. A.; Ulrich, D. O.; and Parker, D. F. (1987). Employee health management programs: Review, critique, and research agenda. *Journal of Management, 13,* 603–615; see also, Erfurt, J. C.; Foote, A.; and Heirich, M. A. (1992). The cost-effectiveness of worksite wellness programs for hypertension control, weight loss, smoking cessation, and exercise. *Personnel Psychology, 45,* 5–27, and Moore, T. L. (1991). Build wellness from an EAP base. *Personnel Journal, 70,* 104.

104. Helmer, D. C., Dunn, L. M., Eaton, K., Macedonio, C., and Lubritz, L. (1995). Implementing corporate wellness programs. *AAOHN Journal, 43,* 558–563; see also, Erfurt, A. E.; Dunham, R. B.; and Heirich, M. A. (1992). The cost-effectiveness of worksite wellness programs for hypertension control, weight loss, smoking cessation, and exercise. *Personnel Psychology, 45,* pp. 5–27.

105. Petersen, C. (1996). Work-hardening program pays big dividends. *Managed Healthcare, 6*(12), 43.

106. Epes, B. (August 1995). Start an employee wellness program. *Training and Development,* pp. 12–13.

107. See note 106.

108. Greenfeld, S. (July 1989). Management's safety and health imperative: Eight essential steps to improving the work environment. *Occasional Paper 2.9.* Cincinnati, OH: Xavier University, Minerva Education Institute. See also, LaBar, G. (1996). Safety gets down to

business. *Occupational Hazards, 58*(8), 23–28; Note 29.

109. Jonas, P. (1996). The missing letter in TQM. *Occupational Health and Safety, 65*(3), 18–19.

110. Nwaelele, O. D. (1996). Prudent owners take proactive approach. *Professional Safety, 41*(4), 27–29.

111. Lamb, M. R. (1996). Safety is all in a day's work at A. M. Castle, *Metal Center News, 36*(10), 42–50.

112. Palmer, M. (1996). Now it's safety first. *Nursing Homes, 45*(8), 29–36.

113. McCurry, J. W. (1996). Milliken & Co.: Textile's king of safety. *Textile World, 146*(11), 76–80.

114. Sand, R. H. (1996). Recent developments: OSHA prosecutions and asbestos class actions. *Employee Relations Law Journal, 22*(3), 149–155.

115. Costello, A. (1996). Your health is your wealth. *Accountancy Ireland, 28*(6), 10–12.

116. Stress in the workplace (May/June 1996). *British Journal of Administrative Management,* pp. 8–9.

117. Ritcy, S. (1996). Psychological job matching. *OH and S Canada, 12*(5), 50–56.

118. Pasquarelli, T. (1996). Dealing with discomfort and danger. *HR Magazine, 41*(10), 104–110.

A P P E N D I X

ASSESSMENT GUIDELINES FOR SELF, PEER, AND DESIGNATED ASSESSORS

Appendix A presents the material necessary for assessments of your performance in the individual and group exercises. Your instructor has elected to use either (1) the "certified assessor" approach, in which certain students are designated to serve as assessors for specific exercises, or (2) the self/peer assessments, which are completed by group members at the conclusion of an exercise.

The certification process usually entails the designated assessors' being examined on the written responses to the exercise before the day on which the exercise is to be done in class. Assessors should receive specific feedback on their written responses and have a clear understanding of appropriate responses to the exercises.

Your instructor may elect to use the self/peer approach to assessment in addition to or as an alternative to the certified assessor approach. Regardless of the approach your instructor uses, students should become familiar with the competencies that are identified and defined in Figure A.2. Research has identified these competencies as critical for success in management. The exercises in this book are designed to enhance these

competencies as you learn, integrate, and apply the HRM content of each chapter. Read the assessor job description in Figure A.1 before you begin. Your instructor will provide additional instructions regarding self and peer assessments.

Prior to Observation

1. Review the materials of the assigned chapter and the exercise to which you are assigned. Get very familiar with the recommended responses/answers and the five competencies defined in Figure A.2.
   —Analytical thinking
   —Leadership
   —Oral communication; presentation
   —Planning and organizing
   —Written communication

2. Review the behavior examples for each competency to gain further understanding of each competency and how each is exhibited in group or written responses (see Figure A.2).

FIGURE A.1
ASSESSOR JOB DESCRIPTION

The job of assessor will entail three major duties: observation, evaluation, and write-up. The actual tasks associated with each of these duties are listed below.

OBSERVATION

Watch participant activities and behaviors during an exercise.

Take notes on what is seen and/or heard.

Classify notes according to predefined competencies.

Write an exercise report that reflects the note-taking activity.

EVALUATION

Assign a numerical performance rating for each competency (based on notes taken).

WRITE-UP

Collect all data on each student's performance for each competency.

Synthesize data for each competency.

Complete a final report, in narrative form, highlighting the participant's strengths and weaknesses.

Instructions for Certified Assessors

After you are assigned to a group in class, review the exercise and competencies, including the behavioral examples for each competency. Before discussion begins, take a seat outside the circle of participants and do not discuss the exercise with group members. (You are strictly an observer/assessor.) Before discussion, quickly review each group member's individual exercise response. Make a note of the name of any group member who has not prepared a written response. Return the exercises to the participants.

3. Once discussion begins, observe the behavior of each discussant, keeping the competencies in mind as a frame of reference.

4. Record your observations on a plain sheet of paper, being careful to note who said what during discussion. Avoid any kind of evaluation at this point. (Do not use a complete sentence format.) Be as precise and complete as possible in recording your observations. Do not try to translate your observations into the competencies until the observation period is over. Your attention should be directed toward making accurate observations and keeping good notes.

5. At the conclusion of the discussion, collect all written responses and, if required, the group's written response. As you review your observations, assign a positive or negative value to each observa-

tion and determine what competency each observation illustrates. Next to each observation, enter the letter of the relevant competency, next to the + or − value.

6. Carefully review and critique each member's written responses, noting and correcting any misspellings, poor grammar, incomprehensible sentences, and so on.

7. Enter your name ("Observer") in the space provided. After reviewing the written responses and your notes on the discussion, summarize your observations in the space provided for feedback. The feedback should be constructive with (it is hoped) both positive and negative comments. Focus on the way in which the member performed in the group and completed the exercise. Be sure to record your name and the name of the participant.

8. After recording your feedback for each participant, make a rating on each student's performance.

To Rate Performance

Use the following scale to make your rating:

7 = Outstanding

6 = Very good

5 = Above average

4 = Satisfactory

3 = Below satisfactory

2 = Well below satisfactory

1 = Poor

NO = Not observed

A very small percentage of students should be rated at the 7 level. *This rating is reserved for only the very best performance for that competency.* **Most ratings should be at or near the 4 level.** Usually, however, when observing a group of about six people, close to the full range of performance levels should be observed and therefore rated. Rate all participants on one competency and then proceed to the next competency. Using the same rating scale, make an overall assessment of each participant.

WHAT IF A GROUP MEMBER DOESN'T PARTICIPATE? How do you rate someone who says virtually nothing in the group exercise? The answer to this question depends on the particular competency. Inactivity in the group would constitute a low score for *leadership* and *planning and organizing.* Inactivity would probably necessitate a rating of "Not observed" (NO) for the other competencies.

FIGURE A.2
CRITICAL COMPETENCIES

BEHAVIORAL EXAMPLES

ANALYTIC THINKING: Identifying the fundamental ideas, concepts, themes or issues that help to integrate, interpret, and/or explain underlying patterns in a set of information or data.

EXAMPLES

Effective

"Let's take turns stating our solution to the problem. We'll write down the points we agree upon and come up with a set of solutions that everyone will be happy with. How does that sound to everyone? Who wants to write them down?"

Gather everyone's ideas, key in on main concept, look for consensus or pattern of responses.

Ineffective

Everyone talks at once, or one person dominates, or no one wants to talk. Instead, socializes with group members.

"We don't know what is wrong with the problem. Let's just put anything down to get a grade," or,

"I skipped that problem because I didn't understand it."

LEADERSHIP: Utilization of appropriate interpersonal styles to stimulate and guide individuals or groups toward goal and/or task accomplishment.

EXAMPLES

Effective

"We've got a lot of great ideas, but we haven't heard from everyone yet. Let's write down what we have and then we'll add the rest of the ideas to our list."

Ineffective

"This case is just too complicated to come up with a solution. There is no way we can find the answer."

"I want to write down the solutions for everyone, that way my ideas will be sure to be included."

ORAL COMMUNICATION; PRESENTATION: Effective expression of ideas or viewpoints to others in individual or group situations (includes gestures, nonverbal communication, and the use of visual aids).

EXAMPLES

Effective

"I wrote down my thoughts on a solution to this problem. Let's take turns giving our ideas so that we can hear how everyone in the group feels about the problem. How does that sound to everyone? Who wants to go first?"

Ineffective

"I am not very good at speaking before a group. Let someone else who has more experience go first."

"I didn't come up with any ideas that the rest of the group hasn't already said. Take their ideas and write them down."

PLANNING AND ORGANIZING: Establishing a course of action for self and/or others to accomplish specific goals; planning proper assignments of personnel and appropriate allocations of resources.

EXAMPLES

Effective

"Our assignment calls for three HRM objectives. Let's talk about each objective individually and reach a consensus for each one. Who will volunteer to write them down. We better hurry, we only have 20 minutes to come up with our final list."

Ineffective

"We have too many opinions to formulate a final list. There is no way that we can decide on the three objectives in 20 minutes."

WRITTEN COMMUNICATION: Clear expression of ideas in writing and in appropriate grammatical form.

Utilized appropriate vocabulary, proper grammar, and correct spelling. Writes legibly.

FIGURE A.3
STUDENT SELF-ASSESSMENT LOG—RATINGS

Name _____

Exer. #	Analytical Thinking	Leadership	Oral Communication, Presentation	Planning & Organizing	Written Communication	Overall Assessment
Average						

Use the following rating scale to make your self-assessment: 7= outstanding; 6 = very good; 5 = above average; 4 = satisfactory; 3 = below satisfactory; 2 = well below satisfactory; 1 = poor.

B

EXERCISES

CHAPTER 1 EXERCISES

EXERCISE 1.1
AN INTERVIEW WITH AN HRM SPECIALIST

OVERVIEW

Chapter 1 presents an overview of the major activities of HR professionals today. As noted, HRM practitioners serve a variety of roles in organizations and are often classified as personnel directors, personnel managers, or HRM staff members. Individuals specializing in specific HRM job activities may be working in departments of training, labor relations, equal employment opportunity/affirmative action, compensation, or personnel research.

LEARNING OBJECTIVES

After completing this exercise, you should be able to:

1. Describe the major HRM responsibilities and activities of HRM professionals.
2. Explain some contemporary problems or difficulties encountered in HRM work.
3. Derive a list of major job activities useful for understanding the HRM domains.

PROCEDURE

Part A: Individual Interviews

Step 1. Read Chapter 1, paying particular attention to the discussion of HRM activities.

Step 2. Identify a practicing HRM or personnel professional or a line manager charged with HR activities and conduct a short interview to gather information about the person's job, his or her background, the organization, and the major job-related problems confronting the individual. An attempt should be made to interview a senior-level HR employee of the organization (e.g., the vice president of human resources or personnel director) either by phone or in person or a line manager who has significant HR responsibilities. Form 1.1.1 should be used as a format for conducting the interview and recording responses.

Part B: Group Discussions

Step 1. Students should assemble in class in groups of about six and review each individual report. The group should then identify common problems identified by the HR professionals. The characteristics of the organization should also be considered in the context of the problems. For example, are there any clear differences in problems confronting HRM professionals from service versus manufacturing organizations, or public- versus private-sector organizations? Students should have a clear understanding of the HRM professional's position and reporting relationships within the organization. The group should also attempt to identify the HRM activities discussed in Chapter 1 that are most related to the problems discussed. The problems should be assessed in the context of the trends discussed in Chapter 1. The group should also discuss the professional's views of how line management views the personnel function (e.g, cooperative, adversarial).

Step 2. A spokesperson should be designated to report each group's findings. After all spokespersons have presented their list of activities and difficulties, the class should suggest HRM strategies and programs that could address the problems raised. Trends related to the relationship between line management and HRM professionals should also be discussed.

FORM 1.1.1
INTERVIEW FORMAT FOR HRM PROFESSIONALS

Interviewer's Name _____   Interview date _____

Interviewee's Name _____   Company _____

1. How would you describe your organization? (e.g., public versus private, size, service/manufacturing, union/nonunion, major competitors, international business, growing, stagnant, downsizing).

2. What is your position title?

3. *a.* How many months/years have you occupied this position?

    b. How many months/years have you been employed by this company?

4. *a.* Briefly, describe your background (education, previous experience).

    b. Which aspects of your background are most directly related to your current job duties?

Name _____

5.   *a.*   How many employees do you directly supervise?

     b.   To whom do you report? What is his or her job title?

6.   Describe the organization's human resource or personnel department. How many employees are in the department? What are their main job duties if different from yours?

7.   What do you regard as your three most significant job responsibilities? Be as specific as possible. (The student may use Figure 1.3 (p. 7) if the HRM professional needs some suggestions.)

FORM 1.1.1 (*Continued*)

Name _____

8. What do you regard as the three most significant and specific HR challenges or difficulties you face in your current job responsibilities? For each, briefly describe the steps you have taken (or are planning to take) to deal with each of the problems.

    Challenges   **Action Strategies**

9. Describe your relationship with line management or if you are in line management, describe your relationship with HR. In general, how would you characterize the relationship (supportive, adversarial, cooperative)? Explain your answer. Give an example of where your interaction with either line management or HR was not favorable. Describe these circumstances in detail. How was the problem resolved? Give an example of a favorable interaction. Describe these circumstances in detail.

EXERCISE 1.2
AN ASSESSMENT OF CUSTOMER SATISFACTION AND THE RELATIONSHIP TO HRM ACTIVITIES

OVERVIEW

Chapter 1 described a variety of new challenges and trends confronting organizations today, many of which include concerns about productivity, product service and quality, and customer satisfaction.

As a practicing manager or an HRM specialist, you are likely to be asked to meet the human resource challenges related to productivity and/or customer satisfaction. Nine out of every 10 jobs are predicted to be in the services sector in the next 20 years. Yet the productivity figures reflect a generally slow rate of productivity growth for the services industry. Assessments of product and service quality are also unfavorable to the United States, and customer service indexes are low in most of the services sector, although they have improved in recent years.

Chapter 1 presents an argument and cites research that shows human resource activities have the potential to enhance customer satisfaction, increase productivity, and improve product and service quality. We emphasized that the most effective HRM programs are those in which the focus is always on the ultimate criterion of customer satisfaction. This exercise will focus on those HRM efforts that are customer oriented and will generate discussion about steps that can be taken to improve customer satisfaction.

LEARNING OBJECTIVES

After completing this exercise, you should be able to:

1. Identify some specific examples of how HRM can affect customer satisfaction.
2. View customer satisfaction from an HRM perspective such as the impact of employee attitudes, the diversity of worker characteristics and the job skills gap and how you as a manager or HRM specialist could improve customer satisfaction through HRM activities.
3. Identify HRM activities that may be useful for tackling problems related to customer satisfaction.

PROCEDURE

Part A: Individual Analysis

Think back over an experience you have had with any product or service. It could even be experiences related to your interaction with the university. Write three examples of what you regard as excellent customer service and three you regard as poor customer service. Write the three negative examples on Form 1.2.1 and the three positive examples on Form 1.2.2. After describing each experience, review the HRM activities discussed in Chapter 1 and form hypotheses as to what particular domains or activities may have been primarily responsible for the excellent or poor customer service. Generate a list of the possible causes. Be creative in your hypotheses and attempt to go beyond simple theories such as a "training" problem as the cause. Bring the completed forms to class for discussion.

On Form 1.2.3, write what you regard as your five absolute favorite products or services that you have actually purchased in any area. For example, both authors of this book consider the Calaway Great Big Bertha Titanium driver to be almost the greatest product ever produced even though they paid more for this one golf club than for their entire set of irons. They would definitely have the Great Big Bertha on the list. This can be any product, large or small, cheap or expensive. If you think a 99 cent Whopper is the best deal going, write this down. In the space provided, write a short explanation of why you regard each particular product or service as your favorite. Bring Form 1.2.3 to class.

Part B: Group Analysis

Approximately six people should be designated to discuss responses on Form 1.2.1 while the same number of students are designated as observers of the group. If possible, each observer should be assigned to observe the group performance of only one group participant. The observer should review the participant's Form 1.2.1 before group discussion. Each observer should use Form 1.2.4 as the context for observing group participation of the participant to whom he or she has been assigned. *Observers should review the directions for observation before the observation period. Form 1.2.4 should be completed by the observer immediately after group discussion is completed while the participant is completing Form 1.2.5 (self-assessment).*

All members of the first discussion group should also read each other's Form 1.2.1 and attempt to discern trends in the incidents. For example, was the dissatisfaction mainly caused for poor product or service quality? Was the product or service representative incompetent and not knowledgeable about the product or service? After identifying any trends in the dissatisfaction, discuss the HRM activities proposed as the major causes of the poor customer service. Generate a list of the most important HRM activities the group believes to be directly or indirectly responsible for the customer service problems. The group should attempt to reach consensus on the top three HRM activities that could be directed at correcting the customer service problems.

After about 15 minutes of discussion, each observer should evaluate the participant's performance in the group and each participant should complete the self-assessment on Form 1.2.5. The pairs should then switch roles and the new discussion group should discuss the responses on Form 1.2.2, also attempting to identify the major HRM activities thought to be the causes of the excellent customer services that were provided and the extent to which HRM was responsible relative to other organizational functions. The second group can use the first group's analysis as a starting point. Again, the group should attempt to reach consensus on the top three HRM activities thought to be responsible for the positive customer satisfaction.

Part C: Self- and Observer Assessment and Feedback Session

After completing the second group exercise, participants should make a self-assessment using the rating scale on Form 1.2.5 while the observer is completing Form 1.2.4. After Forms 1.2.5 and 1.2.4 are completed, students should pair off and take turns reviewing their respective self- and observer assessments. Discussion should then center on each individual's performance in the group, the written responses, areas of strength or weakness, and the rationale of their respective positions regarding HRM activities.

Name _____ Group _____

Think of three situations in which you felt very dissatisfied with the customer service you received. Describe each circumstance in some detail and consider the causes of the service in terms of possible HRM activities. What were you expecting and what did you receive? Answer the questions below for each situation:

1. Describe the organization (e.g., fast food, department store, university setting).
   Situation 1

   Situation 2

   Situation 3

2. Describe the incident and the poor service in some detail.
   Situation 1

   Situation 2

   Situation 3

3. What do you regard as the major causes for your dissatisfaction? To what extent do you believe HRM activities were related to the dissatisfaction? Specifically, which activities are most related to the customer service problem and how could HRM improve the service?
   Situation 1

   Situation 2

   Situation 3

Name _____   Group _____

Think of three situations in which you felt very satisfied with the customer service you received. Describe each circumstance in some detail and consider the causes of the service in terms of possible HRM activities. What were you expecting and what did you receive?

1. Describe the organization (e.g., fast food, department store, university setting).
    Situation 1

    Situation 2

    Situation 3

2. Describe the incident and the good service in some detail.
    Situation 1

    Situation 2

    Situation 3

3. What do you regard as the major causes of your customer satisfaction? To what extent do you believe HRM activities were related to your satisfaction? Specifically, which activities do you believe to be most related to the customer service you have received?
    Situation 1

    Situation 2

    Situation 3

Name _____

1. What do you regard as the most favorite product or service you have ever purchased?

   Explain why you regard this product or service so highly (be specific).

   What (if any) role did human resources have in making this product or service so good?

2. What do you regard as the least favorite product or service you have ever purchased?

   Explain why you regard this product/service so poorly (be specific).

   Do you think human resources had anything to do with the regard you have for this product/service?

Observer's name _____ Discussant's name_____ Group_____

Directions for observation: Get familiar with the 10 behaviors or activities listed below. Observe your designated discussant on the extent to which he or she exhibited these behaviors. *Rate the extent to which the participant exhibited the behaviors described below. Make your ratings in the space provided. Use the following scale to make your ratings:*

1. Not at all

2. To a little extent

3. To some extent

4. To a great extent

5. To a very great extent

x. Does not apply

To what extent did the participant:

_____ 1. Help establish a clear course of action to complete work?

_____ 2. Speak effectively in the group?

_____ 3. Argue persuasively for a point of view?

_____ 4. Present a point of view concisely?

_____ 5. Write clearly and concisely?

_____ 6. Show sensitivity to other group members?

_____ 7. Stimulate and guide group members toward resolution of the assignment?

_____ 8. Listen carefully to other opinions and suggestions?

_____ 9. Analyze all pertinent information carefully before taking a position?

_____ 10. Display a willingness to state a position in a complex situation?

Name _____

Rate the extent to which you exhibited the behaviors described below. Make your ratings in the space provided. Use the following scale to make your ratings:

1. Not at all

2. To a little extent

3. To some extent

4. To a great extent

5. To a very great extent

x. Does not apply

To what extent did you:

_____ 1. Help establish a clear course of action to complete work?

_____ 2. Speak effectively in the group?

_____ 3. Argue persuasively for a point of view?

_____ 4. Present your point of view concisely?

_____ 5. Write clearly and concisely?

_____ 6. Show sensitivity to other group members?

_____ 7. Stimulate and guide group members toward resolution of the assignment?

_____ 8. Listen carefully to other opinions and suggestions?

_____ 9. Analyze all pertinent information carefully before taking a position?

_____ 10. Display a willingness to state a position in a complex situation?

EXERCISE 1.2
ASSESSMENT QUESTIONS

Name _____ Group _____

1. Describe the experience you had in providing feedback on your designated discussant's performance. To what extent did you feel comfortable in that role?

2. How might that role be improved with better directions, better assessment devices, etc.?

3. How did you feel about receiving feedback on your group performance? To what extent did you find the feedback helpful? How might that process be improved?

4. Did this exercise give you a better understanding of the relationship between HRM-related activities and customer satisfaction? Explain your answer.

CHAPTER 2 EXERCISES

EXERCISE 2.1
HUMAN RESOURCE ISSUES AT VALLEY NATIONAL BANK*

OVERVIEW

Chapter 2 introduced you to the human resource issues that HRM professionals and general managers must deal with if they are to assist the organization in becoming competitive and in meeting its goals. This exercise enables you to further develop your analytical skills as you assess the human resource issues affecting competitiveness at Valley National Bank.

LEARNING OBJECTIVES

After completing this exercise, you should be able to:

1. Identify human resource issues that may affect organizational effectiveness and competitiveness.
2. Develop strategies for dealing with human resource concerns.
3. Conduct a SWOT analysis for HR problems.

PROCEDURE

Part A: Individual Analysis

Step 1. Read Chapter 2, paying particular attention to the human resource domains and issues in Figure 2.1 in the context of the discussion on competitive advantage.

Step 2. Read the background information on Valley National Bank provided in Exhibits 2.1 and 2.1.1. Conduct a SWOT analysis based on the information you have been given. Identify the human resource *domains* facing the vice president's department and under which of the HR domains each issue belongs. Outline some strategies for dealing with these issues using Figure 2.1 as a guideline. Develop a rank-ordered *chronological* priority list of the first three issues that require your attention. Provide a written justification for your recommendations. Enter your rank orderings and justifications in the space provided on Form 2.1.1. **Answer the assessment questions *before* class as well.**

Part B: Group Discussions

Step 1. In groups, identify what you believe to be the competitive advantage(s) of the accounting department. Review all individual 2.1.1 forms and the assessment questions and determine the human resource issues of greatest concern to the accounting department. Reach a consensus on the chronology of the top three issues that can affect the competitive advantage. Discuss why these issues must be resolved if the department is to assist the bank in becoming more competitive. Identify the benefits and drawbacks to each recommendation. Also, reach consensus on the four assessment questions as well.

Step 2. A representative from each group should present the consensus recommendations and rationale to the rest of the class.

Part C: (Optional)

Students should complete the self- and peer assessment instrument.

---

*Contributed by Dave Ulrich.

EXHIBIT 2.1
BACKGROUND INFORMATION FOR VALLEY NATIONAL BANK

RECENT BANK HISTORY

Valley National Bank is a relatively young financial institution with close to $10 billion in assets, although it shortly will acquire another bank to bring its size up to about $12 billion in assets. As a whole, there is a wealth of technical talent in the company, yet most of the experiences have been developed within the confines of $1 and $2 billion institutions. The managers and employees have not had much collective experience managing a $12 billion company. Senior managers currently recognize they must make some critical strategic decisions regarding the future of the bank if they are to remain competitive in the next decade.

Accounting Department

The vice president of accounting reports directly to the senior vice president of management accounting, who in turn reports to the controller of the company (see the condensed organizational chart in Exhibit 2.1.1). The vice president, Suzanne Roberts, was promoted into her current position to manage a department that the previous manager had let get out of control. Her job is to provide accounting software to line and staff management throughout the organization so that managers might be able to make better decisions in the daily operations of their respective departments. The software, although difficult to implement, has proven to be very useful in institutions with postures of high growth. The information provided by the programs is financial in nature and, for the most part, is the type of information that VNB bankers are not used to receiving. Therefore, her current charge is twofold: to educate the company in the use of the software so that the bank ultimately benefits in terms of bottom-line results and to use the software to identify those sectors of business in which the bank does exceptionally well so that better and more focused strategic decisions can be made.

As challenging as her stated primary job responsibilities are, Ms. Roberts believes that another issue she currently faces is getting the right people in the right places in her department so that they can accomplish their goals. When she came into the department, she quickly concluded that some of the best contributors in the department were also the lowest paid employees.

Bob Phillips was the former manager of the department.

Through a merger, he came to Valley National Bank to manage the department, having had experience supervising two people at his previous position. In his role as vice president of accounting, he was asked to supervise about 10 people. Over two years, things got so out of hand that his employees did not know what they were supposed to do, except in emergency situations, which seemed to be happening every day. Performance reviews of employees were late by up to six months. Naturally, employee morale was very low and attitudes toward the company became hardened. Good people quit the bank or transferred to other departments. Finding replacements for these individuals was done poorly; often the first person who walked in for the interview was hired. Today, there are several people working for the department who probably should never have been hired. Unfortunately, their options are such that it probably pays for them to stay rather than voluntarily leave.

Bob clearly lacked the organizational and planning skills needed to effectively manage his people. In addition, his weak interpersonal skills have created hard feelings among employees in the department. He usually can arrive at a very good financial/accounting solution to a problem and has an extensive knowledge of the software programs. However, he has a very difficult time working with other people to implement his solutions.

Needless to say, some employees resent that Bob is still paid a very good salary and given a good title to go with his general incompetence and reduced responsibilities. Ms. Roberts believes the company should sever its ties with Bob, but other external factors make this choice difficult. For example, Bob has faced some very severe personal and health problems since transferring to Valley National Bank.

Carla Goodman previously worked for Bob for about 15 years. When the accounting department at Valley National was established, she was placed in charge of several people and given a promotion of two pay grade levels. This decision proved to be disastrous because she could not (or would not) accept the responsibility of supervising and reviewing people. She was quickly relieved of these duties, but her salary grade level remained intact so that today she is overpaid for her overall responsibilities. Her title is such that it implies a lower pay level in the company, but it fools no one. She is somewhat

EXHIBIT 2.1.1
ORGANIZATIONAL CHART

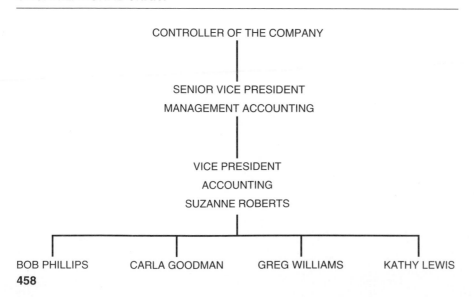

EXHIBIT 2.1 (*Continued*)

above average as a technical worker and understands the flow of transactions quite well. Currently, Ms. Roberts often has Carla working by herself because she doesn't make very good impressions with people. She tends to openly criticize the company, which draws concerns from other employees in the department. In fact, on occasion, she and Bob resort to shouting matches to get their respective points across to each other.

Greg Williams has been with the company about eight years and has worked for Ms. Roberts for about 2.5 years in various capacities. He has progressed in a very normal fashion in the bank, however, he has seen younger people such as Ms. Roberts move ahead of him on the organizational ladder. He expresses concern that his career may be leveling off unless something dramatic happens. He is not the quickest person to catch onto things in a technical sense, and he has a difficult time interacting effectively with people. This reduces his chances for a promotion. In general, he is a conscientious, mild-mannered employee who doesn't normally complain about things. He is good at taking orders, but not very good at handing them out.

Kathy Lewis is the most promising employee in the department today in terms of future potential within the company. She is technically sharp, with considerable knowledge of the new information systems, and has shown some promise in the effective management of people. She has been an employee of the company for a number of years and worked for Bob at the previous bank before the merger. She understands his odd nature. Her skills allow her to get more done than most people, and she is willing to put in extra hours to get things done. She did announce her resignation from the company at one time because of the mounting problems with the department, but a senior vice president talked her into staying by implying changes would be made sometime. Kathy is probably worth more to the bank than her current salary indicates, especially in light of the salaries of Bob and Carla. The normal guidelines should allow her to catch up in the next one to two years. She probably could also gain from receiving experience in other departments, but Ms. Roberts recognizes that she could not afford to let Kathy go because of the lack of depth with the other employees.

Overall, things are probably not as bad as they may appear to be. Ms. Roberts does, however, get concerned from time to time about the general lack of depth in the department as the rest of the bank looks to the department to help the bank become more competitive. Ms. Roberts has met with Mr. Sterrett of the HRM Department, who has recommended that Bob be terminated immediately but that Carla should be retained because of a possible sex discrimination lawsuit.

Name _____   Group _____

First issue in need of attention:

    Justification:

    Action to be taken:

    What is the HR domain?

Second issue in need of attention:

    Justification:

    Action to be taken:

    What is the HR domain?

Third issue in need of attention:

    Justification:

    Action to be taken:

    What is the HR domain?

SWOT ANALYSIS

Name _____   Group _____

List the potential internal strengths at Valley National.

List the potential internal weaknesses at Valley National.

FORM 2.1.1 (*Continued*)

List the potential external opportunities at Valley National.

List the potential external threats at Valley National.

Name _____   Group _____

1. Do you agree or disagree with the recommendation of Mr. Sterrett? Explain your position. How would you respond to Mr. Sterrett's recommendations?

2. What other information would be helpful in preparation for recommending action to be taken?

EXERCISE 2.1 (*Continued*)

3.   What steps would you take to determine the legality of your action?

4.   What is "unique" about VNB and how could the "uniqueness" give the bank a competitive advantage?

EXERCISE 2.2
THE COMPETITIVE ADVANTAGE OF MARRIOTT CORPORATION*

OVERVIEW

In 1997, Marriott Corporation employed approximately 265,000 employees. From 1964 through 1997, Marriott had been one of the most successful firms in the United States and ranked in the top 20 percent of *Fortune*'s 1997 rankings of America's most admired companies. It had established a strong presence in a variety of service industries: hotels, airline food service, business food service, family dining, and contract services. A key to Marriott's success in each of the lines of business came from Marriott's deserved reputation of providing outstanding service to guests and customers. As a result of its excellent service, the Marriott Corporation was considered by customers as the "preferred provider" or the provider customers thought of first when making lodging or food choices.

At a management planning meeting, Marriott executives decided a second major emphasis was necessary for continued success. Along with being the "provider of choice," Marriott decided to become the "employer of choice." It was felt that if Marriott could not continue to attract, retain, and manage its employees, then the rapid growth would slow. As Marriott Corporation approaches the 21st century, managing employees and becoming the employer of choice is not an option; it is seen as central to business success and should be directly linked to the "provider of choice" emphasis. For example, one of Marriott Corporation's central challenges has been to ensure that qualified employees join and stay in the business. Hiring more mature employees, allowing for part-time work schedules, and bussing employees from some distance to the work setting have become staffing practices designed to help enhance Marriott's organizational capability.

LEARNING OBJECTIVES

After completing this exercise, you should be able to:

1. Identify a number of specific HRM practices that can be pursued by Marriott to create and sustain its goal to be the "employer of choice."
2. Understand the connection between the goal to be the "employer of choice" and the "provider of choice."

PROCEDURE

In the context of the discussion on competitive advantage, what specific steps should Marriott take to create and sustain its image as the "employer of choice"?

Part A: Individual Analysis

Step 1. Before class, generate a list of three actions the organization can take that will directly contribute to this goal and fit within the framework of competitive advantage. Bear in mind that competitive advantage does entail labor costs so your recommendations must be made in the context of estimated relative costs for the various actions the organization could take. Try to think of organizational characteristics and policies to which you would be attracted as a recent college graduate. In other words, to what characteristics of an employer and a job are you most attracted? How could Marriott use this information to meet its objectives in the context of cost control, the "provider of choice" emphasis, competitive advantage, and total customer satisfaction?

Step 2. Prepare your priority list on Form 2.2.1 and provide a concise written justification for your rank ordering of actions. **Complete the assessment questions before class.**

Part B: Group Analysis

Step 1. In groups of about six people, exchange your priority lists so that all group members have had an opportunity to review each one. Attempt to reach consensus on a rank ordered list of three specific actions the Marriott Corporation should take to contribute to its goal of becoming the "employer of choice" in the context of one or more principles of competitive advantage and in terms of the "provider of choice" emphasis. How could the HRM systems contribute to the "employer of choice" image while at the same time developing human resource competencies?

Step 2. A group leader will be designated who will present the consensus view of the group. Discussion should focus on the extent to which the various groups agree on the priority list of Marriott activities.

---

*Contributed by Dave Ulrich.

Name _____ Group

Priority 1:

Justification:

Priority 2:

Justification:

Priority 3:

Justification:

1. To what extent do your recommendations generalize to organizations other than Marriott? If they do not generalize, why not?

2. What additional information would assist you in developing the most valid list of HRM activities?

EXERCISE 2.2 (*Continued*)

3. What other preparation could you have done for class discussion on the Marriott Corporation? How would this preparation assist the group in developing its list of corporate actions?

4. What competitive advantage principle(s) did you consider in compiling your priority list?

CHAPTER 3 EXERCISES

EXERCISE 3.1
ZIMPFER V. PALM BEACH COUNTY

OVERVIEW

Chapter 3 presented you with a variety of laws affecting HRM. One of those laws was the Age Discrimination in Employment Act (ADEA). The following case requires you to apply your understanding of the ADEA to provide some suggestions for Palm Beach County.

LEARNING OBJECTIVES

After completing this exercise, you should be able to:

1. Identify the critical issues associated with age discrimination cases.
2. Provide recommendations for a plaintiff filing an age discrimination case and for the employer in defending EEO practices.
3. Outline policies that organizations should adopt to reduce the probability of age discrimination or claims of age discrimination.

PROCEDURE

Part A: Individual Analysis

Step 1. Read the attached background material on Palm Beach County provided in Exhibit 3.1.1.

Step 2. Assume the role of the HR director and respond to the issues described below. Prepare a written report in which you address the issues on Form 3.1.1.

Part B: Group Analysis

Step 1. In groups, attempt to reach consensus on the four questions. Each student should review each other student's Form 3.1.1 before the discussion.

Step 2. The instructor will designate one (or more) representatives to present each group's consensus position.

EXHIBIT 3.1.1
BACKGROUND MATERIAL FOR PALM BEACH COUNTY

Palm Beach County has requested your opinion regarding an alleged violation of the Age Discrimination in Employment Act. Mr. Bryce Zimpfer, age 52, has been an employee of the county for 16 years in the employee relations area. The Department of Human Resources posted a job vacancy for employee relations manager (see Exhibit 3.1.2) and Mr. Zimpfer applied for the position. The department filled the position with Mr. Brad Merriman, age 33, an outside applicant with less experience in employee relations than Mr. Zimpfer.

After filing a timely complaint with the EEOC, Mr. Zimpfer retained Ms. Lynn Szymoniak, an attorney who is now attempting to reach a settlement with the division's legal staff. In preparation for these negotiations, the attorney asked an industrial psychologist, Dr. Marcy Josephs, to examine the résumés of the job applicants and submit a report as to whether Mr. Zimpfer was more qualified for the position than Mr. Merriman. Dr. Josephs submitted a report and concluded that on the basis of her résumé analysis, Mr. Zimpfer was more qualified for the position than Mr. Merriman (see Exhibit 3.1.3).

EXHIBIT 3.1.2
JOB VACANCY

POSITION DESCRIPTION: EMPLOYEE RELATIONS MANAGER

NATURE OF WORK

This is professional personnel and labor relations work developing and managing programs and activities to enhance relationships between management and employees; to promote employee satisfaction, well-being, and quality of work life; to develop greater productivity in the workforce; and to achieve sound labor/management working relationships. Work is of a highly responsible nature, requiring considerable independent judgment and decision making. Work is performed under the direction of the Director, Employee Relations and Personnel, and is reviewed through conferences, reports, and results achieved.

EXAMPLES OF WORK

Initiates and manages programs that aim to improve communication and participation. These may be employee orientation meetings, committees, attitude surveys, suggestion boxes, awards programs, newsletters, newspapers, handbooks, benefits brochures, and other media such as posters or payroll stuffers that communicate policies and practices to employees.

Develops programs that monitor and detect employees' dissatisfactions with policies or working conditions. These include adequate complaint and grievance procedures, communication of these to employees, and adequate follow-up with management to resolve problems.

Initiates procedures for reviewing adverse actions taken by supervisors to insure that such actions are fair. Investigates the facts of the case and determines whether any disciplinary action is appropriate. Directs and trains supervisors in discipline and discharge procedures.

Develops and monitors performance review systems, employee assistance programs, incentive/awards programs, quality circles, and others whose purpose is to motivate workers toward greater productivity.

Initiates programs to improve the quality of supervision, primarily training programs to improve knowledge of effective supervisory practices. May develop and present training programs for supervisors. May write and disseminate supervisors' handbooks or manuals.

Assists the Director in interpreting the provisions of labor contracts to supervisors. May conduct supervisory training sessions in contract administration.

Reviews and recommends policy and benefit changes to the Director that are needed to enhance employee/management relations.

Audits and approves personnel actions when applicable to insure compliance with policies.

May supervise counselors or specialists in carrying out these employee relations activities.

Performs related work as required.

REQUIRED KNOWLEDGE, SKILLS, AND ABILITIES

- Thorough working knowledge of federal and state laws affecting public personnel administration and labor relations.
- Thorough knowledge of merit system principles and policies.
- Knowledge of organization and functions.
- Knowledge of the principles of management and supervision.
- Ability to organize work and supervise professional staff.
- Ability to write and interpret correspondence and reports.
- Ability to speak to a wide variety of groups and present ideas effectively.
- Ability to deal tactfully and persuasively with staff, employees, supervisors, administrators, and union officials.
- Ability to conduct personal and investigative interviews.
- Ability to interpret complex legal cases and documents.
- Ability to conduct independent research and analysis.

MINIMUM ENTRANCE REQUIREMENTS

Graduation from an accredited college or university with major course work in Human Resources Management, Industrial Relations or Labor Relations, or closely related field, considerable progressively responsible experience in employee or labor relations; or any equivalent combination of related training and experience.

EXHIBIT 3.1.3

CULLEN & SZYMONIAK, P.A.

ATTORNEYS-AT-LAW

1030 Lake Avenue

Lake Worth, Florida 33460

(561) 585-4666

MARK A. CULLEN   October 25   LYNN E. SZYMONIAK

Marcy M. Josephs, Ph.D.

10475 Northwest Michigan Avenue

Birmingham, Michigan 48275

Dear Dr. Josephs:

I am very pleased that you are available to assist us with the Bryce Zimpfer case. Please find enclosed the following documents:

1. The job announcement, announcing the position of Employee Relations Manager;

2. A job description for the position of Employee Relations Manager;

3. Copies of the newspaper ads announcing this position;

4. A Referral List listing the candidates chosen for an interview for the position of Employee Relations Manager;

5. The resumes, cover letters, and applications of the applicants listed on the referral list; and

6. The application and resume of Bryce Zimpfer.

Based on your review of the above documents, please advise me:

1. Whether Mr. Zimpfer's qualifications equalled or exceeded the qualifications of the applicants selected for an interview; and

2. In particular, whether Bryce Zimpfer's qualifications equalled or exceeded the qualifications of J. Brad Merriman--the candidate ultimately selected for the position.

The experts' reports are to be exchanged on this case on November 12. Thank you again for your assistance.

Yours truly,

LYNN E. SZYMONIAK, ESQ.

Enclosures

EXHIBIT 3.1.4

MARCY MILLER JOSEPHS, PH.D.

INDUSTRIAL PSYCHOLOGIST

10475 NORTHWEST MICHIGAN AVENUE

BIRMINGHAM, MICHIGAN 48275

November 13

Lynn E. Szymoniak, Esq.

Cullen & Szymoniak, P.A.

1030 Lake Avenue

Lake Worth, FL 33460

Dear Ms. Szymoniak:

The purpose of this letter is to respond to your request for expert opinion in matters related to Bryce Zimpfer. In your letter of October 25, you requested that I render an opinion regarding the following:

1. Whether Mr. Zimpfer's qualifications equalled or exceeded the qualifications of the applicants selected for an interview; and

2. In particular, whether Bryce Zimpfer's qualifications equalled or exceeded the qualifications of J. Brad Merriman--the candidate ultimately selected for the position.

In rendering my opinion, I have reviewed the following documents:

1. The job announcement from Palm Beach County announcing the position of Employee Relations Manager;

2. A job description for the position of Employee Relations Manager;

3. Copies of the newspaper ads announcing this position;

4. A Referral List prepared, listing the candidates chosen for an interview for the position of Employee Relations Manager;

5. The resumes, cover letters, and applications of the applicants listed on the referral list; and

6. The application and resume of Bryce Zimpfer.

Based on my review of the aforementioned documents, I have the following opinions:

1. Mr. Zimpfer's qualifications equalled or exceeded the qualifications of several of the applicants selected for an interview; and

2. Mr. Zimpfer's qualifications exceeded the qualifications of Mr. J. Brad Merriman.

The following is a description of the procedure I followed to arrive at these opinions:

1. Based on a reading of the job announcement, the job description and the newspaper ad, I

EXHIBIT 3.1.4 (Continued)

constructed three applicant/work requirement matrices for purposes of assessing applicant qualifications with regard to program/activities, work examples, and required knowledge, skills, and abilities (KSAs). See Figures 1, 2, and 3. The first column of each matrix represents the critical work requirements of the job as reflected in the job announcement, etc.

2. I read each resume and recorded those work requirements with which each applicant had experience or requisite KSAs. I performed this task on three occasions (for the three matrices), each time evaluating the resumes in random order.

3. I performed the identical task described in Step 2 five days later with no reference to the completed matrices from Step 2. Thus, I made two independent evaluations of each of the three work requirement matrices.

4. I examined the discrepancies in the applicant/requirement cells of each matrix from the Step 2 and Step 3 evaluations and reviewed the resumes for purposes of reconciling the disagreements. The totals in the last row of Figures 1, 2, and 3 reflect the final evaluations I have made of each candidate after reconciling the few discrepancies between the Step 2 and Step 3 evaluations.

5. The opinions rendered above with regard to Mr. Zimpfer are based on the final evaluations of the three matrices.

The matrix analysis on which I have based my opinions represents a content-valid and objective approach to the evaluation of applicant resumes. It is far superior in terms of validity and reliability to a nonquantitative evaluation procedure which calls for a global evaluation of the applicants in terms of suitability for a multifaceted job.

Sincerely,

Marcy M. Josephs, Ph.D.
MMJ:im

EXHIBIT 3.1.4 (*Continued*)

FIGURE 1

PROGRAMS AND ACTIVITIES ANALYSIS

PROGRAMS/ACTIVITIES	ZIMPFER	ATKINSON	BENDER	BLEDSOE	MERRIMAN	SCHWAB
Performance appraisals	X	X		X	X	
Employee assistance	X		X			X
Employee benefits	X	X	X	X	X	
Employee publications	X		X			X
Counseling and discipline	X				X	
Grievance procedures	X		X	X	X	
Attendance and leave policy	X			X		
Layoff policy	X				X	
Unemployment compensation						
Contract administration	X	X	X	X	X	
Totals	9	3	5	5	6	2

FIGURE 2

WORK SAMPLE ANALYSIS

EXAMPLES OF WORK	ZIMPFER	ATKINSON	BENDER	BLEDSOE	MERRIMAN	SCHWAB
Employee orientation	X		X			X
Attitude surveys	X		X			
Suggestion boxes					X	
Awards program			X			
Newsletters	X		X			
Handbooks						
Benefits brochure	X	X				
Grievance procedures	X		X	X		
Disciplinary action			X	X		X
Supervisory training	X	X	X	X		X
Interpreting labor contracts		X	X		X	X
Policy and benefits	X	X	X	X	X	X
Audits and approves personal actions				X		
Totals	7	4	9	5	3	5

FIGURE 3

KNOWLEDGE, SKILLS, AND ABILITIES ANALYSIS

	ZIMPFER	ATKINSON	BENDER	BLEDSOE	MERRIMAN	SCHWAB
State and federal law	X	X	X	X	X	X
Ability to speak to variety of groups	X		X	X		X
Conduct interviews	X	X	X		X	X
Interpret complex legal cases and documents						X
Conduct independent research	X		X			X
Totals	4	2	4	2	2	5

Name _____

1. Does the evidence indicate that Mr. Zimpfer was a victim of age discrimination according to ADEA? Why or why not? (Be specific and cite cases.)

2. What (if any) further information should be ascertained before the county fully understands the legal implications of its actions?

3. Based on what you know, what action do you recommend that the county take in this matter?

4. What policies should the county adopt to reduce the possibility of age discrimination suits in the future?

EXERCISE 3.2
GOEBEL ET AL. V. FRANK CLOTHIERS

OVERVIEW

Many Title VII cases involve the presentation of statistical evidence that is alleged to indicate illegal discrimination. The purpose of this exercise is to review the statistical evidence presented and to assess the implications of the data for the organization.

LEARNING OBJECTIVES

After completing this exercise, you should be able to:

1. Calculate adverse impact for a selection procedure.
2. Provide recommendations for a plaintiff filing a race discrimination case and for the employer in defending EEO practices.
3. Outline the selection procedure the organization should adopt to prevent charges of race discrimination.

PROCEDURE

Part A: Individual Analysis

Step 1. Read the attached background material on *Goebel et al. v. Frank Clothiers* provided in Exhibit 3.2.1.

Step 2. Assume the role of the HR director and respond to the issues described below. Please prepare concise, written responses for the legal division of Frank Clothiers. Answer the questions presented on Form 3.2.1.

Part B: Group Analysis

Step 3. In groups of about six, members should attempt to reach consensus on Question #1. A rationale for the position should be developed that includes relevant court citations.

Step 4. The instructor will designate one member from each group to present the group position and rationale.

Step 5. Students should complete self- or peer assessments of each of their fellow group members.

EXHIBIT 3.2.1
GOEBEL ET AL. V. FRANK CLOTHIERS

The southern California division of Frank Clothiers had 16 openings for assistant store manager last year and, as part of its affirmative action program, filled the vacancies with 10 African-Americans and 6 whites. The selection process was a multiple-hurdle approach that began with an application form and an intelligence test. Applicants who scored 60 (out of 100) or higher on the intelligence test were then given an interview by the store managers. Based on the interview ratings, the 16 vacancies were filled.

The numbers of African-Americans and whites who passed the intelligence test were as follows:

TEST SCORES	AFRICAN-AMERICAN APPLICANTS	WHITE APPLICANTS
Number scoring 60 or higher	25	74
Number scoring less than 60	26	29
Totals	51	103

Dennis Goebel, one of the African-American applicants who scored 39 on the test, filed suit on behalf of all African-American applicants who failed the exam. Mr. Goebel claimed race discrimination based on Title VII of the Civil Rights Act of 1964.

Frank Clothiers has argued that over 62 percent of the actual managerial vacancies were filled with African-Americans (i.e., 10 out of 16). Thus, there is obviously no racial discrimination in the selection process.

Name _____   Group _____

1. Were Mr. Goebel and other African-American applicants victims of illegal racial discrimination because of the hiring policies of the defendant? Explain your position, citing specific cases. If you cannot take a position, what specific additional information do you require?

2. Is there evidence of disparate impact against blacks in the decisions that were made? How did you make this determination?

Name _____   Group _____

3. If disparate impact is evident, what steps should the defendant take next? Provide specific recommendations.

4. An associate of the HR Department is arguing that Frank Clothiers should continue to use the test but that the test scores should be interpreted by the ethnic classification of the test taker. For example, raw scores on the exam would be converted to percentages *within ethnic classification*. With such a procedure, African-Americans taking the test who receive the exact raw score as whites would receive a higher percentage score on the exam because of the ethnic interpretation. He argues that this procedure could enable Frank to continue using a valid and useful test while avoiding adverse impact. Take a position on this recommendation.

5. What additional information is necessary to determine if Frank Clothiers has any other potential EEO problems?

EXERCISE 3.3
COMPLAINT OF MS. SMITH

OVERVIEW

In recent years, the number of lawsuits filed for sexual harassment has steadily increased. As a result, it is becoming more and more important for employers to be familiar with how sexual harassment is defined and what they should do to prevent such instances from occurring in the workplace. This exercise challenges you to think about some of these issues.

LEARNING OBJECTIVES

After completing this exercise, you should be able to:

1. Define what is meant by sexual harassment.
2. Provide recommendations for a plaintiff filing a case charging sexual harassment and for the employer in defending its practices.
3. Outline the policies the organization should adopt to prevent charges of sexual harassment in the future.

PROCEDURE

Part A: Individual Analysis

Step 1. Read the attached background material on the complaint of Ms. Smith provided in Exhibit 3.3.1.

Step 2. As a member of the grievance committee, you have been asked to consider the questions presented on Form 3.3.1. Please prepare concise, written responses to each of the questions presented on Form 3.3.1.

Part B: Group Analysis

Step 1. In groups of about six people, students should attempt to reach consensus on questions 1 through 3 above. Before discussion, each student should read all other group member responses.

Step 2. The instructor will designate one student to present each group's position on questions 1–3.

EXHIBIT 3.3.1
COMPLAINT OF MS. SMITH

Ms. Kathleen Smith has filed a complaint with the internal grievance committee claiming sexual harassment on the job. She has threatened to file a formal complaint with the EEOC if nothing is done about the situation.

A cashier at one of the retail stores, Ms. Smith claims that Mr. Edward Jayjo, a salesman in apparel, has propositioned her on at least three occasions over the last 12 months. These advances have been made in the employee lounge while they were alone and, on at least one occasion, in front of other cashiers who can corroborate her story. Ms. Smith complained to Mr. Joseph Garcia, the store manager, and Mr. Garcia agreed to look into it. However, Mr. Garcia told others that Ms. Smith dressed in a provocative manner and she should expect "to be asked out."

In the 12 months in which the alleged sexual harassment occurred, the following personnel actions were taken at the store:

PERCENT SALARY INCREASES FOR THE YEAR

All cashiers, 5.8% (average)
Ms. Smith, 9 percent

CHRISTMAS BONUSES

All cashiers, $250 (average)
Ms. Smith, $500

PROMOTIONS TO HEAD CASHIER

Total: 4 (including Ms. Smith)

When he finally responded to the complaint, Mr. Garcia stated, "There was no evidence that refusal to submit to sexual advances was related to any negative action against Ms. Smith. She is a good employee and is recognized as such through merit increases, bonuses, and promotions." Garcia also pointed out that Mr. Jayjo has an excellent performance record and that Ms. Smith appears to be unaffected by the alleged events since she is never absent and performs very well.

Name _____   Group _____

1. Based on the above information, does the sexual harassment constitute a violation of the law? Explain your position and cite the pertinent case(s) to support your position. (If you need additional information before you state a position, what do you need?)

2. If you responded "yes" to question 1, is the company legally liable for the violation? Why or why not?

3. What (if any) action do you recommend that the company take in this matter? Should Mr. Jayjo be fired?

4. What specific policies and procedures should be established to prevent such charges in the future? Prepare a detailed outline of your recommendations.

5. How would you advise Ms. Smith to behave given these circumstances? Does she have any time constraints for her options?

EXERCISE 3.4
REVERSE DISCRIMINATION OR LEGAL AFFIRMATIVE ACTION?

OVERVIEW

Chapter 3 presents considerable detail on Title VII of the Civil Rights Act and the evolution of affirmative action programs. This exercise introduces some of the complexities and ramifications of affirmative action programs. Two real cases are described that involve allegations of reverse discrimination.

LEARNING OBJECTIVES

After completing the exercise, you should be able to:

1. Understand the variables that must be considered when determining the legality of affirmative action programs.
2. Know the conditions under which the sex (or race) of an employee may be taken into consideration for personnel decisions.

PROCEDURE

Part A: Individual Analysis (Prior to class)

Each student should study the cases presented in Exhibits 3.4.1 and 3.4.2 and take positions as required. For each case, write a concise paragraph (no more than 150 words) that provides the basis for your position on each case (cite specific cases or material to support your position). Also, answer the questions on Forms 3.4.1 and 3.4.2 after you have taken positions on each case.

Part B: Group Analysis (In class)

Step 1. Students should review each team member's individual report for Exhibit 3.4.1 and Form 3.4.1 and then attempt to reach consensus on a position. Once the consensus is reached, each group should adopt a group position paragraph (no more than 75 words). One group member will be asked to present the group's position to the rest of the class. Follow the same procedure for Form 3.4.2 as well with a second group member designated to present this position.

EXHIBIT 3.4.1

After four tough years working on the road for the Santa Ana County transportation agency, Diane Harrison applied for a less strenuous desk job as a road dispatcher. At that time not one of the California agency's 238 skilled positions was held by a woman. Harrison knew, however, that two years earlier, the county had enacted a voluntary affirmative action policy designed to correct that imbalance.

Harrison has 18 years' clerical experience and almost five years as a road maintenance worker. Another candidate for the position, Edward Jones, had 11 years as a road yard clerk (clerical position) and 4 years as a road maintenance worker. He also had previous experience as a dispatcher in private employment.

The position of road dispatcher required four years of dispatcher or road maintenance work experience with the county. Twelve employees applied for the job. Nine were judged to be qualified and interviewed by a two-person board. Seven of the applicants scored above 70 and were certified as eligible for selection. Jones tied for second at 76 and Harrison ranked next with 72. At a second interview, three agency supervisors recommended that Jones be promoted. At the second interview, one male panel member described Harrison as a rabble-rousing, "skirt-wearing" troublemaker.

The local supervisor picked Jones, but the county's affirmative action coordinator recommended Harrison. When Harrison got the job, Jones got a lawyer. Like Allen Bakke and Brian Weber and countless other white males since the advent of affirmative action programs some 30 years ago, Jones claimed he was a victim of reverse discrimination and filed suit under Title VII of the 1964 Civil Rights Act.

POSITIONS:

A. The Santa Ana plan is consistent with Title VII's purpose of eliminating the effects of past employment discrimination. Given the obvious imbalance in the division and given the agency's commitment to eliminating such imbalances, it was appropriate to consider, as one factor, the gender of Ms. Harrison in making its decision. Thus, the court should decide in favor of Santa Ana County.

B. To decide against Mr. Jones is to complete the process of converting Title VII from a guarantee that race or sex will not be the basis for employment determinations to a guarantee that it often will. Ever so subtly, we effectively replace the goal of a discrimination-free society with the quite incompatible goal of proportionate representation by race and by sex in the workplace. Thus, the court should decide in favor of Mr. Jones.

What position do you support? Write an opinion based on your understanding of Title VII, citing all relevant cases.

Name _____ Group _____

1. What conditions are necessary for an organization to show preference for one group over another?

2. Given the actual wording in *Section 703J* of Title VII, how can an organization show preference to women as in this case?

3. To what extent did you consider the great disparity in the number of male and female dispatchers? What if the four-fifths rule had been violated but the disparity was nothing like that reported in the case? Would you have a different opinion?

4. To what extent did you consider the qualifications of the candidates in taking your position? Did they have to be equally qualified? What if Jones had an interview score that was 10 points higher than Harrison?

EXHIBIT 3.4.2

In 1975, the Board of Education of the Township of Piscataway, New Jersey, developed an affirmative action policy applicable to employment decisions. The board's affirmative action program, a 52-page document, was originally adopted in response to a regulation promulgated by the New Jersey State Board of Education. That regulation directed local school boards to adopt "affirmative action programs," to address employment as well as school and classroom practices and to ensure equal opportunity to all persons regardless of race, color, creed, religion, sex, or national origin. The board also adopted a one-page policy, titled "Affirmative Action-Employment Practices." It is not clear from the record whether the "policy" superseded or simply added to the "program," nor does it matter for purposes of this appeal.

The 1975 document states that the purpose of the program is "to provide equal educational opportunity for students and equal employment opportunity for employees and prospective employees," and "to make a concentrated effort to attract . . . minority personnel for all positions so that their qualifications can be evaluated along with other candidates." A 1983 document states that its purpose is to "ensure [ ] equal employment opportunity . . . and prohibit [ ] discrimination in employment because of . . . race . . ."

The operative language regarding the means by which affirmative action goals are to be furthered is identical in the two documents. "In all cases, the most qualified candidate will be recommended for appointment. However, when candidates appear to be of equal qualification, candidates meeting the criteria of the affirmative action program will be recommended." The phrase "candidates meeting the criteria of the affirmative action program" refers to members of racial, national origin, or gender groups identified as minorities for statistical reporting purposes by the New Jersey State Department of Education, including blacks. The 1983 document also clarifies that the affirmative action program applies to "every aspect of employment including . . . layoffs . . ."

The board's affirmative action policy did not have "any remedial purpose"; it was not adopted "with the intention of remedying the results of any prior discrimination or identified underrepresentation of minorities within the Piscataway Public School System." At all relevant times, black teachers were neither "underrepresented" nor "underutilized" in the Piscataway School District workforce. Statistics in 1976 and 1985 showed that the percentage of black employees in the job category that included teachers exceeded the percentage of blacks in the available workforce.

In May 1989, the board accepted a recommendation from the superintendent of schools to reduce the teaching staff in the Business Department at Piscataway High School by one. At that time, two of the teachers in the department were of equal seniority, both having begun their employment with the board on the same day nine years earlier. One of those teachers was plaintiff Sharon Taxman, who is white, and the other was Debra Williams, who is black. Williams was the only minority teacher among the faculty of the Business Department.

Decisions regarding layoffs by New Jersey school boards are highly circumscribed by state law; nontenured faculty must be laid off first, and layoffs among tenured teachers in the affected subject area or grade level must proceed in reverse order of seniority. Seniority for this purpose is calculated according to specific guidelines set by state law. Thus, local boards lack discretion to choose between employees for layoff, except in the rare instance of a tie in seniority between the two or more employees eligible to fill the last remaining position.

The board determined that it was facing just such a rare circumstance in deciding between Taxman and Williams. In prior decisions involving the layoff of employees with equal seniority, the board has broken the tie through "a random process which included drawing numbers out of a container, drawing lots, or having a lottery." In none of those instances, however, had the employees involved been of different races.

In light of the unique posture of the layoff decision, Superintendent of Schools Burton Edelchick recommended to the board that the affirmative action plan be invoked in order to determine which teacher to retain. Superintendent Edelchick made this recommendation "because he believed Ms. Williams and Ms. Taxman were tied in seniority, were equally qualified, and because Ms. Williams was the only black teacher in the Business Education Department."

While the board recognized that it was not bound to apply the affirmative action policy, it made a discretionary decision to invoke the policy to break the tie between Williams and Taxman. As a result, the board "voted to terminate the employment of Sharon Taxman, effective June 30, 1988."

At her deposition, Paula Van Riper, the board's vice president at the time of the layoff, described the board's decision-making process. According to Van Riper, after the board recognized that Taxman and Williams were of equal seniority, it assessed their classroom performance, evaluations, volunteerism, and certifications and determined that they were "two teachers of equal ability" and "equal qualifications."

At his deposition Theodore H. Kruse, the board's president, explained his vote to apply the affirmative action policy as follows:

> Basically I think because I had been aware that the student body and the community which is our responsibility, the schools of the community, is really quite diverse and there—I have a general feeling during my tenure on the board that it was valuable for the students to see in the various employment roles a wide range of background, and that it was also valuable to the workforce and in particular to the teaching staff that they have—they see that in each other.

Asked to articulate the "educational objective" served by retaining Williams rather than Taxman, Kruse stated:

> In my own personal perspective I believe by retaining Ms. Williams it was sending a very clear message that we feel that our staff should be culturally diverse, our student population is culturally diverse and there is a distinct advantage to students, to all students, to be made—come into contact with people of different cultures, different background, so that they are more aware, more tolerant, more accepting, more understanding of people of all background.

Kruse was asked, "What do you mean by the phrase you used, culturally diverse?"

> Someone other than—different than yourself. And we have, our student population and our community has people of all different background, ethnic background, religious background, cultural background, and it's important that our school district encourage awareness and acceptance and tolerance and, therefore, I personally think it's important that our staff reflect that too.

Following the board's decision, Taxman filed a charge of employment discrimination with the Equal Employment Opportunity Commission. Attempts at conciliation were unsuccessful, and the United States filed suit under Title VII against the board in the United States District Court for the District of New Jersey. Taxman intervened, asserting claims under both Title VII and the New Jersey Law Against Discrimination (NJLAD).

EXHIBIT 3.4.2 (*Continued*)

Following discovery, the board moved for summary judgment and the United States and Taxman cross-moved for partial summary judgment only as to liability. The district court denied the board's motion and granted partial summary judgment to the United States and Taxman, holding the board liable under both statutes for discrimination on the basis of race. *United States v. Board of Educ. of Township Piscataway,* 832 F. Supp. 836, 851 (D.N.J.1993).

A trial proceeded on the issue of damages. By this time, Taxman had been rehired by the board and thus her reinstatement was not an issue. The court awarded Taxman damages in the amount of $134,014.62 for back pay, fringe benefits, and prejudgment interest under Title VII. A jury awarded an additional $10,000 for emotional suffering under the NJLAD. The district court denied the United States' request for a broadly worded injunction against future discrimination, finding that there was no likelihood that the conduct at issue would recur, but it did order the board to give Taxman full seniority reflecting continuous employment from 1980. Additionally, the court dismissed Taxman's claim for punitive damages under the NJLAD.

Title VII makes it unlawful for an employer "to discriminate against any individual with respect to his compensation, terms, conditions, or privileges of employment" or "to limit, segregate, or classify his employees . . . in any way which would deprive or tend to deprive any individual of employment opportunities or otherwise affect his status as an employee" on the basis of "race, color, religion, sex, or national origin." [FN6] 42 U.S.C. 2000e-2(a). For a time, the Supreme Court construed this language as absolutely prohibiting discrimination in employment, neither requiring nor permitting any preference for any group.

In 1979, however, the court interpreted the statute's "antidiscriminatory strategy" in a "fundamentally different way," holding in the seminal case of *United Steelworkers v. Weber,* 443 U.S. 193, 99 S.Ct. 2721, that Title VII's prohibition against racial discrimination does not condemn all voluntary race-conscious affirmative action plans. In Weber, the court considered a plan implemented by Kaiser Aluminum & Chemical Corporation. Before 1974, Kaiser hired as craft workers only those with prior craft experience. Because they had long been excluded from craft unions, blacks were unable to present the credentials required for craft positions. Moreover, Kaiser's hiring practices, although not admittedly discriminatory with regard to minorities, were questionable. As a consequence, while the local labor force was about 39 percent black, Kaiser's labor force was less than 15 percent black and its crafts workforce was less than 2 percent black. In 1974, Kaiser entered into a collective bargaining agreement that contained an affirmative action plan. The plan reserved 50 percent of the openings in an in-plant craft-training program for black employees until the percentage of black craft workers in the plant reached a level commensurate with the percentage of blacks in the local labor force. During the first year of the plan's operation, 13 craft-trainees were selected, 7 of whom were black and 6 of whom were white.

Thereafter, Brian Weber, a white production worker, filed a class action suit, alleging that the plan unlawfully discriminated against white employees under Title VII. The plaintiffs argued that it necessarily followed that the Kaiser plan, which resulted in junior black employees receiving craft training in preference to senior white employees, violated Title VII. The district court agreed and entered a judgment in favor of the plaintiffs; the Court of Appeals for the Fifth Circuit affirmed.

The Supreme Court, however, reversed, noting initially that although the plaintiffs' argument was not "without force," it disregarded "the significance of the fact that the Kaiser-USWA plan was an affirmative action plan voluntarily adopted by private parties to eliminate traditional patterns of racial segregation." The court then embarked on an exhaustive review of Title VII's legislative history and identified Congress' concerns in enacting Title VII's prohibition against discrimination—the deplorable status of blacks in the nation's economy, racial injustice, and the need to open employment opportunities for blacks in traditionally closed occupations. Against this background, the court concluded that Congress could not have intended to prohibit private employers from implementing programs directed toward the very goal of Title VII—the eradication of discrimination and its effects from the workplace:

> It would be ironic indeed if a law triggered by a nation's concern over centuries of racial injustice and intended to improve the lot of those who had "been excluded from the American dream for so long,"[1] constituted the first legislative prohibition of all voluntary, private, race-conscious efforts to abolish traditional patterns of racial segregation and hierarchy.

The court found support for its conclusion in the language and legislative history of section 2000e-2(j) of Title VII, which expressly provides that nothing in the act requires employers to grant racial preferences. According to the court, the opponents of Title VII had raised two arguments: the act would be construed to impose obligations upon employers to integrate their workforces through preferential treatment of minorities, and even without being obligated to do so, employers with racially imbalanced workforces would grant racial preferences. Since Congress addressed only the first objection and did not specifically prohibit affirmative action efforts, the court inferred that Congress did not intend that Title VII forbid all voluntary race-conscious preferences. The court further reasoned that since Congress also intended "to avoid undue federal regulation of private businesses," a prohibition against all voluntary affirmative action would disserve this end by "augment[ing] the power of the Federal Government and diminish[ing] traditional management prerogatives . . ."

The court then turned to the Kaiser plan in order to determine whether it fell on the "permissible" side of the "line of demarcation between permissible and impermissible affirmative action plans." The court upheld the Kaiser plan because its purpose "mirror[ed] those of the statute" and it did not "unnecessarily trammel the interests of the [nonminority] employees":

> The purposes of the plan mirror those of the statute. Both were designed to break down old patterns of racial segregation and hierarchy. Both were structured to "open employment opportunities for Negroes in occupations which have been traditionally closed to them."[2]

> At the same time, the plan does not "unnecessarily trammel" the interests of the white employees. The plan does not require the discharge of white workers and their replacement with new black hires. Nor does the plan create an absolute bar to the advancement of white employees; half of those trained in the program will be white. Moreover, the plan is a temporary measure; it is not intended to maintain racial balance, but simply to eliminate a manifest racial imbalance.

---

[1] 110 Cong. Rec. 6552 (1964) remarks of Sen. Hubert Humphrey
[2] 110 Cong. Rec. 6548 (1964) (remarks of Sen. Humphrey).

Name _____   Group _____

1. Was Ms. Taxman a victim of discrimination under Title VII? Explain your answer, citing pertinent cases and discussion. Was this a violation of Proposition 209?

2. Do you support the argument that a protected class characteristic may be considered in order to meet a goal of "diversity?" If yes, under what circumstances would this be allowed?

3. If you decide that Ms. Taxman was not a victim of illegal discrimination, do you think there could be any unintended consequences to the policy that you have supported with regard to future staffing processes by organizations?

4. If you decide for Ms. Taxman, what do you propose as the remedy? If Ms. Taxman had been awarded the job, would Ms. Williams have redress through Title VII? Explain your answer, citing applicable case law.

5. How is the *Taxman* case different from *Johnson v. Santa Clara Transportation?* Does the *Johnson* decision support the decision to retain Williams? Explain your answer.

EXERCISE 3.5
JOSEPH GARCIA V. HOOTERS
CAMERON V. LAVEILLE MAISON

OVERVIEW

What is allowable as a BFOQ? The Supreme Court has said that BFOQs are allowable if they are "reasonably necessary to the normal operation of that particular business." What if a business has a competitive strategy that appeals to a particular segment of the population that has certain strong preferences for services to be provided by the establishment? (Recall the discussion of the *Pan Am v. Diaz* Supreme Court case.) The 1991 decision in *UAW v. Johnson Controls* stated that the exception to Title VII in the form of BFOQs applies only to policies that involve the "essence of the business." The purpose of this exercise is to present two real cases with characteristics that are hardly unique in an industry. We will ask you to take a position as to the legality of a company policy that the company claims falls under the "business essence" BFOQ exception to Title VII.

PURPOSE

After completing this exercise, you should be able to:

1. Understand the conditions under which a BFOQ is allowable.
2. Know the role of customer preference in Title VII cases.
3. Consider the implications of the case for other similar policies in the industry.

PROCEDURE

Step 1. Before class, read the case histories in Exhibit 3.5.1 and answer the questions on Form 3.5.1.

Step 2. In groups of about six people, each student should review the other group member responses and then attempt to reach group consensus on each of the questions. One person should be designated as the group spokesperson and the group position should be presented.

EXHIBIT 3.5.1

JOSEPH GARCIA V. HOOTERS

Hooters Restaurants had a competitive strategy of appealing to the young, affluent male population through a number of features. Large-screen television for sports events, happy hours, sports celebrity events, and very attractive waitresses were part of the strategy. Joseph Garcia was a waiter from Chicago who had worked at similar restaurants for over 10 years. He heard from a friend that Hooters was hiring. However, he was told he would have to apply in person. When he showed up at one of the 25 franchise establishments, he was told that the restaurant was not hiring. He learned a few weeks later that an attractive female had been hired at the same restaurant. He filed a timely claim with the EEOC.

CAROL CAMERON V. LAVEILLE MAISON

LaVeille Maison is a five-star restaurant in Boca Raton, Florida. Carol Cameron, a waitress with over 10 years' experience in "upscale" restaurants and an esoteric knowledge of wine, applied for a job at LaVeille Maison when the restaurant was hiring waiters in preparation for the heavy winter season. The restaurant employs only male waiters and makes the argument that five-star French restaurants traditionally employ only waiters. After learning that LaVeille Maison had hired three new waiters, Ms. Cameron filed a timely Title VII lawsuit against the restaurant.

Name _____   Group _____

1. Was Mr. Garcia a victim of sex discrimination? Explain your answer in some detail based on your understanding of BFOQs.

2. Was Ms. Cameron a victim of illegal sex discrimination? Explain your answer.

3. In principle, do you see these cases as the same in terms of your interpretation of legal BFOQs?

EXERCISE 3.6
HIRING A BANK TELLER*

OVERVIEW

Chapter 3 discusses the numerous laws that can affect the process of selecting employees. The purpose of Exercise 3.6 is to consider these laws in the context of a hiring situation.

LEARNING OBJECTIVES

After completing the exercise, you should be able to:

1. Recognize the relevance of particular laws for specific situations.
2. Consider the major provisions and key concepts of those laws as they apply to a specific situation.

PROCEDURE

Part A: Individual Analysis (Prior to class)

Before class, read Chapter 3 and the scenario below and complete Form 3.6.1.

Part B: Group Analysis and Class Discussion

In groups, students should review each member's Form 3.6.1 and then attempt to reach consensus on key questions from the form as designated by the instructor. Class discussion will focus on key laws and provisions.

SCENARIO

Applicant Background

Anna has multiple sclerosis. Until 10 months ago she was able to walk with the aid of a cane. Now she uses a wheelchair to get about, but she can stand, unassisted, for very short periods of time. She has recent work experience as a cashier in a local cafeteria, which went out of business a few weeks ago. She worked part time at the cafeteria for six years and was highly regarded by the manager and staff as a pleasant, hardworking person. Anna left when the establishment closed. Before that, she worked part time as a concierge in a local hotel for five years. She speaks English and Spanish although she should brush up on her Spanish. Her credit rating and background are impeccable and she has excellent references.

*Contributed by Lori Spina.

Anna answered the following advertisement in her local newspaper for the position of bank teller with a very large, well-known bank in the Southeast:

TELLER (P/T)

The ideal candidate must be available to work a flexible schedule. Good communication skills, positive customer service attitude, and professional manner a must. Qualified candidates must have min. 1 year recent cash handling experience; 6 month teller experience preferred. Bilingual (Eng/Span) required. We offer a pleasant working environment, competitive salary. Call Monday after 9:00 AM.

Anna called and, after answering a few basic questions about her previous work experience, spoke with Dave, the location manager. He asked her some additional questions about money handling. Dave asked her to come in for an interview.

Bank Background

This bank is a small branch office in a community of 25,000 people. The manager likes to maintain a pool of five tellers, and Dave attempts to schedule them around peak times to best serve the customers. Competition is fierce with five other banks to serve the community. High customer service is a driving force in the organization. The bank's success depends on quality service delivery. The manager prides himself in leading the competition in customer service. Tellers perform a variety of tasks at their stations and also cover the drive-through window. The drive-through window station is two steps below the rest of the floor. Historically, the manager has had difficulty finding qualified people who are bilingual to fill this vacancy.

The Interview

Anna arrives for her appointment 15 minutes early. She is eager to make a good impression and needs to get back into the workforce. She has many ideas and thoughts about how to perform the job.

Dave is under pressure to fill this slot. He has not been impressed by the previous applicants. He is impressed with Anna's résumé and her references. Her work experience appears to be more than adequate. Dave does not know that Anna uses a wheelchair and he has never interviewed a disabled person. Dave's secretary escorts Anna into Dave's office.

Dave: So, you must be Anna. I'm Dave, the branch manager. Come on in.

Anna: Thank you. I hope I'm not too early.

Dave: No, not at all. Let's begin the interview, shall we? You indicated on the phone that your previous job was that of a cashier in a cafeteria, correct?

Anna: Yes, that's right. I usually worked the peak shift from 8:00 A.M. until 2:00 P.M. on my designated days. In addition to the usual register duties, such as keeping track of my cash balance, I also was responsible for the writing and placement of the daily specials menu boards, iced beverage stock count, and the general care and cleanliness of the condiments/register area.

Dave: Tell me, Anna, how did you manage to work at a register for six hours?

Anna: Well, I usually took a break after the coffee break crowd left but before the lunch crowd arrived.

Dave: That's not exactly what I meant. I mean, well, let's talk about the job here as teller. All tellers here have to work their own stations and share the drive-through station. They don't only sit or stand at their stations. They also have to run for signature cards and research items. When a customer arrives at the drive-through, which ever teller is free first automatically moves to that station. During peak times it gets pretty hectic behind the counter. It's hard to imagine your being able to keep up with all of this. We cannot afford to slow the pace.

Anna: If you are asking me how I would be able to perform under the situation you described, I have some ideas about how I can work both stations. I thought about this after we scheduled the interview, and I think that there are some practical ways to work it.

Dave: I'm glad that you've thought about this ahead of time. That is quite commendable. But, on to another demand of the job. We are very proud of our customer service record. In fact, we enjoy the best customer service reputation in the community. We deliver quality work in a timely manner. We know that our customers don't want to waste time waiting in line. So we strive to meet their needs. And we deliver what they have come to expect, great service. That's why we schedule for peak times, even though the hours are somewhat irregular for employees. How do you see yourself fitting into our environment?

Anna: I understand the flexible schedule and don't mind working that way. In fact, after we spoke on the phone to set up this interview, I spoke with a teller at my bank so as to understand what you meant in the ad by a flexible sched-

ule. Also, I don't believe that there was ever a complaint about the quality of my work or my not being able to keep up with the work flow when I worked at the cafeteria. I am very quick with transactions and I enjoy meeting the customers. I got to know most of the regulars pretty well at the cafeteria.

Dave: Well, I think this about wraps up the questions that I have. Is there anything else that I can answer for you before we finish up?

Anna: Do you want to know about my ideas for doing the job?

Dave: I think that might be a bit premature. We can talk about that if you are one of the finalists for the job. Anything else?

Anna: No, I think I am about finished here. Thanks for the appointment.

Dave: Certainly, we will let you know of our decision soon. Good-bye.

Anna: Good-bye.

Dave is in a quandary. He realizes that Anna is qualified for the position, but he does not know how to approach the issue of her using a wheelchair. No other candidate to date is as experienced with both money handling and the language requirement as she. The main office wants Dave to make a decision within the next two to three days. The prospects for the remaining interviews do not look promising. Dave decides to interview everyone who has applied before making a decision.

Over the next two days Dave talks to two of his best friends. They are professionals in their fields and are managers as well. Dave still has not interviewed anyone as highly qualified as Anna, but has reservations about hiring her. Dave's friend Ben is in real estate and owns a small firm. Ben advises Dave to follow his gut feeling and not take the risk. Carl, an insurance actuary, advises Dave to rethink the situation and develop alternatives for Anna since she is most qualified to perform the job. Carl's main point is that the adjustments to the work environment might not be costly and the positive impact to customers could work to the bank's advantage.

Dave decides to hire another person, Nancy. Even though Nancy does not speak Spanish fluently, Dave decides that she can get by and, if necessary, use another teller to handle intricate transactions in Spanish. Dave feels that he has made the right decision and secretly hopes that he does not lose another teller in the near future.

Anna receives a letter of thanks from Dave who states that she is not going to get the job. Anna feels that she did not have the opportunity to explain her ideas about performing the job. She wrestles with the thought of legal action. After a few days she contacts an attorney to discuss the incident. The attorney recommends that they file suit against Dave and the bank.

Name _____   Group _____

1. What, if anything, did Dave do correctly?

2. If Dave determines that Anna cannot perform the essential functions of the job, can he then eliminate her from further consideration?

3. What critical terms must be considered in considering the legal implications of this action? How do they apply in this case?

4. Do you think Anna and her attorney have a case? Explain your reasoning.

5. What barriers would Anna face if hired at your workplace? What barriers could be eliminated to attain reasonable accommodations for Anna?

6. One of Dave's friends points out that multiple sclerosis is a progressive disease and that Anna will almost certainly get worse, creating potential problems of absenteeism and health care costs. Can Dave consider this issue in his decision?

CHAPTER 4 EXERCISES

CHAPTER 4 EXERCISES

EXERCISE 4.1
WRITING A POSITION DESCRIPTION

OVERVIEW

This exercise shows you how to write a position description (PD) that describes either a job you have, have had, or, if you have never worked, the job of someone else. As stated in Chapter 4, job or position descriptions are used for a number of personnel decisions. Many organizations start with job descriptions when they do restructuring and job design. Job descriptions are routinely used to set and adjust wage rates. The information can also be used to assist in recruitment efforts or develop selection devices, work teams, or performance-appraisal systems. To serve HR purposes most effectively, the PD must be current and accurate and it must be consistent with the goals and objectives of the organization, particularly in terms of customer requirements.

LEARNING OBJECTIVES

After completing this exercise, you should be able to:

1. Identify the key components of job descriptions.

2. Prepare a position description report, including data on position objectives, tasks and duties, supervision and guidance, contacts, services and products provided to critical customers, and job qualifications or specifications.

3. Understand the purposes to be served by the position description.

PROCEDURE

Part A: Individual Assignment: Completion of the Position Description

Before class, read the general guidelines for completing the position description (Exhibit 4.1.1). Then complete Form 4.1, the position description. Prior to class, students should also complete the Assessment Questions.

Part B: Peer Review

Step 1. Students should bring their completed Form 4.1 to class. Students should be paired off and first review their respective position descriptions. Each student should serve as an examiner to try to interpret the PD of the other person. The examiner should try to sum up what is involved in the job and whether clear task

statements have been written. The incumbent should clear up any confusion about job duties, requirements, and job specifications. Any needed changes to the PD should be made directly on Form 4.1. The discussion should also focus on any job specifications for the job, particularly those that may cause adverse impact. The examiner should also focus on the identification of the customers with whom the incumbent has contact for products or services that derive from this position and determine whether certain tasks on which the incumbent spends considerable time may be unnecessary in terms of the needs of the internal and external customers. The examiner should continue to seek clarification until he or she is confident the position description is as good as it can be. The examiner should then sign Form 4.1 in the space provided.

EXHIBIT 4.1.1
GENERAL GUIDELINES FOR COMPLETING THE POSITION DESCRIPTION

The position description should be written in your own words—it should not be written in technical "classified language." Basically the position description should be a collection of the tasks that add up to the total work assignment. All major work activities that are performed in the job should be described. The tools and equipment used should be mentioned. Also include the decisions made in performing the job, the outcomes, the products or services, and the relevant customers for each.

Samples of completed position descriptions for the jobs of public health nurse and mechanic helper are also provided in Exhibits 4.1.2 and 4.1.3. Review these samples as you read these instructions. Note the various sections to the position description (see Form 4.1).

PART I: COMPILING ORGANIZATIONAL INFORMATION

Step 1. Following the items listed in Part I (Organizational Information) state the name of the incumbent, the date, and the official job title. In item 5, you should state the working title if this title is different from the official title. Often, employees are given working titles for use. For example, a supervisor on a road crew may officially be a highway maintenance engineer.

Step 2. If possible, ask a supervisor or a personnel officer to complete the information requested from the other items listed in Part I.

Step 3. After reviewing the instructions, complete the items of Form 4.1, Part II: Position Information. This is the most important part of the position description because it provides information on the position's duties.

EXHIBIT 4.1.1 (*Continued*)

PART II: POSITION INFORMATION

Item 11—Objective

Item 11 asks you to state the chief objective of the position. This statement should be no more than two to three sentences. It should state why it is important that the tasks and duties that make up the job are performed. In writing item 11, it may help you to think of this statement as a definition of the position, or perhaps the essential aspect of the job. For example, the objective of a *child welfare supervisor* may be: "To orientate new case workers located in local courts, detention homes, and children's institutions by planning and teaching classes and seminars on social casework principles." This example of a position's main objective was used because: (1) It was *brief* (has no more than several lines); (2) it was *descriptive* (states the main tasks and duties of the position without giving detailed information); (3) it gives the reader an *overview* (what to expect in the more detailed listing of tasks); and (4) it states the *main purpose* for why the position exists.

Item 12—Tasks and Duties

In this section, you are to identify the tasks and duties that are performed in the job. Read the instructions for item 12 on Form 4.1 and write down the tasks on a separate sheet of paper. After you have completed this, arrange the tasks in order of the most important task first and finish with the least important task of the position. When these tasks are listed, decide the percent that each task requires of the total working time. Be sure these percentages total to 100. Writing all the tasks and duties of the position is difficult. Outlined below are some guidelines that should help. Following these are some examples of good and poor task statements.

1. Use action verbs to start each task statement, such as compiles, enters, totals, balances, writes, answers, telephones, or interviews. Avoid nondescriptive verbs such as prepares, conducts, coordinates, processes, or assists—these verbs do not tell the reader what you are really doing.

2. Use task statements to explain: What is done? What actions are you performing? To what or to whom? What is the purpose of this task? What references, resources, tools, equipment, or work aids are you using? Do you write reports? Do you train and supervise employees?

3. Try to group closely related tasks together. This grouping of tasks will help you more clearly define and explain to the reader what you are responsible for in your position.

4. It is important to include all the major tasks and duties of your position. It is not necessary to include minor things such as "sits in chair, pulls open drawer, takes out a pen from desk, begins to write."

EXAMPLES OF GOOD AND POOR TASK STATEMENTS

POOR	GOOD
Ensures that all daily cash is accounted for.	Balances cash in register by comparing it with the total on the register tape; locates and corrects errors in order to account for all cash receipts; writes totals on cash report for approval by head cashier.
Assists with the inspection of construction projects.	Inspects construction operations (erosion control, asphaltic concrete paving, painting, fencing, sign placement); compares visual observations with the construction specifications and plans.
Trains subordinate employees.	Instructs employees under his/her supervision in company policies, office procedures, applicable state and federal laws, and firm report preparation to facilitate improved job performance; distributes firm reading materials, schedules work assignments, and leads staff meetings.

Item 13—Supervision and Guidance

Item 13 asks you to state what work actions and/or decisions are made *without* first getting a supervisor's approval. This decision making is an important element in the evaluation of the job. In answering this question, consider the following examples:

1. If you are a clerk typist, you may edit a memorandum that was drafted by your supervisor in order to make it more grammatically correct.

2. If you are a clerk, you may set up your own filing procedures and reorganize your section's files.

You may also want to list any procedural manuals, laws, and/or standards that are used as guides in the work.

Item 14—Contacts

In many positions, contact with other people is a necessary part of the job. Item 14 requests that you list any contacts you have with individuals, customers, or organizations. Also state the purpose of these contacts, how often they occur (e.g., daily, weekly) and whether they are inside or outside the organization.

Item 15—Most Important Service or Product/Internal and External Customers

Item 15 requests a listing of the most important services or products that are expected from this position and an identification of the internal and external customers who receive them (not by name, just category). Note that managers

EXHIBIT 4.1.2   PUBLIC HEALTH NURSE POSITION DESCRIPTION   **501**

EXHIBIT 4.1.1 (*Continued*)

or supervisors should not be considered customers and their demands may require tasks to be performed that detract from your attention to more important customers (e.g., external customers). Demands from managers should be linked to other internal or external customers.

Item 16—Entry Requirements/Job Specifications

Item 16 asks for information on the KASOCs that an employee must possess on the *first* day of the job. This information will be used in recruiting new employees. There are four sections to be answered.

1. *Knowledge, abilities, skills, and other personal characteristics:* State the KASOCs that a new employee

must bring to the position. Use the definitions provided in Chapter 4.

2. *Special licenses, registration, or certification:* Identify occupational certifications or licenses, if any, that an applicant must hold to comply with laws or regulations.

3. *Education or training:* State the educational background or area of study that would provide the knowledge required for entry into the position.

4. *Experience:* State the level and type of experience an applicant should have to be qualified to fill the position. Examples might include "journey level carpentry with experience in remodeling interiors," or "supervisory experience."

EXHIBIT 4.1.2
PUBLIC HEALTH NURSE POSITION DESCRIPTION

PART I: ORGANIZATIONAL INFORMATION

1. Name (last, first, middle):
   Black, Sandy C.

2. Date:
   Nov. 12

3. Job title:
   Public Health Nurse

4. Position number:
   123456

5. Working title if different:

6. Agency:

7. Work location (county or city) and location code:

8. Agency code:

9. Title and position number of immediate supervisor:

10. Organizational unit:

PART II: POSITION INFORMATION

11. Objective of the position: To ensure that state employees are in good health by providing public health services.

12. Tasks and duties:

PERCENT OF TOTAL WORKING TIME	WORK TASKS AND DUTIES
25%	Evaluates employees' or potential employees' physical condition by taking medical histories and examining the employee using diagnostic tools, such as stethoscope and otoscope, and interprets the results of laboratory tests.
25%	Treats work-related injuries to reduce absenteeism by administering medication and vaccines under the clinical guidance of a physician.
15%	Meets routinely with staff to review existing clinical services in order to improve them.
20%	Reviews accident reports to identify health and safety hazards. Analyzes causes of accidents and makes recommendations to management for eliminating hazards.
5%	Develops programs to educate employees on health-related issues. Uses self-prepared or programmed lesson plans, films, and other audiovisual materials.
5%	Orders supplies to maintain an adequate inventory. Completes requisition forms and sends them to the planning or supply room.
5%	Answers requests for medical status of employees from insurance companies or personnel staff by discussing results of examinations and current medical status over the telephone or by completing medical forms.
100%	

13. Describe work actions and/or decisions you make *without* prior approval and the extent of advice and guidance received from your supervisor:

   I decide how to treat minor injuries—giving first aid. I determine if a laboratory test is within acceptable limits. I plan educational programs.

T 4.1.2 (Continued)

14. Contacts:

CONTACTS	PURPOSE	HOW OFTEN	INSIDE/OUTSIDE ORGANIZATION
Employees	Perform physicals, treat injuries, and obtain information on the workplace	Daily	Inside
Insurance companies	Provide medical claim information	Weekly	Outside
Benefits staff (DPT)	Provide information for worker's compensation claims	Monthly	Inside

15. The most important service or product provided:

    Contact with and treatment of employees.

16. Qualifications for entry into the position:
    A. KASOCs:
       Ability to obtain personal information from people and to determine if they are being truthful. Knowledge of nursing services in the employment setting.
    B. Special licenses, registration, or certification:
       RN
    C. Education or training (cite major area of study):
       Nursing
    D. Level and type of experience:
       Experience in providing nursing services to a wide variety of people.

17. I understand the above statements, and they are complete to the best of my knowledge.

    Sandy C. Black   *Nov. 12*

    Employee's Signature   Date

    Connie Brown   *November 13*

    Examiner's Signature   Date

EXHIBIT 4.1.3
MECHANIC HELPER POSITION DESCRIPTION

PART I: ORGANIZATIONAL INFORMATION

1. Name (last, first, middle):
   Green, Chris M.

2. Date:

3. Job title:
   Mechanic Helper

4. Position number:

5. Working title if different:

6. Organization:

7. Work location (county or city) and location code:

8. Agency code:

9. Title and position number of immediate supervisor:

10. Organizational unit:

EXHIBIT 4.1.3   MECHANIC HELPER POSITION DESCRIPTION   **503**

EXHIBIT 4.1.3 (*Continued*)

PART II: POSITION INFORMATION

11.   Objective of the position:

To maintain highway construction equipment in good operating condition by inspecting and repairing equipment, when necessary.

12.   Tasks and duties:

PERCENT OF TOTAL WORKING TIME	WORK TASKS AND DUTIES
25%	Inspects highway equipment to identify any operating problems by visually checking and listening to the equipment.
25%	Repairs highway equipment, cars, dump trucks, and small engines needed to perform road maintenance work by overhauling motor transmissions and differentials, replacing axles, springs, and wheel bearings using small motorized shop equipment, hand tools, and shop repair manuals.
20%	Maintains equipment to prevent breakdowns by installing spark plugs, starters, distributor caps; changing oil; and greasing equipment using standard mechanic tools.
15%	Tunes up and analyzes gasoline engines to locate minor problems and provide for optimum engine performance by using the Peerless Engine Analyzer.
15%	Helps other mechanics by gathering tools and parts, purchasing, and picking up parts at local suppliers and moving equipment from one place to another as directed by the foreman.
100%	

13.   Describe work actions and/or decisions you make *without* prior approval and the extent of advice and guidance you receive from your supervisor.

I decide how to repair the equipment. If the work is going to take more hours than planned, I tell my supervisor.

14.   Contacts:

CONTACTS	PURPOSE	HOW OFTEN	INSIDE/OUTSIDE ORGANIZATION
Supply stores	Pick up parts or supplies.	Weekly	Outside

15.   The most important services or products provided and the customers:

Perform repair work as assigned. Customer is car owner.

16.   Qualifications for entry into the position:

A.   KASOCs:

Knowledge of gasoline-powered engines.
Ability to drive equipment.
Ability to read and follow instructions in repair manual.

B.   Special licenses, registration, or certification:

Apprentice license for mechanic

C.   Education or training (cite major area of study):

Heavy equipment mechanics

D.   Level and type of experience:

17.   I understand the above statements, and they are complete to the best of my knowledge.

Chris M. Green _____   *April 19* _____

Employee's Signature   Date

Bobby Diangelo _____   *4-20* _____

Supervisor's Signature   Date

FORM 4.1.1
THE POSITION DESCRIPTION

PART I: ORGANIZATIONAL INFORMATION

1. Name (last, first, middle):

2. Date:

3. Job title:

4. How many people in organization have this title?

5. Working title if different:

6. Organization:

7. Work location (county or city)

8. Division within organization:

9. Title of immediate supervisor:

10. Organizational unit:

PART II: POSITION INFORMATION

11. State the chief *objective* of the position in a brief statement:

12. Before filling out the next section, think about the *tasks and duties* performed in the position. Consider the time spent on the tasks and duties, how important they are to achieving the objective of the position, and the processes or ways in which these tasks and duties are performed. After considering these aspects of the position, state the tasks and duties that are performed in the position.

  - State the *most important* duty first and finish with the *least important* duty of the position.

  - Calculate the percent that each duty requires of the total working time. Be sure these percentages total 100.

  - Include *all* tasks, duties and functions that are performed *except* those that occupy 2 percent or less time, unless they are considered very important.

PERCENT OF TOTAL
WORKING TIME   WORK TASKS AND DUTIES

100%   (add additional pages if needed)

504

FORM 4.1.1 (*Continued*)

13. What work actions and/or decisions are made *without* prior approval? To what extent is the advice and guidance from a supervisor received? State examples of the type of supervisory advice and guidance that are received as well as actions or decisions made without prior approval.

14. List and explain the *contacts,* if any, both within and outside the organization, that are a routine function of the work. Do not list contacts with supervisors, co-workers, and subordinates.

CONTACTS	PURPOSE	HOW OFTEN	INSIDE/OUTSIDE ORGANIZATION

15. What are the *most important* services or products expected from an incumbent in the position described and who are the customers with these expectations?

Most Important Service/Product: **Customer:**

Second Most Important:

Third Most Important:

Fourth Most Important:

FORM 4.1.1 (*Continued*)

16. What are the *qualifications for entry* into this position:

    A. What KASOCs should a new employee bring to this position?

    B. Special licenses, registration, or certification:

    C. Education or training (cite major area of study):

    D. Level and type of experience:

17. I understand the above statements, and they are complete to the best of my knowledge.

_____   _____

Employee's Signature   Date

_____   _____

Supervisor's Signature (optional)   Date

_____   _____

Examiner's Signature   Date

Name _____

1. Could you use this job analysis to determine essential functions on the job? How could this be done?

2. When preparing the job description, why is it important to list the critical customers for the products or services and the major tasks and duties of the job? Are there tasks that could be excluded with little or no effect on critical customers?

3. How often should a position description form be updated? Explain your response.

4. Explain how your job description could be used to evaluate your performance or to develop methods for hiring people for the position. Do you think having a highly detailed job description is actually counterproductive for certain jobs? Explain your answer.

EXERCISE 4.2
THE USE OF THE CRITICAL INCIDENT TECHNIQUE TO ANALYZE THE JOB OF UNIVERSITY PROFESSOR

OVERVIEW

The critical incident technique is heralded as one of the best job analysis methods for the development of performance appraisal systems and training programs. You will recall from the chapter discussion that experts in job analysis rated critical incidents as one of the best for these purposes. The purpose of this exercise is to write and critique critical incidents representing the performance of college instructors. The incidents will ultimately be used to develop an appraisal system for professors.

LEARNING OBJECTIVES

After completing this exercise, you should be able to:

1. Know the difference between a good and a bad critical incident.
2. Critique incidents and revise them for purposes of appraisal development.
3. Understand the procedures to be followed in developing work functions from the critical incident technique.

PROCEDURE

Part A: Individual Project

Before class, review the section in the chapter on the criteria for useful critical incidents. Using copies of Form 4.2.1, write five critical incidents (one per form) based on observations and experiences you have had with college instructors. Write at least two examples of effective performance and two of ineffective performance. Also, prior to class, complete the assessment questions.

Part B: Group Analysis and Discussion

Step 1.   Students should be paired off. Each should read and critique incidents written by the other student using the criteria for usefulness presented in the text. Incidents that fail to meet the criteria should be rewritten after consultation with the writer. Make sure each incident is written in the same format (i.e., specific incident or single behavior, active voice, behavioral verb, visible, the action's context, and the

results or outcomes of the incident). Be specific.

Step 2.   In groups, the incidents written by group members should be subjected to a "content analysis." The content analysis identifies common themes or "functions" of behavior. The term *function* implies a category of events or incidents that fit together conceptually. For example, one such function for university professors might be "grading and testing procedures." Students will write many incidents pertaining to the way in which grades are assigned and tests are administered and scored. These incidents might all fit into a function perhaps called "grading and testing procedures." Another example of a function might be "communication skills" where examples of effective and ineffective communication skills are presented. Both positive and negative incidents can fit into the same function as long as they describe something pertaining to that function.

Each group member should read through all the incidents looking for consistencies or common themes running through the ways in which professors perform well or poorly. The group should first develop a methodology to sort incidents into piles representing functions. After the initial sorting, group members should go back through the remaining unsorted examples and try to identify new and different functions underlying these. Continue this process until as many functions are identified as are needed to represent all incidents. Label each of the functions with a short phrase.

After the group members agree on functions, they should then agree into what function each incident belongs and record that function on Form 4.2.1 in the space titled "Possible Job Function." One group member should then write the function titles on the blackboard and indicate the number of critical incidents that represented each function.

Step 3.   The overlap of the functions developed by each group should be determined through class discussion, and the class should attempt to conclude with from 7 to 15 functions that represent all the functions generated for all groups. Function titles should be merged or rewritten to accommodate all perspectives and short definitions of each functions should be written.

Step 4. Students should be regrouped and then given sets of critical incident forms. Each incident should be linked to one of the class functions identified at Step 3. After group discussion and consensus is reached, the function title should be written on each form in the section titled "Final Function Label."

Think back over your observations of various college professors. Try to recall noteworthy examples and things professors did that illustrate either unusually effective or ineffective performance. Write one example on each form.

1. What were the circumstances leading up to this example?

2. Describe exactly what was done that qualifies the example as either effective or ineffective.

3. What were the results or outcomes of the professor's actions? (Be specific.)

Possible function label _____

Final function label _____

Your name _____

Incident number _____

Group number _____

Name _____   Group _____

1. How could the critical incidents be used to prepare professors for the classroom?

2. The book describes the critical incident method as one of the best for developing performance-appraisal systems. How do you propose to get from the incidents and job functions to an actual performance-appraisal system for evaluating professors?

3. Why are results or outcomes requested with CIT? What could be done with this data?

EXERCISE 4.3
JOB ANALYSIS AT COMPTECH

OVERVIEW

Chapter 4 discusses the purposes of job analysis and the derivation of the job description and job specifications as critical products. This exercise explores the methods that could be used to assess job specifications, to solve HR problems, and to consider the implications of the actions recommended.

LEARNING OBJECTIVES

After completing this exercise, you should be able to:

1. Evaluate the processes that could be followed to assess job specifications.
2. Consider the legal and practical implications of the job specifications based on the methods you have recommended and the particular specifications you recommend.
3. Evaluate the best methods for developing training programs based on job analysis information.
4. Explore the use of job analysis to identify problems of high employee turnover.

PROCEDURE

Part A: Individual Analysis

Before class, read the scenario presented below and answer the questions on Form 4.3.1. In the space provided, write down any questions for which you need answers in order to take a definitive position on any of the issues.

Part B: Group Analysis

In groups, students should review each member's Form 4.3.1 and then attempt to reach consensus on the requested positions. You are allowed to ask the professor only three questions so decide what additional information is most important in order for you to address the most critical issues. A designated group spokesperson will present the positions of the group. Class discussion will focus on the positions taken.

SCENARIO

CompTech is a large retailer of computer products. With 442 stores in the United States and a plan for 70 more stores within two years, CompTech is the fastest growing computer retailer in the United States. The company's most important strategic objective is to meet customer requirements and expand the customer base into small-business workstations in order to build a long-term relationship. You have been retained to develop a plan for a "CompTech University" that will provide training for all store managers before taking over a store. In addition, you have been asked to evaluate the hiring process for store managers, to assess problems, and to suggest solutions.

CompTech, in competition with the other retailers, has had some difficulty recruiting store managers and the problem appears to have worsened in recent years. In addition, its turnover rate of store associates is higher than the average in retail although it is offering competitive pay packages. Exhibit 4.3.1 presents the breakdown of management vacancies at CompTech. The retailer's orientation in the past has been to hire experienced store managers from outside the company (approximately 60 percent of store managers are hired from outside the company). However, district managers, responsible for from 8 to 13 stores in a geographical area, are given great discretion in the methods and criteria they use to hire store managers. The company has had to employ a costly employment agency to locate managerial candidates along with an expensive advertising/recruiting campaign, with frequent ads in *The Wall Street Journal* and the *New York Times*. The problem has become more acute in areas with an abundance of retail outlets where retail store managers are in great and increasing demand.

Jamie Carlyle, the vice president of human resources, has three specific requests and would like you to consider two issues in particular: (1) Many district managers have required an MBA or at least three years' ex-

EXHIBIT 4.3.1
COMPTECH MANAGER DEMOGRAPHICS

	ASSISTANT MANAGER	ASSOCIATE MANAGER	STORE MANAGER	DISTRICT MANAGER
WM	612	405	282	25
WF	292	164	56	8
BM	135	85	31	2
BF	115	41	15	0
HM	93	42	19	3
HF	41	20	10	0
Vacancies	20	12	30	3

perience as a store manager as a condition of employment as a store manager. Carlyle would like you to devise a method for evaluating these job specifications. Request any additional data you need to conduct your analysis; (2) Carlyle wants to include training modules for store manager at CompTech University. How would you conduct a job analysis of the store manager job to determine what specific KASOCs are essential or critical for the job? and (3) Carlyle is interested in a more "job-related" approach to selecting managers. How do we proceed with this objective? Carlyle is not certain what type of job analysis method to use and would like your advice on this issue as well. Finally, Carlyle welcomes any opinions regarding the manner in which CompTech is filling managerial positions and any issues related to HRM problems and CompTech's objectives. Use Form 4.3.1 to respond to these issues.

Name _____   Group _____

1. What method(s) of analysis do you recommend in order to evaluate the job specifications for the store manager job?

2. What hypotheses or proposals do you have so far regarding CompTech's situation? What do you regard as the critical SWOTs based on the data you have?

3. Use this space to write specific requests for additional information you need before you can take a definitive position. In the form of "if–then" propositions, take positions based on the possible answers you might receive.

4. If CompTech decides to drop the MBA requirement, what possible effects could such a change in policy have on other human resource activities? What possible advantages do you see by keeping the MBA?

5. Carlyle is partial to the use of the PAQ to set job specifications. What is your position on the use of the PAQ relative to other job analysis methods?

6. Given Carlyle's interest in the training program and the "job-related" selection tests, what job analysis method should be used for the development of these products?

CHAPTER 5 EXERCISES

EXERCISE 5.1
A TURNOVER PROBLEM AT THE FORT LAUDERDALE HERALD*

OVERVIEW

The chapter discusses the importance of using data for better human resource planning and recruitment. The employee matching model is described. This exercise presents some data from a newspaper that documents the problems the company is having recruiting and retaining employees. Your job is to use the data as a basis for recommendations for improving the process and reducing the turnover problem.

LEARNING OBJECTIVES

After completing this exercise, you should be able to:

1. Know how to calculate and use yield ratios for planning.
2. Know how an HR problem (e.g., turnover) can be solved efficiently and effectively using HRP and recruitment.

PROCEDURE

Part A: Individual Analysis

Before class, read the background data on the *Fort Lauderdale Herald*. Using the additional information provided, think about the implications of this information for future recruitment at the newspaper. Then answer the questions at the end of the exercise.

Part B: Group Analysis

In groups, members should review each other's memos and then attempt to reach consensus on the three recommendations to go forward to the director. Analyze those recommendations in the context of the turnover problem, the potential effects on other HR programs, and the cost of implementation. Justify any specific recommendations with relevant research. A group spokesperson will then be designated to present the group consensus recommendations.

SCENARIO

The *Fort Lauderdale Herald* is located in one of the fastest growing regions in the United States. As the migration of new residents from the Northeast and Midwest

has increased the population of south Florida, subscriptions to the paper have risen sharply. The newspaper's increased circulation has generated the need for more customer service representatives. There is also increased competition with two new papers and the expansion of a Miami paper into the metropolitan area.

The advertisement for customer service representative states the following: "Qualifications are: typing 35 WPM, filing, experience in customer contact, answering telephone and referring customer calls to supervisor, some selling of additional services."

The starting salary for customer service reps is $6.65 an hour for a 30-hour workweek. Customer service reps work six days of five-hour shifts per week. They do not receive any fringe benefits.

The majority of the workday is spent talking with subscribers on the telephone regarding account or delivery problems with the newspaper. Billing errors consume about 50 percent of the rep's time. Most of the remaining time is spent responding to customer complaints such as late, improper, or no delivery. Examples of the complaints are: "The newspaper was supposed to be delivered at 7:00 a.m., but did not arrive until 9:00"; "the paper was thrown in a puddle and can't be read"; "the paper was thrown in my neighbor's yard"; and so on. Most of the subscribers who call are not friendly when registering their complaints.

While the newspaper has been able to successfully recruit new customer service reps, turnover in the position is very high. The director of human resources has prepared recruitment data shown in Exhibit 5.1.1. The data show that 200 applicants from all recruiting sources had to be screened to produce 78 who accepted a job offer. Within six months of hiring, 38 percent had resigned from the newspaper. Exit interviews with departing customer service reps revealed many reasons they were dissatisfied with the job (see Exhibit 5.1.2).

The director of human resources has asked you to analyze the recruitment and selection process and the related data and to make recommendations. In the space provided on Exhibit 5.1.1, compute the yield ratios. Compile the yield ratios for each step in the recruitment and selection process from the data presented in Exhibit 5.1.1. Think about the implications of these data for future recruitment at the newspaper. Write a three-page memo to the director of human resources that addresses each of the following issues:

1. Compare the advantages and disadvantages of the various recruiting methods used by the *Fort Lauderdale Herald*.

---

*Contributed by Joan E. Pynes.

2. Recommend recruitment/selection strategies designed to increase the length of tenure for customer service reps. Assume that nothing can be done in terms of employee pay or benefits.

3. Develop three recommendations that could be used to improve the working conditions so that turnover is reduced. Justify your recommendations.

4. What additional studies or data are necessary given the data presented in Exhibit 5.1.1?

EXHIBIT 5.1.1
DATA ON RECRUITMENT SOURCES FOR CUSTOMER SERVICE REPRESENTATIVES, LAST 3 YEARS

Name _____   Group _____

RECRUITMENT SOURCE	TOTAL NUMBER OF APPLICANTS	POTENTIALLY QUALIFIED	INTERVIEWED	QUALIFIED AND OFFERED JOB	ACCEPTED JOB	6-MONTH SURVIVAL	RECRUITMENT COST (TOTAL)
Newspaper ads	122	98	74	66	60	28	$ 465
Walk-in applicants	41	22	14	10	7	3	295
Public employment agency	37	29	17	14	11	7	250
Totals	200[a]	149[b]	105	90[c]	78	38	$1,010

Yield ratios

[a] 115 whites, 60 blacks, and 25 Hispanics.
[b] 91 whites, 43 blacks, and 15 Hispanics.
[c] 65 whites, 20 blacks, and 5 Hispanics.

EXHIBIT 5.1.2
MOST FREQUENTLY GIVEN EXPLANATIONS FOR CUSTOMER SERVICE REP TURNOVER, LAST 3 YEARS

- All customer service reps are required to work on Saturday and Sunday from 7:00 A.M. to 1:00 P.M.
- Seventy-five percent of calling customers are irate about things over which the customer service reps have no control.
- Customer service reps must sit for long periods of time talking with customers on the phone. Physical movement is restricted.
- Customer service reps have little contact with coworkers.
- The work environment is noisy and hectic.
- Customer service reps have not been trained to respond to billing complaints.
- Supervisors monitor a sample of calls taken each day and often contradict what the customer service reps say to customers.

EXERCISE 5.2
AN APPROACH TO DOWNSIZING

OVERVIEW

The chapter discusses the extent of corporate restructuring and downsizing that has occurred in the United States in recent years. Many management experts maintain that overhead reduction and downsizing is required for U.S. corporations to remain competitive. This exercise assesses the effectiveness of downsizing strategies used by a phosphate company and a pharmaceutical company.

LEARNING OBJECTIVES

After completing this exercise, you should have:

1. A better understanding of different approaches to downsizing and the advantages and disadvantages of each.
2. Knowledge of the potential problems that can develop with downsizing programs.

PROCEDURE

Part A: Individual Analysis

Step 1. Before class, review the scenarios below and the notes related to the downsizing/restructuring processes. The Phosphate Company notes were taken by Linda Trudeau, the company president's secretary, who attended the management meeting in which the president (Abbott) announces the need to downsize (Exhibit 5.2.1). Answer the questions on Form 5.2.1.

Step 2. You have been asked to review the documents that were prepared pursuant to a downsizing/restructuring program by Brooks Pharmaceutical. While Brooks had to reduce its workforce, management was very interested in retaining those personnel with the best performance records and also those who had been hired as part of the diversity program. Study these documents and prepare questions of clarification so as to help you understand the entire process of restructuring. On Form 5.2.2, comment on the effectiveness of this restructuring process and point out any potential restructuring scenarios that could pose difficulties for Brooks.

Part B: Group Analysis

Step 1. In groups, attempt to reach consensus on the Form 5.2.1 answers. Organize a group response to items 2 and 3. The instructor will designate one presenter.

Step 2. The group should also generate a list of questions regarding the downsizing and restructuring at Brooks. Prepare scenarios that could indicate future difficulties for Brooks.

EXHIBIT 5.2.1
NOTES FROM DOWNSIZING MEETING

CONFIDENTIAL
STAFF MEETING NOTES

Meeting called by company president Jarold Abbott. All unit managers attended.

The purpose of the meeting was to make preparations for a unit manpower review (UMR) and a "show and tell," which will reduce our manpower by about one-half. We will use UMR, a performance appraisal of each employee, to "clean house." New organization charts are to be drawn up as if we are running all out and then taking every bit of the "fat" out. "Show and tell" will be a reduction in force from half rate to one-third rate. (In preparing the organization charts for the UMR and the "show and tell," early retirement may be an area to look at. Abbott will distribute a list of employees who would be eligible for a program we are considering.)

We have some 30 people in the hourly ranks between 60 and 65 and some 22 people on salary between 55 and up. We want to reduce hourly by 200 people and salary by 60. This includes both the UMR phase and the "show and tell" phase.

Administrative

Presently there are three people in the traffic area. Smith states that at present rates, this is one excess person. This department can function with the supervisor and one clerk, with possibly one-half person from another area in accounting assisting when workload is high.

The purchasing supervisor's position is a training slot. He handles most of the contracts and fills in as a buyer for vacation relief for purchasing agents and storekeeper. He spends a great deal of time supervising warehouse to improve purchasing and warehousing. Abbott stated the warehouse is where we should "stash" maintenance supervisors as storekeepers and storage superintendents. Three people could be used here assuming no warehouse coverage on third shift.

Cost accounting. Messenger can go. Records retention part of that function could possibly be shared by inventory clerk, data processing clerk, or property control clerk.

Laboratory. Will be reorganized with a reduction of seven people.

Projects. Herz supervises project engineers and handles special projects. He, with Andrews, will head the wet rock grinding study. There are three senior project engineers: Valk is handling the absorbing tower and pump tank project; Naberhaus is working on rock wetting project and special projects for production; and Wischmeyer is an electrical engineer.

Plant engineering. Konopnicki is supervising plant engineers with heavy emphasis on vibration analysis and mechanical failures.
There is one senior plant engineer (Lamb).
There are two plant engineers I (Broussard and Martin). Martin is learning vibration analysis and working with Konopnicki. Broussard is an expert on rubber lining materials.
There are three development engineers (Stanton, Neff, and Chamberlin). Neff will be transferred to projects group, and Stanton reassigned to maintenance. Consider eliminating chief plant engineer position and returning Konopnicki to senior plant engineer.

Process. Andrews supervises process engineers and makes sure that environmental government regulations are in force. Andrews will also be working on wet rock grinding study.
There is one chemist I (Riddle), who does all forms on governmental regulations, pond water balances, and any special DAP projects.
There are two process engineers I (Marrone and Katzaras). Marrone will temporarily fill in for Andrews. Katzaras is working on co-generation project.
There is one engineer II (Stone), who is working on DAP projects.

Environmental engineering. One supervisor and three technicians keep track of governmental sampling.
Ken is to draw an organization chart that reflects the number of people he needs with no capital projects and operating at one-third rates (interface with production and maintenance). Possibly eliminate chief plant engineer and move to maintenance. Project can cover both areas.

Production

Presently the production department is structured with four production superintendents and four area superintendents. At one-third rates, Persons would like to restructure to combine areas I and IV and areas II and III. This would eliminate two superintendents and keep four area superintendents. Possibly eliminate area superintendent in area IV (Price) who will be interviewing for a position at Hardee County. Four shift supervisors can be eliminated at one-third rates who could become guards under industrial relations. Some early retirement will be offered.

Maintenance

The department is now staffed by two general superintendents and one superintendent over planning and coordination. The area superintendent position in area III could be eliminated (Garcia is retirement age) and the planner (Card) could be moved over to pick up contractors. One maintenance clerk can also be eliminated. At one-third rates, No. 2 and No. 3 shifts in area I. Eliminate No. 3 shift in area II and possibly Shift No. 1. McDuffie will draw up an organization chart as if Goebel, Garcia, and Lopata were to retire.

Name _____   Group _____

1. How do you evaluate this approach to workforce reduction? What (if anything) did Abbott do right and what did he do wrong? What additional information do you need about the downsizing effort to fully understand the process?

2. Three months after this meeting, Garcia (age 58) and Lopata (age 55) were discharged. Based on the information, were Garcia and Lopata victims of age discrimination? Explain your answer. If necessary, what additional information do you require before you can take a position? Provide a set of "if–then" propositions (e.g., if I know "X," then "Y" follows).

3. How would you have done the downsizing differently? Provide a chronology of steps.

EXHIBIT 5.2.2

TO ALL EMPLOYEES
FROM: DAVID BROOKS, CEO
SUBJECT: EQUAL EMPLOYMENT OPPORTUNITY
DATE: FEBRUARY

On behalf of the management of Brooks Pharmaceuticals Division, I wish to reaffirm our commitment to equal employment opportunity.

It is Brooks' policy to provide equal employment opportunity to all individuals without regard to race, color, religion, age, sex, national origin, Vietnam Era veteran, or handicapped status. This priority covers all phases of employment, including but not limited to: recruiting, hiring, training, promoting, placement, demotion or transfer; layoff, termination or recall; rates of pay or other forms of compensation, fringe benefits, the use of all facilities and participation in all company-sponsored employee activities. We impose only valid requirements to ensure that employment and promotional decisions are made in accordance with equal employment opportunity.

I have appointed Moro Hipple, senior vice president of human resources, to coordinate, implement, monitor, and report on the effectiveness of the Pharmaceuticals Division's affirmative action program. All managers and supervisors are charged with the responsibility of ensuring that any discrimination in employment is avoided. All employees are expected to recognize this policy and cooperate with its implementation.

Our affirmative action plans and programs have been developed to help us achieve full utilization of our human resources. We have made substantial progress in equal opportunity in recent years and with your continued support we will continue to move forward.

EXHIBIT 5.2.2 (*Continued*)

TO: MANAGERS

FROM: MORO HIPPLE

SUBJECT: THE HR DIVERSITY CHALLENGE PROCESS

GOAL: To follow through with our operating principles. Valuing a diverse organization by proactively considering diversity in our restructuring process.

Stages/dates in the process:
* Preliminary ratings   6/5
* Rating sheet discussion   6/6-6/7
* Management/HR review   6/22-6/24
* Adverse impact analysis/challenges   6/28
* Final ratings for decisions   7/1

Rating sheet discussions at the area offices:
* These discussions must include a representative from human resources who will challenge decisions and ensure the integrity of the process.
* HR challengers will receive a report prior to arrival at the area office which details diversity data for personnel in the area.

Management/HR review:
* HR challengers will review retention decisions with respect to diversity. HR challenger will ensure the integrity/objectivity/documentation of the process.

Impact analysis:
The final structure will be assessed against the pre-downsizing structure to test for adverse impact (e.g., 80% rule).
* A report will be generated by HR indicating pre-downsizing (current) diversity data assessed by area and position for comparison to the new organization.
* The result of this analysis may lead to possible further challenges/ratings adjustments.

EXHIBIT 5.2.2 (*Continued*)

- New sales structure
- No relos for reps and DL/minimal relocations for RIs and AIs
- Key job requirements and past performance
- Maintain organizational diversity
- Role of tenure in retention process
- Role of customer constancy
- Role of bumping
- Role of pooling
- Retention of our strongest leaders
- Retention of identified successor candidates

ROLE OF POOLING

Defined as compiling candidate lists based on similar skills, level, and geography.
If an individual's position is affected and a position of similar level is available in the geographical area, this individual will be considered for that position.
- Geographical access is defined as 30 miles or 45 minutes from place of residence to headquarter city.
- Local management can override pooling decision based on geographical constraints.

ROLE OF TENURE

Defined as date of hire at the Brooks Corporation, as indicated in the compensation database.
It should be used as a tiebreaker when two candidates cannot be clearly differentiated.

ROLE OF "BUMPING"

No one has the right to automatically "bump" to a lower level.

RETENTION PROCESS FOR FIELD SALES
ONE GOAL: CUSTOMER CONSTANCY

Balance should be achieved between the needs of customer constancy and the need to retain our best people.

RETENTION PROCESS MISSION:

Maintain Organizational Diversity
- Proactively consider diversity at each stage of the retention process
- Use a diversity challenge at each stage
- Test final structure against pre-downsize structure
- Perform adverse impact analysis

Critical Success Factors
- Retain the best people for the future
- Live within our operating principles (i.e., maintain a diverse organization)
- Ensure a flexible, adaptable organization
- Create a fair process for all employees
- Select a process to minimize adverse effects on new organization

ESTABLISHING POOLS

System support specialists and area office managers will be handled on a case-by-case basis.
- Nonexempt staff will be eligible to compete for positions in the new sales structure but will not be eligible for relocation at the company's expense.
Representatives (HSRs and field reps) in a geographical area will be pooled together and considered for the newly created institutional account manager position.
Field representatives and HSRs will also be pooled in a geographical area and considered for representative positions.
- Those who are not placed will exit the corporation.

DEVELOPING CANDIDATE LISTS

Before creating candidate lists, the following criteria are applied:
- Exit poor performers, defined as:
    Currently on probation, or a performance improvement plan as documented by human resources and before April 14.

Name _____   Group _____

1. Based on what you know so far, evaluate the *Brooks* approach to workforce reduction? What did Brooks do right and what (if anything) did the company do wrong?

2. What additional information do you need about the downsizing effort at *Brooks* to fully understand the legal implications of its restructuring?

3. One month after the restructuring, *Brooks* is informed by the EEOC that, thus far, four complaints have been filed against Brooks for discrimination in the process. What data should you examine to determine the possibility of discrimination? Generate a list of critical questions.

EXERCISE 5.3
PERMALCO'S RECRUITING CHALLENGE

OVERVIEW

Chapter 5 describes the human resource planning (HRP) process and the relationship among resource planning, recruiting, and other human resource activities. Recruiting candidates who will be top performers for an organization requires good planning, targeted strategies, and supportive human resource processes. This exercise formulates a strategy for a company that faces the challenge of recruiting production leaders during a time of change and downsizing.

LEARNING OBJECTIVES

After completing this exercise, you should be able to analyze a company's recruiting challenge and:

1. Identify the company's problems, threats, and opportunities.
2. Identify the impact of other human resource processes on recruiting.
3. Suggest logical, efficient recruiting solutions.

PROCEDURE

Part A: Individual Analysis

Before class, read the scenario. Answer the questions on Form 5.3.1.

Part B: Group Analysis

Working in groups, review each student's answers to Form 5.3.1. Formulate a recruiting plan for Permalco. Include in your plan:

1. Short-term and long-term strategies.
2. Measures of success.
3. Sources of candidates.
4. Recruiting techniques.
5. Recommendations for changes to other human resource systems.

SCENARIO

Tracy Johnson threw open the doors of the storeroom supply cabinet and grimaced at the disarray. She pulled out a few old brochures, dusted them off, and closed the cabinet doors. Shaking her head, she noted that at least half of the people pictured in the brochure were no longer with Permalco.

As she emerged from the storeroom into the aluminum smelting plant she stuffed her long brown hair under her hard hat and donned her safety glasses. Although the early spring weather was cool, the plant was sweltering. Her heavy safety boots clattered against the brick walkway. Here and there someone was tending carbon-lined shells, called pots, where alumina is dissolved into a molten chemical bath. It still amazed her that the electric current that entered the pot and separated the alumina into oxygen and aluminum was so strong that a paper clip chain on the pot would stand straight up like a flagpole. Ahead of Tracy, a crew was siphoning molten metal into a large container called a crucible. The flames and smoke from the pot seemed like hell, but the computer-generated voice from the loudspeaker chanting, "Pot 8. Anode Effect. Pot 8. Anode Effect," reminded Tracy that the smelter was a high-tech facility.

"Hey, sweet thing, how come you don't visit me more often?" shouted Cyrus "Hound Dog" Palmer. Although sexist comments from the crews bothered her, she knew she could accomplish more if she played along. "Hound Dog, I couldn't stand the excitement," retorted Tracy, continuing on her way. She heard the rest of the crew laughing at Cyrus.

Tracy's office was in an area outside the smelter. She had a few minutes to prepare an agenda for the first meeting of the recruiting team. Tracy glanced out the dirty window as a crucible hauler roared by and shook her desk. She recalled her first exposure to Permalco. Permalco's booth at her college career fair proudly displayed pictures of young engineers at work in various parts of Permalco's Landon Works, a smelter located in the mountains of western North Carolina. Landon's recruiter, a young man with a lovely southern accent, was animated as he spoke about Landon Works and Permalco. "The salary and benefits are top notch. You'll have opportunity to advance and transfer to other divisions. You're a mechanical engineer?" Tracy nodded. "We're installing a fume control system in the plant now. It's like playing with Tinker Toys. You'll love it."

And she did. Permalco had recently modernized Landon Works, and Tracy loved working on the high-tech equipment. However, she had accepted an entry-level position at Landon with the thought that she would be able to transfer to a facility closer to a metropolitan area. Although she loved the people in the community, she found it hard to meet other young professionals. Her dream of moving beyond Landon died when the CEO made each division a separate business. She didn't even hear about position openings anymore.

She sighed. The worst part was that after eight years she was worried about her job. Landon had recently laid off 30 percent of its employees, mainly young people.

She walked to the conference room at the end of the trailer. Carbon dust from the plant blanketed the steel table and mismatched chairs. She had just finished writing the agenda on the flip chart when the other members of the recruiting team walked in.

Elizabeth Gomez and Jim Brownwell found seats around the table. Elizabeth pulled off her hard hat to reveal dark hair plastered to her forehead. "I've been taking pot temperature readings all day. I swear I drank two gallons of water from the fountain in the hall. And it's not even summer yet."

Jim responded, "Switch to the graveyard shift. Even though you don't have a life at least it's cooler." Elizabeth laughed.

Jim turned to Tracy, "Can you believe after all the layoffs we're looking for people again? Are the managers crazy?"

"Yes, what is going on, Tracy?" asked Elizabeth.

Tracy paused before she spoke. "There's no doubt about it. This is a challenge. As the managers look at the people in our line organization, they believe there are not enough people to fill our future production leadership positions. They have asked us to begin a recruiting effort focused on future leaders. They asked for both of you because you are good performers and they feel you can talk in a motivated way about opportunities at Permalco."

"Opportunities at Permalco?" snapped Jim. "How can I talk about opportunities when I'm not sure about my future?"

"How many people do they want to hire, Tracy?" asked Elizabeth, sighing.

"Two people this year, if we find people that meet our standards. We need to continue feeding the pipeline with good candidates each year. And by the way, our recruiting focus will be on females and minorities."

Tracy leaned toward them. "Remember, when we were hired, Permalco looked for the best engineer. The engineer with the highest grade point average. The man-

agers hoped that engineers would emerge who had the desire and skills to be a production leader. That strategy won't work today. We must look for a special person. The person who wants to be a leader. The person who was the captain of the football team or head cheerleader. President of the fraternity or sorority. The person whose gleam in their eye says, 'I want to make the million dollar decisions.'"

Jim shot back, "Yeah, the person who wants to do shift work for five years. Shift work used to be a temporary developmental assignment—a way to pay your dues before moving up the ladder. Since the layoffs there isn't anywhere for the production supervisors to go. They're stuck. The good salary and benefits have handcuffed them to Landon."

Elizabeth spoke. "I'm concerned, too. This plant is not the ideal place for a female or a minority. If I hadn't married Bill I imagine I would have left for a different company by now. There are no other Hispanic professionals in the entire town! That's one of the reasons why so many minorities have left Landon."

Tracy nodded, "You're both frustrated with this project. I am, too. But we're going to need people in these critical positions in a few years. Starting now gives us ample time to bring the right people in and develop them. Are you ready to put together a recruiting strategy for the plant manager? By Friday?"

Jim and Elizabeth reluctantly nodded. Tracy grabbed a flip chart marker. "So, where are we going to find these special people?"

"Tracy, you remember what it's like on campus," recalled Elizabeth. "The qualified minorities have been targeted by the large firms before their sophomore year. And for females the competition is intense, too. I had at least three summer internship offers each year. How are we going to attract the top students?"

Jim replied, "Campus isn't the only source of candidates, Elizabeth. Permalco hired me through a recruiting firm when I was leaving the military. Once you've been on a submarine for three months, shift work is no big deal."

Tracy smiled as she began to record the ideas on the flip chart.

Name _____   Group _____

1. Identify the SWOT at Permalco as related to recruiting production leaders?

2. What information must the team gather before it can formulate a recruiting strategy?

3. How might the short-term and long-term recruiting strategies differ?

4. What sources of candidates should the team consider?

5.   What recruiting strategy has the highest probability of paying off for the team?

6.   When planning the recruiting strategy, what other HR systems must the team consider?

7.   What challenges face the recruiting team because of the focus on females and minorities?

CHAPTER 6 EXERCISES

EXERCISE 6.1
SHOULD TENNECO USE THE WONDERLIC TEST?

OVERVIEW

Although cognitive ability tests have been shown to be valid, they are likely to result in adverse impact against minorities because of average test score differences. Recall our discussion in the text regarding the Wonderlic Personnel Test. The purpose of this exercise is to have the student consider the options available for dealing with the problem of a valid test that will probably cause adverse impact.

LEARNING OBJECTIVES

After completing this exercise, you should have a better understanding of the implications of the use of cognitive ability tests and should be capable of developing and articulating a rationale for the use of a cognitive ability test under specific circumstances.

PROCEDURE

Part A: Individual Analysis

Before class, read the scenario presented below regarding the Tenneco Corporation and answer the questions on Form 6.1.1. Be prepared to defend your position in group discussion.

Part B: Group Analysis

In groups, each student should review the written responses of other members to the questions on Form 6.1.1. The group should then attempt to reach consensus on each of the questions. A written group response should be developed for each of the questions, and a group spokesperson should be designated to present the group's positions on the use of the test.

SCENARIO

Tenneco Corporation is considering the use of the Wonderlic Personnel Test as part of its selection process for assistant store managers. Each assistant store manager has management responsibilities for one convenience store. Responsibilities include complete supervision of at least 15 employees, including hiring, firing, and scheduling; budgetary matters; inventory; vendor deliveries; and customer issues. Tenneco hopes to maintain a policy of promotion from within and thus administered the Wonderlic to 300 store employees. The average scores of minorities and whites who took the 100-point exam were as follows: Blacks, 63, Hispanics, 70, and whites, 76 (the standard deviation was 10). The five-week training program at Tenneco headquarters has room for only 20 managerial trainees. The training is required for promotion to assistant store manager. As a new HRM personnel specialist, you have been asked to recommend a specific policy for the use of the Wonderlic. Answer each of the questions on Form 6.1.1.

1. Assuming that only 20 candidates are to be selected for the training program, is adverse impact likely against minorities if the Wonderlic Personnel Test is used as the sole basis for entry into the training? Explain your answer.

2. Given your response to question 1, what are the policy options for this situation? What policy do you recommend that Tenneco adopt for the use of the Wonderlic? Defend your response by considering the job situation, the need for further research, legal and social implications, and *alternative methods of selection*. Provide a detailed recommendation and rationale for action.

3. What if you conducted a *PAQ* analysis which indicated that the Wonderlic was a valid test to use for this job? Do you believe that this result establishes the legality at the Wonderlic? Explain your answer.

EXERCISE 6.2
HIRING A PLANT MANAGER AT DYNAMO INDUSTRIES*

OVERVIEW

Personnel selection decisions are typically made based on a collection of information from several sources. An organization may have test scores, previous performance appraisals, interview ratings, biographical information, and other data on the candidates. This exercise gives the student a feel for making a final recommendation based on such a collection of data. In addition, through the group interaction, students should gain an understanding of the process involved in a leaderless group discussion.

Your assignment is to review candidate credentials for the plant manager positions at Dynamo Industries in Pittsburgh.

LEARNING OBJECTIVES

After completing this exercise, you should be able to:

1. Distinguish between candidate information that is valuable and should be considered in the decision from that which should be ignored.

2. Articulate your rationale for decisions.

3. Suggest ways in which the selection process could be improved.

4. Understand the dynamics of a leaderless group discussion.

PROCEDURE

Part A: Individual Analysis

Before class, review the material presented below. Assume the following:

You are the vice president of personnel. You are to write a report (a one-page executive summary followed by *no more* than three double-spaced pages of supporting information) that includes the following:

  a. A rank ordering of your top four choices for the Pittsburgh job based on the information you have now.

  b. An *in-depth* discussion of how this rank ordering was reached (a rationale for some candidates being ranked higher than others and for others not being ranked).

  c. A brief discussion of how the selection process for hiring a plant manager should be changed in the future (e.g., additional selection devices to use, addi-

tional information to gather, sources to drop or change).

  d. A request for whatever additional information you would like to have regarding the process or the candidates, which could affect your rank-orderings.†

This report will be sent to the vice president of production and to the president of Dynamo Industries. Bring this report to class.

Part B: Group Analysis

Step 1. Groups should be charged with reaching a consensus on the rank ordering of the top four candidates. Each member should be given an opportunity to review the others' written reports. The instructor will designate the time to be allotted to this process and will provide additional information on request. In addition, each group should reach consensus on the changes to be made for hiring the plant manager in the future.

SCENARIO

Dynamo Industries is a medium-sized manufacturer of small electrical motors headquartered in St. Paul, Minnesota. The firm employs 9,800 people. Dynamo Industries has plants in St. Paul; Columbus, Ohio; Atlanta; San Diego; Pittsburgh; Providence, Rhode Island, and Little Rock, Arkansas. All these plants are unionized, although the power of the respective unions varies greatly.

Recently, the company has been trying to hire a new plant manager (see job description in Exhibit 6.2.1) for the Pittsburgh plant (plant managers report directly to the vice president of production). Although Dynamo Industries has experienced slightly above average growth and profit compared to its competitors, the Pittsburgh plant has been a trouble spot. Over the past three years, production costs there have been extremely high and there has been labor strife (e.g., numerous work slowdowns, an excessive number of grievances filed). The most recent Pittsburgh plant manager was terminated although by mutual agreement the company stated he left for a better job with another company. Because of the importance of the plant manager position, Dynamo Industries has used several expensive selection devices.

*Contributed by James A. Breaugh.

† Your instructor may stipulate that requests for additional information may be e-mailed prior to the class meeting.

These devices are detailed below. After a thorough recruitment effort (both within and outside the company) and some initial screening, the list of job candidates has been reduced to eight names. Exhibit 6.2.2 contains extensive information on each of the eight candidates.

Dynamo Industries does not have an established philosophy for filling job openings. In the past, it has favored promotion from within the company. However, the vice president of production was hired externally. Dynamo has no policy on lateral transfers. In the recent past, such transfers have been rare. The key issue seems to be whether the company benefits from the transfer.

EXHIBIT 6.2.1
PLANT MANAGER JOB DESCRIPTION

(Written by the vice president of production)

The plant manager (PM) is ultimately responsible for the operating efficiency of the entire plant. In fulfilling his/her responsibilities, the PM regularly consults with subordinate supervisory personnel (the PM frequently delegates duties). A plant manager must be somewhat knowledgeable of production methods and the capabilities of equipment. Some of the activities the plant manager is directly or indirectly involved in include:

1. Procuring materials.
2. Maintaining the plant.
3. Controlling quality.
4. Using manpower.
5. Establishing budgets.
6. Revising production schedules because of equipment failure or operation problems.
7. Consulting with engineering personnel concerning the modification of machinery to improve production quantity, the quality of products, and employee safety.
8. Conducting hearings to resolve employee grievances.
9. Participating in union–management contract negotiations.
10. Ensuring safety.
11. Establishing community relations.

EXHIBIT 6.2.2
BACKGROUND INFORMATION ON THE CANDIDATES

1. *George Martin*—age 44. Education: B.A., University of Wisconsin; M.A. (Industrial Relations), Cornell University. He is a plant manager of a relatively small (580 nonunion employees) plant (located in Cleveland) of one of Dynamo's competitors. Martin has held that job for the past six years. He has been with that company for 14 years. No reference information was gathered because Martin was concerned about his present employer's reaction.

2. *Tony Caciopo*—age 59. Education: high school graduate. He is an assistant plant manager (Providence). Caciopo has been with Dynamo for 24 years. He has been assistant plant manager in Providence for the past 10 years. He had a severe heart attack four years ago but appears to have recovered. Ten years ago, he was offered a job as plant manager by Dynamo but turned it down because of health problems his wife was having.

3. *Kathy Joyce*—age 36. Education: B.A., Indiana University. She is currently plant manager of the Little Rock plant. She desires a lateral transfer because it would enhance job opportunities for her husband. Joyce has been with Dynamo for five years. She has been plant manager at Little Rock for two years.

4. *Barry Fein*—age 49. Education: associate degree (2 years) from Morehead State University. Until two months ago, Fein was plant manager at a large, unionized textile plant. Two months ago, the company Fein worked for discontinued this product line and he was let go. Fein had been with his former company for 20 years and was plant manager for 5 years. His letters of reference were excellent.

5. *Ron Jackson*—age 33. Education: B.A., Howard University; M.B.A., Northwestern. He is currently an assistant plant manager at the Pittsburgh plant. He has been with the company for four years; he has been assistant plant manager for two years. He has served as acting plant manager at Pittsburgh for the past two months.

6. *Jay Davis*—age 46. Education: B.A., Harvard; M.B.A., Harvard. He is currently assistant plant manager (Atlanta). Davis has been with Dynamo for 10 years; the past 7 years he has been assistant plant manager (6 years in St. Paul, the past year in Atlanta).

7. *Frank Hall*—age 58. Education: B.S. (chemistry), Duke University. He is currently vice president for production for one of Dynamo's major competitors. He says he seeks a demotion so that he is required to travel less. He has been vice president of production for six years. Before that, he was a plant manager for 12 years. The plant was organized. No reference information is available. However, he has received outstanding reviews in trade publications for his performance as vice president.

8. *Tom Doyle*—age 36. Education: B.A., Williams College; M.B.A., University of Chicago. For the past two years, Tom has worked as a special assistant to the vice president of production. Before this he was an assistant PM for two years and a PM (Little Rock) for three years. Tom was the youngest PM ever appointed at Dynamo. He was very ineffective as a PM and after three years was removed from this position.

EXHIBIT 6.2.3   **539**

EXHIBIT 6.2.3
PERSONALITY PROFILE

Each of the eight candidates was examined by a psychiatrist. She utilized personality tests (e.g., 16PF, the Myers-Briggs Type Indicator, and the Thematic Apperception Test) in drawing the following conclusions.

CANDIDATES' RATINGS

	HIGH	MEDIUM	LOW
Ability to handle stress	Martin Caciopo Davis	Joyce Jackson Fein Doyle	Hall
Ability to resolve conflict	Joyce Davis Caciopo	Martin Doyle Hall	Fein Jackson
Interpersonal skills	Martin Joyce	Hall Jackson Caciopo	Davis Fein Doyle
Most likely to succeed as a plant manager	Martin Caciopo Davis	Joyce Doyle Hall Jackson	Fein

EXHIBIT 6.2.4
INTERVIEWERS' RATINGS

	VICE PRESIDENT PRODUCTION	VICE PRESIDENT PERSONNEL	COLUMBUS PLANT MANAGER	ATLANTA PLANT MANAGER
George Martin	6.5	6	5.5	4
Tony Caciopo	5	5.5	4.5	6
Kathy Joyce	6	6.5	5	5.5
Barry Fein	4	4	3	4
Ron Jackson	5	5.5	4.5	5
Jay Davis	4.5	5	3.5	6.5
Frank Hall	6.5	7	Interviewer on vacation day of interview	4
Tom Doyle	5.5	6	4.5	6

Note: Each of the interviewers went through a one-day interview training program. The vice president of production's interviews averaged three hours in length. The other interviews averaged 60 minutes in length. Interview ratings were made on a seven-point scale (1 = poor candidate . . . 7 = excellent candidate). All interviews were semistructured.

EXHIBIT 6.2.5
INTELLIGENCE TESTS AND
HANDWRITING ANALYSES

CANDIDATE	INTELLIGENCE TEST	HANDWRITING RATING
George Martin	119	+3
Tony Caciopo	116	+1
Kathy Joyce	141	−1
Barry Fein	122	0
Ron Jackson	114	+2
Jay Davis	148	+2
Frank Hall	112	+3
Tom Doyle	125	+3

Note: The intelligence test (Wechsler Adult Intelligence Scale) given by Dynamo Industries is commonly used for selecting candidates for management. Individuals scoring below 115 tend not to do well in managerial jobs. Standard error equals 3.5.

The handwriting analyst rated the plant manager candidates in terms of their likelihood of success as the Pittsburgh plant manager (−3 = very poor prospect . . . +3 = very strong prospect).

EXHIBIT 6.2.6
PROMOTABILITY RATINGS, PERFORMANCE RATINGS,
AND WORK SAMPLE SCORES

CANDIDATE	PROMOTABILITY	PERFORMANCE	WORK SAMPLE SCORE
George Martin	Not available	NA	19.5
Tony Caciopo	6	5	15.5
Kathy Joyce	5	6	18.5
Barry Fein	NA	NA	18.5
Ron Jackson	5.5	6	18
Jay Davis	7	7	16.5
Frank Hall	NA	NA	19
Tom Doyle	5.5	6	17.5

Note: A promotability rating was made as part of the annual performance review (7 = ready for immediate promotion . . . 1 = should not be promoted). The performance rating ranges from 1 = poor performance . . . 7 = exceptional performance. As part of the selection process, all applicants went through a series of work sample tests (i.e., in-basket, leaderless group discussion, and production planning exercise). Scoring was done by trained raters from the personnel department (20 = highest possible score).

EXERCISE 6.3
WHAT QUESTIONS CAN YOU ASK IN AN INTERVIEW?*

OVERVIEW

Chapter 6 describes the potential legal liability inherent in the employment interview. Given the subjective nature of the process and the discretion interviewers typically exercise in the interview, there is great opportunity for biases that could be interpreted as violations of any number of state, federal, or local laws on equal opportunity. This exercise explores the potential legal implications of a number of questions often posed by interviewers. The student may want to review Chapter 3 before attempting this exercise.

LEARNING OBJECTIVES

After completing this exercise, you should be able to:

1. Identify those interview questions that are of questionable legality.
2. Know the major laws that may affect the interview process.

PROCEDURE

Part A: Individual Analysis

Before class, check whether each question on Form 6.3 should probably be avoided during an employment interview. For those questions that you consider to be illegal or *potentially* illegal, in the space below the question, provide a justification for your position, citing an applicable law or regulation where appropriate. Rewrite any questions that could yield useful information. Also, before class, do the Assessment Questions.

Part B: Group Analysis

Step 1. In groups, students should compare responses on each item and decide on a group response and justification for each. The items should then be divided among the students so that each group member is prepared to present the group position on the set of 20 items. Also, the group should compose a response to each of the assessment questions for this exercise. Class discussion will focus on group responses to each item and possible discrepancies in the correct answers.

---

*Contributed by Robert W. Eder and M. Ronald Buckley.

FORM 6.3

Name _____ Group _____

QUESTION IS ACCEPTABLE	QUESTION SHOULD BE AVOIDED	
_____	_____	1. Would you mind if I called you by your first name?
_____	_____	2. Are you a citizen of the United States?
_____	_____	3. Are you married or do you live with someone?
_____	_____	4. Have you ever been arrested?
_____	_____	5. What professional societies do you belong to?
_____	_____	6. What kinds of people do you enjoy working with the most?
_____	_____	7. Are you planning to start a family soon?
_____	_____	8. How long do you expect your husband will remain here before changing jobs?
_____	_____	9. I can't help but notice the great shape you've kept yourself in. How do you do it?
_____	_____	10. We're looking for someone who can relate effectively with college students; you're 52?
_____	_____	11. Have you ever been convicted of a crime (beyond traffic violations)?
_____	_____	12. Will your family or personal obligations interfere in your ability to keep the hours of this job?
_____	_____	13. How does your military experience relate to this job?
_____	_____	14. What are your religious beliefs?

———————— ———————— 15. How do you feel about getting personally involved with someone at work?

———————— ———————— 16. Would you be willing to work on Yom Kippur?

———————— ———————— 17. How long have you lived around here?

———————— ———————— 18. Are you a smoker or a nonsmoker?

———————— ———————— 19. Are you a homosexual?

———————— ———————— 20. What plans do you have for taking care of the children if you get this job?

———————— ———————— 21. Do you consider yourself handicapped in any way?

———————— ———————— 22. Is there any history of chronic illness in your family?

———————— ———————— 23. One of your references mentioned that you have a history of depression. Is this still a problem?

———————— ———————— 24. Given that you are in a wheelchair, how do you think you'll be able to do this work?

Name _____

1. How would you design a training program so that future interviewers would understand what can and cannot be asked in an employment interview?

2. If your organizational research had clearly established (with data) that women with children under the age of five are much more likely to be absent from work than others could the company then use this information to make decisions?

3.   How would you design a structured, behavioral interview for an overseas assignment?

4.   Discuss the ethical and legal implications of asking applicants about the health history of family members. Setting aside the possible legal issues, should a company take family health into consideration when evaluating an applicant?

CHAPTER 7 EXERCISES

EXERCISE 7.1
CONDUCTING A NEEDS ASSESSMENT*

OVERVIEW

To determine whether training is needed to address a particular area of concern in an organization (e.g., performance problem), it is first necessary to conduct a needs assessment. As stated in Chapter 7, a thorough needs assessment consists of an organizational analysis, job or task analysis, and a person analysis. This exercise gives the student practice in conducting a needs assessment.

LEARNING OBJECTIVES

After completing this exercise, you should be able to:

1. Understand the various components of a needs assessment.
2. Develop items to conduct an organizational analysis, task analysis, and person analysis.
3. Interpret the results from a needs assessment, describing the implications for designing a training program.

PROCEDURE

Step 1. Before coming to class, each person should review Chapter 7, paying particular attention to the section on needs assessment. Choose a job with which you are very familiar. Collect and review job analysis data (see Chapter 4). From this material, generate a list of "possible training topics" for an individual in that job (i.e., what are the different types of training that might be beneficial for performing that job). For example, if the job is a patrol officer, possible training topics might include: handling firearms, dealing with domestic issues, arrest procedure, teamwork, stress management, legal issues, and investigation. You should generate as long of a list as possible (e.g., 40 to 50 topics).

Step 2. Using Form 7.1, interview employees (at least two) in the job you have chosen. Try to choose a representative sample of employees for the interviews. You may interview them individually or in a group.

Step 3. Summarize your findings from the needs assessment in a one-page report to the vice president of human resources. Offer *specific* recommendations regarding training for the job.

Step 4. Students will be paired. Form 7.1 should be exchanged and critiqued. Reviewers should evaluate the extent to which the responses to Form 7.1 provide guidelines for improving the training functions for this job.

---

*Contributed by Jeffrey D. Kudisch, Stephanie D. Myers, and Joyce E. A. Russell.

FORM 7.1

Job: _____   Organization: _____

Interviewer(s): _____   Date: _____

PART A: BACKGROUND INFORMATION OF INTERVIEWEE

Years in the job: _____   Years in the company: _____

Highest level of education completed: _____

Part B: Organizational Analysis (Attitudes and Climate for Training)

From your perspective, what are the purposes of training?

How successful are current training programs in your firm for achieving these purposes?

If you asked a fellow worker to give his or her opinion regarding training in this firm, what would his or her response likely be?

Do you think trainees are motivated to attend training? Explain your response.

Do you think employees in your job experience any resistance toward attending training? Do you have any suggestions for minimizing this resistance?

What positive consequences are associated with successful completion of training (e.g., increased pay, greater promotional opportunities, recognition)? Are there any negative consequences associated with attending training (e.g., loss of production, loss of status among peers)?

Do you think it is difficult for trainees to apply the skills they learned in training once they return back to the job? Why or why not?

For training programs you have attended, are you asked to provide your reactions to the programs? Are you given learning tests before and after training to assess a change in your learning?

Part C: Task and Person Analysis
Describe the major duties of your job. Rank these in terms of importance.

Take a moment to think about an individual who is especially effective at your job. What knowledges, abilities, or skills does this person possess? Can these skills be enhanced through training?

Looking ahead over the next five years, do you foresee any additional job demands being added to the current responsibilities in your job? If so, what additional skills or abilities will be needed to meet these demands?

Note to the interviewer: Hand the list of "possible training topics" to the interviewee(s). Give them the following instructions.

Step 1: After looking over the list, circle those 10 areas that are most critical to successful performance in your job.

Step 2: Of the 10 items you identified, check those areas in which training would be beneficial to your job performance.

Reviewer's Name _____

Comment on the extent to which this needs assessment provides guidelines for meeting training needs.

EXERCISE 7.2
RAINYDAY INSURANCE ADJUSTERS COMPANY*

OVERVIEW

Often in organizations, new equipment may be installed without designing or offering the appropriate amount or type of training. As a result, productivity and job satisfaction of employees may decline causing business losses for a firm. In some cases, the training problems may also be related to other problems in the organization (e.g., communication, management issues). It is the HR professional's job to diagnose the nature of the problems and offer realistic, timely recommendations. This exercise provides the student with some case information and has the student diagnose the problems with the company and offer recommendations for addressing those problems.

LEARNING OBJECTIVES

After completing this exercise, you should be able to:

1. Understand how to interpret partial needs assessment information to determine the next steps that must be taken in collecting additional information.

2. Use needs assessment information to develop plans for designing or implementing training.

PROCEDURE

Part A: Individual Analysis

Step 1. Read the background material presented in Exhibit 7.2.1. Note that you have been hired by the CEO to help the company interpret its problems and to draft some recommendations. In the first few days, you have collected some information, which is contained in the exhibit.

Step 2. Complete the questions found in Form 7.2.1.

Part B: Group Analysis

Step 1. In groups, discuss your responses to Form 7.2.1

Step 2. As a group, reach consensus on what the company's problems are. Then outline a short-term plan (within the month) and a longer-term plan (over the next six months) to address those problems. Make sure your group includes the timeline for when each recommendation should be implemented and what the benefits and drawbacks are to each suggestion.

---

*Contributed by Steven M. Barnard and Joyce E. A. Russell.

EXHIBIT 7.2.1
BACKGROUND INFORMATION ON RAINYDAY INSURANCE ADJUSTERS COMPANY

Based in South Florida, Rainyday Insurance Adjusters is a medium-sized company with 135 employees and seven managers. They process the claims of insurance holders who have experienced various misfortunes (e.g., hurricanes, floods). Their primary job is to determine the amount to be paid out and process the paperwork for some of the smaller insurance agencies in the area so that final payments can be issued. Although the company is only eight years old, it has done quite well and has seen a large increase in business. It has a reputation for quality work and quick turnaround on claims. Because customers are often eager to move on after misfortunes strike, Rainyday has built a loyal following by the insurance agencies that depend on it. Delayed claims often cost these companies time and money when they have to interact with continuous customer complaints.

To accommodate the increase in customers, six months ago, Rainyday expanded its office in the current building and upgraded all its equipment to make the company more efficient and to allow workers to process claims more quickly. In particular, computers were upgraded to facilitate speedier turnaround and higher capacity from claims processors. The new computers represent a large investment the company cannot afford to underutilize. Since installation of the computers, Rainyday has experienced a number of problems with voluntary turnover among claims processors as well as decreased productivity and increased errors.

Recently, the CEO of Rainyday, Rebecca Stephens, hired you as a consultant to help determine what, if any, training needs the claims processors have. There are 85 processors in the claims department. On your first day, you talked with several employees in the claims department. Fran, one of the more senior claims processors, has been with the company since it started eight years ago. He has become increasingly dissatisfied since the new computers arrived. As he remarked to you, "The managers told us the new computers would make our jobs easier, but they have been nothing but trouble. We spend half of our time printing out the forms and then we have to go back and correct errors on them. Also, some of the newer claims processors have been bugging me to show them how to fill out the forms. I don't have time for that, and besides, they should have learned it themselves in all those hotshot computer classes they have taken. On top of all that, my manager, Paula, stops by every day and tells us we all need to work faster because we are getting behind. I'm telling you, I have had it. I'm about to join the others and quit."

After your conversation with Fran, you decide that before you start drafting an action plan for the training program, you had better meet with Fran's manager to get her perspective. Paula seems friendly enough and is very open about what she

thinks are the reasons for the problems. "Ever since we got the new computers, we have been having problems. Errors have increased, productivity has gone down, and we have had a lot of employees quit. At first, I thought it was just the new computers, but I also noticed a lot of bickering among the claims processors. It seems the more senior processors have resented the new hires, perhaps because some of their buddies quit the firm." After further inquiry, Paula mentioned that when the new computers arrived, she offered to send everyone to the local high school to take a computer class that would teach them how to use the computers and the software. The class was offered early in the morning (6:30 A.M. to 8:00 A.M.) so employees could take the class and still make it to work only one hour later than they normally arrived. They could get to work by 8:30 A.M., which was one hour after their normal start time. Paula also told employees they would be paid for the hour of work they missed. As she noted to you, "I was surprised that the employees did not seem more excited about the idea of the training. In fact, a number of employees told me that they did not want to be going to school with a bunch of teenagers and said they would just train themselves."

After talking with Paula, you asked her to point you in the direction of one of the newer employees who had been experiencing conflicts with the more senior employees. You reserved a conference room and met with Malcolm. He was very talkative and had a lot to complain about, especially regarding the older employees. "I'm having a pretty tough time here. After I took those computer classes at the high school, the computers have been really easy to work with, but I'm still having trouble filling out the claims forms. One of the senior employees, Randall, is supposed to help me, but he seems too busy. I think that he and the other old-timers are just jealous that some of the newer employees know the shortcuts on the computer. It's kind of funny watching them try to format their claims, they get so frustrated because they don't have a clue how to work the computers. I told a few of them I would show them, but they said they didn't need help from 'a youngster.' Fine by me, I have plenty to do."

After meeting with Malcolm, you realize that things don't sound too good. Because of the delays in the work by the claims processors, customers have been complaining to the insurance companies. Consequently, the firms are threatening to drop Rainyday. With all of their expansion efforts, Rainyday needs customers now more than ever. The CEO said to you as you were leaving for the day, "If things don't improve soon, we may be out of business." She encouraged you to develop a training program or whatever you think would help to improve the productivity of the claims department.

BASED ON THE INFORMATION YOU REVIEWED IN EXHIBIT 7.2.1, RESPOND TO THE FOLLOWING QUESTIONS.

Name _____   Group _____

1.   What do you see as the major problems at Rainyday Insurance Adjusters Company?

2.   What are the causes of those problems?

FORM 7.2.1 (*Continued*)

3. What steps should be taken to better understand the performance problems at Rainyday? That is, what would you do to conduct a more thorough needs assessment to better pinpoint the problems?

4. Provide several suggestions for addressing the problems in the claims department at Rainyday.

EXERCISE 7.3
BACKWOODS MAIL ORDER COMPANY*

OVERVIEW

HR professionals are often contacted by an organization to design and deliver a training program to meet a specific problem in the organization (e.g., declining productivity, increasing customer complaints). In some cases, the organization has already conducted a needs assessment and has some idea of what the specific problem is. The HR professional may be asked to review the needs assessment findings and design a training program to meet the specified needs or goals. This exercise provides you with information about a company and the needs assessment findings in order to design a training program.

LEARNING OBJECTIVES

After completing this exercise, you should be able to:

1. Review results from a training needs assessment and design a training plan to address the needs, detailing training objectives, training techniques to use, and the length of training.
2. Outline an evaluation plan to assess the effectiveness of the training program.

PROCEDURE

Part A: Individual Analysis

Step 1. Before coming to class, read Exhibit 7.3.1, which contains the background information on Backwoods Mail Order Company as well as information about the needs assessment that has already been conducted.

Step 2. Complete the questions found on Form 7.3.1.

Part B: Class Discussion and Small Group Analysis

Step 1. As a class, review responses to Form 7.3.1. Discuss the learning objectives of the training program, the training techniques to be used, the duration of the training, and the plan for evaluating the training.

Step 2. In groups, write out ideas for the types of questions that should be included in a reaction form of the training. Each group should draft its own reaction form and share the form with the class.

*Contributed by Steve Long.

EXHIBIT 7.3.1
BACKGROUND INFORMATION ON BACKWOODS MAIL ORDER COMPANY

Backwoods is a telephone and mail-order company that specializes in camping supplies and outdoor clothing. Gerald Banks is the operating manager of Backwoods' customer service department. He is interested in training his 40 employees in the customer orders group to be more effective in filling customers' orders, more helpful in answering customer questions, and more polite in dealing with customer problems and complaints. To familiarize you with the company and the job of customer order representative, an organizational chart and job description are provided below.

BACKWOODS ORGANIZATIONAL CHART

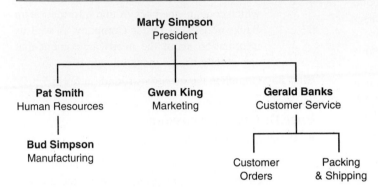

Marty Simpson
President

Pat Smith
Human Resources

Gwen King
Marketing

Gerald Banks
Customer Service

Bud Simpson
Manufacturing

Customer
Orders

Packing
& Shipping

CUSTOMER SERVICE DIVISION

The customer service department consists of 40 employees and four supervisors in the customer orders group and 32 employees and three supervisors in the packing and shipping group. Employees are evenly divided into two shifts: a day shift (7 A.M. to 3 P.M.) and a night shift (3 P.M. to 11 P.M.). Employees in the customer orders group handle incoming calls from customers and record customers' orders on a central computer system that checks the availability of each item ordered. Orders are then transmitted to the shipping department where shipping clerks pull the items from inventory and pack them for overnight delivery.

JOB DESCRIPTION FOR CUSTOMER ORDER REPRESENTATIVES

- Takes customer orders by telephone or direct mail.
- Answers customer questions about product prices, sizing, colors, features, and availability.
- Assists customers on the phone in determining equipment or clothing needs based on season, climate, or use requirements.
- Enters phone and mail orders into on-line order processing computer system.
- Processes returned merchandise, completes a defective merchandise form for quality assurance, and routes serviceable merchandise for repackaging.
- Handles customer complaints about problems or defects in merchandise, wrong sizes, or mistakes on customers' orders (wrong products delivered).
- Responds to questions about orders from employees in the shipping and handling group.

THE TRAINEES

The trainees will consist of the 40 employees in the customer order group as well as their four supervisors. Customer service employees earn about $7 per hour, and supervisors earn about $9 per hour. All employees must receive training, yet service must still be available to customers (i.e., you cannot put everyone through the training at the same time of the day or there will be no one to handle incoming calls from customers).

PROBLEMS IDENTIFIED BY A NEEDS ASSESSMENT

- The majority of merchandise returns (78 percent) are due to problems in size, features, and/or color selection.
- The majority of these errors (54 percent) result from mistakes in entering the order data correctly into the computer system.
- Many of the errors in sizing or features could be avoided if customer service representatives were more knowledgeable about the products' sizing and features (e.g., certain items run larger than standard sizing).
- Incorrect labeling and inventory of products are responsible for fewer than 8 percent of order errors.
- Customer order representatives have never been formally trained in dealing with customer complaints.
- The customer order work area is cluttered and noisy.

GOALS FOR THE TRAINING

- Reduce merchandise returns due to data entry problems.
- Improve the attitude of customer order representatives.
- Help customer order representatives to really understand product features and sizing (e.g., suitable climate range for a sleeping bag).
- Create a positive image of Backwoods Company to customers and employees.
- Reduce sizing errors by having representatives check customer knowledge of differently sized items (e.g., that jacket runs large).
- Encourage representatives to check with mail-order customers on difficult handwriting or potential problems with item sizing or features.

FORM 7.3.1

Name _____   Group _____

Based on the background information provided in Exhibit 7.3.1, respond to the following questions.

1. Write several clear, measurable objectives for the training to be delivered to the employees in the customer order group.

2. Develop a recommendation for the training plan that includes the training techniques that should be used and the length of training.

3. Offer a plan for evaluating the training program. Describe the criteria that will be used and the design you will employ.

EXERCISE 7.4
THE DEVELOPMENT AND EVALUATION OF A TRAINING PROGRAM FOR GRADUATE STUDENT INSTRUCTORS

OVERVIEW

A common practice, particularly in larger, research-oriented universities, is to give graduate students who have only limited training in teaching complete responsibility for teaching an undergraduate class. Thus, while graduate students may possess adequate knowledge to cover the subject matter, many have had little training in organizing a class, teaching techniques, testing, grading, and so on. This exercise develops a training program for graduate students and proposes a design for evaluating the training.

LEARNING OBJECTIVES

After completing this exercise, you should be able to:

1. Outline the steps to be followed in the conceptualization, development, and evaluation of a training program.
2. Discuss the advantages and disadvantages of the various training techniques and the evaluation design options.
3. Develop an approach to determine who should receive the training.

PROCEDURE

Part A: Individual Preparation

Step 1. Before class, review the memo in Exhibit 7.4.1 from the university provost. As a member of the task force to develop and evaluate a new training program, your first assignment is to develop an outline of the steps to be followed to develop the most effective (and practical) training program for graduate student instructors.

Step 2. On Form 7.4.1, write a chronology of the steps you will follow to complete the assignment. Pay close attention to what the provost has requested in the memo.

Part B: Group Analysis

Step 1. In groups of four to six students, each member should review each other members' response on Form 7.4.1

Step 2. The group should attempt to reach consensus on the chronology of events and the position to be taken on the issues raised by the provost. One group member should take careful notes to represent the consensus of opinion and all aspects of the training program, the design of evaluation, and the criteria to be used as a part of the evaluation process.

Part C: Class Discussion

Step 1. One member of each group should present the group's recommendations for the steps to be followed for the training program. Class discussion will follow on the areas where the groups agree and disagree. An attempt should be made to reach consensus on all major points that must be addressed by the task force.

Part D: Self-Peer Evaluation

Step 1. Complete a self- and a peer evaluation form based *only* on the performance in the exercise.

EXHIBIT 7.4.1
THE PROVOST'S MEMO REQUESTING YOUR RECOMMENDATIONS

TO: Students

FROM: Linda Trudeau, University Provost

SUBJECT: Charge to the Training Task Force

Congratulations on your appointment to the task force on graduate student teaching. As you may know, there have been a number of concerns raised about the quality of teaching by graduate students at our university. While the graduate students are highly motivated to teach, most of the students have received very little training or preparation prior to teaching their undergraduate classes. Your job as part of the task force is as follows: (1) to determine if there really is a need for such training; (2) if there is a need, to outline the objectives and the content of the training; (3) to state which graduate students should receive the training (i.e., all students or only those who fail to meet some imposed standard); (4) to identify the specific techniques that are recommended to be used (e.g., lecture, role-plays); and (5) to provide a plan for ensuring that the training will be effective (i.e., specifying the criteria and experimental design that should be used).

Prior to the group meeting, take a position on each of the issues I have raised (and any others you can think of) and provide a detailed chronology using Form 7.4.1. A space is also provided for any questions you might have about this assignment.

I look forward to our meeting.

Name _____   Group _____

Assignment   *Detailed Description of Action to be Taken*

Step   1.

        2.

        3.

        4.

        5.

        6.

        7.

        8.

FORM 7.4.1 (*Continued*)

Critical Questions Related to the Assignment:

1.

2.

3.

CHAPTER 8 EXERCISES

EXERCISE 8.1
ATTITUDES ABOUT OLDER PEOPLE*

OVERVIEW

As noted throughout this book, the workforce is aging. This is due primarily to three factors: (1) the increasing life expectancy of individuals; (2) the aging of the large number of baby boomers; and (3) the decline in birthrates over the past two decades. The aging of the workforce raises the issue of how individuals view older adults and older employees. That is, what stereotypes do they have about older adults, and what are the consequences of these views for older workers. This exercise helps you in understanding your own views about older workers.

LEARNING OBJECTIVES

After completing this exercise, you should be able to:

1. Be aware of the facts of aging.
2. Understand your own views and perceptions of older individuals.
3. Understand how stereotypes about older individuals may influence individuals' behaviors toward them in the workplace.

PROCEDURE

Part A: Individual Analysis

Step 1. Complete Form 8.1.1. Bring your responses to class to be scored.

Step 2. Score your responses in class.

Part B: Group Analysis

Step 1. As a class, address the issues associated with each item on the questionnaire.

Step 2. Address the following questions:

    A. To what extent did the class possess erroneous facts about aging workers?

    B. Why did they possess these inaccurate pictures about older adults?

    C. What are the consequences of stereotypes of older adults for the workplace?

    D. What recommendations would you make for correcting these stereotypes in the workplace? What type of training programs do you recommend and how would you evaluate them?

---

*Contributed by Barbara Haskell.

Name _____   Group _____

Directions. For each item, respond by answering **True** or **False** in the space provided on the left. Be candid in choosing the response that best tells what you believe.

_____ 1. The majority of older people (past age 65) are senile (i.e., have defective memories, are disoriented, or are demented).

_____ 2. All five senses tend to decline in old age.

_____ 3. Most older people have no interest in, or capacity for, sexual relations.

_____ 4. Lung capacity tends to decline in old age.

_____ 5. The majority of older people feel miserable most of the time.

_____ 6. Physical strength tends to decline in old age.

_____ 7. At least one-tenth of the aged are living in long-stay institutions (i.e., nursing homes, mental hospitals).

_____ 8. Aged drivers have fewer accidents per person than drivers under 65.

_____ 9. Most older workers cannot work as effectively as younger workers.

_____ 10. About 80 percent of the aged are healthy enough to carry out their normal activities.

_____ 11. Most older people are set in their ways and unable to change.

_____ 12. Older people usually take longer to learn something new.

_____ 13. It is almost impossible for most older people to learn new things.

_____ 14. The reaction time of most older people tends to be slower than the reaction time of younger people.

_____ 15. In general, most older people are pretty much alike.

_____ 16. The majority of older people are seldom bored.

_____ 17. The majority of older people are socially isolated and lonely.

_____ 18. Older workers have fewer accidents than younger workers.

_____ 19. Over 20 percent of the U.S. population is now age 65 or over.

_____ 20. Most medical practitioners tend to give low priority to the aged.

_____ 21. The majority of older people have incomes below the poverty level (as defined by the federal government).

_____ 22. The majority of older people are working or would like to have some kind of work to do (including housework and volunteer work).

_____ 23. Older people tend to become more religious as they age.

_____ 24. The majority of older people are seldom irritated or angry.

_____ 25. The health and socioeconomic status of older people (compared to younger people) in the year 2000 will probably be the same as now.

_____ 26. Older workers get along well with other employees.

_____ 27. Older workers are less productive than younger workers.

_____ 28. The costs of health care for an older worker are lower than those for a younger, married worker with several children.

_____ 29. Older workers are absent more often because of age-related infirmities and above-average rates of illness.

_____ 30. Mental abilities (e.g., verbal, numerical, reasoning skills) remain stable into the seventies.

Source: Modified from E. Palmore, Facts on aging. *The Gerontologist, 17* (1977), p. 315. Used with permission.

EXERCISE 8.2
CAREER DEVELOPMENT SELF-ASSESSMENT EXERCISE

OVERVIEW

Most career development programs in organizations use self-assessment exercises. In fact, these exercises may be the first activities employees participate in that help them to better understand their personal career interests and goals. Self-appraisal is important for enhancing self-awareness. It generally requires the collection of data about yourself, such as your values, interests, and skills, and the determination of goals and action plans for life and career planning. As an employee you might want to engage in a self-assessment exercise for career planning purposes. As an HR professional, you might be asked to develop a self-assessment exercise to use with employees for career planning purposes. Examples of some of the possible activities that may be included in a self-assessment exercise are included in this exercise.

LEARNING OBJECTIVES

After completing this exercise, you should be able to:

1. Understand your values, skills, interests, experiences, and life and career preferences.
2. Be able to describe your immediate goals, the associated benefits and risks, and the skills you may need to develop to meet your goals.
3. Understand some of your own work attitudes and preferences and the issues associated with making career decisions and changes.
4. Be able to describe some of the activities used in a self-assessment exercise.

PROCEDURE

Part A: Individual Analysis

Step 1. Complete the self-assessment exercise in Form 8.2.1 before coming to class. Be as candid as possible in your responses.

Step 2. Each individual should answer the assessment questions listed in Form 8.2.2.

Part B: Group Analysis

As a class, address the following issues:

A. Discuss the importance of using a self-assessment as a career planning tool. Describe how a self-assessment may be beneficial for individual growth and development as well as for organizational HR purposes (e.g., staffing, training).

B. Explain how you might use a self-assessment tool as part of a career development system you design for an organization.

Name _____

PART A: VALUES AND EXPERIENCES

1. Describe the roles in your life that are important to you. Examples might include your work or career, family life, leisure, religious life, community life, and volunteer activities. Explain why these roles are important to you. Indicate how important each role is to your total life satisfaction. Assign a percent to each role (0 to 100 percent) so that the total adds up to 100 percent.

2. Describe your background and experiences, including:

    a. *Education.* List the names of technical schools or colleges you have attended. List degrees earned or to be earned and your major or minor.

    b. *Work experience.* List any jobs you have held, including part- and full-time jobs, voluntary jobs, internships, cooperative education (co-ops).

    c. *Skills.* Describe any skills that you possess that you feel would be valued in the workplace.

    d. *Extracurricular activities.* Describe any nonwork activities that you engage in for personal development or recreational pursuits.

    e. *Accomplishments.* Summarize any recognition you have received that is related to your education, work experience, skills, or extracurricular activities.

3. Read the following list of skills. Put a + next to those you feel you are particularly strong in and circle those you would like to develop more thoroughly in the future.

    Communication (written or oral communication, listening skills)

    Management skills (supervising, persuading others, planning, organizing, delegating, motivating others)

    Interpersonal skills (working effectively with others)

    Team building (working effectively with groups or teams)

    Creativity (innovativeness, generating ideas)

    Training skills (ability to teach skills and knowledges to others)

    Mathematical skills (computation ability, budgeting, accounting proficiency)

    Sales/promotion (ability to persuade, negotiate, influence)

    Scientific skills (investigative abilities, researching, analyzing)

    Service skills (handling complaints, customer relations)

    Office skills (word processing, filing, bookkeeping, recordkeeping)

4. Rate yourself on each of the following personal qualities or work characteristics. Write one response for each characteristic, using the following scale: 1, very low; 2, low; 3, average; 4, high; 5, very high.

_____	Emotional maturity	_____	Dependability in completing work
_____	Initiative/independence	_____	Flexibility and open-mindedness
_____	Punctuality	_____	Perseverance/willingness to work
_____	Ability to handle conflict	_____	Ability to set and achieve goals
_____	Ability to plan, organize, and determine work priorities	_____	Tolerance for ambiguous, unusual, or different ideas or situations
_____	Ability to work with others	_____	Ability to lead projects
_____	Willingness to do more than is expected (to go above and beyond requirements)	_____	Integrity in work (honesty)
		_____	Ability and interest in coaching others as needed
_____	Tolerance for changes in assignments or team members	_____	Ability and interest in supporting or recognizing others' contributions

PART B: WORK ATTITUDES AND PREFERENCES

1. Describe an ideal job for you. What would it be like? Describe the activities, people, rewards, and other features that would be a part of your job experience.

2. Think about the ideal job you described above. Rank the following values or attributes in terms of how important they are for you in your work (1 = most important; 12 = least important).

VALUES/CONDITIONS	RANK
Independence or autonomy	_____
Financial reward or affluence	_____
Sense of achievement or accomplishment	_____
Helping others	_____
Creating something	_____
Equality, fairness	_____
Loyalty	_____
Job security	_____
Pleasant working conditions	_____
Friendships at work	_____
Variety of tasks	_____
Opportunities for promotions	_____

FORM 8.2.1 (*Continued*)

3. What talents do you wish to use in your work?

4. What type of working relationship with other people do you prefer? That is, do you prefer working alone or with other people? Do you enjoy working with a few people you know well or helping people you don't know?

5. What type of physical work setting is desirable to you (e.g., office, outdoors, plant facility, working at home)?

6. How much freedom and independence do you want in your work? For example, do you want to set your own hours? Determine your own projects? How much guidance or structure by others do you need in your work (i.e., do you need others to outline the scope of your projects and provide deadlines)?

7. Think of one time when you felt like a real professional. What were you doing or what had you just done? Why was this achievement meaningful?

PART C: GOALS AND ACTION PLANNING

1. Describe your career goals for the next several years.

2. What specific things will you need to do to meet your goals?

3. What internal and external obstacles might you encounter along the way toward achievement of your goals?

4. Describe any skills or assistance you will need to meet your goals.

5. How much commitment do you have to your goals? Explain.

1. What did you learn about yourself that you did not realize before?

2. How important is your career and work in your total life? Why is this important for you to realize?

3. How can completing a self-assessment assist you in preparing a résumé or interviewing for a job?

4. What will you do to follow up on this self-assessment?

EXERCISE 8.3
CAREER DEVELOPMENT AT TECHNOCHIP COMPUTERS *

OVERVIEW

As noted in Chapter 8, career development has become an increasingly more important topic with which HR professionals need to be familiar. Organizations have adopted more career programs and have changed the role of managers to reflect more of a coaching function than a traditional supervisory job. As organizations change in terms of structure (more teams, flattening managerial hierarchies), HR professionals face greater pressures in designing effective career programs to meet the needs of a new, more diverse workforce. This exercise presents you with a case that you will need to analyze in order to design a career development system that can be used with the firm's employees.

LEARNING OBJECTIVES

After completing this exercise, you should be able to:

1. Analyze a case to determine the career issues of importance for employees and the types of career programs that are currently in use.

2. Recommend career development tools that can be used for various types of employees and issues.

PROCEDURE

Part A: Individual Analysis

Step 1. Read the background information about the company in Exhibits 8.3.1, 8.3.2, and 8.3.3.

Step 2. Complete the questions found in Form 8.3.1.

Part B: Group Analysis

Step 1. In teams of about five or six people, review each person's responses to the questions found in Form 8.3.1.

Step 2. Discuss your responses and reach consensus on the appropriate career development tools to implement in the sales division at TechnoChip Computers. Be sure to address the following issues:

   a. What is the timeline for implementation of your ideas and recommendations for career interventions?

   b. What are the potential drawbacks as well as advantages to your recommendations?

EXHIBIT 8.3.1
BACKGROUND INFORMATION ON TECHNOCHIP COMPUTERS

TechnoChip Computers is a nationwide computer manufacturing and sales organization. Annual corporate revenue is in excess of $3 billion. Headquarters are located in Troy, Michigan, and there are branch offices in 100 cities across the United States. There are three main divisions within the organization: product development and research, manufacturing and distribution, and sales. This project will focus on the sales division.

TechnoChip has experienced increased competitive pressure in the past three years. This has mainly come from the diversification of products offered in the computer marketplace and rapid technological advancements. While a leader in the computer industry, TechnoChip's annual sales have declined in the past several years, most notably in the past two. Some key indicators of corporate performance are listed below.

PERFORMANCE CRITERIA	1994	1995	1996	1997
Annual sales	3.5	3.4	3.2	2.9
Growth of customer base (new customers)	1%	1%	−3%	−5%
Retention of existing customer base	90%	88%	82%	78%
Customer satisfaction	65%	64%	62%	60%

Notes: Annual sales indicated in billions. Growth of customer base measured as a percentage change from previous year, with positive values indicating an increase, and negative values indicating a decrease. Customer satisfaction percentages indicate the percent of customers rating service and product quality "very good" or "good."

---

*Contributed by Lillian T. Eby and Joyce E. A. Russell.

EXHIBIT 8.3.1 (*Continued*)

To remain competitive in the years ahead, the new CEO of the sales division, Bryan Williams, and a core staff of organizational representatives have refined the mission and strategic objectives for the organization. Their revised mission statement is presented below.

MISSION STATEMENT OF TECHNOCHIP COMPUTERS: SALES DIVISION

Increase TechnoChip's shareholder value and remain the undisputed leader in the computer industry through:

- Satisfying customer needs and exceeding customer expectations
- Improving productivity through employee empowerment and quality principles
- Hiring, developing, and retaining top employees

STRATEGIC OBJECTIVES FOR TECHNOCHIP COMPUTERS: SALES DIVISION

- Grow the existing customer base 3% annually over the next five years.
- Develop specialized sales teams to offer customized service to existing customers.
- Increase customer perceptions of product quality and customer service. Specifically, by 2002, 90 percent of customer satisfaction ratings should be in the "very good" to "good" category.
- Increase customer retention so that in five years, customer retention rates are at 96 percent.
- Increase employee perceptions that TechnoChip is the employer of choice. Key indicators of this will be turnover rates, job satisfaction, and commitment to the organization.

To accomplish the strategic objectives, TechnoChip decided to reorganize work around segmented sales teams in the sales division, instead of continuing the current practice of having individuals try to sell computers to all types of markets. It was believed that the change to teams would allow sales representatives to better meet customer needs by becoming experts in a particular business market. In the new system, sales reps would be better able to develop long-term relationships with customers because they would be servicing the same customers each year. This approach greatly differed from the "old" way of doing things, where sales reps serviced different customers every year. TechnoChip is also embracing employee empowerment by allowing the teams considerable latitude in decision making, work scheduling, and productivity management.

The change to teams occurred six months ago. Within each division, teams were created consisting of 4 to 13 members. Each team was formed to specialize in a particular business segment, and the size of the teams was determined based on the relative size of the business segments. To illustrate this work arrangement, the structure of the Newark, New Jersey, sales division is presented below.

BUSINESS SEGMENT	PERCENTAGE OF TOTAL MARKET SALES	NUMBER OF TEAM MEMBERS
Mainframe computers	15%	10
Management information systems (hardware & software)	35	21
Educational computers and software	10	8
International computer systems	10	8
Personal computers	30	19

NATURE OF THE JOB

Sales representatives can consist of telephone sales representatives who are primarily responsible for calling customers and on-site reps who make actual visits to meet with customers. Each team consists of several telephone reps and several on-site reps. Team members' duties and responsibilities are highly interdependent with one another. Sales calls (phone or on-site) to a customer are typically made by a team of individuals, each of whom has expertise in a certain function (e.g., installation, software, hardware). All team members are expected to have basic knowledge of each others' jobs. For instance, if Allie specializes in installation, then she needs to also have expertise in software and hardware for the particular business segment. In this sense, the teams are expected to be cross-functional. In addition, all team members are responsible for having knowledge specific to their business segment. This is necessary for customer expectations to be exceeded. This can be obtained in a variety of ways, including attending seminars, subscribing to trade journals, and reading current business articles.

CHARACTERISTICS OF THE SALES FORCE

Each city has a sales force of approximately 50 employees, although in larger cities, the sales force may have as many as 80 employees. The total sales force consists of about 7,000 sales reps (4,000 telephone sales reps; 3,000 on-site sales reps) and about 200 managers and 650 team leaders. At least 40 percent of the sales representatives have college degrees and the rest have high school degrees or some college. The average age of a sales rep is about 32, with most reps anywhere from 21 to 58 years old. The average tenure with the company is about 8 years, with most ranging from 1 year to about 25 years of service with TechnoChip.

In the new team environment, former managers have been renamed team leaders or coaches. This individual works side-by-side with the team and acts as a resource for the team by obtaining support for new ideas and facilitating team decision making. The organization is just starting to examine the training needs of its team leaders to help them in their new role as coach. An organizational chart is presented in Exhibit 8.3.2.

OTHER ONGOING INITIATIVES

Consistent with the mission statement, other efforts have also been made to increase employee perceptions of empowerment. This includes instituting a formal suggestion system and starting quality action teams to solve division-wide problems (similar to quality circles). In addition, in the past three months, the sales division, in all locations, has implemented an employee survey system to collect feedback from employees about their views on the changes and other suggestions. The findings from this survey are presented in Exhibit 8.3.3.

EXHIBIT 8.3.3   SURVEY RESULTS FROM SALES DIVISION   **577**

EXHIBIT 8.3.2
ORGANIZATIONAL CHART FOR SALES DIVISIONS
AT TECHNOCHIP COMPUTERS

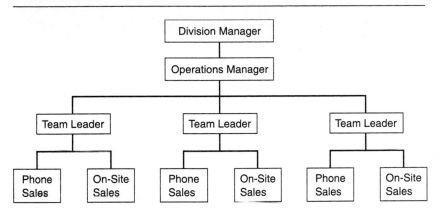

EXHIBIT 8.3.3
SURVEY RESULTS FROM SALES DIVISION

GENERAL RESULTS

Sales representatives responded to a survey in which they indicated whether they were satisfied, neutral, or dissatisfied with various aspects of their jobs. The results for some of the issues are noted below:

- **Job content plateauing:**   55 percent of all sales reps reported *not* feeling plateaued with respect to the nature of the job. In other words, they felt that they were given interesting work and it was not mundane or routine; 10 percent were neutral; and 35 percent felt that they were plateaued and were doing boring work. Telephone sales reps were much more likely to indicate that they were plateaued or bored than were on-site sales reps.
- **Satisfaction with job challenges:**   58 percent of all sales reps reported that they were satisfied with the challenges on their job (i.e., feelings of worthwhile accomplishments, personal growth and development); 12 percent were neutral; and 30 percent reported being dissatisfied with the degree of challenge provided by their jobs. Telephone reps were much more likely than on-site reps to indicate they were dissatisfied.
- **Autonomy:**   70 percent of all sales employees agreed that they were given autonomy in completing their work; 20 percent were neutral; and 10 percent disagreed that they were given autonomy in doing their work. Telephone reps were more likely to indicate they were not given autonomy than were on-site reps.
- **Participation in decision making:**   60 percent of all sales reps agreed that they participated in decision making; 20 percent were neutral; and 20 percent disagreed.
- **Job security:**   55 percent of all sales employees agreed that they were satisfied with their job security or felt secure about their jobs; 10 percent were neutral; and 35 percent felt insecure (or fearful about losing their jobs). No differences were detected between on-site and telephone sales reps in their perceived job security.
- **Promotional opportunities:**   25 percent of all sales reps were satisfied with their chances for promotion or felt that the promotion process was a fair one; 15 percent were neutral; and 60 percent were dissatisfied with the promotion system in place. Note that sales reps could be promoted only one level higher than their current position to the position of team leader. No differences were detected between on-site and telephone sales reps.

- **Career guidance and development system:**   20 percent of all sales reps indicated they were satisfied with the career guidance and development provided to them by the company; 10 percent were neutral; and 70 percent reported being dissatisfied. No differences were detected for telephone or on-site reps.
- **Coaching system:**   25 percent of all sales reps indicated they were satisfied with the coaching provided by their team leader; 10 percent were neutral; and 65 percent reported being dissatisfied. No differences were detected for telephone and on-site reps. Note that 90 percent of all reps reported liking their team leaders. They did, however, feel that their team leaders did not devote enough time to coaching them or providing career assistance.
- **Team leaders' perspective on coaching:**   100 percent of all team leaders felt they did not have enough time to do all their job duties. All indicated that they did not have enough time to coach sales reps. Further, they indicated that in their performance appraisals, their bosses emphasized meeting sales quotas and never mentioned "coaching sales reps" or "career development of reps" as important job duties of team leaders.
- **Role clarity:**   80 percent of all sales reps reported that their roles were clear and that they knew what their job duties were; 10 percent were neutral; and 10 percent reported their roles were not clear. No differences were detected among on-site and telephone sales reps. Seventy-five percent of all team leaders reported that their roles were *not* clear; 10 percent were neutral; and 15 percent felt their roles were clear.
- **Job-induced tension:**   45 percent stated they experienced job-induced tension, while 10 percent were neutral; and 45 percent stated they did not experience job-induced tension. Job-induced tension refers to stress created by the work (having too much to do, conflicts at work, thinking about work-related problems off-duty, experiencing physical symptoms of stress such as ulcers, fatigue, headaches). On-site sales reps were more likely to report higher levels of job-induced stress than were telephone sales reps. Team leaders also reported high levels of job-induced tension.
- **Work–family conflict:**   60 percent of all sales reps indicated they experienced work–family conflict or stress; 15 percent were neutral; and 25 percent reported they did not experience work–family conflict or stress. On-site reps were much more likely to report experiencing work–family stress than were telephone sales reps due to all the traveling the on-site reps do.

FORM 8.3.1

Name _____ Group _____

1. For each of the following groups of employees in the sales division at TechnoChip Computers, first identify their career-related concerns as noted from the survey results. Then provide some recommendations for each group to meet career or job-related needs. Review Figure 8.7 for ideas of tools or programs that can be used to assist employees with career or HR needs.

    A. Telephone sales employees:

        1. Concerns:

        2. Recommendations:

    B. On-site sales employees:
        1. Concerns:

        2. Recommendations:

    C. Team leaders:
        1. Concerns:

        2. Recommendations:

2. Describe the advantages and disadvantages to your recommendations as well as a timeline for when they should be implemented.

3. How would you assess whether the programs you have recommended for employees are perceived positively or improve attitudes after they are implemented? (Hint: Review the evaluation section in Chapter 7.) Should additional surveys be conducted with sales employees and their team leaders? If so, how often and what types of questions should be asked? What would you do with that data?

4. Review TechnoChip's mission statement, strategic objectives, and the survey feedback results. Based on what you learned in Chapter 7, identify the training needs for each of the following groups of employees:

    A. Telephone sales employees:

    B. On-site sales employees:

    C. Team leaders:

5. For each specific training need you identified above, what types of training methods would be appropriate to incorporate into the training? (Hint: Review the description of training methods and techniques in Chapter 7.)

6. Some of the employee attitude problems TechnoChip is facing may be due to the fact that when current employees were hired the job was very different than it is today. What steps can TechnoChip management take before hiring future sales employees and team leaders to be sure the applicants have a realistic assessment of what the job is like? (Hint: Think about what you learned in the previous chapters about job analysis, recruiting, and selecting employees.)

EXERCISE 8.4
THE BIG FIVE AND CAREER DEVELOPMENT*

OVERVIEW

Research supports the proposition that stable personality characteristics are related to not only success in particular occupations but also job satisfaction. The purpose of this exercise is to provide a profile of your personality based on the big five personality structure.

As we discussed in Chapter 6, the big five factor structure has been gaining widespread acceptance by personality researchers and has greatly influenced the research into individual differences. There is also growing evidence that personality measures have utility in providing vocational and career guidance. It is clear that certain big five factors and their combinations are correlated with career choice, success, and satisfaction. While the big five is not as good a measure of career variables as vocational interest questionnaires such as the *Strong* or the Kuder, scores on the big five are nonetheless helpful guides for career development.

OBJECTIVES

After completing this exercise, you should be able to:

1. Understand how your personality as measured with big five dimensions could be related to occupational success;
2. Critique the method for its usefulness in other HR domains.

PROCEDURE

Prior to class, answer the 50 questions below. Based on your answers, a profile from the big five personality factors will be presented. Your instructor will provide the general interpretation of the profile based on your answers.

Answer each question as honestly as you can. The accuracy of your profile depends on honest responses which reflect your true feelings and not how you would like to feel or act.

For each question, try to answer either "yes" or "no." If you cannot decide how to answer, record your answer as "unsure." If your answer to the question is "yes," put a "1" in the space provided to the left of the item number. If your answer is "unsure," put a "2" in the

space provided. If your answer is "no" to the question, put a "3" in the space provided.

Put 1 if your answer is "yes," 2 if your answer is "unsure," and 3 if your answer is "no."

_____ 1. Do you worry about most things?

_____ 2. Are you anxious about your life most of the time?

_____ 3. Do you consider yourself to have low self-esteem?

_____ 4. Are you often depressed?

_____ 5. Are you often embarrassed by your behavior?

_____ 6. Do you feel inferior to most people you know?

_____ 7. Do you often give in to temptations?

_____ 8. Do you have trouble making decisions?

_____ 9. Do you feel vulnerable in many situations?

_____ 10. Do you have difficulty in stressful situations?

_____ 11. Do you prefer working in groups?

_____ 12. Do you really enjoy talking with people?

_____ 13. Do you think you would be good in sales?

_____ 14. Do you prefer being around people than being alone?

_____ 15. Do you prefer work that involves more interaction with people?

_____ 16. Do you consider yourself outgoing?

_____ 17. Would you describe yourself as shy?

_____ 18. Do you tend to dominate most conversations?

_____ 19. Do you often emerge as a leader in a group?

_____ 20. Do you enjoy sports which most people consider to be risky?

_____ 21. Do you like intellectual challenges?

_____ 22. Do you like associating with people who stimulate your mind?

_____ 23. Do you really enjoy good poetry or reading the classics?

_____ 24. Do you have a very active fantasy life?

_____ 25. Are you tolerant of different lifestyles?

_____ 26. Do you like to debate controversial issues of the day?

_____ 27. Do you always like to hear the other side of an issue?

---

*Contributed by Kathleen Bernardin.

_____ 28. Do you often select reading as a leisure activity?

_____ 29. Do you often find yourself daydreaming?

_____ 30. Are you fascinated by art and artists?

_____ 31. Do you have difficulty telling people how you really feel?

_____ 32. Do you trust most people?

_____ 33. Do you think most people are honest?

_____ 34. Do you enjoy a good argument?

_____ 35. Would you describe yourself as stubborn?

_____ 36. Do you prefer cooperating over competing?

_____ 37. Do you like to put people in their place when they deserve it?

_____ 38. Do you consider yourself superior to most people you know?

_____ 39. Would most people describe you as courteous?

_____ 40. Do you hate giving people bad news about themselves?

_____ 41. Do you do well at most things you try?

_____ 42. Do most people consider you to be highly competent?

_____ 43. Do you like to carefully plan things?

_____ 44. Do you have a clear set of objectives when you work?

_____ 45. Do you consider yourself very well disciplined?

_____ 46. Do you always honor the commitments you have made?

_____ 47. Do you consider yourself to be highly effective in your work?

_____ 48. Do you try to do the best that you can every time?

_____ 49. Do you consider yourself well organized?

_____ 50. Do you stick with a job until you're finished?

TO SCORE YOUR RESPONSES

For items 17, 34, 35, 37, and 38 only, change a "1" response to a "3" and change a "3" response to a "1." All other items are scored using the number you have entered (1, 2, or 3). Add up the scores for the big five factors as follows:

1. **ANXIOUS VS. RELAXED** (items 1–10)
2. **EXTROVERTED-INTROVERTED** (items 11–20)
3. **EXPERIMENTAL VS. CONVENTIONAL** (items 21–30)
4. **AGREEABLE VS. SKEPTICAL** (items 31–40)
5. **CAREFREE VS. CONSCIENTIOUS** (items 41–50)

Your instructor will provide the interpretation of your profile and the Internet address for more information.

CHAPTER 9 EXERCISES

EXERCISE 9.1
PERFORMANCE-APPRAISAL FEEDBACK: A ROLE-PLAY EXERCISE*

OVERVIEW

As described in Chapter 9, the performance-appraisal process is a key human resource management function. The face-to-face performance feedback session can be an important part of this process because it allows the rater and ratee to thoroughly discuss the appraisal ratings. It also enables them to derive some developmental suggestions to improve the ratee's performance. This exercise provides an opportunity to role-play a face-to-face performance feedback session.

LEARNING OBJECTIVES

After completing this exercise, you should be able to:

1. Understand and apply general guidelines for providing performance feedback.
2. Understand and apply guidelines for the observation of behavior.
3. Evaluate the effectiveness of a performance-appraisal feedback session.

PROCEDURE

Part A: Analysis

Step 1. Each student should read Exhibits 9.1.1, 9.1.2, and 9.1.3 before class. Based on the discussion in Chapter 9, write a one-page critique on the performance form and the extent to which it will help with the feedback process.

Step 2. In class, the instructor will set up teams of three individuals. You will be assigned one of three roles: feedback giver, recipient, and observer of the feedback giver. If you have been assigned the role of feedback giver (Chris Williams), then carefully review Exhibit 9.1.1 and make notes about the content and message of the feedback you will give to one of your subordinates, Jesse Anderson. Also, review Exhibit 9.1.2, the guidelines for providing feedback. If you have been assigned the role of feedback recipient, then you are Jesse Anderson, the subordinate. Your supervisor, Chris Williams, will be setting up a meeting to discuss your performance. If you have been assigned the role of observer, you should review Exhibits 9.1.2 and 9.1.3 so you can accurately observe and take notes on the feedback giver's behavior in the appraisal session.

Part B: Role-Play

The person assuming the role of Chris Williams, the supervisor, will call Jesse Anderson, the subordinate, into Chris's office and provide the feedback to Jesse in about 15 minutes. The observer will take notes during the feedback session.

Part C: Feedback

After the role-play has been completed, the observer should share his or her observations with the feedback giver. The intent is to give some constructive and positive information to the feedback giver to enhance that person's appraisal skills in the future. Feedback recipients may also want to offer their own perspectives on how comfortable they felt with the feedback session and whether or not they felt motivated to improve their performance after receiving the feedback.

Part D: Class Discussion

The class as a whole should discuss the types of behaviors they observed that were characteristic of effective and ineffective appraisal sessions. The instructor could chart their responses.

---

*Contributed by Sharon L. Wagner, Richard G. Moffett, III, and Catherine M. Westberry.

EXHIBIT 9.1.1
PERFORMANCE-APPRAISAL FORM

SOUTHEAST BANK AND TRUST (CONFIDENTIAL)

Name of Employee:	*Jesse Anderson*	Date:	12/5/97
Name of Supervisor:	*Chris Williams*	Dept:	S-2

Directions: Please rate each factor based on observed behaviors. Answer as honestly and accurately as you can. Provide comments for especially poor or outstanding performance.

Job knowledge: Technical knowledge required to perform the job; skills in implementing policies and procedures; effectively using resources and equipment.

1	(2)	3	4	5
Unsatisfactory	Marginal	Acceptable	Above average	Outstanding

Comments: Has occasionally used the wrong equipment, seems to be uninformed about some of the company's procedures.

Interpersonal skills: Works well with others; displays helpfulness and cooperation with internal and external customers; effectively handles conflict of interests and difficult customers.

1	2	3	(4)	5
Unsatisfactory	Marginal	Acceptable	Above average	Outstanding

Comments: Coworkers and customers have consistently commented on how Jesse gets along with most everyone. A number of situations have arisen in the department that Jesse was instrumental in resolving.

Work quality: The quality of the work including aspects of completeness and thoroughness; adherence to company and organizational standards.

(1)	2	3	4	5
Unsatisfactory	Marginal	Acceptable	Above average	Outstanding

Comments: Has turned in several projects that needed considerable revisions and rework.

Reliability: Can be counted on to attend meetings punctually; turn in assignments when due; and volunteer to assist others in projects.

(1)	2	3	4	5
Unsatisfactory	Marginal	Acceptable	Above average	Outstanding

Comments: Has missed most departmental meetings; has consistently come to work late in the past few months; is difficult to find when help is needed on projects.

Quantity of work: Meets company and departmental standards for production.

1	2	(3)	4	5
Unsatisfactory	Marginal	Acceptable	Above average	Outstanding

Comments: Productivity has been acceptable.

EXHIBIT 9.1.3   GUIDELINES FOR OBSERVING BEHAVIOR   **587**

EXHIBIT 9.1.2
GUIDELINES FOR PROVIDING
PERFORMANCE-APPRAISAL FEEDBACK

1. Inform the employee about the purpose of the meeting. Describe the procedure that you will be following. Attempt to establish rapport with the ratee. You may want to inform the ratee that you may be taking some notes (i.e., ask if that is OK).

2. Focus on describing the ratee's behaviors. Avoid evaluating or blaming the ratee.

3. Be sure to indicate effective behaviors (i.e., praise the employee's strengths) as well as ineffective behaviors. Probe for specific causes of the employee's problem areas (e.g., why she believes she has a particular performance problem).

4. Be sure to make specific references to the appraisal form and ratings.

5. Discuss specific plans of action for improving the employee's deficiencies.

6. Jointly set developmental goals for the employee. Make sure you reach agreement with the employee regarding performance expectations and goals.

7. Strive to make your nonverbal behavior match your verbal message (i.e., maintain eye contact, maintain good posture, avoid use of uhs and uhms).

8. Provide feedback on each behavioral dimension, giving clear behavioral examples of performance to support the ratings.

9. Periodically check the ratee's understanding of the feedback you provide.

10. Answer any questions fully and politely. Remember that the only useful feedback is high-quality feedback.

11. Summarize the content of the feedback session.

12. Set a date for a future meeting to assess progress toward the goals.

EXHIBIT 9.1.3
GUIDELINES FOR OBSERVING BEHAVIOR

1. Focus on observing the behavior of the rater, and secondarily, the behavior of the ratee (i.e., how he/she responds to the rater).

2. Record the behaviors you observe (i.e., things that the role-players do and say). Don't make judgments about the behaviors. For example, write "sat back in his chair with his arms folded," rather than "acted uninterested."

3. Try to record verbatim statements from the role-player whenever possible, particularly statements that indicate exceptionally good or poor performance.

4. In addition to recording statements made by the role-players, be sure to observe and record nonverbal behavior, tone of voice, eye contact, body posture (e.g., leaning forward to show interest).

EXERCISE 9.2
THE HEARTLAND GREETING CARDS CONSULTING PROBLEM*

OVERVIEW

Employee turnover is a costly problem for employers. After spending considerable money recruiting, selecting, and training employees, it is costly to have to replace them. Sometimes the selection process is faulty, allowing the wrong candidates to be accepted, and subsequently leave the firm. Other times, the performance-appraisal system is ineffective at providing valuable feedback to employees, and they become dissatisfied and leave the firm. The current exercise builds from material presented in Chapters 9 and 6 (staffing). Students will have the opportunity to use job analysis information to refine the company's selection and performance-appraisal systems.

LEARNING OBJECTIVES

After completing this exercise, you should be able to:

1. Review job specification and job analysis information to determine the important attributes that a selection tool should be based on.
2. Design a performance-appraisal system given job analysis information and critical organizational goals for the position.

PROCEDURE

Part A: Individual Analysis

Step 1. Read the background information on the company and the job provided in Exhibit 9.2.1. Also, review the job analysis information provided for the merchandiser job provided in Exhibit 9.2.2

Step 2. Referring back to Chapter 6 on staffing, offer some ideas for selection tools that can be used to determine if applicants possess the job specifications. Complete Form 9.2.1.

Step 3. Offer some ideas for the performance appraisal system that can be used for the merchandiser position. Complete Form 9.2.2.

Part B: Group Analysis

In groups, discuss your recommendations for the selection and performance-appraisal systems. As a group,

consolidate your ideas and draft plans for the selection and complete performance-appraisal systems. Be prepared to share your group's ideas with the class. Ask the instructor for information that could affect the positions you take.

EXHIBIT 9.2.1
COMPANY BACKGROUND INFORMATION

Heartland Greeting Cards, Inc., is a national greeting card company that is based out of St. Louis, Missouri. Heartland provides cards, stationery, gift wrap, and party favors to drug, grocery, and retail stores. One of Heartland's main competitors is Hammonds Greeting Cards, which has its own specialty stores as well as accounts in department stores and drugstores. Patriot Greeting Cards, Heartland's other major competitor, also has accounts in department, drug, and grocery stores, and it has recently moved into direct competition with Hammonds by opening its own specialty stores. Heartland has not yet entered into this arena, so it must keep its existing accounts and open new accounts to survive. The competition between these three companies is intense. A common tactic is for one company's sales representative to visit a store with a competitor's account and point out deficiencies in the existing service. Heartland's selling point is "no inventory in the store" guarantee.

The greeting card merchandiser is the employee who interacts most with the store managers (the manager responsible for all the store operations) and store customers. Therefore, it is crucial that each merchandiser maintain his or her card department in top condition to keep the store manager happy.

EXISTING SELECTION PROCEDURES

Most job applicants for the greeting card merchandiser position are recruited through employee referrals. Local newspaper ads are the other major source of applicants. Heartland has experienced the most success with employee referrals. Heartland has always had a serious problem with employee turnover and suspects that poor selection practices may be part of the problem.

EXISTING PERFORMANCE-APPRAISAL SYSTEM

Currently, Heartland has no formal performance-appraisal system. A greeting card merchandiser's performance is evaluated by unannounced spot checks conducted by the area manager (a Heartland employee who manages 23 merchandisers who service 70 stores in a 65-mile radius). These spot checks are often as infrequent as once every three weeks and usually occur when the greeting card merchandiser is not in the store. The merchandiser receives no feedback as to the results of these checks unless there is a problem. Merchandisers often cite lack of feedback about their performance on the job as a major source of frustration. You suspect that the lack of feedback may also be contributing to Heartland's high turnover rate.

---

*Contributed by Esther J. Long.

EXHIBIT 9.2.2
JOB ANALYSIS

Job Title: Greeting card merchandiser   **D.O.T Code:** 299.367-014

DUTIES COMPRISING A ROUTINE SERVICE CALL

(Conducted two to five times a week per store depending on each store's sales volume and seasonal demand.)

1. Contacts the store manager to discuss any problems and determine if any new merchandise has arrived.
2. Checks in all new merchandise according to store procedure so that all items on the invoice are accounted for.
3. Unpacks all new merchandise and prices the soft goods (stationery, party favors, gift wrap, etc.) with a price gun.
4. Returns all cards and merchandise to their designated holders and puts new merchandise on display so that reorder needs can be determined to uphold the "no inventory in the store" guarantee.
5. Orders new merchandise as needed according to Heartland's company procedures and documents any such orders.
6. Fills all empty pockets with discontinued or "extra" cards and merchandise so that a "well-stocked" appearance is maintained.
7. Dusts and cleans card fixtures.

SEASONAL DUTIES

1. Orders seasonal merchandise (e.g., Christmas, Valentine's Day), so it arrives just in time to display on the dates determined by Heartland's company headquarters in St. Louis.
2. Sets up all seasonal displays promptly (there is no place to store excess inventory) and replenishes them as needed.
3. Takes down all seasonal displays the day after the season ends and replaces them with novelty displays.
4. Takes inventory of all leftover seasonal goods and prepares a credit voucher for the store using the SMI forms.
5. Packages all merchandise that needs to be returned to headquarters and mails it.

SUPERVISION RECEIVED

PROXIMITY	FREQUENCY
Visual	Constant
Physical separation	Hourly
Geographical separation X	Daily
	Weekly
	Less than weekly X

PERSONAL CONTACTS

Brief contact on a daily basis with store managers and occasionally with other store employees. No contact with other Heartland employees except the area manager.

WORK SCHEDULE

Hours vary according to the number of stores one is responsible for (usually a minimum of two), sales volume for a particular store, and seasonal demand. Work must be performed during the stores' regular operating hours. A merchandiser sets his or her own work schedule.

PHYSICAL DEMANDS

Standing	X	Note: Must stand for up to three hours at a time.
Walking	X	
Crawling	X	
Stooping	X	
Kneeling	X	
Reaching	X	
Lifting	X	

PHYSICAL ENVIRONMENT

Indoors	X	Note: Typically a merchandiser services two or more stores. A person must provide his or her own
Outdoors		transportation from one store to the next.
Other	X	

EXHIBIT 9.2.2 JOB ANALYSIS **591**

EXHIBIT 9.2.2 (*Continued*)

ORGANIZATIONAL GOALS	JOB PERFORMANCE CRITERIA
1. Heartland's "no inventory in the store" promise is upheld while maintaining a well-stocked appearance.	• New merchandise is on order when a pocket contains less than three items. • No more than 5 percent of the pockets are empty at any given time. • Only merchandise that has arrived within the past four days can be found in the stockroom. Exception: seasonal displays may arrive one week in advance of assembly date. • No inventory is in the under stock drawers except for duplicates that do not fit on the displays.
2. Each store receives the services described in its contract with Heartland Greeting Cards.	• Layout of card department corresponds with blueprint of layout contracted for (training by the area manager is necessary to read the greeting card department blueprints). • Seasonal merchandise is set up according to the procedures provided in Heartland's service manual by Heartland's designated deadline.
3. No lost customer accounts due to poor customer service.	• Contacts store manager every time a service call is made and resolves any problems that may arise. • Is courteous to store manager, employees, and customers. • Prices all soft goods (e.g., stationery, wrapping paper) according to store procedures. • Follows all store procedures (these may vary from store to store) for checking in merchandise, inventory, and returning merchandise. • Fixtures are kept clean and displays are free of stray merchandise from other departments. • Seasonal displays are removed within two days of the end of the season. • Leftover seasonal merchandise is inventoried, packaged, and returned to headquarters within one week of the end of the season.

Identify at least one selection method that could be used to assess whether a candidate possesses each of the job specifications listed below. Refer back to Chapter 6 for guidance and the material presented in Exhibits 9.2.1 and 9.2.2.

Job specifications (minimum qualifications)

1. Mathematical ability to carry out calculations involving addition, subtraction, multiplication, and division of three digits or more including fractions and decimals. Note: Mathematical computations must be carried out when checking in merchandise or completing inventory. Calculators may be used.
   Assessment method:

2. A 12th grade reading level in English. Note: The service manual is written at the 12th grade reading level.
   Assessment method:

3. Ability to attend to details. Note: To minimize the in-store inventory, the company blueprint for each display must be followed precisely. Each set of cards has a pocket where it is supposed to be displayed (the numerical codes on the back of the cards must match the codes on the pocket labels).
   Assessment method:

4. Ability to carry out company procedures while adapting to situational needs. Note: A person must have the ability to make snap decisions on the spot.
   Assessment method:

5. Ability to resolve customer (i.e., store manager) complaints while maintaining good will.
   Assessment method:

6. Basic body mobility (e.g., ability to bend, reach, lift) and ability to stand for up to three hours at a time. Note: A person with a disability (in a wheelchair) could be accommodated.
   Assessment method:

7. Ability to work alone with no supervision for weeks at a time.
   Assessment method:

8. Must provide own transportation to all stores.
   Assessment method:

Name _____   Group _____

Your assignment is to develop plans for a comprehensive performance-appraisal system for the merchandiser job at Heartland Greeting Cards. Decisions you must make include the following:

1.   Choice of person(s) who should be responsible for evaluating the greeting card merchandiser's performance.

2.   Choice of a rating format(s) that will allow you to incorporate the job performance criteria identified in the job analysis directly into the rating form. Explain your answer. Prepare a sample rating form.

3. Techniques to be used to ensure that the greeting card merchandiser is provided with accurate and timely feedback concerning his or her performance. Explain your answer.

4. Other components of the PA system will help make it more legally defensible? Explain your answer.

EXERCISE 9.3
PRICE WATERHOUSE V. HOPKINS

OVERVIEW

This exercise familiarizes students with an important Supreme Court case related to performance appraisal and the implications of the case in terms of appraisal system development, implementation, and administration.

LEARNING OBJECTIVES

After completing this exercise, you should be able to:

1. Understand the importance of performance appraisal for EEO litigation.

2. Suggest methods of performance appraisal that are legally defensible and will result in the most valid results for the organization.

3. Understand what methods could be used to make staffing (e.g., promotion) decisions.

PROCEDURE

Part A: Individual Analysis

Step 1. You have been retained as a consultant to advise Price Waterhouse on matters related to a lawsuit against it and methods that could be adopted to prevent further legal action against the company. Review the actual case, which is summarized in Exhibit 9.3.1.

Step 2. Prepare a one-page report to the vice president of human resources for Price Waterhouse that addresses the following issues: (1) Explain in detail whether you believe that Hopkins was a victim of illegal discrimination; (2) the steps that can be taken with the method of selecting partners to prevent a reoccurrence of this problem. Include a critique of the current system and specific recommendations for change. Be sure to include recommendations for how performance is evaluated for partners and how appraisal data are used for making promotion decisions. Also, complete Form 9.3.1 and bring it to class.

Part B: Group Analysis

Step 1. In small groups, review the written recommendations of each group member and reach consensus on the specific recommendations you would propose for changing the system. Each group member should review responses to Form 9.3.1. One group representative should present the findings to the class.

EXHIBIT 9.3.1
BACKGROUND CASE INFORMATION ON PRICE WATERHOUSE

At Price Waterhouse, a nationwide professional accounting partnership, a senior manager becomes a candidate for partnership when the partners in the local office submit his or her name as a candidate. All the other partners in the firm are then invited to submit written comments on each candidate—either on a long or a short form, depending on the partner's degree of knowledge about the candidate. Not every partner in the firm submits comments on every candidate. After reviewing the comments and interviewing the partners who submitted them, the firm's admissions committee makes a recommendation to the policy board. This recommendation will be either that the firm accept the candidate for partnership, put the application on hold, or deny the promotion. The policy board then decides whether to submit the candidate's name to the entire partnership for a vote, to hold the candidacy, or to reject the candidate. The recommendation of the admissions committee and the decision of the policy board are not controlled by fixed guidelines: A certain number of positive comments from partners will not guarantee a candidate's admission to the partnership, nor will a specific quantity of negative comments necessarily defeat the application. Price Waterhouse places no limit on the number of persons it will admit to the partnership in any given year.

Ann Hopkins had worked at Price Waterhouse's Office of Government Services in Washington, D.C., for five years when the partners in that office proposed her as a candidate for partnership. Of the 662 partners at the firm at that time, 7 were women. Of the 88 persons proposed for partnership that year, only 1—Hopkins—was a woman. Forty-seven of these candidates were admitted to the partnership, 21 were rejected, and 20—including Hopkins—were held for reconsideration the following year. Thirteen of the 32 partners who had submitted comments on Hopkins supported her bid for partnership. Three partners recommended that her candidacy be placed on hold, eight stated that they did not have an informed opinion about her, and eight recommended that she be denied partnership.

In a jointly prepared statement supporting her candidacy, the partners in Hopkins' office showcased her successful two-year effort to secure a $25 million contract with the Department of State, labeling it "an outstanding performance" and one that Hopkins carried out "virtually at the partner level." Despite Price Waterhouse's attempt at trial to minimize her contribution to this project, District Court Judge Gesell specifically found that Hopkins has "played a key role in Price Waterhouse's successful effort to win a multimillion-dollar contract with the Department of State." Indeed, he went on, "none of the other

595

EXHIBIT 9.3.1 (*Continued*)

partnership candidates at Price Waterhouse that year had a comparable record in terms of successfully securing major contracts for the partnership."

The partners in Hopkins' office praised her character as well as her accomplishments, describing her in their joint statement as "an outstanding professional" who had a "deft touch," a "strong character, independence, and integrity." Clients appear to have agreed with these assessments. At trial, one official from the State Department described her as "extremely competent, intelligent," "strong and forthright, very productive, energetic and creative." Another high-ranking official praised Hopkins' decisiveness, broadmindedness, and "intellectual clarity"; she was, in his words, "a stimulating conversationalist." Evaluations such as these led Judge Gesell to conclude that Hopkins "had no difficulty dealing with clients and her clients appear to have been very pleased with her work" and that she "was generally viewed as a highly competent project leader who worked long hours, pushed vigorously to meet deadlines and demanded much from the multidisciplinary staffs with which she worked."

On too many occasions, however, Hopkins' aggressiveness apparently spilled over into abrasiveness. Staff members seem to have borne the brunt of Hopkins' brusqueness. Long before her bid for partnership, partners evaluating her work had counseled her to improve her relations with staff members. Although later evaluations indicate an improvement, Hopkins' perceived shortcomings in this important area eventually doomed her bid for partnership. Virtually all the partners' negative remarks about Hopkins—even those of partners supporting her—had to do with her "interpersonal skills." Both "supporters and opponents of her candidacy," stressed Judge Gesell, "indicated that she was sometimes overly aggressive, unduly harsh, difficult to work with, and impatient with staff."

There were clear signs, though, that some of the partners reacted negatively to Hopkins' personality because she was a woman. One partner described her as "macho"; another suggested that she "overcompensated for being a woman"; a third advised her to take "a course at charm school." Several partners criticized her use of profanity; in response, one partner suggested that those partners objected to her swearing only "because it is a lady using foul language." Another supporter explained that Hopkins "had matured from a tough-talking somewhat masculine hard-nosed manager to an authoritative, formidable, but much more appealing lady partner candidate." As Judge Gesell found, the reasons for the policy board's decision to place her candidacy on hold were to improve her chances for partnership. Thomas Beyer advised, Hopkins should "walk more femininely, talk more femininely, dress more femininely, wear makeup, have her hair styled, and wear jewelry."

Dr. Susan Fiske, a social psychologist and associate professor of psychology at Carnegie-Mellon University, testified at the trial that the partnership selection process at Price Waterhouse was likely influenced by sex stereotyping. Her testimony focused not only on the overtly sex-based comments of partners but also on gender-neutral remarks, made by partners who knew Hopkins only slightly, that were intensely critical of her. One partner, for example, boldly stated that Hopkins was "universally disliked" by staff, and another described her as "consistently annoying and irritating"; yet these people had very little direct contact with Hopkins. According to Fiske, Hopkins' uniqueness (as the only woman in the pool of candidates) and the subjectivity of the evaluations made it likely that sharply critical remarks such as these were the product of sex stereotyping—although Fiske admitted that she could not say with certainty whether any particular comment was the result of stereotyping. Fiske based her opinion on a review of the submitted comments, explaining that it was commonly accepted practice for social psychologists to reach this kind of conclusion without having met any of the people involved in the decision-making process.

In previous years, other female candidates for partnership also had been evaluated in sex-based terms. As a general matter, Judge Gesell concluded, "Candidates were viewed favorably if partners believed they maintained their femininity while becoming effective professional managers"; in this environment, "to be identified as a 'women's libber' was regarded as a negative comment." In fact, the judge found that in previous years "one partner repeatedly commented that he could not consider any woman seriously as a partnership candidate and believed that women were not even capable of functioning as senior managers—yet the firm took no action to discourage his comments and recorded his vote in the overall summary of the evaluations."

Judge Gesell found that Price Waterhouse legitimately emphasized interpersonal skills in its partnership decisions and also found that the firm has not fabricated its complaints about Hopkins' interpersonal skills as a pretext for discrimination. Moreover, he concluded, the firm did not give decisive emphasis to such traits only because Hopkins was a woman; although there were male candidates who lacked these skills but were admitted to partnership. The judge found that these male candidates possessed other positive traits that Hopkins lacked. The judge went on to decide that some of the partners' remarks about Hopkins stemmed from their view of the "proper behavior of women," and that Price Waterhouse had done nothing to disavow reliance on such comments. In fact, Price Waterhouse had given credence and effect to partners' comments that resulted from sex stereotyping.

Source: Price Waterhouse v. Hopkins, U.S. 99 S. Ct. 1775, 49 FEP Cases 954 (1989).

Name _____   Group _____

1. What legal statute applies to this case?

2. What additional data or information would be helpful in order for you to take a definitive position on Hopkins.

3. What steps would you take at Price Waterhouse to prevent a similar legal problem in the future?

4. Is gender stereotyping illegal? If so, does Hopkins prevail in this case?

5. If gender stereotyping is an acceptable legal theory of discrimination, does the theory apply to discrimination against gay people under Title VII? Give an example of what you regard as illegal discrimination against a gay person using this theory.

EXERCISE 9.4
PERFORMANCE APPRAISAL AT DARBY GAS & LIGHT

OVERVIEW

HR professionals are often asked to critique current systems and modify them to meet the changing needs and objectives of the organization. Often, they are also asked to design programs to train raters on using the appraisal systems. This exercise enables you to critique an appraisal system and offer your suggestions for how it should be changed. It also allows you to make some recommendations for a rater training program based on a needs assessment.

LEARNING OBJECTIVES

After completing this exercise, you should be able to:

1. Critique an appraisal system and offer suggestions for revisions.
2. Interpret the findings from a needs assessment report.

PROCEDURE

Part A: Individual Analysis

Step 1. Before class, read the background information on the firm presented in Exhibit 9.4.1. Review the appraisal form currently being used by the firm as illustrated in Exhibit 9.4.2.

Step 2. A survey was administered to 20 managers and to 100 employees at Darby Gas & Light. They were asked to indicate the types of rater training for supervisors that would be most beneficial. Results from the survey are reported in Exhibit 9.4.3. Review these findings. Respond to the questions listed in Form 9.4.1.

Part B: Group Analysis

In class, your group will be asked to revise the Darby form and performance-appraisal system.

EXHIBIT 9.4.1
BACKGROUND INFORMATION
FOR DARBY GAS & LIGHT

Steve Shakely is the CEO of a moderately sized public utility, Darby Gas & Light. He employs about 150 professionals (e.g., engineers, systems analysts) and support staff, including 20 managers. His firm recently started using a new appraisal system that consists of yearly formal reviews between managers and subordinates using the rating form illustrated in Exhibit 9.4.2. All employees are rated by their immediate supervisor once a year, and these ratings are used to make administrative decisions (e.g., promotions, merit increases, transfers, terminations, demotions). Mr. Shakely has hired you as an external consultant to review the appraisal form and offer your recommendations for the form and the system.

Mr. Shakely is also interested in your plans for a rater training program. The managers have never received any formal training in conducting appraisal interviews with their subordinates. The firm's HR director, Linda James, recently surveyed the 20 managers and 100 of the employees to assess the areas in which supervisors needed training for completing appraisals and for conducting feedback sessions. A summary of her findings is presented in Exhibit 9.4.3. The numbers indicate the percentages of managers and employees who agreed that supervisors needed training in those areas.

EXHIBIT 9.4.2

EMPLOYEE EVALUATION FORM

DARBY GAS & LIGHT

Employee's name _____   SSN _____

Supervisor's name _____   SSN _____

Date of review: _____   Date of feedback: _____

Instructions:
This appraisal form is to be used with all employees of Darby Gas & Light, including supervisors. Raters should circle one number on the scales below to indicate the employee's level of performance on the dimension and should provide comments of the employee's performance on that dimension. Dimensions marked with an asterisk must be evaluated for all supervisory employees. After completing the ratings for the employee be sure to schedule a feedback session with the employee to review the ratings.

1. JOB KNOWLEDGE	1 low	2	3 average	4	5 high

Comments: _____
_____

2. DECISION MAKING	1 low	2	3 average	4	5 high

Comments: _____
_____

3. *MOTIVATING OTHERS	1 low	2	3 average	4	5 high

Comments: _____
_____

4. DEPENDABILITY	1 low	2	3 average	4	5 high

Comments: _____
_____

5. *LEADERSHIP	1 low	2	3 average	4	5 high

Comments: _____
_____

6. PROBLEM SOLVING	1 low	2	3 average	4	5 high

Comments: _____
_____

7. COMMUNICATION	1 low	2	3 average	4	5 high

Comments: _____
_____

EXHIBIT 9.4.3 SURVEY RESULTS ABOUT SUPERVISOR APPRAISAL TRAINING NEEDS **601**

EXHIBIT 9.4.2 (*Continued*)

8. *PLANNING AND ORGANIZING   1   2   3   4   5
                                      low   average   high

Comments: _____

_____

9. TEAMWORK/COOPERATION   1   2   3   4   5
                                        low   average   high

Comments: _____

_____

10. *EMPLOYEE DEVELOPMENT   1   2   3   4   5
                                        low   average   high

Comments: _____

_____

11. PROFESSIONAL DEVELOPMENT   1   2   3   4   5
                                        low   average   high

Comments: _____

_____

12. APPEARANCE AND WORK HABITS   1   2   3   4   5
                                        low   average   high

Comments: _____

_____

EXHIBIT 9.4.3
SURVEY RESULTS ABOUT SUPERVISOR APPRAISAL TRAINING NEEDS

AREA FOR TRAINING	PERCENT WHO AGREED TRAINING FOR SUPERVISORS WAS NEEDED	
	SUPERVISORS	SUBORDINATES
	(N = 20)	(N = 100)
Giving specific, constructive criticism to employees	50%	15%
Giving specific, positive feedback to employees	10	50
Identifying available training opportunities for employees	40	40
Identifying employees' skills	40	45
Setting goals for employees' future performance	15	30
Conducting a career development session with employees	10	50
Assigning ratings for employees' performance	10	15
Understanding work-related performance problems	20	60
Administering rewards for good performance	15	55
Administering discipline for poor performance	45	15
Dealing effectively with employees who get upset In the feedback session	60	50
Providing timely praise	15	60
Identifying career paths for employees	40	50

Name _____   Group _____

1. After reviewing Exhibit 9.4.2, list what you regard as the major problems with the form used by the company to evaluate performance.

2. What revisions to the form would you suggest? How specifically should the form or dimensions be changed to make the performance-appraisal system more effective?

3. Suppose the firm wants to use the form for employee feedback (i.e., to provide feedback to employees on their strengths and weaknesses). Do you think the instrument will be useful for this purpose? Why or why not? What, if any, revisions would you suggest so that the form can be used for employee development?

4. Suppose Darby has used this form to both promote people and make merit pay adjustments. Suppose also that Darby has been informed that six African-Americans have claimed discrimination based on promotion and pay policies. What (if any) advice can you give the company? What data should Darby evaluate?

5. Based on the survey data and what you know about performance appraisal, what areas are most important for a rater training program?

6. How would you evaluate the training program? Give specific examples of reactive, learning, behavioral, or results data that could be used.

CHAPTER 10 EXERCISES

EXERCISE 10.1
PROBLEMS IN THE PAY SYSTEM*

OVERVIEW

Chapter 10 discusses the importance of internal and external equity in structuring an effective pay program. This exercise describes a situation in which perceived inequities exist and the organization is already realizing the effects of these perceptions.

LEARNING OBJECTIVES

After completing the exercise, you should be able to:

1. Determine the critical variables that must be considered in assessing the fairness of a pay system.

2. Assess the weights to be given to data related to internal and external equity.

3. Develop a system that can more closely monitor the effects of pay on critical personnel data.

PROCEDURE

Part A: Individual Analysis

After reading the chapter and before class, read the scenario and all exhibits and then answer the questions on Form 10.1.1.

Part B: Group Analysis

In groups of about six, students should first review all of their respective Forms 10.1.1 and then attempt to reach consensus on the questions. The group should prepare a concise, written response to each of the questions on Form 10.1.1.

SCENARIO

Denise Nance is the director of the Computer Center/ User Assistance (CCUA) department of a large manufacturing company in the rural Southeast. Last year's revenue was $23.5 million. Profit was in line with expectations.

Recently, a serious problem has developed in her division. A growing percentage of her employees have left the company in the past year, which has affected unit productivity and costs. While turnover in her department has always been a problem, things appear to have gotten out of hand. Until now, turnover had run around 20 percent per year for lower division staff personnel and 15 percent per year for middle division employees.

However, in the past three months, CCUA has lost five data processors (50 percent of the total) and six (75 percent) computer analysts. Previously, Ms. Nance had no policy regarding exit interviews or turnover control, but informal discussions with the individuals who have left has led to the hypothesis that many employees leave because they feel they are underpaid.

To complicate matters, Ms. Nance's supervisor, Julie Linquist, the vice president in charge of technical services, is becoming increasingly concerned about the costs associated with the human resource function at CCUA. Exhibit 10.1.1 presents a recent memo from Ms. Linquist to Ms. Nance concerning the problem.

Following Ms. Linquist's orders, Ms. Nance conducted phone interviews with 12 former employees (the only ones available) and distributed questionnaires to her current workforce.

The survey results indicated a number of interesting findings, which are summarized in Exhibit 10.1.2. The dominant reason for individuals leaving CCUA was pay. The current workforce also indicated strong dissatisfaction with current pay levels. Although the survey was not limited to data processing IIs and computer analysts Is, both Ms. Nance and Ms. Linquist believe that these two positions are of particular concern. Responses from both current and past employees from both job classifications were similar to those of the entire sample.

The data processor II position currently carries a salary range of $9.00 to $9.70 per hour. The average actual pay of the seven incumbents is $9.20 per hour ($19,136 per year based on their 40-hour workweek). In addition, employees receive 40 hours of paid leave for the first year with an increase of 5 hours every 1,000 hours of service. Health insurance plus basic life insurance are provided by the company at a cost of $750 per year per employee. CCUA usually employs 10 DP IIs, but the current level is only 7.

The computer analyst I position currently carries a salary range of $20,500 to $27,500. The average actual salary paid to the eight incumbents is $26,500. Paid leave for CA IIs is 9 days for the first year of service increasing by 2 days for every following year with a limit of 21 days of paid leave. Health and life insurance coverage costs the company $750 per year per employee.

Recruitment costs for data processor IIs is $250 and $750 for computer analyst Is. Costs are low for the DP

*Contributed by James R. Harris and Lee P. Stepina.

IIs because they have been obtained, primarily, from the local marketplace. Entry-level individuals are hired 75 percent of the time and the organization spends considerable resources to train them. By contrast, the computer analysts are recruited from the regional market. Prime candidates typically possess either considerable experience in a similar position or a college degree in information systems management with light, but related, part-time (or summer) work experience.

Ms. Nance budgets $215,490 for data processing IIs and $243,984 for computer analysts. The company is in the sixth month of its fiscal year. During this fiscal year, the CCUA department has been using a 3.5 percent salary increase budget to reward its performers and to keep pace with the marketplace.

Ms. Nance obtained a pay survey conducted by Decision Sciences, Inc., a reputable, information systems consulting firm. The data are depicted in Exhibit 10.1.3. A compensation analyst at DSI has suggested that, based on the verbal descriptions provided by Ms. Nance, the data processor II position would probably most closely match the survey's "data processor" position, while CCUA's computer analyst I job is most comparable with the survey's "junior analyst and programmer" position.

EXHIBIT 10.1.1

```
To: Denise Nance, Director of CCUA

From: Julie Linquist, Vice President Technical Services

Re: Personnel Problems
```

```
I don't know what's going on down there but Jon Anderson of placement services just informed me
that you requested another listing for a data processing person and another computer analyst.
According to my records, that's the fifth DP person and the sixth computer analyst you have lost
this year! It costs a lot of money to hire new people. This is obviously not the pattern that I
want to see from your department. I want you to investigate this immediately.
```

```
I want you to contact the individuals who you lost and find out why they left. I also want you to
talk to the employees that are still there and find what, if anything, could potentially be causing
the problem. Let's get this problem cleared up now.
```

EXHIBIT 10.1.2 SURVEY RESULTS **607**

EXHIBIT 10.1.2
SURVEY RESULTS

All items scaled 1 (satisfied) to 5 (dissatisfied).

Current employees:	MEAN	SD
Supervision	2.1	1.6
Working conditions	1.9	1.8
Task characteristics	3.0	2.1
Pay	4.2	0.5
Benefits	4.3	1.1
Work hours	3.1	.9
Physical conditions	1.4	1.5
General satisfaction	3.9	0.7

Employees who left:	MEAN	SD
Supervision	1.9	1.5
Working conditions	2.4	1.7
Task characteristics	3.7	2.0
Pay	4.8	1.1
Benefits	4.5	0.6
Work hours	3.0	2.0
Physical conditions	1.7	0.5
General satisfaction	4.2	1.2
Reasons for leaving—		
Not enough money	83.3%	
Spouse left area	8.3%	
Child care problems	8.3%	

EXHIBIT 10.1.3
EXCERPT FROM DECISION SCIENCES

TITLE	AVERAGE WEIGHTED SALARY	MFG./ CONSUMER	MFG./ INDUSTRIAL	BANKING	OTHER FINANCIAL SERVICES	DP SERVICES	WHOLESALE DISTRIBUTION
IS Management							
CIO/VP	106,864	128,611	100,741	124,318	109,130	157,500	130,000
Manager/Supervisor	65,811	83,333	74,821	76,500	67,143	60,000	57,143
End-User Support							
Manager End-User Computing	56,808	74,167	62,667	57,500	58,500	55,000	48,750
Information Center Manager	54,346	56,667	60,833	56,818	53,500	63,333	49,000
PC Specialist Support	38,058	40,000	48,077	39,211	36,250	37,000	38,636
LAN Manager	45,880	55,000	52,857	46,000	46,000	52,000	52,000
WP Supervisor	36,538	55,000	42,500	32,600	34,000	40,000	34,000
Systems Analysis/Programming							
Manager	65,357	83,182	63,913	68,611	64,286	66,364	72,000
Senior Systems Analyst and Programmer	50,345	50,714	53,333	52,143	51,471	56,250	52,000
Systems Analyst and Programmer	43,220	44,000	43,462	45,250	42,647	48,750	60,455
Intermediate Analyst and Programmer	37,517	40,000	38,571	37,750	38,000	38,125	40,000
Junior Analyst and Programmer	30,156	28,750	35,714	30,000	27,143	32,500	26,875
Application/Operating Systems Programming Manager	64,481	79,000	67,667	68,529	71,765	68,750	66,667
Senior Applications/Operating Sys. Prog.	52,434	55,000	55,938	52,353	56,000	55,000	53,125
Applications/Operating Sys. Prog.	44,419	48,571	46,250	46,176	46,563	46,429	40,000
Intermediate Applications/Operating Sys. Prog.	37,150	42,500	40,000	35,000	38,636	35,000	37,500
Junior Applications/Operating Sys. Prog.	29,709	30,000	32,500	29,615	30,455	30,000	28,750
Data Com/Telecom/Connectivity							
Network Manager (LAN-WAN)	57,546	63,750	59,643	59,643	72,500	57,222	58,333
Telecommunications Manager	57,136	58,750	66,111	59,231	67,500	63,125	60,000
Communications Specialist	42,276	37,000	43,000	41,667	46,818	40,000	43,750
Database Manager/Administrator	61,077	71,000	60,500	64,643	70,385	52,500	62,000
Database Analyst	48,194	52,000	55,000	46,000	51,250	42,500	47,500
Microcomputer/Workstation Manager	44,500	35,000	55,000	46,818	43,750	47,500	43,750
Data Processor	22,500	21,000	24,000	23,000	21,500	21,000	22,000

EXHIBIT 10.1.3 EXCERPT FROM DECISION SCIENCES **609**

EXHIBIT 10.1.3 *(Continued)*

GOVERNMENT	MEDICAL/ LEGAL	TRANS./ UTILITIES	EDUCATION	CONSTRUCTION/ MINING	OTHER	AVERAGE SALARY BY COMPANY REVENUE ($ MILLION)				
						LESS THAN $200	$250– $500	$500– $5,000	$5,000– $20,000	$20,000+
71,731	64,500	114,167	103,571	76,667	101,600	82,292	84,697	104,844	128,780	129,700
51,739	42,500	66,667	51,250	52,000	65,104	50,204	61,094	68,534	75,811	73,269
53,750	—	63,462	49,000	43,750	54,310	47,200	46,667	58,871	62,593	60,857
47,500	40,000	61,364	46,000	—	51,500	43,529	46,250	56,957	60,741	56,071
30,455	27,143	41,071	31,429	30,000	38,250	36,053	31,600	39,405	40,429	40,833
42,500	40,000	44,500	34,000	40,000	45,833	42,368	46,667	48,519	46,250	46,172
36,667	40,000	40,000	25,000	25,000	38,846	32,500	40,000	36,667	38,235	37,000
55,294	40,000	67,105	50,000	62,500	65,814	58,958	53,421	65,288	71,216	68,261
45,926	40,000	52,750	40,000	46,000	49,375	46,935	46,250	49,500	53,784	52,843
38,571	35,000	42,727	32,500	40,000	41,667	45,000	39,464	42,750	43,663	44,692
31,316	25,000	39,000	32,500	40,000	38,448	35,000	38,333	38,256	36,250	38,500
27,500	25,000	35,313	25,000	25,000	28,913	32,500	31,000	28,529	28,750	31,667
53,333	47,500	66,875	47,500	62,500	62,027	51,667	51,250	66,395	70,789	68,889
47,105	—	56,875	45,000	47,500	50,286	43,947	46,667	52,391	55,429	57,206
37,500	40,000	47,000	36,000	55,000	43,500	41,500	37,273	44,390	45,571	46,562
33,571	—	38,846	32,500	—	36,250	40,000	30,455	38,448	35,556	39,444
23,125	—	37,273	25,000	26,000	26,875	30,000	26,875	30,192	29,038	31,176
49,231	47,500	68,750	40,000	55,000	60,000	46,154	61,667	54,630	80,000	64,500
46,429	—	54,231	43,750	55,000	55,556	41,538	48,333	57,000	82,258	61,852
36,786	—	49,000	36,250	55,000	41,071	39,000	33,182	39,189	45,825	47,857
51,786	—	69,000	55,033	70,000	55,962	47,778	51,364	60,000	66,818	66,765
42,143	—	50,000	40,000	55,000	46,136	46,000	46,429	46,207	48,500	50,781
43,000	40,000	47,600	40,000	—	38,848	35,714	43,750	45,000	44,412	47,941
20,000	23,000	20,500	20,000	—	23,000	20,000	22,000	23,000	23,500	24,000

Name _____   Group _____

You have been retained as a consultant to evaluate the situation and make recommendations for action. Ms. Nance wants your positions on the following:

1. Are the CCUA department's current pay practices concerning data processor IIs and computer analyst Is externally equitable (i.e., competitive)? Explain your answer.

2. What specific action, if any, do you recommend be taken now? Be specific and justify your recommendations as fully as possible.

3. What specific strategy(ies) do you recommend for the future so that these types of problems can be anticipated and (it is hoped) avoided.

4. As is often the case in business, we typically find that we must make decisions, or recommendations, on the basis of incomplete, imperfect information. What additional information in this situation would have enabled you to improve the quality of your recommendations?

EXERCISE 10.2
SHOULD THE STATE ADOPT A PAY EQUITY POLICY?

OVERVIEW

The chapter discusses the controversial issue of pay equity or comparable worth. Many U.S. states and municipalities and over 100 countries have adopted some form of pay equity policy for government workers. Ontario, Canada, has mandated pay equity for all public and private employers. Many collective bargaining writs now place great emphasis on pay equity adjustments based on studies that find evidence of gender or race-based inequities in the pay system. This exercise examines the issues and implications of pay equity for public and private employers. Students will review the summary of a pay equity study.

LEARNING OBJECTIVES

After completing the exercise, you should be able to:

1. Understand the major components of a pay equity study.
2. Anticipate some of the advantages and disadvantages of a pay equity policy.
3. Discuss the implications of pay equity adjustments on market rates and private-sector employment.

PROCEDURE

Part A: Individual Analysis

Congratulations! You have been appointed to the State University Task Force on Compensation. Your assignment is to review the report (Exhibit 10.2.1) submitted by a consulting firm under contract to an ad hoc committee of the state legislature. After reviewing state compensation information and conducting a pay equity study, this highly credible consulting firm has made specific recommendations to the legislature. As a member of the task force, your job is to take a position on each of the recommendations. On Form 10.2.1, state your position and provide a justification in the space provided. Answer all of the questions on Form 10.2.1.

Part B: Group Analysis

In groups, students should attempt to reach consensus on the three recommendations. Each group should prepare concise justifications for its recommendations.

EXHIBIT 10.2.1
EXECUTIVE SUMMARY OF PAY EQUITY STUDY

The underlying theory of pay equity is that the wages for female- and minority-dominated occupations are artificially depressed due to historical bias against the value of "women's work." The goal of pay equity studies is to use objectively measured criteria to examine the relative value of all jobs to an employer in an effort to correct for any gender- and race-based undervaluation.

Crucial to pay equity policy is the recognition that jobs that require equivalent or *comparable* skill, effort, responsibility, and working conditions should be compensated equally. Once implemented, pay equity policy assures that an employer's classification and compensation systems are administered and maintained objectively and fairly.

To accomplish the above objective, we examined a representative sample of 300 classes in the career service system. This served as the basis of our analysis in determining objectively what job content characteristics the state values when setting pay. The question that guided this study is, in setting pay rates, does the state value work differently (and perhaps in a biased manner) for male-dominated jobs as opposed to female- and minority-dominated jobs? In other words, is there a difference in monetary return for jobs with similar characteristics and requirements?

The state utilizes a position classification system whereby positions are consolidated into job families and these families are assigned to pay grades. This study was designed to provide a model of "equitable compensation" for the state that is based largely on its current pay policy. Using this model, the analysis shows which classes are underpaid due to the influence of female or minority dominance of the job. The recommendations, if adopted, will bring female- and minority-dominated classes in line with equitable compensation.

The approach utilized for this study is called *policy capturing.* Through policy capturing, the relative worth to the state of all jobs in a system is evaluated. As a first step a compensation model is developed in which specific job content features, such as the number of persons supervised, the level of education, the level of analytic reasoning, and the years of prerequisite experience are grouped into compensable factors.

Exhibit 10.2.2 presents a portion of the methodology used. These factors are then weighted in such a way that they statistically "predict" the current wage structure. In other words, the weights for each compensable job content characteristic are derived from a statistical model that makes explicit what is currently valued implicitly within an organization. The relationship between what people do and what they are paid thus becomes clear. Pay equity adjustments are indicated when this relationship is violated simply because the jobs are performed by a high percentage of females and minorities. This methodology was selected because it does not impose outside standards for fair compensation on the state. Rather, it looks at the current compensation policy and simply adjusts the existing system in instances where its own standards are not met. Policy capturing techniques thus allow the state to adjust its salary grades to eliminate any influence of gender or race bias without radically altering its basic philosophy of compensation.

FINDINGS

As a result of the above analysis, it was determined there is substantial undervaluation of female- and minority-dominated classes in the Career Service System. A model of equitable compensation has been developed to adjust for the resulting pay inequities.

Another objective of this study was to assess the cost of correcting gender- or race-based pay inequities for the purpose of budget planning by the legislature. The total cost to the state for making pay equity adjustments to the female- and minority-dominated classes is estimated to be $75,552,000. An implementation model is recommended that suggests an appropriations schedule of $9,552,000 for the first year and $16,500,000 for the next four years.

The wage setting process in the state is not structured in a way that facilitates the maintenance of internal equity. This is primarily because there is no quantitative job evaluation system tied to a unified wage structure that would keep future inequities from occurring. Women and minorities are underrepresented in job classes at the upper end of the wage structure.

EXHIBIT 10.2.2   PART OF POINT FACTOR JOB ANALYSIS METHOD   **613**

EXHIBIT 10.2.2
PART OF POINT FACTOR JOB ANALYSIS METHOD

1. Prerequisite knowledge
    - 11 Doctorate, law, medical, or other degree beyond master's
    - 10 Master's
    - 9 Some graduate education, but no degree
    - 8 B.A. or B.S.
    - 7 Two- or three-year college degree
    - 6 Some business or vocational school courses (such as typing, nursing, or drafting), *after* finishing high school or G.E.D.
    - 5 Some college
    - 4 High school or G.E.D.
    - 3 Some business or vocational courses (such as typing, nursing, plumbing, or drafting) but no G.E.D. or high school degree
    - 2 Some high school
    - 1 Elementary school
    - 0 None

2. Experience
    - 5 5 years or equivalent
    - 4 4 years
    - 3 3 years
    - 2 2 years
    - 1 1 year
    - 0 None

3. Supervision
    - 4 Major program or department
    - 3 Second-line supervision—supervises supervisors
    - 2 First-line supervision—hire, fire, discipline, promote
    - 1 Does not supervise, but coordinates, plans, and schedules, may be team leader or occasional supervisor
    - 0 Does not supervise

4. Mathematics
    - 3 Complex mathematics (statistics, advanced trig, and algebra)
    - 2 Basic math
    - 1 Basic arithmetic
    - 0 None

5. Special certification or license
    - 1 Yes
    - 0 No

6. Writing
    - 10 Technical, legal, scholarly, or policy analysis of length and creativity
    - 9 Formal reports or manual, technical reports/manual, more routine
    - 8 Monthly or annual reports, programs or work plans, technical specs, reports for others to review
    - 7 News releases, speeches
    - 6 Case histories
    - 5 Editing writing of others
    - 4 Writing original letters or memos
    - 3 Taking or writing minutes, dictation
    - 2 Writing (including patient records)
    - 1 Simple recording, tallying
    - 0 None

7. Information Gathering
    - 6 Deciding what information should be gathered (policy decisions)
    - 5 Deciding how information should be gathered (design and planning decisions)
    - 4 Conducting complex information gathering—not routine
    - 3 Conducting data analysis under other's supervision—including lab tests
    - 2 Cataloging or classifying information
    - 1 Collecting or tallying information
    - 0 None

8. Recordkeeping
    - 4 Maintains records and files where confidentiality is required
    - 3 Maintains detailed client, patient, or inmate records, weekly or monthly

EXHIBIT 10.2.2 (*Continued*)

2   Prepares and maintains files and records such as personnel, technical, financial
1   Prepares and maintains daily records such as logs, supply inventory, medical charts, daily calendar
0   None

9.   Organize/prioritize work

5   Set work objectives for agency
4   Responsible for organizing and prioritizing work in unit
3   Responsible for organizing and prioritizing work of projects
2   Organize and prioritize own work and schedule appointments for others (not limited to coworkers)
1   Organize own work only
0   No responsibility for organizing work

10.   Training/teaching (integral part of job)

5   Developing and implementing educational programs at the state level for employees at educational agencies
4   Other employees
3   Clients, inmates, patients
2   Students
1   Training/teaching on occasion
0   None

11.   Budget authority

5   Determine budget priorities for major department
4   Set budget for division within major department
3   Propose or prepare budget or financial projection for unit
2   Propose or prepare budget or financial projection for individual projects (includes assembling data)
1   Authority to spend budgeted money
0   No budget authority

12.   Laws, policies, regulations, administrative codes

		YES	NO
a.	Develop agency position and defend laws or administrative codes	_____	_____
b.	Draft laws or administrative codes for agency use	_____	_____
c.	Insure compliance with law, regulation, or administrative codes with public	_____	_____
d.	Insure compliance within or across agencies	_____	_____
e.	Interpret administrative codes and regulations in order to carry out job responsibilities (i.e. determining eligibility or safety compliance)	_____	_____

Name _____   Group _____

1. The state legislature should appropriate $75,552,000 to cover the costs of the pay equity adjustments indicated by this study. Agree____ Disagree_____ Unsure_____. If you are unsure, what additional information do you require before you take a position?

    Justification:

2. To ensure a systematic and uniform job evaluation and wage setting system, the state should adopt a point factor job evaluation system like the one presented in Exhibit 10.2.2. The outside figure for full implementation of an equitable system is $140,000. Agree_____ Disagree_____

    Justification:

3. Based on the Supreme Court ruling in *Johnson v. Santa Clara Transportation,* the state should establish an affirmative action program for women and minorities because such groups are underrepresented in job classes at the upper end of the wage structure. Agree_____ Disagree_____

    Justification:

4. If the state follows the recommendations, what impact could the policy have on private-sector compensation?

5. To create internal equity faster and more cheaply, the consultants could have recommended reducing the pay of "overvalued" jobs (all male-dominated). Please comment.

6. Explain in your own words how the pay equity study determined that female-dominated jobs were underpaid and that some male-dominated jobs were overpaid. What does the term *policy capturing* mean in terms of this pay equity study?

EXERCISE 10.3
DEVELOPING AN EMPLOYEE BENEFITS PROGRAM*

OVERVIEW

Chapter 10 provides an overview of types of employee benefits programs. The following exercise describes a new business start-up and some key decisions that need to be made if this organization is going to succeed with its planned "preferred employer" strategy.

LEARNING OBJECTIVES

After completing the exercise, you should be able to:

1. Determine the critical issues that must be considered when designing an employee benefits program.
2. Identify the trade-offs that are made when choosing from a wide variety of benefits alternatives.
3. Decide how to judge the effectiveness of a benefits program.

PROCEDURE

Part A: Individual Analysis

After reading the chapter and before coming to class, read the scenario and all exhibits and then answer the questions on Form 10.3.1.

Part B: Group Analysis

In groups, students should first review all their forms 10.3.1 and then attempt to reach consensus on the questions. The group should prepare a concise, written response to each question on Form 10.3.1.

SCENARIO

USA Credit is a major financial services organization with growing interests in the private label credit card area. The organization began three years ago when it successfully acquired the credit card portfolios of five major U.S. retailers that were interested in outsourcing their programs. Since then, the organization has grown to a $1.5 billion business covering 25 retailers with a total of 6 million cardholders. Since its founding, USA Credit has targeted medium-sized retailers that like the customer closeness associated with having their own

---
*Contributed by Christine M. Hagan.

credit card but lack the technical expertise to effectively manage an accounts receivables business. USA Credit's business plan projects that it will double in size in the next two to three years. In addition, it plans to develop a bank card product and aggressively market it to small financial institutions that need this service to compete with the "megabanks" moving into their neighborhoods.

Traditionally, the business has used one of two organization models in its credit card relationships, depending on the needs and the sophistication of the retail client. With its earliest acquisitions, USA Credit simply subcontracted the credit and collections function and staffed the store-based credit offices with its own personnel who processed customers' applications for credit, accepted payments, and assisted customers in the resolution of billing questions and problems. As the business grew, regional processing centers became the more efficient model, facilitated by sophisticated information systems. In recent acquisitions the on-site credit offices have been replaced with a bank of telephones tied directly to the regional processing center. In addition, there is a payment drop box for customer payments and an attractive kiosk containing applications and assorted credit-related information. Recent customer surveys indicate elimination of the traditional, staffed credit office has had no effect on customer satisfaction. In addition, retailers express a neutral attitude concerning whether or not there is a staffed, on-site office. Their major concerns focus on (1) increasing the number of credit card customers; (2) maintaining accurate billing information that is summarized in attractively designed monthly statements to customers; and (3) maximizing collection efforts.

Since its founding, USA Credit's offices (both store-based and regional) have been staffed with part-time employees working 20–25 hours per week. Most employees are full-time students, mothers of school-age children, and senior citizens. Employees have been paid wages similar to those offered by other entry-level employers in the area, such as fast food restaurants and retailers. No employee benefits have been offered, except those required by law.

Several months ago, USA Credit's top management team decided its future goals would best be met by establishing a national service center to replace the regional and in-store credit offices. The firm's information technology is more than capable of supporting such a shift and executives believe that this would effectively position the company for the expected short-term growth, as well as a long-term plan to expand into Mexico and Canada. They wish to attract a full-time workforce in order to provide stability and a level of professionalism as new accounts are added and as strategic services are expanded. Estimates are that the center would initially employee 75 customer service associates and 4 to 7 other individuals, such as managers and technical specialists. If business grows according to plan, the number of customer service associates is expected to double over the next few years.

A lengthy search has been conducted using a cross-functional managerial team, which included Andy Wolfson, USA Credit's HR manager. After months of research, the team recommended locating the center on a two-acre lot just northeast of Las Vegas, Nevada. Real estate values are excellent in the region, the profile of the local worker is very appealing, the tax situation is favorable, and state and local political and community organizations welcome the opportunity to sponsor the opening of a solid, reputable, growing business such as USA Credit. Last week, the recommendation was unanimously approved for implementation. Groundbreaking is scheduled for next month.

Andy Wolfson's main challenge is to assemble an HR plan. A key element of this involves designing a compensation and benefits program for the customer service associates. In addition to its state-of-the-art information systems technology, the competence and courtesy of its associates is expected to be a major source of competitive advantage. If USA Credit is going to continue to be successful in this upcoming growth period, it will be because it didn't lose focus on current customers and the customer service associates at the national service center would be critical contributors to this effort. Andy has requested a variety of information from knowledgeable sources concerning the employee marketplace and the practices of other area businesses. Exhibit 10.3.1 is a copy of a memo concerning local conditions that sums up the vast majority of information that he has compiled from other sources. Based on this information, he has sent a preliminary proposal to the corporate vice president for administration. Exhibit 10.3.2 is a copy of the vice president's response. Working with a number of consultants and with local insurance companies, Andy has developed a list of possible benefit choices and their costs, which are itemized in Exhibit 10.3.3.

EXHIBIT 10.3.1   **619**

EXHIBIT 10.3.1

To: Andy Wolfson, HR Manager

From: Andrea Birch, Senior Consultant

        Human Resources Concepts, Inc.

As requested, I reviewed the information you provided concerning the Customer Service Associate positions planned for your Nevada Service Center.

First, let me tell you that I think you'll be pleased with your decision to locate here. Gambling casinos/hotels are our foremost employers, accounting for 55 percent of the total jobs in the area. Second are tourist-related organizations such as small rental car companies, local motels, and restaurants. From the worker's point of view, these businesses are very cyclical and there is little job security. However, good casino workers are paid very well, both in base salary as well as tips. Needless to say, employee benefit programs are very meager.

It is my belief that, if you position yourself as a solid financial services company with a pleasant, stable work atmosphere, you will have no difficulty finding skilled, reliable workers. In particular, you would represent an excellent opportunity for a "casino spouse" whose concern for stable employment and a comprehensive benefits package--with particular emphasis on spouse and family options--is an important factor in choosing and staying with a job. Even if one or more benefits were contributory, access to the coverage would be valuable to these workers.

Thus, in a market that would normally call for hourly wages of $9.00 and up, we believe that your Customer Service Associate positions could be filled with competent employees in the $8.00 to $8.25 per hour range if the benefits plan were attractive.

As requested, I am also pleased to provide you with some local information concerning paid time off in this area. Most organizations in this market provide two weeks of vacation after one year of service and increase this to three weeks after five years. Typically, firms located here offer 7 to 10 days sick leave per year and 5 to 7 paid holidays. Be aware, however, that there is quite a bit of variance across organizations relating to these practices.

I'll call you next week so that we can identify the next step in this process.

EXHIBIT 10.3.2

To: Andy Wolfson, HR Manager

From: Xavier Ortenzio, VP Corporate Administration

I applaud your efforts to date in constructing a "preferred employer" HR strategy for our National Service Center. Having reviewed the copy of the Birch memo concerning the worker marketplace in Las Vegas, I heartily support your recommendations.

Our original estimates called for a total compensation package for Customer Service Associates of $11.75 to $12.00 per hour. We arrived at this figure by assuming a $9.25 average hourly rate ($19,240 per year) plus 28 percent in fringe benefits. "Fringe benefits" was broadly defined to include mandatory coverages, time off, and various other programs.

Your recommendation--that this amount be redistributed by reducing the average hourly pay rate to $8.50 ($17,680 per year) and by increasing the fringe benefit amount to 38 percent of base rate-- makes sense.

I also have no strong feelings about whether or not some benefits require employee contributions-- provided that this would not interfere with our "preferred employer" strategy. In addition, I read in yesterday's newspaper that cafeteria benefits are becoming increasingly popular. Would such an approach offer us any advantages?

In any event, consider this your go-ahead to draft your benefits program as outlined above. I look forward to receiving your final recommendations and anticipate a speedy Executive Committee approval. The successful staffing and management of the National Service Center is critical to USA Credit's business strategy, future growth, and overall success.

EXHIBIT 10.3.3   LIST OF POSSIBLE BENEFITS   **621**

EXHIBIT 10.3.3
LIST OF POSSIBLE BENEFITS

BENEFIT	COST (Unless where specified, all costs are annual rates)
FICA	
Social Security	6.2% on first $64,900 earned by individual
Medicare	1.45%
FUTA (Federal Unemployment Tax)	.8% on first $7,000 earned by individual
Workers' compensation	$1.50 for every $100 of total payroll
State disability	Not required in Nevada

	EMPLOYEE ONLY	EMPLOYEE AND FAMILY
Health care insurance program		
High plan	$3,000	$5,000
Medium plan	2,500	3,850
Low plan	1,700	3,000
HMO	1,400	2,000
Dental plan		
Regular plan	750	1,400
HMO dental	480	900
Vision care	150	230
Prescription drug	250	425

Life insurance	
1 year's salary	$400
2 years' salary	650
3 years' salary	1,000
Dependent life ($5,000 for spouse; $1,000 per child)	250
Pension plan	
Defined benefit	4.5%
Defined contribution	3.0%
Tuition reimbursement	.7%
Employee assistance program	.5%
Child care subsidy	3.5%
Paid vacation	$62 per day
Paid holidays	$57 per day
Paid sick leave	$52 per day
Long-term disability	
High plan (full salary after five consecutive days absent due to illness)	$1,000
Low plan (60 % of salary after 10 consecutive days absent due to illness)	$550

You have been retained as a consultant to Andy Wolfson.

1. Structure a benefits program that you think would be most effective for the customer service associates to be hired by USA Credit. Assume an average wage of $8.50 per hour and a workweek of 40 hours (average annual salary = $17,680). A benefits budget of 38% of salary has been approved. If needed, assume that 70 percent of the customer service associates will require family coverage.

2. What were the trade-offs you made in deciding on your recommendations?

3. Assume that Andy Wolfson is interested in a cafeteria benefits approach. He has heard, however, that when people are permitted to select their own coverages, unit costs may rise (called "adverse selection"). In other words, in cafeteria benefits, the averaging effect of users versus nonusers across employee populations declines as people opt out of programs that they are not likely to use in favor of benefits that they are very likely to use. How might Andy deal with this problem in designing a cafeteria benefits plan?

4. What additional information concerning this situation would have enabled you to provide better recommendations?

5. How will you decide whether or not your benefits program is an effective one? Describe the procedure that you would use. What specific criteria would you use?

CHAPTER 11 EXERCISES

OVERVIEW

This exercise evaluates the feasibility of different approaches to PFP given the strategic plan of the organization. As discussed in the chapter, the effectiveness of the PFP system depends on a number of factors. This exercise will give the student the opportunity to consider some of these factors in proposing an ideal PFP system.

LEARNING OBJECTIVES

After completing this exercise, you should be able to:

1. Identify the key organizational variables that should be considered in the development and/or revision of a PFP system.
2. Understand the role of and importance of other HRM activities (e.g., job analysis, performance appraisal) in the development of a PFP system.

PROCEDURE

Part A: Individual Analysis

Step 1. Before class, read the scenario.

Step 2. You have been retained as a consultant who must report to Ellen Lennett, director of incentive program development at Mega Manufacturing corporate headquarters. You will be working with the Kanto division. You have been asked to address the five issues raised on Form 11.1.1. Respond to each of the issues and recommend a specific program that supports both Mega's incentive policy and Kanto's situation. Your recommendation should consider *at least* the five points. Also, prior to class, complete the Assessment Questions.

The two memos in Exhibits 11.1.1 and 11.1.2 may be relevant to the recommendations you will make. Ellen Lennett has received the notes, one from Don Walker, vice president, compensation and benefits, and the other from Bill Idrey, a compensation specialist she sent to help the Kanto personnel department.

---

*Contributed by E. Brian Peach and M. Ronald Buckley.

Part B: Group Analysis

Step 1. In groups, each member should review the individual reports and take notes on the most important points. Each member should also devise his or her own strategy for identifying the best group response to make for each of the five questions presented in Form 11.1.1 plus any additional issues the group considers to be relevant. The group should also devise a list of key questions that must be answered by management before a firm position can be taken on the elements of the PFP system.

Step 2. One group member should be designated to make a five-minute presentation of the group's position before the rest of the class. A "free for all" discussion should then focus on the various recommended plans.

SCENARIO

Mega Manufacturing International is a large diversified company with its corporate headquarters in Boston and manufacturing plants, research and development facilities, and distribution and marketing centers in the United States and around the world. Mega Manufacturing is pursuing a long-range strategy of producing high-technology products for three markets: military, industrial, and retail consumer. Because of the intense competitive pressures in its chosen arenas, Mega Manufacturing believes it must obtain the maximum effort from its personnel. In support of this belief, Mega Manufacturing has adopted a policy of paying for performance (PFP). Typically, many of its divisions have incentives comprising a substantial portion of executive pay (40 percent to 150 percent of base pay possible in various types of incentives) and a significant portion of supervisory and employee compensation (5 percent to 25 percent possible).

To expand its capabilities in the new electronic surface-mount technology, Mega Manufacturing acquired GW Industries, which had several plants producing high-quality surface-mount electronic parts. The Kanto assembly plant was part of GW Industries; however, it was an older plant producing electronic parts for an industrial process rapidly approaching obsolescence. Although the products were produced on an assembly line, individual workers had relatively little contact with each other, and the skills required were relatively low.

Kanto had been a profitable operation for GW, but Mega Manufacturing has to switch Kanto to a different product and process or close the plant.

Kanto has a reputation for paying average to below-market wages, but it was viewed as a dependable and stable employer with a good benefits package. As a consequence, Kanto has had a stable and loyal workforce; but with the buyout of GW and the consequent uncertainty surrounding Kanto's future, there has been talk of unionizing and some of the more skilled employees are known to be seeking other jobs.

Mega has decided to offer Kanto the opportunity to manufacture an extremely complex switching device for a military contract. Although the total manufacturing process is complex, it can be broken into steps, with each step consisting of individual skills that can be learned relatively quickly. Groups of individuals, each with a specific skill, will have to work closely together to achieve the required quality levels for each step in the switching device assembly. The nature of the process is such that each individual will have to take an active interest in the success of the assembly or the device will be unsatisfactory.

EXHIBIT 11.1.1

```
TO:       Ellen Lennett
SUBJECT:  Kanto incentive program
FROM:     Don Walker


Ellen,

We need to give Kanto some more help on setting up its incentives to adequately support the new
switching assembly process. We cannot allow the conversion process to delay our completing
switching assemblies as there is a large late delivery penalty. Also, Bids and Contracting
apparently goofed and bid too low on the contract to maintain our usual margins. It appears we
have to make up 3% somewhere.
```

EXHIBIT 11.1.2

```
TO:       Ellen Lennett
SUBJECT:  Kanto Incentive Program
FROM:     Bill Idrey


Just a quick note to advise you of some early problems I'm encountering.
1.  The employees are learning the new skills, but the supervisors are having trouble (resisting?)
    learning the necessary composite skills.
2.  The parts we're getting from our Indonesian plant will sometimes test OK individually, but not
    work in the final assembly. It apparently is not feasible to test the intermediate assembly
    steps.
3.  Although job analysis says the steps and tasks are essentially equal, two of the assembly
    steps are perceived as being more important and thus as having higher status by the workers.
4.  Robert Horne, the plant manager, is complaining that the new final quality check supervisor,
    Beatrice Inggold, is too strict and will slow down production.
5.  Engineers from Design & Fabrication come in and watch, occasionally making suggestions, but
    I'm darned if I can see what they are contributing.
```

Name _____ Group _____

1. Is an incentive program appropriate? Explain your position.

2. If so, should there be one, two, or several plans?

3. Who should be included?

4. What should be the basis for incentive payments?

5. What kind of incentives should be included?

EXERCISE 11.1
ASSESSMENT QUESTIONS

1. What were the key variables you considered in your selection of an individual- or group-based PFP system?

2. What changes in organizational characteristics would seriously affect your recommendations?

3. What circumstances would lead you to conclude that a PFP system would not be in the best interests of the organization?

EXERCISE 11.2
PAY FOR PERFORMANCE AT DEE'S PERSONALIZED BASKETS

OVERVIEW

This exercise provides an opportunity for the student to develop a framework for a PFP system, training for the program, and a framework for the evaluation of the system. The problem is common to many organizations. As discussed in Chapter 11, while pay for performance is the preferred method of compensation for most jobs, there are many problems with such systems, including the apparent inability on the part of evaluators to be critical in their evaluations. Many experts on PFP systems maintain that this is the major problem with most PFP systems in operation today that use ratings as the basis for measurement. This exercise is designed to allow the student to construct a PFP system that would minimize such problems.

LEARNING OBJECTIVES

After completing this exercise, you should be able to:

1. Consider different PFP options.
2. Evaluate the relative advantages and disadvantages of the different approaches to PFP.
3. Consider the various issues related to training for PFP, including transfer, relapse, and cost.
4. Develop an evaluation design that can assess the effects of the PFP system.

PROCEDURE

Part A: Individual Analysis

Before class, read the background material on Dee's Personalized Baskets presented in Exhibit 11.2.1. Answer the questions on Form 11.2.1.

Part B: Group Analysis

Step 1. Assume the role of a team of HR consultants to consider the development of a PFP system. In addition, you have been asked to develop a managerial training program to prepare managers for the new PFP system. You have also been asked to evaluate the effectiveness of the PFP system.

Step 2. Among the critical issues that your team should address include those listed on Form 11.2.1. Review each consultant's responses on Form 11.2.1. Discuss each response and prepare a plan to deal with each.

Step 3. Prepare a short presentation for the vice president that covers your team's ideas regarding the design of the PFP system. Remember that management will weigh heavily both your recommendations as well as your plan for implementation.

EXHIBIT 11.2.1
BACKGROUND MATERIAL FOR DEE'S PERSONALIZED BASKETS

Nancy Harrison, HRM vice-president of Dee's Personalized Baskets in Orlando, Florida, is disturbed by lagging productivity figures and problems of product quality. She is intrigued by the results of a recent attitude survey of her employees. She has decided to experiment with some form of PFP system of compensation. The company's current system of compensation pays either straight hourly rates to nonsupervisory personnel or straight salary to all supervisory/managerial personnel with a year-end bonus that is a percentage of base pay as determined by the board. The attitude survey results indicated employees believed that they would work harder if they perceived a stronger tie between their level of effort and their pay. Each of the 200 employees who would be part of the new pay system prepares individual baskets of gifts (perfumes, fancy soaps, fancy foods, wine, etc.), which are ordered by

customers for clients and potential clients. Some employee discretion is involved in the preparation of the baskets and the finished product can be evaluated for quality and cost-effectiveness.

Few respondents to the survey felt that they were recognized in any significant way for working harder than others. People most disturbed by the failure to recognize greater effort were the same people who indicated they were more likely to seek other employment. The organization has a performance-appraisal system, but the ratings are generally very high. For the last performance-appraisal period, the average rating of effectiveness made by the 20 supervisors was 7.5 on a 9-point rating scale (with 9 representing "highly effective" performance).

Name _____   Group _____

1. What type(s) of PFP system(s) do you recommend for Dee's? Be as specific as possible. What (if any) additional information would help you develop the most effective PFP system?

2. What methods of training (e.g., informational, experiential) do you recommend for the PFP system and why?

3. What is your experimental design for evaluating the effectiveness of the PFP system?

4. What specific criteria will you use to evaluate the results? Provide some examples of criteria.

5. What will be the basis of your final recommendation to the vice president of human resources regarding the implementation of the PFP system? What data will you gather and evaluate?

6. What role (if any) should a PADS score play in the PFP system or training for the system? (See the Critical Thinking Exercise.) To answer this question, the student should complete the PADS and evaluate its usefulness (the instructor will provide feedback on your score on the PADS relative to normative data).

CHAPTER 12 EXERCISES

EXERCISE 12.1
JOB ENRICHMENT AT THE HERDHELM HOTEL*

OVERVIEW

As described in Chapter 12, Hackman and Oldham's Job Characteristics Model is a popular approach to apply for redesigning and enriching jobs. The emphasis is on building into jobs the critical psychological states of experienced meaningfulness, responsibility, and knowledge of results. This is done to improve employees' motivation, satisfaction, and quality of work, and to lower their absenteeism and turnover. This exercise employs the Job Characteristics Model to understand the nature of the job of housekeeper at the Herdhelm Hotel.

LEARNING OBJECTIVES

After completing this exercise, you should be able to:

1. Apply the principles of job enrichment presented in Hackman and Oldham's Job Characteristic Model to a work situation.
2. Identify benefits and constraints associated with job redesign efforts.
3. Evaluate the Hackman and Oldham approach relative to alternative methods of productivity/quality of work life improvements.

PROCEDURE

Part A: Individual Analysis

Before class, read the scenario for the housekeeping department at the Herdhelm Hotel and also read Exhibit 12.1.1. Answer the questions on Form 12.1.1.

Part B: Group Discussion

In groups of about six, each member should read all the other students' Form 12.1.1. The group should then attempt to reach consensus on the questions in Form 12.1.1. Prepare a four-minute presentation with the plan and alternative approaches. A group spokesperson will be designated by the instructor.

Part C: Class Discussion and Assessment

Step 1. Discuss the feasibility of each group's plan. In particular, consider how the recommendations might require changes in the way housekeepers are selected and rewarded, and how the suggestions might necessitate changes in other jobs in the Herdhelm Hotel. The issues of cost and alternative plans should be addressed.

Step 2. Following group discussion, students should complete the assessment questions for this exercise.

SCENARIO

Overlooking the downtown of a southeastern city, the Herdhelm Hotel is a midsized establishment featuring luxury accommodations and a staff of nearly 200 employees. The hotel competes with the finest hotels in the area and focuses on luxury and customer satisfaction in its marketing. The housekeeping department consists of 34 women under the supervision of an executive housekeeper. The staff is responsible for cleaning the hotel's 225 rooms and suites. Throughout the hotel's seven-year history, high rates of absenteeism and turnover have plagued the housekeeping department. Recently, however, complaints from unsatisfied guests concerning the cleanliness of the rooms have prompted management to take action. Hoping to improve the situation, management hired Dr. Katie Bell, a local consultant, to investigate the problem and make recommendations. To gain familiarity with the work of the housekeeping staff, Dr. Bell obtained job descriptions from the HR department. These are provided in Exhibit 12.1.1. After reviewing the job descriptions, Dr. Bell conducted extensive interviews with members of the housekeeping department and identified the following problem areas.

Chief among the housekeepers' list of complaints was the quality of supervision they received. Many comments focused on the executive housekeeper and how she administered performance feedback. "She doesn't tell us if we've done a good job," said Krystal, a 28-year-old employee. In general, housekeepers perceived a lack of performance feedback from the executive housekeeper. However, a more perplexing problem concerned the checkers, a select group of housekeepers whose responsibility it was to inspect the rooms after they were cleaned. Checkers were viewed as applying room cleanliness standards arbitrarily. "I can clean two rooms the same way and get different marks on them from different checkers," reported Gloria, a hotel employee of four years. Such a predicament resulted in housekeepers receiving inconsistent feedback on numerous occasions and created a sense of confusion within the department.

---
*Contributed by Ann M. Herd and Caroline C. Wilhelm.

A second pervasive problem was the perception among housekeepers that their work was not as highly valued as that of other hotel employees. Many housekeepers reported being treated as "second-class citizens" by other employees such as cashiers, bellhops, and managers. "They never smile or speak to us. They don't even say hello. Most times they pretend we're not even here," said Rose, one of the hotel's most tenured employees. Not only did housekeepers feel that they lacked respect from hotel employees, but they also perceived condescension from guests. "Customers are snobbish towards us and act like it's an inconvenience for us to clean their rooms," reported Luanne, who works part-time as a housekeeper. In addition to their esteem concerns, many housekeepers felt alienated from other hotel employees. "We don't know anything about what goes on in the rest of the hotel," said Wanda, whose mother and sister are also housekeepers. Several women said they felt purposely excluded from hotelwide employee meetings, which they were seldom able to attend due to work schedule conflicts. Such exclusion, they believed, was merely another sign that housekeepers were less important than other hotel employees.

Finally, the nature of the work itself was a frequent source of complaints. "Let's face it, making beds all day can get pretty boring," said Krystal. Boredom, however, was a small frustration compared to the exasperation felt by housekeepers when checkers interfered with their work. "They lord over us, watching us like hawks. They tell us what to do and how to do it, as if we don't know anything about our jobs," Krystal continued. Some housekeepers said they would have preferred to conduct their own quality inspections, but management had resisted the idea. Any effort among housekeepers to gain control over their work was doomed, they said, and there was no finer example than the 24-minute time allowance for cleaning each room. Housekeepers had fought bitterly for more time, arguing that their work pace was controlled in such a way that it was impossible to do a good job. "I always feel rushed and worn out trying to meet the deadline, and I end up cutting corners just to get everything done. There's no way I can do this job the way I'd like," said Hazel, one of the hotel's newest hires. The consequence for spending more than the allotted time on rooms was a warning slip from the executive housekeeper. Hoping to avoid such a reprimand, many housekeepers reported that they worked through the 15-minute break allowed each day to make up lost time.

Dr. Bell reflected on the employees' concerns. Consistent with the interview responses, a recent survey of housekeepers had revealed low levels of satisfaction with the present situation. Management was eager to address the problems, as the job performance of housekeepers was critical to customer satisfaction and, therefore, to hotel business. With only two days left before she met with management, Dr. Bell began to prepare her recommendations.

EXHIBIT 12.1.1   JOB DESCRIPTIONS FOR HOUSEKEEPING DEPARTMENT   **635**

EXHIBIT 12.1.1
JOB DESCRIPTIONS FOR HOUSEKEEPING DEPARTMENT

JOB TITLE: EXECUTIVE HOUSEKEEPER

Department: Housekeeping

Immediate supervisor: Assistant hotel manager

Job summary:

Delegates housekeeping duties to employees and sees that they are carried out. Responsible for overall cleanliness of hotel rooms.

Tasks and duties:

1. Obtains number and location of occupied rooms each day and assigns rooms to housekeepers for cleaning.
2. Plans employees' work schedules on a monthly basis.
3. Examines time cards daily and records number of hours worked by each employee on a payroll sheet.
4. Orders cleaning supplies and other housekeeping items as needed.
5. Takes periodic inventory of linens.
6. Inspects a random sample of rooms to ensure that they have been properly cleaned and that all items (e.g., soap) are in the correct place.
7. Notifies housekeepers of substandard work.
8. Holds monthly meeting with housekeepers to discuss work problems and make announcements.
9. Trains new employees to perform housekeeping duties.
10. Performs housekeeping duties as needed.

Working conditions:

Indoor environment
Works at least 60 hours per week, including nights and weekends

Dress requirements:

Uniform required

Minimum qualifications:

Supervisory and motivation skills
Communication skills
Organizational skills

JOB TITLE: HOUSEKEEPER

Department: Housekeeping

Immediate supervisor: Executive housekeeper

Job summary:

Responsible for cleaning hotel rooms and for delivering room linens to laundry.

Tasks and duties:

1. Obtains number and location of occupied rooms from executive housekeeper each morning.
2. Examines cart to ensure that it is adequately supplied with cleaning agents, linens, and toiletries (e.g., soap, shampoo); obtains needed supplies from housekeeping.
3. Strips bed linens and removes towels from bathroom.
4. Cleans shower, sink, and toilet; sweeps and mops bathroom floor; cleans mirrors and counters.
5. Replaces tissue paper, soap, and toiletries in bathroom.
6. Places clean towels in bathrooms.
7. Vacuums carpet.
8. Dusts furniture.
9. Makes bed with clean linens.
10. Empties trash cans.
11. Supplies room with matches and notepaper if necessary.
12. Notifies maintenance department of any needed repairs (e.g., lights).
13. Places linens in laundry chute and empties trash bag from cart.

Working conditions:

Indoor environment
Works at least 40 hours per week, including nights and weekends

EXHIBIT 12.1.1 (*Continued*)

Dress requirements:

Uniforms required

Minimum qualifications:

Ability to operate vacuum cleaner

JOB TITLE: CHECKER/HOUSEKEEPER

Department: Housekeeping

Immediate supervisor: Executive housekeeper

Job summary:

Carries out the requests of the executive housekeeper; examines the quality of housekeepers' work.

Tasks and duties:

1. Assists housekeepers in obtaining supplies for carts.
2. Checks to see that housekeepers have linens and vacuum cleaners.
3. Evaluates the cleanliness of rooms according to established criteria and marks each item inspected on a checklist.
4. Notifies housekeepers if work is substandard.
5. Assists executive housekeeper in planning employees' work schedules and in recording hours worked on time sheets.
6. Performs housekeeping duties as needed.

Working conditions:

Indoor environment
Works at least 50 hours per week, including nights and weekends

Dress requirement:

Uniform required

Minimum qualifications:

Inspection skills
Communication and interpersonal skills
Organizational skills

Name _____   Group _____

1. Evaluate the job of a housekeeper as it is presently designed using the five core job dimensions from the Job Characteristics Model. To what extent is the job enriched?

2. How amenable to job enrichment is the housekeeper's job? What characteristics of the employees should you consider to determine their readiness for job enrichment?

3. Propose a specific, chronological plan to enrich the housekeeper's job.

4. As an alternative to changes based on Hackman and Oldham's model, what other productivity/quality of work life programs might you consider for this job? Would a pay-for-performance system work? If so, what would it look like?

Name _____   Group _____

1. What effects do you expect a redesign of the housekeeper's job to have on the core job dimensions?

2. How do you expect the housekeepers to respond to changes in the core job dimensions?

3. What are the most important features of the Job Characteristics Model for the housekeeper's job?

4. How would you set up an experiment to assess the effects of your new job redesign program for the housekeeper's job? What criteria would you use to assess the effects?

EXERCISE 12.2
PLANNING AN INTERVENTION FOR UNIVERSITY MEDICAL CENTER*

OVERVIEW

As noted in Chapter 12, organizations have increasingly been using the Malcolm Baldrige National Quality Award to assess their effectiveness in terms of quality and business results. It takes organizations years to prepare themselves to be able to apply for the Baldrige award because they need to make changes in a number of important areas. One of the first steps in determining the state of an organization and how close it is to being able to apply comes through analyzing the results from organizational surveys and interviews. This exercise provides some relevant case information regarding one department in a hospital so that students can assess the effectiveness of the department. By applying the criteria of the Baldrige award, particularly the HR Development and Management category, students can learn to employ the criteria to examine the quality of an organization.

LEARNING OBJECTIVES

After completing this exercise, you should be able to:

1. Apply the principles of quality presented in the Baldrige award to a case situation.

2. Identify strategies for collecting additional case information.

3. Offer recommendations to an organization to meet the criteria of the Baldrige award, particularly in the category of HR Development and Management.

PROCEDURE

Part A: Individual Analysis

Before class, read Chapter 12 and the background information found in the exhibits in this case. Answer the questions in Form 12.2.1.

Part B: Group Analysis

Step 1. Working in groups of about four or five, discuss your answers to the questions in Form 12.2.1. The group should reach consensus on their answers to the questions and what group members see as the main problem areas for the nursing department. Discuss what your group would recommend as the next steps to collect any additional information. What suggestions for improvements would your group make? Prepare a short report to present to the class.

Step 2. Following group discussion and any class discussion, students should complete the assessment questions for this exercise.

---

*Contributed by Steve Long and Joyce E. A. Russell.

EXHIBIT 12.2.1
BACKGROUND INFORMATION ON UNIVERSITY MEDICAL CENTER

Your consulting firm has assigned you to develop an organizational intervention to improve employee attitudes and HR systems for the head nurses and assistant head nurses at the University Medical Center, a large regional teaching hospital. Your contact person in the hospital is Peng Tong, director of nursing. Peng is concerned that morale among the nursing staff is low. She has received a number of complaints that head nurses are "overly strict" in supervising the activities of staff nurses, and she senses an increase in the level of friction between head nurses and staff nurses. To familiarize you with the company and the job of head nurse, an organizational chart and a job description are provided.

DEPARTMENT OF NURSING

The nursing department at University Medical Center consists of a director of nursing, six clinical directors, 20 head nurses, 34 assistant head nurses, and approximately 237 staff nurses. Aside from the difference in job title, the actual work performed by head nurses and assistant head nurses is the same. However, head nurses primarily work during the day shift, while assistant head nurses work mostly night and weekend shifts.

DOT JOB DESCRIPTION

075.137-014 NURSE, HEAD (medical service)
Supervises and coordinates nursing activities in hospital unit. Assigns duties and coordinates nursing service. Evaluates nursing activities to ensure patient care, staff relations, and efficiency of service. Observes nursing care and visits patients to ensure that nursing care is carried out as directed and treatment is administered in accordance with physician's instructions. Directs preparation and maintenance of patients' clinical records. Inspects rooms and wards for cleanliness and comfort. Accompanies physician on rounds, and keeps informed of special orders concerning patients. Participates in orientation and training of personnel. Orders or directs ordering of drugs, solutions, and equipment, and maintains records on narcotics. Investigates and resolves complaints, or refers unusual problems to supervisor.

RELEVANT RESULTS FROM A NEEDS ASSESSMENT REPORT

Recently, the HR staff at University Medical Center completed a needs assessment to determine various training needs in the nursing department. The report identified a number of training needs and other issues in the nursing department's operations. This was the first time in the past seven years that a needs assessment was conducted in the nursing department. Some of the findings are noted below.

- *Leadership*—Head nurses and assistant head nurses are "overly strict" in supervising the activities of staff nurses. According to interviews with staff nurses, their supervisors are using an "autocratic leadership style." Staff nurses do not feel that they are ever asked for their views or input on how to improve things despite the fact that they are the ones who work most closely with patients.

- *Training and development*—Some of the staff nurses remarked that they want to attend training programs to get advanced learning on the latest techniques and procedures, yet are not encouraged by their supervisors.

- *Communication*—Head nurses and assistant head nurses are seen as being poor communicators by the staff nurses. As a result, staff nurses often feel confused about what their specific responsibilities. Also, they do not feel well informed about the goals and mission of the nursing department at the hospital.

- *Feedback and coaching*—Head nurses and assistant head nurses need to develop their coaching and counseling skills. Even though one of their responsibilities is to provide performance feedback to staff nurses, most of the head nurses provide feedback only once a year. Staff nurses commented in interviews that they wanted to get more specific feedback in a more timely fashion. They also felt that head nurses could offer them more corrective feedback on how to improve on the job. Head nurses agreed that they should engage in more counseling activities with staff nurses but felt pressed for time.

- *Compensation*—All employees and managers in the nursing department reported feeling underpaid. Each year they receive a merit increase for individual performance, yet in the last five years, everyone has received the same amount. This has been minimal because the hospital has experienced budget problems and cutbacks. The merit increase has barely kept up with inflation and does not motivate employees or reward exceptional or innovative performance.

- *Teamwork*—Staff nurses expressed interest in working in teams so that a small group would be responsible for particular patients and other job duties. To date, head nurses have not assigned any work to be done in teams despite the fact that other hospitals in the area have made these changes.

- *Orientation*—New staff nurses are given an excellent orientation to the hospital and the nursing job by the HR office. Once in the Nursing Department, however, they feel the orientation could be improved. This would help them to better understand the nature of their assignments, who they would be working with, how performance is evaluated, and so on.

- *Work environment*—Staff nurses noted that the work environment is clean, safe, and pleasant. The equipment is state-of-the art, and safety is strongly emphasized by head nurses.

- *Patient complaints*—Recently, there has been a slight increase in patient complaints in the nursing department. This has led to a decline in "business," and more clients going to a nearby hospital for service.

EXHIBIT 12.2.2 UNIVERSITY MEDICAL CENTER ORGANIZATIONAL CHART **641**

EXHIBIT 12.2.2
UNIVERSITY MEDICAL CENTER ORGANIZATIONAL CHART

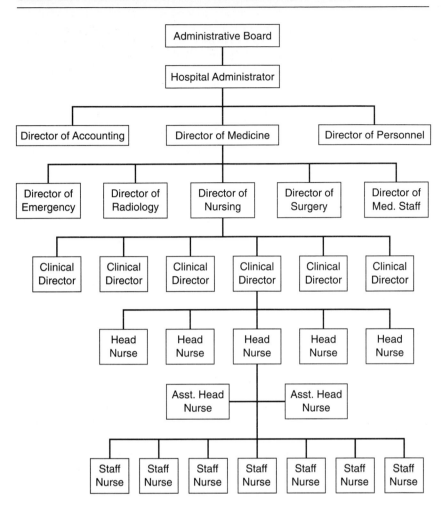

Name _____   Group _____

1. Using the information presented in Chapter 12, analyze the case. How is the nursing department doing with respect to the Baldrige criteria, particularly the criteria specified for "HR Development and Management"? Be specific.

2. What additional information should be collected to better assess the "HR Development and Management" criteria of the Baldrige award?

3. What recommendations for improvements would you make to the nursing department (i.e., changes with the head nurses, assistant head nurses, and staff nurses)? Outline a short-term recommendation (strategies to implement within the next month) as well as a longer-term plan (strategies to implement within the next six months). Indicate the benefits and drawbacks of your proposed recommendations.

Name _____   Group _____

1. How difficult was it to apply the Baldrige criteria to assess the quality of the nursing department? What, if any, additional case information would make it easier to apply the Baldrige criteria?

2. What do you see as the relationship between the Baldrige categories of "Leadership" and "HR Development and Management"? Are there other connections between the Baldrige categories based on the University Medical Center?

3. Suppose the hospital administration decides it wants to try to receive the Baldrige award. What steps must be taken to get the organization ready? What are the advantages and drawbacks associated with this goal?

CHAPTER 13 EXERCISES

EXERCISE 13.1
ORGANIZING A UNION*

OVERVIEW

Research shows that management often neither anticipates nor understands the motivation of employees to organize into unions. This exercise explores an organizing effort from the perspectives of labor and of management.

LEARNING OBJECTIVES

After completing this exercise, you should be able to:

1. Understand the process of starting a union organizing effort.
2. Know the steps involved in the certification process.
3. Be able to consider employee and employer reactions to a union organizing effort.
4. Know the laws and regulations that govern the process of union organizing from management's perspective.

PROCEDURE

Part A: Individual Analysis

Step 1. Before class, read the scenario below and follow the directions of the assignment.

Step 2. Each student will be assigned to either the union organizer role or the general manager role. Each role requires you to write a letter to be used in your arguments. These arguments are described in Exhibit 13.1.1.

Part B: Group Analysis

Step 1. Form small groups in which members are grouped by like assignment (e.g., all union organizers together and all general managers together). The members should first review one another's letters and outlines. One letter should be selected as the most effective, then edited, and submitted as the group response. Each group should also derive a chronology of

steps to be taken by the union organizer to Mr. Cameron.

Step 2. A representative from each group should write the chronological steps on a blackboard or flip chart so that comparisons across groups can be made. The writer of the most effective letter from each group should then read the letter to the class. Discussion should center on the most important elements for each side and the legal implications of various strategies proposed.

SCENARIO

You are a customer service representative for American Rental Car (ARC), a national rental car company. Recently, the employees at the three installations in the southeastern United States, which are managed by the general manager, Scott Cameron, have experienced dissatisfaction. No raises have been given in over a year; employee benefits are sparse; employees' preferences have not been considered in the assignment of work schedules or installations; and an automated employee monitoring system has been implemented.

Many of the 100 full-time employees have been talking about unionization, although many have yet to be convinced that unionization provides the best answer. The average age of the 100 employees is 29; there are 58 females and 41 minorities. Some employees strongly believe that a union can address some of the workers' concerns. Consequently, they have contacted the Customer Service Reps of America (CSRA) for help in organizing the southeastern region of ARC. Despite numerous attempts, the CSRA has been unsuccessful in organizing only three other ARC installations nationwide because the firm engages in a very tough (and often questionably legal) campaign to stop any union organizing efforts. Before the CSRA will send an organizer to your location, it wants to be persuaded that enough employees back the union to merit the expense. Thus, it has suggested that as a first step someone write a letter to the workers convincing them of the benefits of unionization and enlisting their support.

---

*Contributed by Nancy Brown Johnson.

EXHIBIT 13.1.1
UNION ORGANIZER ROLE

Write a letter to your coworkers about the factors involved in the case. You remember from the chapter why people join unions and the benefits of membership, and you want to be sure to include these factors in your letter. Yet you know that your fellow workers will still wonder why the possible costs of unionization (e.g., union dues, getting fired, being permanently assigned to the midnight shift, and being harassed by their supervisor) are worth the benefits. From your speech class you know the importance of providing answers to counterarguments if you wish to effectively persuade your coworkers to support the union.

Prepare a chronological outline for the union organizing effort covering what steps or procedures are to be followed, what data you should gather, what to look for in management's reaction, and what to do if management does not respond fairly. Also, prepare a chronological outline of what you anticipate to be management's reaction to the union organizing effort (i.e., the steps that management will take through the course of the organizing effort).

GENERAL MANAGER ROLE

Assume the role of Scott Cameron and draft a letter to your three supervisors and six assistant supervisors stipulating what can and cannot be done regarding the union organizing effort. For example, you were just informed that one of the supervisors, Meredith Sterrett, has already begun to establish a "paper trail" on one union sympathizer so he can be terminated for poor performance if "things get out of hand." She also told an employee that if a CSRA representative showed up at her installation, she would "call the cops and have him arrested for trespassing." She recently refused to hire a black female applicant because both of the applicant's parents were members of a union. You will need to respond to Ms. Sterrett's actions. You should also prepare an outline of a meeting to be held regarding the union organizing effort and what the firm should do regarding worker concerns. Also, prepare a chronology of steps management should take in response to the organizing effort.

OVERVIEW

Research indicates that general attitudes toward unions are strongly correlated with a number of workplace behaviors. These attitudes, sometimes based on limited facts about unions and their actual effects, can have a profound effect on a number of reactions in the workplace. Research also shows that expectancies regarding union behavior and activities can affect subsequent negotiations and managerial behaviors toward union activity. From the workers' perspective, attitudes can also affect reactions to union organizing efforts, perceptions of the extent to which unions can affect workers' pay and working conditions, and job attractiveness.

This exercise assesses attitudes toward unions in general and the extent to which these attitudes are grounded in fact. Discussion will center on the implications of the attitudes for union–management relations.

LEARNING OBJECTIVES

After completing this exercise, you should be able to:

1. Understand the implications of preconceived attitudes toward union–management relations and managerial behavior.
2. Know some of the myths and truths about the effects of unions.
3. Adopt a more objective perspective on the subject of unions.

PROCEDURE

Part A: Individual Analysis

Before reading Chapter 13 and before class, complete the questionnaire in Form 13.2.1.

Part B: Group Analysis

In class, the instructor will group you according to your scores on Form 13.2.1 and present norms for the data. Group discussion should focus first on the bases for students' responses (i.e., the basis of student opinions expressed on Form 13.2.1). Each group should then attempt to reach consensus on item 1 of Form 13.2.1. Each group should organize a three-minute presentation addressing the consensus point of view on item 1. Support your group's position with specific information. Expect that there will be differences in views among your classmates.

Name _____ Group _____

With regard to unions in the United States today, use the following scale to indicate your opinion about each statement:

        5 = Strongly agree
        4 = Agree
        3 = Undecided
        2 = Disagree
        1 = Strongly disagree

_____ 1. U.S. productivity would be much higher if it weren't for unions.

_____ 2. Unions protect incompetent workers so long as they belong to the union.

_____ 3. Unions interfere with management attempts to increase productivity.

_____ 4. Unions are corrupt.

_____ 5. Unions are mainly responsible for the adversarial relationship that exists between unions and management.

_____ 6. Union wages are not competitive in a global economy.

_____ 7. Union rules and regulations stifle attempts to improve the quality of our products or services.

_____ 8. Unions are a big help to workers.

_____ 9. Unions are violent during strikes.

_____ 10. More protection is needed for replacement workers who are threatened and harassed by striking unionists.

_____ 11. The United States could be more competitive if we could get rid of unions.

_____ 12. Big labor has excessive political power in Washington.

_____ 13. Unions are undemocratic in their organizational structure.

_____ 14. Union workers are less satisfied with their wages and benefits than are nonunion workers.

_____ 15. Unions tend to oppose pay-for-performance (PFP) systems.

_____ 16. Companies should be allowed to screen people based on their general attitudes toward unions.

_____ 17. Union wages have outpaced nonunion wages over the last 10 years.

_____ 18. Management should be allowed to hire replacement workers immediately after a strike action.

_____ 19. I would join a union if I thought it might help me.

EXERCISE 13.3
THE BASEBALL STRIKES: AN EXAMPLE OF COLLECTIVE BARGAINING*

OVERVIEW

We have seen how important collective bargaining is to the resolution of differences between unions and management. Achieving consensus between the two parties is a long and taxing process, often leaving both sides feeling bitter and cheated. Rarely does a collective bargaining session leave both sides feeling good about the overall outcome of the negotiations. Collective bargaining also requires a great deal of preparation and the willingness to be flexible on the issues under debate.

This exercise introduces the collective bargaining process and the difficulties that can arise from the advancement of differing agendas by two parties. This is a team exercise, and each team should attempt to represent its side in good faith and with as much realism as possible. Discussion will probably center on reactions to the differing situations presented in the exercise.

LEARNING OBJECTIVES

After completing this exercise, you should:

1. Understand the difficulties that can arise from two-party negotiations.
2. Understand the preparation involved in collective bargaining.
3. Be able to prepare an argument for the advancement of goals in a collective bargaining situation.
4. Be capable of understanding the process of reaching agreement in negotiations.

PROCEDURE

Step 1. Two teams should be formed—one representing the baseball players union and the other representing the team owners. A student should also be selected as a mediator.

Step 2. The owners and players should be given a few minutes to read over their guidelines and discuss a plan of action. The mediator should read both briefings.

Step 3. The players should present their proposal to the owners, who then provide a counteroffer. Negotiations should continue until 25 minutes have elapsed or a decision is reached.

Step 4. Use of the mediator is optional. If one side asks for mediation, all parties must agree before he or she may be brought in to assist the bargaining. The final decision must still be made by both the owners and the players. The mediator can only provide suggestions or guidelines and help to facilitate the process.

Step 5. Following completion of the exercise, complete Form 13.3.1.

EXHIBIT 13.3.1
BASEBALL PLAYERS' BRIEFING

You represent the National Baseball Player's Union (NBPU). All players from all 28 Major League teams must belong to the union and pay annual dues. Therefore, you represent 700 active players plus players who have paid dues but are currently in the minor leagues and the interests of retired players nationwide. Your primary goals in the negotiations are salary, pension benefits for retiring players, term requirements for benefits, and revenue-sharing issues. The environment with the owners has been difficult in the past. Your union has been forced to strike on three occasions, and lockouts by the owners have occurred on five occasions. The primary issues have shifted over the years, but bargaining has always been fierce and resentment has been high. The owners average a personal wealth of $350 million. Gross revenues from all ballparks average $25 million in ticket sales, $10 million in concession sales, and $22 million in merchandise sales. This does not include licensing rights, city parks, television rights, and other sources of owner income. As the players, the centers of attention, you simply want your fair share of the pie. Your agenda for the coming negotiations is as follows:

- An increase in the minimum salary from $225,000 to $400,000 (citing the similar raises the Canadian Hockey Alliance and the World Roundball Federation both received in their most recent contracts).
- A decrease in the minimum Major League service to earn a pension from five years to three years.
- A decrease in the no trade rule from 10/5 to 7/3 (currently, a player who has been in the majors for 10 years and with the same team for 5 can veto being traded elsewhere).
- An increase in pension benefits for retired players from 25 percent of the minimum salary to 50 percent of the minimum.
- The ability for "marquee" players (i.e., All-Stars, MVPs) to negotiate revenues into their contracts (i.e., a percentage of the ticket sales, etc.) without having to wait for them to be offered by the owners.

These are the basics, but other needs may arise as the negotiations draw near. A poll of the players in the union has shown that the minimum salary increase and the no trade stipulation are the most popular issues. The poll also stated that the players are *very* willing to strike to get what they want. They are still unhappy about the last round of negotiations, in which the owners got the upper hand.

---

*Contributed by Joseph G. Clark, Jr.

EXHIBIT 13.3.2
BASEBALL OWNERS' BRIEFING

You represent the 28 men and women who own Major League Baseball teams in the American Baseball League (ABL). Your primary goal in this negotiation is to keep your shirt. The average salary of a Major League player is $1.1 million. The average team salary is $35 million. Other costs to consider are equipment, travel, pensions, bonuses, stadium rental and city fees, insurance, stadium staff (i.e., groundskeepers, concessions, security, etc.), and taxes. Many owners are barely solvent. If salaries and benefits continue to increase at the current pace, some owners in smaller cities will be forced to sell to corporate alliances, which will surely ruin the integrity of the game. Negotiations with the players' union are always fierce. There is usually a lot of name calling, slander, and bad feelings from the players. This time, something *must* be done to curb the salaries or else the entire sport may be in serious trouble. The owner's agenda is as follows:

- Lower the current league minimum salary from $225,000 to $200,000.

- Increase the minimum league service to earn a pension from five years to seven years.

- Obtain an agreement to at least a five-year contract, rather than the usual three-year contract.

- Obtain a stipulation that the players will not file for arbitration until after a new agreement takes effect (thus minimizing trades and revenue losses during the period when we don't know the future of our own financial status).

- The right to perform surprise drug testing on random or suspected players (with a stipulation for provision of drug and alcohol rehabilitation to be jointly provided by the players' union and the owners).

- The right to renegotiate player vetoed trades to allow them to proceed (a player who has been in the majors for 10 years and with the same team for 5 can veto being traded elsewhere).

These are the key points, but other issues may arise as the negotiations draw nearer. Remember that the future of the game relies on our ability to stay out of bankruptcy court. A poll of the owners has shown that the salary and trade issues are seen as the most important issues (we simply cannot give up any more money). The poll also revealed that a majority (but not all) of the owners are willing to lock the players out if that is the only option. They are still very upset about the last round of talks, in which the players gained a definite victory.

Name _____   Group _____

1.   What were the terms of the final agreement negotiated between the two sides?

2.   What were the difficulties that arose while trying to reach an agreement?

3.   What role can you see the mediator playing during bargaining of this type?

4. During collective bargaining, discussions can become heated. Did this occur during the exercise and, if so, how was this resolved?

5. In the future, what techniques for bargaining might both sides try to better gain their objectives?

CHAPTER 14 EXERCISES

EXERCISE 14.1
THE DEVELOPMENT OF A COMPANY SMOKING POLICY

OVERVIEW

One of the most controversial health issues is smoking in the workplace. Smoking has been taken for granted in most work settings. Little consideration has been given to either (1) the effects of the smoking on the health of both smokers and nonsmokers or (2) the potential cost to the organization. This is so even though smoking is a known cause of cancer, heart disease, and generally bad health. As discussed in Chapter 14, many states now have legislation mandating smoke-free work environments, while some states have taken steps to protect smokers' rights.

LEARNING OBJECTIVES

After completing this exercise, you should be able to:

1. Understand the interpersonal dynamics of policy development, particularly policy that significantly affects (and changes) the work environment.
2. Use negotiating skills in relation to your positions on a controversial matter that has no "correct answer."
3. Use your writing skills in an attempt to assuage readers who may not be easily persuaded to agree with your position.

PROCEDURE

Part A: Individual Analysis

Before class, read the scenario and respond as directed.

Part B: Group Analysis

Step 1. Assemble in groups and compare your developmental strategies. Attempt to reach consensus on the correct approach to take in the formulation of the policy. List all the variables that should be considered and all questions of clarification that must be answered.

Step 2. Either students will be paired off or each student should review all the group members' reports and provide constructive suggestions for improving them. The critiques should focus on the drafts rather than starting from scratch. The feedback from the students should then be used in preparing a second letter. Each student group should select one edited letter considered to be the best.

Step 3. The consensus-derived strategy should then be presented to the rest of the class and the selected letter should be read. Subsequent discussion should focus on the likely reactions of the major constituencies of the law firm and the overall impact of the new policy.

SCENARIO

You have been appointed to a committee charged with the development of a smoking policy for the clerical staff of a law firm. There are no laws or regulations that require the imposition of such a policy and there is currently no such policy. However, several of the younger secretaries and some attorneys have complained about smoke in the work area, which is a large room (2,000 square feet with average ventilation) housing 30 secretaries. Many of the law partners prefer to hire only nonsmokers in the future, and some take the position that current employees who smoke should be told they must quit within six months or they will be terminated. Ten of the secretaries smoke, seven of whom have worked for the firm for over 10 years. Two of the seven have disabilities and have some difficulty getting around. Up to now, all employees have been free to smoke any time and any place they chose.

You have been asked to develop a policy. What steps should you follow in formulating a policy? Review the options, which range from taking no action to imposing a strict ban on smoking for all employees either on or off the job. You have also been asked to take a position on a possible policy specifying that new employees must be nonsmokers and that current employees must stop smoking within six months. Assume you have followed the steps of the developmental plan and are ready to draft a policy. Draft a short letter that explains the policy to all employees including the secretaries. What procedures should be followed for establishing a firm policy? What action should be taken for those who choose to violate the policy? What (if any) additional data do you need to make a specific recommendation?

EXERCISE 14.2
THE DEVELOPMENT OF AN ANTI-DRUG POLICY*

OVERVIEW

As a result of the Drug Free Workplace Act, which went into effect in 1989, all federal contractors are required to provide their employees with a drug-free workplace. The act includes the following guidelines:

1. Furnish a policy statement prohibiting controlled substances in the workplace.
2. Notify employees (regular and contract) of the prohibition and the expected penalties of violating the policy.
3. Establish a drug-free awareness program.
4. Notify employees that conformance to the drug-free policy is a condition of employment.
5. Employees must notify the employer within five days if they are convicted of violating a criminal drug statute while in the workplace.
6. Contractors must notify the contracting agency of any such convictions.
7. For all employees convicted, the contractor must impose a sanction or require the completion of a substance-abuse treatment program.
8. Continue to make a good-faith effort to maintain a drug-free workplace.

LEARNING OBJECTIVES

After completing this exercise, you should be able to:

1. Consider implications of different policies regarding drug testing.
2. Understand the options available for deterrence and enforcement of drug abuse and enforcement of an anti-drug policy.

PROCEDURE

Part A: Individual Analysis

Before class, read the scenario and respond as directed.

Part B: Group Analysis

In groups, each member should review the memos of all other members. Each group should attempt to reach con-

---

*Contributed by Marilyn A. Perkins.

sensus on the recommendation to the board. The recommendation must deal with all the issues raised above. Take a definitive position on random testing for all employees and on what specific steps should be taken if an employee tests positive.

SCENARIO

You are the manager of the HR department of a major federal contractor. Your responsibilities include implementing the drug-free workplace program mandated by the federal government. Your organization is responsible for conducting very costly and sensitive research. The machinery used in the research is complex and could be dangerous if not used properly. Some of the experiments being conducted are risky and could pose a hazard to the environment or a threat to national security. However, not all employees work with the dangerous machinery or on the sensitive experiments.

As part of the drug-free workplace, the position of the security department includes the following:

- Any employee with a substance-abuse problem should be reported to the security department, regardless of whether the substance abuse was detected by management or self-reported.
- Drug testing should be conducted for all individuals filling sensitive positions and randomly for the entire organization.
- All positive test results should be reported to the security department.
- All employees testing positive on the first test should be terminated.
- Any job applicant with a history of drug or alcohol abuse should not be hired.

The EAP representatives have reviewed the security department's position and disagree strongly with the proposed sanctions. In the EAP, 70 percent of the employees sent to employee counseling are self-referred. If the EAP is required to report the self-referrals to the security department, the EAP representatives argue, employees will not seek help from the EAP and will go untreated. The EAP representatives also contend that the termination sanction proposed by the security department is inhumane and may violate the Rehabilitation Act of 1973, the American with Disabilities Act, or inalienable rights of privacy. One board member has stated that mass drug testing as proposed "makes a mockery of the presumption of innocence and strongly implies that someone who refuses to submit to a test is guilty . . . the level of expectations of privacy is diminishing, and we are slowly surrendering our dignity."

The board of directors has requested that you, as a task force member, develop a response to both the security department and to the EAP representatives. Take into consideration the health and safety of the company as well as the rights of the employees. Consider the following components: the Drug Free Workplace Act, an employee's right to privacy, confidentiality of the drug-testing program, and access to the EAP. Prepare a memo to the board of directors in which you take a position on the matter (maximum of five pages). Be prepared to defend your position in group discussion.

EXERCISE 14.3
THE DEVELOPMENT OF A HEALTH AND SAFETY POLICY

OVERVIEW

Chapter 14 discusses the renewed vigor with which OSHA is pursuing violations of the 1970 OSHA Act. This exercise has you consider the implications of health and safety regulation for managerial activities.

LEARNING OBJECTIVES

After completing this exercise, you should be able to:

1. Understand the steps that should be taken under OSHA regulation.
2. Know the rights that employers and employees have with regard to OSHA regulation.

PROCEDURE

Part A: Individual Analysis

Read the following scenario before class. You have been retained as a consultant to implement compliance with OSHA. As a consultant, how would you approach the problem, and what kind of advice and help would you give? Complete Form 14.3.1 and bring it to class.

Part B: Group Analysis

In class, groups should review the completed 14.3.1 forms of individual members and attempt to reach consensus on all three aspects of the report. One group member should report the consensus recommendations to the rest of the class.

SCENARIO

Dynamic Duo, Inc., opened its manufacturing plant several months ago. The company is owned and operated by two enterprising business students from Poedunk University in Poedunk, USA. The company has 50 employees, most of whom work on the floor of the plant and handle the heavy equipment needed to manufacture widgets. One supervisor is in charge. Dynamic Duo, Inc., is concerned about safety, but the owners know nothing about OSHA.

Before you have had a chance to advise Dynamic Duo, the plant is visited by a compliance officer who simply enters the plant and conducts a tour, unaccompanied by either management or employees. At the end of the tour, the compliance officer presents Dynamic Duo with a citation and a penalty. The Dynamic Duo owners call you in as a consultant and ask you what they should do next.

Unfortunately for Dynamic Duo, soon after the compliance officer's visit, five employees are injured or become ill, all on the same day. One is seriously injured, having caught his hand in a conveyor. Another has become mysteriously ill, and three others have suffered minor cuts. The owners call you in again and ask you whether they need to inform anybody of the accidents and the illness or to record them somehow.

Name _____   Group _____

1. What questions would you ask Dynamic Duo's owners?

2. What legal steps would you recommend that Dynamic Duo take?

3. What advice would you give the owners concerning the company's obligations under OSHA to record accidents?

EXERCISE 14.4
THE DEVELOPMENT OF A THREAT MANAGEMENT TEAM
FOR A WORKPLACE VIOLENCE INCIDENT*

OVERVIEW

As described in Chapter 14, incidents of workplace violence are increasing in number and intensity. This exercise describes a situation in which the potential for a violent incident on the job is high. As members of a threat management team, students must decide how to recognize, report, and subsequently deal with the incident.

LEARNING OBJECTIVES

After completing this exercise, you should be able to:

1. Recognize the warning signs and symptoms of a potentially violent situation in the workplace.
2. Record and report threatening behaviors.
3. Construct a plan for assessing an employee's potential for violence and recommend a course of action.

PROCEDURE

Part A: Individual Analysis

Before class, read the scenario. Prepare a written answer to each of the questions presented on Form 14.4.1. Assume you actually observed the situation described in the scenario and complete the Violent Incident Report in Form 14.4.2.

Part B: Group Analysis

Working in groups of about six, review the individual written responses of all group members and develop a new intervention strategy that will handle the potentially violent situation and prevent others from happening. The group should act as a threat management team and reach consensus on the questions in Form 14.4.1.

Part C: Class Discussion and Assessment

Have one member from each group act as a spokesperson to describe the strategies developed by each threat management team. Discuss the feasibility of each team's plan. Recommendations of alternative plans should be addressed.

SCENARIO

Inside a large manufacturing plant in a suburban Midwestern city, a production manager, Rosalyn, just received word that she must lay off eight more people. It's the second time in the last six months that she's had to tell people they are no longer needed. Her head begins to pound and her heart races. She must prepare herself to handle the usual reactions of anger, disappointment, and resentment that will soon follow. This is the third time in the two years since Rosalyn has joined the company that she's had to give employees news about layoffs. It isn't easy, especially since at age 31, she's younger than most of the employees. This time she's particularly afraid that one employee, named Roy, could become a physical threat to the workforce after hearing the news.

Roy is 49 and has worked at the plant for 23 years. He has a large family to support and hopes to remain an employee until retirement. Roy has a record of absenteeism, tardiness, and is viewed as a "loner" by most of his co-workers. No one knows much about him except that he appears to have few interests outside of work besides the shooting range he frequently visits. Some workers have overheard him voicing extremist opinions and attitudes on a variety of issues. For the most part, people leave him alone to do his work.

As expected, Roy was not happy about the layoff. A few days after the layoff, he met with the production manager and a human resource professional to review the severance package offering. During this meeting, Roy began to speak angrily and at one point lost his temper. Shaking his finger at the production manager, he shouted, "I'll be back," and has since been spotted sitting in the parking lot in his truck. No one knows for sure what he's going to do.

Within the hour, Roy's file is on your desk. By the end of the day, you assemble the company's threat management team to assess the potential danger involved. You and the other team members review Roy's records, complete violent incident reports, and discuss options for handling the situation. All collected data will be analyzed and measured against an established criteria for dangerousness to determine whether Roy represents a clear and immediate threat to an identifiable target, namely Rosalyn, the production manager. A course of action must be developed.

---

*Contributed By Susan M. Burroughs.

Name _____   Group _____

1. What warning signs or symptoms were displayed before Roy's blow up?

2. Were proper immediate action(s) taken after this incident?

3. Were time, money, and effort wasted or was a potential crisis averted in the meeting of the threat management team?

4. Discuss five ways in which the threat management team could be more effective.

5. What specific action(s) could be taken to create a security-conscious organizational culture at the manufacturing plant?

6. What, if any, unique challenges may exist in this situation given the differences between Roy and Rosalyn, the production manager, in terms of gender, age, and tenure with the company?

7. What, if any, ethical issues (e.g., privacy) are involved when members of a threat management team seek to identify and report potentially dangerous employees?

FORM 14.4.2
VIOLENT INCIDENT REPORT

Employees who have been victims of violence at work or have observed potentially violent incidents should complete this report as soon as possible. Upon completion, send a copy to your employer and to your threat management team contact person. Be sure to keep a copy for your records.

Please print.

1. **Identifying information**

Name: _____

Job title: _____

Employer: _____

Department/section: _____

2. **Assailant/aggressor**

_____ Worker

_____ Former worker

_____ Supervisor

_____ Customer

_____ Relative

_____ Girlfriend/boyfriend

_____ Spouse/ex-spouse

_____ Patient

_____ Student

_____ Resident

_____ Visitor

_____ Client

_____ Other (specify)

Name (if known): _____

Age: _____

Gender: _____ Male _____ Female

Were you able to identify the assailant/aggressor as one who possessed potential for violence before this incident?
_____ Yes _____ No

If yes, what traits or characteristics did the assailant/aggressor possess? (Check all that apply.)

_____ Anger

_____ Aggressive/threatening

_____ Obsessive

_____ Withdrawn/"loner"

_____ Disgruntled/"troublemaker"

_____ Quiet

_____ Extremist attitudes or opinions

_____ Argumentative/uncooperative

_____ Interpersonal conflict

_____ Real or perceived emotional/mental disorders

_____ Other (explain) _____

3. **Incident and injury information**

Date of incident: _____

Time: _____ (AM) _____ (PM) _____

Type(s) of violence observed (check all that apply):

_____ Gossip/rumors

_____ Verbal abuse/swearing

_____ Arguments with customers, coworkers, supervisors, or other employees

_____ Property damage/vandalism

_____ Fist-fight/physical altercation

_____ Theft

_____ Shooting

_____ Rape

_____ Stabbing

_____ Arson

_____ Murder

_____ Other (specify) _____

Type of weapon(s) used (check all that apply):

_____ Gun

_____ Knife

_____ Club/bat/pipe

_____ Fist

_____ No weapon involved

_____ Other (explain)

_____

Perceived motivation for the aggressive act (check all that apply):

_____ Firing

_____ Layoff

_____ Stress

_____ Feelings of unfairness, injustice, or malice by others

_____ Financial/legal difficulties

_____ Family/marital problems

_____ Emotional problems/mental illness

_____ Drug/alcohol abuse

_____ Personality conflict

_____ Violent criminal history

_____ Don't know/no knowledge of motive

_____ Other (specify)

_____

Medical attention/first aid obtained?	_____ Yes	_____ No	
Workers' compensation forms completed?	_____ Yes	_____ No	
Police called?	_____ Yes	_____ No	
Reported to supervisor?	_____ Yes	_____ No	

Action taken:

_____

_____

4. Other information

Was the assailant involved in any previous violent incidents with staff? _____ Yes _____ No

Are there any measures in place to prevent a similar incident? _____ Yes _____ No

Please provide any other information you think is relevant:

_____

_____

INDEX

SUBJECT INDEX